ISBN 978-1-330-55840-9
PIBN 10078448

1 MONTH OF
FREE
READING

at

www.ForgottenBooks.com

By purchasing this book you are eligible for one month membership to ForgottenBooks.com, giving you unlimited access to our entire collection of over 700,000 titles via our web site and mobile apps.

To claim your free month visit:

www.forgottenbooks.com/free78448

English
Français
Deutsche
Italiano
Español
Português

www.forgottenbooks.com

Mythology Photography **Fiction**
Fishing Christianity **Art** Cooking
Essays Buddhism Freemasonry
Medicine **Biology** Music **Ancient**
Egypt Evolution Carpentry Physics
Dance Geology **Mathematics** Fitness
Shakespeare **Folklore** Yoga Marketing
Confidence Immortality Biographies
Poetry **Psychology** Witchcraft
Electronics Chemistry History **Law**
Accounting **Philosophy** Anthropology
Alchemy Drama Quantum Mechanics
Atheism Sexual Health **Ancient History**
Entrepreneurship Languages Sport
Paleontology Needlework Islam
Metaphysics Investment Archaeology
Parenting Statistics Criminology
Motivational

WAR OF THE REBELLION:

A COMPILATION OF THE

OFFICIAL RECORDS

OF THE

UNION AND CONFEDERATE ARMIES.

PREPARED UNDER THE DIRECTION OF THE SECRETARY OF WAR, BY BVT. LIEUT.
COL. ROBERT N. SCOTT, THIRD U. S. ARTILLERY,

AND

PUBLISHED PURSUANT TO ACT OF CONGRESS APPROVED JUNE 16, 1880.

SERIES I—VOLUME IX.

WASHINGTON:
GOVERNMENT PRINTING OFFICE.
1883.

PREFACE.

By an act approved June 23, 1874, Congress made an appropriation "to enable the Secretary of War to begin the publication of the Official Records of the War of the Rebellion, both of the Union and Confederate Armies," and directed him "to have copied for the Public Printer all reports, letters, telegrams, and general orders not heretofore copied or printed, and properly arranged in chronological order."

Appropriations for continuing such preparation have been made from time to time, and the act approved June 16, 1880, has provided "for the printing and binding, under direction of the. Secretary of War, of 10,000 copies of a compilation of the Official Records (Union and Confederate) of the War of the Rebellion, so far as the same may be ready for publication, during the fiscal year"; and that " of said number, 7,000 copies shall be for the use of the House of Representatives, 2,000 copies for the use of the Senate, and 1,000 copies for the use of the Executive Departments."*

This compilation will be the first general publication of the military records of the war, and will embrace all official documents that can be obtained by the compiler, and that appear to be of any historical value.

---

*Volume I to V distributed under act approved June 16, 1880. The act approved August 7, 1882, provides that—

"The volumes of the official records of the war of the rebellion shall be distributed as follows: One thousand copies to the executive departments, as now provided by law. One thousand copies for distribution by the Secretary of War among officers of the Army and contributors to the work. Eight thousand three hundred copies shall be sent by the Secretary of War to such libraries, organizations, and individuals as may be designated by the Senators, Representatives, and Delegates of the Forty-seventh Congress. Each Senator shall designate not exceeding twenty-six, and each Representative and Delegate not exceeding twenty-one of such addresses, and the volumes shall be sent thereto from time to time as they are published, until the publication is completed. Senators, Representatives, and Delegates shall inform the Secretary of War in each case how many volumes of those heretofore published they have forwarded to such addresses. The remaining copies of the eleven thousand to be published, and all sets that may not be ordered to be distributed as provided herein, shall be sold by the Secretary of War for cost of publication with ten per cent. added thereto, and the proceeds of such sale shall be covered into the Treasury. If two or more sets of said volumes are ordered to the same address the Secretary of War shall inform the Senators, Representatives or Delegates, who have designated the same, who thereupon may designate other libraries, organizations, or individuals. The Secretary of War shall report to the first session of the Forty-eighth Congress what volumes of the series heretofore published have not been furnished to such libraries, organizations, and individuals. He shall also inform distributees at whose instance the volumes are sent."

The publication will present the records in the following order of arrangement:

The **1st Series** will embrace the formal reports, both Union and Confederate, of the first seizures of United States property in the Southern States, and of all military operations in the field, with the correspondence, orders, and returns relating specially thereto, and, as proposed, is to be accompanied by an Atlas.

In this series the reports will be arranged according to the campaigns and several theaters of operations (in the chronological order of the events), and the Union reports of any event will, as a rule, be immediately followed by the Confederate accounts. The correspondence, &c., not embraced in the "reports" proper will follow (first Union and next Confederate) in chronological order.

The **2d Series** will contain the correspondence, orders, reports, and returns, Union and Confederate, relating to prisoners of war, and (so far as the military authorities were concerned) to State or political prisoners.

The **3d Series** will contain the correspondence, orders, reports, and returns of the Union authorities (embracing their correspondence with the Confederate officials) not relating specially to the subjects of the *first* and *second* series. It will set forth the annual and special reports of the Secretary of War, of the General-in-Chief, and of the chiefs of the several staff corps and departments; the calls for troops, and the correspondence between the National and the several State authorities.

The **4th Series** will exhibit the correspondence, orders, reports, and returns of the Confederate authorities, similar to that indicated for the Union officials, as of the *third* series, but excluding the correspondence between the Union and Confederate authorities given in that series.

ROBERT N. SCOTT,
Major, Third Art., and Bvt. Lieut. Col.

WAR DEPARTMENT, *August* 23, 1880.

Approved:

ALEX. RAMSEY,
Secretary of War.

THE

WAR OF THE REBELLION:

A COMPILATION OF THE

OFFICIAL RECORDS

OF THE

UNION AND CONFEDERATE ARMIES.

ADDITIONS AND CORRECTIONS

TO

SERIES I—VOLUME IX.

(To be inserted in the volume. For explanation see General
Index volume, Serial No. 130, page XXVIII.)

PUBLISHED UNDER THE DIRECTION OF

The Hon. ELIHU ROOT, Secretary of War,

BY

BRIG. GEN. FRED C. AINSWORTH,

CHIEF OF THE RECORD AND PENSION OFFICE, WAR DEPARTMENT,

AND

MR. JOSEPH W. KIRKLEY.

Mr. JOHN S. MOODEY, Indexer.

WASHINGTON:
GOVERNMENT PRINTING OFFICE.
1902.

TEXT.

Page   6.   Erase foot-note and insert *See Series I, Vol. 51, Part 1, p. 58.*

Page   15.   Organization table, Roberts' command, erase *Mounted Rifles (2 companies).*

Page   85.   Foster's report, second line, for *observations* read *operations.*

Page   112.   Second line, bottom, for [*General Wise*] read *embarrassments,* and for *marhed* read *marked.*

Page   214.   Twenty-eighth line, top, insert † after *Surg. J. H. Thompson* and add foot-note, † *Medals of Honor awarded to Surg. J. H. Thompson, U. S. Volunteers, and Private John D. Terry, Company E, Twenty-third Massachusetts Infantry, for gallantry in action.*

Page   261.   Ninth line, top, for *Shoffner* read *Shaffner.*

Page   328.   Twenty-seventh line, bottom, for *Nesbet's* read *Nisbet's.*

Page   349.   Sanford's report, caption, for *Twelfth* read *Twenty-seventh.*

Page   431.   First line, for *D. K. Jones* read *D. R. Jones.* Seventh line, top, for *Magruder's* read *McGruder's.*

Page   437.   Erase foot-note *Not found. See Davis to Avery, p. 435,* and insert *See Series I, Vol. 51, Part 2, p. 471.*

Page   447.   Special Orders, No. 53, tenth line, for *L. H. Rogers'* read *S. H. Rogers'.*

Page   460.   Branch's Brigade, insert *Brem's* before *North Carolina Battery.*

Page   469.   Indorsement No. 2, second line, for *necessary* read *unnecessary.*

Page   481.   Insert *March 3, 1862.—Action at Comanche Pass, N. Mex.*

Page   568.   Erase foot-note and insert *Omitted.*

Page   601.   Foot-note, for *inclosure G* read *inclosure No. 1.*

Page   616.   Erase foot-note and insert *Omitted. Shows 4 killed and 19 wounded.*

Page   684.   Thirteenth line, top, for *on* read *over.*

Page   731.   General Orders, No. 1, first line, erase *First.*

INDEX.

Insert all words and figures in *italics* and strike out all in [brackets]. An asterisk (*) following a correction indicates that "Additions and Corrections" to the text should be consulted.

CONTENTS.

CHAPTER XIX.

(v)

CONTENTS OF PRECEDING VOLUMES.

(VI)

CHAPTER XIX.

OPERATIONS IN SOUTHEASTERN VIRGINIA.

January 11–March 17, 1862.

**MARCH 8–9, 1862.—Naval engagement in Hampton Roads, Va., and de-
struction of the U. S. frigate Congress and sloop-of-war Cumberland by the
Confederate iron-clad Virginia (formerly the Merrimac).**

REPORTS.

No. 1.

Extract from Annual Report of the Secretary of the Navy.

DECEMBER 1, 1862.

*　　*　　*　　*　　*　　*　　*

It was the intention and constant effort of the Department and contractors that the Monitor should be completed in the month of January,
but there was delay in consequence of difficulties incident to an undertaking of such novelty and magnitude, and there were also some slight
defects, which were, however, promptly remedied, and she left New York
early in March, reaching Hampton Roads on the night of the 8th.

Her arrival, though not as soon as anticipated, was most opportune and important. For some time the Department had heard with great solicitude of the progress which the insurgents had made in armoring and equipping the large war-steamer Merrimac, which had fallen into their hands when Norfolk was abandoned. On the afternoon of the 8th of March this formidable vessel, heavily armored and armed and fully prepared to operate both as a ram and a war steamer, came down the Elizabeth River, accompanied by several smaller steamers, two of them partially armored, to attack the vessels of the blockading squadron that were in and about Hampton Roads. When the Merrimac and her attendants made their appearance the Congress and the Cumberland, two sailing vessels, were anchored off Newport News, and the remaining vessels were in the vicinity of Fortress Monroe, some 6 miles distant. The Minnesota, the Roanoke, and the St. Lawrence got immediately under way and proceeded toward the scene of action.

The Congress, being nearest to the Merrimac, was the first to receive her fire, which was promptly returned by a full broadside, the shots falling apparently harmlessly off from the armored side of the assailant. Passing by the Congress, the Merrimac dashed upon the Cumberland, and was received by her with a heavy, well-directed, and vigorous fire, which, like that of the Congress, produced unfortunately but little effect. A contest so unequal could not be of long continuance, and it was closed when the Merrimac, availing herself of her power as a steam ram, ran furiously against the Cumberland, laying open her wooden hull, and causing her almost immediately to sink. As her guns approached the water's edge her young commander, Lieutenant Morris, and the gallant crew stood firm at their posts, delivered a parting fire, and the good ship went down heroically, with her colors flying. Having thus destroyed the Cumberland, the Merrimac turned again upon the Congress, which had, in the mean time, been engaged with the smaller rebel steamers, and after a heavy loss, in order to guard against such a fate as that which had befallen the Cumberland, had been run aground. The Merrimac now selected a raking position astern of the Congress, while one of the smaller steamers poured in a constant fire on her starboard quarter. Two other steamers of the enemy also approached from James River, firing upon the unfortunate frigate with precision and severe effect. The guns of the Congress were almost entirely disabled, and her gallant commanding officer, Lieut. Joseph B. Smith, had fallen at his post. Her decks were strewn with the dead and dying, the ship was on fire in several places, and not a gun could be brought to bear upon the assailants. In this state of things, and with no effectual relief at hand, the senior surviving officer, Lieutenant Pendergrast, felt it his duty to save further useless destruction of life by hauling down his colors. This was done about 4 o'clock p. m. The Congress continued to burn till about 8 in the evening and then blew up.

From the Congress the Merrimac turned her attention to the remaining vessels of the squadron. The Roanoke had grounded on her way to the scene of the conflict; and although she succeeded in getting off, her condition was such, her propeller being useless, that she took no part in the action. The St. Lawrence also grounded near the Minnesota and had a short engagement with the Merrimac, but suffered no serious injury, and on getting afloat was ordered back to Fortress Monroe.

The Minnesota, which had also got aground in the shallow waters of the channel, became the special object of attack, and the Merrimac, with the Yorktown and Jamestown, bore down upon her. The Merrimac drew too much water to approach very near; her fire was not therefore particularly effective. The other steamers selected their position, fired with much accuracy, and caused considerable damage to the Minnesota. She soon, however, succeeded in getting a gun to bear on the two smaller steamers and drove them away—one apparently in a crippled condition. About 7 p. m. the Merrimac also hauled off, and the three stood toward Norfolk.

All efforts to get the Minnesota afloat during the night and into a safe position were totally unavailing. The morning was looked for with deep anxiety, as it would in all probability bring a renewed attack from the formidable assailant. At this critical and anxious moment the Monitor, one of the newly-finished armored vessels, came into Hampton Roads, from New York, under command of Lieut. John L. Worden, and a little after midnight anchored alongside the Minnesota. At 6 o'clock the next morning the Merrimac, as anticipated, again made her appearance, and opened her fire upon the Minnesota. Promptly obeying the signal to attack, the Monitor ran down past the Minnesota and laid herself close alongside the Merrimac, between that formidable vessel and the Minnesota. The fierce conflict between these two ironclads lasted for several hours. It was in appearance an unequal conflict, for the Merrimac was a large and noble structure, and the Monitor was in comparison almost diminutive. But the Monitor was strong in her armor, in the ingenious novelty of her construction, in the large caliber of her two guns, and the valor and skill with which she was handled. After several hours' fighting the Merrimac found herself overmatched, and, leaving the Monitor, sought to renew the attack on the Minnesota; but the Monitor again placed herself between the two vessels and reopened her fire upon her adversary. At noon the Merrimac, seriously damaged, abandoned the contest and, with her companions, retreated toward Norfolk.

Thus terminated the most remarkable naval combat of modern times, perhaps of any age. The fiercest and most formidable naval assault upon the power of the Union which has ever been made by the insurgents was heroically repelled, and a new era was opened in the history of maritime warfare.

* *

No. 2.

Report of Maj. Gen. John E. Wool, U. S. Army, commanding Department of Virginia.

HEADQUARTERS DEPARTMENT OF VIRGINIA,
Fort Monroe, Va., March 9, 1862.

GENERAL: Two hours after I sent my hurried dispatch to the Secretary of War last evening the Monitor arrived, and saved the Minnesota and the St. Lawrence, which were both aground when she arrived.

The Merrimac, supported by the Yorktown and Jamestown, commenced an attack on the Minnesota (still aground) early this morning, and after a contest of five hours was driven off in a sinking condition by the Monitor, aided by the Minnesota, and towed by the Jamestown and Yorktown toward Norfolk, for the purpose, no doubt, of getting her, if possible, in the dry-dock for repairs.

It is reported that Magruder is approaching Newport News with a large force of infantry. I have re-enforced that post with three regiments, a light battery of six pieces, and a company of dragoons. The command will consist altogether of over or about 8,000 men. My command consists altogether of 10,000 effective men.

The Cumberland was sunk, and we lost more than one-half of her crew. The Congress surrendered, but the crew was released and the officers taken as prisoners. The Minnesota has got off, but it is reported she is in a sinking condition.

It is to be hoped that I will be largely re-enforced, including two additional light batteries. The Monitor is far superior to the Merrimac. The first has only two guns, while the Merrimac has eight.

I have the honor to be, very respectfully, your obedient servant,

JOHN E. WOOL,
Major-General.

Maj. Gen. GEORGE B. McCLELLAN,
Commanding the Army, Washington, D. C.

[Similar report to Secretary of War.]

No. 3.

Report of Brig. Gen. Joseph K. F. Mansfield, U. S. Army, commanding brigade.

HDQRS. FIRST BRIG., FIRST DIV., DEPT. OF VIRGINIA,
Newport News, Va., March 10, 1862.

SIR: I have the honor to report that in the forenoon of Saturday, the 8th instant, the commanders of the Congress and Cumberland, at anchor in the stream, notified me that the iron-clad Merrimac steamer of the enemy was approaching from Norfolk to attack them, and I immediately telegraphed you to that effect. At about 2 o'clock p. m. she approached very near these vessels slowly. engaged first the Congress and passed on to the Cumberland and ran into her, and all within a mile of our batteries. I immediately ordered Lieut. Col. G. Nauman, chief of artillery, to open our batteries of four columbaids and one 42-pounder James gun to fire on her. It was done with alacrity, and kept up continuously with spirit as long as she was in range, and although our shot often struck her, they made no impression on her at all. I also ordered three of our 8-inch siege howitzers from the land batteries hauled by hand and brought to bear on her from the bank of the river and two of Howard's light battery rifled guns, but no visible serious damage to her from our guns was done, such was the strength of her mail.

As soon as the Cumberland was sunk three steamers, supposed to be the Yorktown, Jamestown, and a tug, came down the river from Day's Point under full head of steam. Our guns were then turned on them, but they kept at a distance and moved rapidly past, and received but little damage from us.

During the sinking of the Cumberland the Congress slipped her cable and hoisted sail and ran ashore just above Signal Point, where many of her men escaped to the shore, and was there followed by the Merrimac, and after two raking shots she hauled down her flag and·

hoisted a white flag and ceased action. The enemy then sent two steamers with Confederate flags flying and made fast on either side of her, with a view to haul her off or burn her. As soon as I saw this I ordered Colonel Brown, of the Twentieth Indiana Regiment, then close at hand, to send two rifle companies (A and K) to the beach. The two rifled guns, under Captain Howard, and a rifled Dahlgren howitzer, manned by Master Stuyvesant and 14 sailors of the Cumberland, went into action from a raking position on the beach, covered by sand banks and trees, against these steamers.

We here had them at about 800 yards to advantage, and immediately they let go their hold on the Congress and moved out of range with much loss. They endeavored to approach her again with a steamer and row-boat, but were beaten off with loss, till finally the Merrimac, finding her prize retaken, approached and fired three shots into her and set her on fire. The remaining men escaped from the Congress over the bows of the ship to the shore, assisted by our boats, and the wounded were removed by dark.

Thus closed the tragedy of the day. The enemy retired at dark toward the opposite shore, and the Congress illuminated the heavens and varied the scene by the firing of her own guns and the flight of her balls through the air till about 2 o'clock in the morning, when her magazine exploded and a column of burning matter appeared high in the air, to be followed by the stillness of death. Through the whole day our troops were under arms, and the officers and men engaged at the batteries and as riflemen on the beach performed their duty well, and the enemy were beaten off wherever we could penetrate them. All was done that it was possible to do under the circumstances to save these ships from the enemy. Some officers and men from the Cumberland, as they escaped to the shore, came forward and volunteered their services at our guns and afforded aid. Toward the close of the day the enemy must have experienced considerable loss. There were none killed of my command, and but one man, private of the Seventh New York Volunteers, severely wounded by a shell from the Merrimac, resulting in the loss of his leg.

The loss on the part of our Navy must have been great by the bursting of shells and the drowning by the sinking of the Cumberland, although our best efforts were made to save them. Our ships were perfectly helpless against the Merrimac, as their broadsides produced no material effect on her.

All of which is respectfully submitted.

JOS. K. F. MANSFIELD,
Brigadier-General, Commanding.

Maj. Gen. JOHN E. WOOL,
Commanding Department of Virginia.

No. 4.

Report of Col. David W. Wardrop, Ninety-ninth New York Infantry.

HDQRS. UNION COAST GUARD, 99TH REGT., N. Y. V.,
Camp Hamilton, Va., March 20, 1862.

SIR: I have this morning received the official report of Capt. William J. McIntire, commanding Company D, of this regiment, who have been doing duty on board of the U. S. frigate Congress from January 13 until March 8, when they were attacked by the rebel iron-clad gunboat Merrimac, or Virginia, and forced to surrender after the ship was ashore and helpless. Captain McIntire reports 9 killed, 10 wounded, 7 missing.*

Respectfully, your obedient servant,

D. W. WARDROP,
Colonel, Commanding Ninety-ninth Regiment, N. Y. V.

Lieutenant CHARLES LORCH,
Post-Adjutant, Camp Hamilton.

No. 5.

Report of Maj. Gen. Benjamin Huger, C. S. Army, commanding Department of Norfolk.

HEADQUARTERS DEPARTMENT OF NORFOLK,
Norfolk, Va., March 10, 1862.

SIR : I telegraphed yesterday to the Secretary of War the fact of the naval engagement on the 8th and 9th instant. As the battle was fought by the Navy, Flag-Officer Forrest will no doubt report to the Navy Department the result of the engagement.

The batteries at Sewell's Point opened fire on the steamers Minnesota and Roanoke, which attempted on the 8th to pass to Newport News to the assistance of the frigates attacked by the Virginia. The Minnesota ran aground before reaching there. The Roanoke was struck several times, and for some cause turned around and went back to Old Point.

The two sailing vessels (Cumberland and Congress) were destroyed— the first sunk and the other burned by the Virginia—and on the 9th the Minnesota, still aground, would probably have been destroyed but for the iron-clad battery of the enemy called, I think, the Monitor. The Virginia and this battery were in actual contact, without inflicting serious injury on either.

At 2 p. m. on yesterday, the 9th, all our vessels came up to the navy-yard for repairs. The Virginia, I understand, has gone into dock for repairs, which will be made at once. This action shows the power and endurance of iron-clad vessels; cannon-shot do not harm them, and they can pass batteries or destroy large ships. A vessel like the Virginia or the Monitor, with her two guns, can pass any of our batteries with impunity. The only means of stopping them is by vessels of the same kind. The Virginia, being the most powerful, can stop the Monitor; but a more powerful one would run her down or ashore. As the enemy can build such boats faster than we, they could, when so prepared, overcome any place accessible by water. How these powerful machines are to be stopped is a problem I cannot solve. At present, in the Virginia, we have the advantage; but we cannot tell how long this may last.

I remain, very respectfully, your obedient servant,

BENJ. HUGER,
Major-General, Commanding.

General S. COOPER,
Adjutant and Inspector General.

---

* Captain McIntire's report not found.

No. 6.

Report of Confederate Secretary of the Navy.

EXECUTIVE DEPARTMENT,
April 10, 1862.

To the Senate and House of Representatives of the Confederate States:

I herewith transmit to Congress a communication from the Secretary of the Navy, covering a detailed report of Flag-Officer Buchanan of the brilliant triumph of his squadron over the vastly superior forces of the enemy in Hampton Roads, March 8 and 9 last.

JEFFERSON DAVIS.

NAVY DEPARTMENT,
Richmond, Va., April 7, 1862.

SIR: I have the honor to submit herewith [a] copy of the detailed report [No. 7] of Flag-Officer Buchanan of the brilliant triumph of his squadron over the vastly superior forces of the enemy in Hampton Roads, on March 8 and 9 last, a brief report by Lieutenant Jones of the battle of the 8th having been previously made.

The conduct of the officers and men of the squadron in this contest reflects unfading honor upon themselves and upon the Navy. The report will be read with deep interest, and its details will not fail to arouse the ardor and nerve the arms of our gallant seamen.

It will be remembered that the Virginia was a novelty in naval architecture, wholly unlike any ship that ever floated; that her heaviest guns were equal novelties in ordnance; that her motive power and her obedience to her helm were untried, and her officers and crew strangers comparatively to the ship and to each other, and yet, under all these disadvantages, the dashing courage and consummate professional ability of Flag-Officer Buchanan and his associates achieved the most remarkable victory which naval annals record.

When the flag-officer was disabled the command of the Virginia devolved upon her executive and ordnance officer, Lieut. Catesby Ap R. Jones, and the cool and masterly manner in which he fought the ship in her encounter with the iron-clad Monitor justified the high estimate which the country places upon his professional merit. To his experience, skill, and untiring industry as her ordnance and executive officer the terrible effect of her fire was greatly due. Her battery was determined in accordance with his suggestions, and in all investigations and tests which resulted in its thorough efficiency he was zealously engaged.

The terms of commendation used by the flag-officer in characterizing the conduct of his officers and men meet the cordial indorsement of the Department, and the concurrent testimony of thousands who witnessed the engagement places his own conduct above all praise.

With much respect, your obedient servant,

S. R. MALLORY,
Secretary of the Navy.

To the PRESIDENT.

No. 7.

Report of Flag-Officer Franklin Buchanan, C. S. Navy.

NAVAL HOSPITAL,
Norfolk, Va., March 27, 1862.

SIR: Having been confined to my bed in this building since the 9th instant, in consequence of a wound received in the action of the previous day, I have not had it in my power at an earlier date to prepare the official report, which I now have the honor to submit, of the proceedings on the 8th and 9th instant of the James River squadron, under my command, composed of the following-named vessels: Steamer Virginia, flag-ship, ten guns; steamer Patrick Henry, Commander John R. Tucker, twelve guns; steamer Jamestown, Lieut. Commanding J. N. Barney, two guns; and gunboats Teazer, Lieut. Commanding W. A. Webb; Beaufort, Lieut. Commanding W. H. Parker; and Raleigh, Lieut. Commanding J. W. Alexander, each one gun. Total, twenty-seven guns.

On the 8th instant, at 11 a. m., the Virginia left the navy-yard (Norfolk), accompanied by the Raleigh and Beaufort, and proceeded to Newport News, to engage the enemy's frigates Cumberland and Congress, gunboats, and shore batteries. When within less than a mile of the Cumberland the Virginia commenced the engagement with that ship with her bow gun, and the action soon became general, the Cumberland, Congress, gunboats, and shore batteries concentrating upon us their heavy fire, which was returned with great spirit and determination. The Virginia stood rapidly on toward the Cumberland, which ship.I had determined to sink with our prow if possible. In about fifteen minutes after the action commenced we ran into her on her starboard bow. The crash below the water was distinctly heard, and she commenced sinking, gallantly fighting her guns as long as they were above water. She went down with her colors flying.

During this time the shore batteries, Congress, and gunboats kept up their heavy concentrated fire upon us, doing us some injury. Our guns, however, were not idle; their fire was very destructive to the shore batteries and vessels, and we were gallantly sustained by the rest of the squadron.

Just after the Cumberland sunk that gallant officer Commander John R. Tucker was seen standing down James River under full steam, accompanied by the Jamestown and Teazer. They all came nobly into action and were soon exposed to the heavy fire of shore batteries. Their escape was miraculous, as they were under a galling fire of solid shot, shell, grape, and canister, a number of which passed through the vessels without doing any serious injury, except to the Patrick Henry, through whose boiler a shot passed, scalding to death four persons and wounding others. Lieutenant-Commanding Barney promptly obeyed a signal to tow her out of the action. As soon as damages were repaired the Patrick Henry returned to her station and continued to perform good service during the remainder of that day and the following.

Having sunk the Cumberland, I turned our attention to the Congress. We were some time in getting our proper position in consequence of the shoalness of the water and the great difficulty of managing the ship when in or near the mud. To succeed in my object I was obliged to run the ship a short distance above the batteries on James River in order to wind her. During all the time her keel was in the mud; of course she moved but slowly. Thus we were subjected twice to the heavy guns of all the batteries in passing up and down the river, but it could not be avoided. We silenced several of the batteries and did much injury on shore. A large transport steamer alongside the wharf was blown up, one schooner sunk, and another captured and sent to Norfolk. The loss of life on shore we have no means of ascertaining.

While the Virginia was thus engaged in getting her position for attacking the Congress the prisoners state it was believed on board that ship that we had hauled off. The men left their guns and gave three cheers. They were soon sadly undeceived, for a few minutes after we opened upon her again, she having run on shore in shoal water. The carnage, havoc, and dismay caused by our fire compelled them to haul down their colors and to hoist a white flag at their gaff and half-mast and another at the main. The crew instantly took to their boats and landed. Our fire immediately ceased, and a signal was made for the Beaufort to come within hail. I then ordered Lieutenant-Commanding Parker to take possession of the Congress, secure the officers as prisoners, allow the crew to land, and burn the ship. He ran alongside, received her flag and surrender from Commander William Smith and Lieutenant Pendergrast, with the side-arms of those officers. They delivered themselves as prisoners of war on board the Beaufort, and afterward were permitted at their own request to return to the Congress to assist in removing the wounded to the Beaufort. They never returned, and I submit to the decision of the Department whether they are not our prisoners. While the Beaufort and Raleigh were alongside the Congress, and the surrender of that vessel had been received from the commander, she having two white flags flying, hoisted by our own people, a heavy fire was opened upon them from the shore and from the Congress, killing some valuable officers and men. Under this fire the steamers left the Congress, but as I was not informed that any injury had been sustained by those vessels at that time, Lieutenant-Commanding Parker having failed to report to me, I took it for granted that my order to him to burn her had been executed, and waited some minutes to see the smoke ascending from her hatches. During this delay we were still subject to the heavy fire from the batteries, which was always promptly returned.

The steam frigates Minnesota and Roanoke and the sailing frigate St. Lawrence had previously been reported as coming from Old Point, but as I was determined that the Congress should not again fall into the hands of the enemy, I remarked to that gallant young officer Flag-Lieutenant Minor, "That ship must be burned." He promptly volunteered to take a boat and burn her, and the Teazer, Lieutenant-Commanding Webb, was ordered to cover the boat. Lieutenant Minor had scarcely reached within 50 yards of the Congress when a deadly fire was opened upon him, wounding him severely and several of his men. On witnessing this vile treachery I instantly recalled the boat and ordered the Congress destroyed by hot shot and incendiary shell. About this period I was disabled, and transferred the command of the ship to that gallant, intelligent officer Lieut. Catesby Jones, with orders to fight her as long as the men could stand to their guns.

The ships from Old Point opened their fire upon us. The Minnesota grounded in the north channel, where, unfortunately, the shoalness of the channel prevented our near approach. We continued, however, to fire upon her until the pilots declared it was no longer safe to remain in that position, and we accordingly returned by the south channel (the middle ground being necessarily between the Virginia and Minnesota, and St. Lawrence and the Roanoke having retreated under the guns of Old Point), and again had an opportunity of opening upon the Minnesota, receiving her heavy fire in return, and shortly afterward upon the St. Lawrence, from which vessel was received several broadsides. It had by this time become dark and we soon after anchored off Sewell's Point. The rest of the squadron followed our movements, with the exception of the Beaufort, Lieutenant-Commanding Parker, who proceeded to Norfolk with the wounded and prisoners as soon as he had left the Congress, without reporting to me. The Congress, having been set on fire by our hot shot and incendiary shell, continued to burn, her loaded guns being successively discharged as the flames reached them, until a few minutes past midnight, when her magazine exploded with a tremendous report.

The facts above stated as having occurred after I had placed the ship in charge of Lieutenant Jones were reported to me by that officer.

At an early hour next morning (the 9th), upon the urgent solicitations of the surgeons, Lieutenant Minor and myself were very reluctantly taken on shore. The accommodations for the proper treatment of wounded persons on board the Virginia are exceedingly limited, Lieutenant Minor and myself occupying the only space that could be used for that purpose, which was in my cabin. I therefore consented to our being landed on Sewell's Point, thinking that the room on board vacated by us could be used for those who might be wounded in the renewal of the action. In the course of the day Lieutenant Minor and myself were sent in a steamer to the hospital at Norfolk.

The following is an extract from the report of Lieutenant Jones of the proceedings of the Virginia on the 9th:

At daylight on the 9th we saw that the Minnesota was still ashore, and that there was an iron battery near her. At 8 [o'clock] we ran down to engage them (having previously sent the killed and wounded out of the ship), firing at the Minnesota and occasionally at the iron-battery. The pilots did not place us as near as they expected. The great length and draught of the ship rendered it exceedingly difficult to work her. We ran ashore about a mile from the frigate, and were backing fifteen minutes before we got off. We continued to fire at the Minnesota, and blew up a steamer alongside of her, and we also engaged the Monitor, and sometimes at very close quarters. We once succeeded in running into her, and twice silenced her fire. The pilots declaring that we could get no nearer the Minnesota, and believing her to be entirely disabled, and the Monitor having run into shoal water, which prevented our doing her any further injury, we ceased firing at 12 [o'clock] and proceeded to Norfolk.

Our loss is 2 killed and 19 wounded. The stem is twisted and the ship leaks. We have lost the prow, starboard anchor, and all the boats. The armor is somewhat damaged; the steam-pipe and smoke-stack both riddled; the muzzles of two of the guns shot away. It was not easy to keep a flag flying. The flag-staffs were repeatedly shot away. The colors were hoisted to the smoke-stack and several times cut down from it.

The bearing of the men was all that could be desired; the enthusiasm could scarcely be restrained. During the action they cheered again and again. Their coolness and skill were the more remarkable from the fact that the great majority of them were under fire for the first time. They were strangers to each other and to the officers, and had but a few days' instruction in the management of the great guns. To the skill and example of the officers is this result in no small degree attributable.

Having thus given a full report of the actions on the 8th and 9th, I feel it due to the gallant officers who so nobly sustained the honor of the flag and country on those days to express my appreciation of their conduct.

To that brave and intelligent officer Lieut. Catesby Jones, the executive and ordnance officer of the Virginia, I am greatly indebted for the success achieved. His constant attention to his duties in the equipment of the ship; his intelligence in the instruction of ordnance to the crew, as proved by the accuracy and effect of their fire, some of the guns having been personally directed by him; his tact and management in the government of raw recruits; his general knowledge of the executive duties of a man-of-war, together with his high-toned bearing, were all eminently conspicuous, and had their fruits in the admirable efficiency of the Virginia. If conduct such as his (and I do not know that I have used adequate language in describing it) entitles an officer to promotion, I see in the case of Lieutenant Jones one in all respects worthy of it. As flag-officer I am entitled to some one to perform the duties of flag-captain, and I should be proud to have Lieutenant Jones ordered to the Virginia as lieutenant-commandant, if it be not the intention of the Department to bestow upon him a higher rank.

Lieutenant Simms fully sustained his well-earned reputation. He fired the first gun, and when the command devolved upon Lieutenant Jones, in consequence of my disability, he was ordered to perform the duties of executive officer. Lieutenant Jones has expressed to me his satisfaction in having had the services of so experienced, energetic, and zealous an officer.

Lieutenant Davidson fought his guns with great precision. The muzzle of one of them was soon shot away. He continued, however, to fire it, though the wood work around the port became ignited at each discharge. His buoyant and cheerful bearing and voice were contagious and inspiring.

Lieutenant Wood handled his pivot gun admirably, and the executive officer testifies to his valuable suggestions during the action. His zeal and industry in drilling the crew contributed materially to our success.

Lieutenant Eggleston served his hot shot and shell with judgment and effect, and his bearing was deliberate, and exerted a happy influence on his division.

Lieutenant Butt fought his gun with activity and during the action was gay and smiling.

The Marine Corps was well represented by Captain Thom, whose tranquil mien gave evidence that the hottest fire was no novelty to him. One of his guns was served effectively and creditably by a detachment of the United Artillery of Norfolk, under the command of Captain Kevill. The muzzle of their gun was struck by a shell from the enemy, which broke off a piece of the gun, but they continued to fire as if it was uninjured.

Midshipmen Foute, Marmaduke, Littlepage, Craig, and Long rendered valuable services. Their conduct would have been creditable to older heads, and gave great promise of future usefulness. Midshipman Marmaduke, though receiving several painful wounds early in the action, manfully fought his gun until the close. He is now at the hospital.

Paymaster Semple volunteered for any service, and was assigned to the command of the powder division, an important and complicated duty, which could not have been better performed.

Surgeon Phillips and Assistant Surgeon Garnett were prompt and attentive in the discharge of their duties. Their kind and considerate care of the wounded and the skill and ability displayed in the treatment won for them the esteem and gratitude of all who came under their charge, and justly entitled them to the confidence of officers and crew. I beg leave to call the attention of the Department to the case of Dr. Garnett. He stands deservedly high in his profession, is at the head of the list of assistant surgeons, and there being a vacancy in consequence of the recent death of Surgeon Blacknall, I should be much gratified if Dr. Garnett could be promoted to it.

The engines and machinery, upon which so much depended, performed much better than was expected. This is due to the intelligence, experience, and coolness of Acting Chief Engineer Ramsey. His efforts were ably seconded by his assistants, Tynan, Campbell, Herring, Jack, and White. As Mr. Ramsey is only acting chief engineer, I respectfully recommend his promotion to the rank of chief; and would also ask that Second Assistant Engineer Campbell may be promoted to first assistant, he having performed the duties of that grade during the engagement.

The forward officers—Boatswain Hasker, Gunner Oliver, and Carpenter Lindsey—discharged well all the duties required of them. The boatswain had charge of a gun and fought it well. The gunner was indefatigable in his efforts. His experience and exertions as a gunner have contributed very materially to the efficiency of the battery.

Acting Master Parrish was assisted in piloting the ship by Pilots Wright, Williams, Clark, and Cunningham. They were necessarily much exposed.

It is now due that I should mention my personal staff. To that gallant young officer Flag-Lieutenant Minor I am much indebted for his promptness in the execution of signals; for renewing the flag-staffs when shot away, being thereby greatly exposed; for his watchfulness in keeping the Confederate flag up; his alacrity in conveying my orders to the different divisions, and for his general cool and gallant bearing.

My aide, Acting Midshipman Rootes, of the Navy; Lieutenant Forrest, of the Army, who served as a volunteer aide, and my clerk, Mr. Arthur St. Clair, jr., are entitled to my thanks for the activity with which my orders were conveyed to the different parts of the ship. During the hottest of the fight they were always at their posts, giving evidence of their coolness.

Having referred to the good conduct of the officers in the flag-ship immediately under my notice, I come now to a no less pleasing task when I attempt to mark my approbation of the bearing of those serving in the other vessels of the squadron.

Commander John R. Tucker, of the Patrick Henry, and Lieuts. Commanding J. N. Barney, of the Jamestown, and W. A. Webb, of the Teazer, deserve great praise for their gallant conduct throughout the engagement. Their judgment in selecting their positions for attacking the enemy was good; their constant fire was destructive, and contributed much to the success of the day. The general order under which the squadron went into action required that, in the absence of all signals, each commanding officer was to exercise his own judgment and discretion in doing all the damage he could to the enemy and to sink before surrendering. From the bearing of those officers on the 8th I am fully satisfied that that order would have been carried out.

Commander Tucker speaks highly of all under him, and desires particularly to notice that Lieutenant-Colonel Cadwallader St. George Noland, commanding the post at Mulberry Island, on hearing of the deficiency in the complement of the Patrick Henry, promptly offered the services of 10 of his men as volunteers for the occasion, one of whom, George E. Webb, of the Greenville Guards, Commander Tucker regrets to say, was killed.

Lieutenant-Commanding Barney reports every officer and man on board of the ship performed his whole duty, evincing a courage and fearlessness worthy of the cause for which we are fighting.

Lieutenant-Commanding Webb specially notices the coolness displayed by Acting Master Face and Third Assistant Engineer Quinn when facing the heavy fire of artillery and musketry from the shore while the Teazer was standing in to cover the boat in which, as previously stated, Lieutenant Minor had gone to burn the Congress. Several of his men were badly wounded.

The Raleigh, early in the action, had her gun-carriage disabled, which compelled her to withdraw. As soon as he had repaired damages as well as he could Lieutenant-Commanding Alexander resumed his position in the line. He sustained himself gallantly during the remainder of the day and speaks highly of all under his command. That evening he was ordered to Norfolk for repairs.

The Beaufort, Lieutenant-Commanding Parker, was in close contact with the enemy frequently during the day, and all on board behaved gallantly. Lieutenant-Commanding Parker expresses his warmest thanks to his officers and men for their coolness. Acting Midshipman Foreman, who accompanied him as volunteer aide; Midshipman Mallory and Newton; captain's clerk Bain, and Mr. Gray, pilot, are all specially mentioned by him.

On the 21st instant I forwarded to the Department correct lists of the casualties on board all the vessels of the squadron on the 8th; none, it appears, occurred on the 9th.

While in the act of closing this report I received the communication of the Department, dated 22d instant, relieving me temporarily of the command of the squadron for the naval defense of James River. I feel honored in being relieved by the gallant Flag-Officer Tatnall.

I much regret that I am not now in a condition to resume my command, but trust that I shall soon be restored to health, when I shall be ready for any duty that may be assigned me.

Very respectfully,

FRANKLIN BUCHANAN,
Flag-Officer.

Hon. S. R. MALLORY,
Secretary of the Navy.

No. 8.

Report of Maj. Gen. John B. Magruder, C. S. Army, commanding Department of the Peninsula, of his co-operation with naval attack.

HEADQUARTERS DEPARTMENT OF THE PENINSULA,
Young's Farm, Va., March 10, 1862.

SIR: I have the honor to acknowledge the receipt, at 9 p. m. on the 8th instant, of your telegram announcing the glorious achievement of the Confederate States war-steamer Virginia, and to report that before daylight I had troops on the way to the immediate vicinity of Newport News, and proceeded in person to join them.

On my arrival I found my advance guard, of one regiment of infantry, Colonel Cumming, Tenth Georgia, and some 300 cavalry (of ours) drawn up in line of battle within 1 mile of Newport News and 600 yards of the enemy's pickets of infantry and cavalry.

As I obtained from all quarters reliable information of the enemy's great strength, which was verified by our observation of the fort and vicinity, amounting to at least 12,000 infantry at Newport News alone, which at any moment could be increased to 18,000 from Fort Monroe, I saw that it was utterly impossible to do anything toward attacking the fort. My own troops, which are obliged to be divided to defend the two roads, Yorktown and Warwick, being when united only about 4,000 infantry, 450 cavalry, and a few pieces of light artillery, the larger number being too heavy to bring over the roads, which are recently worse than ever.

Finding, as I anticipated, that the naval attack produced no effect upon the fort except to increase its garrison, I contented myself with occupying the most advanced posts, Bethel and Young's Mill, where the troops are now.

I believe the enemy's plan was to ascend James River by land and water, to attack and capture, if possible, Jamestown Island, which would cause the fall of Yorktown, and then to occupy Suffolk, Jamestown, and West Point, and leaving Norfolk to fall with the fall of Richmond, if that could be accomplished, and to direct all his energies against the latter place. For the present his plans must be somewhat frustrated; but I consider that the Patrick Henry, Jamestown, and Teazer having gone to Norfolk, and the Virginia into the dock for repairs, affords the enemy an admirable opportunity of fully retrieving his losses by placing the Ericsson battery at the mouth of James River and ascending at once the left bank of that river, attacking, supported by the Ericsson battery, the works of Harden's Bluff and Mulberry Island Point, which are weak, and thus forcing my troops to fall back to protect Jamestown and Williamsburg and isolating and reducing Yorktown. I therefore hope that the steamers Patrick Henry, Jamestown, and Teazer may without delay ascend the James River, and should they require repairs, have them done at Richmond. When the Virginia is repaired they could join her at any moment, as she would be the mistress of the Roads.

I have not had time to report that the troops ordered to Suffolk were embarked from King's Mill wharf immediately after the reception of the orders, as I am informed. A considerable number of the regiments sent were on furlough, and I therefore sent a somewhat larger number than that called for, estimating the number by the aggregate present and absent. I presume those absent will join at once. I sent also two batteries, that of Cobb's Legion and the First Company of Howitzers, the latter being asked for by General Randolph. I have sent 350 cavalry, that number being embraced in Cobb's Legion.

I beg leave respectfully to invite the attention of the Secretary of War to my remarks in relation to the location of the three steamers.

I have at length assembled many negroes, and the defensive works begin again to progress satisfactorily.

I have the honor to be, sir, very respectfully, your obedient servant,

J. BANKHEAD MAGRUDER,
Major-General, Commanding.

General COOPER,
Adjutant and Inspector General.

CORRESPONDENCE, ORDERS, AND RETURNS RELATING SPECIALLY TO OPERATIONS IN SOUTHEASTERN VIRGINIA FROM JANUARY 11 TO MARCH 17, 1862.

UNION CORRESPONDENCE, ETC.

Abstract from return of the Department of Virginia, Maj. Gen. John E. Wool, U. S. Army, commanding, for January, 1862.

Commands.	Present for duty.		Aggregate present.	Aggregate present and absent.	Pieces of artillery.	
	Officers.	Men.			Heavy.	Field.
Department staff..	16	....	16	17	......	......
Fort Monroe..	48	1,280	1,534	1,614	223	23
Camp Hamilton...	164	4,365	5,159	5,941	......	......
Camp Butler...	150	3,301	4,134	4,376	......	......
Fort Calhoun...	7	150	165	184	......	......
Total..	385	9,096	11,008	12,132	223	23

Organizations in the Department of Virginia, January 31, 1862.

FORT MONROE.

Maj. JOSEPH ROBERTS, 4th U. S. Artillery.

10th New York.
99th New York (1 company).
6th Massachusetts Battery.
4th U. S. Artillery, Batteries D and L.
Wisconsin Light Artillery.
Mounted Rifles (2 companies).

CAMP BUTLER.*

Brig. Gen. JOSEPH K. F. MANSFIELD.

29th Massachusetts.
1st New York.
2d New York.
7th New York.
11th New York.

CAMP HAMILTON.†

Col. MAX WEBER, 20th New York.

1st Delaware.
20th Indiana.
16th Massachusetts.
20th New York.
99th New York (6 companies).
11th Pennsylvania Cavalry.
Mounted Rifles (4 companies).

FORT CALHOUN ‡

Lieut. Col. G. B. HELLEDAY, 99th New York.

99th New York (2 companies).

WASHINGTON, D. C., *February* 21; 1862—4 p. m.

Maj. Gen. JOHN E. WOOL, *Fort Monroe:*

The iron-clad steam Monitor and a large frigate will be at Hampton Roads within the time you specify. Do you need troops to replace those intended for General Butler; if so, how many? With the co-operation of the Navy, how many additional troops do you need to take Yorktown, and how many by a subsequent operation to take Norfolk? Send me your best map of Norfolk and vicinity. Please communicate

---

* Newport News.
† Across Mill Creek, near Fort Monroe.
‡ Rip Raps; name changed to Fort Wool.

fully. Let me hear from you every day. Can you take the Sewell's Point Battery? If so, do it and spike the guns.

GEO. B. McCLELLAN,
Major-General, Commanding U. S. A.

WAR DEPARTMENT,
Washington City, D. C., February 22, 1862.

Maj. Gen. JOHN E. WOOL,
Commanding at Fortress Monroe:

GENERAL: Your dispatch of the 20th,* in relation to the expected attack on Newport News, has been received and communicated to the Secretary of the Navy and the General Commanding.

Accept my thanks for your prompt and vigilant attention. It will be the aim of this Department to support you in every particular you may deem essential to the good of the service. You have its perfect confidence and respect.

Yours, truly,

EDWIN M. STANTON,
Secretary of War.

HEADQUARTERS DEPARTMENT OF VIRGINIA,
Fort Monroe, Va., February 23, 1862.

Hon. E. M. STANTON, *Secretary of War:*

SIR: * * * Yesterday I had the honor to receive your telegram, by which I am informed that an iron-clad steamer and a large frigate would be in Hampton Roads within five days, the time stated when the Merrimac, Yorktown, and Jamestown would attack Newport News.

On land I will be prepared for them, and if the steamer and frigate arrive we will be well prepared for them on the water.

I have not time before the mail leaves to give you all the information you desire. I have only time to say, give me 20,000 men, including one regiment of regulars, in addition to those I now have, with two companies of artillery, and four field batteries in addition to the two I now have, which are nearly complete, wanting only a few horses and harness, with boats sufficient to transport several thousand men, and I will, with Burnside's co-operation, take Norfolk, provided I can have aid from the Navy and can be furnished with land transportation. All the boats we had at the post were given to the Hatteras expedition; consequently I have none that will answer for landing of troops.

I have a plan which will be presented to you by Colonel Cram, with a map, who will also be able to explain it to you in detail, and if I can be furnished with the means necessary and the co-operation of General Burnside I have no doubt of success against Norfolk, and, with aid from the Navy, against Yorktown. If we were prepared now it would be more readily accomplished than at a future day. I prefer to have my plan explained by the colonel, because it is less likely to become public.

---

* Not found.

Colonel Cram has a similar dispatch for Major-General McClellan, which is in accordance with his telegram.

I have the honor to be, very respectfully, your obedient servant,

JOHN E. WOOL,
Major-General.

———

HEADQUARTERS DEPARTMENT OF VIRGINIA,
Fort Monroe, Va., February 23, 1862.

Hon. E. M. STANTON, *Secretary of War:*

DEAR SIR: Colonel Cram, my senior aide-de-camp, will present you with a dispatch and a most excellent map, by which he will explain in detail my plans for taking Norfolk, Yorktown, and Richmond.

There has been no time in the last three months until recently that Richmond could not have been taken with 50,000 men, and even with a less force. At all events 50,000 men menacing Richmond would not have failed to have relieved Washington. Fifty thousand men menacing the enemy in the rear and 150,000 advancing in front, the rebel army would have been destroyed.

In conclusion, I would commend to your special attention Col. T. J. Cram. I am in want of another brigadier-general, having but one, who is at Newport News. Colonel Cram would make as efficient a brigadier-general as any other in service.

I have the honor to be, very respectfully, your obedient servant,

JOHN E. WOOL,
Major-General.

P. S.—A steamer has this moment arrived, bringing 372 returned prisoners from the South, of whom 345 are non-commissioned officers, privates, sailors, and citizens; also 10 negroes and 17 commissioned officers, 7 of whom were held as hostages, ranking as follows, viz: Colonels Lee, Cogswell, and Wood; Major Revere; Captains Bowman, Rockwood, and Keffer, all of whom go forward this evening by boat to Baltimore.

———

NAVY DEPARTMENT, *March* 6, 1862—4.10 p. m.

Commodore PAULDING, *Comdg. Navy-Yard, New York:*

Let the Monitor come direct to Washington, anchoring below Alexandria.

GIDEON WELLES,
Secretary Navy.

[Indorsement.]

I never received the above telegram.

JOHN L. WORDEN,
Rear Admiral, U. S. N.

———

WAR DEPARTMENT,
Washington City, D. C., March 7, 1862.

Maj. Gen. JOHN E. WOOL, *Comdg. Fortress Monroe:*

SIR: Your request to be furnished with two gunboats has been referred to the Secretary of the Navy, who informs me that—

Flag-Officer Goldsborough has withdrawn the class of vessels desired by Major-

General Wool for operations in the North Carolina waters. It is presumed he will soon return with most of them. Until that period arrives this Department has no other force to place at Hampton Roads.

Very respectfully, your obedient servant,

EDWIN M. STANTON,
Secretary of War.

NAVY DEPARTMENT,
March 7, 1862—10 p. m.

Capt. JOHN MARSTON,
Senior Naval Officer, Hampton Roads (via boat):

Send the St. Lawrence, Congress, and Cumberland immediately into the Potomac River.

Let the disposition of the remainder of the vessels at Hampton Roads be made according to your best judgment, after consultation with General Wool. Use steam to tow them up.

I will also try and send a couple of steamers from Baltimore to assist. Let there be no delay.

GIDEON WELLES,
Secretary Navy.

NAVY DEPARTMENT,
March 8, 1862.

Capt. JOHN MARSTON,
Senior Naval Officer, Hampton Roads:

The Assistant Secretary will be at Old Point by the Baltimore boat of this evening. Do not move the ships until further orders, which he will carry.

GIDEON WELLES,
Secretary Navy.

HEADQUARTERS DEPARTMENT OF VIRGINIA,
Fort Monroe, Va., March 8, 1862—9 p. m.

Hon. GIDEON WELLES,
Secretary Navy, Washington, D. C.:

Consulting with General Wool, I have ordered the frigates out of the Roads—the St. Lawrence to the Potomac, Roanoke and Minnesota to New York, the latter being disabled. The Monitor, of course, remains. If there are any of those 11-inch gunboats (I think there are two in Boston) please send them at once to this place. They can keep clear of the Merrimac and be of great assistance.

Nearly all here are of the opinion that the Merrimac is disabled. I was the nearest person to her, outside of the Monitor, and I am of opinion she is not seriously injured. I have sent a steamer for Commodore Goldsborough. I cannot see that anything more can be done by the Navy.

G. V. FOX.

WAR DEPARTMENT,
March 9, 1862.

HENRY B. RENWICK, Esq.,
21 *Fifth Avenue, corner Ninth street, New York:*

The Merrimac, an armor-clad vessel belonging to the rebels, issued from Norfolk yesterday, and captured several of the United States blockading vessels, and threatens to sweep our whole flotilla from Chesapeake Bay. Under these circumstances it is of the last importance to capture or destroy the Merrimac, and the whole wealth and power of the United States will be at command for that purpose. As this movement was anticipated and the subject of discussion between you and myself last December, you have no doubt thought of various modes by which it could be met and overcome most promptly. The Secretary of War desires you quietly to call a meeting of from three to nine persons, at your discretion, of the best judgment in naval engineering and warfare, to meet immediately at your father's house or some other convenient and suitable place, and to sit as a committee to devise the best plan of speedily accomplishing the capture or destruction of the Merrimac. I would suggest the name of Abram S. Hewitt as a member of the committee. You will bear in mind that every hour's delay to destroy the Merrimac may result in incalculable damage to the United States, and that the plan or plans for her destruction should be submitted at the earliest hour practicable for the approval of this Department, to the end that their execution may not be unnecessarily delayed a moment. To enable you to communicate hourly with this Department, the telegraphic company is directed to transmit all messages from you at the expense of the Government.

Acknowledge this dispatch the moment you receive it. Spare no pains or expense to get the committee together immediately. Act with the utmost energy. You and each member of the committee will consider this whole matter confidential.

P. H. WATSON,
Assistant Secretary of War.

HEADQUARTERS ARMY OF THE POTOMAC,
Washington, March 9, 1862.

* COMMANDING OFFICERS *Fort Delaware; Fort Mifflin; New York Harbor, N. Y.; Newport, R. I.; Fort Trumbull, New London; Boston Harbor; Portland, Me.:*

The rebel iron-clad steamer Merrimac has destroyed two of our frigates near Fort Monroe and finally retired last night to Craney Island. She may succeed in passing the batteries and go to sea. It is necessary that you at once place your post in the best possible condition for defense, and do your best to stop her should she endeavor to run by. Anything that can be effected in the way of temporary batteries should be done at once.

GEO. B. McCLELLAN,
Major-General, U. S. A.

HEADQUARTERS,
Baltimore, March 9, 1862.

Col. GOUVERNEUR K. WARREN,
Commanding Fort Federal Hill:

COLONEL: The Merrimac has come down from Norfolk and destroyed the Cumberland and the Congress. She may pass Fort Monroe and come here. You will have Forts Federal Hill and Marshall prepared for action, and take every precaution for their security against attack. This is especially necessary in regard to the latter, which has a very small garrison.

You will make the same arrangements which would be necessary if we were in the presence of an enemy.

Very respectfully, yours,

JOHN A. DIX,
Major-General.

WAR DEPARTMENT,
Washington, March 9, 1862.

To the GOVERNOR OF NEW YORK, *Albany;* MASSACHUSETTS, *Boston;* MAINE, *Portland:*

The opinion of the naval commanders here is that the Merrimac will not venture to sea, but they advise that immediate preparations be made to guard against the danger to our ports by large timber rafts, protected by batteries. They regard timber rafts, guarded by batteries, as the best protection for temporary purposes.

General Totten says do not neglect the batteries.

EDWIN M. STANTON,
Secretary of War.

WAR DEPARTMENT,
March 9, 1862.

His Excellency E. D. MORGAN,
Governor of New York, Albany, N. Y.:

The Merrimac was beaten back by the Monitor to-day after a five hours' contest, and is reported to be disabled.

EDWIN M. STANTON,
Secretary of War.

NAVY-YARD,
Washington, D. C., March 9, 1862—2 p. m.

Brig. Gen. HOOKER, *Commanding:*

Please have the following communicated to Captain Wyman as soon as possible:

The Merrimac has got out of harbor, and had pretty much used up our ships at Hampton Roads.

It is impossible to say what she may attempt, but as a proper precaution it is proposed to be ready to block the channel of this river in the event of an attempt to enter it.

By direction of the President it has been agreed on by General McClellan, General Meigs, and myself, the Secretary of War present, to fill some canal-boats and other craft and tow them down near the place where it would be advisable to sink them. I wish you therefore to send up some of the steamers to tow down.

You have no doubt received my dispatch to send a fast vessel to observe the mouth of the Potomac. Let this duty be well looked to.

Will General Hooker please to inform me of this reaching Captain Wyman.

JNO. A. DAHLGREN,
Commandant, Navy-Yard.

WASHINGTON NAVY-YARD,
March 9, 1862—3 p. m.

His Excellency the PRESIDENT OF THE UNITED STATES:

I beg leave to inform you that upon consultation with such pilots as I have in the yard, I find them to be of opinion that a vessel drawing 22 feet water can pass up the Potomac within a hundred yards of the Arsenal. As far as the light-house on Blackistone Island, some 30 miles, there is abundant water for any ship. · About 5 miles higher up is the first obstacle—the Kettle Bottoms. The channel passes among these shoals for 5 miles, and the pilot says 24 feet can be had, which I doubt. The narrowest part about 300 yards wide. From this the channel continues good until just below Aquia, where it shoals, so that 23 feet is considered the best water at common high tide. Having passed this, the water deepens passing the batteries and shoals about Mattawoman Creek, where the depth at common high tide is 22 feet. This obstruction is less than a mile in extent, after which the channel deepens several feet; though it narrows, it runs nearly to the Arsenal, and perhaps some 3 miles from the Capitol.

The actual blocking of the river is only to be resorted to when the exigency arises, the means being at hand. There are three points where it can be done—the Kettle Bottoms, below Smith's Point, and at Mattawoman. I would advise that some heavy ordnance be got ready for placing at the Arsenal, at Giesborough Point, and at Buzzard Point. Fort Washington should also have suitable cannon. I have telegraphed to the flotilla for some steamers to tow down the blocking vessels as soon as General Meigs has them ready. It happens unfortunately that the only two good steamers belonging to the yard are at Fortress Monroe.

JNO. A. DAHLGREN, Commandant.

MARCH 9, 1862—3.40 p. m.

General McCLELLAN, Commander:

I am making arrangements to place an 11-inch gun and some 10-inch mortars on Giesborough Point, which will command at short range the nearest point that a vessel drawing 22 feet can approach the Capitol. The channel passes within 50 yards of this position.

.As I have but a handful of men, it might be convenient to have some assistance from the neighboring regiments. If so, please authorize it.

JNO. A. DAHLGREN.

WAR DEPARTMENT, March 9, 1862—5.30 p. m.

Captain DAHLGREN:

The steamer Sophia will leave G-street wharf in ten minutes, having in tow eight canal-boats loaded with sufficient stone to sink them. Another steamer, with eight more, will leave in the course of the night. The captain of the Sophia bears a letter to the officer in command of the flotilla, stating "that the boats are to be sunk if necessary." This telegram is sent for your information.

By order of General Meigs, Quartermaster-General:

D. H. RUCKER,
Quartermaster and Colonel.

FORTRESS MONROE, March 9, 1862—6.45 p. m.

Hon. GIDEON WELLES, Secretary of the Navy:

The Monitor arrived at 10 p. m. last night and went immediately to the protection of the Minnesota, lying aground just below Newport News. At 7 a. m. to-day the Merrimac, accompanied by two wooden steamers and several tugs, stood out toward the Minnesota and opened fire. The Monitor met them at once and opened her fire, when all the enemy's vessels retired excepting the Merrimac. These two iron-clads fought, part of the time touching each other, from 8 a. m. to noon, when the Merrimac retired. Whether she is injured or not it is impossible to say. Lieut. J. L. Worden, who commanded the Monitor, handled her with great skill, and was assisted by Chief Engineer Stimers. Lieutenant Worden was injured by the cement from the pilot-house being driven into his eyes, but I trust not seriously. The Minnesota kept up a continuous fire, and is herself somewhat injured. She was moved considerably to-day, and will probably be off to-night. The Monitor is uninjured and ready at any moment to repel another attack.

G. V. FOX,
Assistant Secretary.

WASHINGTON NAVY-YARD, *March* 9, 1862—9 p. m.
Hon. GIDEON WELLES, *Secretary of the Navy:*

The proposed measures for guarding the Potomac are in progress. I am informed from the Quartermaster's Department that eight canal-boats, loaded with stone, were about to leave, and eight more would leave during the night. I have sent instructions to the commandant of the flotilla as to their disposition and use at the three places where the channel has the least depth of water.

The only 11-inch gun and 50-pounder which I have will be landed on Giesborough Point before midnight. The platforms will be laid and the guns in position to-morrow morning. The mortars will also be placed. Shot are being cast for all of them, and a full supply will be ready to-morrow.

The Secretary of War has visited the defensive points and given me authority to draw on any of the regiments or forts for men, guns, or munitions. He has also authorized me to take for the while the private steamers plying on the river for present use of the Government, and I have sent around for them. If there should be any use at all for a battery on Giesborough, there ought to be twenty of the heaviest cannon. Shot of 170 pounds at 50 or 100 yards will be apt to do something. A smart steamer has been dispatched to the mouth of the Potomac to observe it.

JNO. A. DAHLGREN, *Commandant.*

BUDD'S FERRY, *March* 9, 1862—9.15 p. m.
Captain DAHLGREN:

I was absent when your telegram for Captain Wyman reached this office; it was, however, duly communicated.

Captain Wyman is of the opinion that the Merrimac cannot ascend the Potomac.

HOOKER, *Brigadier-General.*

EXECUTIVE MANSION, *Washington, March* 9, 1862.
Colonel INGALLS, *Quartermaster, Annapolis:*

Should the Merrimac, which did so much damage at Newport News, attempt anything at Annapolis, it is believed that the best defense would be an attack by a number of swift steamers, full of men, who should board her by a sudden rush, fire down through her hatches or grated deck, and throw cartridges, grenades, or shells down her smoke-pipes; sacrifice the steamers in order to take the Merrimac.

If an overwhelming force can be thus thrown on board there will be little loss of life, though the steam transports may be destroyed. Of course the steamers should be provided with ladders, planks, grapplers, and other means to board with. The Merrimac has iron sides, sloping above water to a deck about 9 feet wide. Said to be an iron-grated deck.

Promotion, ample reward, awaits whoever takes or destroys her.

By order of the Secretary of War:

M. C. MEIGS,
Quartermaster-General.

You, of course, have a swift steamer outside on the look out.

WASHINGTON, D. C.,
March 9, 1862—1 p. m.

Maj. Gen. JOHN E. WOOL, *Fort Monroe:*

If the rebels obtain full command of the water it would be impossible for you to hold Newport News. You are therefore authorized to evacuate that place, drawing the garrison in upon Fort Monroe, which I need not say to so brave an officer is to be held at all hazards as I will risk everything to sustain you should you be attacked by superior force.

From indications here I suspect an intention of the enemy to fall back nearer to Richmond, that they may better concentrate their forces. An attack upon you is not improbable.

If the 15-inch gun is at Newport News I would suggest its immediate removal to either Fort Monroe or Fort Calhoun, unless it will enable you to retain possession of Newport News. By authorizing you to withdraw from Newport News I do not mean to give you the order to do so, but to relieve you from that grave sense of responsibility which every good officer feels in such a case. I would only evacuate Newport News when it became clear that the rebels would certainly obtain complete control of the water and render it untenable. Do not run the risk of placing its garrison under the necessity of surrendering.

You will also please inform me fully of your views and wishes, the practicability and necessity of re-enforcing you, &c. The performances of the Merrimac place a new aspect upon everything, and may probably change my old plan of campaign just on the eve of execution.

GEO. B. McCLELLAN,
Major-General, Commanding.

FORT MONROE, VA.,
March 9, 1862—10.45 p. m.

Major-General McCLELLAN, *Washington, D. C.:*

Your telegram to Major-General Wool received. The performance of the Monitor to-day against the Merrimac shows a slight superiority in favor of the Monitor, as the Merrimac was forced to retreat to Norfolk after a four hour's engagement, at times the vessels touching each other. The damage to the Merrimac cannot be ascertained. She retreated under steam without assistance.

The Monitor is all ready for her to-morrow, but I think the Merrimac may be obliged to lay up for a few days. She is an ugly customer,

and it is too good luck to believe we are yet clear of her. Our hopes
are upon the Monitor, and this days' work shows that the Merrimac
must attend to her alone. Have ordered the large frigates to leave.

G. V. FOX,
Assistant Secretary.

NAVY DEPARTMENT,
March 9, 1862.

Capt. HIRAM PAULDING,
Commandant Navy Yard, New York:

If the Oneida can go to sea, send her to Hampton Roads instantly.
Send any vessels you have. Don't delay a moment.

GIDEON WELLES.

WAR DEPARTMENT,
March 10, 1862.

HENRY B. RENWICK, Esq., *New York:*

Your dispatch of this morning received.* Why not take, say, three
large and swift steamers, drawing not more than 16 feet of water when
loaded, fill their bows, and strengthen them generally, and protect their
machinery with timber? Could not three such vessels be fitted up
and made ready for sea in three or four days, and would they not be
sufficient for the destruction of the Merrimac by running her down, if
managed by volunteer commanders and crews? Telegraph immediately for Carryall to return.

P. H. WATSON,
Assistant Secretary of War.

WAR DEPARTMENT,
March 10, 1862.

Governor ANDREW, *Boston:*

The Merrimac is reported by General Wool as having returned to
Norfolk in a sinking condition, but Assistant Secretary Fox, who is
also at Fort Monroe, reports that it is not known whether she is disabled or not.

My telegram to you respecting your defenses was sent before it was
known that the Monitor had reached Fort Monroe, and it was unknown
what further mischief might be done by the Merrimac. All the information possessed by the War Department respecting affairs at Fort
Monroe is allowed to pass by the telegraph for public information. Any
special information important to public safety will be communicated to
you.

EDWIN M. STANTON,
Secretary of War.

Above dispatch sent to—
Gov. E. D. Morgan, Albany, N. Y.
Gov. John A. Andrew, Boston, Mass.
Gov. Israel Washburn, jr., Augusta, Me.

---

* Not found.

HEADQUARTERS ARMY POTOMAC,
March 10, 1862—1 a. m.
Capt. JOHN. A. DAHLGREN:

You will suspend operations for the present for sinking boats or placing obstructions in the Potomac.

GIDEON WELLES.

NAVY DEPARTMENT,
March 10, 1862—10.27 a. m.
Capt. G. V. FOX,
  Assistant Secretary of Navy, Fort Monroe:

It is directed by the President that the Monitor be not too much exposed, and that in no event shall any attempt be made to proceed with her unattended to Norfolk. If vessels can be procured and loaded with stone and sunk in the channel it is important that it should be done. The San Jacinto and Dacotah have sailed from Boston for Hampton Roads, and the Sabine in tow of Baltic, and a tug from New York. Gunboats will be ordered forthwith. Would it not be well to detain the Minnesota until other vessels arrive?

GIDEON WELLES.

NAVY DEPARTMENT,
March 10, 1862—3 p. m.
Capt. WILLIAM L. HUDSON,
  Commandant Navy Yard, Boston:

Send the Wachusett to Hampton Roads. Have the work on the other gunboats carried on day and night with all the force possible to put on them, and when ready send them to Hampton Roads.

GIDEON WELLES,
Secretary of the Navy.

QUARTERMASTER-GENERAL'S OFFICE,
Washington City, March 10, 1862—3.50 p. m.
Major BELGER, *Quartermaster, Baltimore:*

Hold the steamer Commodore, which was sent to Baltimore from Annapolis yesterday, ready to carry a messenger with dispatches to General Burnside, who will be found in Pamlico or Albemarle Sound.

The messenger accredited from the Secretary of War or Adjutant-General will leave this place on the 5 o'clock train. Have a carriage and conveyance ready to put him on board the Commodore.

Acknowledge receipt of this and report progress. If the Commodore is unfit for the service, consult, by telegraph, Colonel Ingalls, Annapolis, who reports her as swift and drawing only 6 feet of water, as to a vessel for this service.

M. C. MEIGS,
Quartermaster-General.

NAVY DEPARTMENT,
March 10, 1862—9.45 p. m.
Capt. WILLIAM L. HUDSON,
  Commandant Navy Yard, Boston:

If Chocura and Penobscot have not sailed, send them to Hampton

Roads as soon as steam can be gotten up; also the Marblehead or any other gunboat ready.

Answer.

GIDEON WELLES.

___

MARCH 11, 1862—9 a. m.

Brigadier-General MEIGS:

I am now ready to send the only 11-inch gun here to its position on Giesborough Point. It is probably the only heavy gun in this vicinity.

It blew so freshly yesterday that there was danger of the scow foundering on the way if sent. Is it still considered necessary to mount it?

Captain Wyman considers more barges necessary than those to be sent. He wrote me that none of them had reached him at midnight, but they were met going down.

JNO. A. DAHLGREN.

___

QUARTERMASTER-GENERAL'S OFFICE,
Washington City, March 11, 1862—12.27 p. m.

Capt. JOHN A. DAHLGREN,
Commanding Washington Navy Yard:

I take it for granted that all measures of precaution ordered are to be carried out, having no orders to the contrary.

How many more canal-boats should be sent down? I will order eight more made ready and sent as soon as possible, and as many more as you desire.

M. C. MEIGS,
Quartermaster.

___

WAR DEPARTMENT,
March 11, 1862.

General JOHN E. WOOL, *Fort Monroe, Va.:*

Let the name of the gun heretofore known as the "Floyd" be changed, and hereafter be called the "Lincoln." What are you now doing with the two big guns? Can they be mounted on the beach so as to be available for defense? Do you want any aid in mounting them? If there is a carriage for the 12-inch gun, mount the 15-inch gun in that carriage, and let another carriage be prepared for the 12-inch gun.

EDWIN M. STANTON,
Secretary of War.

___

FORTRESS MONROE,
March 11, 1862.

Major-General MCCLELLAN:

Nothing of importance has occurred to-day. The enemy, under the command of Magruder, in some force about 8 miles from Newport News, expecting, no doubt, that the Merrimac, called the Virginia, will again make her appearance.

The Fifty-eighth Pennsylvania Regiment arrived this morning. The First Michigan is expected this evening.

I sent this day a flag of truce to Craney Island. No information was attained in regard to the injury sustained by the Merrimac. She reached Norfolk on Sunday evening.

JOHN E. WOOL,
Major-General.

MARCH 12, 1862—10.45 a. m.

Brigadier-General MEIGS,
    Quartermaster-General:

Captain Wyman informs me that the barges sent down have no arrangement for sinking them, and have so little stone in them that he thinks they would not be very efficient in blocking the channel.

JNO. A. DAHLGREN.

FAIRFAX COURT-HOUSE,
March 12, 1862.

Capt. G. V. FOX, *Fort Monroe:*

Can I rely on the Monitor to keep the Merrimac in check, so that I can make Fort Monroe a base of operations. Please answer at once.

GEO. B. McCLELLAN,
Major-General.

FAIRFAX COURT-HOUSE,
March 12, 1862.

G. V. FOX, *Assistant Secretary of the Navy:*

The possibility of the Merrimac appearing again paralyzes the movements of this army by whatever route is adopted. How long a time would it require to complete the vessel built at Mystic River, working night and day? How long would Stevens require to finish his vessel, so far as to enable her to contend with the Merrimac? If she is uninjured, of course no precaution would avail, and the Monitor must be the sole reliance. But if injured so as to require considerable repairs, these things are important to be considered. The General would desire any suggestion of your own on this subject.

By order of Major-General McClellan:

J. G. BARNARD,
Chief Engineer.

NAVY DEPARTMENT, *March* 13, 1862.

Maj. Gen. GEORGE B. McCLELLAN,
    Fairfax Court-House:

The Monitor is more than a match for the Merrimac, but she might be disabled in the next encounter. I cannot advise so great dependence upon her. Burnside and Goldsborough are very strong for the Chowan River route to Norfolk, and I brought up maps, explanations, &c., to show you. It turns everything, and is only 27 miles to Norfolk by two good roads. Burnside will have New Berne this week. The Monitor may, and I think will, destroy the Merrimac in the next fight; but this is hope, not certainty. The Merrimac must dock for repairs.

G. V. FOX.

WAR DEPARTMENT,
March 13, 1862.

Captain DAHLGREN:

On Sunday I sent down fifteen boats. On Tuesday eight more, making twenty-three in all. Do you want more? If so, notify Colonel Rucker by telegraph and also me.

M. C. MEIGS,
Quartermaster-General.

WAR DEPARTMENT,
March 13, 1862—5.20 p. m.

Captain DAHLGREN:

I ordered yesterday nine barges, and some men to load them, sent down. Does Captain Wyman need more yet? I believe in precaution. I would not trust this city and the fleet you see coming into the river to the strength of a single screw-bolt in the Monitor's new machinery. If one breaks, the Merrimac beats her. The Merrimac, too, is reported able to outrun, neglect her, and pass her.

M. C. MEIGS,
Quartermaster-General.

MARCH 13, 1862—6 p. m.

Brigadier-General MEIGS,
Quartermaster-General:

I have your two telegrams. Captain Wyman writes me that he has placed eight barges on the Kettle Bottoms, eight off Smith's Point, and seven off Mattawoman. He thinks there should be four or six more on Mattawoman, and asks for them, with their anchors.

If it is desired to put the matter beyond doubt, then it will be better to let the two frigates at the mouth of the Potomac enter and proceed to the Kettle Bottoms or Smith's Point, anchor, and prepare to sink them as soon as the Merrimac reaches the Potomac. She cannot get by them. The telegraph at Fort Monroe should give twelve hours' notice; and it would be well to send a fast vessel, like the Metamora, to the mouth of the Potomac to observe and to convey intelligence.

JNO. A. DAHLGREN.

HEADQUARTERS ARMY OF THE POTOMAC,
Fairfax Court-House, March 13, 1862.   (Received 9.40 p. m.)

Hon. E. M. STANTON, *Secretary of War:*

I would respectfully suggest that the Secretary of the Navy be requested to order to Fort Monroe whatever force DuPont can now spare, as well as any available force that Goldsborough can send up, as soon as his present operations are completed.

GEO. B. McCLELLAN,
Major-General.

NAVY DEPARTMENT, *March* 13, 1862.

Hon. E. M. STANTON, *Secretary of War:*

SIR: I have the honor to suggest that this Department can easily obstruct the channel to Norfolk so as to prevent the exit of the Merrimac, provided the Army will carry the Sewell's Point Batteries, in which duty the Navy will give great assistance.

Very respectfully,

GIDEON WELLES.

ADJUTANT-GENERAL'S OFFICE,
Washington, March 13, 1862.

Hon. GIDEON WELLES, *Secretary of the Navy:*

SIR: I am directed by the Secretary of War to say that he places at your disposal any transports or coal vessels at Fort Monroe for the purpose of closing the channel of the Elizabeth River to prevent the Merrimac again coming out.

I have the honor, &c.,

L. THOMAS,
Adjutant-General.

———

FORT MONROE, VA.,
March 13, 1862—2 a. m.

Hon. E. M. STANTON, *Secretary of War:*

I have just sent the following to Major-General McClellan:

Major-General McCLELLAN, *Fairfax Court-House:*

I have just received dispatch from the President, informing me that you are no longer General-in-Chief of the Army. You command the Army of the Potomac. My orders are hereafter to be received from the Secretary of War. I have urged for months Fort Monroe as a base of operations against the army of the rebels at Manassas and the South.

JOHN E. WOOL,
Major-General.

———

FORT MONROE, VA.,
March 13, 1862—2 a. m.

Hon. E. M. STANTON, *Secretary of War:*

I received last evening a dispatch from the President that Major-General McClellan was no longer General-in-Chief of the Army, and that he was assigned to the Army of the Potomac. The Army of the Potomac is not included in my department—the Department of Southeastern Virginia. Since the above telegram I have received the following telegram from Major-General McClellan, viz:

Can I rely on the Monitor to keep the Merrimac in check so that I can make Fort Monroe a base of operations? Please answer at once.

I have answered that he could rely on the Monitor; but if he makes Fort Monroe the base of operations—which should have been done months ago—I will rank him, and must command, for I am now in command by the President according to my brevet rank. Please to answer.

JOHN E. WOOL,
Major-General.

———

FORT MONROE, VA.,
March 13, 1862—3.5 p. m.

Hon. E. M. STANTON, *Secretary of War:*

In reply to Major-General McClellan's desire to know what I wanted for defense of my position, I replied, for immediate defense, as follows, viz: Two thousand regular infantry and 8,000 volunteer infantry; five batteries of light artillery (regulars, if possible); 1,100 horses for the five batteries, to complete the batteries I have here and to mount Dodge's cavalry. I have received only three regiments: First Michigan, Fifth Maryland, and Fifty-eighth Pennsylvania. I require several companies of regular artillery in Fort Monroe. I have only about 110 regulars for Fort Monroe and Newport News. Fort Monroe is too important a position to be neglected. I have never failed to so represent, and ask for troops and other means of defense. .

JOHN E. WOOL,

Major-General.

FORT MONROE, VA., *March* 13, 1862.

Hon. E. M. STANTON, *Secretary of War:*

Major-General McClellan desires by telegraph to know if the channel between Sewell's Point and Craney Island could be blockaded. I reply that it would be impracticable without first taking the battery of thirty guns on Sewell's Point and then sink twenty boats loaded with stone, exposed, however, to a fire of thirty guns on Craney Island. Flag-Officer Goldsborough agrees with me in this opinion. To take the batteries it would require the Monitor. Neither of us think it would do to use the Monitor for that service, lest she should become crippled. She is our only hope against the Merrimac.

JOHN E. WOOL,

Major-General.

WASHINGTON, D. C.,

March 13, 1862—9.15 p. m.

Major-General McCLELLAN:

I have seen Fox. He says the Merrimac is not able to come into the Chesapeake, and is slower than the Monitor. The latter fought under very disadvantageous circumstances, is uninjured, and is capable of mastering her adversary. He seems to regard the operations of the Merrimac as confined to Hampton Roads above the fort. The Secretary has telegraphed concerning Burnside and Wool.* No troops ordered to Frémont from this army.

IRVIN McDOWELL,

Brigadier-General.

WASHINGTON CITY, D. C.,

March 14, 1862—8.45 a. m.

Maj. Gen. JOHN E. WOOL,

Commanding at Fortress Monroe:

The following dispatch from General McClellan has been received by this Department:

FAIRFAX COURT-HOUSE, *March* 13—11 20 p. m.

Hon. E. M. STANTON, *Secretary of War:*

I would be glad to have instructions given to General Wool that the troops and stores now being sent down to Fort Monroe are of my command and not to be appropriated by him.

GEO. B. McCLELLAN,

Major-General.

---

* See Series I, Vol. V, p. 750.

The request of General McClellan is approved, and you are instructed to act in accordance with it, and to acknowledge the receipt of this communication.

EDWIN M. STANTON,
Secretary of War.

———

WAR DEPARTMENT,
Washington, March 14, 1862—10.10 a. m.
Major-General WOOL:

It is represented that a large number of visitors for pleasure, dealers in trade, and other persons not in the public service are now congregating at Fort Monroe, whose presence may embarrass the grave naval and military operations now in progress or in contemplation there. You are authorized, in your discretion, to require the immediate departure of all persons not in the service of the United States whose presence may incommode operations, and to exclude all unauthorized persons from stopping or remaining there, until further orders. You will, from and after this date, exercise the most rigid discipline and police within the territory under your command.

EDWIN M. STANTON,
Secretary of War.

———

WAR DEPARTMENT—12 m.,
(Received March 14, 1862.)
Captain DAHLGREN:

Your telegram relative to barges received. I have ordered eight more sent down. I have seen nothing yet to satisfy me that in the next engagement the Monitor will not be sunk.

M. C. MEIGS,
Quartermaster-General.

———

FORT MONROE, VA.,
(Received March 14, 1862—11.20 a. m.)
Hon. E. M. STANTON, *Secretary of War:*

I beg you will send me more troops. The Merrimac is preparing and they are strengthening her weak points. It is thought she will be prepared to come out in a very few days. If she should overcome the Monitor we would lose Newport News—an important position—unless I have troops enough to meet and repel the rebels before they can reach Newport News.

JOHN E. WOOL,
Major-General.

———

WAR DEPARTMENT,
March 15, 1862.
C. VANDERBILT, Esq., *New York:*

The Secretary of War directs me to ask you for what sum you will contract to destroy the Merrimac or prevent her from coming out from Norfolk—you to sink or destroy her if she gets out?

Answer by telegraph, as there is no time to be lost.

JOHN TUCKER,
Assistant Secretary of War.

NEW YORK CITY, *March* 15, 1862.

Hon. E. M. STANTON:

Mr. Vanderbilt desires me to say he can make no satisfactory reply to the inquiry made of him, but will be in Washington on Monday next to confer with the Department.

W. B. DINSMORE.

WASHINGTON, *March* 15, 1862.

Maj. Gen. GEORGE B. McCLELLAN, *Seminary:*

In reply to your dispatch to this Department of yesterday [13th], which was transmitted to the Secretary of the Navy, he replies as follows:

NAVY DEPARTMENT, *March* 14, 1862.

Hon. E. M. STANTON, *Secretary of War:*

SIR: Yours, inclosing the dispatch of Major-General McClellan, suggesting that the Secretary of the Navy be requested "to order to Fort Monroe whatever force DuPont can now spare, as well as any available force that Goldsborough can send up, as soon as his present operations are completed," has been received. If a movement is to be made upon Norfolk—always a favorite measure of this Department—instant measures will be taken to advise and strengthen Flag-Officer Goldsborough, but unless such be the case, I should be extremely reluctant to take any measure that would even temporarily weaken the efficacy of the blockade, especially at the points under the command of Flag-Officer DuPont. The importance of capturing Norfolk is, I know, deemed almost indispensable by Flag-Officer Goldsborough, who will be happy to co-operate in a movement in that direction, and will, I need not assure you, have the active and earnest efforts of this Department to aid him with all the force that can be placed at his disposal.

I am, respectfully, your obedient servant,

GIDEON WELLES.

The foregoing letter was received late last night.

EDWIN M. STANTON,
Secretary of War.

CONFEDERATE CORRESPONDENCE, ETC.

YORKTOWN, *January* 10, 1862.

His Excellency the PRESIDENT OF THE CONFEDERATE STATES:

DEAR SIR: I understand that my lines of defense are under discussion at Richmond. I know I can expect from you the justice to postpone any decision until I can report at length, which will be in a few days. In the mean time I will venture the remark that I have taken not only the best but the only way of successfully defending this Peninsula with the means at my disposal, and that its defense will be successful. I did not call out the militia, though at one time I had determined to do so, but merely requested to be furnished with the strength of certain regiments, to prepare arms for them, which arms I could procure from the colonels of regiments belonging, as they informed me, to their States. I only desired to prepare for the emergency of a landing in this Peninsula or on the Rappahannock, which I now think more probable, or for an attack on James River. These arrangements required time. I therefore anticipated the emergency. Colonel Randolph informed me that I was authorized by you to do this; that is, to call out all the militia I could arm.

Very respectfully,

J. BANKHEAD MAGRUDER,
Major-General, Commanding.

SPECIAL ORDERS, }   ADJT. AND INSP. GEN.'S OFFICE,
No. 13.   }   *Richmond, January 16, 1862.*

*   *   *   *   *   *   *

V. Authority is granted Major-General Magruder to call upon the commanding officers of all regiments, battalions, and companies, attached to the Army of the Peninsula, for the names of all ship carpenters and joiners in their respective commands, and to grant furloughs to such mechanics, for the purpose of working on gunboats in such numbers and at such times as the public safety may permit. All men so furloughed will be directed to report to the Secretary of the Navy.

*   *   *   *   *   *   *

By command of the Secretary of War:

JNO. WITHERS,
Assistant Adjutant-General.

HEADQUARTERS ARMY OF THE PENINSULA,
Yorktown, January 23, 1862.

General S. COOPER,
Adjutant-General C. S. Army, Richmond:

SIR: I have the honor to acknowledge the receipt last night of a letter from the Secretary of War, expressing his disapprobation of my having impressed the slaves of Chesterfield County, and directing me to countermand it.

In answer I have to state that before the reception of this letter my agent, Mr. Junius Lamb, through whom I communicated my wishes to the people of Chesterfield, had informed me that nine-tenths of that community were willing to send their slaves to work on the public fortifications in this Peninsula, but that some four or five citizens objected, and employed counsel to proceed to Richmond to lay the case before the Secretary of War and President; that the counsel had returned, and stated that the President would issue a proclamation condemning this course and forbidding it for the future. I immediately wrote to you that this last call on Chesterfield and the neighboring counties was made to meet the requisitions of the engineers under my command until the negroes who were being hired by authority of the Government, which I found to be a slow operation, should arrive.

The Government had granted me authority to hire negroes, but I found it occupied more time and was attended with more difficulty than had been represented to me. The unsafe condition of the defenses on James River had been represented to the Department, in a report of the Chief of Artillery, Col. G. W. Randolph, and the engineer here in charge, Mr. St. John, which report was strongly indorsed by myself.

The work at Gloucester Point, ordered by the Engineer Department at Richmond, was not half finished. The works at Yorktown, though trebled in strength in the last two months, were then and still are unfinished, both as regards the protection of the men against the enemy's shell, guns, and mortars by sea, as well as his attacks by land. As the War Department had sanctioned, during the administration of Mr. Walker, my calling on the people for slave labor to work on the fortifications in my charge, and as my instructions were to push these fortifications to completion, I considered it proper in itself and necessary to the faithful obedience of my orders to continue using, as before, this labor until the exercise of the authority granted me by the Government to hire slaves should be successful in procuring the requisite labor. It was intended to be my last call.

The counties of the Peninsula and neighborhood having furnished negroes frequently, I thought it prudent to call upon the counties of Chesterfield and Dinwiddie for this last supply, and I believe I have exercised the power (recognized by the War Department) with discretion. Nevertheless, I immediately directed Mr. Lamb not to take any further steps with reference to the county of Chesterfield, and as he informed me that he had an appointment to meet the negroes from Dinwiddie at Petersburg, I instructed him to keep it, but not to bring any whose masters objected in the least to their coming. This course, pursued before the reception of your letter, I presume meets with the approbation of the War Department and the President. I received a letter last night from Captain Rives, temporarily in charge of the Engineer Department at Richmond, stating in effect that he was not prepared to undertake the hiring of negroes for the works here or their control.

All the negroes are discharged from Yorktown with the exception of 160, about 130 of these being procured from the county of Greenville by calling upon the inhabitants to furnish the labor; it is reported to me that they furnished these men with pleasure. The number required by the works here is about 400. At Mulberry Island, on James River, there are about 30; 200 are required there, and at least 200 at Gloucester Point, where there are, I think, not more than 50, though I have not inquired within the last week.

Under these circumstances I beg that I may be furnished without delay with precise instructions which the War Department, I hope, is well assured will be executed with promptness to the letter and spirit.

I beg that this communication may be laid before the President through the Secretary of War. Inclosed are copies of two letters from General Lee. That containing his original instructions to which allusion is made in one of the inclosed is mislaid, but doubtless will soon be found among the papers in the office.

I have the honor to be, sir, very repectfully, your obedient servant,

J. BANKHEAD MAGRUDER,
Major-General, Commanding.

P. S.—You will also receive a copy of a communication from the War Department fully approving my course in impressing slaves.

[Inclosure No. 1.]

HEADQUARTERS OF THE VIRGINIA FORCES,
Richmond, Va., May 25, 1861.

Col. J. B. MAGRUDER,
Commanding, &c., Yorktown:

COLONEL: Two 12-pounder brass pieces have been directed to be sent you at Yorktown, which may be applied to the land defenses either below Yorktown or Williamsburg, as you may deem best. Two 8-inch columbiads are also sent to you at Yorktown, and if not wanted for the water defense they had better be applied to the land, either there or at Williamsburg.

I again urge upon you the necessity of the line of defenses between the heads of Queen and College Creeks, about which Colonel Ewell has already received instructions. Colonel Ewell had better be directed to apply all the force he can procure to the erection of those lines. Captain Rives and Meade, of the Engineer Corps, are on duty in the Peninsula, and subject to your orders. Should the lines below Williamsburg not have been surveyed and laid out, they had better be put at it directly.

I am, sir, very respectfully, &c.,

R. E. LEE,
Major-General, Commanding.

[Inclosure No. 2.]

HEADQUARTERS OF THE VIRGINIA FORCES,
Richmond, June 10, 1861.

Col. J. B. MAGRUDER,
Commanding, &c., Yorktown, Va.:

COLONEL: In answer to your letter of the 9th instant, just received, I take pleasure in expressing my gratification at the movements and dispositions that you have made, and hope that you may be able to restrict the advances of the enemy and securely maintain your own position.

On the day after my return to Richmond forty-two wagons were ordered to be sent you. Twelve were sent day before yesterday, twelve on yesterday, twelve more will be sent to-morrow, and the others as soon as possible.

As you are aware that it is probable when an effort is made to attack you it will be both by land and water, I take this occasion of urging upon you the importance of pressing the construction of the batteries for water and land defenses.

Very respectfully, your obedient servant,

R. E. LEE,
General, Commanding.

[Inclosure No. 3.]

WAR DEPARTMENT, C. S. A.,
Richmond, September 24, 1861.

Col. J. B. MAGRUDER, *Williamsburg, Va.:*

SIR: In reply to your letter of the 20th instant, referred by the Adjutant-General to this Department, I am directed by the Secretary of War to say that your course in impressing labor for work upon fortifications in cases of absolute necessity and for a fair price is fully approved.

Respectfully,

A. T. BLEDSOE,
Chief Bureau of War.

WAR DEPARTMENT, C. S. A.,
Richmond, Va., January 27, 1862.

Maj. Gen. J. B. MAGRUDER, *Yorktown, Va. :*

SIR: In response to your letter of the 23d instant, on the subject of the impressment of slaves in the counties of Chesterfield and Dinwiddie, I beg to say that you misapprehend the point on which the interference of this Department was invoked. There is no desire or intention of interfering with your discretion in impressing whatever may be necessary for the public defense within your department whenever your wants cannot be supplied by contract, although, of course, this power of impressment should be exercised as sparingly as possible. The point of difficulty was that you went out of your district into the district of another general. You will see at a glance that if a general goes out of his district to exercise such a power he must necessarily come in conflict with the orders of the neighboring commander, and that the inhabitants might have two or more sets of officers all at the same time exercising this very harsh and necessarily odious power. I trust, therefore, that in future you will confine your action, when outside of your district, to contracts, and confine the exercise of the power of impressment to the geographical limits of your own command.

Your obedient servant,

J. P. BENJAMIN,
Secretary of War.

Abstract from return of the Department of the Peninsula, Maj. Gen. John B. Magruder commanding, for January, 1862.

Commands.	Present for duty.		Aggregate present.	Aggregate present and absent.	Pieces of artillery.	
	Officers.	Men.			Heavy.	Field.
Brig. Gen. G. J. Rains':						
Yorktown and vicinity and Ship Point	253	3,728	5,555	6,965	48	29
Brig. Gen. L. McLaws':						
Young's, Harrod's, and Lee's Mills, Mulberry Point, Land's End, &c.	226	4,816	6,137	7,478	......	......
Col. B. S. Ewell's:						
Williamsburg and vicinity.........................	41	588	792	928	......	.
Colonel Crump's:						
Gloucester Point	71	966	1,379	1,846	18	6
Col. Hill Carter's:						
Jamestown	14	265	323	400	20	... ..
Col. Robt. Johnston's :						
Lebanon Church and vicinity	15	262	314	463	......	......
Colonel Bohannan's:						
Matthews County (militia).........................	31	350	391	544	......	4
Total..	651	10,975	14,801	18,624	80	39

Organization of the troops in the Department of the Peninsula, commanded by Maj. Gen. J. Bankhead Magruder, C. S. Army, January 31, 1862.

Yorktown, vicinity, and Ship Point.

FIRST DIVISION.

Brig. Gen. G. J. RAINS, commanding.

13th Alabama.
2d Florida.
6th Georgia.
23d Georgia.
14th Louisiana.
Louisiana Zouave Battalion.
2d Mississippi.
15th North Carolina.
32d Virginia (2 companies).
53d Virginia (8 companies).
115th Virginia Militia.
Maurin's Louisiana Battery.
Nelson's battery.
1st Virginia (3 companies) Artillery.

Bouton's independent company.
De Gournay's independent company.
Duke's independent company.
Ellett's independent company.
Peyton's independent company.
Preston's independent company.
} Serving as heavy artillery.

Mulberry Point Battery, Land's End, &c.

SECOND DIVISION.

Brig. Gen. LA FAYETTE MCLAWS, commanding.

8th Alabama.
Cobb's Legion.
10th Georgia.
16th Georgia.
Greenville Guards.
2d Louisiana.
5th Louisiana.
10th Louisiana.
14th Virginia.
15th Virginia.
32d Virginia (2 companies).
53d Virginia (1 company).
3d Virginia (4 companies) Cavalry.
1st Virginia (5 companies) Artillery.

Gloucester Point.

Col. C. A. CRUMP, commanding.

26th Virginia.
9th Virginia Militia.
21st Virginia Militia.
87th Virginia Militia.
3d Virginia (1 company) Cavalry.
1st Virginia (1 company) Artillery.
Bagby's company Virginia volunteers.
Jordan's company Virginia volunteers.
Montague's company Virginia volunteers.
Otey's company Virginia volunteers.
} Serving as heavy artillery.

Williamsburg and Spratley's.

Col. B. S. EWELL, commanding.

1st Louisiana Battalion.
32d Virginia (2 companies).
53d Virginia (1 company).

Matthews County.

Col. J. G. BOHANNAN, commanding.

61st Virginia Militia.
Captain Todd's company Virginia Cavalry.

Lebanon Church and cavalry camps near Yorktown.

Col. R. JOHNSTON, commanding.

3d Virginia (6 companies) Cavalry.

Jamestown Island.

Col. HILL CARTER, commanding.

52d Virginia Militia.
1st Virginia (1 company) Artillery.
Jordan's independent company Virginia Artillery.
Rambaut's independent company Virginia Artillery.

Abstract from return of the Department of Norfolk, Maj. Gen. Benjamin Huger, command-
ing, for January, 1862.

| Stations. | Troops. | Present for duty. | | Aggregate present. | Aggregate present and absent. | Pieces of artillery. |
		Officers.	Men.			
Smithfield	First (Colston's) Brigade..........	147	2, 752	3, 329	3, 637	46
Norfolk.....................	Second (Mahone's) Brigade.......	231	3, 715	4, 756	5, 224	64
Portsmouth.................	Third (Blanchard's) Brigade......	227	3, 810	4, 776	5, 177	0
Craney Island..............		34	525	687	747	44
Suffolk		40	632	850	903	......
Fort Nelson.		8	140	154	184	16
Fort Norfolk..............	Garrisons.....................	4	82	94	94	14
Pinner's Point.............		4	108	123	132	11
Tanner's Point.............		3	52	61	68	5
Lambert's Point...........		7	93	119	135	10
Navy-yard.................		15	240	278	300	......
	Saunders' artillery battalion.......	3	31	45	47	......
	Young Guard.....................	4	76	80	93	......
Total......................		727	12, 256	15, 352	16, 761	*216

* 24 pieces field and 192 pieces heavy artillery.

HEADQUARTERS ARMY OF THE PENINSULA,
Yorktown, Va., February 1, 1862.

SIR : I have been so constantly occupied since my arrival on this
Peninsula that I have not had time to make to the War Department
the reports necessary, perhaps, to a clear understanding of my operations. When I took command there were no works on the James
River below Jamestown, no fortifications at Williamsburg, Yorktown,
or Gloucester Point, with the exception of one gun at Yorktown and
perhaps two at Gloucester Point. I had to defend a Peninsula 90 miles
in length and some 10 miles in width, inclosed between two navigable
rivers, terminated by fortresses impregnable as long as the enemy commanded the waters. My force was less than 3,000 men, the enemy never
less than 12,000 and sometimes as high as 25,000, and always within
a day's march of us. I had neither adjutant, quartermaster, commissary, nor any staff officer whatever, and an army unfamiliar with the
simplest military duties.

I devoted a day or two to necessary arrangements for subsisting the
army, and, calling on the sheriff of the county as a guide, made a tour
on horseback of the lower part of the Peninsula, in order to get some
knowledge of the country. Seeing at a glance that three broad rivers
could not be defended without fortifications, and that these never could
be built if the enemy knew our weakness and want of preparation, I
determined to display a portion of my small force in his immediate
presence, and upon this forthwith selected Bethel as a place at which
a small force could best give him battle should he advance.

Returning to Yorktown, I called upon Mr. R. D. Lee, who had mills
on that stream, to show me the line of Warwick River, which rises near
Yorktown, flows across the county, and enters James River a little below
Mulberry Point, where there is now a fort. Having made this explora-
tion, I determined to adopt this line to Mulberry Point as the true line
of defense whenever its right flank, on James River, could be protected
by water batteries.

The road to Richmond was open by the York or James Rivers, landing in the latter case below Jamestown. It was therefore necessary to erect defensive works in front of Williamsburg and at Yorktown to oppose an immediate advance. Jamestown Island, having been fortified when I took command, would constitute the right flank; the works at Williamsburg the center, and York River and Yorktown the left flank; but Yorktown being 12 miles farther down the river than Williamsburg or Jamestown, the enemy could land at any time on James River below Williamsburg, march across to York River above Yorktown, and cut it off entirely from its supplies, thus reducing it in a very short time even if it were fortified. Hence it became necessary to erect works as soon as possible at some point on James River below or opposite Yorktown, so that a line across the Peninsula perpendicular to its axis should have both its flanks resting upon water defenses impassable by ships. These two are the lowest points which can be defended against the passage of fleets. · To erect these several works, however, and fortify the lines here indicated would obviously be a work of immense labor, requiring, when prosecuted with the most determined energy, seven or eight months to complete them.

The chances were extremely remote for success in such an undertaking, and there was but one way that furnished the remotest hope that the Peninsula could be defended at all with the means then at the disposal of our Republic, and that was by active and threatening operations in front, to make the enemy fear for himself, while the positions were being most vigorously fortified in rear. This plan was adopted by me, and the enemy on his first advance, with a force of five to one against us, having been repulsed and severely punished, the works were pushed forward with great vigor.

The operations below (in front of) the enemy were, however, always carried on with the liability of having a large force of the enemy thrown in the rear of our forces by the Back or Poquosin Rivers, the former having 10, the latter 18, feet of water. I could not, therefore, hold my position in front without building such works on the most navigable of these rivers as would defend its entrance against the enemy's vessels. Hence the work at Ship Point was built (by the labor of the troops and by my order), and completely commands the entrance to that river. I also felt the great disadvantage, when skirmishing with the enemy so near his fortress, that his re-enforcements were at hand, while mine were at so great a distance. I therefore availed myself of the near approach of the Poquosin River and Deep Creek, on James River, for the establishment of a convenient base of operations from which I could draw re-enforcements and supplies when needed below, and which I could defend with success if attacked by superior numbers by land.

For these reasons, and to prevent the enemy from occupying this strong position himself, I fortified the lines of Harrod's and Young's Mills, the flanks resting, as I before said, upon Poquosin River and Deep Creek, entering the York and James Rivers respectively. I also fortified the mouth of Deep Creek and Warwick River, sinking thirty canal-boats across the channel. This line could still be turned by the enemy landing between Yorktown and Poquosin River, but I hoped to be able to defend a landing between these points by erecting fortifications there before the enemy made the attempt.

In the mean time winter approached and it was necessary to decide where the troops should build winter quarters. I directed them to build on the front line. While this was being done intelligence arrived of

Burnside's preparations for an attack. Indications from the most authentic sources pointed to this region as that on which the attack would be made, and the question arose, Should the army receive the attack on the first or second lines? The engineers were in favor of the second line as the safest, the front line being liable to be turned by the landing of the enemy on York River, on our left flank. Fully appreciating the reasons for this advice, and concurring in the opinion as to the many physical advantages offered by the second line, I nevertheless was satisfied that it would injure the *morale* of the army to fall back from its position at Young's and Harrod's Mills, where winter quarters had been built for some of the regiments. I therefore directed that the heavy baggage and sick be sent to the rear, and that the troops on the front line who had not built their winter quarters should build them, and all on that line should fight where they were, while the rest of the troops who had not built winter quarters should build them on the flanks of the second line, and that good roads, of easy communication, should be made from the first to the second line. By this means, if the enemy attacked in front alone, the troops on the first line could be supported by those from the flanks of the second line, if attacked in front and both flanks.

Our troops in front had as strong a central position on that line as they would have had on the second, and a greater certainty of victory, as they would fight on better ground for us, and the flanks of the second line, resting on the river, would be stronger to resist a naval attack. This disposition was also made to defend the left exposed flank between Yorktown and the Poquosin River, so that if the enemy did land there he would be held in check sufficiently long to give time to our troops on the first line to fall back with deliberation and safety to the second line. Thus all would be accomplished in the end that the advocates of this measure desired and without unnecessary loss of *morale*.

This decision carried with it the additional recommendation, that if the attack were delayed for any considerable time the advance of the enemy, should he land on the left flank, below Yorktown, might not only be checked, but such works erected as would prevent a landing altogether, and thus secure both lines, and make the investment of Yorktown by land highly improbable.

I have the satisfaction to state that this has been the result, and that this position, the left flank, to defend which made it necessary for me to ask for re-enforcements of several thousand men five weeks ago, is now considered one of the strongest of my lines, and can, I think, be successfully defended by the troops which are now there, as I reported to you, before the sailing of Burnside's fleet, would be the case in a few days.

You will perceive by this statement that there are no troops in winter quarters at Bethel, which is held only by a strong picket. It has never been occupied at any time but for a few days at a time, being a convenient stopping place for the troops in their operations below it.

I beg leave to report what remains to be done:

First. The lower defenses on James River are exceedingly weak, and ought to be strengthened without delay by building another battery at Mulberry Point and placing guns in the embrasures of the battery already prepared at Harden's Bluff, opposite. Harden's Bluff and Mulberry Point should then be made impregnable on the land side, which can easily be done.

Second. The number of guns at Yorktown has not yet reached the minimum stated by the engineers to be necessary for the successful defense of the place, and while I differ with them, and think it is strong enough to resist what the United States can bring against them at present, as I lately stated in an order to the troops, yet such formidable preparations are being made at the North—of steel-clad ships and floating mortar batteries—that no time should be lost in preparing adequate means to resist such an attack. For this purpose the 64-pounder 8-inch guns, firing solid shot, of the pattern of one on board the Patrick Henry, placed in casemates at the narrowest part of the river, would be most effective in breaking to pieces the steel-clad ships. Six of them would answer the purpose. In addition to these, there should be at least six of the heaviest mortars cast for this place and six for Harden's Bluff, by means of which the enemy's bomb ships may be reached.

Galleries cut into the side of the ravines leading down to the water are necessary for the protection of the stores and of the troops when asleep or not on duty during a bombardment or siege. These galleries and the casemated batteries for six guns I have directed to be made, and they are now being built; and if the guns asked for, like that on the Patrick Henry, cannot be procured, the ordinary 8-inch columbiad would be the next best, or heavy rifled guns.

The works on the land side at Yorktown are still incomplete, two redoubts being required to command dangerous ravines, and a portion of the river lines are to be completed. The works at Gloucester Point, ordered by the engineers from Richmond, are but half finished, and until finished that post will remain in great danger. If the Government cannot furnish guns at Yorktown and the lower forts on James River, I request that I may be allowed to take without delay the heavy guns from Jamestown Island and mount them at Harden's Bluff and Mulberry Point, and that the command of Harden's Bluff be transferred to me, as it is exclusively a defense of James River and not of Norfolk. The narrow channel of the river at Jamestown Island does not require guns of such heavy caliber as the channel below, at Harden's Bluff.

In connection with this subject permit me to say, that should the expedition of Burnside fail to accomplish the evident purpose of General McClellan, to weaken our army in his front by forcing re-enforcements from it to other points, a landing in force on the Rappahannock might be resorted to by him for the same purpose and might embarrass us greatly. As the York River is broad and difficult to cross between here and West Point inclusive, I do not think it necessary to make any further defenses at the latter place, but think that the formation of an intrenched camp between the Mattapony and Pamunkey Rivers, commanding the main roads leading from Urbana and Tappahannock to Richmond for the reception of troops, should Richmond be threatened in that way, would be highly important. A few thousand troops from this and a few thousand from General Holmes' command could be thrown on the enemy's flanks and embarrass greatly his operations. I might cross over to Gloucester, say with 5,000 men, and march against the left flank of his 25,000 or 30,000 men. He would probably turn aside to crush me, but I should retreat, skirmishing to Gloucester Point, and if that work were finished, he would be obliged to retrace his steps or lay siege to it. If he disregarded my approach and marched forward to Richmond, General Holmes and myself would unite in his rear and cut him off from his base while our troops were being assembled in the intrenched camp in his front. He would thus be defeated.

Should Burnside's expedition march from Edenton to Suffolk, after taking Roanoke Island, to meet Casey's division from Fort Monroe, I might cross the James River with a small portion of my force and assist in preventing a junction of their troops; but the propriety of making either of these movements depends entirely upon the completion of the works on this Peninsula, for if I leave them in their present state, defended with few troops, the enemy will advance from Fort Monroe and carry them; hence my desire to procure negro labor to complete them. I have impressed the negroes of the counties composing my department so often, that it would be oppressive and unjust in the extreme to call upon them again to do the work in which all are interested. I therefore called upon some of the counties out of my department which never had furnished any labor, and a very large majority would have furnished it with pleasure, but a few persons employed a lawyer to raise objections at the War Department, and my orders were disapproved and countermanded; the works are therefore making but little progress. The quantity of labor necessary in this department is greater, perhaps, than that required in all the departments in Virginia put together, and I beg that I may be allowed to repeat my call on the counties in question out of my department in order to save time, which is so precious.

The works on the lower James River being very weak, I desired to have some troops in the fortifications in front of Williamsburg, as the enemy, should he succeed in passing up James River, might occupy those fortifications, now almost without a man, and a great disaster might happen. As my troops were necessary below, I asked for authority to call out the militia of certain counties to man these works, should it become necessary. I procured arms for them from officers who had control of these arms, but were willing to lend them for that purpose. I obtained the authority through Colonel Randolph from the President and Governor Letcher to call out the militia, but did not use it. I desired only that their colonels would send to me an account of the number of men in each regiment and the number of shot-guns which could be procured.

This course seems not to have been acceptable to the War Department, which I regret.

I beg that this communication may be laid before the Secretary of War and the President, and I respectfully invite their attention to what remains to be done in the department under my command.

I have to state, also, that two light batteries, with re-enforcements of infantry to the number of 4,000, are said to have arrived at Fort Monroe as part of the permanent force there, and that on sending a flag of truce to Hampton, a few days since, it was discovered by our officers that soldiers' quarters were being erected in Hampton, showing that more troops were expected, and that they would remain there some time, winter quarters for the troops already there having been previously built.

I am, sir, very respectfully, your obedient servant,

.J. BANKHEAD MAGRUDER,
Major-General, Commanding.

General S. COOPER,
Adjutant-General C. S. Army, Richmond, Va.

WILLIAMSBURG, *February* 7, 1862.

Professor JOYNES, *War Department:*

DEAR SIR: The opportunity of putting the Peninsula in a state of comparative security, by completing the defensive works begun and in part finished, before the spring campaign opens, has not, I regret to say, been improved as it ought to have been. The value of these works in protecting the James and York Rivers, and with the former the Norfolk and Petersburg Railroad (so accessible from many points on the James), whether we look at what may be required or at what they have already accomplished, cannot well be estimated in dollars and cents. As a citizen you are directly interested, and you will, by giving your aid, be doing good, individual and general. Not less than 1,000 or 1,500 negroes ought to be at work, and in six weeks, with this force, would the defenses be finished and rendered well-nigh impregnable. The counties south and west of Richmond can well afford to furnish this labor. General Magruder has so frequently impressed the local labor, that he is not willing to make another call without an order from the War Department to this effect, and thus the works are comparatively at a stand still. He has done all in his power. So important do I consider this, I would at once write to the Secretary did not my position forbid it.

Yours, sincerely,

BENJ. S. EWELL,
Colonel, Virginia Volunteers.

RICHMOND, VA., *February* 15, 1862.

Colonel EWELL, *Commanding, Williamsburg:*

SIR: You will immediately organize, on paper, all the nurses, employés of the Government of every department, to be ready at a moment's notice to defend the works in front of Williamsburg, and lay aside arms and ammunition for the same.

You will also prepare arms for any citizens, of whatever age, who are willing to turn out and assist in holding the works in front of Williamsburg should the lower defenses at Jamestown be passed.

The most important points to be defended are Tetter's Neck and Fort Magruder. You will place the negroes at the service of Mr. Derrick, the engineer, for the purpose, 1st, of preparing without the slightest delay the forts already constructed for the reception of guns; and, 2d, of completing such works as may be unfinished. Infantry must be put on the right of Tetter's Neck to prevent its being turned, and what you may have must be put at once in position. Have men assigned to it and drilled, ammunition prepared, and the pieces fired by the men several times.

Very respectfully, your obedient servant,

J. BANKHEAD MAGRUDER.

Captain Lee's company and the One hundred and fifteenth Regiment Militia are ordered to report to you; you will dispose of them in the best manner possible.

J. BANKHEAD MAGRUDER,
Major-General, Commanding.

HEADQUARTERS DEPARTMENT OF NORFOLK,
February 24, 1862.

Hon. J. P. BENJAMIN, *Secretary of War:*

SIR: I have reliable information that the enemy are sending strong re-enforcements to Old Point as well as to Tennessee, and I hear, for this purpose, are withdrawing large numbers from Manassas. Within the last week several thousand men have been sent up to Newport News and more are to go. General Burnside is also being re-enforced, and the numbers collected on both sides of this place are becoming powerful armies. They threaten such long lines it is difficult for me to tell where to concentrate my forces, and, until I know more than at present, have to keep my forces near the lines of railroad.

The Ericsson (iron-clad) battery has arrived in the Roads, and will probably get one of our batteries to test her resisting qualities. I hear she carries two 11-inch guns.

I write this to call the attention of the Government to the probability of this place being severely threatened by powerful forces, and a general attack may be expected in a week or more. From the same source I hear the mortar fleet, as it is termed, is destined for New Orleans.

I am, very respectfully, your obedient servant,

BENJ. HUGER,
Major-General, Commanding Department.

YORKTOWN, VA., *February* 24, 1862.

General S. COOPER,
Adjutant and Inspector General, Richmond:

SIR: I have the honor to state that on the 21st I received a dispatch from General Huger, stating that four transports, loaded with troops, had been sent to Newport News, and another dispatch from Captain Norris, my signal officer at Norfolk, that three regiments had been landed at Fort Monroe.

I beg leave further to state I reported on the 20th instant that the roads here were in extremely bad order. They are so much worse that it is very doubtful if artillery can be carried down the country, and it will be positively necessary to diminish the usual amount of ammunition by one-half if carried.

I am also satisfied that no one ship can produce such an impression upon the troops at Newport News as to cause them to evacuate the fort. The demoralization to our troops under similar circumstances has been produced by a concentration of fire from many ships at different points. No important advantages can be obtained by the Merrimac further than to demonstrate her power, which, as she is liable to be injured by a chance shot at this critical time, had better be reserved to defeat the enemy's serious efforts against Norfolk and James River.

I have the honor to request that this communication be laid before the President through the Secretary of War.

I have failed in my efforts to get the substance of the above through by telegraph.

I am, sir, very respectfully, your obedient servant,

J. BANKHEAD MAGRUDER,
Major-General, Commanding.

SPECIAL ORDERS, }   ADJT. AND INSP. GEN.'S OFFICE,
No. 45.   }   *Richmond, February* 25, 1862.

*   *   *   *   *   *   *

XVIII. Major-General Magruder will so dispose of the forces under his command and make necessary preparations as to be able to move across the James River all forces that can be spared from his batteries and intrenchments to co-operate in the repulse of the enemy from any threatened attack on Suffolk or other approaches to Norfolk. He will have his forces in readiness to cross the river on receiving further orders.

*   *   *   *   *   *

By command of the Secretary of War:

JNO. WITHERS,
Assistant Adjutant-General.

RICHMOND, VA., *February 26, 1862.*

Maj. Gen. B. HUGER, *Norfolk, Va.:*

MY DEAR GENERAL: I sent Colonel Lee, my aide-de-camp, to converse with you freely and confidentially and to bring to me full and exact information as to your condition and views.

This morning it has been stated to me that you feel restrained by the want of an assurance that the Government has left your action to the guidance of your own judgment. In that regard I have to say that my rule has been to seek for the ablest commanders who could be obtained, and to rely on them to execute the purposes of the Government by such plans as they should devise and with such means as could be made available.

You certainly have not been an exception to that rule. My purpose in your case was the defense of Norfolk, and my confidence in you has been to me a constant source of hope. You will accept assurances of my readiness to sustain you to the full extent of my power, and the expression of·the desire that you would look to success as the only directrix of your course in the discharge of your official duties.

Very truly, your friend,

JEFFERSON DAVIS.

RICHMOND, VA., *February 27, 1862.*

General B. HUGER, *Norfolk, Va.:*

You will place the towns of Norfolk and Portsmouth and their dependencies under martial law. Preparation should be made for the removal of that part of the population who could only embarrass the defense in the event of a siege.

JEFFERSON DAVIS.

RICHMOND, VA., *February 27, 1862.*

Brigadier-General WINDER:

SIR: I have just finished an examination of the field works erected and planned around the city for its defense, and respectfully submit a brief report of their condition for your information.

These batteries, numbering eighteen, and seven outworks, are placed in a circle of about 12 miles around the city. I think their location and design good. The magazines of those on the north side of the river are not in a fit condition to receive ammunition. All of them are more or less damp and some of them have 2 or 3 feet of water in them. I would suggest that they be built above the surface of the ground.

There are eleven long 32-pounders mounted on barbette carriages and nine guns of the same class in the batteries on the north side of the river not mounted. Batteries Nos. 11 and 12 on the north side, and Nos. 17 and 18 on the south side of the river, have not been commenced.

I would respectfully suggest that these last mentioned be completed and armed, as I think that we are most likely to be attacked from that quarter first.

I do not deem it necessary to give a more detailed statement at present. I submit these facts to you in the hope that you will bring the matter before the Engineer and Ordnance Departments.

The accompanying sketch of the works will give you a better idea of them than anything I have written or could write.*

If these works were completed and well armed they would indeed be formidable; yet it seems to me doubtful whether we could supply an army with provisions that would be necessary to defend the city against the force the enemy would likely bring against us. We might possibly be made to experience the fate of General Mack at Ulm. But these are matters for the Government to decide. With these facts and remarks I leave the subject in your hands.

I have the honor to be, very respectfully, your obedient servant,

R. TANSILL,
Colonel, Commanding Second Regiment Virginia Artillery.

P. S.—I should have before observed that it will require 218 guns to fully arm the batteries.

R. TANSILL,
Colonel, Commanding Second Virginia Artillery.

PROCLAMATION.

[FEBRUARY 27, 1862.]

Whereas the Congress of the Confederate States has by law vested in the President the power to suspend the writ of habeas corpus in cities in danger of attack by the enemy:

Now therefore I, Jefferson Davis, President of the Confederate States of America, do hereby proclaim that martial law is extended over the cities of Norfolk and Portsmouth and the surrounding country to the distance of 10 miles from said cities, and all civil jurisdiction and the privilege of the writ of habeas corpus are hereby declared to be suspended within the limits aforesaid.

This proclamation will remain in force until otherwise ordered.

In faith whereof I have hereunto set my hand and seal, at the city of Richmond, on this twenty-seventh day of February, in the year of our Lord one thousand eight hundred and sixty-two.

JEFFERSON DAVIS.

FEBRUARY 28, 1862.

Colonel KEMPER,
Speaker House of Delegates, State of Virginia:

DEAR SIR: I inclose my report on the condition of the defenses of Richmond, as called for by a resolution.

----

* Not found.

Permit me to call your attention to its purport, the better to determine if or not it should be read in open session.

Most respectfully, yours,

C. DIMMOCK,
Colonel Ordnance of Virginia.

[Inclosure.]

Hon. SPEAKER OF THE HOUSE OF DELEGATES OF VIRGINIA:

In compliance with the resolution passed by the House of Delegates, "requesting Col. Charles Dimmock to make a careful and thorough examination of the fortifications and defenses of this city and to report the condition thereof to this House," I respectfully report that I have visited the works referred to, and find that on the north side of James River, commencing on the river below the city and running around to the river above the city, there are seventeen separate batteries and that there are two more about to be thrown up. On the south side of the river, inclosing the town of Manchester, commencing on the river below and running around to the river above the town of Manchester, there are four separate batteries, besides two more about to be thrown up.

The length of line of works on the north side of the river is 7½ miles and on the south side 4½ miles—in all about 12 miles.

If I am to express my opinion, I take the occasion to say that these lines of defense are too near the city, placing it in close siege, if the enemy is to be suffered to approach within reach of the batteries; so near can the enemy come that the city can be shelled and burned before our works are captured, and so near that all intercourse with the country will be cut off, and for the want of subsistence the city would soon be compelled to capitulate without any serious attack by the enemy. The line of defense should be near the banks of the Chickahominy and its tributaries as far as they extend westwardly and thence by a line to James River; and on the Manchester side the works should be thrown out some 2 miles in advance. But as the present batteries are nearly complete, they may be used in the last resort. Yet advanced works should be thrown up as soon as possible upon the lines indicated.

The present works (except their being too near) are well located and of approved ground plan, and when they are completed will make a good defense.

There are several ravines running in between some of the works which are not commanded by their guns. Doubtless it is in contemplation to throw up other small batteries to protect these depressions.

All the batteries are in barbette (without embrasures) and are objectionable, because both the guns and the men who serve them are too much exposed. The guns will be liable to be dismounted and the men disabled.

I think at least some of the most important and assailable ones should be embrasured, and there should be some bomb-proofs within which the men not serving at the guns may find security. There are several lesser defects general to all the works, which I presume the engineer will remedy.

These batteries are from one-half to three-fourths of a mile from each other, between which I think there should be breastworks thrown up, behind which infantry can be posted to prevent any attempt of the enemy to force through and take the batteries in rear, where they are quite open and defenseless.

In each battery there is one or more magazines. With few exceptions these are pits sunk under ground, covered with timber and earth. These I found all very wet and most of them filled with water. These should be made dry by being bricked up or raised above the surface of the ground and drained.

Immediately around some of the works thick forests stand, which should be cut down.

Of cannon I found on the north side but eleven mounted in all the works, and dismounted, lying upon the ground without carriages, there were twelve more, in all within the batteries twenty-three; when the number required is one hundred and forty-three; and on the south or Manchester side I found two mounted (none upon the ground), when the number required is seventy-four.

I could not learn that any, either of guns or carriages, were ready; if they are not, they cannot be obtained and put in place in less time than three months if they are commenced at once.

Of the batteries along James River below the city I only know from report. To remove all fear from the enemy's gunboats, with their almost impenetrable sides and their heavy shells, I suggest that obstructions be gotten ready and floated down about 4 miles below the city, ready to be sunk on the signal of the approach of the enemy.

From what I have said above and especially from the small number of guns (twenty-five of the two hundred and eighteen required) that are ready mounted and dismounted (about two to the mile), I report that Richmond, as far as any reliance is to be placed upon these batteries, is in no state of defense against an enemy likely to approach. The danger from such attack from the north side of the river is greatly lessened by the positions of our armies on the Potomac and on the Peninsula, but I regard an attack from the south side imminent.

Burnside has obtained a permanent landing on the North Carolina coast, at which he is getting re-enforcements. With 15,000 or 20,000 men he can ascend the Roanoke, march to Petersburg, thence to Manchester, and from the commanding hills there shell this city without crossing the river. This he can do in ten days after he is ready.

If to meet this force the assistance of our armies on the Potomac and on the Peninsula are called upon, the answer will be from General Johnston and Magruder, "McClellan and Wool are threatening us (by concert with Burnside) and we can spare no assistance."

If I am right, immediate action should be had toward completing the batteries now projected on the Manchester side and fully arming them.

Respectfully submitted.

C. DIMMOCK,
Colonel Ordnance of Virginia.

Abstract from return of the Department of the Peninsula, Maj. Gen. John B. Magruder, commanding, for February, 1862.

Commands.	Present for duty.		Aggregate present.	Aggregate present and absent.	Pieces of artillery.	
	Officers.	Men.			Heavy.	Field.
Yorktown	158	2,498	3,578	4,553	45	14
Wynn's Mill	58	....	1,410	1,692	.....	.....
Young's Mill	64	1,016	1,254	1,579	4	29
Lee's Mill	27	461	615	683	.....	.....
Harrod's Mill	33	607	789	866	.....	.....
Fort Grafton	33	313	482	665	4	.....
Camp Dudley	37	623	895	1,018	.....	.....
Ship Point	37	686	856	997	.....	.....
Gloucester Point and Matthews County	116	1,089	1,561	2,175	18	4
Williamsburg	22	160	231	404	.....	.....
Jamestown	4	76	90	105	.....	.....
Jamestown Island	7	147	169	184	15	4
Mulberry Point	2	65	78	83	.....	.....
Camp Marion	37	692	886	1,000	.....	4
Warwick Court-House	32	363	543	705	.....	.....
Land's End	36	555	648	704	.....	4
Deep Creek	25	431	595	711	.....	.....
Wall's Farm	23	616	762	945	.....	.....
Spratley's Farm	19	328	458	532	.....	.....
Total	770	11,580	15,900	19,601	86	59

HEADQUARTERS,
Lee's Mill, March 1, 1862.

General S. Cooper,
    Adjutant and Inspector General:

SIR : I received your letter* directing me so to arrange my forces as to send re-enforcements, when I received orders, to Suffolk. You do not state what re-enforcements you intend to send; hence it is impossible to know what arrangements to make. I immediately, however, gave preliminary orders. I can send but one regiment and one field battery, and that with great risk here. The reason why I cannot do more is that, notwithstanding all my efforts to procure negroes, I have received but 11 from the counties in my district, the presiding magistrate referring the call in some cases to the district attorney, who decides that it is illegal, and in other cases no response is made. Two months fully have already been lost in consequence of the War Department disapproving of my arrangements and countermanding my orders.

I fear that it will be a fortnight before the evil following from these causes will have ceased, if ever. The people have got an idea that the influence of the Government will be cast against my efforts. Whilst I was in Richmond 135 slaves from the county of Greenville were discharged, I am informed, by order of the Secretary of War, and without my knowledge. I had expected to have employed these negroes and others—some 800 ready in Henry—in fortifying the second line of my position whilst my troops were occupying and fortifying the front line, where I prefer to fight, but may be forced to leave, as the flanks may

* Not found, but see Special Orders, No. 45, Adjutant and Inspector General's Office, February 25, p. 44.

be turned by the operations of ships of the enemy. I supposed that by this time I would have had negroes enough to have fortified my positions sufficiently to have enabled me to spare temporarily and for a short distance 2,000 men. As I have not had the negroes I cannot spare more troops than I have stated, and for them militia ought at once to be substituted.

I am, sir, very respectfully, your obedient servant,
J. BANKHEAD MAGRUDER,
Major-General, Commanding.

P. S.—I have to request that this communication be laid, through the Secretary of War, before the President.

———

HEADQUARTERS DEPARTMENT PENINSULA,
Yorktown, March 2, 1862.

General S. COOPER,
Adjutant and Inspector General, Richmond:

SIR: The telegraph not being at work, I have the honor to state for General Magruder, who is in the field, in forwarding to you the above [following] copy of telegram, that he recommends that the (Merrimac) Virginia be stationed a little above Newport News, to prevent the gunboats coming up the swash channel leading into Warwick River and turning the right flank of his line of defense.

I am, sir, very respectfully, your obedient servant,
HENRY BRYAN,
Captain and Assistant Adjutant-General.

[Inclosure.]

NORFOLK, *February* 27, 1862.

General J. B. MAGRUDER:

One regiment of infantry landed at Newport News yesterday and to-day six companies of a Massachusetts regiment of light artillery from the Baltimore boat; their horses arrived in transport. I have reliable information that 30,000 men will be landed at Old Point and Newport News before the 5th of March. No arrival or departure of importance to-day.

WM. NORRIS.

———

HEADQUARTERS ARMY OF PENINSULA,
Yorktown, March 3, 1862.

Captain BUCHANAN, C. S. N.,
C. S. Steamer Merrimac, Gosport Navy-Yard, Va.:

CAPTAIN: It is too late to co-operate with my army in any manner below with the Merrimac, even if the roads will admit it, which they will not, for the enemy is very heavily re-enforced both at Newport News and Fort Monroe with infantry and six batteries of light artillery.

It would have been glorious if you could have run into these as they were being landed from a Baltimore boat and a commercial transport.

In addition to the above I have been ordered to make such disposition of my troops as will enable me, in case of necessity, to send re-enforcements to Suffolk, obliging me to fall back to my second line, which I have done.

Any dependence, therefore, upon me, so far as Newport News is concerned, is at an end.

Wishing you every success, I am, captain, very respectfully, your obedient servant,

J. BANKHEAD MAGRUDER,
Major-General, Commanding.

RICHMOND, *March* 4, 1862.

Major-General MAGRUDER, *Yorktown:*

Get 5,000 men and two batteries ready to be thrown across the river as soon as possible. By order of the President. I write to-day.

J. P. BENJAMIN,
Secretary of War.

HEADQUARTERS DEPARTMENT PENINSULA,
Yorktown, March 4, 1862.

Brig. Gen. LAFAYETTE McLAWS,
Custis' Farm:

SIR: I am instructed by the commanding general to inform you that he received a dispatch from the Secretary of War this morning, directing him to send forthwith 5,000 troops to Suffolk, and that he has already given verbal orders for the movement on Thursday to King's Mill of Cobb's Legion, Sixteenth Georgia, and Fifty-third Virginia, and the Second Louisiana and Fifteenth North Carolina on Friday. You will give orders to Colonel Hodges, Fourteenth Virginia, to move early on Friday to King's Mill wharf with all his regiment except the company in charge of the four pieces of artillery. He will take with him his tents, five days' rations, as few cooking utensils as possible, his ammunition, and 20 spades, and axes, turning over the remainder of the same, besides whatever picks and shovels he may have, to the acting quartermaster of the Fifth Louisiana Volunteers, and taking receipt for the same.

You will direct Moseley's battery to proceed also on Thursday early to King's Mill and embark for Suffolk, Va., by way of City Point.

The commanding general desires that these orders be given verbally and kept as secret as possible.

I am, sir, very respectfully, your obedient servant,

HENRY BRYAN,
Assistant Adjutant-General.

HEADQUARTERS ARMY OF THE PENINSULA,
Yorktown, March 4, 1862.

General S. COOPER,
Adjutant and Inspector General C. S. Army, Richmond, Va.:

GENERAL: If 5,000 men are taken from this Peninsula and the enemy should advance in force I fear I will be compelled to leave Yorktown to defend itself with a small garrison, the covering work at Mulberry Island with one regiment to defend it, and that with the rest of the troops I shall be forced back to Williamsburg, as there would be three roads to guard with a force of not more than 4,000 men, after deducting the above-named garrisons. I will do my very best with these against all odds. I have withdrawn the troops from Young's and Harrod's Mills, leaving the cavalry and one regiment of infantry at each of these places, and have nearly completed the concentration of my force on the second line preparatory to this call.

The Quartermaster-General informs me that the Northampton will be ready from Thursday to Saturday, and that a tug and four lighters will be ready on Monday.

The superintendent of the Southside Railroad writes that the most expeditious way to convey troops to Suffolk is to take them from Jamestown by steamer to City Point, thence to Petersburg, and by the Norfolk and Petersburg Railroad to Suffolk. I think this is the best and will also be the most secret, as the troops will have to march as high up as King's Mill at all events and then go down the river to a landing in sight of the enemy, and then have a march of 30 or 40 miles. I shall therefore send them this way.

I have this moment received the Secretary's dispatch and answer by the boat.

I have the honor to be, very respectfully, your obedient servant,

J. BANKHEAD MAGRUDER,
Major-General, Commanding.

P. S.—Not having been previously informed what number of troops would be required to be transported, I could do nothing more than make inquiries and notify the Quartermaster-General of my probable wants in the way of transportation.

J. B. MAGRUDER.

————

WAR DEPARTMENT, C. S. A.,
Richmond, Va., March 4, 1862.
Maj. Gen. J. B. MAGRUDER,
Yorktown, Va.:

SIR: Your letter of March 1 has been submitted to the President, as you desired. The complaints made of the action of this Department in relation to the impressment of negroes were without just foundation. The Department has simply requested that you confine yourself to the impressment of such negroes as are within your command, and has pointed out the utter impossibility of permitting the generals who command in different districts to cross their own lines and encroach on the commands of their neighbors. The slaves from Greenville County were in no sense under your control or authority, and the Secretary was forced, on appeal, to decide that you had no right to retain them.

I regret that the people should have "got an idea that the influence of the Government will be cast against your efforts." I assure you that such an idea is utterly unfounded. It has been my desire, and it is still my most earnest wish, to strengthen your hands and aid your efforts in every possible way, and no one does fuller justice to your zeal, activity, and high soldierly qualities. I pray you to dismiss all such thoughts from your mind as unworthy of us both. In times like these miserable scandal-mongers and panic-breeders ply their vocation of sowing the seeds of mischief among men in office; but we can both afford to scorn such attempts to create distrust between us, and apply ourselves to the sole task of defending our country at this moment of her great need.

I sent you a dispatch to-day, by order of the President, to hold 5,000 men and two batteries ready for crossing the river.

The President says that when in town, a week ago, you proposed yourself to cross and aid, with part of your army, in defense of Suffolk. We do not believe that you are in the slightest danger of an attack at present, either in front or by being outflanked by naval forces. All our intelligence tends to one point. Suffolk is the aim of the enemy. Norfolk is to be cut off, if they can accomplish their purpose. If they succeed in this, then, indeed, your entire flank would be thrown open, and you would be forced to fall back rapidly, for they would get possession of all the defenses on the south side of the James River and cross at pleasure at any point they might select. It is for your own defense, as well as that of Norfolk, therefore, that the President desires you to be ready, at a moment's warning, to re-enforce the army defending Suffolk with at least 5,000 men and two batteries. It is not intended to order you to cross in person or to leave your command, but to send these troops under such general of your command as you may select.

I am, your obedient servant,

J. P. BENJAMIN,
Secretary of War.

HEADQUARTERS ARMY OF THE PENINSULA,
Yorktown, March 4, 1862.

To the Army of the Peninsula:

COMRADES: The time of service for which many of you enlisted is about to expire. Your country, invaded by an insolent foe, again demands your help. Your homes are violated, your firesides polluted by the presence of a mercenary enemy or silent in their desolation; many of your friends in captivity or in exile; our people slain, and the very altars of our religion desolated and profaned. The ruthless tyrants who have dared to invade us have vowed our conquest or our destruction.

It is for you to rise and avenge our slaughtered countrymen or nobly share their fate. Of what worth is life without liberty, peace at the expense of honor, the world without a home?

When our fathers periled life, fortune, and sacred honor to our first war of Independence, was it an empty boast, or was it the stern resolve of freemen, who knew their rights and dared to defend them? The long war of the Revolution culminated at length in victorious triumph on these very plains of Yorktown. These frowning battlements on the heights of York are turned in this second war of liberty against the enemies of our country. You breathe the air and tread the soil consecrated by the presence and heroism of our patriotic sires. Shall we, their sons, imitate their example, or basely bow the neck to the yoke of the oppressor? I know your answer. You remember your wrongs, and you are resolved to avenge them. True to the instincts of patriotic devotion, you will not fill a coward's grave. You spring with alacrity to the death-grapple with the foe, nor relinquish the strife till victory crowns our arms. Cowards die a thousand deaths; brave men die but once, and conquer though they die. It is therefore without surprise that your commanding general has learned of your purpose to re-enlist in this holy struggle, and that you bear with a cheerfulness and constancy worthy of his highest admiration the disappointment of withdrawing from you the furloughs to visit your homes which the Government promised you, and which the present dangers of our beloved country alone forbids it to grant.

When the war is ended, in that hour of triumph you will be proud to remember that by your sufferings and sacrifices, no less than by your valor, you conquered.

Soldiers! though reverses and disasters have recently befallen us, let us remember that trust is eternal and that God is just. His arm is our trust, and the Great Ruler of nations and of men will protect the right and crown with victory the noble and the brave. Let us take courage, then. Our enemy, dead to the spirit of liberty, can only fight while their coffers are unexhausted. Commerce is their king. Their god is gold. They glory in their shame. The war which intensifies our devotion and concentrates our resources scatters theirs. The day of retribution will come. The struggle will not always be defensive on our part. We will yet strike down our ruthless invaders amid smoking ruins of their cities, and with arms in our hands dictate terms of peace on their own soil.

J. BANKHEAD MAGRUDER,

Major-General, Commanding.

HEADQUARTERS DEPARTMENT OF NORFOLK,

Norfolk, Va., March 5, 1862.

Hon. J. P. BENJAMIN, *Secretary of War:*

SIR: I send inclosed a report made to me by Lieutenant Talcott, on engineer duty, who had been sent by me to Roanoke Island, and who assisted in the service of the guns at the Pork Point Battery.

This is the only report I have received from any one. General Wise, as I telegraphed yesterday, has made no official report to me. I had a letter from him on his arrival at Poplar Spring, in Currituck County, informing me of the capture of the island, his information being received from a Sergeant Metzler, who left the island at 5 p. m. on the 8th February, which information I reported at once to the Department.

I remain, very respectfully, your obedient servant,

BENJ. HUGER,

Major-General, Commanding.

[Inclosure.]

ROANOKE ISLAND, *February 9,* 1862.

Maj. Gen. B. HUGER,

Commanding Department of Norfolk:

GENERAL: In obedience to your order of the 1st instant I visited Roanoke Island, and, arriving there on the 4th, commenced the discharge of the duties imposed.

After paying off all the duly-certified claims against the Engineer Department that were presented I made an inspection of the batteries and a general reconnaissance of the position.

On Thursday, the 6th instant, I had taken passage for Elizabeth City, on my return to Norfolk, when the enemy's fleet hove in sight. Believing that very strenuous efforts would be necessary to resist successfully an attack for which the island was still unprepared, I deemed it my duty to return.

On landing I offered my services to Colonel Shaw, the commanding officer of the post, and during the attack which followed rendered such service as I could.

The details of the actions of the 7th and 8th will no doubt be reported by the commanding officer. I merely desire in this to note the facts which may prove important to the department with which I was connected.

The three guns which were alone brought fully into action at Pork Point were all *en barbette*, and although the fire of from sixty to seventy guns was concentrated for six hours on these three, which were mounted close together, without either bomb-proof shelters or traverses between them, no serious damage was sustained and the loss of life was very slight.

Although two of the three guns used were a 41-cwt. and 47-cwt. 32-pounders of short range, considerable damage was done to the enemy's gunboats. One gun in embrasure was used during the early part of the action of the 7th with great effect, but the sod revetment of the cheeks of the embrasure suffered somewhat. These facts should tend to give increased confidence in open batteries and barbette guns. It is also worthy of remark that our force engaged at the causeway, not exceeding 350 men, was enabled, under the partial cover of a breast-work 4½ feet high and less than 100 feet long, to resist for five hours an attack by upwards of 10,000 of the enemy's land forces, aided by artillery at least equal to our own.

Although our arms have been defeated by overwhelming numbers and an important position has been lost to us, I cannot see that we have any reason to be disheartened. The enemy himself confessed to a dear-bought victory and the repulse of his Navy.

I am, sir, very respectfully, your obedient servant,
T. M. R. TALCOTT,
First Lieutenant, Artillery, C. S. Army.

WAR DEPARTMENT, C. S. A.,
Richmond, Va., March 5, 1862.

Maj. Gen. B. HUGER, *Norfolk, Va.:*

SIR: I have your dispatch stating that General Wise had made no report of the capture of Roanoke Island. Congress insists on receiving reports on the subject, and General Wise has sent me copies of his letters of the 10th and 11th ultimo, which he evidently considered as his report.

I am informed by Colonel Shaw that he gave General Wise his report last week. You are therefore instructed to request from General Wise the report of Colonel Shaw, and to make up such report as you can from the material in your possession, whether letters, reports, or other documents, that I may transmit the report to Congress.

We are using every effort to strengthen your command. It seems evident that a great effort is to be made to capture Norfolk, and its defense must be as vigorous as the whole power of the Confederacy can make it. We shall use all our means of concentrating troops for the defense of Suffolk. In the mean time I would be glad to be advised as promptly as possible of your plans of defense. I beg that in determining on this matter you will consider whether it would not be advisable to withdraw to your inner line, or perhaps send to Suffolk such portions of your force as have been heretofore posted on the coast in the neighborhood of Lynn Haven Bay.

The transports recently sent to sea by the enemy are in all probability destined to re-enforce General Burnside and to attack your rear. This is only a suggestion, and is by no means intended to interfere with your own dispositions of your troops.

I trust that, with the aid of Generals Loring and Randolph, recently sent to you, and of General Ransom, who will be at once ordered to join you, you will be enabled to infuse such vigor and activity in your command as to inspire them with confidence in a successful defense. General Ransom has just been nominated, and his regiment of cavalry, which is one of the very finest in any service, is ordered to re-enforce you.

We have also ordered about 2,000 men to aid you from Washington, N. C., and General Magruder will hold in readiness on James River 5,000 men, with the necessary means of throwing them across to your support the instant the movements of the enemy render certain what is now deemed very probable—an attack on Suffolk. Several batteries of field artillery will also be sent to you.

Your obedient servant,

J. P. BENJAMIN,
Secretary of War.

WAR DEPARTMENT, C. S. A.,
Richmond, Va., March 5, 1862.

Maj. Gen. B. HUGER, *Norfolk, Va.:*

SIR: Martial law having been declared in Norfolk under the President's proclamation, he desires me to call your attention to the various measures which he hopes will at once be vigorously executed:

1st. Some leading and reliable citizen to be appointed provost-marshal in Norfolk and another in Portsmouth. In the former city he suggests the mayor, said to be a zealous friend of our cause.

2d. All arms to be required to be given up by the citizens; private arms to be paid for.

3d. The whole male population to be enrolled for military service; all stores and shops to be closed at 12 or 1 o'clock, and the whole of the citizens forced to drill and undergo instructions.

4th. The citizens so enrolled to be armed with the arms given up and with those of infantry now in service at batteries.

5th. Send away as rapidly as can be done, without exciting panic, all women and children, and reduce your population to such as can aid in defense.

6th. Give notice that all merchandise, cotton, tobacco, &c., not wanted for military use, be sent away within the given time, or it will be destroyed.

7th. Imprison all persons against whom there is well-grounded suspicion of disloyalty.

8th. Purchase all supplies in the district that can be made useful for your army, allowing none to be carried away that you might want in the event that the city is beleagued.

In executing these orders you will of course use your own discretion, so to act as to avoid creating panic as far as possible.

Your obedient servant,

J. P. BENJAMIN,
Secretary of War.

HEADQUARTERS DEPARTMENT OF THE PENINSULA,
Yorktown, Va., March 6, 1862.

General S. COOPER,
Adjutant and Inspector General C. S. Army:

SIR: The telegram, informing me that the Baltic, with three regiments on board, had left Newport News, has just been received.

Mr. William Norris, my signal officer at Sewell's, had reported the arrival at Newport News of troops within the last week in large numbers, estimated by me at six regiments, in addition to six companies of light artillery, with their horses.

In pursuance of the orders of the Secretary of War, to so dispose my forces as to throw re-enforcements across to Suffolk, I withdrew the troops from Harrod's and Young's Mills, except the cavalry and one regiment of infantry at each place. It was almost impossible to withdraw the artillery on account of the state of the roads. I have arranged the remaining troops not in garrisons, about 4,000 men, on the second line, and informed Captain Buchanan that for the above reasons I would not be able to have my troops down in the neighborhood of Fort Monroe and Newport News should he attack the two frigates at the latter place. It of course could not have been supposed that I could do so, when the department ordered away from me more than one-half of my force disposable for the field, even if the state of the roads permitted it. The shorter line, which I now occupy, will be defended with a force totally inadequate for that purpose.

The Merrimac will make no impression on Newport News, in my opinion, and if she succeeds in sinking the ships lying there it would do us little or no good, but if she had attacked the Baltic and other transports filled with troops in those waters her success would have been certain and of incalculable advantage to us. Please ask the Secretary of War to impress these views on the Navy Department.

To make up the 5,000 men ordered to Suffolk I have been compelled to send the following regiments and corps, which are now marching to King's Mill, to proceed via City Point and Petersburg, viz : Cobb's Legion, Sixteenth Georgia Regiment, Second Louisiana Regiment, Fifteenth North Carolina, and Fifty-third Virginia Regiments. In Cobb's Legion is included one field battery and about 350 cavalry, and I have sent an additional field battery.

You will perceive that nothing can be done by me in the way of an attack after having parted with so large a portion of my army. Indeed, unless some important object could be attained, the policy of merely being present near Fort Monroe and Newport News when the latter is bombarded is exceedingly doubtful, as it would incur a risk of disaster without any corresponding advantage, and especially as the number of troops at both places is increased, notwithstanding the recent departures, while my own is diminished by more than one-half disposable for field service. In any event I could render no assistance to the Merrimac merely by my presence. These are my views, and I think they are those of every officer under my command. I will execute however with alacrity any orders which may be given.

I have the honor to be, sir, very respectfully, your obedient servant,
J. BANKHEAD MAGRUDER,
Major-General, Commanding.

P. S.—The negroes are coming in pretty rapidly.

HEADQUARTERS DEPARTMENT OF PENINSULA,
Yorktown, March 6, 1862.
General S. COOPER,
    Adjutant and Inspector General, Richmond, Va.:
SIR: I stated in a conversation when in Richmond that I could spare, for a limited period 5,000 men to operate near me, but that their places should be supplied by 5,000 militia.

This statement was made to Mr. R. M. T. Hunter, and the next morning I wrote him that upon reflection I did not think that more than 2,000 men could leave this department with safety, subject to the above conditions, and requested him, I think, to lay the statement before the President. I do not complain, but will abide with cheerfulness by any arrangement made by the Department, knowing the pressure everywhere.

I respond cordially to the friendly assurances of the Secretary of War, and will send him all the support in my power, but fear being misunderstood; hence my explanations of to-day.

I am, sir, very respectfully, your obedient servant,
                    J. BANKHEAD MAGRUDER,
                        Major-General, Commanding.

YORKTOWN, March 6, 1862.
General S. COOPER,
    Adjutant-General C. S. Army:
The troops intended for Suffolk will embark at King's Mill, near Williamsburg, and proceed by steamers to City Point and thence via Petersburg Railroad to Suffolk. This is rendered necessary by the want of wharf facilities at any other point, and will save time as well as a land march of more than 20 miles. The troops will be in readiness to cross to-morrow, 5,000 men and two batteries. When shall they cross? Please answer.
                    J. BANKHEAD MAGRUDER,
                        Major-General, Commanding.

YORKTOWN, March 6, 1862,
(Received Richmond, March 6, 1862.)
General S. COOPER,
    Adjutant and Inspector General:
No answer has been received in reply to my telegram of to-day saying the troops will be ready to embark to-morrow at King's Mill. The horses will be sent by land from the south side, except a few for the officers. The rolling stock of the City Point and Petersburg Railroad will be in place for the transportation of the troops to-day, awaiting the movement.

Detention will be attended with a heavy expense and inconvenience perhaps to the road.
                    J. BANKHEAD MAGRUDER,
                        Major-General, Commanding.

RICHMOND, *March* 7, 1862.
General J. B. MAGRUDER, *Yorktown, Va.*:

Your dispatch received. The command will cross the river and proceed to its destination as soon as you are in possession of the means of transportation, which it is understood you have.

General Cobb is here. Shall he report to you in person or proceed to Suffolk?

S. COOPER,
Adjutant and Inspector General.

HEADQUARTERS DEPARTMENT OF NORFOLK,
Norfolk, Va., March 8, 1862.
Hon. J. P. BENJAMIN, *Secretary of War:*

SIR: I received yesterday your letter of the 5th instant. I have written to General Wise, and directed him to send me the report of Colonel Shaw of the capture of Roanoke Island and any others he may have to submit.

As regards "advising you of my plans and purposes and contemplated mode of defense," I have heretofore had to be only prepared for a front attack. I am now threatened both in front and rear, as the enemy can approach me from James River on my front and Albemarle Sound and the Chowan River in the rear. The principal obstacles to the front attack are the batteries. On the direct approach up the Elizabeth River these batteries are strong and, with the obstructions in the channel, sufficient to prevent their passage. Other points are weaker, but the enemy would be compelled to land and march through a wooded country, intersected with creeks and marshes. He can land at different points at the south, but from any point of landing he must march from 30 to 50 miles before reaching any vitally-important point. My plan is to attack him the moment he attempts to advance on any line, and, if possible, to throw on his flanks and cut his line.

I have thought it necessary to hold Sewell's Point. This battery covers the obstructions in the channel opposite to it. While this barrier remains large vessels cannot approach Craney Island. If the enemy is allowed to remove it, Craney Island could be approached and could be damaged by shells, which can do little injury at Sewell's. I have to keep two regiments and a light battery at Sewell's Point, and a small regiment and some field guns beyond them, to protect them from any landing near Ocean View.

The Third Alabama Regiment and a battery of artillery, which was farther east, toward Lynn Haven Bay, I have withdrawn, and moved across the Elizabeth River. I have kept this regiment on the railroad near Portsmouth ready to proceed to Suffolk or elsewhere as required. Means of transportation for the regiments, wagons, and mules are what I will most require, and I have urged the Quartermaster's Department to provide a sufficient supply as promptly as possible.

Where the move will be must depend upon the enemy, but I see no other plan than to attack him as soon as possible after he attempts to march.

I am, very respectfully, your obedient, servant,
BENJ. HUGER,
Major-General, Commanding.

SPECIAL ORDERS, } HDQRS. DEPARTMENT OF THE PENINSULA,
No. 657. } *Yorktown, March* 9, 1862—3 a. m.

Colonel Winston and Major Phillips will proceed at daylight in the neighborhood of New Market Bridge, sending a party of observation in the neighborhood of New Bridge. It is desirable to approach New Market Bridge through the woods, as the enemy is in great force in the neighborhood of Newport News. Colonel Winston is informed that our cavalry under Lieutenant-Colonel Goode and a regiment of infantry under Colonel Cumming will make a demonstration on the Warwick road on Newport News early this morning, and that the troops and artillery at Ship Point will march at daylight, and also that all the other troops of the Peninsula, except the necessary guards, will take post at Young's and Harrod's Mills.

Colonel Winston will endeavor to surprise any party of the enemy that he may find about New Market Bridge. He will ascertain whether the enemy are on the Scondam road or not, and if not, he will send his dragoons by that road to communicate with Colonel Cumming, who will thereupon advance toward Newport News, displaying his force to the best advantage, but will not engage the enemy if he advances, except that our cavalry will charge their cavalry or their artillery if the occasion offers.

Colonel Winston will keep his troops in ambush, securing for himself a safe retreat; and should the enemy advance he will permit their heads of columns to pass him and fall upon their flanks, and thus annoy him all the way in his advance.

By command of Major-General Magruder:

———— ————.

————

HEADQUARTERS,
Young's Mill, Va., March 10, 1862.

Commodore BUCHANAN, C. S. N.:

COMMODORE: It is with the most cordial satisfaction that I tender you my most hearty congratulations on the glorious and brilliant victory you achieved over the enemy on Saturday and Sunday last. I consider it the greatest achievement of the age, and am delighted beyond expression that it was accomplished under your auspices and that of my friend Lieut. Catesby Ap R. Jones.

I went down in person as soon as I heard of the attack, and had given some orders for the movement of troops and one of my regiments, with 250 cavalry, and remained in front of the works within a mile and a half for some two hours yesterday without artillery, but though very strong—I think at least 15,000—they did not come out to attack us.

I regret to hear that you are wounded, but hope your wound will not prove serious.

I send you this hasty expression of my extreme satisfaction by Sergeant Tabb, whose departure I cannot delay.

With the highest respect, I remain, commodore, very sincerely, yours,

J. BANKHEAD MAGRUDER,
Major-General, Commanding.

ENGINEER BUREAU,
Richmond, March 12, 1862.

Hon. J. P. BENJAMIN, *Secretary of War:*

SIR : The following report is respectfully submitted as a partial reply to the resolutions of Congress of the 24th February, calling for information, surveys, and reports connected with the defenses of Richmond:

In ascending the James River the defenses consist of—

1st. *Fort Boykin, Day's Neck.*—Mounting ten guns; 42-pounders and 32-pounders, hot shot, &c.

2d. *Fort Huger, Harden's Bluff.*—Mounting thirteen guns; one 10-inch columbiad, pattern rifled, *en barbette,* four 9-inch Dahlgrens *en barbette,* two 8-inch columbiads *en barbette,* six hot-shot 32-pounders on ship carriages.

3d. *Mulberry Island Point Battery.*—Five 42-pounder guns *en barbette,* two 8-inch columbiads *en route,* fifteen casemates building rapidly, and large covering work nearly completed.

4th. *Jamestown Island Batteries.*—Thirteen guns; four 9-inch Dahlgrens, four 8-inch columbiads and two more *en route,* five hot-shot long 32s.

5th. *Drewry's Bluff Battery,* coupled with obstructions in the river, is being rapidly constructed, under the direction of Lieutenant Mason, of the Provisional Engineer Corps.

The first is completed, while the second and third are being rapidly and intelligently improved with bomb-proofs, &c., by Captain Clarke, of the Provisional Engineer Corps, who has a force of at least 1,000 hands.

From 20 to 30 miles below City Point there are two positions—Fort Powhatan and Kennon's marshes—which have been thoroughly examined by the ablest officers at the disposition of the department, and reported to be good locations for batteries. If they are placed at either of the above points obstacles should be constructed in connection with them. The final and intelligent selection of a site can consequently not be determined except by a thorough hydrographic survey.

In regard to the Richmond defenses, it was the opinion of General Leadbetter that the works around the city were rather near, but so much had been done at the time he took charge of them, that he directed me, on leaving for Tennessee, to carry out the plans adopted by the Engineer Department of Virginia. This I have sought to do with the means at my disposition, and a large proportion of the leading works are completed. Intermediate secondary breastworks could be thrown up with sufficient rapidity by the troops who are to defend the main works when there is occasion. Labor in that direction at present would seem to be injudicious. Most of the works are closed, and those which are not so can be rapidly protected. Directions have been given to drain the magazines thoroughly, and if necessary to construct new ones.

There are but few guns mounted on the works. A full armament for them would be exceedingly difficult to procure, and the propriety of concentrating so many pieces on a contracted local defense would seem at least doubtful.

The batteries on the Manchester hills are very nearly, if not entirely, constructed, and a force has been called out to repair and complete them. Drewry's Bluff, a most commanding point where the James River is narrowest, about 7 miles below Richmond, has been selected as the best point for a battery coupled with obstructions. In its immediate vicinity also is a strong commanding ridge on the line of approach from Petersburg to Richmond.

In regard to the line of the Chickahominy, I can as yet make no definite report, although an officer is on duty in its examination. The recent calls for engineers by General Johnston and others have left me but limited professional resources. I have heard, however, that Colonel Talcott, Chief of the Virginia Engineer Corps, examined this line, but did not think very favorably of it. It may, however, be possible to erect, in a reasonable time, a series of dams, with properly-constructed covering works, which would add greatly to the strength of the Richmond defenses on the north. As soon as the surveys are completed a full report will be promptly made.

The James River defenses, which are rapidly improving, afford already a good protection against wooden fleets, but not against iron-clad vessels. From recent developments it is evident that nothing but the very heaviest ordnance, and that in connection with obstructions and perhaps torpedoes, can contend successfully with this latter class. It is to such means we are resorting on the James River. In positions similar to those of Fort Huger, Yorktown, and Mulberry Island Point the only course left to pursue seems to be to mount the guns on the bluffs, where they are not liable to be struck, or in well-constructed casemates, to contend with wooden ships, keeping sand bags ready filled to protect them against iron-clad vessels. This class is so excessively expensive and confined as to be ill-adapted to the transportation of troops in large numbers. The effect, however, of passing our lower batteries by preventing the safe navigation of our rivers above them will probably be to force us at no distant day to rely in great measure on land transportation.

A mistaken impression on my part that this report was called for on the termination of the surveys has led to this delay, for which it is the only excuse.

With great respect, your obedient servant,
ALFRED L. RIVES,
Acting Chief Engineer Bureau.

ENGINEER BUREAU,
Richmond, March 12, 1862.

General J. BANKHEAD MAGRUDER,
Commanding Army of the Peninsula:

GENERAL: Colonel Carter, who will hand you this, submitted to me Captain Dimmock's report, approved by himself and addressed to you. From the experience derived in the recent contest between the Virginia and Monitor it is evident to me that water batteries in the immediate vicinity of deep water should be abandoned at once—those at both Yorktown and Gloucester Point. I unhesitatingly recommend such a step, only leaving a masked battery of the smallest pieces to protect the beach and communicating with the works on the bluffs by a covered way.

The sketch below gives the idea roughly:

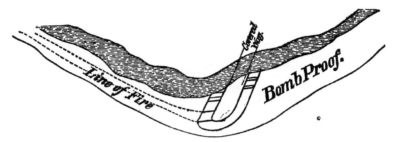

I will send plans promptly, but in case my occupations, which are now very heavy, should prevent, I feel assured the engineers in your command can arrange the details. By keeping sand bags filled, on hand, your guns can in a few minutes be protected against iron-clad boats. These bags could be thrown off rapidly should a wooden fleet attempt to pass with troops, and I believe in that case the bluff batteries fully equal to the water batteries.

You will readily infer from what I have written that I think your water communication with West Point in great danger. I shall exert myself to have the Gloucester Point guns mounted promptly and properly.

Colonel Carter can communicate more fully the result we have arrived at.

With great respect, your obedient servant,

ALFRED L. RIVES,
Acting Chief Engineer Bureau.

HEADQUARTERS,
Young's Mill, March 12, 1862.

General S. COOPER,
Adjutant and Inspector General, Richmond:

SIR: I have the honor to report that I sent Sergeant Tabb, a most intelligent man, who is on signal service in this department and was a volunteer on board of the Virginia in the late action, to reconnoiter Newport News in a boat yesterday afternoon, and he has just returned, stating that whilst in front of Newport News the Ericsson came up from Fort Monroe with some troops on board and landed them at Newport News; that a very large force was at that place and increasing. Their pickets have advanced some mile and a half up the river, and I am satisfied that they mean to march up on the left bank of James River, sending the Ericsson to silence the guns in the river batteries, and thus freeing the river for the passage of transports with other troops and forcing us to fall back by ascending the river. It may require some little time to do this, but they will succeed in the end, unless the Virginia can leave the dock and prevent the Ericsson from coming up. The latter vessel draws, I am informed, much less water than the Virginia, and if she once gets up the Virginia could not follow her, as there is a bar below Day's Neck, I am told by James River pilots, on which there is not more than 18 feet water, and the Virginia draws 22 feet.

I deem it of the utmost importance to make this statement to you for the information of the War and Navy Departments and the President, although the information may already be in their possession.

My cavalry drove in the enemy's pickets last evening, but the advance of their pickets and their increasing force admonishes me of the necessity of arranging my troops on the second line for defense, from which I have advanced them after the naval action, to be ready to take advantage of the effect of that achievement, and at the same time to cover, if possible, the movement of troops from here to Suffolk. They will resume their places to-day, presenting, however, the same line of pickets to the enemy and holding the front line by cavalry and light infantry, with orders to fall back on the second line in case of an advance.

I would recommend that not a moment be lost in again bringing out the Virginia, as I learn from my spies that their officers say the Virginia is much injured and that they have no apprehension from her for the present. I presume that they will advance as soon as possible in the hope that she will not be ready, and the Ericsson once up the river, she cannot follow. Should the Ericsson attack our batteries on James River, the guns on ship carriages will be withdrawn from the effects of the fire and all the other guns and men will be protected as much as possible.

I am, sir, very respectfully, your obedient servant,

J. BANKHEAD MAGRUDER,
Major-General, Commanding.

RICHMOND, VA., *March* 13, 1862.

Maj. Gen. J. B. MAGRUDER,
Commanding, &c., Yorktown, Va.:

GENERAL: I have the honor to acknowledge your letter of the 12th instant, reporting the result of a reconnaissance made by your orders of the condition of the enemy at Newport News and your proposed movements in the event of an advance by him up the left bank of the river. As regards the steamer Virginia, the Secretary of the Navy informs me that she went into the dock upon her arrival at Norfolk, with orders that neither labor nor expense should be spared upon her repair. It is hoped that she will be out at an early day.

I am, &c.,

R. E. LEE,
General, Commanding.

YORKTOWN, *March* 13, 1862,
(Received March 14, 1862.)

General S. COOPER,
Adjutant and Inspector General:

To-day the enemy drove in our pickets 4 miles below Young's Mill. Troops are being again landed at Newport News from the Baltimore boat. Please order at once to Williamsburg by the James River boats the regiment which the Secretary of War said he would send. When will the Virginia be out? The disposition of my troops and the nature of my operations depend upon the answer to this question. Answer by telegraph.

J. BANKHEAD MAGRUDER,
Major-General, Commanding.

[Indorsement.]

MARCH 14, 1862.

The unarmed regiment promised by Secretary of War, to be armed by you with the surplus arms in your command, is expected here soon. It will thereafter be immediately sent to you. It is impossible to say when the Virginia will be in position; it is supposed in a day or two.

S. COOPER.

HEADQUARTERS DEPARTMENT OF NORFOLK,
March 13, 1862.

Hon. J. P. BENJAMIN, *Secretary of War:*

SIR: I have expressed to you my conviction that iron-clad vessels can pass all our batteries with impunity. In barricading the approach to Norfolk it was necessary to leave a narrow passage for our vessels to go out. The Virginia passed through it to get into the Roads the other day.

The question now is, Should not this passage be stopped? If done, it should be with the concurrence of the Navy Department.

I think the channel should be stopped, and our vessels kept inside for the protection of the town. I beg the subject may be considered, and if the work is done, it should be by order of War and Navy Departments.

Very respectfully, your obedient servant,

BENJ. HUGER,
Major-General.

GENERAL ORDERS, }   HDQRS. ARMY OF THE PENINSULA,
No. 159.   }   *Bartlett's Ranche, March* 13, 1862.

All the arrangements having been made for the defense of this Peninsula, and the commanding general, as the troops are stationed at different places, not having it in his power to be at the same time with each body of troops, the following directions are given for the government of all, viz:

When any body of our troops, large or small, meets with any body of the enemy's troops, however large, the commanding officer of our troops will cause the enemy to be immediately attacked, and the men will attack at once and furiously. This is an order easily understood by officers and men and will doubtless be obeyed with alacrity by both.

The above instructions are not intended for those who have special orders under certain named circumstances not to fight.

By command of Major-General Magruder:

JOHN DONNELL SMITH,
Acting Aide-de-Camp.

HEADQUARTERS ARMY OF THE PENINSULA,
At Bartlett's, near Bethel, March 14, 1862.

General R. E. LEE,
Commanding General of the Confederate Armies, at Richmond:

GENERAL: I do not know your adjutant-general, and therefore address you personally.

First, allow me to congratulate you upon the high position to which you have been advanced of being Commander-in-Chief of the Confederate forces, and to predict for you, however long our triumph may be delayed, a career of usefulness to the country and great honor to yourself.

I come again under your command with pleasure, and will execute your orders with alacrity and zeal. I have not time now to write a long letter nor have you perhaps the time to read one, but it is necessary that you should know the state of affairs here at once; and I therefore inform you that the number of my troops is far too small in comparison with the magnitude of the forces in front of me as well as that of the great interests which I have to defend. When in Richmond last the Secretary of War asked me the strength of the garrison at Newport News, and I answered "about 4,000 or 5,000." He desired me, in conjunction with Captain Buchanan, of the Navy, to capture them if possible. I readily assented, and proceeded to make the necessary arrangements. These were based, of course, upon the presumption that the garrison would remain as it was. Subsequently, in a conversation with Mr. Hunter, I was asked what troops I could spare. I answered that I supposed about 5,000. The next morning, after reflection, I wrote a communication to Mr. Hunter, stating that I found upon calculation I could spare but 2,000, and them only to operate for a short time and within convenient distance, and also upon condition that their places would be supplied by militia, from whom I could substitute in some of my works for better-drilled troops.

Soon after my return and before the Virginia was ready troops began to assemble at Newport News, and they have been steadily increasing in numbers ever since, so that now they cannot fall much short of 20,000 men. In consequence of this increase of troops and of the roads being impracticable for artillery I advised the Government against the co-operation. The threatening attitude of Burnside caused them to send about 5,000 troops from my command, which leaves me some 4,500 infantry disposable for the field and about 500 cavalry. With this number there is no line across the Peninsula which I could hope to defend with success. The enemy is fully aware of my having sent troops across the river, though on Sunday last I sent troops in the immediate vicinity of Newport News, and have been operating since with the hope of deceiving him.

A telegraphic communication has been established between Fort Monroe and Washington. All the enemy's ships of war have been sent out of the Roads except the Monitor Ericsson, and I expect an advance on James River every moment, supported by the Monitor, while the Virginia is in dock. No militia can be expected from the counties assigned to my district, as almost all of them have volunteered, the few remaining having been called out long since, not more than a few hundred in all.

I see by the papers that Burnside has landed his troops before New Berne. Under these circumstances is it not absolutely necessary to order back the troops which I sent to Suffolk? I certainly think so, and request that, in view of the above and of the heavy force at Newport News, which threatens the Peninsula, and the changed aspect of affairs at Suffolk, it may be done with the least possible delay. The infantry should come to City Point and by steamboats to King's Mill, and the cavalry, artillery, wagons, and ambulances should march to Carter's wharf and cross over to Jamestown Island. Should the enemy advance I should be compelled to withdraw at once the few troops

I have in front to my main line of defense behind Warwick River, the left resting on Yorktown and the right on Mulberry Island. That line is too long for the few troops I have, being over 8 miles to the mouth of the Peninsula, known as Mulberry Island, and about 14 miles from Yorktown to Mulberry Island Point, which is the corresponding work on James River.

The enemy has at least sixteen companies of good cavalry and about forty pieces of good light artillery. I have about 500 cavalry, all told, and about the same number of light pieces with [as] the enemy, badly mounted and equipped, disposable for the field, the rest being required in the various garrisons. I made requisitions for 50 artillery horses, but have not got them. I have the artillery harness ready.

To meet the enemy's great superiority in cavalry I suggest that the Lunenburg Cavalry, from Fredericksburg, which is armed, and one or two companies from there, if they can be spared, and Capt. B. F. Winfield's company, of Sussex, now at Richmond, armed, be sent to me, also a troop of horse in Petersburg and one in Mecklenburg, neither armed, be ordered to me, and be armed with shot-guns and lances. I think also that there has been an unequal distribution of counties from which militia is to be drawn. The call for the militia will not strengthen me at all, whilst the conflict between the laws of the State of Virginia and the Confederate States and the canvassing for the elections of officers that are to take place is disorganizing and demoralizing to a deplorable extent the twelve-months' regiments and companies with me in this department.

To produce something like order out of this chaos, if possible, I desire to publish an order to the following effect, if it meet with the views of yourself and the War Department:

First. That none shall enlist out of this department in another.

Second. That men who re-enlist shall do so in the same arm of the service to which they now belong.

Third. That the artillery, light and heavy, shall be given only to the artillery officers, or those who have served with artillery who have already proved themselves worthy of having them.

Fourth. That all men who have re-enlisted under the idea that they can choose their arm of service shall organize as infantry, unless they are already artillery or cavalry, and shall afterward be exchanged by the commanding officer of the department, in accordance with their wishes, whenever it can be done without injury to the public service.

I sent a list of artillery officers, according to merit, at the request of the Secretary of War, for the information of the President. Since then some exchanges have occurred. Colonel Randolph has been made a general, and I would like to place the name of [J.] Thompson Brown as colonel instead of Lewis Brown. The latter I recommend to be lieutenant-colonel.

Should the troops sent to Suffolk be wanted there again they could be sent there in time, but unless sent at once here they will not be in time, I think. There is no indication of a possibility of troops crossing over to Suffolk from Newport News except up James River.

I am, General, very respectfully, your obedient servant,

J. BANKHEAD MAGRUDER,
Major-General, Commanding.

We have no more paper here.

WAR DEPARTMENT, C. S. A.,
Richmond, Va., March 15, 1862.

Maj. Gen. B. HUGER, *Norfolk, Va.:*

SIR: I have the honor of acknowledging the receipt of your letter of the 13th instant. The question of closing the harbor of Norfolk, suggested by you, is decided against your views. None of us are of opinion that it would be proper to lose the vast advantages resulting from the enemy's fright at the bare idea of the Virginia reappearing among the wooden ships. The fact of her presence guarantees you against any attempt to blockade the river. It is, however, necessary to keep the necessary means of closing the Elizabeth River ready at hand for use at a moment's warning in case the Monitor should attempt an entrance. The Nansemond River ought to be obstructed without delay.

I inclose you a letter, to be forwarded to General Wise after perusal by you. It explains itself. I also send herewith a voluminous report, 143 pages, sent to me by General Wise, for your remarks. You will find at pages 109 and 116 copies of his letters to you of February 10 and 11, which he evidently regards as his report, and which I asked you to send me, but which you seem not to have received. Congress has made a call for this report; but it cannot be sent in, if at all, without your comments, as it should regularly have been forwarded through you.

l am, your obedient servant,

J. P. BENJAMIN,
Secretary of War.

RICHMOND, VA., *March* 15, 1862.

Maj. Gen. J. B. MAGRUDER,
Commanding, &c., Yorktown, Va.:

GENERAL: As far as I can judge at this distance the plan of constructing a defensive line between Yorktown and Mulberry Island by damming and defending the Warwick River promises the happiest results. I would therefore recommend to you, should you concur in this opinion, to apply as great a force on the work as possible. With your left resting on the batteries on York River and your right defended by the batteries on James River, with the aid of the Virginia and other steamers, I think you may defy the advance of the enemy up the Peninsula, supported as this line would be by your second system of defenses.

I am, &c.,

R. E. LEE,
General, Commanding.

HEADQUARTERS ARMY OF THE PENINSULA,
At Bartlett's, near Bethel, March 16, 1862.

Gen. R. E. LEE,
Commanding Armies of the Confederate States:

GENERAL: The enemy again drove in the pickets to-day on the Warwick road after exchanging fire. He appears to be operating with a considerable advance guard, supported by heavier bodies, between it and Newport News, so that it is difficult to cut off the advanced troops without entangling my handful of men with very superior forces lying in wait. The country is open from the wood to James River, ascending with heavy wood on the right of it all the way. He generally advances a column on the road and one on the beach under the bank, and he occupies the wood in force. . A party sent out by me this morning fell in with what was represented to be a large body of skirmishers in this woods, fired upon them, and one of the enemy fell. Our party consisted of five men, who retired to report the result of their observations.

I immediately sent out about 1,000 men, all I had down here, to support the pickets, but the enemy had withdrawn. I presume this will be repeated daily until he either gains ground or keeps my forces from Yorktown and Mulberry Island, with a view of attacking a more vital point. I cannot keep my troops so far down as this without incurring great risk of losing the vital positions in my rear. So, if the enemy persevere, I shall be compelled in a very short time to withdraw the four regiments which are now in front to the second line, viz, from Yorktown to Mulberry Island. Upon the successful defense of this and its water flanks that of the whole Peninsula entirely depends.

I inclose you a communication from Colonel Cabell in relation to Harden's Bluff. I applied more than three months ago to have this work transferred to my department, and sent Colonel Randolph and Mr. St. John, the engineer then in charge of the works of this Peninsula, to Richmond to press the consideration of the subject upon the consideration of the War Department, but could get no answer. It is too late now probably to effect anything, but I am willing to do what can be done. The battery has been a naval battery, and is now commanded by Captain De Lagnel (late of the Navy, but now temporarily a captain in the Confederate Army). I recommend that the whole be placed under the command of the commanding officer, whoever he may be—at present Colonel Archer—while the guns and the men who serve them should be under the immediate command of Captain De Lagnel, who, however, I believe, is junior to the captains of artillery serving the guns; and, if so, ought to be made a major, as has been done in many similar cases, and as his services at this time cannot be spared.

I recommend that General Colston, who commands that portion of General Huger's department, be ordered to call out forthwith all the negroes, with their axes, spades, &c., for the purpose of executing without delay any work which Captain Rives, in charge of the Engineer Bureau at Richmond, or Captain Clark, the engineer in immediate charge of the work, may require to be done. The decision as respects the rank, relative positions, and responsibilities of the officers at Harden's Bluff I think had better come from yourself or the War Department, as I understand there is some feeling among them on this subject.

Has anything been heard at headquarters of Porter's mortar fleet? I presume that now Yorktown will be the object of attack by the Monitor and that fleet, and I am doing my best to provide against this new danger.

I am, General, very respectfully, your obedient servant,
J. BANKHEAD MAGRUDER,
Major-General, Commanding.

[Inclosure.]

Curtis' Farm, *March* 13, 1862.

Brig. Gen. Lafayette McLaws:

Sir: As directed by Major-General Magruder, I proceeded to-day to Harden's Bluff. Seven of the largest guns have been placed *en barbette,* having been previously placed in embrasure. There are six other guns to be placed *en barbette.* The position I think singularly strong, if further assisted by art. The guns should be immediately placed in position. Traverses should be immediately thrown up. The fort is small, and this could be completed in a very short time. The woods come up immediately to the fort and surround it on all sides, except on the river front. They afford perfect shelter for an attacking force. The forest should be cleared with the utmost possible dispatch. In the woods a very short distance from the fort is a marsh, which nearly surrounds the fort. Over this marsh a road passes leading to the camp of Lieutenant-Colonel Archer. The road can be completely commanded by the fort, but the guns for this purpose are not yet in position. There are several wooden buildings recently erected inside the fort. I think they should be removed at once, with the exception, perhaps, of the one for commissary stores. Of this last I am doubtful. This should be removed as soon as a store-house can be erected in another position. The two artillery companies should be placed under the immediate command of the commander of the fort, and required to occupy their position either in the fort or immediately adjacent thereto. They should be drilled immediately at their pieces. The drill for some time has been suspended, I was informed, partly because some of the guns were being removed *en barbette* from the embrasures.

I do not wish to be understood as interfering in any question existing as to the command between the officers, but the exigencies of the service, the importance of that position as bearing on the defenses of James River, and particularly Mulberry Island batteries, and the batteries on the north side of James River generally justify my allusion to the necessity of its being immediately put in proper state of defense, and that the authority and respective rights and commands of the officers be distinctly defined.

I also recommend that bomb-proofs be erected and the batteries casemated with the utmost possible dispatch.

Respectfully, your obedient servant,

HENRY COULTER CABELL,
Lieutenant-Colonel and Chief of Artillery, P. A. C. S.

[Indorsement.]

MARCH 14, 1862.

Harden's Bluff batteries bear such a close relation to Mulberry Point Battery—the right flank of this department, for if that battery is taken the right flank may be considered as turned—that I feel authorized in calling the attention of the commanding general to the remarks of Colonel Cabell, within, in relation to the condition of that battery, especially as to the drill, the command, and its rear defenses.

L. McLAWS,
Brigadier-General, Commanding.

RICHMOND, VA., *March 17, 1862.*

General J. B. MAGRUDER,
Commanding Army of Peninsula:

GENERAL: I have had the honor to receive your letter of the 14th instant, and regret very much to learn the smallness of the number of your troops. I will endeavor to re-enforce you as soon as possible, but at this time I see no immediate prospect. The pressure of affairs in North Carolina renders it necessary to send there all available forces, even at the risk of hazarding the safety of other points, inasmuch as if the line of railroad through the State is possessed by the enemy it will cause us serious injury.

The object of sending a portion of your command to Suffolk was to prevent the seizure of that point by the combined forces of Generals Wool and Burnside. The latter is now at New Berne, but can easily transfer his troops back to Albemarle Sound, and, unless a change in the supposed original plan of the enemy is more apparent, I think it unnecessary to cross your troops back to the left bank of James River yet awhile. I hardly think he will risk an attack upon you unsupported by his columns in other directions. I know, however, you will be vigilant in watching his movements, and should you ascertain that to be his intention, your troops will be immediately ordered back by the route you designate.

The Quartermaster-General will be informed that the artillery horses you require have not reached you, and be desired to send them as soon as possible. I had hoped that you had sufficient cavalry for your purposes. I have no knowledge of the service on which the companies named by you are placed, but will inquire.

As regards the militia, it is the object of the State to fill up from those enrolled by volunteer or draft its companies and regiments.

The disorganization of the regiments, &c., from the cause you mention is apparent, and some days ago the Military Committee of Congress were appealed to to draft a bill to accomplish what you desire. •It is hoped some measure of relief will be passed.

I am, &c.,

R. E. LEE,
General, Commanding.

GENERAL ORDERS, }   HDQRS. ARMY OF THE PENINSULA,
     No. 161.   }   *Yorktown, Va., March 17,* 1862.

In going into battle commanding officers of companies will call the roll of their companies and in coming out of action the rolls will be called. Any member of the company absent at the latter roll call, unless killed or wounded, will be considered as having been derelict to the highest duty, and will be punished accordingly. The excuse sometimes given that men have left the field to carry off the wounded is inadmissible, as no man will be permitted to leave the ranks for such purpose, but when men are killed or wounded in the ranks their places will be filled by their comrades touching elbows toward the guide.

*   *   *   *   *

By order of Major-General Magruder:

HENRY BRYAN,
Assistant Adjutant-General.

CHAPTER XX.

OPERATIONS IN NORTH CAROLINA.

January 11–August 20, 1862.

SUMMARY OF THE PRINCIPAL EVENTS.*

Jan. 11, 1862.—The Burnside Expedition sails from Fort Monroe, Va.

13, 1862.—Expedition arrives at Hatteras Inlet.

Brig. Gen. Ambrose E. Burnside, U. S. Army, assumes command of the Department of North Carolina.†

22, 1862.—Brig. Gen. Henry A. Wise, C. S. Army, assigned to command at Roanoke Island.

Feb. 8, 1862.—Battle of Roanoke Island.

10, 1862.—Action at Elizabeth City.

18–20, 1862.—Expedition to Winton, and skirmish February 19.

19–20, 1862.—Expedition into Currituck Sound.

Mar. 14, 1862.—Battle of New Berne.

19, 1862.—Brig. Gen. J. R. Anderson supersedes Brig. Gen. R. C. Gatlin in command of the Confederate Department of North Carolina.‡

20–21, 1862.—Expedition to Washington.

23–April 26, 1862.—Siege of Fort Macon.

24, 1862.—Maj. Gen. Th. H. Holmes, C. S. Army, supersedes Brig. Gen. J. R. Anderson.

31, 1862.—Skirmish at Deep Gully.

April 7, 1862.—Skirmish at Foy's Plantation.

Skirmish near Newport.

7– 8, 1862.—Expedition to Elizabeth City.

13, 1862.—Skirmish at Gillett's Farm, Pebbly Run.

19, 1862.—Engagement at South Mills, Camden County.

Skirmish on the Trent Road.

27, 1862.—Skirmish near Haughton's Mill, Pollocksville Road.

29, 1862.—Skirmish near Batchelder's Creek.

May 2, 1862.—Skirmish near Deep Gully, Trenton Road.

7– 8, 1862.—Expedition from Roanoke Island toward Gatesville.

15–16, 1862.—Skirmishes near Trenton Bridge, at Young's Cross-Roads, and Pollocksville.

22, 1862.—Skirmish at the Trenton and Pollocksville Cross-Roads.

30, 1862.—Skirmish at Tranter's Creek.

June 2, 1862.—Skirmish at Tranter's Creek.

---

* Of some of the minor conflicts mentioned in this "Summary" no circumstantial reports are on file.

† This department, to consist of the State of North Carolina, had been created January 7, 1862, by General Orders, No. 2, Headquarters of the Army, of that date.

‡ For General Gatlin's report of operations in his department from August 20, 1861, to March 19, 1862, see Series I, Vol. IV, pp. 573–579.

June   3, 1862.—North Carolina, west of the Blue Ridge, embraced in the Confederate Department of East Tennessee.
        5, 1862.—Action at Tranter's Creek.
       21, 1862.—Confederate Department of North Carolina extended to the south bank of the James River.
       24, 1862.—Reconnaissance from Washington to Tranter's Creek.
July   6, 1862.—Major-General Burnside sails with re-enforcements for the Army of the Potomac, leaving Brig. Gen. John G. Foster in command of the Department of North Carolina.
        9, 1862.—Capture of Hamilton.
       17, 1862.—Maj. Gen. D. H. Hill, C. S. Army, assigned to command of the Department of North Carolina.
   24-28, 1862.—Expeditions from New Berne to Trenton and Pollocksville, &c.
       26, 1862.—Skirmish at Mill Creek, near Pollocksville.
   26-29, 1862.—Reconnaissance from Newport to Young's Cross-Roads, and skirmish 27th.
       28, 1862.—Expedition from Batchelder's Creek, on Neuse River Road.
Aug. 14-15, 1862.—Reconnaissance from Newport to Swansborough.

FEBRUARY 8, 1862.—Battle of Roanoke Island, N. C.

REPORTS, ETC.

No. 1.—Brig. Gen. Ambrose E. Burnside, U. S. Army, with congratulatory orders.
No. 2.—Lieut. Daniel W. Flagler, U. S. Ordnance Department.
No. 3.—Surgeon William H. Church, U. S. Army, Acting Medical Director.
No. 4.—Brig. Gen. John G. Foster, U. S. Army, commanding First Brigade, with sketch.
No. 5.—Capt. Daniel Messinger, Acting Aide-de-Camp.
No. 6.—Lieut. C. Cushing Eyre, First New York Marine Artillery.
No. 7.—Lieut. James H. Strong, Aide-de-Camp.
No. 8.—Lieut. James A. Hedden, First New York Marine Artillery.
No. 9.—Lieut. James M. Pendleton, Aide-de-Camp.
No. 10.—Lieut. Col. Albert W. Drake, Tenth Connecticut Infantry.
No. 11.—Col. John Kurtz, Twenty-third Massachusetts Infantry.
No. 12.—Col. Thomas G. Stevenson, Twenty-fourth Massachusetts Infantry.
No. 13.—Col. Edwin Upton, Twenty-fifth Massachusetts Infantry.
No. 14.—Col. Horace C. Lee, Twenty-seventh Massachusetts Infantry.
No. 15.—Brig. Gen. Jesse L. Reno, U. S. Army, commanding Second Brigade.
No. 16.—Capt. Montgomery Ritchie, Aide-de-Camp.
No. 17.—Lieut. Col. Alberto C. Maggi, Twenty-first Massachusetts Infantry.
No. 18.—Lieut. Col. Charles A. Heckman, Ninth New Jersey Infantry.
No. 19.—Col. Edward Ferrero, Fifty-first New York Infantry.
No. 20.—Col. John F. Hartranft, Fifty-first Pennsylvania Infantry.
No. 21.—Brig. Gen. John G. Parke, U. S. Army, commanding Third Brigade.
No. 22.—Col. Isaac P. Rodman, Fourth Rhode Island Infantry.
No. 23.—Maj. Gen. Benjamin Huger, C. S. Army, with correspondence.
No. 24.—Brig. Gen. Henry A. Wise, C. S. Army, with correspondence.
No. 25.—Col. H. M. Shaw, Eighth North Carolina Infantry.
No. 26.—Capt. James M. Whitson, Eighth North Carolina Infantry.
No. 27.—Col. John V. Jordan, Thirty-first North Carolina Infantry.
No. 28.—Lieut. Col. Wharton J. Green, Second North Carolina Battalion.
No. 29.—Maj. H. W. Fry, Forty-sixth Virginia Infantry.
No. 30.—Lieut. Col. Frank P. Anderson, Fifty-ninth Virginia Infantry.
No. 31.—Maj. G. H. Hill, C. S. Army, commanding Fort Bartow.
No. 32.—Capt. John S. Taylor, C. S. Army, in charge of heavy artillery.
No. 33.—Report of Investigating Committee Confederate House of Representatives.

No.-1.

Reports of Brig. Gen. Ambrose E. Burnside, U. S. Army, with congrat-
ulatory orders.

HEADQUARTERS DEPARTMENT OF NORTH CAROLINA,
Roanoke Island, N. C., February 10, 1862.

GENERAL: I have the honor to report that a combined attack upon
this island was commenced on the morning of the 7th by the naval
and military forces of this expedition, which has resulted in the capture of six forts, forty guns, over 2,000 prisoners, and upward of 3,000
small-arms. Among the prisoners are Colonel Shaw, commander of
the island, and O. Jennings Wise, commander of the Wise Legion.
The latter was mortally wounded and has since died. The whole work
was finished on the afternoon of the 8th instant, after a hard day's
fighting, by a brilliant charge on the battery in the center of the island
and a rapid pursuit of the enemy to the north end of the island, resulting in the capture of the prisoners mentioned above. We have had
no time to count them, but the number is estimated at near 3,000.

Our men fought bravely, and have endured most manfully the hardships incident to fighting through swamps and dense thickets.

It is impossible to give the details of the engagement or to mention
meritorious officers and men in the short time allowed for writing this
report. The naval vessel carrying it starts immediately for Hampton
Roads, and the reports of the brigadier-generals have not yet been
handed in. It is enough to say that the officers and men of both arms
of the service have fought gallantly and the plans agreed upon before
leaving Hatteras were carried out.

I will be excused for saying in reference to the action that I owe
everything to Generals Foster, Reno, and Parke, as more full details
will show.

I am sorry to report the loss of about 35 killed and about 200
wounded, 10 of them probably mortally.* Among the killed are Colonel Russell, of the Tenth Connecticut Regiment, and Lieut. Col.
Joseph A. Viguer De Monteil, of the D'Epineuil Zouaves, both of
whom fought most gallantly.

I regret exceedingly not being able to send a full report of the killed
and wounded, but will send a dispatch-boat in a day or two with full
returns.

I beg leave to inclose a copy of a general order issued by me on the
9th instant.

I am most happy to say that I have just received a message from
Commodore Goldsborough, stating that the expedition of the gunboats
against Elizabeth City and the rebel fleet has been entirely successful.
He will of course send his returns to his Department.

I have the honor to be, General, your obedient servant,
A. E. BURNSIDE,
Brigadier-General, Commanding Department of North Carolina.

Maj. Gen. GEORGE B. McCLELLAN,
Commanding U. S. Army, Washington, D. C.

---

*But see revised statement, p. 85.

GENERAL ORDERS, }   HDQRS. DEPT. OF NORTH CAROLINA,
  No. 7.   }   *Roanoke Island, N. C., February* 9, 1862.

The general commanding congratulates his troops on their brilliant and successful occupation of Roanoke Island. The courage and steadiness they have shown under fire is what he expected from them, and he accepts it as a token of future victory. Each regiment on the island will inscribe on its banner, "Roanoke Island, February 8, 1862."

The highest praise is due to Brigadier-Generals Foster, Reno, and Parke, who so bravely and energetically carried out the movement that has resulted in the complete success of the Union arms.

By command of Brig. Gen. A. E. Burnside:

LEWIS RICHMOND,
Assistant Adjutant-General.

—

HEADQUARTERS DEPARTMENT OF NORTH CAROLINA,
Roanoke, February 14, 1862.

GENERAL: I have the honor to transmit a more detailed report of the events that have transpired in this command since my last dispatch to the General-in-Chief, on the 4th instant, from Hatteras Inlet, stating that I was about ready to move upon Roanoke Island with a portion of this command—of about twelve regiments and a half—the hasty dispatch of the 10th instant only giving the general result of the movement spoken of above.

The difficulty of watering, coaling, and provisioning our vessels in the midst of the gale, after they had crossed the swash, was scarcely less than that of getting our vessels into the sound, owing to the necessity of having to lighten every supply vessel over the bulkhead.

On the evening of the 4th instant I reported to Commodore Goldsborough my readiness to start on the following morning, and accordingly we weighed anchor (the naval fleet leading) at 7 o'clock on the morning of the 5th instant, and arrived without accident off Stumpy Point, some 6 miles from the entrance to Croatan Sound, at 5.30 p. m., when the signal to anchor was given. On the following morning (the 6th) we again weighed anchor at 6.30 a. m., but could proceed no farther than to the entrance of the sound in consequence of a thick fog which had set in. The fleet of the enemy, anchored in line of battle, was discovered off Pork Point before the fog came on, which convinced us that the first battery was probably at that point. The remaining part of that day was used in consultation and arranging the vessels for a general movement on the following day. Five of my armed propellers were lightened of their troops to one company each, and were sent forward with the Picket to anchor in line of battle with the naval fleet, under the direction of Capt. S. F. Hazard, of the Navy. The remaining two propellers I ordered General Parke to anchor some half mile below, as a rear guard to the transport fleet, which consisted of armed and unarmed steamers and sailing vessels.

We weighed anchor early next morning and passed through the narrow channel at the entrance to Croatan Sound in single file, the head of the naval fleet arriving off Pork Point Battery at five minutes past 9 o'clock a. m., when the first gun was fired. By 10.30 o'clock the action became general, the attack continuing in most gallant style until 6.30 p. m. One of the two propellers forming the rear guard, having on board three companies of troops, moved forward and joined Captain Hazard's division.

At 1 o'clock p. m., after ordering preparations to be made for landing, and sending a small boat with Lieutenant Andrews, of the Ninth Regiment New York Volunteers, and six of the Rhode Island Battalion, into Ashby's, to make soundings and examine the landings, I proceeded to the naval fleet, and after consulting with Commodore Goldsborough I determined to attempt a landing before night. After visiting my armed propellers and finding them doing good service, on my return to the troops' fleet I received Lieutenant Andrews' report, which satisfied me that the decision to land at Ashby's Harbor was correct. In leaving the landing Lieutenant Andrews and crew were fired upon by the enemy, wounding one of the crew, Charles Viall, of Company E, Fifth Rhode Island Battalion, in the jaw. The reconnaissance of Lieutenant Andrews was such as reflects great credit upon him as an officer. I accordingly ordered General Foster, who was ready with his first detachment, to attempt a landing at some point in the harbor. I had before ordered General Reno, who was also ready with his first detachment, to halt until the naval-boat howitzers, under Midshipman Porter, could be brought up and placed in position. They were soon taken in tow by General Reno, and in a very few minutes General Foster's boat and his had reached the shore, and were soon after joined by the boats carrying the first detachment of General Parke's brigade. I had before ordered the Picket down to the mouth of the harbor to cover the landing of the troops, and Captain Rowan had also brought his flag-ship, the Delaware, under command of Captain Quackenbush, down for the same purpose. The immediate point of landing at Ashby's Harbor in the original plan was Ashby's Landing, but on approaching it General Foster discovered an armed force in the woods in the rear of the landing, and very wisely directed his leading vessel to another point in the harbor, opposite Hammond's house. This armed force was soon dispersed by a few shell from the Delaware and Picket. In less than twenty minutes from the time the boats reached the shore 4,000 of our men were passing over the marshes at a double-quick and forming in most perfect order on the dry land near the house; and I beg leave to say that I never witnessed a more beautiful sight than that presented by the approach of these vessels to the shore and the landing and forming of the troops. Each brigadier-general had a light-draught steamer, to which were attached some 20 surf-boats in a long line in the rear. Both steamers and boats were densely filled with soldiers, and each boat bearing the national flag.

As the steamers approached the shore at a rapid speed each surf-boat was "let go," and with their acquired velocity and by direction of the steersman reached the shore in line. Capt. Lewis Richmond, assistant adjutant-general, with Mr. W. H. French, one of my secretaries, landed with the Fourth Rhode Island, and Lieut. D. A. Pell, my aide-de-camp, with the Fifty-first New York, Colonel Ferrero. I then went on shore, where I met General Parke, and received from him his report of the disposition of the forces for the protection of the landing of the remainder of the division, which disposition I entirely approved of. Soon after I met General Reno, whom I left in command, General Foster having returned to his vessel to bring up his second detachment.

A position on land having thus been secured, I went on board the commodore's vessel to consult with him in reference to the work of the next day, leaving Captain Richmond, Lieutenant Pell, and Mr. French on shore. The battery at Pork Point was very formidable, and had not been entirely silenced; but when I informed him that the entire force would probably be landed that night, and that we proposed to adhere to the original plan of making an advance early in the morning upon the inland fort in the center of the island, taking it, if possible, and proceeding rapidly up the main road, thus getting in the rear of all the shore batteries, he remarked that it would be dangerous to ourselves for him to renew his attack on the next morning, as his people might fire into our own troops, and I left him with the understanding that the attack would not be renewed without a signal from me.

By 12 o'clock that night the entire division (except the Twenty-fourth Massachusetts, Colonel Stevenson, detained below by the grounding of the steamer), together with Porter's battery of Dahlgren howitzers, had been landed. During the night a careful reconnaissance was made by my three brigade generals and their troops most judiciously posted, the leading regiment, the Twenty-first Massachusetts, Lieutenant-Colonel Maggi, occupying a position at the forks of the road above Hammond's house.

Early the next morning, in pursuance of the plan of action, General Foster ordered an advance. I arrived on the ground after the first three regiments of the brigade had filed through the woods, the other regiments being in line ready to move forward as room was made for them. General Reno's and Parke's brigades were also in readiness for a forward movement.

On reaching a point some mile and a half by the road from Hammond's house, General Foster came upon the battery across the road which, from information received, we had been led to suppose was there, and immediately commenced the disposition of his forces for his attack; and I here beg leave to say that I must refer you almost entirely to the reports of my brigadier-generals for an accurate knowledge of their movements during the day, as the face of the island precluded the possibility of any general oversight of operations on the field. The road from the opening in front of Hammond's house to the battery, some mile and a half, was very narrow and winding, leading through a deep marsh, covered with small pines and thick undergrowth, presenting the appearance of being impenetrable. The battery is not visible until a point some 600 yards from it is reached, when the road takes a turn to the left, and the timber in front is cleared away, that the guns may have full sweep. For more accurate information I beg leave to refer you to the accompanying map of the road.*

Soon after the attack was commenced I ordered General Parke to place a regiment in the woods to the north of Hammond's house and extending up to the main road, to prevent the possibility of the enemy's turning our left. The Eighth Connecticut, Colonel Harland, was detailed for this service. The Fifth Rhode Island Battalion, Major Wright, had been ordered to occupy Ashby's house. I then ordered Captain D'Wolf, with a boat's crew kindly loaned me by the Delaware, which way lying off the shore, to move down and land, and carefully reconnoiter the ground south and east of Ashby's, thus ascertaining that there was no force in the rear or on our right flank. Soon after this the firing indicated that General Foster was very warmly engaged with the enemy. General Reno's brigade was forcing its way up to his relief and General Parke's brigade was ready to follow. I had ordered General Parke to have the Ninth New York, Colonel Hawkins, land their Dahlgren howitzers from their floating battery on the shore, but as the marshy ground would have made it a half-day's work, I counter-

---

* Not found.

manded the order, which was most fortunate, as the regiment moved forward in time to take a most important part in the action.

General Foster commenced the attack by putting six Dahlgren howitzers in position in front of the enemy's battery, supporting it with the Twenty-fifth Massachusetts, Colonel Upton. This regiment was supported by the Twenty-third Massachusetts, Colonel Kurtz, also in line. After the Tenth Connecticut, Colonel Russell, came up, General Foster ordered the Twenty-third Massachusetts and Twenty-seventh Massachusetts, Colonel Lee, to pass into the swamp on the right, for the purpose of getting on the left flank of the enemy. Soon after this the Twenty-fifth Massachusetts exhausted its ammunition, and the Tenth Connecticut advanced to its position. All these movements were performed by the regiments under lead of their respective commanders with the most commendable efficiency. The skill with which the Dahlgren howitzers were handled by Midshipman Benjamin Porter and Acting Master J. B. Hammond is deserving the highest praise, and I take great pleasure in recommending them to the favorable notice of the Navy Department. At this time the number of wounded arriving on litters indicated that the engagement was serious, and two hospitals were established by my brigade surgeon, Dr. W. H. Church, one at Hammond's house and the other at Ashby's, where the wounded were well cared for.

In the mean time, General Reno, coming up, sent word to General Foster that he would try to penetrate the dense wood to the left and thus turn their right flank, which movement was approved by General Foster and was carried out by General Reno, the Twenty-first Massachusetts, Lieutenant-Colonel Maggi, leading, followed by the Fifty-first New York, Colonel Ferrero; Ninth New Jersey, Lieutenant-Colonel Heckman, and Fifty-first Pennsylvania, Colonel Hartranft, each most gallantly led by their respective commanders, and resulting in a complete success. When it is remembered that in addition to the obstacles of thicket and underbrush the men were more than knee-deep in mud and water, it seems a most wonderful feat. Immediately after General Reno's brigade had cleared the road General Parke came up with his brigade, and was ordered by General Foster to support the Twenty-third Massachusetts and Twenty-seventh Massachusetts Regiments, which had by direction of General Foster most gallantly initiated under their colonels a movement to turn the left flank of the enemy, when he at once turned his brigade to the right, the Fourth Rhode Island in advance, gallantly led by its colonel and Capt. Lewis Richmond, my assistant adjutant-general, meeting with obstacles equal to those on the left.

Just as the Ninth New York was entering the woods to follow the Fourth Rhode Island Generals Foster and Parke, discovering that the appearance of General Reno on the enemy's right had staggered him, they decided to order the Ninth New York to charge the battery in front, which was instantly done, and at once the road was filled with a sea of red caps, the air resounding with their cheers. The charge of General Reno's leading regiment, the Twenty-first Massachusetts, and Fifty-first New York was simultaneous with the charge of the Ninth New York, when the enemy broke and ran in the greatest possible confusion, while the cheers of our men indicated to every one on the island that we had carried the battery. The merit of first entering the fort is claimed by the Twenty-first Massachusetts and Fifty-first New York, a few men from each regiment entering at the same time, one regiment hoisting the regimental flag and the other the national flag on the parapet.

Just before the charge the steamer Union arrived with the Twenty-fourth Massachusetts, which I hastened forward, with the exception of three companies, detailed to carry up ammunition. It must be remembered that up to this time there had not been a single horse landed, owing to the impossibility of getting them through the marsh on the shore. All the ammunition and stores had to be transferred by our soldiers, and the general and field officers had to perform their duties on foot. On moving up the road toward the battery I met my aide-de-camp, Lieutenant Fearing, whom I had sent to the front to report progress, when he informed me that an advance was made by General Reno's brigade immediately after the battery was taken, thus anticipating my order sent by Lieutenant Anderson. I had learned from an officer of the Richmond Blues, taken prisoner and brought to me by Capt. William Cutting and Lieut. D. A. Pell, that there were no more batteries on the road.

The Twenty-fourth Massachusetts, Colonel Stevenson, coming up fresh, General Foster pushed on, followed by General Parke. On arriving at the road leading to Pork Point Battery I detailed the Fourth Rhode Island and the Tenth Connecticut from General Foster's brigade, sending them under General Parke down this road to take the battery in the rear, but on their arrival it was found to have been just evacuated. The pursuit was continued by Generals Foster and Reno to the head of the island in rear of Weir's Point Battery, where the entire force on the island had concentrated in two camps. A slight engagement ensued, in which the enemy lost four men killed, after which they surrendered to Generals Foster and Reno at discretion. The entire force of the enemy on the island, in the batteries, and stationed as sharpshooters was about 4,000. Gov. H. A. Wise had a force in reserve at Nag's Head, with which he left as soon as he heard of our victory. Their troops were well posted for defense and their inland battery well masked, so that our men were really fighting against an enemy almost entirely concealed. The force that surrendered to Generals Foster and Reno consisted of 159 officers and over 2,500 men. Among these are two colonels, two lieutenant-colonels, and three majors.

I omitted to mention that the Ninth New York was diverted to the right of the main road by General Reno, where they captured some 60 prisoners in their attempt to escape through Shallow Bag Bay. Among these prisoners was Capt. O. Jennings Wise, who was severely wounded and has since died. The loss of the enemy is unknown, but as many had been removed, but it will not exceed 150 killed and wounded.

By this victory we have gained complete possession of this island, with five forts, mounting thirty-two guns, winter quarters for some 4,000 troops, and 3,000 stand of arms, large hospital buildings, with a large amount of lumber, wheelbarrows, scows, pile-drivers, a mud dredge, ladders, and other appurtenances for military service, of which a careful inventory will be made and sent on, with an accurate list of prisoners, by our next dispatches.

Fort Forrest, on the main-land, opposite Weir's Point, was burned by the rebels on the evening of the 8th instant. It contained eight guns, thus making their loss forty guns in all. The Navy has recovered nearly all from this fort in good condition.

When it is remembered that for one month our officers and men had been confined on crowded ships during a period of unusual prevalence of severe storms, some of them having to be removed from stranded vessels, others in vessels thumping for days on sand banks and under constant apprehension of collision, then landing without blankets or tents on a marshy shore, wading knee-deep in mud and water to a permanent landing, exposed all night to a cold rain, then fighting for four hours, pursuing the enemy some 8 miles, bivouacking in the rain, many of them without tents or covering, for two or three nights, it seems wonderful that not one murmur or complaint has been heard from them. They have endured all these hardships with the utmost fortitude, and have exhibited on the battle-field a coolness, courage, and perseverance worthy of veteran soldiers. The companies left on board the armed propellers during the naval engagement rendered most efficient service, and are highly spoken of by the different brigade commanders. There had been placed on these propellers, by the brigadier-generals, aides-de-camp, who rendered marked service during the action, as did also the officers and men of the Marine Artillery in charge of the guns, headed by Col. William A. Howard.

I desire to tender my thanks to Capt. S. F. Hazard, U. S. Navy, commanding division of armed vessels, for his efficient management of the division. The vessels comprising this division were the Picket, Capt. T. P. Ives; Vedette, Captain Foster; Hussar, Captain Crocker; Lancer, Captain Morley; Ranger, Captain Emerson; Chasseur, Captain West; Pioneer, Captain Baker. The Picket was particularly serviceable in covering the landing of the troops.

I must express to Commodore Goldsborough and the officers of his fleet my high appreciation and admiration of their gallantry, and my thanks for the kind assistance rendered us from time to time in our joint labors.

I have to thank my personal staff for their efficient aid in the work through which we have passed. They are as follows:

Dr. W. H. Church, brigade surgeon; Capt. Lewis Richmond, assistant adjutant-general; Capt. William Cutting, assistant quartermaster; Capt. James F. D'Wolf, assistant commissary; Lieut. D. W. Flagler, ordnance officer; Lieut. D, A. Pell, aide-de-camp; Lieut. G. R. Fearing, aide-de-camp; Lieutenant Andrews, topographical officer. All of these officers have rendered most efficient service in their several capacities.

Mr. D. R. Larned, my private secretary, accompanied me to the shore, and, with Mr. W. H. French, my other secretary, were very serviceable in communicating with the vessels and forces, doing the duty of volunteer aides. I beg leave to refer you to the report of Dr. W. H. Church, brigade surgeon, for list of casualties, which amount to 41 killed and 181 wounded.* Among the killed I regret to record the following officers: Col. Charles L. Russell, Tenth Connecticut; Lieut. Col. Viguer De Monteil, of Fifty-third New York; Second Lieut. John H. Goodwin, jr., Company B, Twenty-third Massachusetts; Lieutenant Stillman, Tenth Connecticut; Capt. Joseph J. Henry, Ninth New Jersey. I refrain from mentioning special cases of heroism in the brigades, as it would be wrong to make distinctions where all behaved so gallantly.

In closing this report I beg leave again to call your attention to Brigadier-Generals Foster, Reno, and Parke, who throughout the action showed the greatest gallantry and directed the movements of the troops with skill and energy. From the moment they joined me I have given them large discretionary powers, and the sequel has shown that I have acted wisely. I especially recommend them to the favor of the Department.

---

* But see revised statement, p. 85.

I have the honor to be, general, very respectfully, your obedient servant,

A. E. BURNSIDE,
Brigadier-General, Commanding Department North Carolina.
Brig. Gen. LORENZO THOMAS,
Adjutant-General U. S. Army, Washington, D. C.

No. 2.

Report of Lieut. Daniel W. Flagler, U. S. Ordnance Department.

HEADQUARTERS DEPARTMENT NORTH CAROLINA,
Roanoke Island, February 20, 1862.

GENERAL: I have the honor to submit for your information the following report of the ordnance and ordnance stores captured on Roanoke Island during the engagement of the 8th instant:

The total number of cannon captured was forty-two. In the inland battery were three, all mounted on field carriages and covered by an earthwork with embrasures. One of these is a heavy 24-pounder boat howitzer; one a 6-pounder brass field gun, model 1846, and the other an 18-pounder brass field gun—probably a Mexican trophy. There were no caissons with these pieces, but the implements and equipments of the pieces were uninjured, and a quantity of ammunition in the ammunition-chest of each of the limbers. In Fort Foster, at Pork Point, were nine guns. Eight of these are heavy 32-pounder navy smoothbore guns and one a banded rifled gun—this last peculiarly rifled, and has been manufactured by the enemy since the beginning of the war. It has seven grooves, the bottom of the groove being cylindrical in form, intersecting at one edge with the surface of the bore. At the other edge the groove is eleven-hundredths of an inch deep. It has thus but one shoulder, which is at the right edge of the groove, as the twist is to the left. The grooves and bands are of equal width, and have a uniform twist of one turn in 32 feet. The gun is manufactured from a 32-pounder navy gun of 61-cwt. A portion at the breech was turned down to a perfect cylinder, and then wrought-iron cylinders shrunk around the breech, similarly to the Parrott gun. The cylinder, when complete, is $24\frac{1}{2}$ inches long and $1\frac{1}{2}$ inches thick. The few experiments I have been able to make with the gun show that it will compare not unfavorably in range and accuracy of fire with the Parrott gun. The only projectiles found for it were shells, ready filled and fused with the navy fuse. It is mounted *en barbette*, with the French navy carriage, on a chassis traversing a semicircle. Two of the other guns at the left flank of the battery are mounted *en barbette*, traversing the entire circle. All the remaining guns have embrasures, and are mounted on the French navy carriage, with platform. The fort has two small magazines. In them and in the fort were found 828 32-pounder round shot, 84 stand of grape, a few shells, and 110 cartridges for the 32-pounder guns. There was also a small quantity of musket ammunition and ammunition for 12-pounder boat howitzers stored in the magazines.

In Fort Parke were found four 32-pounder navy guns mounted *en barbette* on the army 32-pounder barbette carriages, and one spare carriage without the chassis. It had also 440 32-pounder round shot, but all the ammunition had been taken from the magazine and destroyed. The implements belonging to the guns in this fort were not much injured.

In Fort Reno were twelve guns. Of these the two upon the left flank of the battery are rifled guns like the one in Fort Foster which I have already described, and mounted upon the same carriage *en barbette*. All the others are smooth-bore 32-pounder navy guns of 57 and 61 cwt. The two upon the right flank are mounted *en barbette* and the remaining eight on the navy carriage at embrasures. In the fort and magazines were 2,144 32-pounder round shot, 110 shells for the rifle guns, and 42 32-pounder shells. All the ammunition had also been taken from this magazine and destroyed. I found in the water near the shore just outside this fort a 32-pounder gun, which the enemy had apparently let fall in trying to land it. I have hauled it out, and if necessary it can be mounted on a spare carriage. The remaining two guns are in Fort Ellis, opposite Nag's Head.

All of the guns excepting the three field pieces in the inland battery I found had been spiked and other ineffectual attempts made to render them unserviceable. Six of them were spiked with rat-tail files; the remainder with wrought-iron spikes and nails. They were all loaded, some with several shot wedged, and others with charged shells unfused and inverted, so arranged as to explode in the gun if fired. All of these have been removed without accident, and the guns are now ready for service.

In Forts Reno and Foster considerable injury was done to the carriages, implements, and equipments. The guns being mounted on navy carriages, the breechings and tackle-ropes were in most cases cut. With some of the carriages, however, the breechings and tackle were unnecessary, so that with some repairs, using the spare parts and implements that were found, the injuries have been so far repaired that the guns can now be maneuvered and fired without danger. I have made some 400 cartridges for the 32-pounder guns, and so distributed the ammunition found in these two forts as to render them as defensible as possible until larger supplies can be obtained.

The implements and equipments in Fort Parke sustained much less injury. These have all been repaired, but as the magazine of the fort is very damp, and you told me you intended to change the position of the battery, I have done nothing to supply the guns with ammunition.

The small-arms captured were generally of an inferior quality. Of those that have been preserved there are about 1,500. They are principally smooth-bore muskets (caliber .69) made at Harper's Ferry, in 1832, and have either flint-locks or have been altered to percussion. Some of the enemy's troops were armed with fowling-pieces, sporting rifles, and a motley collection of arms nearly useless for military purposes. These were all carried away by our soldiers and people from the transports. The iron parts found among the ruins of the camp near Fort Foster indicate that some 200 or 300 muskets must have been destroyed by fire on the day of the bombardment. I am also satisfied that a quantity of arms and ammunition has been buried or hidden on the island, although we have as yet been unable to find it. Several muskets have been sent as trophies to naval officers of the fleet in accordance with your orders. This must account for the large discrepancy between the number of prisoners and small-arms captured. There are also 1,600 sets of infantry equipments, many of them incomplete. Such of these and of the muskets as will not be required for service in this department I have had boxed, preparatory to any disposition of them the Ordnance Bureau may direct. The greater part of the ammunition found in the cartridge-boxes of the prisoners was sô much injured by exposure to the weather that I do not think it worth preserving. In the magazine at Fort Foster were found in good order 40,000 musket cartridges (caliber .69), 2,200 cartridges for Minie rifles (caliber .54), and 134 rounds fixed ammunition for the 24-pounder boat howitzer. The magazines in the forts are generally not well constructed, affording insufficient protection for the ammunition against dampness. They are bomb-proofs, and built of such light soil that in falling weather the dampness easily penetrates to the magazines. If they are to contain considerable stores or ammunition for any length of time I would respectfully recommend that they be reconstructed or replaced by new ones.

I have the honor to be, general, very respectfully, your obedient servant,

D. W. FLAGLER,
Lieutenant, Ordnance Officer Department North Carolina.
General AMBROSE E. BURNSIDE,
Commanding Department of North Carolina.

No. 3.

Report of Surg. William H. Church, U. S. Army, Acting Medical Director.

HEADQUARTERS DEPARTMENT OF NORTH CAROLINA,
Roanoke Island, February 12, 1862.

GENERAL : I have the honor to submit the following report of the killed and wounded of your command consequent upon the attack upon Roanoke Island :

February 7 a small boat, having been ordered on shore to reconnoiter, was attacked by the enemy, when Charles Viall, a private in Company E, of the Fifth Rhode Island Battalion, received a wound in the lower jaw, causing a compound comminuted fracture, from which he will probably recover.

February 8, upon the advance of General Foster the houses and outhouses at the landing were at once prepared for the reception of the wounded, and placed in charge of Surgeon Storrs, of the Eighth Regiment Connecticut Volunteers, his regiment having been ordered thero to protect the landing of our forces and hold the position. Brigade Surgeon Thompson now advanced with the troops to take charge of the wounded on the field of battle, where he remained until the battery was taken, assisting in the care of the wounded, and sending them with the least possible delay to the hospital. Through the energy of Dr. Thompson much suffering has been avoided.

Finding that there was not sufficient room in these buildings to receive the wounded, we immediately took possession of Ashby's house, a short distance from the first and quite as convenient to the field of action. The Fifth Rhode Island Battalion having been ordered to guard this point, Asst. Surg. A. Potter took charge of it until further assistance could be procured. Surgeon Minis, of the Forty-eighth Regiment Pennsylvania Volunteers (owing to the death of Surgeon Weller, by drowning, at Hatteras Inlet, he was detailed to serve with the Ninth New Jersey Volunteers), was very soon placed in charge of this temporary hospital, where there was sufficient room to receive the wounded not provided for. During the action of this day 32 were killed and 174 wounded.* Col. Charles L. Russell, of the Tenth Connecticut Volunteers, was shot through the lung, and died almost immediately. Lieut. Col. Viguer De Monteil, of the Fifty-third Regiment New York Volunteers, was also killed by a ball passing through his brain.

Accompanying this please find a list of the killed and wounded of each regiment that participated in the engagement.†

The surgical portion of your command has performed its duties faithfully and fearlessly, Surg. J. Marcus Rice, of the Twenty-fifth Regiment Massachusetts Volunteers, having been wounded in the midst of his very arduous duties. The ball grazed his side, fortunately without inflicting a severe wound.

We have found three unusually large, commodious, and well-ventilated buildings erected upon the island for hospital purposes, which will afford ample accommodation for our sick and wounded. The largest hospital at the north end of the island I have placed in the charge of Surg. S. A. Green, of the Twenty-fourth Regiment Massachusetts Volunteers, and Surg. George A. Otis has the management of the two hospitals near the fort at the center of the island.

I would respectfully ask your attention to the fact that the wounded of the enemy have received the same care and attention from the surgeons as our own wounded. Permit me to take advantage of this opportunity to express our gratitude to the officers of the United States gunboat Delaware, the surgeon having dressed a large number of our wounded.

I am, general, very respectfully, your obedient servant and friend,
WM. HENRY CHURCH,
Brigade Surgeon and Acting Medical Director.

---

* But see revised statement, p. 85.
† The revised statement on p. 85 is substituted for that submitted by Dr. Church.

Return of casualties in the Department of North Carolina, commanded by Brig. Gen. Ambrose E. Burnside, at the battle of Roanoke Island, N. C., February 8, 1862.

[Compiled from nominal lists of casualties, returns, &c.]

Commands.	Killed.		Wounded.		Captured or missing.		Aggregate.
	Officers.	Enlisted men.	Officers.	Enlisted men.	Officers.	Enlisted men.	
First Brigade.							
Brig. Gen. JOHN G. FOSTER.							
23d Massachusetts..........................	1	2	....	8	......	......	11
24th Massachusetts *.........................							....
25th Massachusetts	......	6	3	41	......	......	50
27th Massachusetts...........................	.....	4	1	11	......	......	16
10th Connecticut	2	4	2	47	......	......	55
Total First Brigade......................	3	16	6	107	......	......	132
Second Brigade.							
Brig. Gen. JESSE L. RENO.							
21st Massachusetts...........................	......	5	2	37	......	......	44
51st New York	......	3		11	......	9	23
9th New Jersey	1	6	......	28	......	2	37
51st Pennsylvania	......	......	......	1	......	2	3
Total Second Brigade	1	14	2	77	......	13	107
Third Brigade.							
Brig. Gen. JOHN G. PARKE.							
4th Rhode Island * ....*	......	......	......	......	......	......	
5th Rhode Island, 1st Battalion *................... ...	......	......	......	......	......	......	
8th Connecticut *	......	......	......	......	......	......	
9th New York...	......	......	2	15	......	......	17
Total Third Brigade.......................	......	......	2	15	......	......	17
UNASSIGNED TROOPS.							
1st New York Marine Artillery, Detachment *.........	......	......	......	......	......	......	......
99th New York, Company B	......	2	......	5	... ..	......	7
Grand total Department of North Carolina.........	†5	32	10	204	......	13	264

* No loss reported.
† Includes Lieut. Col. Joseph A. Vigner De Monteil, whose regiment, Fifty-third New York, was not engaged.

No. 4.

*Report of Brig. Gen. John G. Foster, U. S. Army, commanding First Brigade, with sketch. ***

HEADQUARTERS FIRST BRIGADE,
Roanoke Island, February 9, 1862.

SIR: I have the honor to report that, in obedience to the orders of the commanding general and in pursuance of the plan of observations previously agreed upon in a council ordered by him, I proceeded to land my brigade on Roanoke Island on the evening of the 7th instant,

* The sketch is taken from his report to the Committee on the Conduct of the War.

while the engagement between the fleet and the enemy's battery on Pork Point was still in progress. I embarked 500 of the Twenty-fifth Massachusetts Regiment on the Pilot Boy, and towing all the boats from the vessels of my brigade loaded with detachments from the different regiments composing it, in all 1,400 men, I headed for Ashby's Harbor, which had been agreed upon as the landing point. As I approached closely I detected with the glass the presence of an ambuscaded force of infantry and artillery, and in consequence immediately headed the boat for the point just above the harbor, in front of Hammond's house, where the force landed without molestation. General Reno, with the Union and Patuxent, and General Parke, in the Phœnix, landed immediately after my detachment, making in all over 4,000 men landed in twenty minutes.

As soon as the force at Ashby's Harbor saw us land at the point above they commenced a hasty retreat, in order not to be cut off by road from Hammond's house, which intersects the main road through the island above its intersection with the road from Ashby's. During the landing Captain Rowan, U. S. Navy, commanding the first division of the fleet, ordered the Delaware, Captain Quackenbush, U. S. Navy, and Captain Hazard, U. S. Navy, ordered the Picket, Capt. T. P. Ives, to run in and cover the landing with their guns. This was handsomely done, although it required but a few shells to accelerate the retreat of the force from Ashby's.

I returned and brought on shore a second load, and then landed, leaving Captain Potter, assistant commissary of subsistence of my brigade, on board the steamer to continue the debarkation. Finding that the general commanding had returned to the fleet, I assumed command as senior officer present. During the night my entire brigade (with the exception of the Twenty-fourth Massachusetts, on board the Guide and aground) were landed, as also the brigades of Generals Reno and Parke. The night was rainy, and the men, wet from their march from the landing, were obliged to bivouac around their fires, but kept in excellent spirits. I made a reconnaissance in the evening with Generals Reno and Parke, to ascertain the position of the enemy, the roads, &c., and made all the proper dispositions for the night.

At daybreak of the 8th I advanced my brigade across the creek in accordance with the plan of operations above referred to, the Twenty-fifth Massachusetts being in the advance. On reaching a clearing I met the enemy's pickets, and was fired upon by them. They then fell back on a run, followed by our skirmishers. We advanced to the main road, and then upon that road until, when near the middle of the island, we came upon the enemy in a strong position prepared for battle. The road at this point was a causeway, flanked on each side by an almost impassable marsh, with thick underbrush on either side. In front of the battery the trees were cut down, so as to give a clear sweep of their guns for a distance of 700 yards in front, for the whole of which distance the advance in front was fully exposed to the fire of three pieces in embrasure, supported by a force of about 2,000 men. Of the seven light pieces from the ships' launches, six were placed on the road so that two could be used at a time, flanked by the Twenty-fifth Massachusetts Volunteers in line. This regiment was supported by the Twenty-third Massachusetts Regiment, also in line. We then advanced to the attack. As soon as the Twenty-seventh Massachusetts and the Tenth Connecticut Volunteers came up I ordered the Twenty-third Massachusetts, supported by the Twenty-seventh Massachusetts, to advance through the morass on our right and endeavor to turn the enemy's left.

The Tenth Connecticut was brought up to support the Twenty-fifth Massachusetts.

General Reno then came up with his whole brigade, and proceeded to turn the right of the enemy's position through the swamp on that side. General Parke next came up with his brigade, and I directed him to push forward to the right, following the Twenty-third and Twenty-seventh Massachusetts in the attempt to turn the enemy's left through the marsh and swamp on that side.

In the mean time the engagement was warm in front. The light pieces having fired all but ten rounds, I ordered their fire to cease, and these rounds to be preserved for an emergency, keeping the pieces in position. The Twenty-fifth Massachusetts had expended its ammunition and suffered considerable loss. I therefore advanced the Tenth Connecticut in front of the Twenty-fifth Massachusetts Regiment, and held the latter in reserve.

After the engagement (which commenced at 8 o'clock) had lasted three and a half hours, the Ninth New York (the last of.General Parke's regiments) coming on the field, followed by the Twenty-fourth Massachusetts, I directed General Parke to order it to charge. The order was given, and the regiment charged at a run with yells, cheered by the other troops, right up the road at the battery. Major Kimball, of this regiment, exhibited marked gallantry, leading the charge by several rods. The enemy left the battery. Their retreat was, however, a necessity from other causes, for General Reno had at this time turned the enemy's right and was firing into the rear of their battery and charging at the same time into them, and the Twenty-third Massachusetts, at the head of General Parke's column, sent to turn the enemy's left, had also made its appearance on the other flank. The enemy retreated in precipitation, leaving three guns unspiked, their caissons, and the dead and some wounded in the battery. General Reno immediately pushed on in pursuit, and I sent to report to the commanding general the result of the battle and the anticipation of another one at the upper batteries. I then followed General Reno with my brigade, the Twenty-fourth Massachusetts, which was fresh, being in front. I soon overtook and passed General Reno, who was busy in securing the fugitives attempting to escape in boats across to Nag's Head, and pushed forward toward the upper end of the island to overtake the retreating regiments of the enemy.

Just before reaching the fort on the upper extremity of the island I was met by a flag of truce, borne by Lieutenant-Colonel Fowle, of the Thirty-first North Carolina Volunteers, who came from Col. H. M. Shaw, of the Eighth North Carolina Volunteers, commanding the enemy's forces on the island, to ask what terms of surrender would be granted. I replied, none but those of unconditional surrender. He asked what time would be allowed for consultation. I replied, just as long as it will take to get to Colonel Shaw and return, and sent Major Stevenson, of the Twenty-fourth Massachusetts, to bring back the answer. Becoming impatient, I advanced with the Twenty-fourth Massachusetts, but when near their camp was met by the flag of truce returning to say that my terms were accepted. I then marched into the main camp and received the surrender of Colonel Shaw as commander of the enemy's forces on the island, with all his forces. I immediately ordered Colonel Kurtz, with the Twenty-third Massachusetts, to advance and secure the camp of the Thirty-first North Carolina Volunteers, near by, but his arrival was anticipated by General Reno, who had already secured their camp, with the regiment it contained.

The camps consisted of well-built quarters, store-houses, and hospitals, all newly built.   The forces surrendered numbered in all about 3,000.

The two forts on the island above the one on Pork Point are well constructed, and mount in all sixteen guns of heavy caliber, with well-stocked magazines.

After securing the prisoners and arms I went to report the result to the general commanding, and found him in the Pork Point Battery, upon which he had advanced with General Parke, supported by the Tenth Connecticut (one of my brigade).

I have only time in this hasty report to notice in general terms the conduct of the troops, and to say that I never saw men stand up more gallantly under a hot fire than did the regiments of my brigade, especially the Twenty-fifth Massachusetts and Tenth Connecticut Regiments, both of which suffered quite severely.   Colonel Russell, of the Tenth Connecticut, fell gallantly at the head of his regiment, and after his fall the regiment was commanded by Lieutenant-Colonel Drake.   I would notice here the gallant conduct of Midshipman Benjamin Porter and Acting Master J. B. Hammond, of the Navy, who commanded the light guns from the ships' launches and were constantly under fire. They both deserve commissions for their admirable conduct on this occasion.

The reports of the several regimental commanders of my brigade, which are herewith inclosed, will show in detail the names of those officers and men who distinguished themselves by their gallant conduct.   They all behaved admirably, both officers and men.

With the exception of Captain Hoffman and Lieutenant Anderson, who were on the field with me, and Captains Potter and Hudson, who were engaged in bringing up ammunition and provisions, my aides were on the gunboats Ranger, Hussar, and Vedette—Captain Messinger and Lieut. Ed. N. Strong on the Ranger, Lieut. James M. Pendleton on the Vedette, and James H. Strong on the Hussar.   Lieutenants Van Buren and Gordon, of the Signal Corps, volunteered as aides at the time and were of great service in carrying orders.

I would mention that Viguer De Monteil, lieutenant-colonel of the Fifty-third Regiment, came up during the action and asked permission to fight as a private.   This I granted, and he passed on in front to the position of the Tenth Connecticut, where he stood coolly aiming and firing his rifle and exhibiting the most marked bravery.   He fell shot dead toward the close of the engagement.

The colonels of the different regiments of my brigade exhibited marked ability, coolness, and daring.

The Twenty-fifth Regiment was commanded by Colonel Upton, the Twenty-seventh by Colonel Lee, the Twenty-third by Colonel Kurtz, the Twenty-fourth by Colonel Stevenson, the Tenth Connecticut by Colonel Russell.

I am, sir, with great respect, your obedient servant,

J. G. FOSTER,
Brigadier-General, U. S. Army.

Capt. LEWIS RICHMOND,
Assistant Adjutant-General.

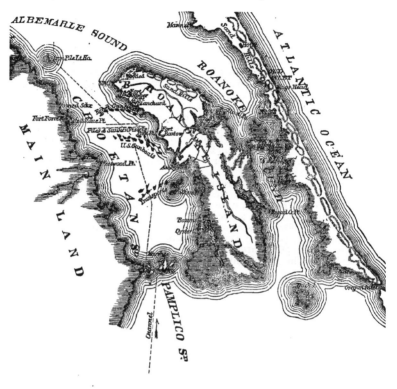

Notes·
Fort Huger........12 guns and hot shot furnace,
Fort Blanchard...4 guns
Fort Bartow........8 guns
Ballast Pt Batt'...2 guns
A . Landing Place
⚔ . Battle was fought.
B . Rebels surrendered.

SKETCH
OF
ROANOKE ISLAND, N. C.

No. 5.

Report of Capt. Daniel Messinger, Acting Aide-de-Camp.

HEADQUARTERS GENERAL FOSTER'S BRIGADE,
On Board Pilot Boy, off Roanoke Island, February 9, 1862.

CAPTAIN: I have the honor to report that by order of Brigadier-General Foster, on the afternoon of February 6, Lieut. E. N. Strong, aide-de-camp, and myself went on board the gunboat Ranger to carry out his instructions. The troops on board the Ranger (the Twenty-seventh Massachusetts Volunteers), with the exception of one company retained as a guard for the boat, and a detail from Company E to serve as gunners, were placed on the steamer New York and schooner Recruit. We then, at 2 o'clock p. m., reported as ready for action to Captain Hazard, U. S. Navy, on steamer Picket.

At 9.30 the next morning a signal from the commodore was repeated to us from the Picket to get under way and follow the fleet into action. At 12.30 we opened fire with one 30-pounder Parrott gun on the battery at Pork Point, and lodged our first shell within the battery. We continued our fire with the Parrott gun and two 12-pounder Wiard guns whenever opportunity was afforded us by the position of the fleet until the order came from the commodore to cease firing at 6.30 p. m. We then had thrown 121 shells, many with effect.

In our endeavor to get within shorter range we ran aground, and thereby lost an hour. Although many of the enemy's shells exploded near us, our vessel was not struck.

On the following day, just after we were ordered into action, we were signaled that the attack had been commenced by our land forces, and we were thus prevented from reopening our fire.

I respectfully call to your notice the zeal and efficiency of Lieutenant Eyre, of the Naval Brigade, under whose immediate direction the Parrott and Wiard guns were served on the gun-deck, and of Lieutenant Dennison, of the Twenty-seventh Massachusetts Volunteers, who had command of the 12-pounder Wiard boat howitzer on the upper deck. I append the report of Lieutenant Eyre, with interesting memoranda as to the service of the guns, and remain, very respectfully, your obedient servant,

DANIEL MESSINGER,
Acting Aide-de-Camp.

Capt. SOUTHARD HOFFMAN,
   Assistant Adjutant-General.

No. 6.

Report of Lieut. C. Cushing Eyre, First New York Marine Artillery.

ROANOKE ISLAND, February 8, 1862.

I have the honor to report the working of the battery of the Ranger during the action at Pork Point Battery on February 7 and 8:

Commenced firing at 12.30 at the distance of 3 miles. As the vessel worked ahead we were several times obliged to wear ship, each time running nearer to the battery. During the afternoon the firing was more effective, owing to the vessel having been brought closer to the enemy's position. During the latter part of the engagement the shell were thrown into the Point battery with accuracy.

Expended during the action, 3 Parrott shell, elevation $17\frac{1}{2}°$, distance about 3 miles; 6 Parrott shell, elevation 15°, distance about $2\frac{3}{4}$ miles; 3 Parrott shell, elevation 16°, distance about $2\frac{1}{4}$ to 3 miles; 12 Parrott shell, elevation 12°, distance about $2\frac{1}{2}$ miles; 2 Parrott shell, elevation $13\frac{1}{2}°$, distance about $2\frac{3}{4}°$ miles,

From Wiard's 12-pounder, expended 20 shell and shot at an elevation of 15° to 17°, distance $2\frac{3}{4}$ miles; 38 shell and shot at an elevation of 8° to 12°, distance $2\frac{1}{2}$ miles.

About 3.30 p. m., being within range for the 12-pounder boat howitzer, commenced firing with it, and expended 45 shot and shell, very

few of them falling short.   This gun was in charge of Lieutenant Den-nison, Twenty-seventh Massachusetts Volunteers.
Respectfully,

C. CUSHING EYRE,
First Lieutenant Marine Artillery.

Capt. DANIEL MESSINGER, *Gunboat Ranger.*

No. 7.

Report of Lieut. James H. Strong, Aide-de-Camp.

HEADQUARTERS GENERAL FOSTER'S BRIGADE,
Pilot Boy, February 10, 1862.

CAPTAIN: I have the honor to report that, in obedience to General Foster's orders, on the afternoon of February 6 I went on board the gunboat Hussar to carry out his instructions.   The troops on the Hussar were distributed on board the Highlander, Skirmisher, and New Brunswick, with the exception of one company, detained on board as a guard for the ship and 18 men detailed for working the guns.   At 7 p. m. we reported, as directed, to Captain Hazard, U. S. Navy, on board the Picket.

At 7 a. m., 8th instant, Captain Hazard came alongside and ordered us to follow the Pioneer on signal from Picket.   This signal we received at 10 o'clock a. m., and as soon as the Pioneer got under way we followed closely.   At 11 o'clock a. m. we received signal, " Prepare for action," and shortly after, "Attack."   We made all ready; as soon as we were within range commenced firing at the battery at Pork Point with one 30-pounder Parrott and sometimes at the gunboats of the enemy when they ventured within range of our 6-pounder Wiard, until a signal from the commodore, "Cease firing," at 6.30 p. m., when we anchored out of range of the battery.

The guns were served with coolness and accuracy by Lieutenant Hedden, of the Marine Artillery, but owing to our draught of water (9 feet 8 inches) we were unable to get as near the enemy as we wished.

Captain Alexander, of the Twenty-third Massachusetts Volunteers, and Mr. Ward, first officer of the Hussar, rendered very material assistance in serving the guns during the action.

I annex report of Lieutenant Hedden, which I requested him to send, in regard to the working of the guns, as it contains some interesting details.

I remain, very respectfully, your obedient servant,

JAMES H. STRONG,
Aide-de-Camp.

Capt. SOUTHARD HOFFMAN, *Assistant Adjutant-General.*

No. 8.

Report of Lieut. James A. Hedden, First New York Marine Artillery.

GUNBOAT HUSSAR,
Roanoke Island, February 10, 1862.

SIR: In answer to your request this morning I herewith inclose you a statement of the working of guns on board the gunboat Hussar at the bombardment of Pork Point, Friday, February 7, 1862: 102 cap shell from two 30-pounder Parrotts; 82 percussion shell from two 30-pounder Parrotts; 52 shot from one 6-pounder Wiard; 6 percussion shell from one 6-pounder Wiard (fell short). The former had an elevation of from 8° to 10° at a distance of from 2¼ to 1½ miles. A portion of the firing was directed to a rebel steamer which came under cover of battery but retired soon, evidently having a few shot through her. The Wiard gun (6-pounder) shot with great accuracy at a distance of 2 miles with as much elevation as we could give her, suppose about 11°. The first shot was fired from the Hussar at 11.45 a. m., and continued firing until a signal from the commodore, " Cease firing," at 6.30 p. m., when we came to anchor out of range of their batteries.

JAMES A. HEDDEN,
Lieutenant.

Lieut. JAMES H. STRONG.

No. 9.

Report of Lieut. James M. Pendleton, Aide-de-Camp.

HEADQUARTERS GENERAL FOSTER'S BRIGADE,
Roanoke Island, February 10, 1862.

I have the honor to report that on Thursday, 6th instant, in obedience to orders from General Foster, I went on board the steamer Vedette, to carry out his instructions. I found the vessel armed with one 30-pounder Parrott gun and one 12-pounder Wiard gun, with ammunition, and three companies of the Twenty-fourth Massachusetts Volunteers, Colonel Stevenson. I transferred two companies to the steamer Guide, Company F, Captain Pratt, remaining on board, and reported to Captain Hazard at 1.30 p. m. The next morning (Friday), at 7 o'clock a. m., Captain Hazard; U. S. Navy, gave orders to follow the propeller Ranger at a signal from the Picket. At 10 a. m. the signal to start was given, when we followed in the wake of the Ranger. At 11.30 prepared for action, and followed the fleet to within about 2 miles of Pork Point Battery. At 12 m. opened fire from the 30-pounder Parrott gun upon the enemy's gunboats. On their retiring and our coming within easy range of Pork Point Battery we fired also from the 12-pounder Wiard gun with accuracy.

By continual sounding we approached the batteries as near as the draught of the vessel would allow, and kept up the fire as often as good aim could be obtained.

At 6.20 p. m. the signal, " Cease fire," was given from the Southfield, when we anchored beyond the reach of the enemy's guns, disappointed at not being able to run nearer the fort. The 30-pounder Parrott gun was well served by Lieutenant Baxter, of the Marine Artillery, not firing except with good aim. The 12-pounder Wiard was faithfully served by Corporal Gilford, of the ——.

Accompanying I have the honor to forward some details of the working of the 30-pounder Parrott gun, drawn up at my request by Lieutenant Baxter.*

I remain, very respectfully, your obedient servant,

J. M. PENDLETON,
Aide-de-Camp

Capt. SOUTHARD HOFFMAN, <i>Assistant Adjutant-General.</i>

* Omitted as of no present importance.

No. 10.

Report of Lieut. Col. Albert W. Drake, Tenth Connecticut Infantry.

HDQRS. TENTH REGIMENT CONNECTICUT VOLS.,
U. S. Steamer New Brunswick, February 11, 1862.

SIR: In obedience to orders of Brigadier-General Foster I beg leave to report the part taken by the Tenth Regiment Connecticut Volunteers in the action of Roanoke Island, February 8, 1862:

The regiment was landed in three detachments during the afternoon, and bivouacked that night near Hammond's house. The next morning at about 7 o'clock the regiment was ordered to fall in, and shortly after moved with the remainder of the First Brigade up the island. We had marched but a short distance before the sound of sharp firing in advance told us that the action had commenced. Arriving on the field the regiment was ordered to form line and commence firing on the enemy, but owing to the dense bushes on our right and the exceedingly swampy nature of the ground there was room only for the right wing to move forward into position. The left wing was held in reserve a short distance in their rear. Firing was immediately commenced by the right wing and was maintained with much steadiness and constancy.

Near the close of the action Colonel Russell was killed. I immediately assumed command, and after the enemy had left the battery formed the regiment, and taking our position on the left of the brigade followed in pursuit. After proceeding up the road some 4 miles I was ordered by General Burnside to march the regiment in rear of the Fourth Rhode Island Volunteers to Pork Point Battery, where we arrived late in the afternoon and found it abandoned. I bivouacked the regiment near the fort until the morning of the 10th, when, in obedience to orders from General Foster, I marched the regiment to the upper end of the island, whence it was transferred to its old quarters on board the steamer New Brunswick.

Before closing this report I feel it my duty to say a word in commendation of the behavior of the officers and men of the regiment during the action and to speak of the noble manner in which they all performed their duty. Captains Pardee, Coit, Leggett, and Jepson, who were in the right wing and hottest of the fire, with their lieutenants, showed great coolness and courage, and merit the highest commendation. Captains Leggett and Jepson were wounded.

Appended is a list of our killed and wounded.*

Yours, very respectfully,

ALBERT W. DRAKE,
Lieutenant-Colonel, Commanding Tenth Regt. Conn. Vols.

Capt. SOUTHARD HOFFMAN,
Asst. Adjt. Gen., First Brigade, Dept. North Carolina.

No. 11.

Report of Col. John Kurtz, Twenty-third Massachusetts Infantry.

HDQRS. TWENTY-THIRD MASSACHUSETTS VOLUNTEERS,
Camp Foster, Roanoke Island, N. C., February 9, 1862.

SIR: I have the honor to report that, in obedience to General Foster's orders, my regiment, at daybreak on the morning of Saturday last, fol-

----

*Embodied in statement on p. 85.

lowed the Twenty-fifth Massachusetts from the ground upon which we bivouacked the night before up the main road of this island. At 8.15 o'clock we arrived at a crotch of the road, and found General Foster, with the Twenty-fifth Massachusetts, already engaged with the rebels at a breastwork which they had thrown across the road in a well-chosen position. I was ordered and formed my regiment in column by division in rear of the Twenty-fifth Massachusetts. I subsequently received an order to march by a flank across the fire of the enemy and through an almost impenetrable swamp and turn his flank, and after an effort of two and a half hours of the most fatiguing and laborious exertion I succeeded in getting four companies into position to rake the left flank of the enemy's lines behind his work. My men introduced themselves to his notice by opening a brisk fusillade, which he did not condescend to return, but immediately commenced to retreat, when the whole line of our troops made a charge which made him accelerate his pace toward his other strongholds, and we took possession of the work.

I cannot speak with too much praise of the conduct of the officers and men of my command for their indomitable perseverance in forcing through the swamp. The undergrowth was a thick bush, entwined by a strong brier, which caused it to close immediately upon the disappearance of a man through it. The water and mud all the way was above the knees of the men, several of whom I saw waist-deep in the mire, and taking into consideration the fact that this was the first time nearly all of them had been under fire, I cannot speak two highly of their conduct, individually and collectively.

After a rest of about half an hour we were ordered to follow the Twenty-fourth Massachusetts, which had just arrived, and pursue the retreating rebels, and after a march of 5 or 6 miles we entered the encampment or winter quarters of the rebels, and found they had surrendered to General Foster, and we were ordered to take up our quarters there with the Twenty-fourth Massachusetts and disarm and guard the prisoners, some 1,900 officers and men, with their arms, equipments, ammunition, and ordnance, quartermaster and commissary stores.

Very respectfully,

JOHN KURTZ,
Colonel, Commanding Twenty-third Massachusetts.

Captain HOFFMAN,
Assistant Adjutant-General, First Brigade, Coast Division.

No. 12.

Report of Col. Thomas G. Stevenson, Twenty-fourth Massachusetts Infantry.

The steamer Admiral, with the Twenty-fourth Regiment on board, having got aground on the afternoon of 7th February, the regiment was not landed until the morning of the 8th. At 7 o'clock in the morning the steamers Union and Eagle came alongside the Admiral and took the troops on board. Two companies—A, Captain Redding, and E, Captain Hooper—were put on board the Eagle, under command of Lieutenant-Colonel Osborn, and seven companies on the Union, under command of myself. Company C, Captain Pratt, had been detailed for service on board the gunboat Vedette, where it remained during the action. The Union landed the troops on board at the same place that troops had been landed the night previous, and about 2 miles below where the action was taking place. After landing I was ordered by General Burnside to advance as rapidly as possible. I accordingly marched the regiment forward, but unfortunately arrived after the battery had been carried. On arriving at the captured fort I reported to General Foster, who ordered us to the front to follow up the enemy.

After marching some distance we met the Fifty-first New York and continued with them until we were halted at the sand hills. From this point we were ordered forward alone to take what prisoners we could, as many were reported to be leaving in small boats. We were accompanied by General Foster. After marching about 3 miles we were met by a flag of truce from the enemy, proposing a suspension of hostilities until the following morning. The reply was given by General Foster, "Unconditional surrender," and time enough given to return to their camp and send back an answer. Major Stevenson, of the Twenty-fourth, was ordered to return with the flag and bring back the reply. After some time he returned with the answer that they surrendered. I was then ordered by General Foster to advance and take possession of their camp. On the way Company H, Captain Daland, and Company B, Captain Austin, were detached and ordered to proceed along the shore and stop any boats that might be leaving with rebels, the remaining five companies numbering about 300 men, and entered their camp, where Colonel Shaw, commanding, delivered up his sword to General Foster, who ordered me to take command. I then ordered the prisoners to be mustered and their arms to be taken possession of. All the muskets were then placed in the quartermaster's building and a guard put over them. While this was being done Private Sanborn, Company K, was wounded in the arm by the accidental discharge of one of the muskets. The officers were allowed to retain their side-arms by order of General Foster. The prisoners were then placed in quarters and a large guard placed over them.

Company B returned from their scouting, having fired upon and brought to a boat containing 10 rebels, including 3 officers. Company H also returned, having captured two boats containing 9 men and 2 officers. They also brought in about 150 prisoners captured in the woods and on the shore. The regiment was joined during the evening by the two companies under Lieutenant-Colonel Osborn. They had been employed in bringing ammunition forward from the landing.

THOS. G. STEVENSON,
Colonel Twenty-fourth Regiment Massachusetts Volunteers.

SOUTHARD HOFFMAN,
Assistant Adjutant-General, First Brigade.

No. 13.

Report of Col. Edwin Upton, Twenty-fifth Massachusetts Infantry.

HDQRS. TWENTY-FIFTH MASSACHUSETTS REGIMENT,
Camp on Roanoke Island, February 10, 1862.

SIR: At about daybreak on the morning of Saturday, the 8th instant, by order of Brigadier-General Foster, my regiment left the bivouac it had occupied the night previous at Hammond's house, and advanced, accompanied by General Foster, in its position on the right of his brigade. Arriving at the ford about one-half mile from Hammond's house, the advance was fired upon by the enemy's pickets. I was immediately ordered by General Foster to throw forward skirmishers, and ordered Company A, Capt. Josiah Pickett, to deploy, supported by Company E, Capt. Thomas O'Neil. The enemy's fire was returned, and his pickets retired rapidly to and down the main road, followed by the skirmishers. Advancing to about a mile from the ford, they reported having discovered the enemy in position, apparently about 2,000 strong. General Foster at once ordered me to form the regiment in line of battle across the road, the right resting on a clearing commanded by the guns of the enemy, the left extending into the woods and thicket. Fire was opened by both parties, our artillery shortly after getting into position, supported by the right wing of my regiment. I was ordered to and did press steadily forward, bringing our line within about 300 yards of the enemy's battery. Fire was kept up by us without intermission for about three hours until about 10.30 o'clock a. m., when, our ammunition being exhausted, I was ordered to form in column by company in rear of our right, which was done in good order. The men rested on their arms, waiting for a fresh supply of ammunition until, the enemy having left his work, I was ordered to advance in company with the remainder of General Foster's brigade. Arriving at the upper end of the island, I was ordered by General Foster to quarter in this camp, then in possession of the Twenty-third and Twenty-fourth Massachusetts Regiments.

Appended is a list of killed and wounded, amounting to 6 killed and 42 wounded.* I would express my great satisfaction with the conduct of the regiment, both officers and men. It was throughout the engagement of the bravest kind, standing as they did for hours in water to their knees and waists, exposed to an incessant fire of musketry, grape, and shell, with no disposition on the part of any man to waver. The skirmishing of Company A, Capt. Josiah Pickett, was performed in a manner that would have done credit to regulars. I can but express my particular satisfaction with the manner in which Lieutenant-Colonel Sprague, Major McCafferty, and Adjutant Harkness performed the duties devolving upon them and the support rendered me by them throughout the engagement.

I am, sir, yours, very respectfully,

EDWIN UPTON,
Colonel, Commanding Twenty-fifth Regiment Mass. Vols.

Capt. SOUTHARD HOFFMAN,
Assistant Adjutant-General, First Brigade.

No. 14.

Report of Col. Horace C. Lee, Twenty-seventh Massachusetts Infantry.

HDQRS. TWENTY-SEVENTH REGIMENT MASS. VOLS.,
In Camp at Dough's Farm, February 10, 1862.

SIR: I would respectfully report the movements of the regiment under my command at the engagement February 8:

We had but nine companies engaged, Company D having been de-

---

* But see revised statement on p. 85.

tailed to serve on board the Ranger. Three of my captains were sick and left on the Recruit. Upon arriving at the scene of action we immediately, by order, filed to the right of the road into the swamp, and formed in line in rear of the Twenty-third. We soon commenced moving to the front and across to the left, firing as we could get an opportunity. As soon as we were uncovered by the Twenty-third, or partially so, being then directly in front of the enemy, we commenced firing. We here met with all the loss sustained. Upon reaching the cover of the woods, finding that we could only fire by company on account of the Twenty-third being partly in front and the Tenth Connecticut partially covering our rear and firing, we formed in that manner, marching out in succession, firing deliberately, then retiring. We were in this manner evidently doing good execution, when orders were received to push on and flank the enemy upon their left. This, on account of the dense undergrowth of vines and bushes, the water and mud being also much deeper, was extremely difficult, and our progress consequently slow. Before we could possibly get through we heard the cheering, and soon learned that the rebels had retreated. After the engagement we, as ordered, followed up the road as rapidly as possible to the rebel encampment. Finding that they had surrendered and were under guard, we encamped on Dough's farm, near there, and now await further orders.

I cannot speak in too strong terms of the good conduct of both officers and men. With scarcely an exception they behaved with the utmost coolness and bravery. Lieutenant Fowler had his sword and sheath deeply indented by a grape shot. Lieutenant Goodale had his sword knocked from his hands and bent nearly double by a ball.

Very respectfully, your obedient servant,

H. C. LEE,
Colonel, Comdg. Twenty-seventh Regiment Mass. Vols.

Brig. Gen. J. G. FOSTER.

No. 15.

Report of Brig. Gen. Jesse L. Reno, U. S. Army, commanding Second Brigade.

HEADQUARTERS SECOND BRIGADE,
LATE CAMP 31ST N. C. REGT., NOW CAMP BURNSIDE,
February 10, 1862.

CAPTAIN: I have the honor to report that in compliance with orders from General Burnside I embarked the Twenty-first Massachusetts Regiment and eight companies of the Fifty-first Regiment New York Volunteers upon light-draught steamboats and proceeded toward Ashby's Harbor. General Burnside coming up, ordered me to wait until the boat howitzers, then being rowed towards my vessels, should arrive. While waiting, General Foster, with a portion of his command, passed ahead. As soon as the howitzers arrived they were taken in tow, preceded by the gunboats Picket and Delaware, and under cover of their fire we effected a landing, no resistance being offered. General Foster first reached the shore, then my command, followed immediately by General Parke's, and within twenty minutes over 4,000 men were landed. I immediately dispatched Captain Neill, assistant adjutant-general, to land the Ninth New Jersey and Fifty-first Pennsylvania, all of whom were landed before 9 o'clock p. m. The general commanding passed me as I was landing, and having given direction to secure and hold the position, returned to the fleet, leaving me in command, General Foster having returned to bring up the rest of his brigade. I sent the Twenty-first Massachusetts Volunteers to occupy the road and woods in front, General Parke having previously sent out skirmishers to hold the woods on the right and left.

General Foster having returned, he, General Parke, and myself proceeded to the front of our lines and made as careful a reconnaissance as circumstances would allow. In accordance with the plan previously adopted in council and ordered by the general commanding, General Foster proceeded at daylight with his brigade, and about 8 o'clock met and engaged the enemy. I followed with my brigade in the following order: The Twenty-first Massachusetts, Fifty-first New York, Ninth New Jersey, and Fifty-first Pennsylvania. As the road was very narrow and the woods and swamp on each side almost impenetrable, we proceeded but slowly, General Foster's brigade occupying the road. Finding it impossible to proceed directly to the front, I sent Lieutenant Morris, my aide, to inform General Foster that I would endeavor to penetrate the woods and swamp, and thus turn their right. General Foster having approved the plan, I proceeded at the head of the Twenty-first Massachusetts Volunteers toward the enemy's right. We were soon hotly engaged, but without stopping I kept moving my flank toward the left, but owing to the depth of water and dense underbrush we could make only slow progress. Finally, after the lapse of about two hours, we succeeded in turning their right. I then ordered a charge, which was most gallantly executed by the Twenty-first Massachusetts, Fifty-first New York, and Ninth New Jersey. The Fifty-first Pennsylvania, owing to their position in the rear, could not get up in time to participate, but they would have been in position in a very short time. Fortunately our charge was successful and the enemy fled precipitately. The honor of first entering the fort is divided between the Fifty-first New York and the Twenty-first Massachusetts, but all charged gallantly, and it was owing only to their position being nearer the fort that enabled them to reach it first. During the engagement, which lasted about four hours, General Foster's brigade most gallantly attacked them in the front, and General Parke was in the act of turning their left when my brigade charged and carried the battery.

During the engagement I proceeded to General Foster's position in front of his brigade, and meeting General Parke, the final plan of the assault was made. From the beginning of the attack until the battery was taken not a regiment or company retired or faltered, but advanced as rapidly as water waist deep and the thick and almost impenetrable underbrush would permit. Within fifteen minutes after the assault I formed my brigade and started in pursuit, the Twenty-first Massachusetts being in advance, followed by the Fifty-first New York, Ninth New Jersey, and Fifty-first Pennsylvania. Colonel Hawkins' regiment (Ninth New York) for some distance accompanied the head of my column, occupying the right. On coming to a road that led to the right I sent my aide, Lieutenant Reno, to direct the Ninth New York to follow it and endeavor to capture those of the enemy that were attempting to escape in small boats. Some 24 wounded prisoners were thus captured, and among others Capt. O. Jennings Wise, who had been mortally wounded. By advancing rapidly we captured a large number of stragglers.

Upon arriving within about a mile of their advanced position I learned from the prisoners that there were some 2,500 of the enemy in advance, and as the Twenty-first Massachusetts was some distance in advance I halted them and sent back one of my aides to hasten up the rest of my brigade. While awaiting their arrival General Foster came up and passed on with the Twenty-fourth Massachusetts, my brigade following immediately. Captain Bradford, commanding Company E, Twenty-first Massachusetts, being in advance, came upon a large body of troops, whom he immediately ordered to lay down their arms, but they opened fire upon him, which he returned, killing 4 of them. The rest then fled precipitately. Immediately after a flag of truce was sent up, and General Foster being in advance, Lieutenant Hovey accompanied it, and an unconditional surrender was made to him. In the mean time I came up, and proceeded immediately to the barracks of the Thirty-first North Carolina Regiment, commanded by Colonel Jordan, who surrendered his entire command. Their arms having been secured, I assigned the prisoners to a portion of the barracks and occupied the remainder with my brigade.

As the command behaved with distinguished gallantry I cannot in justice to the others particularize individuals, but I beg leave to refer you to the accompanying reports of the regimental commanders for the particulars, all of which I most heartily indorse. Lieutenant-Colonel Maggi commanded and led the Twenty-first Massachusetts, Colonel Ferrero the Fifty-first New York, Lieutenant-Colonel Heckman the Ninth New Jersey, and Colonel Hartranft the Fifty-first Pennsylvania. Lieutenant-Colonel Maggi's regiment captured the flag of the fort and raised the first colors (the regimental flag). The Fifty-first New York raised the national flag on the parapet. Lieutenant-Colonel Potter, of the Fifty-first New York, led the three companies of his regiment that first entered the fort and was one of the first in. Captain Neill, assistant adjutant-general, Lieutenant Reno and Lieutenant Morris, my aides, and Lieutenant Marsh, of the Signal Corps, rendered me valuable assistance in carrying orders through the thickest of the fight and in directing the various regiments to their positions. In my brigade the total number killed was 16 and 64 wounded.* The regimental reports give the full particulars concerning the killed and wounded. Captain Henry, Company H, Ninth New Jersey, was killed whilst gallantly leading his company. Captain Foster, Company D, Twenty-first Massachusetts, was severely but not dangerously wounded, and Lieutenant Stearns, adjutant of the Twenty-first Massachusetts, was hit twice in the head and neck, but fortunately the wounds were slight, and he remained, his face covered with blood, with his colonel at the head of the regiment during the whole day. Captain Ritchie, assistant commissary of the brigade, was detailed by me on the 7th instant to go on board the Pioneer and join the naval attack. He gallantly directed the vessel to the thickest of the fight. I beg leave to refer to his report for the particulars. Captain Nichols, of the Naval Brigade, took direction of the Lancer, the other gunboat belonging to the brigade, and participated in the naval attack. Two companies of the Fifty-first New York were on board the gunboats. I have had no report from them, but I have heard that no casualties occurred.

Inclosed I send a list of the prisoners now in my camp.† The list is not complete, but it is all that I have had time to obtain. The names of 30 officers and 493 men are given.

I have the honor to be, very respectfully, your obedient servant,

J. L. RENO,
Brigadier-General, Second Brigade, Burnside's Division.

Capt. LEWIS RICHMOND, *Assistant Adjutant-General.*

---

* But see revised statement, p. 85.   † Omitted.

No. 16.

Report of Capt. Montgomery Ritchie, Aide-de-Camp.

ON BOARD PROPELLER GUNBOAT PIONEER,
February 7, 1862.

SIR : On the 6th instant, in obedience to the orders of General Reno, I proceeded on board and took command of this vessel. At 8.30 a. m. this day got under way and cleared the ship for action. The action became general at 12.30 p. m. between the rebel gunboats, their redoubt on the central part of Roanoke, and the fleet. Opened fire from our 30-pounder Parrott at 25 minutes to 1 p. m., and from the Wiard gun at 10 minutes to 1 o'clock. Owing to her draught of water, though we ran her aground, it was impracticable to approach as near as desirable. We maintained fire during the day until after 5 p. m., expending 95 rounds of ammunition. Captain Baker, of the Pioneer, placed his vessel skillfully in position. The Parrott gun, under command of Lieut. F. W. Tryon, Fifty-first New York Volunteers, and the Wiard gun (12-pounder), under Mr. Griffith, first mate, deserve honorable mention for the manner in which their guns were handled.

I have the honor to be, your obedient servant,

M. RITCHIE,
Captain, Aide of General Reno.

Capt. E. M. NEILL,
Assistant Adjutant-General, Second Brigade.

No. 17.

Report of Lieut. Col. Alberto C. Maggi, Twenty-first Massachusetts Infantry.

HDQRS. TWENTY-FIRST REGIMENT MASS. VOLS.,
Roanoke Island, February 9, 1862.

GENERAL : Friday, the 7th, at 5 p. m., my regiment disembarked. I formed the line rapidly and in good order. Then General Parke came in your name and asked from my regiment a company of skirmishers, in order to go in advance to explore the road which from the place of disembarkation was crossing the woods toward our right side. I gave to him Company D, 90 men strong, commanded by Capt. T. S. Foster. Afterward you came and gave me the order to go to the cross-road and take possession of all that ground, placing my pickets for the night in order to cover the main body. I did so, placing a section of artillery at the cross-road, supported by Company C, and throwing to right and left from water to water two other companies in small pickets, covered by sentries at a distance of 15 paces each, and placing the rest of the regiment at the end of the wood as supports.

During this march the head of the advance guard was fired upon by the advance pickets of the enemy and one of our men wounded. We brought him back. It now being quite dark, the advance guard was called in and one man was found missing. He returned the following day. I had already detailed two sections as a scouting party, who would have relieved each other during the night, in order to explore the ground in front of the pickets and advance as far as possible without giving the alarm, in order to discover the position of the enemy, but at that time you, general, and General Foster, came and gave me the order to change the position of the pickets, concentrating them on the road and place them to the front. I did so. Six companies were in front, with two pieces of artillery, with a prolongation of picket in the two roads which opened through the woods at an angle of about 60°. The other four companies, with the three pieces of artillery, were to the rear precisely at the other cross-road, which lay 500 yards behind the first. Those companies had pickets right and left, but with the order to do no firing to the front and in case of an attack to act as support, we stood all night without fire, it raining all the time. None of the men slept, and every half hour I made the companies fall in in the greatest silence. All officers and men of the regiment, without exception, comported themselves with remarkable patience and endurance during the twelve hours of darkness and raining. Not a word of grumbling, not an expression of weariness.

At 6.30, after a small scouting party which I sent a little beyond my pickets returned, I permitted my men to light fires, in order to dry themselves as much as possible. At 7 o'clock an aide of General Foster came and ordered me to allow the First Brigade to pass through my line of pickets. The brigade came half an hour after, headed by the general himself, in the following order: Twenty-fifth Massachusetts, Twenty-third Massachusetts, Twenty-seventh Massachusetts, Fifth Battalion Rhode Island, and Tenth Connecticut. My regiment was in line, and immediately upon your arrival we followed them. We arrived in time. Following your order to defile through swamp and water to the rear and left of the Twenty-fifth and then halting; I took the two flank companies, D and G, armed with Harper's Ferry rifles and saber bayonets, and having assured myself of the position of the battery of the enemy and by the different shot of their guns of the extension of the ground which they could sweep toward our left (their right), I ordered the two companies to jump into a deep swamp, and commanded them to open fire by file, marching slowly front and toward the left. I forbade those two companies to waste any ammunition, but to aim and fire only when they were perfectly sure of their aim.

We had soon in front the infantry of the enemy, which supported the right flank of the battery. It was then that the fire began to be really hot, and I had many men put *hors de combat.* Among those, I regret to say, Capt. T. S. Foster was shot by a bullet through the left leg. But we steadily kept up the firing for more than two hours, advancing toward the front and left at the same time. At such a moment, the Twenty-fifth Regiment having changed their position, two of my companies joined my line, and a few minutes after all the rest of the battalion proceeded by my order, guided by Major Clark. I was at that moment at the edge of the swamp, and in front of me was an exposed ground of 100 yards.

The regiment once in line, I commanded a general fire. After the charge for all that distance the men lay down and loaded, covered by a small natural elevation. During that march we suffered four or five minutes a very thick fire and lost 15 men, but it was the last of the enemy. The battery was already flanked. You came and said to me, "Charge and take it." We did so. At our left flank were three companies of the Fifty-first New York. Our State color was the first on the battery; afterward the flag of the Fifty-first New York; then, immediately after, our regimental flag. One of our men captured a rebel flag with the motto, "*Aut vincere aut mori.*" After a few moments of joy, by your order I put again the regiment in line in the road behind the battery, and first led by you we proceeded toward Camp Georgia.

Company E, of my regiment, which was in advance, found the enemy retreating. They turned and fired, but soon were repulsed with loss of 3 dead and some wounded. They sent a flag of truce and surrendered.

I am glad to say that I never saw better behavior by any soldiers, young or veterans, and I do not believe it was possible in such a ground—if a continual swamp and ponds of water can be so called— that any one could have surpassed the brilliant and gallant conduct of all my command. I would mention the names of those officers who have distinguished themselves, but I would be obliged to send you the names of all, from the major to the last second lieutenant, as every one of them deserves it. Nevertheless, I shall name two, not because they have been braver than the others, but because both by force of circumstances have been obliged to stand a longer time in the most dangerous position than any other. They are Capt. T. S. Foster, who followed me, leading his company, and my adjutant, F. A. Stearns, who has been during all the fight cool and bravely at my side from the beginning to the end. And also I would call your attention to the faithful services of Surgeons Cutter and Warren and the chaplain, who bravely followed the troops through the fight to bear back the dead and wounded. All our wounded were conveyed at once to the hospital and our dead immediately buried. Both Capt. T. S. Foster and Adjt. F. A. Stearns have been wounded, the first, as I said, by a bullet in the left leg, and the second slightly in the right temple and in the neck. I send you annexed the list of killed and wounded.*

I have the honor to be, your obedient subordinate,

A. C. MAGGI,
Lieutenant-Colonel, Commanding.

* Brigadier-General RENO,
  Commanding Second Brigade, Burnside's Division.

No. 18.

Report of Lieut. Col. Charles A. Heckman, Ninth New Jersey Infantry.

HDQRS. NINTH REGIMENT NEW JERSEY VOLS.,
February 9, 1862.

I hereby respectfully report that the regiment which I command took its position in the brigade about 7 a.m. When we had approached near the field of action we passed, by order of Lieutenant Reno, the Fifty-first Regiment New York Volunteers, and when we had arrived on their right we were met by General Foster, and were ordered by him to enter the swamp to the left by company front. However, finding that our fire would be more effective, I formed them by division. At 9.30 a.m. the first division commenced an oblique fire upon the battery, and the fire was continued until 11.15 a.m. by the successive divisions, when, the fire of the enemy slackening, I ordered the regiment to charge, and in company with the Twenty-first Massachusetts Volunteers we entered the battery.

The officers and men of the regiment conducted themselves with courage and coolness, and I am perfectly satisfied with them. The

---

ground was very swampy, and for most of the time the men were up to their waists in water, though, notwithstanding these discouraging circumstances, they behaved themselves admirably.

There are 35 men missing from the regiment.

C. A. HECKMAN,
Lieutenant-Colonel, Commanding.

Capt. E. M. NEILL,
Asst. Adjt. Gen., Second Brigade, Dept. of North Carolina.

P. S.—All the missing have returned except 14, most of whom probably will.

No. 19.

Report of Col. Edward Ferrero, Fifty-first New York Infantry.

I beg leave to submit the following as the report of the Fifty-first Regiment New York Volunteers at the battle of the 8th of February, 1862, on Roanoke Island, N. C.:

I received an order from General Reno on the morning of Saturday, the 8th of February, 1862, at about .7.30 o'clock a. m., to form line on the right of the Second Brigade. The regiment started about 8 a. m. in rear of the First Brigade. After having marched a distance of about half a mile we met three companies of the Twenty-first Massachusetts Regiment. I halted my column and allowed them to take their position. Following them on the main road up the island and marching a distance of about half a mile, I received an order from General Reno to force our way through a dense jungle in the direction of the fighting. On arriving near the rear of the Twenty-first Massachusetts received an order to advance and take position on their left. Finding the swamp almost impassable, owing to the dense growth of underbrush on the right of my line, I ordered the four companies of the right wing, viz, A, G, D, and I, to push forward toward the left, under command of Lieutenant-Colonel Potter. Said companies advanced and entered the fire on the left of the Twenty-first Massachusetts. During the engagement of the above companies in said position the firing was very galling, but the men and officers replied to it with great vigor. I ordered the companies of the left wing to push forward toward the right. Finding it impossible to engage the enemy on account of the Twenty-first Massachusetts being in front, I ordered the men to lie down to avoid the shower of bullets from our own troops as well as those from the enemy.

The enemy, finding that they were outflanked, commenced to retreat, when the order was given by General Reno to charge. The right wing charged, under command of Lieutenant-Colonel Potter, while I led the left wing. Having advanced a few paces in front of the Ninth New Jersey and the Ninth New York, I feared that their fire would be directed into our ranks, so I halted my men and ordered the signal for cease firing to be sounded by our bugler, which was understood by all the troops in the vicinity. At that moment the cry came to charge, when all charged together, my right wing arriving at the fort first. Captain Wright, of Company A, color company, arrived first with his company, and planted the American flag upon the ramparts in advance of any other regiment. Captain Sims, of Company G, and Captain

Johnson, of Company I, took possession of the guns of the fort. I led the left wing down the main road, followed by the Ninth New York, crossed the moat, and halted inside of the fort. On arriving inside of the fort Lieutenant Springweiler, of Company K, brought me a wounded officer, who was a lieutenant in the Wise Legion of Virginia, who was found lying a short distance off.

After remaining in the fort about fifteen minutes I rallied the men, formed line, and started up the main road in pursuit of the enemy. On arriving at the end of the island I found that two boat loads of the enemy had escaped, but one had been captured, containing O. Jennings Wise, severely wounded, and four others, who were all in charge of the Ninth New York. The four prisoners were transferred to my charge, and I left them in a house which was guarded by our troops. Ascertaining that General Reno had advanced across the island to the left I immediately followed, and arrived in time to receive an order from him to place a chain of sentinels to encircle the grounds and barracks of the captured enemy, which was executed, and remained upon duty until relieved by the Ninth New Jersey.

The men and officers under my command behaved with a coolness that was really surprising for men who were under fire for their first time. On Sunday morning, the 9th, I received an order to detail a company to plant the American flag on one of the captured forts on the sea-shore.

I have the honor to be, your obedient servant,

EDW. FERRERO,
Colonel Fifty-first Regiment New York Volunteers.

No. 20.

Report of Col. John F. Hartranft, Fifty-first Pennsylvania Infantry.

HDQRS. FIFTY-FIRST PENNSYLVANIA VOLUNTEERS,
Camp Jordan, Roanoke Island, N. C., February 9, 1862.

SIR: I have the honor to report that in accordance with orders I yesterday marched my regiment onto the field in rear of the Ninth New Jersey Volunteers. I was ordered by Lieutenant Morris to take my regiment to the extreme left, about 200 yards beyond the temporary hospital. On arriving at the proper place I filed them to the left through the swamp. On account of the depth of water and the extreme thickness of the underbrush I was obliged to conduct them in single file. When two companies had entered, finding it impossible to advance, I returned in person to the road, and I was there ordered to leave two companies already in the morass where they were, under the command of Lieutenant-Colonel Bell, with orders to hold the position he was then in until further orders. I proceeded with the eight companies to the right. I was ordered to follow in rear of the Twenty-seventh Massachusetts Volunteers. In passing to the right we were all very much impeded by the underbrush and water, that reached to our middle. By taking a shorter route I succeeded in coming up side by side with the Twenty-seventh Massachusetts Volunteers. Before any of us succeeded in reaching to cleared ground the battery was taken.

Soon after leaving my first position Colonel Bell received an order to bring his companies toward the main road. Receiving no orders, he marched his companies to the front and joined the companies I was bringing out of the morass. As soon as I could get five of my companies together I moved them forward, leaving orders for the remainder to follow under command of the major. The five companies that were thus left behind were ordered to garrison the battery and are still there.

As far as I have learned, but one man, a private of Company B, has been wounded.

I have every reason to be most pleased with the coolness and bravery of all my officers, and with the patience, bravery, and ready obedience upon the part of my men.

I have two men missing.

I have the honor, general, to be, very respectfully, yours,
J. F. HARTRANFT,
Colonel, Comdg. Fifty-first Regiment Pennsylvania Volunteers.

Brig. Gen. J. L. RENO.

No. 21.

Report of Brig. Gen. John G. Parke, U. S. Army, commanding Third Brigade.

HDQRS. THIRD BRIGADE, DEPT. OF NORTH CAROLINA,
Pork Point Battery, Roanoke Island, February 9, 1862.

CAPTAIN: I have the honor to submit the following report of the operations of the Third Brigade during the 7th and 8th instant from the moment the signal for landing was displayed:

The brigade is composed of the Fourth Rhode Island, Ninth New York, and Eighth Connecticut Regiments, and a battalion of the Fifth Rhode Island Regiment. On the signal being given one wing of the Fourth Rhode Island Regiment was transferred to the light-draught steamer Phœnix, and all the surf-boats, life-boats, and ships' boats belonging to the transports of my brigade filled with men from the Eighth Connecticut and Fifth Rhode Island Regiments, and attached in tow of the steamer. We then proceeded toward the shore as rapidly as safety to the small boats would permit. The steamer was run into the marsh between the steamers of Generals Foster and Reno, and the men immediately sprang into the marsh and were led by their respective commanders out to the firm ground, and there formed in line in the field to the left of Hammond's house. Capt. John N. King, brigade quartermaster, and Lieut. M. A. Hill, aide-de-camp, returned to the transports to superintend the landing of the balance of the brigade.

Orders were then given to the colonels of the Fourth Rhode Island and the Twenty-fifth Massachusetts and Tenth Connecticut Regiments of the First Brigade to send out a force to occupy the woods surrounding the landing place with a continuous line of skirmishers. The commanding general soon appeared on the field, and I reported in person the disposition I had made of the force then on the ground. Brigadier-General Reno came up immediately after and assumed command of the portions of the three brigades then landed. My entire brigade was landed before 11 o'clock p. m. The men bivouacked on their arms.

Soon after daylight on the 8th instant I received orders from General Foster to have my command ready to support his and General Reno's brigades and follow along the road leading through the middle of the island, and to send four companies to occupy Ashby's house, below our camp and on the right of the road. The First Battalion Fifth Rhode Island Regiment was detailed for this latter duty. Firing was heard in our front, and it was soon evident that General Foster had engaged the enemy. Before my brigade could advance on the road, it being still occupied by General Reno I received orders from the general commanding to detach a regiment and hold the landing and bivouac grounds, and prevent the enemy from turning our position by coming through the timber down the beach. The Eighth Connecticut Regiment was detailed for this duty. Before leaving the bivouac the major commanding the First Battalion Fifth Rhode Island Regiment reported Ashby's house and premises occupied by the enemy. I ordered him to throw out skirmishers and hold his position, and if attacked he would be supported. As soon as the last of General Reno's brigade were under way I followed with the Fourth Rhode Island and Ninth New York Regiments.

On reaching the battle-field I found General Foster occupying the road on the edge of the clearing in front of the enemy's battery, and General Reno, with his brigade on the left, endeavoring to turn the enemy's right. The troops of both brigades were exposed to a steady fire from the battery and musketry, but were nevertheless hotly engaging the enemy and gradually gaining upon his flanks. General Foster ordered me to support a portion of his force on his right who were endeavoring to turn the enemy's battery.

The Fourth Rhode Island Regiment, on reaching the boat howitzers, which were in position in the road in the edge of the clearing, bore off slightly to the right, and, exposed to the fire of the enemy's battery and a continuous fire of musketry, were gallantly led by the colonel commanding, I. P. Rodman, and yourself through the clearing, and closing upon the Twenty-seventh Massachusetts Regiment, they encountered an almost impenetrable cypress swamp, through which they worked their way with great difficulty. The Ninth New York Regiment, arriving on the ground, was ordered to follow the Fourth Rhode Island Regiment and turn the left flank of the battery. The regiment, under lead of the colonel, Rush C. Hawkins, entered the clearing with great spirit.

It being now ascertained that the natural obstacles on this line were of so serious a character, and that the delay in the progress of the troops through the swamps was so great, it was decided to change the course of the Ninth New York Regiment, and the order was sent to the colonel to turn to the left and charge the battery directly up the road, and the regiment, with a hearty yell and cheer, struck into the road and made for the battery on the run. "The order was given to charge the enemy with fixed bayonets. This was done in gallant style, Major Kimball taking the lead." The major was very conspicuous during the movement, and I take great pleasure in commending him to your favorable notice. Before reaching the intrenchment the enemy retreated through the timber in great confusion; abandoning their guns, ammunition, and private property.

General Reno started immediately in pursuit, and as soon as the Ninth New York Regiment were reformed they were ordered forward and succeeded in taking "some 40 prisoners. Among them were several of the officers and men of the Richmond Blues, with O. Jennings Wise at their head, who was badly wounded and trying to make his escape in a boat across to Nag's Head."

As soon as the Fourth Rhode Island Regiment was reformed I proceeded with it up to the support of General Reno until he sent me word that he required no more regiments. The commanding general then ordered me to proceed with the Fourth Rhode Island and Tenth Connecticut Regiments, with a boat howitzer, to take Pork Point Battery. A guide being furnished me, we left the main road, and following along a narrow cross-road about a mile, we entered the battery and found that it had been but a short time evacuated, the garrison having retreated up the beach to the northern end of the island. The armament consisted of eight 32-pounder smooth-bore and one 32-pounder rifled gun. They were all spiked and the carriages seriously damaged.

From papers found in the quarters the battery is called Fort Bartow, and commanded by Maj. G. H. Hill, formerly a lieutenant in the United States Artillery. A flag-staff, with the national colors made fast, was immediately raised, and the men had scarcely finished cheering when General Foster rode in to announce to the general commanding that the enemy had surrendered.

At the taking of the masked battery the officers and men, not only of the Fourth Rhode Island and Ninth New York Regiments, but of other regiments that came under my observation, behaved with great gallantry, coolness, and bravery. All seemed imbued with determination to carry the day. Considering the length of time that they have been on board ship, that they bivouacked in the rain on the night of the 7th, and considering the great natural obstacles in front of the battery—a broad swamp surrounded by a dense tangle and thick growth of cypress, through which but a single narrow roadway or trail passed, and that completely raked by the battery—considering all this, it would seem that all engaged are worthy of much praise.

I would respectfully beg to call your attention to the adjutant of the Fourth Rhode Island Regiment, Lieutenant Curtis. He was very conspicuous in conducting and cheering on the men of his regiment while passing through the clearing.

I also wish to pay a just tribute to the officers of my staff for their great gallantry throughout the battle and untiring zeal through the whole day. The staff is composed of the following officers: Capt. Charles T. Gardner, assistant adjutant-general; Capt. John N. King, brigade quartermaster and acting commissary; Lieuts. M. Asbury Hill and Philip M. Lydig, aides-de-camp. Lieut. L. Bradley, of the Signal Corps, was with me, and acted as aide. All of these, including Capt. J. N. King, who volunteered his services as aide early in the morning, were constantly occupied carrying orders, bringing up and conducting the troops into position, and were necessarily greatly exposed. Lieuts. J. W. Hopkins and Anthony Lang, of the Signal Corps, were also actively engaged bringing up the men during the fight. On the morning of the 9th a company of the Fourth Rhode Island Regiment took possession of Fort Blanchard, a small work mounting four 32-pounders. The guns were spiked and the carriages damaged.

A detachment from the Ninth New York Regiment took possession of a two-gun battery on the east side of the island. They found the guns spiked and pointed inland. The battery is surrounded by a marsh and swamp, the only approach to it being by a causeway from the water side. One prisoner was taken in this work, he having been left by his comrades when they evacuated the place.

I regret to have to record the death of Lieut. Col. Viguer De Monteil, of the Fifty-third New York Regiment (D'Epineuil Zouaves). The colonel of the Ninth New York Regiment reports that " he was killed instantly, while urging my men to the charge. He dies greatly lamented by all my officers and men who came in contact with him. His bravery was as great as his patriotism was sincere, and I cannot but feel that had he lived he would have proved a most valuable officer."

The casualties in the Ninth New York Regiment are 2 lieutenants and 15 privates wounded—none likely to prove fatal.

I have the honor to be, very respectfully, your obedient servant,

JNO. G. PARKE,
Brigadier-General Volunteers, Commanding Third Brigade.

Capt. LEWIS RICHMOND,
Assistant Adjutant-General.

No. 22.

Report of Col. Isaac P. Rodman, Fourth Rhode Island Infantry.

FORT BARTOW,
Roanoke Island, N. C., February 10, 1862.

DEAR SIR: I had the honor to write you last from Camp California, Va. Since then the Fourth Rhode Island has been detached from Howard's brigade and assigned to that of General John G. Parke, Third Brigade, Burnside's division, and reported for duty at Annapolis, Md., on the 3d of July [January]. Embarked on the steamer Eastern Queen for Fort Monroe; sailed [January] 9th; arrived the 10th, and sailed for Hatteras Inlet the 11th; arrived the 12th and entered the inlet the 13th, where we were obliged to lay until the 28th before all the fleet had passed over the Bulkhead. The Pocahontas, on which our horses were embarked, was lost on the cape, and all the horses, except 19, perished. I am happy to say that none of the teamsters that were with them were lost, but all succeeded in getting on shore and joining the regiment.

On July [February] 5 the fleet sailed for Roanoke and arrived in sight the same evening.

The gunboats, having completed their preparations, commenced the bombardment of Forts Bartow, Huger, and Blanchard (mounting eight 32s and one 7-inch rifled Parrott on Bartow; six 32s and three 7-inch Parrotts on Huger, and one 7-inch rifled Parrott on Blanchard) on Friday morning at 11.30 a. m., and continued through the day. The troops from different transports were landed the same evening without opposition, with the exception of a small party firing on the sounding party of the Fifth Battalion Rhode Island Volunteers, wounding 2 slightly; the gunboats of the enemy not approaching near enough to do us any damage, of which there were ten in all, with from two to three guns each.

On the morning of the 8th the First Brigade (General Foster's) was put in motion, followed by General Reno's (the second), ours (the third, General Parke) remaining for a short time in reserve. The Fifth Rhode Island Battalion having been deployed on our right and the Eighth Connecticut held in reserve on our left to prevent flank movements, we (that is, the Fourth Rhode Island and Ninth New York) were ordered forward. When the head of General Foster's column had proceeded about 1 mile on the road they were suddenly met by a sharp volley of musketry and the contents of a Dahlgren (12-pounder brass field piece) from behind a masked battery, called by the enemy Fort Defiance, across and commanding the only road for 400 yards, on each side of which was a hitherto-impassable cypress swamp. The First Brigade advancing was supported by Reno, who threw two regiments on their right flank. The Fourth Rhode Island was ordered to follow part of Foster's brigade in turning their left flank, Parke holding the Ninth New York in reserve. Our men at once plunged into the swamp, nearly waste-deep with mud and water, and after almost incredible exertions succeeded in forcing our way through briers, cypress, and a dense mass of birch, &c. When we had nearly succeeded in turning their flank on the left and right General Parke ordered the Ninth New York to charge in front, when the enemy, finding that they were flanked, fled up the island, followed by regiments of Foster and Reno in pursuit, General Parke ordering the Ninth New York to cut off their retreat by the Nag's Head, which they did, taking O. Jennings Wise prisoner, and capturing the battery at that point, with three heavy columbiads. The enemy retreated to Weir's Point, where they did not make any fight, but surrendered to Generals Foster and Reno, about 3,000 all told.

General Burnside ordered the Fourth Rhode Island to proceed to Pork Point and take possession of Fort Bartow, giving us the Tenth Connecticut for our support. We immediately marched for the point and took possession of the place, planting the banner of the Fourth Rhode Island on the ramparts. The Eighth North Carolina was within about half a mile of us, advancing to take possession of it, the battalion of Seventeenth North Carolina having evacuated it about two hours before we took possession. When they saw our flag on the fort they fell back and surrendered to General Reno. The larger fort on the main-land was fired about ten minutes after our arrival and consumed.

We have taken thirty-five to forty pieces of artillery, about 4,000 stand of arms, and camp equipage and stores of four regiments of infantry.

The gunboats of the enemy have escaped up the sound. Four hundred to 500 of the enemy got off the island, and a regiment from Norfolk that were coming to re-enforce the rebels did not land, but got away. The enemy had sunk hulks and driven piles into the channel, which, with their masked batteries and natural advantage of the island, they supposed had made their position impregnable to any force we could bring against them. How we ever got through that swamp I can hardly conceive of now; as it was, we were full two hours in it. Half the time the regiment was under fire, but the distance—300 to 400 yards off the battery—and the enemy being obliged to take uncertain aim from the constant firing of Foster's advance, preserved us from loss.

I don't think we have lost a man, all but one (Corporal Perkins) having joined the regiment, and I think he will be found. A number of our men in the Fourth had balls through their coats and blankets. Our flag being half rolled up, did not present much surface to the fire, and we only got one bullet-hole through it; shall do better when we have a chance. The Fourth was cool and did well. All our force behaved well and gave satisfaction to the commanding· officer of the division.

I must now close this hasty and imperfect sketch, hoping it will give you some idea of the battle of Roanoke. Our regiment is again embarked on board the Eastern Queen, and is to proceed to ———, I suppose. The blank I am unable to fill,

And remain, very respectfully, your obedient servant,

I. P. RODMAN,
Colonel Fourth Rhode Island.

Gov. William Sprague.

No. 23.

Reports of Maj. Gen. Benjamin Huger, C. S. Army, commanding Department of Norfolk, with correspondence.

HEADQUARTERS DEPARTMENT OF NORFOLK,
Norfolk, Va., February 10, 1862.

SIR: I telegraphed last night that a steamer had arrived from Nag's Head and brought the news that Roanoke Island was captured. Men who escaped across Roanoke Sound brought them this information. Lieutenant Pearse brought up his ammunition by this opportunity, but had no communication with Roanoke Island, and got his information from runaways. Such information is not usually correct, but from his statements I had to treat it as true as regards the fact of the capture of all the forces on the island.

I have ordered—

1st. The Sixth Virginia Regiment, some six companies, under Colonel Corprew, to proceed to the Currituck Bridge, near outlet of Chesapeake and Albemarle Canal, to block that avenue to Norfolk. There is a battery of three 32-pounders at Currituck Bridge.

2d. Five companies of the Third Georgia Regiment, under Major Lee, to South Mills, the outlet of Dismal Swamp Canal, to protect that approach, and I have sent orders to Colonel Henningsen, who is at Elizabeth City, to fall back to South Mills and co-operate with Major Lee.

3d. Colonel Hamilton, at Suffolk, is ordered to throw some companies to the Black Water and protect the approach to the railroad bridge on the Black Water, and to obstruct the river.

4th. Lieutenant-Colonel Williams, First North Carolina Battalion, to proceed down the Black Water and Chowan to near Winton, to obstruct the passage of the Meherrin and Chowan, and I have ordered Captain Nichol's light battery to join him and assist in preventing a landing and stopping their boats.

As soon as the enemy hears the news (if true) I expect he will make demonstration in my front, and you will perceive this force can only perform outpost duty.

I will advise you of facts as soon as I can get them, and if the enemy are in strong force on the south of me I must be re-enforced.

I need say nothing now of Roanoke Island. I send you a copy of my instructions to General Wise as soon as he reported to me, dated January 13. These orders have never been carried out. I cannot but regret that Commander Lynch did not come into the Albemarle Canal. We could have supplied him with ammunition and had the use of his boats. I had loaded up a boat with ammunition for him and the island and dispatched it last evening. Soon after it left it met the steamer from Nag's Head with the news of the disaster and returned. These two boats are all I have to forward troops and supplies. Now Commander Lynch is shut up in Elizabeth City I fear he will lose all his boats.

Persons from the south of this report firing in direction of Elizabeth City. Nothing official to 11.30 a. m.

Very respectfully, your obedient servant,

BENJ. HUGER,
Major-General.

General S. COOPER,
Adjutant and Inspector General.

HEADQUARTERS DEPARTMENT OF NORFOLK,
Norfolk, Va., February 11, 1862.

SIR: I telegraphed to you this morning that I had a letter from General Wise, dated 9 a. m. yesterday at Poplar Branch, Currituck County, North Carolina. He would move on to the Canal Bridge and collect all his troops there. I have before reported to you I sent Colonel Corprew, Sixth Virginia Volunteers, to the same point. They left via canal early yesterday morning. I have not yet heard of their arrival. General Wise's account of the capture of Roanoke Island is from the report of a sergeant—Metzer, McCullough Rangers—who left the island at 5 p. m. on the 8th instant. He reports that Lieutenant Selden, in charge of a howitzer, which did great execution, was killed. Capt. O. J. Wise was wounded thrice and carried to the hospital, where it is reported he died, and Captain Coales was killed. All this is only report.

As I heard that Colonel Henningsen had retreated from Elizabeth City toward Edenton, I sent three pieces of Captain Girardey's company (Louisiana Guard) and the Second Battalion of the Third Georgia toward South Mills.

I just have the following report from Sewell's Point: "Three steamers have left the Roads seaward bound. Seventeen schooners are getting under way."

The enemy seem re-enforcing their forces in Albemarle Sound. I cannot detach further. Re-enforcements must be sent to guard the railroad beyond Meherrin. I have telegraphed General Gatlin he must take care of the Roanoke River and Weldon.

I am, very respectfully, your obedient servant,

BENJ. HUGER,
Major-General.

General S. COOPER,
Adjutant and Inspector General.

———

WAR DEPARTMENT,
Richmond, Va., February 23, 1862.

Maj. Gen. B. HUGER, *Norfolk, Va.:*

SIR: I have the honor to inclose herewith copy of a letter addressed by General Wise to the President, with copy of the indorsement by the President. You are respectfully requested to make such remarks thereon as the nature of the case may in your opinion require, and report the same.

Your obedient servant,

J. P. BENJAMIN,
Secretary of War.

[Inclosure.]

CANAL BRIDGE, CURRITUCK COUNTY, N. C.,
February 13, 1862.

His Excellency JEFFERSON DAVIS, *President, &c.:*

SIR: You are aware already, doubtless, of my defeat and disasters. I did my best to prepare for the unequal conflict. Unequal it was. In vain I appealed for re-enforcements; the reply was an order to my post, and that "supplies, hard work, and coolness, not men," were all that was needed. After this there was no election for me but to fight. The lack of time and the storms prevented me from working, and no work had been done. The North Carolina troops had not been paid, clothed, or drilled, and they had no teams or tools or materials for constructing works of defense, and they were badly commanded and led, and, except a few companies, they did not fight.

About 600 of my Legion withstood the enemy for half a day on the 8th without field artillery, except a 24-pounder and 18-pounder with 12-pounder ammunition, and a 6-pounder brass howitzer, which did terrible execution among the enemy. Twice the enemy, at least 8,000 strong, were repulsed with slaughter, and it was not until they passed a dense, deep swamp, thought to be impassable, and outflanked us on the right—and until Lieutenant Selden was killed at his gun sighting the aim of his last round of ammunition, and until the enemy advanced under a white flag, firing at our men as they cheered a supposed surrender—that our artillery pieces were captured and the Legion gave way, but never surrendered.

They fought on all the 8th and continued the fight on the 9th. Never did men do and dare more nobly, but they were unsupported, except by two or three companies of the Eighth North Carolina Regiment. The Thirty-first was hardly in the action at all, and had leave of their colonel (Jordan) to take care of themselves, and some 60 or 70 of them escaped.

The forts on the island were all out of place; they ought to have been at the south end, and they were at the north, leaving several of the landing points on the south end without any defenses against the shot and shell of the heavy steamers, which came quite up and covered the landing of their troops, horses, artillery, and everything required for land forces. We had but four indifferent mules for our pieces and they were killed.

Such were the odds and the deficiencies of our defenses, yet my men fought firmly, coolly, and stubbornly up to the muzzle, to wounds, death, and captivity. Providence sharply prohibited my commanding in person. For nine days I was prostrated at Nag's Head with high fever and a severe attack of pleurisy; but this enabled me to save about 200 of my men. Here we are, a remnant of infantry, a corps of artillery—in all six companies, besides fragments of about 40, who escaped, of the Legion.

I desire your favor now to recruit it. My Third Regiment was, unjustly to me and my men, taken from me and sent to South Carolina. I ask for its return to my command. I ask for the four field pieces taken from me by General Floyd or their equivalent. I ask for the transfer of such troops as seek to join my command and for all facilities to move it under the circumstances. Having obtained my Legion by your good pleasure, having spent it at every risk and sacrifice with honor in the service, I ask your interposition in behalf of its full restoration.

With the highest respect, your obedient servant,

HENRY A. WISE,
Brigadier-General.

[Indorsement.]

Referred to Secretary of War, whose attention is called to the representation of [General Wise] and especially to the order marked by quotation. A copy of the letter will be furnished to General Huger for report.   Authority and all due assistance will be given to recruit and reorganize General Wise's Legion.   My anxiety for the construction of a work on the south end of the island was freely expressed to General Wise, and its importance appears to have been even greater than I supposed, as the north had been reported to me impracticable for the movement of troops.   The Third Regiment was not considered a part of the Legion, and it was only the Legion proper which it was designed to remove, with General Wise, to the coast of Virginia and North Carolina.

JEFFERSON DAVIS.

—

HEADQUARTERS DEPARTMENT OF NORFOLK,
Norfolk, Va., March 5, 1862.

SIR: I beg to submit the following report of facts in regard to Roanoke Island:

1. On hearing of the capture of Fort Hatteras, on August 29 last, I sent troops to hold Roanoke Island and throw up some fortifications as promptly as possible.   Roanoke Island being outside the limits of my command I reported my action to the Department, and was notified that my course was approved by the President.

2. The Third Georgia Regiment continued to garrison the island and the engineer officers I sent there to fortify it.   As the place was so distant and out of my military district, and other troops were sent there from North Carolina, I requested, by letter (dated November 14, 1861), that Roanoke Island be placed entirely under my control and sufficient troops sent me to garrison it, or that I be relieved of the charge of it.   An order dated November 26, 1861, placed the island in the command of Brigadier-General Gatlin.   General D. H. Hill had immediate command.   About December 1 Colonel Wright's Third Georgia Regiment was relieved and ordered to return to this department.   The Thirty-first Regiment of North Carolina Volunteers replaced them.

3. From the time the command was given to Generals Gatlin and Hill until the date of Special Orders, No. 272, December 21, 1861, forming a brigade, commanded by Brig. Gen. H. A. Wise, I had no control over the position, and when Orders, No. 272, were issued I was not certain that it included Roanoke Island, but wrote to inquire on January 2.   Answer received January 4.   General Wise reported to me early in January, and I urged his immediate inspection and examination of the position.   He did visit it, and returned and reported to me.   I addressed him my instructions in a letter of January 13 (copy inclosed).   General Wise went a few days after this to Richmond.   While he was there an order for him to proceed at once to Roanoke Island was issued, and on or about January 29 General Wise arrived at Nag's Head.   On February 7 and 8 the place was attacked and captured by the enemy.

4. The orders of the War Department will show that I had not the control or management of Roanoke Island from the time it was assigned to General Gatlin's command until General Wise was assigned to the command.

My opinion concerning the defenses is expressed in my letter of January 13.   I did write to General Wise that batteries should be so placed as to repel a fleet of gunboats, and that supplies, hard work, and coolness were what was wanted.

I send copies of my letters of January 9 and 13, to which I ask your attention.

I regret that General Wise addressed you directly instead of through me, as it prevented me from sending the above explanations with his letter of February 13.

Very respectfully, your obedient servant,

BENJ. HUGER,
Major-General.

His Excellency JEFFERSON DAVIS,
President of the Confederate States.

[Inclosures.]

HEADQUARTERS DEPARTMENT OF NORFOLK,
Norfolk, Va., January 9, 1862.

GENERAL: I have your letter of the 7th (received last night), and have seen persons who have left you since. The gunboats that have gone to Hatteras are not those which were here. A large number of small vessels and barges are still in the Mill Creek Channel, near Old Point. No number of vessels, but schooners, have left Old Point lately.

I send the steamer Currituck to-day, with Capt. J. S. Taylor and Lieutenant Loyall, to take charge of the batteries at Roanoke Island. I have directed all the supplies asked for by Major Williamson, except the large quantity of shot for which there was no powder sent.

I have got from Richmond to-day an order for a small quantity of powder at Raleigh, and send for it at once. I will send the chief quartermaster with a good pilot down to-morrow. Major Johnston, the quartermaster, will give all instructions necessary in his department. He must have boats and barges enough to get up supplies both for your brigade and the rest of the army. You will find him fully capable to manage the business. The pilot I send, Captain Taylor, informs me that it would be easier to obstruct the channel inside; that is, to the northward and westward of the marshes. He says the water is too deep between some of the marsh islands to block them there; but as soon as you get through, the water shoals and the channel could be obstructed by sinking vessels in some 12 feet of water. I send him, that he may sound out the positions and assist in obstructing them, if you desire it.

Let Major Johnston send back all such boats as you can spare, that we may use them in supplying you with more articles you want. I think you want supplies, hard work, and coolness among the troops you have, instead of more men. If men can help you, you shall have them, if we have boats here to take them. I am most anxious to do all I can to strengthen you. I only want to know how.

Very respectfully, your obedient servant,

BENJ. HUGER,
Major-General, Commanding.

Brig. Gen. HENRY A. WISE,
Commanding Fourth Brigade.

HEADQUARTERS DEPARTMENT OF NORFOLK,
Norfolk, Va., January 13, 1862.

SIR: Your requisition for means to carry on all necessary work at

Roanoke Island will be approved. To secure this important pass, the key of Albemarle Sound, I direct that all efforts be made—

First, to establish batteries at the marshes off south end of the island, one of your own propositions after your personal reconnaissance. If guns at these marshes can prevent the enemy's gunboats from passing they will also prevent any landing, and it will be impossible for them to take the island.

The more permanent battery, as proposed by you, for the marshes may be postponed for the present, and two or more guns mounted on barges or vessels, and placed in position on the different marshes to protect the approaches to the island; this to be the first work done. If it will expedite the work, you are authorized to move one or both of the barges with guns on them now at Redstone Point to the marshes.

Second, one or more wharves appear to be necessary for landing, &c., and should be erected as soon as possible.

I do not consider large forces necessary for the defense of this island. If the batteries can keep off gunboats and transports the infantry will have little opportunity to act. .

Very respectfully, your obedient servant,

BENJ. HUGER,
Major-General, Commanding.

Brig. Gen. HENRY A. WISE, *Commanding Fourth Brigade.*

—

[MARCH 5, 1862.—Huger to Benjamin, inclosing Talcott's report, see p. 54.]

—

HEADQUARTERS DEPARTMENT OF NORFOLK,
Norfolk, Va., March 11, 1862.

Hon. J. P. BENJAMIN, *Secretary of War :*

SIR : I transmit inclosed a copy of a letter received from Brig. Gen. H. A. Wise in reply to mine of 8th instant, requiring, as directed by you, his report of the battle at Roanoke Island.

Very respectfully, your obedient servant,

BENJ. HUGER,
Major-General.

[Inclosure.]

ROLLISTON, NEAR NORFOLK, *March* 8, 1862.

Maj. Gen. B. HUGER, *Commanding, &c.:*

SIR : In reply to yours of this day, I have to inform you that I did not receive the report of Colonel Shaw of the battle on Roanoke Island on the 7th and 8th February until Monday, the 3d instant. It inclosed the reports of Colonels Anderson, Jordan, and Green, Majors Hill and Fry, and Capt. J. S. Taylor, and is dated February 24. As soon as copied, with its accompanying reports, it was sent to the Secretary of War, Wednesday, the 5th instant, the day of the date of the letter of the Secretary of War to you. Before this he has received the report of Colonel Shaw to me and of mine to him. I retain the originals, and if you desire copies will furnish them to you.

At the same time I request to be furnished with copies of all official letters or papers which you have sent to the War Department, and of all letters sent or orders issued by your subordinates commanding departments or other forces in the district assigned to my command in

North Carolina touching or relating to my late command in that district, and especially any of those sent to Colonel Wright at Elizabeth City or elsewhere. I make this request in order to aid the inquiry which I have demanded respecting my command and to subserve the justice due to·you as well as to myself in respect to the defenses of Roanoke Island and their conduct by you and by myself and others and in respect to my retreat to Great Bridge.

Very respectfully, your obedient servant,
HENRY A. WISE,
Brigadier-General, Commanding.

HEADQUARTERS DEPARTMENT OF NORFOLK,
Norfolk, March 17, 1862.

Hon. J. P. BENJAMIN,
Secretary of War:

SIR: I received yesterday by special messenger your letter of the 15th instant,* inclosing a letter to be forwarded to General Wise.† Also a voluminous report (143 pages) sent to you by General Wise, and forwarded to me for my remarks.‡

The letter to General Wise was sent to him at once. I have devoted the night to looking over the voluminous report, which I find is not a report of the battle of Roanoke Island, but a collection of all General Wise's correspondence, with his explanatory remarks, giving his views of the conduct of the War Department, myself, and others. As you remark, no such report should be sent, unless forwarded through me.

It will take much time to examine so voluminous a document carefully, which at this moment I can illy spare from more important duties.

I am, very respectfully, your obedient servant,
BENJ. HUGER,
Major-General, Commanding.

HEADQUARTERS DEPARTMENT OF NORFOLK,
Norfolk, Va., March 18, 1862.

Hon. J. P. BENJAMIN,
Secretary of War:

SIR: I send herewith a letter received from General Wise, dated 16th instant, covering a copy of his report to you of the capture of Roanoke Island and the original reports of his subordinates on the subject, viz: The report of Col. H. M. Shaw and the reports to him of Colonel Jordan, Lieutenant-Colonels Green and Anderson, Majors Hill and Fry, and Capt. J. S. Taylor. Having no personal knowledge of the positions, and uninformed, except by these reports, of. the occurrences there, I have no remark to make upon them.

As I occupied this island the end of August last on my own responsibility, it being without the limits of my command, there seems to be a general impression that I had had entire control of it, which is an error. I did partially fortify and garrison it last summer. I was afterward relieved from all charge of it, and the troops I had sent there were withdrawn and returned to this command. It was, by order of

---

the War Department, the latter part of December, assigned to the immediate command of Brigadier-General Wise and attached to this department, and it is only since then I have had any charge of it.

I am, very respectfully, your obedient servant,

BENJ. HUGER,
Major-General, Commanding.

[Inclosure.]

NEAR NORFOLK, VA., *March* 16, 1862.

Maj. Gen. B. HUGER, *Commanding, &c.:*

SIR: On the 5th instant I sent to the Secretary of War the report of the surrender of Roanoke Island, of which the inclosed is a copy.* At the same time I sent to him copies of the reports of Cols. H. M. Shaw and Jordan, and Lieutenant-Colonels Anderson and Green, and of Majors Hill and Fry, and Captain Taylor.

By a letter dated March 14, just received by me, he corrects my error of sending copies and not the originals and of reporting directly to the Department instead of through you. I deeply regret these errors in form, and now send my report through you, accompanied by the originals.

I respectfully assure you, and through you the Secretary of War, that these informalities were entirely unintentional, as the Secretary does me the justice to suppose. I supposed the originals, addressed to me, were mine, and that I, being changed from your department, was no longer required to report to you. I beg that you will forward this report to the Secretary of War, and believe me, respectfully, your obedient servant,

HENRY A. WISE,
Brigadier-General.

—

RICHMOND, VA., *April* 2, 1862.

Maj. Gen. B. HUGER, *Norfolk, Va.:*

SIR: The committee appointed by the House of Representatives to inquire and report the causes and circumstances of the capitulation of Roanoke Island have instructed me to inclose you the within copy of the comments filed by Brigadier-General Wise with the committee upon the remarks made by yourself upon his report of the battle of Roanoke Island. The committee have thought that you might like to reply to the remarks of General Wise. The committee are delayed in their investigation for the want of the report of Brigadier-General Wise, made on February 21 to the Secretary of War, in relation to the surrender of Roanoke Island, and which was sent by the Secretary of War to yourself, and which has not been returned by you to the War Department. The committee will be greatly obliged if you will return the report to the War Department, so that they can obtain a copy.

I have the honor to be,

B. S. GAITHER,
Chairman.

[Indorsement.]

Respectfully referred to the Secretary of War.

BENJ. HUGER,
Major General.

---

* See No. 24, p. 122.

RICHMOND, VA., *March* 28, 1862.

Hon. Mr. GAITHER, *Chairman, &c.:*

SIR: By permission of a portion of the committee over which you preside I obtained yesterday a copy of General Huger's remarks upon my communication of Colonel Shaw's report of the battle of Roanoke Island.

I beg leave most respectfully to submit some remarks upon the remarks of General Huger.

First. He says that my statement that the artillery of my Legion did not reach me owing to his interruption of my orders to Colonel Henningsen seems to convey the insinuation that the officious interruption of General Huger was the cause of the artillery not arriving, and that his intention was to expedite its arrival, not prevent it, as his paragraph seems to imply. If General Huger, in this paragraph, had left out the word insinuation, and for the word officious had substituted ignorant—had stated that I meant to convey the idea that the ignorant interruption of General Huger was the cause of my artillery not arriving—he would have been nearly correct in his inference, and he would have been relieved of the necessity for any averment of his intention to expedite the arrival of my artillery.

I ordered Colonel Henningsen, commanding a light artillery corps of three companies, six pieces and 213 horses, to have the horses led from Norfolk across what is called the Sand Bridge down the sea-beach to Nag's Head, and to have the field pieces, caissons, and ammunition towed by steam-tugs through the Albemarle and Chesapeake Canal to Roanoke Island. After I left Norfolk he countermanded this order, and commanded Colonel Henningsen to mount the artillery and haul it by horses on land to the nearest point. The nearest point was Powell's Point, about 15 or 20 miles from the island, across the Albemarle Sound, where there was no means of water transportation, except in a small lighter ferry at Gallop's, from the beach to the point.

Colonel Henningsen went to Elizabeth City, 45 miles off, and thence to the island. There was no transportation. Had he been allowed to obey my orders he could have reached me easily in three days, and would have arrived from three to five days before the fight on February 8, leaving Norfolk, as General Huger admits, on the 29th or 30th of January.

On February 8, during the battle, I wrote to General Huger for a boat, and expressed my regret that his change of the route of my artillery prevented its arrival.

On the 9th he replied by note, saying, "You are in error when you say 'Colonel Henningsen was diverted from following the route you ordered him to take by me.' I gave him no order, but not to send one company by the beach, as you ordered. In all other respects he was to obey your orders." Thus he in effect denied making the change in my orders except as to one company, and now he pleads justification of the change of my orders admitted to have been made by him. I required reports of Colonel Henningsen and of my ordnance officer, Lieut. J. H. Pearce. Both officially reported that General Huger had changed my orders, and assigned as reasons for changing the route designated by me that it was impracticable to lead the horses down the beach, owing to the tide, estuaries, inlets, creeks, and deep sands. That was his reason then for doing what he had written he had not done.

Again, when I met him at Great Bridge, February 16, he corrected verbally what he had written to me, alleging error in the statement that he had changed my orders, admitted that he had changed the route of my artillery as ordered by me and assigned the same reasons for so doing that he had given to Colonel Henningsen and Lieutenant Pearce, to wit, "the impracticability of the beach route," &c.   I assured him that I knew it to be not only practicable, but the best route in either Virginia or North Carolina, and referred him to my son, Lieut. R. A. Wise, who had but lately then pursued the route most of the way in a tilt-wagon with a pair of mules, and to Lieut. J. C. Gallop, who had described the route fully to Colonel Henningsen and Lieutenant Pearce at Norfolk in my presence, and who resided at Gallop's Ferry.   He still insisted that the route was impracticable, and said he would order a survey.   That, unfortunately, was impracticable, as the beach then was in possession of the enemy, and I so replied.   But then I aver he was ignorant of the route.   There are no inlets, no estuaries, no creeks to obstruct horsemen from Cape Henry to Oregon Inlet, nearly 100 miles, and the deep sands of the hills are easily avoided by taking the ocean shore at almost any tide.   But now he changes his grounds for changing the route.   In reply to Colonel Henningsen's statement, he says that every tug, barge, and vessel that could be procured was engaged to transport troops, &c., to Roanoke Island.   Unfortunately for General Huger this excuse is as groundless as the former.   I aver that not only every tug, barge, and vessel that could be procured was not engaged to transport troops, &c., to Roanoke Island, but that every one, of every description, was most inopportunely ordered away from Roanoke Island, and imperatively put under orders of General Huger's quartermaster for the transportation of forage to Norfolk.   The only steam-tug I had for transportation was the tug Roanoke and two barges, and these ordered away after the arrival of the enemy at Roanoke Island, as the order, of which the following, delivered to me during the battle, is a copy, will show:

HEADQUARTERS DEPARTMENT OF NORFOLK,
Norfolk, Va., February 3, 1862.

Brig. Gen. HENRY A. WISE,
      Commanding Fourth Brigade, Roanoke Island:

SIR: The steamer Roanoke towed down two barges, which were ordered by the quartermaster to proceed to Scuppernong and bring back corn to this place.   If the Roanoke has been taken for other service, you will, on receipt of this, send her and the barges to carry out the orders of the quartermaster.   I have to charter vessels to bring forage here, and will give vessels so employed by the Quartermaster's Department certificates that they are employed by me, and such vessels are not to be interfered with by any one.   You will direct the captains of all steamboats coming here from your command to report to the chief quartermaster and any officer coming up to report to headquarters.   These orders are imperative.
      Very respectfully, your obedient servant,

BENJ. HUGER,
Major-General, Commanding.

Why General Huger says that "if these men and horses are separated from their guns they would probably never meet again" I cannot conceive.   This blunder may account for his "one" company error in his note to me.   The men were not to be separated from their guns nor from their horses.   One company was to be detailed to lead the horses down to the beach to Nag's Head, and the other two companies, with their guns, &c., were to be towed to the island through the canal, the two ways converging to the same point—the island.   But grant what he says, "that every tug, barge, and vessel that could be procured was engaged to transport troops to Roanoke Island, and therefore none could be got to transport the artillery pieces, caissons," &c., and therefore he sent them by land route. What land route? Not the beach route, for he had ordered them away from that route, and that was the only route by which Roanoke Island could be approximated by land. That route even had to cross Roanoke Sound from Nag's Head. Any other land route had to cross from 15 to 45 miles of the boisterous and broad Albemarle Sound. Then tugs, barges, and vessels would be needed by the route he sent them; and he says there were no tugs, barges, or vessels to be procured for them. Did he know this, and yet did he send them by a route for which there was no water transport? He did; and yet I believe General Huger's intention was to expedite them; that his object, as he says, was to get them there, not to detain them. His intention and object were ever so good, but he was grossly ignorant of the routes and careless in organizing his means of transportation.

For information of the means of transportation and how it was ordered and disposed and how and when it could be procured I refer the committee to Marshall Parks, president of the Albemarle and Chesapeake Canal, and to Mr. Lindsay, of Norfolk. They have furnished most of the tugs, &c., and can tell how many lighters, vessels, and barges could have been procured; if not at Norfolk, in any of the waters of North Carolina nearer to the island than Norfolk. I refer also to Dr. Thomas Warren, of Edenton, N. C.

Second. He says that my remark upon Major Hill's and Captain Taylor's reports about the only three guns brought to bear on the enemy is "disingenuous." This is an offensive term; it means to say that I was not in this remark "frank, free, open, sincere, plain;" but my respect for the military service and for the committee admonishes me to deal with it mildly and forbearingly. I trust, then, it is not unbecoming in me to say that General Huger's reply, showing his reason for using the term, is so *naïve,* so innocent, as to render it innocuous. I stated the fact on the authority of Major Hill. Other guns were fired on the enemy, but because they could not be brought to bear on them ceased firing. But what says General Huger? "The enemy selected a position in which only three guns bore on them." Ah, and were the five batteries so located that an enemy's fleet of thirty-seven sail in attack could select a position in which only three guns bore on them? So says General Huger, and that is all any fair, intelligent mind could have understood me to say. The worst constructed forts in any locality with more than thirty guns could perhaps bring more than three guns to bear if the enemy would let General Huger select his position for him. But in this instance the enemy selected his own position. Where? In the open Croatan Sound. How far off from Pork Point Battery? One thousand yards. Did no guns but three of that battery bear? None. Did the guns of no other battery bear? None. So that General Huger is certainly *naïve,* and I not "disingenuous." His reasoning is like his command, and my statement is in effect admitted by him to be "fair." As far as permitted by the rules of propriety and position I repel his imputation on my sincerity. The committee will maintain decorum and I will observe military discipline.

General Huger's averment that "those three guns did repel their whole fleet" is just simply ridiculous. They did no damage to the enemy's fleet that ever I have been informed of, and why the enemy's fleet did not pass the three batteries—as they could have done in thirty minutes—is not to be accounted for, except upon their supposition that due preparations had been made at the north end of the island, as they found none at the south end. They accordingly ceased firing at insignificant batteries. General Huger's concluding remark under this head forgets his reasoning for the word "disingenuous." There he says but three guns were brought to bear, because the enemy selected a position in which only three guns did bear on them. Here he says that from that position the battery "was exposed to a heavy fire." Then the enemy did fire a heavy fire upon the battery from a position on which but three or four guns could be brought to bear. Material injury was done to the earthworks of the battery. It was materially knocked down by the first day's bombardment, and the night of that day (the 7th) it had to be rebuilt. For proof of this I refer you to Lieutenants Bagwell and Bolton, who are now in this city.

Third. General Huger supposes I meant him and the War Department by the words "my superiors." I meant and mean every superior of every grade and position at all responsible for the lack of defenses at Roanoke Island. I did all I could with the means and facilities allowed to me by them. He coupled himself swimmingly with the War Department. I separate them for the purpose of my remarks on his remarks. He says "we could not control time, weather, or sickness." I say emphatically that he could have taken time by the forelock, which he never did. That he might have worked while the sun shined and not have left everything to be done and undone, too, in the winter's weather of Hatteras; and if he had promptly aided me, as he ought to have done, with men and munitions of war, I could, while in good health, have been preparing at Roanoke Island, and might have saved my command, if it had not been grossly neglected up to the time I was prostrated by a severe illness and up to the arrival of the enemy. Thus, in a very rational sense correlatively with his own use of terms, he might have controlled "time, weather, and sickness." I could not control my command even under his orders. He says that he does not know what available preparation asked for by me could have been made by my superiors. He does know. He has, I believe, now in his hands my letter to the Secretary of War reporting the causes of the disaster at Roanoke Island. It was delivered here by Maj. William B. Stanard on March 1 instant, and the original was forwarded by the Department to him "for his remarks."

That will fully inform the committee of what was asked and what was not allowed. I intend to "accuse" General Huger of nothing! nothing!! nothing!!! That was the disease which brought disaster at Roanoke Island. My purpose is only to fully reply to the committee's inquiries and to his imputations.

Respectfully,

HENRY A. WISE,
Brigadier-General.

HEADQUARTERS DEPARTMENT OF NORFOLK,
April 5, 1862.

General S. COOPER,
Adjutant and Inspector General:

SIR: I return to the Secretary of War "a voluminous document (143 pages), which he sent me for my examination and remarks, stating "Brigadier-General Wise had forwarded this as a report from him direct to the Secretary, instead of sending it through me; that this report had been called for by Congress, but it could not be sent in, if at all, before being submitted to me." This report—as it is called—is, I find, copies of such official letters as General Wise has pleased to select, connected with his remarks, to give his view of the case. I have other employment, and can find no time to examine this voluminous document further. I consider it an improper report, and ought not to be published without other official correspondence, which may not sustain the views here desired to be made history. I return it to the Secretary of War, to be disposed of as he thinks proper. I received on the 3d instant the inclosed reply,* which a committee of Congress received from General Wise, criticising the few remarks I thought proper to make on his report of the capture of Roanoke Island. I considered those remarks proper and just, and regret they do not coincide with General Wise's opinion; but I have no time to discuss the subject with him, and I send his paper to the Secretary of War.

Very respectfully, your obedient servant,

BENJ. HUGER,
Major-General, Commanding Department of Norfolk.

No. 24.

Reports of Brig. Gen. Henry A. Wise, C. S. Army, with correspondence.

GREAT BRIDGE, NORFOLK COUNTY, VIRGINIA,
February 21, 1862.

SIR: I beg leave to make a full report of my command in the District of North Carolina, attached to the Department of Norfolk, under general orders from Major-General Huger.

Upon my return to Richmond from Western Virginia, under orders transferring my command to Brigadier-General Floyd, I was immediately, on September 30 last, stricken down by a severe and protracted illness.

November 18 last I reported for duty to the Secretary of War by letter of which the following is a copy:

ROLLISTON, NEAR NORFOLK, VA., *November* 18, 1861.

Hon. J. P. BENJAMIN, *Secretary of War:*

SIR: I take the earliest opportunity of returning health to report myself officially as ready for duty.

I earnestly request that the forces composing my Legion may without delay be ordered to the point at which the President intends to employ my services. Even the promptest movement on their part will now scarcely enable them to prepare their arrangements for winter before the winter shall be upon them.

In General Lee's absence from Richmond I take the liberty to remind the President and yourself of the disposition which he thought advisable in connection with the Legion, viz: that each western company should decide for itself whether to remain with the Legion or on service in the west; that a certain proportion of the pieces of artillery in possession of the Legion should be retained in the west; and, finally, that all the eastern companies and such of the western companies as shall so elect, with at least one battery of field pieces, should be ordered, with the least practicable delay, to the new field of operations where it is intended to employ them.

In the mean time I also request permission to detail a party to explore the channels of Albemarle and Pamlico Sounds, if it is intended to employ me on the North Carolina coast.

I will await at this place the orders of the President.

My post-office is at Norfolk City.

I have the honor to be, very respectfully, your obedient servant,

HENRY A. WISE,
Brigadier-General.

----

* See Gaither to Huger, April 2, p. 117.

In reply I received from the Secretary of War a letter of which the following is a copy:

CONFEDERATE STATES OF AMERICA,
War Department, Richmond, Va., November 23, 1861.

Brig. Gen. HENRY A. WISE,
　Rolliston, near Norfolk, Va.:

SIR: I have the honor to acknowledge the receipt of your letter of the 18th instant, and am happy to learn that you have been restored to health.

As soon as we are informed of the movements of the enemy consequent upon General Floyd's withdrawal from Cotton Hill orders will be issued in regard to your Legion. Until then, however, it will be impossible to decide.

I have the honor to be, respectfully, your obedient servant,

J. P. BENJAMIN,
Secretary of War.

On December 4, 1861, the following Special Orders, No. 254, extract IV, was issued:

ADJUTANT AND INSPECTOR GENERAL'S OFFICE,
Richmond, Va., December 4, 1861.

Brig. Gen. HENRY A. WISE,
　(Through General Henningsen:)

SPECIAL ORDERS, ⎫
　254. 　　⎬

　*　　　*　　　*　　　*　　　*　　　*

IV. The Wise Legion, under the command of Col. J. Lucius Davis, will repair to Richmond, Va., by the nearest railroad route, and report to Brigadier-General Winder, commanding Department of Henrico.

　*　　　*　　　*　　　*

By command of the Secretary of War:

JNO. WITHERS,
Assistant Adjutant-General.

By Special Orders, No. 272, dated December 21, 1861, from the Adjutant and Inspector General's Office, I was assigned to the command of the military district composed of that part of North Carolina east of the Chowan River, together with the counties of Washington and Tyrrel, designated as the Fourth Brigade, Department of Norfolk. I immediately, from Richmond, ordered Col. J. L. Davis, who was in command of my Legion in Western Virginia, to move with all the forces, arms, ammunition, and equipments of the Legion under his orders to Richmond and report to me.

I then returned home, to prepare for assuming the command assigned me. Again, on January 1 last, I addressed to Col. J. Lucius Davis a letter of which the following is a copy:

ROLLISTON, NEAR NORFOLK, VA.,
January 1, 1862.

Col. J. LUCIUS DAVIS, *Commanding, &c.:*

SIR: General Huger thinks it important that the Legion should reach its place of operation and of quarters as early as convenient and practicable; that the troops should come on to Norfolk, and that the quartermaster and commissary of my brigade should precede the troops to Norfolk, in order to arrange quarters and rations beforehand with the quartermaster and commissary of his division. To these ends, then, you will issue the following orders:

That Quartermaster Cleary and Commissary Thomas will proceed to Norfolk immediately, and report either to General Huger or to myself, in order to arrange for quarters and rations with the quartermaster and commissary of the division; that Lieutenant-Colonel Richardson will proceed, as early as practicable, with the Eighteenth Regiment of Infantry, to Norfolk, procure transportation from the Quartermaster-General, and report either to me, or, if absent, to General Huger; that Colonel Henningsen will, as early as practicable after the Eighteenth Regiment of Infantry has reached Norfolk, proceed with the Second Regiment of Infantry and Captain Wallace's company of the Third and the corps of artillery to join the command at Norfolk, and Major Gibbes will regard this as an order to him to proceed under the command of Colonel Henningsen (Colonel Henningsen will procure transportation from the Quartermaster-General), and that Col. J. Lucius Davis will proceed to Norfolk at the earliest practicable moment with all the cavalry of the Legion and with the two companies of infantry under Colonel Tyler, who will regard this as an order to him to proceed under the command of Colonel Davis. He will transfer Captain Wallace's company of infantry to the Second Regiment, under Colonel Henningsen, to supply the place of the company of Captain Crane, disbanded. Colonel Davis will procure transportation from the Quartermaster-General. In case any of the Legion are still in the west they will be ordered to Norfolk directly, and transportation will be furnished accordingly. Separate orders will be issued to Colonel Green, at Wilmington, N. C., by myself.

Very respectfully,

HENRY A. WISE,
Brigadier-General.

On January 2 I proceeded to Norfolk on my way to Roanoke Island, and Major-General Huger referred to me the letters of which the following are copies:

[1.]

FORT BARTOW, ROANOKE ISLAND,
December 29, 1861.

Col. H. M. SHAW,
Commanding Forces Roanoke Island, Camp Raleigh, N. C.:

COLONEL: I feel it my duty to the cause in which we are engaged to make the following report in relation to the condition of my fort: In the first place, I have only one gun which can possibly bear upon an enemy on the south side of the fort, and an enemy can keep out of the range of that gun, and, with good guns on their vessels, shell us in such a manner as to drive us from our guns without our being able to return her fire, except from this one gun, which is mounted upon a common ship's carriage, and this placed upon a chassis of a columbiad carriage. It is almost impossible to work this chassis so as to traverse the gun, and in its present condition it is my opinion that after firing a few rounds it will become perfectly useless, and in its exposed condition it can be very easily dismounted by the enemy's shot. In the second place, all my other guns are mounted on small ship's carriages and in embrasures, and their field of fire is so limited in extent that I am almost certain if an enemy were to come with a large force, say eighteen or twenty gunboats at a time, they would by a general pressure of steam pass our battery without receiving any perceptible injury. The battery is placed in such a position as to render very little protection to the men and guns from an enfilading fire from the enemy's vessels. My opinion of the battery in its present position is that it affords no protection to the defense of the sound; for if the enemy attempt to pass, I firmly believe they can do so despite all I can do to prevent it. I therefore earnestly recommend that something be done at once to render the fort more efficient.

I am, sir, very respectfully, your obedient servant,

G. H. HILL,
Major, State Provisional Army, Commanding Fort Bartow.

[2.]

HEADQUARTERS FORCES ROANOKE ISLAND,
Camp Raleigh, December 30, 1861.

General HUGER, *Commanding Department of Norfolk:*

GENERAL: Not knowing where to address Brigadier-General Wise, who, as I have learned unofficially, is now in command of this district, I take the liberty of forwarding to you directly the accompanying report of Maj. G. H. Hill, of the Seventeenth Regiment North Carolina troops, commanding battery at Pork Point, and of submitting at the same time some remarks in reference to the defenses of these waters. I am clearly of the opinion that the defensive works on this island are altogether insufficient, as at present an enemy could pass the above-named battery without coming within range of its guns at all, and the others could be passed without much liability to danger. Impressed with this belief, immediately upon assuming command of the forces on this island I urged upon General Gatlin, commanding Department of North Carolina, the necessity of strengthening the lower battery (Pork Point) by the addition of two rifled 32-pounders, so mounted as to give a wide command, and to so obstruct the two channels of the sound as to compel the enemy, should he attempt to pass, to come within easy range of all the guns. (By reference to the map you will see that this battery is not in connection with the others, and can receive no support from either of them.) I also thought, and still think, that it was necessary to obstruct the sound on a line between Weir's Point Battery (Fort Huger) and the floating battery. To that end I directed an agent in Norfolk to call on Commodore Forrest and urge him to send out a steam pile-driver. He agreed to send it, and it was to have been here some time since, but up to this time it has not arrived. I have been very much surprised to hear it has been delayed, because the men desire to have their Christmas holidays. If the plan of obstructing the sound shall meet your approval, I hope you will have the pile-driver in question, and another, if to be obtained, sent out without the least delay. Had this work been undertaken early in the fall it would have been comparatively light, but at this season of the year more than three working days in the week on an average cannot sately be counted on.

I beg leave respectfully to suggest that a competent engineer officer be sent here to examine the works, with a view to such alterations and additions as may be found necessary.

I would also request that a naval officer of intelligence and experience be sent here to give instructions at the several batteries in artillery practice.

The steamboat Wilson, employed for the use of this station, is now, by reason of the carelessness of the captain, ashore here, without any immediate assurance of her being gotten afloat. She will be greatly needed as a tender to the pile-drivers. Permit me to request that you call upon the owner to dismiss the captain and put a more competent man in his place.

The supply of ammunition at this post is altogether insufficient. I hope you will authorize the requisition I have sent by Major Williamson to be filled at once. Major Williamson is an officer of intelligence and high character, and will give you any further information you may desire in regard to this post.

Very respectfully, your obedient servant,

H. M. SHAW,
Colonel, Commanding the Forces on Roanoke Island.

[3.]

HEADQUARTERS FORCES ON ROANOKE ISLAND,
Camp Raleigh, December 30, 1861.

General HUGER,
Commanding Department of Norfolk:

GENERAL: I have to request that you will cause to be returned to this post two 6-pounder boat howitzers, lately taken away by Col. A. R. Wright, formerly commanding on Roanoke Island. I deem it very necessary that we should have those pieces or others of a similar character, and I earnestly hope they will be promptly returned.

I have to report to you, moreover, that one large flat, one two-mast flat-boat, and some five canoes were carried away by Colonel Wright. These flats and canoes were taken in the expedition to Chicamacomico; were of considerable value, and would be of great service at this post. I beg leave to call your attention to the matter, hoping they will be restored.

Very respectfully, your obedient servant,

H. M. SHAW,
Colonel, Commanding on Roanoke Island.

[4.]

HEADQUARTERS OF THE FORCES ON ROANOKE ISLAND,
Camp Raleigh, December 30, 1861.

General HUGER,
Commanding Department of Norfolk:

GENERAL: I beg leave to represent to you the necessity of having this post constantly supplied with at least four weeks' rations for the entire command of about 1,800 men. Should the enemy unfortunately destroy our little navy and get above the batteries, they might, by cutting off our supplies, force us to yield the place without having had the ability to strike a single blow.

This command is now being supplied by a commissary officer (Maj. S. T. Sawyer) stationed, by order of General Gatlin, at Elizabeth City, but the supplies come in very small quantities.

Very respectfully, your obedient servant,

H. M. SHAW,
Colonel, Commanding Roanoke Island.

On the same day (January 2) Major Williamson, under orders from Colonel Shaw, in command of Roanoke Island, called on me and showed to me several requisitions of nearly all kinds of supplies for the defense of the island, which had been largely curtailed by General Huger. I immediately (the same day) addressed to General Huger the letter of which the following is a copy:

NORFOLK, VA., *January 2, 1862.*

Maj. Gen. B. HUGER:

SIR: I return the inclosed papers, which found me this morning in this city, on my way to make reconnaissances of Roanoke Island and other places in my command. They show the sad condition of that post, which I regard as the very key of the rear defenses of Norfolk and the navy-yard. Norfolk and the navy-yard may well then supply its deficiencies, in order to save themselves or their connection with Richmond and the South.

I beg, then, that you, sir, will not scale the requisitions of Colonel Shaw so low as was shown to me this morning by Major Williamson. I have already attended to the two 12-pounder howitzers. They were navy boat howitzers, loaned by Captain Lynch to Colonel Wright; were returned by the latter to the navy-yard, and I am allowed by the authorities of the yard, with the consent of Captain Lynch, to take one of them, while that officer takes the other.

The authorities of the yard have also consented for me to have two 12-pounder iron guns. These pieces need boats and carriages. I beg that I may have assigned to my command at least four boats, of at least fourteen or sixteen oars each, with howitzers, or guns, fitted for both land and water service. As to the batteries, I will have them surveyed and reported upon immediately.

My Legion is ordered to move as early as practicable to Norfolk on their way to join my command, and some of its officers are good artillerists. In the mean time I ask that a competent officer to command batteries may be temporarily assigned to Roanoke Island, in conformity to Colonel Shaw's request.

I request that a commissary and quartermaster—both—be appointed at once for Roanoke Island, to act until my brigade quartermaster and commissary can arrive and report for duty, and that provisions and all supplies be sent directly from Norfolk to the island, and not by way of Elizabeth City. Thirty days' provisions for 2,500 men, at least, ought to be stored on the island at once.

One pile-driver, I am told, was started yesterday for Roanoke Island, and I have ventured to ask the Secretary of War for three more.

I beg that you will order whatever you can to forward the work of obstructing Croatan and Roanoke Channels.

If the captain of the steamer Wilson is not discharged by the owner, when I get to the island I will discharge him myself, and put in his place a substitute.

Any number of rifled cannon required may be got at the navy-yard. I ask to be allowed to have four at least.

I repeat the request, urgently, for a far more ample supply of ammunition.

With the highest respect,

HENRY A. WISE,
Brigadier-General.

On the same day, January 2, General Huger, through Lieutenant Talcott, Acting Chief of Engineers, furnished me with the appended chart of Roanoke Island and its defenses (marked I), which chart I found afterwards to be wholly inaccurate and incomplete.* It was not made by the officer himself, but copied, in part probably, from the Coast Survey, not laying down the marshes correctly, nor the islands of marshes at the south end of Roanoke Island at all.

I proceeded immediately to Roanoke Island, stopping on the way to examine the narrows at Knott's and Crow Islands, and the temporary works constructed at Currituck Canal Bridge. There I found four heavy 32-pounders placed in battery out of range of either end of the canal, one sweeping down the canal toward North River and three covering the road leading up from Powell's Point. The battery and position of the guns were alike futile. They were mounted on navy carriages, were not manned or guarded, and could easily be flanked or enfiladed on either hand.

---

* Not found.

On January 7 I assumed command, in accordance with the order of the War Department, of the district assigned me, just thirty days before the enemy arrived at Roanoke Island. I arrived at the island, I think, late on January 6.

On January 7 I addressed to Colonel Shaw the letter of which the following is a copy:

GENERAL ORDERS, }   HEADQUARTERS ROANOKE ISLAND,
    No. 1.   }   *North Carolina, January 7, 1862.*

Brig. Gen. Henry A. Wise having been ordered to the command of the district lying east of the Chowan River, with the counties of Washington and Tyrrel in addition, in North Carolina, he now announces that he takes command, in accordance with the orders of the War Department of the Confederate States.

HENRY A. WISE,
Brigadier-General.

Col. H. M. SHAW,
    Commanding, &c., Roanoke Island:

SIR: Upon conference with you, immediately on my arrival at Roanoke Island, I have issued the foregoing general order. Under this special order you will continue in command of this island until further orders. You will endeavor to have the two guns lying near Weir's Point placed in battery at Roberts' Fishery; assist by every means in your power the driving of piles across the Croatan Sound; construct a permanent wharf at the most eligible landing near Weir's Point or Northwest Point, on the island; report generally upon the defenses at this point, the number and caliber of guns, and amount of ammunition and provisions, and the location of batteries, and in all respects prepare all the means in your power against any attack of the enemy by sea or land.

HENRY A. WISE,
Brigadier-General.

On January 8, 1862, Colonel Shaw made the report of which the following is a copy:

HEADQUARTERS FORCES ON ROANOKE ISLAND,
Camp Raleigh, N. C., January 8, 1862.

Brig. Gen. HENRY A. WISE,
    Commanding District of Albemarle:

GENERAL: In compliance with your special order I have the honor to submit the following report of the defenses of this island, quantity of provisions and ammunition on hand, the strength of this command, &c.

The defenses at Croatan Sound consist of four batteries, mounting in the aggregate thirty guns, all 32-pounders, as follows: At Weir's Point (Fort Huger), ten smooth-bore and two rifled guns; at Fort Blanchard, four smooth-bore guns; at Pork Point (Fort Bartow), six smooth-bore and one rifled gun, and at Redstone Point (Fort Forrest), seven smooth-bore guns. There is another battery on the Tyrrel side of Croatan Sound, at Roberts' Fishery, already completed, but no guns have been mounted, General Hill having ordered a discontinuance of the work. Its capacity is six barbette guns. The two 32-pounders now lying on the beach at Weir's Point will, agreeably to your orders, be mounted as soon as possible. Upon Roanoke Sound there is a small battery of two smooth-bore 32-pounders, at Midgett's Hommock. The battery at Pork Point ought by all means to be strengthened by the addition of two pivot-mounted guns. Orders have been given for the construction of bomb-proof quarters for the detachment at Fort Blanchard; but up to this time lumber ordered for that purpose has not been received. Quarters should be constructed in the immediate vicinity of Fort Huger for the accommodation of at least one of the companies by which the guns at that battery are manned. There ought also to be built at Fort Forrest quarters not only for the company already there, but for another company necessary at that fort. Most of the guns require sights; nearly all of them have nothing but the dispart sight, which I believe is very unreliable, especially in the hands of inexperienced gunners. I submit that it is very necessary that the most improved sights be obtained at once, and, if needful, an expert artisan sent at once to adjust them.

Of light artillery there are three pieces at this post—one 24-pounder howitzer, one 18-pounder Mexican piece, and one 6-pounder; the latter brought to this place from Elizabeth City, N. C. These pieces are all mounted on carriages, with limbers, but no caissons. For operations upon this island I am not sure that caissons are necessary.

Ammunition on hand.—387 charges for 32-pounder guns; 1,300 round shot; 250 rifle shells; 300 match primers; 83 rounds fixed ammunition (24-pounder howitzer); 1 box percussion wafers; 150 port-fires; 98 rounds 6-pounder shot; 1,000 rounds 6-pounder shot, from Elizabeth City, N. C.; 250 pounds of powder; 315 stand grape (32-pounder); 2,000 friction primers; 500 percussion primers; 150 junk wads; 400 grommet wads; 98 canister (A powder); 38 spherical-case shot; [and] 10 slow matches.

*Ammunition for small-arms —*52,159 ball-cartridges for percussion; 3,320 balls; 16,578 ball-cartridges for percussion (issued one hundred and fifty pounds of lead); 17,183 ball-cartridges for flint and steel; [and] 55,000 percussion caps.

Quantity of provisions on hand.—13,682 pounds of bacon and pork; 3,420 pounds of beef; 20 barrels of beef; 2,158 pounds of hard bread; 598 pounds of lard; 265 barrels of flour; 3,692 pounds of rice; 649 pounds of coffee; 10,554 pounds of meal; 54½ bushels of peas and beans; 3,082 pounds of sugar; 460 gallons of vinegar; 1,570 pounds of candles; 1,348 pounds of soap; 12¼ bushels of salt; 1 barrel of fish; 58 gallons of whisky; [and] 5 boxes of yeast powder.

Aggregate number of entire command.. 1,822
Four cooks allowed to each company,... 92
                                                                             ————
Total to be subsisted.. 1,914
Effective force, officers included, absent and sick being deducted............... 1,435

A call has been made for 250 free negroes, for service in the engineer's department. These will have to be subsisted, as will also the gang of 8 men on the pile-driver.

Horses, mules, and oxen in charge of quartermaster's department.—9 officers' horses, 6 yoke of oxen (hired by quartermaster), 2 pairs of mules (of Eighth and Thirty-first Regiments, property of Government).

The mules and oxen are used for general purposes of land transportation.

Amount of forage on hand.—725 pounds of fodder; 2¼ bushels of corn; 1¼ bushels of oats.

Orders have been given for the construction of a magazine. No regular ordnance officer has been appointed.

Very respectfully, your obedient servant,

H. M. SHAW,
Colonel, Commanding, &c.

On January 8 also I addressed the following orders to Lieutenant Selden and to Colonel Shaw:

STEAMER SEA BIRD, *January* 8, 1862.

WILLIAM B. SELDEN,
First-Lieutenant, Artillery, on Engineer Duty, &c.:

SIR: You will commence piling from Pork Point, on the eastern shore of the channel of Croatan Sound, passing that point to the western edge of that channel or Fulker's Shoal. Place the piles 8 feet apart; wedge with poles 24 feet, alternating from pile to pile or wattling the piles therewith, and then above the poles wattling in the chain the reverse of the poles, thus:*

 *   *   *   *   *   *   *

Please see Colonel Shaw and call for all his available force in assisting at the piling.

Very respectfully,

HENRY A. WISE,
Brigadier-General.

ROANOKE ISLAND, N. C., *January* 8, 1862.

Colonel SHAW, *Commanding, &c.:*

SIR: Lieutenant Selden will call for all your available force to assist in piling the Croatan Channels, which you will order, reserving whatever force may be necessary for equally necessary work—of which you must judge—such as mounting guns, building quarters, &c. You will reserve force enough especially for building wharf. Mr. Selden reports the want of civil laborers. You will please address the Governor of North Carolina on the subject of procuring free black laborers under the laws of the State, and you will take the necessary steps to obtain about 250 common laborers on the works of this island.

Respectfully,

HENRY A. WISE,
Brigadier-General.

————————————————

* Diagram omitted.

I landed on the island, and in company with Colonel Shaw and Major Duffield made a personal reconnaissance to its extreme south end. I noted three successive hommocks of high land between the breastwork for light battery and the south end, each nearly surrounded by marshes and swamps; that the dangerous points were the Hommock Landing at the south end, Pugh's Landing on the southwestern shore, and at Ashby's Landing just on the south side of the swamp south of Pork Point. That swamp on the right and the marshes on the left of Suple's Hill were reported to me by Colonel Shaw to be impassable. T'.ey appeared to be so, but I ordered them to be explored and the earthworks at Suple's Hill to be extended as far as possible on the right and left flanks. The water at Hommock Landing I ascertained to be about 4½ feet. Water at high tide at Pugh's to be from 6 to 9 feet, the channel running between the main and first island of marsh, until it passes Fulker's Island, inside of the sound, and then widening out a mile until opposite Ashby's Landing, up to which a vessel drawing 6 feet of water may run close in to the shore, as a large steamer of the enemy with transports did.

I saw that the enemy might land at Pugh's or Ashby's a portion of their force, pass the batteries with all ease, round the north end of the island, and land another portion of their forces, and gain the rear of all the batteries without exchanging a shot with them, or the least danger of damage. Not a fort was in the right position. They should have been located on the islands of marshes at the south end, with batteries at Hommock and Pugh's Landings.

By the courtesy of Flag-Captain Lynch I passed in the Sea Bird through the channel by the light-house and returned through the channel by the Tyrrel shore. If the five batteries had been placed on those islands of marsh and on the opposite shores every channel would have been guarded and the enemy would have been cut off from landing. As it was, they could have taken the island in two hours easier than they did in two days, if they had landed (as they could easily have done) in front of the breastworks at Suple's Hill and in rear of all the batteries on the north end of the island.

I found no teams for light artillery or for transportation, and no tools, axes, spades, shovels, or hoes for constructing breastworks.

There were two North Carolina regiments, the Eighth and Thirty-first, and a battalion of three companies of the Seventeenth, all under Colonel Shaw. Their entire effective force was less than 1,500 men, and several companies of these were taken from the infantry to man the heavy guns of the batteries and part to man the gunboats of Captain Lynch.

The infantry were undrilled, unpaid, not sufficiently clothed and quartered, and were miserably armed with old flint muskets in bad order. In a word, the defenses were a sad farce of ignorance and neglect combined, inexcusable in any or all who were responsible for them.

Captain Lynch was energetic, zealous, and active, but he gave too much consequence entirely to his fleet of gunboats, which hindered transportation of piles, lumber, forage, supplies of all kinds, and of troops, by taking away the steam-tugs and converting them into perfectly imbecile gunboats. He reported to me the indefensible conditior of what he called the floating battery at Redstone, on the Tyrrel side of Croatan Sound. I accorded with his request by the letter of which the following is a copy:

STEAMER SEA BIRD, *January 9, 1862.*

Capt. W. F. LYNCH, *Flag-Officer, &c.:*

SIR: I received yours of this morning, and regret to be informed of the indefensible condition of the floating battery at Redstone Point, on Croatan Sound. I need not inform you that I have just arrived, and am yet to visit various points of defense at the Roanoke Island. On conference with Colonel Shaw I find that the report of Midshipman Gardner was made December 28 last, and immediately Colonel Shaw (December 29) issued the accompanying order, in which he states that "Midshipman Gardner, having been detailed by Flag-Officer Lynch to instruct and drill Captain White's company, stationed in the naval battery, Captain White will see that strict obedience is given to all orders given by him while in the discharge of that duty. Captain White retains the entire command of his company, except during such hours each day as the men may be under drill by Midshipman Gardner," &c. This order would seem to cover sufficiently all the purposes of Midshipman Gardner's services. But this order to Captain White, you inform me, has been violated by him in not enforcing the obedience of his men under the command of Midshipman Gardner, as verbally reported by the latter to you. My desire and purposes are to co-operate with you in the way to insure the most efficient military and naval service. To that end I have issued the accompanying order, which I trust will be satisfactory.

If you claim the command of this battery as a naval battery, I yield it at once. If it is a military battery, it must be under military command. But in either case, when naval and military officers co-operate in service, the command must depend upon the laws and regulations of rank. In this case I presume that Captain White will command and rank Midshipman Gardner; yet you will observe that under my orders to Captain White, Midshipman Gardner will have ample authority to command the men for drill and instruction in working and fighting the guns and to control the magazine for artillery purposes.

The men need instruction, and I trust Midshipman Gardner will not be taken away from the battery. If you choose to regard this battery under my military command, the accompanying order, if duly enforced by Colonel Shaw in my absence, will effect our mutual desires and efforts to make the battery efficient.

With the greatest respect, your obedient servant,

HENRY A. WISE,
Brigadier-General.

And I issued the following special orders:

SPECIAL ORDERS,   CAMP RALEIGH, ROANOKE ISLAND, N. C.,
No. 2.   *January 9, 1862.*

In constructing the wharf heretofore ordered, the commandant at this post will see that it is a permanent structure, of good, solid materials, capable of bearing the articles of transportation and landing for the army and navy. It should have an outer pier or platform large enough to bear upon it a four-horse wagon, and to accommodate at least one large steamer, with a causeway connecting it from seven feet of water with the dry land. It should be placed where the causeway will be the shortest distance between the requisite depth of water and the dry land. The steam pile-driver will be detained for the wharf.

*   *   *   *   *   *   *

III. The commandant will cause a full and detailed report to be made of all ordnance and ordnance stores, embracing arms and ammunition issued and not issued. He will also report the amount of provisions and the whole number of persons in camp to be supplied with provisions; also the number of teams of horses, mules, or oxen now in charge of the quartermaster, and the purposes for which they are used, and the amount of forage on hand. Also whether there be a proper magazine and ordnance officer in charge, and if not, he will cause temporary magazines to be constructed of logs and earth, as fire-proof as practicable, and detail a proper ordnance officer to take charge thereof, who will receive from the quartermaster all ordnance and ordnance stores and receipt to him for the same, and issue the same upon proper vouchers to the troops. If there are no horses for field artillery, he will make requisition for a sufficient number to serve four pieces and their caissons, and procure caissons for the same—say four caissons and thirty-two horses.

IV. No firing or discharge of pieces will be allowed in camp, for the purpose of cleaning guns or for practice, without special permission or order of the commandant. The ammunition will be carefully economized.

V. No ardent spirits or wine or beer shall be allowed in camp without special order or permission of the commandant, and men or messengers will not be permitted to go to Nag's Head unless under orders. No persons will be allowed to pass to and from the sea-beach and the island without special permission. And to prevent intercourse with the enemy the boats and arms of all suspected persons must be seized, so as to prevent their use by such persons.

HENRY A. WISE,
Brigadier-General.

SPECIAL ORDERS, }   CAMP RALEIGH, ROANOKE ISLAND, N. C.,
No. 6. }   *January 9*, 1862.

Captain White, Seventeenth Regiment North Carolina troops, stationed at the floating battery at Redstone Point, on Croatan Sound, will observe the order of December 29, issued by Col. H. M. Shaw, commanding, &c., in respect to the duties and powers assigned to Midshipman Gardner, detailed by Flag-Officer Lynch to instruct and drill the men at said battery. Captain White will place his men under the command of Midshipman Gardner for the purposes of drill and instruction in working and fighting the artillery pieces; and Midshipman Gardner, for such purposes, will order the men on duty as the service of drill and instruction may require, and Captain White will afford him every facility in the discharge of this duty, making him ordnance officer of the artillery and giving him charge of the magazine for artillery stores. In all other respects Captain White will command his company, and he and Midshipman Gardner (while the latter is on military duty) will report to Colonel Shaw, commanding, &c., at Roanoke Island.

HENRY A. WISE,
Brigadier-General.

On January 9 General Huger addressed to me the following letter,* which I did not receive for some time after it was written.

＊   ＊   ＊   ＊   ＊   ＊   ＊

It was not until January 10 that my Legion was ordered to report to me, and then it was ordered to proceed to Edenton, N. C., and at my request the orders were changed to report to me at Portsmouth, as appears by the following orders and memoranda thereon made by General Huger:

SPECIAL ORDERS, }   ADJUTANT AND INSPECTOR GENERAL'S OFFICE,
No. 8. }   *Richmond, Va., January 10*, 1862.

＊   ＊   ＊   ＊   ＊   ＊

XXVII. All the officers and men of the Wise Legion in this city will immediately proceed to Edenton, N. C., and report for duty to Brig. Gen. H. A. Wise, commanding. By command of the Secretary of War:

JNO. WITHERS,
Assistant Adjutant-General.

[Memorandum.]

JANUARY 11, 1862.

By request of General Wise send the men to Portsmouth, Va., for Roanoke Island.
B. H.

It was not until January 11, twenty-one days after the order was dated at Richmond assigning me to the command of the Chowan District on December 21, 1861, that Special Orders, No. 8, were issued from the headquarters of the Department of Norfolk, announcing my command, as appears by the following order:

SPECIAL ORDERS, }   HEADQUARTERS DEPARTMENT OF NORFOLK,
No. 8. }   *Norfolk, Va., January 11*, 1862.

＊   ＊   ＊   ＊   ＊   ＊

II. Brig. Gen. Henry A. Wise, having reported at these headquarters, is, in obedience to Special Orders, No. 272, Adjutant and Inspector General's Office, Richmond, De-

---

*Printed in General Huger's report, p. 114.

cember 21, 1861, assigned to the command of the military district composed of that part of North Carolina east of the Chowan River, together with the counties of Washington and Tyrrel, which will be designated as the Fourth Brigade, Department of Norfolk. General Wise will establish his headquarters (subject to the approval of the major-general commanding the department) at the most central and accessible point to the forces of his brigade.

* * * * *

By command of Major-General Huger :

S. S. ANDERSON,
Assistant Adjutant-General.

When I went to Roanoke Island on the 6th the pile-driver from the navy-yard reached there about the same time, and on January 2 I wrote to the Secretary of War for authority to procure several others. I received a reply of which the following is a copy :

CONFEDERATE STATES OF AMERICA, WAR DEPARTMENT,
Richmond, Va., January 12, 1862.

Brig. Gen. HENRY A. WISE, *Norfolk, Va.:*

SIR: I have your favor of the 2d instant. On inquiry I find that but one steam pile-driver can be procured, viz, one at the navy-yard in Norfolk, and if that is the one you have, it is the only one to be obtained. I am told, however, that one other exists that is accessible, and was tendered for the service you are now supervising by the owners at Morehead, in North Carolina. The Secretary of the Navy tells me that these two pile-drivers are the only ones that exist in the waters in our neighborhood, and it must be one of the two that is now in your possession.

I have not yet seen your requisition for munitions, but think there can be no difficulty in sending you from here a moderate supply of fixed ammunition for field pieces; but our supply of cannon powder is very limited. At the first indication, however, of an attack on Roanoke Island a supply will be sent you. With the number of batteries now requiring a supply we have a very small reserve, that we can only part with to the point that may be actually attacked. I am in daily hope of the receipt of a handsome importation of powder from abroad, and the instant it arrives you shall be supplied.

Your obedient servant,

J. P. BENJAMIN,
Secretary of War.

While the Secretaries of War and of the Navy were thus uninformed of any but two pile-drivers, three within reach were offered to my command by Messrs. Parks and Culpeper, of Norfolk, and by Dr. Warren, of Edenton.

I had hurried back to Norfolk from Roanoke Island, and made in person the strongest verbal representations of the defenseless condition of the post to General Huger and left a memorandum of the necessary requisitions. I particularly impressed upon him the necessity of making the defenses at the marshes at the south end of the island. On January 13 he gave me the instructions of which the following is a copy.*

* * * * * * *

These were the first instructions, on January 13, which I received from General Huger; he adopted my own proposition to establish batteries on the marshes; he postponed my proposition for several permanent batteries, probably for want of time, but he did not consider that the enemy might probably come before the two-gun batteries he proposed could be begun. The wharves were to be constructed, too, laborers, tools, and machines had to be gotten, and materials transported; he did not seem to calculate upon an early approach of the enemy; he did not appreciate the shortness of time, the want of men and means to do

---

* Printed in General Huger's report, p. 114.

and undo all this work, nor the stormy and inclement season of winter on a Hatteras coast, which cut off more than half of the remaining short time; he wholly overlooked the very contingency which happened, of the enemy's arrival before these batteries at the marshes could be begun, much less completed; nor did he estimate that the enemy might land on the beach north of Oregon Inlet and cross over to the island by wading, as they could the Roanoke Channel, or by barges out of reach of the battery on that sound. In a word, he formed his conclusion that large forces were not required, not from the state of things which did but from that which did not exist, and probably could not exist from shortness of time, stormy winter weather, and want of men and means. The change of defense of batteries on the marshes, instead of at the places where they were put, was all essential—so absolutely necessary that steps ought to have been taken by all means to effect it, in order to make any force effectual, and to reduce the force necessary for defense; but in any event a large force was necessary, and if the change could not be effected, the largest of forces was necessary. What if the enemy came while we were in the act of the change? This they did, and this General Huger did not take into his calculations. Who is responsible for the location of the batteries on the island and their malconstruction and efficiency, I am not informed.

On the same day I addressed to him a letter of which the following is a copy:

NORFOLK, VA., *January* 13, 1862.

Maj. Gen. B. HUGER, *Commanding, &c.:*

SIR: I have left in your office a memorandum of requisitions for additional pile-drivers, for a steam dredging-machine, for steam-tugs and barges for transporting forces, for more ammunition, and for an additional number of large artillery pieces, &c. The items were specified, but will be more formally prepared if necessary or required. Under your orders to make all efforts to carry on all necessary work at Roanoke Island I will proceed at once to employ or procure the laborers necessary, such as free blacks and slaves, under the laws of North Carolina, and to do whatever is necessary without further authority. At the same time, sir, I will refer to you at all times for your orders, advice, and permission, whenever it is practicable to do so. Indeed, I report that Roanoke Island is now in a defenseless condition and in presence of a very formidable enemy's force. My Legion is ordered to report here or at Portsmouth, but has not arrived. I beg you to urge on their movement and have them forwarded as soon as possible.

The Burnside expedition is reported as having sailed. Independent of that, the force now at Hatteras Inlet can pass or take Roanoke Island, and pardon me for saying that I respectfully differ from the opinion you expressed in your orders to-day, that to prevent the enemy's gunboats from passing the marshes at the south end will also prevent any landing. Batteries at the marshes are vitally essential to prevent the gunboats from passing into Croatan Sound, but they will not prevent the landing on the south or east end of the island. At least 3,000 infantry are needed on the island, and a considerable force, say 1,500 more, are needed on the beaches, and if the enemy pass Roanoke, 5,000 at least are necessary to fight them on the tongues of land on the north side of Albemarle Sound. We need on the beach and on the island at least eight field pieces and the carriages and caissons necessary. We require thirty-two horses for the artillery. The guns at Redstone are necessary where they are. We need at least six heavy pieces at the south-end marshes and two at least at Fleetwood Point. The wharves necessary I will proceed at once to have constructed. A large amount of lumber is needed for quarters. You will please bear in mind that as yet the infantry have to man the batteries. There are no trained artillery companies at the island now; therefore it is that I ask for the transfer to my command of Captain Grandy's company of artillery, now at Sewell's Point.

Very respectfully, your obedient servant,

HENRY A. WISE,
Brigadier-General.

And on the same day, January 13, I addressed to the Secretary of War a letter of which the following is an extract:

NORFOLK, VA., *January* 13, 1862.

Hon. J. P. BENJAMIN, *Secretary of War, &c.:*

SIR: It is very important that my Legion should be forwarded as speedily and in as large a force as possible. The defense of Roanoke Island, which is the key of all the rear defenses of Norfolk and its canals and railroads, is committed to my charge, and I have just returned from a reconnaissance of that point. It is now utterly defenseless. No preparations have been made there at all adequate. General Huger has given me a large authority to do whatever is necessary and has advised what he deems proper in my command; but we have very limited means, and not half time enough to prepare to meet an enemy who is now almost in our immediate presence in very formidable force. Twice the number of my Legion is necessary, and I beg that the place of my Third Regiment may be speedily filled or that it may be restored. If that cannot be done, or whether that can be done or not, I ask that the officers of the forces left me may be duly commissioned from the time they were nominated by me and that they have served. The incomplete report of the organization of my Legion, dated August 13 last, is in your office. On it, indorsed in pencil, I found your order for the commissions to be issued according to the report. They were not issued, and I found that the report was not indexed or recorded. The only excuse given me was that the report was not signed by me. It was signed by Assistant Adjutant-General Tabb by my order, and it was recognized by you in your order. That order has not been obeyed, and I ask that the commissions then ordered be issued, not to take effect from their respective dates of nomination and service.

Again, on January 14, I addressed to General Huger a letter of which the following is a copy:

ROLLISTON, NEAR NORFOLK, VA.,
January 15, 1862.

Maj. Gen. B. HUGER, *Commanding, &c.:*

SIR: Yours of January 11, 1862, assigning me to the command of my appointed military district, designated as the Fourth Brigade, Department of Norfolk, was received late last evening.

As reported verbally to you I have already visited the district, assumed command, and issued such orders as I was proud to find met with your approbation. You were also informed by memorandum, and since in writing, of the requisition for my command. I am now awaiting the arrival of a portion of my Legion. As soon as it is moved to Roanoke Island I desire to visit the War Department, to look after that portion of the Legion on its way and to attend to the issuing of commissions for certain of my officers. I am ordered to establish my headquarters, subject to your approval, at the most central and accessible point to the forces of my brigade. Permit me to call your attention, sir, to the fact that the most central are not the most accessible points in my command. Elizabeth City is most central and accessible by land from Norfolk; by water from Roanoke Island 45 miles either way; but there are times in foggy weather when the sound is impassable, and in stormy weather when it is unsafe. Currituck Court-House (called Crawford) is on the line of the Albemarle and Chesapeake Bay Canal and more accessible, but still remote from the main body of forces at Roanoke Island, and the Albemarle Sound has to be passed to and from the island. Hertford, Nixonton, or Edenton are still more remote, with the same objection of delay and danger by water navigation. The key of the whole command is Roanoke Island, and the only quarters yet erected near it are at Nag's Head. With your approval I propose to adopt the latter as my headquarters, to be changed, of course, as necessity or experience may dictate.

I found a long wooden building erected at Roanoke Island for a hospital. The island is unsafe as a medical depot and hospital, and the spot selected is near a marsh and swamp, which must be, and is reported to be, unhealthy and beset in summer by mosquitoes. On consultation with Surgeon-General De Leon I have ordered Surgeon Lyons to proceed at once to Currituck Court-House and examine that place for a hospital site. It is both healthy and safe, and accessible to the forces at Roanoke Island and to medical supplies at Norfolk.

As soon as my forces arrive and I can make the selection I will detail a suitable officer from my brigade to report to your headquarters as acting assistant inspector-general.

I will also examine whether the provision returns of the respective regiments and posts of my brigade correspond with their morning reports, and I will see that the hospital and commissary returns do not exceed the whole force. This, though, can only be done when my forces shall have arrived and been posted.

General Orders, No. 50, shall be strictly observed. General Orders, No. 65, calls my attention to General Orders, No. 46, dated August 1, 1861, of which I have no copy and am not informed. I ask a copy, in order that it may be promptly obeyed. Are these orders explained by the letter of the Assistant Adjutant-General of January 9 instant?

Very respectfully, &c.,

HENRY A. WISE,
Brigadier-General.

On the 15th I again addressed to General Huger a letter of which the following is a copy:

NEAR NORFOLK, VA., *January* 15, 1862.

Major-General HUGER, *Commanding, &c.:*

SIR: I ordered Lieutenant Bagwell to procure a boat, with oars, from the navy-yard fit for sounding the channels of Croatan Sound. He made the within request informally on his friend Captain Lee to save time, expecting to observe official forms afterward. It is absolutely necessary to have a boat belonging to the army, to be immediately and constantly in the sounding service for weeks. It may be sent with the First Regiment of my Legion (just arrived). I beg, therefore, that you will approve of my request to Flag-Officer F. Forrest, to order a proper boat, oars, &c., to be transferred to the army for my command.

There are two brass boat howitzers, mounted as field pieces, at the navy-yard, which Captains Lee and Fairfax (in the absence of Flag-Officer Forrest, with the consent of Captain Lynch) said might be allowed to the commands of Captains Lynch and myself. Captain Lynch agreed that I might have one of them, and the two carriages, harness, &c., for my command, while he would take the other for his boats. They are the guns returned to the navy-yard by Colonel Wright from Roanoke Island; and there are also two 12-pounder guns, which Captains Lee and Fairfax said could be spared to the army, and which can be mounted soon in the yard. Will you please approve of my requisition on the flag-officer for these three guns, carriages, &c., and apprise him thereof. The brass howitzers and two carriages are ready now, and I ask that they may be obtained in time to be sent down with my First Regiment of Infantr .

I am, very respectfully, your obedient servant,

HENRY A. WISE,
Brigadier-General.

On the same day I ordered Col. W. J. Green as follows:

NORFOLK, VA., *January* 15, 1862.

Col. WHARTON J. GREEN, *Commanding, &c.:*

SIR: You will as early as practicable move your whole force from Wilmington, N. C., to Norfolk, Va., and there report to General Huger for transportation to Roanoke Island. Bring with your men all the outfit which you can procure at Wilmington, and make requisitions at Norfolk for deficiencies. Prompt movement is necessary, as the enemy are near in large force.

HENRY A. WISE,
Brigadier-General.

I returned from Roanoke Island to Norfolk on January 11, and on the 15th addressed to the Secretary of War a letter of which the following is a copy:

NEAR NORFOLK, VA., *January* 15, 1862.

Hon. J. P. BENJAMIN, *Secretary of War, &c.:*

Yours of the 12th, in reply to mine of the 2d instant, is just received. I am sure you will not adjudge me importunate when I inform you that I returned from Roanoke Island to Norfolk last Saturday. I hastened back, after a short reconnaissance, to apprise headquarters and the Department that there are no defenses there; no adequate preparations whatever to meet the enemy, and to forward all the means in my reach as speedily as possible to make the key of and the rear of Norfolk, with its canals and railroads, safe. Inside of Hatteras Inlet I found twenty-four vessels of light draught, eight of which, at least, are steamers, said to carry four guns each. They are, at farthest, but 30 miles from Roanoke Island, and can reach there in four hours or less, to attack five small gunboats under Captain Lynch and four small land batteries wholly inefficient. Any boat drawing 7 feet of water or less can pass the Croatan Sound as far off as 1¼ miles from any battery, and the enemy's guns can silence our batteries there in a very short time. Neither battery is casemated, and our men now there are untrained to heavy pieces mounted on navy carriages. The moment the enemy passes Croatan Channel the North Landing River, North River, Pasquotank, Chowan, and Roanoke, Alligator, and Scuppernong Rivers, and the Dismal Swamp and Albemarle and Chesapeake Canals will be blockaded effectually, and Norfolk and Portsmouth will be cut off from supplies of corn, pork, and forage. The force at Hatteras is independent of the Burnside expedition. No matter where the latter is, the former is amply sufficient to capture or pass Roanoke Island in any twelve hours. Let me say, then, sir, that if we are to wait for powder from Richmond until we are attacked at that island, that attack will be capture, and our defeat will precede our supply of ammunition. The case is too urgent for me to delay speaking thus out plainly at once.

We have the navy-yard pile-driver. I took it down and put it to work. It can drive about twenty piles per diem, and can work, perhaps, not three days in the week; drives its piles 8 feet apart, and has at least 3 miles to pile. You can see, then, how slowly we can obstruct the channels with but one pile-driver. I can procure three others—one in a day or two and two in a week or two.

We want also a steam dredging-machine, to fix our floating batteries in the marshes. That I can procure here. We want a number of decked lighters and barges, on which to transport and mount heavy guns in the marshes and to use as " camels" for the pile-drivers. We want also large transport boats and steam-tugs, to throw infantry and artillery across wide channels from the island to the beaches on the main. We want ammunition and men. In a word, almost every preparation has to be made. To make them and to do the least that is necessary I ask, in the emergency, for plenary power, to order what is necessary and to procure what I can get without the delay of observing forms and without making special requisitions for every want. Delay is defeat now at Roanoke Island, and with present means Captain Lynch and I combined cannot guarantee successful defense for a day. I beg, sir, that you will urge this upon the Navy Department, and believe that I am not superserviceable in this urgency.

With the highest respect, your obedient servant,

HENRY A. WISE,
Brigadier-General.

At this time the First Regiment of Infantry of my Legion arrived in Norfolk, numbering nine companies, averaging about 45 men, making a total of about 405 privates ; and on the 16th I issued to Colonel Richardson, of that regiment, the special order of which the following is a copy:

SPECIAL ORDERS, }   NORFOLK, VA.,
    No. 16.   }   *January* 16, 1862.

Colonel Richardson, of the First Regiment of Infantry, Wise Legion, having reported the arrival of his regiment in Norfolk, he will proceed, as early as practicable, by the way of the Albemarle and Chesapeake Canal, to transport his troops to Roanoke Island, N. C. To that end, before moving, he will see that thirty days' rations for at least 1,000 men are forwarded for the Legion and placed in charge of A. Kinney, acting commissary, in the place of Maj. William H. Thomas, during the absence of the latter ; he will see that no provisions are drawn from the commissary of the Legion for more than his actual force, as reported by the morning and hospital returns; he will see the ordnance officer at Norfolk, and ascertain the amount of ammunition and ordnance stores in depot there or at Portsmouth for the Legion, and he will detail some one competent officer to take charge thereof, as acting ordnance officer of the Legion, who will act until further orders, and have the same conveyed to the post at Roanoke Island under guard of Colonel Richardson's command, on its way there, and there put it in a magazine ; he will also see the quartermaster at Norfolk, and ascertain whether the means of transportation have been provided, seeking information from Marshall Parks, the president of the Albemarle and Chesapeake Canal, as to the capacity and comfort of his steam-tugs and barges for transportation, and seeing that they are sufficiently heated and ventilated, and when he arrives at Roanoke Island he will report to Col. Hill Shaw, commanding, &c. ; and if sufficient quarters are not in readiness on the island for his troops, he will land his men at the wharf of Nag's Head, on the beach opposite the north end of the island, and take quarters in the cabins and cottages there erected, occupying such as may be pointed out by the proprietor, Mr. Happer ; he will take command there until further orders as of a separate post for the Legion, and as the east and central portions of the beach can be shelled by the enemy from the sea-side, he will, as far as practicable, occupy the west side of the beach next the Roanoke Channel or Sound ; he will at once establish the strictest discipline of drill, guard, and vedette duty, keeping a vigilant lookout as far down as Oregon Inlet, and as high up as Gallop's, opposite Powell's Point on the main, and keeping up a regular and ample ferry across the Roanoke Channel to the part of the island opposite; he will observe the accompanying orders from headquarters, and allow of no firing or ardent spirits in his camp, except what may be allowed by his own special permission. Owing to the scarcity of powder the order as to firing must be rigidly adhered to, and strong and intoxicating drinks must be issued by the sutlers under the strictest regulations, enforcing moderation and sobriety.

The enemy are near, within a few hours' steaming; attack is hourly expected, and the camp must be in constant order and readiness; and to prevent attracting the enemy's steamers the men must not be allowed to appear in any bodies by daylight, and no fires must be kindled day or night on the sea-side. Fuel must be regularly supplied on the sound side, and covered ways of logs and sand provided against the enemy's shells behind the sand hills on that side. If the enemy attempts to land on either side of the beach north of Oregon Inlet within reach, he must be attacked by all means, and if our forces are obliged to retreat before superior numbers, they will either cross in the ferry to the forts on Roanoke Island or move northward on the western shore of the beach up to Gallop's, and there cross in the ferry over Currituck Sound to Powell's Point on the main. They will never retreat unless compelled, and then in good order, saving all stores and equipage.

HENRY A. WISE,
Brigadier-General.

I then hurried to Richmond to forward the remaining corps of my Legion and to urge upon the War Department the necessity of expediting the defenses of Roanoke Island. I was allowed but a short and cursory interview with the Secretary of War, but pressed upon him the necessity of supplies and re-enforcements and of forwarding the whole force of my Legion; and on January 18 I ordered Colonel Henningsen to visit the Governor of North Carolina in person, with instructions and a letter of which the following are copies:

RICHMOND, VA., *January* 18, 1862.

Col. C. F. HENNINGSEN, *Commanding, &c.:*

SIR: You will take charge of the inclosed letter to His Excellency the Governor of North Carolina. You will confer with him on the defenses of that part of his State confided to my command. You will inform him fully of all the lack of preparations for defense, especially at Roanoke Island. You will impress upon him the importance of those defenses as objects for the enemy to attack. Their main aim is to shut up the rear of Norfolk and the forces there; attack on Wilmington is minor, but the forces of the enemy at Hatteras and with Burnside are ample for invading both Pamlico and Albemarle Sounds. You will urge upon him the necessity to obtain permanent recruits for my Legion, and arms and ammunition, barges, lighters, dredging-machines, pile-drivers, steam tug-boats, negro laborers, &c.

You will look at the within and note its purport as to his executive circular respecting corps formed from the North Carolina Militia, and as to the regret of Colonel Martin, of North Carolina, who, with his men (late prisoners at Hatteras), are now discharged from their paroles, &c. You will, in a word, obtain all the aid you can in any and every form from Governor Clark, and then as early as practicable report to me at Roanoke Island.

In the mean time you will turn over the command of the Second Regiment of the infantry of the Legion to Lieutenant-Colonel Anderson, and issue orders to him to have the Second Regiment in readiness to proceed to Norfolk on Tuesday next, January 28 instant, and toproceed on that day and there report to Maj. Gen. Ben. Huger, commanding, &c., not using his quartermaster and commissary for subsistence and transportation to Roanoke Island, N. C. If he arrives there prior to my return to the island he will report to Colonel Shaw, commanding, &c., at the post, and take quarters, as they can best be provided, either on Roanoke Island or at Nag's Head, on the sea-beach. He will apply to Lieutenant-Colonel Richardson, of the First Regiment, for copies of the general orders of the Legion at Nag's Head.

Very respectfully, your obedient servant,

HENRY A. WISE,
Brigadier-General, Fourth Brigade, Department of Norfolk.

RICHMOND, VA., *January* 18, 1862.

To His Excellency Governor CLARK, *North Carolina:*

SIR: I have made but a brief reconnaissance of the defenses of the counties of your Commonwealth under my command; but, brief as it was, it startled me with the conviction that the large fleet of vessels and steamers inside of Hatteras Inlet can pass Roanoke Island at any hour and blockade all the waters of Albemarle and Currituck Sounds, shutting up the Dismal Swamp and Albemarle and Chesapeake Canals, cutting Norfolk and Portsmouth off from supplies, and North Carolina off from trade, and threatening the Seaboard and Roanoke and the Petersburg and Norfolk Railroads.

Roanoke Island is the key of all these defenses, and is wholly unprepared, in every respect, to repulse an enemy as formidable as that inside of Hatteras Inlet. The fleet there is independent of the Burnside expedition. Eight of the ships are steamers and sixteen sailing vessels, unless those masted have steam propellers also. We want everything in the way both of *personnel* and *materiel*—men, laborers, organization, drill, ammunition, piles, pile-drivers, dredging-machines, barges, boats, steam-tugs, &c. I am here urging and hastening preparations. I appeal to you for aid, and with that view send General C. F. Henningsen, colonel of the Second Regiment of my Legion and commander of my corps of artillery, to confer with you in person.

The Burnside expedition and the fleet at Hatteras may threaten Wilmington, it is true, but my opinion is that the enemy's two fleets are ample to endanger both Albemarle and Pamlico Sounds alike, and as the objects of attack upon the rear defenses of Norfolk and Portsmouth are the more important and vital, it is reasonable to suppose that the enemy will pursue the larger game with the larger force, and the lesser is ample to pass and capture all the present defenses of Albemarle Sound.

By circular, under your orders, I am informed that you gave power to call out the militia of certain counties, including those in my command, taking one-third of each regiment either by enlistment or allotment. Will you please say how I may make requisitions? How the men are to be called out and report for duty? And may I suggest, sir, that unwilling men—not volunteering really—are not reliable, and will you permit me and aid me in inducing companies, battalions, or regiments to enlist in my Legion for the war and to join the Confederate service under the liberal regulations of the late law of Congress? Permit me also to call your attention to the fact that there are three companies belonging to the regiment lately under Colonel Martin, fragments of the North Carolina regiment captured at Hatteras. Colonel Martin and the prisoners of his regiment are now released from their parole as prisoners and may reform their regiment. I saw Colonel Martin at Elizabeth City lately, and I ask that you will, with his consent, assign him to my command, and assent that his regiment may be incorporated in my Legion.

General Henningsen will present you with his views of the defense of North Carolina and with other of my views also, and I beg you to believe that, however much I may lack the ability, I will devote to your defense all my energy, faithfulness, and care.

With great respect, sir, I am, your obedient servant,

HENRY A. WISE,
Brigadier-General, Fourth Brigade, Department of Norfolk and North Carolina.

The Secretary of War replied verbally to my urgent appeals for re-enforcements that he had not the men to be spared for my command. I asked for the restoration of my Third Regiment, which had been taken from me, for the reason that they had been raised to defend Western Virginia and then had been sent to South Carolina. This was not granted. I then urged that General Huger had about 15,000 men in the front of Norfolk, lying idle in camp for eight months, and that a considerable portion of them could be spared for the defense of the rear of Norfolk, and especially as my district supplied Norfolk and his army with nearly or quite all of its corn, pork, and forage; that re-enforcements at Roanoke Island were as absolutely necessary to the defense of Norfolk as forces in its front, and that particular or special posts should not be allowed to monopolize nearly all the men, powder, and supplies. Failing to obtain any definite reply to this appeal, I then resorted to an attempt to procure the addition to my forces of a few men (about 150) at Norfolk, who had escaped from the Eastern Shore of Virginia, and addressed to the Secretary of War a letter of January 19, of which the following is a copy:

RICHMOND, VA., *January* 19, 1862.

Hon. J. P. BENJAMIN, *Secretary of War:*

SIR: The regiment raised for service on the Eastern Shore of Virginia, Accomack, and Northampton Counties, commanded by Col. Charles Smith, has been dispersed, as you know, by the weakness of its local position and the orders of its commander.

A portion of that regiment escaped to York River and Norfolk posts. The number of men would form two, perhaps three, good companies, but they consist of fragments of companies, under different company officers, who cannot or will not unite so as to form full companies, and it is certain that their regiment cannot be reconstructed or reformed. Most, if not all, of these men are assigned to the department of Major-General Huger, in which mine is the Fourth Brigade. Now, these men are natives of my native peninsula, are known to me, and I have a special regard for them, as I have reason to believe they have for me personally. I ask, by way of repairing the damage done to my Legion by taking from it fourteen companies, disbanding one, and nearly destroying two, in all seventeen companies, of which I have been deprived, that these companies may be transferred to my command. I will reorganize them into two or more companies, with the aid of some recruits, and then I propose that they may be discharged from their former service, on condition that they will elect their own company officers and enlist for the war under the late law of Congress. This, I am authorized to say, meets the approbation of General Huger, who will recommend the transfer, and I trust the whole proposition will be at once adopted by you.

Most respectfully,

HENRY A. WISE,
Brigadier-General.

Instead of complying with this request to first transfer them to my command and then to allow them to be mustered out of service on condition that they would re-enlist, the Department ordered that they should first be mustered out of service, and then left it to their option to join my command or not. The consequence was, they were mustered out of service and were entirely disbanded and scattered.

From January 19 to the 22d, at Richmond, I was actively and constantly employed in issuing orders and in urging the forwarding of my artillery and other remaining corps of the Legion.

Dr. Thomas D. Warren, of Edenton, N. C., an active and efficient patriot, having tendered to me his services as a volunteer aide, on January 21 I addressed to him a letter of which the following is a copy:

RICHMOND, VA., *January 21, 1862.*

Dr. THOMAS D. WARREN:

DEAR SIR: Yours of the 17th instant is just received here. You are ordered to be announced as one of my volunteer aides. You will order Colonel Shaw, from me, to have the piles sent for as early and as fast as possible. You can always get a vessel at Elizabeth City. If the piles cannot be driven fast enough he will sink vessels. If the price is too high (the demanded price), he will have them appraised, and at all events will sink enough to obstruct the channels at material points next the piling, taking all he can get for that purpose; and if all are not necessary to be used, he will use first the lowest price vessels. You will see to this, taking post at Edenton and superintending transportation and supplies.

Hastily, yours,

HENRY A. WISE,
Brigadier-General.

Previously I had sent Captain Bolton and Lieutenant Bagwell to Roanoke Island, to superintend the pile-driving and to sound the channals of Croatan and Roanoke Sounds. They were ordered on this duty January 15.

On January 22, in reply to all my urgent appeals for the means of defense, I received the order of which the following is a copy:

SPECIAL ORDERS, } ADJUTANT AND INSPECTOR GENERAL'S OFFICE,
No. 17. } *Richmond, Va., January 22, 1862.*

* * * * * * *

XXXII. Brig. Gen. Henry A. Wise, Provisional Army, will immediately proceed to Roanoke Island, N. C., and assume command of the Confederate States troops at that place.

* * * * * * *

By command of the Secretary of War:

JNO. WITHERS,
Assistant Adjutant-General.

I immediately replied by letter, of which the following is a copy :

RICHMOND, VA., *January* 22, 1862.

Hon. J. P. BENJAMIN, *Secretary of War:*

SIR: Your order of to-day, to "immediately proceed to Roanoke Island, N. C., and assume command of the Confederate States troops at that place," is received. I will proceed immediately, as commanded ; but it is just to myself to say that I had proceeded heretofore to Roanoke Island and assumed command, but finding no adequate preparations whatever to meet an enemy at that place I hastened on to Richmond, to forward that portion of my Legion remaining here and to obtain necessary authority to procure the means of defense.

I am without an ordnance officer or an assistant inspector-general, and various requisitions are delayed here, so that my artillery cannot be forwarded.

I beg respectfully that the Department will expedite the forwarding of my troops and furnish them with the actual necessities of the service.

With great respect, your obedient servant,

HENRY A. WISE,
Brigadier-General.

The next day (January 23) I returned to Norfolk, and hastened home to prepare to execute the order of the 22d, which was peremptory, and left me no election but to go to Roanoke Island, assume command of that post, and defend it as best I could with or without men or means.

In reply to my order to Lieutenant-Colonel Green to report to me as early as practicable, he informed me that he had been detained by Brig. Gen. J. R. Anderson at Wilmington until he could get information from the Secretary of War whether to obey my order or not. I immediately, on January 25, sent him an order of which the following is a copy :

ROLLISTON, NEAR NORFOLK, VA.,
January 25, 1862.

W. J. GREEN, *Lieutenant-Colonel, &c.:*

SIR: I did not, of course, issue orders to you without conferring with the Secretary of War before you were sent to Wilmington as part of my Legion to recruit, and since when I was ordered to North Carolina. In both instances you were acknowledged as part of my Legion, subject to my orders. I therefore report to you the order to at once move from Wilmington to Norfolk, and thence to Roanoke Island, where you will report to me in person.

Your obedient servant,

HENRY A. WISE,
Brigadier-General.

I also the same day addressed a letter to the Secretary of War of which the following is a copy :

NEAR NORFOLK, VA., *January* 25, 1862.

Hon. J. P. BENJAMIN, *Secretary of War:*

SIR: I am detained here by stress of weather and want of transportation to Roanoke Island. To-morrow, probably, or next day, I depart for that post. To-day Lieut. Col. Wharton J. Green reports from Wilmington, N. C., that on reporting to General Anderson my orders to Colonel Green to move to Roanoke Island, General Anderson, commanding the Cape Fear District, objected, until he could communicate with the Secretary of War. I beg that you will at once inform General Anderson that Colonel Green's command was sent to Wilmington simply to winter and to recruit; that they belong to my brigade (the Legion), and that they are essential to the defense of Roanoke Island; a more important point than Wilmington. This hinderance at this time is annoying and might prove fatal. Colonel Green reports to me seven companies, and the probable completion of his regiment in a week from the 23d instant. I have repeated my orders to him to move to Roanoke Island via Norfolk. I hope you will promptly sustain me in this.

With the highest respect, your obedient servant,

HENRY A. WISE,
Brigadier-General.

The Department ordered Colonel Green on, but his arrival at Roanoke Island was on the morning of February 8, while the action was raging, in which his battalion of five companies, about 450 men, were not engaged at all, but they arrived quite in time to be captured. Thus by this interruption I was deprived of this re-enforcement. My Second Regiment, but eight companies (about 350 men), was not forwarded from Norfolk until the evening of January 25, and arrived at Nag's Head on January 27.

On January 26, at home, I received from the Secretary of War a letter, dated January 23, of which the following is a copy:

CONFEDERATE STATES OF AMERICA, WAR DEPARTMENT,
Richmond, Va., January 23, 1862.

Brig. Gen. HENRY A. WISE, *Norfolk, Va.*:

SIR: I have your letter of yesterday, giving me information of your intended immediate departure for Roanoke Island. The terms of your letter imply the idea that you consider the order as being in some way a reflection on your absence from that post at this time. I write therefore to say, as due to you, that nothing was further from my thoughts. I knew you to be here on useful public service connected with your command, and my order was only issued because of receipt of information that an immediate attack was threatened on your post; and I well knew that in such case you would feel grateful for being allowed the opportunity of assuming your command and would be much mortified if accidentally absent. I will take pleasure in attending to your requests and help you to the best of my ability.

Yours, respectfully,

J. P. BENJAMIN,
Secretary of War.

I immediately replied by letter of which the following is a copy:

ROLLISTON, NEAR NORFOLK,
January 26, 1862.

Hon. J. P. BENJAMIN, *Secretary of War:*

SIR: I express to you gratefully my acknowledgments for yours of the 23d instant. Your order to be at my post in the hour of apprehended danger was very proper, yet it relieves my absence from reproach to have it said that I hastened away from it only to return as speedily as possible with the means of its defense. The weather has delayed here the transportation of my Second Regiment of Infantry. They started yesterday for Roanoke Island, and I depart to-morrow, if a steam tug, through the canal, can be found. You, I am certain, would have me succeed triumphantly in my duties, and will excuse even eager, as well as anxious, appeals for the means of victory.

Wherever the Burnside expedition may be, the forces of the enemy already in the Hatteras Inlet are sufficient to overwhelm the present forces and means of defense.

I avail myself of your kindness in attending to my requests and helping me to the best of your ability, by asking that you will order commissions to be issued to the following officers: Maj. C. B. Duffield, of cavalry; Ordnance Officer James H. Pearce; Assist. Inspector-General H. Dugan; Adjutant (of the First Regiment of Infantry) Henry A. Wise, jr., and Second Lieuts. (in the Engineer Corps, Artillery) T. C. Kinney, C. Ellis Munford, and R. A. Wise, &c.

Please order the forces of my Legion under Colonel Green, at Wilmington, N. C., and the two companies at Staunton, assigned to the command of Col. N. Tyler, to be forwarded to me, and order my artillery corps at Richmond to be furnished with guns, carriages, and caissons, and forwarded. I beg you also to order back to me the Third Regiment of Infantry taken from my command.

With the highest respect, your obedient servant,

HENRY A. WISE,
Brigadier-General.

On January 28 I addressed to the Secretary of War a letter informing him that at last I had procured transportation to Roanoke Island; that I would leave that evening at 4 p. m., and begging him to forward my artillery corps and pieces.

I had gone to Norfolk on Monday (the 27th) to start for the island.

The steam-tug could not promise to start before Tuesday evening, the 28th. At 1.30 p. m. we started, and the tug broke down before getting to Portsmouth, and had herself to be towed back to Norfolk by the ferry-boat. We were detained until the evening of the next day (the 29th) for repairs to the tug.

On January 28 I issued various orders in Norfolk to expedite preparations at the island, among others those of which the following are copies:

NORFOLK, VA., *January* 28, 1862.

Lieut. JAMES H. PEARCE, *Ordnance Officer, &c.:*

SIR: You will report to Major-General Huger as the ordnance officer of my Legion. You will ask him for orders to take a gun-carriage and limber, or 12-pounder, or 9-pounder, now at Kempsville. It is one of three artillery pieces, mounted at the navy-yard, and allowed, with carriages, &c., to be issued to me in the spring of 1861 for the defense of Lynn Haven shore. Two of the pieces, I am informed, were taken away from Kempsville, under orders from General Huger. The other is there under no command that I know of, and I desire it to be restored to me. I am personally responsible for all three pieces, as they were issued to me by Flag-Officer Forrest before I was commissioned or had a command, and were taken in my absence at the West. I desire to have all three returned to me, and you will so request of General Huger; but you will especially request to be allowed horses by the quartermaster here to bring the gun from Kempsville to Norfolk, in order that it may be taken to Roanoke Island.

You will also call upon Flag-Officer Forrest, at the navy-yard, and ask for one brass howitzer, allowed to be taken by me, with the consent of Captain Lynch, to whose command it belonged. It is one of two pieces loaned by Captain Lynch to Colonel Wright, and returned by the latter to the navy-yard. Now, Captain Lynch consents that I shall have one of the pieces, with both carriages, caissons, harness, &c.

You will also apply at the navy-yard for two iron 12-pounder pieces, their carriages, caissons, &c. As fast as obtained you will forward these four pieces, &c., to me at Roanoke Island.. To this end you will remain here not more than eight days, and within that time proceed to Roanoke Island as early as you can; and while here you will consider yourself detailed to look after and arrest deserters and stragglers from my command. I am informed that some of my men are now on board the Merrimac. You will take orders and proper steps to arrest them and send them on to Roanoke Island.

Very respectfully, your obedient servant,

HENRY A. WISE,
Brigadier-General.

NORFOLK, VA., *January* 28, 1862.

Maj. F. D. CLEARY, *Quartermaster, &c.:*

SIR: You will proceed as early as practicable to procure for the service at Roanoke Island, its marshes, &c., at Nag's Head, the following implements and materials:

Pile-drivers.—Three can be obtained: one from Capt. M. Parks, and one from Mr. Culpeper, at Norfolk, Va., and one from Dr. Thomas Warren, Edenton, N. C. Each will require a crew of six men.

Dredging-machine.—One; to be procured from the Albemarle and Chesapeake Canal Company, of Capt. M. Parks. They require a double crew of 24 men.

Lighters.—Eight; 50 or 60 feet long, 3½ or 4 feet deep, and 12 or 15 wide, well calked and made water-tight.

Lumber.—Twenty thousand feet of 1-inch plank (sorted), from 12 to 20 feet long; 17,000 superficial, or 42,500 board measure; decking-plank, 2¾ inches thick. Scantling, 6 by 4 inches, 16 feet long; in all 12,000 feet long. Plank for wharves, 12 feet long, 2 inches thick; in all 26,000 feet, board measure. Piles, 1,500, 14 feet long; 1,000, 18 feet long; 500, 22 feet long; 1,500, 20 feet long.

Nails.—Whatever is necessary.

The piles, plank, and scantling you will get best, probably, through Dr. Warren, of Edenton, N. C., and the lighters from the Dismal Swamp Canal.

You will also procure such number of cooking and warming stoves as you may deem necessary for the Legion; and also such an assortment of axes, hoes, spades, shovels, and other implements as are necessary for constructing the works at Roanoke Island, and forward the same as early as possible to that post.

Very respectfully,

HENRY A. WISE,
Brigadier-General.

On the night of January 28 Colonel Henningsen arrived in Norfolk with fragments of three companies of my artillery.

On the 29th, as I was departing from the wharf at Norfolk, I ordered him to send his men and horses by land over the sand bridge to the sea-side beach and thence by the shore to Nag's Head—all except men enough to guard his guns, carriages, caissons, and ordnance stores— and these would be shipped on the barges and towed down to the lower section of the canal at Currituck Canal Bridge, where they would be.met by tugs and barges from the island. This order could have been executed in two or three days at most, and the artillery could have reached me by February 1 or 2. I had previously sent my own private wagon the same route to the point opposite Knott's and Crow Islands, and the beach road the whole way to Nag's Head is not only practicable, but the very best and firmest road in all this section.

I found Lieutenant Gallop, of the Eighth North Carolina Regiment (son of Mr. Gallop, who keeps the ferry between the beach and Powell's Point), on Roanoke Island, and from him got a minute description of the whole route, and gave a memorandum of the way to Lieutenant Pearce and Quartermaster Webb, of the artillery, for Colonel Henningsen, whom I saw at the wharf, and to whom I gave the order and description of the route.

By the reports of Colonel Henningsen and Lieutenant Pearce, of which the following are copies, it seems that General Huger thought differently of the beach route; changed my order to Colonel Henningsen, and attempted to send the artillery by land to Powell's Point, and the fatal consequence was that Colonel Henningsen, with more than 100 men and six field pieces, well mounted, did not reach me at all before the island was captured, and joined me not at all until after I fell back to Currituck Court-House, eight days after the action:

Extract from Colonel Henningsen's report.

On Tuesday, January 28, about 12 p. m., reached Norfolk by rail, with Batteries B, C, and D, of artillery, of Wise Legion, with all the horses, five pieces, and five caissons. Horses fed in the cars that night because too dark to remove them.

On Wednesday morning, January 29, reported to Brig. Gen. Henry A. Wise, and received orders from him to march, with the men and horses of artillery, by a route indicated by him to Lieutenant Pearce, who furnished a copy of these route orders to Captain Webb, quartermaster of artillery of Wise Legion. The guns, caissons, and wagons I was ordered by General Wise to leave in Norfolk, to be transported by water.

I gave marching orders for January 30, the condition of the horses, much injured by the cars, rendering it advisable to rest them twenty-four hours.

On Thursday (30th) was informed by Major Bradford that General Huger could not furnish water transportation for guns, caissons, or wagons, and that I must take them by land. There were now unexpectedly six guns (a sixth iron 6-pounder without caissons having been received at Norfolk), five caissons, and fourteen wagons to be transported by land, with only six horses that had been worked in harness, and between thirty and forty horses and mules which had never been broken to harness. Through consequent accidents occurring it took forty-eight hours before we could move from Norfolk. I ordered a march, however, for next morning, and after receiving General Huger's orders, through Major Bradford, reported to General Huger. General Huger confirmed these orders and also ordered me to change the route laid down by General Wise; that is to say, he ordered me to proceed by the main-land road to Powell's Point, instead of by the beach, he (General Huger) giving as a reason that guns and wagons could not be dragged along the beach, and that, in the then state of the weather, the road would be washed over by the sea. This view, which I have since found to be erroneous, was confirmed by several of General Huger's officers and by others who professed to be acquainted with the locality.

On Friday, the 31st, attempted to march, but had much trouble and several accidents with the teams. One team ran away and damaged the forge wagon, breaking the pole Though the forge wagon was new, being drawn just before leaving Richmond, the wood of the pole when broken was rotten half through. At 2 p. m., when ready to start, found that, on account of the prevailing wind and high tide, the bridge over the East Branch was covered by two feet of water and deep holes reported on the other side. Low water not occurring till after dark, suspended march till next morning, Saturday, February 1. Fresh accidents with teams—one gun-carriage damaged, and harness so insecure, though drawn new in Richmond, that we were obliged to procure bolt-rope. This and waiting for repairs delayed us till 12 m., when we marched from Norfolk City.

C. F. HENNINGSEN,
Colonel Fifty-ninth Regiment Virginia Volunteers,
Commanding Batteries B, C, and D, Artillery, Wise Legion.

NAG'S HEAD, N. C., *February* 6, 1862.

Brig. Gen. HENRY A. WISE:

GENERAL: I have the honor to report that, in obedience to your commands, I read to Colonel Henningsen, in Norfolk, your orders that all the artillery horses and men were to go by the beach route to this place, except such of the latter as were necessary for the protection of the field pieces, &c., which, with their carriages and caissons, were to go in tow of a steam-tug to the lower section of the canal. Capt. L. N. Webb, assistant quartermaster of artillery corps, wrote down, in Colonel Henningsen's presence, the prescribed route, with all the material, as enumerated by Mr. Gallop and embodied in your orders to me. I saw Major Johnson, assistant quartermaster of this department, in order to procure the water transportation for the pieces, caissons, &c. He informed me they were not to go that way. I reported that fact to Colonel Henningsen, and he and I went to General Huger, who ordered Colonel Henningsen to take the horses, pieces, caissons, &c., by the inland route, as the beach was impracticable from inlets, high tides, and the probabilities of being shelled by the enemy's gunboats.

I have the honor to be, general, your obedient servant,

JAMES H. PEARCE,
Lieutenant and Ordnance Officer.

When General Huger met me here on the 19th instant he was still incredulous about the route. I had ordered and promised to order a survey of it. Unfortunately the enemy are now in possession of Nag's Head and the beach; how far up it is not known. I was myself driven in a two-horse wagon on the evening and night of the 8th as high up from Nag's Head as Gallop's Ferry, and was assured by all who knew that it was the only bad part of the beach route up to Cape Henry. The Currituck and other inlets have filled up long ago, and there is not a foot of the way not passable by horses, footmen, carts, and wagons.

On the evening of January 29 I left Norfolk, and reached Nag's Head the night of the 30th. I immediately issued Special Orders, Nos. 12 and 13, of which the following are copies:

SPECIAL ORDERS, }   HDQRS. FOURTH BRIGADE, DEPARTMENT OF NORFOLK,
    No. 12.   }   *Nag's Head, N. C., January* 30, 1862.

The quartermaster, or his brigade agent, for the post at Roanoke Island and Nag's Head will immediately procure twenty lighters, as near 60 feet long, or longer, and 12 feet wide, as he can get them, and have them well calked and water-tight, for the service of ferries and transportation across the Roanoke Sound; to and from the island and the beach and across Currituck Sound; to and from Gallop's on the beach and the shore opposite Powell's Point and across to Croatan Sound; to and from the island and marshes and Tyrrel shore opposite. And to this end he will at once dispatch the steam tug-boat Currituck, Capt. C. Bonton, to such places on the waters of the Albemarle Sound as such lighters can be obtained at, with orders to return as speedily as possible with as many as she can tow to the wharf at Nag's Head; and Sergt. J. C. Gallop, of Company B, of the Eighth North Carolina Regiment, is detailed for the duty of accompanying Captain Bonton as pilot and to assist in obtaining the lighters. He will examine them, and those fit for service he will take at a fair valuation; and if he and the owner or owners cannot agree on the prices he will cause them to be valued by arbitrators, one to be chosen by him and one by the owner, and if they cannot agree, the two to call in an umpire. Upon the return of the steamer and the lighters to Nag's Head he will report to me, or in my absence to the officer of the post there as to the lighters, and also to his commanding officer at Roanoke Island, accounting for his absence by these orders, and Captain Bonton, of the Currituck, will await there for further orders.

> HENRY. A. WISE,
> *Brigadier-General.*

SPECIAL ORDERS, }   HDQRS. FOURTH BRIGADE, DEPARTMENT OF NORFOLK,
No. 13.   }   *Nag's Head, N. C., January 30,* 1862.

The steam tug-boat Roanoke, Captain Hobbs, will proceed as early as practicable to the great bridge over the northern section of the Albemarle and Chesapeake Canal, and there apply to Mr. Parks, the president of the canal company or his agent at that place, for a steam pile-driver and a steam dredging-machine, with their crews, to be employed on the defenses of Croatan and Roanoke Sounds. As soon as he can obtain them he will tow them to Roanoke Island, and report to me at Pork Point Battery for further orders. The brigade commissary, or his agent, will furnish the crews of the pile-driver and dredging-machine with rations for ten days; and if Captain Hobbs finds that either the pile-driver or the machine is ready and the other is not, and cannot be ready for two days or more, he will return immediately with the one which is ready, and report to me for further orders.

> HENRY A. WISE,
> *Brigadier-General.*

The next morning (January 31) I visited Roanoke Island, saw Colonel Shaw, and gave him special orders. The same day I returned to Nag's Head and fixed my quarters.

On the morning of February 1, early, I issued and distributed various orders of my own and of headquarters, when, about 9 a. m. of that day, I was seized with a violent and acute attack of pleurisy, with high fever and spitting of blood, threatening pneumonia, from the bed of which I was taken and placed prostrate in a wagon late on the evening of the 8th instant, after the island was captured. I continued, however, to dictate all orders. The weather was one continual cold rain and high wind, and no work of consequence could be accomplished. I made, however, every disposition in my power.

I could not send to Colonel Shaw, as he requested, any field pieces of artillery, for mine had not arrived; but on the 4th I detailed Captain Schermerhorn and Lieutenant Kinney to report for duty to Colonel Shaw, for drilling and instructing in light artillery practice. Colonel Shaw had reported to me three field pieces of artillery—a 24-pounder, an 18-pounder Mexican piece. and a 12-pounder. I sent him from Norfolk a 5-pounder brass howitzer; but when I arrived there were but three pieces—the 24-pounder, the 18-pounder, and the 6-pounder. It is not yet explained to me how it came that there were but three pieces. For the 24-pounder and the 18-pounder there were no other ammunition than that for a 12-pounder.

On February 3 the Secretary of War addressed to me a letter, in reply to my appeals, of which the following is a copy:

> CONFEDERATE STATES OF AMERICA, WAR DEPARTMENT,
> *Richmond, Va., February 3,* 1862.

Brig. Gen. HENRY A. WISE, *Roanoke Island, N. C.,*
> (*Care of General Huger, Norfolk, Va.*)

SIR: In response to your several letters, which it has not been in my power to answer separately, I now inform you that—

First. The North Carolina Battalion was ordered by me to report to you, and I suppose it is now with you.

Second. I ordered Captain Clement to muster into service his own company of cavalry and to join your command.

Third. In relation to the several commissions asked for your Legion, I beg leave to state what I have done and can do, as follows, viz:

1st. Charles B. Duffield has been nominated for major, and his commission will be sent as soon as he is confirmed by Congress.

2d. Henry A. Wise, jr., has been confirmed as first lieutenant and adjutant, and his commission has been forwarded.

3d. J. H. Richardson will be promoted to colonel of the First Regiment of Infantry of your Legion as soon as the regiment of cavalry is filled up to ten companies, in order to justify the transfer to it of Col. J. Lucius Davis.

4th. M. Dimmock will be appointed adjutant of the cavalry regiment as soon as the ten companies are mustered in. The law does not allow an additional officer as adjutant to a battalion.

5th. You have a right to assign Lieut. J. H. Pearce to duty as ordnance officer if you choose. There is no such office provided by law as ordnance officer, and there can be no appointment. It is a mere assignment to duty.

6th. You cannot have, by law, more than one adjutant-general, who must also act as inspector-general. I cannot, therefore, appoint Hammond Dugan, as you desire; but you have no quartermaster for your cavalry, and you might confer that post on him if you desire.

7th. I will present the name of T. C. Kinney for a second lieutenancy in the Provisional Engineer Corps. This corps is too limited in number for me to be able to yield to your wish for any further nominations in it.

Fourth. I will send your cannon as promptly as possible. I would have had it ready for you before, but I was compelled to direct all my resources in light artillery to aid our army after its recent disaster at Somerset, in Kentucky, where we lost all our artillery.

Your obedient servant,

J. P. BENJAMIN,
Secretary of War.

February 3 General Huger sent to me an order of which the following is a copy:

HEADQUARTERS DEPARTMENT OF NORFOLK,
Norfolk, Va., February 3, 1862.
Brig. Gen. HENRY A. WISE,
Commanding Fourth Brigade, Roanoke Island:

SIR: The steamer Roanoke towed down two barges, which were ordered by the quartermaster to proceed to Scuppernong and/bring back corn to this place. If the Roanoke has been taken for other service, you will, on receipt of this, send her and the barges to carry out the orders of the quartermaster. I have to charter vessels to bring forage here, and will give vessels so employed by the quartermaster's department certificates that they are employed by me, and such vessels are not to be interfered with by any one. You will direct the captains of all steamboats coming here from your command to report to the chief quartermaster and any officers coming up to report to headquarters. These orders are imperative.

Very respectfully, your obedient servant,

BENJ. HUGER,
Major-General, Commanding.

Had I complied with this order I would have had no means of transportation whatever. The steam-tug Currituck had been sent for lighters and never returned to Nag's Head.

February 3 General Huger inclosed to me a letter of the Secretary of War to him, inclosing a letter of Captain Lynch to the Secretary of the Navy:

HEADQUARTERS DEPARTMENT OF NORFOLK,
Norfolk, Va., February 3, 1862.
Brig. Gen. HENRY A. WISE,
Commanding Fourth Brigade, Roanoke Island:

SIR: I inclose herewith copies of a letter, dated January 22, from Commodore Lynch to the Secretary of the Navy, and a copy of a letter of the Secretary of War addressed to me, dated January 31. I am sure you will with pleasure aid the naval officers as far as may be in your power. Without adopting the plans of Commodore Lynch for the defenses of Roanoke Island, I count upon your promptness and energy in rendering the defenses as formidable as possible.

I am, very respectfully, your obedient servant,

BENJ. HUGER,
Major-General.

CONFEDERATE STATES OF AMERICA, WAR DEPARTMENT,
Richmond, Va., January 31, 1862.

Maj. Gen. B. HUGER, *Norfolk, Va.:*

SIR: I have the honor of inclosing for your information a copy of a letter from Captain Lynch to the Secretary of the Navy. This letter has excited the deepest solicitude of the President and myself, and you are requested to take the most prompt and energetic measures in your power to remedy the deficiencies in the defenses at Roanoke Island suggested by Captain Lynch, as well as to furnish him men to man his gunboats, even if necessary to detach temporarily some of the soldiers under your command.

Your obedient servant,

J. P. BENJAMIN,
Secretary of War.

CONFEDERATE STATES STEAMER SEA BIRD,
Off Roanoke Island, January 22, 1862.

S. R. MALLORY, *Secretary of the Navy:*

SIR: I have the honor to report that on the 20th instant, with this steamer and the Raleigh, I started on a cruise in Pamlico Sound and for a reconnaissance of Hatteras. Yesterday afternoon we looked into the inlet and there saw a large fleet of steamers and transports. We counted twenty-one of the former all inside the spit; a fog bank concealed those outside. Two large steamers were outside the bulkhead and one was being lightened over by two schooners. They are evidently prepared for a general movement.

The commanding officer at Middletown, in Hyde County, learned through a deserter that the enemy's force consists of twenty-four gunboats, seven large steamers, and sixteen transports. To meet these I have two old side-wheel steamers and six propellers, the former possessing some speed, the latter slow in their movements, and one of them frequently displacing its shaft; but my greatest difficulty is in the want of men. So great has been the exposure of our crews that a number have been necessarily invalided; consequently the complements are very much reduced, some of them one-half. I have sent to Washington, Plymouth, Edenton, and Elizabeth City for recruits without success, and an earnest appeal to Commodore Forrest brought me only four from Norfolk. To meet the enemy I have not more than a sufficient number of men to fight half the guns.

In a former communication I have informed you of my appeal to Colonel Shaw, commanding the military forces here, for some of the North Carolina Volunteers who had been sailors and wished to enlist in the naval service and of my limited success. Inclosed I send a letter addressed this day to him, asking for 50 men, and detailing Lieutenant-Commander Parker to personally urge compliance. I request the letters to be placed on file, to be referred to in the event of calamity.

My opinion is that the North Carolina Volunteers will not stand to their guns. Men so devoid of energy are incapable of determined and long-continued resistance.

General Wise has sent troops to Nag's Head, upon the sea-beach, where they can be driven from their position by a single gunboat, and is selecting points of defense in Currituck which can scarcely be reached in row-boats, owing to the shallowness of the water. Here is the great thoroughfare from Albemarle Sound and its tributaries, and if the enemy obtain lodgments or succeed in passing here he will cut off a very rich country from Norfolk market. His next aim, I presume, will be to obtain possession of the Seaboard and Roanoke Railroad.

Since the preceding page was written I have received a note from Colonel Shaw, wherein he promises to let me have some men temporarily, but declines increasing the garrison at the floating batteries. Those two batteries mounted together seven guns, manned by 70 men; on my last inspection only three and a half guns' crews could be mustered. Thirty-two-pounders of 500 weight require 13 men each to work them, and when the sick and casualties are taken into consideration, it will be seen how very inefficiently those batteries are manned.

I mention these things to protect in a very probable event the reputation of the Navy. The Army now has the batteries in charge, as General Wise refused to allow the volunteers to remain unless the control was assigned to him. Not having any men to send I was constrained to comply, but have placed an officer there to train the men.

Should General Wise be in Richmond you cannot exert your great influence more patriotically than by urging him to come here at once or at least to send some energetic officer of rank to take command.

I have this moment received your communication of the 17th instant. General Huger is misinformed. When the propeller Powhatan was offered to me, Mr. Parks told me that another party had offered him $10,000 for her, but that he would not take less than $12,000. Understanding him to mean a private person, I told him I would telegraph to you, and that the desire of individuals to purchase should not conflict with the wants of the Government. He did not undeceive me. I did telegraph to you; next day received your authority, and immediately sent my secretary, with a note to Mr. Parks, closing the purchase. Mr. Parks was not in his office, but my note was delivered to his brother, who transacts business for him. In the mean time the Powhatan had left for this island, and I overtook her in the Currituck Canal with Mr. Parks on board. I then told him of my note and claimed the Powhatan. He informed me that Major Johnson, quartermaster at Norfolk, was the one who had offered him $10,000, but that the offer was a conditional one, based upon the approval at Richmond of his application for authority to make the purchase. As Mr. Parks had told me that $12,000 was his very lowest price, and as the quartermaster's offer, if sanctioned, would not be accepted (supposing Mr. Parks to be truthful), I felt justified (as there was a large force at Hatteras) in taking possession of the Powhatan.

If the enemy is coming this way, and there is every indication that such is his intention, his visit has only been delayed by the inclemency of the weather, and I submit to you whether I would not have been derelict to my duty if under the circumstances I had not availed myself of an auxiliary means of defense. The crisis will soon be over, and desirable as it is to keep the Powhatan until some of the new gunboats are ready, I have no wish to detain her unjustly. I do not think the claim of the Army as good as our own; yet, although we were treated unkindly in the matter of the Kahukee, I feel no disposition to retaliate.

I have the honor to be, your obedient servant,

W. F. LYNCH,
Flag-Officer.

No notice was given to me by the Secretary of War of this letter, but I presume it accounts in part for the order to me of January 22. As soon as I could write, and had time and opportunity, I replied to this letter of Captain Lynch by addressing General Huger a letter of which the following is a copy:

GREAT BRIDGE, NORFOLK COUNTY, VA.,
February 17, 1862.

Maj. Gen. B. HUGER, *Commanding, &c.:*

SIR: It has been utterly out of my power heretofore to reply to yours of the 3d instant, inclosing to me a copy of a letter from the Secretary of War, dated January 31 ultimo, addressing to you a copy of a letter from Capt. William F. Lynch, which excited, the Secretary says, the deepest solicitude of the President himself. Justice to myself demands that I should put upon the record a reply to this unwarrantable letter of Captain Lynch.

His report of the enemy's force was wholly inaccurate, and he was not timely apprised of the enemy's approach when they came. They were nearly up to the marshes, at the south end of the island, before his fleet were aware of it, as I have every reason to believe. Captain Lynch took his position opposite or between the batteries, instead of keeping a lookout at the marshes or even far below them.

His information, from the first, I found very inaccurate in respect to the waters of the Croatan Sound. His difficulty in the want of men took away forces from the island twice the number of which were wanted there, and he hindered operations of the army materially. He was furnished by Colonel Shaw with more men than ought to have been spared from the infantry, with which or at the batteries they would have been far more useful than with Captain Lynch's useless and worthless gunboat fleet. The North Carolina Volunteers at the batteries did stand at their guns, and were able to do so much more firmly than did or could Captain Lynch's fleet before the force of the enemy.

His letter was dated January 22, two days after I had sent my first regiment of infantry to Nag's Head. My troops were not upon the sea, but upon the sound beach, where the men could not be shelled from their position by a force much superior to a single gunboat, or to even Captain Lynch's fleet, from the sea. My men were sent there for three princial reasons:

1st. There were no quarters for my men on the island and there were ample quarters for them at Nag's Head, and it was a comparatively safe place for ordnance and other stores; whence, indeed, nearly all were saved in the disaster which came, while none were saved on the island.

2d. It was a necessary position for part of the forces, in order to prevent the enemy from landing on the Roanoke Sound beach and crossing that sound, which they easily could to the island, unless the sound beach was guarded.

3d. It was the only position which could cover a retreat from the island and from which to construct a floating bridge or ferry of lighters, while it was convenient to re-enforce the island.

It was unauthorized intermeddling in Captain Lynch to criticise military positions without better information than he had, and it would have been well for the service to have employed his boats as tugs for transports, instead of vainly trying to turn tugs into gunboats to encounter a Burnside fleet of sixty vessels, any one large steamer of which could easily have taken his seven boats.

He asserts further that I was selecting points of defense in Currituck which could scarce be reached in row-boats, owing to the shallowness of the water. This statement is wholly untrue and without a shadow of foundation. I selected no place whatever for defense in Currituck except the landings of Pugh and Ashby, on the island, and at the latter the enemy did land under cover of the shot and shell of a heavy steamer, which ran in with her train of transports quite up to the landing. Captain Lynch's fleet afforded not the least protection to any landing. He was far above them all. He could not have known where my points of defense were except from some idle rumor. My defenses were wholly on the island, and, weak as they were, for want of men, were incomparably beyond any Captain Lynch's fleet could possibly render. While Captain Lynch was so jealous of the reputation of the Navy he should have been a little careful not to assail that of the Army. The truth is that the greatest assault upon the reputation of the Navy was the want of judgment and skill in getting up a tug-boat fleet of seven to meet a Burnside expedition of sixty vessels.

Captain Lynch does not precisely or accurately state the facts correctly when he says, "General Wise refused to allow the volunteers to remain unless the control was assigned to him." This statement applies to all the batteries. It is not exactly correct as to one of them only. The Redstone Battery, on the Tyrrel side, was constructed of two vessels or barges, embanked in the mud of the marshes. There Captain White, of the North Carolina Volunteers, was posted with his company. A midshipman, Mr. Gardner, had been sent to drill the men at the guns of the battery. Captain Lynch chose to call this a floating battery, and claimed to command it as part of the naval armament, and that Midshipman Gardner should command the company of Captain White.

Colonel Shaw issued what I deemed a very proper order in the case. This he and Captain Lynch submitted to me, the latter claiming for the midshipman the entire command of the battery and the men. I declined to subject a captain of the Army to the orders of a midshipman of the Navy, but ordered Captain White, the officer in command, to submit his men to the drill of Midshipman Gardner and to put him in charge of the keys of the magazine. With this Captain Lynch professed to be satisfied. When he threatened to take his drill-officer away unless he could command a captain of infantry and his company, I offered to give the battery up to him wholly, but said I must remove the company of infantry from the battery rather than have a midshipman of the Navy put in command of a captain of the Army, on the land at least. My record of orders and correspondence will sustain this correction of Captain Lynch's statement. There was no controversy about any other battery. Captain Lynch, it seems, called for me to be sent at once from Richmond to Roanoke Island. This, I suppose, accounts for the sudden order which I received from the War Department to repair to the island. I was on duty in Richmond, urging my Legion to be sent; urging for supplies of ammunition and re-enforcements. It was extraordinary meddling with my movements in this instance also for Captain Lynch, of the Navy, to be asking for my orders from the War Department.

The truth is, I had just left Captain Lynch in Croatan Sound to go to Norfolk and to Richmond and apprise our superiors of the lamentable deficiency of defenses at the island. I was not more zealous in the mission than Captain Lynch was in urging me to go on to hasten supplies and re-enforcements. He was urgent that I should do so. I had gone down in the large and comfortable tug Powhatan, to the surprise of her owner (Mr. Parks), who had already bargained to sell her conditionally to the Quartermaster of the Army. Captain Lynch, immediately on her arrival, sent an officer or agent on board of her to take an inventory of everything belonging to her, and he claimed to have purchased her for $12,000, when the Army had purchased her for $10,000. By his own statement he had not bargained, but said he had been so badly treated by Quartermaster Johnson in respect to another steamer (the Kahukee) that he was determined to have the Powhatan whether the bargain by him for her was legally binding or not. The Powhatan was given up to him, and I returned in the little Roanoke to Elizabeth City, and thence by land to Norfolk.

The truth undoubtedly is, that if Captain Lynch had never attempted to make the futile fleet he did make out of the Canal Company's tugs, we could have had them for the purpose of transportation. The piles could have been brought, perhaps, in sufficient number to obstruct the channels; the wharves could have had timber brought for their construction and repairs, and the transportation of the troops and tools would have been in time. All this was a want of judgment only on the part of Captain Lynch. A braver, more earnest, and active officer is not to be found in either Army or Navy, but he was too vainglorious of the fleet that got the name of the Mosquito

Fleet, and really the enemy did not take time to brush it away while he was bombarding the batteries. It fought bravely and well for its size and construction, but had to run into a trap, where, when pursued, it was nearly destroyed. My only complaint of Captain Lynch is that he was superserviceable and overzealous; grasped at too much command and meddled too much with mine. But this complaint would never have been made by me against so gallant and patriotic an officer except in response to what I deem his injustice to me. I beg that you, sir, will forward this letter, or a copy, to the Secretary of War and President of the Confederate States. As Captain Lynch gave me no notice of his letter, but sent it to his Department, I follow his example by sending this to my Department without notice to him.

With great respect, your obedient servant,

HENRY A. WISE,
Brigadier-General.

On February 5 I ordered requisition to be made for free negro laborers, under the laws of North Carolina, and I required report from Colonel Shaw of the number of men stationed at each of the batteries on Roanoke Island and on the Tyrrel shore, &c. He reported to me on the 7th but 803 men left for infantry duty.

On the 5th I ordered Colonel Henningsen to send my artillery horses to Gallop's Ferry, and to transport them thence by the beach to Nag's Head. The guns were to be left at Elizabeth City, whither he had gone, until I could tow them to Roanoke Island.

On February 6, at 4 p. m., I dispatched Lieut. R. A. Wise to General Huger with my letter of that date, of which the following is a copy:

HEADQUARTERS FOURTH BRIGADE, DEPARTMENT OF NORFOLK,
Camp at Nag's Head, February 6, 1862.

Major-General HUGER,
Commanding Department of Norfolk:

SIR: A messenger from Col. H. M. Shaw, commanding at Roanoke Island, has just arrived (10 p. m.), bearing a dispatch, of which I have the honor to inclose you a copy, by order of General Wise. The officer who brought the dispatch reports that he saw four steamers, about 9 a m. this day, which had passed the marshes, going up Croatan Sound. He likewise brings information that Captain Cook, C. S. Navy, reported seven steamers in sight about the same hour. The general directs me to request that steam-tugs, with lighters suited for the transportation of troops between the island and the beach, may be forwarded as early as practicable.

General Wise has been very sick since Friday last, from a violent attack of pneumonia. He is better to-day, but unable to leave his bed. He is, however, issuing orders, and will do everything in his power, with the means at his command, to repel the advance of the enemy. It is very much to be regretted that the means of communication between the island and beach are so limited and insufficient at this time.

Very respectfully, your obedient servant,

C. B. DUFFIELD,
Assistant Adjutant-General.

On February 6, also, I dictated an order to Colonel Shaw, of which the following is a copy:

HEADQUARTERS FOURTH BRIGADE, DEPARTMENT OF NORFOLK,
Camp at Nag's Head, February 6, 1862.

Col. H. M. SHAW, *Commanding, &c., Roanoke Island:*

COLONEL: Your dispatch dated 2.30 o'clock, inclosing report of Lieutenant Loyall, has been delivered by Lieutenant Simmons. I am directed by the general to say in reply that you will obtain reports from the pickets at Pugh's and Ashby's Landings. You will move all your field pieces to the points commanding these two landings and divide them between the two at your discretion. The general, however, recommends that you place two at Ashby's and the like number at Pugh's. You will move the whole of your infantry, except what is ample for the batteries, stationing one-third at Pugh's, one third at Ashby's, and the remaining third at the breastworks called Suple's Hill. If the enemy attempt to land at Pugh's the force at Ashby's will re-enforce that at Pugh's, and fight every inch of ground at the water's edge as long as prudence will permit. Under no circumstances fail to save your field pieces, retiring them first always and covering their withdrawal with the infantry.

You will fall back to the first eligible position and fight again as long as prudence will allow. Then, if compelled to, retreat to the breastworks, and there make a final stand. If the enemy do not land at Pugh's, but pass the marshes, the force at Pugh's will join the force at Ashby's, and there they will, if possible, prevent the landing of the enemy. There is a point just in the rear of Ashby's house, on the road, where the field pieces may be masked and the enemy may be ambuscaded. If driven from that point, you will fall back to the breastworks and there make your first stand. If the enemy pass the sound without attempting to land, your aim then will be to withdraw the forces to such point on the eastern side of the island as will be most practicable for ferrying them across the Roanoke Sound to the beach. The steamer Currituck is hourly expected; but if she fails to arrive, all the means at our command will be used to prevent their being cut off. There is but one tug now here to do the entire service for the army, and she (the Roanoke) must be kept for the purpose of towing the barges and ferry-boats.

Very respectfully, your obedient servant,

C. B. DUFFIELD,
Assistant Adjutant-General.

At the earliest moment on February 7 I sent to the island ten companies—two of the First and eight of the Second Regiments—and additional orders to Colonel Shaw, of which the following is a copy:

HEADQUARTERS FOURTH BRIGADE, DEPARTMENT OF NORFOLK,
Camp at Nag's Head, N. C., February 7, 1862.

Col. H. M. SHAW, *Commanding Roanoke Island:*

COLONEL: I send you, as promptly as possible, ten small but efficient companies, under Lieutenant-Colonel Anderson, who will hand you this and show to you his instructions, which you will consider, as far as they are pertinent, additions to those sent you yesterday. He is a brave officer, has trained and seasoned men, and you may rely on him implicitly. While you will send a portion of your most efficient men to the south end, who may be relied on to fall back with order and precision, you will be particular in reserving an equally good portion of your best men to maintain the post at Suple's Hill. They must be such picked men as will not fire on our own forces when retreating to that post. At Suple's Hill you will make your breastworks for the infantry right and left by felling trees and brush and covering with earth as sufficiently as time will permit. You will detail a proper reliable officer with a small detachment to mark the best and most solid road over the marsh to the battery on Roanoke Sound, and he will there mark on that sound the narrowest portion of it convenient to the fort at the Hommock where a ferry of lighters may be placed across to the beach. He will on the island side place a signal of the narrowest part of the channel where the ferry ought to terminate on that side. If the enemy's gunboats pass the batteries on the Croatan they may easily prevent our steam-tugs from towing off our troops from Weir's Point or the north end of the island. Your only retreat may be by the ferry of lighters. To establish that ferry you will collect all the lighters and barges you have to spare at Weir's Point and notify me when to send for them. The Currituck is expected to-day with a sufficiency, but may not arrive. Report to me all you know of the enemy this morning and everything new as soon as it occurs. I dispatched to Norfolk yesterday a messenger announcing the approach of the enemy. The road across the marshes and the ferry across the Roanoke Sound are all important. Inculcate upon your men deliberate coolness, and make them work night and day, to hold on until we can re-enforce them or withdraw them in safety. Furnish Colonel Anderson with all needed requisitions. I am still confined to my bed.

Very respectfully, your obedient servant,

HENRY A. WISE,
Brigadier-General.

On the same day, the 7th, I gave the following instructions to Lieutenant-Colonel Anderson:

HEADQUARTERS FOURTH BRIGADE, DEPARTMENT OF NORFOLK,
Camp at Nag's Head, N. C., February 7, 1862.

Colonel ANDERSON:

SIR: On yesterday orders were sent to Colonel Shaw, commanding at Roanoke, as to the disposition of his forces and guns to repel the enemy, who are now in sight of the island in strong force, to which you will refer for your instructions. Have a small but efficient guard at Hommock Landing, at the extreme south end of the island, as the enemy can approach there in the lightest-draught gunboats. The guard must be directed to give the earliest notice of the approach of the enemy at that point to the force at Pugh's Landing. If no enemy is approaching Pugh's for a landing at the same time, the force at Pugh's will re-enforce the guard at the Hommock. If not, the guard at the Hommock will act as vedettes and prevent the enemy from falling in the rear of Pugh's.

Of the artillery, you will leave the heaviest pieces at the breastworks and at Ashby's, and take the lighter pieces to Pugh's and the Hommock, as you will have no artillery horses. Under every emergency save your field pieces, in order to fall back, if compelled, to the breastworks. They will be the only pieces you will have for the defense at Suple's Hill, where the breastworks are. If any fights at the landings, let them be sharp, close, and hot, but not continued too long against great odds. Fall back timely, slowly, and continue to fight and fall back till all the forces at the landings are concentrated at Suple's Hill. There will be in all about 1,350 effective infantry to repel the landing of the enemy and to maintain the post at Suple's Hill. One-third of that force will be posted in reserve at Suple's Hill. That force will at once be employed in constructing right and left flank breastworks at Suple's Hill Battery. To do that work, take with you all the available spades, shovels, and axes, and apply to Shaw for all that he can furnish. You will let the senior captain of the Forty-sixth Regiment take command of the companies from that regiment as a battalion, subject, however, to your command. You will ask Colonel Shaw for the loan of all the spare tents and cooking and other utensils of which you have not sufficient. You will make requisitions upon the quartermaster and commissary at the island for whatever you may need. You will report these instructions immediately on your arrival to Colonel Shaw, and be subject to his orders as commandant.

Very respectfully, your obedient servant,

HENRY A. WISE,
Brigadier-General.

On February 7 I also sent to General Huger and to Colonel Shaw the following letters:

HEADQUARTERS FOURTH BRIGADE, DEPARTMENT OF NORFOLK,
Camp at Nag's Head, N. C., February 7, 1862.

Major-General HUGER, *Commanding, &c.:*

SIR: I send you, by direction of General Wise, copies of the dispatch of Lieutenant Loyall to Colonel Shaw, with the colonel's note forwarding the same to these headquarters, and of the dispatch of Colonel Shaw, received about daybreak this morning. The officer who brought the dispatch first-above mentioned reports that of the enemy's fleet twenty-eight are gunboats, seven are towing steamers, and the rest are transports. A re-enforcement of ten companies was sent from this place this forenoon to Roanoke Island, leaving about 300 men here to cover the retreat of our forces to the beach, should they be compelled to withdraw from the island. Owing to continued sickness the general was unable to accompany the troops sent to Roanoke. He is very much prostrated from the illness which still confines him to his bed, and which, in all probability, will compel him to keep his room for some days to come. At 10.20 a. m. a single gun was heard, which the general supposed to be the signal-gun of Flag-Officer Lynch.

At 11.16½ a. m. of this day firing in the Croatan Sound commenced, and from that time till the period of closing this dispatch from two hundred and fifty to three hundred guns have been heard, showing a furious battle to be raging between our forces and the enemy. It is now 12.25 p. m., and the firing is very rapid and heavy.

Very respectfully, your obedient servant,

C. B. DUFFIELD,
Assistant Adjutant-General.

P. S.—1 p. m. The firing still continues most furious. A cannon is heard every second.

HEADQUARTERS FOURTH BRIGADE, DEPARTMENT OF NORFOLK,
Camp at Nag's Head, N. C., February 7, 1862.

Col. H. M. SHAW, *Commanding, &c.:*

SIR: Your brief dispatch, announcing that the enemy have landed on the island, has been delivered by Captain Robinson. I am directed by the general to say that he very deeply regrets that the enemy were allowed to land without resistance. The orders heretofore given you required that the enemy should be attacked while attempting to land; that you should fight every inch of ground at the water's edge as long as prudence would permit, and, if compelled to fall back, to do so fighting, and make a final stand at the breastworks.

Captain Robinson reports that you expected to be attacked at the breastworks in the morning. The general directs that you will fight until retreat becomes a necessity that cannot be resisted. The very great importance of preventing the enemy from getting possession of the island requires that the most desperate and determined resistance be made, and that you continue to fight as long as there is a possibility of repelling them. If you are compelled to retreat, you will do so in good order, guarding your rear by a sufficient number of your coolest and most reliable men, detailed for that purpose. You will also feel the enemy at Ashby's, and if they are not too strong you will attack them.

The general further directs that you will have provisions conveyed to some point near the breastworks in the morning, and direct that they be cooked, so that the men may refresh themselves during the progress of the anticipated fight.

Lighters will be sent to the battery on Roanoke Sound to facilitate the withdrawal of the troops from the island should the necessity therefor arise.

A re-enforcement of four companies will be sent you in the morning. Keep a vigilant watch on your flanks, and strengthen the breastworks as much as you can.

Very respectfully, your obedient servant,

C. B. DUFFIELD,
Assistant Adjutant-General.

HEADQUARTERS FOURTH BRIGADE, DEPARTMENT OF NORFOLK,
Camp at Nag's Head, N. C., February 8, 1862.

Major-General HUGER, *Commanding, &c.:*

SIR: The dispatch sent you yesterday afternoon announced that a fight was in progress between the enemy's fleet and our batteries at the Croatan Sound. A brief pencil note from Colonel Shaw, dated 7.15 p. m., received during the night, states that the fight commenced at Pork Point Battery, no other batteries being engaged; that at no time could more than four guns of that battery be brought to bear upon the enemy, and that when he left, at 4 p. m., two of the guns there had been disabled. The firing commenced, as announced in my previous dispatch, at 11.16¼ o'clock, and ceased only with the approach of night, having continued six hours and thirty-eight minutes, rapidly and unremittingly, from guns of heavy caliber. It is estimated that about three thousand discharges from cannon took place during the time mentioned, yet our loss at the batteries, so far as ascertained, is only two killed. Nothing is known of the damage sustained by the enemy.

Certain information has been received at these headquarters that the enemy landed on Roanoke Island yesterday afternoon. Colonel Shaw reports that they landed above Ashby's, up a small creek, and it is expected that they will get their field artillery on shore during the night. Orders were given to Colonel Shaw to resist their landing; to fight at the water's edge every inch of ground as long as prudence would permit, and, if compelled, to fall back fighting to Suple's Hill, and there make a stand. Why the enemy were allowed to land without resistance has not been satisfactorily explained by Colonel Shaw. Our forces are now posted at the breastworks at Suple's Hill to receive the attack of the enemy, and orders have been sent to Colonel Shaw to make a most determined and desperate resistance.

There are now about 1,350 infantry on the island to protect the batteries and meet the enemy at the breastworks, who will in all probability advance with from 3,000 to 5,000 men and field artillery likewise. This number of infantry is so entirely insufficient for these purposes that four other companies have been sent to the island, leaving only three small companies at this post, comprising in all about 130 men to guard the commissary stores and construct a ferry for our forces on which to retreat from the island should that necessity occur. Lighters have been collected and will be sent to the redoubt on Roanoke Island this morning to transport our troops across should we be beaten and compelled to retreat. Arrangements have been made to remove to some place of security as much of the stores and equipage as there is transportation for. It is confidently anticipated our men will fight most bravely; yet the very great disparity of numbers renders the result exceedingly doubtful.

The loss of the island, or the passage by the enemy of the Croatan Sound, will enable them to ravage the whole of the Albemarle country, and subject the people there residing to the most terrible of disasters.

The general further directs me to say that a very large additional force is necessary for the successful defense of the district assigned to him. Prostrated by disease, and issuing orders from his sick bed, he is striving with the very limited means at his command to arrest the advance of the enemy. The fleet of Flag-Officer Lynch, doing all that it can, can be of no use to us in the expected conflict. Should the enemy, landing above our breastworks at Suple's Hill take our batteries in the rear, it would prove a most lamentable want of men for the defense of the island. If they defeat us in the anticipated fight at Suple's Hill, or pass the island unless very speedily or strongly re-enforced, he can do but little toward giving protection to the people of the counties on the Albemarle Sound and its tributaries.

On yesterday our men fought with deliberate coolness. All the work that could be has been performed in the time allowed us. The commissary reports that large supplies are on the way. The only want to enable us to drive back the enemy and hold the island is that of more men.

Since the above was written the fighting has recommenced. The enemy's bombardment commenced this morning at 8.47 o'clock with apparent vigor and continued until 9.15 o'clock. Contemporaneously, and since the cessation of the cannonading, volleys of musketry, with the discharges of field artillery, have been distinctly heard from the island. The smoke and firing receding toward the south end of the island, accompanied by cheers, supposed to be from our men, seem to indicate that the enemy are being driven back in that direction.

A steamer is reported as having arrived at the island during the night with troops, supposed to be Colonel Green's regiment; if so, this will furnish, in addition to the four companies sent from this post this day, a re-enforcement of eleven companies since my last dispatch.

The general further instructs me to say that he very deeply regrets that the change made by you of the orders given by him for the transportation of his artillery has entirely deprived him on this occasion of that arm of service.

I have the honor to be, very respectfully, your obedient servant,

C. B. DUFFIELD,
Assistant Adjutant-General.

On February 8 General Huger addressed to me a letter of which the following is a copy:

HEADQUARTERS DEPARTMENT OF NORFOLK,
Norfolk, Va., February 8, 1862—11 a. m.

Brigadier-General WISE, or COMMANDING OFFICER:

Lieutenant Smith has just arrived with your dispatch of yesterday, reporting the attack of the enemy. He reports that firing continued till dark.

The Arrow is just going off, and I write a line. I have no time to send anything by her.

As the firing was stopped by dark, I count the enemy did no damage to signify. Long shot will not destroy batteries. If we keep cool and serve the guns well, light gunboats will get hurt. Stand to the guns. I may communicate later by land.

Respectfully, your obedient servant,

BENJ. HUGER,
Major-General.

On February 9 General Huger addressed to me the following:

HEADQUARTERS DEPARTMENT OF NORFOLK,
Norfolk, Va., February 9, 1862.

Brigadier-General WISE,
Commanding Fourth Brigade:

GENERAL: I have your letter of the 8th. I have ordered the only boat left here to be got ready at once. I will have ammunition ready to go on board, and consult Commodore Forrest as to what he can send. I hope to hear soon what more I can do. I consider every hour you hold out as most favorable to us.

I send Lieutenant Smith back, and have placed a company of cavalry along the route to Powell's Point to carry dispatches.

You are in error when you say Colonel Henningsen was diverted from following the route you ordered him to take by me. I gave him no order, but not to send one company by the beach, as you ordered. In all other respects he was to obey your orders.

Your obedient servant,

BENJ. HUGER,
Major-General.

P. S.—I much regret to hear of your sickness. It is really unfortunate.

In correcting my error General Huger admits that he did change my orders to Colonel Henningsen, and that change did divert him from his true course, and prevented my artillery from arriving at all at Roanoke Island.

On the 9th also the following orders were addressed to me:

HEADQUARTERS DEPARTMENT OF NORFOLK,
Norfolk, Va., February 9, 1862.

To the SENIOR OFFICER,
   Commanding any Troops at Currituck Bridge or Neighborhood:

SIR: I will dispatch a regiment to Currituck Bridge and the mouth of the canal as soon as possible. Obstruct the canal by any means in your power, and get the guns at the battery at the bridge in order. Powder will be sent with the troops for these guns. Order out the militia, and order all the citizens to protect the canal with shot-guns or what they can get.

   Very respectfully, your obedient servant,
                       BENJ. HUGER,
                   Major-General, Commanding.

Send back the steamer Roanoke, with the four barges, at once.
   By order of General Huger:
                       FRANK HUGER,
                   Captain, Aide-de-Camp.

HEADQUARTERS DEPARTMENT OF NORFOLK,
Norfolk, Va., February 9, 1862.

To the SENIOR OFFICER
   At Currituck Bridge or Neighborhood:

SIR: I am directed by the major-general commanding to give you the following instructions:

1. He will dispatch a regiment to Currituck Bridge and the mouth of the canal as soon as possible.

2. Obstruct the canal by any means in your power. Get the guns at the battery and at the bridge in order. Powder will be sent with the troops for these guns.

3. Order out the militia, and get all the citizens to protect the canal with shot-guns or what they can get.

4. Send back the steamer Roanoke, with the four barges.

   I am, sir, very respectfully, your most obedient servant,
                       S. S. ANDERSON,
                   Assistant Adjutant-General.

On the 10th I addressed to General Huger a report in full, of which the following is a copy:

POPLAR BRANCH, CURRITUCK, N. C.,
February 10, 1862—9 a. m.

Maj. Gen. B. HUGER, *Commanding, &c.:*

SIR: I was delayed in Norfolk for want of transportation until Wednesday, January 29, and arrived at Nag's Head on the night of Thursday (30th). My two regiments (the First and Second of the Legion, numbering seventeen companies and less than 800 men) had preceded my arrival, and for want of quarters on Roanoke Island occupied Nag's Head. It was absolutely necessary to maintain some sufficient force there to make and protect a ferry across the Roanoke Sound to the island to secure a comparatively safe depot for provisions, stores, &c., and to guard the beach against the landing of the enemy north of Oregon Inlet. We commenced immediately to procure lighters for the ferry, to repair the bridge, and to make a magazine. Early on Friday I visited Roanoke Island, meeting Colonel Shaw at Weir's Point. I gave him the necessary orders to forward the pile-driving, to construct breastworks at Suple's Hill, and to keep strong guards at Hommock, Pugh's, and Ashby's Landings, on the south end of the island. I returned then to Nag's Head on Friday, and ordered every preparation there. At neither post were any tools to work with. No axes, shovels, spades, nails, &c., and requisitions had been made in vain for them both at Richmond and in Norfolk. Neither place had any teams, except two pairs of broken-down mules at the island and some weak and insufficient ox-carts. The consequence was that men had to carry everything on their shoulders, and no work could be accomplished, and in the evening of Friday a cold, hard rain and storm set in, which lasted until the evening of the 5th instant.

On the morning of Saturday, the 1st instant, I was seized (while attending to duty) with a high fever, resulting in an acute attack of pleurisy, threatening pneumonia, from which I was unable to rise until late on the evening of the 8th instant, but from bed continued to issue orders and to dispatch preparations for the enemy, and on the morning of the 6th the enemy appeared off the southern end of the island. I immediately ordered ten companies (eight companies of the Second Regiment and two companies of the First Regiment), under Lieutenant-Colonel Anderson, to re-enforce Colonel Shaw's force. We had but one tug and two barges for transports. They were landed early on Friday morning. Colonel Shaw was ordered to divide his forces into three divisions. He had for infantry duty, independent of the detachments for the batteries, but 803 men, and the ten companies added made 1,250 effective infantry. He had but three pieces of field artillery—a 24-pounder, an 18-pounder, and a small 6-pounder brass howitzer—with no teams for the guns, and with 12-pounder ammunition only for the 24 and 18-pounders. I sent Captain Schermerhorn and Lieutenant Kinney to assist Lieutenant Selden in commanding these, but there was no artillery company to work them. The artillery of the Legion, under Colonel Henningsen, had not arrived. Colonel Shaw was ordered to leave one-third of his force at Suple's Hill, and to post one-third at Ashby's and one-third at Pugh's Landing, to concentrate his forces wherever the enemy might land, and to fight them at the water's edge as long as prudent, and by all means to save his field pieces, with which to fall back upon Suple's Hill, and there to make his final stand. Colonel Jordan was stationed at Ashby's.

On the morning of the 7th, about 9 a. m., the signal was given of the approach of the enemy, and exactly at 11.16½ a. m. the enemy opened upon our batteries. The fire at first was slow, but rapidly increased to a continued roar of the heaviest artillery, which continued exactly six hours and thirty-eight minutes and until after sundown. But little damage was done to any of the works except those at Pork Point (Fort Bartow). Its walls were dilapidated much, but no guns disabled; 1 man killed and 3 wounded. It was repaired by the next morning. About 3.30 p. m. of the 7th the enemy ran up to Ashby's Landing a three-masted heavy steamer, and covered the landing of their troops with mounted artillery from a long train of transports, and Colonel Jordan retired before them without a struggle to Suple's Hill.

The next morning I got over four more companies of the First Regiment, about 180 men, under Major Fry, and the battalion of Lieutenant-Colonel Green arrived, but neither were in the action; why, is not explained. But the enemy early, on the morning of the 8th, advanced on Suple's Hill, and were met by about 1,250 men only. They brought up a 24-pounder and two 12-pounder howitzers, at least, well mounted and worked. The fight began in earnest between 7 and 8 a. m., and continued unintermittingly until about 1 p. m.; about 10,000 against 1,250. Twice the enemy were repelled with great slaughter, but they fell back and took to the marshes and swamps on either hand, and by wading through mud and water to their knees outflanked us. The fight on the flanks was hot and close, the Richmond Blues, under Captain Wise, leading the left skirmishers, and Lieutenant Haslett leading the Ben. McCulloch Rangers on the right. As soon as the flanks were thus attacked the enemy rallied a third time, charged, and took the three field pieces. Colonel Shaw then ordered a retreat, and the Eighth North Carolina Regiment broke, but the other forces fought on, and the fighting continued irregularly until night.

I ordered Colonel Richardson, with his three companies, to rally and rescue those who escaped. The enemy had cut them off from crossing the Roanoke, and advanced at once on the redoubt at Midgett's Hommock. Its commandant spiked its guns, and with his force escaped to Nag's Beach; a number of others escaped by boats—in all, thus far, about 150. With these we came to Gallop's Ferry, 15 miles above Nag's Head, the night of the 8th, having sent all the heavy baggage, stores, &c., we could by the tugs Roanoke and White in safety (we now know) to the canal bridge. This morning the remnant of my forces will reach there, where I shall await your orders.

It is impossible to state the loss of killed and wounded on either side, but the number must be great. But few of the casualties are yet reported. Sergeant Metzler, of the McCulloch Rangers, escaped about 5 p. m. on the 8th, and has just reported to me that the swamp to our right at Suple's Hill, which Colonel Shaw and all had reported to be impassable to infantry, was easily passed by the enemy in quick-time; that Lieutenant Selden, in command of the 6-pounder brass howitzer, behaved with exemplary coolness and courage, and three times mowed a lane through the ranks of the enemy, killing, he thinks, at least 200 in the three fires, and was killed himself as he was sighting his gun with its last charge; that Captain Wise, on the night of the 7th, was in command of 10 of the Blues and 10 of the Rangers on picket duty; that upon returning from picket he joined the guard to the company of Rangers and drove in the enemy's picket. This was the commencement of the action. On returning from this duty he was ordered in command of his own company of the Blues to prevent the enemy from turning our left flank, Colonel Shaw saying that if the left could be guarded the right was protected by the swamp. Early in the action he was wounded severely, and while wrapped in his blanket, being taken off the field, was struck twice again; was carried to the hospital, and is there reported to have died; that Captain Coles, of the Albemarle Rangers, was killed fighting firmly and bravely; that all the men of the Legion, about 450, in the action were cool and firm and fought to the last; that most of the North Carolina regiments were kept in reserve, and finally fell back under orders of Colonel Jordan; that the artillery exhausted its ammunition before it was taken, and the 24-pounder and 18-pounder were not so efficient as the 6-pounder, owing to having ammunition for 12-pounders only. The Pork Point Battery is said to have discharged every round of ammunition but one. Twenty of the enemy's steamers are said to have passed up the sound yesterday evening, and this morning we hear heavy firing toward Elizabeth City, where it is feared Captain Lynch's fleet retired.

I regret to say that the vessels, with our provisions on board for thirty days, which escaped in safety from Roanoke Island, went to Elizabeth City, and will there, I fear, be taken, unless they can escape by the Dismal Swamp Canal. I am now here with three companies of my First Regiment and about 150 men who escaped and about 200 militia without arms or ammunition. I have called in all their spades, shovels, and tools of all sorts for obstructing the canal. My ordnance officer, Lieutenant Pearce, passed on to Norfolk with many of my ordnance stores, which I hope you will have returned to me and order him to return with them. I await anxiously all the re-enforcements you can send me, and beg you will furnish provisions for, say, 300 men.

Very respectfully, your obedient servant,

HENRY A. WISE,
Brigadier-General.

On February 11 General Huger addressed to me the following:

HEADQUARTERS DEPARTMENT OF NORFOLK,
Norfolk, Va., February 11, 1862.

General HENRY A. WISE, *Currituck Bridge:*

GENERAL: I received this morning your letter from Poplar Springs yesterday. I hope you met Colonel Corprew, with the Sixth Regiment Virginia Volunteers, at Currituck Bridge. I regret you had suffered from so severe an attack of illness. I would recommend you as soon as you have organized your forces to place them under command of Colonel Corprew, and return home and get your health re-established.

Very respectfully, your obedient servant,

BENJ. HUGER,
Major-General.

FEBRUARY 11, 1862—11 a. m.

No further news from Elizabeth City or South Mills. I have sent a battery of artillery and re-enforcements down there.

B. H.

On the same day I replied as follows:

CANAL BRIDGE, N. C., *February* 11, 1862.

Maj. Gen. B. HUGER, *Commanding, &c.:*

SIR: I wrote my report under such inconvenient circumstances that I omitted to add that, on the second day of the bombardment, the enemy, on the 8th instant, opened about 9 a. m.; fired irregularly for an hour and ceased. They opened again about 12 m., and fired for about half an hour and ceased.

The fight with small-arms was continued by the men of my Legion all the day of the 8th, and they renewed the fight again on the 9th. I am now convinced that the defense would have been made better if the troops which had been posted there had been removed out of the way entirely. Colonel Shaw ordered retreat before he was justified in doing so, and Colonel Jordan's Thirty-first Regiment was hardly in the fight at all, and he demoralized them by ordering them to take care of themselves while they were in reserve, and they were never led into the action at all. He is said to have escaped, to be in Norfolk or Portsmouth, and, if so, I ask for his arrest. Colonel Shaw is a prisoner. Colonel Corprew arrived this evening between 3 and 4 o'clock with five companies.

I have obstructed the canal by sinking one old barge across the North River end of it, and will add more obstructions, as the enemy now have the dredging-machine which was taken to Roanoke Island, and may remove easily any ordinary obstructions. I shall try to obstruct the channels at the Narrows of the Currituck Sound, also at Poplar Spring. The militia have been called out, but they have but few indifferent arms and no ammunition. I will feed those who will work efficiently, and send the rest home. They are, in fact, in the way.

Yesterday I sent my official aide, Captain Bacon, and a volunteer, Captain Doland, to Elizabeth City. They were there last night and have just returned, reporting that about two-thirds of the town is burned, and fourteen heavy war steamers are lying off Cobb's Point. The inhabitants have all left and burned the town themselves. Several schooners, with the provisions sent to Roanoke Island, a large supply, are lying up Sawyer's Creek, about 8 miles above the floating bridge. Captain Bacon stationed a picket at the latter, and ordered that, upon the appearance of the enemy, the bridge should be let down, and a schooner all ready to be sunk, so as to obstruct the creek upward.

To-morrow morning I will dispatch him with a detachment of cavalry to procure teams, and have our stores hauled to a place of safety. If the enemy approach to seize them, orders were given to destroy them. This morning, upon her arrival from below, I dispatched the tug Currituck with a flag of truce, in charge of Major Duffield and Captain Robinson, to Roanoke Island, to inquire for killed and wounded; to take clothing and other comforts to the latter, and, if possible, to obtain the bodies of Captains Wise and Coles and Lieutenant Selden, and get all the information they could. I expect the tug back to-morrow evening.

It is reported that Colonel Henningsen, with my artillery, has moved toward Edenton. I shall order him back. He is needed both at South Mills and here. I beg you to order him to join me at Currituck Court-House or Indiantown. I trust also that you will urge the forwarding of my cavalry—they are very much needed to head these streams—with dispatch, and there is a vast amount of forage to supply them which cannot be got to market and is in danger of being taken by the enemy. My artillery and cavalry are needed to prevent the enemy from landing and from reaching Currituck Court-House from Elizabeth City or South Mills and from cutting us off. Indeed, the cavalry is indispensable on these peninsulas.

I thank you, sir, gratefully for the leave, after organizing my forces, to return home for the sake of my health. Providence sharply prohibited me from sharing the fate of my brave, devoted troops, but I can sit in my saddle now. I am happier at the post of duty than I could be at a home now wailing for its best scion, cut down in its full vigor; and, God willing, I never mean to leave the remnant of my men again until I see them recruited again and proudly reanimated. I humbly think that now I may ask your co-operation in building up a corps which more than attempted to obey your orders to be cool, to work, and to fight hard. They have done so nobly and devotedly up to the muzzle, to wounds, captivity, and death, against such odds only as were irresistible by their numbers.

With great respect, your obedient servant,

HENRY A. WISE,
Brigadier-General.

On February 11 I detailed William G. Wilson, esq., of Indian Ridge, Currituck, with a sufficient force of laborers to cut trees across the Indiantown Creek and otherwise obstruct it by all the means in his power 4 miles below the creek bridge. On the 11th also I sent a flag of truce to the enemy, to obtain the bodies of officers killed in action and to ascertain the number of killed and wounded and to take comforts to the latter. Our killed and wounded were 10 of the former and 30 of the latter; the enemy's loss was from 300 to 500 killed and wounded; the former number they admitted.

On the 12th I received orders from the War Department showing that my cavalry was sent to Garysburg. Not a company of mine has joined my command in this district.

February 13 General Huger addressed to me the following:

HEADQUARTERS DEPARTMENT OF NORFOLK,
February 11, 1862.

Brigadier-General WISE:

I have received your letter of the 11th. I am glad to hear you are recovering. I will inform you further what I can do on the several subjects you mention when I get a little more certain information. Captain Tabb reported to me a few days ago, and not being able at this time to forward him to you, I ordered him to collect all the stragglers of your Legion, officers and men, and require transportation and forward them to you. Every one who can is escaping to this town, and I desire to get them back to their duty as soon as possible. Shall I continue Captain Tabb on this service? At this time I have no report from any company of cavalry of your command, and I do not know exactly where Colonel Henningsen is. I hear he is moving toward South Mills. This separation of your troops was one reason why I thought you might assist in collecting and reorganizing them, and I leave it to your judgment at what point you can be most usefully employed. Provisions for ten days for 300 men have been sent to-day.

Respectfully, your obedient servant,

B. H.

CURRITUCK BRIDGE, N. C.,
February 13, 1862—12 noon.

I have received a message from Edenton by a Mr. Haughton, who left there yesterday. He states that the enemy landed at Edenton yesterday morning, estimated 5,000. I have many stragglers of your Legion here. All effective men should move toward Suffolk, and non-effective west of Suffolk, to come back when ready. By this movement up the river they are passing around your position. The report of the landing at Edenton is fully confirmed. I send this by my messenger in haste.

Your obedient servant,

BENJ. HUGER,
Major-General.

P. S.—I hope to hear from your flag of truce this evening or to-morrow.

This gave me full discretion to select whatever position I could occupy most usefully, and intimated that there was apprehension the enemy would, by moving up the river, pass around my position. I immediately replied as follows:

CURRITUCK COURT-HOUSE, N. C.,
February 13, 1862.

Maj. Gen. B. HUGER, *Commanding, &c.:*

SIR: Seeing the position at the Canal Bridge utterly indefensible by my force without field artillery, and that the men had no quarters and the heavy artillery exposed to capture, I this morning shipped them in a schooner, and have ordered them to the Great Bridge, on the Virginia section of this canal, with all my extra ordnance and commissary stores. I have ordered the unarmed escaped men of the North Carolina regiments to Norfolk. They are unfit for service. Just as we were moving from the canal bridge three of the enemy's steamers appeared at the North River end of the canal and opened with a few round shot and shell, which all fell short. We moved slowly away while they were landing at the mouth of the canal. We by land and the transports by water have all arrived here safely. Colonel Henningsen is reported as not far off—some 5 miles—with his artillery. This will give me eleven companies of infantry and artillery and one of cavalry. I have ordered vedettes down to the bridge and westward near to Sawyer's Creek. I shall be governed by the movements of the enemy. I sank a barge at the mouth of the canal and a steam dredging-machine higher up, so as effectually to delay for a day or two, if not to effectually arrest, the entrance or passage of the canal. I beg that Captain Tabb may detail another officer to collect and send to me the stragglers of the Legion. I do not want any of the Eighth and Thirty-first Regiments of North Carolina. Captain Tabb's services as my assistant adjutant-general are needed very much. Please send the Legion men to me, not to Suffolk. The enemy cannot get around my position by passing up the sound and rivers. I fear they mean to move on the Great Bridge. Captain Robinson has taken full report of the flag of truce.

Very respectfully,

HENRY A. WISE,
Brigadier-General.

On the same day I also addressed to him the following:

CANAL BRIDGE, CURRITUCK COUNTY, N. C.,
February 13, 1862.

Major-General HUGER, *Commanding, &c.:*

SIR: The Currituck, with flag of truce, has just returned. She brings the bodies of Captains Wise and Coles and of Lieutenant Selden, and a copy of Major Duffield's report is herein inclosed. Captain Robinson bears to you the letter of General Burnside. I send also the copy of his to me. I beg most earnestly that his proposition be at once accepted and my men released on parole. The messenger must return immediately to Elizabeth City. Send Captain Robinson, if you please, back with a favorable answer. The enemy have about 15,000 men; they landed about 10,000; had 5,000 in the action; 5,000 in reserve. We had not over 500 in action. Our killed, about 15; the enemy's, about 400.

Edenton has fallen. This place is wholly indefensible by the force under my command here. I have determined to move the guns to Currituck Court-House, and, after getting quarters there, to advance toward Elizabeth City and join my forces on the line between Edenton and Currituck. We are to-day throwing more obstructions into the canal and will block it effectually.

Very respectfully, your obedient servant,

HENRY A. WISE,
Brigadier-General.

On February 15 I addressed to General Huger the following:

NEAR NORTHWEST BRIDGE, VA.,
February 15, 1862.

Maj. Gen. B. HUGER, *Commanding, &c.:*

SIR: I have forwarded all extra baggage and stores (saving just what is necessary of commissary stores) to the Great Bridge. Had determined to take post a while at the Northwest River, but finding no quarters, and the weather being very bad in which to expose my men, I concluded it best to fall back to Great Bridge, there to erect quarters, intrench myself, and thence move upon the enemy in case he attempts to penetrate the country and seize on the little canal leading from Northwest River to the Dismal Swamp Canal. I shall try to obstruct Northwest River and Tull Creek, and will fight the enemy at both points. If he passes or crosses south of me before I can obstruct him, I will block the streams and canals behind him and harass his rear.

I beg you to order Col. J. Lucius Davis, at Garysburg, to send three, if he can (two, at all events), of his companies of cavalry, by the shortest route, via South Mills or Sawyer's Creek, to me at North West River Bridge. With his remaining companies (six, if he has them, or as many as he has) he will take the most eligible position northeast of Edenton, as near that place as prudent, so as to communicate both with South Mills or Colonel Wright's command and mine.

Captain Belsches' company is overtaxed in vedette service from Currituck Court-House to Norfolk and to Elizabeth City and South Mills. I ask that you will order Colonel Davis to scout the enemy's cavalry, said to be 150, landed at Edenton, to their saddle-girths. He must not let them penetrate the country beyond cannon range.

The enemy has left the Currituck Canal Bridge and Elizabeth City. No report of them to-day. They said at the bridge their purpose was to attack the rear of Norfolk from several points simultaneously.

I will arrange the defenses of Great Bridge. Send Colonel Henningsen on there to-day. He joined me yesterday. I follow with a rear guard of infantry, in charge of baggage and stores, to-morrow morning.

My march is necessarily scattered to get quarters. As soon as I make matters safe and systematic at Great Bridge I will return and establish a post at Northwest and Falls Bridges, obstruct these streams, and endeavor to join Colonel Davis. Cavalry is our only means of communication now.

I inclose orders to Colonel Davis, which I hope you will approve.

I received your acceptance of General Burnside's proposition, and forwarded it to Elizabeth City immediately, in charge of Captain Belsches, having no steam-tugs to convey it to the island.

With great respect, your obedient servant,

HENRY A. WISE,
Brigadier-General.

P. S.—From personal inspection and all reliable information it is certain there is an abundance of forage and provisions in the country between this and Edenton.

Meeting General Huger here at the Great Bridge on the 19th, he expressed his surprise that I should have fallen back to this point, after having left me full discretion to select whatever position I could occupy most usefully; after warning me that the enemy might pass around my position at Currituck Canal Bridge; after being regularly informed of my intention to fall back, and after knowing that the enemy had already appeared at the North River end of the Currituck section of the canal, might remove the obstructions there, and by passing up Currituck Sound cut me off sure enough, or might attack the Northwest or Little Canal and gain the Dismal Swamp Canal, or land at North Landing and seize this section of the Albemarle and Chesapeake Canal and seriously threaten the rear of Norfolk, and after being informed that there were no quarters for my men at a very bad season, and no defensible position by a small force between this and Currituck Canal Bridge!

The same day (19th) I received an order from the War Department, to which I replied as follows:

GREAT BRIDGE, NORFOLK COUNTY, VA.,
February 19, 1862—5 p. m.

Maj. Gen. B. HUGER, *Commanding, &c.:*

SIR: I was within the current hour surprised by the following order:

"SPECIAL ORDERS, }   "ADJUTANT AND INSPECTOR GENERAL'S OFFICE,
   "No. 40.   }   "*Richmond, Va., February* 18, 1862.

*   *   *   *   *   *   *

"XVIII. Brigadier-General Wise, with the Legion under his present command, exclusive of the eight battery companies, will proceed, with the least practicable delay, to Manassas, and report to General Joseph E. Johnston, commanding the Department of Northern Virginia.

*   *   *   *   *   *   *

"By command of the Secretary of War:

"JNO. WITHERS,
"*Assistant Adjutant-General.*"

It is not for me to murmur at any military order commanding my prompt obedience. I am bound to regard it as not meant to do me any injustice and to obey it implicitly; but I trust that under the circumstances of my case and my command I may be allowed a little reasonable time to make arrangements and inquiries necessary to be made under so sudden and unexpected an order.

1st. My men cannot properly be moved to Manassas until they are provided with clothes, blankets, and outfits generally, of which many were wholly deprived by the late disaster at Roanoke Island.

2d. I require some short time to prepare a full report of my command in the district assigned to me in North Carolina attached to your department.

3d. I desire a few days of time to attend to my private family affairs.

4th. I beg time to inquire of the War Department its purpose in respect to my Legion, and respectfully to protest against detaching the companies of the light batteries. The remnant of the Legion, without these companies, is so small, that it will be inefficient as a distinct force. I wish also to inquire whether by present command the Department means to include the men only whom I have with me here at the Great Bridge, excluding my men to be exchanged as prisoners and my cavalry.

5th. I wish respectfully to inquire whether this order, weakening your defenses in the rear of Norfolk, meets with your approbation, or has been issued at your instance or with your cognizance, and to inquire of the Department whether any censure upon my command here is intended by this order.

With great labor and sacrifice I raised the Legion to 2,850 men, and left 2,400 efficient men at Camp Defiance when my command in the West was transferred to General Floyd. I had the repeated promises of the President and of the Secretary of War to have my Legion restored to me, all except the companies raised in Western Virginia, which were desirous of remaining to defend their homes; but four companies elected to remain in the West. Six were ordered to be left there and ten were taken from both the Legion and from the West, where they were wanting, and sent to South Carolina. Less than 900 men, 750 infantry and 100 artillery, have been forwarded to me: My cavalry has been sent to Garysburg, N. C., and has just been ordered by me to this district. Several of my companies have been left in the West and not furnished with transportation, and nineteen of my companies have been captured and are now prisoners of war. I left nine pieces of light artillery in the West. Four were taken from me, with the express promise of General Lee and the Department that they or their equivalent should be restored to me in the East, and now, if it be the design of this order to take from me all my companies and pieces of artillery, I desire to be so informed distinctly, in order that I may understandingly determine upon the course which self-respect demands of me to pursue.

With the request that you will forward this communication to the War Department, I am, most respectfully, your obedient servant,

HENRY A. WISE,
Brigadier-General.

GREAT BRIDGE, NORFOLK COUNTY, VA.,
February 19, 1862.

His Excellency J. P. BENJAMIN,
Secretary of War:

SIR: The foregoing letter, addressed to General Huger, touching your Special Orders, No. 40, Extract XVIII, 18th instant, I have, as you see, requested time to forward to the War Department for information upon certain points and for answers to certain inquiries which concern my personal rights and self-respect. I protest that my motives are founded upon the most anxious desire to serve my country on terms consistent with a sense of honor and of justice to myself and to the brave and faithful officers and men who have joined my command. They have served arduously and faithfully from one extremity of the State to another, and at last have been compelled to fight against all odds without support of re-enforcements and without adequate means of defense, and have fought well, firmly, and nobly. They have never yet been provided with winter quarters; were removed from the western part of Virginia, where their services were urgently required, at a very inclement season, without a proper allowance of transportation, and now ordered in the depth of winter again to change quarters to Northern Virginia, while their services are again urgently required here.

Very respectfully,

HENRY A. WISE,
Brigadier-General.

To these I have as yet received no reply from either General Huger or the Secretary of War. But yesterday, the 21st, I received the following papers, one of which is not signed:

HEADQUARTERS DEPARTMENT OF NORFOLK,
Norfolk, Va., February 21, 1862.

Brig. Gen. HENRY A. WISE,
Provisional Army Confederate States:

GENERAL: Major-General Huger directs me to say to you that Extract XVIII of Special Orders, No. 40, Adjutant and Inspector General's Office, Richmond, February 18, 1862, renders it necessary that he should make a different arrangement of the brigade in this department. I therefore, by his directions, inclose you an extract of General Orders, No. 14, from these headquarters, for your information and guidance.

I am, general, very respectfully, your most obedient servant,

‾‾‾‾‾ ‾‾‾‾‾,
Assistant Adjutant-General.

[Inclosure.]

"GENERAL ORDERS, ⎫   "HEADQUARTERS DEPARTMENT OF NORFOLK,
    "No. 14.   ⎬   "*Norfolk, Va., February 20, 1862.*

"Until further orders the following will be the arrangement and designation of the brigades in this department:

*   *   *   *   *   *   *

"II. The Second Brigade, the country east of the Elizabeth River (South Branch), and extending southeast of the Dismal Swamp, in Virginia and North Carolina; headquarters Norfolk, Brig. Gen. William Mahone commanding.

"By command of Brigadier-General Huger:

"S. S. ANDERSON,
"*Assistant Adjutant-General.*"

To these I have to-day (the 22d) replied as follows:

GREAT BRIDGE, NORFOLK COUNTY, VA.,
February 22, 1862.

Maj. Gen. B. HUGER, *Commanding, &c.:*

SIR: Yesterday evening late I received the inclosed papers, purporting to come from the headquarters Department of Norfolk. As the letter professing to communicate General Orders, No. 14, is not signed, *non constat* that the order was intended to be issued. But, if it was so intended, I respectfully submit that this has been ordered to be issued before you have replied to mine of February 19, and before a reasonable time has been allowed to receive an answer from the War Department to the same.

I respectfully ask whether I may expect an answer from you to the inquiries of that letter? If not, I will immediately demand a court of inquiry upon my defense of Roanoke Island and upon the previous preparation for its defense. At our last personal interview at this place you said verbally that you would order a survey of the sea-beach on the coast of Virginia and North Carolina, to ascertain whether horses moving from Norfolk could be led down that beach to Nag's Head. In case of such a survey I beg to have notice; and in case of a court of inquiry I claim the justice of not being separated from my artillery corps.

Very respectfully, your obedient servant,

HENRY A. WISE,
Brigadier-General.

I am thus (after obeying all orders to the letter and, without men or means being furnished at all adequate to meet an ordinary superior force, fighting for two days one of the most formidable expeditions ever fitted out on this continent, and giving my men, and more than my men, as martyrs to military law and obedience, and suffering, by sickness, care, and grief more pangs than bullets could inflict) left in an anomalous state of doubt whether I am censured or superseded or not, or am a commander without a command or not.

FEBRUARY 23, 1862.

To-day I received the following letter and order:

HEADQUARTERS DEPARTMENT OF NORFOLK,
February 23, 1862.

Brig. Gen. HENRY A. WISE:

SIR: The general commanding has received your letter, addressed to him, acknowledging the receipt of special order, dated Adjutant and Inspector General's Office, Richmond, February 18, 1862, (paragraph XVIII): As requested by you, it was immediately forwarded to the War Department.

. The general has no reply to make to your letter. The order is imperative, and, being sent through him, it is his duty to see that you obey it, and he directs, if you have not already made the necessary arrangements, that you call at once on the proper departments to provide transportation, &c., and give the necessary orders to move your troops to the point indicated.

The pieces of light artillery and the company or detachment serving them will remain at its present position, unless otherwise ordered by the War Department.

I am, general, very respectfully, your obedient servant,

S. S. ANDERSON,
Assistant Adjutant-General.

GENERAL ORDERS, }   HEADQUARTERS DEPARTMENT OF NORFOLK,
No. 14.   }   *Norfolk, Va., February 20, 1862.*

Until further orders the following will be the arrangement and designation of the brigades of this department:

*   *   *   *   *   *   *

II. The Second Brigade, the country east of the Elizabeth River (South Branch), and extending southeast of the Dismal Swamp, in Virginia and North Carolina; headquarters Norfolk, Brigadier-General Mahone commanding.

By command of Major-General Huger:

S. S. ANDERSON,
Assistant Adjutant-General.

In reply I addressed to Asst. Adjt. Gen. S. S. Anderson a letter of which the following is a copy:

GREAT BRIDGE, VA., *February 23, 1862—1 p. m.*

S. S. ANDERSON, *Assistant Adjutant-General:*

I have just received yours of this day. Please say to the general commanding that I have drawn from his silence in declining to reply to my letter the only inferences which seem to me fair and logical, and I shall immediately demand a court of inquiry upon the defenses of Roanoke Island and his conduct of them as well as mine.*

I have obeyed the imperative order of the War Department, and turned the command of this post and that of the light battery of my Legion over to Brig. Gen. William Mahone.

Very respectfully, your obedient servant,

HENRY A. WISE,
Brigadier-General.

---

* This was forwarded by Major-General Huger with the following indorsement: ·
"Respectfully forwarded for the information of the Secretary of War. Brigadier-General Wise has the right to ask a court of inquiry on himself, but I am not aware of his right to ask the favor for me."

FEBRUARY 28, 1862.

Having forwarded my remaining troops to Norfolk for transportation to Manassas I arrived at home the 26th instant and yesterday received from the Secretary of War the following:

CONFEDERATE STATES OF AMERICA, WAR DEPARTMENT,
Richmond, Va., February 23, 1862.

Brig. Gen. HENRY A. WISE, *Norfolk, Va.:*

SIR: I am in receipt of your letter of the 19th instant, forwarded by General Huger, as well as of a duplicate sent directly to this Department. I have no objection to answering your inquiries in relation to Special Orders, No. 40.

The recent disaster at Roanoke Island, having completely broken up the organization of your Legion, left you without a command sufficient to justify your retaining the office of brigadier-general, the act of Congress having provided that the officer should hold his rank only while his brigade is in service. (Section 6, Act of March 6, 1861.)

General Huger notified the Department that in the organization of the brigades of his department you were supernumerary. General Joseph E. Johnston was urgent with the President to send him additional general officers. Your Legion was reduced to a few companies of infantry, two companies of artillery, and an incomplete regiment of cavalry, not sufficient for an independent command. Under these circumstances the President deemed it advisable that the remainder of your Legion should be sent to the Army of the Potomac, in order to replace a regiment of North Carolina Cavalry, under Colonel Ransom, which it was thought proper to send into North Carolina, and to order you to the same army, in order that General Johnston might assign to you the command of a brigade, thus enabling the President to retain you in the service without loss of rank in the only manner allowed by law.

In regard to your application for a short leave of absence, on the grounds stated in your letter, the Department willingly accords you a leave of twenty days, as it is not believed that during the interval any active operations will occur in the Army of the Potomac.

I am, your obedient servant,

J. P. BENJAMIN,
Secretary of War.

In reply to the foregoing letter, permit me to say that by the recent disaster at Roanoke Island the organization of my Legion was not completely broken up. It was reduced to three companies of the First Regiment of Infantry, under Colonel Richardson, two under Colonel Tyler, two under Lieutenant-Colonel Green (not captured), Captain Lowry's company, which had been attached to the artillery (now a full company), and to the fragments of companies—men who escaped from Roanoke Island, about 70 men, now organized—making in all the equivalent of nine companies of infantry; to two companies of artillery, with five pieces; and to nine companies of cavalry; in all, twenty companies, numbering at least 1,000 men. Besides these there are two companies of infantry still at Lewisburg belonging to my Second Regiment; nineteen companies captured at Roanoke Island, soon to be exchanged, I hope, and my Third Regiment of Infantry, ten companies, which I still claim to be restored to me from South Carolina.

With this force, which can easily be put at once, or soon, under my command, I cannot consent that my Legion is completely disorganized; and especially I insist upon this, when I refer to my first appointment to a brigade. I was commissioned after the act of March 6 was passed, and then had not a single company of the Legion mustered into service. But it may be said that I was assigned to the command of a district. True, but the entire number of volunteers under Colonel Tompkins did not then exceed 600 men, and for months my entire brigade did not number 1,000, the force I now have. If, then, my brigade might exist at first, before a sufficient number was raised for an independent command, I cannot see why it may not continue now, with many more forces than I had at first, and when, too, the Department may speedily restore the Legion, as it was promised me, to its full force. Instead of this I respectfully complain that the two companies and five pieces of artillery have been ordered to be detached from my Legion and to be retained in this department under General Huger. I earnestly insist that I may be allowed to take all my Legion to the command of General Johnston.

I had been assigned to the Chowan District, North Carolina, as an independent command, attached to the department of General Huger. His notification, then, to the Department, that in the organization of the brigades of his department I was supernumerary, was without any meaning, except that he desired a new organization and to exclude my command from his department. He might have taken a more direct and ingenuous way of getting clear of me, and I would have heartily co-operated with him. Nothing could be more agreeable to me than to be removed from his command to that of General Johnston. Please, then, express to the President my grateful acknowledgment for his order for the change of my command to the Army of the Potomac; and when you tell me that the motive of this order is that General Johnston may assign to me the command of a brigade, thus enabling the President to retain me in the service without loss of rank in the only manner allowed by law, it relieves me from much oppression of feeling and from all apprehension of his censure for my part in the defense of Roanoke Island, and I will with alacrity obey his orders and report cheerfully to General Johnston. Indeed, had it been otherwise, and if I had been driven from both rank and command, I would have volunteered in the ranks rather than have been driven from the service; but I deem it my imperative duty to the country, in justice to the President, the War Department, General Huger, and myself to demand a court of inquiry, which I do, as to the defenses of Roanoke Island, involving the conduct thereby of all who are accountable for their conduct, or at least my own responsibility. By the President's late message to Congress I see that he is awaiting official information respecting the humiliating surrender of Roanoke Island. I now, as early as I could, send to you ample official information, and beg you to lay it before him, with my request to give it his critical attention. If I have been lagging or lacking in duty let me be condignly punished. I leave judgment upon the conduct of all others to the proper authorities and tribunals. I ask only for stern justice—court of inquiry—and am ready to make any more sacrifices which may be required of me for the public defense.

For your kind leave of absence for twenty days please accept my thanks. I wish only a few days to protect my family and property from approaching danger, and will at the earliest moment within twenty days report to you in person.

Very respectfully, your obedient servant,

HENRY A. WISE,
Brigadier-General.

Hon. J. P. BENJAMIN, *Secretary of War.*

[Indorsement.]

ADJUTANT AND INSPECTOR GENERAL'S OFFICE,
August 23, 1862.

Respectfully forwarded to the Secretary of War for the information of Congress.

JASPER S. WHITING,
Major and Assistant Adjutant-General.

NEAR NORFOLK, VA., *March* 5, 1862.

SIR: The inclosed report of Col. H. M. Shaw [No. 25] was lately received, and as soon as copied is forwarded. I beg leave to comment upon all the reports so far only as is necessary for explanation and correction.

The first re-enforcements sent by me on the 7th were ten companies, numbering about 450 men. They landed on the north end of the island by beaching the barges and wading the men ashore. They did not stop to take their baggage out of the barges.

My artillery of the Legion not having reached me, owing to the interruption of my orders to Colonel Henningsen by General Huger, I sent to Colonel Shaw the two best artillery officers I had at Nag's Head, Captain Schermerhorn and Lieutenant Kinney, who, notwithstanding the modest disclaimer by the former of "any particular knowledge on the subject" of artillery drill, worked their guns in battle with skill, courage, and great effect.

Colonel Shaw says: "Among these (the prisoners) are the battalions of Lieutenant-Colonel Green and Major Fry, who reached the island too late to participate in the battle." I regret to be obliged to correct this part of Colonel Shaw's report. Both battalions reached Roanoke Island in ample time to have participated for hours in the battle. Colonel Green did not report to me at Nag's Head, but had orders to go, as he did, directly to the island. Had he obeyed my first order to move from Wilmington he would have been at the island more than a week before the battle. Had he not stopped his command on the 7th to go and return 20 miles and back before advancing, he would have been at the island before 7 o'clock on the 8th, and after reaching the island, about 9 o'clock, I think he could have reached the battle ground by 10 or 11 a. m. at furthest, if he had not stopped for several hours at the north end of the island to unload his baggage before advancing. He did not reach the island too late, but advanced too late to participate in the battle.

Major Fry, with his battalion, was sent over very early in the morning of the 8th, and reached the island, I am confident, by 8 or 8.30 o'clock. Instead of beaching his barges and wading to the land, as Lieutenant-Colonel Anderson did, he waited several hours, certainly more than two hours. for lighters and boats to land his men, and thus failed to get into action.

Most of the men who were missing escaped, and were of the Eighth and Thirty-first North Carolina Regiments, chiefly of the latter, and they escaped early in the evening of the 8th.

Col. J. V. Jordan did not obey his orders to fight the enemy at the water's edge and to repel their landing, if possible, and his excuse is not satisfactory, except so far as that he had no teams for his artillery pieces, and he was ordered to save them. In his whole regiment there were but 2 (privates) killed and none wounded. The 70 who were missing escaped to me at Nag's Head and Currituck Bridge, and were forwarded by my orders to Norfolk.

Lieutenant-Colonel Anderson's report is confused and inaccurate in that part in which he says: "I immediately deployed Captain Wise's company (A, Forty-sixth Regiment); Captain Coles' company (Forty-sixth Regiment); and Lieutenant Hazlett's company (A, Fifty-ninth Regiment), on our left, in the swamp." What he should have said is: I immediately deployed Captain Wise's company (A, Forty-sixth Regiment); Captain Coles' company (Forty-sixth Regiment), to our left, in the marsh, and Lieutenant Hazlett's company (A, Fifty-ninth Regiment), on our right, in the swamp, &c.

Major Fry's report was written in pencil and underscored as copied. He does not report when he reached the island nor how long it took him to land nor when he reported to Colonel Shaw. His aggregate was more than 150; he had four companies, which averaged at least 45 men each, making his aggregate 180. He took several hours to land, and reached the island in full time to re-enforce our troops had he advanced at once. We had then but one tug and two barges, and he kept them waiting at least two and a half hours to land in lighters and boats, instead of beaching his barges and wading his men ashore. He, too, did not advance in time, but arrived at the island in full time to be in the battle and at a favorable moment.

Major Hill's and Captain Taylor's reports are clear and intelligible, and show that but three guns of all the batteries located on the island or its sounds could be brought to bear on the enemy. These reports embrace the full official accounts of the surrender of Roanoke Island. Of the causes of our defeat I have heretofore sent to the Department delailed official vouchers.

It is but just to about 400 or 500 of our infantry forces, and to the officers and men in three of the batteries, particularly those at Pork Point, to say that they fought firmly, coolly, efficiently, and as long as humanity would allow, without a sufficiency of means of any kind; to Colonel Shaw to say that he acted bravely, and to myself to say that Providence did not permit me to share the fate of my men. I did all that time, weather, sickness, and my superiors would permit in the way of preparations, and none whatever available were made. The consequence was a defeat, which I had again and again foretold in vain, and which grieves, but does not humiliate or subdue, me.

Very respectfully, your obedient servant,

HENRY A. WISE,
Brigadier-General.

Hon. J. P. BENJAMIN, *Secretary of War.*

[Indorsement.]

There are some remarks on the report of Brigadier-General Wise, dated March 5, which require explanation from me:

First. "My artillery of the Legion not having reached me, owing to the interruption of my orders to Colonel Henningsen by General Huger," seems to convey the insinuation that the officious interruption of General H. was the cause of the artillery not arriving. My intention was to expedite its arrival, not to prevent it, as his paragraph seems to imply. Colonel Henningsen states that he was ordered by General Wise to march with the men and horses of the artillery by a route indicated by him (the sea-beach to Nag's Head). "The guns, caissons, and wagons I am ordered by General Wise to leave in Norfolk, to be transported by water." Now, every tug, barge, and vessel that could be procured was engaged to transport troops, &c., to Roanoke Island, and if the men and horses were separated from their guns they would probably never meet again. I therefore ordered Colonel Henningsen to carry his artillery with him to the nearest point to Roanoke Island. My object was to get it there; not to detain it. This was on the 29th and 30th of January.

Second. The remark that Major Hill's and Captain Taylor's reports show that only three guns of all the batteries located on the island or its sounds could be brought to bear on the enemy is disingenuous. The enemy selected a position in which only three guns bore on them, and these reports show that these three guns did repel their whole fleet, and, though the battery was exposed to a heavy fire, no material injury was done to the battery.

Third. The closing remark, "I did all that time, weather, sickness, and my superiors would permit in the way of preparations, and none whatever available were made." The War Department and myself must be the superiors alluded to. We could not control time, weather, or sickness, but what available preparations asked for by General Wise that could be made by his superiors and refused him I do not know and they are not stated by him. I intended and endeavored to do all in my power to aid and assist him, and am not aware in what particular he intends to accuse me of thwarting him.

Respectfully submitted.

BENJ. HUGER,
Major-General, Commanding.

—

WAR DEPARTMENT, C. S. A.,
Richmond, Va., March 14, 1862.

Brig. Gen. HENRY A. WISE, *Norfolk, Va.*:

SIR: I received on the 7th instant your letter covering copies of the reports of your subordinate officers of the affair at Roanoke Island and immediately called on General Huger for the report, which ought regularly to come through him to this Department.

In return, I learn from General Huger that you have made no report through him, and from your letter to him it seems that you propose to furnish him also copies of the reports of your subordinates. I am much disappointed at the delay which has occurred. Congress is impatient for these reports, and the delay is occasioned by the informality of your proceedings, doubtless entirely unintentional. Under the regulations it is necessary that you should make to General Huger your report of the affair at Roanoke Island, inclosing the original of the reports of your subordinates. You may indorse on these originals or annex to them any remarks you please. General Huger will then forward to me all the originals, including your report, and will indorse on it whatever remarks he thinks proper, and thus the Department will be able to communicate to Congress complete information of what is said by all the officers. The originals of all reports belong to the archives of this office, and when you sent me copies I supposed it was a mere measure of precaution after sending the originals through General Huger. Your letter to him, of which a copy has been forwarded to me, discloses the fact that you retain the originals, and that he has never seen either originals or copies. I beg your most prompt attention to the forwarding now of all these reports in proper form. I have received two calls for them from Congress, and could not, till I received the last letter of General Huger, comprehend the cause of the delay.

Your communication of February 21 was also received by me, but its very great length has prevented my reply. I find, however, that it contains a great deal which ought to have passed through General Huger for his remarks, and have therefore sent it to him.

Permit me, however, to call your attention to the fact that it is not necessary in an official report to copy into its text documents and letters. They may be appended, if necessary. The vast length of your report of the 21st is mainly due to this fact, and the brief moments allowed for reading reports while the war is pressing on us renders it peculiarly necessary to adhere to the rule that a military report is to be a succinct statement of facts. All copies of letters, orders, documents, &c., supposed to be necessary for rendering it intelligible, may be presented in a separate paper or papers as inclosures.

I am, respectfully, your obedient servant,

J. P. BENJAMIN,
Secretary of War.

ROLLISTON, NEAR NORFOLK, VA.,
March 17, 1862.

Hon. J. P. BENJAMIN, *Secretary of War:*

SIR: Yours of the 14th instant was received late last night. I immediately addressed to General Huger a report, and requested him to forward it to you, with the original reports of the surrender of Roanoke Island. I had made reports previously to him, but they preceded the reports of Colonel Shaw to me. These he may not have regarded as full, and copies have been sent to the Department in mine of the 21st ultimo, sending a detailed report of the causes of the disaster at Roanoke Island. I regret the errors on my part of sending copies instead of originals, and of reporting directly to the Department instead of through General Huger. They were unintentional, as you do me the justice to suppose. I thought the originals addressed to me were mine, and that as I had been ordered from the department of General Huger I was no longer required to report to him. I meant no disrespect to him, and especially regret that what I intended as dispatch should have caused delay from mere informality. I trust my report now will conform to your instructions. I forwarded my report to General Huger last night immediately on reception of your orders.

In my communication of 21st February I intended to give a detailed account of the causes of the surrender of Roanoke Island. I endeavored to do so in the shortest way and in a way to insure the reading of the report. To have given a history first and to have appended the vouchers, for the statements, would have increased the volume of the communication. I beg you to remember that I am demanding a court of inquiry, and that I could do no less than state the reasons, and the shortest and fairest possible mode was to state them in the language and order of official correspondence. Besides this, Congress is calling upon all for information, and I deemed it my duty to furnish the fullest in my possession. The mere delay of reading the reports of facts could not excuse the delay or the denial of justice to officials involved in a question of doubt as to their discharge of important duties. The committee of the House of Representatives has called on me for answers to certain interrogatories, and I have requested them to call for this report of the 21st February and that of the 5th March to the Department. You say that you have sent that of the 21st ultimo to General Huger "for his remarks." In case he makes any remarks upon it, I beg to be furnished with a copy of them.

In yours to me of the 23d February you say "General Huger notified the Department that in the organization of the brigades of his department you were supernumerary," &c. I ask for a copy of that notification by General Huger. I ask also that you will order him to furnish me with copies of his orders to Colonel Wright and others of his subordinates touching my command of the district assigned to me east of the Chowan River in North Carolina. I have respectfully applied to General Huger for these copies in vain, and they, involve issues of fact and of responsibility which are important to the public service, to him, and to myself.

The leave of absence given me expires in a day or two, and to-morrow or the next day I will report to you in person at Richmond. I would have reported earlier but for the illness of my wife.

I am, very respectfully, your obedient servant,

HENRY A. WISE,
Brigadier-General.

No. 25.

Report of Col. H. M. Shaw, Eighth North Carolina Infantry.

CURRITUCK COUNTY, N. C.,
February 24, 1862.

GENERAL: I submit the following report of the battles on Roanoke Island on the 7th and 8th instant between the Confederate forces, under my command, and those of the United States, commanded by General Burnside and Commodore Goldsborough. I also transmit herewith the reports of Colonels Anderson, Jordan, and Green, and Majors Hill and Fry, and Capt. J. S. Taylor, who was on detached service at the batteries:

On the morning of the 6th instant the enemy made his appearance, reconnoitering in the neighborhood of the marshes. Four or five steamers could be seen, but the atmosphere was so heavy the exact number could not be made out with certainty. I immediately pushed down two more companies to Ashby's Landing, to support the two pieces of artillery which had been placed at that point some time before; sent off a dispatch to you, informing you of the enemy's movement, and then repaired to the lower part of the island to obtain more definite information. Reaching Ashby's Landing, I discovered a large fleet of the enemy apparently at anchor below the marshes, and at a distance of about 8 or 10 miles from Ashby's. With the aid of a glass about sixty steam and sail vessels could be counted. Returning to camp, preparations were made to move the entire effective force to the southern part of the island, in compliance with your orders received in the evening. Having detailed a sufficient number of men to guard my camp and that of Colonel Jordan, the balance was marched down. A part bivouacked near Ashby's and the rest on the lower end of the island, in the immediate vicinity of Pugh's Landing. Taking Maj. George Williamson and a strong picket guard I repaired at once to Pugh's Landing, where I learned from Captain Pugh that the fleet of the enemy, numbering about seventy vessels, gunboats and transports, was anchored in the sound, about 4 miles from his landing.

The fog being very heavy, it was 9 o'clock in the morning before the fleet could be seen with any sort of distinctness. At about 10 o'clock the movement of the fleet commenced. I remained at Pugh's until several of the steamers had passed through the marshes at the main pass, and as there was no indication of an intention on the part of the enemy to effect a landing at that place, I directed Major Williamson to remain with the picket guard to watch the movements of the enemy, and if he should find that no landing would be attempted at that place to return to Ashby's, taking with him the troops and the field piece, and then, accompanied by Lieutenant Talcott, Provisional Army Confederate States, who had kindly volunteered his services to me, I repaired to Ashby's Landing, and having remained there until it had become apparent to my mind that the enemy designed the reduction of Pork Point Battery before attempting to land his troops, and having repeated to Colonel Jordan the order to fight the enemy at the water should he attempt to land, but to fall back to the redoubt should such a movement become necessary to save the field pieces, I proceeded with Lieutenant Talcott to Pork Point Battery, which we reached at 12 m.

Soon after the battle had begun Major Hill, who was in immediate command at that fort, having given a detailed account of the battle of that day as well as that of the succeeding day at that fort, in his report, herewith submitted, it is not my purpose to add to it further than to indorse all that he has said in praise of the coolness, courage, and persevering efforts of the officers and men of his command, who seemed to be inspired by the noble example set them by Major Hill, as well also by that of Captain Taylor and Lieutenants Talcott and Loyall, who were present at both battles at that place, having been sent to the island a short time before by General Huger on temporary detached service.

At 4.15 o'clock, having observed some indications which induced a belief on my part that the enemy designed landing some troops below the battery for the purpose of making a flank movement upon it by land, and the small-arms of the two companies in the battery having been lost by the destruction of their quarters, I left the battery to rejoin the infantry and send re-enforcements to the battery. Having met Major Williamson, who was hastening to communicate with me, I ordered him to return and move two companies to Pork Point, to be at hand if needed. He did so, taking up Company A, Captain Hinton, and Company G, Captain Yellowley, both of the Eighth Regiment North Carolina troops. Soon after I fell in with Lieutenant-Colonel Anderson, having with him portions of the Forty-sixth and Fifty-ninth Virginia Volunteers—about 400 re-enforcements sent over by you. Reaching the redoubt across the main road, I found, what Major Williamson had already, apprised me of, that Colonel Jordan had withdrawn the artillery from Ashby's without resisting the landing of the enemy and had taken position at the redoubt. He informed me that the enemy had effected a landing above Ahsby's and beyond the reach of the pieces. In his own report you will find his reasons for thus falling back fully set forth.

By this time it was night, and nothing remained but to make a stand at the redoubt. Pickets were put out and the troops bivouacked on the low and wet ground adjacent to the breastwork, where they passed the tedious hours of a cold and rainy night without a single murmur or complaint. About day reconnoitering party was sent out and information obtained of the approach of the enemy in large force.

I then ordered Colonel Anderson to put out a part of his command on the left of the breastwork, and Captain Wise being in command of the companies selected for that service, I instructed him to take position under cover of a small piece of swamp on that flank, and to assail the advance guard of the enemy, directing his fire to the artillery, should the enemy attempt to plant any within reach. Soon after I received a message from that officer saying that a position could not be obtained at the point indicated, and I then directed him to take the most favorable position he could.

At 7 a. m. the battle commenced, and as soon as the enemy gathered in force, which was in a very few minutes thereafter, our battery opened fire. This battery was composed of three pieces—one 24-pounder howitzer, one 18-pounder field piece, and one 6-pounder. For the 18-pounder the only ammunition we had was 12-pounder ammunition. The artillery detachments may be said to have been almost totally uninstructed. Having in my command no officers acquainted with that practice save Major Hill, whose duties confined him to Pork Point Battery, I applied to Colonel Richardson, upon his arrival at Nag's Head, for some officers to instruct the men. He had none. Upon your reaching that place I made a like application to you. Captain Schermerhorn and Lieutenant Kinney were sent. The former disclaimed any particular knowledge upon the subject. They were immediately sent to Ashby's; but the enemy made his appearance so soon, little time was allowed them to drill the men.

Captain Schermerhorn was placed in charge of the 18-pounder, Lieutenant Kinney of the 24-pounder, and Lieut. W. B. Selden, Engineer Department, who had patriotically volunteered his services in the line, was assigned to the 6-pounder, and, notwithstanding the men had received so little instruction, these pieces were handled in such a way as to produce immense havoc in the enemy's ranks; especially that of Lieutenant Selden, whose conduct elicited the unbounded admiration of all who witnessed it. Unhappily at about 11 o'clock that gallant officer received a rifle-ball in his head, and he fell without a groan, a willing sacrifice to a cause which he had espoused with all the ardor of his generous nature.

In the mean time the fire of the musketry had been kept up from the commencement of the action with unabated vigor by the following companies under cover of the breastwork : Company B, Captain Whitson, Eighth Regiment North Carolina State troops ; Company B, Captain Liles, and Company F, Captain Knight, Thirty-first Regiment North Carolina troops ; Company E, Captain Dickinson, and Company K, Lieutenant Roy, Fifty-ninth Virginia Volunteers; and Company E, Lieut. J. R. Murchison, Eighth Regiment North Carolina State troops, whose second lieutenant, N. G. Munro, a promising young officer, fell on his approach near the redoubt.

By the gallant officers and brave men of the above-named companies an unceasing and effective fire was kept up from 7 a. m. until 12.20, when, our artillery ammunition having been exhausted and our right flank having been turned by an overwhelming force of the enemy, I was compelled to yield the place.

The entire available force of my command, exclusive of the companies on duty at the several batteries, amounted to 1,434, rank and file. Of these 568 were of the Eighth North Carolina State troops, 456 of the Thirty-first North Carolina troops, and the balance of the Forty-sixth and Fifty-ninth Virginia Volunteers, commanded by Lieutenant-Colonel Anderson, who, together with Major Lawson, was at the redoubt during the most part of the action, and rendered efficient service. The enemy's force amounted to 15,000 men, with several pieces of artillery. With the very great disparity of forces, the moment the redoubt was flanked I considered the island lost. The struggle could have been protracted, and the small body of brave men which had been held in reserve might have been brought up into the open space to receive the fire of the overwhelming force on our flank, which was under cover of trees; but they would have been sacrificed without the smallest hope of a successful result.

The mules and horses attached to the artillery had been killed during the action; the pieces had to be abandoned, and believing it utterly impossible to make a successful stand against such an overwhelming force, I deemed it my duty to surrender.

A verified roll of the prisoners has gone to General Huger, through Major Allston, Provisional Army Confederate States. The number, I believe, is about 2,500. Among these are the battalions of Colonel Green and Major Fry, who reached the island too late to participate in the battle. Colonel Green, however, had a skirmish with the enemy, an account of which is given in his report.

The loss on our side in killed, wounded, and missing, is as follows: Killed, 23; wounded, 58; and missing, 62. The loss of the Forty-sixth and Fifty-ninth Virginia Volunteers is 6 killed, 28 wounded, and 19 missing; that of the Eighth, Thirty-first, and Second North Carolina troops is 16 killed, 30 wounded, and 43 missing; of the Engineer Department, Lieutenant Selden was killed.

Two companies at Fort Forrest are reported to have blown up the fort and made their escape. A detachment of 17 men, under Lieutenant Pulley, of the Thirty-first North Carolina troops, stationed at the battery at Midgett's Hommock, also escaped.

In addition to the officers killed, whose names have already been mentioned, the country will deplore the loss of Capt. O. J. Wise, of the Forty-sixth Virginia Volunteers, who fell bravely fighting at the head of his company, and whose last utterances as he was borne from the field were words of encouragement to his fellow-soldiers. Captain Coles, of the same regiment, also proved himself a gallant soldier, and was killed upon the field.

While I bear testimony to the bravery and good conduct of the officers and men generally who were under my immediate observation during the long protracted action, it is my duty to express the decided belief that, had an opportunity offered, the officers and men so long held in reserve under the most trying circumstances would have shown themselves worthy the confidence of the country. The loss of the enemy in killed and wounded was very great.

I cannot close this report without giving expression to the deep grief which I feel on account of the disaster which has befallen us, and at the same time expressing the earnest hope that the Great Being who holds the destinies of nations in the hollow of His hand will soon enable us to retrieve the losses we have sustained.

Very respectfully, your obedient servant,

H. M. SHAW,
Colonel Eighth North Carolina State Troops.

Brig. Gen. HENRY A. WISE,
Commanding Fourth Brigade, Department of Norfolk.

No. 26.

Report of Capt. James M. Whitson, Eighth North Carolina Infantry.

FEBRUARY 6, 1862—8 p. m.

Received orders to-night to muster all the available strength of my company, with one day's ration, and march to Pugh's Landing, distant 9 miles from the camp.

At 2 o'clock on the following morning we arrived at the church near the entrance of the road leading to and half a mile from the intended destination of our troops. Here we were halted and ordered to remain till further orders.

At the dawn of day orders reached us to resume our march for the landing. Immediately our forces were under arms and wading through the ponds of water that intercepted our march; but we had not proceeded far when another order from the commanding officer met us, directing us to fall back again to the spot that we had just left, where we remained till 1 p. m.

At 12 o'clock the enemy's fleet engaged our fort on the shore, and one hour after the cannonading commenced our forces were ordered to gain Ashby's Landing with all possible speed, 3 miles in our rear; but before we reached the landing we were again halted. It was now about 4 o'clock, when we saw two or three companies retreating from the landing last mentioned in double-quick time, with two or three field pieces, which I supposed had been previously planted at the landing to prevent the landing of the enemy's troops. Again we were ordered to reform and retire to the little intrenchment at Suple's Hill, a point still farther to our rear.

By the time we reached this last point, after the reception of a few shot and shell from the enemy's fleet, the day had nearly reached its close. While darkness was gathering over us the firmament was becoming thickly condensed with cloud, threatening us with storms of rain, which fell incessantly before day. At the battery, while Colonel Shaw, of the Eighth North Carolina State troops, and Colonel Jordan, of the Thirty-first North Carolina Volunteers, were probably concerting their plans for the defense of the works, our troops were waiting for the next order, and apparently in eager expectation of the arrival of the enemy. At length the conclusion came, when Colonel Jordan, of the aforesaid volunteers, was left in command at the battery. My company having been detached from its regiment by order of Colonel Shaw, to remain with the forces under Colonel Jordan at the battery, was ordered by the latter (Colonel Jordan) to take position on the right of the battery and to defend it, whereupon I immediately moved my men in position, ordering them to stack their arms for the purpose of executing another order from Colonel Jordan to me relative to overlaying the battery with pine bushes, which was soon accomplished in good order; but finding the length of the breastwork from the gun and embrasure on the left of my company to the extreme right totally insufficient to admit my company in two ranks, I applied to Colonel Jordan for spades, that I might both lengthen and turn the battery to the rear so as to facilitate a disposition against a flank movement of the enemy should they attempt it, but unfortunately the spades could not be had. The night passed, and a dark night it was.

The morning came, February 8, and we were all wet with the rain of the previous night, and soon our pickets were driven in and reported they were coming. Scarcely fifteen minutes had elapsed before the balls were whistling thick and fast about our ranks from the long-range rifles of the invaders. A vast number of shots were fired at us, taking but little effect in our lines, before we answered or returned the fire, with the exception of what firing was done by a few of our skirmishers deployed against them.

At length an attempt was made by the enemy as if to charge our battery, but it was at this crisis of the action that we poured a deadly fire into them, repulsing them, as we supposed, with considerable loss, as we did on several other subsequent occasions. Finding it impossible to carry our works by means of charging them in front, the enemy next determined, if possible, to gain the right and left flanks of our line, which they succeeded in doing after a five hours' struggle, having to ford a deep, boggy swamp, which compelled them to move very cautiously and very slowly. During the movement through the swamp to our right Colonels Shaw and Jordan, both being in the latter, urged me to watch the movement, which I did with the utmost precaution, causing my men to fire on the enemy at every opportunity.

Half an hour before the retreat took place, seeing that my company on the right was occupying a critical position, becoming more and more exposed to the fire of the enemy, I passed quickly from my position to Colonel Jordan, informing him of the enemy's movements, and having done this, I passed quickly back to my company. Up to this time I had lost 2 of my men killed and 4 or 5 others wounded.

The fire was now becoming intense, the right flank of my company being the most hotly attacked. Believing that a change of position was really necessary, and that in a few moments more we should be swept with an overraking fire, I threw the right wing of company to the rear, in order to diminish its front. I again went to Colonel Shaw and informed him of the position gained against us.

About this time a retreat had been determined, Colonel Shaw having informed me that we should have to evacuate the works. A few minutes more and all our forces were retreating in the direction of the camp. I had not left the battery but a few paces when I received a slight wound from a ball which passed through the leg of my pants, cutting my leg, but very shallow, though it prohibited me from walking for several days.

Many of my command, being near their homes and thoroughly acquainted and familiar with the vicinity of the island and the region of country around, succeeded in making their escape from the island after the action was over, and some after the surrender was made, before they could be taken prisoners—some leaving their baggage and others carrying both baggage and guns with them. These men, about 35 or 40 in number, are liable to do service, and I have instructed several of them that I have seen to report to those officers of my company who were not taken prisoners for duty. Enoch F. Baxter, brevet lieutenant, Sergts. Lewis N. Simmons and Caleb Toler, and four corporals made their escape. The other commissioned officers and sergeants were made prisoners and paroled.

Respectfully submitted.

JAMES M. WHITSON,
Captain Company B, Eighth Regiment N. C. State Troops.

No. 27.

Report of Col. John V. Jordan, Thirty-first North Carolina Infantry.

STEAMER SPAULDING, *February* 17, 1862.

SIR : I herewith submit to you a report of the part taken by my regiment in the late engagement on Roanoke Island between the forces of the Confederate States and those of the United States.

The first appearance of the enemy was on the morning of the 6th instant, about 8 o'clock, as seen from Ashby's Landing by the forces stationed there, consisting of two companies (B and F, infantry) of my regiment, under command of Captains Liles and Knight, with two pieces of artillery, one 24-pounder navy howitzer, and one 18-pounder field gun, the whole force, including the artillery, under Captain Liles, he being the senior officer present. Under an order from you to proceed to Ashby's Landing I arrived there at 12 m. on the 6th, and discovered by aid of a glass a large number of the enemy's fleet, consisting of steam and sail vessels, then apparently lying at anchor at a point 10 miles below the southern point of the island. I left Ashby's at 2 p. m. and met you, in company with Captain Taylor, of the Navy, and reported the information I had received.

Upon your return to the camp I received an order from you to prepare one day's rations for all the available forces under my command, with the exception of one company, which was to be left in charge of the camp, and that portion of Captain Godwin's company which was then in quarters and which you ordered to be sent to the western side of the sound, at a point called Fort Forrest, then in charge of Captain Whitty, with instructions to Captain Godwin to support Captain Whitty in protecting that point. The remaining portion of my available forces, with one day's provisions, was ordered to take up the line of march to Ashby's Landing or that vicinity. On arriving at Suple's Hill, about a mile and a half above this landing, the forces were ordered to bivouac for the night.

At a very early hour on the morning of the 7th myself, in company with Major Yeates, proceeded to the landing, leaving Lieutenant-Colonel Fowle in charge of the forces at Suple's Hill, with a view of making further preparation to meet the enemy should a landing be attempted at that point.

About 10 a. m. I perceived that the enemy's fleet was in motion, advancing up the sound, and at about 11.45 o'clock the leading steamer opened fire upon Fort Bartow. About 3 p. m. the engagement became general upon the part of the enemy's vessels against Fort Bartow. At about 4 p. m. a small boat, containing about 15 men, left one of the transports of the enemy, apparently with a view of taking soundings at Hammond's Landing, about half a mile above Ashby's. As the boat approached the land I detailed a force of 25, under command of Captain Liles, to intercept it. The party in the boat had effected a landing, when Captain Liles ordered the men under his command to fire upon them, by which fire it has since been ascertained that 3 of the enemy were killed and 1 wounded. The remainder immediately retreated to the vessel in the sound. About 5 o'clock a large steamer and a number of smaller boats, carrying a force estimated at 8,000 or 10,000 men, with several pieces of artillery, and under cover of the gunboats in the sound, was seen approaching Hammond's Landing, between which and the point occupied by my forces lay a large marsh impassable by artillery. Having no horses for our artillery, fearing that we might be cut off, or at least that the shells from the enemy's guns in the sound might confuse and disconcert the men under my command and cause the eventual loss of the field pieces, which you enjoined upon me at all hazards to save, I considered it judicious to order a retreat. The infantry, under command of Lieutenant-Colonel Fowle, was placed in rear of the artillery to protect it, and all the forces retired in good order to a redoubt thrown across the main road one mile and a quarter above Ashby's, where the guns were placed in battery, the 18-pounder on the left and the howitzer on the right, under command of Captain Schermerhorn and Lieutenant Kinney, and a 6-pounder occupying the center, under command of Lieutenant Selden. The gun detachments were immediately ordered to take position at their pieces. A picket guard was thrown out and a detail ordered from each company present, to mask the battery as effectually as the short time rendered practicable. Soon afterward you arrived and took command.

At about 12 o'clock at night I proceeded to obey your order to march all my forces, except those detailed for the support of the battery, in connection with those of Colonel Anderson, to Fort Bartow; but while awaiting at Suple's Hill the arrival of Colonel Anderson I received an order, through Major Yeates, revoking your former order, and remained there during the rest of the night, awaiting further orders, with the following companies of my regiment: Company C, Captain Betts; Company D, Captain Manly; Company G, Captain Picot; Company H, Captain Jones; Company I, Captain McKay; Company K, Captain Whitty.

Early on the morning of the 8th I received orders from you to report myself to you in person at the battery then under your command, which I did, leaving the companies above named to act as a reserve, under command of Lieutenant-Colonel [Daniel G.] Fowle and Major [Jesse J.] Yeates. As you are entirely familiar with the part taken by me and those under my command during the action of the 8th, I deem a further report from me unnecessary. Appended you will find a statement of the number of men of my regiment engaged, killed, wounded, &c.*

I cannot close this report without especially mentioning the acts of coolness and manifest bravery of Captains Liles and Knight, with the officers and men under their command, who were in the fight at the battery. Lieutenant Pipkin, of Company G, was in charge of Fort Blanchard, and, with all of his command, evinced a spirit to faithfully and nobly discharge his duty had an opportunity offered. Lieutenant Pulley, Company H, in charge of Fort ——, at Midgett's, is supposed to have escaped with his command, not having been heard from since our defeat. I doubt not but he remained faithfully at his post, ready to do his duty, till he learned that our battery was flanked by the enemy and a retreat ordered.

Respectfully submitted.

J. V. JORDAN,
Colonel Thirty-first Regiment.

Col. H. M. SHAW,
Commanding Forces Roanoke Island.

No. 28.

Report of Lieut. Col. Wharton J. Green, Second North Carolina Battalion.

ON BOARD STEAMER S. R. SPAULDING,
Off Roanoke Island, N. C., February 18, 1862.

SIR: I herewith submit a report of the skirmish in which my battalion (Second North Carolina) was engaged on Saturday, the 8th instant:

In obedience to orders from Adjutant-General Cooper, received on the evening of January 30, I struck camp in the vicinity of Wilmington

---

* List shows 475 men in action; 2 killed, 8 wounded, and 76 missing.

on the morning of the 1st instant and proceeded hither with all possible dispatch. Owing to the want of transports we were detained two days and upward in Norfolk, leaving that place on Wednesday, the 5th instant, in tow of the canal tug-boat White.

On Friday, when about 30 miles distant from the island, continued discharges of artillery informed us of the progress of a fight between the Federal fleet and Confederate batteries. Being entirely ignorant of the topography of the island, and not knowing where or to whom to report, I left our transports about 20 miles hence and came on in the steamer for information. Having obtained which, I returned to my men and crowded them on the smallest number of transports that would contain them and then started. The night was very dark and stormy, with the wind against us, consequently our progress was slow.

After beating about until midnight our pilot declared that he had lost his reckoning, and as we had only a fathom and a half of water, thought it safer to wait for daylight.

About 2 a. m. Saturday a number of Confederate gunboats passed us from the direction of the island, one of them running into the schooner Beauregard (one of our transports) and seriously injuring her. In reply to our challenge and statement of our condition, all the answer we could get was that one of the boats was the Beaufort, the other the ——. Had they stopped in their flight long enough to exchange pilots with us, or even to give ours the necessary instruction as to his course, my battalion would have reached the island in time to have participated in the entire action.

Failing to do so, it was 10 a. m. when we reached the island, and 12 o'clock before the men, arms, and ammunition could be got on shore, owing to their having to be taken on lighters. Having distributed all of my ammunition I started for the scene of action, but soon met scores of stragglers, who reported everything lost and the Confederate forces entirely dispersed.

Notwithstanding these discouraging reports, my men kept in good spirits and pressed on with animation. On reaching your camp, and having the worst reports confirmed, 1 called upon you for orders, and was told to proceed to a point some mile or two distant, under the guidance of Major Williamson, and take position.

After proceeding about half a mile we came suddenly upon a Federal regiment, which I have since learned was the Twenty-first Massachusetts. The two advanced companies of the respective commands were about 75 paces apart, I being some 20 paces in advance of mine. I gave the command "By company into line," when the officer in command of the Federal regiment threw up his hand and cried out, "Stop, stop, colonel; don't fire; you are mistaken!" Believing it to be a trick, I repeated my command. Thereupon the Federal officer gave the command, "Fire." My advanced companies returned the fire, firing at will after the first volley. Finding that there was some confusion, and not knowing the ground, I soon became satisfied that I could not form my men in line of battle to any advantage on the ground that they then occupied, so I ordered them to fall back a short distance and form behind the log houses occupied by Colonel Jordan's regiment as quarters. This they did in good order. The Federals fell back immediately after. Immediately after forming behind the houses Lieutenant-Colonel Fowle, of the Thirty-first North Carolina, passed by with a white flag, and stated that a surrender had been determined upon.

My loss was 3 men killed and 5 wounded, 2 of whom have since died. I am happy to be able to report favorably of the action of both officers

and men. The enemy's loss, as I learned from themselves, was between 20 and 30.

I marched my entire command, with very few exceptions, in good
order back to your camp.

I am, sir, very respectfully, your obedient servant,   '
WHARTON J. GREEN,
Lieutenant-Colonel, Second North Carolina Battalion.

Col. H. M. SHAW.

No. 29.

Report of Maj. H. W. Fry, Forty-sixth Virginia Infantry.

STEAMSHIP S. R. SPAULDING,
Off Roanoke Island, N. C., February 18, 1862.

In obedience to instructions received from Col. J. H. Richardson,
commanding forces at Nag's Head, I proceeded with my command
(Companies B, D, G, and K, aggregate 150) to Roanoke Island, landed,
and with my command reported to Col. H. M. Shaw, who ordered me
to countermarch my command and save them if possible; but on
arriving at the point where we had landed there was no transportation, the tug and barge that brought us over having left for Nag's
Head.

Respectfully submitted.

H. W. FRY,
Commanding Companies B, D, G, and K, 46th *Va. Regt.*

Col. H. M. SHAW.

No. 30.

Report of Lieut. Col. Frank P. Anderson, Fifty-ninth Virginia Infantry.

ON BOARD STEAMER S. R. SPAULDING,
February 15, 1862.

SIR: I herewith inclose you a report of the part taken by the Fifty-
ninth Regiment Virginia Volunteers in the engagement of the 8th
instant.

In obedience to orders from General H. A. Wise I left Nag's Head
on the morning of the 7th, and not being able to effect a landing at the
wharf, I beached the boats at the north end of the island and there
effected a landing, leaving the baggage and most of the ammunition on
board the transports. My force—consisting of two companies of the
Forty-sixth Regiment Virginia Volunteers and eight companies of the
Fifty-ninth Regiment Virginia Volunteers, amounting in all to about
450 men, officers included—then proceeded to the earthwork, across the
main road, where we arrived about 6 p. m., and found that the enemy
had effected a landing in force at Ashby's Landing.

Colonel Jordan, having fallen back from that point (bringing the
artillery back to the earthwork), I immediately sent scouts to discover
the position and force of the enemy. The scouts returned in fifteen

minutes, having shot one of their advance pickets within 500 yards of the earthwork, and bringing his gun. I immediately sent out a strong picket—10 Rangers, Company A, Fifty-ninth Regiment, and 10 Richmond Light Infantry Blues, Company A, Forty-sixth Regiment, Capt. O. Jennings Wise in command. Nothing occurred during the night.

Early in the morning of the 8th I ordered Company A, Fifty-ninth Regiment, Lieutenant Hazlett commanding, to proceed in the direction of the enemy, to relieve Captain Wise and his pickets. In about fifteen minutes they returned, reporting the advance of the enemy in force. I immediately deployed Captain Wise's company (A, Forty-sixth Regiment), Captain Coles' company (Forty-sixth Regiment), and Lieutenant Hazlett's company (A, Fifty-ninth Regiment) on our left, in the swamp, I having been informed by you that our right was impassable, from reports which you had received. The earthwork not being capable of sheltering more than 200 men, I then marched the rest of my command about 250 yards to the rear, there to be held in reserve.

After getting the reserve placed in position I dispatched scouts to the right for the purpose of discovering, if possible, a road by which we might flank the enemy or be flanked by them. They soon returned, reporting a passage impracticable. I then sent them farther to the right, when a messenger arrived from you requesting me to come to the earthwork. Arriving at the earthwork, I dispatched 10 more men to watch and skirmish on our right flank.

About 9.30 a. m., the firing being very heavy, I dispatched a messenger to Major Lawson to bring three companies to the earthwork to relieve those already engaged. He arrived with Company E, Captain Dickinson, and Company K, Lieutenant Roy, of the Fifty-ninth Regiment, and Company —, Captain Murchison, Eighth Regiment North Carolina State troops. They arrived under a shower of bullets, Lieutenants Miller, Pottier, and Walker receiving wounds. The engagement lasted until 12 o'clock, when, our ammunition being expended and our right flank (which had been reported impassable) being turned, I was obliged to leave the earthwork. My regiment retreated in good order.

After arriving at your quarters, and while in conversation with yourself, Colonel Green engaged the advance of the enemy. I immediately marched my regiment to the woods near the beach, and there placed them in position to receive the enemy. While in this position the report reached me that the white flag had been sent by you to the enemy, and that you had surrendered the forces on the island. I sent an officer to you to inquire into the truth of this report; he returned, informing me that the report was correct. I then countermarched my regiment to your encampment and there surrendered them.

The following is the list of killed, wounded, and missing from my command: Killed, 2 captains and 4 privates; wounded, 4 lieutenants and 24 privates; missing, 19 privates. Those missing are supposed to have escaped from the island.

The officers and privates under my command behaved gallantly against great odds.

I have the honor to be, your obedient servant,

FRANK P. ANDERSON,
Lieutenant-Colonel, Fifty-ninth Regiment Virginia Volunteers.
Col. H. M. SHAW,
Commanding Roanoke Island.

No. 31.

Report of Maj. G. H. Hill, C. S. Army, Commanding Fort Bartow.

STEAMER S. R. SPAULDING,
Croatan Sound, N. C., February 14, 1862.

COLONEL: I have the honor to submit the following report of the engagement between the enemy's fleet and Fort Bartow on the 7th and 8th instant:

On the morning of the 7th, while the men under my command were at drill in the fort, we saw that the fleet of the enemy was coming up the sound. I immediately cleared the fort for action and made every preparation in my power to give them a warm reception.

About 11.30 o'clock their fleet, consisting of about thirty gunboats, advanced within range of the four guns on the left flank of my battery (consisting of No. 6, a 57-cwt. 32-pounder, on a navy carriage in embrasure; No. 7, a rifled 32-pounder, on navy barbette carriage, and Nos. 8 and 9, 41 and 47 cwt. 32-pounders, on columbiad carriages), and opened fire from about sixty guns, throwing 9, 10, and 11 inch shell, with shrapnel, a few round shot, and every variety of rifle projectiles. We answered cautiously and slowly with the four guns that could be brought to bear upon them, and they soon fell back so as to mask gun No. 6, concentrating the fire on the three barbette guns, which now alone bore on them. We fired in all but fourteen shots from gun No. 6 this day.

Early in the action a shell exploded on the platform of the rifled gun, destroying a portion of the traverse circle, diminishing its traverse, so that it could be traversed only on those vessels of the fleet that were advanced farthest to the northward. The enemy maintained an uninterrupted fire for more than six hours, withdrawing at dark. We fired the last shot. The works, however, sustained but little damage. We fired 30 rounds from the rifle gun and 161 rounds from Nos. 8 and 9, making, with the 14 rounds from No. 6, a total of 205 rounds expended. The projectiles used by me were principally round shot.

Early in the action the quarters were fired by the enemy's shells, and, notwithstanding the strenuous efforts of Lieutenant Gilliam, of Company I, who was sent with a detachment to rescue the property contained in them, nearly the whole of it, including the small-arms of my battalion, was destroyed.

While in this service Private Bagley, of Company I, was severely wounded by the explosion of a shell. Private Wilson, of Company L, was killed at the battery early in the action, and Private Baily, of same company, was mortally wounded. Sergeant Graves and Private Green, of Company L, were severely wounded at their guns, making the total of casualties 1 killed and 4 wounded.

The damage sustained by the work was repaired during the night by the negro laborers, under the direction of Lieutenant Talcott, who volunteered his services.

An additional supply of ammunition was sent to us from Fort Huger by Captain Taylor, which gave us, including amount on hand, 42 rounds for the rifled gun and 155 rounds for smooth-bore 32-pounders.

On Saturday, the 8th, my men were at their post by 5.30 a. m. in fine spirits, expecting a renewal of the attack.

At 9 a. m. the enemy's fleet attempted an advance up Croatan Sound, with the apparent intent of cutting off our re-enforcements landing on the north end of the island. I opened fire on them with the rifled gun and gun No. 6, checking their advance and bringing on a desultory engagement, which continued at intervals until 12.30 o'clock, when, receiving the intelligence that our land defenses had been forced and my position consequently turned, I abandoned Fort Bartow, destroying the ammunition and disabling the guns. During the morning we fired about 20 rounds of rifle charges and 20 more from smooth-bore 32-pounders.

In closing, I desire to state that both the officers and men under my command did their duty manfully and with skill and courage. Special commendation is due to Captain Fearing and Lieutenants Elliott and Hinton of Company L, and Lieutenant Gilliam of Company I; also to Sergeant Graves, Privates Black and Dawson of Company L, and Sergeant Barrow and Privates Jacocks and Stokes of Company I.

I here desire also to acknowledge the great service rendered by Captain Taylor, of the artillery; Lieutenant Loyall, of the Navy, and Lieutenant Talcott, also of the artillery. They did great service—cool, calm, and assisting in every way. Their conduct cannot be too highly commended.

I am, sir, very respectfully, your obedient servant,

G. H. HILL,
Major, C. S. Provisional Army, Commanding Fort.

Col. H. M. SHAW,
Eighth Regt. N. C. Troops, Comdg. Forces Roanoke Island.

No. 32.

Report of Capt. John S. Taylor, C. S. Army, in charge of Heavy Artillery.

ROANOKE ISLAND, N. C.,
February 9, 1862.

SIR: On Friday, the 7th instant, at about noon, the enemy's fleet opened fire on our squadron and Fort Bartow. In obedience to your orders I took charge of Forts Huger and Blanchard, and awaited the approach of the enemy; but as they did not come within range of our rifled guns (which I fired eight times) and seemed to concentrate their fire on the left flank of Fort Bartow, I immediately rode to that battery, where I remained until the enemy ceased firing, assisting Major Hill, the commanding officer of that post.

On the morning of the 8th, about 10 a. m., Fort Bartow fired a shot at the enemy's ships, to prevent what seemed to be an attempt to cut off re-enforcements approaching the island from the northward (the other batteries being manned to drive back the enemy should the attempt be persevered in); when their fleet commenced a desultory fire upon Fort Bartow. I immediately repaired to that post, where I remained until the battery was evacuated, in consequence of our land defenses having been forced by the enemy's troops.

I then returned to Fort Blanchard, thinking the fleet would attempt to pass through Croatan Sound, which, however, they did not. Leaving orders to fire upon them should they attempt to pass or come within range, I went to Fort Huger, where I soon received your order to spike the guns and send the men to your encampment. This was done, the powder destroyed, and the gun-carriages somewhat injured, about 2.30 p. m.

I should have entirely dismantled the batteries at Forts Huger and Blanchard but for two reasons: First, because, in doing so, the enemy would have been made aware of it, and would, no doubt, have sent their ships up to take your position in the rear; and, second, because I had not time; for while we were throwing shells into the water a sharp conflict was heard in the direction of the encampment of the Thirty-first Regiment; so I immediately dispatched the companies to go by the beach and through the woods to your support.

While on my way to your headquarters I heard that a flag of truce had been sent out, and received orders not to spike the guns; but it was too late.

I do not hesitate to say, from the service done by the three barbette guns at Fort Bartow (the only guns brought fully into action), and the little damage sustained by that battery, notwithstanding the incessant and terrible fire kept up against it for more than six hours by perhaps sixty guns, that if all our batteries had been brought into action the enemy's fleet would have been destroyed or beaten back.

I desire to say that the officers and men brought under fire behaved in a highly creditable manner, and that they seemed to be in better condition the second day, notwithstanding their fatigue and loss of rest, than they were during the first. I would also say that the officers and men at the batteries not engaged evinced a fine spirit; and I have to regret for them, for myself, and for our cause, that they had not an opportunity to illustrate their skill and patriotism against the gunboats of the enemy.

I understand that the loss in the enemy's fleet was about five times as great as ours in the battery. Ours was 1 killed and 3 wounded. Major Hill will no doubt pay a just tribute to the services of Lieutenant Loyall, of the Navy, and Lieutenant Talcott, of the artillery, which cannot be too highly commended.

Allow me to join in the regret and mortification which I know you feel that our cause should have sustained a defeat while in our hands.

Very respectfully, your obedient servant,

JOHN S. TAYLOR,
Captain, C. S. Army, in charge Heavy Artillery.

Col. H. M. SHAW,
Eighth Regt. N. C. State Troops, Comdg. Forces Roanoke Island.

No. 33.

Report of the Investigating Committee Confederate House of Representatives.

The committee, to whom was referred a resolution of the House of Representatives, instructing them to "inquire and report the causes and circumstances of the capitulation of Roanoke Island," have had the same under consideration, and have given all the facts and circumstances connected with the defenses of the said island and its adjacent waters and of the capitulation on February 8, a most elaborate investigation.

The committee find that on August 21, 1861, Brigadier-General Gatlin was ordered to the command of the Department of North Carolina and the coast defenses of that State. On September 29 Brig. Gen. D. H. Hill was assigned to duty in North Carolina, and charged with the defenses of that portion of said State lying between Albemarle Sound and the Neuse River and Pamlico Sound, including those waters, and was directed to report to Brigadier-General Gatlin. On November 16 Brig. Gen. L. O'B. Branch was directed to relieve Brigadier-General Hill in command of his district in North Carolina. On December 21 that part of North Carolina east of the Chowan River, together with the counties of Washington and Tyrrel, was, at the request of the proper authorities of North Carolina, separated from the remainder and constituted into a military district, under Brig. Gen. H. A. Wise, and attached to the command of Major-General Huger, commanding the Department of Norfolk. At the time, therefore, of the surrender of Roanoke Island, on February 8, 1862, it was within the military district of Brigadier-General Wise, and attached to the command of Major-General Huger.

The military defenses of Roanoke Island and its adjacent waters, on the said February 8, 1862, consisted of Fort Bartow, the most southern of the defenses on the west side of the island—a sand fort, well covered with turf, having six long 32-pounder guns in embrasure and three 32-pounders *en barbette*. The next is Fort Blanchard, on the same side of the island, about 2½ miles from Fort Bartow—a semicircular sand fort, turfed, and mounting four 32-pounders *en barbette*. Next, on the same side and about 1,200 yards from Fort Blanchard, is Fort Huger. This is a turfed sand fort, running along the line of the beach, and closed in the rear by a low breastwork, with a banquette for infantry. It contained eight 32-pounder guns in embrasure, two rifled 32-pounders *en barbette*, and two small 32 pounders *en barbette* on the right

About 3 miles below Fort Bartow, on the east side of the island, was a battery of two 32-pounder guns *en barbette*, at a point known as Midgett's Hommock. In the center of the island, about 2 miles from Fort Bartow and a mile from Midgett's Hommock, was a redoubt, or breastwork, thrown across the road, about 70 or 80 feet long, with embrasures for three guns, on the right of which was a swamp, on the left a marsh, the redoubt reaching nearly between them and facing to the south. On the Tyrrel side, on the main-land, nearly opposite to Fort Huger, was Fort Forrest, mounting seven 32-pounders.

In addition to these defenses on the shore and on the island there was a barrier of piles, extending from the east side of Fulker Shoals toward the island. Its object was to compel vessels passing on the west of the island to approach within reach of the shore batteries, but up to February 8 there was a span of 1,700 yards open opposite to Fort Bartow. Some vessels had been sunk and piles driven on the west side of Fulker Shoals, to obstruct the channel between that shoal and the main-land, which comprise all the defenses either upon the land or in the waters adjacent.

The entire military force stationed upon the island prior to and at the time of the late engagement consisted of the Eighth Regiment of North Carolina State troops, under the command of Col. H. M. Shaw; the Thirty-first Regiment of North Carolina Volunteers, under the command of Col. J. V. Jordan, and three companies of the Seventeenth North Carolina troops, under the command of Maj. G. H. Hill. After manning the several forts on February 7 there were but 1,024 men left, and 200 of them were upon the sick list.

On the evening of February 7 Brigadier-General Wise sent from Nag's Head, under the command of Lieutenant-Colonel Anderson, a re-enforcement numbering some 450 men. This does not include the commands of Lieutenant-Colonel Green and Major Fry, both of whom

marched to the scene of action after the battle was closed. The committee do not think there was any intentional delay in the landing of
the commands of Colonel Green and Major Fry. The former (Colonel
Green) exhibited great anxiety to get into the fight when he did land,
and acted with great gallantry in the skirmish he did have with the
enemy in the vicinity of the camp—the whole under the command
of Brigadier-General Wise, who, upon February 7 and 8, was at Nag's
Head, 4 miles distant from the island, confined to a sick bed, and entirely disabled from participating in the action in person. The immediate command, therefore, devolved upon Col. H. M. Shaw, the senior
officer present.

On February 6 it was discovered by the companies on picket duty
on the south end of the island that the enemy's fleet was in Pamlico
Sound, south of Roanoke Island, and apparently intending to attack
the forces upon the island. Colonel Shaw immediately communicated
the fact to Brigadier-General Wise, and issued orders for the disposition of his troops preparatory to an engagement. The points at which
it was supposed the enemy would attempt to land troops were Ashby's
and Pugh's Landings. Ashby's is situated on the west side of the
island, about 2 miles south of Fort Bartow; and Pugh's on the same
side, about 2 miles south of Ashby's.

On the night of the 6th, or early in the morning of the 7th, a detachment, with one piece of artillery, was sent to Pugh's Landing, and one
with two pieces of artillery was sent to Ashby's, and the remainder of
the forces were stationed in the immediate vicinity of Ashby's.

On the morning of the 7th the enemy's fleet passed by both of the
landings and proceeded toward Fort Bartow, and the detachment of
infantry stationed at Pugh's immediately fell back to the vicinity of
Ashby's Landing and joined the detachments there, all under command of Col. J. V. Jordan.

In the sound, between Roanoke Island and the main-land, upon the
Tyrrel side, Commodore Lynch, with his squadron of seven vessels,
had taken position, and at 11 o'clock the enemy's fleet, consisting of
about thirty gunboats and schooners, advanced in two divisions, the
rear one having the schooners and transports in tow. The advance
and attacking divisions again subdivided, one assailing the squadron
and the other firing upon the fort with 9-inch, 10-inch, and 11-inch
shell, spherical case, a few round shot, and every variety of rifled projectiles. The fort replied with but four guns (which were all that could
be brought to bear), and after striking the foremost vessel several times
the fleet fell back so as to mask one of the guns of the fort, leaving
but three to reply to the fire of the whole fleet. The bombardment
was continued through the day, and the enemy retired at dark. The
squadron under the command of Commodore Lynch sustained their
position most gallantly, and only retired after exhausting all their
ammunition and having lost the steamer Curlew and the Forrest
disabled. Fort Bartow sustained considerable damage from the fire
of the day, but the injuries were partially repaired by the next morning and the fort put in a state of defense.

About 3.30 o'clock on the morning of the 7th the enemy sent
off from his transports about 25 men in a launch, apparently to
take soundings, who were fired upon and retreated; whereupon two
large steamers, having in tow each thirty boats filled with troops,
approached the island, under the protection of their gunboats, at a
point north of Ashby's Landing, known as Hammond's, and did effect
a landing. The point selected was out of the reach of the field pieces

at Ashby's, and defended by a swamp from the advance of our infantry and protected by the shot and shell from their gunboats. Our whole force, therefore, withdrew from Ashby's and took position at the redoubt, or breastwork, and placed in battery their field pieces, with necessary artillerymen, under the respective commands of Captain Schermerhorn, Lieutenants Kinney and Selden. Two companies of the Eighth and two of the Thirty-first were placed at the redoubt to support the artillery. Three companies of the Wise Legion deployed to the right and left as skirmishers; the remainder of the infantry in position 300 yards in the rear of the redoubt as a reserve.

The enemy landed some 15,000 men, with artillery, and at 7 a. m. of the 8th opened fire upon the redoubt, which was replied to immediately with great spirit, and the action soon became general, and was continued without intermission for more than five hours, when the enemy succeeded in deploying a large force on either side of our line, flanking each wing. The order was then given by Colonel Shaw to spike the guns in the battery and to retreat to the northern end of the island. The guns were spiked and the whole force fell back to the camps.

During the engagement at the redoubt the enemy's fleet attempted to advance up Croatan Sound, which brought on a desultory engagement between Fort Bartow and the fleet, which continued up to 12.30 o'clock, when the commanding officer was informed that the land defenses had been forced and the position of the fort turned. He therefore ordered the guns to be disabled and the ammunition destroyed, which was done, and the fort abandoned. The same thing was done at Forts Blanchard and Huger, and the forces from all the forts were marched in good order to the camps. The enemy took possession of the redoubt and forts immediately, and proceeded in pursuit with great caution toward the northern end of the island in force, deploying so as to surround our forces at the camps. Colonel Shaw, having arrived with his whole force at his camp in time to have saved his whole command if transports had been furnished, but none being there, and finding himself surrounded by a greatly superior force upon the open island, with no field works to protect him, and having lost his only three field pieces at the redoubt, had either to make an idle display of courage in fighting the foe at such immense disadvantage, to the sacrifice of his command, or to capitulate and surrender as prisoners of war. He wisely determined upon the latter alternative.

The loss on our side in killed, wounded, and missing is as follows: Killed, 23; wounded, 58; missing, 62. The loss of the Forty-sixth and Fifty-ninth Virginia Volunteers is, killed, 6; wounded, 28; missing, 19. That of the Eighth, Thirty-first, and Second North Carolina State troops is, killed, 16; wounded, 30; missing, 43.

Of the engineer's department, Lieutenant Selden (killed), who had patriotically volunteered his services in the line, was assigned to the command of the 6-pounder, which he handled with so much skill as to produce immense havoc in the enemy's ranks' and to elicit the unbounded admiration of all who witnessed it. Unhappily, however, that gallant officer received a rifle-ball in the head and he fell without a groan.

The loss of the enemy was in killed and wounded at least 900, and the probability is a much larger number.

The foregoing is a brief and concise view of the defenses of Roanoke Island and of the adjacent waters, the number of our troops engaged on February 7 and 8, and the circumstances of the capitulation thereof on February 8. The committee are satisfied that Colonel Shaw held the possession of that post as long as he could have done without a useless sacrifice of human life; that on the 7th and 8th the officers and men in Fort Bartow displayed great coolness and courage and persevering effort to sustain their position and drive back the enemy's fleet.

In the battle of February 8 at the redoubt the officers and men exhibited a cool and deliberate courage worthy of veterans in the service, and sustained their position under an uninterrupted and deadly fire for more than five hours, repulsing the enemy in three separate and distinct charges, and only withdrew from the deadly conflict after exhausting their ammunition for the artillery and being surrounded and flanked by more than ten times their number. Instead of the result being "deeply humiliating" it was one of the most brilliant and gallant actions of the war, and in the language of their absent commanding general, "both officers and men fought firmly, coolly, efficiently, and as long as humanity would allow."

The committee are satisfied that the whole command did their duty, and they do not feel at liberty to designate any particular acts of companies or individuals. But in simple justice to Colonel Shaw—upon whom devolved the command by reason of the extreme illness of his superior, General Wise, and who has been censured for the result—the committee take pleasure in stating that there is no foundation for any just reflection upon him. He, upon February 7, after disposing of his infantry force and finding that the enemy did not intend landing, repaired immediately in person to Fort Bartow, where the bombardment was progressing, and made his way into the fort amid the most imminent danger from shot and shell, and there remained, encouraging the men and assisting, as far as he was able, until he discovered the enemy intended to effect a landing below, when he left the fort under the same dangerous circumstances of the morning, to take command of the infantry in person, and upon the 8th, at the redoubt, he commanded in person, sharing the dangers of his men for more than five hours with a firmness, coolness, and bravery worthy of the position he occupied.

Immediately upon the secession of the State of North Carolina from the Government of the United States and the adoption of the Constitution of the Confederate States of America, the authorities of that State commenced the construction of fortifications at Hatteras and Oregon Inlet and other points upon her coast, which were not completed when the State transferred her forts, arsenals, army, navy, and coast defenses to the Confederate Government. Shortly thereafter the attack was made upon Forts Hatteras and Clark, and they were taken, and the fortifications at Oregon Inlet were abandoned, and the armament, stores, and ammunition were removed to Roanoke Island. The enemy immediately appeared in force in Pamlico Sound, the waters of which are connected with Albemarle and Currituck Sounds by means of the two smaller sounds of Croatan and Roanoke. The island of Roanoke being situated between these two latter sounds, commanding the channels of either, became, upon the fall of Hatteras and the abandonment of Oregon Inlet, only second in importance to Fort Monroe. That island then became the key which unlocked all Northeastern North Carolina to the enemy, and exposed Portsmouth and Norfolk to a rear approach of the most imminent danger.

In the language of Brigadier-General Wise—

That such is the importance and value, in a military point of view, of Roanoke Island, that it ought to have been defended by all the means in the power of the Government. It was the key to all the rear defenses of Norfolk. It unlocked two sounds (Albemarle and Currituck); eight rivers (the North, West, Pasquotank, Perquimans, Little, Chowan, Roanoke, and Alligator); four canals (the Albemarle and Chesapeake, Dismal Swamp, Northwest, and Suffolk); and two railroads (the Petersburg and Norfolk and the Seaboard and Roanoke). It guarded more than four-fifths of all Norfolk's supplies of corn, pork, and forage, and it cut the command of General Huger off from all of its most efficient transportation. It endangers the subsistance of his whole army, threatens the navy-yard at Gosport, and to cut off Norfolk from Richmond, and both from railroad communication with the South. It lodges the enemy in a safe harbor from the storms of Hatteras, gives them a rendezvous, and large, rich range of supplies, and the command of the seaboard from Oregon Inlet to Cape Henry. It should have been defended at the expense of 20,000 men and of many millions of dollars.

The committee are of the opinion that the island of Roanoke was a military post of great importance; that it might have been placed in a state of defense against any reasonable force with the expenditure of money and labor supposed to be within the means of the Government; that the same was not done, and the defenses constructed were wholly inadequate for its protection from an attack either by land or water. And the committee have no difficulty in assigning, as the cause of our disaster and defeat on February 8, the want of the necessary defenses upon the island and the adjacent waters and upon the main-land upon the Tyrrel side; the want of the necessary field artillery, armament, and ammunition, and the great and unpardonable deficiency of men, together with the entire want of transportation, by which the whole command might have been conveyed from the island after the defeat at the battery.

But the committee have had much difficulty in locating the responsibility for the neglect of this exceedingly important point, owing to the fact that the command of that island has been transferred so frequently from one military commander to another between the time that the Confederate Government became responsible for the coast defenses of North Carolina and the attack upon the island on February 7, 1862. That island, upon the fall of Hatteras, was taken possession of by Colonel Wright, under the instruction from General Huger, and the principal defenses constructed under the authority and directions of General Huger, who assumed jurisdiction over the island, although it was within the military command of General Gatlin. Afterward Brig. Gen. D. H. Hill was assigned for a short time to the immediate command of that post, who immediately entered upon his duty, made an examination of the defenses in person, and was making active preparations for putting the island in a state of defense, when he was suddenly superseded, and Brigadier-General Branch given the command. It does not appear in evidence that General Branch ever visited the island or made any move toward its defense. He, however, was superseded by Brigadier-General Wise, about January 1, 1862, who immediately proceeded to the island in person about January 6, spent several days in a reconnaissance of the island and its defenses and in examining the adjacent waters, with a view of constructing obstructions in Croatan Sound and to prevent the passage of a hostile fleet, and from that moment up to February 7 the committee are satisfied that General Wise has devoted his whole time in a zealous, energetic, and indefatigable effort to place that island in a state of defense, and has done all and everything in his power, with the means he had at his command, to effect this important object.

At Norfolk, on January 2, upon his way to Roanoke Island, he met

an express from Colonel Shaw (who was then in the immediate temporary command of the island) to General Huger, informing him of the
defenseless state of the island, and urging the necessity of strengthening Fort Bartow, by mounting other guns, obstructing Croatan Sound,
and making requisitions for ammunition, pile-driver, and other things
necessary. General Wise indorsed and approved of the requisition
and seconded the demands of Colonel Shaw. General Wise arrived at
Roanoke Island upon the 6th and assumed the command at that post
upon January 7. After making a reconnaissance of the island and its
defenses General Wise, on January 13, informed General Huger—

> that Roanoke Island was in a defenseless condition and in presence of a very formi-
> dable enemy's force. The Burnside expedition is reported to have sailed. Independ-
> ent of that, the force now at Hatteras Inlet can pass or take Roanoke Island, and
> pardon me for saying that I respectfully differ from the opinion you expressed in your
> orders to-day, that to prevent the enemy's gunboats from passing the marshes at the
> south end will also prevent any landing. Batteries at the marshes are vitally essential
> to prevent the gunboats from passing into Croatan Sound, but they will not prevent
> the landing on the south or east end of the island. At least 3,000 infantry are needed
> on the island, and a considerable force, say 1,500 men, are needed on the beaches, and
> if the enemy pass Roanoke, 5,000 at least are necessary to fight them on the tongue of
> land on the north side of Albemarle Sound. We need on the beach and on the island
> at least eight field pieces and the carriages and caissons necessary. We require thirty-
> two horses for the artillery. We need at least six heavy pieces at the south end
> marshes and two at least at Fleetwood Point.

On the same day General Wise addressed the Secretary of War, in
which he says that—

> it is very important that my Legion should be forwarded as speedily as possible. The
> defense of Roanoke Island (which is the key of all the rear defenses of Norfolk and
> its canals and railroads) is committed to my charge, and I have just returned from a
> reconnaissance of that point. It is now utterly defenseless. No preparations have
> been made there at all adequate. General Huger has given me a large authority to
> do whatever is necessary, and has advised what he deems proper in my command;
> but we have very limited means, and not half time enough to prepare to meet an
> enemy, who is now in almost immediate presence in very formidable force. Twice the
> number of my Legion is necessary, and I beg that the place of my Third Regiment may
> speedily be filled or that it may be restored.

On January 15, 1862, General Wise writes to the Secretary of War:

> I am sure you will not adjudge me importunate when I inform you that I returned
> from Roanoke Island to Norfolk last Saturday. I hasten back after a short recon-
> naissance to apprise headquarters and the Department that there are no defenses
> there; no adequate preparations whatever to meet the enemy, and to forward all the
> means in my reach as speedily as possible, to make the key of all the rear of Norfolk,
> with its canals and railroads, safe. Inside of Hatteras Inlet I found twenty-four
> vessels of light draught, eight of which are steamers, said to carry four guns each.
> They are at farthest but 30 miles from Roanoke Island, and can reach there any four
> hours or less, to attack five small gunboats, under Captain Lynch, and four small
> land batteries, wholly inefficient. Any boat drawing 7 feet water or less can pass the
> Croatan Sound as far off as 1¼ miles from any battery, and the enemy's guns can
> silence our batteries there in a very short time. Neither battery is casemated, and
> our men now there are untrained to heavy pieces mounted on navy carriages. The
> moment the enemy passes Croatan Channel, the North Landing River, North River,
> Pasquotank, Chowan, Roanoke, Alligator, and Scuppernong Rivers, and the Dismal
> Swamp, and Albemarle and Chesapeake Canals will be blockaded effectually, and
> Norfolk and Portsmouth will be cut off from supplies of corn, pork, and forage. The
> force at Hatteras is independent of the Burnside expedition. No matter where the
> latter is, the former is amply sufficient to capture or pass Roanoke Island in any twelve
> hours. Let me say, then, sir, that if we are to wait for powder from Richmond until
> we are attacked at that island, that attack will be capture and our defeat will pre-
> cede our supply of ammunition. The case is too urgent for me to delay speaking this
> out plainly at once.

And in another part of the same letter he says:

> We want ammunition and men. In a word, almost every preparation has to be
> made. Delay is defeat now at Roanoke Island, and with present means Captain Lynch

and I combined can't guarantee successful defense for a day. I beg, sir, that you will urge this upon the Navy Department, and believe that I am not superserviceable in this urgency.

General Wise, finding that his written appeals for aid in the defenses of the island to headquarters at Norfolk and to the Department at Richmond were neglected and treated with indifference, repaired in person to Richmond and called upon the Secretary of War, and urged in the most importunate manner the absolute necessity of strengthening the defenses upon that island with additional men, armament, and ammunition. The Secretary of War replied verbally to his appeals for re-enforcements that he had not the men to spare for his command. General Wise urged upon the Secretary that General Huger had about 15,000 men in front of Norfolk lying idle in camp for eight months, and that a considerable portion of them could be spared for the defense of the rear of Norfolk, and especially as his (General Wise's) district supplied Norfolk and his army with nearly or quite all of his corn, pork, and forage; that re-enforcements at Roanoke Island were as absolutely necessary to the defense of Norfolk as forces in its front, and that particular or special posts should not be allowed to monopolize nearly all the men, powder, and supplies.

In reply to all his urgent appeals for the means of defense General Wise, on January 22, received the following military order, No. 17:

> Brig. Gen. Henry A. Wise, Provisional Army, will immediately proceed to Roanoke Island, North Carolina, and assume command of the Confederate States troops at that place.
> By command of the Secretary of War:
>
> JNO. WITHERS,
> *Assistant Adjutant-General.*

It is apparent to the committee from [that] the correspondence on file of General Wise with the Secretary of War, General Huger, his superior officer, the Governor of North Carolina, and others, proves that he was fully alive to the importance of Roanoke Island, and has devoted his whole time and energies and means to the defense of that position, and that he is in no way responsible for the unfortunate disaster which befell our forces upon that island on February 7 and 8.

But the committee cannot say the same in reference to the efforts of the Secretary of War and the commanding officer at Norfolk, General Huger. It is apparent that the island of Roanoke is important for the defense of Norfolk, and that General Huger had under his command at that point upward of 15,000 men, a large supply of armament and ammunition, and could have thrown in a few hours a large re-enforcement upon Roanoke Island, and that himself and the Secretary of War had timely notice of the entire inadequacy of the defenses, the want of men and munitions of war, and the threatening attitude of the enemy. But General Huger and the Secretary of War paid no practical attention to those urgent appeals of General Wise, sent forward none of his important requisitions, and permitted General Wise and his inconsiderable force to remain to meet at least 15,000 men, well-armed and equipped. If the Secretary of War and the commanding general at Norfolk had not the means to re-enforce General Wise why was he not ordered to abandon his position and save his command? But, upon the contrary, he was required to remain and sacrifice his command, with no means in his insulated position to make his escape in case of defeat.

The committee, from the testimony, are therefore constrained to report, that whatever of blame and responsibility is justly attributable to any one for the defeat of our troops at Roanoke Island on February 8, 1862, should attach to Maj. Gen. B. Huger and the late Secretary of War, J. P. Benjamin.

All of which is respectfully submitted.

B. S. GAITHER,
Chairman.

FEBRUARY 10, 1862.—Action at Elizabeth City, N. C.

Report of Col. C. F. Henningsen, Fifty-ninth Virginia Infantry.

WINTON, N. C., *February* 12, 1862—12 p. m.

GENERAL : Finding at Currituck Court-House that provision and forage could not be obtained to proceed to Powell's Point, or even to remain at the Albemarle and Chesapeake Canal any nearer than Elizabeth City, [we] marched there on the 3d with artillery of Wise's Legion and remained there till [the] 7th, breaking horses to fire and harness while waiting orders from General Wise. Received on February 7 one order from General Wise to leave guns and wagons at Albemarle and Chesapeake Canal and proceed with horses and men to Powell's Point. Sent quartermaster to make arrangements. Same evening received second dispatch from Brig. Gen. H. A. Wise, dated from Nag's Head, informing me that the Federal squadron in great force was advancing up the sound, and ordering me to remain and do the best I could for the defense of Elizabeth City.

I found a battery (about 2 miles by water and about 3 by land) with four 32-pounders and 28 rounds of ammunition; battery defective (magazine dangerous, if there had been any ammunition to put in it). General Mann promised to call out the militia, and Colonel Starke endeavored to do so, but it seems they would not come. I tried to obtain 150 negroes to throw up traverse (three of the guns being enfiladed) and otherwise improve [the] battery, but could only, by 2 a. m. on the 9th, obtain 30 hands, whom I impressed.

Early on the morning of the 8th Commodore Lynch, with six steamers, arrived; had fought the day before, exhausting all his ammunition. Proposed to man the battery with crew of the lost steamer Curlew; to place therein additional guns, and moor schooner with two guns alongside battery. Colonel Martin received 200 pounds powder from Norfolk and 100 pounds blasting powder was found and made up into cartridges.

On the morning [of the] 9th, Commodore Lynch, having found a few rounds, steamed out with two steamers to reconnoiter enemy. Returned, chased by enemy's steamers, and determined to land crews and fight battery, expecting Captain Hunter with ammunition. It appeared that the militia would not come out without requisition from seven magistrates. This was obtained on the 9th. The naval officers were of opinion that the enemy would not attempt to pass battery until silenced. I undertook, with promise of a regiment of militia and expectation of a few companies, to prevent its being turned for some time.

On the evening of the 9th I moved out four pieces to rear of the battery for that purpose, leaving two pieces and wagons in Elizabeth City ready to move.

Early on the morning of the 10th the enemy's squadron hove in sight, and opened fire on battery, schooner, and steamers, and, as if aware of the helpless condition of all, steamed, after a few minutes, past the battery right up to the city.

Commodore Lynch told me in the battery that he was informed that the enemy had landed below, and a naval officer, galloping up, reported, after I left the battery, that the enemy in large force had landed and formed about a mile below. There were no militia, no one whatever to support the artillery, who have neither fire-locks of any kind nor side-arms. Two pieces were placed to keep the enemy as long as possible at bay, but in a few minutes the Federal steamers were perceived rapidly advancing past the battery toward the city, which they reached before the artillery (now ordered back) had got half way.

As the enemy, after reaching the wharf, had the town at their mercy, I detached Sergeant Scroggs, of Captain McComas' company, with a detail, to aid the citizens in destroying the place by fire, as I had been requested to do by some of the most prominent of them. They only partially succeeded, two blocks only having been burned and a few isolated houses in the suburbs. I retreated with the artillery by the old Edenton road, and halted on the night of the 10th at Newby's Bridge, 2 miles from Hertford, accompanied and guarded by General Mann, of the militia. I opened communication with Edenton and Hertford and sent for some of the transportation of the Fifty-ninth Virginia Volunteers, which was unprotected at the former place. The militia had not been embodied at either place, though the next day I received a dispatch from Colonel Moore, of Edenton, stating that on the requisition of any Confederate general he was ordered to call out his regiment, and could assemble 200 men, armed with muskets and shot-[guns] and with 10 rounds of ammunition each. In this region the militia will not assemble until the enemy is dangerously near. Then it becomes impossible to assemble them until they have attended to the moving of family and property. After that they show a disposition to come out if there is any force to support them.

Generally the population appear to be very true; there are, of course, some traitors, but far less disloyalty than in Western Virginia. A painful instance of the latter occurred a few miles from Elizabeth City on our march to Newby's Bridge. A man by the name of Lester deliberately shot a private who rode into his yard, and then barricaded himself in the upper rooms of his house, refusing to surrender. Captain Webb, quartermaster of artillery, went up to him unarmed and pledged himself to protect him from violence if he came out. After appearing to consent he suddenly and treacherously attempted to fire at the captain, and did fire afterward several times at the men. I ordered the house to be fired. He was driven by the smoke to the window and shot by one of the artillery. The man shot, Private Bransford, is in a very critical condition. Lester, it appears, was a very violent Union man, and had been waited on a month previous by a vigilance committee.

On the morning of the 11th I received a communication from Colonel Wright, of the Third Georgia Regiment, stating that he was 5 miles from Elizabeth City, with 400 of his regiment at South Mills, that 500 more were expected, and that he would wait to hear from me.

I marched on the 11th by what is called the Desert Road to this place with the artillery and a company of the Seventeenth North Carolina Volunteers, which (40 strong), under Lieutenant Lyons, reported to me the preceding night, being part of the force escaped from the naval battery opposite Roanoke Island.

On reaching Winton I found that Colonel Wright had left for Norfolk. This day I remained here, taking up positions and opening communication with Elizabeth City.

The remainder of Colonel Wright's regiment arrived last night, and this afternoon a battery of artillery. I had ordered four companies of Colonel Wright's regiment, with one gun, and was about to make a night reconnaissance of Elizabeth City, when I received the order from Brig. Gen. H. A. Wise to join him at the Albemarle and Chesapeake Canal, whither I proceeded with the artillery in the morning.

At 10 p. m. I received a note from Colonel Wright, informing me that he had arrived at South Mills, and desiring that his companies should not proceed to-night. In consequence of not knowing whether he ranked me or had any special orders from you I have abandoned the reconnaissance, but send a small party of artillery soldiers, with teams, to bring off, if possible, a wagon and caisson which had stalled in Elizabeth City, but had been dragged off and concealed about a mile on this side.

I would beg, respectfully, to call your attention to the case of Sergeant Scroggs. According to the report of the citizens Scroggs was double-ironed on board a Federal vessel in the river, and the Federal officers talked of trying and hanging him as an incendiary. Sergeant Scroggs, son of a Virginia senator, is a gentleman and a soldier, and was acting in obedience to orders from me, of which I am willing to assume the responsibility. I should have sent a flag of truce to-morrow to the enemy but for the fact of having to march. I leave his case, general, in your hands.

Very respectfully,

C. F. HENNINGSEN,
Colonel Fifty-ninth Regiment Virginia Volunteers,
Commanding Artillery of Wise Legion.

General HUGER, *Commanding.*

P. S.—   FEBRUARY 13, 1862—6 a. m.

The artillery detail has returned, bringing back the wagon, with baggage. They report only six Federal steamers in the river. The guns in the battery spiked and carriages burned.

[C. F. H.]

FEBRUARY 18-21, 1862.—Expedition to Winton, N. C., and Skirmish February 19.

REPORTS.

No. 1.—Brig. Gen. Ambrose E. Burnside, U. S. Army.
No. 2.—Col. Rush C. Hawkins, Ninth New York Infantry.

No. 1.

Report of Brig. Gen. Ambrose E. Burnside, U. S. Army.

HEADQUARTERS DEPARTMENT OF NORTH CAROLINA,
Roanoke Island, N. C., February 23, 1862.

GENERAL: Since my dispatch of the 20th, of which I inclose a duplicate,* the expedition up the Chowan has returned, having reached as

* See "Correspondence, etc.—Union," *post.*

far as Winton. On the approach of the gunboat Delaware to the town a negro woman was discovered on the shore motioning the boat to approach. On arriving within 300 yards of the landing a large ambush of from 600 to 1,000 men was discovered, and before the boat could be stopped she was within easy musket range of the men, when they poured a volley into her, literally riddling the wheel-house and the upper joiner work, but fortunately no one was killed; nearly all the men were below. Several of those on deck had ball-holes through their clothes. Captain Rowan, who was on deck, and Colonel Hawkins, in the rigging, made most miraculous escapes. The gunboats in the rear immediately hurried up, and by the use of a few shells dispersed the force, when the Ninth New York, under Colonel Hawkins, was landed. It was ascertained, after landing, that this negro woman had been sent down by her master, one of the captains, for the purpose of deceiving the boats, which was readily done, as it had been reported to the flag-officer and myself that but a few days before 500 loyal people at that place had raised the American flag. It was determined by Captain Rowan and Colonel Hawkins to burn all the military stores that could not be removed, with the store-houses and the quarters occupied by the troops, which constituted almost the entire town, there not being over twenty houses in the place. In one of the store-houses there was a large quantity of bacon, that could not be taken away by our people and it was also burned, together with all the heavy camp equipage, and, in fact, everything that could not be transported by our gunboats. The winds shifting after the fire was started caused the destruction of some few houses not occupied by the soldiers. It was ascertained during the stay at Winton that the Blackwater, the river up which the expedition was destined for the purpose of destroying the railroad bridge, had been effectually blockaded by the falling of trees across it at its narrowest parts, thus rendering it almost impassable. The expedition, therefore, returned, leaving some gunboats at Elizabeth City and at the mouth of the Chowan.

I have two expeditions organized in connection with the Navy to move upon Plymouth, at the mouth of the Roanoke, and Middletown, the outlet of Mattamuskeet Lake, the former commanded by Brigadier-General Foster and the latter by Brigadier-General Parke. They were to have started yesterday morning, but the dense fog that prevails here a greater part of the time prevented the possibility of the vessels moving in the sound. In my next I will send you duplicates of instructions given to these two generals. The enemy is, I learn, very much distracted by these frequent dashes on their coast, and seem to have but little idea where the next blow will be aimed. Before the end of the present week I hope to report to you some important movements, which are dependent upon the arrival of the naval ammunition, which has been hourly expected for several days. The health of the command continues excellent, and the drill and discipline is being perfected by the commanders of brigades.

Our supplies, particularly coal, are not arriving as rapidly as I could desire. Clothing sent to us from Philadelphia is now being issued, and we shall need an additional supply of fully the amount originally sent. The drawers and shirts are said to be very poor.

I have the honor to be, general, respectfully, your obedient servant,

A. E. BURNSIDE,
Brigadier-General, Comdg. Department of North Carolina.

Brig. Gen. LORENZO THOMAS,
Adjutant-General, Washington, D. C.

No. 2.

Report of Col. Rush C. Hawkins, Ninth New York Infantry.

STEAMER VIRGINIA,
Off Roanoke Island, N. C., February 21, 1862.

SIR : Agreeably to your orders of the 17th instant I called upon Captain Rowan, and made arrangements to embark my regiment on board of some of the gunboats of his division for the purpose of proceeding up the Blackwater and Nottoway Rivers and destroying the bridges of the Seaboard and Roanoke Railroad.

At 12 m. of the 18th instant the regiment embarked and the expedition got under way, and that night anchored off the mouth of the Roanoke River, where it remained until 10 a. m. of the 19th instant, and then commenced its journey up the Chowan River. Nothing of importance occurred until about 3.30 p. m. The flag-steamer Delaware was about 1 mile ahead of any of the other boats. I was on the cross-trees of the mainmast, where I had been on the lookout for about two hours. The steamer was within 350 yards of the wharf at Winton when I discovered the high bank, which we were nearing very rapidly, was covered with Confederate soldiers. I immediately gave the alarm, but not in time to change our course until the steamer had got within 100 yards of the shore, when we received the whole fire of about 700 infantry or more, which continued until we had passed out of range up the river, where we turned around and commenced shelling the town, the enemy returning the fire with four pieces of artillery from the shore.

In the mean time the gunboat Perry, having come within range, commenced firing from below. Soon after the enemy was dislodged and retired, when the Delaware returned down the river, receiving four shots as she passed the wharf. The whole fleet came to an anchor about 7 miles below Winton. A consultation was held, and it was agreed to return the next morning and burn the town if found to be occupied by the rebels.

About 11.30 a. m. of the 20th instant our gunboats arrived and took their positions, some above, some below, and others opposite to the town, when our guns commenced firing, and in twenty minutes after my regiment landed, accompanied by three boat guns, under the command of Lieutenant Flusser, of the gunboat Perry. The guns were placed in positions so as to command the approaches to the town; the regiment drawn up in line awaiting the attack of the enemy. In the mean time parties of observation were sent out in all directions. It was soon ascertained that the enemy had retreated as soon as our force appeared in sight that morning, leaving everything behind except their arms and accouterments. Six companies of my regiment took possession of the main approach to the town, and I commenced making a personal inspection of all the buildings. I found that nearly all of them had been taken possession of and had been occupied by the Confederate troops as quarters and store-houses (see Exhibits A and B).*
I then ordered that every building containing stores for the enemy and occupied by them as quarters should be fired, and placed guards in the others to see that they were not disturbed or destroyed. The property destroyed belonging to the Confederate forces consisted of bacon, corn-meal, flour, sugar, powder, mess-pans, camp-kettles, knap-

---

* Omitted as unimportant.

sacks, haversacks, canteens, &c., the whole worth not less than $10,000.

This, I believe, is the first instance during the war on our side where fire has accompanied the sword. It is to be regretted that such severe measures have to be adopted; they can only be justified upon two grounds—first, retaliation for trying to decoy us into a trap at the time of the firing into the Delaware. Evidence of this is that a negress, the property of one of the Confederate officers, was sent down to the wharf by her master to beckon the boat in to the wharf, when we were all to be slaughtered, or in the words of the negress, "Dey said dat dey wan't goin' to let anybody lib at all, but was goin' to kill ebery one of 'em." I infer from this that we were to receive no quarter. Second, the buildings fired had been taken possession of by and were in the use of the rebel forces as store-houses and quarters, which forces had been raised, supported, and used by the States in rebellion for the purpose of subverting the Constitution and the laws of the United States.

From information obtained at Winton we came to the conclusion that it would be impossible for us to accomplish the original object and aim of the expedition, so it had to be abandoned.

The forces at Winton, as near as I could ascertain, consisted of the First Battalion North Carolina Volunteers (six companies), under the command of Lieut. Col. William T. Williams; one battery of light artillery; one company of the Southampton cavalry, and one or two companies of the North Carolina Militia, the whole under the command of Lieutenant-Colonel Williams.

I am happy to inform you that none of our forces were injured. The enemy sustained some loss from the fire of our gunboats on the 19th, but I am not able to state how many were either killed or wounded.

The troops under my command and the officers and sailors on board of the gunboats behaved exceedingly well, and performed all of their various duties with great promptness and alacrity.

I feel greatly indebted to Commodore S. C. Rowan and the lieutenants of the U. S. Navy, in command of the gunboats, for their kind care and attention to the comforts and wants of my regiment, and also for their hearty co-operation in trying to carry out the object of the expedition.

I am, most faithfully, your obedient servant,
RUSH C. HAWKINS,
Colonel Ninth Regiment New York Volunteers.

Brig. Gen. J. G. PARKE.

MARCH 14, 1862.—Battle of New Berne, N. C.

REPORTS, ETC.

No. 9.—Col. Horace C. Lee, Twenty-seventh Massachusetts Infantry.
No. 10.—Brig. Gen. Jesse L. Reno, U. S. Army, commanding Second Brigade.
No. 11.—Lieut. Col. William S. Clark, Twenty-first Massachusetts Infantry.
No. 12.—Lieut. Col. Charles A. Heckman, Ninth New Jersey Infantry.
No. 13.—Col. Edward Ferrero, Fifty-first New York Infantry.
No. 14.—Col. John F. Hartranft, Fifty-first Pennsylvania Infantry.
No. 15.—Brig. Gen. John G. Parke, U. S. Army, commanding Third Brigade.
No. 16.—Col. Edward Harland, Eighth Connecticut Infantry.
No. 17.—Lieut. Col. Charles Mathewson, Eleventh Connecticut Infantry.
No. 18.—Col. Isaac P. Rodman, Fourth Rhode Island Infantry.
No. 19.—Maj. John Wright, Fifth Rhode Island Infantry.
No. 20.—Brig. Gen. L. O'B. Branch, C. S. Army.
No. 21.—Col. Reuben P. Campbell, Seventh North Carolina Infantry.
No. 22.—Lt. Col. Edw. Graham Haywood, Seventh North Carolina Infantry.
No. 23.—Col. S. B. Spruill, Nineteenth North Carolina Infantry.
No. 24.—Col. Zebulon B. Vance, Twenty-sixth North Carolina Infantry.
No. 25.—Maj. John A. Gilmer, jr., Twenty-seventh North Carolina Infantry.
No. 26.—Lieut. Col. Robert F. Hoke, Thirty-third North Carolina Infantry.
No. 27.—Col. James Sinclair, Thirty-fifth North Carolina Infantry.
No. 28.—Col. Charles C. Lee, Thirty-seventh North Carolina Infantry.
No. 29.—Lieut. Col. William M. Barbour, Thirty-seventh North Carolina Infantry.
No. 30.—Col. H. J. B. Clark, Special Battalion North Carolina Militia.
No. 31.—Lieut. J. L. Haughton, Macon Mounted Guards.

No. 1.

Reports of Brig. Gen. Ambrose E. Burnside, U. S. Army, with congratulatory order and communication from the Secretary of War.

HEADQUARTERS DEPARTMENT NORTH CAROLINA,
New Berne, March 16, 1862.

GENERAL: I have the honor to report that after embarking the troops with which I intended to attack New Berne, in conjunction with the naval force, on the morning of the 11th, a rendezvous was made at Hatteras Inlet. Flag-Officer Goldsborough having been ordered to Hampton Roads, the naval fleet was left in command of Commodore Rowan. Early on the morning of the 12th the entire force started for New Berne, and that night anchored off the mouth of Slocum's Creek, some 18 miles from New Berne, where I had decided to make a landing. The landing commenced by 7 o'clock the next morning under cover of the naval fleet, and was effected with the greatest enthusiasm by the troops. Many, too impatient for the boats, leaped into the water and waded waist-deep to the shore, and then, after a toilsome march through the mud the head of the column arrived within a mile and a half of the enemy's stronghold at 8 p. m., a distance of 12 miles from the point of landing, where we bivouacked for the night, the rear of the column coming up with the boat howitzers about 3 o'clock next morning, the detention being caused by the shocking condition of the roads, consequent upon the heavy rain that had fallen during that day and the whole of that night, the men often wading knee-deep in mud, and requiring a whole regiment to drag the eight pieces which had been landed from the Navy and our own vessels.

By signals agreed upon, the naval vessels, with the armed vessels of my force, were informed of our progress, and were thereby enabled to assist us much in our march by shelling the road in advance.

At daylight on the morning of the 14th I ordered an advance of the entire division, which will be understood by the inclosed pencil sketch.* General Foster's brigade was ordered up the main county road to attack the enemy's left, General Reno up the railroad to attack their right and General Parke to follow General Foster and attack the enemy in front, with instructions to support either or both brigades.

I must defer for want of time a detailed account of the action. It is enough to say that after an engagement of four hours we succeeded in carrying a continuous line of field work of over a mile in length, protected on the river flank by a battery of thirteen heavy guns and on the opposite flank by a line of redoubts of over a half a mile in length for riflemen and field pieces, in the midst of swamps and dense forests, which line of works was defended by eight regiments of infantry, 500 cavalry, and three batteries of field artillery of six guns each. The position was finally carried by a most gallant charge of our men, which enabled us to gain the rear of all the batteries between this point and New Berne, which was done by a rapid advance of the entire force up the main road and railroad, the naval fleet meantime pushing its way up the river, throwing their shots into the forts and in front of us.

The enemy, after retreating in great confusion (throwing away blankets, knapsacks, arms, &c.) across the railroad bridge and county road bridge, burned the former and destroyed the draw of the latter, thus preventing further pursuit, and causing the detention in occupying the town by our military force, but the naval force had arrived at the wharves and commanded it by their guns. I at once advanced General Foster's brigade to take possession of the town by means of the naval vessels, which Commodore Rowan had kindly volunteered for the purpose. The city was set on fire by the retreating rebels in many places, but owing to the exertions of the naval officers the remaining citizens were induced to aid in extinguishing the flames, so that but little harm has been done. Many of the citizens are now returning, and we are now in quiet possession of the city. We have captured the printing press, and shall at once issue a daily sheet.

By this victory our combined force have captured eight batteries containing forty-six heavy guns, three batteries of light artillery of six guns each, making in all sixty-four guns; two steamboats and a number of sailing vessels, wagons, horses, a large quantity of ammunition, commissary and quartermaster stores, forage, and the entire camp equipage of the rebel troops, a large quantity of rosin, turpentine, cotton, &c., and over 200 prisoners.

Our loss thus far ascertained will amount to 91 killed and 466 wounded, many of them mortally.† Among these are some of our most gallant officers and men. The rebel loss is severe, but not so great as our own, being effectually covered by their works.

Too much praise cannot be awarded to the officers and men for their untiring exertion and unceasing patience in accomplishing this work. The effecting of the landing and the approach to within a mile and a half of the enemy's work on the 13th I consider as great a victory as the engagement of the 14th. Owing to the difficult nature of the landing our men were forced to wade ashore waist-deep march through mud to a point 12 miles distant, bivouac in low, marshy ground in a rain-storm for the night, engage the enemy at daylight in the morning, fighting them for four hours amid a dense fog, that prevented them

---

* Not found.   † But see revised statement, p. 211.

from seeing the position of the enemy, and finally advancing rapidly over bad roads upon the city. In the midst of all this not a complaint was heard; the men were only eager to accomplish their work. Every brigade, and in fact every regiment, and I can almost say every officer and man of the force landed was in the engagement. The men are all in good spirits, and under the circumstances are in good health. I beg to say to the General Commanding that I have under my command a division that can be relied upon in any emergency. A more detailed report will be forwarded as soon as I receive the brigade returns. The brigadier-generals, having been in the midst of their regiments whilst under fire, will be able to give me minute accounts.

I beg to say to the General Commanding the Army that I have endeavored to carry out the very minute instructions given me by him before leaving Annapolis, and thus far events have been singularly coincident with his anticipations. I only hope that we may in future be able to carry out in detail the remaining plans of the campaign. The only thing I have to regret is the delay caused by the elements.

I desire again to bear testimony to the gallantry of our naval fleet, and to express my thanks to Commodore Rowan and the officers under him for their hearty and cheerful co-operation in this movement. Their assistance was timely and of great service in the accomplishment of our undertaking.

I omitted to mention that there was a large arrival of re-enforcements of the enemy in New Berne during the engagement, which retreated with the remainder of the army by the cars and the country roads.

　　　I have the honor, general, to be, your obedient servant,
　　　　　　　　　　　　A. E. BURNSIDE,
　　　Brigadier-General, Commanding Department North Carolina.

General LORENZO THOMAS,
　　Adjutant-General U. S. Army.

　　　　　HEADQUARTERS DEPARTMENT NORTH CAROLINA,
　　　　　　　　　　New Berne, March 21, 1862.

I have the honor to report the following movements in my department since my hurried report of the 16th instant. The detailed report of the engagement on the 14th is not yet finished, but I hope will be ready to send by the next mail:

As I reported, our forces occupied this city and succeeded in restoring it to comparative quietness by midnight on the 14th, and it is now as quiet as a New England village. I appointed General Foster military governor of the city and its vicinity, and he has established a most perfect system of guard and police. Nine-tenths of the depredations on the 14th, after the enemy and citizens fled from the town, were committed by the negroes before our troops reached the city. They seemed to be wild with excitement and delight. They are now a source of very great anxiety to us. The city is being overrun with fugitives from the surrounding towns and plantations. Two have reported themselves who have been in the swamps for five years. It would be utterly impossible, if we were so disposed, to keep them outside of our lines, as they find their way to us through woods and swamps from every side. By my next dispatch I hope to report to you a definite policy in reference to this matter, and in the mean time shall be glad to receive any instructions upon the subject which you may be disposed to give.

General Foster's brigade is still occupying the city and its suburbs, having pushed his advanced pickets on all the roads leading to Kinston between the Neuse and the Trent, some 9 miles out. I have also sent one regiment of his brigade, in conjunction with a naval force sent by Commodore Rowan, to make a temporary occupation of Washington. Scouting parties from his brigade have visited the country to the north of the Neuse and found everything quiet. Much Union feeling has been expressed, but the people are slow to take the oath of allegiance, evidently 'from a fear that we will not be able to maintain our position here, in which case they would be driven from their homes. Confidence is being restored, however, to a certain extent, and the people of the city are returning to their homes.

I have taken the responsibility, as I did at Roanoke, of issuing provisions to the poor, who were and have been for some time suffering for food. In fact, I have had to order issues made in some cases to persons who have but lately been in affluent circumstances, but who now have nothing but Confederate notes, city shin-plasters, worthless notes of hand, unproductive real estate, and negroes who refuse to acknowledge any debt of servitude. The suffering and anxiety is far beyond anything I had anticipated. It seems strange to me that these people will not perceive that this state of things has been brought about by their own injudicious and disloyal conduct.

General Reno's brigade occupy the south side of the Trent, his advanced pickets extending down the railroad as far as Croatan out to the edge of the swamps and up the Trent some 4 miles to the first bridge above the railroad bridge, the draw of which was destroyed by the rebels, but has since been repaired by our men, thus opening communication with the city to our supply trains and artillery. I have also established a steam ferry, which runs every fifteen minutes, communicating with his headquarters. One of his regiments has been sent up the south side of the Trent, to burn all the bridges on the stream for 30 miles above the one held by us.

I have sent General Parke's brigade to invest and, if necessary, besiege Fort Macon. A personal reconnaissance of Slocum's Creek demonstrated that the railroad could be reached by our light-draught steamers at Havelock Station, thus saving more than one-half the march to Morehead City. The small hand cars brought with the expedition have been of great service in transporting his baggage, stores, &c. He has reached Morehead City by this time, and I shall go down to-morrow, and hope by the next mail to report considerable progress. His instructions are, first, to demand an unconditional surrender of the place, and in case of refusal to begin his work at once and reduce it in the shortest possible time. He has, I think, ample force and means to accomplish it, the General Commanding the Army having instructed me to prepare for it before leaving New York.

And I now beg to say that, in order to move upon the interior of the State, I will require considerable re-enforcements—a regiment of cavalry, two more batteries of artillery, and enough regiments of infantry to make a division out of each one of my brigades. I sincerely hope that the Department may deem it for the interest of the public service to promote each of my three brigadier-generals to either the actual or brevet rank of major-general and place them in command of the divisions. They are eminently qualified for the position, and have, by their untiring industry, their great skill, and conspicuous gallantry under most trying circumstances, earned the right to promotion.

You can scarcely imagine, Mr. Secretary, the amount of patient labor that has been expended in bringing this little command up to this point. If we can have the regiments to make the divisions, we have the material here in the commanders of our regiments to command the brigades.

I see by a recent act of Congress that commanders of departments are allowed an increase of staff. I inclose herewith some nominations for your consideration.

I have the honor to be, sir, your very obedient servant,
A. E. BURNSIDE,
Brigadier-General, Commanding Department North Carolina.

Hon. E. M. STANTON,
Secretary of War, Washington.

P. S.—We shall want with the re-enforcements the usual amount of wagons, horses, clothing, &c.

HEADQUARTERS DEPARTMENT OF NORTH CAROLINA,
New Berne, April 10, 1862.

I have the honor to make the following detailed report of the battle of New Berne, as promised in my hurried report of the 16th ultimo:

After embarking my command, consisting of the brigades of Generals Foster, Reno, and Parke, at Roanoke Island on the morning of the 11th, the transport fleet, in conjunction with the naval fleet, arrived without accident off the mouth of Slocum's Creek, in the Neuse River, some 16 miles from New Berne, on the evening of the 12th, where we anchored for the night. Soon after anchoring I called the three general officers in council, and after consultation with Commodore Rowan we decided to land at the mouth of Slocum's Creek on the following morning under cover of the naval guns, and proceed up the direct road to New Berne, our advance to be designated by signal rockets from the head of the column, thus enabling the Navy and our armed transport vessels to shell the road in advance of us.

At 6.30 the following morning I hoisted the preparatory signal. The naval vessels, with the gunboat Picket, moved in toward the mouth of the creek and shelled the woods some distance in advance of us. A reconnaissance was made to ascertain the depth of water by the gunboat Delaware, Captain Quackenbush, and by Mr. H. H. Helper, with the boat's crew of the Alice Price. After receiving their reports the signal for landing was hoisted, the light-draught steamers and surf-boats having been previously filled with our men, and in twenty minutes some three regiments were on shore. The steamers having grounded, the men on them leaped overboard and waded to the shore, holding their cartridge-boxes out of the water. The enthusiasm with which this work was accomplished cannot be excelled. As the colors of each regiment were planted on the shore the men rallied to them, and their proper formations were soon made. The steamers and boats returned to the fleet for more troops, and the landing was continued, under the direction of my chief quartermaster, Capt. Herman Biggs, until the whole force detailed for the attack had reached the shore except the field artillery and some of the infantry that had not arrived from Hatteras Inlet.

In the mean time I had landed my staff, and detailed Capt. R. S. Williamson, Topographical Engineer, to move on in advance of the column for the purpose of reconnoitering the positions of the enemy. I detailed my aides Lieutenants Pell and Fearing to accompany him, and requested him to call on General Foster for two of his aides, and Lieutenants Strong and Pendleton were detailed to accompany him.

The six naval boat howitzers, under command of Lieutenant McCook, having landed, I ordered a detail of a regiment from General Reno's brigade to assist in hauling them over the road, which was so bad that it was impossible for them to be dragged by the gunners. The Fifty-first Pennsylvania was detailed for this service. I then moved on to the head of the column, and found it had reached the first intrenchment at Otter Creek, some 6 miles up, which had been deserted by the enemy. Captain Williamson, having discovered this fact and previously reported it to General Foster, proceeded on with his party to make a further reconnaissance. After obstructing the railroad at this point, I ordered General Foster to move up the main county road with his brigade and General Reno to move his brigade up the railroad, leaving orders for General Parke to follow with his brigade up the county road. Soon after starting the columns Captain Williamson reported to me that a line of breastworks, broken by a redan for field pieces, along the bank of the river a mile in advance, had also been deserted by the enemy. I visited this work, accompanied by Generals Foster and Reno, where we communicated with the fleet.

Overtaking the head of the column, the march was continued until my own staff officers and those of the different brigades who were acting as escort to Captain Williamson came in contact with the enemy's pickets. It then being nearly 8 o'clock, I ordered a halt, and directed General Foster to bivouac on the right and left of the county road in a line at right angles to it, ordering one regiment to occupy the road leading down to the fortifications on the river. General Reno's brigade occupied a corresponding advanced position across the railroad a half mile to the left and General Parke occupied a position immediately in rear of and parallel with General Foster. It rained all night, as it had done during the day, so that our men passed a most cheerless night. The Fifty-first Pennsylvania, with the naval boat howitzers, under Lieutenant McCook, together with two guns landed from the Cossack and Highlander, under Captains Bennett and Dayton, did not reach my headquarters till 3 o'clock in the morning. Too much praise cannot be awarded to the officers and men who performed this very arduous service, as these eight pieces constituted our entire artillery force during the engagement of the next day.

Soon after leaving the landing I determined not to land the light batteries of Captains Belger and Morris and our wagons at Slocum's Creek, and sent an order to Captain Biggs to move up the river and land them at the deserted intrenchment above the mouth of Otter Creek, but the dense fog that prevailed during the afternoon and night made it impossible to land anything, and it was equally impossible to communicate from shore with the fleet by signals, as agreed upon.

On the following morning I ordered Captain Williamson to move forward and reconnoiter the position of the enemy, which was known to be not far in advance of our pickets, from information obtained during the night from negroes and others, to the effect that they were posted behind a long line of intrenchments leading from the river across the county road to the railroad. The brigades were formed and ordered to advance as follows: General Foster to move up the county road and attack the enemy's front and left, General Reno to move up the railroad and, if possible, turn the enemy's right, and General Parke to move up the county road as a reserve. I also ordered General Parke to detail the Eleventh Connecticut to relieve the Fifty-first Pennsylvania in dragging up the boat howitzers, and their work was done in an efficient and prompt manner. The head of the columns very soon came within range of the enemy's artillery, and the following dispositions were made: General Foster placed the Twenty-fifth Massachusetts, Colonel Upton, and the Twenty-fourth .Massachusetts, Colonel Stevenson, in line of battle on the right of the county road parallel with the enemy's intrenchments; the six navy boat howitzers, under Lieutenant McCook, with the howitzers of Captains Dayton and Bennett, across the road, and the Twenty-seventh Massachusetts, Colonel Lee, and the Twenty-third Massachusetts, Colonel Kurtz, in line of battle on the left of the road.

The enemy then opened fire, both musketry and artillery, upon General Foster's lines. General Reno then, moving briskly forward with his brigade along the railroad, ordered a charge of the right wing of the Twenty-first Massachusetts, Lieutenant-Colonel Clark, on the the brick-kiln, just in the rear of the main line of intrenchments, which was entirely successful. He at the same time ordered the left wing of the Twenty-first Massachusetts, Major Rice; the Fifty-first New York, Colonel Ferrero; the Ninth New Jersey, Colonel Heckman, into line of battle on the left of the railroad, with a view of supporting the Twenty-first Massachusetts, holding the Fifty-first Pennsylvania, Colonel Hartranft, in reserve; but he soon found that instead of the enemy's right being on the railroad it extended to a point some three-quarters of a mile beyond, and they were posted along the whole line in a series of redans separated from him by fallen trees and an almost impassable swamp. He soon found himself engaged along the whole line, and was unable to support Colonel Clark, who was soon after compelled to return from the brick-kiln from the attack of an overwhelming force. General Foster ordered the Tenth Connecticut, Colonel Drake, to interline on the left of the Twenty-third Massachusetts. I then ordered General Parke's brigade to take a position in the intermediate space between General Foster and General Reno, and to support whichever brigade needed it. His brigade was formed in the following order, beginning at the left: The Fourth Rhode Island, Colonel Rodman; the Eighth Connecticut, Colonel Harland; the Fifth Rhode Island, Major Wright. The Eleventh Connecticut, which had brought up the boat howitzers, I held as reserve. Soon after this, learning from General Foster that the Twenty-seventh Massachusetts had exhausted its ammunition, I ordered the Eleventh Connecticut, Colonel Mathewson, to report to General Foster for their support.

The engagement was now general all along the whole line. It had been previously ascertained, by the reconnaissance of Captain Williamson, that the enemy had many pieces of field artillery behind their intrenchments, and on their left flanks there was a river battery with four 32-pounders, pivot guns, which enfiladed our lines. Having ordered to General Foster the last of my reserve, I sent word to General Parke to push on through the timber and pass the enemy's right. I then proceeded to the left of our lines to communicate with General Reno, where I found his brigade very hotly engaged with the enemy.

In the mean time Colonel Rodman, of the Fourth Rhode Island, had met Colonel Clark, of the Twenty-first Massachusetts, who informed him that he could get in rear of the enemy's intrenchments by charging down the railroad directly upon the brick-kiln, which he at once did, under a galling fire from the rifle pits in front of General Reno, and was supported by the remainder of the brigade, by order of General Parke, planting their colors upon the parapet. ·

The brigade then moved rapidly down the line of intrenchments, the Fourth Rhode Island leading, clearing it of the enemy as they advanced and capturing their guns. General Foster, seeing our forces inside of the enemy's lines, immediately ordered his brigade to charge, when the whole line of breastwork between the railroad and the river were by this combined movement of the two brigades most gallantly carried, the enemy retreating in the greatest possible confusion. After the cheers of our men had subsided it was discovered from the sharp firing on our left that General Reno was still engaged with the enemy, upon which General Parke moved back, with a view, if possible, of getting in the rear of the enemy's forces in the intrenchments to the left of the railroad. General Foster also moved foward with one of his regiments farther to the right, with a view to getting in their rear. General Parke, having reached an advantageous position to the right of the brick-kiln and in rear of the redans, by a heavy fire very much staggered the enemy, when General Reno ordered the Fifty-first Pennsylvania, Colonel Hartranft, to charge the enemy's line, which charge was supported by the remainder of his brigade, causing the enemy to desert his works in great confusion.

At this juncture General Foster appeared in their rear with one of his regiments, thus cutting off their retreat, and received from Colonel Avery an unconditional surrender of himself and over 200 men. The Twenty-first Massachusetts was left in charge of the prisoners. The remaining force at that point moved along the railroad directly for New Berne. In the mean time I had conducted the four regiments of General Foster's brigade on the county road in pursuit of the enemy, and at the crossing of the county road and railroad the column came together, General Foster's brigade consolidated and moved on, General Reno's brigade following. I ordered General Parke's brigade to follow the county road, and if possible save the bridge over the Trent from destruction. I then joined the head of General Foster's brigade, and soon after discovered that the railroad bridge and part of the city were on fire. Upon arriving at the head of the bridge I halted the brigades, and after visiting the city, in company with Generals Foster and Reno and consulting with Commodore Rowan, I ordered General Foster to move across to the city and occupy it. Having discovered that the draw of the county bridge had been destroyed, I sent an order to General Parke to proceed no farther, but to bivouac for the night.

Of what has happened since that time I have already sent you detailed accounts. For a more perfect understanding of the exact movements of the different brigades I beg to refer you to the very accurate reports of my brigadier-generals. I also beg to refer you to the report of Captain Williamson and to the accompanying sketch* for a more accurate knowledge of the nature and position of the enemy's intrenchments as well as our own position in the battle. The endurance and courage displayed by our officers and men from the moment they landed at Slocum's Creek until they reached New Berne was beyond anything I could have expected. The road from the landing to Croatan, a distance of 6 miles, was newly cut, and consequently almost impassable, and continually rendered worse by the rain, the march of the troops, and the wheels of the artillery.

I have before mentioned that the rear of the column, with the artil-

---

* Not found.

lery, did not reach our position in front of the enemy's until 3 o'clock in the morning. Both officers and men bivouacked in the open fields and swamps in order of battle, catching such rest as they could, the rain falling constantly during the night. At daylight the next morning the regiments were in line, and soon the brigades commenced filing off to take their positions closer to the enemy's works. When I started from my headquarters for the head of the column I felt that we were going to the fight under most unfavorable circumstances, and expected to find the men fagged and leg-weary, but as I passed regiment after regiment their hearty cheers and firm step convinced me that I had underestimated them.

On reaching the turn in the road where they first came under fire of the enemy's cannon the only change I could perceive in their demeanor was an over-anxiety to keep their ranks well closed, and they filed to their positions, under the direction of their brigadier-generals, with all the regularity and steadiness of veteran soldiers. For more than three hours the contest continued, the fog being so dense at times that the position of the enemy could only be ascertained by the rattle of their musketry and the roar of artillery. The result has proved what work they can do under such trying circumstances. In the midst of all the privations since we left Fortress Monroe the most marked feature that has been demonstrated in the character of these men is their extreme patience. With men of less patience and subordination the work could not have been accomplished.

I cannot mention personal instances of gallantry where all have behaved so nobly. To the reports of Generals Foster, Reno, and Parke, who were always with their brigades in the thickest of the fight, as well as to the reports of the colonels of the regiments, who commanded by example as well as authority, I beg to refer you for details. To them and their brave officers and men the country owes every success which has been obtained during the campaign, and I am sure their services are appreciated.

By the inclosed report of Brigade Surg. W. H. Church, our medical director, it will be seen that our loss was overestimated in my hasty report the day after the battle. The accompanying lists show 88 killed and 352 wounded.[*] Among these names are some of our most valuable officers and men. They are sad losses to us and to their relatives and friends. They nobly gave up their lives in defense of their country, and a debt of gratitude is due from every American citizen to the wives, mothers, and fathers who have laid such sacrifices on the altar of their country. They have my heartfelt sympathy, and I constantly pray that but few more such sacrifices will be required for the breaking up of this unholy rebellion. The memories of the brave dead will ever be green in the hearts of their countrymen and the scars of the wounded will be honorable passports for them through life.

As indicated in the beginning of my report, the plan of attack contemplated the co-operation of the Navy, which was most successfully carried out. As we moved along the road their shells fell in advance of us, and as we approached the rear of each rebel fortification their shells dropped inside the parapets, and by this combined movement the enemy was forced to fly in the greatest confusion. In this instance as well as in every other where it has been needed the most perfect understanding and co-operation have existed between the two arms of

---

* But see revised statement, p. 211.

the service since we joined the naval fleet at Hatteras Inlet. I need hardly say that these brave officers and sailors are bound to us by the strongest ties of friendship and companionship in arms.

The armed transports of the fleet in this instance, as in every other, have shown that they have been most efficiently managèd, and in speaking of the services of this command I always include all the transports of the fleet. The gunboat Picket, Capt. T. P. Ives, rendered marked service in this engagement as well as at Roanoke and elsewhere.

The duties of the officers and attendants of the medical staff have been most arduous both during and since the battle and most nobly have they fulfilled their mission, displaying in all instances both skill and courage.

Some of the results of this battle may be enumerated as follows: The capture of nine forts, with forty-one heavy guns; two miles of intrenchments, with nineteen field pieces; six 32-pounders not in position; over 300 prisoners; over 1,000 stand of small-arms; tents and barracks for 10,000 troops; a large amount of ammunition and army supplies; an immense amount of naval stores, for which I refer you to Commodore Rowan's report; the second commercial city in the State of North Carolina; the entire command of the Albemarle and Pamlico Sounds; the capture of Beaufort, Carolina, and Morehead Cities, and the complete investment of Fort Macon, which we hope soon to reduce. The prisoners belonging to this city I have released on their parole, together with the sick and wounded. The remainder, some 160, I have sent to New York. I hope my course in releasing the sick and wounded and the citizens of this place will meet the approval of the Department, and I should have been glad to have released them all had the enemy fulfilled their engagement made with me when I released the Roanoke prisoners.

I cannot close this report without paying a just tribute of praise to the members of my staff, who have so nobly aided me in every effort in the accomplishment of this work. Dr. Church, after designating the positions for hospitals and performing other duties devolving upon him as medical director, rendered me most efficient service in directing troops and carrying orders. Captain Richmond, my assistant adjutant-general, and Lieutenants Pell and Fearing accompanied me on the field, where they displayed great gallantry and skill.

Capt. Herman Biggs, my chief quartermaster, rendered most important service in directing the debarkation of troops and the movement of our supply transports. From the organization of this expedition in New York last September his work has been arduous and unremitting, and the fact that no call for anything which appertains to his department has been unsatisfied is sufficient evidence of the efficiency with which he has performed his work. He has been and was in this instance most nobly seconded by Captains Cutting and Loring. Capt. R. S. Williamson, chief topographical engineer, made some most daring reconnaissances, and by his skill and courage has commanded the respect of and endeared himself to the whole command. Capt. E. R. Goodrich, my chief commissary, and Captain D'Wolf, in this instance as in all others, have shown marked efficiency in the discharge of the duties of their department under the most trying circumstances. Lieutenant Flagler, my chief ordnance officer, has constantly managed his department with great skill, and rendered most important aid in this instance. My private secretaries, Messrs. Larned and French, here as at Roanoke, accompanied the army on the field, ever ready to perform the duties required of them.

I mentioned in my first dispatch that the loss of the enemy was less than our own, but subsequent information has convinced me that it was much greater; that a large number of their killed and wounded were carried off in the cars there is no doubt, but in the absence of accurate information I refrain from making an estimate. It is never a source of pleasure to me to exaggerate the loss on either side, and could the same results have been obtained without the loss of a man it would have been a source of great gratification. Happily I have the opportunity of decreasing my former estimate of our own loss.

I have the honor to be, your very obedient servant,

A. E. BURNSIDE,
Major-General, Commanding Department North Carolina.

Hon. E. M. STANTON, *Secretary of War, Washington.*

———

GENERAL ORDERS, }   HDQRS. DEPT. OF NORTH CAROLINA,
No. 17.   }   *New Berne, March* 15, 1862.

The general commanding congratulates his troops on their brilliant and hard-won victory of the 14th. Their courage, their patience, their endurance of fatigue, exposure, and toil cannot be too highly praised. After a tedious march, dragging their howitzers by hand through swamps and thickets; after a sleepless night, passed in a drenching rain, they met the enemy in his chosen position, found him protected by strong earthworks, mounting many and heavy guns, and although in an open field themselves, they conquered. With such soldiers advance is victory.

The general commanding directs with peculiar pride that, as a well-deserved tribute to valor in this second victory of the expedition, each regiment engaged shall inscribe on its banner the memorable name, " New Berne."

By command of Brig. Gen. A. E. Burnside:

LEWIS RICHMOND,
Assistant Adjutant-General.

WAR DEPARTMENT,
Washington, D. C., March 22, 1862.

Major-General BURNSIDE:

GENERAL: The report of the late brilliant success of the United States forces under your command at New Berne has afforded the highest satisfaction to the President and to this Department and to the whole nation, and thanks for distinguished service are again tendered to you and to the officers and soldiers of your command.

Inclosed I have the pleasure to transmit your commission as a major-general, so gallantly won.

Re-enforcements have been ordered, and it will be the pleasure of the Department to strengthen and support you to the utmost extent within its power. If anything more than you have be needed for the safety of your command, the success of its operations, or the care, comfort, and attendance of the sick and wounded, you will please communicate to this Department, in order that it may be supplied.

The Adjutant-General has been instructed to communicate with you fully upon other subjects.

Respectfully, yours, &c.,

EDWIN M. STANTON,
Secretary of War.

No. 2.

Report of Capt. Robert S. Williamson, U. S. Topographical Engineers.

NEW BERNE, N. C., *March* 19, 1862.

SIR: In obedience to instructions from the general commanding the Department of North Carolina I have the honor to submit the following report of the reconnaissances made previous to the battle of March 14, near New Berne, together with a sketch of the defenses of that town:*

The fleet arrived near the mouth of Slocum's Creek, about 16 miles below New Berne, on the evening of the 12th instant, and the troops landed the next day on the northern bank of the creek. At 2 p. m. the whole force was on shore, and I was then directed to go in advance, to ascertain the position of the enemy. No cavalry had landed, but I was furnished with a horse, and Lieutenants Pell and Fearing, aides to General Burnside, being also mounted, were directed to accompany me. Taking a northwesterly direction, we soon came to the county road, which leads to the town, and followed it for five or six miles, when we reached the first of the enemy's works, consisting of a long breastwork at right angles to the road. This we found to be deserted. Passing on, we found at the distance of a quarter of a mile a well-traveled cross road leading to the river, about a half a mile distant. This we examined, and found it to terminate at a house near the river bank, on which was a line of breastworks broken by a redan for field pieces. This was also deserted, but according to the statement of a negro at the house it had been occupied by the rebel troops with field artillery during the night previous. I then returned to the head of the advancing column, where I found General Foster, to whom I reported, after which I again advanced on the road.

At various times I was joined by some of the staff officers of the different brigades, among whom were Lieutenants Pell and Fearing, of General Burnside's staff; Captain Potter, Lieut. Ed. N. Strong, Lieut. James H. Strong, and Lieut. James M. Pendleton, of General Foster's staff, and Lieutenant Reno and Lieutenant Morris, of General Reno's staff. There may have been others whose names I have inadvertently omitted, but having been but ten days in this department I have not yet learned the names of all the staff officers. Those whom I have mentioned cheerfully assisted in the reconnaissances. At one time, a little before sunset, Lieutenant Reno and myself rode at a gallop a couple of miles in advance, when suddenly, at a turn of the road, we came within 50 yards of a column of rebels in retreat, upon which we again returned and reported. Finally, when some distance in advance and accompanied by several staff officers, we came upon a small rebel advance guard of 3 or 4 mounted men, who hailed us, when we again returned to the head of the column. It being then after dark, the order was given to bivouac for the night. During the whole day it was cloudy, with rain at frequent intervals. The country traversed was in open pine timber.

In the morning there was a dense fog. Shortly after daylight I again went in advance to reconnoiter, accompanied by several staff officers. After going for a short distance through the pine woods we came to an open place, where the trees had been felled, which gave us a view of the enemy in force. They were in line behind an intrenchment perpendicular to the road, and extended as far as I could see on either hand—that is to say, about a half mile to the left and a quarter

---

* Not found.

of a mile to the right. The distance from them, as shown by a subsequent measurement, was 350 yards. I dismounted and examined them with a glass, but the fog was so dense it was difficult to determine the number of guns in sight, but one brass field piece was plainly to be seen immediately in front, which commanded the road. The number of infantry in sight I estimated to be from 3,000 to 4,000. We therefore turned back, but very soon met General Foster, at the head of the advancing column. In a few minutes General Burnside was on the spot, and immediately arranged for the attack. The firing commenced at about 8 o'clock and continued until about 1 p. m., when the intrenchments were in our possession. During the battle I acted as aide to the generals—particularly to General Burnside.

After the capture of this line of works the enemy was no longer to be seen, and in the afternoon our brigade occupied New Berne. Subsequently I rode with my assistants, Mr. H. C. Fillebrown and Mr. E. S. Walters, over the principal portion of the captured works, and prepared the accompanying hasty sketch of the defenses.

I have the honor to be, very respectfully, your obedient servant,

R. S. WILLIAMSON,
Captain, U. S. Topographical Engineers.

Capt. LEWIS RICHMOND, *A. A. G., Dept. of North Carolina.*

No. 3.

Reports of Surg. William H. Church, U. S. Army, Medical Director.

HEADQUARTERS DEPARTMENT OF NORTH CAROLINA,
New Berne, N. C., March 16, 1862.

GENERAL : I have the honor to submit the following report of the killed and wounded during the action of March 14, 1862 :

I arrived at the rear of the field of action about 8 o'clock a. m., and had just located the hospitals when the wounded made their appearance. Brigade Surg. J. H. Thompson located his hospital in the wood at the rear of the First Brigade, Actg. Brigade Surg. C. Cutter, of the Second Brigade, his on the left of our line, and Actg. Brigade Surg. H. W. Rivers, of the Third Brigade, established his in an open, well-sheltered wood, just to the right of the First Brigade. From the list of casualties you can well understand that the labor of the medical corps has been very severe, especially after the long march and comfortless night before the day of action. The conduct of Surg. George Derby and Asst. Surg. S. E. Stone, of the Twenty-third Massachusetts Volunteers, is deserving of special mention. Before the action opened I located them at a point which proved to be immediately in the range of the enemy's fire. They must have remained there two hours before I thought of their position, when I found them quietly performing their operations with the balls falling thick and fast. I immediately ordered Dr. D. to remove his wounded to a house in a more protected position, where he still remains, in charge of his own and many other wounded.

I submit a full list of each regimental surgeon's report to their respective brigade surgeons.

Of the various staff officers I do not hear of any serious injury, although your aide, Lieutenant Fearing, had a narrow escape from a round shot which struck the earth between his horse's feet, filling his eyes and face with sand and gravel. Lieut. J. M. Pendleton, of General Foster's staff, also had a narrow escape from a ball which passed through the sleeve of his coat. The wounded will be immediately removed to two comfortable hospitals in the city of New Berne. Surgeons Upham, Kneeland, Batchelder, and Clarke, from Massachusetts, joined us at Hatteras Inlet, and have been of great assistance both in the field and hospital.

I am, general, very respectfully, your obedient servant,

WM. HENRY CHURCH,
Brigade Surgeon and Medical Director.

HEADQUARTERS DEPARTMENT NORTH CAROLINA,
New Berne, April 9, 1862.

GENERAL: I herewith submit a revised and correct list of the killed and wounded at the battle of New Berne, on the 14th of March, 1862, compiled from the reports of the various brigade and regimental surgeons. Although the casualties are only reduced to 88, I am happy to find that the number wounded is much smaller than was at first supposed.* A large number of the wounded as they improve have been sent home, and those remaining are comfortably cared for in the Craverstreet Hospital, under the charge of Brigade Surg. J. Bryan, and in the Academy Green Hospital, placed in charge of Surg. George Derby, of the Twenty-third Massachusetts Regiment Volunteers. The wounds were unusually severe, and there have been several remarkable recoveries. The labor of the medical corps has been so great that I would once more respectfully urge upon you the absolute necessity for an increase of our surgical force, as, in addition to the sick of the transports, they are obliged to attend the sick of the town and negroes. The latter are now so numerous that it is necessary to open a hospital for their reception.

I am, general, very respectfully, your obedient servant,

WM. HENRY CHURCH,
Brigade Surgeon and Medical Director.

[Inclosure.]

Return of killed and wounded in action at New Berne, March 14, 1862.*

RECAPITULATION.

Regiment.	Killed.	Wounded.	Aggregate.
8th Connecticut	2	4	6
10th Connecticut	7	17	24
11th Connecticut	6	21	27
21st Massachusetts	16	40	56
23d Massachusetts	7	24	31
24th Massachusetts	10	43	53
25th Massachusetts	4	16	20
27th Massachusetts	9	43	52
9th New Jersey	3	46	49
51st New York	11	60	71
51st Pennsylvania	......	9	9
4th Rhode Island	11	21	32
5th Rhode Island	2	8	10
Total	88	352	440

* But see revised statement, p. 211.

[Addenda.]

Return of casualties in the Department of North Carolina, commanded by Brig. Gen. Ambrose E. Burnside, at the battle of New Berne, N. C., March 14, 1862.

[Compiled from nominal lists of casualties, returns, &c.]

Command.	Killed.		Wounded.		Captured or missing.		Aggregate.
	Officers.	Enlisted men.	Officers.	Enlisted men.	Officers.	Enlisted men.	
FIRST BRIGADE.							
Brig. Gen. JOHN G. FOSTER.							
23d Massachusetts	1	6	3	21	......	......	31
24th Massachusetts	......	10	4	41	......	......	55
25th Massachusetts	......	4	1	15	......	......	20
27th Massachusetts	1	8	2	41	......	......	52
10th Connecticut	......	7	2	15	......	......	24
Total First Brigade	2	35	12	133	......	......	182
SECOND BRIGADE.							
Brig. Gen. JESSE L. RENO.							
21st Massachusetts	1	14	2	40	......	......	57
51st New York	1	10	6	54	......	......	71
9th New Jersey	1	3	4	54	......	......	62
51st Pennsylvania	......	......	......	9	......	......	9
Total Second Brigade	3	27	12	157	......	......	199
THIRD BRIGADE.							
Brig. Gen. JOHN G. PARKE.							
4th Rhode Island	1	10	2	23	......	......	36
5th Rhode Island, 1st Battalion	1	1	......	8	......	......	10
8th Connecticut	......	2	1	3	......	......	6
11th Connecticut	1	5	......	21	......	......	27
Total Third Brigade	3	18	3	55	......	......	79
UNASSIGNED TROOPS.							
1st New York Marine Artillery, detachment	......	......	......	1	......	......	1
99th New York, Company B	......	2	1	6	1	......	10
Total unassigned troops	......	2	1	7	1	......	11
Total Department of North Carolina	8	82	28	352	1	......	471

No. 4.

Report of Brig. Gen. John G. Foster, U. S. Army, commanding First Brigade.

HEADQUARTERS GENERAL FOSTER'S BRIGADE,
Department of North Carolina, New Berne, March 20, 1862.

I have the honor to report that, in pursuance of the orders of General Burnside and in accordance with the plan of operations agreed upon, I proceeded to land my brigade on the 13th instant at Slocum's Creek. I took on board the Pilot Boy about 500 men of the Twenty-fourth Regiment Massachusetts Volunteers, and towing the boats of my brigade, carrying about 600 more, reached the mouth of the creek and landed without molestation. I landed with the first detachment, and instructed Captain Messinger to remain on the Pilot Boy and land the balance of my brigade. I had sent orders to form the Twenty-fourth and advance a short distance on the main road, and on landing I took command and moved on, giving the advance to the Twenty-first Regiment Massachusetts Volunteers, of General Reno's brigade, by order of General Burnside, assigning the advance to General Reno. I left an aide to form the regiments as they landed and to order them to follow.

I advanced on the main road, throwing out skirmishers and an advance guard of the Twenty-first Regiment Massachusetts, and at a distance of 6 miles I heard from Captain Williamson, of the Topographical Engineers, the result of a daring reconnaissance made by him, accompanied by Lieutenants Pell and Fearing, of General Burnside's staff, and by Lieutenants Strong, Pendleton, and Strong, of mine, discovering an abandoned breastwork. I then pushed on and entered the work, accompanied by General Reno, who had shortly before come up and assumed command of the Twenty-first Massachusetts. The work was found to be a breastwork, well constructed, and running in a straight line from the railroad to the river, a distance of about 1 mile, having a flank facing the railroad and a fort on the river flank. There were four flanking bastions for guns, and the fort was prepared for four guns. None were mounted, however. The troops were halted inside the fort to rest and eat. General Burnside then coming up, I, agreeably to his orders, advanced my brigade about 3 o'clock on the county road, General Reno being ordered to take the railroad track, which ran off to the left of the county road. We marched about 4 miles, halted, and bivouacked for the night near the enemy's position.

At daylight on the next morning (the 14th instant) I advanced my brigade, by order of General Burnside, until I came upon the enemy's position. General Parke was ordered to the left by General Burnside, and I made the following dispositions : The Twenty-fifth Massachusetts was thrown to the extreme right, followed in order by the Twenty-fourth Massachusetts in line of battle, their left resting on the county road, just on the left of which I placed the howitzer from the Highlander, under command of Captain Dayton, supported in line of battle on the left by the Twenty-seventh Massachusetts, and opened fire. On the arrival of the navy boat howitzers, under command of Lieutenant McCook, they were placed in line on the left of Captain Dayton's gun, and the Twenty-third was ordered to the left of the Twenty-seventh. The firing was incessant and very severe from the breastwork and within a very short range.

General Burnside arriving, I communicated to him the dispositions I had made, which he approved, sending over to General Parke to push on to the enemy's right, and leaving me to hold the point, he rode off to reach General Reno's position.

The Tenth Regiment Connecticut Volunteers, having arrived, were ordered to the left of the Twenty-third, and to support them, if rendered necessary by want of ammunition. This being the case, they formed on and to the left of the position of the Twenty-third and opened fire. Hearing from the Twenty-seventh that they were very short of ammunition, I ordered the Eleventh Connecticut, of General Parke's brigade, which had just come up, by order of General Burnside, to their support, and sent one of my aides to conduct them to their position. The Twenty-seventh Massachusetts then retired in good order, with orders to lie in a hollow, out of the fire, with fixed bayonets, and wait further orders.

The ammunition of the navy howitzers being nearly exhausted and one piece disabled, the Twenty-fifth Massachusetts were ordered to march by the flank and form so as to support the guns, leaving the Twenty-fourth on the extreme right. About twenty-five minutes from this time the head of General Parke's column, the Fourth Rhode Island, had reached the breastwork at the railroad crossing, and after a brisk fire pushed on and entered the breastwork in an opening left for the railroad track, and where the enemy's fire had much slackened in consequence of the steady and constant fire of the Twenty-third Massachusetts and Tenth Connecticut. This position of affairs being discovered, I ordered an advance along the line,. which was promptly obeyed, the enemy retreating with great precipitation.

On entering the breastworks sharp firing was still heard to the right of the enemy's position, and hearing from General Parke that he was engaged with the enemy's forces in their works to the right of the railroad, I led the Twenty-fifth Massachusetts to his support, and received the surrender of Colonel Avery and 150 men.

The breastwork we had entered was similar in construction to the abandoned one, running from Fort Thompson at the river to the railroad track, a distance of 1¼ miles, and from the railroad track rifle pits and detached intrenchments in the form of lunettes and redans followed each other for the distance of 1¼ miles and terminated by a two-gun battery.

Fort Thompson, a flanking bastion, mounted thirteen guns, all 32-pounders (two rifled), four of which were turned so as to bear upon our line. The breastwork was mounted by two complete field batteries, besides several pieces of heavy artillery, and manned by about 6,000 men. The force in men and artillery of the other defenses I am unable to give, they not coming under my observation.

Pressing forward then with my brigade, I reached the railroad bridge at New Berne, which being burned to prevent our following up the flying enemy, I rested the men on a field on the east bank of the Trent. By order of General Burnside, who had continued up with me, I shortly after crossed with my brigade over the river and encamped the regiments, with the exception of the Twenty-fifth Massachusetts, in the camp of the enemy (at the Fair Ground), the enemy having left all his camp equipage, and from appearances must have fled very precipitately, the Twenty-fifth being quartered in the town for police duty.

The fatigues and hardships of the march from Slocum's Creek I need not mention; the horrible state of the roads, the wearing labor it cost to drag for 12 miles the howitzers, the severity of the storm, and the wet ground of the soldiers' bivouac for the night, you well know.

I must mention in my brigade, where all behaved bravely, with particular praise the Twenty-fourth Regiment Massachusetts Volunteers and the Tenth Connecticut Volunteers. The former, under a severe fire from musketry in the front and exposed to a flanking fire of grape and canister from Fort Thompson, unprotected by the trees, behaved with marked coolness and steadiness. The latter advanced close under the enemy's fire in line of battle, fired with the most remarkable steadiness, and stood steadily up, giving and taking the most severe fire.

The naval howitzers, under command of Lieutenant McCook, Acting Masters Daniels and Hammond, Captain's Clerk Meeker, Captain Rowan's Clerk Gabaudan, Lieutenant Tillotson, Union Coast Guard, and Lieutenant Hughes, Union Coast Guard, were most admirably served during the day, and when the ammunition was exhausted they laid down by their pieces rather than to withdraw from their position.

Captain Dayton volunteered again to land and command the gun from the Highlander. His gun was first in position, and he served it, as before, with steadiness and efficiency. Lieutenant Tillotson, whose gun was disabled, rushed ahead after the action in pursuit with such speed as to be captured by the enemy.

From the joy of victory I must turn to mourn the price it cost in the soldier's death of Lieutenant-Colonel Merritt, of the Twenty-third Massachusetts, who fell early in the action whilst urging and cheering the men on bravely and gallantly, and of Lieut. J. W. Lawton, of the Twenty-seventh Massachusetts, shot dead on the field. Maj. Robert H. Stevenson, of the Twenty-fourth Massachusetts, was wounded in the leg, but stood up encouraging his men till forced to leave the field. Adjt. W. L. Horton, of the same regiment, was severely wounded by a grape shot in the shoulder whilst in the active performance of his duties, and Lieuts. Daniel Sargent and James B. Nichols were each slightly wounded. Capt. V. P. Parkhurst, of the Twenty-fifth Massachusetts, had his leg fractured. Lieuts. J. S. Aitchison and J. W. Trafton, of the Twenty-seventh, were slightly wounded. Capt. R. R. Swift also slightly wounded, and Lieut. George Warner had a foot shot off. Capt. Wesley C. Sawyer and William B. Alexander, of the Twenty-third Massachusetts, were both wounded, the former severely in the leg, rendering amputation necessary, and the latter in the hand. Lieut. T. W. B. Hughes, of the Union Coast Guard, was also wounded. Inclosed I send you a list of the killed and wounded, showing a total of 39 killed and 153 wounded.*

It is with much pleasure that I can report all of my staff as uninjured. They consisted during the day of Brigade Surg. J. H. Thompson, who volunteered in the early part of the fight to carry any order for me, and did so, till called elsewhere by his duties, under the hottest fire; of Capt. Southard Hoffman, assistant adjutant-general; Capt. E. E. Potter, acting commissary of subsistence; Lieut. J. F. Anderson, aide-de-camp; Lieut. J. M. Pendleton, aide-de-camp; Lieut. James H. Strong, aide-de-camp; Lieut. Edw. N. Strong, aide-de-camp; and Lieuts. J. L. Van Buren and R. T. Gordon, of the Signal Corps, who were used by me as aides. I most cordially bear my testimony to the conduct of the above-named gentlemen during the day as most worthy a gallant set of gentlemen. They were indefatigable in carrying orders, urging on men, and in placing the regiments, coolly and correctly obeying every order, and always under the heaviest fire. Without drawing any distinctions in the staff, I would take advantage of this opportunity to mention the names of Lieuts. James M. Pendleton and James H. and Edw. N. Strong as being volunteers who, without commission or enrollment, have acted during the entire campaign as aides, and performed every duty zealously and satisfactorily, and whose conduct during the day I have already spoken of, and to suggest that, under these circumstances, their services deserve a recognition, if not award, from the Government.

I also desire to return my thanks to the colonels of my brigade for the able assistance they rendered me during the day in promptly and correctly obeying, with the regiments under their command, my orders during the day. They were Col. Edwin Upton, Twenty-fifth Massachusetts Volunteers; Col. Thomas G. Stevenson, Twenty-fourth Massachusetts Volunteers; Col. Horace C. Lee, Twenty-seventh Massachusetts Volunteers; Col. John Kurtz, Twenty-third Massachusetts Volunteers; Lieut. Col. Albert W. Drake, Tenth Connecticut Volun-

---

* But see revised statement, p. 211.

teers; Lieut. Col. Charles Mathewson, Eleventh Connecticut Volunteers, and their reports are herewith inclosed.

I am, general, with great respect, your obedient servant,

J. G. FOSTER,
Brigadier-General, U. S. Army.

Capt. LEWIS RICHMOND, *Assistant Adjutant-General.*

No. 5.

Report of Lieut. Col. Albert W. Drake, Tenth Connecticut Infantry.

HDQRS. TENTH REGIMENT CONNECTICUT VOLS.,
New Berne, N. C., March 15, 1862.

SIR: I have the honor to report the part taken by the Tenth Regiment Connecticut Volunteers in the battle near New Berne of March 14, 1862.

At about 7.30 o'clock a. m. on the morning of that day we left our bivouac and advanced up the road leading to the city of New Berne. Although the men were chilled and wet from lying in the rain on the wet, cold ground during the previous night, and were much worn-down with fatigue from their march of the previous day, they advanced with alacrity. Arriving within about one-half a mile from the enemy's intrenchments, we encountered a severe fire from their batteries. I immediately filed the regiment through the woods toward the left, and arriving at a spot of low ground halted and waited orders. After some time had elapsed I received orders to form a line of battle and advance and open fire on the enemy. I immediately formed the regiment in line of battle, and advanced up the rising ground directly in front of their intrenchments, and, halting a little less than 300 yards, opened fire. For a short time we received in return a brisk fire from their artillery and infantry, but it was soon silenced. The men's ammunition getting short and the fire of the enemy having nearly ceased, we ceased firing and remained in our position.

Shortly after the enemy left their works. I followed on with the remainder of the brigade, and without further difficulty reached the Trent River at about 2.30 p. m. That evening the regiment was transported across the river and quartered in a deserted camp of the enemy near the city.

I have to say that all of the officers and men of the regiment did their whole duty during the engagement. Appended is a list of our killed and wounded during the action.*

Yours, very respectfully,

ALBERT W. DRAKE,
Lieutenant-Colonel, Comdg. Tenth Regt. Conn. Vols.

Capt. SOUTHARD HOFFMAN, *Assistant Adjutant-General.*

No. 6.

Report of Col. John Kurtz, Twenty-third Massachusetts Infantry.

HEADQUARTERS TWENTY-THIRD MASS. VOLS.,
New Berne, March 15, 1862.

DEAR SIR: I have the honor to report that at 8 o'clock in the morning of the 13th instant I received the order to disembark my regiment

---

* Embodied in statement on p. 211.

and land upon the shore, 16 miles below this post. Having but five
small boats, and one of my vessels being 3 or more.miles from shore, it
was not completed until near 3 o'clock in the afternoon. My regiment
marched forward with a 12-pounder howitzer as soon as possible after
landing, and arrived at the bivouac of this brigade at 8 o'clock in the
evening, where we slept as comfortably as possible during a night of
drenching rain. At 7 o'clock on the morning of the 14th I was ordered
by General Foster to take up the line of march and follow him. In
the course of half an hour I received an order from him to file into the
woods and form my regiment in line upon the left of the Twenty-seventh
Massachusetts, in front of the enemy's breastwork, and immediately
open fire upon him. The order was promptly executed. The fire was
incessant for one and a half hours within 150 yards of the enemy's
work, &c. My ammunition (40 rounds) was expended. I immediately
sent word to the general of my position and condition, and was assured
that a regiment would be sent to my relief. Accordingly in a few moments the Eleventh Connecticut reported to me. I immediately ordered
them to form in front of my line, and I fell back ten paces in good order,
fixed bayonets, and lay down ready to support the line in front of me.
After remaining in this position about thirty minutes a general charge
was made along the whole front, and we had carried the work and our
glorious old flag floated over it, and we gave nine rousing cheers.
I was immediately ordered by the general to send forward one company as an advance guard, and to follow with my regiment and feel
my way toward the enemy, now in full retreat, and to capture all
belligerents or enemies. We examined the woods, houses, and forts.
We took Dr. West, who reported himself a native of New Rochelle,
New York State, and a surgeon in the Confederate Army. I sent him
to headquarters. In the course of an hour we joined General Foster
with the Twenty-fifth Massachusetts at the railroad, about 2 miles from
this post, and marched along the road until we arrived at the bridge
across the Trent, which was on fire and entirely destroyed. After a
rest of an hour we embarked, crossed the river, and at 5 o'clock occupied the camp of the "chivalry," which appeared to have been left very
hastily, and which was being plundered by the negroes. I stopped the
plundering, took possession, and made myself as comfortable as possible for the night. The officers and men of my regiment behaved in
the most gallant manner, and I take great pleasure in saying that
Captains Brewster, Martin, Center, Howland, Whipple, Raymond, Sawyer, with their officers and men, particularly so Capt. E. G. Dayton, of
the schooner Highlander, volunteered to command the 12-pounder howitzer, and the persevering manner in which he and his men drew the
gun through the mud, in many places knee-deep, and the very gallant
manner in which they served it within a hundred yards of the enemy's
line, met my warmest approbation. They made every shot tell, and had
nearly or quite fired their last charge before they received any support.
My adjutant, Lieut. John G. Chambers, rendered me the most efficient
aid by the prompt and gallant manner in which he carried and executed
my orders, as well as by the alacrity in which he urged the men at the
most necessary points of the line. He comprehends without profuse
explanation my commands, and is a very efficient and gallant officer.
It is with the most sincere regret that I have to report the death of
Lieutenant-Colonel Merritt, who was killed early in the engagement
while urging his men into the line in the most brave and gallant manner.
His loss will be severely felt by the regiment. He was the kindest-
hearted man I ever met with, and I am sensibly affected at his loss.

Captain Sawyer, of Company H, had his left leg taken off by a round shot. Major Elwell behaved in the most gallant manner, and is a most capital and efficient officer, and performs his duty without ostentation, and can be depended upon.

Annexed please find a list of my killed and wounded.*

Very respectfully,

JOHN KURTZ,
Colonel, Commanding Twenty-Third Massachusetts.

Capt. SOUTHARD HOFFMAN, *A. A. G., First Brig., Coast Division.*

No. 7.

Report of Col. Thomas G. Stevenson, Twenty-fourth Massachusetts Infantry.

CAMP NEAR NEW BERNE, *March* 16, 1862.

SIR: I beg leave to report that on the morning of the 13th instant my regiment was on board the transports Guide and Vedette, which were at anchor in Neuse River, off the mouth of Slocum's Creek. Early in the morning I received the signal to prepare to land, and in accordance with the order of General Foster filled the boats belonging to my transports with a part of my men and fastened them to the stern of the steamer Pilot Boy, which came alongside the Guide and took the companies that remained on her. There was no opposition to our landing, and as soon as the men reached the shore I formed them in line of battle. By order of General Foster I then advanced my regiment in rear of the Massachusetts Twenty-first as far as the railroad, when I took the advance on the county road, sending Company E forward as an advance guard. I pushed forward as rapidly as the condition of the road would permit until night-fall, when, in accordance with General Foster's orders, I filed my regiment into the woods on the right of the road and bivouacked for the night. The men were somewhat worn-out by their exhausting march, but made themselves as comfortable for the night as circumstances would permit. I sent forward Companies A, E, K, and F as a picket guard, and we remained undisturbed during the night.

Early in the morning of the 14th instant a small party of the enemy's cavalry appeared within sight of our pickets and was fired upon, whereupon I immediately ordered my regiment to fall in. By order of General Foster I then advanced up the main road, with Company E as an advance guard, until within sight of the enemy's intrenchments, and then filed off to the right of the road, where I formed my regiment in line of battle and advanced forward to within about 50 paces of the edge of the woods, where I halted until my advance guard returned from the road. It was at this time the enemy opened fire, wounding 2 of my men. I immediately advanced my regiment out of the woods, where I ordered them to lie down and open fire. The men behaved very well in this position, keeping up incessant and well-directed fire on the enemy for over two hours.

Owing to the rain and wet to which the guns had been exposed many of my men experienced great difficulty in firing them, and in many cases had to draw the charges before their guns were of any use. Fort Thompson, on our right, which I supposed to have no guns on the land side, opened on us with grape and canister from their guns as soon as

---
* Embodied in statement on p. 211.

we got into position. We afterward found that they attempted to bring one of the guns on the water side of the battery to bear on our line but failed, probably from want of time. Finally I noticed the fire of the enemy's right slackened, as I supposed from the success and advance of our left. I immediately ordered my own regiment forward, and we had advanced but a short distance when the enemy turned, stopping only to give us one volley of musketry and a round of grape. The enemy retreated very precipitately from Fort Thompson as we entered, and I only succeeded in capturing six of them. I immediately raised the American flag on the parapet, to apprise the gunboats of our position.

By order of General Foster I left one company in the fort, selecting for that purpose Company B, and then marched my regiment forward on the county road to the railroad and up the railroad to the Trent River, where I halted them in a large field on the left. After remaining there a short time General Foster ordered my regiment to cross the river in the gunboat Delaware and other boats that he was using for that purpose, and to take possession of the rebel camp in the Fair Ground outside of New Berne. On reaching camp I found my men much exhausted by their severe labors since they had landed, but was pleased to find that there were comparatively few stragglers.

It pains me to close my report by informing you that my regiment lost 55 men in killed and wounded during the action, a list of whom I herewith transmit.*

THOS. G. STEVENSON,
Colonel Twenty-fourth Regiment Massachusetts Volunteers.

Capt. SOUTHARD HOFFMAN, Assistant Adjutant-General.

No. 8.

Report of Col. Edwin Upton, Twenty-fifth Massachusetts Infantry.

HDQR S. TWENTY-FIFTH REGIMENT MASS. VOLS.,
New Berne, N. C., March 17, 1862.

SIR : At about 6 a. m, of Friday, the 14th instant, I was ordered by General Foster to move from the bivouac occupied by my regiments during the night previous, and did so, following the Twenty-fourth Massachusetts Regiment. Proceeding along the main road about a mile I was ordered by General Foster to file to the right of the road, take position on the right of the 24th, and advance. The entire regiment had not cleared the road when the enemy opened fire from his artillery. I passed on to the position assigned me and advanced to the front some distance. Being desirous of ascertaining, if possible, the exact position of the enemy, I dispatched scouts to the right and front. They soon returned, reporting the enemy's earthworks in front, with what appeared to be a three-gun battery directly on our right. The enemy discovering our position and opening fire, we were exposed to a fire from the front and right, and at the same time a fire of shell was opened on us from the rear, which I supposed came from our own artillery or gunboats. We were thus in danger of being badly cut up, with no opportunity to retaliate. The fact being reported, I was ordered by General Foster to move to the support of the Twenty-seventh Massachusetts on the opposite side of the road. Moving in that

---

* Embodied in statement on p. 211.

direction we arrived at the road, and were then ordered by General Foster to support our battery stationed on the road. Taking our position in column by division, we remained there until ordered by General Foster to deploy and charge on the enemy's works. This was done, General Foster leading the charge, the enemy leaving at our approach. Passing into the works, the regiment was formed in line of battle, and I was ordered to move along the road in position for street firing. Having passed the enemy's camp, we filed to the left of the road, flanking. I was ordered to advance in line cautiously, as General Parke's brigade was expected to be on our left and front and General Reno to be turning the enemy's right. We advanced slowly, receiving a fire of musketry, which was at first supposed to come from the other brigades. Deploying two companies as skirmishers, with orders to proceed with caution, they soon discovered a body of the enemy and opened fire upon them. The skirmishers having assembled, the regiment advanced, and the enemy, to the number of about 150, surrendered to General Foster. The general ordered them placed in charge of Company H, Captain Moulton, and then ordered me to proceed down the railroad, which I did, arriving in New Berne at about 5 p. m. Herewith is a list of the casualties, showing 4 killed and 16 wounded.*

In consequence of illness and exhaustion consequent upon the very fatiguing march of the previous day and the night exposure in the drenching rain I was deprived of the assistance of Major McCafferty and Adjutant Harkness, the former of whom was obliged to fall behind just before the close of the action, the latter being left by the road side during the march before the enemy was discovered.

I would again in the highest terms of praise mention the efficiency and bravery of Lieut. Col. A. B. R. Sprague as fully sustaining his former high reputation.

Very respectfully, yours,

EDWIN UPTON,
Twenty-fifth Regiment Massachusetts Volunteers.

Capt. SOUTHARD HOFFMAN, *A. A. G., General Foster's Brigade.*

No. 9.

Report of Col. Horace C. Lee, Twenty-seventh Massachusetts Infantry.

HDQRS. TWENTY-SEVENTH REGIMENT MASS. VOLS.,
In Camp at New Berne, March 15, 1862.

I have the honor to submit the following report:

On Thursday, March 13, at the stated signal, we commenced landing troops, one company at a time (which was all the boat would accommodate), from each vessel—the Recruit and Ranger. Major Bartholomew was sent forward with the first company, and at 11 o'clock, four companies having landed, I went on shore and took command, leaving Lieutenant-Colonel Lyman to come forward with the balance. We marched up the road until night and then bivouacked as ordered and threw out pickets on our left flank, rear and right flank being protected by other regiments of the brigade. Our companies continued to arrive until midnight, when we had about 600 men. At daylight on Friday morning, hearing a rapid firing of musketry in front, I called in the pickets, ordered the men to fall in, and soon after, by order from General Foster, took up the line of march by flank in rear of the 25th. The

---
* Embodied in statement on p. 211.

first intimation we had that we were near the enemy was from a shell thrown directly up the road, but which passed without injury to the right of us. We immediately, by General Foster's orders, formed column by companies and forward into line, and advanced through the woods on the left of the road until we came in sight of the enemy, strongly intrenched directly in front. As soon as near enough to get a good range I gave the order to fire by wing and then by file, and continued in this manner, constantly cautioning the men to take deliberate aim before firing, until from the small amount of ammunition left I thought it best, not wishing to slacken the fire at all, to send to General Foster either for more ammunition or to be relieved. This I did by Captain Pendleton, of your staff, who had been with me from the first fire, and who rendered me good service in keeping the line unbroken. Not hearing from you, I sent Adjutant Bartlett, as we were then reduced to an average of 4 or 5 rounds, many of the men being out entirely. He returned with orders that we were to be relieved by the Eleventh Connecticut and were then to fall back to the rear. As soon as the Eleventh Connecticut came up and were in position I ordered the men to cease firing and lie down. We soon after marched in good order to the rear, and had been there but a few moments when we heard cheering, and having formed again to advance, were met by an aide with orders to form in the fort, the enemy having retreated. My intention had been not to fall back, though the word came to me that we were to do so, but to merely continue lying ready for a charge, if necessary; but at the solicitation of several of my officers I did so. Having come up to the fort, we were at once ordered to follow the Twenty-third, which we did until we arrived at the burning bridge at New Berne. We were soon after taken across the river in boats and established in the camp just vacated by the Seventh North Carolina Regiment. From the position we occupied our loss in wounded is quite large, though fortunately but 5 men killed, which I attribute to the fact that the shot from the rifles and cannon of the enemy passed over our heads; two-thirds of the wounds, so far as I can learn, being caused by balls from smooth-bore muskets. I have not received the surgeon's report, and cannot say for certain that this is so, but think it must be.

I might mention individual cases, as well among men as officers, who displayed unusual bravery and coolness, but where all did so well it is almost impossible, and perhaps impolitic, to do it. I can only say that with very few exceptions I was perfectly satisfied with the manner in which they obeyed my orders and stood up without shrinking to the most terrific fire.

Very respectfully, your obedient servant,

H. C. LEE,
Colonel, Commanding Twenty-seventh Regiment Mass. Vols.
Capt. SOUTHARD HOFFMAN, *Assistant Adjutant-General.*

No. 10.

Report of Brig. Gen. Jesse L. Reno, U. S. Army, commanding Second Brigade.

HEADQUARTERS SECOND BRIGADE,
New Berne, March 16, 1862.

CAPTAIN: I have the honor to report that in obedience to the orders of General Burnside I landed my brigade at the mouth of Slocum's

Creek, some 16 miles from New Berne, and proceeded at once to advance toward the railroad, where we expected first to meet the rebels. After a march of about 4 miles we arrived at a long line of deserted intrenchments, the rebels having abandoned them shortly before. Here I met General Foster, and, agreeably to the general commanding's orders, we awaited the arrival of the rest of the division. The general, soon coming up, ordered me to follow the railroad toward New Berne. The advance was continued until about 8 p. m., when the troops were ordered to bivouac. I was ordered by the general commanding to advance at daylight and attack the right of the rebel lines, but owing to the severe rain of the previous night I found that many of the muskets would not fire, so I ordered that all should discharge their load, drawing such as would not fire. After this my brigade moved forward along the railroad in the following order: Twenty-first Massachusetts, Fifty-first New York, Ninth New Jersey, and Fifty-first Pennsylvania. At about a quarter before 8 a. m. I heard General Foster's brigade hotly engaged, and in a few minutes I saw a large number of the enemy apparently engaged in getting a gun to bear on the railroad. I ordered the skirmishers to fire upon them, at the same time ordering the Twenty-first Massachusetts forward into line. The enemy now opened a brisk fire upon us from near the railroad, the skirmishers in advance replying briskly, and as soon as the right wing of the Twenty-first Massachusetts got into line I ordered Lieutenant-Colonel Clark to charge and take the brick-kiln, which was gallantly executed.

In the mean time I ordered my aides to bring up the balance of my brigade and form in line to the left of the Twenty-first Massachusetts, placing the Fifty-first Pennsylvania in reserve, supporting the extreme left of my line. Owing to the thick fog it was almost impossible to see the rebels, and not knowing that their line extended beyond the railroad, after having ordered Lieutenant-Colonel Clark to advance along the inside of the enemy's intrenchments, I returned across the railroad to bring up the rest of my brigade to his support, but finding the left wing of the Twenty-first Massachusetts and the Fifty-first New York hotly engaged in front and the enemy's lines extending far beyond my extreme left, I found it necessary to attack them in front, and as the ground was quite uneven I directed the regiments to advance as near as possible under cover of the ridges and pick off the enemy whenever their heads appeared above their line of intrenchments.

In the mean time the Ninth New Jersey also came into line and opened a well-directed fire upon a two-gun battery only some 200 yards in front of them, and so accurate was their fire that the enemy could only occasionally fire their guns. The battle now became general along our whole line, and raged fiercely for about three and a half hours. The Fifty-first Pennsylvania was held in reserve during this time, and although exposed to a severe fire, Colonel Hartranft did not allow a single shot to be fired, but directed the men to lie down, and thus saved them from much loss.

It having been reported to me that the regiments engaged had expended nearly all their ammunition, I ordered Colonel Hartranft to send one wing of his regiment to relieve the Fifty-first New York, which had suffered very severely. As soon as they arrived I ordered Lieutenant-Colonel Bell to pass the Fifty-first New York, deliver one volley, and then charge upon the enemy's intrenchments. At the same time I sent orders to the Ninth New Jersey and the remainder of the Fifty-first Pennsylvania to charge. All this was gallantly executed, and the rebels fled precipitately from all their intrenchments. Some 50 prisoners were captured in these works, many severely wounded. Upon reaching the rebel intrenchments I was rejoiced to see our flag waving along the entire line of the enemy's works, General Parke's brigade having previously stormed and captured their center batteries and General Foster's their left.

At the commencement of the action I left Lieutenant-Colonel Clark with his right wing inside of the enemy's intrenchments, ordering him to proceed along their lines toward their left, where General Foster's brigade was engaged, intending to support him immediately, but owing to circumstances previously mentioned was unable to do so. I was, however, confident that he would be able to extricate his command should he meet overwhelming forces, and most gallantly did he do so; for coming unexpectedly upon a light battery of six pieces he charged and captured the entire battery, but was driven out by an overwhelming force of rebel infantry. I beg leave to refer the general commanding to his report of this most daring charge.

In this severely-contested battle both officers and soldiers behaved with distinguished gallantry and nobly sustained the honor of their respective regiments. It would make my report entirely too long to particularize the gallant conduct even of those officers and men who came under my own observation, but I desire that the reports and commendations of the regimental commanders be considered as part of my own.

It is with the deepest regret that I have to announce the death of First Lieutenant Stearns, acting adjutant of the Twenty-first Massachusetts, one of the most accomplished and gallant officers in the Army; of Chaplain Benton, of the Fifty-first New York, who was killed while nobly encouraging the men to do their duty, and of First Lieutenant Allen, of the same regiment, who was shot dead at the head of his company. Also Captain Johnson, mortally wounded, and Lieutenant Walker, of the Ninth New Jersey, who was killed in front of his company. Captain Frazer was wounded and captured in the battery taken by Lieutenant-Colonel Clark, but after it was retaken by the Fourth Rhode Island, and the rebels were retreating with him, he managed to keep in the rear, and drawing his revolver captured the three men left to guard him. Lieutenant-Colonel Potter, of the Fifty-first New York, was wounded early in the action, but he most gallantly continued with the regiment during the entire battle and rendered very important service. Major Le Gendre, of the same regiment, displayed most conspicuous courage until he fell severely wounded. Lieutenants Tryon, McKee, and Coddington, of the Fifty-first New York, also displayed conspicuous courage, and were all wounded, but not fatally. Of the Ninth New Jersey the following gallant officers were wounded, viz: Captains Middleton, McChesney, and Hufty.

I inclose herewith a complete list of the killed and wounded.* In the early part of the battle Lieutenant Reno, one of my aides, made a most daring reconnaissance of the enemy's right, and first informed me of the extent of their lines. They had thirteen finished redans and five guns bearing on my brigade, and an almost impassable morass filled with fallen timber had to be passed over before reaching them. Captain Neill, assistant adjutant-general, was always with me when not carrying orders, and displayed conspicuous courage and coolness. Lieutenants Reno and Morris, aides, rendered highly important service and behaved most gallantly. Lieutenants Reed and Marsh, of the Signal Corps, acted as aides and did their duty well. Captain Ritchie,

---

* Embodied in statement on p. 211.

acting commissary of subsistence, and Lieutenant Hall, acting brigade quartermaster, were present in the battle and behaved gallantly. The surgeons and chaplains of the different regiments did their duty nobly on the field of battle. I desire to return my thanks to Lieutenant-Colonel Clark, commanding the Twenty-first Massachusetts; to Colonel Ferrero, commanding Fifty-first New York; to Colonel Heckman, commanding Ninth New Jersey, and to Colonel Hartranft, commanding Fifty-first Pennsylvania, for the admirable manner in which they brought their regiments into line and for their gallantry on the field. Eight companies of the Fifty-first Pennsylvania, commanded by Lieutenant-Colonel Bell, were detailed to drag up six guns furnished by the Navy, and commanded by Lieutenant McCook, and one from the Cossack, commanded by Captain Bennett, who gallantly volunteered to man it. They succeeded in bringing up the guns, arriving in camp about 2 a. m. on the 14th instant. After almost incredible labor the guns were all brought into action and most gallantly served, but from the nature of the ground they were unable to join my brigade, but served with General Foster, who no doubt will do full justice to their gallantry. The total loss in my brigade was 36 killed, 5 mortally wounded, and 160 more or less severely wounded.*

I have the honor to be, very respectfully, your obedient servant,

J. L. RENO,
Brigadier-General, Commanding Second Brigade.

Capt. LEWIS RICHMOND,
Assistant Adjutant-General.

No. 11.

Report of Lieut. Col. William S. Clark, Twenty-first Massachusetts Infantry.

HEADQUARTERS TWENTY-FIRST MASS. VOLS.,
Camp Reno, New Berne, N. C., March 16, 1862.

CAPTAIN: About 9 o'clock on the morning of the 13th instant the Twenty-first Massachusetts Volunteers, 743 strong, landed at the mouth of Slocum's Creek, and by order of General Reno advanced about 2 miles through the pine woods along the south bank of the river Neuse toward New Berne. Arriving out upon a large open field, the regiment stacked arms, to await the arrival of the general with the rest of the brigade. Company G, under Lieutenant Taylor, formed the advance guard, and discovered a short distance into the woods beyond the cleared space a large number of wooden barracks, which had been evacuated about two hours before by the rebel cavalry, whose equanimity had been disturbed by shells from the gunboats. An advance of 4 miles brought the regiment to Croatan, where we found a very extensive earthwork running at right angles to the highway.

This being unoccupied by the enemy, the colors of the Twenty-first were placed upon the parapet and heartly cheered by officers and men. Near this work a halt of an hour was made for dinner, during which the pioneers tore up the track of the railroad connecting New Berne with Beaufort. From this point the regiment was ordered to move forward upon the railroad track, and Company D, under Lieutenant Barker, was sent forward as advance guard. About a mile of advance brought the regiment to a place where the highway crosses the rail-

---

* But see revised statement, p. 211.

road, and a half a mile to the right of the latter, on the river Neuse, a
deserted earthwork was discovered by Lieutenant Reno, aide-de-camp
to the general. Company H, under Captain Frazer, with the colors,
was detached from the regiment, and under charge of General Reno
visited the work, and waving the Star-Spangled Banner, bearing the
honorable inscription "Roanoke, February 8, 1862," and the spotless
white colors of Massachusetts, with the noble motto, "*Ense petit placi-
dam sub libertate quietem*," gave three hearty cheers and hastily rejoined
the advancing regiment. Proceeding along the railroad about a mile
farther, the advance guard came upon a building containing several
tents, a complete set of artillery harness, and a few boxes of ammunition for 6 and 12 pounder guns. Lieutenant Barker, with Adjutant
Stearns, then made a reconnaissance to the right of the railroad, and
found an extensive encampment, also recently evacuated by·rebel cavalry, where were large quantities of clothing, commissary stores, and
hospital stores, over which a guard was placed. One mile farther on
the regiment bivouacked for the night, throwing out a picket guard of
two companies on the front and left, the right being guarded by the
Twenty-fourth Massachusetts Volunteers and the rear by the Fifty-
first New York Volunteers. The rain, which commenced to fall.about
10 o'clock of the 13th instant, continued in showers through the night,
and on the morning of the 14th mist and fog enveloped everything.
Notwithstanding every precaution on the part of both officers and
men very many of the rifles were rendered quite unserviceable by the
moisture. In some the powder became too wet to ignite, and in very
many of the Enfield rifled muskets the rammers were almost immovable
from the swelling of the stocks. It is a great defect in this weapon
that the friction of the wood along the whole length of the rammer is
relied upon to keep it in place, since it is quite impossible that the rammers be well secured when the musket is dry and sufficiently loose for
service when wet. It is a noteworthy evidence of discipline and courage
on the part of the men that more than 50 went into the battle having
only their bayonets to work with, and it was very hard to hear them,
in the thickest of the fight, while standing helpless in their places, beg
their officers to give them a serviceable musket, and to see them eagerly
seize the weapons of their comrades as fast as they fell beneath the
leaden storm from the enemy's earthworks. Private Sheehan, of Company E, left his company to secure the musket of a man whom he saw
killed in Company K, and when asked by Major Rice why he did not
take the gun of one who had been shot in his own company replied that
it was like his own, good for nothing.

About 7 o'clock a. m. General Reno ordered his brigade forward, the
Twenty-first Massachusetts in the van. The advance guard, consisting
of Company G, was led by Corporal Stratton, who deserves much
credit for his coolness and intrepidity in pushing on through swamps
and thickets and along the track of the railroad both on the 13th and
14th instant, every moment exposed to be fired upon by a concealed
foe. Adjutant Stearns directed the movement of the first two squads
of the advance guard in the most admirable manner during the entire
march from the place of landing to the field of battle. As it was
known that the defenses of the enemy were thrown across the highway to the right of the railroad, the regiment proceeded cautiously
through the woods on the left of the railroad and parallel with it.
After advancing about half a mile a locomotive was seen coming down
the road, and General Reno at once ordered us to file to the left and
advance into the forest, which was no longer a level, open pine wood,

but the ground was broken into hills separated by deep ravines, and the timber was of oak, "white wood," and other deciduous trees, and of the largest description. The First Brigade, under General Foster, having advanced on the highway, came first upon the enemy, and the battle was now raging fiercely upon our right along the whole line of the earthworks from the river to the railroad. The smoke from the rapid firing of more than thirty cannon and several thousand muskets was driven down upon us by the wind, and mingling with the dense fog, so completely shut out the light of day (never more anxiously longed for) that it was impossible to derive any information respecting the position of the rebels except where it was indicated by the noise of battle.

Our skirmishers now reported that we were opposite the right flank of a battery resting at this point on a deep cut in the railroad, and upon several buildings and brick walls in Wood's brick-yard, which was across the road from our position a few hundred yards distant. The regiment was at once formed in line of battle facing the railroad, and Company C, Capt. J. M. Richardson, was ordered forward to reconnoiter. As rapidly as the difficult nature of the ground would allow the other companies formed on the right by file into line, and as soon as the remaining companies of the right wing were ready I moved forward with the colors to the support of·Company C, who were already engaging the rebel riflemen in the trench upon the opposite side of the deep cut on the railroad.

At the moment of their arrival at the cut the enemy were busily engaged in removing ammunition from the cars, which had just come in from New Berne with re-enforcements. At the first volley from Company C the enemy, in great astonishment, fled from the road and the trench to a ravine in the rear of the brick-yard. General Reno now ordered the color-bearer, Sergeant Bates, to plant his flag upon the roof of a building within the enemy's intrenchments. He immediately rushed forward several rods in advance of his company, and, amid a perfect shower of Minie balls clambered to the roof and waved the Star-Spangled Banner presented to the regiment by the ladies of Worcester.

At this moment the noblest of us all, my brave, efficient, faithful adjutant, First Lieut. F. A. Stearns, Company I, fell mortally wounded, the first among the 25 patriotic volunteers of the Twenty-first who laid down their lives for their country at the battle of New Berne. As he was cheering on his men to charge upon the enemy across the railroad he was struck by a ball from an Enfield rifle fired from a redan on the right and rear of the central breastwork, on which we were advancing. The fatal missile entered his left side, and passing through his lungs went out just below the collar-bone on the right breast. Corporal Welch, of Company C, noticing his fall, returned and remained with him during the battle. He lived about two and a half hours, nearly unconscious from the loss of blood, and died without a struggle a little before noon.

General Reno, with Companies C, A, B, and H, of the right wing, dashed across the railroad, up the steep bank, and over the rifle trench on the top into the brick-yard. Here we were subjected to a most destructive cross-fire from the enemy on both sides of the railroad, and lost a large number of men in a very few minutes. The general, supposing we had completely flanked the enemy's works, returned across the road to bring up the rest of his brigade, but just at this time a tremendous fire of musketry and artillery was opened from the redans, hitherto unseen, and which were nine in number, extending from the railroad more than a mile to the right into the forest.

The general, being now obliged to devote his attention to the enemy in front of his brigade, ordered the left wing of the Twenty-first, under command of Major Rice, not to cross the railroad, but to continue firing upon the rebel infantry in the first two redans, with whom they were already engaged. These consisted of the Thirty-third North Carolina and the Sixteenth North Carolina Regiments, and were the best-armed and fought the most gallantly of any of the enemy's forces. Their position was almost impregnable so long as their left flank, resting on the railroad, was defended, and they kept up an incessant fire for three hours, until their ammunition was exhausted and the remainder of the rebel forces had retreated from that portion of their works lying between the river and the railroad.

Having been ordered into the brick-yard and left there with my colors and the four companies above named, and finding it impossible to remain there without being cut to pieces, I was compelled either to charge upon Captain Brem's battery of flying artillery or to retreat without having accomplished anything to compensate for the terrible loss sustained in reaching this point. Accordingly I formed my handful of men, about 200 in number, in line, the right resting on the breastwork of the enemy, and commenced firing upon the men and horses of the first piece. Three men and two horses having fallen, and the other gunners showing signs of uneasiness, I gave the command, "Charge bayonets," and went in to the first gun. Reaching it I had the pleasure of mounting upon the first of the New Berne guns surrendered to the "Yankees." It was a 6-pounder field piece, brought from Fort Macon, and marked U. S. Leaving this in the hands of Captain Walcott and Private John Dunn, of Company B, who cut. away the horses and attempted to load and turn it upon the enemy, I proceeded to the second gun, some 300 paces from the brick-yard.

By this time the three regiments of rebel infantry, who had retreated from the breastwork to a ravine in the rear when we entered the brick-yard, seeing that we were so few and received no support, rallied and advanced upon us. The Thirty-fifth and Thirty-seventh North Carolina Regiments, supported by the Seventh North Carolina, came up from the ravine in splendid style with their muskets on the right shoulder and halted. Most fortunately, or rather providentially, for us, they remained undecided for a minute or two, and then resolved on a movement which saved us from destruction. Instead of giving us a volley at once, they first hesitated and then charged upon us without firing. I instantly commanded my men to spring over the parapet and ditch in front and retreat to the railroad, keeping as close as possible to the ditch. As the enemy could not fire upon us to any advantage until they reached the parapet, nearly all of those who obeyed my order escaped unharmed, though thousands of bullets whistled over us. On the railroad I found Colonel Rodman, with the Fourth Rhode Island, waiting for orders, and informed him of the situation of things in the intrenchments of the enemy, and urged him to advance at once and charge upon their flank, as I had done. Soon after Colonel Harland, with the Eighth Connecticut, came up, and then the two regiments advanced along the railroad to the brick-yard and charged by wing. As soon as the enemy saw them within their lines they instantly retired again to the ravine without firing a gun. It is some satisfaction to those who were obliged to retreat from the battery after once driving the enemy from it that no one of the five brass pieces stationed in this part of their works was ever fired by them after our charge.

Among the incidents of the day perhaps the following may not be out of place here: Capt. J. D. Frazer, of Company H, was wounded in the right arm just before charging, and dropped his sword. He, however, instantly picked it up with his left hand and led on his men with the colors. At the time of the retreat from the battery he was unable to clear the ditch, and fell into the water. As soon as the rebels discovered him they ordered him to get up, took him back over the parapet, and removing his sword, placed a guard of three men over him. When his captors in their turn retreated again he was unable or unwilling to move as rapidly as they, and when he had detained his guard sufficiently long to permit him to attempt it, he drew his revolver and declared he would shoot the first one who stirred. They surrendered to him and were delivered over to the Fourth Rhode Island as prisoners of war. The lieutenant to whom Captain Frazer gave his sword was also captured and the sword returned to its rightful owner. Captain Frazer, before the close of the fight, was again in command of his company. Private J. A. Miller, of Company A, in clambering over the parapet in the retreat, dropped his rifle into the ditch, and rather than leave his pet remained searching for it until captured. He was ordered to the rear of the enemy with a guard, and as the bullets were rather numerous in the air, he laid himself down between two logs and forgot to get up when his captors retreated.

Sergt. A. J. Weatherby, of Company B, was ordered by me to take care of a prisoner captured in the charge, and when obliged to retreat he did not forsake the rebel, but dragging him by the collar over the parapet and through the ditch, compelled him to double-quick with the " Yankees," and after the battle delivered him over to me in good condition. As soon as my men could be collected and the charges drawn from the rifles which had been wet in the ditch I returned along the railroad to rejoin the left wing of my regiment, which, after fighting with great steadiness and effect for three hours in front of the first two redans, were just rushing over the fallen timber of the almost impassable swamp intervening between them and the retreating enemy.

The conduct of my entire command, so far as I can learn, during both the march and the engagement, was worthy of great commendation, and has received it in the assurance of our brigadier that he is satisfied with us.

Having been ordered to occupy the captured works of the enemy, my regiment has been diligently engaged in collecting the arms, ammunition, equipments, clothing, tents, and commissary stores abandoned by them in their precipitate retreat. The prisoners taken by the different regiments have been placed on board the propeller Albany, under charge of Company E, Captain Bradford. There are about 260 of the well prisoners, including 12 officers, and about 40 wounded rebels, who are cared for by their own surgeons and nurses. The dead have been carefully collected and buried under the direction of Acting Brigade Quartermaster Hall. The killed and mortally wounded of my regiment number 25 and the other casualties 31, besides many cases of slight injuries and narrow escapes. The corrected list is herewith inclosed.[*]

During the engagement the killed and wounded were rapidly carried to the rear by the members of the band, under direction of Acting

---

[*] Embodied in statement on p. 211.

Brigade Surgeon Cutter. The men deserve great credit for their attention to duty while their comrades were falling around them, no one attempting to leave the ranks to assist the wounded. This order they obeyed the more cheerfully, because they were certain that Surgeon Cutter, with his hospital corps, was attending to this duty in their very midst. Assistant Surgeon Warren and Hospital Steward Davis have labored with unceasing zeal to render the wounded comfortable since the battle, and their kind care and skillful treatment will never be forgotten by the regiment.

Hoping this report of the part performed by the Twenty-first Massachusetts Volunteers at the memorable battle of New Berne may be satisfactory, I am, captain, very respectfully, yours,

W. S. CLARK,
Lieutenant-Colonel, Commanding Twenty-first Mass. Vols.

Capt. EDWARD M. NEILL,
    Assistant Adjutant-General, Second Brigade.

No. 12.

Report of Lieut. Col. Charles A. Heckman, Ninth New Jersey Infantry.

HDQRS. NINTH REGIMENT NEW JERSEY VOLS.,
Camp Reno, March 15, 1862.

SIR : I have the honor to report the position and part taken by the Ninth New Jersey Volunteers in the action near New Berne, the 14th instant:

At 7 a. m. I received orders from you to form line on the left of the Fifty-first New York Volunteers and follow them up the railroad track toward New Berne. Having arrived within about a mile of the enemy's works we were ordered to file to the left into the timber and approach them under cover, and by the right flank we proceeded until within about 800 yards of their batteries, when on order I formed the regiment into line; but not being able, as I believed, to see the whole of the Fifty-first New York Volunteers, and knowing them to be in the advance, I threw two companies from right to rear in order to avoid firing into their ranks. With the four remaining companies of the right wing I advanced to within about 500 yards and opened a brisk fire on the redan immediately in front, and on another obliquely to the right, adjoining the railroad track. On discovering a third redan obliquely to the left, supported by rifle pits on its right flank, I threw the left to rear, the right of that wing resting on the colors, to avoid a flank attack. I then ordered the advance and to take ground to the left, and on gaining sufficient ground brought the two right companies into line. The whole line advanced, firing until within about 200 yards of the works, pouring a rapid fire into them, the extreme left gaining ground until upon a direct line. Having been firing a long time (about three hours), I examined several boxes and found the ammunition was getting low. I sent a lieutenant, informing you of the fact, and received an order to charge. We charged, and under difficulties (without securing a shot) planted our colors on two redans, capturing two officers and several privates, and a rebel flag with this inscription, "Beaufort Plow Boys." It is in a good state of preservation, and will be kept so by the Ninth, if agreeable to you.

All of the officers and men having performed their duty it is hard for me to particularize. I regret the necessity to add that Lieut. William L. Walker, of Company H, was killed while faithfully discharging his duties as an officer, and also the loss of the services, which I hope is only for a time, of Captains Middleton, McChesney, and Hufty, who were wounded whilst gallantly cheering their men on to victory.

In addition to the above I report the loss of 3 privates killed and 55 wounded, making in all 4 killed in action, 58 wounded; making an aggregate of 62.

Very respectfully, your obedient servant,
C. A. HECKMAN,
Lieutenant Colonel, Comdg. Ninth Regt. New Jersey Vols.

General J. L. RENO,
Commanding Second Brigade, Department of North Carolina.

No. 13.

Report of Col. Edward Ferrero, Fifty-first New York Infantry.

HDQRS. SHEPARD RIFLES, FIFTY-FIRST REGT. N. Y. VOLS.,
Near New Berne, N. C., March 17, 1862.

GENERAL: The regiment under my command landed from the steamers Lancer and Pioneer on the 13th instant about 14 miles below New Berne, N. C. Great difficulty was experienced in landing, on account of the enemy's obstructions by driving spiles, &c., and having finally effected it (my color-bearer being the first to plant the Union colors on the shore) I formed the regiment and took up our line of march, when, having proceeded some 8 miles and night coming on, I ordered the regiment to bivouac in the woods on the line of the railroad.leading to New Berne. The night was very stormy. Most all of my command, being exposed, were saturated by the rain. At 6 a. m. the following morning (14th) I took my line of march up the railroad until within 300 yards of a collection of brick-kilns, where Lieutenant Reno brought me an order from you to turn off in the woods to the left and form in rear of the Twenty-first Massachusetts Regiment. Upon arriving at this point I halted my regiment and threw out Company D as skirmishers. Finding that we could not engage the enemy in this position the lieutenant-colonel and myself proceeded to make a reconnaissance in advance, parallel with the railroad, a distance of some hundred yards. The ground here was undulating, forming a number of deep ravines. We discovered the enemy's batteries and rifle pits extending a distance of a mile and a half, in front of which were deep ravines obstructed by an almost impassable abatis.

Immediately upon the enemy discovering us as we were surveying their works on the brow of the hill they opened a heavy fire upon us, wounding Lieutenant-Colonel Potter. Immediately returned to the position occupied by my regiment and ordered them forward to the summit of the hill, which position we took, firing and lying down in ravine to reload. A continuous fire was then kept up on the enemy, which they returned with great vigor, making sad havoc in our ranks. My loss at this point was very severe, owing to the exposed position of the troops when advancing to fire. The action continued for about three hours, when, we having expended nearly all of our ammunition, I applied for re-enforcements, when the Fifty-first Pennsylvania Regiment was ordered to our support. They having discharged one volley I was ordered to charge, which the men executed gallantly, planting the colors on the ramparts. The enemy fled in great confusion toward New Berne.

The unflinching courage displayed by all of my command cannot be too highly praised, each one vieing with the other to make our victory sure and complete. To particularize those who behaved with gallantry would be unjust where all did so well. The following officers, however, I cannot avoid noticing : Lieut. Col. R. B. Potter, who was wounded in the early part of the action, behaved with great gallantry and coolness. Maj. C. W. Le Gendre, who was dangerously wounded, is deserving of especial notice for his gallantry, contributing no little to our success. Capt. David R. Johnson, of Company I, who was severely wounded, displayed great bravery. Lieutenants Tryon and McKee, of Companies B and C, who were wounded, are also deserving of especial notice.

The bearers of my colors (Sergeants Poppe and Howard) I must also mention, their actions proving them to be possessed of great courage, holding aloft the colors under a very hot fire.

Among the dead I cannot overlook the noble conduct of the Rev. O. N. Benton, my chaplain. In him we have to mourn the loss of a most useful man, one who encouraged my men by word and deed on all occasions, and who did not regard his own life while serving his country. Lieut. George D. Allen, of Company I, who was instantly killed, also conducted himself with great gallantry.

I received an order to march my regiment to the right of the enemy's battery for rest. After remaining there some twenty minutes Lieutenant McCook, of the Marine Artillery, having charge of six howitzers (three of them captured from the enemy), with ammunition, which were to be sent to New Berne, I sent the regiment a distance of a quarter of a mile below to bring up cars for their transportation. Having placed them upon the cars they drew them to the bridge, which upon their arrival was found to have been burned by the enemy after fleeing across, as well as a portion of the city, which was still burning. Here I received an order to bivouac in a corn field to the right of the railroad, where I made my men as comfortable as the circumstances would allow.

I herewith transmit a list of killed and wounded and missing.*

I have the honor to be, general, your very obedient servant,

EDWARD FERRERO,
Colonel Fifty-first New York Volunteers.

General J. L. RENO,
Commanding Second Brigade, Department of North Carolina.

No. 14.

Report of Col. John F. Hartranft, Fifty-first Pennsylvania Infantry.

HDQRS. FIFTY-FIRST REGT. PENNSYLVANIA VOLUNTEERS,
In Cantonment near New Berne, N. C., March 16, 1862.

SIR: I have the honor to report for the information of the general commanding the brigade that after landing three companies of my regiment at Slocum's Landing on the 13th instant I was ordered to follow the Ninth New Jersey. Leaving Lieut. Col. Thomas S. Bell at

---
* Embodied in statement on p. 211.

the place of disembarkation to bring forward the remainder of the regiment as soon as landed, I moved forward after the Ninth up the beach. Finding Captain Bennett's gun (from the steamer Cossack) manned by an insufficient force, I made a detail of my men, who dragged it to the point where we left the river and there left it, with directions to Captain Bennett to apply to Lieutenant-Colonel Bell for assistance when he came up. I soon after overtook Lieutenant McCook, U. S. Navy, with his six-gun howitzer battery from the gunboats, and being so ordered by General Burnside detailed a company to assist in bringing it forward. I then pushed on with the brigade, and bivouacked with it on the railroad about 6 p. m. As soon as the remaining seven companies were disembarked they were marched forward by Lieutenant-Colonel Bell. On reaching Captain Bennett's gun he made the necessary detail to bring it on. He soon after overtook Lieutenant McCook's battery, whose men were very much exhausted, and receiving an order there from General Reno through you to render every assistance in bringing them to the front, took charge of the guns with his seven companies and the one I had left with them.

The ground, before reaching the county road, being very miry, and after reaching it exceedingly heavy, the labor was necessarily very severe and their progress slow. He proceeded with the battery and Bennett's gun, which had overtaken him, until 9.30 o'clock p. m., when an orderly that he had sent on to General Burnside returned with a message that he might bivouac if he thought best, but to have the guns up early in the morning. As the men seemed utterly unable to proceed without some rest, they bivouacked until 1 and 2 o'clock a. m. He then moved them forward and reported his arrival with all the guns to Generals Burnside and Reno at their headquarters at 4 a. m. The companies were again bivouacked until between 6 and 7 a. m., when, in accordance with General Reno's order, they united with me on the railroad. The movement on the enemy commenced almost immediately afterward, and in my position I proceeded up the railroad, and when near the enemy's works filed to the left into the woods with the brigade. I received the order to proceed to the extreme left and support the Ninth New Jersey and resist any attack of the enemy from their works on the left. The Ninth was soon engaged, and under a very heavy fire I brought my regiment into line, supporting the Ninth with my right wing and with my left covering the approaches from that quarter. My regiment remained in this position for some time, and at this point several of my men were wounded, though I sheltered them as much as possible by causing them to lie down. I sent my skirmishers to my immediate left, with orders not to fire, but merely to reconnoiter. They reported to me that the works of the enemy, of the same character as those in our front, extended as far as they could see. The Ninth moving farther to the front, I moved my regiment forward and farther to the left, so as to maintain the interval of about 100 feet between my regiment and the Ninth.

I desire to mention here that Lieutenant-Colonel Heckman, commanding the Ninth, was most persevering and energetic in the management of his regiment throughout the engagement. While in this position I received the order from General Reno to send my left wing to the assistance of the Fifty-first New York (engaged near me on the right), whose ammunition was running short. The left wing, under command of Lieutenant-Colonel Bell, immediately marched on the double-quick to where the Fifty-first New York was engaged, and was formed in line on the crest of the small hill about 125 yards from the enemy, who were firing from behind their breastworks. After delivering a round, which had the effect of causing a slacking of the enemy's fire, General Reno ordered the firing to cease, and directed Lieutenant-Colonel Bell to charge with his companies on the works of the enemy. This was immediately done with loud cheers, and struggling through the abatis and marsh that obstructed the approach through the ravine soon reached the battery and planted their colors inside. The enemy retreated while the charge was being made, leaving the two guns in the battery still loaded. The right wing immediately advanced and joined the left in the battery. The regiment was then formed and marched with the brigade up the railroad and bivouacked for the night.

During the engagement 9 of my men were wounded.

It is with pleasure that I am able to make particular mention of Lieutenant-Colonel Bell, who so gallantly led the charge of the left wing on the enemy's works. I also mention with pleasure the services rendered by Lieutenants Fair, Beaver, and Carman, who were very active from the time of landing, and especially during the engagement. They had been previously detailed to act as aides to me. Lieutenant Bible, my adjutant, was also very active and efficient. All my officers throughout the trying labors of the day of landing and during the engagement were most efficient, and by their patience, coolness, and gallantry inspired their men with confidence. The conduct of the men in forming and maintaining their line of battle under a heavy cross-fire and their gallantry in unhesitatingly charging the works of the enemy over obstacles deemed to be impassable are worthy of all praise. The band of my regiment, which was acting as an ambulance corps, were very efficient in removing my wounded as well as a number of the wounded of the Fifty-first New York and Ninth New Jersey. In conclusion I may say that I have every reason to be fully satisfied with the conduct and discipline of my regiment.

I am, captain, very respectfully, yours,

J. F. HARTRANFT,
Colonel, Comdg. Fifty-first Regiment Pennsylvania Volunteers.

Capt. EDWARD M. NEILL,
Asst. Adjt. Gen. Second Brigade, Coast Division.

No. 15.

Report of Brig. Gen. John G. Parke, U. S. Army, commanding Third Brigade.

HDQRS. THIRD BRIG., DEPT. OF NORTH CAROLINA,
Carolina City, March 22, 1862.

CAPTAIN: I have the honor respectfully to submit the following report of the operations of the troops under my command from the moment the signal for landing was displayed on the steamer of the commanding general on the morning of the 13th instant to the evening of the 14th, when New Berne was taken:

My brigade is made up of the following regiments: Fourth Rhode Island, colonel commanding I. P. Rodman; Eighth Connecticut, colonel commanding Edward Harland; Fifth Rhode Island Battalion, major commanding John Wright; Eleventh Connecticut, lieutenant-colonel commanding Charles Mathewson. At the signal the light-draught steamer Union, with the Fourth Rhode Island Regiment on board, and the tug-boat Alert, with about twenty small boats in tow with detachments from the other regiments, steamed for the shore at the mouth of Slocum's Creek to make a landing at the point indicated by the general commanding in person. Finding obstructions in the mouth of the creek the steamer was unable to reach the bank, and the men were landed in small boats; an operation consuming much time. The men were immediately formed on their respective colors, and as the several regiments were landed they took up their line of march, following for some distance up the right bank of the Neuse River to a point where a company of the enemy's cavalry had been posted on advance-guard duty. Here the road leaves the river, and after passing one or two farm-houses in the pine woods it strikes the main county road leading from Beaufort to New Berne. This we followed for a short distance, and soon came to an extensive line of intrenchments crossing the road and extending to the railroad. This was entirely abandoned by the enemy. Here the railroad crosses the county road at an acute angle, and as the two roads continue on to New Berne in close proximity, the main command was divided. My brigade, by the order of the general commanding, followed General Foster on the county road, while General Reno marched up the railroad. Near night-fall we reached the second crossing of these roads, and as the command continued on in the same order, General Reno's brigade occupied the left. The march was kept up until after dark, when orders were received to halt and bivouac for the night. The regiments were then placed in position on the road-side. The roads generally were in bad order, and the men marched in many localities through water and mud. In addition, heavy showers fell at intervals during the day and night, and although the men had their overcoats and blankets the bivouac was extremely trying.

On the following morning, the 14th, the brigade was under arms and ready for the march soon after daylight. Before starting I detailed, by order of the general commanding, the Eleventh Connecticut Regiment to relieve one of General Reno's regiments in bringing up the boat howitzers and guns which had arrived during the night. Soon the whole command was in motion, my brigade following the guns, which were directly behind General Foster, while General Reno moved up the railroad. It was not long before the advance had engaged the enemy, and it was soon found that in the attack we would be exposed to a flank fire from heavy artillery as well as from field artillery and musketry in our front. The country is generally level and smooth and covered with a growth of pine and occasional clumps of undergrowth, the whole being styled "open piney woods." On the field in front of the enemy this character of ground extends from the river to the vicinity of the railroad, where it becomes broken into shallow hollows and drains, crossing the railroad and running off to the left. Owing to the dense fog that prevailed but little could be seen, although the timber in front of the enemy had all been felled.

As before stated, my brigade followed General Foster's up the county road directly in rear of the howitzers. When the head of the column had nearly reached the edge of the woods, and General Foster's brigade was being placed in position and engaging the enemy, the general commanding directed me to file to the left and take up a position from which I could support either General Foster or General Reno when the occasion required. I directed the brigade through the timber, and guided by the fire of the enemy kept a course nearly parallel to his lines.

After passing General Foster's left and when the head of the column had approached within a short distance of the railroad I halted the brigade, and being exposed to a fire of both artillery and musketry, the regiments were placed in the hollow under as good cover as the ground furnished, and skirmishers were deployed just on the edge of the plateau to observe the enemy. An aide was then sent to the general commanding informing him of my position and that the ground ahead appeared very difficult. The drains spread into a swamp and the timber was felled, making the ground almost impassable.

Before I received a reply from the general commanding the colonel of the Fourth Rhode Island Regiment, finding his regiment too much exposed, moved it over to the railroad, the embankment affording good cover. While in this position I found that the fire in our front was increasing in intensity, and soon discovered some of our men, a portion of the Twenty-first Massachusetts, of General Reno's brigade, were forced to abandon a position they had attained inside the enemy's intrenchments. Lieutenant-Colonel Clark, commanding the Twenty-first Massachusetts, meeting Colonel Rodman, of the Fourth Rhode Island, informed him that he had been in the work, and assured him of the feasibility of again taking the intrenchments. Lieutenant Lydig, one of my aides, then made an examination of the entrance to the intrenchments by the way of the railroad, and finding it quite practicable, so reported it to Colonel Rodman, who assumed the responsibility and at once prepared for the charge. Lieutenant Hill, my other aide, reported immediately the state of affairs. Being thus in position to turn the flank of the intrenchments resting on the railroad and brick-yard, and having just received orders from the general commanding that "we must flank the battery ahead," I approved the course of Colonel Rodman, and at once ordered the Eighth Connecticut and Fifth Rhode Island Regiments to his support. Colonel Rodman reports:

I then gave the order to charge. Passing quickly by the rifle pits (redoubts on our left flank), which opened on us with little injury, we entered in rear of their intrenchments, and the regiment in a gallant manner carried gun after gun, until the whole nine brass field pieces of their front were in our possession, with carriages, caissons, horses, &c., the enemy sullenly retiring, firing only three guns from the front and three others from the fort (Thompson) on their left, which happily passed over our heads.

The Eighth Connecticut and Fifth Rhode Island followed immediately in the rear and in support of the Fourth Rhode Island. We thus broke the enemy's center and drove him from his intrenched position between the railroad and the river. These regiments were immediately formed in line, and were soon joined by the Eleventh Connecticut, the remaining regiment of the brigade. This regiment, being engaged in bringing up the naval howitzers and guns, became detached from the brigade, and by the order of the general commanding was assigned temporarily to the command of Brigadier-General Foster, commanding the First Brigade, and I respectfully refer you to his report of their operations as well as to that of the lieutenant-colonel commanding.

Although now in possession of the entire work of the enemy between the railroad and river, the heavy firing on our left and beyond the railroad proved that General Reno's brigade was still hotly engaging the enemy. Much of the enemy's fire was directed upon us. I ordered the Fifth Rhode Island Battalion and Eighth Connecticut Regiment to advance cautiously and ascertain by skirmishers the ground still occupied by the enemy. The brigade quartermaster and commissary, Capt. J. N. King, then reported to me that the enemy still occupied rifle pits alongside the railroad and back of the brick-yard and a series of redoubts extending beyond the railroad and in General Reno's front. I then had the Fourth Rhode Island Regiment brought up, and ordered the colonel to drive the enemy from his position. This order was executed in a most gallant manner. Although exposed to a heavy and severe fire, killing and wounding most valuable officers and men, the regiment charged the enemy in flank, while a simultaneous charge was made by General Reno in front, thus driving the enemy from his last stronghold.

The brigade then marched directly up the railroad toward New Berne. As we approached it was soon evident, from the dense columns of smoke, that the bridge over the Trent and the city had been fired. By direction of the commanding general I left the railroad at the county-road crossing, and continued up the county road, to secure, if possible, that bridge over the Trent. Before reaching the bridge I received an order to halt the brigade and select ground for a bivouac. In our immediate vicinity I found three encampments just abandoned by the enemy. They attempted to burn their tents, quarters, and stores, but owing to their hasty retreat they only partially succeeded. The fire was soon checked, and I secured good quarters, tents, and shelter for the entire brigade. Property of different kinds—arms, horses, camp equipage, horse equipments, and one caisson—were here captured. I directed the regimental quartermasters to make an inventory of the property and hand it to the brigade quartermaster.

In concluding this report I take great pleasure in expressing my thanks to every officer and soldier in the brigade. During the hard and fatiguing march of the 13th and the trying bivouac of that night not a murmur was heard. On the morning of the 14th all seemed as fresh and as ready as if they had just left the most comfortable encampment. All were under fire, and the officers seemed proud of the men they were leading and the men showed they had full confidence in their officers.

For the details of the movements of the regiments I have respectfully to refer you to the reports of the regimental commanders, to which are appended lists of the killed and wounded. I mourn the loss of the gallant dead and the wounded have my heart-felt sympathy.

My personal staff, Capt. Charles T. Gardner, assistant adjutant-general; Capt. John N. King, brigade quartermaster and commissary; and Lieuts. M. Asbury Hill and Philip M. Lydig, jr., volunteer aides, were indefatigable in their exertions and rendered most valuable aid and assistance. They conveyed orders, brought timely reports, and made reconnaissances of the enemy, and although at times greatly exposed, I am happy to report they all escaped untouched. Acting Brigade Surgeon Rivers entered upon his duties immediately on the commencement of the action and remained on the field throughout the day and night and was unremitting in his care of the wounded.

I have the honor to be, very respectfully, your obedient servant,

JNO. G. PARKE,
Brigadier-General Volunteers.

Capt. LEWIS RICHMOND,
  Asst. Adjt. Gen., Department of North Carolina.

No. 16.

Report of Col. Edward Harland, Eighth Connecticut Infantry.

HEADQUARTERS EIGHTH CONNECTICUT REGIMENT.

CAPTAIN: I herewith submit a report of the movements of the Eighth Regiment of Connecticut Volunteers during the engagement with the forces of the enemy near New Berne on the 14th of March, 1862.

At about 7 a. m. the regiment left the woods where they had bivouacked the night before. In accordance with orders from General Parke I conducted the regiment along the road in the direction of the rebel battery, following the Fourth Rhode Island Regiment. After proceeding for about a mile in this direction we turned to the left and approached through the woods the right of the principal battery. On approaching the edge of the woods in front of the intrenchments of the enemy I received orders from General Parke to remain there with the regiment until further orders. Afterward, being ordered to engage the enemy, I threw forward skirmishers preparatory to advancing in line. Our skirmishers being driven in and it being impossible to advance in this direction, I joined the Fourth Rhode Island, who were then on the railroad, and endeavored, if possible, to turn the enemy's right. We entered the battery in the rear of the brick-yard and found that the enemy had just abandoned it. I formed the regiment in line between the rebel breastworks and the woods and sent skirmishers into the woods. Finding that a direct advance in that direction would bring the regiment in contact with portions of General Foster's brigade, I so reported to General Parke, who ordered me to move more to the left, to the assistance of the Fifth Rhode Island. I filed through the woods, and when we arrived at the railroad the enemy were in full retreat in the direction of New Berne. The regiment then moved toward New Berne and occupied barracks on the right bank of the Trent. Considerable property was taken that had been abandoned by the enemy, though an attempt, partially successful, had been made to destroy it. Lieutenant Alexander, regimental quartermaster, has furnished Captain King, brigade quartermaster, with an inventory of all the property found.

Throughout the day the officers and soldiers of the regiment, though most of them were there under fire for the first time, behaved with commendable coolness and bravery.*

EDWARD HARLAND,
Colonel, Comdg. Eighth Regiment Conn. Vols.

Capt. CHARLES T. GARDNER,
Asst. Adjt. Gen., Third Brigade, Dept. of North Carolina.

No. 17.

Report of Lieut. Col. Charles Mathewson, Eleventh Connecticut Infantry.

ELEVENTH REGIMENT CONNECTICUT VOLUNTEERS.

SIR: On the morning of the 13th the Eleventh Regiment Connecticut Volunteers landed in small boats from the steamer Louisiana, the

---

* Nominal list of casualties reports 2 men killed and 1 officer (Capt. Charles L. Upham) and 3 men wounded.

schooner Eva Bell, and the barges Shrapnel and Grapeshot, and immediately began the march toward New Berne, following the troops who had preceded them. They bivouacked at night, and upon the morning of the 14th, according to order, continued the march, dragging the guns of the Marine Artillery. Owing to the narrowness and the bad condition of the road the progress was slow, and the immense number of troops obstructing the passage caused the companies to become somewhat separated. Upon arriving before the enemy the howitzers were brought into battery by the companies having them in charge. In the absence of orders each company, as it left the guns, fell to the rear and reformed, but owing to a delay of fifteen or twenty minutes in bringing up the last guns the companies arriving first fell back and to the left and formed line of battle. Company C coming up last, and unable after leaving their guns to find the regiment, took position to the right of the Marine Artillery and on the left of the Massachusetts Twenty-fourth. (The denomination of the Massachusetts regiment may be incorrect.)

When the engagement was somewhat advanced the Eleventh Connecticut was ordered to relieve the Massachusetts Twenty-seventh. They formed line of battle 30 paces in advance of them and retained the position until the charge which carried the work was made, when they pushed forward, passed the breastworks, and formed in rear of the Connecticut Eighth. Meanwhile Company C, which had not rejoined the regiment, charged with the Massachusetts troops and placed the colors second upon the battery. The regiment resumed the march upon the left of the Rhode Island Fifth, passed up the railroad, and were assigned quarters in the old rebel cavalry quarters upon the right of the Connecticut Eighth.

Respectfully,

CHARLES MATHEWSON,
Lieutenant-Colonel, Comdg. Eleventh Connecticut Regiment.

No. 18.

Report of Col. Isaac. P. Rodman, Fourth Rhode Island Infantry.

HEADQUARTERS FOURTH RHODE ISLAND REGIMENT,
Camp near New Berne, March 17, 1862.

GENERAL: I have the honor to make the following report of the part taken by the Fourth Rhode Island in the battle of New Berne, March 14, 1862:

Landed from the steamer Eastern Queen, by the aid of the stern-wheeler Union, at a point some 16 miles below this place, on the southern bank of the River Neuse, at 10.30 o'clock a. m. Thursday, the 13th instant, and found the regiment on the marsh and woody land. By your orders took up line of march in rear of the Fifty-first Pennsylvania, continued on through the day, nothing of importance occurring. We bivouacked for the night, which was wet and stormy. The men, being well supplied with blankets and provisions, did not suffer from the exposure. On the morning of the 14th, at 6.30 a. m., we were again ready for a start, when you ordered me to follow the rear of General Foster's brigade, which I did, moving off on the right of our brigade. The road being very heavy, our marching was slow, when at about 8 o'clock a. m. heavy firing was heard ahead and on our left, General

Foster being engaged with the batteries in front, General Reno having engaged the right of the enemy.

Following you by the front of the enemy's lines we filed to the left through the wood for some distance nearly to the railroad, when by your orders the regiment halted while you ascertained where we were most needed. Standing in this position, a few minutes Captain Kenyon's company, D, was deployed to the front as skirmishers, and our position being rather exposed, moved the regiment to the railroad and waited for further orders. While here part of the Twenty-first Massachusetts, Lieutenant-Colonel Clark, was driven back from the battery in a charge they had made before we came up. Colonel Clark assuring me of the feasibility of charging the works from my position, and Mr. Lydig, an aide on your staff, urging me to take the responsibility, I told him if Mr. Hill, your other aide, would inform you, I would go on. Mr. Lydig then promptly started to bring up the Eighth Connecticut to support me. I formed the regiment in a partially-protected hollow, the right wing in front, supported by my left wing, the space and position rendering this, as I judged, the best plan. I then gave the order to charge. Passing quickly by the rifle pits, which opened on us with little injury, we entered in rear of their intrenchments, and the regiment in a gallant manner carried gun after gun, until the whole nine brass field pieces of their front were in our possession, with carriages, caissons, horses, &c., the enemy suddenly retiring, firing only three guns from the front and three at us from the fort on their left, which happily passed over our heads. The enemy forming in the woods—I should judge about the strength of two regiments—I did not think it prudent to attack them. The national flag of the Fourth Rhode Island was planted on the parapet, and the enemy retired from the whole length of their lines on their left flank. I formed the regiment, after resting a few minutes, in rear of the Eighth and Eleventh Connecticut and Fifth Rhode Island.

In about ten minutes, by your orders, I prepared to attack the rifle pits on the right of General Reno's force, where the firing had been and still continued heavy. Countermarched by the right flank and entered the woods near the brick-works, when the enemy opened on us with a severe fire, killing and wounding some of my best officers and men. Seeing this would not do, I ordered the regiment to charge the pits and railroad embankment, which they did in a fine manner, carrying them in about fifteen minutes. At about the same time General Reno's brigade drove the enemy from their front.

Collecting the wounded under the care of my surgeons I prepared to move on, when in a short time by your orders we moved forward on the railroad toward New Berne. On arriving at the county road turned off and sent my right company forward as skirmishers. Marched on without opposition, arriving near New Berne, when you ordered me to take possession of the deserted camp by the road, lately occupied by Colonel Lee's regiment. This I proceeded to do, and took possession of the camp, stores, &c., where my regiment has since remained. The regimental quartermaster, Lieut. C. S. Smith, will render an account of the property found when he has made the inventory.

For the brave men who so gloriously fell I could not say enough. They fell gallantly at their posts—Captain [Charles] Tillinghast at the head of his company; Captain [William S.] Chase, severely wounded, leading on his; Lieutenant Curtis also wounded at his post. Of the living it would be invidious in me to name one officer above another when all did so well.   Every wish and measure was promptly responded to by the officers of field, staff, and line, and this example the men were proud to follow.   Surgeons Rivers, Millar, and Mr. Flanders, the chaplain, were indefatigable in their exertions for the comfort of the men.

*   *   *   *

All of which is respectfully submitted.*
        Your obedient servant,
                                I. P. RODMAN,
                        Colonel, Fourth Rhode Island Volunteers.

No. 19.

Report of Maj. John Wright, Fifth Rhode Island Infantry.

HDQRS. FIFTH REGIMENT RHODE ISLAND VOLUNTEERS,
        Camp Pierce, New Berne, N. C., March 18, 1862.

SIR: I have the honor to submit to you the following report of the operations of the First Battalion of the Fifth Regiment Rhode Island Volunteers in the battle of the 14th instant:

At the signal given from the brigade flag-ship, on the morning of the 13th of March, 1862, the boats of the steam-transports Curlew and Eagle, in which the battalion was quartered, were cleared away, filled with men, and dispatched to the steamer Eastern Queen at about 8 o'clock.   That forenoon I landed with three companies and a half, and with these took my position in line, according to orders, on the left of the Eighth Connecticut.   I continued the march until I received orders to halt and bivouac for the night.   About 2 the next morning the adjutant brought the two remaining companies into camp.   At daybreak the 14th I formed the battalion in line, awaiting orders, which soon came, and were to continue to follow on the left of the Eighth Connecticut.   The column moved about 6.30 o'clock a. m. and passed slowly along the route followed the day before.   Not long after the firing commenced in front, and the orders came to keep well closed up.   Soon after Captain D'Wolf came down the line and ordered us to close up, and we commenced the double-quick.

After following the main road a short distance farther we turned off to the left and entered the woods.   Just after we turned a cannon ball passed over our heads, which showed that we were approaching the battery, and caused us to press forward more eagerly to support the attack.   After passing through a swampy place we came to a halt on the brow of a bluff, where we awaited further orders and the further movements of the Eighth Connecticut.   As the bullets flew very thick over our heads we were ordered to lie down.   When the Twenty-first Massachusetts was driven from the battery and the enemy made a sally the orders came to fix bayonets and prepare to receive a charge.   We formed in line of battle, left in front, but as they were driven back before we saw them, we continued as we were before that.   Our orders were still to continue on the left of the Eighth Connecticut.   At last the orders came to turn the right flank of the enemy.   We passed down into the hollow, filed off still farther to the left, and passed over

---

* A nominal list of casualties omitted above reports 1 officer and 10 men killed and 2 officers and 23 men wounded—total 36.

another elevation, when we came to the railroad, just below the brick-yard. Then, with General Parke at our head, we pushed on, passed in rear of the breastworks of the enemy, and as we came upon the high open ground behind it we came under a raking fire from the rifle pits across the railroad and the brick-yard, where the enemy lay in large force.

We pushed on at the double-quick until we came under cover of the trees, where we formed in line of battle and prepared to charge on the enemy in the battery. As they had retired, I was ordered first to send one company and afterward the whole battalion, and to proceed cautiously and find out what the firing was on our left. I sent the adjutant ahead to find out the direction we should take. As it was pointed out. by the general's aide, Lieutenant Lydig, we passed down into a hollow and ascended the left-hand side cautiously until we reached the brow of the elevation, when we came in view of the enemy and immediately opened upon them a brisk fire, which immediately had an effect, for their fire slackened and stopped when we ceased firing. We opened upon them two or three times afterward until we were afraid of firing upon the Fourth Rhode Island, who were advancing upon them on our right. When the Fourth charged upon them we ceased firing and awaited orders.

It was on this hill that we met with the greater part of our loss. As we had no colors, I was ordered to follow in the rear of the Eighth Connecticut, and leaving a few to take care of the killed and wounded we passed down to the railroad, and at 11 o'clock took up our line of march for the city of New Berne. When we reached the main road, which crossed the railroad, we turned to the left, and continued our march until we received orders to halt and take possession of a rebel* camp off to the right from the road which had been occupied by the rebel artillery.*

I am, very respectfully, your obedient servant,

JOHN WRIGHT,
Major, Comdg. First Bat. Fifth Regt. Rhode Island Vols.

CHARLES T. GARDNER,
Assistant Adjutant-General.

No. 20.

Reports of Brig. Gen. L. O'B. Branch, C. S. Army.

HEADQUARTERS DEPARTMENT OF PAMLICO,
March 15, 1862.

GENERAL: On Wednesday (12th) at 4 p. m. it was made known to me that the enemy were ascending Neuse River in force. Under cover of their gunboats they effected a landing of troops in the rear of the Croatan breastwork Thursday morning, they compelling me to evacuate that position. I instantly threw behind the Fort Thompson breast-work every available man under my command and prepared to wait there the enemy's farther advance.

On Friday morning, at about 7 o'clock, I was assailed by overwhelm-

---

*Nominal list of casualties shows 1 officer (Lieut. Henry R. Pierce) and 1 man killed and 8 men wounded.

ing forces and compelled to yield the breastwork. The evacuation of the river batteries, thus taken in reverse, of course, followed and the enemy is now in possession of New Berne.

From the nature of the position my troops were much scattered in the retreat, and I am rapidly concentrating them at this place.

I have given orders to my chief engineer, aided by Captain Meade, to make an examination into the best means of defending some point which will check the advance of the enemy to the railroad at Goldsborough. I am satisfied that it cannot be done without a large increase of force.

My command is entirely destitute of camp equipage of every description, and can on that account be kept together only with great difficulty.

At an early day I will report more in detail the operations of the two days.

Yours, very respectfully,

L. O'B. BRANCH,
Brigadier-General, C. S. Army.

—

HEADQUARTERS FIRST DIVISION,
In the Field, March 26, 1862.

GENERAL: My report of the battle of the 14th below New Berne has been withheld until I could get a report from Col. R. P. Campbell, who commanded my right wing on that day. It is now submitted, with reports from the commanders of all the regiments on the field.

A brief description of the artificial defenses of New Berne, together with the inclosed sketch, will enable you to comprehend the movements of the day, which were few and simple.

The defensive works were located and constructed before I assumed command. The troops under my command had performed a large amount of work, but it was mainly on the river defenses, which were not assailed by the enemy. They had been originally planned for a force much larger than any ever placed at my disposal, and I was for six weeks engaged in making the necessary changes to contract them, but the failure of all my efforts to obtain implements and tools with which the troops could carry on the work prevented me from making satisfactory progress. I had circulated handbills over the State, calling on the citizens generally to assist me, and received from two counties a small party of free negroes without implements. I then inserted in the newspaper an advertisement calling on the slave owners to hire their slaves, with implements, for a few days, and I got but a single negro.

During all this time I continued the troops at work, and when the enemy came into the river 500 per day were being detailed to construct breastworks, with less than half that number of worn and broken shovels and axes, without picks or grubbing-hoes. If the fate of New Berne shall prevent a similar supineness on the part of citizens, and especially slave owners, elsewhere, it will be fortunate for the country. Ten miles below New Berne, on the south side of the Neuse, is the mouth of Otter Creek. From this creek, 1 mile above its mouth, the Croatan breastwork runs across to an impracticable swamp about three-fourths of a mile. This is a well-planned and well-constructed work, which 2,000 men and two field batteries could hold against a very large force. But from the mouth of Otter Creek to Fort Thompson, the lowest of the river batteries, is a distance of 6 miles of river shore, on any part of which the enemy could, land and take the Croatan work in reverse. It is obvious that the breastwork was useless if I had not sufficient force to hold it and at the same time guard 6 miles of river shore. I have at no time been able to place 4,000 men in the field at New Berne, and at the time of the battle had been seriously weakened by the re-enlistment furloughs.

Coming up the river from the Croatan work you reach the Fort Thompson breastwork. This had been constructed from Fort Thompson to the railroad, about 1 mile, before I assumed command. Finding that, from inadequate force, the Croatan work might be of no avail to me, I determined to extend the Fort Thompson work about one mile and a fourth and rest its right on a swamp. This is the work I was engaged on when the enemy appeared. In order to make the line as short as possible and to avail of a small branch by throwing it in front the line was thrown back about 150 yards on the railroad, and thence a series of small breastworks, conforming to the features of the ground, ran off in the direction of the swamp, making an obtuse angle with the older portion of the line on the other side of the railroad. To guard this gap I directed that the old brick-kiln on the railroad should be loop-holed, and the evening before the battle had ordered two 24-pounder guns to be brought from New Berne and placed in battery there. The enemy's skirmishers drove the laborers from the battery when an hour more would have enabled them to get the guns in position. Of course I lost all the benefit I expected from it. The line of small breastworks from the railroad to the swamp was partially finished for about half the distance.

Running parallel to the river and to each other, and crossing the line at right-angles are, first, after leaving the river, the old Beaufort road and then the railroad; still farther on and near the swamp the Weathersby Road. The railroad and the Beaufort road intersect about 2 miles behind the breastwork, the former crossing the river on a bridge 1,840 feet long at the town of New-Berne and the latter at an indifferent private bridge about one mile and a half above New Berne. Both these bridges are accessible to gunboats, so that when we stood at the Fort Thompson breastwork, fronting the enemy, we had Neuse River on our left, Bryce Creek (an impassable stream) on our right, and the Neuse and Trent in our rear, the only possible mode of escape in case of defeat being across the two bridges I have described, 5 miles in our rear.

I hope this description, with the aid of the map inclosed, will put you in possession of our situation at the opening of the battle.

I omitted to state that the timber had been felled in front of the breastwork for about 350 yards, and the space was swept by ten field pieces, besides three navy 32-pounders, discharging grape and canister from the rear face of Fort Thompson.

It is useless to describe the river defenses, on which the largest amount of labor had been bestowed, as the enemy prudently refrained from attacking the batteries in front and the gunboats did not come within range of their guns until they had been silenced from the rear. I now proceed to detail the incidents of the battle.

On Wednesday, the 12th, at 4 p. m., the approach of the enemy's fleet was reported to me, and at dark I learned that twelve vessels had anchored below the mouth of Otter Creek and about forty-five were ascending the river in their rear.

Orders were issued to Colonel Sinclair, Thirty-fifth Regiment, to proceed immediately with his regiment to Fisher's Landing, which is just above the mouth of Otter Creek, and to resist any attempt of the enemy to land there.   Colonel Avery, Thirty-third Regiment, and Lieutenant-Colonel Haywood, Seventh Regiment, constituting the reserve, were ordered to proceed across the river, so as to be in position at the intersection of the Beaufort road and the railroad at daybreak in the morning. Col. R. P. Campbell, commanding my right wing, was instructed to guard the river shore from the mouth of Otter Creek to Fort Thompson, while Col. C. C. Lee, who commanded my left wing, ·was to guard the remainder of the shore, support the river batteries, and re-enforce Colonel Campbell in case he should be hard pressed. Colonel Campbell was instructed to establish his headquarters at the intersection of the Beaufort road and the breastwork, and to collect his troops around him by daybreak.   Both commanders were instructed that, in case it should be necessary to fall back from the river shore to the breastwork, Colonel Campbell should hold that part to the right of the Beaufort road and Colonel Lee that part to the left of it.

These orders having been dispatched by 9 p. m., the night was spent by the troops in getting into position and other preparations for the contest.

Having given all the necessary directions to staff officers and all others before 3 o'clock Thursday morning, and seen all the men and material forwarded from the camp and depot in New Berne, I proceeded to Colonel Campbell's headquarters.   On the road I met dispatches from Colonel Sinclair and Capt. P. G. Evans, commanding the pickets, informing me that the enemy were landing troops below the mouth of Otter Creek, and Colonel Vance was directed to send his regiment to Croatan breastwork to occupy it.   Railroad trains were on the spot to carry down re-enforcements or to draw off Colonels Vance's and Sinclair's regiments and Brem's battery, as the case might require.

Intelligence was soon brought to me that the enemy's gunboats, having driven Colonel Sinclair's regiment from Fisher's Landing, were rapidly landing troops at that place, and that Colonel Campbell, seeing that the Croatan breastwork was turned, had ordered Vance, Sinclair, and Brem to fall back to the Fort Thompson breastwork.

My force was wholly inadequate to guard the 6 miles of river shore between the mouth of Otter Creek and Fort Thompson.   The result was therefore not wholly unexpected but I had hoped that a line of rifle pits I had caused to be made for a mile along the bluffs at and on both sides of Fisher's Landing would have enabled me to hold the enemy in check and to inflict on him serious loss at the first moment of his placing his foot on our soil.   I was therefore surprised when the position was yielded with a loss of only 1 killed and 2 wounded, all three of which casualties occurred in the retreat.

After the abandonment of Fisher's Landing to the enemy the prompt withdrawal of Vance and Brem could alone save them from being cut off, and the enemy thus came into possession of my strongest work without having received a single shot from us.

The Fort Thompson breastwork now became my sole reliance for resisting his advance, and throughout the remainder of the day and night of Thursday the most active efforts were made to strengthen that unfinished work.   Both officers and men executed my orders with unflagging energy.

I was particularly indebted to Major Thompson and Captain Meade, of the Engineers, to whom I assigned the duty of disposing of the artillery in the most advantageous manner.

In the afternoon the gunboats shelled the breastworks heavily from a position they had taken out of reach of the guns of our batteries.

The composure with which all classes of my troops received this attack from an unseen foe strengthened the confidence I felt in their standing under fire.

No damage was inflicted on us by the shells, but the accuracy with which they were thrown over a thick, intervening woodland convinced me of the necessity of driving traitors and enemies in disguise from all towns and neighborhoods of which we desire to hold military possession.

During the day on Thursday the troops were posted behind the intrenchments, and it was painfully apparent that my force was not sufficient to man them even with a thin line for the finished portions of them. I was compelled to withdraw Lieutenant-Colonel Haywood of the Seventh Regiment from the reserve and place him on the line.

The regiments were posted as follows, commencing on the left:

Lieutenant-Colonel Barbour, Thirty-seventh Regiment, and Major Gilmer, Twenty-seventh Regiment, between Fort Thompson and the Beaufort County road. Lieutenant-Colonel Haywood, Seventh, Colonel Sinclair, Thirty-fifth, and Colonel Clark (Militia), between the Beaufort road and the railroad. Colonel Vance, Twenty-sixth Regiment, to the right of the railroad. A few unattached companies were placed between the regiments. My headquarters were about 200 yards in rear of the intrenchment at the railroad and the reserve was about 200 yards in my rear; the cavalry regiment about half a mile to the rear. In this order the troops slept on their arms.

At 11 o'clock Thursday night Colonel Lee brought me intelligence that signal rockets had just been seen on our extreme right, from which I inferred that the enemy, having found the Weathersby road, were in front of that portion of my line.

Orders were sent to Colonel Vance to extend his regiment so that its right might rest on the Weathersby road, and in an hour a section of Brem's battery was moving by a circuitous route to a position on that road.

On taking my position Friday morning the center appeared so weak that I dispatched my aide-de-camp to Colonel Campbell to say to him that it must be re-enforced if possible.

At about 7.30 o'clock Friday morning the fire opened along the line from the railroad to the river. I soon received a message from Colonel Lee that the enemy were attempting to turn our left. This proved to be a feint, as I replied to him that I thought it would.

The next incident of the battle was the appearance of the enemy's skirmishers in front of Vance, and consequently on the prolongation of the line held by the Militia. It was to drive the enemy from that position that I had directed the 24-pounder battery to be placed there, and supposing it was ready for service, I sent Captain Rodman, with his company, to man it, but they found the guns not mounted, and were ordered into position to act as infantry. The skirmishers of the enemy, finding themselves on the flank of the Militia, fired at them a few shots from their flank files, which caused a portion of them to flee in great disorder.

I instantly ordered Colonel Avery to send five companies to dislodge them. He sent them instantly, under Lieutenant-Colonel Hoke; but before Colonel Hoke had fully got into position, though he moved with the greatest promptness and celerity, I received a message from Colonel Clark, of the Militia, informing me that the enemy were in line of battle in great force on his right. I instantly ordered up the re-maining five companies of Colonel Avery's regiment, and the whole ten opened a terrific fire from their Enfield rifles. The whole Militia, how-ever, had now abandoned their positions, and the utmost exertions of myself and my staff could not rally them. Colonel Sinclair's regiment very quickly followed their example, retreating in the utmost disorder. This laid open Haywood's right and a large portion of the breastwork was left vacant. I had not a man with whom to re-occupy it, and the enemy soon poured in a column along the railroad and through a por-tion of the cut-down ground in front, which marched up behind the breastwork to attack what remained of Campbell's command.

The brave Seventh met them with the bayonet and drove them head-long over the parapet, inflicting heavy loss upon them as they fled; but soon returning with heavy re-enforcements, not less than five or six regiments, the Seventh was obliged to yield, falling back slowly and in order. Seeing the enemy behind the breastwork, without a single man to place in the gap through which he was entering and finding the day lost, my next care was to secure the retreat. This was a critical operation, as the enemy, having pierced our center, had possession of the two shortest roads to the bridges, and besides could approach them at pleasure with their gunboats.

Having dispatched two couriers to Colonel Avery and two to Colonel Vance with orders for them to fall back to the bridges, I moved to the intersection of the Beaufort road and railroad to rally the troops and cover the retreat across the bridges. Here I found a train of cars with the Twenty-eighth Regiment, Lieutenant-Colonel Lowe, who had arrived too late to reach the battle-field, and formed them to hold the enemy in check until all should pass. Colonel Lee was directed to proceed to New Berne and form all the men he could collect in the upper part of town. The Seventh Regiment, arriving in two different parties, was directed to proceed to the Trent Bridge and hold it, while I remained with Lieutenant-Colonel Lowe at the intersection to hold the enemy in check and cover the retreat.

Remaining until there were no more stragglers in sight on either road, I directed Colonel Lowe to fall back to the Trent Bridge, which he did, the enemy showing themselves on the road as his rear guard moved off. Proceeding to the Trent Bridge, I placed Colonel Campbell in command of all the forces there, with instructions to hold the bridge as long as possible for the passage of Avery and Vance, and then to move up the Trent road or join me in town, as I might direct after reaching the town, leaving with him to conduct him that gallant gentleman and soldier Capt. Peter G. Evans, whom I had not allowed to leave my person for two days except to bear orders. The railroad bridge was in flames before I left the intersection.

Arriving in town, I found it in flames in many places and evacuated. Orders written in the street under the lurid glare of the flames were dispatched in every direction through the town to search for Colonel Lee. At Railroad street I learned that a gunboat had already landed at one of the lower wharves. Going up Railroad street to see whether Colonel Lee was at the Fair Grounds, I found, on reaching the depot, that the gunboats were already there and the enemy in the Fair Grounds. Colonel Lee, finding himself in no condition to make resistance, had properly drawn off and marched up the Kinston Road. Following on, and directing all the officers I could overtake to conduct their men to Tuscarora, the nearest railroad depot, I proceeded to that place, and, having made arrangements for the transportation of the troops to

Kinston by railroad and seen most of them off, reached that place myself at 11 o'clock on Saturday.

My loss was 64 killed, 101 wounded, and 413 missing; about 200 are prisoners and the remainder at home. The inclosed tabular statement will show you on which regiments and companies the loss fell.

The horses of Latham's battery and those of four pieces of Brem's battery were killed, and we lost, in consequence, ten pieces of field artillery. There were other pieces at the breastwork, but they were condemned guns from Fort Macon belonging to no company.

The ammunition and ordnance stores at New Berne were saved, and the camp equipage and baggage of the regiments would have been saved but we had not the field transportation with which to haul it to the railroad.

In five days after the battle I had my brigade in camp in advance of Kinston ready for action and but little demoralized.

I had at an early day placed Cols. R. P. Campbell, Seventh Regiment, and C. C. Lee, Thirty-seventh Regiment, in command of the two wings of my brigade. All the troops, except the Thirty-third Regiment and the cavalry regiment, which were in reserve, fought under their immediate command. I could have taken no better security against any errors and oversights I might commit than I did in placing those two trained and experienced officers in immediate command of the troops.

I refer to their reports herewith and the reports of commanders of regiments for particulars as to the conduct of individuals under their command.

As the Thirty-third Regiment was under my own command it is proper for me to say that its conduct was all I could desire. It moved into action with as much promptness and steadiness as I ever saw in its ranks on dress parade and its fire was terrific. It was engaged within 100 yards of my position, and Colonel Avery, Lieutenant-Colonel Hoke, and Major Lewis did their duty fully against an overwhelming force. Its gallant colonel was captured at his post; two different couriers, whom I sent to him with orders to withdraw; having failed to reach him.

With the exceptions noted in a former part of the report all the regiments behaved well. The Seventh and Thirty-third are specially named, because on the former fell the brunt of the battle after its flank was exposed by the retreat of the militia and the Thirty-fifth, and the latter had no other commander except myself through whom its conduct could be made known to you. No troops could have behaved better than the Twenty-sixth, Twenty-seventh, and Thirty-seventh.

Latham's battery was new and was only partially equipped. The horses had not been attached to the guns a week before the battle. Its gallantry and devotion on that occasion show it to be worthy of a new outfit.

My regular staff, consisting of my aide-de-camp, Mr. W. E. Cannady, and assistant adjutant-general, Lieut. Col. W. G. Robinson, rendered me all the assistance I desired. My aide-de-camp in particular bore my orders through the hottest of the fire with unflinching courage and composure.

To Captain Meade, of the Engineers, and Lieutenant Burwell, C. S. Army, and Mr. Francis T. Hawks, who tendered their services for the occasion and were placed on my staff, I was greatly indebted, not only for services in bearing orders and rallying troops, but to the first in an especial manner for counsel and advice.   They remained with me throughout the battle and subsequent retreat.

The panic alluded to in some of the reports occurred after the troops had 'left New Berne.   It was in advance of me and I did not witness it, but the names of officers who contributed to it or participated in it will be reported to you if they can be discovered.   It was soon counteracted by the steadiness of Colonel Lee and some other officers.

Yours, very respectfully,

L. O'B. BRANCH,
Brigadier-General, Commanding.

Maj. Gen. T. H. HOLMES,
. *Commanding Department of North Carolina.*

[Addenda.]

Return of casualties in the Confederate forces at the battle of New Berne, N. C., March 14, 1862.

Command.	Killed.			Wounded.			Missing and prisoners.			Aggregate.	Remarks by compiler.
	Officers.	Men.	Total.	Officers.	Men.	Total.	Officers.	Men.	Total.		
7th North Carolina.	....	6	6	1	14	15	...	30	30	51	
19th North Carolina.	....	....	....	....	....	....	...	....	....	....	No losses reported.
26th North Carolina.	2	3	5	1	9	10	4	68	72	87	
27th North Carolina.	....	4	4	....	8	8	....	42	42	54	
28th North Carolina.	....	....	....	....	....	....	....	6	6	6	
33d North Carolina.	....	....	32	...	....	28	....	....	144	204	Officers and men not separately reported.
35th North Carolina.	1	4	5	....	11	11	....	9	9	25	
37th North Carolina.	....	....	1	....	....	3	....	....	8	12	Do.
Brem's battery......	....	....	1	....	....	8	....	....	7	16	Do.
Latham's battery ...	....	10	10	1	10	11	2	20	22	43	Do.
Independent companies.	....	....	....	...	....	7	...*.	....	73	80	Do.
Total *.........	3	27	64	3	52	101	6	175	413	578	

* For reasons stated in remarks the totals of columns headed "Officers" and "Men" do not prove the "Total" columns.

[Inclosure.]

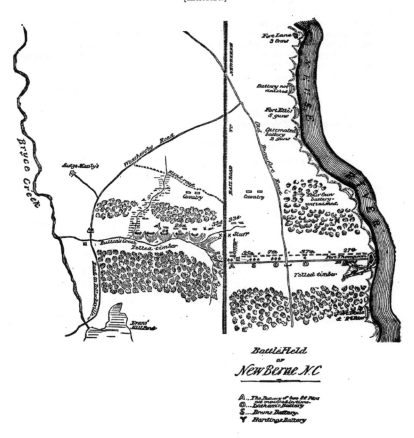

Battlefield
of
New Berne, N.C.

A...The Battery of two 24-Pdrs
        not mounted in time.
O...Latham's Battery
S...Brems Battery.
Y...Hardinge Battery

HEADQUARTERS, *March 28, 1862.*

SIR: I have the honor to request that the inclosed copies of letters may be filed with my official report of the battle of the 14th.

Yours, very respectfully,

L. O'B. BRANCH,
Brigadier-General, Commanding.

General T. H. HOLMES, *Commanding, &c.*

[Inclosure No. 1.]

HEADQUARTERS DISTRICT OF PAMLICO,
New Berne, N. C., March 12, 1862—8.30 p. m.

Col. CHARLES C. LEE:

COLONEL: The following troops have been ordered to report to you, and I presume are in readiness to obey your orders, to wit: The Thirty-seventh North Carolina troops; Sloan's regiment; 'Brem's, Edelin's, Whitford's, Mayo's, Herring's, Leecraft's, and Sutton's companies.

Colonel Campbell is instructed to guard the river shore, and if he should be hard pressed you will send him such re-enforcements as you can spare. I will have two regiments in reserve. My headquarters will be on the Beaufort road, in the rear of the batteries. Have all your troops in position by daybreak. If compelled to fall back from the river shore and occupy Fort Thompson breastwork, you will hold so much of it as extends from the old Beaufort road to the river.

Very respectfully,

———— ————.

[Inclosure No. 2.]

HEADQUARTERS DISTRICT OF PAMLICO,
March 12, 1862—8.30 p. m.

Col. R. P. CAMPBELL, *Commanding:*

It is presumed that the following troops have reported to you, to wit: Colonels Vance's and Sinclair's regiments; Captains Latham's, McRae's, Harding's, and Mallett's companies, and Colonel Spruill's cavalry. Send off couriers to-night, if you have not already done so, and give them orders. Colonel Sinclair's regiment is already at Fisher's Landing. That is the only body of troops that I have moved. Colonel Avery and Lieutenant-Colonel Haywood constitute the reserve, and will receive their orders directly from me.

You had better gather your force near you before daybreak. If the enemy attempt a landing, as he probably will in the morning, resist him with all the force you can bring to bear. If compelled to fall back, occupy so much of the Fort Thompson breastwork as extends from the Beaufort road to an impassable swamp on the extreme right. Guard well the Beaufort road where it crosses the breastwork. If the enemy attempt to land at Fisher's Landing, Sinclair will need strong re-enforcement. Explain to your officers that when they fall back they are to rally behind the Fort Thompson breastwork.

I have just directed that a cavalry company be sent to you immediately, so that you may have abundant couriers by whom to send your orders.

P. S.—My headquarters will be on the Beaufort road, in the rear of the batteries.

[Inclosure No. 3.]

HEADQUARTERS FIRST DIVISION,
March 30, 1862.

Maj. Gen. T. H. HOLMES,
Commanding Department of North Carolina:

GENERAL: I omitted, through inadvertence, to state in my official report of the battle of the 14th a very important movement. When, as stated in my report, an officer came to me from Colonel Clark, of the Militia, and informed me that the enemy were in line of battle in force on his right, I directed him to proceed immediately to Colonel Campbell with the information, and also sent one of my own couriers to guard against a miscarriage.

As soon as the Militia fled my aide-de-camp was sent to Colonel Lee, on the left, with orders to send his own regiment (the Thirty-seventh), if he could possibly spare it, and in any event to send half of it, to the menaced point. Colonel Lee—calling the attention of my aide to the strong body of the enemy along his front with whom he was then engaged, to show how impossible it was for him to send all—promptly disengaged five companies of the Thirty-seventh and ordered them to the right. When they reached there Sinclair's regiment had fled, and they could not retrieve the disaster. I respectfully request that this may be made part of my official report.

    Yours, very respectfully,

L. O'B. BRANCH,
Brigadier-General, Commanding.

No. 21.

Report of Col. Reuben P. Campbell, Seventh North Carolina Infantry.

HDQRS. SEVENTH REGT. NORTH CAROLINA TROOPS,
March 25, 1862.

GENERAL: I have the honor very respectfully to make the following report of the late engagement, 14th instant, at Fort Thompson:

My command, consisting of the Seventh Regiment North Carolina troops, commanded by Lieutenant-Colonel Haywood; Thirty-fifth Regiment North Carolina troops, commanded by Colonel Sinclair; Captain Whitehurst's independent company; some Militia, under Colonel Clark, Captain Latham's battery, and two sections of Captain Brem's battery, were posted along the breastworks from the county road to the railroad. The Seventh Regiment was posted immediately on the right of the county road; Colonel Sinclair's regiment was posted on its right, and Captain Whitehurst and Colonel Clark on his right, extending near the railroad. The batteries were placed at convenient distances along the line.

The battle was commenced by the firing of a Parrott gun belonging to Captain Latham's battery, under command of Lieutenant Wheeler. This shot dispersed a squad of horsemen, who seemed to be reconnoitering under cover of the woods.

Immediately after this, about 7.20 o'clock, the firing became general from the enemy along the whole of my command. It was replied to by both the batteries and small-arms. Shortly after the firing began the Militia under Colonel Clark gave way and left the field in a panic.

About one hour after the firing commenced Colonel Sinclair came to me, and in much excitement said that the enemy had flanked him and was coming up the trenches which had been vacated by the Militia. I ordered him to leave the trenches for the purpose of charging bayonets upon the advancing columns; but he failed to form his men and left the field in confusion. This left the entire space occupied by my command to be defended by the batteries and by the Seventh Regiment North Carolina troops. One section of Brem's battery, left without support by Colonel Sinclair, was taken possession of by the enemy, who had continued his advance on the right. I ordered Lieutenant-Colonel Haywood to have his men leave the breastwork and charge bayonets upon the enemy, who was advancing in column. The charge was made, and the enemy driven over the breastworks with great slaughter, leaving a number of guns and other things in his retreat, which fell into our hands. We also retook the section of Brem's battery which had fallen into the hands of the enemy. With the aid of the Seventh Regiment and the batteries I then held the works until the enemy again appeared on our right with a greatly increased force, some six or eight regiments. The batteries, with the exception of one section, under Captain Latham, had been silenced, so that I had only it and the Seventh Regiment at my command. I ordered the troops to fall back, which they did under a very heavy fire, and formed immediately in rear of Colonel Vance's encampment. After waiting a short time, and seeing no hope of defeating the enemy or offering further resistance to his approach or advancing our cause by meeting, I retired from the field.

The officers and men of the Seventh Regiment North Carolina troops and Captains Latham's and Brem's batteries behaved with coolness and bravery. I cannot speak of the other troops under my command, as they left the field too early in the action for me to say anything about them.

From the report of the officers under my command the following are the casualties: 13 privates and 1 officer killed, 34 privates and 1 officer wounded, and 34 privates missing.*

R. P. CAMPBELL,
Colonel Seventh Regiment North Carolina Troops.

General L. O'B. BRANCH, *Kinston, N. C.*

No. 22.

Report of Lieut. Col. Ed. Graham Haywood, Seventh North Carolina Infantry.

HDQRS. SEVENTH REGT. NORTH CAROLINA TROOPS,
March 25, 1862.

GENERAL: I have the honor very respectfully to report that my command, the Seventh Regiment North Carolina troops, behaved well in the late engagement at Fort Thompson. The command, with the exception of Company F, Captain Turner, was posted on the right of the county road, behind the breastworks, and ordered to defend them and support the artillery. Company F was posted on the left of the road. They held their positions until flanked on the right by the enemy. They were then ordered to leave the trenches and charge bayonets upon the enemy, which they did, driving him beyond the breastworks with great slaughter and retaking a section of Brem's battery which had fallen into the enemy's hands. I then held the breastworks until flanked again by the same direction with a greatly increased force, some six or eight regiments, when I fell back into the woods in rear of Colonel Vance's camp and there formed. Seeing no hope of defeating the enemy, I then, with the command, retired from the field. Major Hall, with three companies, preceded me.

The casualties were 6 men killed, 15 wounded, and 30 missing; among the wounded Capt. W. H. Sanford, regimental commissary.

ED. GRAHAM HAYWOOD,
Lieut. Col., Comdg. Seventh Regt. North Carolina Troops.

General L. O'B. BRANCH.

---

* But see addenda to Branch's report, p. 247.

No. 23.

Report of Col. S. B. Spruill, Nineteenth North Carolina Infantry.

HDQRS. NINETEENTH REGIMENT N. C. STATE TROOPS,
Kinston, N. C., March —, 1862.

On Wednesday evening, the 12th instant, I received information that the enemy had made their appearance in the river and to hold my command in readiness to march at a moment's warning.

On Thursday morning, 13th, I received an order from General Branch to report with my command immediately to the general commanding at the crossing of the Beaufort road and railroad, which was promptly obeyed. My command, consisting of Companies D, E, F, H, and K, proceeded down as far as Colonel Vance's encampment, near the intrenchments, and reported myself for duty. I then received orders to fall back to a convenient position, which I occupied, between the Beaufort road and railroad.

About 2 p. m. I received a verbal order to dismount two of my companies that were best armed, leaving a sufficient number of men to guard the horses, and for them to report to Colonel Vance, then on the extreme right, which I obeyed, by ordering Company A, commanded by Captain Hays, and Company K, commanded by Lieut. William A. Graham, jr., these companies being armed with rifles and carbines. The other companies remained in their same position until about 3 p. m., at which time the enemy were throwing their shells very near us, and I ordered them to move nearer the railroad, and we continued to move until we went a short distance beyond the railroad. There we remained until night, when the firing ceased.

During the time I received an order to send two companies to report to Lieutenant-Colonel Robinson, to act as vedettes for the night, which I obeyed, by detailing Company D, commanded by Captain Strange, and Company H, Captain Randolph. These companies were under the command of Major J. W. Woodfin.

I then ordered Lieutenant Haughton, of Captain Evans' company, which had a short time before joined us, to report to Colonel Campbell, whose immediate command I was then under, and ask of him permission to take my command back to camp for the purpose of feeding my horses. I received in reply to exercise my own discretion. As I had permission to do so, between 9 and 10 o'clock I ordered the remainder of my command, consisting of two companies, and Captain Evans' company, commanded by Lieutenant Evans, taking the horses of the dismounted companies back to camp.

Next morning about 4 o'clock I ordered the two companies to mount, and take with them the horses of the dismounted companies and hold themselves in readiness to march.

Before day I sent Captain Cole's company to relieve the two companies that had been on duty during the night as vedettes. The two companies relieved returned to camp about 4 a. m. I ordered the commanders of these two companies, together with Company C, commanded by Lieutenant Wynn, which had arrived from Washington about 2 o'clock at night, having made the march during the day and part of the night, a distance of 40 miles, to feed and rest until they were ordered by me to report for duty on the field.

When I arrived near the intrenchments on the Beaufort road I ordered a halt. I then reported myself to Colonel Campbell, with my command, for duty. He ordered me to remain ready for duty. I immediately returned to my command, soon after which the enemy's vessels opened a heavy fire, at which time I received orders to dismount the remainder of my command and send them to the right and report to Colonel Vance. I immediately ordered Captain Cole, Company F, and Captain Thomas, Company E, to dismount, and Captain Thomas to take command of the two companies, which he did, and marched off. Soon after Major Woodfin arrived, and I ordered him to proceed and take charge of the two companies then marching to the intrenchments, which he promptly obeyed. I immediately dispatched a courier to order the three companies then in camp to report to me at a point on the railroad for duty; but before reporting to me I was informed that they were ordered to retreat by Lieutenant-Colonel Robinson.

While waiting I perceived that the Militia were giving way and retreating. I immediately rode back where the horses of my dismounted men were held, and found many of them mounted and being mounted by the infantry. Captain Cole, most of his command, and a portion of Captain Thomas' command, succeeded in getting their horses, but Lieutenant Graham's command was left on foot, except those that had charge of his horses; also a portion of Captain Thomas' command, which retreated in company with Colonel Vance's command. I remained a short time, expecting Lieutenant Graham and Captain Thomas to come up, so as to inform them what had become of their horses; but they not arriving, and seeing the infantry retreating from the left of our works, I rode off and overtook my command at Colonel Lee's camp. I immediately proceeded to the head of my command in order to make them march over the bridge by file, fearing that it might break down, which I succeeded in doing in good order, some having however passed over before I arrived at the bridge.

After remaining on the east side of the bridge until about half of my command had passed over I ordered Major Woodfin to remain until they were all over. I then passed over the bridge for the purpose of forming my battalion on the other side. After passing to the other side I found Lieutenant Baker, who I ordered to assist me in forming it. He then informed me that Lieutenant-Colonel Robinson was there attending to the formation of the battalion.

After the whole of my command had passed over, excepting Captain Hays, Company A, I ordered Surgeon Smith to direct Lieutenant Colonel Robinson to march the battalion on the Kinston road a short distance beyond New Berne, and there halt it, and permit the wagons to go on toward Kinston under the directions of the general in command, when a board of officers, composed of the colonels of different regiments, was called, directing us that if we were driven from the intrenchments to fall back on New Berne, which was the only order to retreat I ever received up to that time.

While at the bridge, in company with Captain Strange and Lieutenant Baker, of Company D, Major Barringer rode up, and informed me that he was ordered by the commanding general to direct me to recross the bridge and form my battalion to cover the retreat of the infantry. I told him that I had ordered it to New Berne, but informed him that I would obey the order, and immediately rode rapidly off in company with Major Barringer to do so.

On arriving at New Berne I found my battalion formed and halted on the Kinston road and found Major Woodfin in command. I inquired of him where Lieutenant-Colonel Robinson was, and he informed me that he had rode into New Berne, upon which information we both rode to the railroad. Upon arriving there Major Gilmer gave the order for all the troops to rally around the depot. Major Boone then ordered me to have all the cotton and naval stores in New Berne burned. I asked him by what authority he gave the order. His reply was that it came from headquarters. I then told him it should be executed, and ordered Major Woodfin to make a detail of men to do so, which he promptly did, and left my command for the purpose of executing the same.

I remained with my command halted until the cars left the depot and the enemy were shelling the town, several shells falling near my battalion. I then ordered a retreat, which was continued until some one in the rear gave the order to "Gallop, march." The men then became somewhat excited. I sent back to ascertain who gave the order, but could not find out who gave it, but immediately heard that the enemy were pursuing us with 700 cavalry. Captain Randolph rode up to me and informed me that he had heard that we were pursued with cavalry, and asked me if I did not intend making a stand. I replied that I did intend doing so, and sent him on ahead for the purpose of selecting a suitable place. I was informed there was a bridge some 2 miles ahead, at which place we halted with the intention of giving them battle. Lieutenant-Colonel Robinson then rode up where I was, and I directed him to take his position in the battalion and assist me, as I intended making a stand to resist the 700 cavalry that I understood was in pursuit. He replied that he did not believe that there was any cavalry in pursuit, and that he was ordered to Goldsborough, or had to go to Goldsborough to see General Gatlin. I then told him if he had to go, to go along. He then said to me that I had better form a rear guard to cover the retreat and take command of it myself, and that he should report to General Gatlin that I had done so. He then left. I then ordered 20 men to the bridge and rode along the line and cautioned my men to be cool.

During our halt at the bridge Captain Hays came up with his command, and I invited the captains and lieutenants in command of the companies, with Colonel Crossan, to hold a consultation, and their conclusion was that it would be better for us to proceed on to Kinston that night, for fear of the enemy coming up the river and burning the bridge at Kinston, thereby cutting off our retreat. I then ordered Captain Hays to take command of the rear guard and I took command of the front myself. We continued our retreat to Kinston, arriving there between 11 and 12 o'clock at night.

All the officers under my command, so far as I could discover, obeyed my orders promptly and acted with coolness.

I have submitted one report showing the loss of my horses and baggage. Since that time I succeeded in recovering several of my horses that were missing.

All of which is respectfully submitted.

S. B. SPRUILL,
Colonel Nineteenth Regiment North Carolina State Troops.

Brig. Gen. L. O'B. BRANCH, *Kinston, N. C.*

No. 24.

Report of Col. Zebulon B. Vance, Twenty-sixth North Carolina Infantry.

HDQRS. TWENTY-SIXTH REGT. NORTH CAROLINA VOLS.,
Kinston, N. C., March 17, 1862.

GENERAL: I have the honor to report, in accordance with military usage, the share of my command in the operations of last Friday.

While in temporary command of the post of New Berne, on Thursday, my regiment was ordered to Croatan works, under command of Lieutenant-Colonel Burgwyn, to assist Colonel Sinclair's regiment should the enemy land below those works.

Learning soon after that Colonel Campbell was at his post, I instantly transferred to him my temporary command and proceeded to Croatan to assume command of my regiment. When near there I met Colonel Sinclair retreating, who informed me that the enemy were landing in force at Fisher's Landing, and nearer still to the works I met Colonel Campbell, who had just ordered my regiment to take the cars and return to Fort Thompson. Before my return they had been posted by Lieutenant-Colonel Burgwyn in the series of redans constructed by me, on the right of the railroad, in the rear of Bullen's Branch, extending from the railroad to the swamp, about 500 yards from the road, by Weathersby's.

At this road, as you will remember, I had constructed the night before a breastwork commanding the passage of the swamp, with the assistance of Mr. —— Hawks, a gentleman whose skill in engineering, untiring energy, and zeal I take pleasure in noticing favorably; and there was placed a section of Captain Brem's artillery, lieutenant Williams commanding, and Captain McRae's company of infantry, with a portion of the companies of Captains Hays and Thomas, Second North Carolina Cavalry, dismounted.

About 2 o'clock Friday morning, in compliance with orders received, I pushed companies B, E, and K of my right wing across the small swamp alluded to, so as to make my extreme right rest on the battery at the Weathersby road.

This was our position on Friday morning, which remained unchanged during the day, except that two companies of the Thirty-third Regiment, under Lieutenant-Colonel Hoke, came to my assistance about 9 o'clock, which were placed in the redans vacated by my right companies which were thrown beyond the swamp. You will perceive that my forces covered almost as much ground as all the rest of our troops together. Taking my own position near the center, a little nearer to the right, under Lieutenant-Colonel Burgwyn, about whose position I was considerably uneasy, owing to the unfinished state of our works there, I placed the left under the command of Major Carmichael and awaited the engagement. It began on my left wing about 7.50 o'clock, extending toward my right by degrees until about 8.30 o'clock, when all the troops in my command were engaged so far as the swamp referred to. The severest fighting was on my extreme left, the enemy advancing under shelter of the woods to within easy range of our lines. Whenever they left the woods and entered among the fallen timber of the swamp in our front they were driven back in confusion by the most deadly and well-directed fire from our lines who, with the greatest coolness, watched for their appearance.

The fight was kept up until about 12 o'clock, when information was brought to me by Capt. J. T. Young, my quartermaster, who barely escaped with life in getting to me, that the enemy in great force had turned my left by the railroad track at Wood's brick-yard, had pillaged my camp, were firing in reverse on my left wing, and were several hundred yards up the railroad between me and New Berne; also that all the troops on the field were in full retreat, except my command. This being so, there was no alternative left me but to order an immediate retreat or be completely surrounded by an overwhelming force. Without hesitation I gave the order. My men jumped out of the trenches, rallied, and formed in the woods without panic or confusion, and, having first sent a messenger with an order to Lieutenant-Colonel Burgwyn to follow with the forces on the right, we struck across the Weathersby road for Bryce's Creek, with the intention of getting into the Pollocksville road.   On arriving at the creek we found only one small boat, capable of carrying only three men, in which to pass over.   The creek here is too deep to ford and about 75 yards wide.   Some plunged in and swam over, and, swimming over myself, I rode down to Captain Whitford's house, on the Trent, and through the kindness of Mr. Kit Foy, a citizen, procured three more small boats, carrying one on our shoulders from the Trent, with which we hurried up to the crossing.   In the mean time Lieutenant-Colonel Burgwyn arrived with the forces of the right wing in excellent condition, and assisted me with the greatest coolness and efficiency in getting the troops across, which after four hours of hard labor and the greatest anxiety we succeeded in doing.   Lieutenant-Colonel Burgwyn saw the last man over before he entered the boat.   I regret to say that three men were drowned in crossing.

I must here mention favorably the good conduct of the troops under these trying circumstances, a large Yankee force being drawn up in view of our scouts about 1 mile away and their skirmishers appearing just as the rear got over.

Musician B. F. Johnson, Company B, deserves particular mention for his exertions, having ferried over the greater portion of the troops himself, assisted by a negro boy.

Once over, we were joined by Lieutenant-Colonel Hoke, Thirty-third Regiment, with a large portion of his command, and took the road for Trenton.   We marched night and day stopping at no time for rest or sleep more than four hours.

We arrived at this place safely at noon on the 16th.   The loyalty and hospitality of the citizens greatly facilitated our march, furnishing us cheerfully with provisions, wagons, shelter, and guides.

I regret to say that many of our men, despairing of the boats at the creek and determined not to be taken, threw away their guns to swim over; a serious loss to our Government, but scarcely blamable under the circumstances.

This concludes the narration of the principal matters connected with my command during the engagement and retreat.   The number of my killed and wounded has not yet been ascertained.   Our baggage, of course, was lost, but our sick were safely brought away.

It remains for me to speak of the noble dead we left upon the field. Maj. A. B. Carmichael fell about 11 a. m., by a shot through the head, while gallantly holding his post on the left under a most galling fire. A braver, nobler soldier never fell on field of battle.   Generous and open-hearted as he was brave and chivalrous, he was endeared to the whole regiment.   Honored be his memory.   Soon after Capt. W. P. Martin, of Company H, also fell near the regimental colors.   Highly respected as a man, brave and determined as a soldier, he was equally regretted by his command and all who knew him.   The Twenty-sixth Regiment are justly proud of their glorious fall.   The fate of Captain Rand, of Company D, is yet unknown.   When last seen he was almost surrounded by a large force; but, disdaining to fly or surrender, he was fighting desperately with Lieutenant Vinson and a large portion of his company, who refused to leave him.   Lieutenant Porter, of Company A, was also left behind wounded.   Capt. A. N. McMillan was badly wounded, but got away safely.

In regard to the behavior of my regiment generally, I am scarcely willing to mention particular instances of gallantry where all did their duty. Observing a large portion of the regiment myself, and making diligent inquiry as to the rest, I could learn of but one man in all my command who remembered that he had legs until after the command to retreat was given. They were the last of our troops to leave the field.

I cannot conclude this report without mentioning in terms of the highest praise the spirit of determination and power of endurance evinced by the troops during the hardships and sufferings of our march. Drenched with rain, blistered feet, without sleep, many sick and wounded, and almost naked, they toiled on through the day and all the weary watches of the night without murmuring, cheerfully and with subordination, evincing most thoroughly those high qualities in adversity which military men learn to value still more than courage upon the field.

I have the honor to be, most respectfully, your obedient servant,

Z. B. VANCE,
Colonel, Commanding Twenty-sixth North Carolina Vols.

· General L. O'B. BRANCH,
Commanding District of Pamlico.

No. 25.

Report of Maj. John A. Gilmer, jr., Twenty-seventh North Carolina Infantry.

KINSTON, N. C., *March* 16, 1862.

SIR: I most respectfully submit the following report of the part borne in the engagement of the 14th instant at the breastworks adjoining Fort Thompson, N. C., by the Twenty-seventh Regiment North Carolina troops, then under my command:

On the morning of the 13th, pursuant to orders from your headquarters, I marched the Twenty-seventh Regiment to the river bank, about 100 yards above Fort Thompson, arriving about an hour before daybreak. Forming the regiment in line of battle at that point I awaited orders.

About 7 o'clock I received orders to retire a short distance toward the river, to avoid any shot and shell that might be thrown in the direction of Fort Thompson. The regiment was immediately moved a short distance to the left and rear.

While in this position I received orders to march the regiment to the breastworks and line the same on the left near Fort Thompson, which was immediately done. The regiment remained (covering the breastworks, principally in one rank, for the distance of 300 or 400 yards from Fort Thompson) all the day and night of the 13th; were aroused and placed in position at the works twice during the night. Numbers of shell and shot were thrown from the gunboats of the enemy during the evening of the 13th, most of which, however, passed beyond the works.

On the morning of the 14th the regiment was again placed in position to await the approach of the enemy, whom I supposed to be in force in the woods in front of the works. I was informed by Captain Barden, whose company had been sent out the evening before as a portion of the picket guard, that the enemy was advancing on the county road to our right.

About 6.30 or 7 a. m. the fire of the enemy began beyond our right and continued vigorously during the entire engagement. The fire was immediately returned by the artillery stationed beyond the right of the Twenty-seventh and continued unabated. I commanded the regiment to retain their fire until ordered to fire by me.

A short time after the firing began on the right the bombardment again began from the gunboats of the enemy, directed principally toward Fort Thompson and the portion of the breastworks behind which the Twenty-seventh was stationed. Thus situated, the regiment manfully and cheerfully sustained the shower of shell and shot from the gunboats for two and a half hours, during which but 1 man was killed and 3 stunned.

Between 10 and 11 a. m. I discovered that the troops stationed immediately on the right of the Twenty-seventh were falling back, which movement I discovered was being followed by two or three companies of the Twenty-seventh, on the right. I immediately hastened to my right and ordered the two retreating companies back to the trenches. I then gave my entire command the order to fire by file, designating at the same time the direction in which I perceived the enemy advancing in great numbers.

I then hastened to meet you, whom I perceived advancing along the lines to the left. You informed me that our right had been turned and I must fall back. I then ordered the regiment to retire, which was done in tolerable order by most of the companies on the left. I ordered those companies which were together to march through Camp Gatlin to the railroad bridge, where the greater part of the right assembled and halted. I hastened then to the left, beyond Camp Fisher, to find out what were the plans of our troops, supposing that a stand was to be made at that point. Finding our forces retreating, I returned to the right and passed with them over the bridge to the railroad depot, where the companies were again formed, agreeably to orders I had received from the assistant adjutant-general.

At the depot we were ordered to fall back still farther, when I placed the regiment on the march toward Kinston, under command of my senior captain. I joined the regiment again where the railroad is crossed by the county road above New Berne, and again joined them at Tuscarora, whence I proceeded with them to Kinston, partly on foot and partly by means of the cars which were sent back to take us up.

From the reports of the captains of my command I obtained the following particulars. There were in—

	Killed.	Wounded.	Missing.
Company A	1	....	1
Company B	1	....	1
Company C	1	....	2
Company D	....	....	15
Company E	1	2	22
Company F, all present	....	3	....
Company G	....	*3	1
Company H	....	....	†9
Total	4	8	51

* Slightly injured.   † Reported.

Company I.—The majority of this company followed the captain to Jones County.
Company K.—Two commanding officers and all the company but 30 supposed to be in Goldsborough.

The promptness and cheerfulness with which the officers under my command obeyed every order and the courage with which they took and maintained every position assigned them I cannot too favorably notice. In the retreat I discovered that a few men in each company had either lost or abandoned their guns and cartridge boxes.

Very respectfully,

J. A. GILMER, JR.,
Major, Comdg. Twenty-seventh Regt. North Carolina Troops.

Col. CHARLES C. LEE,
Commanding —— Brigade, North Carolina Troops.

P. S.—It is, perhaps, proper for me to add that about 30 of the Twenty-seventh were detailed to operate Latham's battery in conjunction with Captain Latham's company. These 30 men were in the hottest of the engagement, and several of them seriously injured but none killed.

No. 26.

Report of Lieut. Col. Robert F. Hoke, Thirty-third North Carolina Infantry.

HDQRS. THIRTY-THIRD NORTH CAROLINA REGIMENT,
Kinston, N. C., March 18, 1862.

SIR: In accordance with your orders I respectfully submit the following report concerning our orders received from you and the action of our regiment afterward:

After arriving near the breastworks opposite Fort Thompson and taking up camp on Thursday evening (13th) we were ordered by you to remain in that position for further orders.

At daylight on the following morning you in person ordered Colonel Avery to take position in a line of battle about 400 yards to the rear of the brick-yards, with our right wing resting upon the railroad, and were to remain in that position for further orders, we constituting the reserve; and soon after we had formed our regiment and had them to take off their knapsacks, in order to be ready to move with quickness to any point we might be ordered, we were ordered to move forward about 100 yards immediately to the rear of your position, which in the opinion of the field officers of our regiment was a very exposed one and one well selected, as from that point the movements of the enemy could best be seen. Shortly after we reached that point an order was received from you, through Colonel Robinson to Colonel Avery, to send his right wing, in command of Lieutenant-Colonel Hoke, composing five companies, to occupy the intrenchments on the right of the railroad. I immediately faced the right wing to the right and moved off at a double-quick, going through the woods and down the ravines, in order to protect the men as much as possible, as a forward movement down the railroad would have greatly exposed the command.

I halted them in a ravine, ordered four companies to lie down, and intended to place them in the works by company, as I could in that way save the lives of many, as the firing was very hot at that point. After placing Company A (Captain Cowan) in position, and having returned and was placing Captain Parks' company in position, I received an order from you to return with the command. I immediately faced Captain Parks' company about, and was returning with the four companies, when I was met by Colonel Avery and Major Lewis with the remaining five companies, which composed the left wing, coming up in line of battle and in fine order, and was ordered by Colonel Avery to face about and join him. I did so, and the regiment moved up to the scene of action in fine style, Colonel Avery in command of the center, I of the right wing, and Major Lewis of the left.

Colonel Avery gave the command to fire before we reached the intrenchments, as the enemy were firing upon us and were in full force upon the top of the hill immediately across the swamp. Our fire seemed to have great effect, as the enemy scampered. Major Lewis then moved immediately to the right of the railroad with several companies and engaged the enemy from that time until after 12 o'clock. He behaved most gallantly; was in the hottest part of the whole battle-field. He repulsed the enemy time and again, and twice charged them with detachments of companies, and each time made them flee. Our loss was greater at that point than any other, as he had to fight to his front, right, and left, but still maintained his position, fighting them against greater numbers. No one could have behaved with more coolness, bravery, and determination than he, and he deserves the praise of every true countryman for his actions. He reports his men as having done their duty in every manner.

Colonel Avery was in command of the center, on top of the second hill from the railroad, encouraging his men both by actions and words. He was perfectly cool, and never did man act better upon the battle-field than he. His fire was very destructive, and remarked that if he had his regiment together he would charge the rascals over the fallen timber. He received a shot through the top of his cap, and coolly remarked, "Boys, they liked to have gotten me," but heeded it not, and went on cheering his men.

I was immediately at his right, and finding the enemy were getting in strong force upon our right and were going to turn our right flank, as there were no troops between our regiment and the left of Colonel Vance's companies upon the right flank of the whole troops, a distance of a quarter of a mile, I moved quickly with Captain Parks' company, which I had thrown in the woods in a ravine as a reserve to our regiment, with Lieutenant Poteat adjutant, who displayed great coolness during the action, and finding the enemy in great force did not expose my weakness by firing, but sent a messenger to Colonel Avery for another company. He immediately sent me Captain Kesler's company. I ordered the whole to fire, which did great execution, as the enemy fell and fled, but soon appeared again, and again we drove them back, but soon they again appeared in strong force and engaged us, which continued until 12.30 o'clock. At 12.15 o'clock I saw the United States flag flying upon one of our works, but saw Colonel Avery still fighting, and I, being very busily engaged with the enemy, did not know that Colonel Avery and Major Lewis had fallen back until I saw the enemy upon my left with several regiments (which force caused Colonel Avery and Major Lewis to fall back, as their left was completely turned and the enemy was getting to their rear), and about 50 yards to the rear of the position Colonel Avery had occupied. I then saw for the first time we were driven back, and ordered the men under my command to fall back, but to do so in order. We were hotly fired at when we fell back. I fell back some distance and intended to unite with Colonel Avery and Major Lewis, but found the troops had continued to fall back, so kept on and intended to join my regiment at the bridge, but found it on fire, so had to cross Bryce's Creek; and on getting over learned our troops had made no stand at New Berne; continued the retreat to Trenton, in connection with Colonel Vance, who crossed the creek with me, and learning at Trenton our troops were making a stand at Kinston, made a forced march, and reached that point on Sunday morning about 10 o'clock, which made a march of 50 miles in about thirty-six hours.

Captain Engelhard, quartermaster, Captain Gibson, commissary, and our surgeons, Drs. Baker and Shoffner, all did their duty very well indeed. Dr. Shaffner was of great assistance to me on the march.

We entered the field with 614 men, but lost in killed, wounded, and missing 196. Among this number we have reason to believe our loss in killed and wounded is greater than the number taken as prisoners. Our brave colonel is a prisoner.

Captain Cowan, Company A, was first ordered into the fight and sustained a very heavy loss. His officers acted most bravely, and Private David Phifer is highly spoken of for his bravery before he was killed. He was killed while carrying a message from Major Lewis to Colonel Avery. Private Dolchite is also spoken of in the captain's report for having thrown away his clothing in order to swim the creek and save his gun. He is a boy of sixteen years of age.

Captain Jenkins, Company B, is reported, as also his officers and men, for having acted well in every particular.

Captain Kesler, Company C, and Lieutenant Corzine and men, acted well. Lieutenant Patterson displayed fear. All the officers and men behaved well except Captain Parker, who left the scene of action too soon.

Captain McIntyre, in the retreat, ordered his men to go home, and Lieutenant Rayle did not report himself at all the morning the regiment left for the engagement. Sergeant Babb and Private Daniel Webb are spoken of by Lieutenant Gatling as having acted well.

Very respectfully, yours,

R. F. HOKE,
Lieutenant-Colonel.

General L. O'B. BRANCH.

No. 27.

Report of Col. James Sinclair, Thirty-fifth North Carolina Infantry.

HDQRS. THIRTY-FIFTH REGT. NORTH CAROLINA TROOPS,
Kinston, N. C., March 19, 1862.

COLONEL: I have the honor to inform you that on Wednesday, the 12th instant, at 4 p. m., I received orders to march down to Fisher's Landing, to oppose the landing of the enemy at that place, reported to be in force with his fleet down the river.

I left New Berne, according to orders, at 6.30 p. m., with my command, by railroad, and arrived at the point designated at 8 o'clock that night about 9 miles below the town. At the time I arrived there was sufficient moonlight to enable me to see that the enemy in heavy force was not far distant. I could distinctly hear the music of his bands and even the singing of his men on the fleet. Making Fisher's Landing my center, I posted pickets on each side of the landing, extending 3 miles

from my center.   I posted the balance of my regiment along the rifle
pits and breastworks guarding the landing, holding one company in reserve at the landing proper.   During the night a heavy rain set in,
thoroughly drenching my men, who were without cover or shelter.

Early on the morning of the 13th the enemy commenced landing in
heavy force some 2 or 3 miles below my pickets.   A company of cavalry and a regiment which I was promised would support me did not
make their appearance; consequently, having had orders to oppose the
debarkation of the enemy at Fisher's Landing, I was unable to prevent
him below.   By this means the Croatan breastworks fell into his hands.
During the landing of the enemy his gunboats continued shelling the
woods.

At 10 a. m. he approached Fisher's Landing with his boats, throwing shell and canister as he came, steaming sufficiently nigh to hear the
conversation of 'his men on board.   About this time Colonel Campbell,
of the Seventh Regiment, my senior officer, made his appearance on the
ground (not with his regiment, however), and, having carefully surveyed my position and the force of the enemy, ordered me to fall back
into the woods beyond reach of the enemy's fire, which I did, with my
command in good order, by way of Fisher's avenue.   In retiring I had
3 of my men wounded by the enemy's shells, one of whom has since
been reported dead.

After forming in the woods near the railroad Colonel Campbell ordered me to fall back on the Fort Thompson intrenchments, where I was
ordered to take position on the right of the Seventh Regiment North
Carolina troops.   Here, under a heavy rain, we remained all night of
the 13th instant, without food, after having been all the night previous
exposed to a continuous rain, nearly three hours of the day exposed to
the enemy's fire, besides marching for several hours, having tasted no
food from the evening we left New Berne.   Posted on my right was the
Militia, resting on the railroad by the brick-yard, where the enemy
afterward made his strongest demonstration.

According to the disposition made on the morning of the 14th instant
before the engagement took place, my command was divided by a section of Brem's battery and Captain Whitehurst's independent company
separating my right wing from my center and left wing.   On my right
a space of about 40 yards intervening [between] the Militia and the
railroad was still left vacant; besides, a trench that ran parallel with
the railroad of about 60 or 80 yards was unoccupied by our troops.

In this condition of affairs the battle opened about 7.30 a. m. by the
firing of a gun from the enemy's field batteries planted in front of the
old county road, which fire was replied to by Brem's and Latham's
batteries.   Immediately the enemy opened with musketry from the
county road above referred to, which was replied to by my regiment,
with others to the left.   The enemy advanced twice upon the breastworks occupied by me, which advances were repelled each time.

At 10 a. m. he appeared in force on the railroad and on the right of
my position, and, the Militia having retired and the trench above referred to being occupied by him in force, as also were the buildings in
the brick-yard, I found my command completely flanked.

At this time, however, my second in command, without consulting
me, ordered four of my companies on the right wing to fall back, which
I rallied and ordered back to their post, which they immediately did,
and held it for some time.   The fire of the enemy becoming more galling on my right flank, they again retired, by command of my lieuten-

ant-colonel, who, with one company and portions of other companies at my command, formed in rear of my center.

Meantime I had dispatched my adjutant to Colonel Campbell, my commanding officer, to communicate to him the real condition of my regiment—exposed to the flanking fire of the enemy. The colonel having arrived and having surveyed my position, and the section of Brem's battery near me having by this time ceased to fire, he ordered me to retire with my command in the following words: "You had better take your men out of that as quick as possible"; which order I immediately obeyed. In retiring, however, one of my officers and several of my men were killed and some wounded. This created somewhat of a panic, as the enemy were firing upon us from the railroad and brick-yard; but soon my men rallied and retired in perfect order till we reached that portion of the railroad intersected by the county road, where I formed them into line ready to advance to meet the foe if called upon.

Colonel Lane's regiment, having arrived at this time, relieved me, and I fell back upon New Berne by the railroad bridge.

I again formed my men at the railroad depot, waiting for orders, where Lieutenant-Colonel Barbour, of the Thirty-seventh, having in charge some fragments of his regiment, informed me that the orders were to fall back by the Kinston road. This I did in perfect order, until some officers who were retiring with speed along the road informed me that the enemy's cavalry were in force in the rear. At this juncture Company D, of my regiment, volunteered to become the rear guard of the entire force. Colonel Lee, of the Thirty-seventh, kindly volunteered to command the rear guard, in order to permit me to attend to the balance of my regiment, who were jaded and broken down by exposure, fasting, fighting, and marching since the evening of the 12th instant. My presence was demanded with my regiment by the fact that on the first alarm of the enemy's cavalry being in close proximity my lieutenant-colonel deserted his regiment and sought safety for himself. The alarm proving false the guard was dismissed, and I conducted my regiment to Tuscarora, where I joined portions of the Twenty-seventh and Thirty-seventh Regiments and fragments from the other regiments engaged in the affair of the 14th instant, and took command until the arrival of General Branch.

In conclusion I have only to add that, with the exception above referred to, all my officers and men behaved well.

Special praise is due to Company D, commanded by Captain Lasater, for the alacrity with which they volunteered to defend our retreating columns when the enemy's cavalry was reported to be upon us.

I am indebted for efficient services to Maj. O. C. Pettway and Adjt. Thomas J. Oates.

Casualties of the battle : One officer, Lieutenant Hale, and 4 privates were killed, 11 privates wounded, and 9 missing.

I have the honor to be, colonel, respectfully, your obedient servant,
JAMES SINCLAIR,
Colonel, Commanding.

No. 28.

Report of Col. Charles C. Lee, Thirty-seventh North Carolina Infantry.

MARCH 16, 1862.

GENERAL: In compliance with your orders I herewith submit respectfully to you a report of the left wing at the battle at Johnston's Cross-Roads:

On Wednesday afternoon, at about 5 o'clock, I received from you notice that the enemy were advancing up the river, and later the same information was received by Captain Herring. I rode down to the batteries and ordered everything in readiness.

At 10 p. m. I got notice from you of my command, and immediately issued orders to all to be in readiness and gave them appropriate instructions. Under these Captain Brem packed up his baggage and it has been saved. Captain Brem was afterward transferred to Colonel Campbell's command, and will report through him.

Thursday the enemy spent the day in shelling the woods below, and toward evening some of the men built fires (which were immediately extinguished), when our lines were shelled for about one and a half hours, without injury to any one.

About 8 p. m. notice was sent you of signals on our right flank.

About 7.30 a. m. on the 14th we fired a 12-pounder gun at the enemy, and a few minutes afterward the battle commenced in earnest. A warm attack was made at the Beaufort road; but Captain Latham's artillery was fired with such precision that they made no advance, though they kept up a constant fire here during the whole engagement. The piece on the left hand of the Beaufort road was commanded by Captain Latham in person, and after all his men except 3 were either killed or dangerously wounded and rendered unfit for service, the piece was served effectively for some twenty minutes, until the day was lost, when he barely escaped. After the attempt on the Beaufort road the foe flanked to the right and moved in heavy column toward our left flank; but having given notice to Colonel Crossan of their approach, he opened on them with grape from three 32-pounders with such terrible effect that after about six shots they fell back; and though they kept up a constant and warm fire, they made no advance toward the work.

Some time after this the firing became hotter, when I received from you an order to send some re-enforcements to Colonel Campbell. I ordered the left wing of my regiment to his support and made further arrangements to cover my own flank. The men of the Twenty-seventh and Thirty-seventh Regiments did not fire a shot except a few who were armed with long-range rifles, and this ominous silence was properly appreciated. The men of these regiments, and also of Fort Thompson, appeared always cool and deliberate. While the left wing of the Thirty-seventh moved over to the right they were subjected to a galling fire and suffered to some extent. (See inclosed report of Lieutenant-Colonel Barbour.) Major Gilmer, of the Twenty-seventh, and Lieutenant-Colonel Barbour, of the Thirty-seventh, moved from place to place within the limits of their respective commands, and by their presence and example encouraged their commands very much. One piece—the right piece—in Fort Thompson, which bears on the land, was dismounted, but mounted again by Captain Herring and the carriage properly repaired. Five men in the fort were wounded; none, I believe, dangerously.

Shortly after the left wing of the Thirty-seventh was sent to Colonel Campbell's aid, I observed his regiment moving rapidly to the rear through Colonel Vance's camp. I galloped over and demanded where they were going, when I was informed that they were in full retreat. I hastened back and saw the enemy advancing upon our works. Feeling assured that the regiments which were retreating could not be rallied, I ordered my command to fall back, and passed on to the batteries to look after them. While in Fort Thompson (two and a half minutes) five shots struck the upper portion of the right flank of the works and two shells fell within the works, without effect. The guns were all spiked, but the enemy pressed so closely that there was not time to blow up the magazine, being within about 30 or 40 yards when we had spiked the guns. I then went to the other batteries and had the guns dismounted and the magazines blown up.

In blowing up the magazine at Fort Ellis, Captain Mayo was seriously (I fear dangerously) wounded, and one other man. All the men of the left wing were saved, and retreated over to New Berne in tolerable order. One man of Colonel Sloan's Twenty-seventh Regiment was killed.

When I crossed over to New Berne I found some of the regiments had passed beyond, and I was thus prevented from carrying out your order to form in the upper part of the town. As I advanced up the Trent road to Kinston I overtook Colonel Sinclair's regiment, and a foolish report having got afloat that the enemy had landed cavalry, which were in pursuit, I requested and obtained from Colonel Sinclair a rear guard, which I formed, and we then moved on to the railroad crossing, where it was merged with the regiment, and proceeded up to Tuscarora.

Lieut. C. H. Brown, of Captain Latham's battery, was on several occasions on the left wing, and acted with great coolness; indeed, almost with foolhardiness. Lieutenant Nicholson, my adjutant, and Mr. Noble, who was acting as my aide, also displayed coolness; but no occasion for gallantry presented itself to any one in the left wing.

I am, general, respectfully,

CHARLES C. LEE,
Col. 37th Regt. North Carolina Troops, Comdg. Left Wing.

No. 29.

Report of Lieut. Col. William M. Barbour, Thirty-seventh North Carolina Infantry.

————, —— —, 1862.

I have the honor to submit the following report of the part taken by the Thirty-seventh Regiment in the recent engagement near New Berne:

Pursuant to orders from Brigadier-General Branch I moved with my command at 3 o'clock Thursday morning and occupied that portion of our line on the left of the old Beaufort road. During the day shells were thrown frequently from the enemy's gunboats at our position without any damage to us.

On Friday morning about daylight the enemy appeared in full force in front of our lines, partially concealed by the woods, and immediately opened a heavy fire of artillery and musketry upon us. The fire was promptly returned by Captain Latham's battery, stationed in and near the Beaufort road, with great effect. Immediately the enemy attempted a flank movement on our left, for the purpose of storming Fort Thompson. This movement was at once defeated by a destructive fire from the land batteries of Fort Thompson. During the remaining portion of the action the enemy kept up an incessant fire on the position occupied by my command.

A short time before 12 o'clock I was ordered to send five companies of my regiment to the support of Colonel Campbell's brigade, which was at that time hard pressed. I immediately moved the following companies to the designated point: Company D, under Captain Ashcraft; Company B, under Lieutenant Cook; Company E, under Lieutenant Farthing; Company C, under Lieutenant Gillespie, and Company K, under Captain Rosse. Great credit is due to these companies for the promptness and bravery with which they moved under a very heavy fire of artillery and infantry for some 400 yards. A short time after they marched to the designated point our center near the railroad had given away. After a short and spirited contest these companies were ordered by Colonel Campbell to retire, which was done in good order.

About this time I observed the forces toward our center retreating, but I considered it my duty to hold my position until I was ordered to retreat. Colonel Lee rode toward the center to ascertain the meaning of these movements, and on his return informed me that the center was in full retreat, and directed me at once to fall back. I at once proceeded with my remaining five companies toward the railroad bridge, and at the point where the Beaufort road crosses the railroad I found the five companies which had been sent to the right drawn up in line of battle and awaiting the arrival of the remaining five companies. I inquired of General Branch what I should do with my regiment, and was directed to cross the railroad bridge and form in New Berne across the track. As soon as I reached that point I found this impracticable, for the reason that the houses in that part of the town were built to the water's edge, and I could only have formed a line of battle some 15 feet in length; I therefore moved my regiment to the depot and halted it. I soon afterward saw Colonel Robinson, General Branch's acting assistant adjutant-general, and inquired where he desired me to move my regiment. He directed me to move toward Kinston. I therefore marched my regiment in good order out of New Berne toward Kinston. When we reached the point where the Kinston road intersects the railroad an alarm was raised by some of the cavalry that the enemy's cavalry were in pursuit. Finding a number of men (not in my command) throwing away their guns, I rode to the rear and informed them that it was a false alarm, and begged them to keep the road and act like men. I remained at that point until near sundown, when I proceeded to Tuscarora Depot, 8 miles from New Berne. During the night the troops were brought by railroad to Kinston.

The men under my command behaved with great coolness and deliberation during the entire day, retreated in good order, and brought with them all their guns and ammunition. We could easily have saved our baggage if we had had wagons, but having only two small vehicles, I knew it was useless to attempt it. It was, however, all burned, to prevent it from falling into the hands of the enemy.

When our regiment was ordered to retreat the enemy had crossed the breastworks in the center and in three minutes would have had us completely cut off.

Most of the missing have since been heard from and will rejoin the regiment. *

Respectfully, yours,

WILL. M. BARBOUR,
Lieutenant-Colonel, Thirty-seventh Regiment, N. C. Troops.

----

* Nominal list of casualties omitted; embodied in tabular statement, p. 247.

No. 30.

Report of Col. H. J. B. Clark, Special Battalion North Carolina Militia.

HDQRS. NORTH CAROLINA MILITIA, SPECIAL.BATTALION,
Kinston, N. C., March 17, 1862.

SIR : In compliance with your instructions, received at New Berne 9 p. m. March 13, to report to Colonel Campbell at his headquarters, at Fort Thompson breastworks, I respectfully report that I repaired forthwith to that place, accompanied by Maj. Joseph N. Jones, but did not find Colonel Campbell.

Major Jones called at Colonel Vance's encampment and was informed there that Colonel Campbell had gone in the direction of New Berne. Proceeding thence to New Berne, by way of Colonel Lee's encampment, went to Colonel Campbell's encampment, and reported, in his absence, to Lieut. Col. E. G. Haywood, who directed me to report.for duty at the depot of the Atlantic and North Carolina Railroad in New Berne on the following day, 5 a. m. The company was promptly reported and left New Berne at 8 a. m., and arriving at the breastworks was assigned position.

On the following morning, March 14, my command was placed in line of battle, numbering 264, 20 having been detailed for hospital duty and 45 to aid Lieutenant Hawks in mounting cannon on the right of the breastworks. These last were forced from the works by the enemy's sharpshooters and came to the ranks after the action commenced.

As soon as the firing commenced the ground in front of me was so obscured by smoke that I could see but a short distance, and as firing had commenced on my left with guns of longer range, as soon as I thought the enemy within reach of my guns commenced the fire by file, which order was promptly obeyed with coolness and determination. After firing three rounds I commanded the fire to cease. Soon after the smoke cleared away and the enemy were plainly seen drawn up in force on our right, and a company of sharpshooters commenced pouring a fire into our rear, doing considerable execution and causing confusion in my ranks, but an order to rally and take position was promptly obeyed, and calmness restored by the assurance that you would soon send re-enforcements; but the fire was continued on us and with redoubled energy, while they (the enemy) crossed the railroad, took possession of the rifle pits on our right and rear, and planted the Stars and Stripes.

Previous to this, however, they had fired upon a reconnoitering party I sent in that direction and upon the quartermaster and teamsters I had sent to recover the ammunition.

I at one time intended to leave the breastworks and charge upon the enemy, and for this purpose caused bayonets to be fixed; but when I saw the sharpshooters were supported by so large a force of the enemy, concluded that such attempt would result in great loss of life to my command without being able to effect corresponding good to our cause, and that a failure might have an evil effect on others. At this moment, and just as Colonel Vance poured his first fire into the enemy, a panic seized my command and part of them broke ranks.

Believing it impossible to reform under the fire of these sharpshooters at this moment of confusion I commanded a retreat in order, which was succeeded by a stampede of most of the command. As soon as they had reached a small brush-wood, perhaps 60 yards distant, I ordered a rally and reformation of the line, in which I was promptly aided by every officer present to my view and for the moment thought I should succeed, but the cry was made that the regulars had retreated; the panic was renewed and increased and my influence as a commander gone.

A few, perhaps 20 in all, with their officers, rallied and volunteered to return and obey my orders; but believing it would involve a sacrifice of 'life to them, being untutored, as we were, in the arts of war, I declined to do so, and in my efforts to rally others to join them became separated from these.

In the retreat I joined you at the railroad crossing, when you proposed to rally and cover the retreat. There I rallied a squad of the Athens Guards and Cow Creek Volunteers, with most of their officers; but soon the retreating column came on and this joined with them.

Leaving you there I went, together with Adjutant Roberts and Lieutenant Mitchell, to burn the tents at Colonel Lee's encampment. From this point we went to Trent (Clairmont) Bridge and found Major Hall making an effort to reform a regiment, and at his request took position on the bridge, to prevent soldiers passing, and remained there until an officer, said to be Lieutenant Burrows, took charge. At the close of the day I parted with you at Tuscarora, having received orders to rally my command and report at this place.

I have made as accurate report to Colonel Campbell of the number of my command in action, of the number killed, wounded, and missing, as I could gather from the commanders of companies. It is believed there were certainly 4 killed and 15 wounded, and there are many missing.

Respectfully,

H. J. B. CLARK,
Colonel, Commanding.

Brig. Gen. L. O'B. BRANCH,
District of Pamlico.

No. 31.

Report of Lieut. J. L. Haughton, Macon Mounted Guards.

KINSTON, N. C., *March* 16, 1862.

According to orders from Brigadier-General Branch I left the Thompson breastworks at 8.30 p. m. on the 13th instant with 10 of my men, and proceeded to Evans' Mill to establish a picket guard, which I did, but did not see anything worth reporting.

The next morning a little before day I, with my men, proceeded to the bridge on the road leading from Captain Evans' to Croatan Battery. At light we commenced cutting it away, and after clearing it I then sent my men some 300 yards in a bottom. I then set fire to the abutment of the bridge and all the plank that would have been of service to the enemy.

All the while I was cutting and burning their pickets were firing upon us at a great rate. I encouraged my men all I could, so they stood until I sent them off. After seeing the last of the bridge I then made an attempt to rejoin my company, but was cut off by their picket. I attempted the second time by a new route, but met with like fate. I then made a third trial, and after going for more than a mile I came across a negro, belonging to Dr. Curtis, of New Berne, who was trying to make his escape from the enemy, as he was tired of living with them. I stopped to ask him some questions, and he told me not to go any farther or else I should be taken. I then countermarched my men, and as they turned balls fell around us as fast as hailstones. We retired in perfect order. I had not gone far before we found ourselves surrounded. My only chance then was to charge upon their pickets. It happened just at that time the firing had ceased at the battery, and the picket supposing that we were cavalry in pursuit of them, so they ran from us faster than we from them. I then made my escape through Trenton, reaching Kinston at sunup Sunday morning completely exhausted, both men and horses.

Very respectfully submitted.

J. L. HAUGHTON,
Second Lieutenant Macon Mounted Guards.

Capt. P. G. EVANS, *Kinston, N. C.*

MARCH 20-21, 1862.—Expedition to Washington, N. C.

Report of Col. Thomas G. Stevenson, Twenty-fourth Massachusetts Infantry.

NEW BERNE, *March 23, 1862.*

Agreeably to orders received from General Foster I embarked the Twenty-fourth Regiment Massachusetts Volunteers on the 19th instant on board the steamer Guide, and on the morning of the 20th, at 7 o'clock, got under way for Washington. Followed the gunboats Delaware, Louisiana, and Commodore Barney. At 7 o'clock same evening came to anchor off the mouth of the Pamlico River. The next morning at daylight we again got under way, and at 10 o'clock arrived at within about 6 miles of Washington, when we discovered their deserted batteries without guns, two on the south bank of the river and the other one on the north. We also discovered here a barricade, consisting of piles cut off about 3 feet below the surface. As I found it would be impossible to carry the steamer Guide up to the city even if the barrier was removed, on account of her drawing too much water, I went on board the steamer Delaware and conferred with Captain Quackenbush, who kindly offered to take two companies up in his steamer; and as the mayor, who had come down to meet us, assured us that there were no troops in the city and as all signs confirmed this statement, I placed Companies I and G on board the Delaware and steamed up to the city, where we found a large number of persons on the wharves. I landed the two companies and marched to the court-house, where we nailed the Stars and Stripes to a flag-pole which we found in front of the court-house. The band played national airs and the men cheered. We then marched through some of the principal streets and returned to the boat. While in the city not a man left the ranks or behaved otherwise than as if on drill.

I was glad to notice considerable Union sentiment expressed by the inhabitants. From quite a number of houses we were saluted by waving handkerchiefs, and from one the national flag, with the motto, "The Union and the Constitution," was displayed. A large number of the inhabitants expressed a wish that sufficient force could be sent there to protect them against the rebels.

On returning to the steamer Guide we found that Professor Malle-fert had blown up the barrier, so as to clear a channel some 60 feet wide. At 6 o'clock same evening weighed anchor and started for New Berne, where we arrived on the afternoon of the following day (21st instant).

Your obedient servant,

THOS. G. STEVENSON,
Colonel Twenty-fourth Regiment Massachusetts Volunteers.

Capt. SOUTHARD HOFFMAN,
 Assistant Adjutant-General.

MARCH 23–APRIL 26, 1862.—Siege of Fort Macon, N. C.

REPORTS.

No. 1.—Maj. Gen. Ambrose E. Burnside, U. S. Army.
No. 2.—Brig. Gen. John G. Parke, U. S. Army.
No. 3.—Lieut. Daniel W. Flagler, U. S. Ordnance Department.
No. 4.—Lieut. Merrick F. Prouty, Twenty-fifth Massachusetts Infantry.
No. 5.—Capt. Lewis O. Morris, First U. S. Artillery.
No. 6.—Col. Isaac P. Rodman, Fourth Rhode Island Infantry.
No. 7.—Lieut. William J. Andrews, Ninth New York Infantry, Acting Signal Officer.
No. 8.—Col. Moses J. White, C. S. Army.

No. 1.

Reports of Maj. Gen. Ambrose E. Burnside, U. S. Army.

HEADQUARTERS DEPARTMENT OF NORTH CAROLINA,
New Berne, N. C., April 17, 1862.

I have the honor to report the following movements in this depart-ment since my last dispatch:

Owing to the absence of engines and cars on the railroad and the burning of the bridges by the enemy the work of General Parke at Fort Macon has proved to be exceedingly difficult. The rebuilding of the bridges was necessarily done under the protection of a large guard, and the enemy's cavalry made frequent visits to the road, and I have no cavalry to compete with them. Our losses have been but slight during the work, amounting in all to some 10 or 12 pickets.

On the 7th instant Colonel Egloffstein, One hundred and third New York, was ordered to make a reconnaissance up the Trent in the direc-tion of Onslow County, and I afterward ordered him to continue his reconnaissance down the road leading from Trenton to Core Sound, at the mouth of White Oak River, and then to proceed up the shore of Core Sound and communicate with General Parke at Morehead City. This I did with a hope that we might be able to catch a portion of the enemy's cavalry, the headquarters of which were at Swansborough, from whence they sent detachments over to the railroad, thus making the duty of guarding the 36 miles of railroad from this place to Caro-lina City very onerous. The colonel started with 200 picked men, two days' rations, and no transportation, with instructions to ration his men from supplies found on the route. He yesterday reached Gen-eral Parke's headquarters, having had several skirmishes with the enemy, in which he captured some 23 prisoners, 80 horses, and quite a quantity of pistols, sabers, &c. Among the prisoners captured was Colonel Robinson, formerly of our Army, and son-in-law of Captain Macrae.

I have been thus minute in these details to show you how necessary a regiment of cavalry is to me at this point, and I sincerely hope there will not be a moment's delay in sending me a well-organized regiment.

General Parke has now succeeded in getting on the banks in rear of Fort Macon with the main body of his command and two mortar batteries and one 30-pounder Parrott gun. The enemy's pickets have been driven in and all communication with the garrison from the outside cut off. The enemy's shots thus far have done us but little harm, wounding only 2 men. There are three naval vessels outside co-operating with us, and I hope to reduce the fort within ten days.

The re-enforcements spoken of have arrived, and I have formed the brigades of Generals Foster and Reno into divisions, which now occupy this place and its suburbs. I am building just in rear of the town an inclosed bastioned field work capable of holding 1,000 men and mounting thirty guns, which work will be finished in a few days, after which I propose to build another small four-gun work for two companies to the right of this first work and near the Neuse. These forts completely command the town, and will enable me to leave it with a small force when I move up the country. My advance now on the railroad is at Batchelder's Creek, where we are rebuilding the railroad bridge burned by the enemy, and I have made corresponding advances in the direction of Kinston, on the Neuse and Trent Rivers, which positions have been maintained, with occasional disturbances in the way of picket firing.

On the morning of the 7th some 600 of our men from Roanoke Island were sent to Elizabeth City and succeeded in capturing all the pickets in the neighborhood of that place, amounting to 74 men and 100 stand of arms. Since then the enemy's force has been increased at that point to two regiments and a field battery of four guns. I have organized, in conjunction with Commodore Rowan, an expedition against that place, and if we succeed in capturing or driving the enemy back we shall move up to South Mills and blow up the lock of the canal, and then proceed up to the head of the Currituck Canal and blow in its banks, thus rendering it impossible for the gunboats, which are said to be building at Norfolk, to come into these waters. I hope the expedition will be successful.

The regiments of my original command are much decreased by sickness and casualties in battle, and the recruiting service having been stopped, I shall not be able to fill them up. My command now consists of twenty regiments, one battalion, and a battery, making an aggregate of about 15,000, distributed as follows: Three regiments at Roanoke, a half regiment at Hatteras Inlet, three regiments and a battalion with General Parke and on the road, and thirteen and a half regiments with the battery at this place.

The engines and cars for which we made requisition immediately after the battle have not yet arrived, and as the re-enforcements sent me brought no wagons with them we are absolutely crippled for want of transportation.

I sincerely hope there will be no delay in forwarding me the regiment of cavalry and two batteries of artillery, together with the engines, cars, and wagons already required for.

The enemy continues in force at Kinston, but I feel quite sure I can dislodge them after the fall of Fort Macon.

I have made the above statement in reference to my forces in order that the Department may know what I have to work with, and if in what I may have to do more re-enforcements are necessary they may be sent at once.

I have the honor to be, your most obedient servant,
A. E. BURNSIDE,
Major-General, Commanding Department of North Carolina.

Hon. E. M. STANTON, *Secretary of War.*

—

HEADQUARTERS DEPARTMENT OF NORTH CAROLINA,
New Berne, N. C., April 20, 1862.

I have the honor to state that since my last report I have visited General Parke's force investing Fort Macon and found the work progressing very rapidly, considering the obstructions that have to be overcome. After transporting all the batteries, ammunition, supplies, &c., 36 miles by hand cars, they have to be transported by water some three miles and a half through a tortuous channel, with only 2 feet water at high tide. Flats loaded with supplies are sometimes a day and a half making this short trip. These supplies then have to be loaded on wagons and transported near 4 miles through deep sand to where the trenches are established. The farthest of our batteries, which consists of four 10-inch mortars, is but 1,200 yards from the fort. The battery of 30-pounder Parrott guns and the 8-inch mortar battery are still farther in advance, so that these supplies have all to be transported at night, as the train for a half mile or more would be, if visible, under the direct fire of the fort. The working parties and teams are kept busy every night, and the general has been able to keep some small parties at work during the day under cover of the guard of the trenches, but has had to exercise great care in protecting his men, in which thus far he has been very successful, losing in his whole force—killed, wounded, and missing—but 9 men, and 1 captain wounded (Sheffield, of Fourth Rhode Island*). Some ninety cannon-shot from the fort and considerable musketry fire, which occurred on one morning, wounded but 2 of our men, while we killed and wounded with our rifles 8 of theirs and drove their pickets inside the fort.

On my visit yesterday to the trenches with my staff the ambulance in which we traveled to within a mile of the fort attracted the attention of their lookout on the flag-staff, which caused a battery to open upon us as we passed to and from the batteries, of which I was afterward very glad, as it demonstrated to me that their firing is very wild.

Our batteries, guns, &c., are now about completed and the pieces in position. The work has been most skillfully conducted under the direction of Captain Williamson, topographical engineer, and Lieutenant Flagler, of the Ordnance Corps.

I came up for the purpose of carrying down through Core Sound two of our floating batteries, with four 30-pounder rifled Parrott guns mounted thereon, which I propose to anchor, together with the gunboat Ellis, with an 80-pounder rifled gun, just in front of the fort, opposite the town of Beaufort. The Navy co-operates from the out-

---

* Properly, Eighth Connecticut.

side with three steamers and a sailing vessel. I have ordered General Parke to advance some 400 of his best marksmen in front of the land batteries to within some 500 or 600 yards of the fort, to annoy their cannoneers. The reduction of the fort is, I think, only a question of time.

I sent General Reno up beyond Elizabeth City to destroy the locks in the Dismal Swamp Canal, and to use his discretion as to other operations in the direction of Norfolk, and with a view to creating a diversion in favor of McClellan, and I hope to hear of the successful termination of his expedition within two days.

. General Foster, who is in immediate command here, is pushing his outposts in the direction of Kinston as rapidly as the present force here will admit. He has also, besides building the railroad bridges across the Trent and Batchelder's Creek, fortified this city in the rear, so that it can be held by a small force when we advance up the country or down the coast.

Our sick list is not decreasing. I hope the Governors of States from which my regiments have been drawn may be authorized to fill them up to the maximum number of 1,000 men each. With the present strength of the regiments our men are worked very hard.

I would again urgently but respectfully request of the Department one good regiment of cavalry, two light batteries of artillery, and the transportation required by my chief quartermaster. The engines, cars, and wagons are absolutely necessary to us here.

Captain Cutting, one of my quartermasters, will bear this to you, and explain to you our wants more fully than I can write in this hurried way.

I have the honor to be, your very obedient servant,

A. E. BURNSIDE,
Major-General, Commanding Department of North Carolina.
Hon. E. M. STANTON, *Secretary of War, Washington, D. C.*

—

HEADQUARTERS DEPARTMENT OF NORTH CAROLINA,
New Berne, April 29, 1862. :

SIR: I have the honor to make the following hasty report of the fall of Fort Macon, on Saturday, the 26th instant. The detailed report of the siege will be made in due time by Brigadier-General Parke, who conducted it:

I arrived at the straits leading into Beaufort Harbor on the afternoon of the 23d instant, and immediately after sent the inclosed demand for the surrender of the fort to Colonel White, the answer to which is inclosed herewith.

On the morning of the 24th I communicated with General Parke, and ascertained that a few more preparations remained to be made in the trenches before the firing commenced. The armament in the trenches consisted of four batteries, as follows: Prouty's battery, 1,200 yards from the fort, consisting of four 8-inch mortars; Morris' battery, 1,300 yards from the fort, consisting of three 30-pounder rifled Parrott guns; Flagler's battery, 1,600 yards from the fort, consisting of four 10-inch mortars; Caswell's battery, 1,200 yards from the fort, consisting of one 12-pounder Dahlgren rifled boat howitzer.

On the afternoon of the 24th I sent an order to General Parke to open fire as soon as possible, which he did at 5 o'clock on the morning of the 25th instant and kept it up until 4 o'clock p. m., throwing 1,100 shot and shell, of which 560 struck the fort, dismounting 17 guns, killing 8 men, and wounding 26 others.

About 7.30 in the morning the naval vessels came into action, and continued their fire until the high winds made it so rough outside the bar they were compelled to withdraw. I beg to refer you to the report of the commander of the fleet for more definite information, but I will add that their fire was well directed and was of material aid in the reduction of the fort. The intrepidity with which the vessels were brought within close range of the fort in a sea rolling to a fearful extent commanded the admiration of all who witnessed the sight.

In the mean time the officers and men who accompanied me, aided by Lieutenant Franklin and Midshipman Porter, of the Navy, were getting Nichols' and Baxter's two floating batteries, with four rifled Parrott 30-pounder guns and one Wiard 12-pounder gun into position, but only one of them was able to participate in the conflict in consequence of the high winds.

At 4 o'clock p. m. a flag of truce was hoisted on the parapets, when our batteries ceased firing, and a party coming from the fort bearing a white flag was met by a party from the trenches, when it was ascertained that Colonel White had sent the flag for the purpose of knowing upon what terms he could surrender the fort. General Parke was sent for, and upon coming up he informed the bearer of the flag that the surrender must be unconditional. They informed him of the terms I had offered to Colonel White before the fire had opened and requested a cessation of hostilities until I could be communicated with, which was granted by General Parke; and he sent a message to me stating that Colonel White desired to know on what conditions he could surrender the fort, and without knowing the answer given by him I sent a reply allowing the same conditions I had offered before the firing commenced. There was a very great delay in sending this answer, owing to the fact that it had to be borne part of the way by water, while the wind and tide were so strong that it was almost impossible to move a boat against them.

In the mean time General Parke started for my boat, reaching there at 4 a. m. on the 26th. He had met my answer on the way, but deferred communicating it to Colonel White until he had seen me. Upon consultation we agreed that if an unconditional surrender was demanded the enemy would in all probability stand one day's more bombardment, thereby occasioning an additional destruction of property in the fort, and inasmuch as I have always intended to release them on their parole if they surrendered, as I did the prisoners taken on Roanoke Island, we did not think it wise to allow a technicality in negotiating to prevent us from accomplishing the same result in a less time, and thereby prevent an additional destruction of life and property. The answer was communicated to Colonel White early on the morning of the 26th, soon after which he came on board my boat, where he and General Parke arranged the inclosed terms of capitulation.

We immediately landed at the fort, went up to the trenches, brought the guard that was in them to the fort, and placed them as a guard on the glacis. The garrison of the fort marched out as prisoners of war and stacked their arms on the glacis, after which Colonel White lowered the rebel flag, which was taken possession of by General Parke, who hoisted in its stead an American flag which was found in the fort. The prisoners then signed their paroles and were embarked on vessels with their private property, such as clothing, bedding, &c., and have been transported—some to Wilmington, others to Beaufort, and the remainder to this place.

By this surrender we come into possession of the fort and its armament of 54 guns, 400 prisoners, a large amount of ammunition, commissary, and quartermaster's stores, some 40 horses with their equipments, 500 stand of rifles and muskets with full equipments, and a considerable amount of implements incident to the complete equipment of a fort, besides opening one of the best harbors on the Southern coast.

Of the skill, courage, and endurance displayed in this siege I will allow General Parke to speak in his detailed report. The result proves that the work was conducted by the right man. I inclose my congratulatory order.

I beg to make a further explanation of my reasons for determining to release these prisoners whenever the fort should be taken. I am becoming daily more convinced that the release of our prisoners at Roanoke Island was of material advantage to us; and as a large majority of the men in the fort were from the counties bordering on the sound, which are more strongly Union than any other counties in this State, many of them being Union men themselves and nearly all of them anxious to get to their homes, I felt sure that it would create a much better impression in this community, and thereby strengthen our cause, by releasing them on parole than by sending them to the North. Another important reason for coming to this decision was, the sending them North would deprive me of considerable transportation, which is very valuable to me here now.

During the siege and bombardment I have been aided in communicating with General Parke not only by my own staff, but by almost every member of the staff of Generals Foster, Reno, and Parke.

I am sorry to record the loss of 1 man killed and 2 wounded from our side on the day of the bombardment. The names will be given by General Parke in his detailed report.

I have the honor to be, your very obedient servant,

A. E. BURNSIDE,
Major-General, Commanding Department of North Carolina.

Hon. E. M. STANTON, *Secretary of War.*

[Inclosures.]

HDQRS. DEPARTMENT OF NORTH CAROLINA,
Core Sound, April 23, 1862.

Col. MOSES J. WHITE, *Commanding Fort Macon:*

COLONEL: I have arrived here with additional means of attacking your position. General Parke is now ready, but by my orders there has not been a single shot fired at the fort by the army. I deem it my duty to again summon you to surrender the place in its present condition, in which case you and your garrison will be allowed to return to your homes on parole.

This proposition is made with a view to saving human life. Should you not accept these terms, the consequences of an attack and an assault must rest upon you.

Capt. Herman Biggs, my chief quartermaster, bears this, and will return with an answer. Lieut. E. N. Strong accompanies him.

I have the honor to be, colonel, very respectfully, your obedient servant,

A. E. BURNSIDE,
Major-General Commanding.

HEADQUARTERS, *Fort Macon, April 23, 1862.*

Maj. Gen. AMBROSE E. BURNSIDE, U. S. A.:

SIR : Your letter per flag of truce is received, demanding surrender of Fort Macon. In reply I have to say I decline the surrender.

Lieut. Daniel Cogdell will bear this note to you.

By order of Col. M. J. White :

ROBT. E. WALKER,
Acting Adjutant.

Terms of Capitulation.

The following are the terms of capitulation agreed upon for the surrender to the forces of the United States of Fort Macon, Bogue Banks, N. C.:

ARTICLE 1. The fort, armament, and garrison to be surrendered to the forces of the United States.

ARTICLE 2. The officers and men of the garrison to be released on their parole of honor not to take up arms against the United States of America until properly exchanged, and to return to their homes, taking with them all their private effects, such as clothing, bedding, books, &c.

M. J. WHITE,
Colonel, C. S. Army, Commanding Fort Macon.
SAML. LOCKWOOD,
Commanding U. S. Navy, and Senior Officer.
JNO. G. PARKE,
Brig. Gen. Vols., Commanding Third Division, Dept. N. C.

FORT MACON, N. C., *April 26, 1862.*

GENERAL ORDERS, }   HDQRS. DEPT. OF NORTH CAROLINA,
No. 29.   }   *Beaufort Harbor, April 26, 1862.*

The general commanding takes peculiar pleasure in expressing his thankfulness to General Parke and his brave command for the patient labor, fortitude, and courage displayed in the investment and reduction of Fort Macon.

Every patriot heart will be filled with gratitude to God for having given to our beloved country such soldiers.

The regiments and artillery companies engaged have fairly earned the right to wear upon their colors and guidons the words, " Fort Macon, April 26, 1862."

By command of Major-General Burnside :

LEWIS RICHMOND,
Assistant Adjutant-General.

———

No. 2.

Reports of Brig. Gen. John G. Parke, U. S. Army.

HDQRS. THIRD BRIGADE, DEPT. OF NORTH CAROLINA,
Carolina City, March 23, 1862.

SIR : I have the honor to inform you that I reached this point last evening after a severe march from the landing on Slocum's Creek with a portion of my command.

Hearing that the enemy had burned the railroad bridge over Newport River I hurried off, in order to save the county road bridge. This we succeeded in doing. We also secured some log quarters made for the Seventh Regiment North Carolina troops.

This morning I dispatched Captain Gardner and Lieutenant Flagler with a flag of truce to Fort Macon with a demand to surrender; a copy of my letter, together with the reply of the commanding officer, I herewith inclose.

We have now but one course to pursue, and that is to invest the place; but with the Newport Bridge destroyed this will be a slow operation. I have ordered Major Wright down to that point to rebuild the bridge. This will have to be done before we can bring down the guns. Our supplies can be brought by rail to this point and thence in wagons over a fair road.

The county road from Slocum's to Newport is in one place very bad; will soon be impassable for heavily-loaded wagons.

I have with me about 700 men; the remainder of the Fourth and Eighth are, I presume, now on the way down.

I have sent two companies to Morehead City to prevent any communication with the fort.

At present I have not strength enough to send a force to Beaufort. I believe they communicate with the fort every night.

As far as I can learn the garrison of the fort has but little sympathy, or rather the commanding officer has but little, in either Beaufort or Morehead.

If possible I would like some of the Navy to come around through Core Sound to interrupt communication between Beaufort and Fort Macon.

I have just learned that the officers of the fort communicate with the outer world by running down the beach. My force at present is not sufficient nor have I the means to cut off this communication.

I have just taken a flat-boat, with a mail and a lot of corn, on the way from the fort to Swansborough. I will detain the captain.

Very respectfully, your obedient servant,

JNO. G. PARKE,
Brigadier-General, Commanding.

General AMBROSE E. BURNSIDE.

[Inclosures]

HDQRS. THIRD BRIGADE, DEPT. OF NORTH CAROLINA,
March 23, 1862.

To the Commander of the Garrison of Fort Macon:

SIR: In order to save the unnecessary effusion of blood I have the honor to demand the evacuation of the fort and surrender of the forces under your command.

Having an intimate knowledge of the entire work and an overwhelming force at our command with the means for reducing the work, its fall is inevitable.

On condition that no damage is done to the fortification or armament your command will be released as prisoners of war on their parole.

Very respectfully, yours, &c.,

JNO. G. PARKE,
Brigadier-General, Commanding.

HEADQUARTERS, *Fort Macon, March* 23, 1862.

General J. G. PARKE,
    Brigadier-General, Commanding Morehead City, N. C.:

SIR: Your request is received, and I have the honor to decline evacuating Fort Macon.

Very respectfully, yours, &c.,

M. J. WHITE,
Colonel, Commanding.

HDQRS. THIRD BRIGADE, DEPT. OF NORTH CAROLINA,
    Carolina City, March 24, 1862—11 p. m.

MY DEAR GENERAL: Pell has just arrived. I will detain him until morning, as I have now a move on foot which is of so great importance that I wish you to be apprised of the result.

Since my communication of yesterday's date I have been steadily occupied in cutting off all communication with the fort. I have two companies posted in Morehead City, under Major Allen, with orders to cut off all communication with the fort and Beaufort.

To-day I sent to Beaufort for the town authorities. Captain Gardner met them, and informed them that I required them to stop all communication with the fort. They all have a great horror of Colonel White, and fear that if they communicate with us he will shell their town. However they have determined to hold a town meeting, and I will get their reply to-morrow.

At first I had not the means nor provisions to occupy it. My wagon train has now made two trips to Slocum's Creek Landing, and I have now supplies until Saturday morning; and if the reply is not satisfactory I will send one company over there. The destruction of the Newport River Bridge is a bad business. I hope Field will soon have it in order, and Flagler and Morris will soon have their guns here.

I presume Flagler will inform you of the burning of the hotel at this place, also of the barracks just below here.

Last night Colonel White burnt the prize bark lying under the fort. There are two ships at Morehead, one at the wharf and the other in the stream, purporting to be English, and loaded now with turpentine, cotton, &c. They came in last August, and have not been able to escape. I presume the fact of their flying English colors has secured them against Colonel White's torch.

My work for to-night is to send two companies over to the Banks under a good pilot. I send a boat to be carried across the sand hills to the sea, with a letter to the commanding officer of the fleet informing him of my move and requesting his co-operation.

My transportation is only sufficient to carry over two companies, but it is so very important to occupy the Banks.

We have made two captures, one a schooner load of corn going from the fort to Swansborough, the other a bearer of dispatches from the captain of a picket company on Queen's Creek, beyond Swansborough, to Colonel White. I have the captain of the schooner and the dispatch bearer now confined, and will send them to you by the first opportunity.

O for some of [the] Navy people. Can't you send one or two boat howitzers and ammunition down by rail so that I can send them over to the Banks? One could be mounted on our schooner with all ease.

I am informed that the Union could come through Core Sound with some ship's launches in tow. These could cut off Beaufort and the fort.

Tell the Navy people of these two big ships and cargo.

On this county road there are two points where main roads come in from the Swansborough side, and at these I will establish a guard to protect my wagon train until the railroad is in running order. The enemy may send some cavalry in from that side, but I don't think there is much danger.

MARCH 25—12.45.

Colonel Harland has just reported to me that it is out of the question to get our boats up from Morehead owing to the interference of our old friends the wind, tide, and shoals. I have therefore postponed my trip to the Banks, and it must be all for the best.

Now I will wait for the boat howitzers and their crews and make a lodgment by daylight. Please send them forthwith by rail.

In addition to the schooner I can raise four large boats, but only nine oars. Send some extra ones.

Pell will tell you the condition of the bridge, &c.

As I have not taken steps toward seizing these ships, let Commodore Rowan send an officer down at once to act in the matter. I will furnish him men, and let the howitzers follow as soon as possible.

Let Flagler and Morris have a lot of contrabands, with some teams to carry their ordnance to the railroad, so that it can be run down here on the completion of the bridge.

The people here are all frightened. What shall I do about the oath of allegiance and neutrality?

Please send me the forms and instructions about administering them. I have administered but two oaths of neutrality. Please send some blank passes.

There are some rabid secessionists about here, but they don't make their appearance.

My command is in good health and spirits, excepting the two companies in Morehead; they are bivouacking, but have good shelter.

We expect to supply ourselves with fish, &c.

Very faithfully, yours,

JNO. G. PARKE.

[General AMBROSE E. BURNSIDE.]

●

P. S.—I send the prisoner by Pell, together with the papers found on him.

HEADQUARTERS THIRD BRIGADE,
Carolina City, March 26, 1862.

GENERAL: Yesterday morning I received a visit from Mr. Rumley and Mr. Chadwick on "behalf of the citizens of Beaufort." They expressed the thanks of the citizens for the courtesy and consideration shown them, but were forced to acknowledge that they were powerless in reference to cutting off communication with the fort. They told me that they had communicated with White in reference to my proposition, and he replied that he would not permit us to land in Beaufort; he would shell the town, &c. This of course disgusted the citizens of Beaufort, and I think they express the sentiments of the Beaufort portion of the garrison—about one company.

At the close of the interview Mr. Rumley asked me what course I intended to pursue. I replied that my mind was made up, and that they would soon hear from me. He informed me that there were no supplies for troops in the town; that they had not more than three months, for themselves, and, as all communication with Hyde County was cut off, they were in a sorry plight.

Last night I sent Major Allen, with two companies, over to Beaufort, but as yet I have no report from him, nor have we any *reports* from the fort.

I ordered him to seize all boats, and, if possible, surprise any parties that might be there from the fort. I ordered that no passes be granted unless the parties take the oath of allegiance, excepting passes to come and see me.

I look to-day for some of our Navy people and a boat howitzer.

My two old pilots returned last night from up the Banks. They report a rough sea outside. We can see the enemy's outposts on the Banks opposite in small squads.

I can't learn whether or not they have any small pieces mounted at the salt-works. As that is a good landing I think it possible, and therefore would rather postpone a landing until we can bring at least one howitzer to bear upon them and feel them before we expose too many men.

Very respectfully, your obedient servant,

JNO. G. PARKE,
Brigadier-General Volunteers.

General BURNSIDE.

HDQRS. THIRD BRIGADE, DEPT. NORTH CAROLINA,
Carolina City, March 31, 1862.

GENERAL: I have the honor to report the complete investment of Fort Macon.

Three companies are stationed in Beaufort and two in Morehead City, with instructions to cut off all communications between those points and the fort. The commanding officers at these posts have seized all the boats.

On the 29th I sent a reconnoitering party over to the Banks, consisting of 20 men, with a commissioned officer. Meeting no resistance, the party remained through the night.

During yesterday I sent the remainder of the company over, and to-night I will send over another company.

As soon as the signal officers arrive I will detail an officer for that station and send another to the fleet.

Captain Morris has just arrived with the Parrott guns. The Newport Bridge being finished, they were brought through by rail.

As soon as the boats come over from Beaufort I will send this battery over to the Banks and commence operations.

In my opinion these guns and mortars will be required ultimately, and will do more service on the Banks than they could at Morehead.

The railroad embankment at Morehead will serve us a good purpose in mounting and serving the 100-pounder rifle.

I have now in confinement Mr. Josiah F. Bell, the collector of Beaufort. I will send him up to you, together with papers, &c., and a report.

Very respectfully, your obedient servant,

JNO. G. PARKE,
Brigadier-General, Commanding.

General BURNSIDE.

CAROLINA CITY, *April* 8, 1862—noon.

GENERAL: I sent a dispatch to you yesterday evening, and as the sergeant has not yet returned I fear he may have been intercepted by the rebel cavalry between Havelock and New Berne.

In the dispatch I inclose Colonel Wilson's report* of an attack upon his outside pickets by the rebel cavalry, wounding 1 man and probably taking 1 prisoner.

This morning he reports that not only 1 but 8 are missing; that he increased the picket last night, but nothing further occurred. To-day he sends out four companies to burn the county-road bridges.

This second dispatch I sent you this morning, and fearing that the bearer may be waylaid beyond Havelock, I will send this by Slocum's Creek.

I am informed that Captain King some two or three days ago, heard some cavalry, I believe two, on a cross-road near the deserted battery, Croatan, and shortly after he saw a rocket. Now this may be mere rumor. Still it behooves us to look out. I will write King to make a report to you of the circumstances.

We sent quite a large mail this morning. I sincerely hope it has not been picked up by the enemy.

The balance of the Ninth New Jersey should be sent down to Newport at once. and I think it advisable to have strong pickets posted throughout the railroad; but it is out of the question for me to attend to it from this point.

The stern-wheeler cannot reach the Banks, and taking advantage of the tides is a slow progress.

Morris' company goes over this evening, the Eighth Connecticut during the night, and then I will send all the Fourth Rhode Island, excepting two companies, which I will leave here. The two launches with howitzers are here; these can protect the retreat of the two companies to the stern-wheeler if forced to retire; this is hardly to be expected.

I wish I had some cavalry down here to drive these rebels out of the country. I do not believe there are more than two companies of them.

In haste, yours, faithfully,

JNO. G. PARKE.

General BURNSIDE.

HDQRS. THIRD DIVISION, DEPT. OF NORTH CAROLINA,
Beaufort, N. C., May 9, 1862.

CAPTAIN: I have the honor respectfully to submit the following report of the movements and operations of the troops under my command from the date of their embarking at New Berne, March 19, up to the reduction of Fort Macon, April 26:

On the 19th the Fourth Rhode Island Regiment, Col. I. P. Rodman commanding, and the Eighth Connecticut Regiment, Col. Edward Harland commanding, were embarked, and on the 20th we steamed down the Neuse to Slocum's Creek, and, preceded by the gunboat Picket, followed up this latter stream to the landing place previously determined on by the commanding general.

The Fifth Rhode Island Battalion, Maj. John Wright commanding, marched from New Berne down the railroad, and joined us at Havelock Station, a mile and one-half distant from Slocum's Creek Landing.

---

* See p. 295.

Capt. Lewis O. Morris, First United States Artillery, being assigned to duty with the brigade, was placed in charge of the three 30-pounder Parrott guns, and Lieut. D. W. Flagler, of the Ordnance, had charge of the two mortar batteries.

From Slocum's Creek it was intended to haul the siege train over to the railroad, and thence transport it on cars with horse-power to Carolina City. Immediately on landing at Slocum's Creek I was informed that the enemy had burned the railroad bridge over Newport River, and fearing that a similar attempt would be made on the county-road bridge, I dispatched a company to guard it, and followed with the available force that had landed. We thus secured this bridge, and had an unobstructed route by the common road to Carolina City, which point we reached on the 22d.

The Fifth Rhode Island Battalion was ordered to the crossing of Newport River, and to the major commanding was intrusted the re-building of the railroad bridge. This was accomplished in a few days.

On the 23d a demand was made for the surrender of the fort and garrison. This being refused, steps were at once taken to completely invest the work and preparations made for besieging the place.

Two companies were sent to Morehead City, the terminus of the railway, and three companies to Beaufort, with instructions to the commanding officers at both points to seize all the boats and cut off all supplies for the garrison and stop all communication with the fort. A gunboat served to blockade Core Sound, and by the aid of one or two small boats at Carolina City we were enabled to cut off all communication through Bogue Sound. From Beaufort a communication was opened with the blockading fleet, a party crossing to Shackelford Banks, and thence in a fisherman's boat to the fleet.

Having received a ship's launch and howitzer from New Berne by the way of Clubfoot Canal, a small party on the 29th of March, under cover of this gun, effected a landing on the Banks directly opposite Carolina City, thus completely investing the work.

The enemy now seemed to be very active in and about the fort. The bark Glen, lying under the guns of the fort, was burned; also the Eliason House. The light-house tower and beacon were overturned, and all the outbuildings were destroyed. All parties of our men crossing from Morehead to Beaufort, or anywhere within range of the guns of the fort, were continually fired upon.

Fort Macon is situated upon the eastern extremity of Bogue Banks, a narrow sand island stretching off to the westward a distance of about 25 miles, and separated from the main-land by Bogue Sound, in which the depth of the water is so slight as to permit no navigation other than that of the lightest-draught flats and small boats. From a point on the island opposite Carolina City to the fort, a distance of about 5 miles, the surface of the island is broken, commencing·a short distance from the beach, into irregular knolls of sand, varying in height and extent. Toward the sound these knolls decrease in size until they approach an extensive salt-marsh, through which run numerous creeks. Near the head of one of these creeks, Hoop Pole, our permanent camp and depot was located, and to this point it was necessary to transport all the troops, supplies, siege guns, ammunition, &c., in scows and small boats. On account of the intricacy of the channel and the slight depth of the water, even with the boats which we obtained, no supplies could be transported excepting upon full tide.

Finding that a large force was necessary to guard the Newport

Railroad Bridge, the Ninth New Jersey Regiment, having reported for duty with the brigade, was assigned to that post, with instructions to picket the line of railroad and protect it from encroachments of the enemy from the direction of Swansborough. The Fifth Rhode Island Battalion, being thus relieved, joined me on the 4th of April at Carolina City.

On the 29th of March the first troops were crossed to the Banks, and from that time to April 10 every available hour of night and day was spent in transporting men, siege train, and supplies.

During this period of thirteen days I crossed eight companies of the Fourth Rhode Island Regiment; seven companies of the Eighth Connecticut Regiment; the Fifth Rhode Island Battalion; Company C, First United States Artillery; Company I, Third New York Artillery, Captain Ammon commanding, who reported for duty at Carolina City, and the siege train.

Communication was immediately established with the fleet, a signal officer being placed aboard the vessel of the commanding officer.

On the 11th, aided by Captain Williamson, of the Topographical Engineers, Captain Morris, of the Artillery, and Lieutenant Flagler, of the Ordnance, I made a reconnaissance in force in the direction of the fort. Meeting the enemy's pickets, they were driven in after a slight skirmish, and we advanced to within a mile of the work, when the guns of the fort opened upon us with shot and shell. The men were placed under cover of the sand hills, while Captains Williamson and Morris and Lieutenant Flagler made a careful examination of the ground in our front, and selected sites for our batteries ranging from 1,300 to 1,700 yards from the fort. The force was then withdrawn, no casualties having occurred from the fire of the enemy. In the reconnaissance we received great assistance from the blockading fleet, Capt. S. S. Prentiss commanding. The gunboats engaged the fort and shelled the beach in our front. For this and other timely aid rendered us I desire to express my acknowledgments and thanks.

On the 12th a permanent advance guard of five companies was organized and work on the approaches was commenced. During this day a skirmish occurred with the enemy, in which Captain Sheffield and a private of the Eighth Connecticut Regiment were wounded. The enemy were driven back, and although more than seventy shot and shell were fired on our advance guard and fatigue parties, not a man was injured by them. From this date the regular work on the approaches, trenches, batteries, and rifle pits was vigorously pushed forward by all our available force both night and day, in spite of the desultory fire kept up by the enemy.

The road along the beach being in full view of the lookout on the flag-staff of the fort, it became necessary to transport our guns, mortars, and ammunition to the batteries and magazines under cover of the night. The enemy made two ineffectual attempts at night to dislodge us from our advanced position, in one of which Lieutenant Landers and a private of the Fifth Rhode Island Battalion were slightly wounded, and in the other Major Appleman and a private of the Eighth Connecticut Regiment received severe contusions from a discharge of grape while digging rifle pits within 750 yards of the fort.

On the morning of the 24th the two mortar batteries were prepared to open fire, and the Parrott-gun battery was ready, with the exception of the opening of the embrasures, which was delayed until the moment of opening fire was arranged, so that the enemy might not discover our position.

In selecting sites for our batteries advantage was taken of the sand hills previously spoken of. By cutting down the natural slopes of these hills to a sufficient depth to lay the platforms for our guns and mortars and revetting the interior faces with sand bags excellent epaulements were formed. Embrasures for the Parrott guns were cut directly through the sand hills, and revetted with sods taken from the salt-marsh close at hand. During the night of the 24th the embrasures of the Parrott-gun battery were opened, and at 5.40 o'clock on the morning of the 25th the first shot was fired upon the fort. Immediately all three of our batteries opened, and our fire was vigorously answered.

Owing to the high wind and rough sea it was impracticable to communicate with the blockading fleet our intention of opening fire on the morning of the 25th. As soon, however, as the commanding officer, Capt. Samuel Lockwood, discovered our movements he brought all his vessels into action, and for a time attracted the enemy's attention to such an extent as to greatly facilitate the officers in charge of the mortar batteries in correcting their range and length of fuse, but owing to the extreme roughness of the sea the fleet was compelled to withdraw. At 4.30 in the afternoon a white flag was displayed upon the ramparts of the fort and the firing ceased upon both sides. After communicating with the general commanding during the night of the 25th, on the morning of the 26th, at 9.30 o'clock, I received the surrender of the fort and garrison.

A copy of the terms of capitulation is herewith transmitted.*

For the detailed operation of the three batteries I have to refer you to the very interesting reports of Captain Morris and Lieutenant Flagler.

The fort and armament bear evidence not only of the great skill with which these batteries were served, but also of the wonderful effects produced by the introduction of rifled guns into our siege trains. The number of guns disabled and the effect produced upon the scarp-wall, although not, exposed to view from our position, are sufficient proof of the great value of the 30-pounder Parrott as a siege gun.

In truth, the result of the ten and a half hours' firing from our three batteries exceeded my most sanguine expectations, and they reflect the highest credit upon the officers and men engaged in their location and construction, as well as the working of the mortars and guns.

To Capt. R. S. Williamson, of the Topographical Engineers, I am under lasting obligations. His bold and daring reconnaissances to within 800 yards of the fort gave us full and complete knowledge of the ground up to the very foot of the glacis. He so located the batteries that the sand hills themselves served as epaulements, rendering but little work necessary to prepare them for the guns and mortars and the construction of the magazines.

Captain Morris and Lieutenant Flagler were untiring in their zeal and energy in superintending the construction of the batteries. The work was carried on both by day and night under their supervision by the men of Company C, First United States Artillery, and Company I, Third New York Artillery, and such details as could be spared from the infantry force.

The Parrott-gun battery was commanded by Captain Morris, First United States Artillery, assisted by Lieutenant Gowan, Forty-eighth Pennsylvania Regiment, and Lieutenant Pollock, First United States Artillery.

---

* See p. 276.

The 10-inch mortar battery was commanded by Lieutenant Flagler, of the Ordnance, assisted by Captain Ammon, Third New York Artillery, and Captain Pell, aide-de-camp to the general commanding, who volunteered his services. The 8-inch mortar battery was commanded by Lieutenant Prouty, of the Twenty-fifth Massachusetts Regiment, assisted by Lieutenants Thomas and Kelsey, of the Third New York Artillery. The result shows the efficiency with which the batteries were worked, and I take great pleasure in acknowledging my thanks to these officers.

From the time of our first occupying the ground immediately in front of the fort very severe and onerous duty was performed by the officers and men of the Fourth Rhode Island, Eighth Connecticut, and Fifth Rhode Island Battalion. Owing to companies being detached from the first two regiments and their otherwise weak condition the tour of duty in the trenches and on advance picket guard returned every third day. This, in connection with a march of 3½ miles through heavy sand to and from camp and occasional fatigue duty, was beginning to tell fearfully on both officers and men; still they bore it all without complaint, and it gives me pleasure to commend them as soldiers of true grit.

The Ninth New Jersey Regiment guarded our route of supplies, and rendered most efficient service in completely protecting our line of communication from raids of the rebel cavalry, who were constantly prowling about the country.

During the investment of the work and active operations of the siege I kept up constant communication with my force by means of the officers of the Signal Corps. From favorable positions previously determined upon these officers were enabled to report to the commanding officers of the batteries the effect of their shot and shell.

During the action I have to report the following loss: 1 killed and 2 wounded. Killed, Private William R. Dart, Company I, Third New York Artillery. He fell, struck by a round shot, while in the performance of his duty resetting a pointing stake on the parapet of the 10-inch mortar battery. Wounded, Sergeant Hynes and Private Bonnet, of Company C, First United States Artillery.

The reported killed and wounded in the fort is as follows: Killed, 8; wounded, 20.

I have the honor to be, very respectfully, your obedient servant,

JNO. G. PARKE,
Brigadier-General, Commanding Third Division.

Capt. LEWIS RICHMOND,
Assistant Adjutant-General.

No. 3.

Report of Lieut. Daniel W. Flagler, U. S. Ordnance Department.

FORT MACON, N. C., *April 29, 1862.*

SIR: I have the honor to submit for your information the following report of the disposition made of the siege batteries used in the attack upon Fort Macon:

I was detailed for duty with the Third Division in the Department of North Carolina on the 19th of March, and, in accordance with an order from General Parke, turned over a Parrott-gun battery of three rifled

30-pounders to Captain Morris, of the First Artillery, and also loaded a
battery of four 10-inch siege mortars upon a bark, holding them in
readiness to proceed with the division whenever it should move. When
the division arrived at Slocum's Creek, as it was not sure there would
be occasion to use these batteries, they were left on board the vessels
at that point.

I came on with the division to Carolina City, and after the general
had communicated with the commanding officer of the fort I received
an order from him (General Parke) to return immediately and attend
to the transportation of the batteries. Fearing we had not artillery
enough I went to New Berne and loaded another battery of four 8-inch
mortars upon a barge, and Lieut. M. F. Prouty, of the Twenty-fifth
Massachusetts Regiment, having reported to me for artillery duty, I
left him to bring this battery to Slocum's Creek. From the head of
this creek to Carolina City the artillery had to be transported by land.

The quartermaster could furnish very little transportation, as nearly
all that could be procured was engaged in bringing down baggage and
stores for the troops.

There were no men with the batteries to unload and move them, and
the labor had to be performed by negroes, whom I obtained from Captain King, the division quartermaster. The batteries were hauled to
Havelock Station in quartermasters' wagons and there loaded on cars,
and hauled to Carolina City with horses and mules. The large quantity of heavy shell necessary for the mortar batteries, and the lack of
men, wagons, and cars to transport them, must account for the delay
of these batteries in reaching Carolina City.

At the latter point only one scow could be obtained suitable for carrying purposes across Bogue Sound to the Banks, and owing to tides
and the difficulties of a shallow, intricate channel not more than one
trip could be made daily.

A magazine was established in a deserted building at the point of
landing, and again all the materials had to be hauled a distance of 4½
miles along a sandy beach.

On the 12th instant, the day after the enemy's pickets were driven
into the fort, I went with Captain Williamson, Corps of Topographical
Engineers, and selected positions for the batteries. The first of these,
the 10-inch mortar battery, was at a distance of 1,680 yards from the
fort, and behind a natural sand hill, which was sufficiently high to protect it from the direct fire of the enemy's cannon. It was near the
marsh, on the left side of the island.

Captain Morris' battery of Parrott guns was placed about 200 yards
in advance of this and a little to the right. The position of 'the sand
hills was such and the strip of available land so narrow that the latter
had to be put more nearly in front of the mortars than was desirable
in order to distract the enemy's fire. The 8-inch mortars were placed
still 200 yards farther in advance, and on the right, near the sea-shore.

The work of moving the ordnance, building the mortar batteries,
constructing roads, &c., was all performed by details from the regiments
of infantry of the division and from Captain Ammon's company of the
Third New York Artillery. The men were often at work before they
were rested from the fatigue of twenty-four hours' picket duty, the
pickets themselves often volunteering to assist, and always with a
cheerfulness which evinced their determination to accomplish the end
we had in view. While at work the men were often annoyed by
artillery firing from the fort, but no one in the batteries was even hurt,
the sand hills affording good protection. On the evening of the 23d

instant the batteries, magazines, and roads leading to them were all completed. Wagons had been engaged for several nights previous hauling shells to the mortar batteries, and on the night of the 23d I had the magazines filled with ammunition and reported to General Parke that we were ready to open fire.

The following day at 2 o'clock I received orders from him to commence firing that afternoon, if possible. I obtained details of men for the mortar batteries from Captain Ammon's company of the Third New York Artillery. The men, having a march of 4 miles to the batteries, did not arrive there till late in the afternoon. Captain Morris reported that he would not be able to open fire till the next morning, as he had still some work to do upon the embrasures. As I was confident that the enemy was ignorant of the nature and position of our batteries and as we would be able to fire only a few shells before dark, while obtaining our ranges, I thought it better to wait till morning, keeping the enemy in ignorance till we,were ready to open fire upon all the batteries simultaneously and to continue it. The men slept in the batteries that night, and all commenced fire shortly after sunrise in the morning.

Lieutenant Prouty commanded the 8-inch mortar battery, and I took charge of the 10-inch, and was assisted by Captain Ammon, and by Captain Pell, aide-de-camp to General Burnside. The first few discharges were from the Parrott guns, which were followed soon by the mortars, and the fire was continued without interruption till 5 p. m. It was returned from the fort with twenty-one guns, among which were one 8-inch and two 10-inch columbiads and six 32-pounders mounted as mortars. At first the enemy's fire was very rapid, principally shells and shrapnel, and the fort was so enveloped in smoke that it was difficult to tell whether our shells were falling within or beyond them. At 9 o'clock I received a dispatch from the signal officer at Beaufort, saying the mortars were " firing too far." The error was corrected immediately, and shortly after the enemy's fire was somewhat slackened.

The smoke cleared away, and I could observe the effect of every shell distinctly. The bolsters of the 10-inch and one of the 8-inch mortar-beds were split during the day. The platforms of the 10-inch mortars were badly injured, as the soil was too light to afford a firm foundation. These were all repaired, stopping fire from one piece at a time for that purpose. During the afternoon we fired very carefully, but slowly, as I wished to reserve ammunition enough for night firing if necessary.

After 11 o'clock more than five-eighths of the shells fell within the fort. The epaulement of the 10-inch battery was considerably injured by round shot and the explosion of a few 10-inch columbiad shells from the fort. The pointing stakes were several times displaced. At about 5 o'clock the enemy hoisted a white flag and we ceased firing. During the night the batteries were completely repaired and the magazines replenished. The men slept in the batteries, that they might open fire again if necessary.

But one man was killed in my battery and none wounded. I received most valuable assistance from Captains Pell and Ammon, and I cannot speak in too high terms of the men. The detachments from Captain Ammon's company were without previous knowledge of mortar practice except what they had gained from a drill the preceding day, yet they served the pieces efficiently and without accident throughout the day. The gunners detailed from Captain Morris' company, Privates Carlin, McKinstry, Reising, and McKenna were invaluable.

I take particular pleasure in calling your attention to the management of the 8-inch mortar battery. It was under the charge of Lieutenant Prouty, who, as a volunteer officer of infantry, has had no practical experience in artillery practice and no knowledge on the subject except what he has gained since he reported to me. His success is the result of his own industry and energy. I inclose his report. I have since examined the fort, and find that of the 1,150 shots fired from our three batteries about 500 took effect within the works of the enemy, not counting the shells that were exploded over the fort. The fire of the Parrott guns was most destructive, these three pieces having disabled nineteen of the enemy's guns. Only about 3 feet in width along the tops of the scarp-wall of the western face could be reached by their fire, yet in this narrow portion 41 shots had taken effect, some of them penetrating the brick masonry to a depth of 2 feet. Comparing the angle at which the guns were fired with the angle of fall necessary for the shot to reach this wall, I am confident they could not have reached it without having been partially spent by passing through the crest of the glacis.

Barricades for the casemates have been formed within the fort by standing bars of railroad iron up against the casemate inside walls. Several traverse circles were blown up by mortar shell, but they did not seem in any other way to have disabled guns. Forty-eight of the same shell exploded in the bottom of the ditch and a large number on the parade. One of the latter broke through into the drain of the fort.

The choice of the kind and caliber of the artillery used in the attack upon Fort Macon was certainly a good one. The object to be effected with the siege mortars was, at first, by exploding the shells at short distance above the fort, to drive the cannoneers from the guns or prevent them from being efficiently served; afterward, by exploding the shells at or after striking, to disable guns. In both respects they were successful. The destructive and accurate fire of the 30-pounder Parrott guns has shown that the work of dismounting or disabling guns with them is not a matter of chance, but of certainty. There was no exposed wall on which to try their breaching power.

During the enemy's fire since the first commencement of operations I have often had occasion to observe the want of effect in the explosion of their shells. I have examined a few of those left in the fort and find them filled with cannon powder.

I have the honor to be, very respectfully, your obedient servant,

D. W. FLAGLER,
First Lieutenant of Ordnance.

Capt. CHARLES T. GARDNER,
Assistant Adjutant-General.

No. 4.

Report of Lieut. Merrick F. Prouty, Twenty-fifth Massachusetts Infantry.

SIR: I have the honor to report that on Thursday, April 24, 1862, at 1 p. m., I was ordered by you to move to the 8-inch mortar battery of four pieces, which was planted 1,280 yards from Fort Macon, and open fire on the fort.

Lieutenants Thomas and Kelsey and 15 men of the Third New York Artillery and 5 men of Captain Morris' battery were detailed to man the mortars, but owing to the distance of the camp from the battery and hard walking in the loose sand we did not reach there till 3.30 p. m., and before we could open fire I was ordered by you to await further orders before doing so. The men remained in the battery during the night, and I opened fire, as you ordered, about 5.30 a. m. The first shells falling short, the charges were increased and a good range was obtained in a short time. A steady and effective fire was kept up from each piece until 11 a. m., when the bolster of No. 4 was broken by the recoil, and that was not worked until about 1 p. m., when, having been repaired, it was again opened. At 3 p. m. I received an order from you that a reserve of ammunition should be kept for contingencies during the night, and from 3.20 p. m. to 5 but two pieces were used. At that time firing was suspended, the enemy showing a white flag. The firing during the afternoon was very fine, nearly every shell bursting within or over the fort. During the night of the 25th shell and ammunition were brought, and at daylight of the 26th the men were at their posts, and everything in good order to open fire, had it been necessary.

Very efficient service was rendered me by Lieutenants Thomas and Kelsey, and the conduct of the men was beyond praise.

I am happy to report that no casualties occurred; but two of the enemy's shell bursting in or over the battery.

Very respectfully,

M. F. PROUTY,
Lieut. Co. C, 25th Mass. Vols., Comdg. 8-inch Mortar Battery.

Lieut. D. W. FLAGLER.

No. 5.

Report of Capt. Lewis O. Morris, First U. S. Artillery.

FORT MACON, N. C., *April 28, 1862.*

SIR: I have the honor to submit the following report of the operations of Company C, First Artillery, during the siege and reduction of Fort Macon:

As you are aware, I was ordered to leave my light battery at New Berne and report to you with three Parrott 30-pounder guns as part of the siege train for the reduction of Fort Macon, and that they did their work well the sequel has proved.

After the investment of the fort and a careful reconnaissance it was decided to place my battery at a distance of 1,500 yards from the fort, the 10-inch mortar battery about 200 yards in rear, and the 8-inch mortar battery about 200 yards to the right and front. As these batteries were constructed under fire, much of the work was done at night, which, added to the fact that guns, ammunition, and materials were transported through deep sand some 3½ miles, will prove that it was no light labor which the men performed so cheerfully and so well.

The company, having worked all night, completed the battery on the morning of the 25th of April, and at 5.30 I opened fire on the fort, the first shot striking the parapet. The mortar batteries followed immediately, and shot and shell were poured rapidly into the fort, which returned the fire with spirit. For several hours the fire from the fort was rapid and well sustained, and 8 and 10 inch shell and shot, 32-pounder shot and shell, 24-pounder shot and rifled projectiles were ploughing the ground in furrows before the battery, striking the parapet or exploding in front and rear. After that time they served a less number of guns.

Six 32-pounder shot passed through my embrasures, one of which struck the Parrott gun on the left of the battery, but fortunately did not disable it. The piece was struck on the chase and wrought-iron band, carrying away the breech sight. About the same time a 10-inch shell fell upon the wheel of a limber and shattered it. This was all the damage to my battery by the enemy's fire.

About 9 o'clock in the morning the blockading fleet engaged the fort and withdrew after an hour's firing. During the afternoon the fire from the batteries was rapid and effective, so much so that about 5 o'clock a white flag was displayed from the fort and a proposition to surrender was made. The following morning the flag of the Union was floating over another rebel fortification. There was fired during the day from my three guns 450 shot and shell, and the effects of these projectiles are seen everywhere in disabled guns and broken walls. One shot disabled two guns, 8 and 10 inch columbiads ; another passed through a bar of railroad iron and buried itself in the wall. The scarp-wall was protected by the glacis, but occasionally a shot would strike this wall and penetrate over 2 feet. Had this wall been exposed to a direct fire from these guns it could have been breached in a few hours. Nineteen guns were disabled by my fire. From rapid and continued firing the vents of all my guns were enlarged, one of them so much so as to render the gun unserviceable.

To the officers and men of my command I am indebted for the coolness and skill with which they served the pieces. First Lieut. G. W. Gowan, Forty-eighth Pennsylvania Volunteers, attached to my company, and Second Lieut. W. K. Pollock, First Artillery, each had charge of a piece, which they pointed themselves during most of the day and disabled many of the enemy's guns. Sergeant Reynolds and Corporal Leahy rendered efficient service as gunners and made some fine shots. Sergeant Thompson did good service in the magazine, filling and fusing shell and serving out ammunition. Nine of my men were detailed to serve as gunners in the two mortar batteries, which service they performed to the satisfaction of the commanders of these batteries. These men were replaced by nine men from Captain Ammon's company, I, Third Regiment New York Volunteer Artillery, who did their duty well. It gives me pleasure to report that during the day only two men, Sergeant Hynes and Private Bonnet, were slightly wounded.

I am, respectfully, your obedient servant,

LEWIS O. MORRIS,
Captain, First Artillery, Commanding Company C.
Capt. CHARLES T. GARDNER, *A. A. G., Third Division.*

No. 6.

Report of Col. Isaac P. Rodman, Fourth Rhode Island Infantry.

HDQRS. FOURTH REGIMENT RHODE ISLAND VOLS.,
DEPARTMENT OF NORTH CAROLINA,
Beaufort, N. C., May 1, 1862.

SIR: I have the honor to report the action of the Fourth Rhode

Island in the reduction of Fort Macon, which surrendered to our forces on the 26th ultimo:

After a march, which was necessarily a forced one, the Third Brigade of this department, or a portion of it, arrived and invested Fort Macon on March 26. The Fourth Rhode Island had two companies in Beaufort, one in Carolina City, and seven on the Banks. The labor of those on the Banks was very arduous, as much so as we could well endure, which was cheerfully performed without flinching. Five companies of the Fourth alternately relieved the Eighth Connecticut and Fifth Rhode Island Battalion in the trenches for fifteen days, exposed through the day to the fire of the enemy, during which time our siege batteries were planted. Not a day passed that the enemy did not open on us, firing from 30 to 50 shells, none of which, I am happy to say, injured any of my regiment.

The exposure and fatigue incident to our duty has largely increased our sick list, and we have lost 6 men by death since we arrived. Their names will appear in the adjutant's report to General Mauran, which we have at last completed.

Our batteries opened on the morning of the 26th, and in two or three hours told with fearful effect on the enemy's works. They held out for about ten hours, when by a flag of truce they requested a cessation of hostilities preparatory to a surrender. General Burnside granted this, and on the morning of the 27th Fort Macon was ours. The Fifth Rhode Island Battalion, being on duty in the trenches, received their arms, and five companies of my regiment relieved Major Wright, guarding the prisoners until they were shipped off. The fort is much damaged by our fire and some twenty-six guns were rendered unfit for service. The flag that was flying on the fort General Parke has requested General Burnside to send to you.

Nine companies of the Fourth are now quartered here, and we have a fine building for a hospital, where, I do not doubt, our men will rapidly improve. Dr. Millar assures me that they are better already. I hope soon to have the most of them able for duty.

All of which is respectfully submitted.

I have the honor to remain, your obedient servant,

I. P. RODMAN,
Colonel Fourth Rhode Island Volunteers.

Gov. WILLIAM SPRAGUE, *Providence, R. I.*

No. 7.

Report of Lieut. William S. Andrews, Ninth New York Infantry, Acting Signal Officer.

BEAUFORT, N. C., *May* 1, 1862.

MAJOR: Fort Macon fell on the 25th of April. I believe that never in the history of warfare have signals been used with more complete success or to greater advantage than during the siege of that place. When operations were commenced against Fort Macon, between four and five weeks ago, I was ordered to open a station at this place to communicate with General Parke's headquarters via Morehead City and with the blockading squadron. From that time until the 25th instant all orders were sent and received by signals. At times no other communication was had with headquarters, it being unsafe for boats to cross the harbor except under cover of the night. From my station (less than 2 miles distant from the fort) I could with the aid of glasses observe distinctly the movements of the enemy, as, for instance, should a force go out to attack our troops at work on the siege batteries or any alteration be made in the position or bearing of guns or any movement made important to be immediately known at headquarters, and of which our men could have no knowledge from their position. On my representing this fact to General Parke he ordered a station to be open by day on Bogue Banks, near our batteries, to receive official messages only, having reference to observations made from my station (this station was at different times worked by Lieutenants Marsh, Lyon, and Palmer, and was several times fired upon by the enemy). By this arrangement the enemy were held under a complete surveillance during daylight. I was the only officer on the Beaufort station until the 21st instant, when Lieut. Marvin Wait reported for duty.

On the night preceding the bombardment a number of important official messages were sent and received in communication between General Burnside's headquarters on board the steamer Alice Price (lying in Core Sound back of Beaufort) and General Parke.

The bombardment commenced on the 25th instant at 6 a. m. I had expected to receive special instructions to watch and report the accuracy of fire; but not receiving them, I determined to act upon my own responsibility. My station was at very nearly a right angle with the line of fire, so that I was enabled to judge with accuracy the distance over or short that the shot fell. The 10-inch shell were falling almost without exception more than 300 yards beyond the fort. Lieutenant Wait and myself continued to signal to the officer in charge until the correct range was obtained. The 8-inch shell were falling short; we signaled to the officer in charge of that battery with the same effect. The same was the case with the battery of Parrott guns, which were much elevated. From the position of our batteries it was impossible for the officers in charge of them to see how their shot fell; but owing [to] the observations made by Lieutenant Wait and myself and signaled to them from time to time, an accurate range was obtained by all the batteries, and was not lost during the day. *After 12 m. every shot fired from our batteries fell in or on the fort.* The accuracy of fire astonished ourselves equally with the enemy. From that time until 4 p. m., when a white flag appeared upon the fort and the firing ceased, a greater amount of execution was done than could have occurred in twenty-four hours further bombardment without the aid of signals.

The proposition to surrender and the reply, with terms of capitulation, were sent to and from General Burnside through this station by Lieutenant Wait and myself. I saw General Parke immediately after the occupation of Fort Macon by our forces. He spoke in the highest terms of praise of the system of signals used, and extended his thanks to the signal officers for the services they had rendered.

Constant signaling during a period of over four weeks across a sheet of glaring water has injured my eyes somewhat.*

Very respectfully,

W. S. ANDREWS,
Second Lieutenant, Ninth N. Y. Vols., Acting Signal Officer.

Maj. ALBERT J. MYER,
Signal Officer, U. S. Army.

---

* Some personal matter omitted.

No. 8.

Report of Col. Moses J. White, C. S. Army.

GOLDSBOROUGH, N. C., *May* 4, 1862.

GENERAL: I have the honor to submit the following report of the defense of Fort Macon, which you will find to be imperfect. As my adjutant has mysteriously disappeared with his papers, I have no means of giving you a full report:

A demand was made for the surrender of Fort Macon on March 23 last by Brigadier-General Parke, U. S. Army, which demand was refused. General Parke then, having collected a large force at Carolina City, took possession of Beaufort and Shackelford Banks, thus cutting us off from any communication without the range of our guns.

Having established his camp 8 miles from the fort, on Bogue Banks, the enemy drove in our pickets on April 10, and established themselves just without the range of our guns and their pickets within 1 mile of the fort. In retiring before them our pickets showed great coolness, and forced the enemy to advance with caution, although flanked by a fire from the sea. The enemy, after fully establishing themselves, commenced their advance on the fort by means of ditches, using the sand hills as a covering for their working parties.

With their larger force (being well protected by the sand hills) they were able by April 22 to establish their batteries within 1,400 yards of Fort Macon.

Only one sortie was made during their advance, which consisted of an attempt made with two companies to drive in their working parties and pickets on April 11, but, they being largely re-enforced from their camp, our companies were forced to retire. Occasional firing took place between our pickets and those of the enemy at night, but without any casualties on our side. We could only annoy the enemy by the fire of our artillery, which. fired horizontally, could do them no damage and only force them to keep behind the sand hills. Not having a mortar in the fort, we mounted six old 32-pounder carronades, which had been placed in the fort for defending the ditch, with 40° elevation, and used them for throwing shell behind the enemy's coverings. Two 10-inch guns were also used for the same purpose. They were, however, so completely concealed that we could seldom ascertain the position of their working parties, and when driven from them we could not see when they returned, and from scarcity of shell could not keep up a continued fire. Had the fort been built and armed for defense from a land attack the siege might have lasted longer; but as neither was the case, the enemy were able to complete their batteries, completely masked, in a shorter time than I had hoped for. During the siege some discontent arose among the garrison, which ended in several desertions. The men complained of their fare, although furnished with full rations, and seemed to be dissatisfied with being shut up in such a small place, so near their relations and friends, but unable to communicate with them. I am sorry to say that the officers did not act in a proper manner to suppress the difficulty. The health of the troops did not seem to be good, although we lost but one man by sickness. Nearly one-third were generally on the sick list.

On April 22 General Burnside arrived with several boats and anchored about 4 miles down the sound, but was forced by the fire of a rifled gun to retire and take up a position near Harker's Island.

On the 23d a demand was made by General Burnside for the sur-render of Fort Macon, which being refused, a request was made that I should meet him in person the next day on Shackelford Banks on very important business.

At 8 a. m. on the 24th I met General Burnside, as he requested. He then attempted by persuasion to produce a change in my deter-mination, but was told that the fort would be defended as long as possible.

At 6 a. m. on the 25th the enemy's land batteries opened upon the fort, and at 6.30 a. m. their vessels, consisting of three war steamers and one sailing vessel, commenced a cross-fire with rifle and 11-inch shell. The fire from both directions was immediately returned, and at 7 a. m. the ships retired—one disabled and two others in a damaged condition. The attack from land was kept up with great vigor, the enemy having immense advantage from their superior force, being able to relieve their men at the guns, while our morning reports showed only 263 men for duty. Our guns were well managed, but being able to do little damage to water batteries and siege guns, firing through very narrow embrasures. The enemy kept up a very vigorous and ac-curate fire from both rifles and mortars, dismounting guns, disabling men, and tearing the parade, parapet, and walls of the fort.

At 6.30 p. m., finding that our loss had been very great, and from the fatigue of our men being unable to keep up the fire with but two guns, a proposition was made to General Parke for the surrender of Fort Macon. General Parke demanded an unconditional surrender, which was refused, and the general informed that the firing would be renewed immediately. He then requested that the firing should cease until the next morning in order that he might consult with General Burnside, and that the general should meet me the next morning at Shackelford Banks. This proposition was accepted.

On the 26th, at 7 a. m., I met General Burnside, as proposed, and a surrender was agreed to on terms shown in the inclosed paper.* The Southern flag was hauled down at 12 m. and the men left the fort as soon as means could be furnished. A portion crossed to Beaufort.

Captain Guion's company started for New Berne on the 27th, and on the same day 150 men, consisting of parts of several companies, started for Wilmington on the United States gunboat Chippewa, arriving at Fort Caswell at 7 p. m. on the 28th.

Our loss during the fight was 7 killed and 18 wounded—2 danger-ously. Privates Langston and Jewel I was forced to leave in the fort. All other of the wounded were brought off. A nurse was left with the two men. The fort was very much damaged and fifteen guns disabled. Two days more of such firing would have reduced the whole to a mere mass of ruins.

Respectfully submitted.

M. J. WHITE,
Colonel, C. S. Army.

Maj. Gen. T. H. HOLMES,
Commanding Forces North Carolina.

---

* See inclosures to Burnside's report, p. 276.

APRIL 7, 1862.—Skirmish near Newport, N. C.

REPORTS.

No. 1.—Lieut. Col. James Wilson, Ninth New Jersey Infantry.
No. 2.—Capt. John Boothe, C. S. Army.

No. 1.

Report of Lieut. Col. James Wilson, Ninth New Jersey Infantry.

NEWPORT BARRACKS, N. C.,
April 7, 1862—2.30 p. m.

GENERAL: I have to inform you that our outside pickets on the Cedar Point road were attacked this noon at about 1 o'clock by a force of about 40 cavalry mounted and about 20 on foot, who made a sudden dash upon our post.

In skirmishing we had 1 man shot, wounded, and are fearful 1 made prisoner. This information I have from courier sent in.

Our men stood the attack and returned the fire, killing one horse, but are unable to learn any other damage, as the enemy retreated at a rapid rate, but suppose they must have killed or wounded some.

I have sent forward another company to strengthen this post, who arrived there soon after the attack.

Awaiting your orders,* I remain your most obedient servant,

JAMES WILSON,
Lieutenant-Colonel, Comdg. Ninth Regiment New Jersey Vols.
Maj. Gen. J. G. PARKE.

——————

No. 2.

Report of Capt. John Boothe, C. S. Army.

JONES COUNTY, N. C., *April* 8, 1862.

SIR: According to your instructions I make the following report of my progress since Saturday last:

I took my march toward Carteret County on Saturday, and reached Mr. Foscue's, on the Beaufort road, 20 miles below Trenton.

Sunday I was joined by Captain Hill and 50 of his men and proceeded toward Beaufort. At sunset I halted, and sent forward to ascertain the number and position of the enemy's advance reported to be ahead. At 1 o'clock in the night my scouts came in, not able to find anything, and I proceeded to Eli Saunders' and fed my horses and men.

Monday morning I was joined by Lieutenant Humphreys with about 30 men. By agreement with Captain Hill and Lieutenant Humphreys I divided the whole force into four platoons of about 30 men each, placing the men with the best arms in the first platoon. This platoon I placed under command of Lieutenant Eure and sent it forward as an advance down the road from Saunders' toward Newport. I followed with the other three platoons and their commanders a short distance behind the advance. After going within 5 miles of Newport the

————————————
* See Parke to Burnside, April 8, in "Correspondence, etc," *post.*

advance saw a squad of 5 of the enemy and charged them, capturing 3 and killing 2. About 200 yards in advance of the first squad there was another squad of 12, which being discovered, Lieutenant Eure rallied his platoon and charged them, killing 1 and capturing 6. Most of the enemy fired their muskets without injuring a horse or man on our side. In five minutes after the firing ceased two companies of the enemy came in sight and fired upon us and fell into the marsh. By their fire the only damage done was the killing of my horse under me. I ordered the men to retire down the hill, as there was no chance to charge them from a miry causeway. With our 9 prisoners I retraced my steps to this place last night.

As the first platoon did the principal work, I deem it sheer justice to say that they behaved with great bravery.

I let Lieutenant Humphreys take charge of 3 prisoners, Captain Hill 3, and I send the remainder to you and through you to General Ransom.

I am very anxious that you should recall me forthwith, as my horses and men are completely exhausted and tired out.

I also send 7 muskets captured from the enemy and Captain Hill took two.

The number of the enemy at Newport and stationed at intervals from Newport to the place we encountered them is about 600 or 700 from the best information. At and about Morehead City one regiment.

All praise is due to Lieutenant Eure and Orderly Jordan, who led the charge of the advance guard.

Your obedient servant,

JNO. BOOTHE,
Captain, Commanding.

Col. W. G. ROBINSON.

P. S.—Since writing the above one of my pickets has come in from Haughton's, about 4 miles from Pollocksville, toward Wilmington, saying the enemy had fired upon him and killed or taken the 2 pickets that were with him, and that there was 500 or 600 of the enemy.

APRIL 7–8, 1862.—Expedition to Elizabeth City, N. C.

Report of Col. Rush C. Hawkins, Ninth New York Infantry.

HEADQUARTERS ROANOKE ISLAND, N. C.,
April 11, 1862.

SIR: On the morning of the 7th instant a detachment of 600 men left here on board of the steamers Virginia, Putnam, Ceres, and Eagle for Elizabeth City, under the command of Lieutenant-Colonel Griffin, of the Sixth New Hampshire Volunteers. At 4 o'clock a. m. of the 8th instant they landed two companies of the New York Ninth at the city and four companies of the New Hampshire Sixth 6 miles above the city. They surprised two companies of the enemy's forces, who ran without firing a shot. Our forces pursued and succeeded in capturing 73 of the rebels, belonging to the First Brigade of North Carolina Militia, who are now here and await your orders. Unless I hear from you to the contrary I shall release them on their parole and send them back.

Our forces killed a noted rebel scout by the name of Tim. Gregory and wounded a rebel vedette. These were the only 2 killed or wounded on either side.

Fifty stand of arms, 2 drums, 4 horses and saddles, and 1,000 rounds of cartridges were captured and brought away.

Trusting that this little transaction will meet with your approval, I am, most faithfully, your obedient servant,

RUSH C. HAWKINS,
Colonel, Commanding Fourth Brigade and Post.

Maj. Gen. AMBROSE E. BURNSIDE,
Comdg. Dept. of North Carolina, New Berne, N. C.

P. S.—I have just heard that the enemy are building flats in a creek about ▉miles above Currituck Court-House. If I can get the Navy to co-operate and you will send me the Picket, I will organize a party to break up the rebel forces at the Court-House and at the creek. This can be done without running any great risk. I wish you would let me have the Picket. She would be of very great use here in running about in these shallow waters.

APRIL 13, 1862.—Skirmish at Gillett's Farm, Pebbly Run, N. C.

REPORTS, ETC.

No. 1.—Baron Egloffstein, Colonel One hundred and third New York Infantry.
No. 2.—Brig. Gen. Robert Ransom, jr., C. S. Army, with letter from General Robert
E. Lee.

No. 1.

Reports of Baron Egloffstein, Colonel One hundred and third New York Infantry.

HDQRS. SEWARD INFANTRY, 103D REGT. N. Y. S. V.,
Hdqrs. 9th N. J. Regt., near Newport, April 15, 1862.

SIR: With this I have the honor to report to you the partial success of my expedition against the Second Regiment North Carolina Volunteers.

I brought all the available forces of that regiment to battle last night at Th. Gillett's farm. The regiment was commanded by its colonel, William G. Robinson, formerly of the Regular Army, an old Indian fighter, like myself. I made him prisoner. I could not recapture the Ninth New Jersey boys, they having been transported to Kinston before I reached Young's. Th. Gillett's farm, the battle ground is situated 6 miles south of Young's, at the fork of the Onslow and Carolina City roads. I made many prisoners. The wounded enemies number considerable.

I will have the honor to report to you in full on my arrival at New Berne.

I have the honor to be, most respectfully, your obedient servant,

BARON EGLOFFSTEIN,
Colonel, Seward Infantry, 103d Regt. N. Y. S. V.

Maj. Gen. AMBROSE E. BURNSIDE,
Commanding Department of North Carolina.

P. S.—Most of my men are mounted on the horses captured from the enemy and beg to serve as cavalry on similar expeditions. The regiment of Col. William G. Robinson was perfectly routed, but owing to the absence of cavalry on my part I could not reap the full advantages of the victory gained in pursuing the rebels.

—

HDQRS. SEWARD INFANTRY, 103D REGT. N. Y. S. V.,
Camp Burnside, New Berne, N. C., April 19, 1862.

April 5.—In obedience to Special Orders of Headquarters Second Division, Department of North Carolina, No. 66, a detachment of 141 men left April 5 in order to occupy Evans' Mill; distance, 6 miles; course south.

April 6.—The party, being re-enforced, left Evans' Mill at midnight, under command of Colonel Baron Egloffstein, leaving a small garrison to protect both the grist and the lumber mill.

April 7.—Breakfasted at Tippe's plantation. Reached Noah Jackson's plantation, where we were informed of the presence of pickets, stationed 1 mile farther west, on Christopher Foy's farm, the owner of which had been instrumental in carrying away N. Jackson the day before and burning several thousand bales of cotton. Arriving on Christopher Foy's plantation, the colonel was fired at by the pickets, Foy being reported as taking part in the skirmish. I retaliated by driving the pickets off the ground and securing 50 head of cattle for the use of the Government. We captured 3 horses on the premises, and commenced mounting our infantry, encamped on Foy's plantation. The next morning a detachment of 25 men, commanded by Captain Schuckhart, was sent to Camp Burnside in charge of the cattle. Left late in the evening for Haughton's Mill. When near Mill Creek arrested a lone traveler on horseback, who was returning in the direction from Kinston. Through his instrumentality we made the first rebel prisoner at Haughton's Mill. Major Quentin, with a small detachment, acted as a surprise party with great promptitude.

April 8.—Encamped at Haughton's residence at 1 o'clock at night. Sent out another surprise party to Crooked Run. Two rebels crossing the run at 9 o'clock in the morning, one of them was made prisoner; the other, having been shot at, escaped through the woods in a southerly direction. From Evans' Mill we traveled 1 mile south to the fork of the Trenton and Beaufort road; took the Trenton road running west for 10 miles; changed course 2½ miles south to Haughton's Mill. Later in the afternoon 6 men (pickets) ran in our trap on Crooked Run, but returned post-haste on the road they came, owing to one of the inexperienced soldiers firing too soon. Left the mill at 10 o'clock p. m., having sent the prisoners back to New Berne with a strong escort of cavalry.

April 9.—After a severe march in rain and storm we arrived at Mr. E.. Foy's farm before daybreak—course, west 3 miles, south 2½ miles. Captain Schuckhart rejoined us here, bringing orders for the colonel to return to New Berne for further instructions, Major Quentin remaining in command under instructions to return on the road we came, but securing his position and retreat by scouting parties to the plantations of Cummings, William and Henry McDaniel, by means of which we were informed that 9 prisoners of the Ninth New Jersey Regiment, under an escort amounting nearly to 100 men of cavalry, had passed on their way to Kinston.

April 11.—Colonel Baron Egloffstein returned from New Berne the next evening. The column moved on to Cummings' farm during the night, reaching Jones' Mill, where a picket of 11 rebels was posted.

April 12.—The column was halted, and Major Quentin marched stealthily with a small body of men through the swamps surrounding the enemy, who, on discovering our men, sought their safety in flight, taking the Onslow road. The major made 1 rebel prisoner in person. We proceeded to the Jones' estate, superintended by Thomas Garrock; course south, 7 miles. I ordered the major to conduct the infantry through the swamps and across White Oak River, guided by an experienced negro, to Thomas Gillett's farm, on Pebbly Run. With a view to mislead the enemy I marched the cavalry back to Cummings' plantation, the fork of the Onslow and Hadnot road, marked Young's on old geographical maps.

April 13.—To draw the attention of the enemy to the movement of the cavalry I made a number of secessionists prisoners on this road during the night. Marched 6 miles on the Hadnot road, course southeast, to Thomas Gillett's farm, where we joined the infantry in the afternoon. Foske's and Bell's farms were occupied by our own pickets south of Pebbly Run, and a strong picket posted north of Gillett's plantation to apprise us of the approach of the enemy. The whole cavalry was sent on picket duty in the immediate neighborhood.

At 11 o'clock p. m. our northern picket was driven in by the advance guard of the Second Regiment of Cavalry (Nineteenth Regiment North Carolina Volunteers), led by their colonel, William G. Robinson. Rapid firing on the part of the advancing enemy, chiefly directed to the windows of the room occupied by Colonel Baron Egloffstein, roused our men to prompt action. The inclosures of Gillett's farm were simultaneously attacked by 300 men—well-mounted cavalry. Gallant conduct was shown on the part of our officers and men. Three charges were repulsed with the greatest firmness, after which the enemy fled in confusion and disorder in all directions, leaving 1 dead, their colonel, and 2 privates as prisoners in our hands. Twelve horses of the enemy we found dead on the battle-field and 5 more *hors de combat.*

Col. William G. Robinson exhibited much boldness, and deserving of being better sustained by his followers. He was wounded in the thigh heading the third attack in person. Two of our *élites*, Captain Langner, Prussian artillery, and Lieutenant Martinez, adjutant to General Garibaldi, wrested the colonel from his command.

Our loss was Sergt. Adolph Grossmann, of Company F; Capt. Th. Schuckhart, shot through the heart; Sergt. Henry Bopp, Company B, Captain Muller; Privates Morgenstern, same company, and Muhsam, Company F, wounded, and since recovering.

In the morning pistols, sabers, and guns were found lying about the fields and along the road to Cummings' and several stray horses were captured.

The *élite* Geiger was promoted to an honorary lieutenancy on the battle-field. Lieut. Arthur von Brand rendered valuable services. Capt. Th. Schuckhart proved an efficient officer. Drs. John Kraeuter and Marc Boecking deserve credit for giving prompt medical attention to the wounded. First Sergt. Niemetz von Rottenberg, Company K, defended the entrance to the inclosure with much energy and coolness and is deserving of promotion. He was well seconded by Corp. Franz Ebner, same company. Sergeant Krauth, of Company E, acted promptly. Sergeant Wettstein and Corporal Schrag, Company F, behaved bravely. Private Durr, of Company K, was bold and cool. Private Polguere, of Company K, remained on guard during the whole engagement like an old soldier. Sergt. Martin Hacker, of Company K, acted well. *Élites* Bernhard von Schmidt and Louis von Waldeck acted well. Sergt. Valentine Horst was instrumental in securing the gates against the boldest cavalrists, and prevented the disaster which might have followed an early success on the part of the enemy. Privates Muhsam, Ohnesorg, Rieke, Glyckherr, and Nagel, of Company F, fought bravely at the same post. Sergeant Leither, same company, exhibited much courage and electrified our men when most needed. Sergeants Zimmermann and Baumann were active in resisting the main charge directed to the rear of the premises.

April 14.—For the purpose of delivering Col. William G. Robinson to headquarters without running the risk of another engagement the colonel determined to march without delay to the encampment of the Ninth New Jersey Regiment at Newport. This was accomplished by marching 27 miles our fatigued and brave men. We destroyed the bridge at Jones' Mill to prevent the enemy from following close to our heels. We reached Carolina City and reported to General J. G. Parke, meeting Capt. D. A. Pell, aide to General Burnside, who directed the immediate delivery of the prisoner colonel to New Berne, where Mrs. William G. Robinson had arrived with a flag of truce to welcome him.

April 18.—By means of railroad and steamer we reached Camp Burnside without further incidents.

BARON EGLOFFSTEIN,
Colonel 103d Regt. N. Y. S. V., Seward Infantry.

No. 2.

Report of Brig. Gen. Robert Ransom, jr., C. S. Army, with letter from General Robert E. Lee.

HDQRS. FIRST BRIG., ARMY [DISTRICT] OF THE PAMLICO,
April 20, 1862.

SIR: In compliance with instructions from General Holmes I have the honor to make the following report of the circumstances attending in attack made by Lieutenant-Colonel Robinson, with a part of the Second North Carolina Cavalry (Nineteenth North Carolina Volunteers), upon a detachment of the enemy's infantry, near White Oak Run, on the night of the 13th instant:

Colonel Robinson's command was composed as follows: Company D, Captain Strange, Lieutenants Baker and Williams, 54 men; Company I, Captain Bryan, Lieutenant Blasingame, 45 men; Company K, Captain Turner, Lieutenants Graham, Lockhart, and Moore, 45 men; Company B, Lieutenant Allison, 14 men, Company F, Lieutenant King, about 15 men; Company E, 25 men; Company A, 4 men. Total, 1 lieutenant-colonel, 3 captains, 8 lieutenants, and 202 men.

About 2 miles before reaching the house in which the enemy was known to be Colonel Robinson called the three captains together and consulted about a plan of attack. At first it was agreed to dismount two companies, who were to attack in flank and rear while the rest were to charge in front. This mode was, for some unexplained cause, abandoned, and it was determined to charge the premises mounted, and the following arrangement was made:

Captain Bryan, with his company, and the detached portions of Andrews', Thomas', and Cole's (B, E, and F) companies, was to charge down the lane to the front of the house. Strange, with his company, was to throw down the fence on the left, and Turner, with his company, was to do the same on the right, and each to charge on the flanks and rear.

The moon was at the full and the night cloudless. A negro belonging to the premises was taken, and from him and·'Lieutenant Nether-cutt, of the Twenty-seventh North Carolina Volunteers, the exact local-ity of the premises was ascertained and information minute in detail collected.   Before getting close an advanced party of 6 privates (4 from Company A and 2 from Company D) was thrown forward to draw off any guard protecting the front.   It was concerted that when this party fired the whole command was to move in the direction indicated, each party taking the route previously determined.   Near the mouth of the lane a small guard was found and the sentinel shot by the advance party.   The lane is about 100 yards long.   Immediately upon hearing the shot Colonel Robinson ordered the charge.   The advanced party and Captain Bryan and Lieutenant Blasingame, with a small portion of Bryan's company, obeyed, and reached the yard fence while many of the enemy were yet lying down.   Being feebly sustained, they, after discharging their pieces, fell back near the mouth of the lane, where by far the greater portion of all had halted and were wildly and waste-fully throwing away their fire.   No effort up to this time had been made by either Captains Turner or Strange to reach the flanks and rear of the house.

By some means or other a second charge was made up to the yard gate (which was only about 20 feet from the house), and Captain Bryan and several men state that an officer came out of the house and begged to have the firing cease, offered to surrender, and Captain Bryan gave the order to cease, and for an instant it was obeyed; but some person cried out, "Shoot the d——d rascal!" and at once the firing recom-menced on each side.

By this time 2 or 3 of the men had been wounded and 1 or 2 killed, and again the party fell back.   Colonel Robinson was all this time try-ing to urge the men up to their work, but in vain.   A large number took to the woods; nearly all hesitated and refused to charge.   By dint of personal effort and the assistance of a few others Colonel Robinson threw down the fence on the left, and with about 20 or 30 men (among whom was Captain Strange) charged to the left and rear.   Captain Bryan says he joined the party.   When nearly in rear of the house the men fell off behind a low hill and left Colonel Robinson almost alone close to the paling.   Here he was wounded and fell off his horse.   Captain Bryan says he saw and recognized the horse and tried to catch him.

The whole party that had gone into the field toward the rear now gal-loped entirely around and passed into the road some 200 or 300 yards in rear of the mouth of the lane.   Lieutenant Allison says he was not close to the house, as his horse run away with him.   About the time that the second charge was made up the lane Captain Turner's horse was seen to turn back and move off with him.   When Colonel Robinson took the field to the left Lieutenants Graham and Moore say that they pulled down the fence on the right, rode into the field, and tried to get their men to follow, but all effort was futile.   The whole, except the small party who had gone with Colonel Robinson, either remained in the road, took to the woods, or retired by the way they had come. When those who had pretended to follow Colonel Robinson reached the road all seemed to have become confused and perfect disorder prevailed for 15 miles.   Lieutenant Baker says he remained with a small number near the mouth of the lane for more than an hour after the rest had gone.   At any rate some reached camp two or three hours sooner than others.   No effort was made by any one after Colonel Robinson was wounded to rally the men and renew the fight.   It is apparent that a success was completely and with scarcely an effort won and afterward lost by folly and cowardice.

Captain Turner was found about 200 yards from the mouth of the lane, lying wounded and stunned in the road. Some suppose that he was wounded in the head and thrown by his horse. As I examined the wound I am satisfied all his injuries were caused by the fall from his horse.

The casualties are Colonel Robinson and Captain Turner wounded; 2 privates killed, 5 wounded, and 5 taken prisoners—probably all wounded.

It is impossible to express too harsh terms toward the men for their dastardly behavior, and we can hardly justly [sic] apply his severe disapprobation to officers who could permit their commander to fall into the hands of the enemy without an effort to rescue him, and who exhibited scarcely the first quality which ought to entitle them to command.

It is but right to remark that the enemy's numbers have been variously estimated at from 50 to 200. I cannot determine the real strength, but suppose a mean between the two numbers would be just.

To keep such troops in the presence of the enemy would be useless [and] criminal, and I respectfully suggest that the officers and men who have on two occasions covered themselves with shame and our arms with dishonor be debarred the privilege of combatting for our liberties. The officers should be reduced, never to hold commissions; the men should be dismounted and disarmed and placed at hard labor during the war, and the second in command should be made an especial example for the benefit of our country and its cause. It may, perhaps, appear severe that the few who seemed willing to do their duty should suffer with the multitude of those who failed in all that becomes the officer or soldier, but they are so inextricably mingled that human ingenuity would fail to make the just discrimination.

I respectfully recommend that all but one squadron of the regiment be transferred to the rear and there be placed in a school of instruction under competent officers. Ignorance, idleness, and incapacity so strongly characterize a large number of the officers that a thorough purging is required.

I am, sir, very respectfully, your obedient servant,

R. RANSOM, JR.,
Brigadier-General.

Maj. ARCHER ANDERSON,
Assistant Adjutant-General, Department of North Carolina.

P. S.—I inclose a rough map, which will explain the report.

[Indorsements.]

HEADQUARTERS,
Goldsborough, N. C., April 21, 1862.

This report is respectfully referred to the Secretary of War, with a recommendation that General Ransom's suggestion be complied with.

TH. H. HOLMES,
Major-General.

APRIL 23, 1862.

Respectfully referred to General Lee.

S. COOPER,
Adjutant and Inspector General.

[Inclosure]

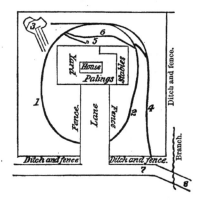

1. Route which Strange ought to have taken at first and which was taken by Colonel Robinson.
2. Route which Turner ought to have taken but did not.
3. Low hill behind which the men skulked.
4. Route taken by Strange and party.
5. Robinson wounded.
6. Bryan's retreat and pursuit of Robinson's horse.
7. Turner's fall from his horse.
8. Road going and returning.

—

HEADQUARTERS,
Richmond, Va., April 25, 1862.

Maj. Gen. T. H. HOLMES,
   Commanding, &c., Department, &c., Goldsborough, N. C.:

GENERAL: The report of Brig. Gen. Ransom of the circumstances attending an attack by Colonel Robinson's command upon the enemy's infantry, with your indorsement, recommending that the suggestions of General Ransom be complied with as regards the men and officers who have on two occasions covered themselves with shame and our arms with dishonor, has been referred by the Department for my action.

While deeply mortified at the conduct of the men, as reported by General R., I cannot see how his suggestions to reduce the officers and disarm the men and condemn them to hard labor can be carried out, unless charges be properly preferred and the matter submitted for investigation to a court-martial, when it could be ascertained how far they were culpable and what punishment is merited. If in your judgment it is deemed advisable, the whole companies might be disbanded and their arms given to others. But it would appear from the report of the detachments engaged that but a few men from some of the companies were present. For the bad behavior of a few it would not appear just to punish the whole. I would suggest that these men be stationed at some point, if possible, where their drill could be perfected, as it would seem that their unfortunate behavior was attributable in a great measure to lack of drill and discipline.

I am, very respectfully, your obedient servant,

R. E. LEE, *General.*

APRIL 19, 1862.—Engagement at South Mills, Camden County, N. C.

REPORTS, ETC.

No. 1.—Maj. Gen. Ambrose E. Burnside, U. S. Army.
No. 2.—Brig. Gen. Jesse L. Reno, U. S. Army.
No. 3.—Col. William A. Howard, First New York Marine Artillery.
No. 4.—Col. Rush C. Hawkins, Ninth New York Infantry, commanding Fourth Brigade, with resulting correspondence.
No. 5.—Lieut. Col. Thomas S. Bell, Fifty-first Pennsylvania Infantry, commanding Second Brigade.
No. 6.—Lieut. Col. William S. Clark, Twenty-first Massachusetts Infantry.
No. 7.—Maj. Edwin Schall, Fifty-first Pennsylvania Infantry.
No. 8.—Maj. Gen. Benjamin Huger, C. S. Army, with communications from General R. E. Lee.

No. 1.

Report of Maj. Gen. Ambrose E. Burnside, U. S. Army.

HEADQUARTERS DEPARTMENT OF NORTH CAROLINA,
New Berne, April 29, 1862.

SIR: I have the honor to inclose General Reno's report of the movement made by him, in accordance with my order, for the purpose of accomplishing certain objects already indicated in a former dispatch, the main one of which was most succesfully accomplished. General Reno's report gives a detailed account of the movement, and I need only add that I feel an increased confidence in the brave officers and soldiers who accomplished so much in so short a time.

Our loss in the engagement was 14 killed and 96 wounded and 2 taken prisoners.* The enemy's loss must have been much greater, as the chaplain of the Ninth New York, left in charge of the wounded, reports having seen on the field 30 killed, besides several wounded, the main body of the wounded having been taken from the field when they retreated.

Our forces drove the enemy from the field in a most gallant style, buried our dead, bivouacked on the field for seven hours, transported all the wounded, except 14 so severely wounded that they could not be moved, but were comfortably provided for and left in charge of a surgeon and chaplain.

General Reno then, in obedience to orders, returned to his fleet and embarked his men. He felt less reluctance in leaving behind these 14 wounded with the surgeon and chaplain from the fact that I had but a few days before released some 80 wounded, with the surgeons, who were left by the enemy in New Berne, and the commanding officer in that neighborhood would be less than human were he to refuse to release these wounded as soon as they can be transported safely.

I beg to inclose my congratulatory order with the report of General Reno; also the correspondence between the general and the commanding officer at South Mills.

I have the honor to be, your obedient servant,
A. E. BURNSIDE,
Major-General, Commanding Department of North Carolina.
Hon. E. M. STANTON, *Secretary of War, Washington.*

---

* But see revised statement, p. 307.

No. 2.

Report of Brig. Gen. Jesse L. Reno, U. S. Army, with congratulatory order.

HEADQUARTERS SECOND DIVISION,
New Berne, N. C., April 22, 1862.

CAPTAIN: I have the honor to report that, in obedience to the order of Major-General Burnside, I proceeded from New Berne with the Twenty-first Massachusetts and Fifty-first Pennsylvania Regiments to Roanoke, and was there joined by part of the Ninth and Eighty-ninth New York and Sixth New Hampshire.

We proceeded directly to Elizabeth City and commenced disembarking on the 19th instant at midnight, at a point about 3 miles below, on the east side. By 3 p. m. Colonel Hawkins' brigade, consisting of the Ninth and Eighty-ninth New York and the Sixth New Hampshire, were landed and ready to move. I ordered Colonel Hawkins to proceed at once with his brigade toward South Mills for the purpose of making a demonstration on Norfolk. I remained to bring up the other two regiments, they having been delayed by their vessels getting aground at the mouth of the river. They came up at daylight and were landed by 7 a. m. I proceeded directly toward South Mills, and about 12 miles out met Colonel Hawkins' brigade, who, it seems, lost his way, either by the treachery or incompetency of his guide, he having marched some 10 miles out of his way. As his men were very much jaded by their long march, I ordered them to follow the Second Brigade.

Proceeding about 4 miles farther, to within a mile and a half of South Mills, the rebels opened upon us with artillery before my advance guard discovered them. I immediately reconnoitered their position, and found that they were posted in an advantageous position in a line perpendicular to the road—their infantry in ditches and their artillery commanding all the direct approaches, their rear protected by a dense forest. I ordered the Fifty-first Pennsylvania immediately to file to the right and pass over to the edge of the woods to turn their left. I also ordered the Twenty-first Massachusetts to pursue the same course, and when Colonel Hawkins came up with his brigade I sent him with the Ninth and Eighty-ninth New York to their support. The Sixth New Hampshire were formed in line to the left of the road and ordered to support our four pieces of artillery.

Owing to the excessive fatigue of the men they could not reach their position for some time. In the mean time the enemy kept up a brisk artillery fire, which was gallantly responded to by our small pieces under charge of Colonel Howard, of the Coast Guard, who during the entire engagement displayed most conspicuous gallantry and rendered very efficient service both during the action and upon the return, he bringing up the rear. As soon as the Fifty-first Pennsylvania and Twenty-first Massachusetts had succeeded in turning their left they opened a brisk musketry fire, and about the same time the Ninth New York, also coming in range and being too eager to engage, unfortunately charged upon the enemy's artillery. It was a most gallant charge, but they were exposed to a most deadly fire of canister, grape, and musketry, and were forced to retire, but rallied immediately upon the Eighty-ninth New York. I then ordered both regiments to form a junction with the Twenty-first Massachusetts. In the mean time the

Fifty-first Pennsylvania and Twenty-first Massachusetts kept up an incessant fire upon the rebels, who now had withdrawn their artillery and had commenced to retire in good order. The Sixth New Hampshire had steadily advanced in line to the left of the road, and when within about 200 yards poured in a most deadly volley, which completely demoralized the enemy and finished the battle. Our men were so completely fagged out by the intense heat and their long march that we could not pursue them. The men rested under arms in line of battle until about 10 o'clock p. m., when I ordered a return to our boats, having accomplished the principal object of the expedition, conveying the idea that the entire Burnside expedition was marching upon Norfolk.

Owing to the want of transportation I was compelled to leave some 16 of our most severely wounded men. Assistant Surgeon Warren, of the Twenty-first Massachusetts, was left with the men. I sent a flag of truce the next day to ask that they might be returned to us, Commodore Rowan kindly volunteering to attend to it. We took only a few prisoners, some 10 or 15, most of whom belonged to the Third Georgia Regiment.

The Ninth New York suffered most severely, owing to their premature charge, our total loss in killed and wounded being about 90, some 60 belonging to that regiment.*

The officers and men of the several regiments all behaved with their usual gallantry and many are worthy of particular mention, and I presume the brigade and regimental commanders will do justice to their respective commands. I will forward their reports as soon as received.

The return march was made in perfect order, and few if any stragglers were left behind. Considering that during the advance the weather was intensely hot and that on the return a severe rain rendered the roads very muddy, and that a portion of the command had to march 45 miles and the other 35 and fight a battle in the mean time, and that all this was accomplished in less than twenty-four hours, I think that the commanding general has every reason to be satisfied with his command.

I desire to return my thanks to Commodore Rowan and the officers and men under him for their untiring energy in disembarking and re-embarking my command, and also to Lieutenant Flusser for the gallant manner in which he assisted us by proceeding up the river and driving the enemy out of the woods along the banks. Colonel Hawkins, commanding the First [Fourth] Brigade, and Lieutenant-Colonel Bell, commanding Second, both displayed conspicuous courage, as did also the regimental commanders. Lieutenant-Colonel Clark commanded the Twenty-first Massachusetts, Major Schall the Fifty-first Pennsylvania, Lieutenant-Colonel Kimball the Ninth New York, Colonel Fairchild the Eighty-ninth New York, and Lieutenant-Colonel Griffin the Sixth New Hampshire. Captain Fearing, aide-de-camp to General Burnside, accompanied me as volunteer aide, and rendered efficient and gallant service; also Captain Ritchie, commissary of subsistence, and Lieutenants Gordon and Breed, of the Signal Corps. My own aides, Lieutenants Reno and Morris, behaved with their usual gallantry. As soon as the brigade and regimental reports are furnished I will forward them, together with a complete list of killed and wounded.

The enemy's loss was considerable, but they succeeded in carrying off most of their wounded. Several, however, were left on the field, one of whom was a captain of the Third Georgia Regiment. The color-bearer of the Third Georgia Regiment was shot down by the Twenty-

---

* But see Addenda following.

first Massachusetts while waving defiantly his traitorous flag. The enemy had from six to ten pieces of artillery and from 1,800 to 2,000 men. We approached to within 30 miles of Norfolk, and undoubtedly the defeat of one of their best regiments, the Third Georgia, produced considerable panic at Norfolk.

I have the honor to be, very respectfully, your obedient servant,

J. L. RENO,
Brigadier-General, Commanding Second Division.

Capt. LEWIS RICHMOND, *Assistant Adjutant-General.*

[Addenda]

Return of casualties in the United States troops in the engagement at South Mills, N. C.,
April 19, 1862.

[Compiled from nominal lists of casualties, returns, &c.]

Command.	Killed.		Wounded.		Captured or missing.		Aggregate.
	Officers.	Enlisted men.	Officers.	Enlisted men.	Officers.	Enlisted men.	
6th New Hampshire Infantry	......	1	......	2	......	1	4
21st Massachusetts Infantry	......	1	......	15	......	1	17
1st New York Marine Artillery, detachment *	......	......	......	......	......	......	
9th New York Infantry	1	7	7	54	......	6	75
89th New York Infantry	......	......	1	3	......	2	6
51st Pennsylvania Infantry	......	3	1	18	......	3	25
Total	1	12	9	92	......	13	127

*No loss reported.

—

GENERAL ORDERS, }   HDQRS. DEPT. OF NORTH CAROLINA,
No. 30.   }   *April 26, 1862.*

The general commanding desires to express his high appreciation of the excellent conduct of the forces under command of Brigadier-General Reno in the late demonstration upon Norfolk. He congratulates them as well upon the manly fortitude with which they endured excessive heat and extraordinary fatigue on a forced march of 40 miles in twenty-four hours as upon the indomitable courage with which, notwithstanding their exhaustion, they attacked a large body of the enemy's best artillery, infantry, and cavalry in their own chosen position, achieving a complete victory. It is therefore ordered, as a deserved tribute to the perseverance, discipline, and bravery exhibited by the officers and soldiers of the Twenty-first Massachusetts, Fifty-first Pennsylvania, Ninth New York, Eighty-ninth New York, and Sixth New Hampshire, on the 19th of April—a day already memorable in the history of our country—that the above regiments inscribe upon their respective colors the name, "Camden, April 19."

The general commanding desires to express his approbation of General Reno's strict observance of orders when the temptation to follow the retreating enemy was so great.

By command of Maj. Gen. A. E. Burnside:

LEWIS RICHMOND,
Assistant Adjutant-General.

No. 3.

Report of Col. William A. Howard, First New York Marine Artillery.

HEADQUARTERS MARINE ARTILLERY,
On Board Steamer Virginia, Croatan Sound, April 20, 1862.

GENERAL : I have the honor to report that in accordance with your instructions of the morning of the 18th instant I took the schooner Edward Slade, with Professor Maillefert and corps in her, and proceeded to the mouth of the Pasquotank River and anchored. On the arrival of the gunboats and troop ships I proceeded up the river and anchored with the fleet. Two launches, with boat howitzers and crews, under command of Lieutenants Gerard and Avery, of Marine Artillerymen, landed, and joined the advancing column, under command of Colonel Hawkins, Ninth (Zouaves) New York Volunteers. The launches were employed landing troops. The steamers Northerner and Guide, with the Twenty-first Massachusetts and Fifty-first Pennsylvania, not appearing, I dispatched by your orders the steamers Virginia, Ocean Wave, Massasoit, and Phœnix down the river to bring up the troops, which was done about daylight. The troops were landed, also two howitzers (one smooth, one rifled) belonging to the Ninth New York Volunteers, and were attached to the column under your immediate command, Lieutenant Herbert, with a detachment of the Ninth, in charge. By your orders I assumed command of the advance guard and guides and moved into the interior. Having marched several miles, it was observed that a picket of 8 horsemen were watching our movements, giving us, however, only one opportunity of firing upon them. We had marched about 14 miles when dense black smoke was seen to arise from burning buildings, and sweeping across the road concealed the enemy from our sight. On arriving at the line of smoke the advance was arrested by the unmasking of a battery of 12-pounders, which opened fire with shell and grape. Having examined its position as far as possible I reported to you, and was directed to bring up the howitzers, which was done. You had previously, however, directed a flanking movement made by your column. The column of advance, under Colonel Hawkins, not having made its appearance, it was evident we had been misled by his guide. It became necessary, therefore, to keep the enemy in play until its arrival. In forty-five minutes or thereabouts that brigade appeared. The two howitzers and men belonging to the Marine Artillery reported and asked for orders; also Lieutenant Morris, with 15 men of the Ninth New York, to serve with the guns, which were immediately run into position, the range and direction given them, when a very hot fire was opened and continued until the enemy withdrew his pieces, which I reported to you.

On the near approach, however, of the Ninth New York and Eightyninth New York on their left flank their guns were again run into position, and severe fire of grape and canister opened upon the charging troops. Our battery was immediately advanced and opened with grape and shell and continued until their final retreat. Our forces, having quiet possession of the field, rested. A reconnaissance made by your instructions showed the object of the movement had been accomplished.

Having given the men sufficient rest and food, at 10 o'clock we commenced our return. By your direction I assumed command of the rear guard with two pieces, supported by the Twenty-first Massachusetts and one company of the Fifty-first Pennsylvania. The rain in the evening having made the roads very bad, our progress was somewhat retarded, but on arriving at our place of landing at 6 o'clock, finding our boats ready to receive us, we embarked on board our proper transports, proceeded to this anchorage, landing the detachment belonging to Roanoke, and those destined for New Berne proceeded to their stations.

I cannot close this report without bearing testimony to the gallant officers and men under my command. Lieutenants Gerard and Avery, Marine Artillery; Lieutenants Morris and Herbert, Ninth (Zouaves) New York Volunteers, deserve all I can say for their coolness and courage. Mr. Albert E. Hand, formerly clerk of this vessel, attached himself to my command, and behaved in the most gallant manner. Captain Child, temporarily on duty in this vessel, S. C. D., and Mr. Moore, pilot, were indefatigable in landing the troops, piloting the vessel, &c. When it is considered that our men marched nearly all night, fought a hard battle of three hours' duration, and marched the same distance the second night without sleep through deep mud cheerfully, without a murmur, too much praise cannot be awarded them.

Respectfully submitted.

W. A. HOWARD,
Colonel Marine Artillery.

Brigadier-General RENO, U. S. A.,
New Berne, Department North Carolina.

No. 4.

Reports of Col. Rush C. Hawkins, Ninth New York Infantry, commanding Fourth Brigade, with resulting correspondence.

HEADQUARTERS,
Roanoke Island, N. C., April 21, 1862.

SIR: In accordance with orders from department headquarters I, on the 18th, at about 11 a. m., embarked on board of the transports about 2,000 men of my brigade from the following regiments: Ninth New York Volunteers, 727; Eighty-ninth New York Volunteers, 625, and Sixth New Hampshire Volunteers, 600. In this force was included two boat guns belonging to Company K, Ninth New York Volunteers.

About 11 o'clock the same evening my brigade commenced landing at a place opposite Cobb's Point, about 4 miles below Elizabeth City, on the Pasquotank River.

By 2.30 o'clock on the morning of the 19th the landing of my brigade had been completed, including two field pieces from the steamer Virginia; this through the water where it was more than knee-deep, which the men were compelled to wade.

At 3 a. m. the whole brigade was on the march, and continued for the next twelve hours on its weary way through a long, circuitous route of 32 miles, beneath the terrible heat of the sun, amid the constantly-rising dust.

At about 3 p. m. I succeeded in arriving in sight of the enemy's position with about one-half of the men who had commenced the march, when we were immediately ordered into action, the Sixth New Hampshire Volunteers going to the left of the enemy's position, the Ninth and Eighty-ninth New York going to the right through the woods to outflank the enemy on each side. Up to this time the part of a battery from the Ninth New York, worked by Lieutenant Herbert, assisted by

5 men (the rest having been worn out by fatigue), received and sustained the whole fire of the enemy's battery.

After marching about 2 miles through a swamp covered with thick undergrowth I arrived within about three-eighths of a mile of the enemy's position, where they were concealed in the woods. After a short tour of observation I came to the conclusion that it would be impossible to outflank them on the right the undergrowth and swamp being almost impenetrable. A charge through an open field directly in front of the enemy's position was thought to be the only way in which they could be dislodged. I then returned to where I had left the Ninth New York and found them lying on the ground completely exhausted. I stated to the regiment what I proposed to do, and asked the men if they felt equal to the task. Their answer was, "We will try, colonel, and follow wherever you may lead us." Immediately the command, "Forward!" was given, the Ninth New York taking the lead, followed by the Eighty-ninth New York. We had proceeded to within about 200 yards of the enemy's concealed position when the Ninth New York received the full and direct fire from the enemy's infantry and batteries. This completely staggered the men, who were before completely exhausted, and the order was given for the regiment to turn to the right, where it would be partly sheltered from the fire. This order was executed, but slowly. Soon after the Eighty-ninth New York commenced to move forward, supported by the Ninth New York, when the enemy retreated. When this commenced the Sixth New Hampshire poured a volley into the right wing of the Third Regiment Georgia Volunteers, which completely cut them to pieces. The troops then bivouacked on the field, where they remained until 10 p. m., when they were ordered to fall in and return to their transports.

It is seldom, if ever, that men have been called upon to perform so much in so short a time as those were who composed the Fourth Brigade under my command. Marching 50 miles and fighting a battle all in twenty-six hours you will admit is no small undertaking, and yet this was done without a murmur or a complaint.

In the charge of the Ninth New York that regiment lost 9 killed and 56 wounded. Among the former was Lieut. Charles A. Gadsden, adjutant, who fell at the head of his regiment. He was a kind, considerate man and a most excellent soldier, and dies greatly lamented by all of his companions.

Colonel Howard, of the steamer Virginia, who was in command of the artillery, has not yet made his report, consequently I am unable to give any particulars concerning his part in the engagement, but believe that he behaved with great coolness and bravery, as well as all of the men and officers under him.

Soon after the troops had returned to Roanoke Island the Rev. T. W. Conway, chaplain of the Ninth New York Volunteers, returned, bringing with him about 50 stragglers and some of the wounded left behind on the field of battle. He remained to bury the dead and to assist the wounded. On the morning of the 20th he started out to find the rebel pickets, and after going some distance he was informed that the rebels had left the night before—re-enforcements which they had only a few moments before received included—for Suffolk, thinking that our forces were by a flank movement getting in their rear to cut them off; returned to the hospital by the way of the battle-field, where he counted 30 of the enemy's dead. After the dead were buried and the wounded who could not be brought away cared for, all the stragglers who could be found armed themselves and started for the place of debarkation and arrived here in safety the next morning.

In this enterprise you have received another evidence of the courage and enterprise of the troops under your command. Although the results of this expedition may seem disastrous on account of the loss of life, still the reconnaissance cannot fail to be of great value to you when connected with future operations.

In justice to other regiments I cannot say what I should like to about the officers and men of my own, consequently would only say that all alike did their duty faithfully and well.

I regret to add that, owing to our limited transportation, we were compelled to leave behind 14 of our wounded in care of Dr. Warren, of the Twenty-first Massachusetts, 2 or 3 of which were brought away by the chaplain of the Ninth. I have to-day sent a flag of truce by Major Jardine, who was accompanied by the surgeon, chaplain, and 10 privates, of the Ninth New York, for the purpose of bringing back the wounded and the bodies of Lieutenant Gadsden and our dead who were buried on the field.

Herewith you will find a complete list of the killed, wounded, and missing of the Fourth Brigade in the action of the 19th.*

Respectfully, your obedient servant,
RUSH C. HAWKINS,
Colonel, Commanding Fourth Brigade and Post.

Maj. Gen. AMBROSE E. BURNSIDE,
Comdg. Dept. of North Carolina, New Berne, N. C.

[Indorsement No. 1.]

HEADQUARTERS,
New Berne, N. C., May 1, 1862.

Respectfully referred to General Reno, to whom it should have originally been addressed.

By order of Major-General Burnside:
LEWIS RICHMOND,
Assistant Adjutant-General.

[Indorsement No. 2.]

HEADQUARTERS SECOND DIVISION,
May 2, 1862.

I beg to inclose the following indorsement.
J. L. RENO,
Brigadier-General, Commanding Second Divison.

[Indorsement No. 3.] .

HDQRS. SECOND DIVISION, DEPT. OF NORTH CAROLINA,
New Berne, N. C., May 1, 1862.

Capt. LEWIS RICHMOND,
Assistant Adjutant-General:

CAPTAIN: I have the honor to indorse upon the report of Colonel R. C. Hawkins, Ninth New York Volunteers, which you this day caused to be referred to me, the following remarks and statements, viz:

In the first place I beg leave to call your attention to the fact that this report was rendered by Colonel Hawkins directly to you instead

---

* Embodied in statement on p. 307.

of to me, his immediate commanding officer, which is in violation of the
Army Regulations and Rules of Service, as also that the spirit of the
report indicates a disposition to ignore me, the commanding officer of
the expedition, as well as the rest of my command not embraced in
Colonel Hawkins' brigade. No mention is made by Colonel Hawkins
in his report of the orders received on the march and during the engagement from me personally and through my aides. He gives no
explanation of the way in which my orders were carried out, nor why
some of the orders given him were not obeyed. To be more explicit,
I will state in detail that the whole force under my command, consisting of the Sixth New Hampshire, Ninth and Eighty-ninth New York
Volunteers (which three regiments composed the brigade of Colonel
Hawkins), the Fifty-first Pennsylvania, and Twenty-first Massachusetts, set sail from Roanoke Island by my orders, and debarked near
Elizabeth City by my order and under my personal direction, and that
the march toward South Mills was executed by though not according
to my express orders, as Colonel Hawkins took his brigade by a most
circuitous route. The orders I gave Colonel Hawkins on landing were
to proceed directly to the bridge across the Pasquotank, about a mile
this side of South Mills, and to occupy it. This order he did not obey
promptly, and I sent two aides in succession to order him to proceed,
and finally was obliged to go in person to force obedience to my order.
Four hours after this I landed with the remaining two regiments, which
had been delayed in disembarking by the steamers Northerner and
Guide getting aground at the mouth of the river. We passed Colonel
Hawkins' brigade about 12 miles out and before he had got upon the
direct road, he having marched some 10 or 12 miles out of the way.
The road to South Mills was open, plain, and perfectly direct, known
to every resident in the country, and nothing but design or negligence
could have caused him to miss the road. With respect to the statement
in Colonel Hawkins' report to you that "at about 3 p. m. I succeeded
in arriving in sight of the enemy's position with about one-half of the
men who had commenced the march, when we were immediately ordered
into action, the Sixth New Hampshire Volunteers going to the left of
the enemy's position, the Ninth and Eighty-ninth New York Volunteers
going to the right through the woods to outflank the enemy on each side,"
I have to state that at about 1 o'clock I arrived with my whole command in front of the enemy's position, the Fifty-first Pennsylvania Volunteers, followed by the Twenty-first Massachusetts Volunteers, with
Colonel Howard's artillery, being in advance, the brigade under Colonel
Hawkins following. I immediately sent the Fifty-first Pennsylvania
Volunteers and Twenty-first Massachusetts Volunteers to the right with
orders to turn the enemy's left, and at once sent orders to Colonel
Hawkins to move forward with his whole brigade. This order not
being promptly obeyed, I went back and found that he had halted his
command and had not prepared to move. I immediately ordered him
forward, with directions to follow (with two regiments) the Twenty-
first Massachusetts Volunteers and Fifty-first Pennsylvania Volunteers,
to aid in turning the enemy's left. I then went forward and placed the
two latter regiments in proper position, and, returning, met Colonel
Hawkins, and again giving the orders above named, I pointed out to him
the position of the Twenty-first Massachusetts and Fifty-first Pennsylvania Volunteers. The way was through an open pine wood, which
had already been passed over by the above-named regiments. It is
thus shown that the time at which the engagement commenced was
before the time which the said report would lead one to suppose, and

that the time consumed by Colonel Hawkins in coming under fire was due to unnecessary delay on his part, and that the studious avoidance of the mention of orders received by him from me was calculated to cover this delay and convey the impression that he acted by his own authority.

With respect to the statement that "after marching about 2 miles through a swamp covered by thick undergrowth I arrived within about three-eighths of a mile of the enemy's position, where they were concealed in the woods, I came to the conclusion that it would be impossible to outflank them on the right, the undergrowth and swamp being almost impenetrable," I have to state that the route pursued by the command of Colonel Hawkins did not lead through a swamp or almost impenetrable undergrowth, as is shown by the fact that two regiments (the Twenty-first Massachusetts and Fifty-first Pennsylvania) had already passed over this ground, and that I had been over the ground myself and found it dry and perfectly practicable for passage.

As to the statement that "a charge through an open field directly in front of the enemy's position was thought to be the only way in which they could be dislodged," I have to state that if the intention be to convey the idea that I, the commanding officer, thought so, it is untrue, as it was directly contrary to my opinion. If the intention be to convey the idea that he or other officers thought so and that he acted upon that conclusion, it was an act of insubordination, as it was contrary to my orders.

As to the statement that "soon after the Eighty-ninth New York commenced to move forward, supported by the Ninth New York, when the enemy retreated," &c., I have to state that it is calculated to give the false impression that this movement caused the retreat of the enemy, when in reality it was caused by the enemy's flank being turned by the Twenty-first Massachusetts and Fifty-first Pennsylvania Volunteers.

In conclusion, I have to state that Col. R. C. Hawkins, in making his report directly to you instead of his commanding officer, has been guilty of a breach of military usage and discipline, and that the spirit of said report is calculated to ignore my presence as commanding officer, to ignore orders received from me, as well as to ignore the presence of those regiments which principally fought the engagement, and that the report tends to convey a false impression of the circumstances arising during the engagement and of the part which he played in it, and that it contains a perversion of truth in the statements concerning the obstacles to his progress in moving to turn the enemy's left. I beg leave also to state that the principal loss in killed and wounded is due to the unauthorized and unnecessary charge made by the Ninth New York, under the immediate command of Colonel Hawkins.

I have the honor to be, very respectfully, your obedient servant,

.J. L. RENO,
Brigadier-General, Commanding Second Division.

—

HEADQUARTERS,
Roanoke Island, N. C., April 21, 1862.

SIR: In accordance with orders from the department headquarters, and under your immediate orders I, on the 18th, at about 11 a. m., embarked on board of the transport about 2,000 men of my brigade from the following regiments: Ninth New York Volunteers, 727;

Eighty-ninth New York Volunteers, 625, and Sixth New Hampshire Volunteers, 600. In this force was included two boat guns belonging to Company K, Ninth New York Volunteers.

About 11 p. m. the same evening my brigade commenced landing at a place opposite Cobb's Point, about 4 miles below Elizabeth City, on the Pasquotank River.

By 2.30 o'clock on the morning of the 19th the landing of my brigade had been completed, including two field pieces from the steamer Virginia; this through the water where it was more than knee-deep, which the men were compelled to wade.

At 3 a. m. the whole brigade was on the march, and continued for the next twelve hours on its weary way through a long, circuitous route of 32 miles, beneath the terrible heat of the sun, amid the constantly-rising dust.

At about 3 p. m. I succeeded in arriving in sight of the enemy's position with about one-half of the men who had commenced the march, when we were immediately ordered by yourself into action, the Sixth New Hampshire Volunteers going to the left of the enemy's position, the Ninth and Eighty-ninth New York going to the right through the woods to outflank the enemy on each side. Up to this time the part of a battery from the Ninth New York, worked by Lieutenant Herbert, assisted by 5 men (the rest having been worn out by fatigue), received and sustained the whole fire of the enemy's battery.

After marching about 2 miles through a swamp covered with thick undergrowth I arrived within about three-eighths of a mile of the enemy's position where they were concealed in the woods. After a short tour of observation I came to the conclusion that it would be impossible to outflank them on the right, the undergrowth and swamp being almost impenetrable. A charge through an open field in front of the enemy's position was thought to be the only way in which they could be dislodged. I then returned to where I had left the Ninth New York, and found them lying on the ground completely exhausted. I stated to the regiment what I proposed to do, and asked the men if they felt equal to the task. Their answer was, "We will try, colonel, and follow wherever you may lead us." Immediately the command forward was given, the Ninth New York taking the lead, followed by the Eighty-ninth New York. We had proceeded to within about 200 yards of the enemy's concealed position when the Ninth New York received the full, direct, right-oblique, and left-oblique fires from the enemy's infantry and batteries. This completely staggered the men, who were before quite exhausted. The order was then given for the regiment to turn to the right, where it would be partly sheltered from the fire. This order was executed, but slowly. Soon after the Eighty-ninth New York commenced to move forward, supported by the Ninth New York, when the enemy retreated. When this commenced the the Sixth New Hampshire poured a volley into the right wing of the Third Georgia Volunteer Regiment, which completely cut them into pieces. The troops then bivouacked on the field, where they remained until 10 p. m., when they were ordered to fall in and return to their transports.

It is seldom, if ever, that men have been called upon to perform so much in so short a time as those were who composed the Fourth Brigade, under my command. Marching 50 miles and fighting a battle all in twenty-six hours you will admit is no small undertaking, and yet this was done without a murmur or complaint.

In the charge of the Ninth New York that regiment lost 9 killed and

60 wounded. Among the former was Lieut. Charles A. Gadsden, adjutant, who fell at the head of his regiment. He was a kind, considerate man and a most excellent soldier, and dies greatly lamented by all of his companions.

Colonel Howard, of the steamer Virginia, who was in command of the artillery, has not yet made his report, consequently I am unable to give any particulars concerning his part in the engagement, but believe that he behaved with coolness and bravery, as well as all of the men and officers under him.

Soon after the troops had returned to Roanoke Island the Rev. T. W. Conway, chaplain of the Ninth New York Volunteers, returned, bringing with him about 50 stragglers and some of the wounded left behind on the field of battle. He remained behind to bury the dead and to assist the wounded. On the morning of the 20th he started out to find the rebel pickets, and after going some distance he was informed that the rebels had left the night before—re-enforcements which they had only a few moments before received included—for Suffolk, thinking that our forces were by a flank movement getting in their rear to cut them off. He returned to the hospital by the way of the battle-field, where he counted 30 of the enemy's dead. After the dead were buried and the wounded who could not be brought away cared for, all the stragglers who could be found armed themselves and started for the place of debarkation, and arrived here in safety the next morning.

In this enterprise the commanding general has received another evidence of the courage and enterprise of the troops under his command. Although the results of this expedition may seem disastrous on account of the loss of life, still the reconnaissance cannot fail to be of great value to him when connected with future operations.

In justice to other regiments I cannot say what I should like to about the officers and men of my own, consequently would only say that all alike did their duty faithfully and well.

I regret to add that owing to our limited transportation we were compelled to leave behind 14 of our wounded in care of Dr. Warren, of the Twenty-first Massachusetts, 2 or 3 of which were brought away by the chaplain of the Ninth New York. I have to-day sent a flag of truce by Major Jardine, who was accompanied by the surgeon, chaplain, and 10 privates of the Ninth New York, for the purpose of bringing back the wounded and the bodies of Lieutenant Gadsden and our dead who were buried on the field.

Herewith you will find a complete list of the killed, wounded, and missing of the Fourth Brigade in the action of the 19th.*

Respectfully, your obedient servant,

RUSH C. HAWKINS,
Colonel Ninth New York Volunteers, Comdg. Fourth Brigade.

Brig. Gen. JESSE L. RENO,
Comdg. Second Div., Dept. of North Carolina, New Berne, N. C.

[Indorsement.]

HDQRS. SECOND DIV., DEPT. OF NORTH CAROLINA,
New Berne, N. C., May 15, 1862.

This amended report of Colonel Hawkins, made to me in obedience to your express orders, exhibiting the same inconsistencies and misstatements as the first or original report, is not deemed satisfactory, and

---

*Embodied in statement on p. 307.

I can see no reason for altering or suppressing my original remarks or indorsement. I therefore recommend that his original report, with my indorsement, be forwarded.

J. L. RENO,
Brigadier-General.

HEADQUARTERS,
Roanoke Island, N. C., April 23, 1862.

SIR: Doubtless the unfortunate occurrence of the 19th has been brought fully to your notice. No one can regret the result more than myself. First, because of the loss of life; second, the object of the expedition not being accomplished after all the obstacles in our way had been removed. It seems that both parties were badly frightened. The enemy ran like quarter-horses toward Norfolk, and we as fast as our weary legs would carry us toward Roanoke, leaving quite a number of our wounded and destroying the bridges behind us. In this connection I will only add our retirement was discretion, our valor having been wholly spent on the field of battle. There is one satisfaction, that we whipped them in their own well-chosen position like the devil. They acknowledged to have had three companies of the Georgia Third completely cut to pieces, and from this acknowledgment it is but fair to infer their loss was much greater. Their force, as near as I can ascertain, was the Georgia Third, 1,165 strong; a battery of Henningsen's artillery of four pieces, and some North Carolina Militia, number not known, and a full squadron of Suffolk and Southampton cavalry. This statement of the enemy's forces I believe to be very nearly correct.

I most cordially join in the recommendations of the surgeons that the wounded be removed North as soon as possible, and that a steamer, made comfortable by the necessary beds, &c., be sent here for that purpose at the earliest moment. They can be of no service here and will recover much more rapidly at the North, besides relieving our surgeons, who are already worn-out by their arduous labors. Owing to the little wound received in my left arm in the affair of the 19th I am compelled, by the advice of surgeons, to lay up in ordinary for repairs, much against my desire or inclination. They say it will be eight weeks before I am fit for service. Under such circumstances, being forbidden to perform any labor, I would ask for leave of absence until such time as I am able to return to duty, which will be at the earliest possible moment. But still, if you cannot spare me, I will remain and render such service as I am able to perform lying on my back. I know and can dictate what ought to be done.

I should be very happy to see you here, as I have much to say to you that I cannot write.

Most faithfully, your friend and servant,
RUSH C. HAWKINS,
Commanding Post.

Maj. Gen. AMBROSE E. BURNSIDE,
Commanding Department of North Carolina.

NEW BERNE, N. C., *April 24,* 1862.

MY DEAR GENERAL: Foster showed me the letter of that infernal scoundrel Hawkins, and he and other rascals have been circulating reports concerning my conduct and the command at the recent battle of Camden which are calculated to do me and the gallant men with me great injustice. You remember that my orders were not to risk any disaster, and that I did not go prepared to remain absent more than two days. After ascertaining that the Navy could not make a junction with me at the bridge, and hearing from a variety of sources that I considered reliable that re-enforcements were on the way, I deemed it for the best to retire, and no man more highly approved that course than the rascal Hawkins. In fact, it was his bad conduct in placing his regiment in a position to get whipped and demoralized that principally induced me to change my first intention, which was to remain on the field and proceed to South Mills in the morning. The commanding officers of both the Twenty-first and Fifty-first came to me to urge that course, stating that they had not sufficient ammunition to risk another battle. The doctors also stated that the wounded could be moved more easily then than at any other time, and not being able to divine the future or imagine that they would abandon a 32-pounder battery, which I knew they had at South Mills, I believed I was carrying out your wishes in returning. If such was the fact, I think that out of justice to me and the command you should publish an order to that effect. You have no idea how industriously some scoundrel has been spreading reports that we were badly whipped, and how dissatisfied the officers and men of the Twenty-first and Fifty-first are that no official contradiction of such lying reports has been made. •

All well here. We will keep up a sharp lookout for our secesh friends. I think that I will send the One hundred and third New York to Parke. My love to him, yourself, and others.

Yours, truly,

J. L. RENO.

General AMBROSE E. BURNSIDE.

No. 5.

Report of Lieut. Col. Thomas S. Bell, Fifty-first Pennsylvania Infantry, commanding Second Brigade.

CAMP FIFTY-FIRST REGIMENT PENNSYLVANIA VOLS.,
New Berne, N. C., April 23, 1862.

SIR: I have the honor to report, for the information of the general commanding the division, that on the landing of the Fifty-first Regiment Pennsylvania Volunteers and Twenty-first Regiment Massachusetts Volunteers at the point on the Pasquotank River about 3 miles below Elizabeth City, between the hours of 6 and 7 a. m. on the 19th instant, I by his order took command of the two regiments and formed them in line in the open field. Sending forward Company A, of the Fifty-first Pennsylvania, as an advance guard to the column, the wagons hauling the cannon and loaded with the ammunition, &c., were next put in line. These were followed by the Fifty-first Pennsylvania Volunteers and Twenty-first Massachusetts. Everything being in readiness, the march was commenced about 7.30 o'clock.

Colonel Hawkins (Ninth New York), commanding the First [Fourth] Brigade, composed of the Ninth New York, Eighty-ninth New York, and Sixth New Hampshire Volunteers, had marched from the point of landing between the hours of 2 and 3 a. m., and was supposed to be in possession of the bridge near South Mills at the time of our marching. The road was in most excellent marching condition, and the men pushed forward as rapidly as could be desired. The extreme heat of the sun, though, soon began to exhaust them very much. After having marched a distance of about 10 miles we were unexpectedly joined from the right by Colonel Hawkins' command, who, through an unfortunate mistake upon the part of his guide, had taken the wrong road and been misled some 10 miles from his course. His brigade fell in rear of the column, and as rapidly as possible we moved forward.

Company F, of the Fifty-first, was now sent forward to strengthen the advance guard. The heat of the sun was most oppressive, the road dusty, the men hungry. About noon General Reno, who was in advance, was just about to call a halt, in order that the men might dine and rest themselves, when, most unexpectedly, the enemy opened upon us with cannon, the position of which was well masked by a burning house and some cedar trees. They kept up from the first dis-charge a vigorous fire. By order from General Reno I directed the Fifty-first Pennsylvania Volunteers to move by the right flank across the field to the woods on the enemy's left, in order to flank the battery and troops supporting it. The Twenty-first Massachusetts, having halted to rest before the enemy opened, was some distance in rear. The enemy kept up an incessant fire at the Fifty-first Regiment as it crossed the field toward the woods, but the range being too great for canister they were obliged to confine themselves to solid shot, and these did no damage. After reaching the woods they were moved toward the enemy's position. On account of the extreme exhaustion of the men and the thickness of the underbrush their advance was necessarily slow and tedious. The enemy followed the movement with his cannon, but not until we had approached sufficiently near for him to use canister did he do any injury. By the canister 1 man was killed and several wounded.

I ordered Major Schall, commanding the Fifty-first, to put out his skirmishers and advance on the enemy's left to where the Third Georgia Volunteers were posted in the woods and engage them and sent back to bring up the Twenty-first Massachusetts. On their arrival I conducted them, by order of General Reno, along the edge of the woods in the course taken by the Fifty-first. On coming up with the Fifty-first the skirmishers of the enemy showed themselves in the field and woods, and fire was immediately opened upon them by Company B, of the Fifty-first. That regiment, by my order, immediately advanced to the fence on the edge of the open field and opened an enfilading fire on the Third Georgia and other troops of the enemy, who were drawn up in the woods skirting the open field at right angles to our position. Our fire was warmly responded to. I ordered the Twenty-first Massachusetts farther to the right, in order to guard against any attack on our flank or rear. They were immediately engaged with the enemy.

Soon after we had opened fire the Ninth New York (Hawkins' Zouaves) started to charge the position of the enemy across the open field in front, but by heavy discharges of canister they were repulsed with considerable loss. Many of the men of the regiment joined us in our position. After the firing had been vigorously kept up from half to three-quarters of an hour I ordered a charge across the field on their position. This was most gallantly done by the Fifty-first Pennsylvania and Twenty-first Massachusetts, the Sixth New Hampshire advancing up the left of the road and the Eighty-ninth and Ninth New York from the woods. The enemy broke and fled from the field precipitately, leaving us in undisputed possession of it. Our troops being too much fatigued from the long march and the battle to pursue the enemy farther, they were, by order of the general commanding, bivouacked in the woods.

On account of the ease with which the enemy could be re-enforced from Norfolk, distant only about 28 miles, and the probability that he had already been largely re-enforced, thus accomplishing the chief object of the reconnaissance, and because of the smallness of our force, the lack of ammunition and provisions, it was deemed prudent by the general commanding and all the officers consulted by him to retire to our vessels. Accordingly, between 9 and 10 o'clock p. m., large camp-fires having been built, the column moved off. The Twenty-first Massachusetts brought up the rear, Company D, under Lieutenant Barker, and two guns, under the command of Colonel Howard, of the Marine Artillery, and the Pioneer Corps of the Fifty-first Pennsylvania, under Lieutenant Ortlip (to destroy the bridge), acting as our guard.

On account of a heavy rain which had fallen the roads were in a miserable condition, but the arduous march to the landing was accomplished by between 6 and 7 o'clock a. m. on the 20th.

On account of the lack of transportation and the severity of their wounds the medical director of the column, Dr. Humphreys, of the Ninth New York, was obliged to leave about 20 of the wounded in charge of Dr. Warren, assistant surgeon of the Twenty-first Massachusetts, in the hospital established in the houses about the field. Some few from exhaustion failed to reach the place of landing in time to embark in the transports, but it is confidently expected that they have all been taken on board the gunboat sent up to the creek above Camden Court-House, and will soon rejoin their regiments. On arriving at the landing the troops were placed on board the transports and soon sailed. The Twenty-first and Fifty-first arrived at New Berne about 12 o'clock on Tuesday, the 22d instant.

I transmit herewith the reports of Lieutenant-Colonel Clark, commanding Twenty-first Massachusetts, and Major Schall, commanding the Fifty-first Pennsylvania, with their list of casualties. Though both regiments were almost utterly exhausted before the commencement of the action, both attacked the enemy with great vigor, and by their gallant charge completely routed them.

I desire to mention particularly the assistance rendered me during the march and on the field by my acting aides, Lieutenant Harlow, quartermaster of the Twenty-first Massachusetts, and Lieutenants Beaver and Fair, of the Fifty-first Pennsylvania.

I am, captain, very respectfully, yours,

THOMAS S. BELL,
Lieut. Col., 51st Pa. Vols., Comdg. Brig., Reconnoitering Expedition.
Capt. EDWARD M. NEILL, *A. A. G., Second Division.*

No. 6.

Report of Lieut. Col. William S. Clark, Twenty-first Massachusetts Infantry.

HEADQUARTERS TWENTY-FIRST MASSACHUSETTS VOLS.,
Steamer Northerner, Pamlico Sound, April 21, 1862.

CAPTAIN: I have the honor to report that, in accordance with orders from Acting Major-General Reno, the Twenty-first Massachusetts Volunteers embarked on board the transport-steamer Northerner at 5 o'clock p. m. on the 17th instant, and proceeded to the mouth of the Pasquotank River, in Albemarle Sound, where we arrived about sunrise on the 19th.

The regiment was here transferred to the light-draught steamers Ocean Wave and Massasoit, and afterward to small row-boats and launches, which were run in as near shore as possible at a point on the north bank of the river about 3 miles below Elizabeth City. Officers and men now cheerfully sprang into the water and waded to land, where the line was immediately formed and muskets loaded. We numbered 500 picked men, and were furnished with two days' rations and 60 rounds of ammunition.

Three regiments, the Ninth and Eighty-ninth New York Volunteers and the Sixth New Hampshire Volunteers, had been landed about 2 o'clock a. m. and sent forward, under command of Colonel Hawkins, to take possession of a bridge near South Mills, where are extensive stone locks on the Dismal Swamp Canal.

A little before 7 o'clock General Reno followed with the Fifty-first Pennsylvania Volunteers and the Twenty-first Massachusetts Volunteers, which regiments had been delayed about four hours by the want of suitable pilots to bring up the transports. The column advanced rapidly along an excellent road through a level and fertile district, halting a few minutes occasionally for water and rest. About 10 o'clock, as we were lying by the road-side, we were astonished to see a large body of troops coming down upon our left flank. "Attention" was immediately sounded by the bugle and the general rode out to reconnoiter. He was not a little chagrined to find that Colonel Hawkins, with his command, having been misled by his guide, had marched 10 miles farther than was necessary to reach this point, and instead of having surprised the enemy by an early arrival at the bridge had nearly exhausted his men by a wearisome march. The weather was now very oppressive, and the men began to suffer greatly from the heat and the want of water, as their canteens were emptied early in the day and there had been no opportunity of refilling them. As no halt had been made for breakfast, and hard bread and salt beef could not well be eaten without water, they were also faint from the want of food.

Before noon large numbers had fallen out from all the regiments, utterly unable to proceed, and General Reno, who was now in advance, with the Fifty-first Pennsylvania and the Twenty-first Massachusetts, was just about to order a halt for dinner, when most unexpectedly a brisk fire of round shot and canister was opened upon us.

The battery of the rebels was skillfully masked by the smoke from a dwelling-house and outbuildings on the highway, which had been set on fire for this purpose, and our advance guard was close upon it when the cannonade commenced. General Reno at once ordered the Fifty-first Pennsylvania to take shelter in the woods on the left of the enemy's position, and sent back for the remaining regiments and the four howitzers which were under command of Colonel Howard of the Marine Artillery.

In consequence of the extreme exhaustion of the men considerable time elapsed before they could be brought into position for the attack, and the artillery of the rebels continued for more than an hour without interruption from us and without doing us much damage, as they had no shells and the range was too great for canister. Many trees and a few men were injured by their round shot, which were thrown with considerable accuracy.

The rebels had one light battery stationed on the main road behind the burning buildings, and another one about 50 yards to the right of the first, upon a road running in that direction. The batteries were supported by two regiments of infantry, numbering about 1,800 men, and 200 cavalry. The Third Georgia Volunteers was formed in line of battle in a grove of young pines some 300 yards behind and to the left of the burning buildings, and their skirmishers were thrown far into the swampy forest on their left to prevent us from getting in their rear.

By command of General Reno I advanced with my regiment as rapidly as the greenbrier and tangled underbrush would permit, marching by the flank toward the line of the Third Georgia until fired upon by their skirmishers. Two companies were then ordered into line and to fire several volleys into the swamp from which the bullets came, when the rebels retired. My regiment was now entirely in the rear of the batteries and very near the Third Georgia, whose traitorous flag was distinctly seen through the pines.

Company K, under Captain Davis, was sent forward into the swamp to follow up the rebel skirmishers and prevent any attack upon our rear. Company G, commanded by Lieutenant Wheeler, was then ordered to advance to the fence between the woods and the cleared field and open fire upon the Georgians. This difficult task was performed in the most admirable manner amid a perfect storm of bullets, and the company gallantly formed along the fence and drove out the skirmishers of the enemy, some of whom fired upon them from a distance of not more than 20 yards. The entire regiment was now ordered to form in line behind the fence and commenced firing as rapidly as possible, and the battle was fairly opened.

The position of my regiment was all that could be desired, as we were well protected by the fence and bushes were in the rear of the batteries and immediately upon the left of the Georgians, our line being at right angles to theirs, so that our fire was constantly right-oblique. Upon our left was the Fifty-first Pennsylvania, then the Ninth New York, and then the Eighty-ninth New York. About half an hour after the firing commenced the Ninth New York (Hawkins' Zouaves) charged across the open field toward the enemy, but were repelled by a destructive volley from the Third Georgia Volunteers. The Twenty-first Massachusetts, being thus temporarily relieved from their fire, immediately sprang over the fence into the open field and killed the color sergeant, who was defiantly waving his rebel flag several yards in front of his regiment.

Our entire line now advanced from the woods and charged with shouts and cheers across the cleared ground, while the Sixth New Hampshire, which had supported our howitzers in front of the enemy's position, poured in a tremendous volley by command of General Reno, who happened to be with them at the moment. The rebels fled precipitately to the woods and were seen no more.

As it was now nearly night and our forces were quite exhausted and as we had no cavalry, it was impossible to pursue them. The Twenty-first was at once formed in line, and having stacked arms, sat down upon the battle ground to rest. Squads were now sent out from each company to pick up the killed and wounded and their weapons. Our hospital was established in a house near by, and the regiment prepared to bivouac on the very spot in the forest which they had occupied during the fight, the fence which had served so well as a protection by day furnishing excellent fuel for camp-fires at night.

In consequence of the unfortunate delay referred to in the first part of the report it was impossible to carry out the original plan of the expedition. Accordingly, as we had neither provisions nor ammunition enough to do another day's work, the general reluctantly decided to return to his vessels, and, considering that the night was rainy and the men without tents or blankets and that the enemy might receive re-enforcements before daylight from Norfolk, which was only 30 miles distant, and harass us on our return with their cavalry and flying artillery, he resolved to make the march by night. Orders were therefore issued to build large fires around the battle-field and to provide transportation for such of the wounded as were able to be moved. About 30 of them were unavoidably left behind, in charge of Dr. O. Warren, assistant surgeon of the Twenty-first Massachusetts, who cheerfully remained, subject to the tender mercies of the rebels. The choice of surgeon for this duty was made by lot. Chaplain Ball labored as usual most assiduously to promote the comfort of the wounded both on the field and at the hospital, and especially on the return to the transports and on the voyage to New Berne, when, in the absence of any surgeon, he kindly dressed their wounds and administered such remedies as their circumstances required.

At 9 o'clock Lieutenant Reno, aide-de-camp, started with the Ninth New York Volunteers to take possession of a draw-bridge near Camden Court-House and prevent its destruction in case the enemy should attempt it. The other regiments silently left their places in the woods and moved along the road past the hospitals; the wagons, with their wounded, took their position in the center of the column, and the general followed with the Twenty-first Massachusetts as the rear guard.

Company D, under Lieutenant Barker, performed in the most efficient manner the very arduous and unpleasant duty of rear guard to the regiment. Not only were they obliged to be constantly on the lookout for the enemy, but they were compelled to labor incessantly to urge and assist forward the numerous stragglers who fell out from the various regiments. Between Company D and the rest of the Twenty-first Colonel Howard was placed with two howitzers.

A more wearisome march has been seldom made by any troops. The night was dark, the soft, clayey mud from 3 to 12 inches in depth, and the men worn out by the labors of the day, having marched 16 miles and most of them 26, besides passing through the excitement and fatigue of the battle. Nevertheless the greater part of them bore up manfully, and though terribly exhausted moved steadily to the landing, where the head of the column arrived about 5 o'clock in the morning.

I am happy to report that while the Twenty-first was unable to do much damage to the enemy they suffered a comparatively slight loss. Not a man was injured by artillery and but 15 by infantry, owing to our excellent position. Only two others failed to come up with the regiment, although the Twenty-first constituted the rear guard on the return march, and these both fell out before the battle. Notwithstanding the difficulties of the march every rifle taken from the camp was returned to it in good condition, including those of the killed and wounded, except one thrown away by an exhausted man and the two in the hands of the missing men.

On the whole I think I may safely say that nearly every officer, non-commissioned officer, and private did his duty to the extent of his ability. The members of the Twenty-first will remember with peculiar pride that on the 19th of April, 1862, just one year after the blood of Massachusetts men was first shed by the rebels of Baltimore, we conquered them at the battle of Camden, and we shall be no less proud of this name inscribed upon our war-worn banner than that of "Roanoke" and "New Berne."

I am, captain, very respectfully, your obedient servant,

W. S. CLARK,
Lieutenant-Colonel, Comdg. Twenty-first Massachusetts Vols.

Capt. EDWARD M. NEILL,
Assistant Adjutant-General.

No. 7.

Report of Maj. Edwin Schall, Fifty-first Pennsylvania Infantry.

HDQRS. FIFTY-FIRST REGIMENT PENNSYLVANIA VOLS.,
New Berne, N. C., April 22, 1862.

SIR: For the information of the colonel commanding the Second Brigade I submit the following report:

After the landing of the regiment below Elizabeth City, on the 19th instant, I immediately formed it, and by your orders detailed Company A as an advance guard. When we got some distance into the enemy's country Company F was sent forward to the support of Company A. While moving forward along the main road the enemy suddenly opened fire upon us, their position being masked by the dense smoke arising from burning buildings. I immediately filed to the right with the regiment and formed in an open field. In compliance with your orders I conducted the regiment into the woods and moved forward to get on the left of the enemy. While advancing through the woods I received orders from you to send forward a body of skirmishers. I at once ordered Company D forward, which after some delay returned and reported to me the position of the enemy and his battery. I then ordered the regiment forward with the intention of coming on his left and rear; but the thicket being so dense and orders having just been received from you to make no delay in getting into position, I ordered a halt, and determined to move forward, left in front. Going to the left, I ordered Company B to reconnoiter immediately to our front and right.

Having definitely learned the position of the enemy by reports and personal observations I ordered Company B to advance to the right along the edge of the woods, taking position behind the fence. The remaining companies of the regiment followed and got into position. After being exposed to a heavy fire for some time you in person ordered a charge, the men with cheers responding as they advanced across the field in face of a hot fire, driving the enemy before them and obtaining full possession of the ground occupied by them. After this successful charge and termination of the battle I formed the regiment in the open field, and by your orders marched the regiment to the woods occupied by us during the engagement, and threw out as pickets Company B. A detail also was made to bury the killed during the battle.

Early in the evening I received orders from you to hold the regiment in readiness to retire from the field. Shortly after 9 o'clock I had the soldiers noiselessly awakened and formed the regiment as quietly as it was possible to do. The pickets were called in, and the Pioneer Corps, under command of Lieut. Abraham L. Ortlip, sent to the rear to destroy the bridge as we retired.

We moved off between 10 and 11 o'clock, and reached the place of disembarkation the day previous at 6 o'clock on the morning of the 20th instant. The march was long and the rain and mud were well calcu-lated to exhaust the men. Few, however, were left behind, as the stronger very generously assisted the weaker comrades. After some delay the men were re-embarked on steamer Guide.

It is with pain I announce that Lieut. Lewis Hallman, in command of Company E, fell wounded on the field while gallantly leading on his men and is now a prisoner in the hands of the enemy, it being impossible, in consequence of his weakness, to bring him with us. With him are 5 more of our men, who by reason of their wounds and the lack of transportation we were compelled to leave behind. As already stated, the number killed is 3; 19 are wounded and 3 are missing. Of the wounded 4 are supposed to be mortally, while the remainder have received but slight injuries. The missing, it is believed, will yet make their appearance.

It gives me pleasure to mention the excellent services rendered me by Actg. Adjt. Lieut. George Shorkley on the 19th and 20th instant. For his activity and courage during the engagement he deserves and has my warmest thanks. I also feel indebted to the quartermaster, Lieut. John J. Freedley, for conveying orders, and he deserves well for the prompt and faithful manner in which he had the wounded cared for. Surgeon Hosack was untiring in his attendance upon the wounded, whose wounds he carefully dressed and administered to their every want up to the hour of our departure. Nor can I forget to mention Sergeant-Major Iredell, who was constantly by my side during the engagement, carrying orders and giving me valuable information by his gallant reconnoitering.

The officers and men all, I may say, behaved well and acquitted themselves in a creditable manner. Too much praise cannot be awarded them for the manner in which they bore up under the fatigue of the long and dusty march. It was well calculated to weary them, yet all behaved most gallantly.

In conclusion, I can only say I endeavored, as far as possible, to carry out all your orders on the 19th and 20th instant.

I am, very truly, yours,

EDWIN SCHALL,
Major, Commanding Fifty-first Pennsylvania Volunteers.
THOMAS S. BELL,
Lieutenant-Colonel, Commanding Second Brigade.

No. 8.

Reports of Maj. Gen. Benjamin Huger, C. S. Army, with communication from General R. E. Lee.

HEADQUARTERS DEPARTMENT OF NORFOLK,
Norfolk, Va., April 21, 1862.

I informed you by telegraph yesterday that the enemy had on the 19th instant attacked Colonel Wright in his position near South Mills,

N. C.   He reports they advanced on him in strong force (estimated by him at 5,000) and commenced the attack at 11.45 a. m.   He had in a strong position, with an open space in front of some 600 yards over which they had to advance, some 400 men and four pieces of artillery. The enemy were held in check till 5 p. m.

At 4 p. m. Captain McComas, who commanded the battery, was killed.   Colonel Wright speaks of his gallantry and good conduct in high terms.

The ammunition in the limber-boxes was exhausted and the caissons not at hand.   There was some confusion and the pieces went after the caissons, and at 5 p. m. Colonel Wright retired a mile or so.

Early yesterday morning he moved all his forces back to Northwest Lock (about half way on the Dismal Swamp Canal), at which point Brigadier-General Blanchard joined him yesterday with the Thirty-second North Carolina and First Louisiana Regiments.

Lieutenant Sloan, aide-de-camp, returned from Northwest Lock last night.   Up to 3 p. m. they had heard of no movement of the enemy.

Colonel Wright reports his total loss of killed, wounded, and missing at 73.   He does not give other numbers.   I make out from the wounded who have arrived at the hospital that the number killed was 7 or 8; wounded, 20; only 10 severely enough to be sent to the hospital.   Colonel Wright mentions that he fears Lieutenant Wilson is killed.   He was wounded and is missing.

Whether the enemy intend to occupy Elizabeth City and neighborhood or whether this was only an expedition to capture the troops there, I cannot yet tell.

Colonel Wright estimates the killed and wounded of the enemy as very large.   At all events, he did not pursue our troops at all.

Since writing the above I have received the inclosed letter from General Blanchard, covering copy of one from Brigadier-General Reno, from which it appears it was Reno's brigade, of Burnside's army, which made the attack, and they were evidently severely handled and defeated.

I am, general, very respectfully, your most obedient servant,

BENJ. HUGER,
Major-General, Commanding.

General R. E. LEE, *Commanding General.*

[Inclosure No. 1.]

SOUTH MILLS, N. C., *April 20, 1862.*

GENERAL: I inclose a copy of a letter from General Reno, U. S. Army, relative to wounded men, by which you will see that he recognizes a defeat.   It appears that the enemy were entirely defeated, and if our forces could have pursued them we could have made many prisoners. Two are sent with this dispatch.   Our people are gathering many guns, &c., left on the field by the fleeing foe.   A return will be made of the property captured.

I am in doubt what answer to make about the wounded enemy (about 14), now in hospital, under charge of their surgeon.   Please advise me without delay, as I am not sure it is not a plan to find out where we are.   I shall send troops down the country toward Elizabeth City early to-morrow.

Respectfully, your obedient servant,

A. G. BLANCHARD,
Brig. Gen., Prov. Army C. S., Commanding Third Brigade.

General B. HUGER, *Commanding Department.*

HDQRS. SECOND BRIG., DEPT. OF NORTH CAROLINA,
April 20, 1862.

SIR: In the recent engagement near South Mills, owing to a lack of transportation, I was compelled to leave a few of my wounded under the charge of one of our surgeons. As it has been invariably our practice to release the wounded on parole, I confidently anticipate that you will pursue the same course, in which case you will please inform Commodore Rowan at what time and place they can be received. I also request permission to remove the body of Lieutenant Gadsden, of the Ninth New York. The surgeon will point out the place of his interment.

Very respectfully, your obedient servant,

J. L. RENO,
Brigadier-General, U. S. Army.

To the COMMANDING OFFICER
At Elizabeth City or at South Mills, N. C.

—

HEADQUARTERS DEPARTMENT OF NORFOLK,
April 22, 1862.

GENERAL: I have heard but little from South Mills and Elizabeth City since my letter of yesterday. I have a dispatch from General Blanchard, from South Mills, dated yesterday. The enemy had returned to their boats and destroyed the bridges behind them on their retreat.

A small steamer came in last night and brought 1,100 pounds of powder, and I am informed we have collected a good many muskets and tools.

A diary and letter to his wife from one of the band were picked up on the field of battle. He belonged to a Massachusetts regiment, and left New Berne under orders for a short expedition, embarked on board the steamer Northerner, and was told by Colonel Clark they were to go via Roanoke Island to Elizabeth City and thence to blow up the locks to a canal from Norfolk, to prevent the rebels from coming down with their iron-clad steamers to destroy our fleet at New Berne. He said the rebels had two regiments and four cannon to guard the canal, and we would have five regiments and eight cannon to fight them, if they should fight. * * * We have been lying here near Roanoke Island pretty much all day, and the report is after dark we have got to land and march from 12 to 20 miles. Dated April 18.

The captured powder, other reports, and this letter confirm the opinion that their intention was to capture the forces at South Mills and destroy the locks of the canal to prevent our use of it. When they retire I will withdraw our troops, keeping only a guard at South Mills, and make Deep Creek the position for the main body to re-enforce them.

[BENJ. HUGER.]

General R. E. LEE, *Commanding.*

—

HEADQUARTERS DEPARTMENT OF NORFOLK,
Norfolk, Va., April 28, 1862.

GENERAL: I have received through Brigadier-General Blanchard, commanding Third Brigade, the reports of Cols. A. R. Wright and

Ferebee, commanding the drafted North Carolina Militia, and Lieut. D. A. French, who succeeded to the command of the battery of artillery after the death of its gallant captain, McComas.

I would forward these reports to you at once, but there are some discrepancies and omissions in them which I desire first to have corrected, and will therefore try to make a brief statement from these reports, to give you and the War Department information concerning this severe and well-fought action, which was successful, inasmuch as the enemy failed to accomplish his object and was obliged to retire to his vessels with great loss.

I send herewith a sketch of the country between South Mills and Elizabeth City, showing the position of the battle.

All the forces under the command of Colonel Wright were the Third Regiment Georgia Volunteers, some drafted militia, under Colonel Ferebee, of North Carolina (Colonel F. omits to state in his report how many he had on duty), McComas' battery of artillery (one rifled piece and three bronze 6-pounders), and one company of cavalry, Captain Gillett's Southampton company.

On Friday, the 18th, I had ordered forward the Thirty-second North Carolina Regiment (Colonel Brabble's) and the First Louisiana Regiment (Colonel Vincent's), but they did not arrive until after the battle.

On Friday, the 18th, Colonel Wright occupied South Mills with three companies of his regiment (160 strong) and the drafted North Carolina Militia, two companies at the intrenchments at Richardson's Mills (125 effectives) and five companies (about 300 men) and McComas' battery of artillery at Elizabeth City.

On Friday evening, anticipating the enemy's advance and in compliance with my instructions to concentrate his forces at or near South Mills, he ordered the companies at Elizabeth City to retire 9 miles to Richardson's Mills. From some cause not yet explained these companies did not leave Elizabeth City until after daylight on Saturday morning.

The cavalry company from Camden Court-House reported at 8.30 o'clock.

On the 19th, the enemy approaching, having then passed the Court-House, Colonel Wright moved forward with his three companies, and at 9.30 o'clock was met by Colonel McComas with his battery. After advancing 3 miles from South Mills the road emerged from the woods, and the field on the right and left extended 160 to 180 yards to thick woods and swamp. On the edge of the woods, on both sides of the road and perpendicular to it, was a small ditch, the earth from which was thrown up on the south side in a ridge, upon which was a heavy rail fence. From this point the road led through a narrow lane (Sawyer's) for 1 mile, with cleared land on both sides of it. Here he determined to make his stand.

About 300 yards from the woods ran a deep, wide ditch parallel with the one first mentioned and extending to the woods on either side of the road, and a short distance beyond it were dwellings and outhouses which would give cover for the enemy. Colonel Wright therefore ordered them burned. The large ditch in his front he filled with fence rails and set them on fire, his object being to have this ditch so hot by the time the enemy came up they could not occupy it. (This ditch is marked on sketch as "Roasted Ditch.")

Two pieces of artillery (the road was too narrow for more) were placed in the road just where it emerged from the woods, which commanded the road—the range of the guns. He also threw down the fences for

300 yards on each side of the road for 300 yards in front of the guns, and tossed the rails into the road to destroy the effect of the enemy's ricochet firing and to deprive him of the cover of the fences. The fences on the sides of the woods were taken down and laid in heaps on the embankment in front of his men.

All these arrangements were made, and it was 11 o'clock before he was joined by Lieutenant-Colonel Reid and the seven companies from below. Two of these, under Major Lee, were placed at River Bridge, with one piece of McComas' artillery, with directions to destroy it and stop the enemy there if he should attempt to get into our rear by coming up the west side of the river. Lieutenant-Colonel Reid and three companies of the Third Georgia (and by Colonel Ferebee's report the North Carolina Militia) were placed about a mile in the rear at the meeting of an old road, to protect that passage and serve as a reserve. The remaining five companies were deployed in open order across the road on the right and left of the artillery, protected by the ditch and fence rails on the banks.

The smoke from the burning buildings and fences was rolled toward the enemy, thus masking the position. At 11.45 a.m. the front of a heavy column of the enemy was seen passing through the smoke and Captain McComas opened a destructive fire upon it, which checked its advance for half an hour, when it again approached under the fire of a 12-pounder, but soon retired entirely out of sight in considerable confusion. Up to 3 o'clock thrice had the heavy columns of the enemy been beaten back by the heavy fire of Captain McComas' artillery, and our only casualties were one man wounded and one wheel injured.

At 3.15 p.m. the enemy again advanced and deployed two regiments to their right, our left. These regiments, after advancing toward us, were driven back by the well-directed fire of Captain McComas' artillery and Captains Nesbet's, and Musgrove's companies. Captain McWhorter's fire also caused the Zouaves on our right to retire, and this attack ceased by 3.35 p.m. Our loss up to this time was very slight, while that of the enemy was very severe, as we could plainly see them fall, and they had raised the hospital flag on a building in rear of their line.

They soon advanced again, two regiments skirting the woods on our left, and approached near enough to engage the skirmishers. One company from the right was moved over and Colonel Reid ordered to send one company from the reserve. The enemy deployed in the open field and bore down rapidly, but the heavy fire of musketry caused them to waver, and they fell back to the fence. Three regiments and a field piece were in the center and the Ninth New York Regiment on the right. The fire was now brisk from one end of the line to the other, and the enemy were held in check, when just at this moment Captain McComas was killed by a Minie ball, and his men, who for four hours had fought with most indomitable courage, became panic stricken and left the field, taking their pieces with them. Colonel Wright succeeded in rallying them and getting two pieces and a few men in position, and the enemy had advanced so close that canister was fired on them with effect and they again fell back. The ammunition in the limber-boxes was exhausted, and during the temporary absence of Colonel Wright the artillery left the field.

The enemy made a charge upon our line, but the steady fire at close distance (Colonel Wright estimates it at 50 yards) caused them to break in confusion and they fell back. Taking advantage of their confusion Colonel Wright now fell back in good order to the intrenchments on Joy's Creek, about 2 miles in his rear, and called in Lieutenant-Colonel Reid's and Major Lee's commands, and there awaited the enemy, who it appears were so badly injured that they made no advance, but at about 8 p. m. began to retreat to their boats. At this time I am informed that several companies of the Thirty-second North Carolina Regiment joined Colonel Wright, who during the night retired from this position to the Northwest Lock.

Colonel Wright states his loss at 6 killed, 19 wounded, and 3 taken prisoners. The enemy's loss he estimates as very large, as high as 300. Colonel Wright states that the regiments opposed to him were the Ninth, Twenty-first, and Eighty-ninth New York, and the Twenty-first Massachusetts, Sixth New Hampshire, and Fifty-first Pennsylvania Regiments (we have prisoners or wounded of five of these regiments), the whole commanded by Brigadier-General Reno. Among the killed he is grieved to announce the loss of Captain McComas, an estimable gentleman and brave and skillful officer, whose conduct throughout the action elicited the highest praise.

All the command engaged behaved in the most gallant manner, standing firmly against overwhelming odds until ordered to fall back to our intrenchments. They maintained their position over five hours, and killed and disabled more of the enemy than we had in action.

On returning to the field next day we recovered 1,100 pounds of powder, and the arms, accouterments, tools, &c., left by the enemy. I have already reported his leaving such wounded as he could not remove, and I have sent them to Fort Monroe on parole. Some 10 or 12 stragglers were taken on the 20th and held as prisoners of war. I will forward the original reports as soon as they are corrected, and meanwhile submit this as a summary.

Very respectfully, your obedient servant,

BENJ. HUGER,
Major-General, Commanding.

General R. E. LEE, *Commanding, &c.*

[Inclosure.]

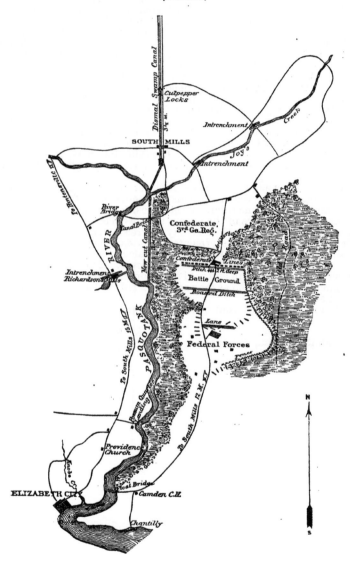

HEADQUARTERS,
Richmond, Va, April 20, 1862.

Maj. Gen. B. HUGER, *Comdg. Dept., Norfolk, Va.:*

GENERAL: I have received this morning your telegram of the 19th instant, reporting the landing of the enemy at Elizabeth City and his attack upon the Third Georgia Regiment near South Mills. It is presumed this is but a feint or predatory excursion made from his reserve at Roanoke Island. Not knowing the advantages of the position at South Mills, it seems to me to be too far removed from your line of operations and calculated to invite an attack of the enemy, inasmuch as the strength of your party would be reported by the disaffected, and they would reasonably hope to cut it off. A corps of observation would seem only to be necessary for such an advanced point, and your force should·be stationed nearer to you, at some strong point behind the Dismal Swamp, which could be more readily re-enforced. By pursuing this system on other points your troops could be more rapidly concentrated to strike a blow whenever the enemy showed himself within your reach.

I am, very respectfully, your obedient servant,

R. E. LEE,
General.

HEADQUARTERS,
Richmond, Va., April 22, 1862.

Maj. Gen. B. HUGER, *Comdg., &c., Norfolk, Va.:*

GENERAL: I am directed by General Lee to acknowledge the receipt of your letter of the 21st, with its inclosures, reporting the result of the attack by the enemy at South Mills and his subsequent action concerning his captured wounded, and to say in reply that he is much gratified at the determined resistance made by Colonel Wright to so largely superior force, but regrets the loss of Captain McComas, whom he knew to be a gallant officer. As regards the wounded prisoners of the enemy, he is under the impression that General Burnside has generally pursued the course indicated in the letter of Brigadier-General Reno, and sees no objection to releasing the wounded prisoners on their parole as an offset to some of our men liberated under similar circumstances.

I am, very respectfully, your obedient servant,

W. H. TAYLOR,
Assistant Adjutant-General.

—

HEADQUARTERS,
Richmond, Va, April 24, 1862.

Maj. Gen. T. H. HOLMES, *Comdg., &c., Goldsborough, N. C.:*

GENERAL: General Huger reports that Colonel Wright, with 400 men and four pieces of artillery, was attacked near South Mills by the enemy on the 19th instant. Colonel Wright estimates the enemy's force at about 5,000 men, and it appears from a letter received by Colonel Wright from Brigadier-General Reno, U. S. Army, asking permission to remove the body of an officer and that his wounded might be released on parole, that the attacking force was composed of the Second Brigade. A letter and diary written by a soldier, which were picked up on the field, show that his force consisted of five regiments and eight pieces of artillery, and that it left New Berne on a short expedition to destroy the locks of the canal. A quantity of powder and some tools captured by our forces seemed to confirm this account. The enemy were repulsed by Colonel Wright with considerable loss and retired to their boats, burning the bridges behind them in their retreat. This is probably the force reported by you as having left New Berne on the 16th and 18th instant.

I am, general, very respectfully, your obedient servant,
R. E. LEE,
General.

HEADQUARTERS,
Richmond, Va., April 29, 1862.

Maj. Gen. B. HUGER,
Commanding, &c., Yorktown, Va.:

GENERAL: General Lee directs me to acknowledge the receipt of your letter of the 28th instant, together with the report of the brilliant affair at South Mills, which he has read with much interest and pleasure, and which reflects so creditably upon the officers and men engaged. As regards your request that additional troops be sent to Suffolk, which you represent as being particularly weak, he instructs me to say that the call for troops from every department is urgent, and it is impossible to re-enforce points more seriously threatened than Suffolk. He wishes it was in his power to meet your requisition, but had hoped that with the addition of the Militia (2,000 or 3,000 of which have been reported to him to be inactive and unassigned in your department) your command would be materially strengthened and the approaches to your rear rendered more secure, inasmuch as this acquisition to your force would enable you to increase the number of troops protecting Suffolk and vicinity.

I am, general, very respectfully, your obedient servant,
W. H. TAYLOR,
Assistant Adjutant-General.

APRIL 27, 1862.—Skirmish near Haughton's Mill, Pollocksville Road, N. C.

Report of Baron Egloffstein, Colonel One hundred and third New York Infantry.

HDQRS. SEWARD INFANTRY, 103D REGT., N. Y. S. V.,
HELEN'S PLANTATION, 3 MILES SOUTH OF POLLOCKSVILLE,
April 27, 1862.

SIR: Agreeably to orders from General J. L. Reno, a detachment of 40 men (cavalry) and three officers left New Berne for Pollocksville on the 26th instant, in the evening. Passed through Evans' Mill at midnight. To secure the line of communication to Pollocksville 70 men of infantry followed in the rear. Passed Haughton's Mill to cross Mill Creek 2 miles south of Pollocksville road, the bridge on the Pollocksville road being destroyed. About 3 o'clock in the afternoon the first rebel picket was seen on the Onslow and Pollocksville road. Major Quentin and myself chased the advance guard of the enemy on an open plain a quarter of a mile to Helen's mansion, gradually followed by our cavalry. I gave the order for immediate firing to prevent the enemy from running away. They were 30 men strong, located in and around a frame house. We wounded and killed several by means of revolvers and rifles, our cavalry having dismounted with a view to cut off the retreat of the enemy from the premises at as small a loss on our side as possible. When the infantry came up we charged bayonets and made ourselves masters of the position. The enemy, having a more perfect knowledge of the premises, succeeded in taking away some of their wounded, killed, and horses in the direction of Kinston during the hottest fight.

The loss of the enemy was 2 men killed by bullets, 1 by bayonet, 8 wounded, 9 horses, 3 prisoners—N. W. Collins, James H. Kelly, and G. Battle, privates of Company C, Second Regiment of Cavalry North Carolina Volunteers. A number of arms captured—carbines, sabers, pistols, double-barreled shot-guns—and 5 fine horses, with equipments.

Our loss was Private Sanders killed and Lieutenants Von Seldeneck and Von Vogt, of the cavalry, wounded—since recovering; 4 more slightly wounded—flesh wounds. Col. Baron V. Egloffstein was wounded in the leg in dismounting, his horse having been killed under him. Besides, 2 of our cavalry horses killed.

Our cavalry distinguished themselves in their first fight by rapid action and good firing. Had we prepared a slow attack on the cavalry they would have fled from us as on former occasions. The wound of the colonel being of a more serious character than first imagined, we halted and reconnoitered the surrounding country by means of cavalry patrols. Several encampments in the direction of Trenton were discovered. I determined to return after this successful reconnaissance, drawing in the boards at Haughton's Mill for the purpose of securing said mill for the Government.

I beg to propose to station several hundred men at once at Haughton's Mill as an advance guard, to prevent the enemy from occupying this valuable military position situated within 2 miles of Pollocksville.

I will have the honor, general, to report the details on my arrival at New Berne.

Remaining, most respectfully, your obedient servant,

BARON EGLOFFSTEIN,
Colonel of Seward Infantry.

Brig. Gen. JESSE L. RENO,
Commanding Second Division, Department of North Carolina.

APRIL 29, 1862.—Skirmish near Batchelder's Creek, N. C.

Report of Maj. Andrew Elwell, Twenty-third Massachusetts Infantry.

HDQRS. TWENTY-THIRD REGIMENT MASS. VOLS.,
Railroad Bridge, Batchelder's Creek, April 30, 1862.

The picket established by Special Brigade Order, No. 7, was attacked yesterday. They were posted in accordance with the above-named order one-half mile in advance of the bridge, deployed on either side of the railroad to the distance of one-fourth of a mile. About 12 o'clock m. a body of rebel cavalry emerged from the woods and attacked the extreme right flank, passing between the right group and the rest of the picket, thus cutting them off. As far as can be ascertained the enemy numbered about 70. The picket opened fire upon those of the enemy who were in the advance, while the enemy returned the fire with a volley of some 20 or 30 shots, killing 1 man, three shots penetrating his body. The remainder of the picket instantly rallied to the spot, but the enemy had fled, taking with them probably the other 3 belonging to the group, as they are missing.

Upon hearing the report in camp sufficient force was immediately sent to the assistance of the picket. This re-enforcement made an advance some 2 miles through the woods, but nothing could be heard from our missing men or the enemy. The affair has given rise to exaggerated stories, but it was not deemed of sufficient importance to give any alarm or call for any assistance. The picket force has been increased to treble its former numbers, and everything has been quiet since the attack.

The names of the killed and wounded are Edward B. Braley, private Company E, killed; Corp. Hiram J. Lauman, Privates Edward Smith and John Taylor, of the same company, missing.

Respectfully submitted.

A. ELWELL,
Major, Commanding Twenty-third Massachusetts.

Lieut. E. T. PARKINSON,
  A. A. A. G., First Brigade First Division.

MAY 2, 1862.—Skirmish near Deep Gully, Trenton Road, N. C.

Report of Lieut. Charles H. Pope, First Rhode Island Light Artillery.

HDQRS. BATTERY F, RHODE ISLAND ARTILLERY,
New Berne, N. C., May 2, 1862.

SIR : I have the honor to inform you that our pickets, stationed on the Trenton road, about 1 mile from the Deep Gully, were attacked by a body of rebel infantry, supposed to be about 40 in number. They came into the Trenton road by the cross road from the Red House, firing upon our pickets, instantly killing Corporal Martindale and severely wounding Private Vincent, who has not been found yet.

C. H. POPE,
First Lieutenant First R. I. Art., Comdg. Battery F.

Brig. Gen. J. G. FOSTER,
  Commanding First Division.

MAY 7–8, 1862.—Expedition from Roanoke Island toward Gatesville, N. C.

Report of Col. Rush C. Hawkins, U. S. Army.

HEADQUARTERS,
Roanoke Island, N. C., May 10, 1862.

SIR: Having ascertained that the rebels had a large amount of stores, consisting of bacon, corn, salt, flour, &c., at a place about 8 miles south of Gatesville, on the 7th instant I sent Captain Parisen's company (C, Ninth New York Volunteers), on board of the gunboat Shawsheen, for the purpose of destroying these stores.

This force landed about 1 a. m. on the morning of the 8th instant 2 miles up Catherine's Creek, which empties into the Chowan River opposite to Holliday's Island. After marching about 8 miles they came to the place where the stores were, set fire to the building in which they were contained, and destroyed the whole. The estimated value of the stores (so the officers in charge of the forces was informed) was $50,000.

On the return of the force to the gunboat the rear guard was attacked by a small body of cavalry which had been concealed in the woods. They (the cavalry) were repulsed with a loss of one of their number, who was shot through the breast.

Captain Parisen, in charge of his company, and Captain Woodward, of the gunboat Shawsheen, both deserve great praise for the manner in which they carried out their instructions and the dispatch with which the work was performed.

I am, respectfully, your most faithful servant,

RUSH C. HAWKINS,
Colonel, Commanding Fourth Brigade and Post.

Maj. Gen. AMBROSE E. BURNSIDE,
Commanding Department of North Carolina, New Berne, N. C.

MAY 15–16, 1862.—Skirmishes near Trenton Bridge, at Young's Cross-Roads, and Pollocksville, N. C.

REPORTS.

No. 1.—Col. Thomas J. C. Amory, Seventeenth Massachusetts Infantry.
No. 2.—Lieut. Col. J. Eugene Duryée, Second Maryland Infantry.
No. 3.—Col. Simon H. Mix, Third New York Cavalry.

No. 1.

Report of Col. Thomas J. C. Amory, Seventeenth Massachusetts Infantry.

HDQRS. FIRST BRIGADE, FIRST DIVISION,
New Berne, N. C., May 15, 1862.

CAPTAIN: I have the honor to report that in accordance with the instructions of General Foster I proceeded this morning at 2.30 o'clock on a reconnaissance in the direction of Trenton. My command, consisting of the Third New York Cavalry, the Seventeenth and Twenty-fifth Regiments Massachusetts Volunteers, and two pieces of artillery, was attacked 5 miles this side of Trenton. Not having as yet received the official reports of regimental commanders, I can state generally from my personal knowledge that our loss consists in the wounding of 3 privates and 1 officer (Major Fitzsimmons), of the Third New York Cavalry, Lieutenant Mayes and 1 man, of the same regiment, missing. Six of the enemy found dead on the field and 2 prisoners—1 mortally wounded. I consider the original plan and purpose of this movement frustrated by the late arrival of the cavalry last night, owing to the storm.

To surprise the enemy at Trenton being under those circumstances impossible, and having but limited transportation for my wounded, with only twenty-four hours' rations, I deemed it advisable to return.

I am, sir, your obedient servant,

THOS. J. C. AMORY,
Colonel Mass. Vols., Comdg. First Brig., First Div.

Captain HOFFMAN,
Asst. Adjt. Gen., First Div., Dept. North Carolina.

No. 2.

Report of Lieut. Col. J. Eugene Duryée, Second Maryland Infantry.

CAMP OF THE SECOND MARYLAND REGIMENT,
Near New Berne, N. C., May 18, 1862.

CAPTAIN : I have the honor to submit the following report:

On Wednesday, the 14th, about noon, I received from Lieutenant Morris Brigadier-General Reno's order to move my regiment at 5 o'clock that afternoon, with two days' rations. In obedience to his directions I at once reported to Brigadier-General Foster and Colonel Amory for instructions. I was ordered by them to march at 5 o'clock in the after-noon to occupy Pollocksville, the bridge across the Trent, and Young's Cross-Roads, 5 miles from Pollocksville, and hold these points until I received further orders from Colonel Amory. Between 4 and 5 o'clock I started with the regiment in the midst of a violent thunder-storm, which turned into a steady rain, making the roads almost impassable.

I reached Haughton's Mill about 5 o'clock on Thursday morning [15th], when for the first time we encountered the pickets of the enemy. When fired upon by two of the advance guard they galloped away at full speed, part in the direction of Pollocksville and part toward Young's Cross-Roads. Immediately after rapid firing was heard in the woods in the direction of Young's Cross-Roads,' probably to give notice of our arrival. I immediately sent three companies (D, F, and K), under the command of Capt. M. Wilson, to Young's Cross-Roads, and with the rest of the regiment marched to Pollocksville. I found the bridge across the Trent had been burned, but nevertheless stationed sentinels there. During the remainder of the day (Thursday) everything re-mained quiet at Pollocksville, but at Young's Cross-Roads, where I had stationed Captain Wilson, with three companies, a body of cavalry made their appearance about 1 p. m. They approached by the road leading from Onslow Court-House. When within about 200 yards our men fired upon them. One officer was badly wounded, but his comrades managed to keep him in his saddle and escaped with him. The citizens in the neighborhood say that the name of the officer was Col. William Cotton, and that he was dangerously wounded. About 11 o'clock that night the enemy began to annoy our pickets, driving them in twice, and during the remainder of the night Captain Wilson kept his whole command under arms. Lieutenant Fleckenstein, of Company K, made a reconnaissance for about 2 miles beyond our lines and returned in three hours, having ascertained that the enemy had retreated over White Oak River Bridge, on the road leading to Onslow Court-House.

About 2 o'clock next morning the report of a musket was heard near my headquarters at Pollocksville. The long roll was sounded and the regiment immediately turned out under arms. From the state-ments of the prisoners whom we captured on Friday afternoon I am satisfied that the enemy was moving forward to surprise us under cover of the darkness, but on hearing the long roll beat, and perceiving the promptness with which the regiment turned out, they concluded to defer the attack until the next day.

About 12 o'clock on Friday [16th] our pickets were driven in and there was quite a smart skirmish at two of our outposts. Two or three of the enemy were killed, a number wounded, and two prisoners were captured. I was every moment expecting an attack in force, which I had made every preparation to receive. From the circumstances I supposed that the enemy were in full retreat from Colonel Amory's attack, and were attempting to escape by the roads I was guarding. I felt perfectly confident of my ability to stop their retreat and hold them in check until Colonel Amory should overtake them.

Things remained in this condition until between 2 and 3 p. m., when Lieutenant Morris arrived with a squadron of cavalry, with orders that we should return immediately. I at once sent two companies, under command of Captain Bigelow, and a detachment of cavalry to Young's Cross-Roads, with orders to Captain Wilson to join the regiment immediately with the three companies under his command.

By about 8 p. m. they arrived, and the regiment at once commenced its march homeward. The incessant rain of the previous forty-eight hours had rendered the roads still worse than during the advance, and Mill Creek, which we reached about 9 o'clock, was swollen to such a degree that the mounted officers had to swim their horses to cross it. Although the men had but partially recovered from the fatigues of their previous march, yet they plunged in without a moment's hesitation at the word of command and crossed the stream. They bore this and all the other hardships and exposures of their march through the mud and rain like veterans.

Between 1 and 2 o'clock on Saturday morning I destroyed the bridge at Haughton's Mill, having heard from our pickets in the rear that they had encountered the pickets of the enemy on this side of Mill Creek.

About 11 o'clock I reached Evans' Mill, where, through the kindness of the Twenty-first Massachusetts Volunteers, we were supplied with rations and hot coffee, which supply was very gratefully received, as, having been ordered by Colonel Amory to take only two days' rations, we had been without food for many hours. I reached camp about 4 p. m.

From a reconnaissance made by Captain Bigelow, who approached within 400 yards of the enemy's camp, I learned there was between 800 and 900 cavalry in our immediate vicinity. I also received information that there is no regular encampment between that at Wambleton's Bridge, which is 8 miles from Young's Cross-Roads, and Kinston; that some days there would be in Trenton and vicinity 1,000 or 1,500 troops and other days not more than 500 or 600. I was also informed that they came from Kinston into the neighborhood of Trenton foraging and pressing horses and men into their service; also to watch and obtain information of the movements of our troops.

I have lost several men who strayed beyond our lines contrary to orders how many I am unable at present to say, as 5 whom I have already reported as prisoners have just returned, and perhaps what few others are missing may return to camp. There are now but three men missing.

In addition to the officers already spoken of I wish also to mention the names of Captain Brunner and Lieutenants Martin, Dougherty, and Gault as worthy of special commendation. But where all the officers did their duty so nobly it seems invidious to single out any as specially deserving.

In conclusion, I have only to say that my orders from General Foster and Colonel Amory were to hold the points assigned to me till I received further instructions from Colonel Amory, and although the two days' rations I was instructed to take had been entirely consumed (much of it having been spoiled by the rain during our night's march), I was determined not to quit my post until I was ordered to do so. I had commenced to collect what few cattle, swine, and fowls had escaped the rebel foraging parties, and had already obtained a sufficient quantity to supply the regiment with meat (such luxuries as coffee, bread, and salt being altogether too extravagant for soldiers) for at least a week. My men, though weary and foot-sore from their long march over most horrible roads were nevertheless in the best possible spirits, eager for the fray, and burning with anxiety to vindicate the ancient glory of Maryland.

I have the honor to be, very respectfully,

J. EUGENE DURYÉE,
Lieutenant-Colonel, Commanding Second Maryland Regiment.

Capt. EDWARD M. NEILL,
Assistant Adjutant-General.

[Indorsement.]

HEADQUARTERS SECOND DIVISION,
New Berne, N. C., May 20, 1862.

Respectfully forwarded. I am happy to state that Lieutenant-Colouel Duryée executed his part of the plan in a gallant and skillful manner.

J. L. RENO,
Brigadier-General, Commanding Second Division.

No. 3.

Report of Col. Simon H. Mix, Third New York Cavalry.

HDQRS. THIRD NEW YORK VOLUNTEER CAVALRY,
New Berne, N. C., May 19, 1862.

COLONEL: I have the honor to report that, in obedience to your order dated May 14, I marched this regiment at 10 p. m. of that day, taking the Trent road in the direction of Trenton. Having arrived at your headquarters I halted by your order about two hours.

At 2 a. m. May 15 I took up the line of march from that point. After proceeding along the direct road about 8 miles I sent the First Squadron of my regiment, under command of Lieut. Col. John Mix, by a by-road, in order to cut off a party of the enemy supposed to be quartered at what is called Merritt's house. The remainder of the regiment proceeded on the direct road, which passed by the aforesaid house. The instructions given to Lieutenant-Colonel Mix were to proceed along the by-road to its intersection with the main road, a distance of about 4 miles, and by a countermarch rejoin the regiment at Merritt's house.

These instructions were strictly complied with. On reaching Merritt's house I found it evacuated, no trace of the enemy being discovered. I then pushed on, sending in advance the Fourth Squadron of my regiment (Companies C and F), under command of Maj. Charles Fitzsimmons. One mile and a half beyond Merritt's house 4 mounted vedettes of the enemy were discovered, one of whom was captured by Captain McNamara (Company F). The advance guard, composed of 18 men, under command of Lieut. John Mayes (Company C), was ordered to pursue the remainder. Major Fitzsimmons, seeing that the advance guard were getting too far from his squadron, rode forward to check it. He, however, did not reach it until it was at least a third of a mile ahead of the squadron. He here halted and sent an order to Captain Stearns, commanding the squadron, to close up at a gallop. Before the order was executed a mounted party of the enemy, in number about 60, came into the main road from a by-path on the left between our advance guard and the squadron. They immediately opened fire on the squadron, causing it to halt. The advance guard now charged them from the rear and gallantly cut their way through the enemy and rejoined the squadron. I had in the mean time dismounted 50 of my men, armed with carbines and Belgian rifles, and deployed them in the woods to the right and left as skirmishers. The enemy, however, on seeing our force, retreated in confusion and scattered through the woods, leaving their dead and wounded, 10 in number, on the field. My skirmishers, having been relieved by infantry, were called in, and by your order my regiment countermarched and returned to New Berne, reaching here at 4 p. m. May 15.

My command behaved most gallantly throughout the affair. Major Fitzsimmons was wounded by a rifle-ball in the left shoulder at the outset of the engagement, which had the effect to dislodge him from his saddle. His horse was subsequently shot. While dismounted he received a slight wound from a rifle-ball on the back of his head, which stunned and threw him to the ground, when he was made a prisoner. He shortly recovered and made his escape, but was soon retaken. While being taken away by a rebel soldier he was struck on the forehead by the breech of a rifle in the hands of a rebel who rushed out of the woods, which was observed by a private in Company K (Thomas Maine), who rode forward and shot the assailant, thereby releasing Major Fitzsimmons.

The following is a list of the casualties in my regiment: Wounded— Maj. Charles Fitzsimmons slightly; Private William Bellows, Company C, seriously, left arm amputated; and Private Robert Craig, Company C, slightly. Missing—Lieut. John Mayes and Privates Matthews Sullivan, Joseph Carson, Benjamin Corsout, and William Hithree, all of Company C.

I am, colonel, with much respect, your obedient servant,

SIMON H. MIX,
Colonel, Commanding Third New York Volunteer Cavalry.

Col. THOMAS J. C. AMORY,
Seventeenth Mass. Vols., Comdg. First Brig., First Div.

MAY 30, 1862.—Skirmish at Tranter's Creek, N. C.

Report of Capt. George F. Jocknick, Third New York Cavalry.

WASHINGTON, N. C., *May 31, 1862.*

SIR: I have the honor to submit to you the following report of the fight which occurred yesterday between a mounted patrol of my company and a body of rebel troops laid in ambush:

In accordance with our daily routine of duties Second Lieutenant Allis started early in the morning with a detail of 15 men to reconnoiter the Greenville road as far as Tranter's Creek, about 8 miles from here. Having received information that only a small body of rebel troops, invariably estimated at from 12 to 15 men, were in advance, Lieutenant Allis deemed it expedient to cross the bridge over the said creek, leaving a few men to secure his retreat, but had only proceeded a short distance when he was attacked by about a dozen men, mounted and on foot. After discharging their fire-arms and receiving our fire in return they fled to the woods, closely followed by Lieutenant Allis and his men, who succeeded in taking two prisoners. These prisoners he was subsequently compelled to let go after having secured their arms. Finding himself surrounded by a large body of infantry concealed in the woods Lieutenant Allis gallantly cut his way through the crowd, and returned here with his command about noon, with only one man— Private Ogden Harrison—badly wounded and 2 horses killed. The enemy had 3 men killed besides those wounded, supposed to have been 5 or 6. A fine horse, valued at $200, fell in our hands, which will partly make up for the two lost.

Lieutenant Allis speaks in the highest terms of the bravery and coolness displayed by our men, and I am happy to say that this little affair has reflected much credit on all concerned.

The wounded man has good medical attendance and is doing well.

I have the honor to be, very respectfully, your obedient servant,

G. F. JOCKNICK,
Captain Company I, Third New York Cavalry.

Col. E. E. POTTER, *Commanding.*

JUNE 5, 1862.—Action at Tranter's Creek, N. C.

Report of Lieut. Col. Francis A. Osborn, Twenty-fourth Massachusetts Infantry.

HDQRS. TWENTY-FOURTH REGIMENT MASS. VOLS.,
Washington, N. C., June 6, 1862. ·

CAPTAIN : In obedience to orders received from Colonel Stevenson in person I embarked three companies of the regiment under my command on board the steamer Pilot Boy, bound for this place, at 11.30 p. m. of the 3d instant, and left instructions with Captain Maker to follow with the four companies on board the Lancer as soon as possible. Lieut. W. B. Avery came on board with a battery of three pieces and reported to me for orders.

The Pilot Boy got under way early on the morning of the 4th (Wednesday), and arrived at this place at 6 p. m. In the course of the evening Colonel Potter informed me that the enemy's force under Colonel Singeltary was between this place and Pactolus, a village about 12 miles distant, on the Greenville road, and suggested the propriety of attacking them at once before they should hear of the arrival of re-enforcements. I therefore determined to take eight companies of the Twenty-fourth Regiment, after the arrival of the four companies left at New Berne, two pieces of artillery, and the company of the Third New York Cavalry stationed here, under command of Captain Jocknick, and to march as early as possible the next morning toward Pactolus. Colonel Potter gave orders to Captain Nichols, of the gunboat Picket, to go up Tar River to the same place, throwing shells into the woods between the river and the road as he proceeded. He also ordered him to take two scows in tow in which to bring down the troops in case they should reach Pactolus. This arrangement would leave two companies of infantry, one 12-pounder howitzer, and one mountain howitzer for the defense of the town, besides the usual pickets and provost guard.

As the four companies under Captain Maker did not arrive until 6 a. m. Thursday the expedition was not able to take up the line of march until 9.15 a. m. I got information from contrabands as we proceeded that the enemy was posted at two bridges which crossed Tranter's Creek, one being on the road which we were pursuing and the other about half a mile distant from the first to the right of the course we were following. I further learned that the first had been rendered impassable, but that the second, though only a slight bridge, running through a mill, was probably in order or could easily be made so. I therefore turned off to the right a mile this side of Tranter's Creek, and after marching 2 miles came in sight of the mill. There were three buildings, about 30 feet apart, open in the lower story, through which the bridge ran. Our advance, on approaching the first of these around a turn in the road, found that the floor of the third had been torn up and made into a barricade on the opposite side, behind which was placed the advance of the enemy. Our men on seeing them immediately fired upon them and received a volley in return, which caused them to fall back and which wounded Lieut. H. D. Jarvis, who was in command of the advance. I then ordered up the artillery, which took up its position near the entrance of the first building and commenced firing in the direction in which the enemy was supposed to be, their advance having retired. This was at 2.45 p. m.

Company A, Captain Redding, was disposed on the left of the artillery, under cover of the logs and beams of the mill, and Company F Captain Clark, was ordered to advance to the support of the artillery; but owing to a misconception of the order the whole regiment approached much nearer than I had intended, inasmuch as from the conformation of the ground, which ran to a point at the mill, only about 50 or 60 men could be placed to fire with effect. I accordingly ordered all to lie down and await orders. The cavalry retired to the rear to guard against the possibility of an attack in that direction.

The firing of the enemy was at this time very rapid and well directed, and we discovered from the flash of their guns that they were distant not more than 50 paces from us. This placed our artillery at a great disadvantage, for at so short a range it could not do its best execution. It was, however, admirably managed by Lieutenant Avery, and as it seemed still to be doing good service I felt unwilling to change its position.

During the first fifteen minutes the enemy's fire continued steady, and most of the wounds on our side were inflicted at that time. After that time it began to slacken, and when we had discovered a large number of men in trees just on the opposite bank and had poured a few rounds of canister into them it wholly ceased. At this time we could see a large number of men running along the opposite bank at some distance from us, and were satisfied that they were totally routed.

The leading companies then advanced to the third building and relaid the floor, which could not have been done until the enemy had been driven from their position, as any one attempting it would have prevented our own fire while within 30 paces of that of the enemy.

The bridge being repaired sufficiently for foot passengers, the infantry, excepting Company K, Captain Maker, which was left for the support of the artillery, crossed; and marched about 100 paces beyond the position which the enemy had occupied, forming line of battle there. Having remained there a short time and examined the position, after consultation with Colonel Potter I deemed the object of the expedition had been gained in giving the enemy a severe lesson, and that it would be better to return to Washington rather than to go on to Pactolus, particularly as it would take some hours to make the bridges strong enough for the passage of the cavalry and artillery. I therefore ordered the infantry to recross, and returned to Washington, bringing the dead and wounded.

The battle lasted forty-five minutes, and the troops arrived at Washington at 8.30 p. m., having made a march of 18 miles in the heat of the day. During the march we constantly heard the Picket throwing shells a long way on our left.

Our force consisted of eight companies of the Twenty-fourth Massachusetts Regiment (Company D, Captain Prince, and Company C, Lieutenant Bell commanding, having been left at Washington), numbering about 430 men; two 12-pounder howitzers of the Marine Artillery, Lieut. W. B. Avery, manned by 12 men each, and Company I, of the Third New York Cavalry, Captain Jocknick, numbering 40 men.

The enemy's force must have been quite equal to our own to judge from the firing. From what information I could gain I estimated it at 450 infantry and 70 cavalry, under command of Colonel Singeltary, of the Forty-fourth North Carolina Volunteers, now acting brigadier-general.

We have learned that information of our approach was conveyed to Colonel Singeltary by a man living on the road, so that he was able to concentrate all of his force upon us. His position was a very superior one, which could easily have been defended against us by a small body had we not had artillery.

Our loss, considering the length of the action and the small number engaged, was severe, there having been in the Twenty-fourth Massachusetts 3 men killed, 3 mortally wounded, who have since died, 1 lieutenant and 1 man severely wounded, 1 captain and 3 men slightly wounded. In the Marine Artillery there was 1 man killed, 1 severely and 1 slightly wounded. The cavalry suffered no loss, as they were not able from the nature of the ground to be brought into action.

The enemy's loss must have been heavy, as we found 5 dead bodies and saw a large quantity of blood in every direction. Since the action I have heard rumors of a very large loss on their side, including the death of Colonel Singeltary, but I cannot trace them to any reliable source.

I regret to say that the wound of Lieut. Horatio D. Jarvis, of Company A, is quite severe. He had been skillfully conducting the advance during the day, and I felt heavily the loss of so capable and energetic an officer. In the beginning of the affair Capt. William F. Redding, of Company A, received a buck-shot in his right wrist, but without leaving the field continued attending to his duties with his usual promptitude.

I desire to mention with the highest commendation the conduct of Lieut. William B. Avery, of the Marine Artillery, Colonel Howard. Placed in the midst of the hottest of the fire, he managed his battery with the greatest coolness and skill and contributed much to the success of the day. As I have said above, I think that but for his battery and the determination with which it was worked the enemy with a moderate amount of courage could have maintained their position. His men also deserve high praise for their courage and zeal. Of my own officers I am proud to say that they displayed the same coolness and courage that have distinguished them heretofore.

Capt. R. F. Clark, Company F, was particularly noticed by me as being in the advance with the foremost of the men, directing their fire and animating them by his example.   Capt. C. H. Hooper, acting lieutenant-colonel; Lieut. Albert Ordway, acting adjutant; Capt. W. F. Redding, Company A; Lieut. J. C. Jones, Company F; Capt. John Daland and Lieut. Charles G. Ward, of Company H; Capt. E. C. Richardson and Lieut. J. M. Barnard, Company G, being near the head of the battalion, and their companies being at various times engaged in firing, were conspicuous for their coolness and prompt attention to their duties.   The officers of the companies in rear of these proved by their bearing an equal degree of courage and determination, but were debarred from the opportunity [of doing] anything but remaining passive with their companies under fire which they could not return.

While, under the peculiar circumstances of the case, it may seem invidious to mention the names of some officers to the exclusion of the rest, I cannot but feel that justice demanded that they should receive the credit of what they actually did, though I believe that the others in their position would have done equally well, and I know from their urgent request to be allowed to do something that they were equally desirous of being in the front.   My men behaved remarkably well, situated as they were in the hardest position that a soldier can be called upon to remain in—that of not being allowed to do anything.

Col. Edward E. Potter, of First Regiment North Carolina Volunteers, [Union] military governor of this city, and Lieut. J. M. Pendleton, of his staff, accompanied me, and I have to thank them for valuable assistance and advice.

As I stated above, the conception of the plan of the expedition was due to Colonel Potter, and to his energy was it greatly indebted for being so efficiently carried out.

Respectfully, your obedient servant,

F. A. OSBORN,
Lieutenant-Colonel, Comdg. Twenty-fourth Regt. Mass. Vols.

Capt. WILLIAM PRATT,
Act. Asst. Adjt. Gen., Second Brig., First Div., Dept. of N. C.

JUNE 24, 1862.—Reconnaissance from Washington to Tranter's Creek, N. C.

Report of Capt. George F. Jocknick, Third New York Cavalry.

WASHINGTON, N. C., *June 25, 1862.*

SIR: Having within the last few days received a number of reports from various sources in regard to certain fly-trap contrivances made by the rebels on the Greenville road for the purpose of catching my mounted patrols whenever they should venture beyond their usual limits of 4 miles, I made yesterday a reconnaissance with my company to Tranter's Creek, a distance of 8 miles, where they were said to have a large force on each side of the stream.   I advanced cautiously, with my advance guard dismounted and acting as skirmishers, but could discover no signs of the presence of an enemy until we struck the bridge where our late engagement took place.   Here, within reach of our rifles and partially concealed behind the trees, we could just discover in the bend of the road on the other side of the stream two mounted pickets, whom my men were exceedingly anxious to relieve from all further troubles in

the world, but as I did not want to make any noise until the object of
my reconnaissance was accomplished their lives were spared. I found
the bridge partially destroyed, the mill where they made their last stand
entirely deserted, and no traces whatever of the presence of a large
force.

In the direct road to Greenville, about a mile from this point, is
another bridge, which Lieutenant Allis crossed at the time of his engagement; but although I made a careful reconnaissance of that locality,
no rebel pickets could be seen. About 12 feet of the center of this
bridge has been sawed off and a breastwork of logs and lumber erected
on the other side, but, as I said before, no indications of the presence
of rebel troops could be found.

I mention these little particulars merely to show that our late battle
at Tranter's Creek has had a very salutary effect on the enemy, and
that we shall probably not be molested here for some time to come.

Very respectfully, your obedient servant,

G. F. JOCKNICK,
Captain, Commanding Company I, Third New York Cav.

First Lieut. R. M. HALL,
Adjutant Third New York Cavalry, New Berne, N. C.

P. S.—I hand you inclosed requisitions for ordnance and stationery
and extra return for salt, which after being approved by the colonel
commanding please hand to the quartermaster, with my request to have
the articles forwarded to me per next steamer. I also hand you a letter
to the Adjutant-General United States Army and a private letter, both
to be mailed at your post-office.

**JULY 24–28, 1862.—Expeditions from New Berne to Trenton and Pollocks-
ville, N. C., etc.**

REPORTS.

No. 1.—Brig. Gen. John G. Foster, U. S. Army.
No. 2.—Col. Horace C. Lee, Twenty-seventh Massachusetts Infantry.
No. 3.—Second-Lieutenant Byron W. Gates, Third New York Cavalry.

No. 1.

Report of Brig. Gen. John G. Foster, U. S. Army.

HDQRS. DEPARTMENT OF NORTH CAROLINA,
New Berne, N. C., July 28, 1862.

SIR: I have the honor to report that everything is going on well in
this department. I sent on Friday last four reconnaissances, with the
object of ascertaining the force of the enemy near. this town, taking
prisoners for the purpose of acquiring information and to acquire a
more thorough knowledge of the topography of the neighboring counties. I am happy to say that the three parties heard from were perfectly successful and with very little loss. One detachment made a
circuit of 50 miles by way of Trenton and Pollocksville. Another proceeded to Pollocksville by another road. A third went some 18 miles
up the Neuse road and broke up the main post of the pickets on that

road. The fourth, not yet reported, were to occupy Young's Cross-Roads, situated about 14 miles distant from and at right angles with the Atlantic and North Carolina Railroad, half way between Beaufort and this place. We have taken several horses and prisoners and learned much concerning the enemy's force.

A more detailed report I shall have the honor of sending by the steamer hence on the 30th proximo.*

I have the honor to be, sir, very respectfully, your obedient servant,

J. G. FOSTER,

Brigadier-General, U. S. Army, Commanding Department.

Hon. E. M. STANTON, *Secretary of War, Washington, D. C.*

No. 2.

Report of Col. Horace C. Lee, Twenty-seventh Massachusetts Infantry.

HDQRS. FIRST BRIGADE, FIRST DIVISION,
DEPARTMENT OF NORTH CAROLINA,
New Berne, N. C., July 28, 1862.

DEAR SIR : I have the honor to report the movements of a reconnoitering body of troops under my command, consisting of six companies of the Seventeenth Massachusetts, Lieutenant-Colonel Fellows; nine companies of the Twenty-fifth, Lieutenant-Colonel Sprague ; seven companies of the Twenty-seventh, Lieutenant-Colonel Lyman ; five companies of cavalry, Major Lewis, and one battery of artillery, Lieutenant Pope.

We left New Berne at 5 p. m. of the 24th instant, the six companies of the Seventeenth and one company of cavalry going up on the south side of the Trent River toward Pollocksville, the balance up the north side toward Trenton. We encamped that night at Deep Gully, throwing our pickets forward to the right toward the Red House and on the left down to the creek.

We moved at daylight the next morning, two companies of cavalry acting as advance guard. When within 3 or 4 miles of the forks of the Kinston and Trenton road two companies of the Twenty-fifth Massachusetts were sent in advance and deployed as skirmishers. Rebel vedettes were from time to time in sight about 1 mile in advance. When within 1½ miles of the forks I ordered Major Lewis to dash on with the cavalry and clear the road. He did so, and drove 6 or 8 of the enemy up the Kinston road, firing upon them and killing, as reported, 1 man. The fire was returned, but without injury to us.

Arriving at the forks, we left two companies of the Twenty-fifth, two companies of the Twenty-seventh, one section of battery, and 20 cavalry, under command of Captain Moulton ; then pushed on rapidly for Trenton. The cavalry, being in the advance, discovered a small number of the enemy firing the bridge across Trent River. They fired upon and dispersed them, and extinguished the fire, saving the bridge. The whole force were soon up and halted, and, it being 12 o'clock, the men had their dinner and horses were fed. The bridge was soon repaired and a guard stationed to prevent the men from crossing into the village.

The force left at the forks was ordered back, and at 3.30 o'clock, the

---

* Not found.

cavalry having rode up two or three of the roads leading from Trenton without discovering an enemy, we marched through the village and on toward Pollocksville, halting at 8 o'clock and spending the night at a plantation belonging to Mr. McDaniel, who we learn left it in March last. It was now the headquarters of the rebel cavalry scouts or pickets. The artillery and baggage train found some difficulty in fording a small creek near this place, but all got safely through in the course of the evening. It rained very hard most of the night, but the men were well sheltered in the large barns and sheds, the officers occupying the house. Picket guards were thrown out, the guns of the battery stationed so as to command the different roads, and the baggage train well secured within the yard. Just previous to arriving here four prisoners were taken, who reported themselves as conscripts from Swansborough on their way to Trenton to join their company.

As we were about to move the next morning I discovered that a large grist-mill by the side of the road, below the house, was in a blaze, having been fired by some one or more of the men. It was completely destroyed. The house was also set on fire in the attic, together with a small house in the rear. By my orders a party of the Twenty-fifth, headed by Adjutant Harkness, succeeded in stopping the flames and saving the house. Although I should not have given my consent to the burning of the mill and should have prevented it had I supposed it in danger, I think it may, perhaps, have been well to have had it destroyed, as it must have been extensively used by the enemy and contained quite a quantity of grain, which could not be brought away. A guard was left to prevent any more burning, and we proceeded on to Pollocksville, being obliged to build a small bridge on the way for the artillery and baggage. Arriving at 10.30, we found there the six companies of the Seventeenth and Captain Cole's company of cavalry, who had arrived the day before. They had lost 4 men of the cavalry; six of them on a foraging tour having been fired upon by a party of guerrillas in ambush, 2 were killed, and 2 wounded and taken prisoners. Lieutenant-Colonel Fellows immediately sent out three companies of infantry, but did not succeed in discovering the rascals. Two prisoners were taken the morning we arrived, who were suspected of being concerned in the affair. We were delayed until nearly 3 o'clock on account of the bridge built by Lieutenant-Colonel Fellows' command across Mill Creek not proving strong enough for the artillery. It was strengthened. The artillery and baggage train got safely across, and we arrived in New Berne at 10 p. m.

Although we did not meet with as many of the enemy as we should have been glad to, I feel very well satisfied with the result. From information given us by citizens on the road and at Trenton I am satisfied that there is no force this side of Kinston, with the exception of about 100 rebel cavalry and parties of citizens acting as guerrillas. These are divided into small squads and scour the country from Deep Gully to Pollocksville.

The troops behaved extremely well throughout the entire march, and notwithstanding the heat of the weather and the many streams to be forded, some of them 3 and 4 feet in depth, there was no murmuring and but few stragglers.

The heavy rain had made the roads in many places very bad for artillery, but they came safely through, Lieutenant Pope managing them with much skill and with little bluster.

I am greatly indebted to Captain Hoffman, of General Foster's staff, who accompanied me, and by his advice did much to make the reconnaissance successful; also to Lieutenant Dennison, of the Twenty-seventh, who acted as aide.

The bridge built at Mill Creek was not destroyed as directed, because it would have delayed us so long that we could not have arrived at New Berne that night, and because I considered it of very little if any benefit to the enemy.

Very respectfully,

H. C. LEE,
Colonel, Commanding First Brigade.

Lieut. J. F. ANDERSON, *Acting Assistant Adjutant-General.*

No. 3.

Report of Second Lieut. Byron W. Gates, Third New York Cavalry.

CAMP RENO, *near New Berne, N. C., July* 29, 1862.

SIR: In compliance with your request I have the honor to report the movements of my company, as follows:

In obedience to orders received from General Foster I joined my company with the Seventeenth Massachusetts. Marched July 26 toward Pollocksville, taking the road leading past the University. Soon after reaching Mill Creek the work of bridging was commenced, when the commanding officer, ordered me to have vedettes stationed along the road leading to Haughton's Mill. I ordered a sergeant to take 5 men—went myself and posted the first, then directed him to station the next in sight of the first, that they might communicate with each other readily, and to observe the same order in posting the rest. They had proceeded about 400 yards, after stationing the second vedette, when they were fired upon by a party in ambush. I think there were 50 shots discharged. Two or three companies of infantry moved immediately to the spot, where they found the sergeant and 1 of [the] men killed, the other 2 missing. Skirmishers were deployed; the enemy's trail followed into the woods; how far I don't know. They soon returned, however.

As soon as the bridge was completed we moved on to Pollocksville, where we remained overnight, returning to camp next day. On our return I dismounted a portion of my men and searched the woods for the two missing men. I took the trail, which led directly to the creek, where there was a log lying across, which bore the appearance of having been used a long time by footmen to cross. I then returned to the regiment.

Very respectfully, yours,

BYRON W. GATES,
Second Lieutenant, Commanding Company K.

Lieutenant-Colonel MIX.

JULY 26–29, 1862.—Reconnaissance from Newport to Young's Cross-Roads, N. C., and skirmish 27th.

Report of Col. Charles A. Heckman, Ninth New Jersey Volunteers.

HDQRS. NINTH REGIMENT NEW JERSEY VOLS.,
Newport Barracks, July 31, 1862.

SIR: I have the honor to report the following as the result of a reconnaissance made in force from this point to Young's Cross-Roads:

The expedition consisted of six companies of the Ninth New Jersey Volunteers, under Major Zabriskie; three companies of the Third New York Cavalry, under Captain Stearns, and one section of the Rocket Battalion, under Lieutenant Graham. We started from this point on Saturday, the 26th instant, at 4 a. m., and after building two bridges proceeded as far as Davis' Mill, 26 miles distant, where we bivouacked for the night.

At daylight on Sunday, 27th, we started for the Cross-Roads, where we arrived at 10 a. m. At 1 p. m. I started one company of cavalry toward Pollocksville and one toward Trenton for the purpose of communicating with the expedition from New Berne. With one company of cavalry I started on a reconnaissance toward Onslow. We had proceeded about 1¼ miles when we came to a sharp curve in the road. As soon as the advance had made the turn a volley of musketry was poured into us from the opposite side of the creek, the bridge over which had been destroyed. I immediately ordered a halt, and those of the cavalry who were armed with rifles to dismount and deploy as skirmishers, and sent back for re-enforcements. The re-enforcements arriving promptly, I deployed them as skirmishers, and a brisk fire was opened upon the enemy. I also had a piece of artillery placed in position, and opened on them with grape and canister. Under cover of our fire I had the bridge rebuilt and crossed after them, but they had been completely routed, leaving behind several sabers, shot-guns, &c., taking with them, however, all their killed and wounded, the exact number of which I could not ascertain. Our loss was 6 wounded, 1 seriously. The rebels numbered about 300, under Captains Ward, Humphreys, and Perkins. I brought in 3 prisoners, 2 of whom belonged to rebel cavalry and were home on furlough.

My orders being to proceed to Young's Cross-Roads and if possible communicate with the expedition from New Berne, on Monday, 28th, I started, with one company of cavalry for Pollocksville, where I found the expedition had been, and left on Sunday afternoon. The distance being less from the Cross-Roads to New Berne than to Newport, and the roads I had passed over being almost impassable, I concluded to go on to New Berne and obtain transportation from there to Newport. We left the Cross-Roads on Monday at 3 p. m., and at night bivouacked at the Seminary, near Pollocksville. Tuesday morning at daylight we started, and arrived at New Berne at noon and at Newport the same evening.

I am deeply indebted to Captain Stearns, of the cavalry, and Lieutenant Graham, of the artillery, for valuable services rendered, and the prompt and energetic manner with which they executed every order. The officers and men of the infantry performed their duties nobly, and where all did their duty it is impossible to particularize.

I regret the necessity of reporting the burning of Mr. Foy's property, 8 miles from the Cross-Roads. The column had passed the house, when I perceived smoke ascending in that direction. I returned and found the house in flames. I have been unable to find out the cause of the fire or by whom it was done.

I am, general, very respectfully, your obedient servant,

C. A. HECKMAN,
Colonel, Commanding.

Brigadier-General STEVENSON,
Commanding Second Brigade, First Division,
Department of North Carolina.

JULY 28, 1862.—Expedition from Batchelder's Creek, on Neuse Road, N. C.

Report of Capt. Charles D. Sanford, Twelfth Massachusetts Infantry.

—— —, 1862.

SIR: I have the honor to report that, having received orders from General Foster to make a reconnaissance on the Neuse road and if possible break up a company of guerrillas stationed there, I left Batchelder's Creek with the following force at 2.45 a. m. July 28:

Company H, Twenty-seventh Massachusetts Infantry	44
Company D, Twenty-seventh Massachusetts Infantry	38
Company G, Twenty-seventh Massachusetts Infantry	2
Company C, Third New York Artillery	11
Company G, Third New York Cavalry	10
Total	105

Reaching the Neuse road and passing through Jumping Run Swamp (a small brook running through a dense swamp and crossed by a small log bridge), supposed to be a guerrilla rendezvous, we reached the house of White, when we were met by the outer guard of the enemy, who attempted to fire, but missed, and immediately ran into the woods. A mile farther and we reached Keith's, at the forks of two roads, where some 15 or 20 were charged on, but escaped through the corn fields. The house was searched and a few cartridges only found. The roads were carefully watched meanwhile by infantry and cavalry in every direction. Ascertaining from the residents that French's, a notorious rebel nest, was only a mile and a half farther on, I immediately moved forward and came on the house very suddenly, it being almost entirely concealed by trees. Sending Company D to the right and the cavalry forward, we nearly surrounded the house. We expected to meet the entire rebel force in that section there, and I therefore ordered a charge and a fire while charging (before Company D came within range of our guns on the right), considering it the shortest manner of ending the affair. The whole was well executed and promptly by the men. They fired a volley through the windows and yard, the volley being the first intimation the rebels had of our presence. They ran quickly, but only 4 escaped, 1 of them being wounded in the leg. The prisoners were brought in from the swamp and placed under guard and the house searched. Nothing was found of any value but a few sabers, the rifles and pistols being mostly worthless and condemned. Some 20 good horses were captured, only 4 escaping. The wounded of the enemy were placed in a wagon and sent under charge of the cavalry to the railroad. Everything having been cleared out of the house, it, together with most of the outbuildings, were fired, and were burning finely when we left.

We took 10 prisoners, 1 dead man being unintentionally left behind unburied, and 1 dying (Corp. Grier Black, of Mecklenburg County, North Carolina) on the return home. One with his arms shattered was immediately sent to the hospital; the remainder, by General Foster's order, being sent to the provost-marshal. The prisoners belonged to Company G, Second North Carolina Cavalry, and had been at French's some three weeks.

We reached Batchelder's Creek at 9.15 a. m., having been absent six hours and a half. When we surprised the enemy at French's the sun had but just risen.

No wounds or injuries were received by any of our men.

Lieutenant Randolph, of the Third New York Artillery; Lieutenant Skinner, commanding Company D; Lieutenant Joslyn and Sergeant McKay, of Company H, rendered valuable aid in searching the houses, scouting the woods, &c.

I desire especially to mention Sergeant Safford, of the Third New York Cavalry, Company G, for his brave conduct under all circumstances. He was especially cool and daring, leading off in two charges in a most gallant manner.

I am, sir, yours, very truly,

CHARLES D. SANFORD,
Captain, Commanding Guard at Batchelder's Creek, N. C.

Col. HORACE C. LEE,
Commanding First Brigade.

AUGUST 14–15, 1862.—Reconnaissance from Newport to Swansborough, N. C.

Report of Col. Charles A. Heckman, Ninth New Jersey Infantry.

HDQRS. NINTH REGIMENT NEW JERSEY VOLS.,
Newport Barracks, N. C., August 16, 1862.

GENERAL: I have the honor to report that in accordance with your order I left camp on the evening of the 14th at 7 p. m. with one squadron of cavalry and 100 infantry on a reconnaissance. I took the White Oak road, crossed the bridge over Pettigrew's Creek, and continued on this road until we arrived within 2 miles of Peletier's Mill, where I found a good road leading to the mouth of Pettiford's Creek, at which point I expected to find means of transportation across the White Oak River, which would bring me in the rear of Swansborough, and enable me to capture at least the pickets of the enemy. But I was sadly disappointed, the boats having been destroyed the week previous, as I was informed by a person whose slumber I was compelled to disturb for the night. I could not find anything in the shape of a boat and again took up the march for Cedar Point.

I took possession of Mr. E. Hill's plantation, opposite Swansborough, at 4 a. m. Hill's place is on high ground, separated from the village by White Oak River, about 2 miles wide, and having over 5 feet water in the channel. The only transportation that I found here was one yawl and a canoe, capable of carrying 16 persons. I dispatched Captain McChesney, with 12 men, in the yawl, followed by 4 men in the canoe, armed with rifles and Colt's navies, with orders to reconnoiter and secure two flats, but not to attempt a landing.

On his return he reported that on his getting within a half mile of the shore a gun was discharged, and instantly a body of armed men, numbering from 250 to 300, made their appearance from the heavy timber in the rear of the village. They started three boats to capture him, but altered their minds on receiving a volley from his little party, and skedaddled for the timber. Not deeming it prudent to run in nearer the shore with so small a force, the captain returned.

Having done all that was possible with our limited transportation, I took up the return march by another route. When about 8 miles from the Point, a sailor with a fowling-piece, was picked up, who informed me that two steamers (stern-wheelers) were aground in the sound, and had been there since early morning. By him I sent information as to matters in and about Swansborough. Knowing that I could not assist them in their difficulty, I continued my march, arriving in camp at 10 p. m. of the 15th in a drenching rain.

I have the honor to be, general, with high regards, your obedient servant,

C. A. HECKMAN,
Colonel, Commanding.

Maj. Gen. J. G. FOSTER, *Comdg. Dept. of North Carolina.*

CORRESPONDENCE, ORDERS, AND RETURNS RELATING TO OPERATIONS IN NORTH CAROLINA FROM JANUARY 11 TO AUGUST 20, 1862.

UNION CORRESPONDENCE, ETC. *

GENERAL ORDERS, }   HEADQUARTERS COAST DIVISION,
     No. 14.   }   *Annapolis, January 3,* 1862.

The vessels for the transportation of this division are assigned to the different brigades, as follows:

To the First Brigade (Brig. Gen. J. G. Foster), New Brunswick, steamer; Vedette, propeller; New York, steamer; Zouave, propeller; Guide, steamer; Guerrilla, bark; Ranger, propeller; Highlander, schooner; Hussar, propeller; Recruit, schooner.

To the Second Brigade (Brig. Gen. J. L. Reno), Northerner, steamer; Kitty Stimpson, ship; Cossack, steamer; Ann E. Thompson, ship; Lancer, propeller; Dragoon, brig; Pioneer, propeller; Scout, schooner.

To the Third Brigade (Brig. Gen. J. G. Parke), Eastern Queen, steamer; Arrican, ship; Sentinel, propeller; H. D. Brookman, bark; Chasseur, propeller; Voltigeur, bark; John Trucks, ship; Skirmisher, schooner.

The troops will have three days' cooked rations on hand, and be prepared to embark at twelve hours' notice. Orders for the details of embarkation and quarters will be issued by the brigade commanders.

By command of Brig. Gen. A. E. Burnside:
LEWIS RICHMOND,
Assistant Adjutant-General.

GENERAL ORDERS, }   HEADQUARTERS COAST DIVISION,
     No. 15.   }   *Annapolis, January 4,* 1862.

1. General Foster will embark at the city wharf to-day and to-morrow the horses and teams of his brigade. The troops will be marched on board on Monday from the upper wharf at the Naval School yard.

2. General Reno will embark at the city wharf to-day and to-morrow the horses and teams of his brigade. The troops will be marched on board on Monday from the lower wharf at the Naval School yard.

3. General Parke will embark at the city wharf to-day and to-morrow the horses and teams of his brigade. The troops will be marched on

* Some correspondence had in 1861, relating to the preparation of this Burnside Expedition, will be found in Series III, Vol. I.

board on Monday from the small wharf north of the hospital at the Naval School yard.

By command of Brig. Gen. A. E. Burnside:

LEWIS RICHMOND,
Assistant Adjutant-General.

HEADQUARTERS OF THE ARMY,
Washington, January 7, 1862.

Brig. Gen. AMBROSE E. BURNSIDE,
Commanding Expedition:

GENERAL : In accordance with verbal instructions heretofore given you, you will, after uniting with Flag-Officer Goldsborough at Fort Monroe, proceed under his convoy to Hatteras Inlet, when you will in connection with him take the most prompt measures for crossing the fleet into the "Bulkhead" into the waters of the sound. Under the accompanying general order, constituting the Department of North Carolina, you will assume the command of the garrison at Hatteras Inlet, and make such dispositions in regard to that place as your ulterior operations may render necessary, always being careful to provide for the safety of that very important station in any contingency.

Your first point of attack will be Roanoke Island and its dependencies. It is presumed that the Navy can reduce the batteries on the marshes and cover the landing of your troops on the main island, by which, in connection with a rapid movement of the gunboats to the northern extremity as soon as the marsh battery is reduced, it may be hoped to capture the entire garrison of the place.

Having occupied the island and its dependencies you will at once proceed to the erection of the batteries and defenses necessary to hold the position with a small force. Should the flag-officer require any assistance in seizing or holding the debouches of the canals from Norfolk, you will please afford it to him.

The commodore and yourself having completed your arrangements in regard to Roanoke Island and the waters north of it you will please at once make a descent upon New Berne, having gained possession of which and the railroad passing through it you will at once throw a sufficient force upon Beaufort, and take the steps necessary to reduce Fort Macon and open that port. When you seize New Berne you will endeavor to seize the railroad as far west as Goldsborough, should circumstances favor such a movement. The temper of the people, the rebel force at hand, &c., will go far toward determining the question as to how far west the railroad can be safely occupied and held. Should circumstances render it advisable to seize and hold Raleigh, the main north and south line of railroad passing through Goldsborough should be so effectually destroyed for considerable distances north and south of that point as to render it impossible for the rebels to use it to your disadvantage. A great point would be gained in any event by the effectual destruction of the Wilmington and Weldon Railroad.

I would advise great caution in moving so far into the interior as upon Raleigh. Having accomplished the objects mentioned the next point of interest would probably be Wilmington, the reduction of which may require that additional means shall be afforded you. I would urge great caution in regard to proclamation. In no case would I go beyond a moderate joint proclamation with the naval commander, which should say as little as possible about politics or the negro. Merely state that the true issue for which we are fighting is the preservation of the Union and upholding the laws of the General Government, and stating that all who conduct themselves properly will as far as possible be protected in their persons and property.

You will please report your operations as often as an opportunity offers itself.

With my best wishes for your success, I am, &c.,

GEO. B. McCLELLAN,
Major-General, Commanding-in-Chief.

P. S.—Any prisoners you take should be sent to the most convenient Northern post. You can, however, exchange any of them for any of your own men who may be taken.

GENERAL ORDERS, }   HDQRS. OF THE ARMY, A. G. O.,
No. 2.   }   *Washington, January 7,* 1862.

The State of North Carolina will hereafter constitute a separate military command, known as the Department of North Carolina, under the command of Brigadier-General Burnside.

By command of Major-General McClellan :

L. THOMAS,
Adjutant-General.

GENERAL ORDERS, }   HDQRS. DEPT. OF NORTH CAROLINA,
No. 1.   }·   *Hatteras Inlet, January 13,* 1862.

In accordance with General Orders, No. 2, from the Headquarters of the Army I hereby assume command of the Department of North Carolina.

A. E. BURNSIDE,
Brigadier-General, Commanding.

NAVY DEPARTMENT,
January 18, 1862.

Maj. Gen. GEORGE B. McCLELLAN,
Commanding-in-Chief :

SIR: I inclose herewith copy of letter received from Commander Glisson, and by him from Lieutenant Braine, in relation to affairs at Wilmington, N. C.

Yours, very respectfully,

G. V. FOX,
Assistant Secretary.

[Inclosure.]

U. S. STEAMER MONTICELLO,
Off Wilmington, N. C., January 5, 1862.

Commander OLIVER S. GLISSON,
Senior Officer of Wilmington Blockade, U. S. S. Mount Vernon :

SIR: On December 30, 1861, two contrabands came off from the batteries at New Inlet and they gave me the following information as regards the state of affairs here and up at Wilmington, N. C.:

At New Inlet in and about the fortifications (which consist of one battery of twelve guns, one earth casemate of six guns, one small battery of three guns, and one battery on Zeeke's Island of four guns) there are stationed about one regiment and a half (1,400 men) also four field pieces, horse artillery. All the guns in these batteries are short 32-pounders. One of these contrabands, named Kent Newton, has worked for several years on the ferry-boats that cross the river at Wilmington. He says that on Friday, the 27th day of December, 1861, the steamer Gordon or Theodore arrived at Wilmington from Cuba with a cargo of coffee and fruit, and that she was partially disabled, having been struck by a shot, passing through the wheel-house.

The crew of the Gordon or Theodore left on the 28th instant for Charleston, S. C., by land; he, Kent Newton, ferried them across the river. While crossing they told him that they left their guns at Charleston, S. C., before going to the West Indies, and that they sailed under the English flag.

There are very few soldiers at Wilmington. About the 25th of December, 1861, three regiments arrived from Manassas Junction per railroad. He also states about the middle of December the rebels towed down by steamer Uncle Ben four large heavy wooden cribs, diamond shape, about 40 or 50 feet wide and 12 feet deep, which they moved on the shoal and in the channel-way close together at the northwestern end of Zeeke's Island, and filling three of them, as he saw, with rocks, sunk them, and completely blocked the channel of New Inlet at that point, and the fourth one they said was to be sunk alongside.

This man's statement appears to be very correct. I have questioned him closely, given him the map to look at, and had him mark exactly where these cribs were sunk, and admitting his statement is true (and he appears to be a very intelligent, active "nigger"), New Inlet is at least for the present effectively blockaded, as you will see by referring to a harbor chart of that place. During the month of November that we blockaded this place we frequently saw a small steam-tug come past Zeeke's Island out in the channel-way to the [eastward] toward the outer bar, where she would lay under the cover of the batteries.

During this period of our blockade in the months of December and January, covering a period of over three weeks, although we have seen the same steamer repeatedly in Wilmington River and on the western side of Zeeke's Island, she has never come to the eastward of Zeeke's Island or in the outer channel-way, as she did during the month of November. This fact has been the subject of comment among the officers, and now that we are aware of the fact that these cribs have been sunk in the channel at Zeeke's Island, I know that it is an impossibility for her to pass or any other vessel drawing 9 feet of water. I make this statement for your information.

I am, respectfully, your obedient servant,

D. L. BRAINE,
Lieutenant, Commanding U. S. S. Monticello.

HEADQUARTERS DEPARTMENT OF NORTH CAROLINA,
Hatteras Inlet, January 26, 1862.

Maj. Gen. GEORGE B. MCCLELLAN,
Commanding U. S. Army, Washington:

GENERAL: I beg leave to give you herewith a report of our progress thus far. We left our anchorage at Annapolis on Thursday, the 9th instant, and after a protracted passage, owing to dense fogs, arrived at Fort Monroe Friday night at 12 o'clock.

Leaving Fort Monroe on Saturday at 10 p. m. we proceeded at once to sea, but owing to fogs on Sunday and Sunday night our progress was very slow.

Monday, the 13th, the weather cleared; but a very heavy wind and rough sea caused many of our vessels to labor very heavily, and some were obliged to cut loose from the vessels they were towing. Most of them, however, came over the bar and anchored inside the harbor about 12 m. on the 13th, just in time to escape the severe gale of Monday night and Tuesday.

The propeller City of New York ran onto the bar at the entrance to the harbor, and owing to the severe weather and want of small boats we could render her no assistance. She was laden with supplies and ordnance stores, and both vessel and cargo have proved a total loss.

I had been led to suppose, from conversation with Colonel Hawkins, that we should find pilots here whose experience in navigating the harbor would be of great service, but I find great difficulty in accomplishing my work for want of proper accommodations. The harbor with our fleet at anchor is so much crowded that we have suffered much from collision and running aground, and the want of tow-boats of light draught has been and still is one of our most serious hinderances. The boats chartered in Baltimore have none of them arrived. The reason of this delay I am utterly at a loss to comprehend. The channel to the sound is very crooked and shallow, there being on the bar at full tide only 8 feet, while many of our vessels are drawing from 8 to 10 when not loaded. I confess to having been deceived as to the depth of water in the channel and on the bar, and had supposed that any vessel in the fleet could easily pass over, but, on the contrary, it has taken every vessel that has gone over from one to two days to cross, and some it will be entirely impossible to get over. It is positively necessary that we have sent us at once powerful tug-boats, drawing not over 6 or 6½ feet. The strength of the tide and the heavy winds that prevail here incessantly render it impossible to accomplish anything without these boats. All our transport vessels have to be lightened of their troops before crossing, and many of the gunboats are also obliged to be relieved of every possible weight. In order to do this we need the tugs, and it is necessary that they be of such draught as to be able to run in any part of the harbor.

I took the precaution to arrange for a supply of water to be forwarded from Baltimore before I left, ordering one schooner to leave each day till further orders, but not one has yet arrived. Our supply of water is nearly out, and unless we can receive additional supplies our troops must suffer. I have made requisition on Col. A. B. Eaton for additional rations for my command and on Colonel Tompkins for transportation. I shall to-day commence to build a wharf for the landing of supplies, &c. This has been considered impracticable, but the necessity of the case leads me to the effort, though I am by no means sure of success. Here, too, we find the necessity of having the tug-boats of light draught. In landing our troops from transport vessels much time is necessarily consumed for want of these boats that can come alongside the vessel. The numerous shoals and bars render it impossible for larger vessels to move from their anchorage without danger of grounding. With the greatest exertion, and amid obstacles that have seemed insurmountable, we have succeeded in getting into the sound six of our armed vessels and three of the transports. These vessels will carry some 4,000 to 5,000 men. Several of the other vessels are now hard aground, and it is impossible to see how they are to be got off without the aid of more powerful tug-boats than we now have at our command. The enemy have full knowledge of our present position, and have already been down with one or two vessels on a reconnoitering expedition, but our boats soon gave chase and drove them back. I shall not feel warranted in making any advance upon the enemy till I have from 7,000 to 8,000 men in full position for battle.

It is not possible for any one not on the spot to conceive the difficulties I have to encounter in accomplishing the duties assigned me. The utter barrenness of the shore, there being only a sand spit, which the high tides often cover, prevent any permanent landing. There is no timber to be had even for fuel, and the great difficulty in transporting men and baggage to and from the shore causes great delay. Notwithstanding all these difficulties our men are cheerful and patient, and if we soon receive the necessary aid in the way of tug-boats and supplies of water I shall proceed with much confidence. Let me urge the immediate necessity of having these tug-boats forwarded with all possible haste. I send these dispatches by Mr. F. Shelden, who has been with us from the first, and who is entitled to my entire confidence. He will give you in detail any additional information you may require.

I also send Quartermaster Loring to Baltimore by the same boat for the purpose of forwarding with all possible speed the boats and water schooners from there. I trust you will instruct your chief quartermaster to grant him every facility in aid of his duties.

I am, general, your very obedient servant,

A. E. BURNSIDE,
Major-General.

HEADQUARTERS DEPARTMENT OF NORTH CAROLINA,
Hatteras Inlet, January 29, 1862.

Maj. Gen. GEORGE B. McCLELLAN,
Commanding U. S. Army, Washington:

GENERAL: Since my last report on the 26th instant we have been incessantly engaged in getting our vessels over the bar into the sound. They have all had to be lightened of their cargo in order to bring them to the necessary draught for crossing. This has necessarily consumed much time, owing to the limited means for towing and discharging. We have, however, at anchor in the sound this morning transportation for twelve regiments.

All the necessary arrangements for a considerable movement having been made, I shall, in conjunction with Commodore Goldsborough, at once make an advance upon Roanoke Island. These arrangements have all been made in the best spirit and we have received much valuable assistance from the commodore's vessel. Of the eight tug boats ordered from Baltimore only one has arrived; the other seven are still at Old Point Comfort, afraid to go out to sea. The want of these boats has been a most serious hinderance to our progress. I have never undertaken a work that has presented so many obstacles.

Since our last dispatch four water schooners have come in, affording us much relief. We look for others daily. The inclosed list of vessels will show you our strength now at anchor in the sound.

The health of the troops has been and still is very good, considering their long confinement on shipboard, and the men are all eager for a forward movement. I have landed at this point, and shall leave in charge of General Williams the Eighty-ninth New York, Sixth New Hampshire, Eleventh Connecticut Regiments, with the Rhode Island Battery. I find I cannot use so many men to advantage upon the island, and these regiments, under the care of General Williams, will be ready and accessible at all times.

In my last I made mention of Colonel Hawkins in a way that may convey to you a wrong impression.

The pilots were engaged for service in the harbor and in the sound, but failed to fulfill their contract, either from unwillingness or incompetency, and we have suffered much for want of experienced men in towing the vessels.

I neglected to mention in my last dispatch a painful occurrence that happened on the 15th during a heavy blow. A boat containing Colonel Allen and Surgeon Weller, of the Ninth New Jersey Regiment, with a boat's crew, was upset in the breakers while returning from this ship to his own vessel, he having come on board to report the arrival of his command. The colonel and surgeon were both drowned. Their bodies were recovered and will be sent home by the Suwanee to-day.

The bark John Trucks, with Fifty-third Regiment New York Volunteers, Col. L. J. D'Epineuil, arrived here after a long passage, but owing to the great draught of the vessel and the consequent impossibility to bring her over the bar and the difficulty of landing her troops she was ordered back to Fort Monroe on the 26th to report to General Wool.

The brigadier-generals have all been incessant in their labors, and the best of feeling pervades the whole command, both among officers and men. The weather for the last two or three days has been bright and clear, and everything evinces a much more cheerful aspect than at the time of my last dispatch.

FRIDAY, *January* 31.

Yesterday afternoon five of the tug-boats from Baltimore came in and anchored inside the bar. We immediately put them to work in towing over the remainder of the vessels, and with their assistance we now have at anchor in deep water all the vessels we intend to take up the sound. Having had to lighten these vessels of their troops and of everything that could be taken from them, some time will be required to re-embark the troops and reload them. We are busily engaged now in this work and in supplying them with water and provisions, ready for a forward movement, and hope very soon to be under way. The Eastern State returned from Fort Monroe last evening, bringing a large mail. Owing to her drawing so much water we shall not attempt to take her over the bulkhead, but leave her for other purposes in the harbor.

Early this morning a sail was seen approaching as from the opposite side of the sound. One of the picket gunboats was sent out to meet her and soon brought her in. She proved to be a small schooner from Middletown, a point nearly opposite where we are now lying. She was laden with pine wood and had on board 5 men, deserters from the camp at Middletown. They report about 600 men at Middletown under arms. These are all poorly equipped and armed with smooth-bore flint-lock muskets, and not at all inclined to resist the landing of the Federal forces. The men have been detained and are now on board this vessel.

I have the honor, General, to be your obedient servant,

A. E. BURNSIDE,
Brigadier-General.

Abstract from return of the Department of North Carolina for the month of January, 1862.

| Troops. | Present for duty. | | | | Aggregate present. |
| | Infantry. | | Artillery. | | |
	Officers.	Men.	Officers.	Men.	
1st (Foster's) Brigade...	168	3,973	......	......	4,363
2d (Reno's) Brigade..	141	3,364	......	......	3,697
3d (Parke's) Brigade..	116	2,613	......	.	2,867
Williams' brigade..	66	1,603	6	165	1,902
Total............................	491	11,553	6	165	12,829

Organization of troops in the Department of North Carolina, January 31, 1862.

Brig. Gen. AMBROSE E. BURNSIDE commanding.

First Brigade.

Brig. Gen. JOHN G. FOSTER.

10th Connecticut, Col. Charles L. Russell.
23d Massachusetts, Col. John Kurtz.
24th Massachusetts, Col. Thomas G. Stevenson.
25th Massachusetts, Col. Edwin Upton.
27th Massachusetts, Col. Horace C. Lee.

Second Brigade.

Brig. Gen. JESSE L. RENO.

21st Massachusetts, Lieut. Col. Alberto C. Maggi.
9th New Jersey, Lieut. Col. Charles A. Heckman.
51st New York, Col. Edward Ferrero.
51st Pennsylvania, Col. John F. Hartranft.

Third Brigade.

Brig. Gen. JOHN G. PARKE.

8th Connecticut, Col. Edward Harland.
9th New York, Col. Rush C. Hawkins.
53d New York,* Col. L. J. D'Epineuil.
4th Rhode Island, Col. I. P. Rodman.
5th Rhode Island (battalion), Maj. John Wright.

Williams' Brigade.

Brig. Gen. THOMAS WILLIAMS.

11th Connecticut, Lieut. Col. C. Mathewson.
6th New Hampshire, Col. Nelson Converse.
89th New York, Col. H. S. Fairchild.
48th Pennsylvania, Col. James Nagle.
1st Rhode Island Artillery, Battery F, Capt. James Belger.
1st U. S. Artillery, Battery C, Capt. Lewis O. Morris.

HEADQUARTERS DEPARTMENT OF NORTH CAROLINA,
Pamlico Sound, February 3, 1862.
Maj. Gen. GEORGE B. McCLELLAN, *Comdg. U. S. Army, Washington:*

GENERAL : Owing to the many difficulties I have met with in the transportation of troops and supplies into the sound, together with the want of more vessels that could be of service in shallow water, I have felt compelled to avail myself of all the resources within my reach to forward my command as speedily as possible. I have therefore detained for service here the steamer S. R. Spaulding, having been assured that she was well suited to the navigation of the waters of this sound. The ·result has proved the correctness of this statement, as

* Absent.

she has been brought over the Bulkhead with less difficulty than any of my transport vessels.

I feel confident that this step will meet with your approval, when you are fully informed as to the emergencies of the case. As soon as I can make a permanent landing of a portion of my forces I shall return the Spaulding to Fort Monroe.

For the same reasons as in the above case I have also detained the propeller Virginia, being confident that the necessities of the case and the good of the public service warranted me in so doing. She will be returned to Old Point as soon as I can possibly dispense with her services.

The weather for the last two or three days has been such as to retard our progress very considerably. The winds have been so fresh and the sea so rough that it has been with the greatest difficulty that we could, even with the assistance of the tugs, pass from one vessel to another; we have, however, been constantly at work, and the preparations for an advance are now rapidly drawing to a close. The vessels that have suffered from collisions and other causes we are endeavoring to repair, and with one or two exceptions have succeeded in rendering them again serviceable. Having understood that a force of some 5,000 of the enemy were at Nag's Head, opposite Roanoke Island, orders were issued by Commodore Goldsborough for the Chippewa, now of the blockading force off Wilmington, to proceed at once to Nag's Head for active service. These orders were forwarded by the Eastern State on Saturday, the 1st of February, and the return of the vessel is now hourly expected.

The storm has considerably abated, and we are now in hopes to be under way by to-morrow or at farthest the day after. Our vessels are nearly ready, and nothing but violent weather will now prevent our getting off.

I am, General, your very obedient servant,

A. E. BURNSIDE,
Brigadier-General.

List of vessels now at anchor in Pamlico Sound.

TRANSPORTS.	Men.	GUNBOATS.	Men.
S. R. Spaulding	400	Picket	....
Guide	700	Vedette	300
Cossack	700	Lancer	450
Geo. Peabody	800	Pioneer	400
Northerner	1,000	Ranger	450
New Brunswick	700	Hussar	400
New York	700	Chasseur	400
Virginia	500	Sentinel	450
Eastern Queen	875		
Brig Dragoon	300		

GENERAL ORDERS,　}　　HDQRS. DEPT. OF NORTH CAROLINA,
　No. 5.　　　 }　　　　*Pamlico Sound, February 3,* 1862.

This expedition being about to land on the soil of North Carolina, the general commanding desires his soldiers to remember that they are here to support the Constitution and the laws, to put down rebellion, and to protect the persons and property of the loyal and peaceable citizens of the State. In the march of the army all unnecessary injury to houses, barns, fences, and other property will be carefully avoided, and in all cases the laws of civilized warfare will be strictly observed.

Wounded soldiers will be treated with every care and attention, and neither they nor prisoners must be insulted or annoyed by word or act. With the fullest confidence in the valor and character of his troops, the commanding general looks forward to a speedy and successful termination of the campaign.

By command of Brig. Gen. A. E. Burnside:

LEWIS RICHMOND,
Assistant Adjutant-General.

HEADQUARTERS OF THE ARMY,
February 10, 1862.

Brig. Gen. AMBROSE E. BURNSIDE,
Commanding Department of North Carolina:

GENERAL: Major-General McClellan directs me to acknowledge the receipt of your letters of January 29 and February 3, and to say in reply that he deeply regrets that you have had so many difficulties to contend with; he is glad, however to learn that you have overcome them. You have succeeded much better than he could expect and he is perfectly satisfied. He has heard to-day several rumors of an action at Roanoke Island, and is confident that he will hear to-morrow or the next day of your complete success.

I am, sir, very respectfully, your obedient servant,

A. V. COLBURN,
Assistant Adjutant-General.

WASHINGTON, D. C., *February* 10, 1862.

General AMBROSE E. BURNSIDE:

MY DEAR OLD BURN.: Your dispatches of 29th January and 3d February received yesterday, together with your private notes. I feel for you in your troubles, but you have borne yourself nobly in difficulties more trying than any that remain to you to encounter, and the same energy and pluck that has carried you through up to the present will take you through to the end.

We hear various rumors to-day about firing at Roanoke Island. I hope to hear to-morrow that you have taken it. In any event I shall feel sure that you have done all that a gallant and skillful soldier can accomplish. We are *in statu quo* here; have gained a great point in Tennessee by the capture of Fort Henry, which opens the road to us into Tennessee.

Everything is bright except the roads.*

*   *   *   *   *

God bless you, old fellow, and give you success.

Ever yours,

GEO. B. McCLELLAN.

---

* Some personal matter omitted.

GENERAL ORDERS, ⎰　　HDQRS. DEPT. OF NORTH CAROLINA,
　　No. 10.　　 ⎱　　　　*Roanoke Island, February* 10, 1862.

The names of the forts and batteries captured on this island in the action of the 8th of February are hereby changed as follows:

I. Fort Huger, at the head of the Island, to Fort Reno.

II. Fort Blanchard to Fort Parke.

III. Fort Bartow to Fort Foster.

IV. The inland battery is named and will be called Battery Russell.

V. The battery on Shallow Bag Bay is named and will be called Battery De Monteil.

By command of Brig. Gen. A. E. Burnside:

LEWIS RICHMOND,
Assistant Adjutant-General.

ANNAPOLIS, *February* 11, 1862.

General [J. P.] HATCH, *Commanding Post:*

GENERAL: I have the honor to inclose my statement of my unavoidable delay on board the John Trucks and of the events which took place during that time.

When General Burnside's expedition was about to sail for Hampton Roads our general determined on placing my whole command on board the John Trucks—sailing bark of about 800 tons, commanded by Captain Collins. The men would be crowded, but as they were (according to General Burnside's own statement) only to remain on board for five or six days at most, I made no objection, but simply obeyed, embarking my men on the 5th January, 1862.

On the 9th of the above month we left Annapolis, towed by the gunboat Sentinel, Captain Conellard, and then began the series of misfortunes which have pursued us ever since.

On the 10th of January, during a thick fog, we went ashore at Cove Point, and did not reach Fort Monroe until the 13th, just one day after the departure of our expedition to Hatteras Inlet.

We were detained until the weather cleared, and were for ten days endeavoring, but in vain, to reach Hatteras, where we arrived at last in a pitiable condition, after ten days spent at sea battling against the elements, in an overcrowded vessel with 700 men on board.

We were barely anchored at about 6 miles from shore and in sight of the fleet when a furious storm of northwest wind arose and blew for. ten days, after which I at last got to shore and reported to Generals Parke and Burnside.

The fleet was then inside the inlet as ready for action as it was possible to be after a fortnight of storms and gales which had dispersed or at least delayed eleven vessels, of which we were, after all, the first that arrived safely. The water schooners were not yet in sight, nor had the tug-boats, so indispensable to the speedy communication of orders, arrived.

General Burnside had no lightening vessels at his disposal on board of which to place us, and as the John Trucks drew too much water to pass the bar, he found it impossible for my men to be put on shore, and consequently ordered us back to Fort Monroe, pledging me his word and honor that he would send us a steamer to fetch us thence and enable us to join the expedition.

In accordance with the above order we sailed and reached ——

———— six days after, but my men being in great need of landing, and there being no ground fit for them to do so, we again sailed, and reached Annapolis on the evening of Wednesday, 6th February, 1862.

By remaining for thirty-four days, 700 on board, which if intended to sail is only calculated to carry 300, and which was consequently over-crowded by double the number, the Fifty-third Regiment New York Volunteers has undergone fatigue and miseries a thousand times harder to bear than ten battles, and more demoralizing than ten battles or even a defeat. Let us call to mind the English pontoon, between the decks of which an enormous number of prisoners, deprived of all means of cleaning themselves or the ship, were gathered and overcrowded; let us remember that besides this we were, if not exactly short of rations, at least compelled to the strictest economy in order to avoid becoming so; that besides we had not soft water enough even to dream of giving any to the men for the purposes of corporeal cleanliness; let us con-sider all, and I think that we shall still have a very inadequate idea of what the sufferings of my poor men have been.

I should be completely misunderstood if it was thought that I in any way meant to complain. No; we have been the victims of circumstances, hard, undoubtedly, but unavoidable, and in our misery we ought to thank God for not having sent to destroy us some of those fearful con-tagious diseases which are the natural consequences of men being, as we were, overcrowded in a small place.

In making the above picture of our misfortunes I have only in view to state the fact that my men, although submitted to the hard disci-pline, which is so needed in such cases, behaved in the most admirable manner; that they were ever obedient, calm, and resigned to their fate. Like faithful soldiers, which they are, they have strictly obeyed the orders of our general, and are worthy of the highest consideration.

I shall perhaps have to bear the blame of public opinion for not hav-ing protested here or there; for not having done this or that, and many will perhaps think that the colonel could have avoided much suffering by acting in such or such a way. Let them think so. Let even my men be dissatisfied with me now. Time will clear up all those clouds, and if the Fifty-third Regiment has not been yet of any utility to the country, the admirable patience and abnegation displayed by the officers and men during their long sojourn on board has at least shown what may be expected from their bearing when they are at last able to go into the field.

Very respectfully, &c.,

L. J. D'EPINEUIL,
Colonel Fifty-third New York Volunteers.

————

HEADQUARTERS OF THE ARMY,
Washington, February 12, 1862.

Brig. Gen. AMBROSE E. BURNSIDE,
Commanding Department of North Carolina:

GENERAL: We are all rejoiced to hear, through rebel sources, the gallant capture of Roanoke Island and the rebel gunboats. I hope to receive your account of it in a day or two, and take it for granted that your success has been at least as decisive and brilliant as indicated by rebel accounts.

I am glad to see that Commodore Goldsborough and yourself have pushed the enemy so rapidly and so far. I hope that the effect has been produced of drawing the attention of the rebels toward Norfolk, &c., so that, after having fully secured what you have gained, you will, by a rapid counter-movement be enabled to make the second attack with every chance of success. I still hope that you will be able to seize and hold Goldsborough, as well as gaining possession of the seaport in view.

You will have heard of our marked success in Tennessee—the capture of Fort Henry—and the trip of our gunboats into Alabama.

Everything goes well with us, but your success seems to be the most brilliant yet. I expect still more from you. While in the sound, please gain all possible information as to the possibility of attacking Norfolk from the south; that *may* prove to be the best blow to be struck. Although, as I am not yet quite prepared to secure it as it should be, it may be our best policy to defer that until you have accomplished all the original objects of the expedition, when with suitable re-enforcements you may attack Norfolk to great advantage.

I regret that the special messenger is waiting and that I must close this.

Very truly, yours,

GEO. B. McCLELLAN,
Major-General, Commanding U. S. Army.

GENERAL ORDERS, }   HDQRS. DEPT. OF NORTH CAROLINA,
No. 8.   }   *Roanoke Island, February* 15, 1862.

1. In this department, whenever possible, Divine service will be held by the chaplains on Sunday, and on that day all work will cease excepting such as is absolutely necessary for the public service. The great trials and labors which have lately prevented the proper observance of this day being over, it is hoped that, in thankfulness for our preservation through the storms and the dangers we have passed and for the great victory granted us, all will join in the endeavor to keep it sacred.

2. In order to preserve the health of the command the brigade commanders will direct their troops to avoid as much as possible the swampy parts of the island, not to bathe in the sound before 9 o'clock in the morning or later than 3 in the afternoon, and not bathe or wash their clothes in swamp water, this practice engendering chills and fever.

By command of Brig. Gen. A. E. Burnside:

LEWIS RICHMOND,
Assistant Adjutant-General.

Proclamation made to the People of North Carolina.

ROANOKE ISLAND, N. C., *February* 16, 1862.

The mission of our joint expedition is not to invade any of your rights, but to assert the authority of the United States, and thus to close with you the desolating war brought upon your State by comparatively a few bad men in your midst.

Influenced infinitely more by the worst passions of human nature than by any show of elevated reason, they are still urging you astray to gratify their unholy purposes.

They impose upon your credulity by telling you of wicked and even
diabolical intentions on our part; of our desire to destroy your freedom,
demolish your property, liberate your slaves, injure your women, and
such like enormities, all of which, we assure you, is not only ridiculous,
but utterly and willfully false.

We are Christians as well as yourselves, and we profess to know full
well and to feel profoundly the sacred obligations of the character.

No apprehensions need be entertained that the demands of humanity
or justice will be disregarded.

We shall inflict no injury unless forced to do so by your own acts,
and upon this you may confidently rely.

Those men are your worst enemies. They in truth have drawn you
into your present condition, and are the real disturbers of your peace
and the happiness of your firesides.

We invite you in the name of the Constitution and in that of virtu-
ous loyalty and civilization to separate yourselves at once from their
malign influence, to return to your allegiance, and not compel us to
resort further to the force under our control.

The Government asks only that its authority may be recognized,
and, we repeat, in no manner or way does it desire to interfere with
your laws constitutionally established, your institutions of any kind
whatever, your property of any sort, or your usages in any respect.*

A. E. BURNSIDE,
Brigadier-General, Commanding Department N. C.
S. C. ROWAN,
Commanding Naval Forces in Albemarle and Pamlico Sounds.

WASHINGTON, *February* 20, 1862.

General AMBROSE E. BURNSIDE:

GENERAL: I have only time to write a few hasty words. Everything from the West is thus far satisfactory, and your victory has
created a profound impression. I still hope that you will be able to
seize Goldsborough, though, in the uncertainty that exists in regard to
the force of the enemy in front of you, I do not feel able to give you
definite instructions. I feel sure that you will gain Beaufort. We
have from rebel sources a rumor, yet unconfirmed, to the effect that
[T. W.] Sherman has taken Savannah.

In great haste, very truly, yours,

GEO. B. McCLELLAN,
Major-General, Commanding U. S. Army.

HEADQUARTERS DEPARTMENT NORTH CAROLINA,
Roanoke Island, February 20, 1862.

GENERAL: I have the honor to present the following statement of
events that have transpired in my department since my last dispatch
on the 12th instant:†

After the occupation of this island by our troops a few irregularities
occurred in the way of destruction of property, such as burning of

---

* Other copies of this proclamation appear to have been signed by Flag-Officer L.
M. Goldsborough and Brigadier-General Burnside.
† Not found. Reference is probably to his report of February 14, see p. 75.

fences, taking furniture and food from houses, killing stock, &c., but in no case has personal violence or indignities been offered. I have ordered an investigation to be made, and find the amount of damage done will not exceed $2,000, and this includes the stock killed for food, which seemed to be almost a necessity, as many of the troops were entirely out of rations after the battle and it was impossible to land subsistence stores that night in consequence of the storm. In every instance these irregularities were committed on places that had been temporarily deserted, the occupants having fled to distant parts of the island. I have ordered payment for these damages to be made to those who seem well disposed to our Government and have taken the oath of allegiance. These islanders as a body are ignorant and inoffensive, and I am quite sure have not aided in this rebellion more than they were forced to do by the forces that were quartered upon them, and which has left them in a very destitute condition, impressing their horses and cattle, eating their provisions, giving them in return worthless shin-plasters. They have also been prevented from fishing, which constitutes their chief source of living, from fear of their visiting our port at Hatteras Inlet with information of the strength and movements of the enemy at this place. I have given them protection and granted them permission to pursue their work unmolested. They seem to be delighted at the arrival of our troops, and nearly every man on the island has taken the oath of allegiance, as well as large numbers from the neighborhood of Nag's Head, Powell's Point, and many from the main-land. In cases of absolute want of food among the women and children subsistence stores have been issued. This, I trust, will meet the approval of the General Commanding.

Our troops are fast improving the roads on the island, and have materially improved in point of cleanliness and comfort the winter barracks, camp grounds, and hospitals. A wharf some 500 feet long has been built at Pork Point Battery out to 8-foot water, on which we can readily embark our troops and land our stores, &c. All the guns of the forts, with two exceptions, have been unspiked and their carriages repaired. Cartridges have been made, and the forts are now in good condition. All of this work has been superintended by Lieut. D. W. Flagler, who has proved himself a most competent ordnance officer. Small-arms and equipments have been boxed and stored, an inventory of which will be forwarded with this report. Advantage has been taken of the few days' rest here to repair several of our vessels and to clean out their boilers, &c. The health of the command is excellent. The wounded are all doing well under the unwearied attention of the medical staff, which has proved itself all that could be desired. The troops are encamped by brigades, the commanders of which are perfecting them in brigade drill.

On the 10th instant I sent the Picket, Capt. T. P. Ives, with two companies of the Ninth Regiment New York, Col. R. C. Hawkins, to make a reconnaissance in the neighborhood of Nag's Head. They found that General Wise left there with the remnant of his troops on the day of the battle, burning the large hotel, to prevent its use by our troops, and destroying a considerable amount of public property that could not be removed. We, however, secured a large steam mud-scow, a blacksmith forge, and some open boats and flat-boats loaded with wood.

On the 12th I again sent a smaller party, under my aide-de-camp, Lieutenant Pell, which succeeded in bringing back several Sibley tents and a large box of medical stores. Frequent scouting parties have been sent over the island, bringing in a considerable quantity of military stores concealed by the rebels.

On the 18th I joined Flag-Officer Goldsborough in ordering an expedition up the Chowan River, for the purpose of destroying the bridge over the Norfolk and Weldon Railroad, detailing for this service the Ninth New York, Colonel Hawkins, who were transported by the gunboats of Captain Rowan, detailed by the flag-officer for this purpose. I hope to hear from them by to-morrow.

On the 19th we dispatched a joint expedition, consisting of the Fifth Rhode Island Battalion, on the steamer Union and three naval launches, under the immediate direction of Captain Jeffers, of the Navy, up Currituck Sound, for the purpose of reconnoitering the shores and destroying some salt-works that were reported in operation on the coast. The expedition returned this evening, and report that the importance of the works was very much exaggerated; in fact, there is no organized establishment there. A few iron kettles, owned by different individuals, have been used from time to time to boil down the sea-water to obtain a supply for immediate or local use. They found the inhabitants very much alarmed, but after assuring them that our purpose was not to harm them they became more communicative, and were free in the expression of their opinion that they had been deceived as to our intentions.

I have ordered General Williams' brigade, with the exception of the Forty-eighth Pennnsylvania and Captain Morris' company, First Artillery, to this place, and shall as soon as the expedition from the Chowan River returns make some rapid movements in the direction indicated in my instructions. I am satisfied that our best policy is to dismantle the small fortifications at different points on the sound and destroy the means of transportation, immediately after which I shall try to do the more important work which I know is expected of me. But I beg here to say that, in order to be perfectly secure in my movements, it would be well to have my force increased to double its present strength. I shall not, however, hesitate in going forward, and will leave the matter of re-enforcements to your better judgment. But one of the light-draught steamers sent for some time since has arrived, but we are expecting more daily, when I shall establish a line from here to Old Point Comfort, by way of Oregon Inlet, in the following manner: By steamers of from 3½ to 4 feet draught from here to the inlet, and by sea-going propellers of from 6 to 7 feet draught from there to Old Point Comfort. I hope the Quartermaster's Department will hasten to send me at once five of the former and six of the latter. By this route we shall avoid the passage of Cape Hatteras, and thus save over 100 miles, which is of the greatest importance.

Roanoke Island must continue to be the central point from which all naval and military movements in these sounds must be made.

I have issued an order changing the names of the forts on the island as follows: Fort Bartow, at Pork Point, to Fort Foster; Fort Huger, at Weir's Point, to Fort Reno; Fort Blanchard, the intermediate fort, to Fort Parke; the fort on south point of Shallow Bag Bay to Fort De Monteil, and the battery in the center of the island to Battery Russell. I propose to remove the guns from Fort Parke to a fort of the same name to be built at North Point, and the guns from Battery Russell to a battery of same name to be built on Dolby's Point, on the north point of Shallow Bag Bay. I also propose to build a battery either at Broad Creek Point or Indian Shells Bank. For this purpose I have ordered up Lieutenant Farquhar, of the Engineers, from Fort Hatteras.

We shall need a supply of ammunition for these guns; at least 300 rounds to a piece. I inclose herewith requisition of Lieutenant Flagler for the same. ·

Our supplies of commissary stores have been ample, and with what is now on hand and ordered we have enough for sixty days. I am not so sure of forage and coal. It has been ordered, but does not arrive as promptly as I had hoped for. The steamer S. R. Spaulding, of which I wrote to you, will be returned to Old Point Comfort in two days.

I beg to inclose the correspondence with General Huger in reference to exchange of prisoners,* which will explain itself, and I hope my course will meet with the approval of the General-in-Chief. I was induced to pursue this course for the reason that the sending of these prisoners to the North would have deprived me of transportation for at least three regiments, and also of a considerable force, which would have been necessary to guard them on their way thither; besides, if they had been sent North there would have been a delay in the exchange of some days, thus prolonging the confinement of our prisoners in the hands of the rebels, who it will be seen by the terms of exchange are to be released at once.

Although this is not in obedience to the letter of my instructions, I am sure the General-in-Chief will feel that I am observing the spirit of them. Inclosed please find an accurate list of the prisoners, with a recapitulation. The original parole I still hold, but will forward it by the next mail. The prisoners were all embarked for Elizabeth City, under the direction of Lieutenant-Colonel Osborn, Twenty-fourth Massachusetts Regiment, at 1 o'clock p. m. to-day, and are by this time handed over to Major Allston, who represents General Huger.

The flag-officer has kept his fleet constantly engaged upon the most important and effective service, the details of which I do not mention, for I know he will keep his Department thoroughly informed of his movements.

I beg to close by assuring you that my command is in most excellent discipline and spirits and anxious for another forward movement.

I have the honor to be, general, very respectfully, your obedient servant,

A. E. BURNSIDE,
Brigadier-General, Commanding Department N. C.

Brig. Gen. LORENZO THOMAS,
Adjutant-General, U. S. Army, Washington, D. C.

U. S. FLAG-STEAMER PHILADELPHIA,
Croatan Sound, N. C., February 24, 1862.
Brig. Gen. AMBROSE E. BURNSIDE,
Commanding Department of North Carolina:

SIR: I am directed by the flag-officer to forward to you the inclosed, which is a copy of a dispatch received by him this day from the Secretary of the Navy.

I am, very respectfully, your obedient servant,
HENRY VAN BRUNT,
Secretary to the Flag-Officer.

---

* To appear in Series II. Burnside's action was approved by dispatch of February 22, from McClellan.

[Inclosure.]

NAVY DEPARTMENT, *February* 14, 1862.

Flag-Officer L. M. GOLDSBOROUGH,
  Commanding North Atlantic Blockading Squadron :

SIR: Your dispatches of the 9th and 10th instant, by the hands of your private secretary, communicating the great success that has thus far attended the expedition into the waters of North Carolina, were received this morning, and I hasten, in the name of the President, to thank you for the service you and the brave men connected with you have rendered the country.   These successful achievements of our Navy and Army in North Carolina come to swell the current of cheering tidings that reach us from the West, where the gallant Foote, with his flotilla, has co-operated with the Army in a successful demonstration against the rebel forces in Tennessee.

Our brave and patriotic men on the coast and in the interior are earning a debt of gratitude from their country.

The hearts and best wishes of the nation have been with you through the long trials you have endured, and most sincerely do we rejoice with you in the success which you have obtained.

In congratulating you and the officers and men of your command the Department would also extend congratulations to General Burnside and the Army.

I am, respectfully, your obedient servant,
                              GIDEON WELLES.

HEADQUARTERS OF THE ARMY,
              Washington, March 4, 1862.

Brig. Gen. AMBROSE E. BURNSIDE, U. S. A.:

GENERAL: The General-in-Chief has read your dispatches of the 14th, 20th, and 23d February.   Your course merits his full approval, and he desires me to say your wants are at once attended to.   The subject of re-enforcements will meet with immediate attention.

I am, sir, very respectfully, your obedient servant,
                              L. THOMAS,
                                Adjutant-General.

HEADQUARTERS DEPARTMENT OF NORTH CAROLINA,
              Roanoke Island, March 5, 1862.

Brig. Gen. LORENZO THOMAS,
  Adjutant-General, Washington, D. C. :

GENERAL: I have the honor to report for the information of the General Commanding that I have now embarked, preparatory to a movement designated by his instructions, the whole of General Reno's brigade and half of each of the brigades of Generals Foster and Parke. I had hoped to have finished the entire embarkation of the three brigades to-day, but the severe gale now prevailing will prevent.   It is impossible to calculate upon the time necessary to make movements on this coast.   At this season of the year there are either gales or fogs five or six days in a week.

The necessary delay here has probably done us no material harm, as we have been making a few minor movements, which have served to distract the enemy. Colonel Hawkins, of the Ninth New York, with his regiment, together with the Eighty-ninth New York and the Sixth New Hampshire, will be left to garrison the island. I have some movements on foot with a view to breaking up the communications of the enemy, the result of which I had hoped to report to you, but the severe weather doubtless delayed the return of the expeditions. If possible I shall leave here with three brigades to-morrow night and make a hasty descent upon New Berne, the result of which will be reported to you at once by a dispatch ship.

I send to New York by the vessel carrying this dispatch all the sick and wounded that will not be fit for duty in sixty days. The command generally is in good health. I have moved since my last dispatch from Hatteras Inlet the three regiments and Belger's battery of light artillery, leaving there the Forty-eighth Pennsylvania and Captain Morris' company of First Artillery. I propose to take with me a portion of this company, which has been used to man two 32-pounder field howitzers, for which horses and harness were issued a month since, and it is now a very efficient section of artillery.

The order relieving General Williams from this department has been received, and he will leave Hatteras Inlet for his new field of duty by the first opportunity.

I have the honor to be, general, your very obedient servant,

A. E. BURNSIDE,
Brigadier-General, Commanding Department N. C.

HEADQUARTERS OF THE ARMY,
Washington, March 10, 1862.

Brig. Gen. AMBROSE E. BURNSIDE, U. S. A.:

GENERAL: Your letter of the 5th instant has been received. I am instructed to inform you that in consequence of information just received that the enemy is abandoning his position at Centerville and toward Manassas, and that he has retreated from his batteries near Aquia Creek, a forward movement of the Army of the Potomac has been ordered this day, to seize upon any advantage that may offer. You can make your arrangements accordingly.

I am, &c.,

L. THOMAS,
Adjutant-General.

GENERAL ORDERS, }　　　HDQRS. ROANOKE ISLAND, N. C.,
No. 2.　　　 }　　　　　　　　　 *March 12,* 1862.

The contrabands at this post will hereafter be placed in the employ of the Government upon the following terms, viz:

1. Men will receive $10 per month, one ration, and soldier's allowance of clothing.

2. Women will receive $4 per month, one ration, and allowance in money equal to and in lieu of soldier's allowance of clothing.

3. Boys between the ages of twelve and sixteen will receive $4 per month, one ration, and soldier's allowance of clothing.

4. All children under the age of twelve will receive one ration and remain with their parents.

5. The above regulations apply only to contrabands in the public service. When in the employ of officers or any other persons, as servants or in any other capacity, they will be paid by the person in whose employ they are an amount in money equal to the sum total of the clothing allowance, rations, and money expressed in the above regulations.

All persons at this post having contrabands in their employ or under their control will report in writing to these headquarters their names, ages, sex; where they come from; the names of their owners, and how long and by whom they have been employed.

In all cases they will be treated with great care and humanity. It is to be hoped that their helpless and dependent condition will protect them against injustice and imposition.

By order of Col. R. C. Hawkins, commanding the post:

JOHN E. SHEPARD,
Acting Assistant Adjutant-General.

WAR DEPARTMENT,
Washington City, D. C., March 13, 1862.

Major-General BURNSIDE, *Roanoke Island :*

GENERAL : Dispatches to inform you of the state of military operations on the Potomac will be sent you by this steamer.

It may chance that it will be important for you to co-operate with contemplated movements of Major-General McClellan, and, if so, you will place your command under his direction and obey his instructions.

By the return of this steamer, or earlier, if possible, you will make full report to this Department; 1st, of the state of your command ; 2d, the operations you are carrying on or contemplate; 3d, your wants, if there be any.

Nothing will be spared that can be furnished by this Department that may contribute to the safety and success of your operations.

Accompanying this you will find a communication by General McClellan respecting your operations, to which you will conform according to your circumstances and judgment.

Yours, truly,

EDWIN M. STANTON,
Secretary of War.

[Inclosure.]

FAIRFAX COURT-HOUSE,
March 13, 1862.

Adjutant-General THOMAS :

In doubtful uncertainty as to General Burnside's position and how far he may now be engaged in his final operations, it is difficult to give him very precise orders at present. I think it would be well that he should not engage himself farther inland than at New Berne, and should at once reduce Beaufort, leaving there a sufficient garrison in Fort Macon. He should at once return to Roanoke Island, ready to co-operate with all his available force either by way of Winton or by way of Fort Monroe, as circumstances may render necessary. I advise this on the supposition that Captain Fox is correct in his opinion that Burnside will have New Berne this week. If he has become fairly engaged in the movement I would not stop him.

GEO. B. McCLELLAN,
Major-General.

•

WAR DEPARTMENT, ADJUTANT-GENERAL'S OFFICE,
Washington, March 15, 1862.

Brig. Gen. AMBROSE E. BURNSIDE,
U. S. Volunteers, Comdg., &c., Roanoke Island, N. C.:

SIR : On Sunday last the iron-clad steamer Merrimac, called by the rebels the Virginia, ran out from Norfolk, attacked our blockading squadron, destroyed two frigates and two gunboats. She was subsequently beaten back in a severe battle with our steamer Monitor, and has not since attempted to come out.

The rebel army has retreated from Winchester and Manassas, and retired, without fighting a battle, beyond the Rappahannock. The batteries on the Potomac have also been abandoned. These movements were made evidently in great haste, as they left behind pieces of artillery and other stores which they had not time to destroy.

The President's Order, No. 3, herewith inclosed,* relieves Major-General McClellan from the command of the Army, and confines him to the Army of the Potomac. The Secretary of War directs that you make your reports also returns to him. He also directs that you forward dispatches to him on the return of the dispatch vessel, and permit no officer to detain her on any pretext whatever.

I inclose herewith a copy of a dispatch from Major-General McClellan, dated the 13th instant.†

I am, sir, very respectfully, your obedient servant,

L. THOMAS,
Adjutant-General.

HEADQUARTERS DISTRICT OF PAMLICO,
March 15, 1862.

OFFICER COMMANDING U. S. FORCES AT NEW BERNE:

SIR: Lieutenant-Colonel Crossan, who bears this flag of truce, is instructed to propose to you on my behalf a cessation of hostilities, so far as he and the men under his command are concerned, for such length of time as may be necessary to enable him to have interred the bodies of those of my command who were killed in the action of yesterday.‡

Very respectfully, your obedient servant,

L. O'B. BRANCH,
Brigadier-General, Commanding.

SPECIAL ORDERS, ⎰   HDQRS. DEPT. OF NORTH CAROLINA,
No. 51.   ⎱   *New Berne, March 15, 1862.*

*   *   *   *   *   *   *

4. Brig. Gen. J. G. Foster is hereby appointed military governor of

---

* See Series I, Vol. V, p. 54.
† See inclosure to Stanton to Burnside, March 13, 1862, p. 370.
‡ Answer, if any, not found.

New Berne and its suburbs, and will be obeyed and respected accordingly.

5. Brig. Gen. J. G. Foster, military governor of New Berne, will direct that the churches be opened at a suitable hour to-morrow, in order that the chaplains of the different regiments may hold Divine service in them. The bells will be rung as usual.

By command of Brig. Gen. A. E. Burnside:

LEWIS RICHMOND,
Assistant Adjutant-General.

GENERAL ORDERS, }   HDQRS. DEPT. OF NORTH CAROLINA,
  No. 19.   }   *New Berne, March 19, 1862.*

1. The brigade commanders will direct that their men have 40 rounds of ball cartridges in their cartridge-boxes at all times, ready for immediate use.

The post will be guarded as follows :

General Foster will guard the approaches to the town, throwing his pickets out some 4 or 5 miles, with strict instructions to them to carefully watch every way of entrance. General Reno will guard the line of the Trent and railroad as far as the brick-yard, throwing out his pickets in the same manner. General Parke will guard from Croatan down his line, throwing out his pickets in the same way.

2. No officer or soldier will, except on duty, be allowed outside the lines under any pretext whatever.

The pickets must be watchful, strong, well pushed out, and thoroughly instructed as to their duty.

By command of Brig. Gen. A. E. Burnside:

LEWIS RICHMOND,
Assistant Adjutant-General.

SPECIAL ORDERS, }   HDQRS. DEPT. OF NORTH CAROLINA,
  No. 56.   }   *New Berne, March 20, 1862.*

1. General Foster will move five companies toward Kinston up the main road bordering the railroad till they come to the fork of the road between the railroad and the river Neuse. They will then divide, and move up both roads till they come to Batchelder's Creek, and will burn both bridges over the creek. The force will then retire and occupy the fork of the roads and a point on the railroad immediately opposite, the pickets in communication with each other visiting occasionally with sufficient force the bridges and the bridge previously burned by the enemy. It may be well to have a patrol occupy the fork of the road, visiting occasionally the river Neuse. General Foster will also detail four companies of the same regiment to move up what is called the Trent road to the line dividing Craven and Jones Counties and occupy that position, keeping a constant patrol from the swamp on the right to the Trent River on the left, distance probably 2 miles. He is authorized to direct his quartermaster to employ such labor as he may require to throw up field works. The remaining company will remain in camp as a camp guard. The regiments in this service will be changed as often as the general thinks necessary.

2. General Reno will order a regiment up the road on the south of the Trent River, with instructions to burn the bridge 10 miles above

this place, which leads to Pollocksville. The force will then proceed to the town of Trenton, and burn the bridge across the river at that place, and then proceed to a point 5 miles above, and burn the bridge at that place. The regiment will then return to its camp, instructing the people that all communication with New Berne must be by the road on the south side of the Trent and over the ferry and bridge at the city.

The intention of this order is to destroy all the bridges over the Trent except the one near the city, where a strong guard must be kept. Personal instruction will be given to the brigadier-generals as to the orders to be given to the pickets.

By command of Brig. Gen. A. E. Burnside:

LEWIS RICHMOND,
Assistant Adjutant-General.

HEADQUARTERS DEPARTMENT OF NORTH CAROLINA,
New Berne, March 27, 1862.

Hon. E. M. STANTON,
Secretary of War, Washington:

I have the honor to state that since my dispatch of the 21st instant we have been organizing and sending to General Parke batteries and ammunition for the siege of Fort Macon. He now occupies with his brigade Morehead City and Beaufort. Considerable delay has occurred from the weather and the burning of bridges over the railroad by the rebels immediately after the taking of New Berne. The bridge over Newport River has required a great deal of labor to reconstruct it. It will be finished, I think, by Saturday night, when we shall be able to forward things with much greater facility. The roads are very bad, and it requires an immense amount of labor to haul the heavy articles from the head of Slocum's Creek to the railroad. Yesterday I made a visit to General Parke's brigade, and gave him some more definite instructions as to his mode of proceeding. I hope when the enemy sees the ample means we have for the reduction of the fort he will conclude to surrender.

The expedition to Washington, mentioned in my last, was entirely successful, and productive, I think, of most excellent results. The enemy deserted the batteries, but the obstructions were still in the river. A passage-way for our steamers was, however, very soon made by our submarine engineers. The mayor of the city and some of the most respectable citizens met the vessels some distance below the town and conducted them up. The troops landed, under the command of Colonel Stevenson, of the Twenty-fourth Massachusetts Regiment, marched through the streets of the city, then re-embarked, after hoisting the Stars and Stripes on the court-house, and then returned to this city. One or two naval vessels were left there for a short time. The light belonging to the Hatteras light-house, which had been in Washington for some time, was removed up the Tar River in a very light-draught steamer, owned by one of the citizens, who was a large property-owner there. Notice has been given him that he must return the light or his property will be seized or destroyed.

The negroes continue to come in, and I am employing them to the best possible advantage; a principal part of them on some earth fortifications in the rear of the city, which will enable us to hold it with a small force when it becomes necessary to move with the main body. The enemy have been remarkably quiet; in fact, we have had but one meeting of the outposts, when we drove their pickets from their position.

There is nothing now of which we stand in so much need as cavalry. I have had to take the pieces from Captain Belger's battery and organize it into a cavalry company in order to keep up communication with my outer line of pickets, as it was impossible to do it with infantry.

In my last I gave an estimate of the number of troops necessary to make a rapid move into the interior, and I hope the Department will find it convenient to send among the first of his troops a good regiment of cavalry. 1 believe I mentioned in my last that these regiments should bring with them a requisite number of horses and wagons, clothing and ammunition, at least 100 rounds per man.

I beg to thank the Department for the kind and too liberal appreciation of my services by recommending me for promotion.

I have the honor to be, sir, very respectfully, your obedient servant,

A. E. BURNSIDE,
Brigadier-General, Commanding Department of North Carolina.

HEADQUARTERS ARMY OF THE POTOMAC,
Steamer Commodore, April 2, 1862.

Maj. Gen. AMBROSE E. BURNSIDE,
Commanding Department of North Carolina:

GENERAL: I expect to reach Fort Monroe to-day, to take control of active operations from that point. The line of operations will be up the Peninsula, resting our line on the York River and making Richmond the objective point. In the course of events it may become necessary for us to cross the James below Richmond and move on Petersburg. It has now become of the first importance that there should be frequent communication between us, and that I should be informed of the exact state of things with you and in your front. Four additional regiments should have reached you by this time.

I am entirely in the dark as to the condition of your operations against Beaufort, the force of the enemy there and at Goldsborough. Will you please at once inform me fully, stating how soon you expect to be in possession of Fort Macon, what available troops you will then have for operating on Goldsborough, what can, in your opinion, be effected there in the way of taking possession of it, of neutralizing a strong force of the enemy there, and of doing something toward preventing the enemy's retreat from Richmond. On the other hand, please inform me what you can do in the way of a demonstration at Winton on Suffolk.

You will readily understand that if I succeed in driving the enemy out of Richmond I will at once throw a strong force on Raleigh and open the communication with you via Goldsborough; after which I hope to confide to you no unimportant part of subsequent operations.

Taking all things into consideration, it appears probable that a movement in the direction of Goldsborough would be the best thing for you to undertake, as you can make it in larger force than that on Winton, for as soon as you have possession of Fort Macon nearly all your force will be available. Great caution will, however, be necessary, as the enemy might throw large forces in that direction. The main object of the movement would be to accomplish that, but it would not do for you to be caught. We cannot afford any reverse at present. I wish your opinion in regard to the whole affair.

Very truly, yours,

GEO. B. McCLELLAN.

GENERAL ORDERS, No. 23. } HDQRS. DEPT. OF NORTH CAROLINA, *New Berne, April 2, 1862.*

1. The corps d'armée now in occupation of this department will at once be organized into three divisions, to be commanded, according to seniority of rank, as follows, viz:

First Division by Acting Major-General Foster.

Second Division by Acting Major-General Reno.

Third Division by Acting Major-General Parke.

2. The commanding general takes great pride in presenting to his soldiers extracts of letters received from distinguished sources, which express the anxiety with which their motions are watched by the Government and the nation, the appreciation of the suffering they have endured, and a grateful acknowledgment of the brilliant victories they have won.

The General Assembly of the State of Ohio have forwarded resolutions passed by them:

Proffering their heartfelt thanks and hearty congratulations on the brilliant victories in North Carolina, which they regard as the beginning of what all patriots hope may be the speedy end of the great rebellion.

General Thomas, Adjutant-General United States Army, writes:

The President and Secretary of War have specially instructed me to express their high appreciation of the bravery and skill displayed by the * * * commander of the Department of North Carolina and his troops in achieving successes at once brilliant and fruitful. They have not failed to notice also a sure sign of high discipline in the cheerful spirit with which obstacles briefly alluded to in reports have been overcome in the field.

Hon. Edwin M. Stanton, Secretary of War, writes:

The report of the late brilliant successes of the United States forces under your command at New Berne has afforded the highest satisfaction to the President and to this Department and to the whole nation, and thanks for distinguished service are again tendered to you and the officers and soldiers of your command. * * * It will be the pleasure of the Department to strengthen and support you to the utmost extent within its power.

By command of Maj. Gen. A. E. Burnside:

LEWIS RICHMOND,
Assistant Adjutant-General.

HEADQUARTERS DEPARTMENT OF NORTH CAROLINA,
New Berne, April 3, 1862.

Hon. E. M. STANTON,
Secretary of War, Washington, D. C.:

SIR: I have the honor to thank the President and yourself for the very complimentary way in which you have chosen to mention the services of my command. I have had your kind letter published to every regiment as a general order, and I am sure it is as gratifying to every officer and soldier in my command as it is to myself. I must apologize for making this dispatch very short, as some requisitions from my chief quartermaster for transportation, &c., render it necessary that a vessel should be dispatched at once for Hatteras Inlet to communicate with a vessel bound North from that place.

To-morrow I shall dispatch the E. S. Terry direct to New York with the convalescent wounded, and will send by her a more full account of our movements since our last.

Four regiments of re-enforcements have arrived, the Third and One hundred and third New York, Seventeenth Massachusetts, and Second Maryland. I have assigned them to the different brigades. Their arrival was very opportune, as the enemy are concentrating a very large force at and near Kinston. All deserters that have come within our lines report the intention of the enemy to move upon this place. We are as well prepared for them as we can be with our present force, and as soon as sufficient re-enforcements and transportation arrive I shall move upon them, unless I receive instructions from you to make the attack on Weldon and Gaston instead of Goldsborough and Raleigh. You will remember I mentioned this subject in one of my dispatches from Roanoke Island.

We suffer very much for want of cavalry, and I hope the Department will send me a good regiment at once. It is very difficult with our present means to keep ourselves posted as to the movements of the enemy, and in the absence of accurate information we are constantly receiving most fabulous reports of their great strength and rapid movements. That they are concentrating in large numbers at and near Kinston there is no doubt. My force here, as you know, is weakened by the absence of General Parke's brigade and the necessity of guarding the 36 miles of railway between here and Beaufort. Our lists of wounded and sick are very large, but I hope it will decrease under the constant skillful care of our surgeons. I beg here to say that we are much in need of more surgeons, which you were kind enough to say would be forwarded if required. I hope the Surgeon-General's Department will find it for the interest of the public service to see that any brigade surgeons that may be sent are junior to Brigade Surg. W. H. Church, as he is my medical director, and it would be a very serious disappointment to have to give another surgeon his position.

General Parke is progressing but slowly with the siege of Fort Macon. We find it very difficult, with the limited means of transportation, to transport the heavy siege batteries and supplies, but I hope to report good progress within a week.

I hope the Quartermaster's Department will not fail to send at once the transportation required by my chief quartermaster. The horses and wagons can be sent on light-draught schooners, such as we used when we moved from Annapolis.

We have suffered very much for want of fresh meat, which was to have been sent from Baltimore, but not a single head has arrived.

I have the honor to be, your very obedient servant,

A. E. BURNSIDE,
Brigadier-General. Comdg. Department of North Carolina.

HEADQUARTERS DEPARTMENT OF NORTH CAROLINA,
New Berne, April 7, 1862.

Hon. E. M. STANTON,
Secretary of War, Washington, D. C.:

I have the honor to report that a well-authenticated rumor has reached the commander of the naval fleet here to the effect that the rebel authorities at Norfolk are fitting out two small iron-clad gunboats for these waters. The exact state of progress is not known. It is said by some persons recently from that neighborhood that they will be finished within ten or twelve days, but I cannot believe but that this is an exaggeration.

The preparation to meet these boats is a duty devolving upon the

Navy Department, but as I cannot learn of any important steps being taken in that direction I deem it my duty to make the statement of the case to you, in view of the fact that we have so large a number of army vessels in these waters. The naval commander here will doubtless use all the means at his disposal to prevent any disaster, but the vessels of this fleet are but frail things at best, and have been much shaken up by constant service for three stormy months. I do not feel any serious apprehension in reference to this matter, but we certainly need two or three gunboats of a better class to make us perfectly secure. The armed vessels in my fleet will be put in the best possible condition to meet such an emergency, and I shall very soon try to land a force at the head of North River and try to permanently obstruct Currituck and Albemarle Canal. The locks of the canal leading from Elizabeth City are said to be too narrow to admit of a passage for these vessels, which I hope is true.

I have received nothing from General Parke this morning, but hope to report his progress by next mail. The commander of the fort seems disposed to make an obstinate resistance, but we have the means at hand to effect its reduction, but an Engineer officer, with a corps of Sappers and Miners, would be of great service.

The enemy in our front still continue in force, but we do not hear of them making any important advances in this direction. The outposts occasionally meet, but thus far there has been no important results from their meeting. We have lost but one man during the week, he being taken prisoner, and have killed one and wounded another of the enemy.

There is nothing of which we stand so much in need now as a regiment of cavalry, and I hope the Department will find it convenient to send one at once.

I hope you will excuse me for suggesting that the Van Alen Cavalry be sent, if, as I understand, it is in Washington.

Our sick lists are increasing slightly, but I hope to report a decrease very soon, as our beef cattle begin to arrive and they will have a change of diet.

I have the honor to be, your very obedient servant,

A. E. BURNSIDE,
Major-General, Commanding Department of North Carolina.

HEADQUARTERS DEPARTMENT OF NORTH CAROLINA,
New Berne, April 17, 1862.

Maj. Gen. GEORGE B. MCCLELLAN,
Commanding the Army:

GENERAL: I have the honor to state the following movements in this department since the battle of New Berne:

Immediately after the battle I started General Parke, with a portion of his brigade, to take possession of Morehead City, Carolina City, and Beaufort, and to invest Fort Macon.

This work has proved to be exceedingly difficult, owing to the absence of engines and cars on the railroad and the burning of the bridges by the enemy. The latter work was necessarily done under the protection of a large guard, and the enemy's cavalry made frequent visits to the road, and I had no cavalry to compete with them.

Our losses have been but slight during the work, amounting in all to some 10 or 12 pickets. On the 7th instant Colonel Egloffstein, of

the One hundred and third New York, was ordered to make a reconnaissance up the Trent in the direction of Onslow County, and I
afterward ordered him to continue his reconnaissance down the road
leading from Trenton to Core Sound, at the mouth of White Oak
River, and then to proceed up the shore of Core Sound and communicate with General Parke at Morehead City. This I did with a hope
that we might be able to catch a portion of the enemy's cavalry, the
headquarters of which were at Swansborough, from whence they sent
detachments over to the railroad, thus making the duty of guarding
the 36 miles of road from this place to Carolina City very onerous.

The colonel started with 200 picked men, two days' rations, and no
transportation, with instructions to ration his men from supplies found
on the route. He yesterday reached General Parke's headquarters,
having had several skirmishes with the enemy, in which he captured
some 23 prisoners, 80 horses, quite a quantity of pistols, sabers, &c.
Among the prisoners captured was Colonel Robinson, formerly of our
Army, son-in-law of Captain McCrae.

I have been thus minute in these details to show you how necessary a regiment of cavalry is to me at this point, and I sincerely hope
there will not be a moment's delay in sending me a well-organized regiment.

General Parke has now succeeded in getting on the banks in rear of
Fort Macon with the main body of his command, with two mortar
batteries and one 30-pounder Parrott gun. The enemy's pickets have
been driven in and all communication with the garrison from the outside cut off. The enemy's shots thus far have done us but little harm,
wounding only 2 men. There are three naval vessels outside co-
operating with us, and I hope within ten days to reduce the fort.

The re-enforcements you spoke of in your letter have arrived, and I
have formed the brigades of Generals Foster and Reno into divisions,
which now occupy this place and its suburbs. I am building just in
rear of the town an inclosed bastioned field work capable of holding
1,000 men and mounting thirty guns, which work will be finished in a
few days. After which I propose to build another small four-gun work,
with two companies, to the right of this first work and near the Neuse.
These forts completely command the town, and will enable me to leave
it with a small force when I move up the country. My advance now
on the railroad is at Batchelder's Creek, where we are rebuilding the
railroad bridge burnt by the enemy, and I have made corresponding
advances in the direction of Kinston, on the Neuse and Trent Roads,
which positions have been maintained with occasional disturbances in
way of picket firing.

Some days ago I sent, in conjunction with the Navy, a regiment to
Washington, to temporarily occupy that place, destroy the batteries,
and remove the obstacles in the river, which was successfully accomplished, and the troops have returned.

Some 600 of our men from Roanoke Island were sent to Elizabeth
City last week, and captured all the pickets in the neighborhood of
that place, amounting to 74 men and 100 stand of arms. Since then
the enemy's force has been increased at that point to two regiments
and a field battery of four guns.

I have organized an expedition, in conjunction with Commodore
Rowan, against that place, and if we succeed in capturing or driving
the enemy back, we shall move up to South Mills and blow up the
lock of the canal at that place, and then proceed to the head of the
Currituck Canal and blow in its banks, thus rendering it impossible

for the gunboats which are said to be building at Norfolk to come into these waters. I hope the expedition will be successful.

The regiments of my original command are much decreased by sickness and casualties in battle, and the recruiting service having been stopped, I shall not be able to fill them up. My command now consists of twenty regiments, one battalion, and a battery, making an aggregate of about 15,000 men, distributed as follows: Three regiments at Roanoke, one-half of a regiment at Hatteras Inlet, three regiments and a battalion with General Parke and on the road, and thirteen and one-half regiments with the battery at this place. The engines and cars, for which we made requisition immediately after the battle, have not yet arrived, and as the re-enforcements sent me brought no wagons with them, we are absolutely crippled for want of transportation. I sincerely hope there will be no delay in forwarding me the regiment of cavalry and two batteries of artillery, together with the engines, cars, and wagons already required for.

The enemy continues in force at Kinston, but I feel quite sure I can dislodge them after the fall of Fort Macon.

I have the honor to be, General, very respectfully, your obedient servant,

A. E. BURNSIDE,
Major-General, Commanding Department of North Carolina.

HEADQUARTERS ARMY OF THE POTOMAC,
Near Yorktown, April 20, 1862.

Maj. Gen. AMBROSE E. BURNSIDE,
Commanding Department of North Carolina :

GENERAL: I have information, which I regard as entirely reliable, that on the 25th of March a movement of troops commenced from Richmond for North Carolina to operate against your command. These regiments came from Fredericksburg and Gordonsville, having formed part of the Army of Manassas. They are Fourth, Tenth, and Fourteenth Alabama regiments, two Virginia regiments, two North Carolina regiments, Sixth and Sixteenth Mississippi, Eighth Georgia, two other Georgia regiments, one or two Louisiana regiments, Thomas' artillery (four batteries), Ransom's regiment of North Carolina cavalry, the heavy guns formerly at Leesburg, said to be from twenty to twenty-five in number, and generally large rifled guns. I think the number and caliber of these guns exaggerated; there were probably ten to twelve. The total being thirteen or fourteen regiments of infantry, one regiment of cavalry, and four light batteries.

The railways in the South are represented to be in miserable condition, both as regards tracks and rolling stock, so the progress of these troops was probably slow.

It is represented that the energetic steps taken by the rebel Government in reference to the conscription have filled their regiments.

I learn to-day that General R. E. Lee commands in front of me, having Johnston under him, Lee being now Commander-in-Chief of the rebels, and that their force in and around Yorktown numbers more than 80,000 men.

I would recommend to you to make no offensive movement beyond New Berne until you have secured Fort Macon; also to be well on the alert against an attempt to turn your left flank.

I hope the Department may be able to let you have some of the heavy guns used in the siege of Fort Pulaski.

GEO. B. McCLELLAN,
Major-General.

WAR DEPARTMENT,
Washington City, D. C., April 25, 1862.

Major-General BURNSIDE:

GENERAL: Your dispatches by Major Sherman and by Captain Cutting have been received, and you will please accept my thanks for your very full and satisfactory report of the operations under your command.

The Van Alen Cavalry [Third New York] are under orders to join you. Two batteries are embarking here to-day. These comprise all the re-enforcements you asked for.

The President as well as the country at large feels great interest in everything concerning the safety and success of your expedition, and no effort of the Department will be spared in supporting you.

Appointments of your staff were ordered, as you desired, immediately upon the receipt of your letter naming the persons you desired appointed. We hope soon to hear that Fort Macon is in your possession. The operations at Yorktown and Corinth are now the subjects of great interest. No doubt is entertained that Generals McClellan and Halleck will be entirely successful. Your limited force and the inability to increase its numbers at present will necessarily prevent your engaging in active operations to any great extent until the issue is determined at Yorktown. From your communications we are led to believe that you feel yourself entirely secure in your present position.

I shall be glad to hear from you as often as it is possible for you to report, and with sincere regard remain, truly, yours,

EDWIN M. STANTON,
Secretary of War.

GENERAL ORDERS, }   HDQRS. DEPT. OF NORTH CAROLINA,
No. 28.   }   *New Berne, April 28,* 1862.

Whoever, after the issue of this order, shall, within the limits to which the Union arms may extend in this department, utter one word against the Government of these United States, will be at once arrested and closely confined. It must be distinctly understood that this department is under martial law, and treason, expressed or implied, will meet with a speedy punishment.

The military governor of New Berne is charged with a strict execution of this order within the bounds of his control.

By command of Maj. Gen. A. E. Burnside:

LEWIS RICHMOND,
Assistant Adjutant-General.

Abstract from return of the Department of North Carolina, Maj. Gen. Ambrose E. Burnside commanding, for April, 1862.

Troops.	Present for duty.		Aggregate present.	Aggregate present and absent.
	Officers.	Men.		
1st Division	184	4,836	6,010	7,083
2d Division	152	4,381	5,335	6,099
3d Division	83	2,210	2,649	3,259
4th Brigade	80	2,128	2,534	2,701
Total	499	13,555	16,528	19,147

Organization of troops in the Department of North Carolina April 30, 1862.

Maj. Gen. AMBROSE E. BURNSIDE, commanding.

FIRST DIVISION.

Brig. Gen. JOHN G. FOSTER.

First Brigade.

17th Massachusetts, Col. T. J. C. Amory.
23d Massachusetts, Maj. A. Elwell.
25th Massachusetts, Col. Edwin Upton.

Second Brigade.

10th Connecticut, Lieut. Col. I. W. Pettibone.
24th Massachusetts, Col. T. G. Stevenson.
27th Massachusetts, Lieut. Col. L. Lyman.

ARTILLERY.

3d New York, Col. J. H. Ledlie.
1st Rhode Island, Battery F, Lieut. C. H. Pope.

SECOND DIVISION.

Brig. Gen. JESSE L. RENO.

First Brigade.

2d Maryland, Lieut. Col. J. E. Duryée.
103d New York, Col. F. W. Egloffstein.
48th Pennsylvania, Col. James Nagle.

Second Brigade.

11th Connecticut, Lieut. Col. Charles Mathewson.
21st Massachusetts, Lieut. Col. W. S. Clark.
51st New York, Col. Edward Ferrero.
51st Pennsylania, Col. J. F. Hartranft.

THIRD DIVISION.

Brig. Gen. JOHN G. PARKE.

8th Connecticut, Col. Edward Harland.
9th New Jersey, Col. Charles A. Heckman.
4th Rhode Island, Col. I. P. Rodman.

5th Rhode Island (battalion), Maj. John Wright.
1st U. S. Artillery, Battery C, Capt. L. O. Morris.

FOURTH BRIGADE.

Col. RUSH C. HAWKINS.

6th New Hampshire, Lieut. Col. S. G. Griffin.

9th New York, Lieut. Col. E. A. Kimball.
89th New York, Col. H. S. Fairchild.

U. S. STEAMER STATE OF GEORGIA,
May 1, 1862.

General AMBROSE E. BURNSIDE,
Commanding Department of North Carolina, New Berne:

GENERAL: I am now having four companies Eighth Connecticut placed on board the Highland Light, and expect to have him start for New Berne this p. m. The other companies have not yet reached Morehead City.

The Union has not yet arrived. As soon as she does I will start the balance of the regiment.

The Fourth Rhode Island is now quartered in Beaufort.

I have made Colonel Rodman military governor of the Beaufort district, and Major Allen provost-marshal.

Captain Morris' and Captain Ammon's companies are now in the fort.

The guns and mortars from our batteries have been brought to the fort.

Our camp on the Banks is by degrees being broken up. I am having everything there brought down to the fort and everything at Carolina City brought down to Morehead.

I keep the two launches on picket duty up Bogue Sound toward Swansborough.

I am informed that the rebel cavalry are still in that vicinity, and I would particularly request that a gunboat be sent through Bogue Inlet into White Oak River, and directed to keep a lookout for the rebels in that quarter.

The Chippewa has returned, having delivered her prisoners to a rebel steamer near Fort Caswell. While there Captain Bryson learned that the Nashville had run into New Inlet on the 26th. On the 24th she started in and ran aground, and for some unaccountable reason she was permitted to remain there until sufficiently lightened to pass inside the bar. She is reported to have 16,000 stand of arms and a tremendous quantity of gunpowder. Awful, is it not?

Well, can't we take Fort Caswell and the adjacent batteries? I believe we can.

Captain Bryson, of the Chippewa, has furnished me with a copy of the statement of two deserters from Fort Caswell. I inclose copy.

1 p. m.—The Union has just arrived, with the cattle and potatoes. The Highland Light has not got under way as yet. There is much trouble in bringing the troops and baggage over from the Banks to Morehead City. I will start her off as soon as she gets four companies on board.

To-morrow the Chippewa goes to Cape Fear River. The State of Georgia follows in a day or two and the bark Gemsbok goes to Hampton Roads. This will leave only one vessel here, the Daylight, Captain Lockwood. Now, I sincerely hope Commodore Rowan will send one of his vessels to the White Oak and Swansborough district. It will be of immense service all around.

The citizens of Beaufort are after me on the negro question. They want me to prevent the slaves from coming within our lines. I tell them I can use no force to aid them in recovering their negroes; at the same time, if they can prevail on the negroes to go home, I am perfectly willing and satisfied. I can furnish them no aid or assistance, and at the same time will not permit any disturbance in camp.

Yours, faithfully,

JNO. G. PARKE.

P. S.—The Chippewa and State of Georgia both go to Cape Fear, and the Gemsbok goes North. This will leave only one steamer here. The gunboats will take all the coal now here.

Please have another schooner sent.

HEADQUARTERS DEPARTMENT OF NORTH CAROLINA,
New Berne, N. C., May 3, 1862.

Hon. E. M. STANTON,
Secretary of War, Washington, D. C.:

SIR: I have the honor to report that the only thing of moment that has occurred since the fall of Fort Macon was a skirmish that occurred between three or four companies of the enemy's cavalry and 30 or 40 of our men, temporarily mounted, under the command of Colonel Egloffstein, of the One hundred and third New York, which resulted in a loss on our side of 1 private killed and Colonel Egloffstein and 2 privates wounded. The colonel was shot in the leg just below the knee, making a painful wound, which will probably disable him from service for some three months. The rebels were dispersed, with a loss of 3 killed, 8 wounded, and 3 taken prisoners. We captured 5 horses with full cavalry equipments. Our pickets are constantly annoyed by the enemy's cavalry, and we have this week lost 2 killed and 3 prisoners. Our losses in these little rencounters are more than compensated for by the losses of the enemy. Our infantry pickets compete remarkably well with the enemy's cavalry, and had we one cavalry regiment here I feel sure that we could keep the two cavalry regiments of the enemy which are now in our front at a respectful distance, and at the proper time would drive in every one of their outposts. We look with great anxiety for the arrival of the cavalry and light artillery ordered here. All the troops destined for this department can be transported to Beaufort Harbor in large vessels and landed at the wharf at Morehead City, where there is some 17 or 18 feet of water. We are repairing Fort Macon as rapidly as possible, and I am gradually withdrawing General Parke's (First) brigade to this place, with a view to leaving some five companies in Fort Macon and five in the town of Beaufort and Morehead City as guards. The main fort on the outskirts of this town is now about finished, and the smaller fort, which will complete the line of fortifications, is commenced. These forts are built not only with a view to hold the place with a small force, but to give occupation to the hundreds of negroes that are flocking to us. They will make our base more secure, and thereby add greatly to our strength in an advanced movement into the interior.

By the next mail I hope to forward you the detailed report of General Parke of the siege of Fort Macon, and at the same time I will forward to the Department a more intelligible statement of our condition, strength, and resources.

The three definite objects of my expedition have been accomplished, and the remaining ones were necessarily left to a certain extent to my discretion, as it was impossible to predict all the changes that might occur in the mean time. Of course I do not consider my work as finished, and shall be glad to receive more definite instructions, if the interests of the service require it. My own view is, that a movement upon Goldsborough and Raleigh in force is the proper one, and I am quite sure that General McClellan is of the same opinion. With these two places in our possession, Wilmington and Fort Caswell will surely be taken in time; but I will speak of this matter more fully in my next.

The health of the command is improving, but our ranks are still slim, and I hope the Department will deem it for the interest of the service to request the Governors of the States of New Hampshire, Massachusetts, Connecticut, New York, New Jersey, Pennsylvania, Maryland, and Rhode Island to send us recruits enough to fill our regiments to the maximum standard.

I have the honor to be, sir, very respectfully, your obedient servant,
                                    A. E. BURNSIDE,
        Major-General, Commanding Department of North Carolina.

HEADQUARTERS DEPARTMENT OF NORTH CAROLINA,
                                    New Berne, May 5, 1862.
Hon. E. M. STANTON,
        Secretary of War, Washington, D. C.:

SIR: I have the honor to report that since my last dispatch one of General Parke's regiments, the Eighth Connecticut, has been transferred to this place from Beaufort, and I shall at once order up the Fourth Rhode Island, leaving the Fifth Rhode Island Battalion at Beaufort and Fort Macon as garrison.

From information obtained through our spies I am satisfied that the force in the neighborhood of Kinston and Goldsborough is diminishing rather than increasing, and had we to-day a cavalry regiment and two batteries of artillery, and the locomotives, cars, and wagons required for, I should initiate a movement in that direction. We are expecting them hourly, and are convinced that nothing but the heavy requisitions upon the different Departments has necessarily delayed their arrival.

General Ransom, formerly of the United States Cavalry, is posted 6 miles this side of Kinston with two regiments of infantry, two of cavalry, and one or two batteries of artillery of six pieces each, with no intrenchments other than abatis. General Branch is posted at Kinston and its neighborhood with four regiments of infantry and one or two batteries of artillery; he and Ransom together having just three batteries of artillery, but we have not been able to ascertain positively which has the two batteries.

General Holmes, late of the U. S. Army, commands the department, and has his headquarters at Goldsborough. The force in that neighborhood is variously estimated at from 5,000 to 15,000. I am satisfied that the lower number is the nearest to the absolute fact.

The possession of Beaufort Harbor renders the transportation of troops to this department very easy, and if a movement in force into the interior, with a view to occupying Goldsborough and Raleigh and thereby cutting off the retreat of the rebels, who will in all probability be dispersed by General McClellan, be desirable, the necessary force can easily be brought to this point, and I am not sure that the object cannot be accomplished with the re-enforcements of cavalry and artillery already ordered to this point; but I shall make no hazardous movement until I hear more definitely from the Department or of the result of the movement before Yorktown.

Your kind letter of the 25th ultimo warrants me in remaining on the defensive until such time as I think that my force here can be used as an auxiliary or a diversion. In the mean time I would be glad to receive any re-enforcements that it may be found for the interests of the service to send me, in order that I may carry out more active field operations. I am becoming more convinced every day of the importance of occupying Goldsborough and Raleigh; you will readily see the reason for this conviction; but I would not, if I could, disturb the organization of the forces of the different columns now moving upon the enemy, unless it was for the interest of the public service.

In the first part of my dispatch I stated that I believed that the force in front of us was diminishing rather than increasing. My reason for coming to this conclusion is that one of our spies informed me this evening that General Branch was to leave with a considerable portion of his brigade for Virginia. If this statement should be confirmed and the cavalry and artillery should arrive I may make a movement in that direction, and I hope that whatever the result may be the Department will not consider that I am transcending my orders.

Another mail will leave here to-morrow, by which I will send a dispatch.

We are very much in need of the locomotives, cars, and wagons required for, all of which can now be sent to Beaufort Harbor in heavy-draught vessels.

Should it be deemed advisable to send re-enforcements to this department I hope it will be done with a view to leaving Generals Foster, Reno, and Parke in command of divisions. By their untiring industry and gallantry they deserve to remain as permanent commanders in this department; without them the work that has been done here could not have been accomplished. I have already recommended them to the Department for promotion, and hope it may be found for the interest of the public service to grant the request.

I have authorized the organization of the First North Carolina Union Volunteers. The movement was initiated by the Union men in and about Washington, and I have encouraged it to the extent of feeding, clothing, and arming the ——— vicinity, and have promised to recommend to the Department that they be mustered and paid. Captain Potter, General Foster's chief commissary, has been appointed colonel, and Mr. Respess, whose father was mayor of Washington and is now in prison in Richmond, has been appointed lieutenant-colonel. I hope that the regiment will be filled up within a very short time, but would not for a moment try to impress the Department with the idea that it will be done. I shall do all in my power to accomplish it, and trust my action will meet with the approval of the Government.

I have the honor to be, your obedient servant,

A. E. BURNSIDE,
Major-General, Commanding Department of North Carolina.

BEAUFORT, *May* 5—9.30 p. m.

[General AMBROSE E. BURNSIDE:]

MY DEAR GENERAL: The adjutant of the Ninth New Jersey has just come in with a man from near Newport Bridge, who brings in the report that the enemy is crossing the White Oak Creek in force from Swansborough.

I wrote you by the adjutant, who has started on his return to Newport, and directed him to forward the letter to you.

As the Allison did not get off to-day, as was expected, I will dispatch her early to-morrow morning with this.

The man who brings the report is a Union man, named Gainer, and he gets his information from a paroled prisoner by the name of Jones, who lives about 6 miles to the westward of Newport Bridge.

Jones says: "We will see hot work about Newport Bridge before Saturday night; that 10,000 troops are crossing from Swansborough."

Now I can't believe any such story, but I should like to feel sure that it is all false. I have requested the colonel of the Ninth New Jersey to send out a scout and inform you directly of the result.

I will see Commander Lockwood and request him to keep his steamer near Morehead City, and I told the Ninth New Jersey that if they were too hotly pressed to fall back on Morehead.

It may be that the rebels at Wilmington have armed the militia and drafted men with the arms brought in by the Nashville, and are marching there in hopes of again destroying the Newport Bridge.

I will send the Little Union up the Sound to-morrow. A gunboat in White Oak Creek would fix this whole business and make me feel perfectly easy, and a squadron of cavalry would now be of infinite service.

A paroled officer applied to me to-day for permission to go with his wife to Swansborough. In course of conversation he said that he expected to be exchanged in a week. It may be that this fellow has heard of a probable advance from Swansborough.

Faithfully, yours,

JNO. G. PARKE.

FORT MONROE, VA., *May* 11, 1862.

Major-General BURNSIDE:

DEAR SIR: You will be pleased to learn that yesterday General Wool advanced with 5,000 men on Norfolk. The city surrendered, General Huger having withdrawn his force. We are now in possession of Norfolk and Portsmouth. This morning the rebels set fire to the Merrimac and blew her up. General Wool will throw an additional force of 2,000 men into Norfolk without delay.

I send you a copy of the last dispatch received—at 5 o'clock last evening—from General McClellan. We have been aware for some days that the enemy were contemplating the abandonment of Norfolk. General Huger continued there until yesterday with 5,000 men. Three days ago Commander Rodgers, with the Galena and two other gunboats, were sent up the James River toward Richmond to co-operate with McClellan. When last heard from yesterday they were "picking their way slowly up." The Monitor and Stevens will be sent up to-day.

General Wool proposes without delay to move on to Suffolk, and would be glad to co-operate with you by your advancing, if you deem it prudent, to Weldon and seizing the railroad there.

We have no certain intelligence in respect to the movements of the rebels southward. A large force is no doubt in front of General McClellan. Whether they will give him battle at or in front of Richmond you can as well judge as any one else. The co-operation of yourself and General Wool must undoubtedly produce favorable results, and communication between you and him should be established at the earliest possible moment.

My last advices from Corinth were three days ago, at which time a severe battle between the forces of Beauregard and Halleck was impending. It has no doubt taken place by this time. Such, at least, is my impression.

Captain Richmond informs me that the cavalry you sent for were arriving, and that you need more infantry. I regret to say that the Government has not at this moment any troops that can be sent you. Generals McClellan and Halleck are both urgent for re-enforcements, which cannot be given. When your cavalry and artillery arrive nothing further can be sent until the recruits are raised.

The co-operation of yourself and General Wool and the operations to be conducted by you are left to your discretion under the circumstances in which you may be placed. Frequent advices are desired. The President, Secretary Chase, and I have been here five days, and expect to return to-day.

Yours, truly,

EDWIN M. STANTON,
Secretary of War.

[Inclosure.]

CAMP 19 MILES FROM WILLIAMSBURG,
May 10, 1862.

Hon. E. M. STANTON, *Secretary of War :*

I have fully established my connection with the troops near West Point, and the dangerous movement has passed. The West Point Railway is not very much injured; materials for repairs, such as rails &c., cars, and engines may now be sent to me. Should Norfolk be taken and the Merrimac destroyed I can change my line to the James River and dispense with the railroad. I shall probably occupy New Kent in force to-morrow and then make my first preparations for battle. As it is, my troops are in advance of their supplies. I must so arrange my depot that we can follow up success. When at New Kent I will be in position to make a thorough examination of the country, so as to act understandingly. General Johnston cannot well be in front of Frémont for two reasons: First, he has no business there; Second, I know that I fought him on Monday, and that he is now on the Chickahominy. I have used his vacated headquarters from day to day. He is certainly in command here with all the troops he can gather. Two or three more of the cavalry regiments I left on the Potomac would be very acceptable. I am overworking what I have.

GEO. B. McCLELLAN,
Major-General.

HEADQUARTERS DEPARTMENT OF NORTH CAROLINA,
New Berne, May 16, 1862.

Hon. E. M. STANTON,
Secretary of War, Washington, D. C.:

SIR: I have the honor to acknowledge the receipt of yours of the 11th instant by the hand of Captain Richmond.

After dispatching him to Old Point Comfort from Oregon Inlet I visited Elizabeth City, and sent other spies up through the country, from whom I learned that Norfolk had been evacuated and occupied by General Wool, and upon the receipt of your dispatch I immediately returned to this place with a view to making arrangements for a move upon Weldon by way of Winton. I expected to find the horses and wagons for which I had required at this place, but as yet none have arrived. They are absolutely necessary to me in order to move into the

interior either from Winton or from here.   From the loss of horses dur-
the storms at Hatteras our means of transportation were much reduced,
and we could not move now with more than 20 to 25 wagons after the
different posts occupied by me have been supplied.   You will readily
see that this would be entirely inadequate, as it would not carry the
ammunition necessary, to say nothing of the cooking utensils, commissary supplies, and forage.   I should not wait for means of transporting
tents, baggage, &c., as at this season of the year they could easily be
dispensed with.   Had we the cars and engines that have been required
for, a movement might be initiated in the direction of Goldsborough
and Raleigh. None of the re-enforcements sent to me brought any means
of transportation. You will remember these requisitions were sent in
immediately after our arrival in New Berne.

I beg you will not think these remarks are made in a complaining
spirit, for I am fully conscious of the heavy draughts that have been
made on the different bureaus in your Department, and often wonder
how you have accomplished so much.

Forces like mine, which are occupying position to hold the enemy in
check or to create diversions, should be entirely subservient of course
to the great armies in the East and West that are now in front of the
enemy, and I again beg that you will not feel that my frequent requisitions for re-enforcements and transportation are made in any other
spirit than that of a desire to be useful.

I am on the eve of ordering some small movements, in conjunction
with the Navy, up the Chowan River, thus threatening the enemy's communications, and have already ordered a reconnaissance through the
Dismal Swamp Canal with a view to opening communication with
General Wool through that channel.   There are no troops along it, except a few militia pickets, but it is understood that the banks have
been cut and the water let out between some of the locks.   As it has
turned out, it is very fortunate that the locks were not destroyed by General Reno, as they will prove useful to us now in communicating with
Norfolk.

I shall write General Wool by this mail, and if upon hearing from
him it may be deemed advisable for us to make a junction or co-operate
with each other I will act accordingly. Everything depends, however,
upon the position occupied by General McClellan's forces. If, as I believe,
he is in Richmond, and the enemy in full retreat southward—the transportation necessary for a movement into the interior will not be so great,
as a junction will very soon be formed with the main body, unless the
enemy should retreat in such force as to drive us back. We are anxiously waiting dispatches from Old Point Comfort.

Day before yesterday I sent out two parties in the direction of Trenton and Kinston—one on the north and one on the south side of the
Trent River—for the purpose of driving in the enemy's pickets and outposts and ascertaining their strength. A brisk skirmish ensued on the
north side, upon which we killed 1 lieutenant and 9 privates and took
2 prisoners.   Our loss was 1 lieutenant and 4 privates taken prisoners
and 1 officer wounded—Major Fitzsimmons, of the Third New York Cavalry. Their outposts were driven in, and quarters, stables, &c., destroyed. The party on the south side of the river met with a large force
of cavalry, and a skirmish, ensued in which we killed 1 rebel captain
and wounded several of their men, without sustaining any loss on our
side. The force is just returning to its camp, but I have not yet learned
the exact result of the reconnaissance.

In my next I will give you the details of this reconnaissance. I have not been well for a few days past, otherwise would have sent this mail off before. To-morrow I hope to be out as usual.

I have the honor to be, your very obedient servant,

A. E. BURNSIDE,
Major-General, Commanding Department of North Carolina.

HEADQUARTERS DEPARTMENT OF NORTH CAROLINA,
New Berne, May 17, 1862.

General GEORGE B. MCCLELLAN,
Commanding the Army of the Potomac:

GENERAL: I heard of your victories at Williamsburg and West Point, the evacuation of Norfolk, and the destruction of the Merrimac while I was on a visit to Roanoke Island and Elizabeth City, and I immediately returned to this place with the hope of finding the engines cars, and wagons required for immediately after the battle of New Berne, but none have yet arrived.

I am very much crippled for want of land transportation. I could not to-day muster a train of 25 wagons, which you know would not be sufficient to carry my ammunition, and, as you see, it would be almost fatal for me to make a move into the interior before they arrive.

I am anxiously awaiting dispatches from you before attempting another move. Everything is quiet in this vicinity, and I think the rebel force at Kinston, Raleigh, and Goldsborough are about the same as when I last wrote. The health of the command is improving.

Capt. Thomas P. Ives will bear this dispatch to you.

Most heartily congratulating you on your brilliant success, I remain, general, your most obedient servant,

A. E. BURNSIDE,
Major-General, Commanding Department of North Carolina.

HEADQUARTERS DEPARTMENT OF NORTH CAROLINA,
New Berne, May 19, 1862.

Hon. E. M. STANTON,
Secretary of War, Washington, D. C.:

SIR: I have the honor to report that since the sending of my last dispatch I have received accurate reports from the commanders of the reconnoitering parties in the direction of Kinston. Our exact loss was 2 wounded and 7 prisoners. That of the enemy was 11 killed and 15 or 20 wounded and 4 prisoners.

It was ascertained by this reconnaissance that the enemy had on the south side of the Trent River, in the neighborhood of Trenton, about 1,500 cavalry. The road from that place to Kinston is very heavily picketed, the main body being in and beyond Kinston, under the command of Ransom.

The force at Kinston and Goldsborough will probably concentrate, in case we advance up the country, at Falling Creek, about 7 miles above Kinston, on the railroad, at which point they are building some light breastworks, but are putting no heavy guns in position. Goldsborough is not being fortified at all, but we learn that Raleigh has been. The force on this line at this time, as near as we can learn, is two regiments of cavalry, four light batteries, and some fifteen regiments of infantry. This does not include any of the force along the Weldon and Wilmington Railroad, which just now is very considerable, all the bridges being very heavily guarded.

Our engines, cars, &c., have not yet arrived. A portion of the wagons have come in, but none of the horses or harness.

I have heard nothing from Roanoke Island or that neighborhood for two or three days.

My medical director is establishing a general hospital at Beaufort, to which point all the serious cases will be transported as soon as possible. The location is much more healthy than this, and by concentrating the sick in one general hospital there it will require fewer surgeons to attend them. A large hotel there has been appropriated to that purpose. Could I have known that the delay here in the arrival of transportation would have been so great, I think I would have made a demonstration against Fort Caswell which might have resulted in its fall. However, both Wilmington and Fort Caswell can easily be taken if we once get possession of Goldsborough and Raleigh.

I have been on the eve several times of expressing the opinion to you, which if correct is of great importance, but have hesitated to do it, fearing that I may not be correct. It is this: The Convention in this State is divided in opinion as to the present mode of action to such an extent that it failed to take any action at all when it last met, preferring to await the issue of the great events that are now transpiring. I am satisfied that, if the rebel army in Virginia is either captured or dispersed or forced to retreat beyond the lines of this State, the State will at once return to its allegiance through its Convention by a considerable majority. There is much true loyalty here, and all the people are heartily sick of the war, and are very much exercised lest their own State should be made the next battle ground. They have been taught that the institution of slavery, which their leaders have made them believe is a great element of strength, is in fact an element of weakness. Wherever the Union arms have made a lodgment they have lost the entire control of their slaves, and they are quite convinced that, if the slave States formed a recognized government independent of the North, we would not make war upon them with the same leniency that we do now, but would use this element against them with very great success.

The arrival of Governor Stanley will, I hope, do a great deal of good. You are looking at this subject of course in all its bearings upon the different sections of the country, and will give to these opinions only the weight they deserve.

In the absence of definite instructions upon the subject of fugitive slaves I have adopted the following policy:

First. To allow all slaves who come to my lines to enter.

Second. To organize them and enroll them, taking their names, the names of their masters, and their place of residence.

Third. To give them employment as far as possible, and to exercise toward old and young a judicious charity.

Fourth. To deliver none to their owners under any circumstances, and allow none of them to leave this department until I receive your definite instructions.

To-morrow I shall go to Beaufort and Fort Macon, if I am well enough, and from thence to Roanoke and the Chowan River, unless I should hear something definite from Fortress Monroe which requires my immediate attention here.

I was not as well when I last wrote you as I thought, and have consequently had to remain indoors, but I feel now that I am quite recovered.

I have the honor to be, very respectfully, your obedient servant,

A. E. BURNSIDE,
Major-General, Commanding Department of North Carolina.

HEADQUARTERS FIRST BRIGADE,
Pamlico, May 19, 1862.

General AMBROSE E. BURNSIDE,
Commanding U. S. Troops, New Berne, N. C.:

GENERAL: In reply to your letter of yesterday (but dated 17th instant *) I have the honor to state that your request shall at once be communicated to the General Commanding our troops, and, if acceded to, the parties desiring to return to New Berne will be speedily forwarded by flag of truce. Permit me to state that I have no doubt that every act consistent with public safety will be reciprocated on our part.

I have the honor to be, very respectfully, your obedient servant,

R. RANSOM, JR.,
Brigadier-General, C. S. Army.

WAR DEPARTMENT,
Washington City, D. C., May 20, 1862.

Major-General BURNSIDE, *Commanding, &c.:*

GENERAL: I have the pleasure of presenting to you the Hon. Edward Stanley, who has been appointed Military Governor of the State of North Carolina.

The nature and extent of Governor Stanley's authority and jurisdiction are expressed in his commission, which will be exhibited to you. Between him and yourself the President expects cordial co-operation for the restoration of the authority of the Federal Government. The province of Governor Stanley is to establish and maintain, under military form, the functions of civil government until the loyal inhabitants of North Carolina shall be able to assert their constitutional rights and privileges.

In order to maintain peace and enforce respect the Governor must be supported by a sufficient military force, to be detailed by you from your command, and report to him and act under his direction.

You will please detail such force as may be adequate for this purpose, to be designated as a Governor's Guard, and to be commanded by a competent officer. You will also, at all times, upon the Governor's requisition, support his authority and enforce his orders by a military force competent for the occasion.

The well-known patriotism and discretion for which the Governor and yourself are distinguished render it superfluous to give any further general instructions. The President expects from your harmonious and intelligent action the most favorable results.

With great respect, I am, yours, &c.,

EDWIN M. STANTON,
Secretary of War.

---

* Not found.

HEADQUARTERS OF THE ARMY,
Tunstall's Station, May 21, 1862.

Maj. Gen. AMBROSE E. BURNSIDE,
Commanding Department of North Carolina :

·MY DEAR BURN. : Your dispatch and kind letter received. I have instructed Seth to reply to the official letter and now acknowledge the kind private note. It always does me good, in the midst of my cares and perplexities, to see your wretched old scrawling. I have terrible troubles to contend with, but have met them with a good heart, like your good old self, and have thus far struggled through successfully. Our progress has been slow, but that is due to ignorance of the country (we have to feel our way everywhere; the maps are worthless), the narrowness, small number, and condition of the roads, which become impassable for trains after a day's rain, of which we have had a great deal.

I feel very proud of Yorktown; it and Manassas will be my brightest chaplets in history; for I know that I accomplished everything in both places by pure military skill. I am very proud and grateful to God that he allowed me to purchase such great success at so trifling a loss of life. We came near being badly beaten at Williamsburg. I arrived on the field at 5 p. m. and found that all thought we were whipped and in for a disaster. You would have been glad to see, old fellow, how the men cheered and brightened up when they saw me. In five minutes after I reached the ground a possible defeat was changed into certain victory. The greatest moral courage I ever exercised was that night, when, in the face of urgent demands from almost all quarters for re-enforcements to hold our own, I quietly *sent back* the troops I had ordered up before I reached the field. I was sure that Johnston would leave during the night if he understood his business, or that I could be able to thrash him in the morning by a proper use of the force I had. It turned out that Jo. left ! Hancock conducted himself magnificently ; his charge was elegant !

I expect to fight a desperate battle in front of Richmond, and against superior numbers, somewhat intrenched. The Government have deliberately placed me in this position. If I win, the greater the glory. If I lose, they will be damned forever, both by God and men.

Well, I have bored you long enough, old fellow. I will merely add that my light troops have crossed the Chickahominy at Bottom's Bridge this morning, 10 miles from Richmond, and that the advanced guard, under Stoneman, has driven in everything upon New Bridge (on my right), 6 miles from Richmond. The crisis cannot long be deferred. I pray for God's blessing on our arms, and rely far more on his goodness than I do on my own poor intellect. I sometimes think now that I can almost realize that Mahomet was sincere. When I see the hand of God guarding one so weak as myself, I can almost think myself a chosen instrument to carry out his schemes. Would that a better man had been selected.*

       *   *   *   *   *   *   *

If I thrash these rascals we will soon be in direct communication, and I shall then wish to give you a command from this army to add to the noble men you now have.

Good-by, and God bless you, Burn. With the sincere hope that we may soon shake hands, I am, as ever, your sincere friend,
McCLELLAN.

---

*Some personal matter omitted.

HEADQUARTERS ARMY OF THE POTOMAC,
Camp near Tunstall's Station, Va., May 21, 1862.

Maj. Gen. AMBROSE E. BURNSIDE,
Commanding Department of North Carolina, New Berne:

GENERAL: By direction of the general commanding I have the honor to acknowledge the receipt of your dispatch of the 17th instant and to communicate the following in reply:

Assuming your force to be about 15,000, in the event of a movement on Winton, &c., you would probably have to leave at least 5,000 in New Berne, 1,000 as a railway guard, 1,000 at Beaufort and Fort Macon, 500 at Hatteras Inlet, and 1,000 at Roanoke, making 8,500 in all, and leaving not more than 6,000 to 6,500 men for active operations, a force too small to do much good; but by operating on Goldsborough, you would have to leave only, say, 1,000 at Roanoke, 500 at Beaufort, and 1,000 at New Berne, giving you 12,500 available in the field. The general, therefore, thinks that a cautious yet bold advance on Goldsborough as soon as the necessary transportation arrives would produce a better effect, and would neutralize a larger portion of the enemy's force than any other movement you could make.

We are moving on steadily and as rapidly as the state of the roads hitherto, supplies, and the necessity for extended reconnaissances have allowed. Our light troops crossed the Chickahominy early this morning at Bottom's Bridge and the railway bridge (both of which had been burnt) without meeting the enemy, but we have as yet no reliable intelligence of his position or movements. A heavy force will be thrown across without delay.

Everything goes to show that the enemy is before us in superior force, perhaps double our own available strength at present, and the general is still of the opinion that they will make a decided stand this side of Richmond, as is evidently their best policy. But even should they abandon Richmond, it may well be to offer battle at some point farther South in Virginia and off the navigable streams.

We command the navigation of the James River up to Wall's Bluff, on the other bank, about 8 miles below Richmond, where the gunboats were repulsed on the 15th.

You are probably informed that General McDowell was ordered on the 17th to move on Richmond by the line of the Fredericksburg Railway and to effect a junction with this army on our right, keeping his forces always so as to cover the line of approach to Washington. McDowell will bring from 35,000 to 40,000 men with him.

Very respectfully, your obedient servant,
S. WILLIAMS,
Assistant Adjutant-General.

HEADQUARTERS DEPARTMENT OF NORTH CAROLINA,
New Berne, May 28, 1862.

Hon. E. M. STANTON,
Secretary of War, Washington:

SIR: I have the honor to report that Governor Stanley arrived at this port night before last, and is fast making his arrangements to assume the duties assigned to him. He handed me your letter of instructions to me, which I will most cheerfully obey to the best of my ability. I have consulted fully with the Governor, and find that our views in reference to the course that should be adopted in this State by the General Government are remarkably coincident, and you may be sure that I will grant him every facility in my power to carry out these views. His arrival here is a source of very great relief to me, as there are many civil cases here that require early attention. In a few days I will be able to report to you more definitely the arrangements made to carry out the instructions to the Governor and myself.

You will have seen in the papers that his brother was arrested by my forces a few days ago. Upon investigation of the charges upon which he was arrested I was very glad to find they were not of a sufficiently serious nature to require his detention, and I therefore released him the day before the Governor's arrival. The prisoners brought by him from Washington City have been sent to their homes under a flag of truce. We are now receiving our prisoners from Salisbury, N. C., at the rate of 200 per day. They will be forwarded to New York with the least possible delay. There will be some 1,300 non-commissioned officers and privates in all. General Holmes, the rebel commander in this State, has no authority to release the commissioned officers confined in Salisbury, among whom are Colonels Corcoran and Willcox. I shall continue my efforts in their behalf, and do not despair of obtaining for them an early release.

I shall send by the steamer carrying the prisoners duplicate rolls, one to yourself, the other to Colonel Tompkins, chief quartermaster, New York City. Would it not be well to send from your office by telegraph instructions to Colonel Tompkins to furnish these men with immediate transportation to their homes?

Nothing of importance has occurred in a military way in this department since my last dispatch. We are anxiously waiting the result of General McClellan's movement before Richmond.

None of our teams or locomotives have yet arrived.

I have the honor to be, sir, very respectfully, your obedient servant,
A. E. BURNSIDE,
Major-General, Commanding Department of North Carolina.

HEADQUARTERS DEPARTMENT OF NORTH CAROLINA,
New Berne, May 30, 1862.

Hon. E. M. STANTON,
Secretary of War, Washington, D. C.:

SIR: I have the honor to report that during the last week the naval force in these waters has been reduced by sending two vessels (the Underwriter and the Valley City) North for repairs, and by ordering two (the Delaware and Southfield) to join Flag-Officer Goldsborough on the James River.

I am not disposed to question the wisdom of these orders, but I deem it my duty to remind you that we hold, by means of the military and naval force here, all the towns in these waters, and if the number of naval vessels is to be diminished, it will be necessary to vacate some of the places. In every place that has been visited by either the Army or Navy some Union feeling has been displayed, and in some of the places the American flag has been hoisted upon the public buildings by citizens of their own volition, and it would be manifest injustice to leave these people without a protecting force to the oppression of the rebel Government.

Without wishing to complain of the Navy Department, which has done so much for our cause in these waters, I beg that you will remind the Secretary of the Navy of these facts, and request that, as far as the interest of the public service will allow, the naval force under Commodore Rowan be strengthened rather than weakened.

In my previous communication I rather exceeded my province by stating that Governor Stanley's views and my own, as to the policy the Government wished to adopt in this State, "were remarkably coincident." It would have been quite enough for me to have said that Governor Stanley, being the representative of the Government here, will be sustained by all the force under my control. You will readily see that the civil policy to be adopted by him will cover a very wide range, and may in many cases not be in accordance with the views of a majority of the people under my command; but we are here to sustain the Government, and as long as Governor Stanley is its representative his wishes shall be carried out at any cost.

I avail myself of the departure of one of the naval vessels to send you this hasty dispatch, and I beg that you will not understand by it that any disagreement has occurred between the Governor and myself, for I simply want to avoid the trouble that may arise from an uncalled-for indorsement of future events, of which I necessarily know so little.

I am sorry again to report that none of our engines, cars, &c., have arrived.

I have the honor to be, your obedient servant,

A. E. BURNSIDE,
Major-General.

————

WASHINGTON, *June* 3, 1862.

Major-General BURNSIDE,
  Care of General Dix, New Berne via Fort Monroe:

Your dispatches of May 19, 23, and 30 have been received. A copy of the last-mentioned dispatch has been communicated to the Secretary of the Navy and also to the President. The Quartermaster-General informs me that the locomotives and cars, to wit, four locomotives and fifty cars, have been shipped to you from Baltimore on fifteen schooners. General Wool has been transferred to Baltimore. General Dix takes his place. The troops at Old Point are probably taken by General McClellan. You will please place yourself in communication with General Dix. I will communicate more fully by mail.

EDWIN M. STANTON,
Secretary of War.

————

WAR DEPARTMENT,
Washington City, June 3, 1862.

Hon. EDWARD STANLEY,
  Military Governor of North Carolina, New Berne, N. C.:

SIR: The House of Representatives of the United States on the 2d instant adopted a resolution of which the following is a copy:

Resolved, That the President of the United States be requested to communicate to this House— .

First. What powers have been conferred upon Hon. Edward Stanley, as Military Governor of North Carolina, or as the agent of the Government in said State, under the appointment of the President.

Second. Whether the said Edward Stanley has interfered to prevent the education of children, white or black, in said State; and if so, by what authority, if any?

Third. If the said Edward Stanley has been instructed by the Government to prevent such education, to what extent and for what purpose were such instructions given.

The President has referred the resolution to this Department for reply, but as it has no information touching the matter covered by the second of the above inquiries, you are hereby requested to furnish the Department with a full and immediate answer to the same.

I am, very respectfully, your obedient servant,

EDWIN M. STANTON,
Secretary of War.

————

NAVY DEPARTMENT,
June 4, 1862.

Hon. E. M. STANTON, *Secretary of War :*

SIR: I have the honor to acknowledge the receipt of your letter of the 2d instant, inclosing copy of a part of a dispatch from General Burnside, commanding the Department of North Carolina.

It is not known at this Department what places in North Carolina are occupied by General Burnside and therefore liable to be vacated by him upon the withdrawal of part of the naval force, but it is believed that the enemy's force both naval and military in those waters is dispersed and destroyed, and the large number of steamers used to accomplish this cannot now all be required there, more especially as an urgent call has been made upon this Department for an increase of force in the Virginia waters. There remain in the North Carolina waters, after the withdrawal complained of by General Burnside, seventeen naval vessels.

I am, respectfully, your obedient servant,

GIDEON WELLES.

————

WAR DEPARTMENT,
Washington City, D. C., June 4, 1862.

The PRESIDENT:

SIR: In answer to a resolution of the House of Representatives, dated on the 2d of June, in relation to the power conferred on the Military Governor of North Carolina, I have the honor to state:

1. That a copy of the letter of appointment and instructions to Governor Stanley are hereto annexed.

2. That Governor Stanley has not been instructed by the Government to prevent the education of children, white or black, in the State of North Carolina.

3. That this Department has no official information that Governor Stanley has interfered to prevent the education of white or black children in said State, but that a copy of the resolution of the House has been transmitted to him for report upon his action on the subject, which, when received, will be communicated to you.

Your obedient servant,

EDWIN M. STANTON,
Secretary of War.

[Inclosure No. 1.]

WAR DEPARTMENT,
May 19, 1862.

Hon. EDWARD STANLEY, *&c., &c., &c.,*
Washington, D. C. :

SIR: You are hereby appointed Military Governor of the State of North Carolina, with authority to exercise and perform, within the limits of that State, all and singular the powers, duties, and functions pertaining to the office of Military Governor (including the power to establish all necessary offices and tribunals and suspend the writ of habeas corpus) during the pleasure of the President or until the loyal inhabitants of that State shall organize a civil government in conformity with the Constitution of the United States

EDWIN M. STANTON,
Secretary of War.

[Inclosure No. 2.]

WAR DEPARTMENT,
Washington City, D. C., May 20, 1862.

Hon. EDWARD STANLEY,
Military Governor of North Carolina :

SIR: The commission you have received expresses on its face the nature and extent of the duties and power devolved on you by the appointment [as] Military Governor of North Carolina.

Instructions have been given to Major-General Burnside to aid you in the performance of your duty and the extent of your authority. He has also been instructed to detail an adequate military force for the special purpose of a governor's guard and to act under your directions.

It is obvious to you that the great purpose of your appointment is to re-establish the authority of the Federal Government in the State of North Carolina and provide the means of maintaining peace and security to the loyal inhabitants of that State until they shall be able to establish a civil government.

Upon your wisdom and energetic action much will depend in accomplishing the result. It is not deemed necessary to give any specific instructions, but rather to confide in your sound discretion to adopt such measures as circumstances may demand. Specific instructions will be given when requested.

You may rely upon the perfect confidence and full support of the Department in the performance of your duties.

With respect, I am, your obedient servant,

EDWIN M. STANTON,
Secretary of War.

FORT MONROE, *June* 9, 1862—1.30 a. m.

Hon. E. M. STANTON, *Secretary of War :*

I learn here that Commodore Goldsborough has ordered two more gunboats out of our department, the Hunchback and Commodere Perry, two of our best vessels. When the other boats were taken away it created much alarm among the Union people who had made demonstration in our favor in the towns occupied by these boats. It will be disastrous to the Union cause in North Carolina if this policy is carried out. We should have more gunboats instead of less, but will be satisfied with what we have. Seven have already left us. I hope the President will deem it proper to direct by telegraph that this order be revoked; if sent here to me I will transmit it. I am sorry to learn that there is much feeling against Governor Stanley, but I hope the Government will await further developments before condemning him. He is doing much good. I wish I could communicate with you personally, and would, but for going so far from my department. General Dix has not troops enough now to co-operate with me against Weldon.

BURNSIDE.

FORT MONROE, *June* 9, 1862—8.05 a. m.

Hon. E. M. STANTON, *Secretary of War:*

In accordance with your dispatch, requesting me to communicate with General Dix, I thought it best to see him in person. Left my department at 5 p. m. yesterday and came through canal. Shall leave in two hours unless I get other orders from you. I meet General Dix in a few minutes and will telegraph result of conference. In the mean time will be glad to hear from you, and will give any information you may desire.

All quiet in my department. We had a small fight at Washington on Friday last, in which we were victorious.

A. E. BURNSIDE,
Major-General.

WASHINGTON, *June* 9, 1862.

Major-General BURNSIDE, *Fort Monroe:*

The President is now with me in the Department. We have nothing to communicate, but leave it to you and General Dix to make such military arrangements as you may deem expedient. We would be glad to be informed of the result of your conference. I wish also to know whether there is anything you desire that can be furnished by this Department. Have the cars and locomotives reached you? I would like to know confidentially from you by letter of Governor Stanley's operations and your opinion of them and what the facts really are.

EDWIN M. STANTON,
Secretary of War.

FORT MONROE, *June* 9, 1862—1 p. m.

Hon. E. M. STANTON:

Your telegram received. I have already telegraphed in reference to the co-operation of General Dix and myself. I also referred to Governor Stanley's policy. It is evidently misunderstood by the Northern people. Mr. Colyer has misrepresented the matter, if newspapers are correct. Governor Stanley is as sound on the Union question as you or I. In answer to a dispatch from me to General McClellan, stating that I was here, he says: "Can you not come up to see me in a special boat?" Shall I go?

A. E. BURNSIDE,
Major-General.

WASHINGTON, *June* 9, 1862.

Major-General BURNSIDE:

I think it would be desirable for you to see and confer with General McClellan, and you have the permission of the Department to do so if your own command does not require your presence. You will advise me before leaving Fort Monroe for New Berne, if convenient to do so.

EDWIN M. STANTON,
Secretary of War.

WASHINGTON, *June* 9, 1862.

Major-General BURNSIDE,
        Fort Monroe: .
    Your dispatch in relation to the gunboats has been laid before the President. He has directed the Hunchback and Perry to remain where they are, and that Goldsborough's order for their removal be countermanded. This I understand to be satisfactory to you. I should be glad to have a detailed statement of your force and its position.
                        EDWIN M. STANTON,
                                Secretary of War.

FORT MONROE, *June* 9, 1862—5 p. m.

Hon. E. M. STANTON,
        Secretary of War:
    Three regiments on Roanoke Island, one at Washington, one at Newport on railroad, and one and a half at Beaufort and Fort Macon; fourteen at New Berne. One regiment artillery and one regiment cavalry and three batteries divided along the different commands. A large portion of the force at New Berne is on picket duty. Regiments average 600 effective men. I leave for McClellan's at once. Will telegraph you before I return to New Berne.
                                BURNSIDE.

FORT MONROE, *June* 11, 1862—10.30 a. m.

Hon. E. M. STANTON,
        Secretary of War:
    I have just returned from McClellan's headquarters, where I passed about six hours. It stormed very hard all day. The roads are in the most wretched condition. I was four and a half hours traveling 9 miles. It is impossible to move artillery whilst they are so bad. But for the railroad, the army could not be subsisted and foraged. The general health was improving. The officers and men are in good spirits. I will write you fully of our consultation about co-operating. I would very much like a personal interview, but feel that I cannot remain away from my department any longer unless you desire it. I would be glad to get any instructions you may have by telegraph.
                                BURNSIDE.

    P. S.—Since writing the foregoing I have just heard from my department by a boat which left Roanoke at 7 o'clock last evening. Everything quiet.

HEADQUARTERS DEPARTMENT OF NORTH CAROLINA,
        New Berne, June 12, 1862.

Hon. E. M. STANTON,
        Secretary of War:
    SIR: Your letter of the 3d instant has not received the immediate answer you requested, because I was absent in Beaufort when it arrived. You send me a copy of the resolution adopted by the House of Rep-

resentatives on the 2d instant, and desire I should furnish the Department with a full and immediate answer to the following part of said resolution:

Second. Whether the said Edward Stanley has interfered to prevent the education of children, white or black, in said State; and, if so, by what authority, if any.

On the 31st day of May last I addressed you a letter, which I presume had not been received when you wrote on the 3d instant. In that letter of the 31st, in reference to matters here, I made the following observations:

The perplexing question of what is to be done with the negroes is constantly presenting itself. I have thus far managed it with discretion. Upon all occasions I say I have no hope of affording redress to the enemies of our country; that the Union is to be restored, cost what it may in blood and treasure, and this is a matter not to be argued.

One person came to me yesterday who had four slaves taken from him, and told they were free by a rude soldier, who cursed his wife. I suggested, first, he must take the oath of allegiance; this he agreed to do. Then I gave him authority to look for his property, advising him to use mildness and persuasion. He did so, and one servant voluntarily returned to the home of a kind master. This has already excited some evil-disposed persons and will be misrepresented.

Almost all the inhabitants have gone away and the belief still exists that it is dangerous for them to return.

The Confederates refuse to allow any persons to come to this place, keeping away even women and children. Unless I can give them some assurance that this is a war of restoration and not of abolition and destruction, no peace can be restored here for many years to come. I am making efforts to induce Union men to come and talk with me. I feel confident I shall be successful in a few weeks.

One person ventured to give me advice. I gave him at once permission to go to New York. The person whose impertinent meddling I rebuked is Mr. H. H. Helper.

A gentleman of good Samaritan inclinations and acts had established a school for negro children. He called and informed me what he was doing, and asked my opinion. I approved all he had done in feeding and clothing the destitute white and black, but told him I had been sent to restore the old order of things. I thought his negro school, if approved by me, would do harm to the Union cause. In a few months we shall know the result of the war. If by Southern folly emancipation comes, their spiritual welfare would not suffer by the delay, for I desired he would give such oral instructions in religious matters as he thought best.

Another reason I urged was, that by one of the cruel necessities of slavery the laws of North Carolina forbade slaves to be taught to read and write, and I would be most unsuccessful in my efforts if I encouraged the violation of her laws. He acquiesced, I thought, cheerfully. If the old residents ever return, those negroes who have been taught to read and write would be suspected and not benefited by it.

You have no idea how happy the influence has been on the minds of the excellent and severely-punished people of this lonely town. This school affair has already been much misrepresented.

This extract might be sufficient to answer the resolution, but as you request not only an immediate "but a full" answer, it may be proper to add something more.

To the extent mentioned I did interfere, and would most assuredly do so again under the same circumstances.

My authority for so doing was the only instruction given me in your communication of May 20, 1862, in the following words:

It is obvious to you that the great purpose of your appointment is to re-establish the authority of the Federal Government in the State of North Carolina and to provide the means of maintaining peace and security to the loyal inhabitants of that State.

I had these instructions in view when I made the suggestion relative to the negro school.

And in your letter to General Burnside, of date 20th of May, to which you referred me, you state:

The province of Governor Stanley is to re-establish and maintain, under military form, the functions of civil government, until the loyal inhabitants of North Carolina shall be able to assert their constitutional rights and privileges.

I ask to be instructed what "civil government" is here meant, and what are the "constitutional rights and privileges" of the loyal inhabitants of this State? If their property is destroyed or removed before peace is restored, what "rights and privileges" are they to expect?

In the interview with the manager of the schools I made use of no threats, used no discourteous language, and treated the gentleman referred to with all kindness. He called the next morning and informed me he had suspended teaching the negro children. I approved what he had done, but nothing approaching unpleasantness occurred during the interview, nor did the thought enter my mind I had given him offense. Not a word was said, nor any intimation given, of any intention to "enforce" the laws of this State. No such thought was in my mind nor ever can be.

I do not intend to be guilty of disrespect to the Secretary nor to betray too much sensitiveness, and will not therefore comment upon what seems to me to be unusual language in requesting an "immediate" answer.

My position is one of great responsibility. I am ready to meet it. I hope it is an honorable one. It certainly can bring no profit and is not unaccompanied with peril. I have great difficulties to overcome—greater than you suppose—and am entitled to all the confidence and support which I was assured I should have.

I believe the President to be sincere in his various public declarations, and wish to make the people of North Carolina believe him to be sincere and patriotic.

But I am grieved to say that some of the most eminent and influential of our citizens, from listening to oft-repeated slanders, have been persuaded and charge the Southern country is invaded by "an enemy who come to rob us, to murder our people, to emancipate our slaves, and who is now preparing to add a new element to this most atrocious aggression, and involve us in the direful horrors of a servile war. He proposes nothing less than our entire destruction, the total desolation of our country—universal emancipation; to crush us, to wipe out the South, to involve us in irredeemable misery and hopeless ruin."

Though I know all this is the effect of long-continued excitement, and not words of truth and soberness, but of passion and altogether incorrect in every particular, still they are the words of sincerity, from men of irreproachable lives, who denounced secession as treason down to the day when the North Carolina Convention passed the ordinance of secession.

If this idea, so monstrously incorrect, be in the minds of men of standing and influence, how must the large body of the people regard the action of the General Government?

In view of this most deplorable condition, I avail myself of the privilege I understood from you I should have of asking instructions upon the following points:

1. When slaves are taken from the possession of their loyal masters by violence offered by armed men and negroes, what redress shall be afforded to the owners and what protection for the future?

2. When persons connected with the Army prevail on negroes to leave their masters, shall the loyal master or mistress have permission to prevail on them to return and be protected while so doing?

3. When steamers and vessels are almost daily leaving this State,

and negroes, the property of loyal citizens, are taken on board without the consent of their owners, who are sometimes widows and orphans, will authority be given to prevent their being removed?

4. In cases where aged and infirm people, who have been always loyal inhabitants and treated with cruelty by secession soldiers because of their loyalty, have had their able-bodied slaves taken away, their barns robbed and fences destroyed, themselves unable from age and infirmity to labor, shall any effort be made, either by persuasion, by the civil authority, or otherwise, to have them delivered up?

5. If the Military Governor shall interfere with any action which it is known will violate the long-established law of North Carolina, and a person connected with the Army on the Sunday following shall make inflammatory appeals to a crowd of several hundred negroes, exhorting them to resort to violence and bloodshed, what action shall be taken by the Governor, if any, to prevent the recurrence of such conduct?

6. When the slaves of loyal citizens, who have never given aid and comfort to the rebellion and sometimes suffered because they did not, are employed by the authorities of the United States in various kinds of labor, can any steps be taken to secure a portion of what is due for their labor to their owners?

These are not cases of imagination; they have occurred and are most of them coming before me for action daily. I will not weary or distress you by the details.

I hope I am not exceeding the duties of my place while I urgently, but most respectfully, request an answer to these questions.

When I receive that answer I shall be able, without delay, to inform the Department how far I can be relied upon to carry out its wishes.

Every day's experience impresses more forcibly on my mind the conviction, felt by abler and better men than myself, that some course of policy must be adopted as to the disposition of slaves within our lines.

If the Army advances, and their numbers, already large, shall be increased, what is to be done with them? Who will support them or their owners, often loyal and true men, already reduced to want by the rebellion, who can make no crops without their aid?

The expense of feeding the negroes will be enormous. It is estimated that each negro man employed by Government will require in wages and subsistence $40 per month to support himself and family, who generally accompany him.

It is my heartfelt desire to restore to my native State the countless blessings conferred by the Union. I am ready to make any sacrifice a gentleman and patriot can make to do so. But if I cannot rely upon the "perfect confidence and full support of the War Department," which was promised me, I desire to know it.

The loss of my humble abilities will not be felt by this great country.

If I am to act without instructions and not to be supported when I pursue the deliberate dictates of my judgment and conscience, then I ask—the only favor I ever asked for my personal benefit of any administration—to be allowed to tender my "immediate" resignation, and to be restored as early as possible to the honor of a private station.

I have the honor to be, your obedient servant,

EDWARD STANLEY,
Military Governor of North Carolina.

HEADQUARTERS DEPARTMENT OF NORTH CAROLINA,
New Berne, June 24, 1862.

Hon. E. M. STANTON,
Secretary of War, Washington, D. C.:

SIR: I have the honor to report that Governor Stanley arrived at this place yesterday, after having made an extended visit to Washington, N. C., which has, in my opinion, resulted in very great good to the Union cause. He has no doubt given you a detailed account of his visit. I had a lengthy conversation with him last evening, in which I gave him as accurate a statement as I could of the interview which I had the pleasure of having with the President, yourself, and other distinguished gentlemen, and he expressed himself highly pleased with the result of the interview.

He very frankly said to me that he was much annoyed by the course that had been pursued by a portion of the Northern press and the criticisms of some distinguished Senators, all of which were caused by the statement of a very insignificant person, who had seized upon an accidental expression of his opinion, and taken decided action on the ever-agitated negro question, and then ran off to the North for the purpose of creating an excitement and thereby gaining a little temporary notoriety, without thinking of the embarrassment it would cause the Government. Like all men who are working for the restoration of the Union, he has ceased to think of the matter, and when Mr. Colyer returned to the department this morning he received him as kindly as if nothing had happened; in fact, the mild course which he pursued toward a man who had done all he could to injure him had the effect to cause me to change my determination to dismiss Mr. Colyer if he again came into the department. We both of us feel that we had rather be annoyed by an over-officious person than to do any act to embarrass the Government by causing discord among the members of Congress at a time when harmony should prevail and all should unite in sustaining the policy of the Government at any sacrifice of opinion, comfort, or means.

I sincerely hope that you will find it for the interest of the public service to sustain the Governor.

The military affairs of this department are in a fair condition, the health of the command is improving, and we now have near 15,000 men for duty. The infantry regiments are in fine spirits and discipline, have excellent arms and plenty of ammunition, a good supply of clothing and camp equipage, and are abundantly and well provided for by the Commissary Department. The cavalry regiment is also in fine condition, and are equally well supplied, their only want being hair saddle blankets, which are very necessary in this climate, and which have already been required for. I hope the Quartermaster's Department will forward 1,000 of the same at once.

You will remember that this regiment was only armed with sabers and pistols, which I am convinced is a most excellent general rule to adopt in any cavalry, but in this thickly-wooded country a great portion of the skirmishing has to be done on foot, which renders carbines very necessary, and I would be very glad if you would authorize General Ripley to issue 1,000 good carbines, with the cartridge-boxes and slings, and a good supply of ammunition.

You will, I am sure, pardon a very natural prejudice when I say that I would prefer what is called the "Burnside carbine," if the Ordnance Department have them, but I would much prefer "Sharp's" or any good carbine rather than delay the shipment even for one week.

Our field artillery force is also in good condition, having been increased by the fitting up of new batteries of captured pieces to over thirty guns now ready for the field, only fourteen of which belong to the regularly-organized batteries of the command. A few more horses and a small supply of harness would be of service to us, and Colonel Sibley has gone North for the purpose of procuring them, but they are now, as I before stated, in a fair condition to move.

You are so perfectly conversant with the length of line and number of places that we have to hold in these waters that I will not enter into details as to the garrisons that it will be necessary to leave behind in case we receive an order to move, but will simply give you the answer which I gave in reply to a dispatch from General McClellan, and am expecting an answer from him to-morrow night:

I can place 7,000 infantry in Norfolk ready for transportation to White House in five days, but with no wagons, camp equipage, artillery, or cavalry, or I can place at a point on the Chowan River, with a view of co-operating in an attack on Petersburg, 7,000 infantry, twelve pieces of artillery, three companies of cavalry, and wagons enough for the ammunition, and five days' subsistence, at five days' notice. (Of course I can move on Weldon with the same force), or I can move on Goldsborough at sixty hours' notice with 10,000 infantry, twenty pieces of artillery, and five companies of cavalry.

Either one of these moves can be made, and at the same time leave the places which we now hold tolerably secure. Several miles of railroad between here and Goldsborough have been torn up and many of the bridges and culverts destroyed, but I am convinced that we can take the place, but would not like to guarantee that it can be held with this small force. If, however, it should be deemed advisable, after hearing from General McClellan, to make either one of these moves, I shall avail myself of the very great confidence which you have placed in me by allowing me the discretion of co-operating with the Army of the Potomac without waiting for special instructions from the Department.

Of the four engines started to us two were lost at Hatteras Inlet in a gale, and two are now running on the road between here and Fort Macon. The cars, wagons, and horses are arriving rapidly, and are being put in movable condition. I heard of the loss of the two engines while at Fort Monroe, and Mr. Tucker, your Assistant Secretary, promised to send us two more at once.

I have the honor to be, very respectfully, your obedient servant,
A. E. BURNSIDE,
Major-General, Commanding Department North Carolina.

WASHINGTON, *June 28*, 1862.
General BURNSIDE:
I think you had better go, with any re-enforcements you can spare, to General McClellan.
A. LINCOLN.

WAR DEPARTMENT, *June 28*, 1862.
Major-General BURNSIDE, *New Berne:*
We have intelligence that General McClellan has been attacked in large force and compelled to fall back toward the James River. We are not advised of his exact condition, but the President directs that you shall send him all the re-enforcements from your command to the

James River that you can safely do without abandoning your own position. Let it be infantry entirely, as he said yesterday that he had cavalry enough.

EDWIN M. STANTON,
Secretary of War.

FORT MONROE, *June* 28, 1862.
ECKERT:

The following was sent to Burnside on the 25th. If it decides the President not to send his of this date telegraph me to Norfolk. I will be there in an hour and half:

HEADQUARTERS, *June* 25, ——.
Maj. Gen. AMBROSE E. BURNSIDE:

Reports from contrabands and deserters to-day make it probable that Jackson's forces are coming to Richmond, and that a part of Beauregard's force have arrived at Richmond. You will please advance on Goldsborough with all your available forces at the earliest practicable moment. I wish you to understand that every minute in this crisis is of great importance. You will therefore reach Goldsborough as soon as possible, destroying all the railroad communications in the direction of Richmond in your power.

If possible, destroy some of the bridges on the Raleigh and Gaston Railroads and threaten Raleigh.

GEO. B. McCLELLAN.

SHELDON.

WAR DEPARTMENT,
June 28, 1862—6 p. m.
Major-General BURNSIDE, *New Berne:*

Since the dispatches of the President and myself to you of to-day we have seen a copy of one sent to you by General McClellan on the 25th, of which we were not aware.* Our directions were not designed to interfere with any instructions given you by General McClellan, but only to authorize you to render him any aid in your power.

EDWIN M. STANTON,
Secretary of War.

ON BOARD THE ALICE PRICE,
Pamlico Sound, June —, 1862.
Maj. Gen. GEORGE B. McCLELLAN:

We can put 7,000 infantry in Norfolk in five days, but no artillery, cavalry, or wagons, and will require transportation from Norfolk. We can land at a point on the Chowan to attack Petersburg with 7,000, twelve pieces of artillery, 240 cavalry, and enough wagons for ammunition, and four days' provisions in five days. We can move on Goldsborough at sixty hours' notice with 10,000 infantry, twenty pieces of artillery, and five companies of cavalry.

From my present information I think that we can take Goldsborough and hold it for the present, although 13 miles of railroad between here and Kinston have been destroyed. At all events we can go to Kinston and repair the railroad and bridges between here and there. We have already built the bridges over the Trent and Batchelder's Creek,

---

* See Sheldon to Eckert, immediately preceding.

and will probably have to build one more bridge of 80 feet at Cane Creek and one of 400 feet at Kinston, although the latter is not yet destroyed and we may save it.

BURNSIDE.

Abstract from return of the Department of North Carolina, Maj. Gen. Ambrose E. Burnside commanding, for June, 1862.

Station.	Troops.	Present for duty.		Aggregate present.	Aggregate present and absent.	Pieces of field artillery.
		Officers.	Men.			
New Berne....................	First (Foster's) Division:					
	Infantry....................	168	4,469	5,109	6,343	....
	Artillery....................	49	1,024	1,265	1,532	30
	Cavalry....................	33	534	629	760	....
	Second (Reno's) Division:					
	Infantry....................	148	3,549	4,169	4,938	....
	Artillery....................	4	61	76	79	4
	Third (Parke's) Division:					
	Infantry....................	95	2,033	2,127	2,784	....
	Artillery....................	2	44	55	57	....
Roanoke Island	Hawkins' brigade (infantry).	56	1,407	1,603	1,750	....
Newport Barracks	Garrison (infantry)...........	25	670	749	1,091	....
	Total....................	580	13,791	15,782	19,334	34

HEADQUARTERS DEPARTMENT OF NORTH CAROLINA,
New Berne, July 3, 1862.

Maj. Gen. GEORGE B. McCLELLAN:

GENERAL: I embarked 7,000 infantry and was on my way to join you, at the suggestion of the Secretary of War, when I met a messenger, informing me of your important success before Richmond, which, if true, rendered it unnecessary for me to join you. I accordingly brought my fleet to an anchor, and have sent a steamer through to Norfolk to ascertain the exact state of affairs, and shall hold myself in readiness to move in any direction.

The movement up the country in the direction of Goldsborough will be pushed as rapidly as possible. The railroad bridges and culverts, as you know, are all destroyed, but we are rapidly repairing them, and to-morrow we will make an advance of some 10 or 12 miles beyond our present outposts. I had already commenced a movement with my entire force, when I received a dispatch from the President and Secretary of War requesting me to do anything in my power to assist you before Richmond.

I have the honor to be, general, very respectfully, your obedient servant,

A. E. BURNSIDE,
Major-General.

HEADQUARTERS DEPARTMENT OF NORTH CAROLINA,
New Berne, July 3, 1862.

Hon. E. M. STANTON, *Secretary of War:*

SIR: In accordance with the suggestion of your dispatch, I embarked 7,000 infantry, and was proceeding to the point designated by you, when I met a dispatch from Colonel Hawkins, commanding at Roanoke Island, stating that there was information from Fort Monroe of some very important successes to our arms in front of Richmond, which, if true, renders our proceeding further unnecessary; in fact, renders it almost necessary that the original suggestions of General McClellan to me should be carried out. I accordingly ordered my fleet to come to anchor, and sent a messenger to Norfolk to ascertain the exact state of affairs, and shall hold myself in readiness to proceed in either direction.

I have the honor to be, sir, very respectfully, your obedient servant,

A. E. BURNSIDE,
Major-General.

I hope this action will meet with your approval.

FORT MONROE, *July* 3, 1862—3 p. m.

Hon. E. M. STANTON, *Secretary of War:*

I have just received the following dispatch from Colonel Hawkins. I do not quite understand why General Burnside should not have sent it in his own name, if it comes from or is authorized by him. The officer who brought it says Colonel Hawkins sent it, with the assurance that General Burnside would approve it:

HEADQUARTERS, *Roanoke Island, July* 2—6 p. m.

General DIX:

I wish you would telegraph immediately to President Lincoln if he has any orders other than the last sent some three days ago for General Burnside. We are almost ready to move in obedience to that order. If Richmond be taken, the President may wish to change his instructions. Please give me General McClellan's position when last heard from. Please return the dispatch boat immediately, as the news which it brings will, I think, govern the operations in this department.

Very respectfully, your obedient servant,

RUSH C. HAWKINS,
Colonel, Commanding Fourth Brigade and Post.

P. S.—We shall be ready to move in twenty-four hours.

JOHN A. DIX,
Major-General.

WAR DEPARTMENT, *July* 3, 1862.

Colonel HAWKINS,
Commanding at Roanoke Island:

Your telegram of July 2 to General Dix has just been received. Richmond is not taken. General McClellan has been compelled to fall back to Harrison's Bar, on the James River. It is the opinion of the President, and he so directs, that General Burnside in person, with all the infantry force he can spare, move by way of Hampton Roads and the James River to General McClellan's headquarters, to re-enforce him immediately.

EDWIN M. STANTON,
Secretary of War.

FORT MONROE, *July* 3, 1862.

The PRESIDENT:

Soon after sending you Colonel Hawkins' dispatch I received from General McClellan an order to General Burnside to bring on all the troops he could spare. I sent it off immediately, with a letter from myself, describing to General Burnside the position of General McClellan's army. The steamer having gone, I cannot send your dispatch to Colonel Hawkins until morning. I will do so then, if you desire it.

JOHN A. DIX,
Major-General.

———

HEADQUARTERS DEPARTMENT OF NORTH CAROLINA,
New Berne, July 5, 1862.

Hon. E. M. STANTON,
Secretary of War, Washington:

SIR : I have the honor to report that the dispatch boat which I sent through the canal to Norfolk for information and instructions has not yet returned. In the mean time we hear most startling rumors of disasters to General McClellan's army, which are in sad contrast to the dispatch from Colonel Hawkins, on Roanoke Island, on the night of the 2d instant. We have Richmond papers giving information, or rather their version of the events, up to 10 o'clock of the night of the 1st. After making due allowance for the exaggerations, we are led to hope that General McClellan has made a successful retreat to some point on the James River nearly opposite City Point, thereby securing a new and better base of operations; in which case he can, I imagine, after resting his army and receiving proper re-enforcements, work his way up the James River to Richmond. In view of the great uncertainty of the actual state of affairs in the Army of the Potomac, I beg to make the following statement :

First. We can move with 7,000 infantry (which were started the other day for the James River) at once, at the same time holding with tolerable security all the points now in our possession, together with the railroads from this place to Beaufort.

Second. Or we can send 8,000 infantry and hold all these points, but cannot protect either the railroad or Beaufort. The latter, however, can be protected by the Navy, while we hold Fort Macon. This movement will require two days' notice.

Third. Or we can move from here with from three to five days' notice with the entire command, except the garrisons for Hatteras Inlet, Fort Macon, and Roanoke Island, placing our sick at the latter place, leaving this place to be protected by the Navy, as Elizabeth City and other places on the Albemarle Sound are held. This will involve the dismantling of the two very strong forts on the outskirts of the city, which have been erected with great care and labor with a view to holding the place as a base of operations. This movement can be made without exciting the suspicions of the enemy in this neighborhood, and we can thus add to the Army of the Potomac a force of 11,500 infantry, one regiment of cavalry, twenty pieces of light artillery, and, if necessary, 100 wagons and a supply of ambulances; all in good condition.

All these propositions presuppose that the rebel army are still occupied in Richmond by the establishment of the Army of the Potomac at some point on James River near City Point.

If such is the case, General McClellan would, I imagine, cut off their communication with North Carolina by taking Petersburg, thus rendering it unnecessary for the present to cut the two lines in the interior of this State.

If, as the rebel papers assert, the Army of the Potomac is demoralized and broken to pieces, which we do not credit, the rebel army in front of

Richmond will be relieved, and this place will be liable to an attack by a very large force; but I think, with the aid of the forts and gunboats, we can hold it, and we will remain subject to your orders.

I omitted to state that the execution of this last proposition might create some suffering among a few Union people in this city, but the other towns in these waters would not be affected so long as the naval forces here remain undiminished. The proposition contemplates leaving garrisons at Hatteras Inlet, Fort Macon, and Roanoke Island large enough to furnish as much protection to these other towns as they now receive, and as the Union sentiment in this place is remarkably limited, it should not be taken into consideration in devising plans for the public good.

We hope and pray that the condition of the Army of the Potomac is not as has been represented by the rebel accounts, but in any event we hold ourselves in readiness to stand by the Government, and perform any duties that may devolve upon us to the best of our abilities.

The adoption of the third proposition will involve the necessity of sending to Beaufort from the North transportation for six regiments of infantry, one regiment of cavalry, four batteries of light artillery, and also for 200 wagons and ambulances, with teams, if they are required; if not, they can be left in the depot at Morehead City, near Beaufort, with the engines and cars.

I have the honor to be, very respectfully, your obedient servant,

A. E. BURNSIDE,
Major-General, Commanding Department of North Carolina.

WAR DEPARTMENT, *July 5*, 1862.
Major-General BURNSIDE, *via Fortress Monroe :*

The Department has no further orders to give, but hope you will with all speed reach General McClellan with as large a force as possible.

EDWIN M. STANTON,
Secretary of War.

FORT MONROE, *July 7*, 1862—4.40 p. m.
Hon. E. M. STANTON, *Secretary of War :*

Arrived here safely with the advance of my command. I bring near 8,000 good men. Please give me any instructions you may have. I shall leave as soon as the bulk of the command arrives. It takes some time for all the vessels to pass the swash. If necessary I will go right up.

A. E. BURNSIDE,
Major-General.

WAR DEPARTMENT, *July 7*, 1862.
Major-General BURNSIDE, *Fort Monroe :*

The President is on the way to meet you at Fort Monroe. Please remain, and do not send your troops forward until you see him.

EDWIN M. STANTON,
Secretary of War.

HEADQUARTERS DEPARTMENT OF NORTH CAROLINA,
New Berne, July 8, 1862.

Hon. E. M. STANTON, *Secretary of War:*

SIR: I have the honor to report that General A. E. Burnside left this department on the morning of the 6th day of July with the Second and Third Divisions of this corps d'armée to join the Army of the Potomac under General McClellan, leaving me in command of this department.

My force, comprising the First Division, consists of seven regiments and one battalion of infantry, one regiment of cavalry, one of artillery, and the Marine Artillery.

One regiment of infantry guards the railroad from here to Beaufort, one battalion at Beaufort, and one-half of the Marine Artillery as garrison on Roanoke Island. The balance of the forces are stationed at this point, under my immediate command.

I am at present engaged in strengthening and fortifying the place at every possible point of attack, and consider myself abundantly able to hold the position against almost any force that may be brought against it.

I have the honor to be, very respectfully, your obedient servant,

J. G. FOSTER,
Commanding Department.

HEADQUARTERS DEPARTMENT OF NORTH CAROLINA,
New Berne, N. C., July 15, 1862.

Hon. E. M. STANTON,
Secretary of War, Washington, D. C.:

SIR: I have the honor to report that everything has remained quiet in this department since the date of my last letter, July 12 [8th?]. I am progressing quite well in strengthening the field works around the city, and am also erecting block-houses at all the exposed points, such as bridges, stations, &c., on the line of the railroad, so as to enable a comparatively small force to hold the road with tolerable security. A fortified car, arranged to carry two guns, with loop-holes for musketry, and manned with a crew from the Marine Artillery, is run with every train between this city and Beaufort.

The city is quite healthy at this time, and I find by a personal examination of the hospitals that most of the patients are convalescing.

I go to Beaufort to-day to inspect the hospital there and to arrange for placing it under the efficient care of some Sisters of Charity who are expected from New York.

Commodore Rowan left here at night on the 12th, in obedience to his orders. I had the honor to write in relation to him in my letter of that date.

I have the honor to be, very respectfully, your obedient servant,

J. G. FOSTER,
Brigadier-General, U. S. Army, Commanding Department.

HEADQUARTERS DEPARTMENT OF NORTH CAROLINA.
New Berne, July 21, 1862.

Hon. E. M. STANTON,
Secretary of War, Washington, D. C.:

SIR: I have the honor to report that all has been quiet in this department since the date of my last report, July 15.

The work on the defenses of this town is progressing very favorably, and before long I expect the town to be sufficiently fortified to be held by a small force.

The construction of the works for the defense of Washington is rapidly approaching completion.

The work on block-houses on the line of the Atlantic and North Carolina Railroad is going on with proper dispatch.

There are now three light batteries, of four guns each, organized and mounted, taken from the Third Regiment New York Volunteer Artillery. They are being drilled assiduously, and will soon reach that state of proficiency that will enable them to be most useful in attack or in defense.

There is from the same regiment another battery of six guns organized, which will be mounted from the horses arrived by the Cahawba (100 in number). I look forward to having a comparatively large and efficient corps of light artillery.

The health of the department, I am very happy to say, is improving, the new cases being mostly of milder form than before, but I have deemed best to establish a general hospital at Portsmouth, so as to remove as much as practicable the sick from the hospital in this town to the sea-breezes and purer air of Portsmouth. I have used the Marine Hospital built by the United States Government for the purpose.

I have to report that, at the request of Major-General Burnside, nine Sisters of Mercy have arrived from New York, to take charge of the hospital at Beaufort, and under their kind and educated care I hope for a rapid improvement in the health of the patients. The Rev. Mr. Bruehl, their priest, accompanied them, and, in consideration of the worthiness of this gentleman and of the large number of Catholics in the New York regiment attached to my command, I most earnestly recommend that he be appointed chaplain of the United States hospital at Beaufort, N. C.

Chaplain James Means has arrived at this place, and having presented his appointment as chaplain for the United States hospital at New Berne, has been assigned to duty accordingly.

I am, sir, with great respect, your obedient servant,

J. G. FOSTER,
Brigadier-General, U. S. Army, Commanding Department.

HEADQUARTERS DEPARTMENT OF NORTH CAROLINA,
New Berne, N. C., July 29, 1862.

Hon. E. M. STANTON,
Secretary of War, Washington, D. C.:

SIR: I have the honor to report that all is well in this department. The work on the fortifications at this point and at Washington is progressing well. At the latter place the fort is ready to receive its guns. This work, with the block-houses being erected and with the gunboat in the river, will make the place secure against any small force. The block-houses on the line of the Atlantic and North Carolina Railroad, between here and Beaufort, are going on well. The health of the troops continue about as last reported.

The condition of the hospital at Beaufort is improving, and the comforts of the men are being admirably looked after by the Sisters of Mercy, recently arrived from New York.

The hospital at Portsmouth is being prepared for the reception of patients, and I expect to send there on Thursday next the requisite number to fill it. The diseases incident to this climate are of such a debilitating nature that all cases require the tonic of salt air to recuperate. I had the honor to send you, under date the 28th instant, a brief report of several reconnaissances ordered by me.

The first, under command of Colonel Lee, of the Twenty-seventh Massachusetts Volunteers, and in command, temporarily, of the First Brigade of my division, consisted of nine companies of the Twenty-fifth Massachusetts, under Lieutenant-Colonel Sprague; seven companies of the Twenty-seventh Massachusetts, under Lieutenant-Colonel Lyman; four companies of Third New York Cavalry, under Major Lewis, and Belger's Rhode Island Battery, under Lieutenant Pope. They left Deep Gully, the limit of our pickets, at daylight of Saturday, and marched up the Trent Road, driving in the enemy's pickets as they advanced. Arriving at the fork of the roads (one fork leading to Kinston and one to Trenton) we came upon the picket station and surprised them, but were unable to catch them, as they took to their horses, leaving everything behind, and started for Kinston.

At this point a force of four companies infantry, a section of artillery, and a platoon of cavalry were left, the remaining force pushing on for Trenton.

On reaching the bridge over the Trent at this place it was found on fire and a small force of the enemy on the other side. A dash of our cavalry and a volley forced them to leave; the fire was extinguished, the bridge replanked, and the force entered the town without opposition.

After a halt the column was started for Pollocksville, marched till night, camped for the night at a deserted plantation, and started for Pollocksville the next a. m. This place was reached at 10 a. m. and there met the second reconnaissance, under Lieutenant-Colonel Fellows, and consisting of six companies Seventeenth Massachusetts and one company Third Cavalry. This detachment started from their camp the other side of the Trent River Saturday morning at daylight, with orders to march to Pollocksville, building all the necessary bridges on the line of their march, take and hold Pollocksville until communicated with by Colonel Lee. This they did without opposition, though as the command neared Mill Creek, which it was necessary to cross to reach Pollocksville, the cavalry vedettes, 4 in number, were fired upon from the bushes, 2 killed and 2 wounded and taken prisoners. Infantry skirmishers were immediately thrown forward to the right and left of the road by Colonel Fellows, who was at the head of the column some 500 paces in rear. The skirmishers deployed through the swamp and wood on either side of the road, but were unsuccessful in their efforts to find the firing party. The perfect knowledge of all the by-paths, serpentine roads, &c., possessed by these small parties of the enemy, renders pursuit almost hopeless. Colonel Fellows, crossing the creek, occupied the town till met, as before said, by Colonel Lee, when both commands uniting, under command of Colonel Lee, started for New Berne, and arrived at 10 o'clock Sunday night. The circuit made by Colonel Lee was about 50 miles in circumference.

The third detachment, under Colonel Heckman, of the Ninth New Jersey Volunteers, consisted of five companies of that regiment, two companies Third New York Cavalry, and Battery B of the New York Rocket Battalion, consisting of three pieces. This command started from Newport, the headquarters of this regiment, on picket duty on the railroad, on Saturday morning, and marched for Young's Cross-Roads, a point 25 miles distant (about), and on the direct road from Pollocks-ville to Wilmington, and distant 8 miles from the former place. On arriving at a creek just between them and the Cross-Roads the bridge was found taken up and the enemy showed themselves by firing a volley from the other side, which wounded 3 of our men, 1 mortally. The fire was replied to and one piece of artillery brought up and opened fire on them with canister, and when they retreated they were followed up by shell. The people in the neighborhood represent that they carried off two wagon loads of killed and wounded. The bridge was then rebuilt and the command bivouacked there for the night, and the next morning started for New Berne, via Pollocksville, reaching here without opposition.

The fourth detachment consisted of two companies Twenty-seventh Massachusetts, 10 cavalry, and 20 Third New York Artillery, with muskets, under command of Captain Sanford, of Twenty-seventh. Started Sunday a. m. up the railroad to break up the picket headquarters on the Neuse road. They moved up with great expedition for about 5 miles from Batchelder's Creek, our picket limits on that road, and then branched off toward the Neuse road, off of which was the headquarters. They drove in the vedettes and moved on with such speed as prevented the alarm being given. They reached the house and partially surrounded it, announcing their presence by a volley, wounding 3 and killing 1, and succeeded in capturing 10 soldiers of the Second North Carolina Cavalry and about 20 horses. The party then returned, having destroyed the house, to New Berne in safety.

· By the foregoing we have learned much of the topography of the surrounding country and ascertained somewhat the force and position of the enemy. They have a very small force this side of Kinston. Only some two companies of cavalry and perhaps three companies of militia—guerrilla bands or roving rangers, as they are called. At Kinston there is about one small brigade, supported by a larger force with artillery at Blackwater, some 8 miles beyond Kinston, on the road to Goldsborough. The Wilmington road is picketed by about 500 men.

Capt. E. E. Potter, of my staff, acting colonel of the First North Carolina Union Volunteers, started from Washington, his headquarters, with a company of Third New York Cavalry, and rode across to Plymouth, a distance of 36 miles, meeting with no opposition, and hearing of no rebel force this side of Jamesville, at which place he estimates the force at some 400 or 500 men, more for defense than offense. At Halifax there are several regiments, probably two or three.

Col. William A. Howard, of the Marine Artillery, in command of the post of Roanoke Island, has succeeded in destroying the salt-works on Currituck and so breaking up that source of supply. I shall hope soon to advise the breaking up two others on the peninsula, about 20 miles above Roanoke Island. Colonel Howard is now endeavoring to break up some of the trade with Richmond, carried on by way of the Perquimans and Chowan Rivers. This trade is represented as being carried on to a considerable extent, and, if so, a blow struck in that way might be severely felt.

I am, sir, with great respect, your obedient servant,

J. G. FOSTER,
Brigadier-General, U. S. Army, Commanding Department.

Abstract from return of the Department of North Carolina, Maj. Gen. John G. Foster commanding, for month of July, 1862.

Stations.	Present for duty.		Aggregate present.	Aggregate present and absent.	
	Officers.	Men.			
Beaufort............	12	285	369	383	5th Rhode Island.
Fort Macon	1	41	52	• 56	1st U. S. Artillery, Battery C.
Hatteras Inlet.....					Three companies 103d New York. No report.
New Berne.........	190	4,985	6,494	7,804	10th Connecticut; 17th, 23d, 24th, 25th, and 27th Massachusetts; 3d New York Artillery; New York Rocket Battery A; 3d New York Cavalry; and Battery F, 1st Rhode Island Artillery.
Newport Barracks.	36	799	955	1,102	9th New Jersey, and New York Rocket Battery B.
Plymouth..........		64	76	89	Company F, 9th New York.
Total	239	6,174	7,946	9,434	

HEADQUARTERS DEPARTMENT OF NORTH CAROLINA,
New Berne, August 7, 1862.

Hon. E. M. STANTON,
Secretary of War, Washington, D. C.:

SIR: I have the honor to report that everything in this department is progressing favorably. The fortifications are approaching completion and the block-houses on the Atlantic and North Carolina Railroad are nearly finished.

The health of the troops is as good as reported in my last. The hospital at Portsmouth is ready to receive patients, and some invalids are at present being removed there, and in a short time I expect to have the greater portion of my sick at the general hospitals at Beaufort and Portsmouth on the seaboard.

Since my last report I have made three more reconnaissances in force, the first by the Marine Artillery, on the transport steamer Massasoit, armed for the occasion with guns. The boat proceeded up the Neuse as far as Swift Creek, when, seeing a party of the enemy, they fired a few shells and landed, capturing 2 prisoners, with their horses and equipments complete. They then proceeded about 14 miles up the Neuse River, when, in consequence of orders to be at New Berne the same night, they returned.

The second consisted of the same boat, accompanied by the Pilot Boy and the Navy gunboat Ellis, under command of Lieutenant Porter, and proceeded up the same river to within 7 miles of Kinston, meeting with few, if any, obstructions on the way, but at this point the obstructions were more serious, consisting of sunken piles, which were indicated by ripples on the surface of the water; also a four-gun battery on the left bank of the river. The officers of the expedition landed on the opposite side of the river and reconnoitered the place thoroughly. The boats also threw a few shells into the battery, with what result is not known. The battery, however, did not return the fire of the boats. The object of the reconnaissance being accomplished, the expedition returned to New Berne.

The third expedition was started in conjunction with the second. This proceeded by land up the Trent road, under command of Lieutenant-Colonel Mix, of the Third New York Cavalry, and consisted of nine companies of cavalry, six companies of infantry in wagons, under Lieutenant-Colonel Pardee, of the Tenth Connecticut Volunteers, and two sections of artillery, under Lieutenant Pope, of the Rhode Island Artillery. On reaching the forks of the Trenton and Kinston road, after driving in the enemy's pickets, they turned toward Trenton, where, after a skirmish with a company of the enemy's cavalry, routing them and capturing several of their number, they burned the bridge over the Trent. The force then countermarched to the forks of the road and advanced about 5 miles in the direction of Kinston, capturing on the way about 15 of the enemy's pickets, when, upon signals received from the boats that the river expedition was on the return to New Berne, this force also returned.

The expeditions having returned only a few hours ago, this report is necessarily without particulars and brief; in my next I shall be able to give a more complete account of the same.

I have the honor to be, very respectfully, your obedient servant,

J. G. FOSTER,
Major-General, Commanding.

HEADQUARTERS DEPARTMENT OF NORTH CAROLINA,
New Berne, August 10, 1862.

Hon. E. M. STANTON,
Secretary of War, Washington, D. C.:

SIR: I have the honor to inform you that since my report of the 7th instant the health of the command has continued to improve, notwithstanding the great heat of the weather.

A brief mention was made of the three last reconnaissances in my last communication. The subsequent and full reports have demonstrated that the reconnaissances, both by land and water, were complete, obtaining full and correct information of the position of the enemy without the loss of a single man. These reconnaissances have had the effect of causing the enemy to withdraw their pickets to within 5 miles of Kinston, thereby putting an end to the harassing practice of picket firing.

Owing to the heat of the weather it will be impossible for the next month or six weeks to make any more expeditions except by means of night marches and by water. These expeditions I shall keep up continually in order to draw as much as possible from the forces at Richmond, as it is of importance for them to preserve their security in this State.

I am now organizing two expeditions, one, to be composed of a party of horsemen, aided by the gunboats, to go into Hyde County, to arrest some violent secessionists, who have been persecuting the Union citizens; the other, to be composed of light-draught gunboats and transports, to go through Bogue Sound and to White Oak River, to scour those waters and to break up all the salt-works which are at present known to be in active operation there.*

I have the honor to be, very respectfully, your obedient servant,

J. G. FOSTER,
Major-General, Commanding.

_____

*Some matters of detail omitted.

HEADQUARTERS DEPARTMENT OF NORTH CAROLINA,
August 17, 1862.

General H. W. HALLECK,
Commander-in-Chief U. S. Army, Washington, D. C.:

GENERAL: I have the honor to report that generally everything is quiet in this department. The reconnaissance now out in the direction of Wilmington, with orders to destroy the salt-works on the coast, has been much delayed in its operations by the northerly winds that have prevailed since Friday last. I have no fears for its safety or the success of its operations.

Recruits are arriving rapidly for the regiments now here (seven and one-half of infantry, one of artillery, one of marine artillery, and one of cavalry). I have organized and horsed four field batteries from the artillery regiment (the Third New York Artillery), and these, with those previously here, make seven field batteries (two of six pieces each, three of four pieces each, and two of three pieces each). I am drilling these batteries constantly to make them efficient, with the view of making an artillery fight in case it becomes necessary to advance up the country with a small force of infantry. I am aware of the infantry force between here and Goldsborough (eight regiments of infantry) and of the light artillery force (three field batteries), and am confident that I can advance at any time that the General-in-Chief commands and whip these two arms of the rebel force. I will also venture to advance and destroy the railroad as near Raleigh as I can go with my force.

In any case of an advance I shall not expect to occupy the places that I capture up the country, but rather to have for an object to destroy the railroad bridges, &c., so as to cut off the communication of the army at Richmond with the South.

At most the force that I could take with me and leave everything safe at New Berne would be 5,000 men. If it be desired by the General Commanding that an attack be made on the works at the mouth of the Cape Fear River, and those works taken, I shall require that my force be increased by seven regiments of infantry.

I beg leave respectfully to ask that this be done at any rate, because I am confident that I can employ my division to so good purpose as to keep employed much more than an equal number of the enemy.

Captain Williamson, of the Topographical Engineers, and Lieutenant Flagler, of the Ordnance Corps, having been relieved from duty here to report at General Burnside's headquarters, I am left without any regular officers in those departments. I would respectfully ask that officers from both those corps or from the Engineers be sent to replace them.

Although the sickly season will continue for a month, and thus disable many otherwise effective men, I shall stand ready at any moment to make any movement or diversion that the Commander-in-Chief may order or consider necessary to divert attention from the more important operations against the army in front of Richmond.

I have the honor to be, very respectfully, your obedient servant,

J. G. FOSTER,
Major-General, Volunteers.

HEADQUARTERS DEPARTMENT OF NORTH CAROLINA,
New Berne, N. C., August 20, 1862.

Maj. Gen. H. W. HALLECK,
Comdg. Armies of the United States, Washington, D. C.:

GENERAL: I have the honor to report that all is well within this department.

The health of the men is remarkably good, considering the unhealthfulness of this climate at this season. The convalescents are rapidly brought up by a short stay at the general hospital at Beaufort.

I started a reconnaissance on the 16th instant toward Wilmington for the purpose of destroying some salt-works known to be in operation at or near Bogue Inlet, and to ascertain the force of the enemy in that section, the character of the country, depth of water in the sounds, inlets, and rivers, &c. I have now the honor to report their return and the successful accomplishment of their object and without resistance. One man was slightly wounded by a guerrilla's shot and we took one prisoner.

The reconnaissance was under command of Colonel Stevenson, commanding the Second Brigade of my division, and consisted of seven companies of the Twenty-fourth Massachusetts Volunteers, Riggs' battery Third New York Artillery, and a large detachment of the Marine Artillery, Colonel Howard. The force was embarked on seven light-draught steamers, five of which proceeded to Bogue Inlet from Beaufort outside, and two through Bogue Sound to the same point. The vessels rendezvoused at the mouth of White Oak River, Swansborough, landed, and took possession of the town. The next day the two lightest-draught steamers started up Stumpy Sound, and, having proceeded 2 miles, landed a detachment of troops, who, marching down the banks of the sound, found and destroyed the salt-works of a Mr. Hawkins, with a store-house partially filled. These works were quite extensive and well filled up, and had a capacity of about 7,000 bushels per annum. The force then proceeded to the works of Colonel Saunders (capacity about 2,500 bushels per annum), which they destroyed, and hearing of no other works of any consequence, the detachment returned to their vessels.

During their absence Lieutenant Porter, commanding the naval gunboat Ellis, kindly furnished me by Lieutenant Colhoun, the senior officer at this station, found and destroyed two small works on Queen Creek.

Having destroyed all the known works in this part of the country and obtained much information the forces started for their return, first destroying a well-constructed unarmed fort built to protect the entrance to Bogue Inlet, the guns of which had been taken (six in number) to New Berne to aid in the defense of that point and were there captured by us, and had not since been replaced.

Before closing this report I must make my acknowledgments of the promptness, willingness, and efficiency of Lieutenant Colhoun, of the Navy. His cordial and ever-ready co-operation with me in any move I may make, joined with his high character as an officer and a gentleman, convinces me that he is one of the most worthy and deserving of those ex-officers of the Navy who at the call of their country re-entered the service, hoping and wishing to be reinstated in the Regular Navy of the United States. Than Lieutenant Colhoun none are more worthy.

I am, General, with much respect, your obedient servant,

J. G. FOSTER,
Major-General, Commanding.

CONFEDERATE CORRESPONDENCE, ETC.

HEADQUARTERS FORCES ON ROANOKE ISLAND,
Camp Raleigh, January 8, 1862.

Brig. Gen. HENRY A. WISE,
Commanding District of the Albemarle:

GENERAL: In compliance with your special order, I have the honor to submit the following report upon the defenses of this island, quantity of provisions and ammunition on hand, strength of this command, &c.

The defenses of Croatan Sound consist of four batteries, mounting in the aggregate thirty guns, all 32-pounders, as follows: At Weir's Point (Fort Huger), ten smooth-bore and two rifled guns; at Fort Blanchard, four smooth-bore guns; at Pork Point (Fort Bartow), six smooth-bore and one rifled gun; at Red Stone Point (Fort Forrest), seven smooth-bore guns. There is another battery on the Tyrrel side of Croatan Sound, at Roberts' Fishery, already completed, but no guns have been mounted, General Hill having ordered a discontinuation of the work. Its capacity is six barbette guns. The two 32-pounders now lying on the beach at Weir's Point will, agreeably to your orders, be mounted as soon as possible. Upon Roanoke Sound there is a small battery of two smooth-bore 32-pounders at Midgett's Hommock. The battery at Pork Point ought by all means to be strengthened by the addition of two pivot mounted guns.

Orders have been given for the construction of bomb-proof quarters for the detachment at Fort Blanchard, but up to this time lumber ordered for that purpose has not been received. Quarters should be constructed in the immediate vicinity of Fort Huger for the accommodation of at least one of the companies by which the guns at that battery are manned. There ought also to be built at Fort Forrest quarters not only for the company already there, but for another company necessary at that fort. Most of the guns require sights; nearly all of them have nothing but the dispart sights, which I believe is very unreliable, especially in the hands of inexperienced gunners. I submit that it is very necessary that the most improved sights be obtained at once, and, if needful, an expert artisan sent at once to adjust them.

Of light artillery there are three pieces at this post, one 24-pounder howitzer, one 18-pounder Mexican piece, and one 6-pounder; the latter brought to this place from Elizabeth City, N. C. These pieces are all mounted on carriages, with limbers, but no caissons. For operations upon this island I am not sure that caissons are necessary.

Ammunition on hand.—Three hundred and eighty-seven charges for 32-pounder guns, 1,300 rounds shot, 250 rifle shell, 300 match primers, 83 rounds fixed ammunition (24-pounder howitzers), 1 box percussion wafers, 150 port-fires, 98 rounds 6-pounder shot (1,000 rounds obtained from Elizabeth City, N. C.), 250 pounds powder, 315 stand grape (32), 2,000 friction primers, 500 percussion primers, 150 junk wads, 400 gromet wads, 98 canister (6-pounder), 28 spherical-case shot, 10 slow matches.

Ammunition for small-arms.—Fifty-two thousand one hundred and fifty-seven ball cartridges for percussion (16,578 ball cartridges issued), 17,183 ball cartridges for flint and steel, 3,320 balls, 150 pounds lead, 5,500 (about) percussion caps.

Quantity of provisions on hand.—Thirteen thousand six hundred and eighty-two pounds bacon and pork, 3,420 pounds beef, 598 pounds lard, 3,692 pounds rice, 649 pounds coffee, 1,570 pounds candles, 12½ bushels salt, 1 barrel fish, 20 barrels and 2,158 pounds hard bread, 265 barrels flour, 10,554 pounds meal, 54½ bushels pease and beans, 3,082 pounds sugar, 400 gallons vinegar, 1,348 pounds soap, 58 gallons whisky, 5 bushels yapon [a kind of wild tea].

Aggregate number of entire command	1,822
Four cooks allowed to each company	92
To be subsisted	1,914

Effective force, officers included, absent and sick being deducted, 1,435.

A call has been made for 250 free negroes for service in the engineer department. These will have to be subsisted, as will also the gang of 8 men on the pile-driver.

Horses, mules, and oxen in charge of quartermaster's department.—Nine officers' horses, 6 yoke of oxen hired by quartermasters of Eighth and Thirty-first Regiments, 2 pair mules, property of the Government. The mules and oxen are used for general purposes of land transportation.

Amount of forage on hand.—Seven hundred and twenty-five pounds fodder, 2½ bushels corn, 1¼ barrels oats.

Orders have been given for the construction of a magazine. No regular ordnance officer has been appointed.

Very respectfully, your obedient servant,

H. M. SHAW,
Colonel, Commanding.

RICHMOND, *January* 12, 1862.

Gov. HENRY T. CLARK, *Raleigh:*

Please order at once two of your regiments now at Raleigh to rendezvous at Goldsborough. Give them what arms you can, and we will complete their armament.

It seems probable that the expedition is against your coast, but I do not yet rely on the information hitherto received. Act as promptly as possible.

J. P. BENJAMIN,
Secretary of War.

ROANOKE ISLAND, N. C., *January* 15, 1862.

SIR: In compliance with your orders, Lieutenant Loyall and myself have reported at this place for duty connected with the heavy batteries, and up to this time have inspected and frequently exercised them, with the exception of Fort Forrest, on the other side of the sound. This we have not visited, in consequence of the weather, which has not been favorable for the past few days. We find the batteries well constructed and arranged, except that at Pork Point, which requires a flank to the southward, to prevent its being enfiladed. This has been recommended to Colonel Shaw, and orders have probably been given to have the work done. The equipment of the guns is incomplete, only one gun on the island being sighted, and the rifled guns (three in number) are mounted on navy barbette carriages, which are very unwieldy. The instruction is indifferent, but the officers and men evince such a good disposition to learn, that we hope, with the facilities offered us, to be able in a short time to report very favorably of their proficiency. I would here state that I found Major Hill in command at Pork Point Battery. He was an old Army officer, and is no doubt a better artillerist than I am; and, as I did not desire to supersede a superior and could not suppose that you wished it, I placed myself under his command, and offered my services to him to assist in instructing his men, and detailed Mr. Loyall for that particular duty. None of the guns have locks, nor are any of them drilled for either locks or sights; but this could be very easily done here if locks and sights should be furnished. I presume they know at the navy-yard exactly what guns are here, and could make sights for them without the measures of the guns being sent. We have no shells for any but the rifled guns, and there is no shot furnace fit for use. The engineer officer assures me that the furnace at Fort Huger (the only one constructed) is worthless, and that he tried it for five hours without any other effect than to burst it. He recommends one for each battery here, after the pattern of Mr. Singleton's, of the engineer's office at Norfolk. The amount of ammunition on hand is not more than twenty rounds for each gun.

Very respectfully, your obedient servant,

JOHN S. TAYLOR,
Captain, C. S. Army.

General HUGER,
Commanding Department of Norfolk, Va.

RICHMOND, *January* 16, 1862.

General GATLIN, *Goldsborough, N. C.:*

Huger telegraphs nine transports, with troops aboard, headed for the capes this morning.

S. COOPER,
Adjutant and Inspector General.

GOLDSBOROUGH, *January* 20, 1862.

General L. O'B. BRANCH, *New Berne:*

MY DEAR GENERAL: I would come down to-night, but I hardly think they would dare to leave Roanoke Island in their rear; so in my opinion you can proceed with deliberation, though zealously, in your defenses.

I am fearful that our northeastern counties are lost. It is sad to think how obstinate the authorities at Richmond have been in regard to the destination of the fleet.

Your friend,

R. C. GATLIN.

RICHMOND, *January* 21, 1862.

Maj. Gen. B. HUGER, *Norfolk:*

The President would approve of your taking or sending from Norfolk into North Carolina all the forces you can spare without endangering the safety of your command.

J. P. BENJAMIN,
Secretary of War.

SPECIAL ORDERS, }   ADJT. AND INSP. GEN.'S OFFICE,
    No. 17.   }   *Richmond, January* 22, 1862.
  *   *   *   *   *   *   *

XXXII. Brig. Gen. Henry A. Wise, Provisional Army, will immediately proceed to Roanoke Island, N. C., and assume command of the Confederate States troops at that place.
  *   *   *   *

By command of the Secretary of War:

JNO. WITHERS,
Assistant Adjutant-General.

HEADQUARTERS DEPARTMENT OF NORTH CAROLINA,
Goldsborough, January 24, 1862.

General S. COOPER,
    Adjutant and Inspector General, Richmond, Va.:

GENERAL: I have the honor to report that a storm of great violence has been prevailing upon our coast since early on the night of the 22d instant; it has doubtless damaged the enemy at Hatteras, and it may be well deranged his plans for some days.

As there can be no doubt but that the Burnside expedition is intended to operate in our sounds, it becomes a matter of vital importance to us to consider the means in our power to resist his advance upon the main-lands, and if the force now in the State is insufficient, to try to provide for the deficiency and that speedily.

The principal points in my department accessible from the sound are New Berne, Washington, and Hyde County.

New Berne being the most important, I have concentrated in that neighborhood all the available force at my disposal, save a new regiment held in reserve at this point. In consequence of the great amount of sickness, prevailing principally among the new regiments, that force does not exceed 4,000 effective men.

For the defense of Hyde County the effective force does not exceed 700 men, and for the defense of Washington 1,200 men. The militia called into service are not taken into consideration, as I have no reports of the number that may be expected from the adjacent counties.

Satisfied that the expedition is of such a magnitude that to resist it successfully we ought to have a large increase to our present force, I am constrained to renew my application of the 3d instant, viz, that a large reserve, with an experienced commander, be at once sent to this point and placed at my disposal.

Hoping that the War Department will take speedy action in the matter, I remain, sir, very respectfully, your obedient servant,

R. C. GATLIN,
Brigadier-General.

HEADQUARTERS DISTRICT OF THE CAPE FEAR,
Wilmington, N. C., January 24, 1862.

Hon. J. P. BENJAMIN,
    Secretary of War, Richmond:

SIR: I have the honor to inclose extracts from the report of Captain Ward, in command of the Coast Guard in the northwestern part of this district.

You have already been advised of the stranding of the British ship York on our coast near Bogue Inlet. It now appears that she has been burnt by the enemy's blockading squadron.

I have the honor to be, your obedient servant,
J. R. ANDERSON,
Brigadier-General, Commanding.

[Inclosure.]

HEADQUARTERS GATLIN DRAGOONS,
Swansborough, N. C., January 17, 1862.

ROSCOE B. HEATH,
Assistant-Adjutant-General :

DEAR SIR: On yesterday morning about 9 o'clock my pickets reported two blockaders off this place, one a steamer, supposed to be the Albatross; the other a bark. After reconnoitering off and on until about 2 o'clock they came to anchor about one-fourth of a mile from the wreck of ship York (before reported); lowered six boats, containing each about 15 men. Three of the boats came close alongside of the wreck and threw over into it some combustible matter, which soon had the wreck in flames.

This morning early I took a detachment of 20 men and went over to the wreck and found it still burning—no vessel in sight. The enemy did not land at all. We had succeeded in securing only one flat load of rigging; the balance was ready on deck to be taken off as soon as the weather would permit the wreckers to go alongside. The captain of the wrecked ship, before leaving here, made an assignment of everything pertaining or belonging to the wreck, by power of attorney, to parties here, for the benefit of the underwriters. There are a great many tons of wrought iron about her, but will now be hard to save, if at all. I am now [convinced], and have been ever since seeing the crew and papers, that the wrecked ship York was a genuine British ship.

*   *   *   *   *   *   *

Very respectfully,
EDW'D W. WARD,
Captain, Commanding.

RICHMOND, VA., *January* [*March*] 25, 1862.
Hon. GEORGE W. RANDOLPH, *Secretary of War :*

SIR: Yesterday I addressed a letter to Hon. J. P. Benjamin, dated the 22d instant,* calling for the copy of a report† to the Department from General Huger, stating that my brigade was "supernumerary" in his department, and giving a succinct history of my Legion from its first organization to its present state, and putting certain questions, which I respectfully asked for information. I beg to call your attention to that letter and ask its early consideration. I have now under my orders five companies of infantry under Lieutenant-Colonel Richardson, two under Col. N. Tyler, and nine companies of cavalry under Col. J. L. Davis, in all sixteen companies, numbering, I suppose, 1,100 men. The two companies of the Second Regiment of Infantry at Lewisburg have been ordered to remain there for the present, under General Heth. But my two companies of artillery, with five field

---

* See Series IV.   † See p. 434.

pieces, which by order of the Secretary of War were left at Great Bridge, under command of Brigadier-General Mahone, in General Huger's department, I ask may be restored to my command, which, if done, will increase the Legion to about 1,300 men.

With this force, ordered to join me here, I can easily recruit the Legion to its original number, and if my third regiment be restored to me, now under Colonel Starke, at Goldsborough, N. C., it will have its complement of men of over 2,000 at once.

I ask, then, that my Legion may be preserved as a distinctive and independent force, under General Lee's definition of its character whilst under his command in the West; that my third regiment and corps of artillery may be restored to my command, and that I may be allowed to recruit and organize new companies for my Legion.

I am now awaiting a reply to my call for a court of inquiry; for the arrival of my command, when relieved from special orders here and at Murfreesborough, N. C.; for further orders from the Department since the last to report to General J. E. Johnston at Manassas; and for the call of a committee of the House of Representatives of the Confederate Congress.

I am, with great respect, your obedient servant,

HENRY A. WISE,
Brigadier-General.

COOSAWHATCHIE, S. C., *January* 28, 1862.
General JOSEPH R. ANDERSON,
Commanding District of Cape Fear, Wilmington, N. C.:

GENERAL: I have had the honor to receive your letter of the 24th instant.* and can sympathize in your anxiety to make a successful resistance to the landing of the enemy on the coast of North Carolina. You may be assured that nothing will be wanting on my part to give you all the aid in my power, and I should be pleased to be able to send you my whole force if required, but I beg that you will not rely upon it, but endeavor to organize a sufficient force for your purpose independent of any re-enforcement from this department. The enemy is in great strength on this coast; has command of all the communications by water, and by means of his immense fleet and the net-work of sounds, rivers, and creeks spread over the Carolina and Georgia coast, a disembarkation of a large force can be made under cover of his floating batteries at any time. Scarcely a day passes that a demonstration is not made on some point, which obliges us to keep troops always ready to oppose him. You will see, therefore, how impossible it may be for me to send you succors at the time you may most need them, as it may be expected that when an attack is made on a part of the coast the adjacent country will be imposingly threatened.

As regards the two North Carolina regiments and light battery, I understood they were to form a permanent part of the troops assigned to this department, and would be replaced in your district by [receiving ?] other regiments from the State into the service. This I had hoped had been done, as it is necessary to be prepared along the whole line. The want of arms has prevented my receiving troops that have offered their services from beyond the limits of the department, and has also prevented troops from the State coming into the service. I am sorry

---

* Not found.

to say.that I am not in a condition to spare any troops, but am using every means in my power to organize additional force for service in the department.

I am, &c.,

R. E. LEE,
General, Commanding.

Abstract from return of District of the Cape Fear, commanded by Brig. Gen. Joseph R. Anderson, for January, 1862.

Troops.	Present for duty.		Total enlisted present.	Aggregate present and absent.	Pieces of artillery.	
	Officers.	Men.			Heavy.	Field.
Wilmington, N. C	45	677	943	1,042	......	......
Camp Grant	4	69	78	84	......	......
Camp Davis	4	64	76	102	......	6
Camp Heath	4	77	85	91	......	
Camp Wyatt	43	637	746	891	......	
Fort Fisher	15	232	310	356	25	4
Zeeke's Island	2	73	91	99	3	......
Fort Johnston	41	593	711	794	......	
Fort Caswell	14	217	312	348	34	1
Camp Hopkins	4	70	74	79	....	
Swansborough	3	64	75	102	....	
Huggins' Island	4	64	64	68	....	
Total	183	2,837	3,565	4,056	62	11

Abstract from return of the District of Pamlico, commanded by Brig. Gen. L. O'B. Branch, for January, 1862.

Troops.	Present for duty.		Total enlisted present.	Aggregate present and absent.	Pieces of artillery.	
	Officers.	Men.			Heavy.	Field.
Fort Macon, Shell Point, and Harker's Island	32	434	660	749	......	......
Camp Vance	42	766	905	976	......	......
Camp Graham	29	497	592	684	......	......
Camp Fisher	26	470	595	705	......	......
New Berne	62	705	992	1,315	......	......
Post of Washington	64	1,034	1,305	1,457	......	......
Hyde County	27	464	584	651	......	......
Post of the Neuse	97	1,585	1,883	2,137	......	......
Total	379	5,955	7,516	8,674	......	......
District of the Cape Fear brought forward	183	2,837	3,565	4,056	62	11
Goldsborough, N. C., 34th Regiment North Carolina troops	37	709	792	910	......	......
Grand total	599	9,501	11,873	13,640	62	11

Abstract from post return of Fort Bartow,* Roanoke Island, N. C., commanded by Maj. G. H. Hill, for January, 1862.

Troops.	Present for duty.		Total present.	Aggregate present.	Total present and absent.	Aggregate present and absent.
	Officers.	Men.				
Field and staff..	3	2	2	5	2	6
17th North Carolina troops:						
Company E...................................	3	67	70	73	77	81
Company I....................................	3	52	76	79	82	86
Company L...................................	3	57	74	77	81	87
Total...............................	12	178	222	234	244	260

STATE OF NORTH CAROLINA, EXECUTIVE DEPARTMENT,
Raleigh, February .1, 1862.

Hon. J. P. BENJAMIN, *Secretary of War:*

SIR: The various and conflicting rumors about the destination of the Burnside expedition is now settled by its rendezvous at Hatteras. It has no doubt suffered from the late storm, but not enough to divert its object or its means of successful assault. If you will glance at the map you will readily perceive the extent of injury both to North Carolina and the Confederacy by an expedition into the interior from any part of Albemarle or Pamlico Sound. And I regret again to allude to our inability to check so formidable an expedition, whatever route it may select, and I have refrained as long as I could from alluding to re-enforcements. I am aware of the zeal you devote to the immense labors before you, and of the great strain pressing on you from every quarter, and that you would send re enforcements unasked if you had them to spare.

But I will respectfully tender a suggestion, and be gratified if it coincides with your views; that is, to spare us two or three regiments from the Peninsula, particularly the Fifth North Carolina Volunteers. I make the suggestion on the ground that General Magruder has had every facility in men and good, skillful officers for seven months to fortify the Peninsula; that it has been successfully done; that his intrenchments, fortifications, and guns have been so successfully and extensively done [*sic*] that they can now be defended with one-half of the men required some months ago; that the place will only allow a defensive warfare, and he is prepared for that, and he can now spare some of his force. A commanding general always asks for more, and never consents to give up a single company. Upon these grounds I refer you to this position, where I hope you can spare at least our own regiment.

I thank you for aid of General Wise's Legion to the Albemarle country, but I regret to say that Roanoke, not having the benefit of engineers and skillful officers, is not much benefited by the last four months' occupancy of [it] by the Confederate Government. General Wise writes to me that it needs everything, whereas it should have been an impregnable barrier to the Yankees and a protection for a great extent of North Carolina and Virginia. There has been culpable neg-

---

* Fort Bartow and Fort Forrest were one command. Nine heavy pieces of artillery were in the first and seven in the latter.

ligence or inefficiency at this place. I hope Colonel Clarke's (Twenty-fourth Regiment North Carolina Volunteers) regiment, now stationed at Petersburg, will have sufficiently recruited to be serviceable. '

I have now to rely on an unarmed and undrilled militia for protection, and a draft which has been made for one-third of them has, I regret to say, developed or occasioned much dissatisfaction.

I tender these suggestions to you most respectfully. Should they fail in enlisting your favor, I shall regret to believe that there are other places besides our coast which claim your protection from overwhelming forces and need more help than we do, for I feel assured of your assistance if it could be spared.

Very respectfully, yours,

HENRY T. CLARK.

[FEBRUARY 2, 1862.—The Confederate authorities make requisition upon the State of North Carolina for twenty-six regiments "for the war." For requisition and the Governor's response, of February 11, see Series IV, Vol. I.]

WAR DEPARTMENT, C. S. A.,
Richmond, Va., February 3, 1862.

GOV. HENRY T. CLARK, *Raleigh, N. C.:*

SIR: I have received your favor of the 1st instant, and assure you that you but do me justice in confiding in my earnest desire to do everything in my power to aid in the defense of your coast. Most fortunately the enemy's fleet has been crippled much more seriously than you seem to be aware, and we are thus allowed some time for preparation beyond what we could otherwise have hoped.

In regard to re-enforcements, my thoughts had already been turned on the Peninsula, but there is a serious difficulty in the way there of which you are not aware. Four or five of the regiments on the Peninsula are twelve-months' men, whose term of service is on the eve of expiring; others will expire a little later, and nothing can induce the men to re-enlist unless they have a furlough. But for this I could withdraw a few regiments from the Peninsula. We are reaping the bitter fruits of the blind folly of short enlistments, against which I have struggled with unremitting energy from the day the first shot was fired at Fort Sumter.

However all is not as bad as you supposed. I have just ordered two batteries of artillery to your aid, and have instructed General Huger to see in person to the defenses at Roanoke. He will also send 2,000 or 3,000 men, perhaps more, that can be spared from Norfolk. I have ordered a detail of men to give full efficiency to the gunboats under Commodore Lynch and to the floating battery. The regiment at Petersburg ought now to be able to move, and I will order it at once to report to General Gatlin.

I am sure I could organize the defenses of our country, wherever attacked, if I only had munitions; but, in addition to the heavy superiority in numbers of the enemy, we have to struggle on with a very inadequate supply of materials of war. Your people may suffer somewhat at points where the enemy's superior water forces enable them to ravage the country within reach of their guns, but I do not fear, and am sure you need not, that they can do more than this; and even this shall not be done if every possible precaution in our power can suffice to prevent it.

I am, your obedient servant,

J. P. BENJAMIN,
Secretary of War.

P. S.—I was compelled by stress of occasion to send 1,000 flint-locks to your last two regiments, but will immediately replace them by better arms.

CONFEDERATE STATES OF AMERICA,
NAVY DEPARTMENT,
Richmond, February 3, 1862.

Hon. J. P. BENJAMIN, Secretary of War:

SIR: In compliance with your indorsement upon the letter of Maj. J. A. Johnston, quartermaster, in relation to Albemarle and Chesapeake Canal, I have the honor to state that Mr. Parks· has not yet submitted his bills for tolls against this Department,·but from data before me I infer that since the North Carolina vessels were transferred these tolls amount to about $700 per month.

I know nothing of the condition of the canal or of the work necessary to keep it in order, but I regard it of vital importance to the defenses of North Carolina. I would suggest that a reliable officer be sent to examine the canal and to report the probable expense of maintaining it in navigable condition, which will have to be done by the Confederate States if the canal company and the State of North Carolina will not do it, and I think that the sooner the subject is acted· upon the better.

I presume that with twenty-five gunboats in the waters of North Carolina the tolls would not exceed $2,000 per month, but I think that the work should be kept up without regard to this consideration. The papers are herewith returned.*

With much respect, your obedient servant,

S. R. MALLORY,
Secretary of the Navy.

[Indorsement.]

ASSISTANT SECRETARY:

Have copy made of this entire correspondence, to be forwarded to General Huger, with request that he will send a reliable officer to examine and report on the whole subject.

HDQRS. FOURTH BRIGADE, DEPARTMENT NORFOLK,
Camp at Nag's Head, February 7, 1862.

Major-General HUGER, Commanding, &c.:

SIR: I send you, by direction of General Wise, copies of the dispatch of Lieutenant Loyall to Colonel Shaw, with the colonel's note forwarding the same to these headquarters, and of the dispatch of Colonel

----

* Not found.

Shaw, received about daybreak this morning. The officer who brought the dispatch first above mentioned reports that of the enemy's fleet twenty-eight are gunboats, seven are towing steamers, and the rest transports.

A re-enforcement of ten companies was sent from this place this fore-noon to Roanoke Island, leaving about 300 men to cover the retreat of our forces to the beach, should they be compelled to withdraw from the island.

Owing to continual sickness the general was unable to accompany the troops sent to Roanoke. He is very much prostrated from the illness which still confines him to his bed, and which will in all proba-bility compel him to keep his bed for some days to come.

At 20 minutes past 10 a single gun was heard, which the general supposed to be the signal gun of Flag-Officer Lynch. At 16½ minutes past 11 o'clock of this day firing on Croatan Sound commenced, and from that time to the period of closing this dispatch from 250 to 300 guns have been heard, showing a furious battle to be raging between our forces and the enemy. It is now 25 minutes past 12 o'clock, and the firing is very rapid and heavy.

Very respectfully, your obedient servant,

> C. B. DUFFIELD,
> *Assistant Adjutant-General.*

P. S.—1 *o'clock p. m.*—The firing still continues most furious. A cannon is heard ever second.

> C. B. DUFFIELD,
> *Assistant Adjutant-General.*

[Inclosure No. 1.]

PORK POINT, *February* 6—1 p. m.

COLONEL : The fog has cleared away from below, and I can distinctly see that the enemy is about 8 miles from us, in full force. I can make out more than fifty vessels, either at anchor or under way in tow of steamers. I believe that they are at anchor. I am of opinion that they have stopped to consider, but it requires a bright lookout to keep the run of them.

Very respectfully,

> B. P. LOYALL,
> *Lieutenant, C. S. Navy.*

[Indorsement.]

GENERAL : This was received at half past 2 o'clock. I am now leav-ing for the lower end, having ordered four companies down.

> H. M. SHAW,
> *Colonel, Commanding.*

Brigadier-General WISE.

[Inclosure No. 2.]

HEADQUARTERS ROANOKE ISLAND,
February 6, 1862—8 p. m.

Brig. Gen. HENRY A. WISE,
Commanding Fourth Brigade, Department of Norfolk :

GENERAL : Your dispatch by Lieutenant Simmons has been received, and I hasten to report that I myself have been to Ashby's. The enemy is in full view and about 7 or 8 miles below that point. The atmosphere is so thick that I could not positively determine their number; between fifty and sixty, of which the larger part I think are sailing vessels. Two of the pieces of artillery are already at Ashby's, where it has been for several days; the 6-pounder was moved down to another point this afternoon, and four companies of infantry under a field officer.

The orders contained in your dispatch will of course be carried out. I have to report to you that the available force at my command, exclusive of the detachments on duty at the batteries, is only about 800—808 by last report. The enemy numbers 10,000 men probably. I ask you to send re-enforcements. I forgot to say you are mistaken in supposing I have four pieces of light artillery. The number here is three.

I send this by Lieutenant Cooper.

Very respectfully, your obedient servant,

H. M. SHAW,
Colonel, Commanding.

———

HEADQUARTERS DEPARTMENT OF NORFOLK,
February 8, 1862.

Colonel SHAW,
Eighth Regiment North Carolina Troops:

SIR: Lieut. A. D. Smith, Company G, First Regiment Wise Legion, arrived 10.30 a. m., crossed at 12.30 from Nag's Head by Gallop's to Powell's Point, and rode all night. He heard the same heavy firing all day. It ceased at night.

Respectfully, yours,

BENJ. HUGER,
Major-General.

———

NORFOLK, *February* 9, 1862.

President JEFFERSON DAVIS:

Ammunition was dispatched to Commodore Lynch, who is at Elizabeth City. On the afternoon of the 9th, on meeting the boat stating Roanoke Island was captured, the steamer returned. Commodore Forrest will try and send it by Dismal Swamp Canal, the lower end of which is broken.

I have no news of the enemy. I have ordered troops to move at once and protect the different approaches. Should the enemy attack in front I must be re-enforced.

BENJ. HUGER.

———

RICHMOND, *February* 10, 1862.

Major-General HUGER, *Norfolk:*

Take measures for destroying all supplies at Elizabeth City as soon as satisfied that they cannot be saved from seizure by enemy.

J. P. BENJAMIN,
Secretary of War.

———

RICHMOND, *February* 10, 1862.

Brigadier-General GATLIN, *Goldsborough:*

I am informed there are about 15,000 bales of cotton ready for shipment at Roanoke River. Give orders to burn all that is not immediately moved into the interior out of enemy's reach.

J. P. BENJAMIN,
Secretary of War.

———

HEADQUARTERS DEPARTMENT OF NORTH CAROLINA,
Goldsborough, February 10, 1862.

Hon. J. P. BENJAMIN,
Secretary of War, Richmond, Va.:

SIR: I have the honor to acknowledge the receipt of your dispatch of this date, directing all the cotton on the Roanoke River not removed to a safe distance into the interior to be burned. The dispatch has been replied to by telegraph.

The only troops at my disposal, a regiment of infantry, will be sent up to Halifax to-night, with instructions to march down the Roanoke as far as Jamesville. I will place another regiment on that river, should it be placed at my disposal by Governor Clark. In my dispatch I begged that a light battery be sent to Halifax to join the infantry. This force might answer to check the advance of the enemy should he undertake the ascent of the Roanoke in force, but is not sufficient to do more than retard his progress. I would therefore respectfully suggest that large re-enforcements be sent into that section of the country.

Very respectfully, your obedient servant,
R. C. GATLIN,
Brigadier-General, Commanding.

———

RALEIGH, *February* 10, 1862.

J. P. BENJAMIN, *Secretary of War:*

Roanoke Island has fallen; its garrison captured. We must organize another army for that section. I have only two regiments, which will go down forthwith to Weldon. Avenues to our railroads must be guarded. Send what assistance you can.

HENRY T. CLARK.

———

RICHMOND, *February* 11, 1862.

Gov. HENRY T. CLARK, *Raleigh:*

Your dispatch received. I am glad to hear of your two regiments ordered to Weldon. We are making every possible effort for your defense, and feel confident we can prevent access to the railroad.

J. P. BENJAMIN,
Secretary of War.

———

SPECIAL ORDERS, }   ADJT. AND INSPECTOR GENERAL'S OFFICE,
    No. 35.   }   *Richmond, February* 12, 1862.

*   *   *   *   *   *   *

II. Brig. Gen. R. H. Anderson, Provisional Army, will proceed to Manassas, Va., and report to General Joseph E. Johnston, commanding, for assignment to the command of the South Carolina Brigade, now under Brig. Gen. D. K. Jones, the latter to be assigned to the command of the Georgia Brigade lately commanded by Brig. Gen. S. Jones.

*   *   *   *   *   *   *

IV. Col. J. L. Davis, Wise Legion, will proceed without delay to Garysburg, near Weldon, N. C., with the following companies of the Legion, to act as circumstances may require, under the direction of the commanding officer: Captains Z. S. Magruder's, Caskie's, Rosser's, Timberlake's, and Phelps'.

*   *   *   *   *   *

By command of the Secretary of War:

JNO. WITHERS,
Assistant Adjutant-General.

SPECIAL ORDERS, }   HDQRS. DEPT. OF NORTH CAROLINA,
No. 29.   }   *Goldsborough, February 12,* 1862.

*   *   *   *   *   *

III. Col. William J. Hoke, Thirty-eighth Regiment North Carolina troops, will proceed with his regiment to Weldon, N. C., and take such measures as the force at his command will permit for the defense of the bridge at that place.

He will consider himself still under the command of Colonel Leventhorpe, Thirty-fourth Regiment of North Carolina troops.

By order of Brigadier-General Gatlin:

R. H. RIDDICK,
Assistant Adjutant-General.

NORFOLK, *February* 13, 1862.

General S. COOPER.

I have ordered 1,000 men, Third Alabama, to Suffolk. This weakens front very much indeed. I must have more troops.

BENJ. HUGER,
Major-General.

RICHMOND, *February* 13, 1862.

General HUGER, *Norfolk, Va.:*

Col. W. J. Clarke's North Carolina regiment is ordered to Garysburg, N. C., from Petersburg, subject to your orders for disposition of the regiment on the line of the Weldon and Portsmouth Railroad wherever deemed best. He has been so advised and ordered to report.

S. COOPER,
Adjutant and Inspector General.

HEADQUARTERS DISTRICT OF THE CAPE FEAR,
Wilmington, N. C., February 13, 1862.

General S. COOPER,
Adjutant and Inspector General, Richmond, Va.:

GENERAL: In my letter of 24th September last* I gave you an estimate of the least amount of force I regarded requisite to hold this place

----

* See Series I, Vol. IV, p. 656.

and the railroads terminating here. I beg leave respectfully to ask your attention to that letter, and to say that I now deem a very considerable increase of force here indispensable to the safety of this command if it should be attacked by a large force by land, as it probably will be, if attacked at all.

This is the only point of importance on our Atlantic coast not hitherto threatened by the enemy, and it is reasonable to expect, in view of other expeditions, now fitting out by the enemy at the North, that an effort against this place will not be much longer postponed. That you may exactly appreciate the wants of this command I desire to call your attention to the disposition of the forces now here.

My attention has been directed principally to the defense of the approaches by water. In the works erected for this purpose I have a good degree of confidence, although I have been unable to procure all the armament required. Fort Caswell, on the south side of the Cape Fear River, about 30 miles from Wilmington, is manned by three unattached companies and one company of the Twentieth Regiment North Carolina Volunteers; aggregate strength of the garrison, 350 men. Fort Caswell is supported by the remaining nine companies of the Twentieth Regiment North Carolina Volunteers, stationed at Smithville or Fort Johnston, numbering in the aggregate 765 men.

At the Northern or New Inlet of the Cape Fear River the defenses consist of a battery on Zeeke's Island, manned by one company, of the aggregate strength 99, and Fort Fisher, manned by two unattached companies and one company of the Thirtieth Regiment North Carolina Volunteers, aggregate 250, supported by nine companies of the Thirtieth Regiment, aggregate of which is 770, and a battery of light artillery of four 12-pounders.

The coast of the district is watched by five companies of cavalry, of which three are "local defense" companies, and four are only partially or indifferently armed. Fort Fisher is about 25 miles from Wilmington; the road very difficult, on account of deep sand.

I have at Wilmington the Twenty-eighth Regiment North Carolina Volunteers, aggregate 933, and one battery of light artillery of six 6-pounders.

There are several points east of Wilmington within 10 miles of the city where the enemy might land if he should choose not to attempt to pass the main batteries, but to cross with a large land force the narrow strip of land which separates the city from the ocean.

You will thus see that I have only one regiment and a light battery to oppose such a march of the enemy. Before I could withdraw the two regiments from the mouth of the river by land or water the enemy could reach the city or the railroad to Weldon, having to accomplish only 8 miles, while my regiments would have to move 30.

In this reference to my exposed line I leave out of view the coast south of Fort Caswell, on which he may land, march against Smithville and thence to Wilmington, on the right bank of the river. But were I able to concentrate all the men I have instantaneously at the point of attack which the enemy may select, you are still aware that my strength would not be sufficient to resist the force he will probably bring against us, judging by the past.

I therefore beg that Clingman's and Radcliffe's regiments and Moore's battery of the North Carolina troops, placed here for the defense of this point and sent by me to Port Royal, by direction of the honorable Secretary of War, under peculiar circumstances, be ordered back immediately. These troops were sent there with the belief that they were necessary to prevent a sudden invasion, and were expected to remain only "till they could be replaced by other troops." And I should be doing injustice to the interest confided in me if I did not most respectfully urge that they be sent back, now that we learn a large force has come to the defense of that coast, whilst this is comparatively defenseless as to men.

I will advise General Lee of my expectations, and beg you will inform him that I have stated the case correctly, and order the return of the troops. My force would still fall very much short of what I estimated 24th September. Still, with the return of these troops and the aid of the militia, I believe we can defeat any force he will probably send.

The city is defended by intrenched works on the east, but I have no men to man them, nor is there any force in the vicinity which could be sent to my aid. I have felt it necessary to make this statement to you in order to enforce my application for re-enforcements and that you may see clearly the necessity therefor.

I have the honor to be, your obedient servant,

J. R. ANDERSON,
Brigadier-General, Commanding.

P. S.—In the enumeration of my forces I have given the aggregate, which must be abated 30 or 40 per cent. for the sick.

[Indorsement.]

HEADQUARTERS DEPARTMENT OF NORTH CAROLINA,
Goldsborough, February 15, 1862.

Respectfully forwarded, and urgently request that the troops asked for be ordered to Wilmington without delay.

R. C. GATLIN,
Brigadier-General, Commanding.

RALEIGH, *February* 13, 1862.
J. P. BENJAMIN, *Secretary of War:*

Weldon and the Sea-board Railroad must be defended. I am calling together the militia for that purpose, but that is very insufficient. We must be aided by your regiments from the Peninsula or elsewhere. The danger of cutting off Norfolk is great and a large supply of provisions stored in that section.

HENRY T. CLARK,
Governor of North Carolina.

RICHMOND, VA., *February* 14, 1862.
Gov. HENRY T. CLARK, *Raleigh:*

Your dispatch received. We are hard at work for you, and you will see the result in a very few days. Keep your people in good heart. The danger is greatly exaggerated

J. P. BENJAMIN,
Secretary of War.

HEADQUARTERS DEPARTMENT OF NORTH CAROLINA,
Goldsborough, February 15, 1862.
General S. COOPER,
    Adjutant and Inspector General, Richmond, Va.:

GENERAL: I have the honor to report that Colonel Leventhorpe, with the Thirty-fourth Regiment North Carolina troops, is at this time on the Lower Roanoke, to prevent the boats of the enemy ascending that stream; that Colonel Hoke, with the Thirty-eighth North Carolina troops, is in the vicinity of Weldon, to protect the bridge and railroad at that point; and that Bouldin's section of a light battery has just left for the latter place. I hear from persons passing that Colonel Clarke's regiment and other troops are at Weldon, sent from Virginia, but cannot credit the statement, inasmuch as I have received no intimation of the movement of these troops into this department from your office, nor have the commanders reported to me.

    Very respectfully, your obedient servant,
R. C. GATLIN,
Brigadier-General, Commanding.

FEBRUARY 15, 1862.
WELDON N. EDWARDS,
    President of North Carolina Convention, Raleigh:

Your dispatch received. The defense of North Carolina occupies my anxious attention. I am sending there all the aid I can procure. I prefer not to send back the North Carolina troops referred to. The exigency which caused them to be sent to South Carolina is not less pressing now than at the time of their assignment to the defense of that locality, and they could only be withdrawn by substituting others. To be successful, the common means must be employed for the common defense, as its necessities require.*

JEFFERSON DAVIS.

HEADQUARTERS DEPARTMENT OF NORFOLK,
Norfolk, Va., February 16, 1862.
General S. COOPER,
    Adjutant and Inspector General:

SIR: I submit for the consideration of the Secretary of War a proposed arrangement of the brigades of this division, rendered necessary by the movements of the enemy.

I had sent the Sixth Virginia Regiment, Colonel Corprew, to the Currituck Bridge, with orders to hold that point and prevent the enemy from passing through the South Branch of the Chesapeake and Albemarle Canal.

General Wise, on his retreat from Nag's Head, came to Currituck Bridge, assumed command, removed the battery of three 32-pounders erected there, and began abandoning the place before any enemy appeared. Soon after two or three gunboats came up, fired a few rounds, which fell short, and our troops left. The enemy have not advanced since, and our cavalry pickets are still there.

I had no report from General Wise for two days, but heard he was

---

* See Davis to Avery, February 18, p. 435.

falling back on Norfolk. I sent yesterday to establish batteries near Great Bridge, on the North Branch of Albemarle and Chesapeake Canal, to block that passage, and visited that place to-day. I found General Wise there, with the five companies of the Sixth Virginia Regiment, five pieces of artillery, under Colonel Henningsen, and about four companies of his Legion, under Colonel Richardson. I inquired of General Wise why he abandoned his position at Currituck Bridge without orders, but could get no satisfactory answer. He said he intended to occupy a position on Northwest River, but on reaching there in a snow-storm, found no quarters for his men. He fell back to Great Bridge, 12 miles south of Norfolk, where he now is.

I must be allowed to consider General Wise supernumerary with this army, and relieve him from duty. His Legion has no doubt fine material, but I consider it entirely disorganized, and I shall feel stronger if it is removed.

I am, sir, very respectfully, your most obedient servant,

BENJ. HUGER,
Major-General, Commanding.

RICHMOND, *February* 16, 1862.

Brig. Gen. GEORGE W. RANDOLPH, *Richmond, Va.:*

SIR: The Secretary of War directs that you proceed forthwith to Suffolk, Va., and report for duty to Major-General Huger, under whom you will immediately proceed to fortify and defend the approaches to Norfolk and provide for the protection of the Portsmouth and Weldon Railroad between Suffolk and Weldon. To effect these objects you are authorized to call out a sufficient negro force and adopt such measures as may be necessary.

Capt. I. M. St. John, Engineers, will be directed to report to you for duty.

You will arrange with the Commissary General for the rations of the negroes before leaving the city.

Very respectfully, &c.,

S. COOPER,
Adjutant and Inspector General.

RICHMOND, VA., *February* 18, 1862.

Hon. W. W. AVERY, *Richmond, Va.:*

MY DEAR SIR: Your note of yesterday,* in reference to the conversation I had with yourself and other Representatives from your State, in consequence of the resolutions of the North Carolina Convention, has been received.

I have already replied to the Convention by telegraph† that I prefer not to send back the North Carolina troops referred to, for the reason that the exigency which caused them to be sent to South Carolina is even more pressing now than at the time of their assignment to the defense of that locality. The enemy seriously threatens Savannah, and occupying, as he does, a secure position on the islands in its vicinity, where, protected by his gunboats, he can mature his plans and

---

* Not found.   † See Davis to Edwards, p. 434.

make his arrangements without our being able to obtain any information as to his designs or movements, he may at any moment make a sudden attack upon either Charleston or Savannah.

It will require all the ability for disposition of troops and engineering skill of our generals there to thwart his purposes and defend that portion of our extended coast.

The North Carolina troops could only be withdrawn by the substitution of others, and this change would necessarily, to a greater or less degree, disorganize for a time that portion of our line from which they are drawn and add to the burden of our overtaxed railroad transportation.

The defense of North Carolina occupies my serious attention, and I am sending there all the aid at my disposal. General Randolph has been sent to protect the railroad which connects Weldon with Norfolk, with orders to assemble the troops for this purpose at points on the road convenient for concentration at any point which may be threatened.

It may not be possible, with our limited means, to protect every point which the enemy can attack by means of his fleets, but every effort will be made to hold those positions which are of vital interest to the State and to our common cause.

Our ability to defend is limited by the supply of arms, powder, and other munitions of war. Efforts were made, as you are no doubt aware, at an early period of our troubles, to purchase arms from abroad. Some have been received from this source and we have hopes of more.

I have received no official reports of the disastrous affair at Roanoke Island. The newspaper accounts indicate that the greater portion of our men there behaved very badly. I will wait for more accurate and full reports before forming a judgment as to the cause of our signal defeat.

When the island was first occupied by our troops after the fall of Hatteras, realizing the importance of the position to us, I sent one of my aides-de-camp to make a personal examination of its condition and capabilities for defense. From his report I concluded that the condition of affairs was such as to justify a reasonable hope of successful resistance to any force the enemy could then bring to bear against it, and capable, with proper dispositions and energetic efforts in preparation, of making a creditable, if not successful, defense against any force that would be prepared for the purpose. To this end it was attached to the department of General Huger. After it became probable that the expedition under Burnside would attack this position General Huger was directed to re-enforce it to the extent of his means.

I am not sufficiently informed as to what was done after the inspection of my aide to enable me to say whether the preparation was defective or whether the fault was in the troops.

Very respectfully and truly, yours,

JEFFERSON DAVIS.

HEADQUARTERS DEPARTMENT OF NORTH CAROLINA,
Goldsborough, February 20, 1862.
General S. COOPER,
Adjutant and Inspector General C. S. Army, Richmond, Va.:

GENERAL: On the 15th instant I sent my aide-de-camp to Weldon to ascertain what troops were in that vicinity other than those sent there by my orders. He found Colonel Clarke at Garysburg. with the Twenty-fourth Regiment of North Carolina troops, together with a number of detached companies. Colonel Clarke informed him that he was there by orders from your office, and was instructed to report to Major-General Huger, commanding the Department of Norfolk, and that he was then acting under his orders. As Garysburg is within the Department of North Carolina, I am at a loss to know why troops are sent there and placed under the orders of the commander of another department and I not even officially informed of it.

Already a conflict of jurisdiction has arisen between the officers acting under my orders and those acting under General Huger. I hope immediate steps will be taken to restore order. I have given orders, but they may not be obeyed. I beg to call your attention to my letter of the 15th instant in relation to the defense of the Roanoke, some portion of which is germane to this matter.

Very respectfully, your obedient servant,

R. C. GATLIN,
Major-General, Commanding.

[Indorsement.]

Inform General Gatlin that the troops sent to Garysburg were not intended for his command, but were camped there temporarily, until General Huger could send for them.

J. P. B.

———

RICHMOND, VA., *February* 21, 1862.

Hon. WELDON N. EDWARDS,
President Convention of North Carolina, Raleigh, N. C.:

MY DEAR SIR: Your communication of the 13th instant,* with the accompanying resolutions of the Convention, has been received.

The North Carolina delegation in Congress had presented a copy of the resolutions before the receipt of your letter, and have received a reply, the substance of which has, I suppose, been already delivered to the Convention by them.

I am, very truly, yours,

JEFFERSON DAVIS.

———

RICHMOND, VA., *February* 21, 1862.

A. J. BATTLE, Esq., *Wilson, N. C.:*

MY DEAR SIR: The President has received your letter of the 12th instant,† in reference to the defense of North Carolina, and instructs me to say in reply that inadequate means have limited preparations in that State, as elsewhere, and that he had not doubted the sobriety of General Gatlin, although General Loring, an officer of higher rank, had been sent to North Carolina.

Very respectfully,

G. W. C. LEE,
Colonel, and Aide-de-Camp.

---

* Not found. See Davis to Avery, p. 435.   † Not found.

STATE OF NORTH CAROLINA, EXECUTIVE DEPARTMENT,
Raleigh, February 22, 1862.

Hon. J. P. BENJAMIN, *Secretary of War:*

SIR: I have heretofore drawn your attention to the situation and defenses of Wilmington and the Cape Fear River. The defenses on the north side of the inlet, at mouth of Cape Fear River, were put up by the local authorities. There are several batteries on the river below the town of Wilmington, with some guns, but are without garrison. So you may readily see that a fleet can pass the inlet and ascend the river and destroy Wilmington. They can also land north of the inlet, and are within a march of 10 miles, with only two volunteer regiments to oppose them. The possession of Wilmington commands the Great Northern and Southern Railroad, with all its valuable machine-shops.

But the most attractive feature for that expedition in the eyes of the enemy is the Fayetteville Arsenal, a day's journey up the river. The destruction of that arsenal would be a heavy blow, and would give peculiar gratification, in the Yankee eye, as the recapture of the Harper's Ferry works.

I have just received a memorial from the town authorities of Fayetteville, asking for assistance and urging a system of defense by blocking the channel of the Cape Fear, which is necessary [*sic*] enough to be effected very easily.

The defense of Wilmington cannot be delayed much longer. Moore's light battery, Clingman's regiment, 1,100 strong, and Radcliffe's regiment have been taken from the defense of Wilmington and sent to Port Royal. They are not permitted to return and no efforts are known to be made to supply their places, and there is the most painful anxiety for the safety of Wilmington and Fayetteville. If you have any disposable force, they could not be sent to any position where they are more needed or where they could render more valuable service.

Most respectfully, yours,

HENRY T. CLARK.

DEPT. OF NORFOLK, HDQRS. THIRD BRIGADE,
Portsmouth, Va., February 24, 1862.

Lieut. Col. S. S. ANDERSON,
Adjutant-General, Norfolk:

COLONEL: I have the honor to report that I returned to Suffolk and continued the works on Nansemond River and held correspondence with the different commands. On the 20th instant the news of the first attack on Winton reached me, and I moved Colonel Armistead's Fifty-seventh Regiment of Virginia and one section of Girardey's battery to Franklin to defend the Blackwater and block it up. He is still there. I regret to say that the three companies of South Carolina Volunteers at the mouth of Blackwater had fallen back from that position. I inclose Captain Butler's report.* At the request of many citizens I carried the cotton (500 bales) lying at Franklin to Portsmouth. On the 21st Major-General Huger and Brigadier-General Randolph came to Suffolk and relieved me from duty. At the request of General Randolph I remained with him. The news of Lieutenant-Colonel Williams' retreat reached me, and that Colonel Clarke had arrived at Franklin. We

---

* Not found.

started with a train of cars, and found the Fifty-seventh Virginia and Fourteenth North Carolina down the river on scout. The North Carolina regiment was recalled, and an order sent to Lieutenant-Colonel Williams to return forthwith to Winton. I send copy of his report.* I can see no reason or excuse for his retreat. His men have lost all except their arms and what they wore. He is under command of Colonel Clarke. He left Newsom's for Murfreesborough on the 22d. Colonel Clarke's regiment also went there.

The want of cavalry is excessive. I have ordered the detachment of Captain Gillett's company, which was relieved at Winton by the Nansemond cavalry, to stay with Colonel Armistead until further orders.

I have sent Captain Brewer's Nansemond cavalry toward Edenton to co-operate with the militia in getting off the provisions in that section.

Major Brabble, First North Carolina Battalion, went into Edenton, and arrested Messrs. Norcom and Bland as traitors, in dealing with the enemy. They are sent to Raleigh. The Union men south of Chowan were arrested by Colonel Williams' order, but escaped during the retreat. The whole country south of Chowan is more or less disaffected. I send Colonel Moore's report.*

These two reports of mine will partially show that I have not been idle since my command was extended and that no point in the district was neglected. I must therefore respectfully ask that General Order, No. 14, of 20th February, 1862, reducing my command to a small brigade, while the youngest brigadier in the Army has charge of two brigades, be so modified as to express the opinion of the general that the service required such action and was not done from any disapproval of my conduct.

Colonel Wright, Third Georgia Regiment, has acted separately, and his reports have been sent in.

Respectfully, your obedient servant,

A. G. BLANCHARD,
Brigadier-General, P. A. C. S.

HEADQUARTERS FIFTH BRIGADE, HUGER'S DIVISION,
Murfreesborough, N. C., February 24, 1862.

Hon. J. P. BENJAMIN,
Secretary of War, C. S.:

SIR: Having been placed in command of the forces covering the large territory between the Chowan and the Roanoke Rivers, consisting of my own regiment, numbering less than 600 effective men; Colonel Williams' Battalion North Carolina Volunteers, 400; one company of cavalry of Wise's Legion, only 40 of whom are with me, and Nichols' battery of four small pieces, I hasten to inform you that these forces are wholly inadequate to the important services required of them, and respectfully, but most urgently, request that an additional force of cavalry and artillery may be immediately placed at my disposal. I am using my utmost endeavors to raise a small body of mounted men in this vicinity to act as couriers and vedettes, but being wholly undisciplined and but poorly armed, they will be incompetent to meet the enemy in the field, even should I be able to raise them, which is doubtful.

---

* Not found.

My artillery consists of four light pieces, insufficient, both in range and caliber, to defend the rivers against the heavily-armed gunboats of the enemy. An order received from you stopped the march of two companies of cavalry of Wise's Legion, who were at Garysburg, N. C., and were about moving to re-enforce me. I have detained Lieutenant Tucker, who was ordered to proceed to Manassas, until you could be informed of the indispensable necessity of his remaining with me until some other cavalry force should relieve him. My only means of obtaining information and keeping up communication is by means of vedettes, and these should be men that have seen service, that I may not be misled by erroneous reports. Instead of depriving me of cavalry my force should be strengthened, for if ten times as strong it would not be sufficient for the service necessary in the territory committed to my charge. By means of one cavalry company I was enabled a few days ago to secure a large amount of Government property, which otherwise would most probably have fallen into the hands of the enemy.

Permit me to inform you that my command embraces a highly productive tract of country, which now contains provisions sufficient to subsist the whole Army of the Confederate States for at least half a year, and it is of the first importance that it should not be ravaged by the enemy. The white population is sparse, and they have been so long neglected that they are perfectly demoralized. An exhibition of force, which I made a few days ago, has been of inestimable value in inspiring our people with confidence and in intimidating our foes.

I expect to be able to obstruct this (the Meherrin) river effectually by the time this reaches you, and with two 18-pounders and two 24s or 32s I could destroy any vessels that should attempt to come up to this place and at the same time effectually protect the bridge of the ·Seaboard and Roanoke Railroad over this river.

With two more regiments of infantry and 500 cavalry, in addition to the force now present, I could keep the enemy from advancing inland in my department.

I beg that you will countermand the order removing Wise's cavalry, and that the whole battalion will be ordered here, and also artillery and experienced artillerists.

Very respectfully, your obedient servant,

WM. J. CLARKE,
Colonel, Commanding Fifth Brigade, Huger's Division.

HEADQUARTERS DEPARTMENT OF NORTH CAROLINA,
Goldsborough, February 27, 1862.

General S. COOPER,
Adjutant and Inspector General, Richmond, Va.:

GENERAL: I received last night the following telegram from the Secretary of War, viz:

Send a statement as promptly as possible of your forces, their disposition, and your means and plans of defense.

I inclose herewith an imperfect return of the troops within the department.* It may answer for present purposes, but 1 hope to be able to forward a more complete one in a few days.

For a detailed report of the defenses of the Cape Fear District, the

---

* Not found.

location of the troops, &c., I beg to refer to the report of Brigadier-General Anderson, dated the 13th instant,* and which was forwarded to you through these headquarters. As General Anderson will be in Richmond to-day, he will be able to explain in person anything not understood in that communication. In case he is attacked, his defenses destroyed, and his troops driven from their positions, it is understood that he is to fall back in the direction of Fayetteville, with the view of checking the advance of the enemy in that direction. It is hoped and believed that his defenses are sufficient, but he is sadly deficient in troops.

Conceiving the town of New Berne, the point most likely to be attacked, I have assembled in its vicinity as large a body of troops as in my power. They are under the command of Brig. Gen. L. O'B. Branch, who also commands the District of the Pamlico. Batteries have been erected on the Neuse below the town and the river effectually blocked. These batteries are open and the guns mounted in barbette, but it is hoped they will not fail to drive off the fleet of gunboats should they attempt to reduce them. Below these batteries are breastworks running from the river to the swamps on Bryce's Creek, which are believed to be impassable. The breastworks are thought to be strong enough to enable our troops to resist and hold them against a large force of the enemy. I regret that I have no sketch of these works to transmit. You will perceive that a large increase to the force at New Berne should be made to place them upon an equality with such a force as attacked Roanoke Island.

In case they are driven from their positions they are to fall back upon the line of the Atlantic and North Carolina Railroad, and take up the first defensible position, not yet determined upon, which may confine the enemy as close to New Berne as practicable.

The batteries at Harkers' and Huggins' Islands have been withdrawn, and the garrison at Fort Macon reduced to five companies of artillery, the largest number that could be sheltered inside the fort in case of siege. The fort has a supply of seven months' provisions, and its commander is of opinion that he can hold it as long as powder and his provisions last. A large supply of powder is required to meet the contingencies of a siege.

The Pamlico River is protected by batteries some 8 miles below the town of Washington. They are considered sufficient to beat off the gunboats, but the force there is not adequate to contend with a large land force. In case of the loss of the batteries the troops will retreat up the Tar River in the direction of Greenville.

The troops heretofore stationed in Hyde County have been withdrawn, as it was considered imprudent to keep them there, there being but one road leading out of the county which could readily be seized by the enemy, thus cutting off all retreat. A local company still remains for such service as it may be able to render in preventing servile insurrection. Five companies taken from Hyde have been sent to New Berne; the remainder are at Washington.

You will perceive that the force under my command is very inadequate to the defense of so extensive a coast against an enemy who has possession of our sounds and can direct his large columns against any point he may elect.

Very respectfully, your obedient servant,

R. C. GATLIN,
Brigadier-General, Commanding.

* See p. 431.

RICHMOND, VA., *March* 2, 1862.

Brigadier-General GATLIN, *Goldsborough, N. C.:*

The President directs that the troops be withdrawn from the defense of Washington [N. C.], and sent immediately to General Randolph, at Suffolk, to aid in defense of that point. The artillery can be withdrawn to the line of railroad, to be disposed of as may be found best hereafter.

J. P. BENJAMIN,
Secretary of War.

GENERAL ORDERS, } HDQRS. DEPT. OF NORTH CAROLINA,
No. 4.   }   *Goldsborough, March 9,* 1862.

By direction of the Secretary of War, all cotton, tobacco, and naval stores within this department must be removed west of the Wilmington and Weldon Railroad; or, if distant from any railroad or navigable stream, put in such places of security that they cannot be reached by the enemy. Such of the above-mentioned products as are in exposed positions must be removed at once, and those less exposed removed or secured by the 25th instant; otherwise they will be destroyed by the military authorities.

The generals commanding the Districts of the Cape Fear and Pamlico will see that these orders are carried into effect.

It is hoped that the owners themselves will apply the torch rather than see the enemy gain possession of these much-coveted products.

Whenever it shall become necessary for an officer or citizen to destroy private property to prevent its falling into the hands of the enemy he will make a report of the facts and circumstances to these headquarters, accompanied with a statement of the property destroyed and to whom it belonged, and furnish the owner with a copy of the statement.

By order of Brigadier-General Gatlin:

JOHN W. GRAHAM,
Acting Assistant Adjutant-General.

GOLDSBOROUGH, *March* 13, 1862.
(Received Richmond, March 13, 1862.)

General S. COOPER,
Adjutant and Inspector General:

The enemy are in large force in Neuse River—ten steamers and one transport; are about 12 miles below New Berne. The pilot reports fifty vessels coming up. This is General Branch's report, date 9 p. m. yesterday.

R. C. GATLIN,
Brigadier-General.

RICHMOND, VA., *March* 13, 1862.

Brigadier-General GATLIN, *Goldsborough:*

The two North Carolina regiments of Radcliffe and Clingman have been ordered to New Berne. In the mean time draw re-enforcements from Wilmington, if practicable.

J. P. BENJAMIN,
Secretary of War.

RICHMOND, VA., *March* 13, 1862.

Major-General PEMBERTON, *Pocotaligo, S. C.:*

Send Radcliffe's and Clingman's regiments to New Berne, N. C., to report to General Branch. Will be replaced by two regiments from Georgia.

J. P. BENJAMIN,
Secretary of War.

RICHMOND, VA., *March* 14, 1862.

Brigadier-General GATLIN, *Goldsborough:*

What have you done about destroying cotton? What re-enforcements have you sent to New Berne? What are your plans? Keep us constantly advised.. Have you established a line of signals to New Berne?

J. P. BENJAMIN.

GOLDSBOROUGH, *March* 14, 1862.

Hon. J. P. BENJAMIN:

An officer has just arrived from New Berne, who reports that the town fell into the hands of the enemy at 10 or 11 a. m. to-day, and that the troops are falling back in the direction of Kinston. I will try to hold the line of railroad between New Berne and this place, but to prevent the advance of the enemy large re-enforcements will be required. A general order was issued in regard to cotton on the 9th instant.

R. C. GATLIN,
Brigadier-General, Commanding.

HEADQUARTERS DEPARTMENT OF NORTH CAROLINA,
Goldsborough, March 14, 1862.

General S. COOPER,
Adjutant and Inspector General, Richmond, Va.:

GENERAL: I had the honor to send to-day to the honorable Secretary of War a telegram announcing the fall of New Berne. I have received no report from Brigadier-General Branch, who commanded, and I learn was on the railroad 10 miles this side of New Berne at sunset this evening with a part of his forces. I design to collect at Kinston all those who have passed General B., as at that point the several roads on which they may have retreated join. No re-enforcements reached New Berne in time to take part in the action. I have summoned General Anderson to my assistance, and will place the troops in such position as may seem best. In the mean time I will telegraph General Lee for advice as to the best line of defense it will be advisable to adopt.

My health for some time past has not been such as to warrant my taking the field, and for a few days past have been confined to my room; otherwise I should have been present to have conducted the operations in person.

A telegram from the Secretary of War to-day would indicate that he had not seen my report, accompanied by a return of the troops in General Branch's district. If such is the case, I beg that it may be laid before him.

Very respectfully, your obedient servant,

R. C. GATLIN,
Brigadier-General, Commanding.

SPECIAL ORDERS, ⎰　　HDQRS. DEPT. OF NORTH CAROLINA,
No. 51.　　⎱　　　*Goldsborough, March* 14, .1862.

I. Col. James H. Lane, Twenty-eighth Regiment North Carolina troops, will assume command of all troops in this vicinity, who have escaped from New Berne, and proceed with them to Kinston.

*　　　*　　　*　　　*　　　*　　　*

By order of Major-General Gatlin:

JOHN W. GRAHAM,
Aide-de-Camp.

RICHMOND, VA., *March* 14, 1862.

General JOSEPH R. ANDERSON,
Wilmington, N. C.:

Send such re-enforcements as you can, to report to General Gatlin immediately. Halt, if necessary, in their stead Radcliffe's and Clingman's regiments, on way from North [South] Carolina.

J. P. BENJAMIN,
Secretary of War.

RICHMOND, VA., *March* 15, 1862.

Gov. HENRY T. CLARK, *Raleigh:*

Large re-enforcements are immediately requisite for the defense of your State. The regiments of Clingman and Radcliffe have been ordered back to Wilmington. Call on your people to arm in defense of their homes. Send all the men you can to Weldon as rapidly as possible. 1 will find means to arm them all. I pray you to allow no time to be lost.

J. P. BENJAMIN,
Secretary of War.

STATE OF NORTH CAROLINA, EXECUTIVE DEPARTMENT,
Raleigh, March 15, 1862.

Hon. J. P. BENJAMIN,
Secretary of War, Richmond:

SIR: On Wednesday, the 12th, the Burnside expedition appeared in large force below our batteries on the Neuse, opened fire on the next morning about 8 o'clock a. m., and in latter part of the day effected a landing of a large body of troops, estimated about 25,000.

On Friday our force, about 5,000, engaged them in the morning, and after a severe conflict of two or three hours were outflanked and nearly surrounded.

In the mean time the fleet had passed the river batteries and entered the Trent River off the town and behind our troops, who were on the opposite bank from the town. Our troops, thus overpowered and nearly surrounded, made such an escape as they could, and many no doubt were captured, but I have no reliable knowledge of this or of the casualties on either side.

New Berne being in possession of the enemy, we have no communication there, except from some refugees or stragglers.

The hard fighting that took place disposes me to believe that there was considerable mortality on both sides.

I suppose you will soon have official reports.

I hear much complaint and criticism among the people of the absence of General Gatlin from the field of battle and his entire neglect and inattention to the coast defenses of his command for the last five months, and they judge of this neglect and inattention from the alleged fact that he has not during that period visited and examined the fortifications and inspected the troops more than once, if at all, during his command of six months, notwithstanding his headquarters are in easy railroad communication of both Generals Anderson's and Branch's commands.

I am only stating what I hear constantly around me. Perhaps his headquarters is the proper place for him, but the people so deeply interested in their own homes and interests expected the benefit of his military knowledge and experience, and [are] greatly distressed that they have not had it, and regard with much anxiety his want of attention to their safety and interest and what they believe was his special business.

The present prospect is that we shall soon have our quota, five regiments, and probably more, and I am looking to you for the supply of arms.

In connection with the formation of these regiments I will take the liberty of suggesting to you some regulation or legislation to inquire by examination or otherwise into the qualification of the commissioned officers.

It seems now that there is manifest want of attention to the proper requisite for an officer. In the great number there must necessarily be many that are not qualified, but still there should be some means of ascertaining the fitness of at least commanding officers of companies, regiments, and brigades, and regulations, general in their application, would or ought to prove acceptable. Too much has to be intrusted to the commanding officer.

Very respectfully,

HENRY T. CLARK.

SPECIAL ORDERS,   ADJT. AND INSP. GENERAL'S OFFICE,
No. 60.   Richmond, March 15, 1862.
*   *   *   *   *   *

XIV. Brig. Gen. Richard C. Gatlin is relieved from duty in North Carolina on account of ill health, and will be succeeded in the command of the Department of North Carolina by Brig. Gen. Joseph R. Anderson.

XV. Brig. Gen. Samuel G. French will repair to Wilmington, N. C., and relieve Brigadier-General Anderson in the command of that district.*

---

*See General Orders, No. 13, dated at Wilmington, N. C., March 22, 1862, p. 450.

XVI. Brig. Gen. Carter L. Stevenson will report to Major-General Huger for assignment with troops on the line of railroad near Weldon, N. C.

By command of the Secretary of War:

JNO. WITHERS,
Assistant Adjutant-General.

●

RICHMOND, VA., *March* 17, 1862.

Gov. HENRY T. CLARK, *Raleigh:*

I did not request that militia should be called out. If not armed, they would be of no service. I will arm all the volunteers you send. If you have more than two regiments, send the remainder to Goldsborough. Tents, camp equipage, and blankets will be sent immediately to Goldsborough.

JEFFERSON DAVIS.

STATE OF NORTH CAROLINA, EXECUTIVE DEPARTMENT,
Raleigh, March 17, 1862.

His Excellency JEFFERSON DAVIS,
President of the Confederate States:

SIR: I have the honor to present to you the inclosed memorial and resolutions of the people of Wilmington, which have just been handed to me, and I feel a deep anxiety that it should receive your attentive consideration. I would not press it on your attention if I could grant them assistance myself, but I have no troops at my disposal, and a call for militia, with their tardiness of action, destitution of arms, and the requisite of a soldier, leaves no hope of benefit from them.

The only troops at Wilmington are the few that I could put there, and insufficient as they were, they have been removed by Confederate officers to other positions, till there are less than 1,500 left, which could not resist even a fourth of the Burnside expedition.

Wilmington has the great machine-shops, the railroad connections (our only means of getting salt), furnishes the materials, support, and access for the Confederate States Arsenal. Any one of these presents sufficient claims to be defended by the Confederate States, and it must be done quickly or not at all; for it is doubtless the next move of Burnside, which will destroy the last connection of North Carolina with the ocean.

The people of Wilmington must know in time what to depend on, either to be defended or to seek safety in flight. If the great public interests will not secure a defense for them, they must secure their private interests as far as possible by removal to some more secure spot. . I will take the liberty of further adding that the adjacent counties to Wilmington have sent out an unusual number of volunteers, who are now absent on duty elsewhere, and presents the great difficulty of procuring within reach any amount of militia.

I take pleasure in introducing to you the committee who present these resolutions, Messrs. Strange, Thomas, and De Rosset, and hope they will enlist your attention in behalf of a cause which so much interests both you and them.

I have the honor to be, most respectfully, yours,

HENRY T. CLARK.

[Inclosure.]

OFFICE OF THE COMMITTEE OF SAFETY,
FOR THE TOWN OF WILMINGTON,
Wilmington, N. C., March 15, 1862.

At a meeting of the Committee of Safety held this day the following resolutions were adopted:

Resolved, That Maj. Robert Strange, A. J. De Rosset, and W. G. Thomas, as representatives from the Committee of Safety of the town of Wilmington, forthwith proceed to the city of Raleigh, and confer with the Governor of this State on the subject-matter of the defenses connected with this portion of the State of North Carolina, representing to him the present condition of these defenses, the amount of the forces connected with them, and all such facts in relation to this subject-matter necessary to a full knowledge of our true condition.

Resolved, That said committee ascertain from the Governor what are his views as to the defense of this portion of the State, and if his purpose be to make such defense, that he be requested, without delay, to provide a competent force, with necessary munitions of war, for that purpose.

Resolved, That said committee, after conferring with the Governor, proceed to the city of Richmond, and ascertain, if practicable, the intentions of the Confederate States in reference to the defenses of the town of Wilmington.

S. D. WALLACE,
Secretary.

SPECIAL ORDERS, }   ADJT. AND INSP. GENERAL'S OFFICE,
No. 61.   }   *Richmond, March* 17, 1862.

*   *   *   *   *   *   *

XV. Brig. Gen. Robert Ransom will proceed without delay to Goldsborough, N. C., and report to Brig. Gen. Joseph R. Anderson, commanding, for duty with the troops in the field.

By command of the Secretary of War:

JNO. WITHERS,
Assistant Adjutant-General.

SPECIAL ORDERS, }   HDQRS. DEPT. OF NORTH CAROLINA,
No. 53.   }   *Goldsborough, March* 17, 1862.

*   *   *   *   *   *   *

II. Brig. Gen. Samuel G. French, C. S. Army, having reported for duty in this department, agreeably to Special Orders, No. 1, from Headquarters, Richmond, Va., March 14,* 1862, is hereby assigned to the command of the District of the Pamlico, which district embraces the counties of Edgecombe, Wilson, Pitt, Greene, Wayne, Lenoir, Duplin, Jones, Carteret, Craven, Beaufort, and Hyde.

The troops in the field in that district will be formed into two brigades, as follows:

The First (or French's) Brigade will consist of the Seventh, Twenty-sixth, Twenty-seventh, Thirty-fifth Regiments, and Maj. L. H. Rogers' battalion of infantry, North Carolina troops; Captains Sutton, Tripp, Rodman, Lane, Harding, Mallett, and Whitehurst's companies of foot artillery, which will be formed into a battalion, under the command of Capt. William Sutton; Captains Jones and Grisham's batteries, and Colonel Spruill's cavalry.

The Second (Branch's) Brigade will consist of the Eighteenth, Twenty-fifth, Twenty-eighth, Thirty-third, and Thirty-seventh Regiments North

---

* (March 15th.) See Special Orders, No. 60, March 15, 1862, from Adjutant and Inspector General's Office, Richmond, p. 445.

Carolina troops; Captains Whitford's, Mayo's, Leecraft's, and Herring's companies of foot artillery, which will be formed into a battalion, under the command of Capt. John N. Whitford; Latham's and Bunting's batteries, and Captain Evans' cavalry.

Any other companies or parts of companies not embraced in the foregoing will be assigned to brigades by Brigadier-General French, who will immediately report the same to these headquarters.

*   *   *   *   *.   *

By order of [Brig. Gen. J. R. Anderson]:

R. H. RIDDICK,
Assistant Adjutant-General.

GENERAL ORDERS, }   HEADQUARTERS,
　　No. 1.   }   *Kinston, March* 18, 1862.

In accordance with Special Orders, No. 53, Headquarters Department of North Carolina, dated March 17, the undersigned assumes command of the troops in the field in the District of Pamlico, which district embraces the counties of Edgecombe, Wilson, Wayne, Lenoir, Duplin, Jones, Carteret, Craven, Beaufort, Pitt, Greene, and Hyde.

S. G. FRENCH,
Brigadier-General, C. S. Army.

HEADQUARTERS DISTRICT OF PAMLICO,
Kinston, March 18, 1862.

General R. E. LEE, *Richmond:*

GENERAL: I. I have not given this section of country, as regards defense, any consideration until within the last two days, but from what I have seen of the country and the force of the enemy I have drawn certain conclusions.

II. This place cannot be defended, because it is an open, level country, with roads enabling the place to be flanked. A column of the enemy approaching by the road on the left bank gains our left flank. The stage road and railroad cross about a mile from each other in our front, and then another crossing at White Hall, some miles above us, gaining our rear; besides, wagon roads numerously intersect them. The river is also boatable.

III. If the rail of the road be taken up, which I would advise, it would prevent its use by the enemy hereafter, and he could, if he advances, be better and more successfully fought near Goldsborough, farther from his base of operations and in a more defensible country. Further, the country abandoned is sterile and destitute of supplies.

IV. The force concentrated at or near Goldsborough would be in a strategic position, and available for Wilmington and Suffolk.

V. From numerous sources, especially Captain Meade, Engineers, and other officers, I am informed that, should the expedition depart for Wilmington, they can land readily on the land which forms the sound south of Sandy Hall Inlet, and, as it connects with the main-land, get to the rear of the city.

The sound also is at the south end easily forded; after which it becomes deep and the main shore easily approached by boats; hence a land force in strength is necessary for the defense of the place. This might probably be sent in time from Goldsborough.

VI. Hence I recommend the destruction of this road to Goldsborough and concentration of forces at that point. I know, however, that you have better means of knowing the ease with which a force can be landed for the attack on Wilmington than I have collected in the two days I have been here, amidst a press of business.

The defenses against attack on Wilmington by water are represented as being good. You will excuse my making these suggestions to you, who have doubtless considered them. I have thought they could do no harm in any event. One of the surgeons who went to New Berne has returned. He reports that General Burnside told him candidly that he had 27,000 men, and that he knew every regiment and the exact nature of the fortifications at New Berne before the attack, and he named all the regiments with perfect familiarity.

Yours, very truly,

S. G. FRENCH,
Brigadier-General, C. S. Army.

RICHMOND, VA., *March* 20, 1862.
Governor HENRY T. CLARK, *Raleigh, N. C.:*

Call on every man in your State that can come with arms to rally with the utmost dispatch to defend your line of railroad.

JEFFERSON DAVIS.

HEADQUARTERS DEPARTMENT OF NORFOLK,
March 20, 1862.
General R. E. LEE,
General, Commanding:

SIR : As I reported by telegraph, I have dispatched to Goldsborough, to report to Brigadier-General Anderson, the Louisiana Battalion, the Georgia Battalion, Major Hardeman, and Col. D. H. Hamilton's regiment South Carolina Volunteers.

This latter regiment has eleven companies, one of which (Captain McIntosh's) has a battery of field artillery (four guns).

I last night received your dispatch to send to Goldsborough Colonel Leventhorpe's regiment from Hamilton, N. C., Colonel Hoke's regiment from Weldon, N. C., and Brig. Gen. Howell Cobb's brigade from Suffolk. The orders were dispatched at once and receipt acknowledged, except from Colonel Leventhorpe, who cannot be reached so soon. The railroad has been notified and transportation arranged.

Very respectfully, your obedient servant,

BENJ. HUGER,
Major-General.

HEADQUARTERS,
Richmond, Va., March 21, 1862.
Maj. Gen. B. HUGER,
Commanding Department Norfolk, Va.:

GENERAL : I have had the honor to receive your letter of the 20th instant, reporting the execution of orders for the movement of troops in your department to Goldsborough. The battalions of Louisiana and Georgia Volunteers which you forwarded, to report to General Anderson, it is presumed were sent in lieu of the regiments of Colonels Clarke and Armistead; it was not intended that more should be sent than were specified in telegrams of 19th. As regards the regiment of Colonel Leventhorpe, stationed at Hamilton, about which you yesterday telegraphed, I do not see that much can be gained in keeping him at that place. Should the enemy attack him, so small a force could do but little to resist him, and would afford no material impediment to his further progress. It would seem much more desirable to concentrate the troops nearer the railroad and keep them light and movable, so as to re-enforce readily any point of the road he might seriously threaten. The guns and all other munitions at Hamilton should of course be removed, and could be devoted to the strengthening of other points of defense in your department.

I am, very respectfully, your obedient servant,

R. E. LEE,
General, Commanding.

Unless wanted elsewhere in your department, it is suggested to send the section of Captain Bruce's artillery which was at Hamilton to Goldsborough, where it is likely to be much needed.

GENERAL ORDERS, }   HDQRS. DISTRICT OF THE CAPE FEAR,
No. 13. }   *Wilmington, N. C., March 22, 1862.*

The undersigned, by virtue of Special Orders, No. 60, Adjutant and Inspector General's Office, Richmond, dated March 15, 1862, hereby assumes command of the District of the Cape Fear, embracing the counties of New Hanover, Onslow, Brunswick, Robeson, Cumberland, Bladen, Columbus, and Sampson.

S. G. FRENCH,
Brigadier-General, Commanding.

HEADQUARTERS,
Richmond, March 23, 1862.

Maj. Gen. T. H. HOLMES,
Commanding, &c., Richmond, Va.:

GENERAL: You will proceed with the troops under your command to Goldsborough, N. C., and take command of the operations in that department. It will be your object to make arrangements to ascertain whether the enemy will advance upon Goldsborough or Wilmington, and to use your whole force to repel them and to protect the railroad. Orders will be issued placing you in command, and the troops from the Department of Northern Virginia will be forwarded to you as soon as possible.

Very respectfully, your obedient servant,

R. E. LEE,
General, Commanding.

SPECIAL ORDERS, }   ADJT. AND INSP. GENERAL'S OFFICE,
No. 67. }   *Richmond, March 24, 1862.*

*   *   *   *   *   *

XXVI. Maj. Gen. Theophilus H. Holmes is assigned to the command of the Department of North Carolina, and will proceed to Goldsborough and relieve Brig. Gen. Joseph R. Anderson.

XXVII. The following troops will proceed at once to Goldsborough, N. C., and report for duty to the commanding general of the Department of North Carolina:

First Regiment North Carolina Volunteers, Colonel M. S. Stokes.
Second Regiment North Carolina Volunteers, Colonel C. C. Tew.
Third Regiment North Carolina Volunteers, Colonel G. Meares.
Third Regiment Arkansas Volunteers, Colonel V. H. Manning.
Thirtieth Regiment Virginia Volunteers, Colonel R. M. Cary.
Captain Cooke's battery.

XXVIII. The troops composing General Wilcox's brigade will be forwarded immediately on their arrival in this city to Goldsborough, N. C., and will report for duty to Major-General Holmes, commanding Department of North Carolina.

*   *   *   *   *   *   *

XXX. Brig. Gen. J. G. Walker will proceed with his brigade, and the battery attached, to Goldsborough, N. C., and report for duty to Maj. Gen. Theophilus H. Holmes, commanding Department of North Carolina.

By command of the Secretary of War:

JNO. WITHERS,
Assistant Adjutant-General.

HEADQUARTERS DEPARTMENT OF NORTH CAROLINA,
Kinston, March 25, 1862.
General S. COOPER,
Adjutant and Inspector General, Richmond, Va.:

GENERAL: As I advised you by telegraph, I arrived here yesterday. I found some confusion in the army, arising from the recent events at New Berne. In a few days I trust order and system will be restored.

The accounts I am able to get as to the plans of the enemy are conflicting naturally, but that he will move forward in this direction or on Wilmington I presume there is no doubt.

Under these circumstances I thought it best for General French to proceed to Wilmington and assume command, though I regretted much to lose his services here. I also concluded to halt Starke's regiment and Moore's battery at that point for the present, and the forces coming from the north at Goldsborough, from which point they may be moved quickly, as the emergency may require.

I have the honor to forward a letter from General French, written while he was in command.* I concur in his views as to this position, and while I push my pickets down to feel the enemy's within 3 or 4 miles of New Berne, and will send down large scouting parties with a view of annoying his progress if he commences a march, it is my opinion that it will be better to fall back gradually some 10 or 15 miles before fully testing our strength, with a view of finding more favorable ground.

Still, there is no ground between this and Goldsborough on which we can intrench without being likely to have our flanks turned by a superior force, so level and firm is the ground, intersected by various roads.

---

* See French to Lee, March 18, p. 448.

I will be pleased to have the advice of the Commanding General. In the mean time we will do our best to watch and protect both points, Goldsborough and Wilmington.

I have the honor to be, your obedient servant,

J. R. ANDERSON,
Brigadier-General, Commanding.

SPECIAL ORDERS, }   ADJT. AND INSP. GENERAL'S OFFICE,
No. 68.   }   *Richmond, March* 25, 1862.

*   *   *   *   *   *   *

VI. General Wilcox's brigade will be halted at Weldon, N. C., until the object of the enemy is disclosed.

*   *   *   *   *   ..

By command of the Secretary of War:

JNO. WITHERS,
Assistant Adjutant-General.

GENERAL ORDERS, }   HDQRS. DEPT. OF NORTH CAROLINA,
No. 6.   }   *Goldsborough, N. C., March* 25, 1862.

I. Under instructions from the President, the undersigned assumes command of the Department of North Carolina.

II. Maj. Archer Anderson is announced as assistant adjutant-general.

TH. H. HOLMES,
Major-General, P. A. C. S.

GENERAL ORDERS, }   HDQRS. DEPT. OF NORTH CAROLINA,
No. 7.   }   *March* 25, 1862.

The enemy are before us and must advance at an early day. If we do not defeat him North Carolina will be under his worse than vandal despotism. Let us all, then, give ourselves up, body and mind, to the sacred duties of her defense. To effect this the strictest discipline must be preserved, and the commanders of companies, regiments, and brigades are required to enforce the most exact obedience to all orders and regulations. Until further orders no furloughs will be granted, nor will any officer or soldier be permitted to leave his camp without permission from his brigade commander. The most active system of drills will be instituted, and every commanding officer is held responsible that his command is ready to march at a moment's notice.

By order of Maj. Gen. T. H. Holmes:

WM. NORWOOD,
Assistant Adjutant-General.

GOLDSBOROUGH, *March* 27, 1862.

General R. E. LEE:

MY DEAR SIR: There appears to be no disposition on the part of the enemy to advance in this direction. From the best information I have I doubt if he has more than three or four regiments in New Berne, and on Monday last there were but five or six steamers at the wharves. It is believed by General Branch that their army is encamped below the town and across the Trent, which is 2,000 yards wide, and on which they have destroyed the bridges as high up as Trenton. They have established a ferry over it at New Berne, but permit no citizen, under any pretense, to pass over. I have sent secret agents to ascertain, if possible, whether they are there or not. I am waiting most anxiously their report. The inclosed sketch will show you the supposed position of the enemy and its surroundings.*

I went yesterday to examine into the position and condition of the army under General Branch. I was assured by the colonels that there was no demoralization, and that the men were tolerably well supplied and most anxious to advance. The position they occupy, 7 miles this side of Kinston, is too far from the enemy, and I shall order General Ransom, with his brigade, to advance 5 or 6 miles beyond Kinston to some point from whence he can more closely watch the enemy. Instead of sending General Anderson back to Wilmington I have given him a brigade. I did so because General French was already there, and perfectly acquainted with the particular kind of duty required there. If Wilcox's brigade and the First North Carolina Cavalry are subject to my orders I shall let them remain at Weldon for the present, and authorize the commanding officer of that department to use them if the enemy makes his appearance in that direction. I have ordered six companies who have been drilled at heavy artillery to report to General French in Wilmington. This will make the batteries there secure against their Navy, and I hope to have timely notice before they can land to send troops from here to give him battle.

The Governor of North Carolina has detained the arms sent to me until he can hear from you on the subject of using them for arming certain regiments that he has organized in Raleigh. It would be a thousand times better if those regiments were sent to me here, in order that they may be properly brigaded and instructed. If possible, send General Whiting to report to me.

I am, General, very respectfully,

TH. H. HOLMES,
Major-General, Commanding.

GOLDSBOROUGH, *March* 28, 1862.

General R. E. LEE, *Commanding:*

MY DEAR SIR: Every appearance indicates that the enemy does not design to advance in this direction at present, but rather that he is seeking to possess himself of the counties along the coast and to invest Fort Macon. If an attack is made on Wilmington I believe it will be by other troops than those under Burnside, for I am assured that their transports draw too much water to cross the Swash Channel when loaded, and that they were three weeks entering the sound, having been obliged to unload them before doing so. I have very little doubt that the force here is able to retake New Berne, but I fear to move until it is ascertained that they will not be required at Wilmington or some other new point of attack. Please inform me what you think and wish about it. I am oppressed with the responsibility upon me. The

---

*Omitted as of no present value.

tremendous issue involved makes it necessary that a more able brain than mine should direct. Please, therefore, my dear General, come and straighten out this tangled yarn.

Since writing the above your telegram is received.* I can drive the enemy out of New Berne, because I can transport the troops by rail; but their main army is below, and I can only reach it by crossing the Trent high up and marching down, which can only be done after I have collected transportation enough to carry provisions. See the sketch I sent you two days ago. I am making every effort to procure transportation, but my quartermaster wants experience and is inefficient. Please send me Major Cone or some other who knows and will do his duty. If you think I can attack New Berne without the fear of being out of place when another point is attacked I will do so at once, though from the best evidence I have there are not more than 4,000 men there, and they can retire beyond the Trent without my being able to follow.

The people here are to a certain extent reassured. They are loyal and true-hearted, but a deep and dangerous despondency, even among the members of the Convention, had taken possession of them, and hence the great necessity of some able man to command here, for if this army should meet with a reverse the political consequences would be disastrous in the extreme. If you cannot come and G. W. Smith's health will permit it, please send him. I will assist him in every way possible, and will be pleased to serve under him if he is a good general.

I am, General, yours, very respectfully,

TH. H. HOLMES,
Major-General.

HEADQUARTERS,
Richmond, Va., March 29, 1862.

Maj. Gen. T. H. HOLMES,
Commanding, &c., Goldsborough, N. C.:

GENERAL: I am directed by General Lee, commanding, to acknowledge the receipt at these headquarters of the letter of General French of March 18, 1862, from Kinston, N. C., forwarded by and inclosed in one of the 25th instant from General Anderson, in reference to the disposition of the forces at Goldsborough and Wilmington, copies of which are doubtless in your possession; also of your two telegrams of the 27th instant.*

In reply the General wishes me to say that it now rests with you to assume such a line with your army as may to your judgment appear best for the protection of the railroad and the security of Goldsborough and Wilmington; and should there be no indications to lead you to infer that the enemy intend to threaten seriously either of those places, you should so dispose your command as to re-enforce Suffolk, as it is not unlikely the enemy may turn their attention to that point, with a view of carrying out a combined movement upon Portsmouth and Norfolk. Being on the ground, however, you have the best opportunity of observing the enemy's movements and divining his intentions. Circumstances must, however, in some measure control your actions.

I am, general, very respectfully, your obedient servant,

T. A. WASHINGTON,
Major and Assistant Adjutant-General.

---

* Not found.

Abstract from report of the troops of the Department of North Carolina, commanded by Maj. Gen. T. H. Holmes, Goldsborough, N. C., March 31, 1862.

Troops.	Present for duty.		Effective total.	Aggregate present.	Aggregate present and absent.	Artillery.	
	Officers.	Men.				Horses.	Pieces.
Infantry	921	15,909	16,436	19,848	23,574		
Cavalry	70	1,364	1,400	1,581	1,833		
Artillery	114	1,994	2,088	2,601	3,167	481	142
Grand total	1,105	19,267	19,924	24,030	28,574	481	142

HEADQUARTERS,
Richmond, Va., April 1, 1862.

General T. H. HOLMES,
Commanding Department of North Carolina:

GENERAL: From your telegraphic dispatches I learn that the enemy • apparently is making no forward movement, nor do you appear to be able to discover that he is making any preparations with that view. That leads me to fear that while making demonstrations in that quarter and on the Peninsula against General Magruder, his real object is to attack Norfolk from both sides, with the force now collecting at Hampton and neighborhood on one side and that under General Burnside on the other. I desire you, therefore, to watch the movements of the enemy vigilantly, and at the same time so to post your troops that while restraining his operations you may readily re-enforce any point attacked. If Wilmington should be the point, you must concentrate there. If Norfolk, it will be necessary to move all your disposable force there.

With this view it might be well to hold a portion of your troops at Weldon. This will depend upon your facilities for moving, and of this you may judge.

I am, with high respect, your obedient servant,
R. E. LEE,
General, Commanding.

HEADQUARTERS,
Goldsborough, April 2, 1862.

General R. E. LEE, *Commanding Army:*

GENERAL: From information received from a Federal prisoner and from Dr. West, C. S. P. A., just returned from New Berne, I have very little doubt that General Burnside will confine his present operations to the coast from New Berne to Fort Macon. Hoping to reduce the latter, he is fortifying New Berne, and has divided his forces between the two places. I am convinced that none of his command have left the coast, and every appearance indicates that he is striving to conciliate the people and designs a permanent possession. His transports have been sent off, and it may be they have gone for re-enforcements, or rather for troops with whom to make an expedition up the Albemarle Sound or against Wilmington. I much doubt if they will make any attack requiring land transportation.

Your telegram is received. I will hold my disposable force ready to march at a moment's notice, though I do not believe it should be moved until it is certain it will all be required elsewhere. It has reassured the people here, and to a certain extent restored confidence where I grieve to say, despondency was fast generating indifference to our cause, and if the troops are removed without a necessity, perfectly apparent to the people, it will produce a panic that will be most serious in its effects. I shall therefore make no move until further instructed by you.

I am, General, very respectfully,

TH. H. HOLMES,
Major-General, Commanding.

HEADQUARTERS,
Goldsborough, April 6, 1862.

General R. E. LEE,
Commanding Army, C. S. A.:

GENERAL: I telegraphed you yesterday that I should not send the troops to Suffolk until further developments of the enemy's intentions. General Burnside's whole force is available for an invasion in this direction, and my efficient force (12,000), including the troops that were defeated near New Berne, is not more than would be required to resist him.

A serious panic will result if it be materially diminished, and as there is a general feeling that North Carolina has been neglected by the Government, the steps I have taken to reassure the people and restore confidence would be to a great extent nullified, and hence it is that I shall wait until I am certain that a blow will be struck at another point, or until, in your superior wisdom and better information, you shall direct me otherwise.

The Georgia regiments have not arrived, and yesterday the Governor of North Carolina ordered Rogers' battalion of five companies back to Raleigh to complete its organization as a regiment. I permitted it to go, because it had not been turned over to the Confederate Government and had been ordered here only to meet an emergency.

I have ordered a large amount of transportation to be collected here, so as to throw the command in the shortest time possible to any point where it may be required.

There are in Raleigh five or six regiments organized, or partially so, but as they have not been turned over to the Government I have no authority over them. Would it not be well to receive them as they are, in order that I could arrange for their proper instruction while waiting to be armed?

I thank you, General, for the kind confidence you so blindly repose in me, and can only pray that God will give me strength to justify it.

I am, General, very respectfully,

TH. H. HOLMES,
Major-General.

P. S.—I received a letter from General Burnside, saying that he had released on parole our sick and wounded, and requested me to release certain of his prisoners. As the United States Government acted in bad faith with us in reference to an exchange of prisoners, I did not answer his letter or take other action on it than to send to Washington for the released sick.

TH. H. HOLMES,
Major-General.

HEADQUARTERS,
Richmond, Va., April 9, 1862.

Maj. Gen. T. H. HOLMES,
 Commanding, &c., Goldsborough, N. C.:

GENERAL: Your letter of the 6th instant is received. Your views with reference to the disposition of the troops of your command are approved. I recommend the utmost diligence in getting information as to the movements of the enemy, and that you hold yourself fully prepared to move rapidly to any threatened point.

General Huger, by telegram, dated the 8th, informs me that Colonel Ferebee, North Carolina Militia, reports to him that the enemy have landed some 2,000 men at Elizabeth City.

Your attention is specially directed to this report and to any movement in that direction. I think that if an attack be made on Norfolk it will be from the south side. The presence of the Virginia will, in my opinion, deter the enemy from attempting a movement on Norfolk from the direction of Fort Monroe or by way of Elizabeth River.

I have directed the Georgia regiments to be sent to you at once, and as soon as they arrive you will do everything in your power to arm and prepare them for service. I am informed by Major Ashe, of North Carolina, that large numbers of country rifles and other arms can be collected in that State, and I have directed him to get all he can. You will also do everything in your power to collect arms for the troops that you will receive.

With reference to the North Carolina troops, I am desirous that you should have them as soon as possible, and the Governor of North Carolina has been written to on the subject. I desire that you shall do whatever may be in your power to expedite the matter, and as soon as the troops arrive proceed to organize and prepare them for service, and after arming the Georgia troops, those from North Carolina that are unprovided with arms can be supplied with such as remain from what Major Ashe or yourself may collect or any others that may be sent to you.

With reference to the exchange of prisoners, I would state that while I believe the enemy have acted in bad faith in the matter, it is not desirable to follow a bad example. If you have any sick or wounded prisoners of the enemy I would advise their release in return for the release of ours by General Burnside.

I am, general, very respectfully, your obedient servant,

R. E. LEE,
General, Commanding.

HEADQUARTERS,
Goldsborough, April 10, 1862.

General R. E. LEE, Commanding Army:

GENERAL: The enemy were re-enforced at New Berne on Thursday last by about 4,000 men; whether they were from the North or his reserve brought up from Hatteras and Roanoke Island I don't know. He has taken possession of Beaufort, and Fort Macon is invested; he is also fortifying New Berne by a line of intrenchments extending from one river to the other.

I see no signs of an advance in this direction. As near as I can ascertain, his present position is, viz: 2,000 men about Beaufort, 4,000 in New Berne, and the remainder of his army across the Trent, opposite. If I attack New Berne, he can concentrate and fight me if he thinks proper, or he can cross over the Trent and leave me to be shelled out of the town from both rivers by his gunboats. This would also imply the destruction of the town, which would not only cause great misery among the poor people who remained there, but would add to the luke-warmness that threatens to culminate here into indifference to the cause. I have no words to express my disappointment and distress at this feeling, particularly as I can expect comparatively little sympathy beyond my power to protect property.

I am, general, very respectfully,

TH. H. HOLMES,
Major-General.

HEADQUARTERS,
Richmond, April 15, 1862.

Maj. Gen. T. H. HOLMES,
Commanding Department, Goldsborough, N. C.:

GENERAL: I have had the honor to receive your letter of 13th instant,* inclosing reports of the disposition and movements of the enemy in your front and of the state of affairs in Fort Macon. I am deeply grieved to hear of the discontent and insubordination which is reported to exist among the troops in Fort Macon. In addition to other matters, Lieutenant Fenrose tells me they complain of their fare. This is much to be regretted, but I suppose is now beyond remedy. Indeed from the accounts given me I very much doubt whether even a tolerable resistance would be made if the fort were attacked, and you are authorized, if it be possible, to withdraw the garrison and secure such of the public property as can be brought off, if you think it advisable.

I am, very respectfully, your obedient servant,

R. E. LEE,
General Commanding.

HEADQUARTERS,
Goldsborough, April 15, 1862.

Maj. Gen. R. E. LEE:

MY DEAR GENERAL: The letters I sent you by Lieutenant Primrose showed the strength of the enemy. On this coast he has twenty regiments in the immediate vicinity of New Berne and three near Fort Macon. His only reserve is about 3,000 men at Roanoke Island. His effective force is probably about 20,000, with ten gunboats in the Neuse and Trent Rivers.

My effective force is about 14,000, three of the regiments being raw recruits.

_____
*Not found.

I am having accurate maps made of all the country between here and New Berne, as the last service I can render to the general you must send here to command. Believe me, my dear General, this is not false modesty on my part; I know my deficiencies, and I love the cause too much to permit its vital interests to be intrusted to my management. All my life has been passed in executing the orders of others; send therefore a superior to me, or else change me for another who is capable, or who has his own as well as your confidence.

Do not ascribe this to a want of ambition or to diffidence, but rather believe that I know myself and have the honesty to sacrifice my vanity to the interest of my country. I can execute, but I cannot originate.

I am, general, yours very faithfully,

TH. H. HOLMES,
Brigadier-General.

HEADQUARTERS,
Richmond, Va., April 19, 1862.

General J. G. MARTIN,
*   Adjutant-General of North Carolina, Raleigh:*

GENERAL: Your letter of the 16th instant to Major-General Holmes, in reference to the condition, &c., of the new North Carolina troops at Raleigh, has been referred to me. I regret very much to hear of the great reduction in their strength by sickness and of the inability on the part of the State to furnish them with arms. All arms that were available have been forwarded to General Holmes, to be placed in the hands of the unarmed troops in his department. It was hoped that the State would succeed in collecting numbers of private arms for the new regiments and by this time have them ready for the field. I have been compelled to remove one regiment from General Holmes' command and may have to deprive him of more. I had relied upon the new regiments to replace those removed. It is earnestly requested that you will spare no efforts to get them in condition for active field service.

I am, very respectfully, your obedient servant,

R. E. LEE,
General.

Abstract from statement of the troops serving in the Department of North Carolina, commanded by Maj. Gen. T. H. Holmes, April 19, 1862.

Troops.	Effective total.	Aggregate present.	Aggregate present and absent.
1st (Ransom's) Brigade	4,295	4,954	6,211
2d (Branch's) Brigade	3,169	3,820	4,795
3d (Anderson's) Brigade	2,873	4,080	4,665
4th (Walker's) Brigade	3,693	4,520	5,373
District of the Cape Fear (French)	3,623	4,369	4,962
Fort Macon (White)	294	375	427
Total	17,947	22,068	26,433

Organization of the troops serving in the Department of North Carolina, commanded by Maj. Gen. T. H. Holmes, April 19, 1862.

FIRST BRIGADE.*

Brig. Gen. R. RANSOM, commanding.

25th North Carolina
26th North Carolina.
27th North Carolina.
35th North Carolina.
Battalion North Carolina.
  9th North Carolina (1st Cavalry).
19th North Carolina (2d Cavalry).
Evans' North Carolina Troop.
Grisham's Mississippi Battery.
Jones' North Carolina Battery.

SECOND BRIGADE.*

Brig. Gen. L. O'B. BRANCH, commanding.

7th North Carolina.
18th North Carolina.
28th North Carolina.
33d North Carolina.
37th North Carolina.
North Carolina Battery.
Bunting's North Carolina Battery.
Latham's North Carolina Battery.

THIRD BRIGADE.

Brig. Gen. J. R. ANDERSON, commanding.

45th Georgia.
49th Georgia.
3d Louisiana Battalion.
34th North Carolina.
38th North Carolina.
1st South Carolina (Hamilton's).
Battery (section of), Lieutenant Bouldin.
Battery (four pieces), Captain McIntosh.

FOURTH BRIGADE.

Brig. Gen. J. G. WALKER, commanding.

3d Arkansas.
44th Georgia.
1st North Carolina.
2d North Carolina.
3d North Carolina.
30th Virginia.
French's Virginia Battery.

DISTRICT OF THE CAPE FEAR.

Brig. Gen. S. G. FRENCH, commanding.

20th North Carolina.
30th North Carolina.
60th Virginia.
20 companies infantry, cavalry, and heavy artillery.

GARRISON OF FORT MACON.†

Col. M. J. WHITE, commanding.

Official.

ARCHER ANDERSON,
Assistant Adjutant-General.

HEADQUARTERS,
Goldsborough, April 20, 1862.

General R. E. LEE,
  Commanding C. S. Army:

GENERAL: I have little doubt that the force of the enemy that landed at Elizabeth City was taken from Roanoke Island, where four days ago they had a reserve of 3,000 men. I am almost certain that they have withdrawn no men from New Berne. They have repaired a bridge that we burned 7 miles this side of New Berne, and have advanced three regiments there, but as they have no transportation, I doubt if they intend a serious advance.

I have directed Colonel Deshler to make an estimate for funds to

* The First and Second Brigades constituted a division under Branch's command.
† Composition of garrison not indicated.

pay for private arms. None can be had unless they are paid for at the time.

I am deeply pained and mortified at the apathy that pervades the people, and have utterly failed in my efforts to arouse them.

Relative to the Enfield rifles, I had issued them, according to your instructions, to the three Georgia regiments. There was a small overplus, which I gave to the flank companies of other regiments. If I should take them from the Georgia regiments it would produce discontent, and as most of the flank companies have rifles of one sort or another, I think it best not to disturb them.

If you do not insist on it I will not send a regiment to Wilmington for the present to take the place of Colonel Starke's, as there is no indication of danger in that direction.

I am, General, very respectfully,

TH. H. HOLMES,
Major-General.

HEADQUARTERS,
Richmond, Va., April 20, 1862.

Maj. Gen. T. H. HOLMES,
Commanding, &c., Goldsborough, N. C.:

GENERAL: The demand for arms from all sides is so great and their scarcity so keenly felt, that I deem it proper to call your attention to the importance of making a judicious distribution of the rifles recently sent you. By a letter from General Martin to you, of the 16th instant, I am advised of the inability of the State of North Carolina to arm the regiments now in camp at Raleigh. I have written to him, urging that the State make all possible efforts by procuring private arms, &c., to arm them. The rifles sent you were of a very fine quality, and I suggest that you place them in the hands of the flanking companies of the regiments, and give the balance muskets or such private arms as can be procured. The rifles will thus be made to do much towards enhancing the efficiency of each regiment. If you can use them and desire it, I can order a number of pikes to be sent you. Owing to the lack of fire-arms some of these have been sent to nearly every army in the field, and, if well handled and wisely distributed, will undoubtedly do good service.

I am, very respectfully, your obedient servant,

R. E. LEE,
General.

HEADQUARTERS,
Richmond, Va., April 20, 1862.

Maj. Gen. T. H. HOLMES,
Commanding Department, Goldsborough, N. C.:

GENERAL: I am directed by General Lee to acknowledge the receipt of your letter of the 18th instant, wherein you state that you cannot recommend the withdrawal of Colonel Starke's regiment from your department, and to say that, the necessity having become urgent for additional troops between Fredericksburg and this city, he on yesterday telegraphed you to send this regiment, at the same time ordering one from the departments of South Carolina and Georgia to this place. No other consideration influenced him in doing this except the necessities of the service, and he hopes that you will soon be able to replace the regiment taken from you by one of the new regiments now at Raleigh.

I am, very respectfully, your obedient servant,

W. H. TAYLOR,
Assistant Adjutant-General.

If the regiment has not started, the General desires you to send it immediately.

HEADQUARTERS DEPARTMENT OF NORTH CAROLINA,
Goldsborough, April 21, 1862.

General R. E. LEE, *Commanding, &c.:*

GENERAL: The enemy show a disposition to remain entirely quiet at New Berne. They have thrown up works extending from the Neuse to the Trent, and have cut down the forest in front of them. Their purpose there seems to be only to defend themselves.

On the 16th instant two regiments, and on the 18th instant three regiments, were sent by water from New Berne, as I think, to re-enforce the troops engaged in the investment of Fort Macon. I may be mistaken, however, as to their destination, my opinion of it being based mainly on the fact that the enemy's force near Fort Macon has recently been represented to me as much larger than it was previously reported.

This information reached me this evening. If you think it advisable under it to withdraw any of the troops from here please do not designate them, but permit me to do so.

I respectfully request authority under the conscript law to order a board of examination upon the officers newly elected in the volunteer regiments; otherwise many very inferior officers will come into the service, greatly to its injury.

Very respectfully, your obedient servant,

TH. H. HOLMES,
Major-General, Commanding.

HEADQUARTERS,
Richmond, Va., April 22, 1862.

Maj. Gen. T. H. HOLMES,
Commanding Department, Goldsborough, N. C.:

GENERAL: General Lee directs me to acknowledge the receipt of your letter of the 21st instant, brought by General Anderson, stating that the enemy exhibited no intention of an immediate advance, and to say that on the strength of it he has ordered by telegraph to-day that you send a brigade at once to Fredericksburg, where troops are much needed. The enemy are reported to be 5,000 strong on the opposite side of the river from Fredericksburg, and a heavy force between that and Aquia Creek, under McDowell. [If] it is [true], the necessity to re-enforce General Field is urgent. One brigade has been ordered up from your department. The General would like much to have another brigade, and wishes to know if you cannot spare an additional one from your command. You will designate the troops that are to move. Instructions based upon the conscript law are being prepared by the Secretary of War for the guidance of all concerned, and will be forwarded to you as soon as ready for distribution.

I am, very respectfully, your obedient servant,

W. H. TAYLOR,
Assistant Adjutant-General.

SPECIAL ORDERS, }   HDQRS. DEPT. OF NORTH CAROLINA,
    No. 88.   }   Goldsborough, April 22, 1862.
*   *   *   *   *   *   *

IV. The First Regiment South Carolina Volunteers and the Third Louisiana Battalion will move to-night by rail to Richmond. The remainder of Brigadier-General Anderson's brigade, with the exception of the Forty-ninth Georgia Regiment and Lieutenant Bouldin's section of battery, will be held in readiness to move at a moment's notice.
*   *   *   *   *   *   *

By command of Maj. Gen. T. H. Holmes:

ARCHER ANDERSON,
Assistant Adjutant-General.

HEADQUARTERS,
Richmond, Va., April 23, 1862.

Brig. Gen. S. G. FRENCH,
    Commanding, &c., Wilmington, N. C.:

GENERAL: In reply to your telegram of yesterday,* I am directed by General Lee to say that all available arms have been given to General Holmes for distribution to the troops under his command. There are none now on hand for issue save pikes. He thinks you might arm the regiment at Wilmington by placing pikes in the hands of the men at the heavy batteries, and giving their muskets, as far as they will go, to the unarmed regiment, and make up deficiency by arming some of the center companies with pikes, the flanking companies having the rifles. This is the best arrangement that can now be made.

I am, very respectfully, your obedient servant,

W. H. TAYLOR,
Assistant Adjutant-General.

SPECIAL ORDERS, }   HDQRS. DEPT. OF NORTH CAROLINA,
    No. 89.   }   Goldsborough, April 23, 1862.

I. The Thirty-fourth North Carolina, Forty-fifth Georgia, and Thirty-eighth North Carolina Regiments will move to-day, with three days' rations, by rail, to Richmond, in the order in which they are mentioned. The baggage transported will be strictly limited to the necessary cooking utensils and tents and the field allowance for officers. The time of the departure of each train will be fixed by the chief quartermaster, Major Cone, who will make the necessary arrangements for the prompt transportation of the troops as far as Richmond. Upon the arrival of each regiment at that place its commanding officer will receive orders from Brig. Gen. J. R. Anderson.
*   *   *   *   *   *

By command of Major-General Holmes:

ARCHER ANDERSON,
Assistant Adjutant-General.

HEADQUARTERS DEPARTMENT OF NORFOLK,
April 24, 1862.

General R. E. LEE, *Commanding:*

GENERAL: My reports from South Mills, N. C., up to 3 p. m. last

---
* Not found.

evening, represent all quiet. The enemy had not returned there, and the reported landing of the day previous at Canal Bridge, Currituck County, turned out to be only a small party, who soon retired.

General Blanchard sent the wounded prisoners up here, and I forwarded them (19) yesterday to General Wool at Fort Monroe. The surgeon I released unconditionally.

You are aware that no forces have replaced Colston's brigade, and our batteries and the country along James River (Burrell's Bay) are undefended.

Very respectfully, your obedient servant,
BENJ. HUGER,
Major-General, &c.

HEADQUARTERS DEPARTMENT OF NORFOLK,
Norfolk, Va., April 26, 1862.

General R. E. LEE, *Commanding:*

GENERAL: My report from South Mills up to 3 p. m. yesterday states all is quiet. The enemy had not returned.

I conversed yesterday with one of the North Carolina Militia (Stephen Williams), who was captured by the enemy near Elizabeth City some two weeks since (with 72 others), and has been on Roanoke Island. He was forced to act as guide to the expedition, and landed them at 12 at night 2 miles below Elizabeth City. In the dark and during the confusion of landing he made his escape. He states he was in the cabin with General Reno and Colonel Hawkins and other officers, and they spoke openly of their intention of seizing the south end and destroying the lock of the canal so we could not pass iron-clad boats into the sound, and that they would fortify and hold the position and re-enforce it to any amount and threaten Norfolk in the rear, while McClellan attacked it in front. Several of the regiments sent on this expedition came from New Berne.

If the attack is renewed troops will no doubt be sent from there. Is General Holmes strong enough to threaten them from Goldsborough? If he can, it would be well to occupy them.

Very respectfully, your obedient servant,
BENJ. HUGER,
Major-General, Commanding.

HEADQUARTERS,
Richmond, Va., April 26, 1862.

Maj. Gen. T. H. HOLMES, *Goldsborough, N. C.:*

GENERAL: The arrival of arms in Wilmington enables me to distribute some to the troops organized in North Carolina. If I am correctly informed as to the numbers received I will assign to you 2,400, which, with the arms of the country, which I hope have been collected by the Governor for these troops, will enable you to arm six regiments. We can only now, in the present scarcity of arms, distribute 400 to a regiment, which will enable you to arm the flank companies with the improved arms and the center companies with the State arms.

In distributing the arms you are authorized to issue to the flank companies of the old regiments those improved arms, and take from them the arms they now have and issue them to companies of the new regiments.

An officer of the Ordnance Department goes on to Wilmington to receive and distribute the arms, and you are desired to give him any assistance he may require. Should the equipments accompany the arms they will be issued to the troops in proportion to their quantity, as compared with the whole number of arms. The troops thus armed will re-enforce your army and enable you to send another brigade to Fredericksburg, which I desire you to do as soon as possible. The selection of the brigade I leave to you, but should you have more transportation than is required for the troops in your department, I desire that you will forward such as can be spared for service with the troops in this. Should you have an engineer and an ordnance officer whose services can be spared, I request that they be ordered for duty with the troops near Fredericksburg.

I am, very respectfully, your obedient servant,

R. E. LEE,
General.

HEADQUARTERS DEPARTMENT OF NORTH CAROLINA,
Goldsborough, April 27, 1862.
General R. E. LEE,
    Commanding C. S. Army :

GENERAL : Your favor of yesterday is received. As soon as the arms are received I will organize a brigade out of the troops in Raleigh, and I will be much obliged if you will send me a brigade general to command it. I greatly fear it will be some time before the country, arms can be collected, in sufficient numbers to arm six regiments, as the Governor has but 1,400 of all sorts, and Major Ashe thus far has sent none. I will order Major Thompson to report to you as an engineer. Colonel Deshler is the only ordnance officer I have, and he cannot be spared, as he is also my chief of artillery. I will send Ransom's brigade to Fredericksburg as soon as I can relieve it, unless you will be satisfied with the new one to be organized out of the troops at Raleigh. I shall be left with but two brigades (Walker's and Branch's) that can be at all relied on if Burnside advances.

I am, General, very respectfully and truly,

TH. H. HOLMES,
Major-General, Commanding.

P. S.—If it be possible please send me General Pettigrew; he is from North Carolina, and I need his strength to discipline new recruits rapidly.

HEADQUARTERS DEPARTMENT OF NORTH CAROLINA,
Goldsborough, April 27, 1862.
Maj. W. H. TAYLOR,
    Assistant Adjutant-General, Richmond :

MAJOR : I send herewith, for the information of General Lee, a copy of a letter just received from Capt. W. S. G. Andrews, who commands a small body of troops near Tarborough. The intelligence it contains is corroborative of accounts from other sources.

Very respectfully, your obedient servant,

TH. H. HOLMES,
Major-General, Commanding.

[Inclosure.]

HEADQUARTERS,
Tarborough, N. C., April 26, 1862.

Maj. Gen. T. H. HOLMES,
Commanding Department of North Carolina:

GENERAL: James A. Corey and W. G. Andrews, two men who were wounded at Hatteras and have been prisoners at Annapolis, arrived inside our lines from New Berne last night. They left New Berne on Wednesday last. They have been confined in the jail there for two weeks, but have been permitted to converse freely with the soldiers and to walk about for a limited time each day. They were furnished by General Burnside with passports to cross the river, which they did at New Berne, and saw no enemy's pickets on this side. What they relate is not of their own knowledge, but the substance of numerous conversations with the soldiers. They were examined separately and agree in nearly every particular. Their statement is, General Burnside left New Berne on Wednesday morning with all the gunboats but two, and 1,300 men. There is but one regiment in the town. About 9,000 troops around the town at Fair Grounds, across Trent, and at Deep Gully. They were expecting an attack from the Confederate forces. The opinion expressed was that General Holmes could take the town, but could not hold it. General Burnside declared his intention to be to reduce Fort Macon at once, making a "breakfast spell" of it, and then to go immediately to Kinston and Goldsborough. This was spoken of by every one they conversed with. Never heard Wilmington mentioned; the talk was always Fort Macon, Kinston, Goldsborough. No re-enforcements but those previously reported by me. The small-pox was spreading among the troops and many were dying with it.

These men are reliable and honest in their intentions. They have served under me, and I know them well. I have a man in an oyster boat gone to Core Island, and hope to hear direct from Fort Macon by Wednesday next.

Very truly, your obedient servant,

W. S. G. ANDREWS,
Captain, Tenth Regt. North Carolina Artillery, Comdg.

P. S.—Since I wrote the above my messenger has got in from Albemarle Sound. Six gunboats are still at Elizabeth City with the expedition to destroy the canal. They are probably awaiting re-enforcements to attack Colonel Wright again. No increase in gunboats or troops at Roanoke Island. Some of the citizens went from Washington County to Roanoke Island to get the enemy to send forces to Plymouth. They have not returned. A company of cavalry is needed there to arrest such men and keep the people quiet. Eight citizens went. No gunboats in the sound except those at Elizabeth City.

Very truly, yours,

W. S. G. ANDREWS,
Captain, Tenth Regt. North Carolina Artillery, Comdg.

HEADQUARTERS DEPARTMENT OF NORFOLK,
April 28, 1862.

General R. E. LEE, *Commanding:*

GENERAL: I have tried to make out a report of the battle near South Mills on 19th.* I have given a detailed account of the arrangement of

---
*See p. 326.

the ground, which seemed to me judicious and showed resources. At last accounts, yesterday, the enemy, with an increased number of boats, were still on board their vessels off Elizabeth City, thus threatening our line from Powell's Point to the Blackwater. He may land at Elizabeth City or any other point on the Chowan he pleases. I am too weak to scatter troops. Suffolk is particularly weak. If any additional force can be spared from anywhere it should be sent there.*

Very respectfully, your obedient servant,

BENJ. HUGER,
Major-General.

HEADQUARTERS,
Richmond, Va., April 28, 1862.

Maj. Gen. T. H. HOLMES,
Commanding, &c., North Carolina, Goldsborough, N. C.:

GENERAL: I have had the honor to receive your letter of the 25th instant relative to the removal of a brigade from your command, and giving your objections to a further decrease of your force. You will have learned since the date of your letter, as I informed you in mine of the 26th, of the arrival of arms at Wilmington, and the assignment of a portion of them to your order, for the purpose of arming the new troops within your department. The number turned over to you, together with those collected by your agents and those of the State, will enable you to arm, it is hoped, six new regiments. The need for troops in the vicinity of Fredericksburg is very urgent, and they can contribute to the defense of North Carolina as materially at that point as they would in assisting to prevent an advance from the enemy now occupying the eastern waters of the State.

In view of the pressing necessity for re-enforcing the army operating in Northern Virginia, and of the assignment of arms to troops in your department, I determined to order a brigade of your forces to the vicinity of Fredericksburg, as you were advised on the 26th. You will please forward the command you may select without unnecessary delay, and lose no efforts to supply their places by some of the new regiments at Raleigh. I would also request that, if it can possibly be spared, you will forward some of the land transportation heretofore used by the troops which have been withdrawn from North Carolina. Wagons and teams are much needed by the army collecting near Fredericksburg.

I am, very respectfully, your obedient servant,

R. E. LEE,
General.

HEADQUARTERS,
Richmond, Va., April 30, 1862.

Maj. Gen. T. H. HOLMES,
Commanding, &c., Goldsborough, N. C.:

GENERAL: Your letters of the 27th instant and telegram of 29th are received. Information received by General Huger confirms the report of Captain Andrews with regard to the continued presence of the enemy at Elizabeth City. It does not seem to me that there are any indications of an advance toward Goldsborough by General Burn-

---

* Further correspondence between Lee and Huger will be printed in Series 1, Vol. XI.

side at this time. I think your force will enable you to prevent such a movement, and in the mean time I hope you will be able, with the improved arms that have been sent you and the country arms, to prepare a sufficient number of the new regiments to supply the place of the troops that have been withdrawn from you. It would not be well to send the new brigade to be organized at Raleigh to Fredericksburg instead of Ransom's. The new men would no doubt suffer greatly, and their efficiency be much impaired by the usual diseases of the camp. They would suffer less if retained in North Carolina.

General Johnston writes that the situation of affairs in the Peninsula is such that it is impossible for him to spare General Pettigrew.

With reference to the promotion of Colonel Daniel the Secretary is unwilling at this time to increase the number of brigadiers. There are two now without commands, Generals Wise and Pryor, either of whom can be ordered to you if you desire it.

I am, general, very respectfully, your obedient servant,

R. E. LEE,
General.

HEADQUARTERS,
Goldsborough, April 30, 1862.

General R. E. LEE,
Commanding C. S. Army:

GENERAL: I telegraphed last night, asking permission to retain the brigade ordered from me to Virginia.

I know you will not consider me importunate when I tell you that it will be better to withdraw all the troops from North Carolina except a few regiments for the defense of Wilmington than to reduce this command, because that would give you material aid in Virginia, and the demoralization of the people here would be scarcely less than it will be if I am deprived of the means of fighting Burnside.

General French has made a positive and stern demand on me for troops and I must send them, because the great uncertainty and mismanagement of the trains will not justify me in trusting to them for defending Wilmington by the troops that are here.

As for the troops at Raleigh, it is doubtful when I shall get them and still more doubtful when they will be armed. The military camp there is a sort of hobby with the authorities, and they require all the arms they have to exercise their men.

I wrote immediately on the receipt of your letter for six regiments. This was three days ago, and yet I have had no word in answer and no evidence the regiments are coming, and if they do come they will be nothing better than raw militia.

Immediately on the receipt of your order yesterday I sent to the railroad authorities for transportation for the brigade, and was informed it could not be furnished before to-morrow, the 1st May.

I am, General, very respectfully and faithfully,

TH. H. HOLMES,
Major-General, &c.

P. S.—The common council of Wilmington has sent a committee to the Governor and to me begging for help.

Abstract from monthly report of the troops of the Department of North Carolina, commanded by Maj. Gen. T. H. Holmes, for April, 1862.

Troops.	Present for duty.		Effective total.	Aggregate present.	Aggregate present and absent.	Artillery present.	
	Officers.	Men.				Pieces.	Horses.
Cape Fear District..........................	179	3,003	3,153	3,890	4,502	......	......
Greenville................................	6	94	94	116	132	......	......
Infantry.................................	593	10,258	10,680	13,396	15,006	......	......
Cavalry.................................	69	1,450	1,524	1,751	2,068	......	2,058
Artillery................................	24	579	501	669	753	129	543
Grand total....................	871	15,384	16,042	19,822	22,461	129	2,601

HDQRS. FIRST DIVISION, DEPARTMENT OF NORFOLK,
Suffolk, May 1, 1862.

Col. S. S. ANDERSON, *Adjutant-General:*

COLONEL: As the enemy is threatening the coast throughout this division I respectfully request to know whether the troops stationed at Roanoke River and ordered to Goldsborough have been asked for again. That portion of the division is more exposed than any other, and is at the same time important, as several roads meet at Weldon, and nothing to prevent the enemy from coming up the river with their gunboats except an obstruction now in progress of construction below Hamilton.

There can be no doubt but that troops have left New Berne for Roanoke Island, and General Holmes can doubtless spare those sent him from this division.

I inclose to-day a dispatch from below, showing that the enemy are now near Edenton and Roanoke River.

Respectfully, your obedient servant,

W. W. LORING,
Major-General, Commanding.

I have to-day sent Captain Poor, engineer, to the Roanoke, to select a place for a battery near Halifax.

Respectfully, your obedient servant,

W. W. LORING,
Major-General, Commanding.

[Indorsement No. 1.]

HEADQUARTERS DEPARTMENT OF NORFOLK,
Norfolk, Va., May 2, 1862.

Respectfully forwarded. A similar application was sent from these headquarters on 14th April.

BENJ. HUGER,
Major-General.

[Indorsement No. 2.]

RICHMOND, *May 3, 1862.*

Respectfully returned to General Cooper. The movement of General Johnston renders re-enforcements to General Huger necessary if they were available.

R. E. LEE.

HEADQUARTERS,
Richmond, Va., May 3, 1862.

Maj. Gen. T. H. HOLMES, *Goldsborough, N. C.:*

GENERAL: That you may better understand the movements of General Burnside I must explain to you that it is in contemplation to withdraw the troops from Norfolk. As soon as he learns it I think he will move in that direction. Be prepared to strike at him if he offers the opportunity. I do not think it advisable therefore to move your troops to Wilmington until the indications are such as to induce you to believe that he is preparing to attack that city.

I have the honor to be, your obedient servant,

R. E. LEE,
General.

HEADQUARTERS,
Richmond, Va., May 3, 1862.

Maj. Gen. T. H. HOLMES,
Commanding, &c., Goldsborough, N. C.:

GENERAL: I am directed by General Lee to acknowledge the receipt of your letter of the 30th ultimo, and to say that it was with great reluctance and regret that he found himself compelled still further to reduce your command. Such, however, is the strength of the enemy near Fredericksburg, and threatened as the rear of the Army of the Peninsula would be by a column advancing from the Rappahannock, it was imperatively necessary to re-enforce our army operating in that quarter, in order to enable it successfully to resist any advance from that direction. He has to-day telegraphed Governor Clark, requesting that he would send you the unarmed regiments from Raleigh, and he trusts that with the arms you now have, with such additional as he hopes to be able to give you, you will soon have a number of armed troops sufficient to replace the brigade of General Ransom ready for active service.

I am, general, very respectfully, your obedient servant,

W. H. TAYLOR,
Assistant Adjutant-General.

HEADQUARTERS,
Richmond, Va., May 7, 1862.

Maj. Gen. T. H. HOLMES,
Commanding, &c., Goldsborough, N. C.:

GENERAL: I have instructed General Huger to have Colonel Clarke's regiment in North Carolina, with others, to report to you. The withdrawal of General Huger's command from the Department of Norfolk renders the transfer necessary. With the accession of this regiment you will, I hope, be able to afford some protection to the railroad and aid the citizens of the counties adjacent to the sound in their endeavors to move their grain and provisions to places of security.

It will be advisable also to send a regiment to Weldon if you can spare one for that purpose.

Very respectfully, your obedient servant,

R. E. LEE,
General.

HEADQUARTERS,
Richmond, Va., May 8, 1862.

General J. G. MARTIN,
Adjutant and Inspector General North Carolina, Raleigh:

GENERAL: Your letter of the 1st instant is received, and I am much gratified to hear of the six regiments already ordered to move, and hope the others will soon be ready also. The President is not authorized by law to accept troops in larger organizations than regiments. He is required to organize the brigades and divisions and appoint the commanding generals. You will perceive that he has no authority to accept the troops referred to in your letter as a division. In organizing them into brigades and divisions the necessity of the service may require the separation of these troops and their distribution among the different divisions in the field. You will thus perceive that it is not in the power of the President to receive these troops as a division with yourself as major-general, and that the question of their organization into a single division must be determined by the exigencies of the service.

From these facts you will understand that the President is unable to appoint you as a major-general to command these particular troops, as you request. My impression, derived from a conversation with the President, is that he does not consider it expedient to appoint another major-general at this time. The law to which I have above alluded is the act approved March 6, 1861, No. 48.

I am, general, very respectfully, your obedient servant,

R. E. LEE,
General.

————

HEADQUARTERS,
Richmond, Va., May 13, 1862.

Maj. Gen. T. H. HOLMES,
Commanding Department, Goldsborough, N. C.:

GENERAL: I have received your telegram of yesterday reporting that the enemy was being re-enforced at New Berne, and asking if it was desired that you should keep Colonel Clarke's regiment at Murfreesborough. As well as can be judged from this distance, this seems to be a good point to hold in defending that line of road, and it would appear advisable to retain it in that vicinity. It is thought that the movements of Burnside are merely intended to divert our attention from other seriously-threatened points, and that no advance in force is contemplated by his column. Such is the pressure in Virginia that it is imperatively necessary to concentrate our forces to enable us successfully to meet the heavy columns of the enemy. It may be necessary to draw still further from your department, and you are to make every exertion to get the State troops down from Raleigh and do all in your power toward arming them. All that we can hope is to hold and protect the line of road leading south through Weldon, Goldsborough, and Wilmington. Whatever force may not be necessary for this purpose should be advanced to Virginia and united with the army north of Richmond. The re-enforcements reported at New Berne are in all probability some force returning which has been moving about the sounds. Burnside has received none, as far as can be ascertained, from any other quarter.

I am, very respectfully, your obedient servant,

R. E. LEE,
General.

HEADQUARTERS,
Richmond, Va., May 13, 1862.

Maj. Gen. T. H. HOLMES,
    Commanding Forces in North Carolina:

GENERAL: I fear it will be necessary to draw still further from the troops under your command for the defense of Richmond and its neighboring approaches. You are being weakened much more than is desirable, but the necessity is unavoidable. The troops which have been withdrawn from you will be replaced by the new levies now being organized in North Carolina. It is highly important that these should be brought to the field with as little delay as possible. General James G. Martin and Colonel Clingman will be appointed brigadier-generals, and will report to you. Their brigades will be formed from the North Carolina regiments. Enjoin upon them the importance of speedily organizing and equipping the new levies that may compose their brigades.

I am, very respectfully, your obedient servant,
                                        R. E. LEE,
                                            General.

———

HEADQUARTERS,
Richmond, Va., May 19, 1862.

Maj. Gen. T. H. HOLMES,
    Commanding, &c., Goldsborough, N. C.:

GENERAL: I am directed by General Lee to say that all of General Huger's command will be withdrawn in this direction, and that it will be necessary for you to replace the regiment now stationed at Weldon. Col. S. R. Harrison, commanding First Louisiana Volunteers, is now there in command. As soon as practicable you are desired to send a regiment to relieve him, that he may proceed with as little delay as possible to join the balance of General Huger's division.

I am, very respectfully, your obedient servant,
                                    W. H. TAYLOR,
                                    Assistant Adjutant-General.

———

HEADQUARTERS,
Richmond, Va., May 22, 1862.

Brig. Gen. S. G. FRENCH,
    Commanding, Wilmington, N. C.:

GENERAL: I have received your letter of the 20th instant, reporting attack on Fort Fisher, and asking for additional guns of long range. Colonel Gorgas has been directed to send to you as soon as possible two 32-pounder rifled guns, which are the only suitable ones that are available at this time.

Very respectfully, your obedient servant,
                                        R. E. LEE,
                                            General.

———

RICHMOND, VA., May 23, 1862.

His Excellency HENRY T. CLARK, Raleigh, N. C.:

You know the importance of maintaining communication South. Will you send a brigade, under General Martin, to Petersburg for that purpose, the whole line of railroad to Wilmington being under General Holmes! By taking arms from ineffectives here I can add to the arms you have already furnished to four of your regiments enough to complete their armament. Will send arms to Petersburg to meet troops and will add two light batteries to brigade. Urgent.

JEFFERSON DAVIS.

SPECIAL ORDERS, }   ADJT. AND INSP. GENERAL'S OFFICE,
   No. 127. }   Richmond, Va., June 3, 1862.

* * * * * * *

XIV. That part of North Carolina west of the Blue Ridge, and adjoining East Tennessee, will be embraced within the Department of East Tennessee, under Maj. Gen. E. K. Smith.

* * * * * * *

By command of the Secretary of War:

JNO. WITHERS,
Assistant Adjutant-General.

HDQRS. FIRST BRIGADE, ARMY OF THE PAMLICO,
Camp Johnston, June 17, 1862.

Maj. Gen. T. H. HOLMES,
   Comdg. Department of North Carolina, Goldsborough, N. C.:

GENERAL: On the 1st of this month I assumed command of this brigade, consisting of four regiments of infantry, one of cavalry, three batteries of light artillery, and two independent companies of cavalry; also Captain Whitford's company of heavy artillery, acting as Partisan Rangers, and Captain Nethercutt, with about 20 men, on the same duty, the whole force making an aggregate of 5,329, of which only 3,928 were reported present for duty.

The rest of the command were sick in hospitals in camp, some absent sick, with a few on detached service and furloughs.

My first attention was called to the large amount of sickness in camp and the probable cause, with the view to remedy it if possible. The ground on which the troops were camped was low, without any drainage, and a swamp on the side of each regiment.

After careful examination in every direction in the vicinity of Kinston I found it necessary to remove my camp to Falling Creek, where there is a high and dry encampment on the railroad, and to all appearances healthy, at least as much so as any place in this section of the country. There is an excellent drill ground at the camp, large enough for the entire brigade.

I left one regiment of infantry on picket around and 6 miles in advance of Kinston. The cavalry pickets extend to within a few miles of New Berne, nearly to Deep Gully, on the Trent road, and from the railroad near Tuscarora, running across to the Neuse. This duty was done by five companies of cavalry, which I intend to strengthen by three more.

On the other side of the Neuse, on Swift Creek, Captain Carraway's company of cavalry and Captain Whitford's Partisan Rangers picket and keep the enemy close to New Berne in that direction. Captain Tucker's cavalry company picket on the Tar River from Greenville to within a short distance of Washington. Captain Nethercutt, with his

Partisan Rangers, operates with the cavalry near Deep Gully and across the Trent River, in Jones County.

On account of retiring 6 miles from Kinston I desire to strengthen my cavalry pickets by a regiment of infantry and a battery of artillery to support it, should there be any necessity for it. There is also another reason: There is a large amount of grain and meat in that section of the country which I want to secure. As soon as the three additional companies of cavalry are sent there instructions will be given them to collect all the grain and provisions possible and send them to a safe place to the rear, from which point I expect to haul it to Kinston.

The most reliable information that can be received of the enemy's forces at New Berne estimates it from 8,000 to 10,000. The balance of General Burnside's forces are with General McClellan in Virginia. Should the enemy take Richmond or withdraw from the Peninsula, Burnside's forces will doubtless return to him, and he will at once commence his onward march through North Carolina. He has a large number of wagons and means of transportation at New Berne. He is also making arrangements for railroad transportation and is rebuilding the railroad bridge across the Trent. Several engineers have already been sent to him, and it is supposed some engines and cars are at Beaufort. He is building at New Berne two iron-clad cars or batteries, to carry six guns each.

The railroad track was taken up from Core Creek to the Dover road, about 10 miles, when I took command. Since then I had strong parties to work on it. The ties have been burned and the iron bent so as to render it useless. Several additional miles of the track are being taken up and the iron taken to a safe place by the railroad. This would render the enemy's advance by railroad, should he attempt it, slow and laborious. In his advance, should he take either of the roads along the Neuse or Trent Rivers, I could offer but feeble resistance with my present force. An advancing column can march on both sides of the roads for any distance that its strength will permit it to extend. Should he take the Trent Road it would be extremely hazardous to go below Kinston with my command, as there is only one bridge, and that a very poor concern, and the river not fordable. If the enemy should march on the south side of the river, instead of crossing at Kinston, little or no resistance could be offered to him to White Hall.

The river is at present navigable to Kinston, and is higher than it has been for years. The obstructions placed in the river below Kinston are entirely covered by several feet of water, and I fear damaged, if not washed away.

As far as I have been able to examine, this section of the country is level and intersected by many roads, making it extremely difficult to defend. The enemy can only be met with any degree of safety by a force equal to his own and well supplied with transportation.

Since I assumed command of this brigade it has been increased by two small new infantry regiments, who report less than 400 men each present for duty. My aggregate effective infantry force to-day fit for duty is 3,887 men—cavalry, 648, and 212 artillery. The cavalry are deficient in arms and equipments, and I have been informed by the ordnance officer at Goldsborough, in answer to a requisition made on him, that he cannot supply any.

The batteries are greatly in need of men. In their present weak condition they cannot be expected to render good service. A few days ago one of them did not have a sufficient number of men for duty to drill with four pieces. An officer should be detailed from each of these batteries to recruit, and furnished with money to pay the men their bounty.

The entire command is deficient in transportation. About one-half of what is on hand has been furnished by the State, for which the Confederate States have refused to refund the State or give a per diem.

I will make requisitions on the depot quartermaster at Goldsborough for the amount of transportation required, and hope you will order it to be furnished. As the Tar River district has only been attached to my command temporarily (as I understand it), I will say nothing of that section, or the troops there, in this letter.

I thus explain my position as far as I can at present, so that you may clearly understand it, and, in case of the enemy's advance, that you may have a sufficient force with which to meet him.

I am, general, very respectfully, your obedient servant,

J. G. MARTIN,
, *Brigadier-General.*

[Indorsement.]

HEADQUARTERS DEPARTMENT OF NORTH CAROLINA,
Goldsborough, June 19, 1862.

This report is respectfully referred to the Adjutant and Inspector General, with the remark that General Martin's force has since been reduced by ordering three of his infantry regiments to Petersburg.

TH. H. HOLMES,
Major-General.

SPECIAL ORDERS, }   HDQRS. DEPT. OF NORTH CAROLINA,
No. 134.   } .   *Goldsborough, June 19, 1862.*

I. Brig. Gen. J. G. Martin will assume command of the troops on Tar River, and direct the operations in that vicinity.

*   *   *   *   *   *   *

By command of Major-General Holmes:

ARCHER ANDERSON,
Assistant Adjutant-General.

GENERAL ORDERS, }   HDQRS. DEPT. OF NORTH CAROLINA,
No. 30.   }   *Petersburg, June 21, 1862.*

The following order is published for the information of the troops:

SPECIAL ORDERS, } HEADQUARTERS DEPARTMENT OF NORTHERN VIRGINIA,
No. 140.   }   *June 21, 1862.*

*   *   *   *   *   *   *

VII. The department of Maj. Gen. Theo. H. Holmes is hereby extended to the south bank of the James River, including Drewry's Bluff. He will establish his headquarters at Petersburg, or at such other point as he may deem more convenient.*

*   *   *   *   *   *   *

By command of General Lee:

A. P. MASON,
Assistant Adjutant-General.

By command of Major-General Holmes:

ARCHER ANDERSON,
Assistant Adjutant-General.

---

* Correspondence relating to operations on the James River will appear in Series I, Vol. XI.

SPECIAL ORDERS, }   HDQRS. DEPT. OF NORTH CAROLINA,
    No. 143.   }   *Drewry's Bluff, July* 5, 1862.

II. Brigadier-General Martin will move with two of the regiments near Kinston, and the Forty-fourth Regiment North Carolina troops without delay by rail to Petersburg. He will report his progress *en route* to these headquarters, so that orders may reach him on the arrival of the first regiment of his command at Petersburg.

By command of Major-General Holmes:

                              ARCHER ANDERSON,
                                   Assistant Adjutant-General.

Abstract from the report of the troops of the Department of North Carolina, commanded by Maj. Gen. T. H. Holmes, for July 15, 1862.

Troops.	Present for duty.		Effective total.	Aggregate present.	Aggregate present and absent.	Artillery present.	
	Officers.	Men.				Pieces.	Horses.
Daniel's brigade	125	1,943	2,009	2,454	3,488		
French's brigade	77	1,344	1,429	1,800	2,123		
Martin's brigade	186	2,092	2,113	2,528	3,413		
Ransom's brigade	153	2,538	2,675	3,109	4,708		
Walker's brigade	199	3,028	3,165	4,133	4,762		
District of the Cape Fear	130	2,265	2,465	3,049	3,379	87	
Drewry's Bluff	12	157	163	211	261		
Near Kinston	51	1,015	1,098	1,304	1,441	14	196
Near Petersburg	117	1,934	1,971	2,452	2,986	40	
Near Weldon	12	127	129	158	227		
Grand total	1,012	16,493	17,217	21,196	26,826	141	196

SPECIAL ORDERS, }
    No. 165.   }   JULY 17, 1862.

XVI. Maj. Gen. D. H. Hill is assigned to the command of the division and district lately commanded by Major-General Holmes.

By command of the Secretary of War:

                              JNO. WITHERS,
                                   Assistant Adjutant-General.

                    GOLDSBOROUGH, N. C., *August* 7, 1862.

Maj. Gen. D. H. HILL:

GENERAL: There are some matters in relation to which, before acting, I should like to be instructed.

From the condition of things on this side of New Berne, and more particularly of Washington, I think the enemy have no difficulty in getting information through our lines.

Captain Lawrence, stationed in Pitt, says that the enemy get the Richmond papers and other news regularly.

Satterthwaite, a member of the State Convention, lives within the enemy's lines unmolested, and has been allowed to come through our lines to Greenville whenever he wishes it. This is only one of many cases.

I fear, as you suggest, that Colonel Williams is not in all respects fully qualified for the position he holds, but the other two colonels there are much less so. In fact, Williams complains of their want of discipline, &c. The greatest difficulty, however, arises from the small force on the lines. In Pitt there are two cavalry companies, divided by the Tar River, and they are not sufficient to prevent intercourse, even if the officers were efficient, which they are not.

Negroes are escaping rapidly, probably a million of dollars' worth weekly in all. It is estimated that one-third of the negroes in the State are east of this line of railroad, and gentlemen complain, with some reason, that that section of the State is in danger of being ruined if these things continue.

It strikes me that, if we had force sufficient to accomplish the object, negroes and other movable property of value within or near the enemy's lines should be brought away and intercourse prohibited. I think it unwise to attempt it, however, until there is an effective force, because an alarm might cause the enemy to run away negroes more rapidly than they are doing. If the force could be had, a regiment of infantry might be well employed in the vicinity of Greenville, Pitt. I think Washington could be taken; but probably the best line of attack would be from Williamston, in Martin, there being no stream to cross.

If there were two or three reliable regiments here they might be moved by rail to Tarborough, Kinston, Wilmington, and Weldon, and could thus aid either in striking or defending those points.

If the separate cavalry companies could be united into regiments or battalions under proper officers, they might be made effective, while at present they are almost useless.

I had written the above, general, when your dispatch reached me.

If the companies of Partisan Rangers are collected at this place they leave a number of the richest counties (eastern) entirely unprotected, and those having most slaves. If the enemy are allowed to establish themselves within 30 miles of the railroad, they can by cavalry dashes constantly interrupt it; whereas if we can confine them to the coast, we save the negroes and the growing corn crop, as well as secure the road.

I suppose I must send all applications for furlough to your headquarters, no matter how urgent the case.

The telegraph wire to Kinston has been interrupted for an hour; what I get I will send by telegraph, if worth it. I have felt it my duty, general, to lay before you the late dispatches from Kinston, as they come from persons said to be reliable. While I hope there may not be a formidable attack, yet if one were made, I fear that it would not be successfully resisted.

My anxiety is increased because I cannot just now either ride a horse or walk. Coming from Petersburg inflamed my foot somewhat, but it is getting better, and, unless hurt again, in three days I can be on horseback, I think. I then hope to get matters in better shape.

I hope you will excuse the frequency and length of my letters.

Very respectfully, your obedient servant,

T. L. CLINGMAN,

Brigadier-General.

WIIMINGTON, N. C., *August* 7, 1862.

Hon. GEORGE W. RANDOLPH:

I have just received the following from Goldsborough yesterday: ·

Enemy's gunboats made their appearance in the Neuse, 25 miles above New Berne, this morning. They are 6 miles below Kinston. One is iron-clad. Shelling the woods near the obstructions.

I write you to-day.

W. S. ASHE.

HEADQUARTERS DEPARTMENT OF NORTHERN VIRGINIA, ·
August 8, 1862. ,

His Excellency HENRY T. CIARK,
Governor of North Carolina:

SIR: I have the honor to acknowledge the receipt of your letter of the 4th instant.* I have been an eye-witness of the outrages and depredations upon private property committed by the enemy in this State, and can fully appreciate what you say of the injuries sustained by the people of North Carolina; nor am I unmindful of the importance of protecting the line of railroad and, as far as practicable, the valuable private interests in the section of country to which you refer. But it is impossible, with the means at our command, to pursue the policy of concentrating our forces to protect important points and baffle the principal efforts of the enemy and at the same time extend all the protection we desire to give to every district. The safety of the whole State of North Carolina, as well as of Virginia, depends in a measure upon the result of the enemy's efforts in this quarter, which, if successful, would make your State the theater of hostilities, far more injurious and destructive to your citizens than anything they have yet been called upon to suffer.

To prevent effectually the enemy's gunboats from ascending navigable rivers would require not only batteries, but adequate land forces to defend them, which would lead to a subdivision of our forces, from which we could anticipate nothing but disaster. The selection of the troops to be withdrawn from North Carolina was made by General Holmes, who brought the most serviceable because there was most probability of their being used, the enemy being known to be here in great force and it being believed that most of his troops had been withdrawn from North Carolina. The raw troops were left for the additional reason that it was thought they would stand the usual camp diseases better at home than if removed. General Holmes and part of his army left North Carolina before the late battles and participated in them. He brought the brigades of Generals Martin and French because, the enemy being in and upon James River, it was thought proper to provide against any attempt he might make to·penetrate North Carolina and cut the railroad from the north, which might have been among his designs. With this view General Holmes was ordered back to the south side of the river immediately after·the battles, where he was joined by Generals Martin and French. The information received by General Holmes led him to believe, as I do, that the principal part of General Burnside's command had been transferred to Virginia, where I believe they now are.

Maj. Gen. D. H. Hill is in command of the district lately commanded by General Holmes, as you will perceive from the inclosed copy of the

---

* Not found.

order* assigning him to it. He will no doubt be very glad to confer with you as to the best means of protecting the country you refer to, and I should be most happy if your plan of retaking the places on the coast now held by the enemy can be carried out. I am most anxious to do all in our power to accomplish so desirable a result and extend the best protection to the people our means will permit.

I regret to hear what you say of the character of the officers appointed to command the troops in North Carolina.

I have the honor to be, very respectfully, your obedient servant,

R. E. LEE,
General.

HEADQUARTERS DEPARTMENT OF NORTHERN VIRGINIA,
August 12, 1862.

His Excellency HENRY T. CLARK,
Governor of North Carolina, Raleigh, N. C.:

SIR: I have the honor to inform you that Brig. Gen. J. G. Martin has been assigned to the immediate command of the troops in the State of North Carolina. It is hoped and believed that his position as an officer of the Confederate States Army will in no way interfere with the discharge of the duties devolving upon him in his capacity as Adjutant and Inspector General of the State, and that under his immediate supervision the troops in the State will reach a high degree of efficiency and nothing be neglected which can advance and protect the interests of North Carolina. I have desired that he will render such aid as he can toward collecting and enrolling the men liable to military duty, so that the regiments from the State may be speedily and fully recruited.

I am, very respectfully, your obedient servant,

R. E. LEE,
General.

HEADQUARTERS DEPARTMENT OF NORTHERN VIRGINIA,
August 12, 1862.

Brig. Gen. J. G. MARTIN, *Commanding, &c.:*

GENERAL: I am informed by the Adjutant and Inspector General that your resignation has not been accepted, and that you have been directed to report to me for duty. You will report for further orders to Maj. Gen. D. H. Hill, commanding the Department of North Carolina. I trust you will be enabled to perform the duties, devolving upon you as an officer of the State as well as of the Confederate States. I particularly desire that you will render such assistance as may be in your power, as commanding officer of the Confederate troops in the State, toward collecting and enrolling the men liable to military duty under the act of Congress of April 16, 1862, as it is all important that the ranks of the regiments so reduced by sickness and battle shall be filled. After the old regiments have been recruited the surplus men should be collected in camps of instruction and there organized and prepared for service in the field.

I am, very respectfully, your obedient servant,

R. E. LEE,
General.

* See p. 476.

SPECIAL ORDERS,) ¹ HDQRS. DISTRICT OF NORTH CAROLINA,
    No. 180.   )   (*Petersburg, Va., August* 18, 1862.

. . . .

III. Brig. Gen. J. G. Martin is assigned, in accordance with instructions from the General Commanding the Army, to the District of North Carolina, extending from the right banks of the Roanoke to the South Carolina line.

Brig. Gen. J. J. Pettigrew will relieve General Martin of the charge of his brigade.

Brig. Gen. T. L. Clingman will assume command of the troops at Wilmington, N. C.

Brigadier-General Martin will render all the assistance in his power toward collecting and enrolling the men in the State subject to military duty, so that the ranks of the North Carolina regiments may be speedily recruited.

After this duty has been done the surplus should be collected at camps of instruction and organized and prepared for active service in the field.

By command of Maj. Gen. D. H. Hill:

                    ARCHER ANDERSON,
                    Assistant Adjutant-General.

                    PETERSBURG, *August* 19, 1862.

General S. COOPER:

Tell General D. H. Hill that Clingman, reports enemy landing at Swansborough from transports. Have been joined by cavalry and artillery.

                    S. G. FRENCH.

CHAPTER XXI.

OPERATIONS IN TEXAS, NEW MEXICO, AND ARIZONA.

February 1–September 20, 1862.

SUMMARY OF THE PRINCIPAL EVENTS.

Feb.   —, 1862.—The Confederate forces enter New Mexico.

    11–13, 1862.—Operations at Aransas Pass, Tex.

    21, 1862.—Engagement at Valverde, N. Mex.

    22, 1862.—Engagement in Aransas Bay, Tex.

Mar.   2, 1862.—Albuquerque, N. Mex., abandoned by the Union forces.

    3, 1862.—Capture of Cubero, N. Mex.

    4, 1862.—Santa Fé, N. Mex., abandoned by the Union forces.

    26, 1862.—Skirmish at Apache Cañon, N. Mex.

    28, 1862.—Engagement at Glorieta, or Pigeon's Ranch, N. Mex.

April   5– 6, 1862.—Affair at San Luis Pass, Tex.

    8, 1862.—Skirmish at Albuquerque, N. Mex.

    13–22, 1862.—Pursuit of the Confederate forces, including skirmish at Peralta, N. Mex., April 15.

    13–Sept. 20, 1862.—Expedition from Southern California, through Arizona, to Northwestern Texas and New Mexico.

    15, 1862.—Skirmish at Peralta, N. Mex.
              Skirmish at Picacho Pass, Ariz.

    22, 1862.—Capture of Union launches in Aransas Bay, Tex.

    25, 1862.—Affair at Socorro, N. Mex.

May   15, 1862.—Naval demonstration upon Galveston, Tex.

    20, 1862.—Tucson, Ariz., occupied by Union forces.

    21, 1862.—Affair at Paraje, N. Mex.

    23, 1862.—Affair near Fort Craig, N. Mex.

    26, 1862.—Texas embraced in Confederate Trans-Mississippi Department.

    30, 1862.—Martial law proclaimed in Texas.

June   8, 1862.—Martial law proclaimed in Arizona.

    18, 1862.—Brig. Gen. Paul O. Hébert, C. S. Army, assumes command of the District of Texas.

July   4, 1862.—Attack on United States vessels near Velasco, Tex.

    7–17, 1862.—Operations in Aransas Bay, Tex.

    15, 1862.—Skirmish at Apache Pass, Ariz.

Aug.   10, 1862.—Affair on the Nueces River, near Fort Clark, Tex.

    11, 1862.—Affair at Velasco, Tex.

    12, 1862.—Capture of the Breaker and destruction of the Hannah in Corpus Christi Bay, Tex.

    16–18, 1862.—Bombardment of Corpus Christi, Tex.

    20, 1862.—Texas and Arizona embraced in Trans-Mississippi Department.

Sept.   —, 1862.—Proclamation declaring martial law in Texas annulled.

    13–14, 1862.—Operations at Flour Bluffs, Tex.

    18, 1862.—Brig. Gen. James H. Carleton, U. S. Army, supersedes Brig. Gen. E. R. S. Canby in command of the Department of New Mexico.

FEBRUARY 11–13, 1862.—Operations at Aransas Pass, Tex.

REPORTS.

No. 1.—Maj. C. G. Forshey, C. S. Army, Engineer of Coast Defenses.
No. 2.—Maj. Daniel D Shea, C. S. Army, commanding Battalion of Artillery.

No. 1.

Report of Maj. C. G. Forshey, C. S. Army, Engineer of Coast Defenses.

CAMP ESPERANZA, PASS CAVAILO, TEX.,
February 15, 1862.

MAJOR : As this command does not report directly to headquarters, at Houston, I take the liberty to report the matters of much interest transpiring on this portion of the coast. The bark reported to you in my letter of the 5th took her position at Aransas Pass, and, landing in two boats her small parties of 20 or 30 men, scared off, it would appear, the companies posted there, assumed many liberties, took beef and mutton at their pleasure, burned several houses, shelled the neighboring islands and sand hills in the moorings, to test the presence of a possible rebel arrival during the night, and made themselves at home there.

Major Shea, with detachment of mounted men, went to Aransas, arriving stealthily, with a hope of capturing the party and relieving the citizens from their great annoyance and peril. In this he was not successful. His presence was discovered, and the commander of the bark Afton came into the Pass with three boats and 28 men, out of range of rifles, his splendid rifled guns from the ship shelling the village and Major Shea's command quite across the island. Major Shea protected his men as well as possible in rear of the sand mounds and avoided any serious casualty, though their well-directed shells (thrown directly, and not as from mortars) burst over their heads several times. At a signal from the boats his guns ceased firing, a flag of truce was sent ashore, and a parley asked with Major Shea.

The commander then came up and held a long and quite communicative interview with the major; wished to send letters and packages from his prisoners, taken on the McNeill (already reported by me as captured near this pass), to their families; delivered the letters to Judge Talbot's family and others residing in the vicinity; said the prisoners were well and kindly treated, messing at his table, &c. He informed the major that he was well informed of all the defenses, could reach the whole coast with his guns, but was not there to fight, but to stop the trade he saw running by the Pass, and that he would do; that his ship could enter that Pass, and he intended to command it and the bays within; would have the small vessels for the important purposes he had in view, with many other saucy remarks needless to relate. The most mortifying remark, however, was that " if Texans were like those he had seen run away on his approach his handful of men could whip five hundred of them."

Major Shea told him that he did not command those men, in answer to the question, but would offer to fight him then, man for man, on shore, and would thank him for the opportunity. He told him, further, that his profession that " he did not want to hurt the people or their property " was belied by the bombardment of the village, with women and children, burning houses &c.

Major Shea left Aransas early yesterday morning and returned with his command at 3 p. m. to-day. He reports to Colonel Garland, and sends a messenger at once for advice as to what steps are next to be taken, if any, to protect the interests at stake. As he came up the large schooner that passed here yesterday was hugging the shore, apparently bound for Aransas, doubtless having supplies on board and perhaps forces. She was lined with surf-boats along her deck.

The light-house there, like this at Pass Cavallo, furnishes the enemy with many advantages. The line of trade for the present is destroyed. No boats will be allowed to pass below this point in future. I have been thus circumstantial, that you may lay before General Hébert the weakness of the forces and the defenses on this portion of the coast.

Very respectfully submitted.

C. G. FORSHEY,
Major of Artillery and Engineer of Coast Defenses.

Maj. SAMUEL BOYER DAVIS,
Assistant Adjutant-General, C. S. Prov. Army, Houston, Tex.

No. 2.

Report of Maj. Daniel D. Shea, C. S. Army, commanding Battalion of Artillery.

CAMP ESPERANZA, NEAR SALURIA, TEX.,
February 16, 1862.

COLONEL: I have the honor to report to you the result of my excursion down the island and the information it furnished for the public service:

As already reported to you by Major Forshey, I took a detachment of mounted men, 32 in number, under Lieutenants Patton and Preston, and went down to Cedar Bayou, 35 miles, in hopes to capture the parties landing from the blockading bark Afton.

On my arrival there I learned that she was at Aransas Pass, and the citizens in great alarm from the precipitate retreat of Captain Neal's command, the capture of the sloop that his pickets were using, and the impudence of the enemy making his landings, getting such supplies as he chose, and reconnoitering the vicinity. I therefore pushed directly on to Aransas, and took a position on the rear of the island, remote as possible from the ship.

Immediately after my arrival it was reported that the crew were on Light-House Island, and that Captain Neal had landed a force of 200 men the night before on Mustang Island, and would attack them. I waited on the point of San Joseph's Island with my force to act in concert with the party on the opposite side of the Pass; but when the enemy's boats were going out of the harbor only about 6 men fired at them from the hills on Mustang. I perceived this mode of attack was attempted by a party of civilians, and not regular troops; therefore, I kept my party secreted. The enemy's four boats, manned by only 28 men, passed out over the bar without sustaining any damage. I drew my party off to await the landing on San Joseph's. They, however, returned to their ship.

Wednesday, 12th, the ship made sail and came to off Mustang Island about 10 a. m. and commenced shelling. I could not find a boat of any character to cross me on the island. I intended to take command of Neal's companies. The shelling from the ship ceased, when I succeeded in getting a boat. On approaching the land I discovered a house on fire (Mr. Clubb's residence), and saw the sailors of the enemy on the island, and on closing up on the land they went into Mercer's house and set it on fire. Then I was fully convinced that Captain Neal had vacated the island and that it was occupied by Lincoln. I turned back disgusted with the spirit of our men in that section, and immediately sent a letter to Neal's camp, 10 miles on the main-land, demanding 50 volunteers. I had taken up a position out of sight of the ship with my cavalry detachment and watched the movements of the enemy. ·

Thursday, 13th, about 2 a. m., 22 men and 3 lieutenants reported to me. This small number was inadequate to carry out my plan of capturing the crew, and therefore kept them secreted on San Joseph's Island, hoping the enemy would land. I had caused this detachment to be divided into two parties, one commanded by Lieutenant Conklin, stationed in Mercer's store, at the head of his wharf; the other by Lieutenant Canfield, at the town. I drew off the cavalry from picket and secreted them in the town. All kept quiet.

About 1 o'clock three boats of the enemy started down towards the Pass with the intention to land at some point. I immediately disposed of my force to engage them when they should land. They came inside the Pass and continued to advance up Aransas Bay toward the town. When within 1,000 yards of my position the ship opened fire on us with shell. They were thrown with remarkable precision at a distance of $3\frac{1}{2}$ miles and bursted over our heads. I saw that I could not use my men mounted, and ordered the detachment to dismount, sent the horses to the rear; but the ship continued firing, the shells bursting in our midst. Some of the horses and 2 of the men were struck, but not wounded.

I saw no chance of engaging the boats from under the ship's fire; the horses became unmanageable, and I ordered my men to fall back and take shelter close to the town; also the lieutenant and 10 men, of Neal's command, I had secreted in the house that was bombarded by the enemy, to retreat toward the sand hills and concentrate close to the town, where I waited for the approach of the enemy in his boats. I expected he would land his force, and I could get a chance to engage him from under his ship's fire. I expected he would fire the store and dwelling of Mr. Mercer, but he passed it and advanced toward my little force.

I was informed by the citizens that Captain Neal fell back in the presence of the enemy's force, numbering only 28 men, and I expected this captain would follow up his former successes. He came within rifle-range and 3 men landed; the other two boats stood off. Immediately one of the three advanced with a white flag. Some of the citizens were at a short distance in the rear. I ordered one of them to ascertain what he wanted. I still hoped to draw him from under the fire of the ship. The person bearing the white flag stated that there were prisoners on board the ship, and wished to communicate with some persons on shore. The bearer of the white flag requested the citizens (Mr. Mercer and Captain Wells) to see the captain of the ship, who was on shore and near his boats. He (captain) asked who commanded, and they said I commanded. He asked if I would respect a white flag; he wished to see and speak with me, and one of the citizens, Captain Wells, came to me and delivered the message. I advanced toward him within 50 yards and stood. He then came toward me and both advanced and met. He stated to me he did not come here to make war on women and children; he was sent to blockade this harbor, and he would carry out his orders. To which I replied that his causing to be destroyed the dwellings of Messrs. Mercer and Clubb, on Mustang Island, and killing of cattle and sheep, the property of inoffensive citizens, looked to me that his mode of warfare was of a promiscuous character. He said when he went on shore on Mustang Island he met Mr. Mercer's son, and thought that Mercer and himself had understood each other. Mercer was one of the party that fired on his boat when passing out of Aransas Pass, and he was compelled to retaliate. He said he captured a schooner off Pass Cavallo. He sent some of the crew prisoners on the prize to New York. He had Judge Talbot and Captain Hopper and wife on his ship. He said they had the liberty of the ship and dined at his table.

The surgeon, white flag bearer, remarked that the captain had treated them kindly, and endeavored to make them feel easy on the vessel. The captain continued, and said he sent Captain Coffin to New York, and handed to me two letters and a package directed to Mrs. Smith, Coffin's daughter, and a package from Judge Talbot, directed to George Bunkmark, at Matagorda. He requested me to say to Judge Talbot's friends and relatives that the old gentleman was well, and he would intercede for his release with the commodore at Ship Island. The captain asked me if I commanded the troops on this island. I answered, "I command a detachment of cavalry." The surgeon inquired if I commanded the troops on Mustang Island and vicinity. I said, "No, sir." The captain remarked, "You perceive I can shell this island. I can hold and command this coast with my ship." I said, "I perceive that, and we could not hold this portion of the coast, from the fact we had no ordnance here to defend it; but I would like to have the pleasure of meeting you on main-land or with equal numbers from under the fire of your ship." He replied, "Let that be as it may; I admire your gallantry." He inquired if the people on the coast would respect a white flag. I answered, "I presume they would; but the white flag was not respected on the Atlantic coast by his party." He said he would not do any harm to citizens. He wanted fresh provisions occasionally, and would pay for what he would take. The surgeon remarked naively they only wished to come on shore and get some oysters and fish. The captain said he would come on shore again, and bring with him Judge Talbot's trunk and some other packages and forward them to my care at Pass Cavallo. We bid each other adieu, and when at the distance of about 50 yards he called and asked if Captain Nichols still lived at Pass Cavallo. I answered, "Yes." He asked if he was at home. I answered in the affirmative, and he then went on board his boat.

One of the boats had a mast rigged and signalized the ship when to open fire and when to cease. The surgeon stated to K. A. Mercer, jr., a few days previous, when they landed on Mustang Island, that he was a Texan and his name is Osborne. He is a large man, about forty-seven to fifty years old. The captain is a small, light man, sallow complexion, about thirty-five years old. He told Mercer he intended to break up the commerce now carried on through the bays, and he intends to go to Lamar, and would have the pilot schooner Twin Sisters. He is very anxious to capture small boats. He said he could take his ship to Lamar and his crew and boats could take Corpus Christi. He said two of the crew captured by him joined his ship; these, of course, have given him all the information he requires.

I must state that the captain is a brave and daring officer, and is putting himself in the way of being captured by a small party of good men. If this man is not stopped immediately, before he can capture the small boats now in the lower bays and salt-works, he will command our whole western coast.

When returning from Aransas I saw a three-masted schooner sailing to the westward. I suppose her to be a supply vessel. She had launches slung along her sides and more men than a vessel of her class requires for her own purposes.

It gives me pleasure to testify to the good conduct of the whole party under my command, and specially to compliment Lieut. I. A. Patton and his detachment of Beaumont's cavalry for their coolness and soldierly behavior under a heavy fire of shells. Lieutenant Conklin and a small party of Captain Neal's command were also under the same fire and conducted themselves with commendable coolness.

I would close this communication by stating my conviction that nothing short of immediate and energetic action, under a prudent and skillful commander, can prevent the enemy from getting a foothold at Aransas and destroying the commerce of the bays, and thus rescue the vast interests at this moment periled in that region.

I have the honor to be, very respectfully, your obedient servant,

DAN. D. SHEA,
Major, Prov. Army C. S., Comdg. Batt. Art., Pass Cavallo.

Col. R. R. GARLAND. C. S. Army,
Comdg. Sixth Regiment Texas Infantry, Victoria, Tex.

P. S.—I forgot to embody in the above report that Capt. B. F. Neal reported to me about 60 men for duty on the morning after the parley with the commander of the blockading vessel. I had concluded to return to my post and lay before you the above report, in order to prepare a proper military force to protect our commerce west, and advised him to retire from the island.

FEBRUARY 21, 1862.—Engagement at Valverde, N. Mex.

REPORTS, ETC.

No. 1.—Col. Edward R. S. Canby, Nineteenth U. S. Infantry, commanding Department of New Mexico.
No. 2.—Col. Benjamin S. Roberts, Fifth New Mexico Infantry.
No. 3.—Maj. Thomas Duncan, Third U. S. Cavalry, and resulting correspondence.
No. 4.—Col. Christopher Carson, First New Mexico Infantry.
No. 5.—Col. Miguel E. Pino, Second New Mexico Infantry.
No. 6.—Lieut. Col. José M. Valdez, Third New Mexico Infantry (mounted).
No. 7.—Findings of Court of Inquiry on conduct of Capt. R. S. C. Lord, First U. S. Cavalry.
No. 8.—Brig. Gen. Henry H. Sibley, C. S. Army, commanding Army of New Mexico, including operations from January — to May 4, 1862.
No. 9.—Maj. Charles L. Pyron, Second Texas Cavalry.
No. 10.—Lieut. Col. William R. Scurry, Fourth Texas Cavalry.
No. 11.—Maj. Henry W. Raguet, Fourth Texas Cavalry.
No. 12.—Col. Thomas Green, Fifth Texas Cavalry.
No. 13.—Col. William Steele, Seventh Texas Cavalry.
No. 14.—Capt. Powhatan Jordan, Seventh Texas Cavalry.
No. 15.—Capt. Trevanion T. Teel, Texas Light Artillery.

No. 1.

Reports of Col. Edward R. S. Canby, Nineteenth U. S. Infantry, commanding Department of New Mexico.*

HEADQUARTERS DEPARTMENT OF NEW MEXICO,
Fort Craig, N. Mex., February 22, 1862.

SIR: I have the honor to report that a battle was fought yesterday at Valverde, a few miles above this place, between the Union troops under my command, and the Confederate force under General Sibley. The battle commenced at an early hour in the morning and was continued with unvarying success until about 5 o'clock in the evening, when, in a desperate charge of the Confederates, McRae's battery was taken, the supporting party repulsed and thrown into confusion and driven from the field at the moment that success seemed certain. The battle was fought almost entirely by the regular troops (trebled in number by the Confederates), with no assistance from the militia and but little from the volunteers, who would not obey orders or obeyed them too late to be of any service. The immediate cause of the disaster was the refusal of one of the volunteer regiments to cross the river and support the left wing of the army.

The contemporary operations of the right wing were eminently successful, but the confusion produced by the loss of the battery could not be remedied in season to retrieve the fortunes of the day. The retreat was effected in good order and without further loss.

Under a flag the killed and wounded have been removed from the field and properly cared for. The absolute loss cannot yet be ascertained. It will probably reach 40 killed and 150 wounded, with perhaps a few prisoners.† Large numbers of the militia and volunteers have deserted, but this adds to rather than diminishes our strength. Among the killed are Captain McRae, Captain Bascom, and Lieutenant Mishler. Among the wounded, Captain Wingate, Captain Stone, and Acting Second Lieutenant McDermott.

The troops are not dispirited by this result, as all are satisfied that we have inflicted greater losses upon the enemy than we have suffered ourselves and that the ultimate result of the contest will be in our favor.

I will report more in detail in a few days.

Very respectfully, sir, your obedient servant,

ED. R. S. CANBY,
Colonel Nineteenth Infantry, Commanding Department.

The ADJUTANT-GENERAL OF THE ARMY,
Washington, D. C.

HEADQUARTERS DEPARTMENT OF NEW MEXICO,
Fort Craig, N. Mex., March 1, 1862.

SIR: In submitting my report of the battle of Valverde I have thought it necessary for a proper appreciation of the battle itself to include a connected history of the events that immediately preceded and followed it.

---

* See also Canby to Adjutant-General U. S. Army, February 23, in "Correspondence, etc," *post.*

† But see revised statement on p. 493.

You were advised by previous reports that the advance of the enemy made its appearance in the neighborhood of this post as early as the 12th ultimo. His force consisted of Riley's and Green's regiments, five companies of Steele's and five of Baylor's regiments, Teel's and Riley's batteries, and three independent companies, making a nominal aggregate, as indicated by captured rolls and returns, of nearly 3,000 men, but reduced, it was understood, by sickness and detachments to about 2,600 when it reached this neighborhood.

To oppose this force I had concentrated at this post five companies of the Fifth, three of the Seventh, and three of the Tenth Infantry, two companies of the First and five of the Third Cavalry, McRae's battery (G of the Second and I of the Third Cavalry), and a company of Colorado volunteers. The New Mexican troops consisted of the First Regiment (Carson's), seven companies of the Second, seven of the Third, one of the Fourth, two of the Fifth, Graydon's Spy Company, and about 1,000 hastily-collected and unorganized militia, making on the morning of the 21st an aggregate present of 3,810.

Having no confidence in the militia and but little in the volunteers, I had determined from the first to bring on a battle if possible in a position where the New Mexican troops would not be obliged to maneuver in the presence of or under the fire of the enemy. Several days were spent in the endeavor to accomplish this object, which failed, for the reason that several officers of the Confederate force had lived or served in New Mexico and thoroughly understood and appreciated the character of its people.

On the 19th the enemy fell back from his advanced position and crossed to the east bank of the river, about 7 miles below the post, with the evident intention of reaching the country above without fighting or of forcing us to attack him upon ground of his own choice. On the 20th the first movement for turning the post or occupying a point within range which commanded it was commenced, and in order that the operations of this and the subsequent day may be understood it is necessary to give a short topographical sketch of the country embraced in these operations.

From Paraje, 7 miles below, to a point immediately opposite the post, the valley of the Rio Grande is bounded on the east by a basaltic mesa from 40 to 80 feet in height, accessible at a few points by bridle-paths, and at only one point by a road practicable for artillery. Immediately opposite the post a point of the pedregal projects into the valley, and at the distance of 1,000 yards has a slight command over the post, which would be tenable only by preventing the establishment of batteries on the point. Two and a half miles above the post the Mesa del Contadero, about 3 miles long and 2 wide, rises to the height of 300 feet above the level of the valley. At the southern and northern ends of this mesa the valley of the river is accessible, and at both points was favorable for the establishment of a camp beyond the reach of our artillery and covered in front by the river itself.

The mal pais, or pedregal, is traversed by ridges of drifting sand, broken in places by protruding beds of lava, and parallel in their general direction to the valley of the river. The ravines between these ridges are natural covered ways, affording the enemy great advantages, by concealing his movements and securing him from attack by the impracticable character of the country between them and our position.

On the 20th the main force of the enemy moved up one of these ravines, and at 4 o'clock in the afternoon had reached a position in which it was possible to attack him, although the ground in his front was exceedingly difficult for the operations of cavalry or artillery. For the purpose of attacking him while on the march the main body of our force had already been thrown across the river and advanced into the neighborhood of the ravine up which he was moving. Preparations for the attack were made, and skirmishers thrown forward for the purpose of drawing the fire of his batteries and developing his position. This was accomplished, but one of the volunteer regiments (Pino's) was thrown into such utter confusion by a few harmless cannon-shots that it was impossible to restore them to any kind of order. This and the near approach of night rendered it inexpedient to continue the attack. To mask our intentions and keep the enemy in his position as long as possible a demonstration upon his right flank was made by Colonel Roberts with all the cavalry force, under cover of which the troops were withdrawn, the infantry posted so as to prevent his effecting a lodgment during the night on the point opposite the post, and the artillery and cavalry crossed the river to the fort.

These movements had the intended effect, and on the morning of the 21st the enemy was found in the position he had occupied on the previous evening. During the night many of his animals stampeded from the want of water and between 200 and 300 horses and mules were captured and brought into the fort.

At 8 o'clock his advance was seen moving in the direction of the upper ford, and Colonel Roberts was detached with the regular and volunteer cavalry to occupy and hold the ford. He was followed immediately by two sections of McRae's battery and Hall's 24-pounder howitzers (two), supported by Brotherton's company of the Fifth, Ingraham's of the Seventh, and two (Mortimore's and Hubbell's) selected companies of volunteers. Graydon's Spy Company and 500 mounted militia, under Colonels Pino and Stapleton, had already been sent to the eastern side of the river to watch the movements of the enemy, threaten his flanks and rear, and impede his movements as much as possible.

As his movement in the direction of the upper ford became more determined, Selden's battalion, eight companies of regular infantry, and one of Colorado Volunteers, were recalled from the opposite side of the river and sent forward to re-enforce Colonel Roberts. Carson's regiment (eight companies of New Mexican Volunteers) followed immediately afterwards. Soon after noon the object of the enemy was fully developed, and his whole force, with the exception of about 500 men, was moving in the direction of the upper ford. Leaving two companies of volunteers, a regiment of militia under Colonel Armijo, and some detachments from the regular troops to garrison the post, I ordered Pino's regiment from its position on the opposite bank, and moved with Company G, First Cavalry, and the remaining section of McRae's battery, to the upper crossing. On reaching the field I learned that the advance of the enemy had gained the crossing before our own advance, and endeavored to effect a lodgment that would command the ford. Major Duncan, Third Cavalry, in command of the immediate advance, promptly crossed the river, dismounted his men, and in a sharp and spirited skirmish drove the enemy from the position he had seized, enabling Colonel Roberts to establish his batteries in positions to drive the enemy from the heavy bosques in rear of the ford.

After a contest of two hours with artillery and small-arms, during which the Confederate forces fought with great determination and made several desperate efforts to obtain command of the crossing, this was accomplished, and they were driven from all the points near the ford. At 12 o'clock Selden's command reached the field, and under

Colonel Roberts' direction immediately crossed the river, attacked the enemy in his new position, repulsed a desperate charge of his cavalry, drove him with great loss from this position, and remained master of the field. The batteries were now crossed to the east bank of the river, and the effective fire of McRae's and Hall's batteries, aided by the small-arms of Selden's and Duncan's commands, dislodged the enemy from all the positions and forced him to take shelter behind the sand hills. Three of his guns were disabled and left on the ground traversed by our troops, but were too much injured to be removed.

The position now occupied by the enemy was one of great natural strength, behind a sand ridge nearly parallel to the course of the river, which covered his guns and men from our fire, and in a great measure concealed his movements. Up to this time our loss in the Regulars and Colorado Volunteers had been 10 killed and 63 wounded. The arrival of the cavalry company and section of McRae's battery (94) actually added but 21 men to our effective strength, while the enemy, abandoning a large portion of his train, had just brought upon the field an additional force of 500 men.

The reports of the several commanders and a personal reconnaissance satisfied me that a direct attack upon his position would be attended with great loss, and would be of doubtful result. I determined to attempt to force the left of his line, and the disposition of the troops to effect this was at once commenced, McRae's battery, resting on the river and strongly supported, forming the left, Selden's regular infantry and Carson's volunteers the center, Hall's battery, with its infantry support and Duncan's cavalry (dismounted riflemen), the right of our line; Pino's volunteers, a squadron of the First Cavalry, and Valdez's volunteers the reserve.

With this arrangement I hoped by advancing the right and center, turning upon the left as a pivot, to force the left of his line, enfilade his position behind the sand hill, and drive him from the field. Accordingly Carson's regiment, which at his own request had not hitherto been brought into action, was ordered to cross the river. Captain Lord was ordered to unite his own with Claflin's company, and report to me as the cavalry reserve. The support of McRae's battery was increased by Plympton's battalion (four companies of regulars and one of Colorado Volunteers), and Pino's regiment, then just coming up, was ordered to cross the river as the reserve for our left and an additional support for the battery. While these arrangements were in progress Hall's battery was attacked by a large force of the enemy's cavalry. Receiving from Major Duncan urgent and repeated messages, I detached first Ingraham's company of the Seventh Infantry to support the battery, and then Wingate's battalion of the Fifth to aid in repelling the attack. This was soon accomplished, and Carson's regiment, which had just crossed the river, attracted by the firing, joined in the pursuit, and by a well-directed fire added to the discomfiture of the enemy, who fled precipitately, and did not stop until he had passed beyond the second range of sand hills.

At this moment a formidable storming party, supported by several infantry columns and four pieces of artillery, the whole estimated at more than 1,000 men, suddenly made its appearance from behind the sand ridge, and moved rapidly upon McRae's battery. Perceiving that Plympton's command was entirely unsuspicious of the danger that threatened the battery, I hastened in person to point it out and make arrangements for its defense, but before this could be fully accomplished the volunteers that formed a part of its support gave way, and in passing through Plympton's battalion communicated their panic, and carried with them a part of his men. The main body of his command, however, rushed into the battery and engaged in a gallant and desperate attempt to repel the enemy. The advance of the storming party was driven back, and under cover of this repulse the first fugitives from the battery crossed the river with but little loss. Lord's squadron coming up from the right (where he had been ordered for the purpose of uniting his company with Claflin's), was ordered to charge, but on approaching the battery became exposed to the fire of our own men as well as that of the enemy, turned to the left, and for reasons that are not entirely satisfactory fell back without making the charge. The storming party proper was deployed as skirmishers, enveloping the left. front, and a part of the right of the battery by a circular segment nearly half a mile in length. Armed with double-barreled fowling-pieces and revolvers, and converging as they approached, a rapid and destructive fire was poured into the battery. From the moment that it made its appearance the storming party was met by a terrible fire of grape and double canister from the battery and of musketry from its infantry support. This contest was continued in and about the battery long after its guns had been silenced, the gunners with their revolvers and the infantry with their muskets in desperate and often hand-to-hand conflicts, until, overwhelmed by superior numbers, this gallant band was driven from the field, but not until it had lost in killed, wounded, and prisoners nearly one-half of its effective force.

At this moment Wingate's battalion, coming up at the double-quick, poured upon the Confederates a rapid and destructive fire, under which they recoiled in disorder. So great was the confusion produced by this sudden and to them unexpected attack that for some moments I entertained the confident hope that the battery, and with it the fortunes of the day, would yet be saved; but the rapidly-gathering re-enforcements of the enemy and the distance to which our troops on the right (though promptly recalled by Colonel Roberts, commanding on that flank) had pursued the flying enemy, convinced me that to prolong the contest would only add to the number of our casualties without changing the result. Orders were accordingly sent to Captain Selden to fall back slowly and cover the retreat, and to the other commanders to recross the river. The movement of Selden's column (four companies of the Fifth Infantry), in the immediate presence and under the fire of the enemy, was admirably executed, the command moving with deliberation, halting occasionally to allow the wounded to keep up with it, and many of the men picking up and carrying with them the arms of their dead or wounded comrades. The other columns, under the personal superintendence of Colonel Roberts, crossed over without disorder, confusion, or loss. The ammunition wagons, a disabled gun, and all the material except the captured battery and a part of the arms of the killed and wounded, were safely passed over.

On the west bank of the river the troops that had escaped from the battle were found to be much scattered, but the regular troops were easily collected and sent forward in the direction of the fort. Pino's regiment, of which only one company (Sena's) and part of another could be induced to cross the river, was in the wildest confusion, and no efforts of their own officers or of my staff could restore any kind of order. More than 100 men from this regiment deserted from the field. Under cover first of Selden's column and afterwards of the regular cavalry the stragglers were collected, arrangements made for the removal of the dead and the care of the wounded, the beef herds driven in, and the public property collected and removed. Nothing was abandoned on the field except some tents and fixtures of the field hospital left behind to make room for wounded men, and one wagon, from which the escort (volunteers) had cut the mules and fled to the mountains. With the cavalry as a rear guard the command marched in without confusion or loss.

Besides the superiority in numbers the Confederate Army possessed a great advantage over us in the superior mobility of its force, which was all mounted. Occupying on the morning of the 21st a position which threatened two points of vital importance to us, he was able to evade the attacks directed against him and to concentrate superior numbers at any other point. Our infantry, which in the morning held him in check at the lower end of the mesa, was obliged to march 7 miles and to ford twice a deep and rapid stream in order to reach the field he had finally chosen. In all the earlier conflicts of the day, as in the final struggle, our troops were always encountered by superior numbers, never less than two and sometimes four to one.

Although defeated, my command is not dispirited. All feel that greater injuries have been inflicted upon the enemy than we have sustained ourselves, and that what we have lost has been without loss of honor.

With deep sorrow I transmit the list of our killed, wounded, and missing, amounting in the aggregate to one-fourth of the effectives we had on the field. On the list are the names of several accomplished officers and many brave and noble men, who have exhibited the last and highest example of devoted loyalty and patriotism. Their memory is commended to the respect, and their relatives and friends to the sympathy, of our countrymen. Among these, however, is one, isolated by peculiar circumstances, whose memory deserves notice from a higher authority than mine. Pure in character, upright in conduct, devoted to his profession, and of a loyalty that was deaf to the seductions of family and friends, Captain McRae died, as he had lived, an example of the best and highest qualities that man can possess.

I desire to bring to your notice Colonel Roberts, Third Cavalry, for some time past the energetic and efficient commander of the troops at Fort Craig, and on the 21st the immediate commander of the troops at Valverde, until 2.30 o'clock. He was then, as he has always been, distinguished for coolness, gallantry, and efficiency.

The officers whose conduct came under my own observation or is reported by subordinate commanders are Captains Selden, Wingate, and Brotherton, Lieutenants Anderson and Cook, of the Fifth Infantry; Captain Plympton, of the Seventh Infantry; Lieutenant Hall, of the Tenth Infantry; Captains Morris and Howland, Third Cavalry; First Lieutenant Bell, Second, and Captain Mortimore, Third New Mexico Volunteers. These names are presented because the officers were isolated by command, by position, or by peculiar circumstances, and I adopt as my own the commendation bestowed by other commanders upon the officers and men of their commands. The names of the non-commissioned officers and men who were distinguished have been called for, and will be presented hereafter.

My thanks are especially due to the members of my staff, Major Donaldson, Captains Archer, Evans, and Nicodemus, and Lieutenant D'Amours, all of whom were much exposed, and exhibited the greatest coolness and zeal in the performance of their duties.

Higher thanks than any I can bestow are due to the medical officers of the command, and especially to Assistant Surgeons Norris (medical director), Clements, and Bill, upon whom the chief labors fell, for their untiring devotion to the comfort of our wounded men. Assistant Surgeons Shout and Rankin, of the volunteer service, and Doctors Arnold and Belt are specially noticed by the medical director.

Colonels Pino and Carson, Lieut. Cols. J. F. and Manuel Chavez, and many other officers of the New Mexican Volunteers, were noted for their zeal and energy.

I have the honor to be, very respectfully, sir, your obedient servant,

ED. R. S. CANBY,
Colonel Nineteenth Infantry, Commanding Department.

The ADJUTANT-GENERAL OF THE ARMY,
Washington, D. C.

[Addenda.]

Return of casualties in the United States troops, commanded by Col. Edward R. S. Canby, at the battle of Valverde, N. Mex., February 21, 1862.

[Compiled from nominal lists of casualties, returns, &c.]

Command.	Killed.		Wounded.		Missing.		Aggregate.	Remarks.
	Officers.	Enlisted men.	Officers.	Enlisted men.	Officers.	Enlisted men.		
1st New Mexico Infantry		1		1		11	13	
2d New Mexico Infantry		1		3			4	
3d New Mexico Infantry		6	1	3		1	11	
4th New Mexico Infantry								No loss reported.
5th New Mexico Infantry		3		1			4	
Graydon's company, New Mexico								No loss reported.
Dodd's company, Colorado		2		28		9	39	
1st U. S. Cavalry, Companies D and G.		1		9		1	11	
2d U. S. Cavalry, Company G		9		9		2	20	
3d U. S. Cavalry, Companies C, D, G, I, and K.	1	5		14			20	
5th U. S. Infantry, Companies B, D, F, I, and K.	1	9	2	33		1	46	
7th U. S. Infantry, Companies C, F, and H.	1	18		39		4	62	
10th U. S. Infantry, Companies A, F, and H.		10		17	1	5	33	
Total	3	65	3	157	1	34	263	

NOTE.—McRae's battery (provisional) was composed of Companies G, Second, and I, Third, U. S. Cavalry.

No. 2.

Report of Col. Benjamin S. Roberts, Fifth New Mexico Infantry.

HEADQUARTERS SOUTHERN MILITARY DISTRICT,
Department of New Mexico, Fort Craig, February 23, 1862.

CAPTAIN: I have the honor to report, for the information of the department commander, the operations of my command at the battle of Valverde, near Fort Craig, N. Mex., on the 21st instant.

Conforming to his orders, I proceeded with one company of the First and four of the Third Cavalry and the four companies of mounted volunteers, commanded by Lieutenant-Colonel Valdez, to watch the movements of General Sibley's Confederate forces, supposed to be attempting to reach the river near Valverde, and to prevent their effecting that object. This mounted force was supported by Captain McRae's field battery of four pieces, Lieutenant Hall's, Tenth Infantry, two 24-pounder howitzers, Captain Brotherton's company of the Fifth, Captain Ingraham's of the Seventh Infantry, Captain Hubbell's company of the Fifth Regiment, and Captain Mortimore's of the Third Regiment New Mexico Volunteers.

On reaching the crossing at the foot of the mesa of the Contadero I discovered that the Confederate forces had already reached the river and occupied the large bosques in the Valverde bottom with quite heavy forces of cavalry and several guns. Major Duncan, commanding the regular cavalry, in advance, promptly crossed the ford, and dismounting his force, commenced the action by skirmishing on foot, and in a spirited and sharp skirmish with the Confederates cleared the bosque of their forces, enabling me to establish the batteries to cover the crossing and to shell the enemy from the heavy timbers he had already seized.

A careful examination of the field of battle made by me some months ago impressed me with the importance of seizing and holding the thick bosque at the lower ford the moment I discovered the Confederate forces had reached the river. For this reason I directed all the strength of my command toward the accomplishment of that object. But the enemy had discovered it was the strength of their position, and they struggled with desperation to keep it. It was of paramount consequence to lose no time in gaining this point, as re-enforcements were rapidly increasing the Confederate forces, and their possession of this bosque in force gave them the command of the ford. They were first driven from it by the dismounted cavalry. Three times afterwards, with accumulated strength, they swarmed into it, but they were three times driven out by the slaughter of McRae's and Hall's guns, that disabled, in their last attempt to establish a counter-battery, one of their pieces and destroyed one caisson. My anxiety to gain this position was extreme, and three times I sent orders to Major Duncan to take it and hold it at all hazards. It was my intention to place McRae's battery there, and had the dismounted cavalry, conforming to my orders, vigorously supported the advance of Brotherton, with his company of bayonets, and held the position twenty minutes, McRae's guns and Hall's howitzers could have been crossed over and placed in battery on this key of the field. The disorder of the Confederates was very great at that time. Their re-enforcements were swarming down from the mesa in confusion, and the effect of our guns from this commanding point I had hoped to gain would have forced them back on the mesa and kept them from the river.

I cannot withhold my expression of regret that the commanding officer of the cavalry made no efforts to take and hold this bosque after my reiterated orders had been conveyed to him to do so. The success of my plan seemed to me beyond peradventure at the time I crossed Captain Brotherton's company over and reiterated the order to Major Duncan to support him and clear the bosque. Colonel Carson's regiment and Captain Selden's command of regulars would then have been crossed at the lower ford and thrown upon the Confederates' left flank with an assurance of victory as certain as the laws of nature.

The failure to secure this position in the early part of the action forced upon me the subsequent operations on the Confederates' right wing, by crossing Captain Selden's command higher up the river, which I was only enabled to do in consequence of the low stage of the water. No fords were known above, but the regulars took the water and crossed, selecting step by step their foothold among quicksands and against the strong current of the Rio Grande up to their arms in its water.

The fire of our batteries commenced at 10 o'clock, and under the admirable serving of Captain McRae, Third Cavalry, Lieuts. L. Mishler, Fifth Infantry, I. McC. Bell, Second New Mexico Volunteers, and Robert H. Hall, Tenth Infantry, drove the enemy's forces from all their main positions. But they were constantly receiving re-enforcements, and having established their guns at different points within twenty minutes after Captain McRae's first shot, replied with well-directed and rapid returns of shot, shell, and grape, making the most desperate efforts to regain the ground from which they had been driven by Major Duncan's skirmishers. This contest of artillery and rifles was continued for more than two hours with a desperation on the part of the Confederates well worthy of a better cause. At about 12 meridian I had driven them from all the positions they had taken, forced them to withdraw their guns, and take a position higher up the river.

Captain Selden's battalion of regular infantry, including Captain Wingate's and Captain Plympton's battalions and Colonel Carson's regiment New Mexican Volunteers, reported to me at this juncture. I directed Captain Selden with his command to cross the river higher up, in the direction the enemy had been driven, and engage them with the bayonet.

Having received information that 500 Confederate cavalry had crossed the river above and threatened my rear, I placed Colonel Carson's regiment in a bosque higher up, near the main road to Valverde, to observe that direction, and to prevent any attempts on my left and rear. Captain Selden promptly formed after fording the river, and in the most gallant manner attacked the large forces that had been driven from their first positions and taken a still stronger one higher up the river. He drove them with great slaughter from the bosque they had then seized, repulsed a determined charge of their Lancers, made with audacity and desperation, and was master of the field.

I had intended Major Duncan's dismounted cavalry and Captain Brotherton's regular infantry to press the enemy's left at the same time Captain Selden attacked their right, and had sent my aide-de-camp, Lieutenant Meinhold, to the major with the order to do so, and it is to be regretted that Major Duncan conceived that his small force justified a non-compliance with my order. I am undoubting in my conviction that if the dismounted cavalry and Brotherton's infantry had vigorously pushed the enemy's left while Captain Selden was successfully forcing their right wing their rout would have been complete.

I now felt secure in crossing the batteries, and having posted them on Captain Selden's right, with the support of Captain Brotherton's and Captain Ingraham's companies of regular infantry and Captains Hubbell's and Mortimore's companies of volunteers, opened fire again on the other parts of the field still held by the enemy. This movement forced the Confederates to change the positions of their guns, and they renewed the artillery combat with activity and spirit, but the superior service of our guns, under the skill and conduct of Captain McRae, again silenced their batteries, and seemed to assure us of victory.

In this manner I continued the combat until 2.30 p. m., when information reached me that Colonel Canby was arriving with re-enforce-ments. The commands were fatigued with five hours' constant action, and while waiting the arrival of the commanding colonel the men were permitted to lunch and ordered to replenish their cartridge-boxes. During this time the batteries continued to operate on the enemy when-ever he displayed himself until Colonel Canby reached the field, fifteen minutes before 3 o'clock p. m. The heavy bosques in our front were terminated by a drift of sand extending from the high bluff of the Con-tadero to the river. Behind this drift the enemy, concealed from my observation, rallied all their forces abandoning wagons on the sand hills, tents, and other supplies, including ammunition, with the desper-ate resolve to storm our batteries. Hiding their design, they formed two strong parties of stormers, that were undiscovered until they fell with great fury on McRae's battery on our left and Lieutenant Hall's 24-pounder howitzers near Major Duncan on our right. Major Duncan's cavalry on foot and Captain Brotherton's company of the Fifth Infantry, re-enforced promptly by Colonel Carson's regiment of volunteers and Captain Wingate's battalion of regulars, opened a destructive fire on the charging columns on the right and repulsed them with great slaugh-ter. McRae's battery, though held with unexampled determination after the loss of every horse and more than half the gunners disabled and killed, was carried, and fell into the enemy's hands. Captain Mc-Rae, Third Cavalry, and Lieutenant Mishler, Fifth Infantry, were killed at their pieces, and illustrated a courage and conduct that will render the battle of Valverde memorable among the glories of American arms. It is due to the memories of the dead who served this battery and to the survivors, whose gallant and heroic service commends them to the praise of the country, to mention them as deserving honor and thanks.

The supporting columns of McRae's battery and the left wing having retired across the river, I ordered the cavalry forces to recross, and they fell back in good order into this post.

It is with a heavy heart I inclose you a list of the killed and wounded of my command, exceeding in the regular forces one-fifth of all that command in the field—a loss unexampled, it is believed, in any single battle ever fought on this continent.

The officers whose conduct came under my own observation and were distinguished above praise are Capt. H. R. Selden, Fifth Infantry; Capt. B. Wingate, Fifth Infantry, badly wounded; Captain Mortimore, Third New Mexico Volunteers, three times wounded; Lieut. I. McC. Bell, Second New Mexico Volunteers, serving with McRae's battery; Lieutenant Anderson, Fifth Infantry, acting adjutant to Captain Selden's battalion; Lieut. F. Cook, Fifth Infantry, and Lieut. R. H. Hall, Tenth Infantry, serving the 24-pounder howitzers. These names are not mentioned to lessen the great praise due to many other officers who served in my command, and who are deserving honor and grati-tude. I refer the commanding officer of the department to the reports of battalion commanders for their names, and present them as especially entitled to distinction.

I mention with pleasure Lieuts. Charles Meinhold and William W. Mills, of the Fifth Regiment of Volunteers, who served as my aides on the field, and who executed every duty gallantly, rendering most im-portant and valuable service. Capt. James Graydon, with his inde-pendent Spy Company, rendered me eminent service by his vigilant watch of the enemy's movements, and great energy, enterprise, and daring during the entire day. Assistant Surgeon Bill, in charge of ambulances on the field, was distinguished for his energy and admirable arrangements for the relief of the dying and care of the wounded.

I am, captain, very respectfully, your obedient servant,

B. S. ROBERTS,
Colonel, Volunteers, Commanding.

Capt. WILLIAM J. L. NICODEMUS,
12th Infantry, Act. Asst. Adjt. Gen., Dept. New Mexico.

No. 3.

Reports of Maj. Thomas Duncan, Third U. S. Cavalry, and resulting correspondence.

HEADQUARTERS THIRD REGIMENT OF CAVALRY,
Fort Craig, N. Mex., February 23, 1862.

SIR: I have the honor to make the following report of the operations of the troops under my command at the battle of Valverde, on the 21st ' instant:

On leaving here at about 8 o'clock on the morning of that day my command was composed of Companies C, D, G, and K, Third U. S. Cavalry, and Company G, First U. S. Cavalry. After marching a short distance up the river I was directed by Col. B. S. Roberts, commanding column, to leave my rear company as an escort and to proceed rapidly with the other four to the upper end of the Mesa del Contadero, and, if possible, to cross the river and hold the bosque on the opposite side, so as to prevent the enemy from reaching the water.

On arriving at the ford I found two companies of Colonel Valdez's mounted volunteers. These, as well as my own command, were crossed over as promptly as possible; but we had no sooner arrived on the river bank than a large force of the enemy's cavalry could be seen in the woods a few hundred yards to our front. It was soon discovered that his squadrons of cavalry were moving rapidly to our left under cover of the timber, and I immediately ordered Lieutenant Claflin, with his company (G, First U. S. Cavalry), to proceed up the river, in order to observe the enemy's movements. In a few minutes this officer returned and reported that the enemy's cavalry had reached the river about 1,000 yards above us, watered their horses, and were returning to their position in front of us. As the enemy was greatly superior in numbers, had the advantage of a thick cover of timber, and by this time had brought up a piece of artillery and put it in position at close range to my front and right, I saw that it would be folly to move forward and attack him. I therefore dismounted my command, had the horses and horse-holders concealed as well as possible behind a low sand ridge, about 80 yards from and parallel to the river, and deployed the remainder of the men behind some small sand hills, logs, and a few scattering trees, about 100 yards in advance of the horses, determined, if possible, to hold the position and keep the enemy back from the ford until our artillery and infantry could arrive and cross. The enemy constantly sent forward small reconnoitering parties to examine the nature of the ground and the number and kind of my force, but the accurate aim of our sharpshooters as often prevented them from getting near enough to ascertain my real weakness.

32 R R—VOL IX

Directly after I had gotten my command in position a 6-pounder to the front of my right flank opened upon us with vigor and kept up the fire with an occasional cessation until about 1.30 p. m., when it was either disabled or driven from its position by two or three well-directed shells from Hall's 24-pounder howitzer. Very soon after the enemy's 6-pounder gun had opened its fire a heavy force of his cavalry, soon followed by a piece of artillery, moved down through the timber toward the Mesa del Contadero, with the evident intention of assailing our right flank and resting his left on the river below the ford. Colonel Roberts, who was waiting on the opposite bank of the river to place McRae's battery, which was then approaching, in position, discovered this move of the enemy through an opening, promptly advised me of it, and directed me to throw some skirmishers into the thick timber immediately to my right and below the ford to drive the enemy back. Companies C and D, Third U. S. Cavalry, under the command of Captains Howland and Treacy, were dispatched for this duty.* After a spirited skirmish for several minutes the enemy was driven back, but soon rallied and renewed the assault with vigor, and although several times repulsed, he as often returned.

By this time, which I think was not far from 10 o'clock, McRae's battery opened a deadly fire of shot and shell into the bosque, supported by my skirmishers and Captain Brotherton's company of the Fifth U. S. Infantry, which Colonel Roberts had sent across the river to their support. Our fire soon became so galling that the enemy was driven from the woods in great disorder and with heavy loss, abandoning their gun, but soon rallied and carried it off by hand, the animals all being killed or crippled. From this until about noon a fire was kept up by McRae's battery and Hall's howitzer upon every party that showed itself, as well as upon the enemy's battery, which had for some time turned its attention from my cavalry to our guns across the river. Our infantry arrived soon after this, and crossing the river at the upper ford, just above my left flank, deployed through the thick woods up the river. Colonel Roberts followed with the artillery, taking McRae's battery with him up to the left, and at my request sending Hall's 24-pounder howitzer down to the right.

After silencing the gun which had been playing from 9 o'clock in the morning alternately on my command and upon the battery, Lieutenant Hall was sent to the right with his gun to dislodge a large party of the enemy reported by Captain Morris, commanding skirmishers in the bosque, to be directly in his front. As soon as Lieutenant Hall could ascertain the exact position of the enemy he commenced shelling it with such precision as to entirely clear the woods in a few minutes. After this no part of the enemy's force was seen on our right for some time and all remained quiet.

Before the arrival of Colonel Canby on the field I had asked for and received authority from Colonel Roberts to move my whole force through the timber on our right whenever I should discover that a general movement was being made against the enemy's right.*

Being informed soon after 3 o'clock that a concerted movement by our whole left flank was soon to be made against the enemy's right, I sent a request that one more company of infantry might be sent to join Brotherton's, as a support to Hall's howitzer, in order that I might be able to throw the whole of my dismounted cavalry forward as skirmishers. Captain Ingraham was promptly sent to me, and Colonel Carson soon followed with his regiment, deploying on my left. Soon after we

---

* See inclosure to Duncan to Roberts, March 7, p. 500.

commenced the forward movement a terrific cannonading and roar of small-arms was heard on our left flank, and immediately a large force of the enemy's cavalry came charging down, with the evident intention of seizing Hall's howitzer at the same time of the attack on McRae's battery; but before they could get nearer than 150 yards a deadly discharge of rifles and musketry by my skirmishers, the two companies of infantry, Graydon's Spy Company, and part of Colonel Carson's regiment was poured into their column, causing the enemy to wheel about in full retreat. Just then Lieutenant Hall dropped a shell in the midst of them, and so increased the panic which the enemy had just received from our volley of small-arms that he retreated entirely out of sight. At this moment, and when I was hurrying Hall's howitzer forward to place it in an advantageous position about 300 yards in advance, I was informed by an aide-de-camp that McRae's battery had been taken, and was ordered to recross the river without delay. My whole command, including the howitzer and infantry support, was immediately put in motion in the direction of the lower ford and crossed over in perfect order.

It only remains for me to say that during the whole of the day I was nobly supported by all the officers and men under my command.

The conduct of Captains Morris, Howland, Tilford, and Treacy, commanding companies, and Lieutenants Falvey, Texter, Wall, and Ewing, was characterized by the greatest zeal and coolness. The conduct and deportment of the non-commissioned officers and men were equally commendable.

I am, sir, very respectfully, your obedient servant,

THOMAS DUNCAN,
Major, Third U. S. Cavalry, Commanding Regiment.

Acting Second Lieut. C. MEINHOLD, *Third U. S. Cavalry,*
Acting Assistant Adjutant-General.

—

HEADQUARTERS SOUTHERN MILITARY DISTRICT,
Fort Craig, N. Mex., March 5, 1862.

MAJOR: On reading your report I discover that you say on pages 4 and 5:

After this no part of the enemy's force was seen on our right for some time and all remained quiet. Before the arrival of Colonel Canby on the field I had asked for and received authority from Colonel Roberts to move my whole force through the timber ●n our right whenever I should discover that a general movement was being made against the enemy's right.

If you sent any request of this kind to me I did not receive it; but as I had sent reiterated orders to you to take and hold the bosque on the enemy's left and had used McRae's battery to aid you in that object, your report should be so corrected as [to] show that fact.

I am, sir, very respectfully, your obedient servant,

B. S. ROBERTS,
Colonel of Volunteers, Commanding.

Maj. T. DUNCAN,
Commanding Third U. S. Cavalry, Fort Craig.

—

HEADQUARTERS THIRD U. S. CAVALRY,
Fort Craig, N. Mex., March 7, 1862.

COLONEL: Herewith I have the honor to inclose a copy of my report of the part taken by the troops under my command in the battle of

Valverde, corrected in accordance with the suggestion contained in your letter of the 5th instant. You will observe that I have made another slight correction in regard to the time that Captain Treacy's company was first sent into the bosque as skirmishers and also an allusion to Lieutenant Claflin.

I am, sir, very respectfully, your obedient servant,

THOMAS DUNCAN,
Major Third U. S. Cavalry, Commanding Regiment.

Col. B. S. ROBERTS,
. *Fifth Regiment New Mexico Volunteers, Commanding District.*

[Inclosure.]

HEADQUARTERS THIRD REGIMENT OF CAVALRY,
Fort Craig, N. Mex., February 23, 1862.

SIR: I have the honor to make the following report of the operations of the troops under my command at the battle of Valverde, on the 21st instant:*

*   *   *   *   *   *   *

Directly after I had gotten my command in position a 6-pounder to the front of my right flank opened upon us with vigor and kept up the fire with an occasional cessation until about 1.30 p. m., when it was either disabled or driven from its position by two or three well-directed shells from Hall's 24-pounder howitzer. Very soon after the enemy's 6-pounder gun had opened its fire a heavy force of his cavalry, soon followed by a piece of artillery, moved down through the timber toward the Mesa del Contadero, with the evident intention of assailing our right flank and resting his left on the river below the ford. Colonel Roberts, who was waiting on the opposite bank of the river to place McRae's battery, which was then approaching, in position, discovered this movement of the enemy through an opening, promptly advised me of it, and directed me to throw some skirmishers into the thick timber immediately to my right and below the ford, to drive the enemy back. Company C, Third U. S. Cavalry, under Captain Howland, was immediately dispatched to re-enforce Captain Treacy's company (D), which I had thrown into the bosque as skirmishers to keep out some small reconnoitering parties that had been seen to our right previous to the colonel's arrival. After a spirited skirmish for several minutes the enemy was driven back, but soon rallied and renewed the assault with vigor, and although several times repulsed, he as often returned.

*   *   *   *   *   *   *

After silencing the gun which had been playing from 9 o'clock in the morning alternately on my command and upon the battery, Lieutenant Hall was sent to the right, with his gun, to dislodge a large party of the enemy reported by Captain Morris, commanding skirmishers in the bosque, to be directly in his front. As soon as Lieutenant Hall could ascertain the exact position of the enemy he commenced shelling it with such precision as to entirely clear the woods in a few minutes. After this no part of the enemy's force was seen on our right for some time and all remained quiet.

After the arrival of our infantry, and before Colonel Canby had reached the field, I sent several messages to Colonel Roberts, requesting authority to move my whole force through the timber on our right

---

* So much of this as is a repetition of the report on p. 497 is omitted.

whenever I should discover that a general movement was being made against the enemy's right. I was finally informed by one of my messengers that the request was granted; but it is proper to state that I have since been informed by Colonel Roberts that he received no such request.

*   *   *   *   *   *   *

It only remains for me to say that during the whole of the day I was nobly supported by all the officers and men under my command.

The conduct of Captains Morris, Howland, Tilford, and Treacy, commanding companies, and Lieutenants Falvey, Texter, Wall, and Ewing was characterized by the greatest zeal and coolness.

Lieutenant Claflin also obeyed the orders given him with alacrity, but before the most important events of the day occurred he had been detached from my command.

The conduct and deportment of the non-commissioned officers and men were equally commendable.

I am, sir, very respectfully, your obedient servant,

THOMAS DUNCAN,
Major, Third U. S. Cavalry, Commanding Regiment.

Acting Second Lieut. C. MEINHOLD, *Third U. S. Cavalry,*
Acting Assistant Adjutant-General.

HDQRS. SOUTHERN MILITARY DIST., DEPT. OF N. MEX.,
Fort Craig, N. Mex., March 8, 1862.

MAJOR: I have received your report, corrected, as you state, in accordance with the suggestion contained in my letter of the 5th instant. You have not, however, in that alteration removed the clear repugnancy of your statement that—

After the arrival of our infantry, and before Colonel Canby had reached the field, I sent several messengers to Colonel Roberts, requesting authority to move my whole force through the timber to our right, &c.

That position through the timber to your right is the very one I had repeatedly ordered you to take and hold, and you had three times justified your non-execution of the order by saying your force was insufficient, the ground did not permit it, &c. From the beginning of the action I was directing all my forces to drive the enemy from his position in this bosque and to move McRae's battery to that point, as I knew that the position enfiladed the line of sand drift and commanded every position on the field where the Confederates could find shelter and prepare any plan of battle.

The contradiction of your report, major, is this: That you sent several messages to me requesting permission to take position where I had repeatedly ordered you [to] go, and you had as often declined even to make the attempt. An officer must have strong reasons for any justification of non-execution of orders on the field of battle, and I am constrained to confess that after a good deal of reflection I am convinced that, had you attacked vigorously with all your force after I re-enforced you with Brotherton's company of bayonets, you would have carried and held the enemy's left with little loss, and the subsequent misfortunes of the day would not have occurred.

I will thank you for the names of the messengers you sent me with the requests referred to, as I wish to arrest and punish them, whoever they may be, for not conveying your orders.*

I am, major, very respectfully, your obedient servant,

B. S. ROBERTS,
Colonel of Volunteers, Commanding.

Maj. T. DUNCAN,
Commanding Third U. S. Cavalry.

No. 4.

Reports of Col. Christopher Carson, First New Mexico Infantry.

HDQRS. THIRD COLUMN TROOPS IN THE FIELD,
Near Fort Craig, N. Mex., February 26, 1862.

COLONEL: I have the honor to make the following report of the operations of the third column, composed of eight companies of the First Regiment of New Mexico Volunteers, under my command, during the battle of Valverde, on the 21st instant, and prior to the arrival on the field of Col. E. R. S. Canby, U. S. Army, commanding department:

Pursuant to the order of the department commander my command marched from Fort Craig and arrived on the battle ground about 9 o'clock in the morning, soon after the batteries had opened fire. I remained on the west side of the Rio Grande, gradually moving up the bank of the river as the enemy extended his right in the same direction, until after the arrival of Colonel Canby, commanding, upon the field, when I was ordered to cross the river, which I did at once. My after operations will, as directed, be made to him.

I am, colonel, very respectfully, your obedient servant,

C. CARSON,
Colonel First New Mexico Vols., Commanding Third Column.

Col. B. S. ROBERTS,
Fifth Regt. N. Mex. Vols., Comdg. Fort Craig, N. Mex.

HDQRS. THIRD COLUMN TROOPS IN THE FIELD,
Camp near Fort Craig, February 26, 1862.

CAPTAIN: I have the honor to make the following report of the operations of the third column, composed of eight companies of the First Regiment New Mexico Volunteers, under my command, during the battle of Valverde, on the 21st, and subsequent to the arrival on the field of Colonel Canby, commanding department, until which time my column had remained on the west side of the river and taken no part in the battle:

About 1 o'clock in the afternoon I received from Colonel Canby the order to cross the river, which I immediately did, after which I was ordered to form my command on the right of our line and to advance as skirmishers toward the hills. After advancing some 400 yards we discovered a large body (some 400 or 500) of the enemy charging diagonally across our front, evidently with the intention of capturing the 24-pounder gun, which, stationed on our right, was advancing and doing much harm to the enemy. As the head of the enemy's column

---

* Answer, if any, not found.

came within some 80 yards of my right a volley from the whole column was poured into them, and the firing being kept up caused them to break in every direction and retreat. Almost at the same time a shell from the 24-pounder was ·thrown among them with fatal effect. They did not attempt to reform, and the column, supported by the gun on the right, was moving forward to sweep the wood near the hills, when I received the order to retreat and recross the river. This movement was executed in good order. The column, after crossing the river,· returned to its station near Fort Craig, where it arrived about 7 o'clock in the evening.

I am, sir, very respectfully, your obedient servant,

C. CARSON,
Colonel First N. Mex. Vols., Commanding Third Column.

Capt. WILLIAM J. L. NICODEMUS,
A. A. A. G., Hdqrs. Dept. of N. Mex., Fort Craig, N. Mex.

No. 5.

Report of Col. Miguel E. Pino, Second ·New Mexico Infantry.

HDQRS. SECOND REGIMENT NEW MEXICO VOLS.,
Camp near Fort Craig, N. Mex., February 26, 1862.

SIR: I have the honor to report, for the information of the department commander, the operations of the column under my command on the 21st February, 1862, in the field, viz:

The column, being stationed on the eastern bank of the river opposite Fort Craig, received orders to cross the river and escort the ammunition train to the field of battle. The column crossed and proceeded with the train to the crossing of the river in rear of the engagement, where orders were received to cross and form on the eastern bank. While this movement was being executed we were ordered back to form on the western bank, where we took our position and fired upon the enemy until ordered to return to Fort Craig and occupy our former encampment.

I am, sir, very respectfully, your obedient servant,

MIGUEL E. PINO,
Colonel Second Regiment New Mexico Volunteers.

Captain NICODEMUS,
Assistant Adjutant-General.

No. 6.

Report of Lieut. Col. José M. Valdez, Third New Mexico Infantry.

FORT CRAIG, N. MEX., *February* 26, 1862.

I have the honor to make the following report of the conduct of the companies under my command of the Third Regiment New Mexico Volunteers during the battle of Valverde, on the 21st instant, against the Confederate troops, according [to] the reports of the commanders of said companies:

Capt. Pedro Sanchez, Third Regiment New Mexico Volunteers, reports that his company (C) fought gallantly during the battle without making any retreat without orders; that his company, with some other companies, under the direction of the gallant Major Duncan, did commence the attack against the enemy before the battery and troops of ours could reach the camp of battle, but he makes special mention that Corp. Antonio Chawn, Privates Jesus Archuleeta and Pastor Archuleeta did act on that occasion with such encouragement and valor that they killed some men of the enemy's battery.

Capt. Juan A. Sarracino, Third Regiment New Mexico Volunteers, reports that Company G, under his command, acted in the battle in good spirits at all times during the war, and that they did not make any retreat without orders.

Capt. Rafael Chacon, First Regiment New Mexico Volunteers, reports that his company did fight well and with valor during the battle, and that when the company was ordered to retreat they were satisfied of having obliged the enemy to retreat in all their charges, and that his company, when retired from camp of battle, was in good and quiet spirits.

Capt. Ricardo Branch, Third Regiment New Mexico Volunteers, reports that his company (B) was in the camp of battle acting as well as they could, fighting all the time with valor and activity, and that the company did not make any retreat without orders.

The commander of the company of Capt. William Mortimore, Third Regiment New Mexico Volunteers, reports that the following non-commissioned officers and privates, viz, First Sergt. J. W. Lewelling, Sergts. Edward Watters and Trancer Moore; Corps. Biter Terreme, José Leyra, S. C. Miller, C. A. Reisden, George Beker, Henry York, Marceline Martinez, and José Anartaico Crespin, with others that are killed and missing, fought in the battle the 21st instant gallantly and sustained the battery to the last moment.

I certify in honor that the above is correct and just.

JOSÉ M. VALDEZ,
Lieutenant-Colonel Third Regiment New Mexico Mounted Vols.
ACTING ASSISTANT ADJUTANT-GENERAL,
Southern Military District, Fort Craig, N. Mex.

No. 7.

Findings of Court of Inquiry on conduct of Capt. R. S. C. Lord, First U. S. Cavalry.

GENERAL ORDERS, }   HDQRS. DEPT. OF NEW MEXICO,
    No. 92.   }   *Santa Fé, October 13,* 1862.

I. At the request of Capt. R. S. C. Lord, U. S. First Cavalry, a Court of Inquiry, consisting of Maj. Henry D. Wallen, U. S. Seventh Infantry, Surg. Elisha I. Baily, medical director, U. S. Army, and Surg. James M. McNulty, First Infantry, California Volunteers, with Capt. Andrew W. Evans, U. S. Sixth Cavalry, was assembled at Santa Fé, on the 2d of October, 1862, to investigate certain allegations made against the official reputation of the applicant.

The court was ordered to report the essential facts and its opinion in the case, and the following is the result of the investigation:

The court is of the opinion that the statement in the Santa Fé Gazettc of the battle of Valverde is incorrectly given. The evidence of First Sergeant Walker, of Captain Lord's company, goes to show that the battery was charged by Captain Lord's order, and that he led the charge. The evidence of Lieutenant Meinhold is that Colonel Donaldson was not dressed in uniform, and therefore the soldiers of Captain Lord's command were not bound to recognize his orders. Lieutenant-Colonel Donaldson did not give that order to Captain Lord in person, nor did he see him on the battle-field.

In reference to the second allegation, the court is of the opinion that the orders, as sworn to by Lieutenant Meinhold, may have been given to Captain Lord, but from the fact that they were not heard or understood by the officer on duty with Captain Lord, nor by First Sergeant Walker, who was by his side, they may likewise have been misunderstood or lost by him in the confusion of the battle.

The evidence given by Acting Second Lieutenant Bernard is that Captain Lord's command, while proceeding to join Colonel Donaldson, had lost their guides, and were out of provisions, and that their horses were broken down, and that they were ignorant of the country, and they found themselves under these circumstances between two superior forces of the enemy. The court is of opinion that the evidence places the conduct of Captain Lord in its true light, and exonerates him from all censure on that allegation.

The evidence before the court goes to show that the company did not flee ingloriously from the field, but that it did charge the battery, did cover the men, and form in good order on the opposite side and open fire on the enemy, and all this was in obedience to the orders of Colonel Canby.

The court is of opinion that this investigation should have been granted Captain Lord months since, and that, in denying this opportunity to vindicate his character, much injustice has been done him. The evidence now presented before the court acquits him of all censure or blame for the loss of the battle of Valverde.

The court is further of opinion that no further action should be taken in the case of Capt. R. S. C. Lord, First Cavalry, U. S. Army.

II. The proceedings of the court of inquiry are approved. Captain Lord will proceed to join his company in the East.

III. The court of inquiry, of which Maj. Henry D. Wallen, U. S. Seventh Infantry, is president, is hereby dissolved.

By order of Brigadier-General Carleton:

BEN. C. CUTLER,
Captain and Assistant Adjutant-General.

No. 8.

Reports of Brig. Gen. Henry H. Sibley, C. S. Army, commanding Army of New Mexico, including operations from January — to May 4, 1862.

HEADQUARTERS ARMY OF NEW MEXICO,
BATTIE GROUND OF VALVERDE,
February 22, 1862.

GENERAL: I have the honor to report to you, for the information of the President, that 1 encountered the enemy at this point (6 miles above Fort Craig) in force at 11 o'clock yesterday morning, and after one of the most severely-contested actions, lasting until 5 p. m., the enemy was driven from the field with a loss, as estimated, of 4 captains of the Regular Army and some 300 killed and wounded, and the capture of his entire field battery, the disabling of, one 24-pounder, and the abandonment of another in the river. We have but few prisoners; among them is Capt. William H. Rossell, of the Tenth Infantry.

The enemy had upon the field about 3,500 men, 1,200 of whom were old regulars. We never had more than 1,500 engaged. For the first time, perhaps, on record batteries were charged and taken at the muzzle of double-barreled shot-guns, thus illustrating the spirit, valor, and invincible determination of Texas troops. Nobly have they emulated the fame of their San Jacinto ancestors.

Our loss was severe—40 killed, including Maj. S. A. Lockridge, of the Fifth Regiment, and Capt. M. Heuvel, of the Fourth. I have no reports of the wounded, but I think 100 will cover it.

Before closing this report it is especially due to Col. Thomas Green, of the Fifth, to say that, in consequence of severe and prolonged illness and weakness resulting from it, I could only keep my saddle until 1 o'clock, and at that hour I relinquished to him the full direction of active operations. His coolness under the heaviest fire and intrepidity under the most trying circumstances are sufficiently attested by the results. I cannot commend Colonel Green too highly to the favorable consideration of the Executive.

Where so much gallantry was displayed I cannot, before reaching the reports of commanders, particularize individuals.

It will be necessary, to secure our purpose, to re-enforce me largely from Texas at as early a day as possible. The force we had to contend against amounted to near 6,000 men.

I beg leave, in conclusion, to bring to your notice the intelligence and valor of the members of my staff, Maj. A. M. Jackson, assistant adjutant-general; Maj. R. T. Brownrigg, commissary of subsistence; Lieutenant Ochiltree, aide-de-camp, and Col. W. L. Robards, Major Magoffin, and Capt. J. Dwyer, volunteer aides.

I am, sir, very respectfully, your obedient servant,
H. H. SIBLEY,
Brigadier-General, Commanding.

General S. COOPER,
Adjutant and Inspector General, Richmond, Va.

P. S.—Lieut. Col. J. S. Sutton, of the Seventh Regiment (Col. William Steele's), in command of his battalion, and Capt. Willis L. Lang, of the Fifth, greatly distinguished themselves, and were both severely wounded; and I should not omit Lieut. D. M. Bass, of Captain Lang's company, who was also severely wounded in front of the charge leading the Lancers upon the enemy.

I am, sir, very respectfully, your obedient servant,
H. H. SIBLEY,
Brigadier-General.

HEADQUARTERS ARMY OF NEW MEXICO,
Fort Bliss, Tex., May 4, 1862.

GENERAL: I have the honor to report, for the information of the Secretary of War, the operations of this army during the months of February, March, and April, ultimo: ·

This report is made to cover the whole campaign, for the reason that the special reports of the various commanders, herewith inclosed, enter sufficiently into detail to elucidate the various actions in which the troops were engaged during the campaign.

It is due to the brave soldiers I have had the honor to command to premise that from its first inception the "Sibley brigade" has encountered difficulties in its organization and opposition and distaste to the service required at its hands which no other troops have met with.

From misunderstandings, accidents, deficiency of arms, &c., instead of reaching the field of its operations early in September, as was anticipated, I found myself at this point as late as the middle of January, 1862, with only two regiments and a half, poorly armed, thinly clad, and almost destitute of blankets. The ranks were becoming daily thinned by those two terrible scourges to an army small-pox and pneumonia. Not a dollar of quartermaster's funds was on hand or ever had been to supply the daily and pressing necessities of the service, and the small means of this sparse section had been long consumed by the force under the command of Lieutenant-Colonel Baylor, so that the credit of the Government was not as available a resource as it might otherwise have been.

Having established a general hospital at Doña Aña, I determined to move forward with the force at hand. Accordingly, during the first week in January [February?], the advance was put in march for old Fort Thorn; thence on the 7th of February the movement was continued to a point 7 miles below Fort Craig, where the Santa Fé papers boasted we were to be met and overwhelmed by Canby's entire army.

On February 16 a reconnaissance in force was pushed to within a mile of the fort and battle offered on the open plain. The challenge was disregarded, and only noticed by the sending out of a few well-mounted men to watch our movements. The forces of the enemy were kept well concealed in the bosque (or grove) above the fort and within its walls.

The reconnaissance proved the futility of assaulting the fort in front with our light metal, and that our only hope of success was to force the enemy to an open-field fight. It was accordingly determined by a partial retrograde movement to cross the Rio Grande to the east bank, turn the fort, and force a battle for the recrossing. To do this involved, first, the hazardous necessity of crossing a treacherous stream in full view of the fort; second, to make a "dry camp" immediately opposite and remote from the fort, only a mile and a half, and the next day to fight our first battle. The enemy seemed to have been so confounded by the boldness and eccentricity of these movements that the first was accomplished without molestation, save a demonstration on the afternoon of the 20th, as we were forming our camp by the crossing, of some 2,500 infantry and cavalry, with the purpose apparently of making an assault upon our lines. Here the spirit and courage of our men were evidenced by the alacrity shown in getting into line to confront the enemy. A few rounds from our well-directed guns, under the management of Captain Teel, Lieutenants Riley and Woods, checked his advance and drove him to the cover of his sand-revetted mud walls.

It is proper to state here that these operations, approved by me, were conducted by Col. Thomas Green, of the Fifth Regiment, the state of my health having confined me to the ambulance for several days previous.

On the morning of the 21st, considering that the impending battle must decide the question at issue, though still very weak, I took the saddle at early dawn to direct in person the movement. Green's regiment, with a battalion of the Seventh, under Lieutenant-Colonel Sutton, and Captain Teel's battery, were ordered to make a strong, threatening demonstration on the fort, while Scurry, with the Fourth, well flanked by Pyron's command on the left, should feel his way cautiously to the river.

This movement was unfortunately delayed by the loss during the night, by careless herding, of 100 mules of the baggage train of the Fourth Regiment. Rather than the plan should be defeated a number of wagons were abandoned, containing the entire kits, blankets, books, and papers of this regiment, and, meanwhile, what was left of the trains was kept in motion over the sand hills, which the enemy had deemed impossible.

On reaching the river bottom at Valverde it was ascertained that the enemy, anticipating our movement, had thrown a large force of infantry and cavalry up the river to dispute the water with us. Pyron immediately engaged him with his small force of 250 men, and gallantly held his ground against overwhelming odds until the arrival of Scurry with the Fourth Regiment and Lieutenant Riley's battery of light howitzers.

At 12 m., the action becoming warm and the enemy evidently receiving large re-enforcements, I ordered Green's regiment and Teel's battery to the front. These in the course of an hour gallantly entered into action and the battle became general. Subsequently Lieutenant-Colonel Sutton, with his battalion, was ordered forward from the rear and did right good service, leading his men even to the cannon's mouth.

At 1.30 p. m., having become completely exhausted, and finding myself no longer able to keep the saddle, I sent my aides and other staff officers to report to Colonel Green. His official report attests the gallantry of their bearing and his final success, resulting in the capture of their battery and driving the enemy in disorder from the field, and thus evidencing his own intrepidity and the indomitable courage of all engaged.

From information derived from reliable sources, the forces opposed to us could not have been less than 5,000 men, with a reserve of 3,000 at the fort. Ours did not exceed 1,750 on the field, viz: the Fourth Regiment, 600; Fifth, 600; Seventh, 300; and Pyron's command (of Second Mounted Regiment Rifles), 250. This signal victory should have resulted in the capture of the fort, as fresh troops had been brought forward to pursue and follow the discomfited column of the enemy. A flag of truce was opportunely dispatched by the Federal commander before he reached the gates of his fort, and which was for two hours supposed by our troops to be a proposition to surrender.

This flag had for its object the burying of the dead and removal of their wounded; and I regret to state here, for the sake of old associations, that, under this flag and another sent next day, the enemy, availing himself of our generosity and confidence in his honor, not only loaded his wagons with arms picked up on the battle-field, but sent a force up and actually succeeded in recovering from the river one 24-pounder which had been left in our hands. Even a guidon and a flag, taken in the same way, under the cover of night, and a white flag were boastingly pointed to, in an interview under a flag of truce between one of my aides and the Federal commander at the fort, as trophies of the fight.

The burying of the dead and care of the wounded occasioned a delay of two days on the field, thus leaving us with but five days' scant rations. In this dilemma the question arose whether to assault the fort in this crippled condition or move rapidly forward up the river, where supplies of breadstuffs and meat could be procured. The latter course, in a council of war, was adopted.

Depositing our sick at Socorro, 30 miles above Fort Craig, the march was uninterruptedly made to Albuquerque, where, notwithstanding the destruction by the enemy of large supplies by fire, ample subsistence was secured. A very considerable quantity of supplies and ammunition was also obtained at Cubero, a temporary post 60 miles west of Albuquerque. Other supplies were also taken at Santa Fé, and upon the whole we had a sufficiency for some three months.

It is due to the Fourth Regiment to mention at this place an action of devotion and self-sacrifice worthy of high praise, and the more commendable because they are Texans.

In the action at Valverde many of their horses were killed, thus leaving them half foot and half mounted. The proposition being made to them to dismount the whole regiment, without a dissenting voice, a cavalry regiment, which had proudly flaunted its banner before the enemy on the 20th, took the line of march on the 24th a strong and reliable regiment of infantry.

Having secured all the available stores in and about Albuquerque and dispatched Maj. Charles L. Pyron with his command to Santa Fé to secure such as might be found there, I determined to make a strong demonstration on Fort Union.

With this view Col. William R. Scurry, with the Fourth and the battalion of Colonel Steele's regiment, under Maj. Powhatan Jordan, was pushed forward in the direction of Gallisteo, while Colonel Green, with his regiment (Fifth), being somewhat crippled in transportation, was held for a few days in hand to check any movement from Fort Craig.

Meanwhile the enemy (having received re-enforcements at Fort Union of 950 men from Pike's Peak, on or about March 12) took the initiative and commenced a rapid march on Santa Fé.

Major Pyron, re-enforced by four companies of the Fifth Regiment, under Major Shropshire, receiving notice of this movement, advanced at once to meet him on the high road between Santa Fé and Fort Union.

On March 26th a sharp skirmish ensued, described in detail by that officer, wherein many acts of daring heroism were enacted. The company of "Brigandes" (independent volunteers), under the command of Capt. John Phillips, is said to have done good service. One of their number, Mr. Thomas Cator, was killed and 2 wounded. On this occasion, as on every previous one, this company showed a devotedness to the cause which has elevated them and inspired confidence throughout the army.

Colonel Scurry reached the scene of action at daylight next morning, and the next day fought the battle of Glorieta, driving the enemy from the field with great loss.

His report is respectfully referred to for the details of this glorious action. Pending this action I was on my route to Santa Fé, in rear of Green's regiment, which had, meanwhile, been put in march for that place, where, on my arrival, I found the whole exultant army assembled. The sick and wounded had been comfortably quartered and attended; the loss of clothing and transportation had been made up from the enemy's stores and confiscations, and, indeed, everything done which should have been done.

Many friends were found in Santa Fé who had been in durance. Among the rest General William Pelham, who had but recently been released from a dungeon in Fort Union.

After the occupancy of the capital of the Territory for nearly a month from the time of our first advance upon it, the forage and supplies obtainable there having become exhausted, it was determined to occupy, with the whole army, the village of Manzano, intermediate between Fort Union, Albuquerque, and Fort Craig, and securing as a line of communication the road to Fort Stanton.

This plan was disconcerted, however, by the rapid and continuous expresses from Albuquerque, urging the necessity of re-enforcements to hold the place (the depot of all our supplies) against the advancing forces of Canby from Fort Craig.

The entire force was accordingly moved by forced marches in the direction of Albuquerque, arriving too late to encounter the enemy, but time enough to secure our limited supplies from the contingency of capture.

In our straightened circumstances the question now arose in my mind whether to evacuate the country or take the desperate chances of fighting the enemy in his stronghold (Union), for scant rations at the best. The course adopted was deemed the wisest.

On the morning of April 12 the evacuation commenced by the crossing of Scurry's (Fourth) regiment, the battalion of Steele's regiment, Pyron's command, and a part of the artillery, by ferry and ford, to the west bank of the river. Green's regiment was ordered to follow; but finding the ford to be difficult, he encamped for the night on the east bank, hoping to be able on the ensuing morning to find a better ford lower down the river.

Accordingly on the next day that officer proceeded with his regiment as low down as Peralta, opposite Los Lunas, the point at which I had halted the balance of the army to await his arrival.

In the mean time Canby, having formed a junction with a large force from Fort Union, debouched through a cañon after night-fall to the neighborhood of the river, taking a commanding position in close proximity to Green's camp, and in the morning opened a furious, but harmless, cannonade.

On being notified of the critical situation of this detached portion of the army the whole disposable force at Los Lunas, reserving a sufficient guard for the train, was dispatched to its relief. The passage of the river by this force and the artillery was successfully effected, under the direction of Colonel Scurry.

Following shortly after with a portion of my staff to assume the immediate command, and having crossed the river, I was notified by several officers who had preceded me some hundred yards of the rapid approach of a large number of the enemy's cavalry. Finding myself completely cut off, I had no other alternative than to recross the river amid a shower of balls. The day was occupied at Peralta in ineffectual firing on both sides.

After night-fall I gave orders for the recrossing of the whole army to the west bank of the river, which was effected without interruption or casualty, and on the next morning the march down the river was resumed. The enemy followed on the opposite bank, and both armies encamped in full view of each other, the river alone intervening.

The transportation and artillery had by this time become such an incumbrance on the heavy, sandy road, without forage or grass, that the abandonment of one or the other became inevitable. My original plan had been to push on by the river route in advance of the enemy, having the start of him two whole days from Albuquerque to Fort Craig, attack the weak garrison, and demolish the fort. This plan was defeated by Colonel Green not finding a crossing of the river at a convenient point.

Colonels Green and Scurry, with several other practical officers, here came forward and proposed, in order to avoid the contingency of another general action in our then crippled condition, that a route through the mountains, avoiding Fort Craig and striking the river below that point, should be pursued, they undertaking with their respective commands to push the artillery through at all hazards and at any expenditure of toil and labor. Maj. Bethel Coopwood, who had familiarized himself with the country, undertook the difficult and responsible task of guiding the army through this mountainous, trackless waste.

The arguments presented in favor of this course were potent. Besides having the advantage of grass and a firm road, with very little difference in distance, the enemy would be completely mystified, as afterwards proved to be the case. Accordingly, all the wagons which could possibly be dispensed with were ordered to be abandoned on the ground, seven days' provisions to be packed on mules, and the entire force put in march after night-fall. The route was a difficult and most hazardous one, both in respect to its practicability and supply of water. The successful accomplishment of the march not only proved the sagacity of our guide, but the pledge of Colonel Scurry that the guns should be put over every obstacle, however formidable, by his regiment, was nobly fulfilled. Not a murmur escaped the lips of these brave boys. Descents into and ascents out of the deepest cañons, which a single horseman would have sought for miles to avoid, were undertaken and accomplished with a cheerfulness and ability which were the admiration and praise of the whole army. Thus in ten days, with seven days' rations, a point on the river where supplies had been ordered forward was reached. The river, which was rising rapidly, was safely crossed to the east bank, under the direction of Colonel Green, and at this moment, I am happy to repeat, the whole force is comfortably quartered in the villages extending from Doña Aña to this place.

My chief regret in making this retrograde movement was the necessity of leaving hospitals at Santa Fé, Albuquerque, and Socorro. Everything, however, was provided for the comfort of the sick, and sufficient funds, in Confederate paper, provided them to meet every want, if it be negotiated. It has been almost impossible to procure specie upon any terms. One thousand dollars is all I have been able to procure for the use of hospitals and for secret service. The ricos, or wealthy citizens of New Mexico, had been completely drained by the Federal powers, and, adhering to them, had become absolute followers of their army for dear life and their invested dollars. Politically they have no distinct sentiment or opinion on the vital question at issue. Power and interest alone control the expression of their sympathies. Two noble and notable exceptions to this rule were found in the brothers Rafael and Manuel Armijo, the wealthiest and most respectable native merchants of New Mexico. The latter had been pressed into the militia, and was compulsorily present in the action at Valverde. On our arrival at Albuquerque they came forward boldly and protested their sympathy with our cause, placing their stores, containing goods amounting to $200,000, at the disposal of my troops.

When the necessity for evacuating the country became inevitable, these two gentlemen abandoned luxurious homes and well-filled storehouses to join their fate to the Southern Confederacy. I trust they will not be forgotten in the final settlement.

In concluding this report, already extended beyond my anticipations, it is proper that I should express the conviction, determined by some experience, that, except for its political geographical position, the Territory of New Mexico is not worth a quarter of the blood and treasure expended in its conquest. As a field of military operations it possesses not a single element, except in the multiplicity of its defensible positions. The indispensable element, food, cannot be relied on. During the last year, and pending the recent operations, hundreds of thousands of sheep have been driven off by the Navajoes. Indeed, such were the complaints of the people in this respect that I had determined, as good policy, to encourage private enterprises against that tribe and the Apaches, and to legalize the enslaving of them.

As for the results of the campaign, I have only to say that we have beaten the enemy in every encounter and against large odds; that from being the worst armed my forces are now the best armed in the country. We reached this point last winter in rags and blanketless. The army is now well clad and well supplied in other respects. The entire campaign has been prosecuted without a dollar in the quartermaster's department, Captain Harrison not having yet reached this place. But, sir, I cannot speak encouragingly for the future, my troops having manifested a dogged, irreconcilable detestation of the country and the people. They have endured much, suffered much, and cheerfully; but the prevailing discontent, backed up by the distinguished valor displayed on every field, entitles them to marked consideration and indulgence.

These considerations, in connection with the scant supply of provisions and the disposition of our own citizens in this section to depreciate our currency, may determine me, without waiting for instructions, to move by slow marches down the country, both for the purpose of remounting and recruiting our thinned ranks.

Trusting that the management of this more than difficult campaign, intrusted to me by the Government, may prove satisfactory to the President, I have the honor, general, to be, your obedient servant,

H. H. SIBLEY,
Brigadier-General, Commanding.

General S. COOPER,
Adjutant and Inspector General, Richmond, Va.

No. 9.

Report of Maj. Charles L. Pyron, Second Texas Cavalry.

SOCORRO, N. MEX., *February* 27, 1862.

MAJOR : On the morning of the 21st instant I left our camp, opposite Fort Craig, with 180 men of my command, under Captains [James] Walker and [Isaac C.] Stafford, Lieutenant Nicholson, of Captain Coopwood's Spy Company, and Lieutenant [William G.] Jett, Company B, Second Regiment Mounted Volunteers, to reconnoiter the road leading to the river near Valverde. Upon reaching the river I could see the water, with none of the enemy intervening. I immediately dispatched a note to the general commanding, stating the road was clear and the water in sight, and proceeded leisurely to the river to water our horses, they having been over twenty-four hours without water.

When I reached the woods I discovered a body of cavalry, which I supposed to be about four companies, and immediately gave chase, they withdrawing to my left. I followed until reaching the bank of a slough in the bottom, when I found myself in front of a large force of all arms. Immediately my men were formed along the bank, when the action commenced, and for over one hour, by the courage and determination of the men, I was enabled to maintain the position in the unequal struggle, when I was relieved by the Fourth Regiment Texas Mounted Volunteers, under the command of Lieut. Col. W. R. Scurry.

For nearly two hours our joint commands held our position against odds of three to one, checking every attempt to outflank us and checking every effort to drive us back. The arrival of Teel's battery of artillery was the first re-enforcement we received, but it was soon followed by Major Lockridge's battalion, of the Fifth Regiment Texas Mounted Volunteers, and about 1 o'clock Colonel Green reached the field and took command.

Late in the afternoon a general charge was made along our line, by which a battery of artillery, consisting of six guns, was taken and their left driven back.

Following rapidly up our successes, the enemy were driven back at all points, and the field of Valverde was won.

It is proper to state that all the officers and men of my command behaved in the most gallant manner, and where all were equally brave it would be invidious to particularize. It is sufficient to say that it was a day on which deeds of personal valor were continually occurring.

I cannot consent to close this report without bearing my testimony to the gallant bearing and personal valor of Colonels Green, Scurry, and Sutton, and Majors Ragnet and Lockridge, and others equally courageous.

I have the honor to be, sir, yours, most respectfully,
C. L. PYRON,
Major Second Texas Mounted Rangers.

Maj. A. M. Jackson,
Assistant Adjutant-General, Army of New Mexico.

No. 10.

Report of Lieut. Col. William R. Scurry, Fourth Texas Cavalry.

Valverde, N. Mex., *February* 22, 1862.

Major : Early on the morning of yesterday, while the army was encamped on the east side of the Rio Grande, opposite Fort Craig, I received orders to march with my command, Fourth Regiment Texas Mounted Volunteers, and take possession at as early an hour as practicable of some point on the river above Fort Craig at which water might be obtained. By 8 o'clock the regiment took up the line of march, accompanied by Capt. George M. Frazier, of Major Pyron's battalion, with his company acting as guide for the command. Supposing that we were the advance of the army, to prevent surprise I ordered Major H. W. Ragnet to take the advance, with four companies and Captain Frazier's company, throwing out at the same time front and flank patrols. In a short time I learned that Major Pyron, with 180 men, was in our advance. Aware of the great vigilance of that active officer, I recalled Major Ragnet and reunited the regiment. A report was received from Major Pyron that the road was clear of the enemy and the river in sight; but in a short time a second message was received, through Capt. John Phillips, from the major, informing me that large masses of the enemy were in his front and threatening an attack. As his force was but small,.I was fearful that he would be overpowered before we could reach him, and accordingly pushed forward, guided by Captain Phillips, as rapidly as our horses could carry us, to his relief, and found him gallantly maintaining a most unequal contest against vastly superior numbers. Dismounting my command, we formed on his right and joined in the conflict. For near two hours we held our position in front of an enemy now known to be near 5,000 strong, while our own forces were not over 700 in number. Immediately upon reaching the field Captain Frazier joined.the command to which he belonged, where he did good service during the remainder of the day.

Upon opening fire with the light howitzer battery, under Lieut. John Riley, it was found to be ineffectual against the heavier metal of the enemy. It was therefore ordered to cease firing and be withdrawn under cover.

At about 1 o'clock Captain Teel, with two guns of his battery, reached the ground. Being placed in position on our right he opened a galling fire upon the left flank of the enemy, whereupon the enemy commenced a furious cannonade upon him from their entire battery, consisting of eight guns. So heavy was their fire that the captain soon found himself with but five men.to work the two guns. A bomb exploding under his pieces had set the grass on fire; still, this gallant officer held his position and continued his firing upon the enemy, himself seizing the rammer and assisting to load the piece.

Seeing his situation, I ordered Lieutenant Riley, with his command, to join him and assist in the efficient working of the guns. During the balance of the day this brave little band performed the duty assigned them. Judging by the heavy firing on the left that Major Pyron was hard pressed, Captain Teel, with more of his guns, which had just reached the ground, was dispatched to his relief. Major Raguet, with four companies of the regiment, was ordered to maintain our position there. I remained on the right with the balance of my command and two pieces of Teel's battery, under Lieut. J. H. McGinnis, to hold in check the enemy, who were moving in large force in that direction to turn our flank. About this time Major Lockridge, of the Fifth Regiment, arrived on the field and reported himself with a portion of that command. He was ordered to join our troops on the left. During all this time the fire of the enemy had been extremely heavy, while, owing to the shorter range of most of our guns, our fire was reserved until they should approach sufficiently near our position to come within range of our arms, when they were invariably repulsed with loss. Soon after the arrival of Major Lockridge Colonel Green reached the field and assumed command.

At about 3 o'clock in the afternoon, in extending our line to prevent the enemy from turning our right, I found myself with only two companies, Captain [William P.] Hardeman's and [James M.] Crosson's, opposed to a force numbering some 400 men, the other four companies being several hundred yards to my left. It was there that that daring charge was made by Captain Lang, of the Fifth Regiment, with a small body of lancers. But desperate courage was ineffectual against great odds and superior arms, and this company there sustained the greatest loss of life of any company of the brigade. This charge, otherwise unfortunate, had the effect of bringing the enemy within range of our guns, when the two pieces of Captain Teel's battery and the small-arms of Captains Hardeman's and Crosson's companies opened an effective fire upon them, before which they rapidly retreated with considerable loss. Just before sunset Lieut. Thomas P. Ochiltree, of General Sibley's staff, brought an order to prepare for a charge all along the line. All prepared for its prompt execution, and when the words "Up boys, and at them!" were given, straight at their battery of six guns supported by columns of infantry and cavalry, some 700 yards in front of our position, went our brave volunteers, unmindful of the driving storm of grape and canister and musket balls sent hurling around them. With yells and ringing shouts they dashed on and on, until the guns were won and the enemy in full retreat before them. After carrying the battery, their guns were turned upon themselves, Captains Hardeman and Walker manning those on the right. Lieutenant Ragnet, of Riley's battery, being on the ground, I placed one gun in his charge, manning it with such of the men as were nearest. The rammer being gone, a flag-staff was used in its stead. Captain Teel coming up, an effective fire was kept up as long as the enemy was in reach. In the mean time a most timely and gallant charge was made by Major Ragnet from our left, thus effecting a favorable diversion at the moment of our charge upon their battery. This charge by Major Ragnet and his command was characterized by desperate valor.

In the last brilliant and successful charge, which decided the fortunes of the day, there were six companies of the Fourth Regiment Texas Mounted Volunteers, under their respective captains, Hardeman, Crosson, [Charles M.] Lesueur, [W. W.] Foard, [George J.] Hampton, and [D. A.] Nunn. Besides those, I saw Captains [John S.] Shropshire, [J. G.] Killough, and [H. A.] McPhaill, of the Fifth Regiment, and Captain Walker, of Major Pyron's battalion.

The brave and lamented Major Lockridge, of the Fifth Regiment, fell almost at the muzzle of the enemy's guns.

Major Pyron was also in the thickest of the fray, and contributed much by his example to the success of the charge, as did also Lieutenant Ochiltree, of the general's staff.

There were others there whom I now regret my inability to name. Where all, both officers and men, behaved so well it is impossible to say who is the most deserving of praise. The enemy retired across the river, and were in full retreat when Major Ragnet, Captains Shannon, Adair, [W. L.] Alexander, [Charles] Buckholts, and Lieut. A. S. Thurmond reached the field with their companies, mounted. I asked and obtained permission from Colonel Green to cross the river with these companies to pursue the flying foe.

When the head of the column reached the opposite shore we were ordered to return. Night closed in on the hard-won field of Valverde. This brilliant victory, which, next to Heaven, we owe to the heroic endurance and unfaltering courage of our volunteer soldiers, was not won without loss. Of the regiment which I have the honor to command there were 8 killed and 56 wounded, 2 of which were mortal.

It affords me great pleasure to be able to bear testimony to the calm, cool, and discriminating courage of Col. Thomas Green during the fight. Major Pyron also deserves great credit for his soldiery bearing from the commencement to the close of the battle. Of the general's staff, Major Jackson was early on the ground, as was also Major Brownrigg, Captain Dwyer, and Lieutenant Ochiltree, actively engaged in the discharge of the duties assigned them. Each of these gentlemen exhibited that high courage which I hope will ever distinguish the officers of the army. To Majors Jackson and Brownrigg I am under obligations for valuable aid in the early part of the action.

It is due to the adjutant of this regiment, Ellsberry R. Lane, that I should not close this report without stating that he was actively and bravely engaged in the discharge of his duties on horseback until his horse failed, when, taking a gun, he entered the ranks of Captain Hampton's company, and did duty as a private during the remainder of the day.

I have the honor to be, very respectfully, your obedient servant,

W. R. SCURRY,
Lieutenant-Colonel, Comdg. Fourth Regt. Texas Mounted Vols.

A. M. JACKSON,
Assistant Adjutant-General, Army of New Mexico.

No. 11.

Report of Maj. Henry W. Ragnet, Fourth Texas Cavalry.

CAMP VALVERDE, ARMY OF NEW MEXICO,
February 23, 1862.

MAJOR: About sunrise on the 21st instant, while in camp opposite Fort Craig, I was ordered by Lieutenant-Colonel Scurry to take four companies of the Fourth Texas Mounted Volunteers, to which would be added Captain Frazier's company, from Major Pyron's battalion, and march as an advance to the river at the best point for approaching it above the fort, supposed to be about 6 miles distant. After marching about 3 miles I was ordered to halt and join Lieutenant-Colonel Scurry, who was approaching with other companies of the regiment and Lieutenant Riley's artillery.

Our course was then changed for a nearer point on the river. After a half-hour's march, while descending a cañon, the rapid advance of the head of our column gave notice that we were approaching the enemy, and, emerging into the valley, the firing of skirmishers told that Major Pyron, who had been marching on our left flank, was already engaged with the enemy. A half-mile gallop brought us within range of the enemy's artillery, when Lieutenant-Colonel Scurry ordered us to dismount and advance, when we were soon within range of their small-arms, and took position on the right of Major Pyron, behind a low bank, about 9 a. m.

After we had taken this position about half an hour the enemy moved up on our right, with the evident intention of flanking us, which at the time would have been fatal, when Lieutenant-Colonel Scurry, dividing the command, assigned that position to me, and moved up to the position occupied by him during the day, and checked their advance.

The troops at this time with me were Major Pyron, with his battalion of 180 men, under Captains Walker, Stafford, and Frazier, and Lieutenants Nicholson and Jett, and four companies of the Fourth Regiment, under Captains [A. J.] Scarborough, Buckholts, Heuvel, and Alexander.

About noon one piece of Captain Teel's battery, under Lieutenant [James] Bradford, was added to my position, which did good service until the heavier metal of the enemy silenced it. Soon after the arrival of this gun Major Lockridge arrived with three companies of the Fifth Regiment Texas Mounted Volunteers, under Captains [John S.] Shropshire, [G. W.] Campbell, and [Daniel H.] Ragsdale, and Major Pyron, and Lieutenant Bradford's commands were withdrawn to the right. Major

Lockridge called my attention to the gun, which had been partly disabled and silenced, on our left, at the foot of the mesa, where it had been placed in an endeavor to disable the enemy's battery on the west bank of the river. I ordered Company B, Fourth Regiment, Captain Scarborough, to the rescue, and with part of that company, under their captain and Sergeant Nelson, of Company H, Fourth Regiment, Captain Alexander, and some of that company, I succeeded in drawing the gun by hand from its perilous position amid the hottest cannonading on that part of the field, losing only 1 man killed and a few wounded.

The horses of this gun had nearly all been killed by the enemy's artillery. This gun was then used by three of Lieutenant Riley's company, assisted by a few others, until I ordered the fire discontinued for want of gunners, leaving it double-shotted, to await an anticipated charge of the enemy. The enemy threatened us in such great numbers and their fire was so heavy that Major Lockridge and myself each sent messengers to Colonel Green for re-enforcements; failing to get which, Major Lockridge deemed it prudent to fall back to a sand bank, about 100 yards in our rear, which was done by companies, after the artillery and the wounded had been removed. This gave us a better position, as the ground was somewhat broken in front.

The section of Teel's artillery was now withdrawn to the right, leaving only one howitzer, under Lieutenant Woods, who had arrived at our new position. Lieutenant-Colonel Sutton now arrived on the field, approaching in our rear, when a messenger was dispatched asking that he be ordered to remain by us.

He soon marched up to the right and then returned. Major Lockridge now told me that we were to move up and join the forces on the right for a charge; that he would cover any movement to get my horses, which were on the left and rear. Ordering the companies of the Fourth Regiment to horse, I soon marched up on the right in the rear of the rest of the command, dismounted, and ordering the companies then with me, under Captains Buckholts, Heuvel, and Alexander, of the Fourth, and Captain Ragsdale, of the Fifth, into line to advance.

Colonel Green rode up and ordered me to reserve my command for a charge as cavalry. No sooner were we mounted than an order came by Major Pyron to move down on the left and menace the enemy, now flanking us in large force. Marching down to within 600 yards I dismounted my command under cover, when I was joined by Captain Scarborough, of the Fourth, and received an order through Captain Dwyer to charge the enemy.

Aligning in single rank, I charged to within about 100 yards of the enemy's lines, composed of infantry, supported by cavalry on each flank and in the rear and by artillery on their right, when, looking back, I saw great confusion from the wounded and fallen horses, for we had aligned and advanced under the heavy fire of their infantry and artillery. I thought we could not break their lines, and ordered my command to fall back and rally at the sand bank which we had left on our rear and left. When I had arrived at the sand bank I found that most of my command had passed it for some others still on their left, and that the position was untenable, as the enemy's artillery now raked it. I ordered those there to follow those yet in advance, and, rallying, we could return.

Finding Lieutenant Woods, with one howitzer, uselessly exposed under the enemy's fire, I ordered him to a position between the enemy and the train, to protect it as well as he could, and ordering such of my command as I met to join in the action on the right, I galloped down, then too late, however, to participate in that brilliant charge which gave us the victory.

A few moments after reaching the river bank Lieutenant-Colonel Scurry asked permission of Colonel Green to cross and pursue the enemy with some fresh companies that had just come up, which permission being granted, I joined with my command who were present, and as the head of our column gained the opposite shore we were ordered back. Shortly after the arrival of the flag of truce ended the battle of Valverde after sunset.

During the entire day my position on the left was under a constant fire of the enemy's heaviest artillery, and their small-arms, whose longer range enabled them to keep out of our small-arm range. When they threatened an advance and would reach our aim they were repulsed.

The gallant Major Lockridge, of the Fifth, while in command of the left, won the admiration of all who saw him, and whose regrets are now mingled with those of his other friends at his death. The brave Heuvel, of this command, who fell in the charge he had so impatiently waited for, added another to the list of our gallant dead at Valverde.

For the officers and privates whom I had the honor to command on that day I can well say that they have never faltered in their dangerous duty; and for those, less than 200, whom I led to the charge against more than eight times their numbers, together with artillery, the recital of the act is their praise. This charge, though at the cost of nearly one-fifth the men and horses in killed and wounded, succeeded in checking the flank movement of the enemy in time to enable the charge which won the day to be made.

Very respectfully, your obedient servant,

HENRY W. RAGNET,
Major, Fourth Regiment Texas Mounted Volunteers.

A. M. JACKSON,
Assistant Adjutant-General, Army of New Mexico.

No. 12.

Report of Col. Thomas Green, Fifth Texas Cavalry.

CAMP VALVERDE, N. MEX.,
February 22, 1862.

SIR: I have the honor of submitting to you the following report of the battle of Valverde, fought on yesterday by a part of the brigade of General Sibley, under my command:

While in the act of turning Fort Craig, on the east side of the Rio Grande, Major Pyron, with 200 men, was sent to reconnoiter, early on the morning of the 21st, the route around the mesa, north of the fort, and secure a footing on the river above. While Major Pyron was approaching the river with his command the enemy appeared in considerable numbers between his command and the river on the north of the mesa, and opened on him, about 8 o'clock, a heavy fire of artillery and small-arms. The gallant Pyron, with his brave little force, kept up the unequal contest for an hour or two, until the arrival of Lieutenant-Colonel Scurry with a part of his regiment, and Lieutenant Riley's howitzer battery. Scurry took position on the right of Pyron, and both kept up the contest and maintained their position behind a low line of sand hills. About this time one section of Captain Teel's battery came up and took position and replied to the fire of the enemy.

At 12 o'clock, while, under the orders of the general, I was threatening the fort on the south side of the mesa, I received his orders to move up, with all my disposable force, to the support of Lieutenant-Colonel Scurry and Major Pyron, after leaving a sufficient force to protect the train which was then moving from our late camp around the mesa to the battle ground, and which was stretched out for several miles. Our train was threatened by a considerable body of troops of the enemy, who made their appearance on the mesa. Detaching Lieutenant-Colonel Sutton's command and a detachment from my own regiment to protect the train, I moved up, with as much speed as practicable, with eight companies of my regiment, sending forward Major Lockridge, with the two companies of lancers, under Captains Lang and [Jerome B.] McCown. My companies were placed in the line of battle, between Pyron on the left and Scurry on the right, except three, which were sent by me, under Lieutenant-Colonel [H. C.] McNeill, to drive the enemy from the north point of the mesa, where they were annoying our left and threatening our train.

After these dispositions I moved up to the line of battle myself, and by the orders of the general took command of the forces present. The enemy during the day, and, with little intermission, kept up a brisk cannonade upon us, to which our 6-pounders, under Captain Teel, replied with effect. The enemy repeatedly advanced with their skirmishers to near our lines, killing many of our horses tied in the rear.

About 3 p. m. a most galling fire was opened upon Lieutenant-Colonel Scurry's command, on our right, by 300 or 400 of the enemy's riflemen. Captain Lang, of the Fifth Regiment, with about 40 of his lancers, made at this time one of the most gallant and furious charges on these light troops of the enemy ever witnessed in the annals of battles. His little troop was decimated, and the gallant captain and Lieutenant Bass severely wounded—the latter in seven places. The enemy were repulsed by this gallant charge, and our right was for some time unmolested.

Large bodies of the enemy's infantry having crossed the river about 3.30 p. m., bringing over with them six pieces of splendid artillery, took position in front of us, on the bank of the river, at a distance of 600 yards. In addition to this body of troops two 24-pounder howitzers were placed on our left flank by the enemy. These were supported by a regiment of infantry and a regiment of cavalry. The heaviest fire of the whole day was opened about this time on our left, which was under the command of the gallant Lockridge. Our brave men on that part of the line maintained the unequal fight with desperate courage, though overwhelmingly outnumbered. Lieutenant-Colonel Sutton, now coming up with part of his battalion, took position on our left.

The enemy, now being on our side of the river, opened upon us a tremendous fire of round shot, grape, and shell. Their force in numbers was vastly superior to ours; but, having the most unbounded confidence in the courage of our troops, I ordered a charge on their battery and infantry of regulars in front, and at the same time Major Ragnet, of the Fourth, with four companies of the same, and Captain Ragsdale's company, of the Fifth, were directed by me to charge as cavalry upon the infantry and Mexican cavalry and the two 24-pounder howitzers on our left flank.

Our dismounted troops in front were composed of parts of the Fourth

and Fifth Regiments Texas Mounted Volunteers and parts of Lieutenant-Colonel Sutton's and most of Pyron's battalions, and Teel's, Riley's,
and Wood's batteries of artillery, numbering about 750 on the ground.
Major Ragnet's cavalry numbered about 250, making about 1,000 men
in the charge.

At the command to charge, our men leaped over the sand bank, which
had served as a good covering to them, and dashed over the open plain,
thinly interspersed with cottonwood trees, upon the battery and infantry of the enemy in front, composed of United States Regulars and
Denver City Volunteers, and in a most desperate charge and hand-to-
hand conflict completely overwhelmed them, killing most of their gunners around their cannon and driving the infantry into the river. Never
were double-barreled shot-guns and rifles used to better effect. A large
number of the enemy were killed in the river with shot-guns and six-
shooters in their flight.

While we were occupied with the enemy in front Major Ragnet
made a gallant and most timely charge upon the infantry and cavalry
of the enemy on our left flank. This charge was made against ten
times the number of Raguet's force, and although we suffered severely
and were compelled to fall back, he effected the object of his mission,
and occupied the attention of our powerful enemy on the left, while our
dismounted men were advancing upon those in front and running them
into the river.

So soon as the enemy had fled in disorder from our terrible fire in
front we turned upon his infantry and cavalry and 24-pounders on our
left flank, just engaged by Major Ragnet. We charged them as we had
those in front, but they were not made of as good stuff as the regulars,
and a few fires upon them with their own artillery and Teel's guns, a
few volleys of small-arms, and the old Texas war-shout completely dispersed them. They fled from the field, both cavalry and infantry, in
the utmost disorder, many of them dropping their guns to lighten their
heels, and stopping only under the walls of the fort. Our victory was
complete. The enemy must have been 3,000 strong, while our force actually engaged did not exceed 600. Six splendid pieces of artillery and
their entire equipage fell into our hands; also many fine small-arms.

This splendid victory was not achieved without severe loss to us.

Major Lockridge, of the Fifth, fell at the mouth of the enemy's guns,
gallantly leading our brave troops to the assault.

Lieutenant-Colonel Sutton, of the Seventh, fell mortally wounded at
the head of his battalion while assaulting the enemy's battery.

Several of our officers were desperately wounded; some of them no
doubt mortally. Among them are the gallant Captain Lang, of the
Lancers, and Lieutenant Bass, both of Company B, and Lieut. D. A.
Hubbard, of Company A, Fifth Regiment.

Captain Heuvel, of the Fourth, fell in the gallant cavalry charge of
Major Ragnet. He was one of the most distinguished of the heroes of
the day. Like the gallant Lang, of the Fifth, he could not appreciate
odds in a battle.

I cannot say enough in praise of the gallantry of our surviving officers and men. It would be invidious to mention names. Were I to do
so, the rolls of captains, lieutenants, and men would have to be here inserted. I will only mention the principal field and staff in the engagement. The cheering voice of Lieutenant-Colonel Scurry was heard
where the bullets fell thickest on the field. Lieutenant-Colonel McNeill,
and the gallant Major Pyron, who has been before mentioned, displayed
the most undaunted courage. Major Ragnet, of the Fourth, though

wounded, remained at his post, and retired not until the field was won. These were the field officers present, as I have just stated. The captains, lieutenants, and men in the action displayed so much gallantry that it would be invidious to make distinctions. They fought with equal valor and are entitled to equal credit with the field and staff here mentioned.

I will not close this report without a just meed of praise to the general staff, who served me as aides-de camp during the day. Col. W. L. Robards was in the dashing charge of the gallant Lang, and wounded in several places.

Capt. Tom P. Ochiltree, aide-de-camp to General Sibley, was exceedingly useful to me on the field and active during the whole engagement. He assisted me in the most critical moment to cheer our men to the assault. He deserves the highest praise for his undaunted chivalry and coolness, and I recommend him to the general for promotion.

Captain Dwyer was also very useful, gallant, and active during the whole action.

I cannot close without the mention of Captain Frazier, of the Arizona Volunteers. To him, more than all others, we are indebted for the successful turning of Fort Craig. He led us over the high ground around the mesa to the east of the fort, where we at all times had the advantage of the enemy in case he had attacked us in the act of turning the fort.

I will only personalize further by the mention of my own regimental staff.

Sergt. Maj. C. B. Sheppard shouldered his gun and fought gallantly in the ranks of Captain McPhaill's company in the charge. Lieut. Joseph D. Sayers, adjutant of the Fifth, during the whole day, reminded me of a hero of the days of chivalry. He is a gallant, daring, and dashing soldier, and is as cool in a storm of grape, shell, canister, and musketry as a veteran. I recommend him, through the general, to the President for promotion.

Our killed and wounded are as follows:

	Killed.	Wounded.	Missing.
2d Regiment Texas Mounted Volunteers, Major Pyron's command................	4	17	1
4th Regiment Texas Mounted Volunteers, Lieutenant-Colonel Scurry's command..	8	36	......
5th Texas Mounted Volunteers, Colonel Green's regiment........................	20	67	......
7th Regiment Texas Mounted Volunteers, Lieutenant-Colonel Sutton's command..	2	26	......
Teel's battery...	2	4	......
Total..	36	150	1

Since which time Lieutenant-Colonel Sutton, of the Seventh, and 2 privates of the Fifth, and 2 of Teel's battery, have died from wounds received in battle.

The enemy's loss was far greater than ours. The precise number cannot be ascertained by us, as many were killed in the river, and as the enemy's white flag, asking permission to gather up their dead and wounded, came almost before the sound of the last cannon had ceased to reverberate in the hills. It is confidently asserted and believed by many of our officers and men that the enemy, under the flag of truce, picked up many small-arms and carried them off with the dead-wagons;

that they also carried off their two 24-pounder howitzers which were left by them in the river. It is certain that during the cessation of hostilities they picked up a company flag and guidon of my regiment, left on the field during our charge, while they were gathering up their wounded and dead; and it is said these are considered by them as trophies. I do not believe that the commanding officer of the enemy is aware of these facts, as he would not have spoken of stolen flags as trophies.

I think, from the best information in my possession, that the enemy's loss must have been in killed and wounded at least 350 or 400. Among their killed were several gallant officers. The gallant McRae fell at his guns. Several other captains and lieutenants were killed. Captain Rossell, of the Tenth U. S. Infantry, and several privates of the Fifth and Tenth Infantry and Denver City Volunteers, were taken prisoners.

Respectfully submitted.

THOMAS GREEN,
Colonel Fifth Regiment Texas Mounted Volunteers.

Maj. A. M. JACKSON,
 Assistant Adjutant-General, Army of New Mexico.

No. 13.

Report of Col. William Steele, Seventh Texas Cavalry.

CAMP NEAR FILLMORE, N. MEX.,
March 1, 1862.

GENERAL: I have received a verbal express from General Sibley, the numerous parties of Mexicans in the employ of the enemy rendering it dangerous to write. Our forces turned the enemy's position by crossing the river to the east side, which drew him out of his intrenchments, and an engagement ensued just above Fort Craig, which commenced about 9 o'clock on the morning of February 21, and lasted, with little intermission until near sunset, when the enemy was driven in confusion from the field. We captured seven pieces of artillery and a considerable number of small-arms were picked up. Much of the Mexican portion of the enemy fled to the hills. The regulars and Pike's Peak Volunteers returned to the fort. Our forces were encamped on the field when my informants left. Our loss is stated at 38 killed and 106 wounded. Major Lockridge is recollected as one of the killed. General Sibley had been sick some days previous to the action, and the command devolved upon Col. Thomas Green, who was in command most of the day, General Sibley being unable to remain long upon the field.

This account agrees with the information I had a few days previous as to the contemplated movement. I received this intelligence the day after the stage left for San Antonio and have delayed writing, hoping to get some more particulars, but as yet have none.

Very respectfully, your obedient servant,

WM. STEELE,
Colonel Seventh Texas Mounted Regiment.

General S. COOPER, *Adjutant-General.*

No. 14.

Report of Capt. Powhatan Jordan, Seventh Texas Cavalry.

IN CAMP NEAR SOCORRO, N. MEX.,
February 27, 1862.

GENERAL: I have the honor to report the First Battalion of the Seventh Regiment Texas Mounted Volunteers in the battle of Valverde, N. Mex., on February 21. The First Battalion of the Seventh Regiment, under command of Lieut. Col. J. S. Sutton, with Companies C and H of the Fifth Regiment, were detailed as a guard for the transportation on the morning of the 21st. Before the train had gotten fairly out of camp we were apprised of the fight having commenced at Valverde Crossing of the Rio Grande by hearing the sullen roar of cannon. The train being in danger of attack, we were kept in position as the guard, and all thought for a time the Seventh would have no share in the conflict; but in about two hours after the commencement of the battle an officer appeared with the order for us to move on to the battle-field. Colonel Sutton detached from his command Companies A and F, of the Seventh, and Company C, of the Fifth, to remain, and then gave the order to forward, when the remainder of his command, consisting of Companies B, F, and I, of the Seventh, and F, of the Fifth, moved on to the scene of action. We went at a gallop, and were met on the field by Major Lockridge, who ordered us to take position on the left. We were here held for an hour or more, running the gauntlet by countermarch under a most galling and destructive fire from their batteries.

While in this position we lost 2 men and some 3 horses killed. The battle having now continued several hours, the charge was ordered, and the Seventh was most gallantly led in the charge by Lieutenant-Colonel Sutton, who fell mortally wounded when within 20 paces of the enemy's battery. The battle was now soon ended, and victory was ours, though purchased by the Seventh with the death of the heroic Sutton. The Seventh did its duty bravely, nobly, all acting gallantly.

To make mention of individuals would be unjust. They all shared equally the dangers of the field, and all deserve equal praise. To Capt. Redden S. Pridgen and his company (H, of the Fifth), who acted with our command, we must give great credit for their coolness and gallantry, and wish himself and company to share with us whatever credit may fall to our command.

Accompanying is the list* of killed and wounded, together with the horses killed in the battle, as furnished me by captains of companies.

I have the honor to be, very respectfully, your obedient servant,

POWHATAN JORDAN,
Captain, Comdg. First Battalion,
Seventh Regiment Texas Mounted Volunteers, Army of N. Mex.

General H. H. SIBLEY, *C. S. Army.*

No. 15.

Report of Capt. Trevanion T. Teel, Texas Light Artillery.

CAMP LOCKRIDGE, N. MEX., *February 27, 1862.*

SIR: I have the honor to report to the general commanding the

---
* Not found.

Army of New Mexico the operations of the light battery which I had the honor to command in the battle of Valverde, N. Mex., on February 21.

I received orders on the morning of the 21st, at camp, 5 miles below the battle-ground, and opposite Fort Craig, to detach one section of the battery, under Lieutenant [James] Bradford, to march in the front of the column and head of the train to Valverde, and place the other section and remain myself in rear with the Second Regiment of Sibley's brigade, which orders were executed.

About an hour after the head of the column had moved I received intelligence that a large body of the enemy's cavalry, infantry, and artillery had taken up the line of march for Valverde.

I then placed the section of the battery in command of Lieutenants [Jordan W.] Bennett and [Joseph H.] McGinnis, and went to the head of the column; before reaching the head of the train I heard the firing of the advance at Valverde.

I found Lieutenant Bradford, with his section, at the head of the train, and ordered the pieces to the place of firing at a gallop, and in a few minutes it was placed in battery about the center of Lieutenant-Colonel Scurry's regiment, and commenced firing upon the battery of the enemy and his line in a few minutes. I lost 1 man killed and 2 wounded, which left but 5 cannoneers to man the two pieces. I then kept up the fire alternately with the pieces. Finding it impossible to use the pieces with steady and effective fire, I called upon Lieutenant-Colonel Scurry for men to fill up the detachments of the guns, which were immediately sent from Lieutenant Riley's company of howitzers. After sustaining the action for some time the enemy changed his front. I then placed the section in another position.

Lieutenants Bennett and McGinnis having by this time reached our line, I ordered them to place their section in battery, which they did, and opened upon the enemy with good effect.

From the great length of the enemy's line and his superior number I found it necessary to detach the pieces. Lieutenant Bradford was sent to the extreme left flank with his piece to support Majors Lockridge and Pyron's commands, which had been engaged with the enemy for more than an hour; Lieutenant McGinnis, with his gun, on the right of Major Lockridge's battalion; Lieutenant Bennett at the center of the right flank, and the other piece at the extreme right flank; Lieutenant Riley, with his battery of howitzers, on the left wing, and Lieutenant Woods, with his battery of howitzers, on the right wing. The different pieces and howitzers changed positions, however, during the action as circumstances required, and were used with effect whenever the enemy presented a front or his battery in view.

Having received orders that our troops were about to charge the enemy, I placed the guns in battery upon the extreme right flank as a reserve, in case the charge was unsuccessful, so that I could open the line of the enemy with raking shots or engage his battery until our troops would prevent my firing by their closing with the enemy. The charge was made by our line, and in eight minutes his battery was captured and his troops completely routed. Lieutenant Ochiltree, aide-de-camp, rode back and ordered the guns forward, which order was executed, and soon the enemy's guns, as well as ours, were opened on his retreating forces. Firing was kept up from our guns until the enemy's rear was out of range of them; I then ordered the firing to cease.

I lost 4 men killed, including 2 who died the day after the battle, and 6 wounded; 25 horses killed and wounded, one gun partially disabled, and eight sets of harness rendered unserviceable.

I refer with great pleasure to the gallant conduct of Lieutenants Bennett, McGinnis, and Bradford, of my company, as well as Lieutenants Riley, Woods, Ragnet, and Falcrod, of the batteries of howitzers; also of the non-commissioned officers and privates of all the batteries.

I cannot close my report without bearing testimony to the bravery and coolness of the officers under whom I acted during this sanguinary and well-contested battle. Colonel Green, and especially Lieutenant-Colonel Scurry, who so promptly manned my guns from his regiment (the First), and who was present with my guns under the heavy fire in the morning, and whose voice was heard above the din of battle, and smoke, and flame, and death, encouraging the men to stand by their posts. Also the lamented Lockridge; Major Jackson, assistant adjutant-general; Major Brownrigg, brigade commissary; Lieutenant-Colonel McNeill and Lieutenant Ochiltree, aide-de-camp, who were rallying the men to the charge and were in the line leading on the troops; also Captain Dwyer, of the staff, Colonel Robards, and Major Ragnet. Also the deep obligations I am under to Lieutenant-Colonel Scurry, and Captain Scarborough and his company, who hauled out a disabled piece by hand under a hot fire; to Captains Campbell, McPhaill, and Killough, and their respective companies, for the promptness and willingness with which they replaced the killed and wounded at my guns, many of their comrades having been killed and wounded while aiding in manning the battery during the action.

Very respectfully, your obedient servant,
T. T. TEEL,
Captain, Artillery.

Maj. A. M. JACKSON,
Assistant Adjutant-General, C. S. Army.

FEBRUARY 22, 1862.—Engagement in Aransas Bay, Tex.

REPORTS.

No. 1.—Col. H. E. McCulloch, C. S. Army, commanding Western Military District.
No. 2.—Capt. B. F. Neal, C. S. Army, commanding.

No. 1.

Letter of Col. H. E. McCulloch, C. S. Army, commanding Western Military District.

HEADQUARTERS WESTERN MILITARY DISTRICT,
San Antonio, Tex., February 27, 1862.

SIR: I inclose a report from Capt. B. F. Neal, commanding at Aransas.

Major Yager, with his two cavalry companies, are there before this time. I sent the ammunition required by Captain Neal with Major Yager's cavalry when they went down. This re-enforcement and ammunition will be sufficient, I hope, to enable them to defend that section until better can be done.

I regret that the 18-pounders sent from Galveston have been delayed.

Most respectfully, your obedient servant,

H. E. McCULLOCH,
Colonel, Commanding Western Military District.

Maj. SAMUEL BOYER DAVIS, *Assistant Adjutant-General.*

No. 2.

Report of Capt. B. F. Neal, C. S. Army, commanding.

HEADQUARTERS CAMP ARANSAS, TEX.,
February 22, 1862—9 p. m.

COLONEL: I have just returned to camp this moment, and hasten to communicate to you the movements of the enemy this evening. At 3.30 o'clock this evening the enemy appeared within 3 miles of our camp with two launches, captured a sloop boat bound for Corpus Christi, and took from her a lot of medicines and other articles for the Government—I presume this command. Two or three of my men were oystering and gave the alarm. I immediately ordered out my command, got aboard all the boats I could raise, and went in pursuit. We overtook one of the launches in Aransas Bay and engaged them. The wind was ahead, consequently we were prevented from capturing them, as they could out-travel us with their horses. They returned our fire, but none of our men were injured. We drove them within range of their guns. Night coming on, we retired.

I do not know what effect our Minie rifles had upon them, but I presume some one must have been hurt.

We should have re-enforcements and powder. I made a requisition, through Major Yager, when at San Antonio, for ammunition, but it has not arrived yet. All we want is powder for our two pieces of ordnance—6-pounders.

The enemy is becoming quite bold and daring, and will destroy the commerce of these bays unless checked in their buccaneering. I shall do all I can to annoy them and keep them back until we are better prepared. They have the advantage of us, possessing better boats and being more accustomed to them than we are.

Excuse this hastily-written letter. I shall give further particulars of our skirmish this evening.

Yours, respectfully,

BENJ. F. NEAL,
Captain, Commanding Troops near Shell Bank.

Col. H. E. McCULLOCH,
Comdg. Western Military District, Department of Texas.

MARCH 2-4, 1862.—Evacuation of Albuquerque and Santa Fé, N. Mex., by Union forces.

REPORTS.

No. 1.—Maj. James L. Donaldson, Quartermaster, U. S. Army, commanding District of Santa Fé, N. Mex.

No. 2.—Ca t. Herbert M. Enos Assistant Quartermaster. U. S. Army.

No. 1.

Report of Maj. James L. Donaldson, Quartermaster, U. S. Army, commanding District of Santa Fé, N. Mex.

HEADQUARTERS,
Fort Union, N. Mex., March 10, 1862.

COLONEL: I have the honor to report that in consequence of the near approach of the enemy, and his not having troops to defend the place, Captain Enos, assistant quartermaster, abandoned Albuquerque on the 2d instant, having first loaded up a train with his most valuable stores, started it to Santa Fé, and destroyed the rest. His report is herewith inclosed. On the 4th instant I deemed it necessary to pursue the same course, as Santa Fé was not defensible, being commanded on all sides by hills, and the safety of the train, composed of 120 wagons, loaded with the most valuable stores in the department, required a strong escort. Its value could not have been less than a quarter of a million of dollars, and its safety was a matter of paramount importance. I am glad to say that it has arrived under the guns of Fort.Union, and that the enemy has gained nothing of importance along the line. The force I brought from Santa Fé consists of Captain Lewis' company, Fifth Infantry; Captain Ford's company, Colorado Volunteers; Lieutenant Banks' company (E), Third Cavalry, and two mounted howitzers, under Lieut. C. J. Walker, Second Cavalry. Some volunteers also accompanied me, under Lieut. Col. Manuel Chavez, but all of them except the lieutenant-colonel and some officers deserted on the march. I beg to call your attention to Capt. W. H. Lewis, Fifth Infantry, whose efficiency was of great service to me in evacuating the town and in conducting the train to Union.

Very respectfully, your obedient servant,

J. L. DONALDSON,
Major, Commanding District Santa Fé.

Col. G. R. PAUL, *Commanding Fort Union.*

No. 2.

Report of Capt. Herbert M. Enos, Assistant Quartermaster, U. S. Army.

ASSISTANT QUARTERMASTER'S OFFICE,
Fort Union, N. Mex., March 11, 1862.

MAJOR : I have the honor to make the following statement relating to the abandonment and destruction of the public property under my charge at Albuquerque, N. Mex.:

On the afternoon of the 1st instant I received reliable information that a body of Texans, about 400 strong, supposed to be the advance guard of the enemy, had reached the town of Belen, 35 miles below Albuquerque. Upon this intelligence I ordered that every preparation be made for destroying the public stores, both quartermaster's and subsistence, which could not be carried off. At about 6 p. m. one of my express riders came in and reported that a party of about 50 had reached the town of Los Lunas and captured a citizen train, carrying public stores. I had in the mean time loaded what ammunition and ordnance stores the ordnance agent, Mr. Bronson, deemed important to secure, and started them on the road to Santa Fé. I had all the teams that were left, some eight or nine, harnessed and ready for moving at a moment's warning, for the purpose of carrying the baggage of some militia and volunteer companies and 12 regular soldiers. The latter were my only dependence, and I had assumed command of them.

The night passed without the appearance of the enemy, but believing that he would soon be upon me, and not hearing of any troops being on the way from Santa Fé to hold the town, I gave the order to fire the property at about 6.30 on the morning of the 2d instant. The destruction would have been complete had it not been for the great rush of Mexican men, women, and children, who had been up the whole night, waiting anxiously for an opportunity to gratify their insatiable desire for plunder. The only property that was not burned consisted of molasses, vinegar, soap, and candles in the subsistence department, and a few saddles, carpenter's tools, and office furniture in the quartermaster's department. Most of these articles were carried off by the Mexicans. The destruction of the stores involved the destruction of the buildings containing them, as it would have been impossible with the force and the short time at my disposal to have removed the property from the buildings in order that it might then be burned. Had I attempted to carry out this plan I am of the opinion that the native population would have overpowered me and saved the property for the enemy.

The last wagons, five in number, which left the town were escorted by Mexican volunteers and militia. While in camp near the puebla of Sandilla the train was attacked by deserters from the militia and volunteers, when the escort was thrown in confusion, and the robbers succeeded in carrying off three wagons, with a portion of the mules. Much credit is due to Wagon-master Reilley for getting away with the remainder.

Six wagons and teams which had been sent to the mountains for fuel on the morning of the 1st instant, and afterwards ordered to move by the way of Gallisteo to Santa Fé, are missing, and I have been informed that they were attacked by Mexican robbers and the train carried off.

H. M. ENOS,

I am, major, very respectfully, your obedient servant,

Captain and Assistant Quartermaster.

Maj. JAMES L. DONALDSON,
   Quartermaster, U. S. A., Comdg. East. Dist. N. Mex., Fort Union.

MARCH 3, 1862.—Capture of Cubero, N. Mex.

Report of Capt. A. S. Thurmond, Third Regiment, Sibley's Brigade.

CUBERO, N. MEX., March 19, 1862.

SIR: In making an official report of my entry into this place, &c., I will furnish a transcript of the notes handed me by men whom I have myself found to be sound.

NOTE 1.—At 9 a. m. March 3, Dr. F. E. Kavenaugh, in command of three Americans, demanded of Capt. Francisco Aragon, U. S. Army, commanding military post of Cubero, the surrender to him for the Confederate States of himself and command, consisting of Dr. Boyd, surgeon of post, 42 New Mexican soldiers, and 3 Americans, one of whom was

Sergeant Wahl, bugler, U. S. Army, together with the post, and all stores, arms, ammunition, and property, of whatsoever description, belonging thereto. Captain Aragon was allowed ten minutes to decide whether he would peaceably comply with the demand or resist. At the expiration of the time, he not having returned an answer, one of Kavenaugh's party was 'sent to receive the arms, which were formally demanded. The following correspondence will show the formal surrender of the post to Dr. Kavenaugh and his regiment, to hold the same in the name of the Confederate States of America, which said correspondence I herewith inclose.*

The amount of property turned over will be accurately shown by the quartermaster's invoices, which show a large and valuable lot of quartermaster's, commissary, and ordnance stores. The surgery is also well supplied with valuable medicines, &c. There was not less than 60 arms and 3,000 rounds of ammunition turned over. Captain Aragon and company were furnished with arms and transportation sufficient to take and protect them to Albuquerque upon promise to deliver the Government property furnished them to the Confederate States Army officer commanding there.

Upon taking command of the post Dr. Kavenaugh dispatched Mr. Richmond Gillespie, one of his party, to take information to Albuquerque of the surrender of the post, and to procure assistance in holding it. This trip was performed by Mr. Gillespie greatly to his credit, he having voluntarily risked his life a second time in passing without protection through a most dangerous portion of hostile Indian country to a post where he was not certain but what he might fall into the hands of the enemy. The successful execution of this hazardous trip brought to the protection of the post Capt. A. S. Thurmond, C. S. Army, with 25 men of his command; arrived at Cubero on March 5, at 2 p. m.

Next day the command was turned over to him by Dr. Kavenaugh.

George Gardenhier, one of Dr. Kavenaugh's party, has rendered most valuable services as assistant quartermaster and commissary, working incessantly in saving and protecting property belonging to those defenses.

Mr. R. T. Thompson has, not only at the capture of the post, but always, been truly Southern, being a Virginian by birth, and certainly his services were most efficient in carrying out the duties of adjutant, treating the enemy always with much leniency, but with the sternness and decision of a true Southern gentleman.

In conversing with both friends and enemies I have found the above to be substantially true; yea, more than true, for such an act of bravery, under the circumstances, could not be expected from the number of men. Dr. Kavenaugh and Messrs. Thompson, Gillespie, and Gardenhier constituted the whole reliable force on the side of the Confederate States, and they, too, men who had been persecuted by the Federal Government. They were not only suspected but were known to be friends of the Confederate States, consequently there was but one game to play, and they did play it with profit to the Confederate States and great credit to themselves. The game would be in other countries called bluff, though it was not intended so by them, although it had that effect.

---

* Omitted as unimportant.

34 R R—VOL IX

Dr. Boyd is also among us, a gentleman of high medical attainments, and is at this time doing us valuable service, as I have quite a number of cases of pleurisy in my company.

This at Cubero, March 20.

A. S. THURMOND,

Comdg. Co. A, Third Regt., Sibley's Brig., Army of N. Mex.

To the OFFICER COMMANDING C. S. FORCES,

Albuquerque, N. Mex.

MARCH 26, 1862.—Skirmish at Apache Cañon, **N. Mex**

REPORTS.*

No. 1.—Maj. John M. Chivington, First Colorado Infantry.
No. 2.—Capt. Charles J. Walker, Second U. S. Cavalry, including engagement at Glorieta, March 28.

No. 1.

Report of Maj. John M. Chivington, First Colorado Infantry.

CAMP LEWIS, NEAR PECOS CHURCH, N. MEX.,

March 26, 1862.

GENERAL : I have the honor to submit to you the following report of the troops under my command on the 26th of March, 1862, at the battle of Apache Cañon :

The force consisted as follows : Company A, 60 men, Captain Wynkoop ; Company E, 60 men, Captain Anthony, and 60 men of Company D, Captain Downing, of the First Regiment Colorado Infantry Volunteers, and 28 men of Company C, 6 men of Company D, 6 men of Company —, 10 men of Company K, Third Cavalry, under Captain Howland and Lieutenants Wall and Falvey ; 50 men of Company E, Third Cavalry, commanded by Captain Walker and Lieutenant Banks ; 50 men of Companies D and G, First Cavalry, under Captain Lord and Lieutenant Bernard (all of the U. S. Army), and 88 men of Company F, First Regiment Cavalry Colorado Volunteers, under Captain Cook and Lieutenants Nelson and Marshall ; making the total force on our side 418 men. We marched from Bernal Springs for Santa Fé at 3 o'clock p. m. of the 25th instant, intending to surprise the enemy in small force at that place. After a march of 35 miles, and learning we were in the vicinity of the enemy's pickets, we halted about midnight, and at 2 o'clock a. m. on the 26th Lieutenant Nelson, with 20 men, was sent out to surprise their pickets, which they did, and captured them at 10 o'clock a. m. The detachment again moved forward, and just as we entered the cañon (Apache) discovered the advance guard of the foe and captured two lieutenants. In a few minutes they planted their battery and began to throw grape and shell among us. In double-quick Companies A and E, First Colorado Volunteers, were deployed as skirmishers to the left and on the mountain side, and Company D, First Colorado Volunteers, was deployed as skirmishers to the right on the mountain side, and an order was given that the cavalry be held

---

* This skirmish is also mentioned in Slough's and Scurry's reports of engagement, March 28, at Glorieta, N. Mex.

in readiness to charge whenever the cannon were about to retreat. Soon our men from the mountain sides made it too hot for their gunners, and they fell back about 1½ miles and took another and more advantageous position, completely covering the sides of the mountains with their skirmishers to support their guns in the cañon below them.

Having mean time assembled our skirmishers in the cañon, we again deployed Company D, First Colorado Volunteers, on the right, and Companies A and E, First Colorado Volunteers, on the left, and dismounted all the cavalry and deployed them as skirmishers, except Company F, First Colorado Volunteers, Captain Cook, who was ordered to charge them the moment they gave way before the fire of our infantry. After a contest of an hour they began to prepare for another retreat, and by this time Company D, Captain Downing, had well-nigh flanked them, so as to cut off their retreat, Captain Cook and Lieutenants Nelson and Marshall leading the way. Company F now made a flying charge on the enemy, running over and trampling them under the horses' feet. Captain Downing with his men, and Lieutenant Bernard with Company C, Third Cavalry, poured into him a sharp fire from the right, which drove him up a cañon on the left side of the main cañon, when Companies A and E, First Colorado Volunteers, took a large number of prisoners. It now being sundown..and we not knowing how near the enemy's re-enforcements might' be, and having no cannon to oppose theirs, hastened to gather up our dead and wounded and several of the enemy's, and then fell back to Pigeon's Ranch and encamped for the night.

Our loss was 5 killed and 14 wounded. The loss of the enemy was, as we ascertained from their own accounts, 32 killed, 43 wounded, and 71 taken prisoners.

I am, sir, with much respect, your obedient servant,

J. M. CHIVINGTON,
Major, First Regiment Colorado Volunteers.

Brig. Gen. E. R. S. CANBY, U. S. A.,
Commanding Department New Mexico, Santa Fé, N. Mex.

No. 2.

Report of Capt. Charles J. Walker, Second U. S. Cavalry, including engagement at Glorieta, March 28.

FORT CRAIG, N. MEX., *May* 20, 1862.

SIR: In compliance with orders from the Headquarters of the South Military District, Fort Craig, N. Mex., of May 18, 1862, requiring a detailed report of the operations of my company or command in the recent actions of Apache Cañon and Pigeon's Ranch, I have the honor to state that on the morning of the 26th of March last my company, forming a part of the cavalry command under Capt. G. W. Howland, Third Cavalry, moved from Gray's Ranch, near the old Pecos Church, in the direction of Johnson's Ranch, in Apache Cañon, a point near which we reached about 2 o'clock p. m. We here discovered the enemy, about 250 or 300 strong, some 400 or 500 yards in front of us. They had two pieces of artillery in position on the road, and were awaiting us. As soon as our column appeared they opened fire with their battery, and, though they kept it up between five and ten minutes at close range, did us no damage. They then retired with their guns, and our

entire force, infantry and cavalry, advanced about 600 or 800 yards farther on the road. At this point my company was ordered to dismount
and assist Captain Wynkoop's company of Colorado Volunteers in
clearing the hills to the left and front of our position. Some little skirmishing occurred after this at long range, but the enemy fell back so
rapidly that we scarcely got sight of them.

By this time the firing had ceased at every point of the field and
the troops were recalled to the road, where my company remained
until about 9.30 o'clock that night, when I retired to Pigeon's Ranch
and rejoined Colonel Chivington. Next morning we marched to old
Pecos Church, at which place Colonel Slough united all of the forces.
On the following morning (March 28) the entire command, my company in advance, moved to Pigeon's Ranch, where we halted about
an hour and a half, after which we started on. We had not, however,
proceeded more than 600 or 700 yards before we discovered the enemy
in force immediately in front of us. They, as on the 26th, had their
artillery (three pieces) in the road, ready to receive us. As soon as I
learned the position of their guns I at once moved into the timber on
our left, and dismounted my company and commenced skirmishing on
foot. About this time Captain Ritter's battery arrived, and, supported
by the infantry, took position in the road on my right. As soon as he
opened on the enemy's guns my company was ordered to mount and
follow the colonel commanding. I followed Colonel Slough, in obedience to this order, for a half or three-quarters of an hour, by which
time the action had become general. I was then ordered to occupy
the high ridge running obliquely back from the road and on the right
of Pigeon's house. I did so, and held that position during the remainder of the day, or at least until our forces had retired from the field.
While in this position we at several times during the day had some
skirmishing with the enemy in small parties. The company, though
under fire a great part of the day, accomplished nothing that I remember of special importance, though they did all that the position assigned
them required. The officer (Lieut. Sidney Banks) and men behaved
handsomely whenever brought under the enemy's fire, and gave every
evidence of a willingness and determination to do any duty that might
be required of them. The strength of the company (E, Third U. S. Cavalry) during these two actions was one officer (Lieut. Sidney Banks,
Third Cavalry) besides myself and about 40 or 45 enlisted men.

I am, sir, very respectfully, your obedient servant,

C. J. WALKER,
Second Cavalry, Commanding Company E, Third Cavalry.

Lieut. N. M. MACRAE,
Fourth New Mexico Volunteers, Act. Asst. Adjt. Gen.

MARCH 28, 1862.—Engagement at Glorieta, or Pigeon's Ranch, N. Mex.

REPORTS.

No. 1.—Col. John P. Slough, First Colorado Infantry.
No. 2.—Lieut. Col. Samuel F. Tappan, First Colorado Infantry.
No. 3.—Maj. John M. Chivington, First Colorado Infantry.
No. 4.—Capt. John F. Ritter, Fifteenth U. S. Infantry, commanding light battery.
No. 5.—Brig. Gen. Henry H. Sibley, C. S. Army.
No. 6.—Col William R. Scurry, Fourth Texas Cavalry.

No. 1.

Reports of Col. John P. Slough, First Colorado Infantry.

KOZLOWSKI'S RANCH, *March* 29, 1862.

COLONEL : Learning from our spies that the enemy, about 1,000 strong, were in the Apache Cañon and at Johnson's Ranch beyond, I concluded to reconnoiter in force, with a view of ascertaining the position of the enemy and of harassing them as much as possible ; hence left this place with my command, nearly 1,300 strong, at 8 o'clock yesterday morning. To facilitate the reconnaissance I sent Maj. J. M. Chivington, First Regiment Colorado Volunteers, by a road running to the left of the cañon and nearly parallel thereto, with about 430 officers and picked men, with instructions to push forward to Johnson's. With the remainder of the command I entered the cañon, and had attained but a short distance when our pickets announced that the enemy was near and had taken position in a thick grove of trees, with their line extending from mesa to mesa across the cañon, and their battery, consisting of four pieces, placed in position. I at once detailed a considerable force of flankers, placed the batteries in position, and placed the cavalry—nearly all dismounted—and the remainder of the infantry in position to support the batteries.

Before the arrangement of my forces was completed the enemy opened fire upon us. The action began about 10 o'clock and continued until after 4 p. m. The character of the country was such as to make the engagement of the bushwhacking kind. Hearing of the success of Major Chivington's command, and the object of our movement being successful, we fell back in order to our camp. Our loss in killed is probably 20, including Lieutenant Baker, of Company I, Colorado Volunteers; in wounded probably 50, including Lieutenant Chambers, of Company C, Colorado Volunteers, and Lieutenant McGrath, U. S. Army, who was serving with Captain Ritter's battery; in missing probably 30. The enemy's loss is in killed from 40 to 60 and wounded probably over 100. In addition we took some 25 prisoners and rendered unfit for service three pieces' of their artillery. We took and destroyed their train of about 60 wagons, with their contents, consisting of ammunition, subsistence, forage, clothing, officers' baggage, &c. Among the killed of the enemy 2 majors, 2 captains and among the prisoners are 2 captains and 1 lieutenant. During the engagement the enemy made three attempts to take our batteries and were repelled in each with severe loss.

The strength of the enemy, as received from spies and prisoners, in the cañon was altogether some 1,200 or 1,300, some 200 of whom were at or near Johnson's Ranch, and were engaged by Major Chivington's command.

The officers and men behaved nobly. My thanks are due to my staff officers for the courage and ability with which they assisted me in conducting the engagement.

As soon as all the details are ascertained I will send an official report of the engagement.

Very respectfully,

JNO. P. SLOUGH,
Colonel, Commanding Northern Division, Army of New Mexico.

Col. E. R. S. CANBY,
Commanding Department of New Mexico.

HEADQUARTERS NORTHERN DIVISION, U. S. FORCES,
San José, N. Mex., March 30, 1862.

SIR: As the department commander is at Fort Craig, beyond the lines of the enemy, I have the honor to submit direct a synopsis of the military operations of the division since it̀s organization at Fort Union. When an opportunity occurs a complete report will be submitted through the proper channels.

After the arrival of the First Regiment Colorado Volunteers at Fort Union I found that Colonel Paul, Fourth Regiment New Mexico Volunteers, had completed the preliminary arrangements for throwing a column of troops into the field, and by seniority of volunteer commission I claimed the command. Accordingly the following division was organized and I assumed the command of the whole: First Colorado Volunteers, aggregate 916; Captain Lewis' battalion Fifth Infantry and Captain Ford's company volunteers (Fourth New Mexico), three companies, 191; Captain Howland's cavalry detachment of First and Third Cavalry and Company E, Third Cavalry, 150; Captain Ritter's battery, four guns, 53; Lieutenant Claflin's battery, four small howitzers, 32. Total, 1,342.

The movement commenced from Fort Union on Saturday, the 22d March, and the command encamped at Bernal Springs, 45 miles from Union, on Tuesday, the 25th instant. On Wednesday, the 26th instant, a command of 200 cavalry and 180 infantry, under Major Chivington, was advanced toward Santa Fé, with a view of capturing or defeating a force of the enemy reported to be stationed there. The enemy in force was engaged near Johnson's Ranch, Apache Cañon, about 15 miles on this side of Santa Fé. The result was victorious to our forces. The enemy was defeated, with some 20 to 25 killed, more wounded, and about 70 prisoners, who fell intò our hands. Our loss was small—3 men killed in battle, 2 since died, and some 8 others wounded. Among the wounded is Captain Cook, Colorado Volunteers, badly. I regret to report that Lieutenant Marshall, Colorado Volunteers, accidentally shot himself while breaking a loaded musket which he held in his hand by the muzzle. Having accomplished this, Major Chivington's command took position on the Pecos, at Kozłowski's Ranch, 27 miles from Santa Fé.

About noon on the 27th I left Camp Paul, at Bernal Springs, and about 2 o'clock next morning I had posted my entire force at Kozłowski's. On the 28th a movement was made upon the enemy in two columns, with a view of reconnoitering his position at Johnson's Ranch. For this purpose an infantry force of regulars and volunteers, under Major Chivington, was directed to move off on the Gallisteo road, attain the principal heights upon the side of Apache Cañon, and occupy them, while the main body, under my command, moved directly into the cañon. It was known before this movement was made that the enemy had been strongly re-enforced, and his estimated strength was from 1,200 to 1,400.

At 9 o'clock we left our encampment, and at 10.30 a. m. we arrived at Pigeon's Ranch, 5 miles distant, the command uǹder Major Chivington having flanked off at a point about 2 miles beyond Kozłowski's. We had just reached Pigeon's when I directed Captain Chapin, Seventh Infantry, adjutant-general, to proceed forward with the cavalry and reconnoiter the position of the enemy. He had proceeded but about 300 yards when our pickets were driven in, and the enemy opened a fire of grape and shell from a battery carefully placed in position upon the hill-side above. The batteries were brought forward and the infantry thrown out upon the flanks. The cavalry, with an addition of infantry, supported the batteries, and the firing became general. The battle continued over five hours. The fighting was all done in thick covers of cedars, and having met the enemy where he was not expected the action was defensive from its beginning to its end. Major Chivington's command continued on toward Johnson's, where some 200 of the enemy were posted, and fell upon the enemy's train of 60 wagons, capturing and destroying it and capturing and destroying one 6-pounder gun, and taking 2 officers and about 15 men prisoners. The loss of this train was a most serious disaster to the enemy, destroying his baggage and ammunition, and depriving him of provisions, of which he was short. Much praise is due to the officers and men of Major Chivington's command.

About 5 o'clock p. m. a flag of truce came from the enemy, and measures were taken by both forces to gather up the dead and take care of the wounded. Our loss is not great. We have 1 officer (Lieutenant Baker, Colorado Volunteers) killed and 2 (Lieutenant McGrath, U. S. Army, and Lieutenant Chambers, Colorado Volunteers) wounded; 28 men killed and 40 wounded. We lost some 15 prisoners. The loss of the enemy is great. His killed amount to at least 100, his wounded at least 150, and 1 captain and several men prisoners. He is still burying his dead. It is claimed in the battles of the 26th and 28th together that we damaged the enemy at least 350 killed, wounded, and prisoners, and have destroyed their entire train and three pieces of artillery—one by Major Chivington and two by our batteries. We have killed 5 of their officers—2 majors, 1 captain, and 2 lieutenants—and have captured 5 more—2 captains and 3 lieutenants. This has been done with the purpose of annoying and harassing the enemy and under orders from Colonel Canby, commanding department. But as the instructions from him are to protect Fort Union at all hazards and leave nothing to chance, and as the numbers and position of the enemy in a mountain cañon are too strong to make a battle with my force, I shall now occupy a position to protect Fort Union and at the same time harass and damage the enemy.

Officers and men, regulars and volunteers, all acquitted themselves handsomely during both engagements. It is especially proper that praise should be accorded Captain Ritter and Lieutenant Claflin, U. S. Army, for the efficient manner in which they handled their batteries during the battle of the 28th instant.

I desire to notice the members of my staff for the efficient manner in which they assisted me in the battle of Pigeon's Ranch, and especially Captain Chapin, U. S. Army, assistant adjutant-general; Lieutenants Bonesteel and Cobb, of the Colorado Volunteers, and Mr. J. Howe Watts, volunteer aide, upon all of whom fell the heavier portion of dangerous duty during the battle, and whose intelligent, courageous, and prompt action contributed much towards the result attained.

In conclusion, I would add that to Captain Chapin, whose connection with me was the most intimate, and upon whom fell the burden of duty, I owe and return especial thanks.

I have the honor to be, with much respect, your obedient servant,

JNO. P. SLOUGH,
Colonel First Regiment Colorado Volunteers, Commanding.

The ADJUTANT-GENERAL U. S. ARMY,
Washington City, D. C.

No. 2.

Report of Lieut. Col. Samuel F. Tappan, First Colorado Infantry.

SANTA FÉ, N. MEX., *May* 21, 1862.

In compliance with orders just received from department headquarters I have the honor herewith to submit report of engagement at Glorieta, or Pigeon's Ranch, on the 28th March last, between the forces of the enemy, under Colonel Scurry, and Colonel Slough's column of Colorado Volunteers, Howland's cavalry, Ritter's and Claflin's batteries, of four guns each.

On the morning of the day last mentioned I was assigned to the immediate command of a battalion of infantry, consisting of Companies C, Captain Sopris; D, Captain Downing; G, Captain Wilder; I, Captain Maile, and K, Captain Robbins, First Colorado Volunteers. A battery of four guns—two 12-pounders and two 6-pounders—Captain Ritter, Regular Army, and four 12-pounder mountain howitzers, Lieutenant Claflin, U. S. Regular Army, were attached to my command. We marched out of camp near the Old Pecos Church, Howland's cavalry in advance, and proceeded about 5 miles down the road toward Santa Fé to Glorieta, situated in a deep, narrow, and thickly-wooded cañon. While my command was at a rest information of the immediate presence of the enemy was brought by some pickets falling back on Captain Howland's advance. They reported the enemy in position in the timber about 800 yards in advance. My command was immediately formed, and in obedience to the orders of Colonel Slough I advanced half that distance at a double-quick, where the batteries were stationed on a slight elevation in and to the left of the road. Company D deployed to the left and Company I to the right, to occupy the hill-sides as skirmishers; Company C was assigned to the support of Ritter's and Company K Claflin's batteries. The enemy were concealed among the trees, and opened fire upon us with their batteries, which was promptly returned by ours, and our skirmishers from the hill-sides discharged volley after volley among the enemy with telling effect.

Company I, in deploying to the right, passed an opening commanded by the enemy's batteries and suffered severely. They, however, reached the position assigned them and did excellent service. Occupied this position for nearly half an hour, when the order was given to fall back to a new position in front of and near the house of Mr. Pigeon. Claflin's battery took position on an eminence to the left and Ritter's occupied the road. At this juncture Company G, that morning detailed as rear guard, came up, and were assigned with Company C to support Ritter's battery. Subsequently the first platoon of this company, commanded by Captain Wilder, was ordered by Colonel Slough to deploy to the right as skirmishers. The enemy advanced and occupied the position we had left, and the firing was renewed and kept up a considerable time. Then our batteries fell back to their third position.

While the batteries occupied their second position Captain Chapin and myself were requested to accompany Colonel Slough up the hill to the right to reconnoiter. It was there suggested to the colonel the necessity of occupying the hill to the left with skirmishers, to prevent the enemy from outflanking us in that direction, to fall upon our rear, and destroy our train, and it would also afford support to our batteries. He thereupon ordered me to take 20 men from Captain Sopris' company and take position on the hill. These men were furnished, and not considering them sufficient I took the police guard, not yet assigned to any special duty, numbering about 70 men, and with them took position in front of and to the left of the batteries on the summit of the hill, extending my line of skirmishers for nearly three-quarters of a mile in a half circle and at nearly a right angle from the road occupied by our train of 100 wagons. This position commanded the valley in part, and the irregularities of the surface afforded excellent protection for the men from the fire of the enemy. Remained here for about four hours. Occasionally small parties of the enemy would attempt to ascend the hill toward my line, but were driven back as often as they made their appearance.

Before the batteries had fallen back to their third position I noticed 200 or 300 of the enemy nearly a mile off assembling. Apprehending that they were preparing to charge our batteries, I descended to the valley and communicated my apprehensions to Colonel Slough. Soon after, returning to the position assigned me on the hill, I received information from Colonel Slough that the enemy evidently intended to charge my skirmishers to get my position, from which they could assault our battery and train; was ordered to hold it at all hazards, for all depended upon it; also to be in readiness to advance and attack the enemy's flank when he should charge him in front, which he designed doing as soon as Major Chivington should attack him in rear, which he expected every moment. About half an hour afterward a party approached my line, dressed in the uniform of the Colorado Volunteers, requesting us not to shoot, as they were our own men. They were allowed to come within a few paces of us, when, not giving satisfactory answers to interrogations in reference to their commanders and recognizing them as Texans, my men were ordered to fire. The enemy suddenly disappeared, leaving several dead and wounded. Apprehending at this time the arrival of Major Chivington with his command to attack the enemy's rear and that some of his men might get in our front while deployed as skirmishers, I was therefore extremely cautious not to give the order to fire on parties approaching until they were near enough to be recognized.

At the time the enemy charged our battery a battalion of the enemy made its appearance among the trees before us, approaching the center of my line, Major Shropshire and Captain Shannon at head of column. When they had arrived to within a few paces of my skirmishers, Private Pierce, of Company F, Colorado Volunteers, approached them, killing and disarming the major and taking the captain prisoner. He returned to our main body and delivered over his prisoner to Captain Chapin, U. S. Army. The fire of my skirmishers was directed against the head of the still advancing column with such rapidity and effectiveness that the enemy were compelled to retire, with the loss of several killed and wounded. They once again appeared in the valley, but were repulsed and driven back. Our column had fallen back from the valley to my right a considerable distance. The enemy occupied the place we had left. Considering it extremely hazardous to remain longer, and thereby enable the enemy to get in my rear and cut me off from support of our battery and protection of our train, I ordered my men to fall back and close in in the rear of the retiring column, which they did in good order at a point nearly 2 miles back, and then returned to the camp we left in the morning.

Not having at my command at this time the several reports of commanders of companies engaged in the battle I am consequently unable to particularize individual acts of heroism, and the exact number of killed, wounded, and missing. Therefore my report must necessarily be incomplete. I would, however, remark that an estimate was made after the battle of the casualties of my command, and, if my memory serves me, 29 killed, 64 wounded, and 13 missing. Companies D and I, First Colorado Volunteers, were the greatest sufferers. Several of the wounded have since died from the effects of their wounds, making the number killed 38. The missing were taken prisoners by the enemy, one of whom escaped. The others were released on their paroles. Lieutenant Baker, of Company I, was severely wounded during the early part of the engagement, and afterward beaten to death by the enemy with the butt of a musket or club and his body stripped of its clothing. He was found the next morning, his head scarcely recognizable, so horribly mangled. He fought gallantly, and the vengeance of the foe pursued him after death. Lieutenant Chambers, of Company C, Colorado Volunteers, was also severely wounded, from which there is but little hope of his recovery. He proved himself a gallant officer.

Suffice it to say that officers and men acted with great gallantry, and where all did so well to particularize and refer to individuals becomes unnecessary.

I have the honor to remain, yours, with respect,

SAM. F. TAPPAN,
Lieutenant-Colonel, First Regiment Colorado Infantry Vols.

Capt. G. CHAPIN,
7th Inf., U. S. A., A. A. A. G., Dept. Hdqrs., Santa Fé, N. Mex.

No. 3.

Report of Maj. John M. Chivington, First Colorado Infantry.

CAMP LEWIS, NEAR PECOS CHURCH, N. MEX.,
March 28, 1862.

GENERAL: I have the honor to submit to you the following report of the troops under my command on the 28th of March, 1862, at the battle of Pigeon's Ranch:

In obedience to General Orders, No. —, issued to me on the morning of this day, with the following command: 1st, Captain Lewis' battalion, assisted by Captain Carey, consisting of 60 men; Companies A and G, Fifth Infantry, in charge of Lieutenants Barr and Norvell; Company B, First Regiment Colorado Volunteers, 78 men, in charge of Capt. S. M. Logan and Lieutenant Jacobs, and Capt. James H. Ford's company, Second Colorado Volunteers, in charge of Captain Ford and Lieutenant De Forrest. 2d, Captain Wynkoop's battalion, consisting of Company A, First Regiment Colorado Volunteers, in charge of Lieutenant Shaffer, 68 men; Company E, First Regiment Colorado Volunteers, in charge of Capt. Scott J. Anthony and Lieut. J. A. Dawson, 71 men; Company H, First Regiment Colorado Volunteers, in charge of Capt. George L. Sanborn and Lieut. B. N. Sanford, numbering about 80 men, I left Camp Lewis at 8.30 o'clock a. m., and at 9.30 o'clock a. m. we left the main road and took the trail leading to Gallisteo, which we kept for 8 miles, and then without road we traveled about 8 miles, and about 1.30 o'clock p. m. we reached an eminence overlooking Johnson's Ranch.

After reconnoitering the position it was ascertained that there were corraled in the cañon 80 wagons and one field piece, all in charge of some 200 men. The command was given to charge, and the troops started upon double-quick. Captain Wynkoop, with 30 of his men, were deployed to the mountain side to silence their guns by picking off their gunners, which they did effectually, Captain Lewis capturing and spiking the gun after having five shots discharged at him. The remainder of the command surrounded the wagons and buildings, killing 3 and wounding several of the enemy. The wagons were all heavily loaded with ammunition, clothing, subsistence, and forage, all of which were burned upon the spot or rendered entirely useless. During the engagement one of the wagons containing ammunition exploded, severely wounding Private Ritter, of Company A, First Colorado Volunteers; the only person injured. We retook 5 privates, who had been taken in the forenoon in the battle between Slough's and Scurry's forces, from whom we gleaned our first intelligence of the general engagement, and upon reaching the summit of the mountain we were met by Lieutenant Cobb, bringing an order from Colonel Slough for our advance to support the main column, which we hastened to obey. We also took 17 prisoners, and captured about thirty horses and mules, which were in a corral in the vicinity of the wagons.

Both officers and men performed their duty efficiently. Captain Lewis had the most dangerous duty assigned him, which he performed with unfaltering heroism. I repeat, all, ALL did well. The command returned to Camp Lewis about 10 o'clock p. m. the same day.

I am, general, with much respect, your obedient servant,

J. M. CHIVINGTON,
Major, First Regiment Colorado Volunteers.

P. S.—I ought in justice to say that a Mr. Collins, in some way connected with Indian affairs in this Territory, and one of Colonel Slough's volunteer aides, by his own request and Colonel Slough's desire accompanied the command, and gave evidence that he was a brave man, and did us good service as a guide and interpreter, though he did not burn the train or cause it to be done.

J. M. C.

27 killed; 63 wounded. Total, 90.

No. 4.

Report of Capt. John F. Ritter, Fifteenth U. S. Infantry, commanding light battery.

FORT UNION, N. MEX., *May* 16, 1862.

SIR: Pursuant to a letter dated Headquarters, Department of New Mexico, Santa Fé, N. Mex., May 15, 1862, I have the honor to submit the following report:

The light battery which I commanded in the action of Pigeon's Ranch was composed of two 12-pounder howitzers and two 6-pounder guns, without caissons, there being none then in the department. Its total strength consisted of 3 commissioned officers, 4 non-commissioned, and 46 enlisted men present. The commissioned officers, besides myself, were First Lieut. P. McGrath, Sixth Cavalry, and Second Lieut. R. S. Underhill, Fourth New Mexico Volunteers. The order for the formation of this battery was dated March 9, 1862, and on March 23 it was ordered with Colonel Slough's column into the field. On March 28 the enemy was reported in advance, and the battery was ordered to the front to a position in the road a few hundred yards west of

Pigeon's Ranch, where it commenced fire upon the enemy. After firing a number of rounds I was ordered to take position farther to the rear and south of the road, some distance from it. Here I was exposed to a galling fire without being able to return it effectually, the enemy being some distance off and entirely sheltered by trees, &c., and I was also some distance from my ammunition wagons. The supports to the battery were all ordered away with the exception of about one platoon of Colorado Volunteers, and I deemed it proper to return to the road, which I did after firing a few rounds. It was here that Lieutenant McGrath was fatally wounded. I then took position nearly in front of Pigeon's Ranch, and established one 6-pounder in the road, while the limber-boxes of the pieces, two at a time, went to the rear to be replenished. Here one of the enemy's pieces was dismounted by a round shot striking it full in the muzzle, and another was disabled and a limber-box was blown up by a case shot striking it. Private Kelly, Company E, Fifth Infantry, was gunner at the piece which did this execution.

From here I was ordered by Captain Chapin to cross the ravine to the other side of the cañon and take up a position there, which I did. Lieutenant Claflin's mountain howitzer battery joined and took position with me. The enemy here made a desperate charge on the batteries, and was repulsed with, I think, great loss. The enemy then got on the rocky hill on my right flank, and was pouring a destructive fire of small-arms in the batteries and killed two horses, so that I deemed it proper to withdraw from my position. Private G. H. Smith, Company E, Fifth Infantry, was killed, and Privates Raleigh and Woolsey, same company, and Private Leddy, Company I, Second Cavalry, were wounded at this place. I then took position some distance farther to the rear (this position was selected by Capt. G. Chapin, Seventh Infantry) in front of a deep ravine, where the supports were entirely sheltered from the enemy's fire. The supply train was in the road about 40 yards from the left of the battery. The enemy here made another desperate charge on the battery, and apparently also the train, but was again repulsed, with, I think, great loss and in great disorder. This was my last position, and I heard no more firing from either side afterwards. The command then retired for the day to Kozlowski's.

I wish to state in conclusion that I had made a night march the night before the action, and did not get into camp until 4 a. m., and officers and men were necessarily much fatigued. I was very much impeded in my movements by reason of the deficiency of caissons.

I am, sir, very respectfully, your obedient servant,

JOHN F. RITTER,
Captain, Fifteenth Infantry, Commanding Light Battery.

Capt. G. CHAPIN,
Seventh Inf., A. A. A. G., Dept. of N. Mex., Santa Fé, N. Mex.

No. 5.

Report of Brig. Gen. Henry H. Sibley, C. S. Army.

HEADQUARTERS ARMY OF NEW MEXICO,
Albuquerque, N. Mex., March 31, 1862.

GENERAL: I have the honor and the pleasure to report another victory.

After the battle of Valverde our advance was uninterrupted to this city. Here sufficient supplies were secured for sixty days, while from Cubero, a village 60 miles distant, large supplies have been drawn from the enemy's depot. We have been surrounded with every description of embarrassment, general and individual. Whole trains had been abandoned, and scantily provided, as they had originally been, with blankets and clothing, the men had, without a murmur, given up the little left them. More than all this, on the representation of their officers that forage could not be procured with one accord the regiment agreed to be dismounted.

These preliminary facts are stated because it is due to the brave men under my command that they should be known and the hand-to-hand desperate contests duly appreciated.

The battle of Glorieta was fought March 28 by detached troops, under the command of Lieutenant-Colonel Scurry, and Federal forces, principally Pike's Peakers, under the command of Colonel Slough; the one having 1,000 men and the other estimated at 1,500 or 2,000. Glorieta is a cañon 23 miles east of Santa Fé.

Pending the battle the enemy detached a portion of his forces to attack and destroy our supply train, which he succeeded in doing, thus crippling Colonel Scurry to such a degree that he was two days without provisions or blankets. The patient, uncomplaining endurance of our men is most remarkable and praiseworthy.

Our loss was 33 killed and 35 wounded. Among the killed are Majors Ragnet and Shropshire and Captain Buckholts. Colonel Scurry had his cheek twice grazed by Minie balls, and Major Pyron had his horse killed under him.

In consequence of the loss of his train Colonel Scurry has fallen back upon Santa Fé.

I must have re-enforcements. The future operations of this army will be duly reported. Send me re-enforcements.

I have the honor to be, very respectfully, your obedient servant,

H. H. SIBLEY,
Brigadier-General, Commanding.

General S. COOPER,
Adjutant and Inspector General, Richmond, Va.

No. 6.

Reports of Col. W. R. Scurry, Fourth Texas Cavalry.

SANTA FÉ, N. MEX., *March* 30, 1862.

GENERAL: I arrived here this morning with my command and have taken quarters for the present in this city. I will in a short time give you an official account of the battle of Glorieta, which occurred on day before yesterday, in the Cañon Glorieta, about 22 miles from this city, between the Confederate troops under my command and the Federal forces, commanded by Colonel Slough, of the Colorado Volunteers, (Pike's Peakers), when another victory was added to the long list of Confederate triumphs.

The action commenced at about 11 o'clock and ended at 5.30, and, although every inch of the ground was well contested, we steadily drove them back until they were in full retreat our men pursuing until from sheer exhaustion we were compelled to stop.

Our loss was 33 killed and, I believe, 35 wounded. Among the killed was that brave soldier and accomplished officer Major Ragnet, the gallant and impetuous Major Shropshire, and the daring Captain Buckholts, all of whom fell gallantly leading the men around against the foe. Major Pyron had his horse shot under him, and my own cheek was twice brushed by a Minie ball, each time just drawing blood, and my clothes torn in two places. I mention this simply to show how hot was the fire of the enemy when all of the field officers upon the ground were either killed or touched. As soon as I can procure a full report of all the casualties I will forward them.

Our train was burned by a party who succeeded in passing undiscovered around the mountains to our rear. I regret to have to report that they fired upon and severely wounded Rev. L. H. Jones, our chaplain, of the Fourth Regiment. He was holding in his hand a white flag when fired upon.

The loss of the enemy was very severe, being over 75 killed and a large number wounded.

The loss of my supplies so crippled me that after burying my dead I was unable to follow up the victory. My men for two days went unfed and blanketless unmurmuringly. I was compelled to come here for something to eat.

At last accounts the Federalists were still retiring towards Fort Union.

The men at the train blew up the limber-box and spiked the 6-pounder I had left at the train, so that it was rendered useless, and the cartburners left it.

Lieutenant Bennett writes for more ammunition. Please have it sent. As soon as I am fixed for it I wish to get after them again.

From three sources, all believed to be reliable, Canby left Craig on the 24th.

Yours, in haste,

W. R. SCURRY.

P. S.—I do not know if I write intelligently. I have not slept for three nights, and can scarcely hold my eyes open.

W. R. S.

SANTE FÉ, N. MEX., *March* 31, 1862.

MAJOR: Late on the afternoon of the 26th, while encamped at Gallisteo, an express from Major Pyron arrived, with the information that the major was engaged in a sharp conflict with a greatly superior force of the enemy, about 16 miles distant, and urging me to hasten to his relief. The critical condition of Major Pyron and his gallant comrades was made known to the command, and in ten minutes the column was formed and the order to march given. Our baggage train was sent forward under a guard of 100 men, under the command of Lieutenant Taylor, of the Seventh Regiment, to a point some 6 miles in the rear of Major Pyron's position, the main command marching directly across the mountains to the scene of conflict. It is due to the brave men making this cold night march to state that where the road over the mountain was too steep for the horses to drag the artillery they were unharnessed, and the men cheerfully pulled it over the difficulties of the way by hand.

About 3 o'clock in the morning we reached Major Pyron's encampment at Johnson's Ranch, Cañon Cito. There had been an agreed cessation of hostilities until 8 o'clock the next morning. Too much praise cannot be bestowed upon the courage of the officers and men engaged in the affair of the 26th.

As soon as daylight enabled me I made a thorough examination of the ground, and so formed the troops as to command every approach to the position we occupied, which was naturally a very strong one. The disposition of the troops was soon completed, and by 8 o'clock were ready to receive the expected attack.

In this position we remained until the next morning. The enemy still not making their appearance, I concluded to march forward and attack them. Leaving a small wagon guard, I marched in their direction with portions of nine companies of the Fourth Regiment, under their respective officers, Captains [George J.] Hampton, Lesueur, Foard, Crosson, Julius Giesecke, Alexander, Buckholts, [J. M.] Odell, and Lieutenant Holland, of Company B, Captain Scarborough being unwell; four companies of the Seventh Regiment, under Captains [Gustav] Hoffman, [J. W.] Gardner, [J. F.] Wiggins, and [Isaac] Adair; four companies of the Fifth Regiment, under Captains [Denman] Shannon and [Daniel H.] Ragsdale and Lieuts. Pleasant J. Oakes and John J. Scott; three pieces of artillery, under Lieutenant Bradford, together with Captain Phillips' company of independent volunteers.

From details and other causes they were reduced until (all combined) they did not number over 600 men fit for duty. At about 6 miles from our camp the advance guard gave notice that the enemy were near in force. I hastened in front to examine their position, and found they were about 1 mile west of Pigeon's Ranch, in Cañon Glorieta. The mounted men who were marching in front were ordered to retire slowly to the rear, dismount, and come into action on foot. The artillery was pushed forward to a slight elevation in the cañon and immediately opened fire. The infantry was rapidly deployed into line, extending across the cañon from a fence on our left up into the pine forest on our right.

About the time these dispositions were made the enemy rapidly advanced in separate columns both upon our right and left. I dispatched Major Pyron to the right to check them in that direction, and placing the center in command of Major Ragnet I hastened with the remainder of the command to the left. A large body of infantry, availing themselves of a gulch that ran up the center of an inclosed field to our left, were moving under its cover past our left flank to the rear of our position. Crossing the fence on foot, we advanced over the clearing some 200 yards under a heavy fire from the foe, and dashed into the gulch in their midst, pistol and knife in hand. For a few moments a most desperate and deadly hand-to-hand conflict raged along the gulch, when they broke before the steady courage of our men and fled in the wildest disorder and confusion.

Major Pyron was equally successful, and Major Ragnet with his force charged rapidly down the center. Lieutenant Bradford, of the artillery, had been wounded and borne from the field. There being no other officer of the artillery present, three guns, constituting our battery, had been hastily withdrawn before I was aware of it. Sending to the rear to have two of the guns brought back to the field a pause was made to reunite our forces, which had become somewhat scattered in the last rencounter. When we were ready to advance the enemy had taken cover, and it was impossible to tell whether their main body was stationed behind a long adobe wall that ran nearly across the cañou or had taken position behind a large ledge of rocks in the rear.   Private W. D. Kirk, of Captain Phillips' company, had taken charge of one of the guns, and Sergeant Patrick, of the artillery, another, and brought them to the ground.

While trying by the fire of these two guns to ascertain the locality of the enemy, Major Shropshire was sent to the right, with orders to move up among the pines until he should find the enemy, when he was to attack them on that flank.   Major Ragnet, with similar orders, was dispatched to the left.   I informed these gallant officers that as soon as the sound of their guns was heard I would charge in front with the remainder of the command.   Sending Major Pyron to the assistance of Major Ragnet, and leaving instruction for the center to charge as the fire opened on the right, I passed in that direction to learn the cause of delay in making the assault.   I found that the gallant Major Shropshire had been killed.   I took command of the right and immediately attacked the enemy who were at the ranch.   Majors Ragnet and Pyron opened a galling fire upon their left from the rock on the mountain side, and the center charging down the road, the foe were driven from the ranch to the ledge of rocks before alluded to, where they made their final and most desperate stand.   At this point three batteries of eight guns opened a furious fire of grape, canister, and shell upon our advancing troops.

Our brave soldiers, heedless of the storm, pressed on, determined if possible to take their battery.   A heavy body of infantry, twice our number, interposed to save their guns.   Here the conflict was terrible. Our men and officers, alike inspired with the unalterable determination to overcome every obstacle to the attainment of their object, dashed among them.   The right and center had united on the left.   The intrepid Ragnet and the cool, calm, courageous Pyron had pushed forward among the rocks until the muzzles of the guns of the opposing forces passed each other.   Inch by inch was the ground disputed, until the artillery of the enemy had time to escape with a number of their wagons.   The infantry also broke ranks and fled from the field.   So precipitate was their flight that they cut loose their teams and set fire to two of their wagons.   The pursuit was kept up until forced to halt from the extreme exhaustion of the men, who had been engaged for six hours in the hardest contested fight it had ever been my lot to witness.   The enemy is now known to have numbered 1,400 men, Pike's Peak miners and regulars, the flower of the U. S. Army.

During the action a part of the enemy succeeded in reaching our rear, surprising the wagon guard, and burning our wagons, taking at the same time some 16 prisoners.   About this time a party of prisoners, whom I had sent to the rear, reached there, and informed them how the fight was going in front; whereupon they beat a hasty retreat, not, however, until the perpetration of two acts which the most barbarous savage of the plains would blush to own.   One was the shooting and dangerously wounding of the Rev. L. H. Jones, chaplain of the Fourth Regiment, with a white flag in his hand; the other an order that the prisoners they had taken be shot in case they were attacked on their retreat.   These instances go to prove that they have lost all sense of humanity in the insane hatred they bear to the citizens of the Confederacy, who have the manliness to arm in defense of their country's independence.

We remained upon the battle-field during the day of the 29th to bury our dead and provide for the comfort of the wounded, and then marched to Santa Fé, to procure supplies and transportation to replace those destroyed by the enemy.

Our loss was 36 killed and 60 wounded. Of the killed 24 were of the Fourth Regiment, 1 of the Fifth Regiment, 8 of the Seventh Regiment, and 1 of the artillery.

That of the enemy greatly exceeded this number, 44 of their dead being counted where the battle first opened. Their killed must have considerably exceeded 100.

The country has to mourn the loss of four as brave and chivalrous officers as ever graced the ranks of any army. The gallant Major Shropshire fell early, pressing upon the foe and cheering his men on. The brave and chivalrous Major Ragnet fell mortally wounded while engaged in the last and most desperate conflict of the day. He survived long enough to know and rejoice at our victory, and then died with loving messages upon his expiring lips. The brave, gallant Captain Buckholts and Lieutenant Mills conducted themselves with distinguished gallantry throughout the fight and fell near its close. Of the living it is only necessary to say all behaved with distinguished courage and daring.

This battle proves conclusively that few mistakes were made in the selection of the officers in this command. They were ever in the front, leading their men into the hottest of the fray. It is not too much to say that, even in the midst of this heroic band, among whom instances of individual daring and personal prowess were constantly occurring, Major Pyron was distinguished by the calm intrepidity of his bearing. It is due to Adjt. Ellsberry R. Lane to bear testimony to the courage and activity he displayed in the discharge of his official duties, and to acknowledge my obligations for the manner in which he carried out my orders.

I have the honor to be, very respectfully, your obedient servant,

W. R. SCURRY,
Colonel, Commanding Army of New Mexico.

Maj. A. M. JACKSON,
Assistant Adjutant-General, Army of New Mexico.

APRIL 5–6, 1862.—Affair at San Luis Pass, Tex., including destruction of the Columbia.

REPORTS.

No. 1.—Col. J. Bates, Thirteenth Texas Infantry.
No. 2.—Maj. S. S. Perry, Thirteenth Texas Infantry.
No. 3.—Capt. S. L. S. Ballowe, Thirteenth Texas Infantry.

No 1.

Reports of Col. J. Bates, Thirteenth Texas Infantry.

HEADQUARTERS BATES' REGIMENT,
Velasco, Tex., April 6, 1862.

SIR: I have the honor to report as follows:

Information reached my headquarters at 7 p. m. on yesterday that at 4 p. m. of that day a large steamer anchored off San Luis Pass, displaying an English and a Confederate ensign and what seemed to be from the shore a white flag. I immediately dispatched a detachment of 25 mounted men from Captain Moseley's company, under the command of Maj. S. S. Perry, with instructions to watch the enemy closely and prevent depredations in case of their attempting to land.

When about half way to San Luis, which is 16 miles from this post, Major Perry met an expressman, who stated that Lieut. O. W. Edwards, of Captain Ballowe's company, and 7 of his men, with Mr. Alexander Follett, residing near the Pass, had been decoyed out to the steamer and captured; that the enemy had then taken the boat in which Edwards and his men had gone out and had passed our battery (one 18-pounder) on San Luis Island, and were between the island and the main-land; that it was supposed that they had captured the schooner Columbia, lying in the rear of the island, loaded with cotton; that their force was unknown, and Captain Ballowe's command was in danger of being cut off.

I immediately dispatched Lieut. Col. R. R. Brown, with the remainder of Captain Moseley's artillery company and two field pieces, to the scene of action. [Lieutenant] Colonel Brown arrived at San Luis at daylight this morning. The Columbia was then in flames and nearly consumed, the enemy having retired to their vessel.

At daylight an action commenced between our battery, under Lieutenant-Colonel Brown, and the enemy's vessel, in which a few shots were exchanged and the enemy drew off. As she steamed down the coast she sent the crew of the destroyed cotton schooner ashore in a small boat, retaining Lieutenant Edwards and his men as prisoners. No other casualties on our side.

Captain Ballowe was absent from his command when the vessel arrived, and did not reach there until late in the night. The night was very dark and the force of the enemy in the bay was unknown. Our best boat was captured and the others were too frail to risk a night attack from the small force on the island.

Further particulars will be reported as soon as information can be received, with a list of the prisoners.

J. BATES,
Colonel, Commanding.

Col. SAMUEL BOYER DAVIS,
  Acting Assistant Adjutant-General, Department of Texas.

HEADQUARTERS BATES' REGIMENT,
Velasco, Tex., April 13, 1862.

Col. SAMUEL BOYER DAVIS,
  Acting Assistant Adjutant-General, Department of Texas:

SIR: I have the honor to submit to you copies of reports made by Major Perry and Captain Ballowe, of my command. These reports are in reference to the unfortunate capture of Lieutenant Edwards and 7 of Captain Ballowe's company and the burning of the schooner Columbia and her cargo of cotton.

It seems to me that the conduct of Captain Ballowe on that occasion, as represented by Major Perry, deserves a court-martial. However, the reports are respectfully submitted for your consideration.

  Very respectfully,

J. BATES,
Colonel, Commanding.

No. 2.

Report of Maj. S. S. Perry, Thirteenth Texas Infantry.

HEADQUARTERS BATES' REGIMENT,
Velasco, April 7, 1862.

SIR: I have the honor to lay before you for your consideration the following report:

According to your order, issued to me April 5, I detailed Lieutenant Duff and 25 men of Captain Mosley's company, and proceeded down the coast to San Luis. When about 6 miles from this place I met Mr. Follett with an express from Captain Ballowe, who informed me that the enemy had decoyed off Lieutenant Edwards, Orderly-Sergeant Westervelt, Sergeant Carville, and 5 privates of Captain Ballowe's company, and Alexander Follett, citizen, and that they had passed into the bay in small boats from the steamship, which lay about 2 miles from the fort and near the bar, and he (Mr. Follett) supposed their object to have been to capture the schooner Columbia, loaded with cotton, which was lying in the bay near San Luis Island, or attack the said island. I then ordered one of my party to return immediately and report the above facts to Colonel Bates. I then proceeded to San Luis at a very rapid gait, and arrived there about 10.30 p. m., and immediately ordered out and posted scouts on the east end of the peninsula, and went to the fort and had an interview with Captain Ballowe. During said interview he informed me that the schooner Columbia was captured by the enemy, and that there must have been at least 100 of the enemy on board of her. They also captured a small sail-boat with passengers (the number I did not ascertain), which had been sent by the enemy out to the steamship, and that he expected to be attacked by the enemy with about 300 men, and that he wanted 100 more men.

I will also state, sir, that the enemy set the schooner on fire, and that it was burning when I got to San Luis. Thus matters stood when I arrived. I detailed a scout from my party, on ascertaining the above, to proceed to Velasco, to report the condition of affairs to Colonel Bates. I went from the island to the mainland for said purpose, and sent Lieutenant Duff with 5 men to re-enforce Captain Ballowe, and also sent orders to Captain Ballowe to have all his small boats concentrated at a point designated by me, intending to follow immediately when I had made the necessary arrangements with my pickets on the mainland.

During my absence, after those arrangements were made, I went to the beach to cross over to the island, at which time I was informed that Captain Ballowe had not concentrated his boats, but had made arrangements for abandoning the island, having sent back Lieutenant Duff, with the 5 men that I sent him and his entire company, under command of his first lieutenant, reserving only 13 men on the island, all of which acts were contrary to my orders, and in my opinion premature and not necessary; and on the arrival of the first lieutenant he informed me that Captain Ballowe and 13 men were coming off the island at once. I then ordered the first lieutenant (having waited some time for the arrival of Captain Ballowe) to collect all the small boats that he could, and after considerable delay he succeeded in collecting three or four small boats, which would have only carried about four men each. I then waited with the boats and the men under my command on the east end of the peninsula, momentarily expecting Captain Ballowe's arrival, expecting some information from him. Not daring to trust my command to any person else in case of an attack by the enemy, and while thus waiting, Lieutenant-Colonel Brown, with the balance of Captain Moseley's men, arrived. After consulting with [Lieutenant] Colonel Brown I went over to the fort, and found Captain Ballowe, Lieutenant Taylor, and a few men at the fort; the balance of his command were scattered about.

I remained at the fort until daylight, at which time I discovered four boats, two of which belonged to the enemy, and two with the passengers and crew of the Columbia, that had been captured. They were then lying about one mile and a half from the fort. As soon as I discovered them I ordered Captain Ballowe to fire on the enemy's boats, which he did, this being the first cannon-shot fired, though the steamer had been lying since 1 o'clock the previous day within firing distance of the fort. After firing [Lieutenant] Colonel Brown arrived at the fort, when our shot was answered by one from the steamship. [Lieutenant] Colonel Brown then took command and fired again, exchanging some six shots, none of which took effect. The captured passengers and crew of the Columbia having been sent on shore from the steamer, she weighed anchor and put to sea.

Colonel, I will say, in conclusion, that had the orders I issued to Captain Ballowe on my arrival been carried out, I have not the slightest doubt but that I could have got between the steamer and the party sent to burn the cotton schooner and captured every one of them; but my orders being disregarded, all my efforts proved abortive.

I am, sir, very respectfully, your obedient servant,

S. S. PERRY,
Major, Bates' Regiment.

Col. J. BATES, *Commanding Bates' Regiment.*

No. 3.

Report of Capt. S. L. S. Ballowe, Thirteenth Texas Infantry.

FORT SAN LUIS, TEX., *April 5, 1862.*

SIR: I have to report to you the capture of Second Lieut. O. W. Edwards and 7 others of my command off this post on yesterday by the Federal screw propeller Montgomery, Captain Hunter, under the following circumstances, viz: She appeared off the bar with English colors, with a signal for a pilot, and fired a blank cartridge and anchored. After some time Lieutenant Edwards sent the life-boat out to the bar, with instructions to anchor inside and hoist a white flag and wait for them to meet them with a boat from the steamer. The crew obeyed instructions, but the steamer refusing to send a boat, as expected, they raised anchor and returned to the fort. By this time Mr. A. G. Follett arrived at the fort with the intention of getting the life-boat and a crew and going out to her, and was so well satisfied that she was an English vessel, that he induced the lieutenant to take a boat and go out. They went aboard about 3 p. m. I returned to my quarters at 3.30 p. m. and watched their movements until night. About this time I saw one boat leave the steamer and come in the direction of the fort, and as soon as she arrived inside the bar I discovered that there were two instead of one, and supposed their destination to be the schooner Columbia, lying in the bay and laden with cotton, or else that they intended an attack on this island. It soon grew so dark, however, that I could not see them, and made my arrangements as best I could with my small force to receive them, but the sentinel placed near the entrance to the canal saw them going to the schooner and fired on them. My first intention was to throw 15 or 20 men on the schooner, but it would have taken all the boats I had to do so, and only left me with about that number of men and no means of retreat in case I should be compelled to do so. Believing it to be unwise and unsafe to attempt to save her and sustain myself on the island, I concluded to let her go, knowing that it was impossible for them to get her out, the wind and tide both being against them. I had also sent to Major Perry for re-enforcements, by the aid of which I hoped to be enabled not only to hold my position, but to take the crew that had been sent to the schooner. As soon as they got possession of her they made a signal-light on her, which was answered by the steamer. After about an hour the sentinel nearest the schooner saw three boats leave and pull over near the Galveston shore, returning to the steamer, the signal-light still burning on deck and no evidences of her being on fire, which forced me to the conclusion that they had left a crew on board and went after a force to attack me.

About 11 o'clock Major Perry arrived and reported re-enforcements to the number of 25 men on the main-land, but that there were only 5 or 6 of them armed, and that he had sent for 40 or 50 more. I requested him to return to his men and as soon as the others arrived to bring them over.

[I] waited until 1.30 o'clock and no assistance came, and expecting an attack every moment, and knowing that I had only boats enough to take off 25 or 30 men, I deemed it prudent to send off a portion of my men, and did so, with instructions that if re-enforcements came up to return to the island. Lieutenant-Colonel Brown arrived with re-enforcements on the opposite side of the channel on the main-land about half an hour before day.

At 2.20 o'clock I discovered the schooner to be on fire. I continued on my lines from dark until daylight.

The names of my men taken are as follows: Second Lieut. O. W. Edwards, a native of Texas; Orderly Sergt. C. H. Westervelt, a native of New York; Third Sergt. James Carville, a native of Indiana; First Corp. William Turner, a native of England; Privates A. Metcalf, R. W. Silk, and Samuel Gibson, natives of England, and P. Cornyn, a native of Ireland.

This report has assumed much greater length than I intended, but I have been unable to give all the circumstances without entering into detail.

With high respect, your obedient servant,

S. L. S. BALLOWE,
Captain, Commanding Post San Luis.

Col. J. BATES, *Commanding, Velasco, Tex.*

APRIL 8, 1862.—Skirmish at Albuquerque, N. Mex.

Report of Col. Edward R. S. Canby, Nineteenth U. S. Infantry, commanding Department of New Mexico.

HEADQUARTERS DEPARTMENT OF NEW MEXICO,
San Antonio, N. Mex., April 11, 1862.

SIR: I have the honor to report that in pursuance of the intention reported in my communication of the 31st ultimo my command (860 regulars and 350 volunteer troops) left Fort Craig on the 1st instant, and arrived before Albuquerque on the afternoon of the 8th. I immediately made a demonstration upon the town, for the purpose of ascertaining its strength and the position of the enemy's batteries. This demonstration was made by Captain Graydon's Spy Company, supported by the regular cavalry, and developed the position of the batteries. In the skirmish Major Duncan, Third Cavalry, was seriously but it is hoped not fatally wounded. No other casualties were sustained.

It was my wish to have made a junction if possible below the Confederate troops in order to cut off their retreat, but the state of our supplies and the inferiority of our force rendered this inexpedient, and it was determined to continue the demonstration before Albuquerque in order that the Confederate forces might be withdrawn out from Santa Fé, and then by a night march place my command in a position from which the junction could be effected without danger of opposition to either column. Accordingly the demonstrations against the town were continued, and during the night of the 9th and the succeeding day the command marched to this place. I am now in communication with the commander of the troops from Fort Union, and can effect a junction at any point.

My spies from Santa Fé report that the entire Confederate force left that city and moved rapidly to Albuquerque upon the news of our appearance before that place. Their preparations indicate the intention of leaving the country. I shall therefore remain at this place to watch their movements and instruct Colonel Paul to join me here.

Very respectfully, sir, your obedient servant,

ED. R. S. CANBY,
Colonel Nineteenth Infantry, Commanding Department.

To the ADJUTANT-GENERAL OF THE ARMY,
Washington, D. C.

APRIL 13–22, 1862.—Pursuit of Confederate forces, including skirmish at Peralta, N. Mex., April 15.

REPORTS.*

No. 1.—Col. Edward R. S. Canby, Nineteenth U. S. Infantry, commanding Department of New Mexico.
No. 2.—Col. Gabriel R. Paul, Fourth New Mexico Infantry, commanding district.
No. 3.—Col. Benjamin S. Roberts, Fifth New Mexico Infantry, commanding district.

No. 1.

Report of Col. Edward R. S. Canby, Nineteenth U. S. Infantry, commanding Department of New Mexico.

HEADQUARTERS DEPARTMENT OF NEW MEXICO,
Fort Craig, N. Mex., April 23, 1862.

SIR: I have the honor to report that a junction with Colonel Paul's command was effected at Tijeras on the evening of the 13th instant. I had in the mean time received information that the Confederate force

---

* See also Sibley's report of engagement at Valverde, p. 506.

had left Albuquerque, moving down the river, and during the day and night of the 14th the united command was marched to Peralta, 36 miles distant, arriving there before the Confederates had any suspicion of the movement. On the morning of the 15th a mountain howitzer, and a train of 7 wagons, loaded with supplies and escorted by a lieutenant and 30 men, were captured. In the conflict 6 of the Confederates were killed, 3 wounded, and 22 captured. To cover this movement Colonel Paul, with his column and three companies of cavalry, under Captain Morris, Third Cavalry, had been detached, and, after completing it, received permission to clear the bosque in front of Peralta of the enemy's force that then occupied it. After some sharp skirmishing, in which our loss was 1 killed and 3 wounded, this work was handsomely executed, and the bosque in front and rear of the town occupied by our troops.

The point occupied by the Confederate troops was known to be the strongest (except Fort Union) in New Mexico, and as nearly all the men had been twenty-four and many of them thirty-six hours without food, no general attack was designed until after the approaches to the place had been thoroughly reconnoitered and the troops allowed time to obtain food and rest. This reconnaissance was made on the afternoon of the same day, the points and direction of attack selected, and the camp of the command advanced to a point nearer the town, and where the trains could be guarded by a smaller number of men. During the night the enemy abandoned his position and crossed to the right bank of the river, leaving his sick and wounded behind him, without attendance, without medicines, and almost without food.

After detaching the staff officers attached to department headquarters to make arrangements for future operations and the train that could be spared for supplies the pursuit was continued down the left bank of the river (the shortest route), with the intention of crossing at La Joya, Polvadera, Sabino, or Fort Craig, if the enemy should not be overtaken sooner. On the night of that day our camp was 5 miles in his rear. On the 16th we had nearly overtaken the rear of his column, and the march was continued during the remainder of the day in sight and almost within cannon range, but on opposite sides of the river. At night our camps were directly opposite, but during the night he abandoned a large portion of his train, 38 wagons and the supplies that they contained, and fled into the mountains. After making arrangements for securing the property abandoned by the enemy the march was continued to Polvadera. At this place the command was halted for a day, in order to assure myself of the position and movements of the enemy and to secure the safety of a supply train in our rear. These objects having been accomplished, the march was resumed and continued until we reached this post on the afternoon of the 22d (yesterday).

The Confederate force is still in the mountains west of us. If they have taken the route by the Miembres it will be impossible to overtake them. If they have taken that by Cañada Alamosa I am not without hopes of intercepting them, although my scouts report that they have abandoned everything that would encumber them in their flight.

Very respectfully, sir, your obedient servant,

ED. R. S. CANBY,
Colonel Nineteenth Infantry, Commanding Department.

The ADJUTANT-GENERAL OF THE ARMY, *Washington, D. C.*

No. 2.

*Report of Col. Gabriel R. Paul, Fourth New Mexico Infantry, command-
ing district.*

HEADQUARTERS SOUTHERN DISTRICT NEW MEXICO,
Fort Craig, N. Mex., May 1, 1862.

GENERAL : I have the honor to report that I left Fort Union, N.
Mex., on the 6th of April, 1862, in command of a column to form a
junction with Col. E. R. S. Canby, who had left Fort Craig on the 31st
March, 1862. The junction was made at Tijeras, and our combined
forces moved against the enemy, who retreated before us. On the 15th
April, at Peralta, we had several skirmishes with the enemy, and during
the night he evacuated Peralta and continued his retreat. The pursuit
was kept up until our arrival at this post, when from want of provisions
we halted; the enemy in a disorganized state, leaving behind him
wagons, sick, &c., is making his way out of the Territory. I was left
temporarily in the command of this district, with my headquarters at
Fort Craig.

I am, sir, very respectfully, your obedient servant,
G. R. PAUL,
Colonel Fourth Regiment New Mexico Vols., Comdg. Dist.

The ADJUTANT-GENERAL U. S. ARMY,
Washington, D. C.

No. 3.

*Report of Col. Benjamin S. Roberts, Fifth New Mexico Infantry, com-
manding district.*

HDQRS. CENTRAL, SANTA FÉ, AND NORTHERN MIL. DIST.,
DEPARTMENT OF NEW MEXICO,
Santa Fé, N. Mex., April 23, 1862.

GENERAL : I have the honor to report myself in command of the
Central, Santa Fé, and Northern Military Districts, Department of
New Mexico, and that I have established and garrisoned the posts at
Albuquerque and Santa Fé, recently occupied by Confederate troops
of General Sibley's brigade. It will gratify you to know that the
Texan troops are in retreat out of the country, having been compelled
by our operations to abandon most of their supplies of all kinds and to
take the mountain route behind the Socorro range to avoid the capture
of their small remaining force of the 3,000 troops that invaded the
Territory. They have abandoned their sick and wounded everywhere
on their line of retreat, and are leaving in a state of demoralization
and suffering that has few examples in any war. The long line of their
retreat over Jornada and wastes of country without water and that
furnish no supplies will render their march extremely difficult and
aggravate the ordinary sufferings of a disorganized army under defeat.
The broken-down condition of all our animals, the want of cavalry, and
deficiencies of all our supplies will make a successful pursuit equally
impracticable, if not impossible.

My reports of the operations of my division in the field from the 1st
to the 16th instant will reach you in time through the proper channels.

I effected a junction with Colonel Paul's command at San Antonio on the 13th, after a demonstration on Albuquerque and artillery combats there on the 8th and sharp skirmishing on the 8th and 9th. The last engagement was at Peralta, on the 15th. That drove the main Confederate forces from that position and put their army in utter rout.

We have great numbers of their prisoners, but I am unable to give the figures with accuracy, and some 60 wagons of their supply train and two pieces of artillery have fallen into our hands.

Colonel Canby is on the pursuit with both the northern and southern divisions of the army, and this information is communicated indirectly, because it will be many days before his official reports can be made.

According to the most reliable information General Sibley has not left 1,200 men of the army of 3,000 that appeared before Fort Craig on February 13th, and his retreat is the complete annihilation of his remaining forces.

I am, general, very respectfully, your obedient servant,

B. S. ROBERTS,
Colonel, Commanding.

General LORENZO THOMAS,
Adjutant-General U. S. Army, Washington, D. C.

APRIL 13-SEPTEMBER 20, 1862.—Expedition from Southern California, through Arizona, to Northwestern Texas and New Mexico.

REPORTS.

No. 1.—Brig. Gen. James H. Carleton, U. S. Army, commanding expedition.
No. 2.—Lieut. Col. Edward E. Eyre, First California Cavalry.
No. 3.—Surg. James M. McNulty, U. S. Army, Medical Inspector.

No. 1.

Reports of Brig. Gen. James H. Carleton, U. S. Army, commanding expedition.

HEADQUARTERS COLUMN FROM CALIFORNIA,
Fort Barrett, Pima Villages, Ariz., May 25, 1862.

MAJOR: The advance guard of this column, under Lieut. Col. Joseph R. West, First California Volunteer Infantry, took possession of Tucson, in this Territory, on the 20th instant, without firing a shot. All the secession troops who were in the Territory and all of the secessionists, so far as we can learn, have fled—the troops to the Rio Grande, the citizens to Sonora. Our arrival is hailed with great joy by all the people who remain. We shall doubtless be able to get some forage, flour, and beef, and perhaps sugar, from Sonora; but of this I will write you in detail from Tucson in a few days. A rumor comes from the Rio Grande that Sibley has met with a serious reverse.

I am, major, very respectfully, your obedient servant,

JAMES H. CARLETON,
Colonel First California Volunteers, Commanding.

Maj. RICHARD C. DRUM,
Asst. Adjt. Gen., U. S. Army, San Francisco, Cal.

MAJOR: In my letter to you, dated June 18, I informed you that I had sent Expressman John Jones, Sergeant Wheeling, of Company F, First California Volunteer Infantry, and a Mexican guide named Chavez, with communications for General Canby.

These men started from Tucson on the evening of June 15. On the 18th they were attacked by a party of Apaches, and Sergeant Wheeling and the guide (Chavez) were killed, and Jones, almost by a miracle, succeeded in getting through the Indians, and after a hot pursuit on their part made out to reach the Rio Grande at a point known as Picacho, 6 miles above Mesilla. He was taken prisoner by the secessionists, who brought him before Colonel Steele (William Steele, late Second Dragoons), who examined him, took his dispatches, and threw him into jail. He managed, however, to get word to General Canby that he was there and that the Column from California was really coming—an achievement that was considered absolutely impracticable. However, as soon as Steele ascertained this matter as a fact, hurried preparations were made to abandon the country. Meantime General Canby had sent a large force to Fort Craig to move on Mesilla as soon as transportation could be provided. A strong reconnoitering force, under Lieutenant-Colonel Eyre, left Tucson on June 21, and after a hard march arrived on the Rio Grande near Fort Thorn on July 4.

On the 5th this force occupied that work, it having been abandoned by the enemy. Here the colors were run up by the California troops. Lieutenant-Colonel Eyre was then re-enforced by a squadron of the Third U. S. Cavalry, and having constructed a raft and built a boat, was at the last advices about to cross the river to march on Fillmore and Fort Bliss, in Texas. Steele, meanwhile, had abandoned Mesilla and was making his way to Texas. The Mexican population was rising on every hand and were killing his men and running off his stock. It is said that Teel's battery, C. S. Army, the one taken from Canby at Valverde, had been attacked some 30 miles below Fort Bliss and taken by the people, who had hovered around it to the number of 1,500. It was believed that neither Steele nor Teel would ever reach Texas. Sibley and Colonel Reily had fallen back on Texas in May, leaving Steele with what was considered force enough to hold Arizona.

All this news came last night. It was brought by Captain McCleave, who had been exchanged for two lieutenants, one of whom was Steele's adjutant, who had been taken by Captain Fritz, First California Volunteer Cavalry. Captain Fritz went after Colonel Steele with a flag of truce to effect the exchange. He overtook Colonel Steele 20 miles below Fort Fillmore in full retreat.

As you have been informed, the uncommon drought of this summer had so dried up the country that it was impracticable to move a large force in the direction of the Rio Grande until the rains commenced falling. Usually this occurs by June 24, but this year there has been but little fall even yet. The column, however, has been taking the road by installments, commencing with Roberts' company of infantry and Cremony's cavalry, which was sent with 25,000 pounds of corn and thirty days' rations for Eyre in case he was obliged to fall back to the Rio de Sauz, 128 miles from Tucson, starting on July 9. (See letter to Colonel West, marked A,* herewith inclosed.) I also inclose Colonel Eyre's report,† dated at Fort Thorn, July 6, 1862. This officer deserves great credit for his enterprise. I trust the Governor will notice the conduct

---

* Not found. †See report No. 2, p. 585.

of himself and men. This report is marked B.† I also send a subsequent report of Colonel Eyre's, dated July 8, 1862 (C†), and also one still later, dated July 11, 1862, marked D,* and still another, dated July 14, 1862, marked E;† also a letter from Colonel Chivington, marked F;* also a letter from General Canby, marked G,* and letters* from General Canby to Colonel Chivington, dated June 9, 16, 18, 27, and July 1 and 4, 1862. I also inclose General Orders, Nos. 10 and 11, from these headquarters.

The troops marched on the days specified. I shall leave this post to-morrow and move rapidly to the front. If a demonstration on Northwestern Texas will serve as a diversion in favor of forces landing on the coast that State will soon be ours. The country is still dry, but we shall do our best.

Respectfully, your obedient servant,

JAMES H. CARLETON,
Brigadier-General, U. S. Army.

Maj. RICHARD C. DRUM,
Asst. Adjt. Gen., San Francisco, Cal.

[Inclosure No. 1.]

GENERAL ORDERS, }   HDQRS. COLUMN FROM CALIFORNIA,
No. 10.   }   *Tucson, Ariz., July 17, 1862.*

The Column from California will move to the Rio Grande in the following order:

I. On the 20th instant Col. Joseph R. West, First California Volunteer Infantry, with Companies B, C, and K, of his regiment, and Company G, of the Fifth California Volunteer Infantry. This command at the Rio de Sauz will receive the addition of Company E, of West's regiment, and Thompson's mountain howitzers. Maj. Theodore A. Coult, of the Fifth California Volunteer Infantry, is assigned to duty with this command. Colonel West will take 40,000 rounds of rifle-musket ammunition.

II. On the 21st instant a second command, consisting of Shinn's light battery, Third U. S. Artillery, and Companies A, First, and B, Fifth California Volunteer Infantry, will take up its line of march for the Rio Grande. This command will be supplied with all the artillery ammunition now here which pertains to Shinn's battery and 17,000 rounds of ammunition for the rifle musket.

III. On the 23d instant a third command, under Lieut. Col. Edwin A. Rigg, consisting of Companies I, F, D, and H, First California Volunteer Infantry, will start for the Rio Grande. This command will have 28,000 rounds of ammunition for the rifle musket.

IV. Each of these commands will be supplied with subsistence for thirty days, with at least two tents for each company and with a good supply of intrenching tools. Each command will also have one hospital tent complete and an ambulance for the sick and wounded, and will have a forge and material for shoeing horses and mules, and also a water-tank and a good supply of water-kegs.

V. On the 31st instant a train of wagons laden with forty days' supplies of subsistence for the whole command hereby ordered forward, with the following ammunition, viz, 40,000 rounds of the rifle musket, 30,000 rounds for the Sharp's carbine, and 20,000 rounds for the navy size Colt's revolver, together with such other supplies of clothing,

---

* Not found.   † See report No. 2, p. 585.

tents, tools, spare wagon timbers, leather, wagon grease, horseshoes, mule-shoes, horseshoe-nails, stationery, &c., as may be required, will leave Tucson for the Rio Grande, escorted by Companies A, Fifth California Volunteer Infantry, and A, First California Volunteer Cavalry, each furnished with sixty days' rations. This command will have an ambulance, forge, and water-tank, and such other articles as may be required to render it efficient.

VI. Company D, First California Volunteer Cavalry, will move from Tubac directly for the crossing of the San Pedro, where it will arrive on the 22d instant. From that point it will form the advance guard of the column, and habitually, unless otherwise ordered, will march one day in front of West's command.

VII. Captain Cremony's company (B, of the Second California Volunteer Cavalry) will march near the head of the column, to serve as flankers or as vedettes, as occasion may require.

VIII. The staff officers attached to these headquarters, except the chief commissary, will, until further orders, move with West's command. Surgeon Prentiss, First California Volunteer Cavalry, will move with the second command, and Surgeon Wooster, Fifth California Volunteer Infantry, will move with Rigg's command.

IX. The chief quartermaster, chief commissary, and medical director are charged with giving the most perfect efficiency possible to all matters pertaining to the public service in their several departments, keeping in mind the fact that this column is presumed now to move forward prepared at all points to engage the enemy at any moment by night or by day. Let nothing be omitted or neglected which will give due effect to this idea, whether on the march or on the field of battle.

X. That every soldier may move forward with a light, free step, now that we approach the enemy, he will no longer be required to carry his knapsack.

XI. This is the time when every soldier in this column looks forward with a confident hope that he, too, will have the distinguished honor of striking a blow for the old Stars and Stripes; when he, too, feels in his heart that he is the champion of the holiest cause that has ever yet nerved the arm of a patriot. The general commanding the column desires that such a time shall be remembered by all, but more particularly by those who from their guilt have been so unfortunate as to be prisoners on such an occasion. He therefore orders that all soldiers under his command who may be now held in confinement shall be at once released.

By command of Brigadier-General Carleton:

BEN. C. CUTLER,
First Lieutenant, First Cal. Vol. Inf., Asst. Adjt. Gen.

[Inclosure No. 2.]

GENERÁL ORDERS, }   HDQRS. COLUMN FROM CALIFORNIA,
        No. 11.   }   *Tucson, Ariz., July* 21, 1862.

I. All of the Territory of Arizona west of a meridian line running through what is known as Apache Pass, on the Butterfield Mail Route, hence to Mesilla, will constitute a military district, to be known as the District of Western Arizona, the headquarters of which shall be Tucson, Ariz. Maj. David Ferguson, First California Volunteer Cavalry, is hereby placed in command of this district, as well as of the post and town of Tucson.

II. The duties which devolve upon Major Ferguson by this order are additional to those he is required to perform as chief commissary of this column. He is also empowered to make estimates of all funds necessary to be used in the quartermaster's department and subsistence department, so far as the wants and necessities of those departments may be concerned direct to the proper officers at the headquarters Department of the Pacific. Major Ferguson will disburse and direct the disbursement of these funds when received to the best interests of the public service, having reference first to having on hand an adequate supply of all articles of prime necessity, such as food and forage; likewise all that will insure mobility to the column by having its means of transportation always in as good order and good repair as practicable.

III. Great vigilance will be exercised by Major Ferguson to see that no successful attack is made on his trains within his district by secessionists or Indians. The troops in the district are to be kept in fighting condition, and the public animals and public stores so carefully guarded as to secure against loss by surprise or by depredation and secure against destruction by fire or by flood.

By command of Brigadier-General Carleton :

BEN. C. CUTLER,
First Lieutenant, First Cal. Vol. Inf., A. A. A. G.

HEADQUARTERS COLUMN FROM CALIFORNIA,
Ojo de la Vaca, Ariz., August 2, 1862.

GENERAL: General George Wright, U. S. Army, commanding the Department of the Pacific, recommended to the General-in-Chief that a force from California, to consist of a battery of four guns (Company A, U. S. Third Artillery), the First Regiment of Infantry California Volunteers, and five companies of the First Cavalry California Volunteers, should cross the Yuma and Colorado Deserts, and recapture the posts in Arizona and Southern New Mexico, then supposed to be in the hands of the rebels, and open the Southern Overland Mail Route.

These recommendations or suggestions were approved by the General-in-Chief, and arrangements were set on foot to carry them into effect. But what with unprecedented floods in California and uncommon drought on the Yuma and Colorado Deserts, and other serious difficulties which had to be encountered, it has been quite impossible to bring forward the force above indicated in a fighting condition at an earlier date than the present.

I was baffled in every effort I attempted to communicate with you. My first note, marked A, after many days came back to me, the messenger not being able to ascend the Salt Fork of the Gila on account of high water. My second note, marked B, after several days was returned from Sonora, as the Mexican expressmen were too much afraid to encounter the dangers of the journey through Chihuahua to El Paso and so on to your headquarters. Of the 3 men whom I sent with my third notes, marked C and D, 2 were killed by the Apache Indians near the Chiricahua Mountains on the evening of the 18th of June last. The third, after a miraculous escape and a perilous ride, arrived on the Rio Grande at sunset on the evening of the 20th, 160 miles from where his companions were murdered. Here, in an exhausted, half-delirious state, he was captured by secessionists, and, together with his dispatches, taken to Colonel Steele, C. S. Army. On the 17th of June I directed Lieutenant-Colonel Eyre, First Cavalry, California Volun-

teers, with a small command from his regiment, to make a forced reconnaissance toward the Rio Grande. He started from Tucson on this duty
on the evening of June 21. (See my letter to him, marked E.)

On the 8th of July I directed some supplies to be forwarded half way
to the Rio Grande, to provide for the emergency of Eyre's being obliged
to fall back. (See letter to Colonel West, marked F.) Roberts' command, which acted as a guard to these supplies, had a fight with the
Apache Indians at Apache Pass, in which he lost 2 killed and 2 wounded,
but in which he succeeded in driving the Indians, as he reports, with a
loss of 9 killed on their side.

From June 7 until July 17 I was busily employed in repairing trains,
in getting supplies up from Fort Yuma and from Sonora, and in regulating somewhat the affairs of Western Arizona. On the 17th July,
without yet having heard from the Rio Grande, I made the order for
the advance to that river. It is herewith inclosed, marked G.*

On the evening of the 21st of July, after the second detachment of
the column had started from Tucson, I received your note of the 4th
ultimo, together with copies of some orders and instructions to the
commander of the Southern Military District, Department of New
Mexico.

I left Tucson on the 23d ultimo and arrived at this point on the 1st
instant. I left 100 men at Apache Pass. (See General Orders, No. 12;
marked H.†)

Colonel West's detachment will arrive here to-morrow; Captain
Willis' the next day; Lieutenant-Colonel Rigg's on the 5th. I shall
halt two or three days on the Miembres to recruit and let the column
close up, and shall then proceed by the stage route to Mesilla.

I received your letter of the 9th of July day before yesterday.

It was not the intention of General Wright to throw a command
into your department which would embarrass you to keep it supplied.
The troops from California were to draw nearly all their stores from
Fort Yuma, to which point they are shipped from San Francisco.
Some were to be bought in Sonora. My supply train, which leaves
Tucson to-day, will have forty days' rations for the whole command
from the 20th instant. Even those rations of yours consumed by
Eyre's cavalry I had hoped to replace, learning to what straits you
had been put for subsistence for your own command. I am happy to
know that you have now such an abundance of stores, and should I
fall short of anything, I will cheerfully avail myself of your authority
to draw on your depot at Fort Craig for what I need.

A train of about 50 wagons will ply between Fort Yuma and Tucson,
starting from Tucson, say, the 12th instant, to accumulate and keep up
a good supply at that point. A contractor has given bonds to keep
the Column from California supplied with fresh beef at 9 cents a pound.
Stores can be hauled by private trains from the port of Guaymas to
Tucson for five cents a pound. This latter information may be of
service to you. I have no subsistence funds here; the paper marked
I† will exhibit the condition of those in the quartermaster's department.

The paper marked K† will tell you of my means of transportation
after the arrival of the train which leaves Tucson to-day, minus, say,
three teams left at Fort Bowie, Apache Pass, Chiricahua Mountains.

All my troops except one company of cavalry have pay due from
February 28, 1862. It will be a great kindness to have them paid, if

---

* Inclosure G is a duplicate of General Orders, No. 10, p. 555.
† Omitted as of no present importance.

it can be done without inconvenience to the troops of your own department. I have no paymaster with me, and was not counting on the troops being paid by your paymaster. The men are sadly in want of small stores, tobacco, &c. We have no sutler, and of course, on the desert, the soldiers have exhausted what few necessaries they happened by chance to have.

I have, say, 100 rounds of ammunition for small-arms per man, and can soon have more from Fort Yuma, and I have for the four pieces of artillery the ammunition named in a letter to Lieutenant Shinn, U. S. Third Artillery, marked L.*

The men have only fatigue clothing and that somewhat worn, but I expect some up from Fort Yuma very soon. Can you spare any?

Capt. Tredwell Moore, assistant quartermaster, is the only staff officer belonging to the army with me, and he will be relieved from duty in this column shortly after my arrival at Mesilla. I have with me two surgeons, one assistant and one acting assistant surgeon, all of the volunteer service. For the state of my medical supplies, see Surgeon McNulty's letter, marked M.*

The strength of the command when it arrives at Mesilla will be approximately:

Field and staff	25
Say of artillery, aggregate	73
Of infantry	825
Of cavalry	350
Total fighting force	1,273
Of employés	127
Total requiring subsistence	1,400

I will send you an accurate field return as soon as the command under Captain McCleave reaches Mesilla.

I inclose herewith a letter from Maj. Richard C. Drum, assistant adjutant-general Department of the Pacific, marked N; also a copy of General Orders, No. 29 [1862], from the War Department, on the same sheet.

I beg to be fully instructed by you in all measures wherein myself or the California Column can be of the most service. We have not crossed the continent thus far to split hairs, but with an earnest resolution to do our duty whatever be our geographical position; and so the marches of this column tend always toward the heart of the rebellion; the men will forget their toils and sufferings on the Great Desert in their hope ultimately to reach the enemy.

In all this I am sure I but express the sentiments of General Wright.

As the gallantry of the troops under your command has left us nothing to do on the Rio Grande, it would be a sad disappointment to those from California if they should be obliged to retrace their steps without feeling the enemy.

I hope I do not ask too much when I inquire whether a force could not profitably be thrown into Western Texas, where it is reported the Union men are only waiting for a little help to run up the old flag.

I have the honor to be, general, very respectfully, your obedient servant,

JAMES H. CARLETON,
Brigadier-General, U. S. Army.

Brig. Gen. E. R. S. CANBY, *Comdg. Dept. of New Mexico.*

-----

* Omitted as of no present importance.

[Inclosure A.]

HEADQUARTERS DISTRICT OF SOUTHERN CALIFORNIA,
Fort Yuma, Cal., May 3, 1862.

Col. E. R. S. CANBY,
Commanding Department of New Mexico :

COLONEL : Having no means of getting reliable information from you except by a special express, I send the bearer of this to you for that purpose. He will be able to tell you about this part of the country, and will bring to me any communication you may desire to write.

I have a force of light battery (Company A, Third Artillery) of two 12-pounder howitzers and two 6-pounder guns, and fifteen companies of infantry and five companies of cavalry, California Volunteers, well armed and provided for, and the men are as fine material as any in the service. I can move on from Tucson or Fort Breckinridge as soon as I hear from you. I am ready and anxious to co-operate with you.

If necessary I can be followed by still another regiment or more of infantry, to be sent by steam to the mouth of the Colorado.

It will afford me pleasure to enter into any plan you may suggest, so my force can be of service to you and to the cause.

Let me know your strength, your situation, your purposes ; the strength, situation, and probable purposes of Sibley and his troops.

Please send an escort with my messenger, to get him safely through the Apaches.

I have the honor to be, very respectfully,
JAMES H. CARLETON,
Colonel First California Volunteers, Commanding.

[Indorsement.]

At the time this letter was written it was the intention of General Carleton to move forward to the Rio Grande five companies of the Fifth Infantry, California Volunteers. Some of those companies are now serving in Western Arizona.

BEN. C. CUTLER,
First Lieut., First Infantry, Cal. Vols., A. A. A. General.

[Inclosure B.]

HEADQUARTERS COLUMN FROM CALIFORNIA,
Tucson, Ariz., June 11, 1862.

General E. R. S. CANBY, U. S. A.,
Commanding U. S. Forces in New Mexico :

GENERAL : I had the honor to write to you on the 3d ultimo from Fort Yuma, Cal., that I was on my way to Arizona, and desired to co-operate with you in driving the rebels from New Mexico. My messenger was unable to reach you via the Salinas Fork of the Gila on account of high water. I therefore dispatch another through Mexican territory.

I am ordered to recapture all the works in New Mexico which had been surrendered to rebels. This I shall proceed to do, starting from here as soon as the rains have filled the natural tanks, say early in July.

What number of troops can find subsistence, say at twenty days' notice, at Mesilla and Fort Bliss, in Texas ? I can start from here with sixty days' supply for one battery of artillery, one regiment of infantry, and five companies of cavalry. With this force I desire to co-operate with you. This will enable me to hold this country besides.

I have placed Arizona under martial law, and shall continue it so until the civil officers come. I can bring more force if necessary. Let me know by the bearer your wishes, purposes, strength; the strength, position, and apparent purposes and condition of Sibley and his forces.

I am, general, your obedient servant,

JAMES H. CARLETON,
Colonel First California Volunteers, Commanding.

[Inclosure C]

HEADQUARTERS COLUMN FROM CALIFORNIA,
Tucson, Ariz., June 15, 1862.

General E. R. S. CANBY,
Comdg. Department of New Mexico, Fort Craig, N. Mex.:

GENERAL: I have the honor to inform you that I have advanced thus far from California with a force of regulars and volunteers sufficient in numbers to occupy this Territory.

I have assumed to represent the United States authority, and for the time being have placed the Territory under martial law.

Inclosed herewith please find a proclamation to this effect. I send this to you by express, that you may not go to the expense of sending troops from your department to occupy Arizona.

I congratulate you on your success against the Confederate forces under Sibley. If you can send an escort to the expressman who takes this I shall feel greatly obliged.

I am, general, respectfully, ,

JAMES H. CARLETON,
Colonel First California Volunteers, Commanding.

[Inclosure to C.]

To all whom it may concern:

The Congress of the United States has set apart a portion of New Mexico and organized it into a Territory complete of itself. This is known as the Territory of Arizona. It comprises within its limits all the country eastward from the Colorado River, which is now occupied by the forces of the United States known as the Column from California; and as the flag of the United States shall be carried by this column still farther eastward, these limits will extend in that direction until they reach the farthest geographical boundary of this Territory.

Now, in the present chaotic state in which Arizona is found to be, with no civil officers to administer the laws—indeed, with an utter absence of all civil authority—and with no security of life or property within its borders, it becomes the duty of the undersigned to represent the authority of the United States over the people of Arizona as well as over all those who compose or are connected with the Column from California. Thus, by virtue of his office as military commander of the United States forces now here, and to meet the fact that wherever within our boundaries our colors fly there the sovereign power of our country must at once be acknowledged and law and order at once prevail, the undersigned, as a military governor, assumes control of this Territory until such time as the President of the United States shall otherwise direct.

Thus also it is hereby declared that until civil officers shall be sent by the Government to organize the civil courts for the administration of justice the Territory of Arizona is hereby placed under martial law. Trials for capital offenses shall be held by a military commission, to be composed of not more than thirteen nor less than nine commissioned officers. The rules of evidence shall be those customary in practice under the common law. The trials shall be public and shall be trials of record, and the mode of procedure shall be strictly in accordance with that of courts-martial in the Army of the United States. Unless the public safety absolutely requires it, no execution shall follow conviction until the orders in the case by the President shall be known.

Trials for minor offenses shall be held under the same rules, except that for these a commission of not more than five nor less than three commissioned officers may sit, and a vote of a majority determine the issue. In these cases the orders of the officer organizing the commission shall be final.

All matters in relation to rights in property and lands which may be in dispute shall be determined for the time being by a military commission, to be composed of not more than five nor less than three commissioned officers. Of course appeals from the decisions of such commissions can be taken to the civil courts when once the latter have been established.

There are certain fundamental rules for the government of the people of this Territory which will be rigidly enforced:

I. No man who has arrived at lawful age shall be permitted to reside within this Territory who does not without delay subscribe to the oath of allegiance to the United States.

II. No words or acts calculated to impair that veneration which all good patriots should feel for our country and Government will be tolerated within this Territory or go unpunished if sufficient proof can be had of them.

III. No man who does not pursue some lawful calling or have some legitimate means of support shall be permitted to remain in the Territory.

Having no thought or motive in all this but the good of the people and aiming only to do right, the undersigned confidently hopes and expects, in all he does to further these ends, to have the hearty co-operation of every good citizen and soldier in Arizona. All this is to go into effect from and after this date, and will continue in force, unless disapproved or modified by General George Wright, U. S. Army, commanding the Department of the Pacific, under whose orders the Column from California has taken the field.

Done at the headquarters Column from California, in Tucson, Ariz., this 8th day of June, A. D. 1862.

JAMES H. CARLETON,
Colonel First Cal. Vols., Major Sixth U. S. Cavalry.

[Inclosure D.]

HEADQUARTERS COLUMN FROM CALIFORNIA,
Tucson, Ariz., June 15, 1862.

Brig. Gen. E. R. S. CANBY, U. S. A.,
Comdg. Department of New Mexico, Fort Craig, N. Mex.:

GENERAL: I have forwarded by another express the originals of the notes numbered 2, which the bearer of this takes to you.

My wagons are so shrunk in coming over the desert that I am obliged to delay here until the 1st proximo, when from the rains having fallen I hope to be able to move to the Rio Grande. I hope I can count on getting meat and bread there. Mesilla is far removed from my source of supply. Pray advise me of all this.

I am anxious to co-operate with you. My men are the finest material I have ever seen and anxious to strike a blow for the cause.

Have you a plenty of rifled-musket ammunition ?

We can be on the Rio Grande in fifteen days from this post.

Respectfully, &c.,

JAMES H. CARLETON,
Colonel First California Volunteers, Commanding.

P. S.—I am straining every point to get up supplies so as to leave July 1.

[Inclosure E.]

HEADQUARTERS COLUMN FROM CALIFORNIA,
Tucson, Ariz., June 17, 1862.

Lieut. Col. EDWARD E. EYRE,
First Cavalry, California Volunteers, Present:

COLONEL : It is important that a forced reconnaissance be made in advance of the column from the Rio Grande, and you are selected for this delicate and at the same time hazardous duty.

You will take with you for this purpose a squadron of your regiment, to be composed of all the effective officers and men of Companies B and C now here.

For transportation you will have three six-mule teams. Take six aparejos in the wagons for packing purposes when necessary. Take, say, four days' pork, and dried beef and pemmican, and flour, coffee, sugar, salt, and vinegar for thirty days. Take 70 rounds of ammunition for the Sharp's carbines per man, and 30 rounds per man of navy-revolver ammunition. You should have at least 6 pick-axes and 12 long-handled shovels as intrenching tools.

Acting Assistant Surgeon Kittredge will accompany you.

All other essentials of your outfit will readily suggest themselves to you. When you bear in mind that you are always to be ready to fight, with your horses in the best possible condition, all, and only all, you will want practically to fulfill these requirements will come to your mind.

You go to watch the road in the direction of the enemy. If possible you will capture or drive in his pickets, and observe and report upon his situation, strength, movements, and apparent purposes. To do this successfully the greatest prudence, sagacity, forecast, and boldness are necessary. I hardly need assure you that I have the fullest confidence in your ability to carry the purpose of your reconnaissance to the most useful results.

Avoid collision with the Indians. Of course you will report back to me all that it is necessary for me to know.

Wishing you success, I am, colonel, very sincerely, yours,

JAMES H. CARLETON,
Colonel First California Volunteers, Commanding.

[Inclosure F.]

HEADQUARTERS COLUMN FROM CALIFORNIA,
Tucson, Ariz., July 8, 1862.

Col. JOSEPH R. WEST,
First Infantry, Cal. Vols., Comdg. at Tucson, Ariz.:

COLONEL: You will order a sergeant and 9 trusty infantry soldiers and 3 first-rate cavalry soldiers to the crossing of the San Pedro, to guard some forage which the quartermaster will send to that point.

You will order Roberts' company, of the First Infantry, California Volunteers, to the San Simon, *en route* to the Rio Grande, where they will make an intrenched camp, if possible, near the mail station, and there await further orders.

A train will accompany these troops with thirty days' rations for Colonel Eyre's command, commencing on its arrival at the San Simon, and thirty days for the troops who are to remain at the San Pedro.

Each soldier will have 110 rounds of ammunition, and the party at the San Simon will have some intrenching tools and also some scythes.

These troops are sent to guard these supplies until the column reaches them on its march to the Rio Grande. They also go to observe the road and to form a support to Colonel Eyre in case he falls back.

You cannot be too minute in your instructions to them, having in view the furtherance of these ends. They are to have scouts all the time well to the front, unless menaced, say 50 or more miles; they are to keep me informed of movements in their vicinity of the enemy, and if attacked they are not to surrender on any terms. They are to be uncommonly watchful that Indians do not run off their stock, and at the same time are not to attack the Indians unless the latter are the aggressors.

I am, colonel, respectfully,

JAMES H. CARLETON,
Brigadier-General, U. S. Army, Commanding.

[Inclosure N.]

HEADQUARTERS DEPARTMENT OF THE PACIFIC,
San Francisco, Cal., May 30, 1862.

Col. JAMES H. CARLETON,
First Infantry, Cal. Vols., Comdg. Column from California:

SIR: Inclosed I have the honor to transmit, by direction of the general commanding the department, General Orders, No. 29, from the War Department. It is probable that your command may enter the Department of New Mexico. You will nevertheless act under the orders of the general commanding the Department of the Pacific, and make your returns as usual to these headquarters.

Very respectfully, your obedient servant,

R. C. DRUM,
Assistant Adjutant-General.

[Sub-inclosure.]

GENERAL ORDERS, } WAR DEPARTMENT; ADJT. GEN.'S OFFICE,
No. 29.　　　　 } 　　　　*Washington, March* 22, 1862.

In the changes recently made in the boundaries of department commands it may happen that troops belonging to one department may either be in, or may unavoidably pass into, another. In such a case the troops so situated will continue under the command of the general

under whose orders they may have been operating; but it is expected that they will be withdrawn as soon as the position they may occupy comes within the control of the proper commander of the department.
. By order of the Secretary of War:

L. THOMAS,
Adjutant-General.

[Indorsement.]

· ·AUGUST 10, 1862.

Respectfully forwarded. I have supposed that General Orders, No. 29, of 1862, applied to troops passing through, even temporarily within, the limits of a department to which they did not belong, but it will be seen that General Wright has given it a more extended application. This is not immediately material, as no question of command or personal consideration will be allowed by me to interfere with the interests of the service. It is ·proper, however, that its status should be fixed by superior authority.

If this force is to return to the Department of the Pacific, that fact will modify materially the recommendations made in my report of the 6th instant.

HEADQUARTERS COIUMN FROM CALIFORNIA,
Santa Fé, N. Mex., September 20, 1862.

COLONEI: I wrote to you on July 22, informing you of all the important events connected with the Column from California from June 18 to that date. I then inclosed copies of General Orders, Nos. 10 and 11, from these headquarters, which prescribed the manner in which the column should march across the desert from Tucson to the Rio Grande.

I left Tucson myself on July 23; passed Colonel West, with most of the troops encamped on the San Pedro, on the 24th, and led the advance of the column from that point to Las Cruces, N. Mex., with one company of infantry and two of cavalry. From the hostile attitude of the Chiricahua Indians I found it indispensably necessary to establish a post in what is known as Apache Pass. It is known as Fort Bowie, and garrisoned by 100 rank and file of the Fifth California Volunteer Infatnry, and 13 rank and file of Company A, First California Volunteer Cavalry. This post commands the water in that pass. Around this water the Indians have been in the habit of lying in ambush and shooting troops and travelers as they came to drink. In this way they killed 3 of Lieutenant-Colonel Eyre's command, and in attempting to keep Captain Roberts' First California Volunteer Infantry away from the spring a fight ensued, in which Captain Roberts had 2 men killed and 2 wounded. Captain Roberts reports that the Indians lost 10 killed. In this affair the men of Captain Roberts' company are reported as behaving with great gallantry.

Two miles beyond Apache Pass I found the remains of 9 white men, who had been murdered by the Indians. They were a party traveling from the Pino Alto mines to California. One of them had been burned at the stake; we saw the charred bones and the burnt ends of the rope by which he had been tied. The remains of 7 of these men were buried on that spot.

From the Rio de Sauz to Ojo de la Vaca there was a great dearth of water. At the latter place I addressed a letter to General Canby, giving him all the elements going to make up the column, the object of its march, and the wishes of General Wright. A copy of that letter is herewith inclosed, marked A.*

Having been informed that a large number of men, women, and children were in a destitute and starving condition at Pino Alto mines, 40-odd miles northeastward from the Ojo de la Vaca, I directed Colonel West to furnish them with some subsistence stores as a gratuity. (See letter of instructions to Colonel West, marked B, and Captain Shirland's report on the starving condition of these people, marked C.)

I arrived on the Rio Grande on August 7 at a point 3 miles above Fort Thorn, and immediately communicated with General Canby by letter, marked D.

On August 9 I passed the Rio Grande at the San Diego Crossing, 18 miles below Fort Thorn. The river was still very high and very rapid, but the men stripped off their clothes and dragged the wagons through by main force; the baggage, subsistence stores, ammunition, &c., were crossed in two small, leaky boats. At this point we built a larger and better boat for the use of the detachments of the column still to come up.

The head of the column arrived at Las Cruces on August 10. Here I found the advance guard, under Lieutenant-Colonel Eyre, First California Volunteer Cavalry, strengthened by four companies of the Fifth U. S. Infantry, which had been sent down from Fort Craig. Two companies of regular cavalry had also been sent down to re-enforce Colonel Eyre; but these had been recalled and had started back to Fort Craig on August 9.

Unfortunately Colonel Eyre had been forbidden by Colonel Chivington and Colonel Howe to proceed in the direction of Texas below Las Cruces; otherwise I believe he would have captured the whole of Steele's force of Confederate troops. (See his report † on this subject, marked E.) The energy, enterprise, and resources of Colonel Eyre, as exhibited in his rapid march from Tucson to the Rio Grande; his crossing of that river, and his unlooked-for presence directly upon the heels of the retreating rebels, cannot be too highly appreciated. He exhibited some of the finest qualities of a soldier, and had he not been fettered by orders from higher authority than himself, he would, without a doubt, have achieved advantages over the enemy creditable to himself and to the Column from California. But for his timely arrival on the Rio Grande, Las Cruces and Mesilla would have both been laid in ashes by the enemy. Hampered as he was by orders, he nevertheless managed to hoist the Stars and Stripes upon Fort Thorn, Fort Fillmore, Mesilla, and Fort Bliss, in Texas.

On August 11 General Canby wrote me a very handsome letter, in which he liberally offered to furnish the column with all the supplies it might need, together with $30,000 subsistence funds. General Wright will be gratified to read it; it is marked F. It will be seen by that letter that the medical supplies and ordnance stores in the Department of New Mexico are so abundant as to preclude the necessity of any more of these stores being purchased or shipped in the Department of the Pacific for any of the troops east of Fort Yuma belonging to the Column from California.

On August 11 General Canby sent to me another communication, in which he treats of the impracticability of an invasion of Texas from

---

* See Carleton's report to Canby of August 2, p. 557.
† No. 2, dated August 30, 1862, p. 585.

this direction, and in which he speaks of removing the regular troops from New Mexico and of receiving other re-enforcements from California. As the views it sets forth seem to be of great value, I submit it for the perusal of General Wright; it is marked G.

On August 12 General Canby wrote still another letter, in which he authorized me to use my own judgment in regard to the disposition of troops in Arizona and Southern New Mexico; it is marked H. My letter to General Canby, dated August 15, together with General Orders, Nos. 14 and 15, herewith inclosed, will inform General Wright of the distribution of the troops along the Rio Grande. These communications are marked I.

On August 16 I started with three companies of cavalry for Fort Bliss, in Texas. At the town of Franklin, opposite El Paso, I found a surgeon of the Confederate Army and 25 sick and disabled soldiers, whom I made prisoners of war by order of General Canby. I also found that a large amount of hospital stores and quartermaster's property, which once had belonged to the United States, was in store-rooms connected with the custom-house at El Paso, in Mexico. These stores I managed to recover; there were 12 wagon loads of them. I sent them to the depot at Mesilla, which I had established. I then proceeded 100 miles farther down the valley of the Rio Grande into Texas. The object of my march was to restore confidence to the people. They had been taught by the Texans that we were coming among them as marauders and as robbers. When they found we treated them kindly and paid them a fair price for all the supplies we required they rejoiced to find, as they came under the old flag once more, that they could now have protection and will be treated justly. The abhorrence they expressed for the Confederate troops and of the rebellion convinced me that their loyalty to the United States is now beyond question.

On August 22 the troops of the Column from California hoisted the Stars and Stripes over Fort Quitman. This was done by Capt. John C. Cremony, with his company (B, Second California Volunteer Cavalry). On the same day Captain Shirland, First California Volunteer Cavalry, was directed to proceed to Fort Davis, 140 miles still farther into Texas, and hoisted the national colors over that post. (See General Orders, No. 16, marked K.) How well Captain Shirland performed this duty and how gallantly he and his men behaved in a fight with the Indians will be seen by his report, a copy of which is herewith inclosed, marked L.

Captain Roberts' company, which whipped the Indians in Apache Pass, is from Sacramento. Lieutenant-Colonel Eyre, who led my advance guard to the Rio Grande and hoisted the colors over Forts Thorn, Fillmore, Bliss, and Mesilla, is from Sacramento, and so is Captain Shirland, who hoisted the Stars and Stripes 240 miles farther into the State of Texas; and also whipped the Indians in that neighborhood. This speaks nobly for the men from that city.

I inclose a telegraphic communication from General Canby to the Adjutant-General of the Army, dated August 10, in which he requests that a regiment more of infantry and five companies of cavalry be sent into the Department of New Mexico from California, so as to relieve the regular troops now here; it is marked M.

On August 21 I was instructed to arrange the affairs of the District of Arizona so as to turn over that district to the officer next in rank to myself, and to hold myself in readiness to repair to the headquarters Department of New Mexico. I also received Special Orders, No. 148, from the headquarters of that department, directing me to send an officer as bearer of dispatches to the commander of the Department of the Pacific. Copies of these documents are herewith inclosed, marked N.

On September 2 I received Special Orders, No. 153 (marked O), directing me to relieve Brigadier-General Canby in the command of the Department of New Mexico. Previous to this order I had published General Orders, No. 17, which posted a company of infantry at Franklin, Tex., and another one at Hart's Mill, Tex. It is herewith inclosed, marked P.

On September 1 I put the Texan prisoners of war whom I found at Franklin on their parole, and sent them on their way to San Antonio, Tex., escorted by Company D, First California Volunteer Cavalry. (See my letter to the commanding officer of the Confederate forces, San Antonio, Tex., marked Q.) I then returned to Las Cruces, N. Mex., where I published General Orders, No. 20 (marked R), regulating the affairs of the District of Arizona and transferring the command of that district to Col. Joseph R. West, First California Volunteer Infantry. (I still retain the command of the Column from California, and shall cause all the reports which you require in your letter to me, dated at San Francisco, May 30, to be sent to the headquarters Department of the Pacific, until I am otherwise ordered by competent authority.) I then proceeded to Santa Fé, arriving here on the 16th instant.

General Canby relinquished the command of the Department of New Mexico on the 18th instant. (See General Orders, No. 83, marked S.) I assumed command of the department on the same day. (See General Orders, No. 84, marked T.)

Some additional changes have been made of the troops pertaining to the Column from California, which are indicated in a letter to Colonel West, dated September 8 (marked U), and in another dated September 9 (marked V); also two others, dated September 14 (marked W and X, respectively).

I inclose for your information three communications (marked Y).[*] I also inclose a copy of an order directing Lieut. Col. Edward E. Eyre, First California Volunteer Cavalry, to bear these dispatches to the headquarters Department of the Pacific; it is marked Z.

These various communications will give General Wright a pretty good idea of the operations of the troops composing the Column from California from July 22, of this year, to the present time.

I find that the supply of provisions in this department is adequate to the wants of all the troops from California now serving here, and therefore respectfully recommend that no more subsistence stores be purchased for the Column from California until further advices on this subject. I propose to transport from Fort Yuma to Tucson during the cool weather of the fall and winter a large quantity of subsistence stores now in excess at the former post, so as to provide for the contingency of other troops being ordered to New Mexico from California; to provide for the troops already stationed in Arizona, and to form a magazine in case of any reverses here which may lead to the destruction of our present stores or oblige the California or other troops to retire towards the Pacific. When these supplies have been accumulated at Tucson by a train now employed for that purpose that train will be required for service in this department; meantime it can be used as transportation from Fort Yuma to the Rio Grande for any troops which General Wright may order from the Department of the Pacific into Arizona or New Mexico.

---

*Not found.

omitted

The Southern Overland Mail Route has been opened, and the military posts in Arizona, Southern New Mexico, and Northwestern Texas have been reoccupied by troops composing the Column from California. Thus far the instructions of the general commanding the Department of the Pacific have been carried out.

It was no fault of the troops from California that the Confederate forces fled before them. It is but just to say that their having thus fled is mainly to be attributed to the gallantry of the troops under General Canby's command. That they were hurried in their flight by the timely arrival of the advance guard of the Column from California, under Lieutenant-Colonel Eyre, there cannot be a doubt. The march from the Pacific to the Rio Grande by the Column from California was not accomplished without immense toil and great hardships or without many privations and much suffering from heat and want of water.

The amount of labor performed by Col. Joseph R. West, the second in command, was immense and of the greatest practical importance. Much of our success was dependent on his energy, perseverance, cheerfulness, and high soldierly qualities. I cannot too strongly recommend that this officer be promoted to the grade of brigadier-general of volunteers as a reward for these services, and particularly as he now commands the most important district in this department. I trust that General Wright will urge the necessity of this advancement of Colonel West, and set forth to the General-in-Chief his eminent fitness for the office of brigadier-general. This will promote Lieutenant-Colonel Rigg, which will be a reward for his important services as commanding officer at Fort Yuma during the past winter and for his efficient labors in the column while crossing the Great Desert. I regard Colonel Rigg as one of the finest soldiers in the Column from California. Those who knew the troops from California as I knew them will consider this a high compliment.

Lieut. Col. Edward E. Eyre, First California Volunteer Cavalry, deserves a regiment. The zeal he has manifested in the discharge of his duties and the alacrity and cheerfulness he has always shown when called upon for any hazardous enterprise distinguished him as one eminently fitted for the profession of arms. If five companies more of cavalry are to be sent from California, as requested by General Canby, I trust they will be added to the five which now compose the First California Volunteer Cavalry, and that Lieutenant-Colonel Eyre will be commissioned as full colonel.

The services of Major Coult, Fifth California Volunteer Infantry, and of Major Ferguson, First California Volunteer Cavalry, and of Major McMullen, First California Volunteer Infantry, have been most arduous and are deserving of reward.

The officers and men of the Second California Volunteer Cavalry and of the Fifth California Volunteer Infantry shared alike in all the privations and toil encountered by the First California Volunteer Infantry and the First California Volunteer Cavalry. As soldiers, in the highest acceptation of that word, they were all equally subordinate, patient, energetic, and patriotic. If I should select the names of some of them to be rewarded for these high qualities it would be an invidious distinction.

Capt. John B. Shinn and First Lieut. Franklin Harwood, of the Third U. S. Artillery, for their incessant toil by night and by day to bring the battery of light artillery which is attached to the Column from California through the Yuma and Gila Deserts, should each receive the compliment of a brevet—Captain Shinn to be brevetted as major and First Lieutenant Harwood as captain. Unless these young men are rewarded by a compliment of this kind I shall always feel that the passage of a battery of light artillery, always in fighting condition, over such an inhospitable waste, in the midst of the heats of summer, is a matter of such trivial importance in the profession of arms as not to be worthy of notice. Theirs was the first battery that ever crossed the desert. I am sure that he who crosses the next one will be considered an accomplished soldier.

I trust that General Wright will call the attention of the General-in-Chief to the credit which is eminently due these young gentlemen for their services in this column. I have already asked for promotion of my adjutant-general, Lieut. Benjamin C. Cutler; for my medical director, Surg. James M. McNulty, and for my regimental quartermaster, First Lieut. Lafayette Hammond, all of the First California Volunteer Infantry. Their merits are too well known at the headquarters Department of the Pacific to need any further words of commendation from myself.

In conclusion, I beg to thank General Wright for the confidence he always reposed in me. In carrying out his orders and instructions I have endeavored to do my best, yet, as it was a new and very extended field of operations, my judgment about what was best to be done under emergencies as they arose was doubtless not always of the soundest character; yet I feel that General Wright has kindly overlooked all imperfections of this nature, and saved me the pain of many rebukes, which no doubt I have deserved. For this I feel very grateful.

The march of the column from California in the summer months across the Great Desert, in the driest season that has ever been known for thirty years, is a military achievement creditable to the soldiers of the American Army; but it would not be just to attribute the success of this march to any ability on my part. That success was gained only by the high physical and moral energies of that peculiar class of officers and men who composed the Column from California. With any other troops I am sure I should have failed.

I send you a set of colors which have been borne by this column. They were hoisted by Colonel West on Forts Breckinridge and Buchanan, and over Tucson, Ariz.; by Colonel Eyre over Forts Thorn and Fillmore, and over Mesilla, N. Mex., and over Fort Bliss, in Texas. They were hoisted by Captain Cremony over Fort Quitman, and by Captain Shirland over Fort Davis, in Texas; and thus again have those places been consecrated to our beloved country.

All of which is respectfully submitted.

JAMES H. CARLETON,
Brigadier-General, U. S. Army, Commanding.

Lieut. Col. RICHARD C. DRUM,
Asst. Adjt. General, U. S. Army, San Francisco, Cal.

[Inclosure B.]

HEADQUARTERS COLUMN FROM CALIFORNIA,
Miembres River, Ariz., August 6, 1862.

Col. JOSEPH R. WEST,
First California Volunteer Infantry, Comdg. Camp:

COLONEL: I have been credibly informed that there are some 20 families of men, women, and children at the Pino Alto mines, some 40 ·

miles from this camp, who are nearly perishing for want of food, the Indians having robbed them of what they had, and the secessionists having captured and appropriated to themselves a train of supplies which was on the way some time since to their relief. You will send Capt. E. D. Shirland, First California Volunteer Cavalry, and Lieut. D. C. Vestal, First California Volunteer Infantry, with a sufficient escort of cavalry and infantry, to the Pino Alto mines with some provisions for these starving people. Send them 5 beeves, 600 pounds, more or less, of pemmican, 3,000 pounds of flour, and 1,500 pounds of panoche (Mexican sugar). These provisions will be given to the most needy. If it be not practicable to distribute them all at once, they will be left in the hands of some responsible man for this purpose, proper receipts being taken therefor. I instruct Captain Shirland particularly on these points, and direct him and Lieutenant Vestal to make a joint report on the number and sufferings of the people at Pino Alto, and whether they are strong enough to protect themselves from further harm from the Indians.

I am, respectfully, your obedient servant,
JAMES H. CARLETON,
Brigadier-General, U. S. Army.

[Inclosure C.]

CAMP ON RIO MIEMBRES, ARIZ.,
August 10, 1862.

Col. JOSEPH R. WEST,
First California Volunteer Infantry:

COLONEL: Pursuant to instructions received on the 6th instant we left this place on that day for the Pino Alto mines, taking with us a quantity of provisions for distribution among the inhabitants of that place, represented to be in a starving condition. We arrived there on the 7th, and called upon the principal men of the place to assist us in ascertaining the names, ages, business, condition, number, &c., of the inhabitants. We found about 30 Americans, French, Germans, &c.; two of the Germans with families; all the rest were Mexicans. Most of them were extremely poor and destitute, there being scarcely any ore at all in the mines. They had received some little assistance previous to our arrival, before which time they had been living on purslane and roots, and several had become insane from hunger.

*　　*　　*　　*　　*　　*

Number of families in the mines, two—Mr. Schneider's and Mr. Holtz's; number of Mexican families living in the mines, about 30, all extremely poor.

All the people seemed to be loyally inclined, although several of them had belonged to the Arizona Rangers, a company formed for the purpose of fighting the Indians in the Territory. The Indians were represented as being extremely hostile and in the habit of committing depredations upon the settlers whenever they had anything to steal. At the time of our visit there were no Indians in the neighborhood, but every one thought that as soon as trains with supplies commenced their trips the Indians would begin to commit depredations. All were extremely anxious to have the Government extend to them sufficient protection and station at least one company in their neighborhood.

Very respectfully, your obedient servant,
E. D. SHIRLAND,
Captain, First California Volunteer Cavalry.

[Inclosure D.]

HEADQUARTERS COLUMN FROM CALIFORNIA,
CAMP ON THE RIO GRANDE, ARIZ.,
Three and a half miles above Fort Thorn, August 8, 1862.

Brig. Gen. E. R. S. CANBY,
    Comdg. Department of New Mexico, Santa Fé, N. Mex.:

GENERAL: Before arriving at Cooke's Wells I learned that there was not any water to speak of between that point and El Picacho, on the Rio Grande, 55 miles from Cooke's Wells and 6 miles above Mesilla. The Rio Grande had divided in the great flood and broken across the country, so as to leave the town of Mesilla on an island, difficult of access from the west, and that the facilities for grazing in the neighborhood of Mesilla were bad. This information decided me to strike the Rio Grande at or near Fort Thorn, a distance of not less than 35 miles, nor more than 40, from Cooke's Wells, but destitute of water the whole way.

I arrived here last evening with two companies of cavalry and one of infantry, having left Cooke's Wells at 8 a. m. The other detachments—West's, Willis', and Rigg's, a day apart—will reach this point, commencing with West's, to-morrow evening. I leave to-day for the San Diego Crossing, at the foot of the Jornada, and I shall pass the Rio Grande at that point.

I have this day written to Colonel Howe, that if they have not already left Fort Craig, to go up the river. The Colorado Volunteers can leave at once, agreeably with your Special Orders, No. 128, current series.

I inclose for your information a copy of a note to Colonel West, First California Volunteer Infantry, in relation to sending some provisions to some destitute men, women, and children at the Pino Alto mines.

If I have authority to occupy posts in the northwestern portion of Texas, *i. e.*, Forts Bliss and ——, will you permit me to have my headquarters, say, at Hart's Mill, on the Rio Grande, some 3 miles above Fort Bliss?

I am, general, very respectfully, your obedient servant,
            JAMES H. CARLETON,
                Brigadier-General, U. S. Army.

NOTE.—My command did not use tents in crossing the desert. I had a few (two to a company) when I left Tucson, but 13 of these were left to shelter the garrison at Fort Bowie, Apache Pass, Chiricahua Mountains. I have sent to Fort Yuma to have all the tents at that post repaired and sent on as soon as possible. Should I need them, can you lend me some?

I left Tucson July 23; stopped one day at the Cienega de Sauz, and four and a half at Ojo de la Vaca, and arrived here on the 7th.
                                                J. H. C.

[Inclosure F.]

HEADQUARTERS DEPARTMENT OF NEW MEXICO,
        Santa Fé, N. Mex., August 11, 1862.

Brig. Gen. JAMES H. CARLETON,
    Commanding Column from California, District of Arizona:

GENERAL: I have just received your interesting communication of the 2d instant and the accompanying papers.

The chief quartermaster, Lieutenant-Colonel Donaldson, has been instructed to send an additional supply of clothing to the depot at Fort Craig to meet your immediate wants. He will communicate with your chief quartermaster in relation to the wants of your command and the supplies that can be furnished from the depots under his charge.

I have directed the chief commissary to place $30,000 subsistence funds in the hands of the commissary at Fort Craig, subject to your order. This course has been adopted in consequence of the insecurity of the mails below Fort Craig. He also will communicate with your commissary in relation to his branch of the service.

The statement of your medical director has been referred to the medical director of the department, who will send to you such medical and hospital supplies as appear to be needed. The medical supplies and ordnance stores in the department will be largely in excess of the wants of the troops, and as both classes are liable to deterioration, it will be advisable to exhaust those on hand before drawing again from the east or the Pacific coast. If you have not already ordered these supplies from Fort Yuma, please make your requisitions upon the depots in this department.

The depot at Fort Craig will be subject to requisitions, and any supplies that are not there now will be sent there as soon as advised that you need them. A part of the supplies will be late in reaching that point, having been detained by the commander of the Department of Kansas until he could provide an escort for them, and subsequently delayed by the unusual floods in the Arkansas.

I have heretofore recommended that all posts in Arizona west of the Rio Grande should be supplied by the way of the Gulf of California and Guaymas. From the information contained in your letter the cost of transportation from Guaymas to points on the Rio Grande below Fort Craig will be about the same as to the depot at Fort Union.

One of the paymasters in this department has been ordered to the East for the purpose of renewing his bond and the commission of another has expired, leaving but one for the payments now in progress. Another is expected by the next mail from the East, and as soon after he arrives as possible arrangements will be made for the payment of your command.

The wants of your men in tobacco and sutler's stores will be made known to the merchants in this city, who will no doubt be very glad of the opportunity of supplying them.

General Wright has given a more extended application to War Department General Orders, No. 29, than I have understood it to warrant. That, however, is of no material consequence. We are here in the same cause and for a common purpose, and nothing shall be wanting on my part to insure the harmony of action which is essential to efficiency, and I feel assured from your character that I may count upon your co-operation in everything that has for its object the advancement of the honor and interest of our country.

Please communicate with me freely, and be assured that whatever I can do, either officially or personally, to advance the interests or add to the comforts of your command will be done with the greatest pleasure.

Very respectfully, sir, your obedient servant,

ED. R. S. CANBY,
Brigadier-General, Commanding Department.

HEADQUARTERS DEPARTMENT OF NEW MEXICO,
Santa Fé, N. Mex., August 11, 1862.

Brig. Gen. JAMES H. CARLETON,
  Commanding Column from California, District of Arizona:

GENERAL : At an early period of last year I reported that an invasion of Texas from New Mexico, although practicable, was not a practicable undertaking ; the length of the march, the desert character of
the country to be traversed, the scarcity of supplies on the route, the
necessity of bringing from the Missouri River or from the Pacific coast
every article of equipment and munition and much of the food, all con-
spired to make it an undertaking of great magnitude and of questionable value; and that the troops that would be required for the expedition
could be more usefully employed at points that are not only near the
sources of supply but near the points to be attacked. The same views
appeared to have been entertained at the Headquarters of the Army, as
before my report could have reached Washington I received instructions
to withdraw first a part and afterward the whole of the regular force
then in New Mexico. These last instructions were subsequently so
modified as to direct the withdrawal of these troops "at such time and
in such manner as would not expose the Territory to conquest or invasion before the volunteer troops of New Mexico are properly organized,
armed, and posted."

At a later period I reported that it would be difficult, if not impracticable, to raise the additional force authorized for this Territory ; nor
do I think it desirable that it should be done if it is practicable to send
one or two volunteer regiments from the East to replace the regular
troops when they are withdrawn. The New Mexican Volunteers, unless
supported by regular troops or by volunteers drawn from some other
section of the country, cannot be relied on to resist invasion of the
Territory if one is attempted.

When a force from the Department of the Mississippi was under
orders for this department I received instructions from the Secretary
of War to disband the New Mexican Volunteers whenever I thought
proper. The force from the Department of the Mississippi was subsequently diverted from its destination, and soon after information was
received that your command was on the march. I have coupled these
changes with the instructions for the movement of the regular troops,
and supposed that your command was intended for service in New
Mexico. Acting upon this supposition, I have reported that " the near
approach of General Carleton's force justifies the opinion that the regular troops may now be withdrawn, as originally intended, without
detriment to the service," and have already made some arrangements
for the movement; but as there have been some material changes since
these instructions were given, I do not intend to put any of the regular
troops beyond the reach of recall until I receive further instructions.
I have been thus particular, not only for the purpose of answering your
question, but to indicate the policy and instructions under which I have
been acting, and which I suppose will devolve upon you when the regular troops leave the country.

In the arrangements that were made for the reoccupation of Arizona
it was my intention to restore the sovereignty of the United States in
its original integrity, post the troops so as to protect the inhabitants
and guard against invasion, and, in addition, to occupy such points in
Texas as could be reached without throwing the troops so employed

beyond the reach of support. This has been directed in general terms in the instructions given to the commander of the Southern Military District, and who would also have been the commander of the expedition organized for that purpose. Copies of these instructions have already been furnished you. The retreat of the rebels and the approach of your command rendered it unnecessary to send this force below the Jornada, and, with the exception of the infantry battalion and the cavalry force with Lieutenant-Colonel Eyre, it has been recalled. The detachments will also be recalled, but the movement will not be commenced until your arrangements are so far perfected that it can be done without inconvenience.

I do not think that an invasion of New Mexico will again be attempted by the Rio Grande; but if our troops in the Southwest should meet with any serious reverses, it may be by the Canadian or attempts may be made to interrupt our communications with the East. This last I have regarded as the most probable danger, and some time since requested the commander of the Department of Kansas to place a sufficient force on that line (within his department) to secure it. The renewal of the disturbances in Missouri has prevented this, and I am now putting some of the Colorado troops on the line.

If there should be no change in the order for the removal of the regular troops a part of your command will probably be needed at and above Fort Craig. I have estimated the force required at that post and the Rio Grande as far as Fort Bliss at 2,000 men. I infer from your letter of May 3 that you can readily be re-enforced from California, and there is no doubt that troops can better be spared from that State than from any other quarter. I make these suggestions now for your consideration, and will be pleased to hear from you in relation to them before any general movement of the regular troops takes place.

Very respectfully, sir, your obedient servant,
ED. R. S. CANBY,
Brigadier-General, Commanding Department.

[Inclosure H.]

HEADQUARTERS DEPARTMENT OF NEW MEXICO,
Santa Fé, N. Mex., August 12, 1862.
Brig. Gen. JAMES H. CARLETON,
Commanding Column from California, District of Arizona :

GENERAL : I have just received your communication of the 8th instant. It is my wish that you should exercise your own judgment both with regard to the distribution of your troops and the point at which your headquarters will be established. My instructions to Colonel Chivington of June 22 and subsequent dates were predicated upon the supposition that he would meet with some resistance, and were more in detail than I should have considered necessary with an officer of more experience.

In my letter of yesterday I gave the general tenor of my instructions, in order that you might use your discretion in carrying out the policy of the Government with reference to this department. Directions will be given to send tents to Fort Craig for the use of your command, and I trust that you will not hesitate in asking for anything that will add to the comfort of your command. If not already at Fort Craig, it will be sent there, and if not now in abundance, we will share what we have, and renew our supplies when the trains come in. It will probably be necessary for a time to send your own transportation to Fort Craig for any supplies that you may need from that place.

Very respectfully, sir, your obedient servant,

ED. R. S. CANBY,
Brigadier-General, Commanding Department.

[Inclosure I.]

HEADQUARTERS DISTRICT OF ARIZONA,
Las Cruces, N. Mex., August 15, 1862.

Brig. Gen. E. R. S. CANBY,
Commanding Department of New Mexico, Santa Fé, N. Mex.:

GENERAL: I wrote to you a letter from Ojo de la Vaca on the 2d instant advising you of the strength of the forces under my command then *en route* to the Rio Grande. Since then I have not received any letters from your headquarters advising me of the receipt of that communication. The inclosed general orders (Nos. 14 and 15, from these headquarters) will give you an idea of the force stationed at Mesilla. In Las Cruces there are four companies of the Fifth U. S. Infantry; at Fort Fillmore there are Shinn's light battery, Third U. S. Artillery; Companies A and E, First California Volunteer Infantry; Company B, Fifth California Volunteer Infantry, and Companies B and D, First California Volunteer Cavalry, and Company B, Second California Volunteer Cavalry. I placed all the cavalry and nearly all the quartermaster's wagons and teams at Fort Fillmore on account of the good grazing in that vicinity and the abundance of mesquite beans now in that neighborhood, which for the present precludes the necessity of purchasing much forage. As there are sufficient quarters at La Mesilla for the four companies of the Fifth U. S. Infantry I shall establish them in that town, unless otherwise directed by yourself, at least for the present. The emulation which will naturally spring up between them and the volunteers, as to who shall best perform their duties, will, in my opinion, be of great service to both; besides, there is a fine building there, where the supplies—quartermaster's and subsistence—can be kept free of expense, and the town of Mesilla is said to be a cooler and healthier locality than Las Cruces. Colonel Howe wrote to me desiring that I would send these four companies to Fort Craig, but this I do not feel authorized to do unless you order it.

Mr. Woods, the beef contractor, wrote me a note in relation to furnishing beef for my command. It is herewith inclosed,* together with my reply. I hope my decision in this case will meet with your approval. I have not yet learned officially whether Mr. Woods will or not supply beef for only the four companies of regulars; I have heard that he would not.

To-morrow I leave for Fort Bliss, in Texas, with Companies B, of the First, and B, of the Second, California Volunteer Cavalry. Company C, First California Volunteer Cavalry, is already at Hart's Mill, as you had doubtless heard previous to my arrival. There are many matters of moment which require my attention, as I have heard, in the neighborhood of Fort Bliss.

I am, general, very respectfully, your obedient servant,

JAMES H. CARLETON,
Brigadier-General, Commanding.

---

* Not found.

[Inclosure K.]

GENERAL ORDERS, } HDQRS. COL. FROM CAL., CAMP ON RIO GRANDE,
    No. 16.   }   Near Fort Quitman, Tex., August 22, 1862.

I. At 12 m. to-day Capt. John C. Cremony, with his company (B, of the Second California Volunteer Cavalry), will proceed to Fort Quitman and hoist over it the national colors, the old Stars and Stripes. By this act still another post comes under its rightful flag and once more becomes consecrated to the United States.

II. Capt. Edmond D. Shirland, First California Volunteer Cavalry, will proceed without delay, yet by easy marches, to Fort Davis, Tex., and hoist over that post the national colors. If Captain Shirland finds any sick or wounded soldiers there he will make them prisoners of war, but put them upon their parole and let them proceed without delay to Texas. If they are unable to travel, Captain Shirland will report to these headquarters by express what they need in the way of surgical or medical attention; what they need in the way of food or transportation, and all other essential facts connected with them which it may be necessary to have known to have them properly cared for. If the fort is abandoned, Captain Shirland will retrace his steps and report in person to these headquarters.

III. Twenty effective men will be ordered from Company B, First California Volunteer Cavalry, to report to Captain Shirland for detached service to Fort Davis, Tex.

By order of Brigadier-General Carleton:

BEN. C. CUTLER,
First Lieut., First Cal. Vol. Infantry, A. A. A. G.

[Inclosure I.]

CAMP ON RIO GRANDE, September 2, 1862.
Lieut. BENJ. C. CUTLER,
    Actg. Asst. Adjt. Gen., Franklin, Tex.:

LIEUTENANT: I have the honor to state that, in pursuance to instructions received from General James H. Carleton, commanding Column from California, I left this camp at 3 p. m. August 23 en route to Fort Davis. Encamped at 8 o'clock the same evening, having marched 15 miles.

Started at daybreak of the 24th and arrived at Eagle Springs at 9.30 a. m., 17 miles; found the springs filled with rubbish and carrion; by cleaning them out found water for men and animals. There being no grass in the vicinity, I left the springs at 4 p. m.; marched about 5 miles and made a dry camp; grass abundant and good.

Started at daybreak and marched 20 miles to Van Horn's Wells; found these wells entirely filled up; cleared out one of them, but found it impossible to obtain sufficient water for the men. Many of the horses being unfit to proceed farther, I thought it best to go on from here with 20 men and picked horses, taking the ambulance with me. Accordingly I directed Lieutenant Haden to retrace his steps to Eagle Springs with the remainder of the detachment, to clean out the springs thoroughly, and to remain there eight days, unless he received other orders from me. If at the expiration of eight days I should not have returned or sent back an express, I directed him to return to the river and wait for me there two days and then proceed up the river and report to General Carleton.

37 R R—VOL IX

I left Van Horn's Wells at about 4 p. m. and arrived at Dead Man's Hole at about 2 a. m.; found sufficient water there for the animals, but not enough for a company; distance 35 miles.

Started at 6.30 a. m. and arrived at Barrel Springs at 3 p. m., having halted on the road to graze the animals. Found water enough at these springs for one company. Remained here that night, and on the next afternoon sent forward Corporal Bartlett, with one private and the Mexican guide, to find out the condition of affairs at Fort Davis, distant 18 miles. They returned about noon the next day, having performed their duty in such a manner that if the fort had been occupied by the Confederate States troops their (Corporal Bartlett and party) presence could not have been discovered. They reported the fort unoccupied, and I, thinking it best not to send back for the company on account of the scarcity of water, proceeded to the fort. I found it entirely deserted, but in one of the buildings of the Overland Mail Company I found the dead body of a man lying on the floor. He had been shot through the body with a bullet and had an arrow wound on the head and one on the arm. From the appearance of the room I think that it had been used by the Confederate troops as a hospital, and this man left there sick and afterward killed by the Indians. I had the body buried. The fort appears to have been garrisoned by the Confederate States troops since their first appearance in the country by at least a portion of one company. It also seemed to have been used as a rendezvous for sick soldiers, but they had all left with the last detachment for San Antonio.

The following is a description of the buildings at the fort: Five company quarters, about 80 by 25 feet; one story high; built of stone; thatched roof. Four of these buildings are in fair condition. The roof, doors, and windows of one have been burned. One guard-house, about 80 by 25 feet; building stone; roof, doors, and windows burned. One quartermaster's store-house, about 100 by 20 feet, built of stone; roof, doors, and windows entirely destroyed; surrounded by several small buildings; use not known. One wooden or slab building, 30 by 16 feet; thatched roof; used as an adjutant's office. One wooden building, 36 by 27 feet, with kitchen and several small outbuildings; supposed to have been the commanding officer's quarters. On this building the flag was raised and kept up one day. One wooden building, 48 by 22 feet, with kitchen and outhouses attached; supposed to have been officers' quarters. One wooden building, 22 by 12 feet, with one small outbuilding, 10 by 14 feet. One wooden building, 36 by 18 feet; one outbuilding, 14 by 12 feet; one slab building, 40 by 15 feet; one slab building, 50 by 14 feet; one slab building, 20 by 12 feet; one slab building, 20 by 12 feet; one slab building, 30 by 15 feet; one outhouse, 10 by 12 feet; seven small slab outhouses; one slab stable, 50 by 14 feet; one stone and mud house; three small slab buildings. These are estimated measurements, as I had no other means of doing. One Overland Mail station, consisting of house, store-house, shop, stable, saddlery, granary, &c.; one adobe building, formerly used as a store. Many of the doors and windows have been destroyed. Some seem to have been hauled off; others burned. One wagon stands loaded with lumber. I have heard a report, in fact, that the entire fort was sold by the Confederate States officers to some party at Del Norte, Mexico. Property consists of some iron in quartermaster's store-house, some 100 horseshoes, two old citizen wagons, several wagon and cart wheels, empty barrels, several chains, many hospital bedsteads, but all broken or in a dilapidated condition.

I started from the fort on my return at daylight of the 30th and marched to Dead Man's Hole; watered the animals, and made a dry camp in the prairie.

Left camp at 9 a. m. and marched about 10 miles, when an Indian made his appearance with a white flag, followed by 5 others, all mounted. I tried to hold a talk with them, but they seemed unwilling to have anything to say, they being followed by 25 or 30 more mounted men, and still farther behind was a large party on foot, and it being evident that their only intention was to gain time and delay us until they could surround us, coming towards us in every direction, a large proportion of them mounted. Wishing to get rid of the footmen, I made a running fight of it, expecting the mounted men to follow, which they did for a short distance; but finding it too hot for them, they returned. They left 4 men dead on the field, 2 of them the leaders, respectively, of the mounted and footmen. I have good reason to believe that at least 20 were wounded. I had 2 men wounded, 1 slightly and 1 painfully, by a pistol-ball in the shoulder. I had also 1 horse wounded.

I then came on to Eagle Springs, where I arrived at 11 p. m., watered all my animals, and found that Lieutenant Haden, with the remainder of the command, had left for the river several days before. Encamped for the remainder of the night, and on the next day proceeded to the river, arriving there about 5 p. m., and found Lieutenant Haden, with the remainder of the command, he stating that he could not find sufficient water at Eagle Springs for the use of the animals.

I omitted in the foregoing report to state that about 10 miles from Van Horn's Wells I met two Mexicans coming this way. I arrested them and brought them to this camp, where I released them, and they went on up the river and will report to General Carleton in person.

I am, sir, very respectfully, your obedient servant,

E. D. SHIRLAND,
Captain Company C, First California Volunteer Cavalry.

[Inclosure M.]

HEADQUARTERS DEPARTMENT OF NEW MEXICO,
August 10, 1862.

To the ADJUTANT-GENERAL,
Washington, D. C.:

General Carleton's force in the Mesilla will be less by 700 men than is stated in my report of the 6th. He reports that he can be followed by another regiment of infantry or more. I recommend that one regiment of infantry and five companies of cavalry be ordered from California. The regular troops can be ready to leave as soon as the answer to my report of the 6th is received, or earlier if I find it safe to move them.

ED. R. S. CANBY,
Brigadier-General.

[Inclosure N.]

HEADQUARTERS DEPARTMENT OF NEW MEXICO,
Santa Fé, N. Mex., August 21, 1862.

Brig. Gen. JAMES H. CARLETON,
Commanding District of Arizona, Fort Bliss, Tex.:

GENERAL: The commanding general desires that you will arrange the affairs of your district so that the command may be turned over to

the officer next in rank as soon as practicable, and hold yourself in readiness to repair to the headquarters of the department.
Very respectfully, your obedient servant,
GURDEN CHAPIN,
Captain, Seventh U. S. Infantry, Actg. Asst. Adjt. Gen.

[Inclosure O.]

SPECIAL ORDERS, } HDQRS. DEPARTMENT OF NEW MEXICO,
No. 153.   }   *Santa Fé, N. Mex., August 26, 1862.*
Brig. Gen. James H. Carleton, U. S. Army, will repair without delay to Santa Fé, for the purpose of relieving Brigadier-General Canby in the command of the Department of New Mexico.
By order of Brigadier-General Canby:
GURDEN CHAPIN,
Captain, Seventh U. S. Infantry, Actg. Asst. Adjt. Gen.

[Inclosure P.]

GENERAL ORDERS, } HEADQUARTERS DISTRICT OF ARIZONA,
No. 17.   }   *Franklin, Tex., August 27, 1862.*
*   *   *   *   *   *   *

II. Captain Roberts' company (E, First California Volunteer Infantry) and Captain Pishon's company (D, First California Volunteer Cavalry) will be ordered by Colonel West to proceed without delay to Franklin, Tex., where Captain Roberts' company will take post, and whence Captain Pishon's company will march to Fort Stockton, in Texas, as a guard to some prisoners of the Confederate Army who are to be sent to Texas on parole.
Each of these companies will be rationed from the depot at Mesilla to include the 30th proximo. Besides these rations Colonel West will send, escorted by Roberts' company, 6,000 rations of subsistence stores from the Mesilla depot to Franklin, Tex.
By order of Brigadier-General Carleton:
BEN. C. CUTLER,
First Lieutenant, First Cal. Vol. Infantry, A. A. A. G.

[Inclosure Q.]

HEADQUARTERS DISTRICT OF ARIZONA,
Franklin, Tex., September 1, 1862.

COMMANDER OF CONFEDERATE TROOPS, SAN ANTONIO, TEX.:
SIR: I found on my arrival here some 20-odd sick and wounded soldiers of the Confederate States Army, whom I was ordered by General Canby, commanding the Department of New Mexico, to make prisoners of war. These men, at their earnest solicitation, I sent to San Antonio on their parole. They have been furnished with rations of subsistence for forty days and with such medicines and hospital stores as were necessary for them for the road. I have also furnished two wagons for the transportation of those who are unable to walk, and I have sent an escort of 1 lieutenant and 25 rank and file of the First California Volunteer Cavalry to guard them from attack by Mexicans or Indians until a sufficient force from your army is met, to whom they may be transferred, or until they reach some point near San Antonio, where from thence onward they can travel with safety. From that point the lieutenant is ordered to return with his party and all

the means of transportation belonging to the United States with which he is intrusted for the use of his escort and benefit of these prisoners.
I have the honor to be, very respectfully, your obedient servant,

JAMES H. CARLETON,
Brigadier-General, U. S. Army, Commanding.

[Inclosure R.]

GENERAL ORDERS, } HEADQUARTERS DISTRICT OF ARIZONA,
No. 20.   }   *Las Cruces, N. Mex., September 5, 1862.*

I. Maj. Theodore A. Coult, Fifth California Volunteer Infantry, will proceed without delay to Tucson, and relieve Maj. David Ferguson, First California Volunteer Cavalry, in the command of the District of Western Arizona.

II. Maj. David Ferguson, First California Volunteer Cavalry, is hereby relieved from duty as chief commissary of the Column from California, and will immediately transfer all funds, property, records, &c., pertaining to the subsistence department to Capt. Nicholas S. Davis, First California Volunteer Infantry, who is hereby appointed acting chief commissary of the Column from California. Having done this, Major Ferguson will proceed, via Arivaca and Altar or Cubero, without delay, to a point at or near Lobos Bay, on the Gulf of California, known as Libertad, and examine the intermediate country, with a view to the transportation of supplies. He will ascertain the resources of the country on this route; also the availability of Lobos Bay as a port where the military supplies destined for Arizona may be landed. Major Ferguson will then repair in person to the headquarters District of Arizona, and make a report of his examination of the Port Lobos route to the general commanding the Column from California. As soon thereafter as practicable Major Ferguson will assume command of his regiment, the First California Volunteer Cavalry.

III. Capt. Nicholas S. Davis, chief of transportation of the Column from California, will discharge all mechanics from Government employment at Tucson, except such as may be necessary to keep the train that plies to Fort Yuma in repairs. This train and any other quartermaster's property in Western Arizona for which he is responsible may, if the exigencies of the service so require it, be transferred by Captain Davis to the depot quartermaster at Tucson. Captain Davis and Lieutenant Lysander E. Hanson, First California Volunteer Infantry, with Mr. George C. Alexander, clerk to the chief commissary of the Column from California, will report by the first opportunity to the commander of the District of Arizona.

IV. Surg. John H. Prentiss, First California Volunteer Cavalry, will relieve Surgeon McNulty as medical purveyor of the District of Arizona, and will receipt for the medical supplies appertaining to the same.

V. Estimates for medical supplies and ammunition required at Fort Bowie and Tucson will be made upon the proper officers at the headquarters of the District of Arizona.

VI. Brigadier-General Carleton having been ordered to Santa Fé, to relieve Brigadier-General Canby, in the command of the Department of New Mexico, he hereby relinquishes the command of the District of Arizona to Col. Joseph R. West, First California Volunteer Infantry. Brigadier-General Carleton still retains the command of the Column from California, and his staff—Actg. Asst. Adjt. Gen. Benjamin C. Cutler, Surg. James M. McNulty, Lieutenant-Colonel Eyre, chief quartermaster, and Lieut. Joseph F. Bennett, acting assistant adjutant-general—will accompany him to Santa Fé, starting to-day.

VII. The District of Arizona comprises the Territory of Arizona and that portion of New Mexico which lies south of an east and west line drawn through Fort Thorn and also Northwestern Texas. The executive powers assumed by Brigadier-General Carleton in his proclamation, dated at Tucson, June 8, 1862, will, until further orders, be retained by that officer.

By order of Brigadier-General Carleton :

BEN. C. CUTLER,
First Lieutenant, First Cal.Vol. Infantry, A. A. A. G.

[Inclosure S.]

GENERAL ORDERS, }   HDQRS. DEPARTMENT OF NEW MEXICO,
    No. 83.   }   *Santa Fé, N. Mex., September 18, 1862.*

The undersigned hereby relinquishes the command of this department to Brig. Gen. J. H. Carleton, and is gratified in announcing as his successor an officer whose character, services, and experience in this country entitle him to the confidence of the people of New Mexico.

In taking leave of the troops he has for some time had the honor to command he desires to leave with them the assurance of his high respect and admiration and his best wishes for their happiness and advancement.

ED. R. S. CANBY,
Brigadier-General, U. S. Volunteers.

[Inclosure T.]

GENERAL ORDERS, }   HDQRS. DEPARTMENT OF NEW MEXICO,
    No. 84.   }   *Santa Fé, N. Mex., September 18, 1862.*

I. The undersigned hereby assumes command of the Department of New Mexico.

II. The following staff officers are announced: First Lieut. Ben. C. Cutler, First California Infantry, acting assistant adjutant-general; Maj. Henry D. Wallen, Seventh U. S. Infantry, acting inspector-general; Capt. A. W. Evans, Sixth U. S. Cavalry, acting assistant inspector-general; Capt. John C. McFerran, U. S. Army, chief quartermaster; Capt. A. F. Garrison, U. S. Volunteers, chief commissary of subsistence; Surg. E. I. Baily, U. S. Army, medical director. Surg. James M. McNulty, of the First California Volunteer Infantry, in addition to his duties as medical director of the Column from California, is assigned to duty as acting medical inspector of the Department of New Mexico, and will be governed in the performance of these duties by such instructions as he may receive from these headquarters. Maj. William J. Martin, U. S. Army, chief paymaster. Capt. William H. Rossell, Tenth U. S. Infantry, will continue to perform the duties of disbursing officer of the fund for collecting, drilling, and organizing volunteers. Capt. William R. Shoemaker, military store-keeper of ordnance, will perform the duties of chief of ordnance at Fort Union.

III. The orderly hours at department headquarters will be from 9 to 10 a. m. for chiefs of staff departments and officers on duty, and from 11 a. m. to 12 m. for citizens on business.

IV. All orders and instructions from headquarters Department of New Mexico, unless hereafter modified or repealed, will remain in full force; and particular attention is directed to department General Orders, No. 62, of July 7, 1862; its requirements will be strictly observed.

JAMES H. CARLETON,
Brigadier-General, U. S. Volunteers, Comdg. Department.

[Inclosure U.]

HEADQUARTERS COLUMN FROM CALIFORNIA,
Jornada del Muerto, N. Mex., September 8, 1862.

Col. JOSEPH R. WEST,
Commanding District of Arizona, Mesilla, Ariz.:

COLONEL: I met this morning some paroled prisoners of war. I have heard there are 93 of them. They are on their way to Texas. Surgeon Covey, of the C. S. Army, who goes with them, informs me that they have some arms belonging to the United States, with which to defend themselves *en route* to San Antonio. Give orders so that Lieutenant French, First California Cavalry, whom I sent towards Texas with other prisoners, may bring these arms and this transportation back, escorted by his men. I have not received one word of instruction in relation to these prisoners, and know nothing about them except what I gleaned from orders in Lieutenant Bennett's possession and from what Surgeon Covey told me. Having these arms they will need no escort from you, and it will not be well to have our men and animals broken down without good cause. Keep them moving. Have no delays at Fillmore. Let them camp down near, but not at, the grazing camp. Do not let them delay at all at Franklin. If care is taken the brigands and others in El Paso will attempt to communicate with them and may be caught. Surgeon Covey should not know the full extent of our force now *en route* from California.

*   *   *   *   *   *   *

Be sure and have Wagon-master Veck report at Peralta with 15 wagons and the ambulance and team and driver which went below with me (Truett's).

Assistant Wagon-master Francis will be placed in charge of the train of 25 wagons which are to go to Tucson. No soldier teamster will go with that train, and no man who is mustered as teamster who does not drive a team; nor will any such men be permitted to remain with any train, whether in camp or on the road. All such men will at once be provided with teams, and a like number of soldiers be relieved from extra duty. I desire that you will see that this rule goes into effect at once. Should a teamster become sick in camp or on the road, his place will be supplied temporarily by a soldier. It follows, therefore, that there will not be a single man mustered as teamster who does not drive a team, nor will any extra man be allowed as a cook for the teamsters. They must cook for themselves. If you can swoop up other people about you who had better travel to Texas, now is a good opportunity to send them to that country.

You must discharge every civil employé whose services are not indispensably necessary.

Please make me a report of the amount of provisions you have on hand and the number of troops, &c., to be rationed, as soon as the Texans have gone.

I am, colonel, very respectfully, your obedient servant,
JAMES H. CARLETON,
Brigadier-General, U. S. Army, Commanding.

NOTE.—Ask Colonel Bowie to do me the favor to release and send to California a political prisoner named J. S. Bratton on his taking the oath of allegiance.

J. H. C.

HEADQUARTERS COLUMN FROM CALIFORNIA,
Fort Craig, N. Mex., September 9, 1862.

Col. JOSEPH R. WEST,
Commanding District of Arizona, Mesilla, Ariz.:

COLONEL: Captain Archer, commissary of subsistence at this post, informs me that he sent $5,000 subsistence funds to Lieutenant Baldwin at the time the Confederate prisoners went below a few days since. This must be transferred to your depot commissary or be disbursed under your direction. He informs me that he can send, on your estimate (dated September 1, 1862), for $19,986.66, $10,000 in drafts on the assistant treasurer in New York. The remainder will be sent to you as soon as Captain Garrison gives him further authority to make additional drafts. I have placed in his hands your estimates for stores, for expenditures, veterinary tools, and horse medicines, carpenter's tools, stationery, miscellaneous tools, and for blank forms, and asked him to fill them as far as he can and send them on to me, to be completed at other depots when Veck comes up. The articles from Fort Craig will be sent down on the train which came up with me.

*   *   *   *   *   *   *

Your arrangement about sending Swilling as an expressman is a good one, and I have given Colonel Steen a memorandum of it, and will endeavor to have the time so fixed for other expressmen that there will be no delay in the transmittal of letters up and down the river.

Please give Azbon C. Marcy, who took the oath of allegiance to Colonel Eyre, a free pass to California.

I inclose herewith a list of the quartermaster's property on hand at this post. I have asked Captain Archer to send one also of the subsistence stores, which will embrace many things received to-day.

*   *   *   *   *   *   *

Whatever you want to make your command efficient you shall have. Only bear in mind not to get a thing you do not need. I wish to accumulate but little of public stores below the Jornada.

Very respectfully, your obedient servant,
JAMES H. CARLETON,
Brigadier-General, U. S. Army, Commanding.

HEADQUARTERS COLUMN FROM CALIFORNIA,
Albuquerque, N. Mex., September 14, 1862.

Col. JOSEPH R. WEST,
First Cal. Vol. Infantry, Comdg. Dist. of Arizona:

COLONEL: By the same express which carries this letter you will receive an order from department headquarters, directing you to send troops to Fort Craig to relieve the garrison now at that post. The general commanding directs that you send for this purpose Lieut. Col. Edwin A. Rigg, First California Volunteer Infantry, with about 200 rank and file, so selected as not to take from your command more than three companies.

Captain Fritz, First California Volunteer Cavalry, will proceed to Tucson, as previously directed, with 25 wagons. If Wagon-master Veck has not already started for Peralta with 15 wagons, as directed, the general commanding orders that his train be increased to 35 wagons.

If he has already started, send 20 additional wagons when Colonel Rigg goes to Fort Craig. Wagon-master Francis will go with Captain Fritz to Tucson, and Winston will remain with the rest of the wagons.

I am, colonel, very respectfully, your obedient servant,
BEN. C. CUTLER,
Acting Assistant Adjutant-General.

[Inclosure X.]

HEADQUARTERS COLUMN FROM CALIFORNIA,
Albuquerque, N. Mex., September 14, 1862.

Col. JOSEPH R. WEST, *Comdg. Dist. of Arizona, Mesilla, Ariz.:*

COLONEL: It is presumed, from advices lately received from Maj. David Ferguson, First California Volunteer Cavalry, commanding District of Western Arizona, that about 1,000 head of cattle will shortly be at Tucson *en route* to the Rio Grande for the use of the Column from California. The general commanding directs that you give to the commanding officer at Tucson such detailed instructions as will insure the arrival in this valley of these cattle at an early day. After deducting a sufficient number for the use of the troops in the District of Western Arizona, the cattle should be sent forward in small herds, so that too many may not arrive at the watering places at any one time—say, one portion with Greene's company and another with Wellman's cavalry and so on.

The general commanding directs that you arrest one Manuel Barella, a brother of Anastacio Barella, of Mesilla, and send him up the country as far as Fort Craig.

I am, colonel, very respectfully, your obedient servant,
BEN. C. CUTLER,
First Lieutenant, First Cal. Vol. Infantry, A. A. A. G.

[Inclosure Z.]

SPECIAL ORDERS, }   HDQRS. COLUMN FROM CALIFORNIA,
No. 36.   }   *Santa Fé, N. Mex., September* 17, 1862.

*   *   *   *   *   *   *

II. Lieut. Col. Edward E. Eyre, First California Volunteer Cavalry, will proceed without delay to San Francisco, Cal., as bearer of dispatches to the commander of the Department of the Pacific, in accordance with Special Orders, No. 148, from Headquarters Department of New Mexico, dated August 22, 1862. Having performed this duty, he will rejoin his regiment at the earliest practicable moment.

By order of Brigadier-General Carleton:
BEN. C. CUTLER,
First Lieutenant, First Cal. Vol. Infantry, A. A. A. G.

No. 2.

Reports of Lieut. Col. Edward E. Eyre, First California Cavalry.

HDQRS. FIRST CALIFORNIA VOLUNTEER CAVALRY,
Fort Thorn, Ariz., July 6, 1862.

LIEUTENANT: In compliance with orders received from the colonel commanding, dated June 17, 1862, I have the honor to make the following report:

. June 21, left Tucson at 3 a. m. with Captain Fritz, Lieutenants Haden and Baldwin, First California Volunteer Cavalry, and 140 men; marched 35 miles to Cienega de los Pinos, and encamped at 12.30 p. m.; water and grazing abundant. The road to-day is very good, with the exception of two or three hills. At a distance of about 28 miles the road descends into the cienega, then 7 miles to water near the burned station, which stood on the hill to the right of the road. Course, southeast; 35 miles.

June 22, left Ciénega at 6 a. m.; marched over a high, rolling country, but good wagon road, and splendid grazing all the way for a distance of about 22 miles, when the road descends through a cañon for 1 mile, and then opens on the San Pedro Valley. Two miles farther the river is reached at the Overland Mail Station; strong bridge over the river; water and grass abundant; wood very scarce. Course, northeast; 25 miles. There found the name of Jones, the expressman..

June 23, left camp at crossing of the San Pedro at 7.30 a. m. The road at once leaves the river and enters a valley about 1 mile wide and 4 miles long, when it terminates at the foot of the mesa, which is gained through a narrow cañon, in which is a long but not very steep hill. The cañon is about 1½ miles, when the top of the mesa is reached; then about 14 miles to Overland Mail Station at Dragoon Spring, at which place we arrived at 12.30 p. m. and encamped; found water sufficient, by digging, up the cañon 2 miles, the trail to which is difficult in some places to lead animals over. Course, northeast; 19½ miles.

June 24, left Dragoon Spring at 10.30 a. m.; was detained in consequence of scarcity of water. Marched 25 miles over an excellent road to Ewell's Station, arriving there at 5.30 p. m.; sent Captain Fritz and 6 men with spades to examine the spring in the mountain north of station. He had returned to station by the time the command arrived and reported only enough water for the men. Encamped at 6 p. m. Course, northeast; 25 miles.

June 25, left Ewell's Station at 1 a. m.; marched 15 miles over a very hilly and in places a very rocky road to station in Apache Pass, and encamped at 6 a. m.; water scarce; no grass. Course, northeast; 15 miles.

About 12 m.—I being engaged at the spring superintending the watering of animals, it being necessary to dip it with tin cups—four shots were heard in the vicinity of where the horses that had been watered were being grazed under a strong guard. Immediately thereafter it was reported that Indians were in sight and that the guard had fired to give the alarm. Almost immediately thereafter it was reported to me that the Indians were waving a white flag. I at once started for them, taking with me a white flag, and Mr. Newcomb, as interpreter. At the end of about one hour I succeeded in getting sufficiently near one of them to be understood. I explained to him what I desired and asked for the chief. At this time at least 75 to 100 Indians were in sight, many of them mounted on good-looking horses and all of them armed with fire-arms, some with rifles and six-shooting pistols. Of the latter I observed a great number and occasionally single-barreled shotguns. When the chief came forward I told him we were Americans, and that our Great Captain lived at Washington; that we wished to be friends of the Apaches; that at present I was only traveling through their country, and desired he would not interfere with my men or animals; that a great captain was at Tucson with a large number of soldiers; that he wished to have a talk with all the Apache chiefs and to make peace with them and make them presents. He professed a great desire to be friendly with the Americans, and assured me that neither my men nor animals should be molested. He asked for tobacco and something to eat. I gave him all that could possibly be spared, and we parted, with a request on his part that I would meet him at the same place at sunset. On my return it was reported to me that 3 of the men were missing. A party of 30 were at once sent out in the vicinity of where the firing was heard, and after an hour's search the bodies of the missing men were found stripped of all their clothing and two of them scalped. Each was shot through the chest with fire-arms and lanced through the neck. They were victims to their own imprudence, the entire command having been repeatedly warned by me not to wander from camp. It appears they had started, leading their horses from the spring where the watering was being done, over the ridge into another gulch, when they came on the Indians and were murdered. The Indians succeeded in getting one horse. When the bodies of our murdered men were found instant pursuit of the Indians was made, some of whom were seen on a hill half a mile distant; but being unable to come up with them a return to camp was ordered, carrying in the dead bodies, which were buried, the entire command being present. The animals now being all watered, or as much as could be obtained for them, and there being very little grass in the pass, at 6 p. m. left camp; marched out and made a dry camp on the plain 2 miles beyond the cañon. Course, east by northeast; 4 miles.

At 11 p. m. a volley of six or eight shots was fired into camp, wounding Acting Assistant Surgeon Kittredge in the head and killing one horse at the picket line.

June 26, left Dry Camp No. 1 at 3.30 a. m.; marched 15 miles over an excellent road to San Simon Station, then turned square to the right and marched 13 miles up the dry bed of the river to a large cienega and encamped at 2 p. m. Course, east, northeast, and southeast; 28 miles. This is a splendid camping place—water and grass in the greatest abundance. The proper road to the cienega turns to the right from the stage road about 6 miles from Apache Pass and around the point of the mountain. It comes on the San Simon 1 mile below the water.

At 12, midnight, camp was alarmed by a shot fired by one of the guard. On examination it was found to be a coyote, which he mistook in the dark for an Indian crawling through the scattered bushes, but which he instantly killed. This was a very hard day's march on men and animals, being obliged to leave Dry Camp without breakfast owing to the scarcity of water, having but eight five-gallon kegs in which to carry water for the men, and not being able to get at the pass as much water as the animals required.

June 27, laid over.

June 28, left camp at Cienega of San Simon at 4 p. m.; marched 5 miles north-northeast to the pass in the mountains; road heavy. On arriving at the pass, found the road through it very good and the pass wide. Marched 15 miles from San Simon, and made Dry Camp No. 2 at 10.15 p. m. Course, north-northeast; 15 miles.

June 29, left Dry Camp at 4 a. m.; marched 9 miles to Lightendorffer's Well, in Round Mountain Cañon; good road; well on right of and close to the road. It is about 8 feet square and 7 feet deep; rock bottom. Halted at well one hour and obtained a very limited supply of water for my command. This is a tolerably good camping place for three companies of infantry. By care they could obtain sufficient water, which is good. Left Lightendorffer's Well at 8 a. m.; marched 22 miles to Densmore's Station (Soldier's Farewell) and halted at 5 p. m. Discovered here a small spring about 2 or 3 miles up the arroyo, north of station, and a hole of bad water 800 yards south of station. Left Densmore's Station at 8 p. m.; marched 14 miles to Cow Springs, and encamped at 12, midnight; water and grazing abundant. The road from the Cienega of San Simon to this place is good for loaded teams, excepting 4 or 5 miles to the pass. Course, northeast; 46 miles.

Soon after leaving Densmore's Station found 2 men on the side of the road under rather suspicious circumstances; took three letters from them, one directed to the commander of Federal forces at Tucson or *en route;* put the men in charge of guard and brought them back. (Letters herewith inclosed, marked Nos. 1, 2, and 3.*) There discovered 9 men encamped, who proved to be a party sent by Colonel Chivington, commanding Southern Military District of New Mexico, at Fort Craig, with a letter to Colonel Carleton, with verbal orders to deliver it to the commander of the advance of his column when met with, and return to Fort Craig. Read the communication, and returned Mr. Milligan and one of his party with the answer to Fort Craig at 3 p. m. on the 30th instant, at which place he would arrive on the evening of the 2d proximo. Letter of Colonel Chivington and my answer thereto herewith inclosed.* From Mr. Milligan I learned of the capture of Jones, the expressman, by the secessionists at the Picacho, near Mesilla, his two companions having been killed by Indians at Apache Pass and himself chased by them for a great many miles. This information was brought to Fort Craig by a friendly Mexican, who was present at the capture of Jones.

June 30, laid over.

July 1. This morning a number of men were discovered by the look-out approaching from the direction of the Pino Alto gold mines; sent out a party and brought them into camp. They proved to be a party of 30 Mexican miners, returning to Sonora in consequence of the almost total absence of provisions at the mines; allowed them to proceed on their journey. Left Cow Springs at 8 a. m.; arrived at the Rio Miembres at 1 p. m. and encamped 2 miles above station; water and grazing abundant and of the best quality; road good. Course, northeast; 16 miles.

July 2, laid over. At 1 o'clock this morning one of the pickets discovered persons approaching camp. They were arrested and brought in—12 men and 2 women, one a German, the others Mexicans. They also were from the mines *en route* for Mesilla. Ordered them confined, in order to secure the secrecy of my movements. At 9 a. m. sent out party of 20 men to examine Cooke's Cañon, with orders to arrest, if possible, all persons they may meet with, and remain at Cooke's Spring until the command came up.

July 3, left Miembres River at 6.30 a. m.; marched 12 miles over a good road to Cooke's Pass. From here to summit road hilly. A long, rocky, but not very steep, hill brings you to the top of the pass; from there the descent to the spring is good; distance from pass to spring 6 miles. Course, north-northeast and northeast; 18 miles. There came up with the party sent in advance yesterday; they reported no person in sight and no fresh traces.

July 4, left Cooke's Spring at 6.30 a. m.; took Fort Thorn road, which keeps a north-northeast course, while the Mesilla road turns to the right immediately at the springs and bears east-northeast, passing the

---

* Not found.

Overland Mail Station, which is seen on the hill about half a mile distant. Marched 13 miles to Mule Spring; good road. Here no water could be found even by digging, having sent a party in advance with spades for that purpose. Left Mule Spring at 12 m.; marched 22 miles to the Rio Grande, and encamped at 7 p. m. near Fort Thorn. Course, north-northeast and northeast; 35 miles.

The road for about 8 miles after leaving Mule Spring is very good, when it enters a rolling country, the hills becoming more and more abrupt for a distance of about 6 miles, when it descends into a broad cañon, which is followed on a good road to the river. Immediately on making camp the national colors were raised amid the loud and continued cheers of the assembled command. This was the first time the Stars and Stripes floated on the Rio Grande below Fort Craig since the occupation of the country by the Confederate troops, and it being the anniversary of our National Independence, was not calculated to dampen the ardor of the command.

We are now within 35 miles of the enemy, which the prisoners whom I have taken variously estimate from 200 to 800 strong. As soon as the horses have a little recruited (they being considerably reduced on a march of about 300 miles through a broiling sun and over a country utterly destitute of water for distances ranging from 35 to 60 miles) will reconnoiter his position and endeavor to ascertain his strength, which I have but little doubt of accomplishing, and in case he does not greatly outnumber me will give him a fight.

July 5, moved 3 miles down the river to and reoccupied Fort Thorn; 3 miles.

I am, lieutenant, very respectfully, your obedient servant,

E. E. EYRE,
Lieut. Col., First California Volunteer Cavalry, Commanding.

Lieut. BENJ. C. CUTLER,
A. A. A. G., Column from California, Tucson, Ariz.

———

HDQRS. FIRST CALIFORNIA VOLUNTEER CAVALRY,
Fort Thorn, Ariz., July 8, 1862.

LIEUTENANT: I have the honor to report the reoccupation of Fort Thorn by the squadron of First California Volunteer Cavalry, under my command, on the evening of the 5th instant. Immediately thereafter the national colors were run up and the old flag once more floated over the garrison.

On the morning of the 6th instant an express arrived from Fort Craig, with a communication from Colonel Chivington, First Colorado Volunteers, commanding Southern Military District of New Mexico, a copy of which is herewith inclosed.* He also sent a communication addressed to Colonel Steele, C. S. Army, empowering me to negotiate an exchange for Captain McCleave and the men who were made prisoners with him. Soon after the express from Colonel Chivington arrived a party of men were seen approaching from the direction of Mesilla. One of them proved to be Captain McCleave, on his way to Fort Craig, bringing with him a proposition from Colonel Steele for an exchange for Captain Gardner, C. S. Army. Having learned from the expressman just arrived that Captain Gardner died a few days since, I

_____
* Not found.

at once sent Captain Fritz, First California Volunteer Cavalry, to Fort Fillmore, with a request to Colonel Steele to name any other captain General Canby had made prisoner in exchange for Captain McCleave; also proposing an exchange for the men taken with him, as well as an exchange for our expressman (Jones) and a Mr. John Lemon, of Mesilla, who was extremely kind to Captain McCleave during his confinement, and who had horses ready saddled and hid out for Jones' escape. He was ordered to be hung, and was taken to a tree for that purpose, but after hanging a Mr. Marshall, who was taken out with him, his execution was postponed. Captain Fritz will probably be back to-night, when I will at once send Captain McCleave with a party of 25 men through to Tucson. It is not safe for a less number to travel that road on account of the Indians, and even then with the utmost caution.

If it is the desire of the colonel commanding to keep open communication between Tucson and the Rio Grande I would respectfully recommend that a company of infantry be stationed at Dragoon Spring and two companies at the Apache Pass. That corps would be far more effective against the Indians in the rugged mountains at the points above named than cavalry; besides, horses could not be kept in flesh on the dry grass alone; they would be utterly useless in two weeks' riding. At this season of the year sufficient water and of a good quality can be obtained for two companies of infantry at the foot of the mountain, four miles north of Ewell's Station. The spring is prominently marked by a large, white spot on the mountain, which is directly over the water.

The Rio Grande has been unusually high this summer, almost the entire bottom between Fort Craig and Mesilla being still overflowed. It is impossible at this time to approach Mesilla on the west side of the river, a new channel having been washed out on that side of the town, through which the largest portion of the water flows; besides, the bottom for a long distance is overflowed, and, the soil being of a loose nature, animals mire down in attempting to get through it. This morning I sent Captain McCleave with a small party to examine the San Diego Crossing, 18 miles below here, to ascertain if the river can be forded at that point. The moment a crossing can be effected it is my intention, unless otherwise ordered by General Canby, to move on Mesilla and reoccupy Forts Fillmore and Bliss. When that is done that portion of the proclamation of the colonel commanding will not only have been carried out, but the sacred soil of Texas will have been invaded. Captain McCleave reports Colonel Steele with the rear of Sibley's brigade making hurried exertions to get away from Texas. He is pressing every team, both mule and oxen, he can find into service, compelling the owners (generally Mexicans) to take Confederate scrip in payment therefor. The same mode is resorted to by him in regard to provisions.

Captain Howland, Third U. S. Cavalry, in advance of his squadron, has just arrived; his command (100 men) will probably be here this evening. His horses are in shocking condition. Should we come up with Colonel Steele and a mounted charge be made, it must be done by the squadron of my regiment.

On the capture of Jones greatly-increased exertions were made by Colonel Steele to get away. Mesilla was evacuated, and Captain McCleave, who was at the time on parole to the limits of the town, immediately confined under a strong guard. Mr. White, of the Pima Villages, has been released, and will probably be here with the return of Captain Fritz.

The horses are out grazing (under a strong guard) from daybreak until dark, then tied up to the picket line, with as much grass as they can eat during the night. They are doing very well, but have not yet recovered from the effects of the very distressing march from Tucson here.

Captain McCleave has just returned, and reports the road down the river almost impassable for loaded wagons and the river swimming at the crossing.

July 9 [7th?] sent Captain McCleave, with an escort and two wagons, to Fort Craig for supplies.

The squadron of Third U. S. Cavalry (100 strong) arrived and gone into quarters at this post.

Captain Fritz returned this evening, having effected an exchange for Captain McCleave and the others named in my communication to Colonel Steele, a copy* of which is herewith inclosed. Two lieutenants were given in exchange for Captain McCleave, as Colonel Steele affected to know of no captain of theirs for that purpose, although there are a number. His real object was to exchange for officers of his own regiment only.

About 6 o'clock this evening an express arrived from Captain McCleave, informing me of an attack on his party, as they were moving up the river, by the Navajoes ,60 or 70 strong; that he had made camp, but was being surrounded by them. I immediately sent Captain Howland, with Lieutenant Baldwin and 40 men, to his relief.

I forward herewith, for the information of the colonel commanding, all communications* received or written by me since my arrival on the Rio Grande.

I am, lieutenant, very respectfully, your obedient servant,

E. E. EYRE,
Lieutenant-Colonel, First Cal. Vol. Cavalry, Comdg.

Lieut. BENJ. C. CUTLER,
A. A. A. G., Column from California, Tucson, Ariz.

—

HDQRS. FIRST CALIFORNIA VOLUNTEER CAVALRY,
Fort Thorn, Ariz., July 14, 1862.

LIEUTENANT: I have the honor to report the arrival here on yesterday of another express from General Canby, the second one alluded to in Colonel Chivington's communication of the 7th instant.

*   *   *   *   *   *   *

I leave here to-morrow morning with my command for Mesilla. On examination found the road from here to Rough and Ready Station impracticable, and have determined to make a road to the San Diego Crossing, and then pass the river on a raft, which I am now having made for that purpose, and which will be floated down to the crossing. The road on the east side of the river from San Diego to Mesilla is good. It is my determination, unless otherwise ordered, to hoist the national colors over Mesilla and Forts Fillmore and 'Bliss before the end of the present month.

*   *   *   *   *   *   *

---

* Not found.

I neglected in my report of the march to this place to give the names of the men killed by the Indians at Apache Pass. Their names are Privates James F. Keith, Peter Maloney, and Albert Schmidt, of Company B, First California Volunteer Cavalry.

I am, lieutenant, very respectfully, your obedient servant,

E. E. EYRE,
Lieutenant-Colonel, First Cal. Vol. Cavalry, Comdg.

Lieut. BENJ. C. CUTLER,
A. A. A. G., Column from California, Tucson, Ariz.

HDQRS. FIRST CALIFORNIA VOLUNTEER CAVALRY,
Las Cruces, Ariz., August 30, 1862.

Lieut. BENJ. C. CUTLER,
Actg. Asst. Adjt. Gen., Column from California, Franklin, Tex.:

LIEUTENANT: In compliance with verbal orders received from the general commanding the column, I have the honor to report that immediately after my arrival on the Rio Grande, July 4, I sent a scouting party down the river as far as the San Diego Crossing, for the double purpose of ascertaining if the enemy had pickets within that distance of my camp, and also whether the high stage of water in the river rendered it impracticable to move my command that far for the purpose of crossing, it being my intention to follow and, if possible, overtake the retreating Texans under Colonel Steele. On their return they reported it impracticable to get to the crossing with wagons, but that the river was falling fast, and that in a short time—say one week—I would be able to accomplish my purpose of moving on Fort Fillmore, where a portion of the Texans were then quartered. I therefore determined to remain at Fort Thorn for a short time longer, to recruit the men and animals and to receive re-enforcements from Fort Craig, which I had asked for from Cow Springs, having sent an express from that point on June 28.

On the 8th ultimo Captain Howland, Third U. S. Cavalry, with 100 men, arrived at Fort Thorn and reported to me for duty. I was now still more anxious to pursue the enemy, being confident of my ability to successfully cope with his disorganized and disheartened troops, although they outnumbered me more than two to one.

On the morning of the 10th ultimo I received a communication from Colonel Chivington, commanding Southern Military District of New Mexico, of which the following is an extract:

> You will do all you can to learn the enemy's strength, position, and purpose, but General Canby does not design an advance from where you are until he can go in force. I am under orders to advance to Santa Barbara or thereabouts with sixteen companies of infantry and a battery of four 6-pounder guns and two 24-pounder howitzers and an additional cavalry force, to support the advance of General Carleton and to co-operate with the forces under him in the reoccupation of the valley of Mesilla.

Although this was not a positive order to remain where I was, yet it intimated too clearly the desire of the district commander to lead the advance on Mesilla and Fort Fillmore, that I felt exceedingly embarrassed as to whether I would be authorized in leaving Fort Thorn until the arrival there of Colonel Chivington; but on consultation with Captains Howland, Tilford, and Fritz I determined, unless more positively ordered, to remain, and to move down to the San Diego Crossing as soon as the water would permit.

Accordingly, on the 13th ultimo, I sent Wagon-master Black, with a party, to the crossing, to ascertain if it was yet practicable to get the train of thirteen wagons to that point. On his return the same day he reported favorably, and on the 15th ultimo I left with my command and arrived at the crossing on the 16th ultimo, a distance of 18 miles.

On the 17th ultimo I had succeeded in crossing successfully my command in a small boat, which I caused to be made for that purpose before leaving Fort Thorn.

On the 19th ultimo I received from Lieut. F. Van Vliet, acting assistant adjutant-general, the following communication:

> I am instructed by the colonel commanding the district to inform you that your troops will not cross the river until further orders.

This was from Colonel Howe's acting assistant adjutant-general, he then being in command of the Southern Military District of New Mexico; but having crossed the river before its receipt, and having received supplies from Fort Craig, I determined to push on to Robledo or Doña Aña and there await his further orders, and so wrote him. But on my arrival at the latter place I found neither forage nor grazing for the animals, and pushed on to Las Cruces, where quarters were found for the command in unoccupied houses belonging to notorious secessionists.

On my arrival at Las Cruces I at once made inquiry as to the whereabouts of the Texans, and learned from reliable authority that a portion of them were yet at Franklin, Tex.; that they were collecting at that point a large amount of Government property which had been by them secreted at different places on their march up the river, and that they designed selling it to a citizen of El Paso, Tex. This property I could undoubtedly have taken, and in all probability have captured the Texans then at Franklin, had I at once pushed on to that point; but the strong intimation not to leave Fort Thorn which I received from Colonel Chivington, and the positive order not to cross the river which I received from Colonel Howe, and my letter to him that I would await his further orders at Las Cruces, compelled me to remain at the latter place. Indeed, by moving farther down the river I would have run counter to the expressed wishes of the district commanders of the Southern Military District of New Mexico, if not against their positive orders.

On the 28th ultimo I received a positive order from Colonel Howe not to leave Las Cruces until further orders.

Subsequently, while accompanying the general commanding on his march to Fort Quitman, I learned that Colonel Steele greatly feared he would be overtaken by the California troops, and in his hurried retreat burned a number of his wagons and destroyed a large amount of ammunition. I also learned that so much were his men disheartened and so thoroughly disorganized, that had they been attacked by even a small force they would have at once surrendered. Certainly it is an opportunity would have been given them to do so had it not been for the orders received from Fort Craig, for I should certainly have followed and as certainly overtaken them before they left the river at Fort Quitman.

I am, lieutenant, very respectfully, your obedient servant,

E. E. EYRE,
Lieutenant-Colonel, First California Volunteer Cavalry.

No. 3.

Report of Surg. James M. McNulty, U. S. Army, Acting Medical Inspector.

SANTA FÉ, N. MEX., *October* —, 1863.

Brig. Gen. W. A. HAMMOND,
    Surgeon-General U. S. Army, Washington, D. C.:

GENERAL: Agreeably to the wish conveyed in your letter of July 27, 1863, I send you the following history of that portion of the California Volunteers known as the Column from California.

The march of this column from the Pacific Ocean to the Rio Grande is somewhat remarkable, from the fact that almost the entire distance is a desert waste, with great scarcity of water and that of the worst quality.

Men marching day after day through the burning sands and nearly suffocated with alkali dust required to be made of stern stuff—of such were the men composing this column. Men inured to mountain life in California, pioneers and miners; men self-reliant and enduring; men equal to any emergency, if guided by a firm hand and clear head. That they were equal to a great emergency is evinced by the fact that they conquered vast deserts, and accomplished a march not equaled in modern times, traversing a distance of nearly a thousand miles and almost the entire route over a sterile waste.

I am, sir, very respectfully, your obedient servant,

JAMES M. McNULTY,
    Surgeon, U. S. Volunteers, Acting Medical Inspector.

On the 22d of July, 1861, the President of the United States approved "An act to authorize the employment of volunteers to aid in enforcing the laws and protecting public property." Under this act was raised in California one regiment of infantry and five companies of cavalry. These were called respectively the First Infantry and First Cavalry, California Volunteers. The troops were raised for the protection of the Overland Mail Route between California and the Eastern States, by way of Salt Lake City. The force was placed under the command of Bvt. Maj. James H. Carleton, First U. S. Cavalry, with the rank of colonel. The regiments rendezvoused at Oakland, opposite San Francisco, Cal. During the latter part of August and the month of September they had acquired nearly their full complement of men. Active preparations were making to put the command in the best condition for active field service, and by the 1st of October everything was in readiness for the movement of the troops. About this time the spirit of rebellion became manifest in California. "Treason stalked abroad." In the southern part of the State an open rupture was apprehended. In consequence of this condition of affairs the command of Colonel Carleton was diverted from its original destination by General Sumner, department commander, and moved to the infected district. About the 1st of October the troops moved down the coast and formed a camp near Los Angeles, called Camp Latham.

On the 14th three companies of the First Cavalry, California Volunteers, under the command of Major Eyre, of the same regiment, were ordered to relieve the regular troops stationed at San Bernardino. This place was the hot-bed of secessionism in California. On the same day orders were received to send three companies of the First Infantry, California Volunteers, under the command of Lieut. Col. J. R. West, to relieve the regulars stationed at Fort Yuma. Regular troops stationed at different parts of the State were ordered to rendezvous at two points, viz, San Diego and San Pedro, for the purpose of embarkation, orders having been issued by the War Department that all regular troops on the Pacific coast be sent to the seat of war in the East. Brig. Gen. E. V. Sumner, at that time in command of the Department of the Pacific, was also ordered in. On the departure of General Sumner, Col. George Wright, Ninth U. S. Infantry, assumed command of the department. The Southern District of California was turned over by Colonel Wright to the command of Colonel Carleton.

During the two succeeding months quiet and order were restored throughout the southern part of the State. The distribution of the troops indicated to the disaffected the determination of the authorities to keep California firm and steadfast to the Union.

On the 12th of January Colonel Carleton was summoned to San Francisco, to consult with Colonel Wright in reference to the movement of troops into Utah. About this time rumors reached California that Van Dorn, of the rebel service, was fitting out an expedition for the invasion of California by way of Arizona. The fact was well-established that Arizona and a portion of New Mexico were occupied by Confederate troops, and it was apparent to all that California was more accessible through Arizona by way of Fort Yuma than any other point. Fort Yuma, located on the Colorado River, on the southeastern line of the State, is our extreme outpost. Surrounded as it is by a vast desert, if once in the possession of an enemy the key to the State was lost.

In view of all these threatened dangers to the State and coast General Wright suggested to the War Department that perhaps the Government would be better served by throwing the California troops into Arizona and driving the rebels from that Territory. A double object would thus be gained: first, an effectual guard would be kept against any invasion of the Pacific coast from that quarter; second, the California troops would fall in the rear of the Confederate forces then in New Mexico and assist the Federal forces in expelling them from that Territory.

The suggestions of General Wright were favorably received by the War Department. The feasibility of the movement was so apparent, that the consent of that Department was at once obtained.

On the receipt of the decision of the War Department authority was granted to Colonel Carleton to organize and fit out the expedition. The Fifth Infantry, California Volunteers, under the command of Col. George W. Bowie; also Company A, Third U. S. Artillery, with a light battery, under command of First Lieut. John B. Shinn, of the U. S. Army, were added to Colonel Carleton's command; also Captain Cremony's company, Second Cavalry, California Volunteers.

Active preparations were at once made for the movement of the column. It was important that the troops should move as soon as possible, in order that they might receive the benefit of the cool winter weather while passing over the Gila and Colorado Deserts. The great distance from the Pacific Ocean to the Rio Grande, the entire and complete desolation of nearly the whole route, presented obstacles almost insurmountable to marching a column of over 2,000 men and the same number of animals. It was well known that forage and provisions could be obtained but at two points between Fort Yuma and the Rio Grande in time of peace, and then in limited quantities, viz, at the Pima Villages and at Tucson; and it being well known that the enemy occupied one, if not both, of these points, it was necessary that transportation should be made entirely independent of them. The greatest difficulty appeared to be in subsisting animals. Unless this could be done rations could not be furnished the troops, and the expedition would necessarily fall to the ground.

With the commencement of preparations came unlooked-for difficulties. Not for twenty years had a winter of such severity occurred in California. The whole country was flooded; hundreds of horses and cattle mired down in the open plains and were lost. For weeks it was almost impossible to move a vehicle of any kind, and the movement of baggage trains was out of the question.

In the mean time commissary stores and forage were sent by sea to Fort Yuma, making this point a general depot and base of operations.

The troops during this terrible winter lived in tents. As the rain subsided and the ground became more settled the troops were gradually moved toward Fort Yuma by companies of twos and threes. A sub-depot was formed at Oak Grove, near the edge of the Yuma desert, 120 miles from Los Angeles, called Camp Wright. From this point to Fort Yuma, 180 miles, it is a continuous desert, entirely destitute of vegetation; water very scarce, and generally of bad quality. Before moving the troops on this desert Colonel Carleton sent out parties and had the wells cleaned out and new ones dug, in order that every drop of water might be available. Forage for the animals was deposited at different points between Camp Wright and Fort Yuma. The troops were marched across by companies, one day apart. At some of the wells there was so little water that it was necessary to dip it out in a pint cup, thus consuming nearly a whole night in watering 100 animals.

In order that this desert may be more thoroughly understood I quote from the notes of Lieutenant-Colonel West, of the First Infantry, California Volunteers, who marched the first three companies over. The description of the route commences at Oak Grove, Camp Wright, near the edge of the desert:

Left Camp Wright, near Warner's Ranch, at 7.30 a. m.; marched 5 miles over pleasant rolling roads and well-wooded country to La Puerta, at which place found mountain stream, but no place for a camp ground; thence by fair road, without water, to San Felipe, 8 miles; pasturage good, but no wood; water neither overabundant nor good; camp ground inferior.

Left San Felipe at 3.30 a. m. by heavy, hilly roads to Vallecito. Road sandy through bottom land to first hill, 7 miles; thence broken road, 6 miles, a great portion of which is a cañon, with but one wagon track, winding between cliffs. A very small force could oppose an enemy of far superior numbers. The latter part of the road more level. On the left side and about half a mile from the road is a spring, that affords water enough for 50 men; thence a small rugged hill is surmounted and a valley reached, 5 miles in length, by sandy road to Vallecito; water in fair supply; no wood but mesquite bushes; pasturage fair.

Left Vallecito at 3.30 a. m.; marched 9 miles by heavy, sandy road to Palm Springs; water in limited supply, and required to be prepared for a command. The locality can be used for a camp. Thence by a heavy, sandy road to Cariso Creek; no pasturage. The country has now become a complete desert of most forbidding aspect. The creek is a small stream, affording an abundant supply of water of an inferior quality. The bottom land is filled with a stunted growth of mesquite and arrow bushes.

Left Cariso Creek at 11.30 a. m., following the stream and constantly crossing it; road heavy and sandy; thence over a level road, with somewhat improved traveling, 4 miles, to a short, steep hill; thence to a level plain, with desert brush, to Sackett's Wells. Last part of the road fair traveling; the desert complete; water good, but uncertain; in dry weather it certainly disappears.

Left Sackett's Wells at 5.45 p. m., through a continuous desert; first 5 miles sandy; thence better traveling to Indian Well.

Indian Well is some 30 feet deep; water good, but in small quantities. Signal

Mountain is a prominent landmark; bears southwest about 15 miles; reached camp at 11 p. m.; distance, 15 miles. Left at 5 p. m. for New River Station; road a perfect level, over an alkali plain, with a few patches of mesquite bushes; road dusty and heavy for wagons; well deep; water scarce and of inferior quality.

Started at 5 p. m. for Alamo; road heavy, over barren flat; there is a well some 30 feet deep, affording some water. Left at 4 p. m. for Gardner's Wells; no water; 9 miles; thence, by same character of road and country, to Salt or Seven Wells; water plenty, but brackish. Started at 4 p. m., 9 miles, to Cooke's Wells. First 2¼ miles bad road. At Cooke's Wells water and wood abundant and good; thence, 15 miles, to Pilot Knob. Camped on the bank of the Colorado at foot of mountain. From Cooke's the road is generally good, through mesquite flat, and latter part through Indian Gardens; distance 25 miles. Started at 1.30 p. m. The road follows the Rio Colorado to Fort Yuma; distance 10 miles; road much broken. Reached Fort Yuma at 4.30 p. m.

I have been thus minute in detail in order that a correct idea may be had of some of the difficulties encountered in marching troops across this desert.

It will be seen that nearly every march was made in the night-time. By starting at 4 or 5 in the afternoon the march would be accomplished before daylight, thus enabling men to sleep a part of the night.

The ground did not become sufficiently settled for the movement of Shinn's battery until the 13th April. Previous to this nearly all the command had been moved toward Fort Yuma, one company only remaining to accompany the battery. Colonel Carleton arrived at Fort Yuma on the 29th of April. Active preparations were made to move the command eastward without delay. Water-tanks, holding 600 gallons each, were prepared to accompany each detachment. Contracts were made at Fort Yuma to have hay cut and deposited at different points between the fort and the Pima Villages.

It was ascertained that Tucson was still in the hands of the Texans. Their pickets extended down the Rio Gila till within 50 miles of Fort Yuma. Hay deposited at different points by Colonel Carleton's agents was burned. The Pima Indians are an agricultural people, and cultivate large quantities of wheat. Knowing this fact and the importance of securing as much as possible, Colonel Carleton had for some time been in communication with an American living at these villages. He was directed to purchase all the wheat the Indians had. A considerable quantity was thus accumulated; but before the advance of the column reached that point the Texans had destroyed it all, with the exception of a small quantity the Indians had cached. This was a serious loss, but the growing crops had not been molested, and Colonel Carleton was enabled to secure a considerable amount for his animals. Two companies of infantry and one of cavalry were sent forward toward the Pima and Tucson. As our forces advanced the Texans fell back to Tucson. The command followed them to within a short distance of that place; but not feeling sufficiently strong to attack them, fell back to the Pima. Lieutenant-Colonel West was then ordered forward with four companies of infantry. The following itinerary was made by Lieutenant-Colonel West:

To Gila City, 17 miles; no grass, wood; camp on river; thence to Mission Camp, 11 miles; wood, water, and a little grass; wood, water, and grass 4 miles farther on. From Mission Creek to Fillibuster is 6 miles; thence to Antelope Peak, 9 miles; grass within three-fourths of a mile; camp at station. From this place to Mohawk Station, 12 miles; no grass; camp on the river. To Texas Hill, 11 miles; a little grass on the hill station, one-half mile back from the river. Lagoon Camp; fine water, wood, grass, and shade; thence to Burwell's Ranch, 11 miles; very dusty and disagreeable; men nor animals cannot recruit much. At Grassy Camp, 3 miles distant, they do much better. From Grassy Camp to Berk's Station, 6 miles; a very poor camp; little better at Oatman Flat, 11 miles farther. From Oatman Flat to Kenyon Station, 11 miles; poor camp; no grass. To Shady Camp, 10 miles; everything good. From Shady Camp to Gila Bend, 4 miles; wood and water, but no grass; thence to Desert

Station, 22 miles: good wood; no water or grass. To the Tanks, 7 miles; same as Desert Station. To Maricopa Wells, 11 miles; plenty of brackish water; some salt grass; and from thence to the Pima Villages, 11 miles; road fair, with some sloughs.

The march from Fort Yuma to the Pima Villages was fatiguing in the extreme. The intense heat and alkali dust was almost unbearable; both men and animals suffered very much. As fast as possible the troops were pushed forward. On the 14th of May Lieutenant-Colonel West was sent forward by way of Fort Breckinridge with four companies of infantry. This fort was reoccupied, and the Stars and Stripes again floated to the breeze. Fronf Fort Breckinridge Colonel West proceeded to Tucson by way of Cañada del Ora. A description of the route is taken from the notes of Colonel West:

May 14, left Fort Barrett, Pima, at 7 a. m.; road tends toward the river on the left hand; detached and irregular mountains, from 5 to 9 miles, to the right; soil becomes sandy and the country desert. Greasewood and mesquite wood abounded, but no thickets. The river is gradually approached and touched at Sacaton Station; there plenty of sacaton grass; a poor article for pasturage; good camp on the river; road fine for marching and transportation. Course, east-northeast.

15th, left Sacaton Station at 5.40 a. m. Road parts from the river and leaves it from 1 to 2 miles to the left; mountain spurs trend off southeast; a lone peak about 1½ miles long is detached from the main range. The Butterfield road to Tucson passes between the peak and main mountain. A picket there can effectually watch both roads. A small lagoon of water is found at the north base. The Picacho is plainly visible throughout the day's march. Dense mesquite thickets; road fine for marching and transportation. Camp on the river in a cottonwood grove, one-fourth mile below White's; good grazing and fine. Course, east by south.

May 16, left White's at 5.50 a. m. Road leaves the river and takes the mesa; the ascent is gradual and road good for 20 miles. Thickets of cactus and palo verde. At 20 to 31 miles a steep descent leads to Dry Camp, a basin in the hills of some 30 acres in area; a trail makes out of this due north to Ojo Verde Springs, 4 miles; the Gila River is 3 miles farther in the same direction. Ojo Verde can be used; the water is inferior and not abundant; the quality and perhaps the quantity could be improved. The spring is 4 miles off the road, and the return must be made by the same track. Left Dry Camp at 6.40 p. m.; road turns off southeast up an arroyo; very heavy sand for about 6 miles; then gradual ascent of 5 miles; then more abrupt and up high hills.

At 15 miles from Dry Camp a finger-post, marked "Water," points to the right.

Cottonwood Spring is distant half a mile, in a ravine. The grazing is fine and water abundant for such a body of troops as this. A lone cottonwood tree prominently marks the spring. Course, east by south-southeast.

May 17, laid by.

May 18, left Cottonwood Spring at 5 a. m.; road over rolling hills 5 miles; good grass, then pass the summit, and the descent commences towards San Pedro River. Sandy arroyo for 8 miles and heavy traveling; the road becomes a cañon. A walnut tree, 3 miles west of Fort Breckinridge, marked "Water," stands in the middle of the road. At this point the road to Tucson turns off square to the right; thence to the San Pedro and Fort Breckinridge. Colonel Carleton changed the name of this fort, and called it Fort Stanford, in honor of Leland Stanford, Governor of California. The fort is 3 miles up a cañon; rocks from 100 to 300 feet high; pass from 20 to 70 yards wide; road extremely heavy. At this fort fine stream, good grazing, and abundance of wood. Course, east by south.

19, left Fort Breckinridge at 5.45 a. m. Returned by the cañon to the walnut tree; thence turned abruptly to the left and south up a similar cañon, which gradually expands to open country; road for 12 miles excessively heavy and sandy; thence gently rolling hills until the foot of a mountain is reached on the left, about 17 miles from the walnut tree. Next 3 miles the hills are sidling and difficult. A steep descent of 1 mile leads to Cañada del Oro. Camp on a fine mountain stream; grazing very fine and wood abundant. This is a very difficult day's march. Course, northwest and south.

20th, left Cañada del Oro at 2 p. m.; road follows a ravine between the mesa on the right and a mountain range on the left; a good deal of sand, but mainly a fair road; fine grass along the road.

At 11.55 the road forks, the left-hand leading 1 mile to the Rincon, a small, running stream; fine camp; grass immediately under the mountain. Course, southwest.

May 21, left Rincon at 5 30 a. m. Road turns round the point of the mountain on the left; traveling rather heavy. Sandy arroyo, and then the ground becomes rolling. About 8 miles from Rincon a mesa covered with cactus and mesquite is reached; traveling improves. Course, southwest and south by east.

Our troops entered and occupied Tucson without firing a shot. At our approach the Texans made a precipitate retreat. Colonel Carleton determined to collect the troops at this point for rest, drill, &c. Men and animals required rest; wagons wanted repairing. The dryness of the atmosphere and the intolerable heat had shrunk them to the point of falling to pieces. Communication was opened with Sonora for the purchase of flour, grain, &c.

In the first part of June all the troops composing the column were in and about Tucson, with the exception of a part of the Fifth Infantry, left to garrison Forts Yuma and Barrett. There is another and more direct road leading from the Pima Villages to Tucson. This road was taken by Lieutenant Shinn and two companies of infantry. A description of the road by Lieutenant Shinn is appended.

SPECIAL ORDERS, }   HEADQUARTERS COLUMN FROM CALIFORNIA,
    No. 15.   }   Tucson, Ariz., June 16, 1862.

The following itinerary of the marches from Fort Barrett (Pima Villages) to Tucson, Ariz., via Picacho Mountain, made by Captain Shinn, Third Artillery, U. S. Army, is published for the information of all concerned:

June 1, left camp at Fort Barrett at 4.15 p. m., with battery, one ambulance, one water and eight transportation wagons (loaded to 3,600 pounds with ammunition, flour, and forage), 87 men, and 153 animals. Road on Gila River fine for transportation of heavily-loaded wagons. No water; no grass; vegetation mesquite and greasewood. At Sacaton Station very dirty; encamped on river at 8 p. m.; 11.8 miles.

June 2, filled water-tank (600 gallons), and left camp at Sacaton at 4.20 p. m. Road leaves the river and sweeps round from southeast by south to south by east, with gradually ascending slope to summit, 5¼ miles between mountain spur and detached peak on left, 2 miles of road dusty, then soil changes from the alkali dust of Gila River bottom to mixture of sand and gravel, very hard and quite smooth. From summit Casa Grande in sight on desert to left and the Picacho straight ahead south by east 31 miles; desert continues to Oneida Station; road continues good; at 8 miles gravel replaced by hard alkali clay; vegetation, mesquite, greasewood, and cactus; no water or grass on road; wood plenty and sufficient for cooking near Oneida Station, which is on the left; well on the right of road; depth 29 feet, with 5 feet of water; encamped there at 7.45 p. m.; train all in 10 minutes later.

One hundred and seventy-five buckets (equal to 700 gallons) was taken from the well, at the rate of 10 gallons per minute, apparently without diminishing the supply. The water is excellent, cold, and sweet; the best this side of Fort Yuma; arrived and departed during the night; found no grass near station; 11.1 miles.

June 3, left camp at 4 a. m. Old marks of surface water show a gradual rise of the desert toward Blue Water Station; road fine for marching; very little sand. At 6 miles halted from 5.45 to 6.45 for grass, which may be found in considerable quantity 100 yards to the left of road in the belt of mesquite or arroyo leading east from that point, and said to extend 4 or 5 miles in the same direction; obtained sufficient for a good night's feed. This grass is gramma, with some little gaeta. The gaeta was also observed on the left of the road 1 mile farther on; no water; vegetation, desert plants, mesquite, and greasewood. Arrived and encamped at Blue Water Station at 7.45 a. m.; well (69 feet in depth, with 2¼ feet of water) and station both on right of road; drew water at the rate of 6 gallons per minute for 1¼ hours; watered 90 horses at same time, 4 gallons each; mules in the p. m. and horses again in the p. m. Took from this well in ten hours over 1,600 gallons of water and left the depth of water as found. It will probably afford 4.000 gallons of water in twenty-four hours; quality good and water cool. At 4 p. m. sent a detachment forward to clean out well at the point of mountain; wood plenty; some gramma and a little gaeta reported to exist in the mesquite 500 yards northwest of the station; 9.7 miles.

June 4, left Blue Water Station at 2.10 a. m. and expected to march to Tucson, 54 miles, in the next twenty-four hours, as there is no water on the road, and not enough with company to encamp on; some wagons remain loaded with 3,600 pounds; morning quite cool and very fine for marching; road continues to rise to the Picacho; at 4.40 a. m. 9.6 miles from Blue Water; soil, clay, water-washed, and very hard and smooth, extends for miles on either side of the road; considerable dry gramma grass in the immediate vicinity and mesquite sparde● At 13.9 miles passed graves of Lieutenant Barrett and two soldiers on the left of road. The chalcos or water-holes, now dry, are in the mesquite, on the right of the road; here quite a thicket; some gra , but dry. The road is now level, or nearly so, for 3 or 4 miles. At 6.45 a. m. halted at the Picacho Station on the right, and distant from Blue Water Station 14.9 miles; saw a band of antelope near foot of peak; no water at this point; consumed about 200 gallons of water in tank, for which had to wait half an hour; resumed march at 7.45 a. m.; road begins to descend towards the south 2 miles beyond the Picacho and so continues to point of mountain, a very excellent road all the way. At 25.5 miles passed a deep well; dry on right; no water ever found here; high mountains on right; distant from 30 to 100 miles, and between mountain and road valley of Santa Cruz River, here only an arroyo, which road crosses near point of mountain; at 12 m. and 29 miles halted one-half hour; met a messenger at 1.30 p. m. and received notice of water in abundance at point of mountain, where company arrived and encamped at 4.15 p. m.; station on right and well on left of road; water plenty; no grass; no wood at well, and but little on last 8 miles of road; used water brought from Tucson on wagons, and did not thoroughly test the capacity of the well, which is 39 feet deep, with 4 feet of water; all agree in pronouncing it the best on the desert and say it cannot be dipped dry; 39.1 miles.

June 5, left camp at 3 a. m., about 5 miles from point of mountain; dense mesquite thicket a good cover for Indians; at 6 miles crossed arroyo of Santa Cruz River, descending to left; quite dry; a little sand and some more at 11 miles, one-half mile of it this time; remainder of road very good; numerous cottonwood trees on road this day and much mesquite; no water; between 7 and 10 miles from point of mountain much salt grass; poor stuff for forage. First 5 and last 3¼ miles of to-day's march very fine; road of hard gravel; arrived at Tucson at 8.45 a. m.; 15 miles. Total, 86.7 miles.

Tucson is about half way between Fort Yuma and the Rio Grande, and contains a population of 400, or perhaps 500, mostly Mexicans. A few Americans and foreigners were living here, principally gamblers and ruffians, traitors to their country—secessionists.

Colonel Carleton received his promotion to brigadier-general of volunteers while on the desert in the early part of June. On his arrival at Tucson the Territory of Arizona was at once placed under martial law, and the following proclamation issued.*

*   *   *   *   *   *   *

A number of notorious characters were arrested, examined by military commissions, and sent to Fort Yuma. Order sprang from disorder, and in a short time a den of thieves was converted into a peaceful village.

In the mean time General Carleton was making active preparations to move his command to the Rio Grande; wagons were repaired; stores collected from Sonora, and everything put in as good condition as circumstances would permit after the severe march over the Yuma and Gila Deserts.

No communication up to this time could be had with our forces in New Mexico. The strength of the rebels and their locality entirely unknown. The great difficulty in communicating with General Canby, at that time in command of the Department of New Mexico, was on account of hostile Indians. The Apache Nation occupying the whole country between the Rio Grande and the Colorado River, the great distance to be traversed through their country, rendered it hazardous if not impossible for any small party to get through it.

General Carleton endeavored to send an express to General Canby from Tucson. This was carried by 3 men. The party was attacked near Apache Pass, and 2 of the men were killed by the Indians; the survivor was pursued some 40 miles and barely escaped death. He was captured by the Texans near Mesilla and the dispatches to General Canby fell into their hands. From these they learned the exact strength of General Carleton's command and the intended movement of the column.

On the 22d of June General Carleton sent forward Lieutenant-Colo-

---

* See inclosure C to Carleton's report of August 2, p. 561.

nel Eyre, of the First Cavalry, California Volunteers, with 140 men. This was the advance guard of the column. With the exception of frequent skirmishing with Indians and the loss of 3 men killed and several wounded at Apache Pass, the party met with no other enemy before reaching the Rio Grande.

Apache Pass is about midway between Tucson and the river. The pass is through a spur of the Chiricahua Mountains, about 3½ or 4 miles long. In this pass is a fine spring of water, and a favorite haunt of the Indians. A company of infantry and a part of a company of cavalry, with two mountain howitzers, fought the Indians at this spring for four hours. A number of the savages were killed in the fight. Our loss was 3 killed and several wounded. On either side of this pass extends a plain from 30 to 40 miles in width. The Indians can see parties approach and lay in wait for them.

On the 17th of July, preparations for the movement of the command having been completed, General Carleton issued the following general order:*

*   *   *   *   *   *   *

No report had been received from Colonel Eyre. The strength and locality of the Confederates was unknown; consequently the column was kept well in hand, the companies marching only one day apart.

For a description of the country I quote from the notes of Colonel Eyre.†

*   *   *   *   *   *   *

As soon as the arrival of Colonel Eyre on the river was known the Texans made a hasty flight. Their army was completely demoralized, and Colonel Eyre's force magnified fourfold. What they could not carry with them they destroyed. One hundred and fifty sick and wounded were left in hospital at Franklin, Tex., and above.

Colonel Eyre crossed the river near Fort Thorn and pushed down toward the retreating rebels. He entered Las Cruces, opposite Mesilla, and raised our national colors. Franklin was also occupied by a detachment of his command. General Carleton, with the head of the column, reached the river on the 8th of August, the time consumed in the march being eighteen days. The sight of this beautiful stream after the many days of toil and suffering gladdened the hearts of all. The last day's march was particularly severe; over 40 miles had been made by the infantry without water without a murmur. The desert had been conquered, and the command arrived on the river in good fighting condition. No deaths had occurred between Tucson and the river, and but few remained on the sick list.

General Carleton crossed the river at the point where Colonel Eyre crossed. The river was so high that it could not be forded, and the only boats were two small scows, made by Colonel Eyre. First the animals were swum over. This was successfully accomplished; none were lost. A rope was attached to both sides of the boats and extended to either bank of the river. A number of men were stationed on both flanks. By this means they were enabled to pull the boat from shore to shore, being constantly in the water. The wagons were unloaded; their contents ferried across in the boats, which were hauled across by ropes. In this manner each command as it came up was crossed in safety. Nothing was lost or injured.

General Carleton moved the column down the river as far as Las

---

* See inclosure G to Carleton's report, p. 555.
† Surgeon McNulty here quotes Eyre's entire report of July 6, see p. 585.

Cruces, La Mesilla, and Franklin. Taking with him two companies of cavalry, he proceeded on down as far as Fort Quitman, Tex.; from there he dispatched a company of the First Cavalry as far as Fort Davis, distant from Fort Quitman —— miles. The Texans had abandoned this post. One man, much reduced, was found dead, his body being pierced in many places with arrows. This man had evidently been left behind sick. The sick and wounded Texans left behind at Franklin were sent with an escort to San Antonio.

General Canby, at this time in command of the Department of New Mexico, had been ordered East, and on the 16th of September, 1862, General Carleton arrived in Santa Fé, and on the 18th assumed command of the department. Before leaving the lower country he published the following general order:

GENERAL ORDERS, }   HEADQUARTERS DISTRICT OF ARIZONA,
    No. 15.   }   *Las Cruces, N. Mex., August* 14, 1862.

I. Commanders of towns will at once establish sanitary regulations, and require them to be observed by the inhabitants and by the troops, so far as the policing of the streets and the keeping of their dwellings, quarters, stores, corrals, &c., in a state of cleanliness may be necessary to their health and comfort. Frequent inspections will be made by commanding officers or by a medical officer under his direction, to see that in all respects these regulations are followed.

II. It is expected that all of the inhabitants living along the Rio Grande southward from the Jornada del Muerto to Fort Bliss, in Texas, will, at the earliest practicable moment, repair their dwellings and clean up their streets.

The people may now rest assured that the era of anarchy and misrule—when there was no protection to life or property, when the wealthy were plundered, when the poor were robbed and oppressed, when all were insulted and maltreated, and when there was no respect for age or sex—has passed away; that now, under the sacred banner of our country, all may claim and shall receive their just rights. Therefore let the burden of anxiety be lifted from their hearts, and once more let them pursue their avocations with cheerfulness, and with the full confidence that the protection which now shelters them from injustice will always be stronger in proportion as they shall be powerless to protect themselves.

The success of the march of this column was dependent upon two things: First, the endurance of the men; second, the care taken of them. From the first organization of the column the constant care of General Carleton was given it; the health of the men first, discipline next. Constantly watchful, the minutest detail received his personal attention. Every movement was based upon calculation; nothing avoidable left to chance. To conduct this expedition successfully required a clear head, sound judgment, indomitable will, and perseverance. All these General Carleton possesses in an eminent degree.

It will not be too much to say that there are probably few men in the United States Army so well fitted to command an expedition of this kind. A military experience of more than twenty years, a great portion of it spent on our frontiers, has made him familiar by experience with the wants and requirements of men in desert marching.

In this march everything was reduced to the smallest possible compass. No tents were used by officers or men during the whole march. Two wagons were allowed to a company. In these were carried camp and garrison equipage, ten days' rations, mess furniture—everything belonging to a company. Every article was weighed. Officers, from the general down, carried but 80 pounds of baggage, including bedding, mess kit, &c.

The troops suffered very little from sickness. The mortality was very small. Not one single death occurred on the march of the column from the Pacific Ocean to the Rio Grande, from the 13th of April to the 8th of August, and but five deaths from disease in hospital during this time—two at Fort Barrett and three at Tucson.

Every possible care was observed to guard against sickness. This, together with the splendid material of the men, will account for the success of the expedition and the slight mortality from disease attending it.

General Carleton, on relinquishing the immediate command of the column, published the following general order, viz:

GENERAL ORDERS, }   HEADQUARTERS DEPARTMENT OF NEW MEXICO,
     No. 85.   }   *Santa Fé, N. Mex., September* 21, 1862.

In entering upon the duties that remove him from immediate association with the troops constituting the Column from California the commanding general desires to express his grateful acknowledgment of the conduct and services of the officers and men of that command. Traversing a desert country, that has heretofore been regarded as impracticable for the operations of large bodies of troops, they have reached their destination, and accomplished the object assigned them, not only without loss of any kind, but improved in discipline, in *morale,* and in every other element of efficiency That patient and cheerful endurance of hardships, the zeal and alacrity with which they have grappled with and overcome obstacles that would have been insurmountable to any but troops of the highest physical and moral energy, the complete abnegation of self and subordination of every personal consideration to the grand object of our hopes and efforts, give the most absolute assurance of success in any field or against any enemy.

California has reason to be proud of the sons she has sent across the continent to assist in the great struggle in which our country is now engaged.

The commanding general is requested by the officer who preceded him in the command of this department to express for him the gratification felt by every officer and soldier of his command at the fact that troops from the Atlantic and Pacific slope, from the mountains of California and Colorado, acting in the same cause, impelled by the same duties, and animated by the same hopes, have met and shaken hands in the center of this great continent.

JAMES H. CARLETON,   •
Brigadier-General, U. S. Army, Commanding Department.

Very respectfully,

J. M. McNULTY,
Surgeon, U. S. Volunteers.

APRIL 22, 1862.—Capture of Union launches in Aransas Bay, Tex.

Report of Maj. William O. Yager, commanding Camp Aransas.

HEADQUARTERS CAMP ARANSAS, TEX.,
April 25, 1862.

SIR: On the 22d instant intelligence reached Shell Banks that the enemy had run two of their launches through Cedar Bayou and captured three sloops, one of which, the Democrat, they stripped of her sails and left the captain and mate to pole their way to land. With the other two they bore down toward Shell Banks, with the purpose of running past the fort under friendly appearance, and thence out the Aransas Pass to the blockader. They had approached within 6 miles of the fort, and were tacking back and forth as if waiting for night before attempting to pass. When, with two sloops carrying 32 men, Captain Neal, myself, and Lieutenant Canfield set out after them, they put back in haste. But having no place where they could get out of the bay with their prizes without passing us, they quit them and took to their launches. They made directly for Blind Bayou and soon entered it. We left our boats and hurried across by land to intercept them. Finding themselves thus headed off, they reluctantly abandoned their launches and made off to the sand hills, firing upon our men, who were now kept from pursuing them by the depth of the water in the pass at the point where we approached it. (We could have swum across, but would then have been on the wrong side, with wet ammunition. Their fire was returned with spirit for several rounds, but without damage to either party.) The blockading vessel, meantime, was within 2 miles of the scene, an interested spectator. I wonder that she did not shell us. It may be she did not fully understand the situation of parties, and may have mistaken our boats for their prizes. The Yankees, 22 in number, soon disappeared among the sand hills, and the folly of groping about in the dark after them being manifest, we returned with their launches and contents to Shell Bank. Our prizes are cutters or launches—one pulling five and the other four oars—capable of carrying 10 or 14 men, respectively, with sails; a fine mariner's compass, a pennant, three pairs of handcuffs, and two guns belonging to the men, taken by them on the two sloops; the sails of the Democrat, some rations, one boarding-pistol, and other trifles.

On our return to the bank we met Major Forshey and Lieutenants Aspinwall, Conklin, and Russell, with parties, on three other boats; but darkness prevented any attempt at further proceedings.

The captain of the bark (Kittredge) was in the party. They left the bark with five days' rations; handcuffed the men taken on the Swan and Mustang, more for humiliation than to secure them.

Some of the Yankee soldiers expressed great dissatisfaction with their commander; said they would not fight for him if they could avoid it.

The men of the Swan and Mustang seemed very grateful for their release.

On the 21st the Burkhart was chased by these launches for several hours; but want of knowledge of the channels on the part of the enemy prevented them from overtaking her.

I have not been able to engage suitable schooners for guard boats in the bays. Chartered a sloop (the Rebecca) to lay about Blind Pass, but for some cause she has not returned from Saluria according to contract. I sent an armed party up to Saluria yesterday to carry some returning boats and to escort Major Forshey.

I have the honor to be, very respectfully, your obedient servant,

WM. O. YAGER,
Major, Mounted Battalion, Comdg. Camp Aransas, Tex.

Lieut. B. E. BENTON,
A. A. A. G., Southern Military District of the Rio Grande.

P. S.—The compass taken from the enemy was sent by Major Forshey to General Hébert, to be presented, with his permission, to Commodore William Hunter, chief naval commander of the Department of Texas, from the officers engaged in the expedition.

Respectfully,

W. O. Y.

APRIL 25, 1862.—Affair at Socorro, N. Mex.

Report of Maj. Charles E. Wesche, Second New Mexico Militia.

SANTA FÉ, N. MEX., *May 5, 1862.*

GENERAL: In accordance with your verbal order I herewith report to you the movements and surrender of that part of the Second Regiment New Mexico Militia which, under command of Col. Nicolas Pino, left Fort Craig the night of February 22 last:

The morning of the 24th said detachment, consisting of 280 men, passed through Socorro *en route* to Polvadera. Not far from Limitar we met Lieutenant Cooley, with letters from General O. P. Hovey, ordering Colonel Pino to fall back on Socorro, and to station his militiamen at or below said place. A halt was made to refresh our animals, and early in the afternoon Second Major Rivera, with a file of deserted volunteers and militiamen whom we had picked up on the road the day before, started for Polvadera, while the detachment countermarched to Socorro. Lieutenant-Colonel Baca and myself went ahead and selected the place where to establish quarters. As soon as our detachment arrived Colonel Pino ordered an advance guard of 14 mounted men, under Captain Gutierrez, below the town, and the animals were to be sent to graze under a strong guard, but had scarcely gone five minutes when Captain Gutierrez sent word that a picket of the enemy was approaching. By this time it grew dark. Colonel Pino ordered out two companies afoot, with Lieutenant-Colonel Baca, to reconnoiter the force of the advancing enemy. At the same time our animals were ordered back and to be guarded in a corral near by. Immediately below the town, under the cover of some adobe walls, Lieutenant-Colonel Baca had posted his two companies, when Captain Gutierrez pointed out to him the place where the enemy's advance guard were ambushed. Lieutenant-Colonel Baca ordered Captain Gutierrez to dislodge them. The Gutierrez picket had moved on a short distance when the Texans fired a shot, whereupon Lieutenant-Colonel Baca's party discharged their rifles in the direction whence they saw the flash of the enemy's gun. This made the Texan picket retreat to their main body, and Lieutenant-Colonel Baca came back to our headquarters and reported the above-stated facts to Colonel Pino, who ordered the different captains under his command to keep their men under arms and to be ready for immediate action. Small parties of our men were sent to cover such points as appeared most important.

Meantime a part of the Texans, under Lieutenant-Colonel McNeill, had taken position on an elevation southwest of Socorro, while Captain Frazier went around the town and intercepted the road north. It was about 8 p. m. the enemy fired a cannon-ball over the town, and from that moment our men began to desert and to hide themselves away. I sent Ygn° Montoya to Camp Connelly with a note, addressed to the commanding officer there, asking for re-enforcements. Accompanied by Adjutant Gonzales I visited the houses of some of the influential Mexicans, and tried my best to make them take up arms in defense of their Government, their homes, and firesides. Vain endeavor! No one responded to the call. Don Pedro Baca went even so far as to say that the United States Government was a curse to this Territory, and if the Texans would take and keep possession of New Mexico the change could only be for the better.

I went back to headquarters, and having reported to Colonel Pino the revolting ingratitude of Don Pedro Baca and the stupid indifference of other citizens, the alcalde of Socorro made his appearance, and told us that a Texan officer who came to his house had sent him to bring about an interview with our commanding officer. Colonel Pino sent me to see who the Texan officer was and to find out his intentions. The alcalde conducted me to a house not far from the church, where I found Lieutenant Simmons, who told me that by order of

Colonel McNeill he had come to ask the unconditional surrender of
the town; moreover, he manifested the desire to speak to Colonel
Pino himself. I replied that, although only an inferior militia officer,
I could assure him that Colonel Pino would not listen to such a demand, and that if he had no other business with my colonel he could
save himself the trouble of going to our headquarters; but as Lieutenant Simmons again expressed his wish to see Colonel Pino, I conducted him to our quarters.   Here the Texan messenger made the
same request as he had stated to me, and Colonel Pino answered about
in the same way as I had anticipated, when Lieutenant Simmons added
that Colonel McNeill would be sorry to attack Socorro and sacrifice
the lives of innocent families; to which Colonel Pino replied that he was
as anxious to spare the innocent families as Colonel McNeill could be,
and that at daybreak he (Colonel Pino) would meet the Texans and
give them battle in the plain south of Socorro.   Lieutenant Simmons
promised to inform Colonel McNeill of that proposition and to return
his answer.   I mounted my horse to accompany the Texan officer
through our pickets, but our pickets had disappeared, and the enemy's
pickets extended to the very houses of Socorro.   At a short distance I
met several Texan officers, and among them Colonel McNeill, who,
after having listened to Lieutenant Simmons' report, went with me to
our headquarters.   At the conference which now commenced Colonel
Pino, Lieutenant-Colonel Baca, and myself attended from our side, and
Lieutenant-Colonel McNeill, Major Ragnet, and Interpreter Stewart
from the rebels.   Colonel Pino repeated he was willing not to expose
the town, but to fight next morning in the open field.   Colonel McNeill
wanted to take possession of the town at once.   Our object was to gain
time, as we expected that on my message to the commander of Camp
Connelly, Governor Connelly, General Hovey, and Adjutant-General
Clever, who at the time were at Polvadera, would come to our relief with
the volunteers stationed at that place.   The discussion between Pino and
McNeill was interrupted by some of our officers, who wanted to speak
to Colonel Pino alone.   The latter went out, returned after a few
minutes, and then taking me aside ordered me to inquire into the state
of affairs at the quarters, inasmuch as the officers complained that all
their men had absconded.   At the principal door of the quarters I
found Capt. Mercedes Sanchez as sentinel, which place he had taken,
he told me, because the militiamen on guard had abandoned their posts
and no soldiers were left to replace the sentinel.   Inside I met Capts.
Ramon Sena y Rivera and Cruz Gutierrez, Lieutenants Garcia, Her-
rera, Homberger, Ortiz y Tafoya, Sergeant Martinez, and several
others, amounting to 37 persons in all.   This deplorable state of things
I reported to Colonel Pino, and then the conference was continued.
Colonel McNeill would not wait until next morning, he said, because he
knew he had the advantage at that moment; but if Colonel Pino could
give his word of honor that we had not written to anybody or otherwise given notice of the approach of the Confederates, in such case he
would consent that hostilities should not be commenced until daylight.
As Colonel Pino replied indirectly the conference was considered concluded.

Colonel McNeill had invited Colonel Pino several times to visit his
camp and persuade himself that the Confederates largely outnumbered
us, and Colonel Pino now determined to go.   Colonel Pino, Lieutenant-
Colonel Baca, and myself rode along with our visitors, and after having
looked at the long line of rebels and seeing that no relief came from
Camp Connelly, then, at 2 a. m. April 25, Colonel Pino surrendered.

If it had been disgusting to us to see our militiamen abscond in the hours of trial, it was more provoking to see them come out of their hiding places when the danger was over. There were at least 150 militiamen who at 10 a. m. took the oath of neutrality. Colonel Pino, Lieutenant-Colonel Baca, and myself were paroled.

I am, general, your obedient servant,

CHAS. EMIL WESCHE,
First Major, Second New Mexico Militia.

MAY 15, 1862.—Naval Demonstration upon Galveston, Tex.

Report of Col. Joseph J. Cook, commanding Military District of Galveston.

HDQRS. FIRST BRIG. TEX. VOLS., MIL. DIST. GALVESTON,
Galveston, Tex., May 15, 1862—6 p. m.

SIR: I beg most respectfully to report to the commanding general that about 3 p. m. to-day the schooner Sam Houston approached South Battery from westward, a brisk sea-breeze blowing, and stood down within a mile and a half of the battery, ostensibly for the purpose of drawing our fire or making an attack. Captain Schneider, thinking that he could cripple or sink her, fired four shots, striking very close, and thinking that one shot struck. She tacked after the first fire. Finding that she was too close in, she stood off and returned to her anchorage near the frigate. Captain Schneider and his officers have had repeated verbal orders from me to send me word if approached by any vessel and not provoke an attack; also a written order from Col. E. B. Nichols, under date of December 6, 1861, viz :

Should appearances indicate an attack, you will immediately telegraph to me at the office of E. B. Nichols & Co., where my headquarters are established.

Captain Schneider failed to inform me of the approach, and had I been present I should not have allowed the firing. Captain Schneider, however, justified himself under Post Order, No. 1, dated July 25, 1861, issued by Col. J. C. Moore, paragraph IV, viz :

Should any of the enemy's vessels come within effective range of either battery, the officer in charge will open fire without hesitation and give him the warmest reception his metal will afford.

After the firing at the schooner the movements on board the frigate indicated her intention to move, whereupon orders were issued for extraordinary vigilance on the part of the vedettes.

I have the honor to be, very respectfully, your obedient servant,

JOS. J. COOK,
Colonel, Commanding Military District.

Capt. SAMUEI BOYER DAVIS,
Acting Assistant Adjutant-General.

MAY 16, 1862—6 a. m.

All passed quiet during the night.

J. J. C.

MAY 21, 1862.—Affair at Paraje, N. Mex.

Report of Capt. Joseph G. Tilford, Third U. S. Cavalry:

PARAJE, N. MEX, *May* 30, 1862.

SIR: I have the honor to report that on the 21st, about sunup in the morning, a person was brought me by my guard bearing a white flag. On being questioned as to his business, he replied that his commanding officer (Lieutenant Bowman, I think) demanded a surrender of the town. On my declining to surrender and instructing him to inform Lieutenant Bowman that a compliance with his demand depended altogether on his ability to enforce it, he left, and I immediately proceeded to place my small command (45 men) in the best positions to resist an attack. None, however, was made. A few straggling shots at long ranges were made, and the Texans commenced a retreat down the Jornada. My spies reported them to be about 100 strong. My horses were so very poor and weak, and not knowing but that they had a stronger force below and were only attempting to draw me out, I did not deem it prudent to follow. I saw no more of them.

At about the time the demand for a surrender came a smaller party was seen, and near where my horses had been, until a few days previous, herded day and night, which leads me to believe, as my party was very small and about half with the herd, that simultaneous with their attack on me they would run off my herd; but finding the herd in, they declined the attack. I believe the white flag that came up with Lieutenant Taylor's party some time since covered a party of spies. I had only about 20 men then and herded my animals day and night.

In conclusion, I beg to say that I regret that they approached so near before I had notice of their coming, as I might then have been enabled to have so disposed my force as to have done them some injury. I had every confidence in my spies, as they were highly recommended to me, but they entirely neglected their business on that occasion, which I reported to you on the next day.

I am, sir, very respectfully, your obedient servant,

JOS. G. TILFORD,
Captain, Third U. S. Cavalry.

Lieut. A. L. ANDERSON,
A. A. A. G., Southern Mil. Dist., Fort Craig, N. Mex.

MAY 23, 1862.—Affair near Fort Craig, N. Mex.

Report of Brig. Gen. Edward R. S. Canby, U. S. Army, commanding Department of New Mexico.

HEADQUARTERS DEPARTMENT OF NEW MEXICO,
Santa Fé, N. Mex., May 25, 1862.

SIR: I have the honor to report that one of our pickets, 8 miles below Fort Craig, was attacked by a superior force of the enemy on the 23d instant, and repulsed, without loss on our side and a loss of 4 on the part of the assailants. With this exception there has been no change in the state of affairs since my last reports. Supplies are being accumulated at Fort Craig and Peralta as rapidly as possible, but the great flow in the Rio Grande continues to be a serious embarrassment to all our operations.

Very respectfully, sir, your obedient servant,

ED. R. S. CANBY,
Colonel Nineteenth Infantry and Brig. Gen. Comdg. Dept.

The ADJUTANT-GENERAL OF THE ARMY,
Washington, D. C.

. JULY 4, 1862.—Attack on U. S. Vessels near Velasco, Tex.

Report of Col. J. Bates, Thirteenth Texas Infantry.

HEADQUARTERS BATES' REGIMENT,
Velasco, Tex., July 5, 1862.

SIR: On the 3d instant, at dusk, I received information from Capt. William Saunders that there was a vessel outside, near San Luis. It was the impression of the pilots that she had some designs upon a cotton schooner in the canal, intending to capture or burn her. At Captain Saunders' request I issued him an order to take 40 of his men, without delay, repair to the cotton schooner, and defend her.

On the morning of the 4th a schooner was reported near shore this side of San Luis, on the peninsula, and soon afterwards I saw a large steamer coming from the west. When near the steamer the steamer opened fire. I started immediately for the scene of action. The schooner was about 6 miles east of this place. When about half way to the schooner I met Captain Saunders and his command. I halted them, ascertained that the schooner had been beached, and was out of gun-shot of the shore. Our men had been driven off by a constant fire of shot and shell. I felt that Captain Saunders and his men had performed all that was in their power and with much hazard to their lives. I perceived, also, that the cotton schooner was in line with the steamer and beached; schooner with her sails lowered. Captain Saunders informed me that he thought her crew had abandoned her. I at once ordered a forward movement of Captain Saunders' company as skirmishers, and sent an order back to Velasco to Lieutenant Moss to move forward; with Captain Clark's infantry company as a reserve, to defend the schooner in the canal, and have no doubt that the presence of Captain Saunders and his men saved the schooner from conflagration. Fire was now seen to be raging on the beached schooner and shells were thrown at all who attempted to approach her. Captain Saunders disposed of his men in detachments near the scene of action, and advanced with a few of his men under fire to the burning schooner. Soon afterwards the steamer got under way, apparently abandoning all designs upon the schooner in the canal, and I ordered Captain Clark's company back to Velasco, and some of Captain Saunders' men also commenced to return, when, to my surprise, the steamer put back, came close in to shore near the cotton schooner, and landed three boats full of men under a brisk fire. Such of Captain Saunders' men who were within reach I ordered rapidly forward, with instructions to attack; others voluntarily returned, and shots were exchanged between the enemy and our force. The fire from the steamer upon our men became very galling, they firing round shot and shell at the rate of six per minute, and scattering our men whenever

they formed. The enemy made no attempt to advance inward from the
beach, and after remaining some time on shore retreated hastily to the
steamer and put to sea.

We sustained no loss, although under a fire at times very heavy, and
continued at intervals seven or eight hours, and saved from the burning schooner some $2,000 worth of stores, principally medicines.

I have the honor to be, your obedient servant,

J. BATES,
Colonel, Commanding.

JULY 7–17, 1862.—Operations in Aransas Bay, Tex.

REPORTS.

No. 1.—Col. Charles Livenskiold, C. S. Army, Provost-Marshal, &c.
No. 2.—Capt. B. F. Neal, C. S. Army.

No. 1.

Report of Col. Charles Livenskiold, Provost-Marshal, Corpus Christi.

CORPUS CHRISTI, TEX., *July* 17, 1862.

GENERAL: Your letter of the 11th instant, by express, came duly to
hand, but only this day. From its tenor I see that my communication
in relation to the appearance of the enemy off Aransas Bay and his entrance in the bay had not then been received. I will therefore report
to you in full since the 7th instant, the date of his first appearance.

On the 7th a bark, with a 100-ton schooner and one large frigate
(second-class cutter), came off the bay. The schooner and cutter, with
six launches, entered the bay and proceeded to take a position near the
Shell Bank, and so as to rake and control the ship channel leading from
Aransas [Bay] to Corpus Christi Bay. Upon receiving this news I
sent the dispatch-boat Breaker, under Captain Rose, with Captain Ware
and 10 men, to make a reconnaissance, and, returning, they reported the
enemy's force to be as before represented—all well armed and probably
some 225 men. Next Captain Harrison, in command of gunboat General Bee, of Major Shea's command (here present on recruiting service
for a crew of sailors), went down and reconnoitered the enemy very
closely, say within 200 yards. His report was to the effect that the
schooner was heavily armed with cannon, about 125 tons burden, evidently a fine sailer, sharp and deep, and drawing at least 6 feet of water.
The cutter was thirty-oared and armed with one 24-pounder howitzer,
the launches four-oared whale-boats. The force was deemed too formidable, on account of its superiority in artillery, to warrant any attack or
action on the offensive. Three prizes had already been taken by the
enemy, say sloop Bella Italia, of 10 or 12 tons, with corn and bacon;
schooner Reindeer, of about 15 tons, with 52 bales of cotton, and a lug-
ger, with corn, name unknown. The schooner Monte Christo had been
visited, and the cotton at Lamar (some 47 bales) taken off to Saint Joseph
and stored near Johnson's house.

I received a communication from Captain Neal upon the subject,
which I inclose, marked No. 1*. From its tenor I concluded that he
was undecided as to what he should do, and desired advice from me.

---

*See p. 720.

I wrote him at once that there could be no danger for his command, as from my information the numerical strength of the enemy must be insignificant; that I deemed it of great importance that he should retreat or fall back no farther, but, on the contrary, maintain his position, and that, if practicable, without too great a risk of life or public property, he should endeavor to tease the enemy, so as to draw his fire and ascertain range and caliber of guns of the armed schooner.

I inclose subsequent communications from Captain Neal, marked Nos. 2 and 3, which will throw further light on proceedings up to this date.

The rapid movements of the enemy, the numerous exaggerated reports, and the absence of the commanding officer, together with want of experience in the officers present and unwillingness to assume responsibility for fear of consequences, all tended to create a perfect panic at the very beginning; and to put this down and take all necessary steps for the proper defense of the town and the protection or rescuing of a large amount of cotton and tobacco, with the cargo just landed from the schooner Penelope, it became necessary that some one should command and take the lead. As the officers all seemed to look to me for guidance, advice, and orders, and showed themselves willing and anxious, with their men, to obey me, under the circumstances, I did not shrink from the great responsibility, and at once made all necessary suggestions.

All the necessary ammunition was at once prepared, and finding the troops without caps for their arms, almost barefoot, very small quantity of serviceable powder on hand, and in want of clothing, I took from the cargo of the schooner 20,000 percussion caps, 400 pounds of fine powder, the necessary shoes, 1½ dozen flannel overshirts, and 2 pieces ditto; also—as the company of Captain Ware needed them—I took for them 15 double-barrel shot-guns and 3 five-shooters. Thereupon I obtained the requisite transportation, and forwarded the remainder of said cargo to Victoria, and sent all the cotton and tobacco on hand to its places of destination. There have been sent off from the 7th until date 421 bales of cotton, 500 bales of tobacco, also about 7,600 pounds of powder. If the enemy should be able to pay us a visit here he will not find anything worth plundering or carrying away. The records of the county and district clerk I have caused to be made ready for packing in chests made for the purpose, ready to be moved at a moment's warning.

From the passengers referred to by Captain Neal as sent from on board the enemy's bark, and whom I critically examined, assisted by Captain Ware, Lieutenant-Commanding George, and Mr. Robert Mott, late of New Orleans, and known as an able lawyer, we learned that the enemy's forces did not number 125 men, all told, and that the men on the gunboat, cutter, and launches were supplied from the bark, leaving this latter with only about 20 men or less. Captain Kittredge is in command inside on board gunboat, which carries two 32-pounder Dahlgrens and one large caliber gun amidships. She was a pleasure yacht in New Orleans, built by Robinson, owned by Story, and lastly taken and fitted up by and for General Lovell, and brought out as one of the enemy's trophies of war, about 125 tons burden, and about 6 feet draught of water. The cutter carries 30 oars, one 24-pounder howitzer, and is manned from the schooner. The greatest number of men ever seen on these vessels, including the prizes, does not exceed 87. The cotton taken by the enemy is piled, as before stated, on Saint Joseph's Island, opposite Captain Johnson's house. The conclusion as to the prisoners was unanimous that Andres Roeg and wife were citizens of Matamoros, caught in New Orleans by the enemy on his taking possession, and that as a matter of kindness Captain Kittredge had carried them as passengers. But in relation to Mr. Cavaños, a doubt as to his true status and feelings was created, and hence I released the former two and detained the latter, to be sent to Colonel Luckett, whom he claims to be well and intimately acquainted with, for final disposition.

Owing to the information received as above—that from Captain Neal, the results of several reconnaissances, and reports brought in from various quarters as to the designs of the enemy and his expecting re-enforcements within a few weeks—I called the officers together for consultation and to decide as to what ought to be done to oppose and prevent the further encroachments of the enemy. It was unanimously decided—

1st. To send the gunboat General Bee, Capt. Thomas Harrison, with a picked crew, and the dispatch-boat Breaker, Capt. J. Harding, with a detachment from Captain Ireland's company, to guard the ship channel.

2d. To obstruct the ship channel by sinking in the narrowest point such number of "come-at-able" vessels as were requisite, the vessels to be loaded with stone.

3d. To take possession of the schooner Elma and fit her for a gunboat at once, arm and man her, and place her at Corpus Christi Pass, to prevent the enemy's cutters or launches to force [from forcing] an entrance to our bay from said point.

4th. To send 40 picked men, as well armed and mounted as possible, under a proper guide, and commanded by Lieut. W. Mann, around by the reef, avoiding the coast until above Lamar, and thence crossing to Saint Joseph's Island, to burn and destroy the cotton taken by the enemy and piled at Johnson's house in the night.

5th. To fit out an expedition by water, to make a feint upon the enemy at the Shell Bank, to divert his attention from Saint Joseph's Island, while Lieutenant Mann's forces attempt to destroy the cotton.

6th. To appoint Capt. John Dix to superintend and direct the arming, equipping, and fitting out of the vessels to be employed.

Under the second head the schooners Relief and Confederate, after appraisement, were taken, loaded with concrete, and sunk in the night unobserved by the enemy, and the sloop Iowa is now in like manner being loaded for the same purpose. These will effectually prevent the enemy's gunboat from coming into Corpus Christi Bay through the ship channel. All the other heads have been acted on, and are either executed or in progress of execution. I inclose you slip from Captain Ware,* and will report final results as soon as possible. Captain Ware, with his party, attacked the enemy near the Shell Bank and drove him back, firing with rifles at 200 yards, and causing the enemy to seek shelter in the hold of his boat. The prize Bella Italia now fitted up by him as a small gunboat. There is no doubt that the Corpus [Christi] Pass is now blockaded by the prize-schooner Reindeer, and that the entrance thence must be guarded. I will see that the proper steps are taken for preventing a surprise. The cotton at the Flour Bluffs and the salt trade along the Laguna de la Madre are the objects sought by the enemy.

I trust that my action in the foregoing may meet with your approbation. Should it be otherwise I should feel much chagrined. I send you English paper and a New Orleans Delta of the 1st, in which see

---

* Not found.

an infamous special order from Butler in relation to Mrs. Philips. I have not had time to answer your letter in relation to McKinney. He lies basely if the messenger reports him correctly. I thank you for having taken notice of it, and will furnish proper refutation as soon as the present excitement is over.

I must not forget to say that all here is harmony and perfect union among all officers, men, and myself, and all vie with one another in zealously obeying orders.

In haste, very truly, yours,

CHAS. LIVENSKIOLD.

General H. P. BEE,
    Comdg. Mil. Dist. of the Lower Rio Grande, San Antonio, Tex.

P. S.—I trust you will at once send Major Shea to assume command of the operations or return Captain Ireland.

No. 2.

Reports of Capt. Benjamin F. Neal, C. S. Army.

CAMP NEAR DREDGE-BOAT, *July 13, 1862.*

SIR: To-day, about 11 o'clock, the picket guard reported a launch coming down the cut toward the dredge-boat. I immediately ordered the company down, and observed that they were approaching the dredge under a flag of truce. I notified them to land on the opposite side of the channel, some 200 or 300 yards from the dredge, when I took a boat, accompanied by Captain Ware and Lieutenant Conklin, and went over to them. The interview lasted some half an hour. The officer, second in command I presume, stated that his object was to pass to Corpus Christi Cavaños and another Mexican gentleman and his lady, who was then at Saint Joseph's Island. I consented that they should go down on board the Rebecca, and have given orders to Lieutenant Russell to carry them down and report them to you. I had no opportunity of asking or ascertaining how Cavaños got on board the bark, further than he was in [New] Orleans when that city was taken by the enemy. I therefore leave it for you to investigate the whole matter when they arrive in Corpus [Christi]. Sergeant Bradley has just arrived from Lamar, and says that the enemy held Captain Brown for the purpose of piloting the schooner down to Corpus Christi. They also say that Kittredge, who is in command of the expedition, stated at Lamar that 15,000 troops would be landed on Saint Joseph's Island in a few weeks. I think that is only bombast. I have sent a party of men to Lamar to-night to burn the Monte Christo, as they are going up for her on Monday for the purpose of carrying out the cotton they have captured. I presume you can get more accurate information from Cavaños. I shall hold my position here until ordered or driven away.

Very respectfully,

BENJ. F. NEAL,
Captain, Commanding Camp Aransas.

Colonel LIVENSKIOLD.

CAMP NEAR DREDGE-BOAT, *July 16, 1862.*

SIR: I received your note per Mr. Hooper, and willingly comply

with your request, believing that his services would be more valuable
to the public interest in some other capacity. Mr. Hooper is truly
patriotic and true to the Southern interest, and his services, considering
his age, should be appreciated.

I committed an error in my letter of Sunday in stating that the officer
with whom I had the interview was second in command. I misunderstood him. I have learned since he was only purser of the blockading
squadron.

We have had some little excitement in camp to-day. For the purpose of obtaining better water I had to move my command nearer and
in front of the enemy. This morning the Bella Italia, one of the captured boats, came into Shell Bank, and, from her movements, I supposed she was coming down the cut, but she only went down the Corpus
Christi channel some 200 or 300 yards below the cut and returned.
Shortly afterward the schooner got under way and took a position as
near our camp as she could, and has been throwing shell occasionally
ever since, but nothing has come near enough to us to create any apprehension. She is some 3 or 4 miles from us. She evidently had not
given us the full strength of her guns, as I observe the fuse in every
case was too short. What she may do hereafter can only be determined
by future experiments. I intend to hold my position at this point until
driven or ordered away, unless I deem it necessary to aid some other
point. I must have more transportation to remove all of my guns and
camp equipage, besides ammunition.

On yesterday the bark and captured schooner left and sailed up the
coast. This morning the bark returned, but without the schooner. I
was apprehensive she was going down toward Corpus Christi Pass,
but I think she did not. If I observe her going down the coast I will
send an express.

Very respectfully,

BENJ. F. NEAL,
Captain, Comdg. Company of Artillery, Coast Defense.

Col. C. LIVENSKIOLD.

AUGUST 10, 1862.—Affair on the Nueces River near Fort Clark, Tex.

Report of Lieut. C. D. McRae, Second Regiment Texas Mounted Rifles.

SAN ANTONIO, TEX., *August 18, 1862.*

SIR: I have the honor to report, for the information of the general
commanding, the result of a scout under my command, consisting of
detachments from Captain Donelson's company, Second Regiment
Texas Mounted Rifles; Captain Duff's company, Texas Partisan
Rangers; Captain Davis' company of State troops, and Taylor's battalion; amounting in the aggregate to 94 men, rank and file.

I left camp on the morning of the 3d instant on the Perdinalis and
proceeded up the South Fork of the Guadalupe River.

On the morning of the 6th instant struck the trail of a party of
horsemen, numbering, as I suppose, from 60 to 100; pursued the trail
in a southwesterly direction four consecutive days, and on the evening
of the 9th instant, about 3 o'clock, my advance guard reported a camp
in sight on the headwaters of the Western Fork of the Nueces River.
I immediately diverged from the trail to the right, secreting my com-

mand in a cañon about 2½ miles from the enemy, and at once proceeded, in company with Lieutenants Homsley, Lilly, Harbour, and Bigham, to make a careful reconnaissance of the position of the enemy's encampment, which we were fortunate enough in effecting without being discovered. Returned to camp, and proceeded to make my dispositions for an attack at daylight on the following morning.

Accordingly, at 1 o'clock that night, I moved my command to within 300 yards of their camp, where I divided my command into two equal divisions, placing one under the command of Lieutenant Homsley, whom I directed to take position on the right of the enemy, in the edge of a dense cedar-brake, about 50 yards from their camp, which he succeeded in doing without detection. In the mean time I had had equal success in obtaining another cedar-brake with my division within about 40 yards of the enemy, on their left. These movements were accomplished about an hour before daylight. Shortly after having secured our positions a sentinel on his rounds came near the position of Lieutenant Homsley's division, which he had the misfortune to discover; whereupon he was shot dead by Lieutenant Harbour, which caused an alarm in the enemy's camp, and a few shots were exchanged between the parties, and all became quiet again for the space of half an hour, when another sentinel hailed us on the left, and shared the fate of the first. It being still too dark for the attack, I ordered my men to hold quietly their positions until daylight. The enemy in the mean time were actively engaged preparing to resist us. The moment it became light enough to see, I ordered the attack to be made by a steady and slow advance upon their position, firing as we advanced until within about 30 paces of their line, when I ordered a charge of both divisions, which was executed in fine style, resulting in the complete rout and flight of the enemy.

They left on the field 32 killed. The remainder fled, scattering in all directions through the many dense cedar-brakes in the immediate vicinity. From the many signs of blood I infer many of those escaping were seriously wounded.

We captured 83 head of horses, 33 stand of small-arms, 13 six-shooters, and all their camp equipage, and provisions for 100 men for ten days. The arms I turned over to the commanding officer at Fort Clark. The horses are *en route* to this place. The provisions were consumed by my command.

Although the surprise and rout of the enemy was complete, I regret to state it was not unattended with loss on our part. We had 2 killed on the field and 18 wounded.

The fight occurred about 20 miles north of Fort Clark, to which point I sent for assistance, both surgical and transportation, for my wounded, which was promptly forwarded by the commanding officer, Captain Carolan, and Assistant Surgeon Downs, to whom I am greatly indebted for many kind attentions to myself and command, as also to Mr. D. H. Brown. My wounded are all well provided for and are doing well.

I have learned from one of the party whom we fought, captured some four or five days subsequent to the fight, that the party was composed of 63 Germans, 1 Mexican, and 5 Americans (the latter running the first fire), all under the command of a German by the name of Fritz Tegner. They offered the most determined resistance and fought with desperation, asking no quarter whatever; hence I have no prisoners to report.

My officers and men all behaved with the greatest coolness and gallantry, seeming to vie with each other in deeds of daring chivalry. It would be invidious to attempt to draw any distinctions when all did their part most nobly and gloriously.

Inclosed find a list of killed and wounded of each company.*

I remain, with great respect, your obedient servant,

C. D. McRAE,
First Lieut., Second Regt. Texas Mounted Rifles, Comdg. Scout.

Maj. E. F. GRAY,
        A. A. A. G., Sub-Military District of the Rio Grande.

AUGUST 11, 1862.—Affair at Velasco, Tex.

Report of Col. J. Bates, Thirteenth Texas Regiment.

HEADQUARTERS BATES' REGIMENT,
                Velasco, Tex., August 16, 1862.

SIR: I have the honor to report operations at this post, resulting in a collision with the enemy, on the afternoon of the 11th instant:

About 4 p. m. of that day a screw-propeller of about 800 tons burden, two-masted, and marked with a figure 5 on her smoke-stack, steamed slowly in from the eastward, and when opposite the battery at this place, immediately outside the bar, opened fire, without showing colors or giving any notice of her intentions. Her fire was promptly responded to, and after firing four times and receiving five shots from us she drew out of range and disappeared down the coast. It is believed that our third shot took effect. We sustained no damage. A 13-inch shell, which failed to explode, was picked up by our men. One other shell exploded in our camp; the others went overhead and struck some distance out in the prairie. I am confident that if we had had even a single piece of heavy ordnance she could have been disabled. Of late the vessels which pass here have been coming much nearer the shore than formerly. This may result from their having adopted more hostile intentions, but I think it is due in part from a knowledge (how acquired I know not) of our defenseless condition. A late freshet in the Brazos River has considerably deepened the water on the bar at the mouth. Vessels are constantly receiving permits to proceed to sea from this port, and lie in the river above awaiting a favorable opportunity to run the blockade, and a well-sustained attack from the sea might well result in great loss both to Government and individuals.

Allow me to respectfully urge upon your consideration that there are quite a number of heavy pieces of ordnance now in this department dismounted and not in use, which, if placed in battery here, could defend my position and our foreign trade, and save my command from this now constant source of annoyance, which, although as yet resulting in no damage, might at any time become fraught with humiliation and disaster. I have but one 18-pounder gun in battery at this place. I ask, if compatible with the interests of the service, a 32 rifled cannon, a 64-pounder, or both. If granted, they will do good service ere long, should we continue to be menaced and insulted by our vaunting foe.

---

* Not found.

If they are needed at more important points they can be promptly forwarded.

Very respectfully,

J. BATES,
Colonel, Commanding.

Capt. C. M. MASON,
Acting Assistant Adjutant-General, San Antonio, Tex.

AUGUST 12, 1862.—Capture of the Breaker and destruction of the Hannah in Corpus Christi Bay, Texas.

REPORTS.

No. 1.—Capt. John Harding, of the capture of the Breaker.
No. 2.—Capt. Jack Sands, of the destruction of the Hannah.

No. 1.

Report of Capt. John Harding, of the capture of the Breaker.

CORPUS CHRISTI, TEX., *August 27, 1862.*

On the evening of August 11 I was directed by Maj. A. M. Hobby to take on board of the Breaker Captain Jones and a party of men from his battalion. On Captain Jones, accompanied by Lieutenant Vinyard and party, coming on board, he informed me that he was sent in charge of the boat for the purpose of watching the movements of the enemy, then engaged in removing the obstructions in the channel. Got under way and proceeded to McGloin's Bluffs, where we anchored for the night.

Next morning got under way and stood down in the direction of the enemy; discovered them at work on the obstructions; stood down about three-quarters of a mile from them, took a look, came around, and stood back about a quarter of a mile and came to anchor. Just as we came to, discovered that they had removed the last of the obstructions. Their large schooner made all sail and stood up the channel. I immediately got under way and made all sail for Corpus Christi. Soon discovered that the enemy were overhauling us, and thought it best to make for the nearest shore (Indian Point), being about 6 miles distant. Just after passing McGloin's Bluffs they commenced firing on us, and continued to do so until the boat was beached and this party landed from her. I gave orders to have the boat fired some time before she was beached, knowing that at the rate she was sailing no injury could result to the party on board; but there was a clamor raised against me by the officers on board, who told me that Major Hobby gave them the command of the boat, and that they would not allow her to be fired until she was beached. A few minutes before she struck she was set on fire, and all of the party left as fast as they could, leaving me alone on board. I did everything that I could think of to aid in her destruction, but the enemy were too close after me and I had to leave, as I would have been killed or captured by staying longer. The enemy sent a boat alongside, put out the fire, and towed her off.

Respectfully,

JOHN HARDING,
Captain.

No. 2.

Report of Capt. Jack Sands, of the destruction of the Hannah.

CORPUS CHRISTI, TEX., *August* 27, 1862.

A few days before the arrival of the enemy at this place I solicited Maj. A. M. Hobby to allow me to get my boat to a place of safety in Nueces Bay, there being at the time plenty of water on the reef for her to get over. He said that he wanted the Hannah and the Breaker to remain at this place as spy boats, but assured me that none of the larger boats should attempt to cross the reef before mine. Accordingly I remained at the wharf.

On the afternoon of August 12, when the enemy were in full sight, distant about 7 miles of the town, I was ordered to get over the Nueces Reef with all speed. Got under way immediately and stood for the reef. The Elma, or Major Minter, had been run into the channel the previous day, where she grounded, leaving only a narrow place for vessels to pass. On arriving off the reef discovered that she had been fired, and seemed to be on fire fore and aft. Hearing that she had powder on board, did not like to attempt to pass her. An explosion would have killed us all. Came around and stood back for the town, intending to run on the flats, where the boat could have been hauled out and been safe from capture, but was ordered back, and the boat was run on shore above the town on a bold bank. Major Hobby said that he would send men to haul her out, a thing that was impossible without ways, as the bank at that place was at least 4 feet in height. A party of 15 unarmed men came down and were at work on her, when the enemy came abreast of the boat and fired a shot at the party. They all immediately left. The enemy then came to anchor, distant about 400 yards, and commenced manning a boat. Fearing that they would cut her out, I immediately fired her and she was consumed.

Respectfully,

JACK SANDS, *Captain.*

AUGUST 16–18, 1862.—Bombardment of Corpus Christi, Tex.

REPORTS.

No. 1.—Brig. Gen. Hamilton P. Bee, C. S. Army.
No. 2.—Maj. A. M. Hobby, C. S. Army.

No. 1.

Reports of Brig. Gen. Hamilton P. Bee, C. S. Army.

HDQRS. SUB-MIL. DIST. OF THE RIO GRANDE,
Corpus Christi, Tex., August 21, 1862.

SIR: I reached this place yesterday, and have the honor to report that I find all things quiet. The enemy attacked the town on Saturday and again on Monday, firing between 200 and 300 shell and shot. They were bravely resisted by our forces, and after being struck a number of times by the shot from our battery (which was planted during the night of Friday) he was forced to retire, we believe in a crippled condition.

On Tuesday morning the enemy left, and is now lying at his old anchorage near the Shell Bank. His return is looked for, as his discomfiture was a source of great mortification. A more full report will be forwarded at an early day. The damage to the town is inconsiderable. We had but 1 man killed.

Very respectfully, your obedient servant,

H. P. BEE,
Brigadier-General, Provisional Army.

Capt. O. M. MASON,
   A. A. A. G., Dept. of Texas, San Antonio, Tex.

—

HDQRS. SUB-MIL. DIST. OF THE RIO GRANDE,
Corpus Christi, Tex., August 26, 1862.

SIR : I have the honor to report that I proceeded to within 4 miles of the anchorage of the fleet of the enemy on yesterday, and, except witnessing the arrival of a large schooner from sea, found the fleet all quiet. There are now eight vessels of all sizes lying within the bar at Aransas Pass. It was impossible to ascertain anything about the new arrival. She seemed to be a large merchant schooner, probably loaded with supplies and men, but may be a mortar boat. I have sent a spy onto Mustang Island to ascertain her character and hope to report it for this mail.

There has been no movement by the enemy since their repulse from this place. The steamer was much injured, as her steam-pumps were heard during the day and night she consumed in passing through the canal. I examined the Shell Bank and found that it would be untenable even if cannon could be placed on it, which, from its proximity to the fleet and in full view of them, would be impossible, it being 3 miles from water and the guns of the enemy covering its approach; nor is there any other point adjacent to the canal on which guns can be erected, owing to the low, marshy approaches; therefore all hopes of defending the narrow bayou and canal must be abandoned. The obstructions placed there proved no obstacle, as with the steam-power of their boat they were easily removed. I am making another effort to sink more permanent obstructions, which, if successful, will prevent at least any sudden attack, but if unsuccessful forces me to rely on the naturally-strong position of this place for its defense. The battery used in the late fight on the north side of the town was thrown up by General Taylor in 1845, of shell and sand, which, being solid and impenetrable to 32-pound shot, has proved an admirable defense. Another work of similar character is now complete on the south side of the town, both being on the water's edge. I shall at once erect another on the bluff overlooking the water batteries, and distant, say, 400 yards, which, completed, will be all that can be done.

I found great confusion existing in the quartermaster's, commissary, and ordnance departments here, owing to the inexperience of the officers, and deeming it indispensable for the public interest, I have appointed H. A. Gilpin, who distinguished himself in the late engagement and is a man of experience and business habits, to act as quartermaster and commissary at this point, subject to the approval of the general commanding, and respectfully request that the appointment may be confirmed. I have also appointed (subject to like approval) F. Blucher, major of Engineers, and charged him with the erection of the necessary defenses of this place. He is a nephew of Marshal Blucher, and an educated soldier, and as civil engineer has resided many years at this place. The services of Major Blucher were indispensable and the rank was temporarily given him to facilitate his labors. With great satisfaction I tendered to Mr. William Mann the position of captain of artillery, vacated by the declension of Captain Livenskiold. This mark of my appreciation for his gallant services I felt satisfied would meet the approval of the general commanding. But he declines the commission, owing to the shattered state of his health from exposure at Island No. 10; but he accepts the position temporarily, and will command his battery until this emergency passes over, when he will retire.

Captain Willke's battery of light artillery, from Ringgold Barracks, will be here to-morrow. His guns are four 12 and two 24 pounder howitzers, and will add materially to our defenses, but the fact of his company being well-drilled artillerists is the most pleasant reflection attending his arrival. A delay of a few more days on the part of the enemy (which seems probable) will enable me to meet him with satisfactory results.

Very respectfully, your obedient servant,

H. P. BEE,
Brig. Gen., Prov. Army, Comdg. Sub-Mil. Dist. of the Rio Grande.

Capt. C. M. MASON,
Acting Assistant Adjutant-General, Department of Texas.

———

HDQRS. SUB-MIL. DIST. OF THE RIO GRANDE,
Corpus Christi, Tex., August 26, 1862.

SIR: I have the honor to inclose the official reports of Maj. A. M. Hobby, commanding this post, of the bombardment of Corpus Christi. It is with great satisfaction that I call the attention of the general commanding the Department of Texas to the judgment and gallantry of Major Hobby, as well as to the satisfactory manner in which he discharged his duty under the trying circumstances in which he was placed. The enemy brought into action seven pieces of heavy artillery, adapted to and using all the modern improvements in projectiles. Our force was two 18-pounder and one 12-pounder guns, manned by inexperienced artillerists, and supported by volunteers but a few days in the service; yet the furious fire of shot and shell by the enemy, after the first few rounds, served but to inspire the men, and their spirit and bravery are worthy of all praise.

After several hours of incessant fire on our little battery, without effect, a force of about 40 men, with a rifled gun, was landed on the beach about a mile from the battery (which, having but a water front, was not able to resist their approach), and slowly advancing, endeavoring to flank it, the three heavy gunboats being within 400 yards of the shore, covering their advance with a continuous fire of grape and canister. So completely did the guns of the boats cover their approach that the advancing force may fairly be considered as equal to two batteries of 24 and 32 pounders. To charge through such a formidable fire seemed hopeless; yet, when almost within musket-range of the battery, Major Hobby led a charge of 25 men and put the marines to flight. At this moment Captain Ware's fine company of cavalry came dashing into the plain, and but for the peremptory order from Major Hobby in person would in another moment have cut them to pieces and captured their gun; but, when it is considered that this charge would have been made through a flank fire of heavy guns, loaded with grape and canister, at 400 yards distance, and must have resulted in the sacrifice of most of the men, I approve of the order of Major Hobby in restraining them, considering the object to be gained as not commensurate with the almost certain loss.

It is due to Captain Ware and his command to say that, with all its probable consequences, they were not only ready for the work and actually under fire, but were bitterly disappointed at losing the opportunity thus presented.

Foiled in all his plans, the enemy vented his spleen on the defenseless houses of the town for a short time and then withdrew, with his fleet badly crippled, but with what loss we have no means of knowing. Between 400 and 500 shot and shell were fired by the enemy.

One man killed and 1 wounded constitute the casualties among our troops. Major Hobby was struck on the head by a glancing ball, which inflicted but a slight wound. A great many houses in the town were struck, but the damage is slight.

Too much praise cannot be given to the patriotic citizens of Corpus Christi. They removed out into the woods with their families out of fire, and in tents and under trees calmly and confidently awaited the result. They have suffered many inconveniences and privations, especially for want of water, as the drought of this section has been unprecedented, yet they have set a laudable example to their countrymen and added another to the many instances of patriotism which this war has elicited. It is worthy of remark that the citizens of the surrounding counties, for a distance of 100 miles, attracted by the fire of the cannon, with their rifles in hand, repaired to the scene and tendered their services to the commanding officer, demonstrating that when the emergency arises their country can depend on them.

The defenses of the town have been materially strengthened and heavier guns added to the batteries, and should the enemy renew the attack I feel confident of reporting equally as successful a result.

The attention of the general commanding is specially called to the service rendered by Mr. William Mann, a young gentleman of this place, who, having served at Belmont, Columbus, and Island No. 10, brought all the experience of those well-fought fields to the assistance of his native city, and materially contributed by his gallantry and skill to the discomfiture of our enemies.

Major Buckner, a citizen of Corpus Christi, but an experienced soldier from the Old World, rendered useful service.

Judge H. A. Gilpin, chief justice of Nueces County, was much exposed, and rendered good service, as did many other citizens of the town.

Very respectfully, your obedient servant,

H. P. BEE,
Brig. Gen., Prov. Army, Comdg. Sub-Mil. Dist. of the Rio Grande.
Capt. C. M. MASON, *A. A. A. G., Department of Texas.*

No. 2.

Reports of Maj. A. M. Hobby, C. S. Army.

HDQRS. SUB-MIL. DIST. CORPUS CHRISTI AND ARANSAS,
Corpus Christi, Tex., August 16, 1862.

SIR: In my communication of yesterday I reported the arrival of four Federal vessels in Corpus Christi Bay, they having removed the obstruction placed in the ship channel—the yacht Corypheus, Reindeer, Bella Italia, and steam gunboat. The yacht appeared off Ingleside at 4 p. m., chasing the Breaker, a pilot-boat in the Confederate service, which was just returning from a reconnoitering expedition, with a detachment of men under Capt. R. E. Jones. To prevent her capture by the enemy she was run on shore at Indian Point, and the reconnoitering party effected their escape. The Breaker was fired some distance from shore, but unfortunately not in time to prevent her from falling into the hands of the enemy, who extinguished the flames. Eleven shots were fired at her during the chase. The Breaker is a small boat, carrying a crew of 3 men. The yacht then steered for Corpus Christi, standing close along the shore, and fired a shot at a detachment of Captain McCampbell's company, hauling a boat upon the beach. She came to anchor opposite the city, and was joined during the night by the remainder of the fleet.

At 9 o'clock this morning Captain Kittredge, in a launch, approached the wharf with a flag of truce, at which point I met him. He informed me that he had been ordered by the United States Government to examine the public buildings in the city and make an official report of their condition. I informed him that the United [States] Government owned no property in Corpus Christi, and that he should not be allowed to land. He replied that it was his prerogative to land when and where he pleased, under what he called the national ensign. I told him the Confederate Government recognized no such right, and I was here to prevent him from placing his foot upon our soil. He then desired to accompany me ashore or go alone under a white flag. Every proposition to land, under whatever pretext, was peremptorily rejected. He then demanded that the women and children should be removed beyond the limits of the town in twenty-four hours, as he intended to land with a force and execute his orders. I demanded forty-eight hours, which was finally agreed upon. He requested that the matter again be taken into consideration. The second interview resulted as did the first. One of the conditions of the armistice was that the forty-eight hours be exclusively devoted to the removal of the families from town, which I strictly complied with.

On the evening of the 15th the Federal fleet took position opposite the northern suburbs of the city in line of battle, within range from the shore. Immediately after dark I planted a battery of two guns (a 12 and 18 pounder) behind a strong fortification near the water's edge, and supported it by a detachment from Captain Ireland's company and my battalion, they furnishing also an extra detachment to move the guns.

At daylight on the 16th we opened on the enemy. Six shots were fired at the fleet before they replied. The enemy shelled the battery and the town furiously, doing, however, but little damage. At 9 o'clock we drove him from his position. Beyond the reach of our guns he repaired damages and mended sails rent by our shot. At 3 o'clock he again returned, and when within reach of our battery it opened on him, striking both yacht and steamer, and compelled them to withdraw beyond the reach of our guns. They contented themselves with shelling the battery during the remainder of the day.

Mr. William Mann volunteered his services in the battery, and I placed him in charge of the guns. By his coolness, courage, and judgment he elicited the admiration of all, and I herein acknowledge the value of his services in our gallant attack upon the enemy's boasted gunboats. With guns of inferior caliber and a smaller force than their own they were twice driven from their position, and resulted in their discomfiture. Five shots were seen to do execution. The enemy fired 296 times.

The casualities on our side were inconsiderable. Private Steiner, of Captain Ireland's company, was slightly wounded in head by a spent ball. To Judge Gilpin and Major Blucher I am indebted for valuable services. To-night all is quiet. We do not need more troops.

I have the honor to be, very respectfully, your obedient servant,

A. M. HOBBY,
Major, Commanding.

Maj. E. F. Gray,

Acting Assistant Adjutant-General, San Antonio, Tex.

HEADQUARTERS,
Corpus Christi, Tex., August 18, 1862.

Sir: On the morning of the 18th the enemy again opened on our battery, bringing his whole force to bear on it. Failing to silence our guns, a portion of his fleet withdrew and landed a 12-pounder rifled gun, supported by 30 or 40 well-armed men, who approached our battery by the beach, close under cover of their gunboats, firing continuously. They attempted to enfilade our battery, their balls passing just above our intrenchments. I immediately ordered 25 men to charge the gun, which they did in gallant style. When from under cover of the breastworks they entered an open plain and rapidly neared the gun, the gunboats of the enemy opened a heavy fire upon them. Undaunted they pressed onward, and when within range of small-arms I ordered them to fire, which they did, still advancing, the enemy in the mean time retreating in double-quick, carrying with them their gun. They left in the retreat their ammunition-box, hatchet, rat-tail files, (intended, I presume, to spike our guns); a hat and rifle-cartridges were scattered along the road. We chased them to their gunboats, to which they retreated without delay. Whenever a ball from the battery would strike the boats of the enemy they would rise and cheer, regardless of the fire to which they were exposed. The enemy withdrew, and taking position in front of the city, avenged themselves upon a few unoffending houses. A few shots from our guns drove them off, and on the following morning stood away for Aransas Pass.

Our loss in the engagement was one killed—Private Henry Mote, in Capt. R. E. Jones' company. He was shot through the head among the foremost in the charge. Captain Ware's fine cavalry company was present and eager for the fray.

I have the honor to be, very respectfully, your obedient servant,

A. M. HOBBY,
Major, Commanding.

Maj. E. F. Gray,
Acting Assistant Adjutant-General, Corpus Christi, Tex.

SEPTEMBER 13–14, 1862.—Operations at Flour Bluffs, near Corpus Christi, Tex.

REPORTS.

No. 1.—Brig. Gen. Hamilton P. Bee, C. S. Army.
No. 2.—Maj. E. F. Gray, C. S. Army.
No. 3.—Capt. John Ireland, C. S. Army.

No. 1.

Reports of Brig. Gen. Hamilton P. Bee, C. S. Army.

HDQRS. SUB-MIL. DIST. OF THE RIO GRANDE,
San Antonio, Tex., September 24, 1862.

SIR: I have the honor to report that Lieutenant Kittredge, command-ing United States fleet in the waters of Aransas Bay, arrived at Corpus Christi under a flag of truce on the 12th instant, asking permission to convey the family of E. J. Davis, a renegade traitor of Texas, to New Orleans. Maj. E. F. Gray, commanding at that post, received the flag, and refusing to allow Mrs. Davis to comply with the request until permission should be received from headquarters, notified Lieutenant Kittredge that ten days would elapse before an answer could be given; whereupon Lieutenant Kittredge withdrew, and proceeded down the bay some 15 miles toward the salt-works, on the Laguna de la Madre. On the same night Major Gray dispatched Captain Ireland, with 50 men and one piece of artillery, to watch his proceedings, accompanied by Captain Ware, of the cavalry. Captain Ireland posted a portion of his men under Captain Ware at a vacated house near the shore, and within a short distance of where it was known that the fleet of the enemy was anchored for the night, the piece of artillery being well masked in the sand hills.

Early in the ensuing morning the enemy shelled the houses and sur-rounding points for some time; then, the ground being apparently unoccupied, Lieutenant Kittredge, accompanied by 7 men, landed and approached the house. Our men being concealed, the adventurous lieutenant fell gracefully into the trap set for him, and, with his whole party, were taken prisoners. The report of Captain Ireland of this well-conceived and successful plan is herewith inclosed for the information of the general commanding.

It is worthy of note that as soon as the gunboats of the enemy be-came aware of the fate of their officer they opened a rapid fire of shell and grape on the command, which fell alike on soldiers and prisoners, but without damage to either.

Maj. E. F. Gray immediately forwarded Lieutenant Kittredge, under escort of Major Hobby, to this place, where he arrived on the 20th instant, and having given his parole, now awaits the order of the gen-eral commanding. The 7 seamen are also *en route* to this place.

It gives me great satisfaction to announce this creditable sequel of the defense of Corpus [Christi] by the capture of the bold and ener-getic leader of the enemy, and the end of the campaign for the present, as the fleet have all retired to their usual place of anchorage near Aransas Bar.

It is also proper to state that the course of Lieutenant Kittredge, while for many months in command on our coast, has been that of an honorable enemy, and as such he is entitled to the consideration due to his situation by the terms of civilized warfare.

With great respect,

H. P. BEE,
Brigadier-General, Provisional Army.

Brig. Gen. P. O. HÉBERT,
Commanding Department of Texas.

—

HDQRS. SUB-MIL. DIST. OF THE RIO GRANDE,
San Antonio, Tex., September 26, 1862.

CAPTAIN: I have the honor to forward to the general commanding the Department of Texas a flag of the enemy, captured by a detachment of Confederate troops under command of Captain Ireland, on the waters of the Corpus Christi Bay.

I have the honor to be, very respectfully, your obedient servant,

H. P. BEE,
Brigadier-General.

Capt. O. M. MASON,
Acting Assistant Adjutant-General, San Antonio, Tex.

———

No. 2.

Report of Maj. E. F. Gray, C. S. Army.

CORPUS CHRISTI, TEX., *September 16, 1862.*

SIR: I have the honor to report that the expedition under Capt. John Ireland, of which I notified you in my last communication, has returned to this place successful. Inclosed I forward a copy of his official report, which will explain itself. I request that the special recommendations contained in his report may be considered as my own, without a repetition, as I am firmly satisfied they are merited.

Major Hobby has been directed to accompany Lieutenant Kittredge to San Antonio and to be governed by your further directions. The other prisoners will be forwarded to-morrow with an escort. I inclose you Lieutenant Kittredge's parole.* I have informed him that he would be forwarded across the lines without delay. I would most respectfully request that my assurance may be complied with, or, rather, verified; yet he understands that everything remains subject to your decision. After his capture I communicated with his vessels under a flag of truce for the purpose of obtaining wearing apparel for him and for his men, which has been done. I consented that the vessels should approach and retire under a flag of truce.

Everything is progressing here to my satisfaction, and I hope to send you additional good news ere long. I will write again by mail.

I have the honor to be, very respectfully, your obedient servant,

E. F. GRAY,
Major, Commanding.

Brig. Gen. H. P. BEE,
Comdg. Sub-Mil. Dist. of the Rio Grande, San Antonio, Tex.

———
*Omitted.

No. 3.

Report of Capt. John Ireland, C. S. Army.

CORPUS CHRISTI, TEX., *September* 15, 1862.

SIR: In obedience to your orders I left Corpus Christi at 8 p. m. on the 13th instant. I took with me one small piece of Captain Willke's battery, under Lieutenant Johnson, a detachment of 50 men from my own company, and Capt. J. A. Ware. I proceeded to Flour Bluffs, 15 miles south of this place. Arrived there at 1.30 o'clock same night. I took two positions within half a mile of the enemy's gunboats, three in number. At one place I stationed Captain Ware with a detachment of 20 men, and the other I occupied with the remainder of my force. The positions were selected with a view of commanding the channel leading to [Point] Penascal and of cutting off any force that might attempt to land. After throwing a number of shells at some unoffending citizens on shore the enemy landed, which he effected near the point where Captain Ware was posted. When the enemy were within musket-range Captain Ware advanced, and without firing a gun captured the party, consisting of Captain Kittredge, commanding blockading fleet off this coast, and 7 of his men. This occurred at 11 o'clock of the 14th.

It now being certain that they would not then attempt to enter Laguna de la Madre, and there being nothing further that I could accomplish by remaining, the line of march was resumed for this place. The enemy then threw some 40 or 50 shells, but without effect. I also captured 8 stand of arms—Enfield rifles, Colt's six-shooters, and 2 cutlasses.

I take great pleasure in calling your attention to the efficient service and gallant conduct of Captain Ware, who obeyed orders with alacrity and executed them with great judgment. I desire also to call your attention to the gallantry of Private William Saffold, who in person captured Captain Kittredge. I have also to acknowledge valuable services rendered by four of Captain Ware's cavalry as guides.

The enemy's boats immediately left the bay.

All of which is respectfully submitted.

I am, sir, your obedient servant,

JNO. IRELAND,
Captain, Commanding Expedition.

Maj. E. F. GRAY, *Commanding.*

CORRESPONDENCE, ORDERS, AND RETURNS RELATING TO OPERATIONS IN TEXAS, NEW MEXICO, AND ARIZONA FROM FEBRUARY 1 TO SEPTEMBER 18, 1862.

UNION CORRESPONDENCE, ETC.

HEADQUARTERS DEPARTMENT OF NEW MEXICO,
Belen, N. Mex., January 28, 1862.
MEMORANDUM, No. 116.]

As the bulk of the enemy's force is mounted, it is to be expected that his principal efforts will be directed to attempt to cripple the means of transportation by attacking the trains, or impede the operations of the troops by stampeding the animals, or subjecting the men to the annoyance of night attacks. These will, of course, be guarded against by the usual precautions, but the colonel commanding desires that commanders will impress upon their men that these attacks are to be feared only when they succeed in throwing a portion of the command into confusion and in forcing their way within the lines, and that in this event they should be enjoined to repel the enemy by the use of the bayonet or clubbed musket, and not by firing, which is more likely to endanger their friends than enemies. In any encounter with the enemy's horsemen the main reliance of the infantry should be in their bayonets. An infantry soldier who is cool is more than a match for a horseman, and in groups they are safe against any number.

Four days' rations will habitually be carried in the company wagons and the remainder in the supply train.

By order of Col. E. R. S. Canby:

WM. J. L. NICODEMUS,
Captain, Twelfth Infantry, Acting Assistant Adjutant-General.

HEADQUARTERS DEPARTMENT OF THE PACIFIC,
San Francisco, January 29, 1862.

Brig. Gen. LORENZO THOMAS,
Adjutant-General U. S. Army, Washington, D. C.:

GENERAL: Inclosed herewith is a copy of a telegraphic dispatch which I had the honor to transmit to you yesterday; also copy of extract from a letter from Mr. Thomas Robinson, a resident of Guaymas, Sonora. This extract was presented to me by Mr. Flint, of this city, a gentleman of standing and reliability, connected with the steamship line between this place and Guaymas. From the best information in my possession at this moment I am disposed to believe that the views taken by Mr. Robinson as to the intended movements of the rebel forces are in the main correct. The large force I am assembling in the southern portion of this State, preparatory to an advance from Fort Yuma, will doubtless cause the rebel leaders to deflect from their line of operations and, if possible, gain the port of Guaymas. To frustrate all such attempts I deem it of the first importance that a strong force should be thrown into that city, aided by the presence of a few ships of war. I propose to open a correspondence with the Governor of Sonora on this subject, and I am assured by the best authority that our temporary occupation of Guaymas or any portion of the State, to protect it from the inroads of the rebels, would be cheerfully acquiesced in by the authorities and people of that country.

The storm has somewhat abated for a few days past. To-day it is raining again, and the roads are not in a condition to advance my expeditionary forces to Fort Yuma. However, it is only a question of time. We will be successful.

I have no special news from the District of Oregon. All was quiet in that quarter when last heard from. The winter has been unusually severe, and the navigation of the Columbia River entirely obstructed by ice.

The Legislature of California is now in session in this city, compelled to abandon Sacramento temporarily.

Very respectfully, your obedient servant,

G. WRIGHT,
Brigadier-General, U. S. Army, Commanding.

HEADQUARTERS DEPARTMENT OF THE PACIFIC,
San Francisco, Cal., January 28, 1862.
Brig. Gen. LORENZO THOMAS,
Adjutant-General U. S. Army, Washington, D. C.:

From the latest and most reliable information I am more strongly than ever impressed with the importance of an early and prompt occupation of Guaymas.

G. WRIGHT,
Brigadier-General, U. S. Army, Commanding.

Copy of letter from Thomas Robinson, Esq.

* * * * * * *

Immediately on the receipt of this please call upon General Wright, and state to him, in my name, that by express received by me to-day from Arizona, and from most reliable source, I have the following statement:

The Southern troops, under Colonel Baylor, Military Governor, are expected at Tucson within ten days, numbering 900 men. It is said they will immediately make a strong and continued campaign on the Apaches. Reports say (which, I fear, is very probable) they march into Sonora. In the mean while their headquarters will be at Calabazas, on the line. Agents to purchase flour, corn, &c., are actually in the Territory under escort. Contracts for hay have already been given out. Brigadier-General Sibley, C. S. Army, with 3,000 men, takes command in Arizona and New Mexico, and will immediately attack the United States forces in New Mexico. The Southern soldiers are full of fight. Only the other day 100 crossed the Jornada del Muerto, drove in the pickets of the United States forces, and made 40 prisoners.

These same reports were afloat here three days since, when I arrived, and to-day they are confirmed. There is no doubt in my mind as to the desires and intentions of these Southern forces. What the devil do they care for Arizona, without 100 souls in it, and nothing worth having there? They wish to march into Sonora, as is intimated from many sources, and take quiet possession, for we are not at present in condition to resist, having just passed through a very sore trial, although with success. If they once get possession of this State and its ports, the North may just as well give up the complete line through from Gulf of Mexico to Gulf of California, and it will require a supreme effort then to rout them.

This is no newspaper talk, but something certain, and the only way to avoid a most serious and difficult position is for the United States Government to send, without a moment's delay, the necessary forces to act.

Let me request of you to urge upon General Wright the necessity of this step. Let 1,000 men, properly equipped, be sent immediately to Guaymas, officered by gentlemen of prudence and judgment, and I will see that they get through immediately to Arizona. The Governor and people will be too happy to see such a friend coming to their rescue. If necessary, let the general telegraph to Washington for the necessary powers, but he must act promptly, and I will guarantee his full success, and by adopting these measures he will have acquired a victory which will be more than galling to the South.

* * * * * * *

I will take the contract for transporting troops and equipments to Arizona and furnishing everything necessary. You are aware the Congress of Mexico has given a cordial permit for transit of troops through Sonora, and our State will be pleased to forward the views of the United States Government or its representatives. You can assure General Wright that all my influence and that of my friends will be used in favor [of] his forces.

Yours, sincerely,

THOS. ROBINSON.

———

WAR DEPARTMENT,
Washington City, D. C., February 3, 1862.
Hon. W. H. SEWARD, *Secretary of State:*

SIR : I am directed by the Secretary of War to acknowledge the receipt of your communication of the 29th instant, inclosing copies of letters from the Secretary of the Navy and the United States consul at Havana, and suggesting that, should the exigencies of the public service permit, a military force of observation be posted opposite to or near Matamoros, on the Rio Grande; that he referred your communication and inclosures to Major-General McClellan, who reports as follows, viz:

The occupation of Brazos de Santiago and Brownsville is important and desirable for many reasons. It would not be prudent, however, to attempt it without force sufficient to hold points farther north and east. We have not the disposable force at the present moment, nor would it do to risk a detached force in so remote a position, without retreat or succor, until certain that our foreign relations are entirely satisfactory.

I have the honor to be, very respectfully, your obedient servant,

P. H. WATSON,
Assistant Secretary of War.

———

DEPARTMENT OF STATE,
Washington, February 7, 1862.
Hon. E. M. STANTON, *Secretary of War:*

SIR: I inclose for your information a copy of a letter of the 11th ultimo, addressed to this Department by the Governor of the Territory of New Mexico.

I have the honor to be, your obedient servant,

F. W. SEWARD,
Acting Secretary.

[Inclosure.]

EXECUTIVE DEPARTMENT,
Santa Fé, N. Mex., January 11, 1862.
Hon. W. H. SEWARD, *Secretary of State, Washington, D. C.:*

SIR : Since my last, of the 4th instant, there has nothing taken place in relation to the Texans that merits attention. They retired precipitately from the settlement of Alamosa, 30 miles below Fort Craig, and have made no demonstration against that place. Since Colonel Canby has divided his forces, leaving about one-half at Craig, and has or is about to take a position midway between Craig and the Pecos River, so as to enable him to act in conjunction with the forces at Union on the Pecos, or with those at Craig on the Rio del Norte, as circumstances may require, I am of opinion that there are no Texan forces on the Pecos; but this is merely an opinion, the truth of falsehood of which will be revealed within a few days.

The spy companies sent in that direction ten or twelve days since have not returned. We have no fears of any armed force that Texas can send against this Territory. We have now in the service of the Government and under fair discipline something more than 4,000 volunteers and militia of this Territory; also, say, 1,500 regular troops. With this force and what I could call into the field of the organized militia in a few days' notice I am sure we can repel any force that will be sent against this Territory.

We are in great want of arms and ammunition, and hope that by the early spring trains our requisition will be filled.

The Navajo and Apache Indians still continue their depredations to an alarming extent, altogether in robberies. Few deaths occur, but a continual spoliation of property. The losses of the Territory the past year will not fall short of half a million of dollars. The Texans keep us in such continual uneasiness that we can make no effective campaign against those hostile tribes.

Very respectfully, your obedient servant,

HENRY CONNELLY,
Governor of New Mexico.

HEADQUARTERS DEPARTMENT OF KANSAS,
Fort Leavenworth, Kans., February 10, 1862.

To His Excellency ACTING GOVERNOR OF COLORADO,
Denver City, Colo.:

Send all available forces you can possibly spare to re-enforce Colonel Canby, commanding Department of New Mexico, and to keep open his communication through Fort Wise. Act promptly and with all the discretion of your latest information as to what may be necessary and where the troops of Colorado can do most service.

D. HUNTER,
Major-General, Commanding.

CIRCULAR.]   HDQRS. DEPARTMENT OF NEW MEXICO,
Fort Craig, N. Mex., February 14, 1862.

The following arrangements of the columns for field operations will govern the chiefs of the staff departments in making the necessary provisions for supplying the troops:

First column.

Headquarters, Company D, First Cavalry, and detachment....................	86
First column: Capt. H. R. Selden, Fifth Infantry.	
First Battalion: Capt. B. Wingate.	
Headquarters and Companies B, D, F, and I, Fifth Infantry	306
Second Battalion: Capt. P. W. L. Plympton.	
Companies C and F, Seventh Infantry; A and H, Tenth Infantry, and Colorado Volunteers..	310
	616
McRae's battery...	130
Hall's battery...	37
	167

Second column.

Col. B. S. ROBERTS.

Headquarters and Companies C, D, G, and K, Third Cavalry, Major Duncan..	210
Companies B, E, and G, Third New Mexico Volunteers, Lieutenant-Colonel Chavez..	234
Barriento's company, Fifth New Mexico Volunteers...................	63
Four companies New Mexico Mounted Militia, Lieutenant-Colonel Otero.	200
	707

Third column.

Col. C. CARSON.

First Battalion, four companies, First New Mexico Volunteers, Lieutenant-Colonel Chavez.. 254
Second Battalion, four companies, First New Mexico Volunteers, Major Morrison... 258
                                                                            ——— 512

Fourth column.

Col. M. E. PINO.

First Battalion, four companies, Second New Mexico Volunteers, Lieutenant-Colonel Chavez.. 252
Second Battalion, two companies, Second and Third New Mexico Volunteers, Major Pino.. 238
                                                                            ——— 490

Fifth column.

Six companies First New Mexico Militia, Colonel Armijo; four companies Second New Mexico Militia... 272

The ambulances and wagons (hospital) and an ammunition wagon for each column will be kept in readiness to move with the column whenever it marches.

Three days' cooked rations, to be carried in the haversacks, are required to be kept constantly on hand.

If any of the columns leave the post permanently the amount of supplies and the transportation to be taken will be specially directed.

By order of Col. E. R. S. Canby:

WM. J. L. NICODEMUS,
Captain, Twelfth Infantry, Acting Asst. Adjt. General.

GENERAL ORDERS,   }   HEADQUARTERS OF THE ARMY, A. G. O.,
· No. 14.   }   *Washington, February* 14, 1862.

I. Fort Garland, Colorado Territory, is transferred from the Department of Kansas to the Department of New Mexico.

*   *   *   *   *   \~   \~

By command of Major-General McClellan:

. L. THOMAS,
Adjutant-General.

EXECUTIVE DEPARTMENT, COLORADO TERRITORY,
Denver, February 14, 1862.

Brig. Gen. E. R. S. CANBY,
Commanding Department of New Mexico:

GENERAL: Orders have been received from Maj. Gen. David Hunter, commanding the Department of Kansas, to which this Territory is attached, to send all the available forces of the Territory to your support. I have therefore ordered the seven remaining companies of the First Regiment to march immediately to Santa Fé, under command of Col. John P. Slough.

The other three companies of the regiment are stationed, as you are aware, at Fort Wise, under command of Lieut. Col. S. F. Tappan. I have written to Colonel Tappan to hold himself in readiness to join his regiment in case you desire it. I think that in the present state of things at that post it might be easily held by a detachment of Mexican troops; in which case three very efficient companies, two of infantry and one of cavalry, could be added to your force.

Feeling that it was possible that you might desire these troops, I have written to Colonel Tappan to consider himself under your orders. I trust that this course will be agreeable to you.

You will find this regiment, I hope, a most efficient one and of great support to you. It has had, of course, no experience in the field, but I trust that their enthusiasm and patriotic bravery will make amends, and more than that, for their lack of active service in the past.

I have the honor to be, with great respect, your obedient servant,

LEWIS WELD,
Secretary and Acting Governor of Colorado Territory.

HEADQUARTERS DEPARTMENT OF NEW MEXICO,
Fort Craig, N. Mex., February 14, 1862.

To the ADJUTANT-GENERAL OF THE ARMY,
Washington, D. C.:

SIR: I have the honor to state that since my report of the 10th instant* the Confederate forces have been moving slowly up the river, and are now about 20 miles below this place. From spies captured yesterday by our pickets their entire force is estimated at 3,000 men. I have now at this post, including the New Mexican Volunteers and Militia, nearly 4,000. The Mexican population appear to be animated by a very good spirit.

Very respectfully, sir, your obedient servant,

ED. R. S. CANBY,
Colonel Nineteenth Infantry, Commanding Department.

HEADQUARTERS ARMY OF NEW MEXICO,
Camp near Fort Craig, N. Mex., February 22, 1862.

Col. E. R. S. CANBY,
Commanding U. S. Forces in the Territory of New Mexico:

COLONEL: I desire hereby to accredit to you Lieut. Col. William R. Scurry, of the Fourth, and Capt. D. W. Shannon, of the Fifth, Regiment of Texas Mounted Volunteers, in the service of the Confederate States.

These gentlemen are dispatched under flag of truce, to hold communication with you upon matters pertaining to the military service of our respective Governments, in regard to which they will express to you my views and purposes.

I commend them as officers and gentlemen to your highest esteem and confidence.

I am, colonel, your obedient servant,

H. H. SIBLEY,
Brig. Gen. Army of C. S., Comdg. Army of New Mexico.

*Not found.

HEADQUARTERS DEPARTMENT OF NEW MEXICO,
Fort Craig, N. Mex., February 23, 1862.
The ADJUTANT-GENERAL OF THE ARMY,
Washington, D. C.:

SIR: After the battle of the 21st instant there remained for the troops at this post but three plans of operation:

1. To retain this post to the last extremity, await the arrival of the re-enforcements that had previously been asked for, and upon their arrival, by concerted operations in the direction of the Pecos and the Rio Grande, defeat the enemy and force him to retreat down that river, and in that event cut off his retreat with the force at this point. This post is regarded as of paramount importance, not only for the purpose above indicated, but to intercept any re-enforcements that might be sent from Texas, and with a view to ulterior operations against the Mesilla Valley.

2. To abandon the post and endeavor to throw the force now here above the enemy, impede his further progress up the river, and then unite with any force that might be found above. This course would involve the loss of the supplies on hand, the abandonment of an important strategic point, and of the sick and wounded who could not be transported.

3. To bring on a second battle with the Confederate Army, and submit this portion of our Army and New Mexico to the chances of that battle. The organized Confederate force in the battle of the 21st was above 2,500 men. Our own force on the field was 2,200, of whom more than half were volunteers and militia. Our loss in killed, wounded, and prisoners was 222 in the regulars and Colorado Volunteers; in the New Mexican Volunteers about 15.* The loss of the Confederates was somewhat greater, but independent of the loss of our battery the proportional disparity of force was increased by the results of the battle.

The first of these plans was in my judgment best calculated to secure the ultimate success of our operations, and was concurred in by the several commanders and functionaries of the Territory who were consulted. It was adopted, and measures immediately taken to carry it into effect.

I have disembarrassed myself of the militia by sending them away, and have arranged with the officers of that force to impede the operations of the enemy, obstruct his movements if he should attempt to advance, and cut off his supplies, by removing from his route the cattle, grain, and other supplies in private hands that would aid him in sustaining his force. I have also sent away all the public animals not required for the immediate service of the post.

I am now organizing a partisan force from the volunteers, for the purpose of operating on the flanks of the enemy. This force will be composed of picked men, and I anticipate some good results from their action. If there be any consistency of purpose or persistence of effort in the people of New Mexico, the enemy will be able to add but little to his resources from a temporary occupation of the country.

If the enemy should determine to advance, I will send a part of the regular cavalry now here to re-enforce our troops in the northern part of the Territory, as they are now deficient in that class of troops.

On the night of the 21st instructions were sent to the commander above to remove or destroy any public property that might fall into the hands of the enemy. Major Donaldson, quartermaster, having volun-

* But see p. 493.

teered for the purpose, was detached last night with the militia, and charged with the duty of superintending the removal of the public property, procuring supplies, and collecting troops for future operations.

. The enemy still occupies a position near the battle-field. His intentions are not yet developed; but as a demand for a surrender has been made, I anticipate, of course, an attempt to enforce it. If it should be made, I have no apprehensions as to the result.

Our loss in killed, wounded, and missing is somewhat greater than I supposed when my report of yesterday was made. The wounds, however, are generally of a light character, and the proportion that will terminate fatally will be small.

Very respectfully, sir, your obedient servant,

ED. R. S. CANBY,
Colonel Nineteenth Infantry, Commanding Department.

HEADQUARTERS DEPARTMENT OF NEW MEXICO,
ACTING INSPECTOR-GENERAL'S OFFICE,
Santa Fé., N. Mex., February 28, 1862.

Maj. Gen. H. W. HALLECK,
Comdg. the Dept. of the Missouri, Saint Louis, Mo.:

DEAR SIR: I wrote to you fully and freely, as acting inspector-general of this Territory and a member of Colonel Canby's staff, in order that you may have a proper view of the situation of affairs here.

This communication would have been sent to General Hunter, as a nearer military commander, had it not suggested itself that possibly he would be absent on the field when this communication should have reached his headquarters.

You will probably learn from the telegraph, from rumor, and from other sources that we have had a most desperate and bloody struggle with the Texans, and that, notwithstanding the great loss upon their part, we have lost one light battery and retreated to Fort Craig. Colonel Canby did everything which man could do to retake his battery and thus save the day. He beseeched and begged, ordered and imperatively commanded, troops to save his guns, and a deaf ear met alike his supplications and commands. Our loss is great; 4 officers killed—Captains McRae and Stone, Lieutenant Mishler, and Captain Bascom. Stone was first wounded and has since died; Captain Wingate, leg shattered; Lieutenant McDermott, volunteers, killed. Our loss, as far as ascertained up to the present moment, is 62 killed and about 140 wounded.*

The loss of the enemy is 150 killed and 450 wounded. Major Donaldson thinks they lost over 100 killed in front of McRae's battery. The enemy is now above Colonel Canby, on the Rio Grande, and of course has cut him from all communication with his supplies. It is needless to say that this country is in a critical condition. The militia have all run away and the New Mexican Volunteers are deserting in large numbers. No dependence whatever can be placed on the natives; they are worse than worthless; they are really aids to the enemy, who catch them, take their arms, and tell them to go home.

A force of Colorado Volunteers is already on the way to assist us, and they may possibly arrive in time to save us from immediate danger; but, my dear sir, we must look to the future. The conquest of it (New

---

* But see p. 493.

Mexico) is a great political feature of the rebellion. It will gain the rebels a name and a prestige over Europe, and operate against the Union cause. It therefore should not only be checked, but it should at any future period during the spring or summer be rendered impossible.

These Texans will not rest with the forces they have already with them, but they will have large additions to their command here, in order to extend their conquest toward old Mexico and in the direction of Southern California. I therefore beg you, in the name of Colonel Canby, who is fighting two to one, and laying valuable lives upon this issue, to send at once—lose not a day—at least two regiments infantry and a battery of rifled cannon to Fort Union. These troops cannot serve the Government better than by saving this Territory. Do not depend on the New Mexican regiments serving in Kansas; they are not filled up nor ready for the field. Send us troops already organized; they can start by the time this reaches you.

Believe no reports you may hear of the number of troops Canby has. I have given you a true picture of the state of this country, and if you wish to save it, you, I hope and pray, will act immediately in its favor.

I remain, sir, very respectfully, your obedient servant,

GURDEN CHAPIN,
Captain, Seventh Infantry, Acting Inspector-General.

Colonel Canby has but 1,100 men, exclusive of his volunteers, and the Texans have at least 2,200, all mounted.

Please inform the headquarters Department of New Mexico, Santa Fé, what you can do for this country, and if you cannot help us, be kind enough to acknowledge the receipt of this communication.

Abstract from return of the Department of New Mexico, Col. Edward R. S. Canby, Nineteenth Infantry, commanding, for the month of February, 1862.

Commands.	Present for duty. Officers.	Present for duty. Men.	Aggregate present.	Aggregate present and absent.	Aggregate last monthly return.	Pieces of field artillery.
Department staff	5		5	5	5	
Abo Pass					145	
Albuquerque					162	
Camp Connelly					167	
Cubero					74	
Fort Craig and vicinity	110	2,130	2,677	2,892	1,208	
Fort Garland	3	37	48	51	130	
Fort Marcy*					221	
Fort Union and depot	14	267	359	601	780	15
Hatch's Ranch	6	57	73	102	261	
In the field					1,775	
Total	138	2,491	3,162	3,651	4,928	15

* No return.

HEADQUARTERS DISTRICT OF SANTA FÉ,
Santa Fé, March 1, 1862.
General LORENZO THOMAS, *Adjutant-General, Washington, D. C.:*

GENERAL: In obedience to an order from Colonel Canby, commanding the Department of New Mexico, I respectfully inclose his report[*] of the battle of Valverde, which took place near Fort Craig, on the 21st instant.

The colonel is sanguine that he will succeed in holding the enemy in check, but having been in the battle, and having succeeded in getting through the enemy's line from Craig on the night of the 22d with the view of turning back any trains that may have been on the road, as well as to secure the public property on the river below Albuquerque, I may be allowed to express the opinion that I consider the colonel's situation as critical, and would most earnestly advise that no time be lost in sending re-enforcements to this country. Four regiments of infantry, some cavalry, and a battery of rifled cannon at least should be sent. The enemy numbers about 2,000 men, all mounted, and is expecting re-enforcements. He suffered severely in the battle, and is now encumbered with a large number of wounded. This may prevent him from moving up the river at present, but his foraging parties have already come within 60 miles of Albuquerque. No reliance can be placed on the New Mexican Volunteers or Militia, and I advise their being disbanded. They have a traditionary fear of the Texans, and will not face them in the field.

I will not anticipate Colonel Canby's detailed report, but I must say that he made every exertion to save Captain McRae's battery.

Very respectfully, your obedient servant,

JAS. L. DONALDSON,
Quartermaster, Brevet Major, Comdg. Dist. Santa Fé.

HEADQUARTERS DISTRICT OF SANTA FÉ,
Santa Fé, March 1, 1862.

General LORENZO THOMAS,
Adjutant-General, Washington, D. C.:

GENERAL : I am in receipt of a letter from Lieutenant-Colonel Tappan, of the Colorado Volunteers, informing me that General Hunter had ordered his regiment immediately from Denver City to Santa Fé to re-enforce Colonel Canby, who, as you will see by his report, has had a severe conflict with the Texans near Fort Craig. This order of General Hunter is most seasonable, and may perhaps save the Territory. Colonel Tappan is stationed at Fort Wise with two companies of his regiment and a mounted company, the rest of the garrison being a regular company, under Lieutenant Warner. I have not hesitated to order Colonel Tappan to Santa Fé by special express to join the other companies (seven) coming by way of Garland, and if Colonel Canby can hold the enemy in check for fifteen or twenty days I am in hopes of marching to his assistance with 1,000 men, 100 of whom will be regulars, under Captain Lewis, Fifth Infantry.

I have dates from Colonel Canby to the 25th instant. I sent a trusty messenger to him last night, urging him to delay the enemy as much as possible, and communicating the fact of a Colorado regiment being on the road to his relief. Nothing as yet has fallen into the hands of the enemy. When I left Craig, which I did the evening after the battle, Colonel Canby authorized me to use his name and to take such steps as I deemed best. If disaster happens to the colonel before re-enforcements arrive I shall throw myself into Union, but I need hardly urge the importance of at once putting *en route* to Union a force that will overwhelm the enemy.

---

[*] See Canby's report of February 22, on p. 487.

I send a copy of these letters to General Halleck, Saint Louis, being apprehensive that General Hunter has gone South.

Very respectfully, your obedient servant,

JAS. L. DONALDSON,
Brevet Major, Commanding District of Santa Fé.

HEADQUARTERS DISTRICT OF SANTA FÉ,
Santa Fé, March 1, 1862.

General H. W. HALLECK,
Commanding Department of Missouri, Saint Louis:

GENERAL: I have the honor to inclose a copy of the official report* of a battle between the Union troops under Colonel Canby and the Texans, near Fort Craig.

The loss was heavy on both sides, that of the enemy being at least double that of ours.

The enemy have possession of the road above Craig, and may march up, as Colonel Canby is embarrassed with his wounded, as well as having lost McRae's battery.

Everything will be done here to succor him. You will see by my letter to the Adjutant-General of the Army that a regiment of Colorado Volunteers is on the march to this city from Denver and Fort Wise, but the snow is deep on the Taos Mountains and they may not get through in time.

I urgently recommend that four regiments of infantry, some cavalry, and a battery of rifled cannon be at once put *en route* for Union.

Very respectfully, your obedient servant,

JAS. L. DONALDSON,
Quartermaster, Commanding District of Santa Fé.

EXECUTIVE DEPARTMENT,
Santa Fé, March 1, 1862.

SECRETARY OF STATE, *Washington, D. C.:*

SIR: Since my last communication from Fort Craig I have been unable to write you until this day, in consequence of the commotion and excitement that have existed from that day to the present. On the 19th of February the enemy retrograded from their position, 5 miles below Craig, to the place called Paraje, where they crossed to the opposite or east side of the river. On the 20th he advanced up the river, but at the distance of 4 or 5 miles from it, until about opposite the fort, when Colonel Canby marched out to give him battle. The ground over which the enemy passed, and over which our forces had to pass in order to reach him, was a bed of sand, covered generally with loose volcanic rocks, which impeded the progress of our train of artillery, and made it quite late in the evening before the position of the enemy was reached. This position he had taken with great labor on a sandy height somewhat inaccessible to our heavy artillery. After some fifty or sixty shots fired by the enemy with their largest guns without effect our forces retired again to the fort, arriving some time after dark.

On the 21st the enemy were met 5 miles above the fort, having during the night and the next morning made their way to the river at

---

* Canby's report of February 22, p. 487.

that distance above the fort. The action commenced about 10 o'clock, with artillery across the river at a distance of 1,000 yards and in a forest of cottonwood trees, which gave the enemy greatly the advantage, as it shielded them from our artillery and even the small-arms that were used at that distance.

About 1 o'clock our whole force passed the river, having previously driven the enemy from his position near the river to the foot of and into the sand hills. The battle now raged with increased fury, and the enemy was to all appearances in the act of retreating from the ground, when, to hasten his retreat, one of our batteries of six guns, light artillery, was advanced some 200 yards nearer their position, which was in a degree covered by a ridge of sand, behind which they had taken momentary refuge, when, to the surprise of all, about 500 men came forth from that position and advanced steadily on to and finally captured the battery. This was not done without great loss to the captors, for of the 500 men that left the position of concealment not more than 200 arrived at the battery.

It is painful to relate that of the forces in position for the protection of the battery not one company advanced to its relief or even fired upon the enemy as he approached. The force consisted of two or more companies of regular troops and one regiment of volunteers. The regulars were ordered—nay, implored—to charge the enemy, by Colonel Canby, Major Donaldson, and Colonel Collins, superintendent of Indian affairs, who were all three present in immediate contact with the troops and within 10 or 20 yards of the battery when it was taken. The regulars having refused to advance, the volunteers followed their example, and both retired from the field, recrossing the river and leaving the battery in possession of the enemy. There was no flight, and the enemy gave no pursuit. He was evidently greatly crippled, and chose as the more prudent course to close the day with the advantage gained. Colonel Canby now ordered all our forces to recross the river, and marched into the fort some time after dark. Thus ended the bloody day of the 21st February.

A cessation of hostilities intervened the next day, for the purpose of burying the dead and removing the wounded from the field. On the following day, 23d, a deputation of two officers waited upon Colonel Canby, asking a surrender of the fort, and indicated that very honorable terms would be granted. The proposition was peremptorily refused. The day following it was thought that the fort would certainly be attacked by the enemy. A council of war was held, in which it was determined rather to await the attack of the enemy in the fort than to attack him again in his strong position. The number of men in the fort was more than could be usefully employed, and it was ordered by Colonel Canby that the militia lately called into the service should withdraw from the fort and make a detour that would place them in advance of the enemy. This had to be done by a night march, which was effected without much difficulty and with no loss, except in the dispersion of the militia, but few of whom have been embodied since they emerged from the mountains and reached the settlements upon the Rio Grande. In fact, the enemy gave but little time for rallying.

On the morning of our arrival on the river in advance of the enemy, and before all had reached the place of rendezvous, it was ascertained that a body of the enemy, 400 strong, with two pieces of artillery, was in our neighborhood, and advancing at the rate of 30 miles per day. This they had done in order to capture a depot of provisions that was at Polvadera, 50 miles from Craig. The provisions, however, had been sent off in advance, and the enemy captured nothing or very little. Under this state of things I saw that my presence out of the capital would be of no further utility, and therefore came in company with a few militia officers, and arrived here on the 27th of February.

Colonel Canby is, or was at last accounts (25th), still at Craig. The enemy had not attacked the fort, as was expected, but had crossed to the west side of the river, and was encamped 8 miles in advance of the fort. It is supposed that Colonel Canby will attack him so soon as he leaves the strong position he occupies, and his forces are quite sufficient to defeat the enemy. He has yet 1,000 regular troops, with five pieces of artillery, among them two 24-pounder howitzers, and a volunteer force of not less than 1,500 men. His stock is in much better condition than that of the enemy, and we are expecting the result of a decisive action daily.

The advance party of the enemy mentioned had not progressed farther at last accounts than the depot of provisions spoken of before. Whether they will continue to advance with their small number will be known in a short time. Albuquerque is defenseless as to any armed force in that place, and if the enemy advance it is very likely that they will succeed in taking that place. All the Government stores have been removed, however, and are far on their way to this place and to Fort Union. We are making some efforts here to repel any small force that may arrive in advance, and we will be able to do so; but all will be determined by the result of the operations of Colonel Canby upon the enemy. If he defeats him, or even be not routed and dispersed by the enemy, we will be able to expel the invaders from the Territory.

Our loss consisted of 46 killed and 160 wounded.* Among the former were several valuable officers. Captain McRae, commanding the battery, died at his guns, with one or two other officers. The 80 men at the battery defended it with a heroic valor worthy of better success, of whom 43 were either killed or wounded. The loss of the enemy, it is ascertained by deserters from their camp, was very large—at least 300 killed, and the wounded in proportion. The deserters say that a consultation was held two days after the battle in regard to an attack upon the fort, and that the more daring officers were in favor of an attack, but that the men utterly refused to put their lives in such imminent danger, which would lead to certain defeat and dispersion of the whole invading force. There was some talk of their trying to effect a retreat, as it was thought that the conquest of the Territory could never be effected by the force then in the Territory.

I have been absent from the capital one month, and am sorry to be able to give no better account of the operations of our army. I had anticipated a very different result. Through the official reports you will be informed more in detail as to the cause of our repulse.

March 2. An express has just arrived, giving information that nearly or quite the whole force of the Texans are on their march up the river and have reached the town of Socorro. No news of Colonel Canby having moved from Craig. Under these circumstances Major Donaldson, commander of this district, has ordered all the Government stores from this place to Union, and most likely will leave himself with the three companies of troops that have arrived here within the last two days. Should this be the case I shall follow him to Union, and even to the States,

*But see p. 493.

should the Territory be abandoned to the enemy; for I feel no disposition to be taken prisoner by them.

Very respectfully, your obedient servant,

HENRY CONNELLY.

DEPARTMENT OF STATE,
Washington, D. C., March 4, 1862.

Hon. E. M. STANTON, *Secretary of War:*

SIR: I transmit for your information a copy of a letter of the 31st of January last, addressed to this Department by Henry Connelly, esq., the Governor of the Territory of New Mexico.

I have the honor to be, your obedient servant,

WILLIAM H. SEWARD.

[Inclosure.]

SOCORRO, N. MEX., *January* 31, 1862.

Hon. W. H. SEWARD,
Secretary of State, Washington, D. C.:

SIR: I wrote you on the 25th instant that I should leave the day following for the theater of war, Fort Craig, having left the major-general of divisions of the militia actively engaged in organizing and sending into the field all the disposable militia force in the Territory. I have daily intelligence from them, and from appearances there will be an additional force of 1,500 men with us within five days. The forces of Texas have fallen back to Fort Thorn, 75 miles below Fort Craig, and I think it very doubtful whether they will give us battle this side of that place. Colonel Canby left here yesterday with 1,500 men for Craig, 35 miles distant, and will increase the number of men at that place to 3,000. We have now no fears of any serious reverse to our arms. The whole Texan force is concentrated at and near Fillmore, Robledo, and Thorn, distant from each other 25 miles. We have a force at Craig equal to theirs, and with the militia now *en route* will have fully 1,000 men more. Whether Colonel Canby will advance upon them I have no idea, but think he will pursue a prudential course until he is sure of success. The proclamation of General Sibley to the people of this Territory,* which has been found in considerable numbers scattered through the villages in this part of the Territory, has, when found, been universally delivered to the military commander, without having circulated among the people any number of copies. I have none by me, or I would inclose you one. It will have no effect, even if circulated. I am sure the Territory is safe at present, and only by re-enforcements, which the enemy in all probability will never obtain, can there be any danger of a great disaster to our arms. A great inconvenience will always be felt by having to keep so many men under arms to meet and repel this force of the enemy which is threatening our borders. Perhaps a few days or weeks may lead to new developments, and teach us more of their plans and their means of executing them.

I have remained at this place a few days to await the arrival of the militia now *en route* from the counties above. When they arrive much more will be known as to the position and intentions of the enemy than we now know, and then, in co-operation with Colonel Canby, will be

---

*Reference is probably to proclamation printed on p. 89, Series I, Vol. IV.

able to determine upon the course most prudent to be pursued. I will keep you advised of anything worthy of note that may take place. The enemy is in straitened circumstances, both as to subsistence and forage, and will have to advance upon us with a hope of success, or forage upon Mexico for the means of subsistence. It is said they are in doubt which course of the two presents the fairer prospect of success.

Very respectfully, your obedient servant,

HENRY CONNELLY,
Governor of New Mexico.

DEPARTMENT OF STATE,
Washington, D. C., March 11, 1862.

Hon. E. M. STANTON, *Secretary of War:*

SIR: I have the honor to inclose herewith a copy of dispatch No. 3, received on the 7th instant, from Franklin Chase, esq., United States consul at Tampico, recommending the capture and occupation of Brownsville, Tex., by our forces. Believing as I do that such occupation is necessary to prevent the injury to our Government which would ensue from the unrestricted intercourse between Tampico and the Southern States, I beg to commend the subject to your consideration, and to suggest that you confer with the Secretary of the Navy in regard to it, to whom I have also written and inclosed a copy of Mr. Chase's dispatch.

I have the honor to be, sir, your obedient servant,

WILLIAM H. SEWARD.

[Inclosure.]

CONSULATE OF THE UNITED STATES OF AMERICA,
Tampico, January 24, 1862.

Hon. F. W. SEWARD,
Asst. Secy. of State of the United States, &c., Washington, D. C.:

SIR: I have the honor to report to you that since the commencement of this month the military and civil authorities have been busily engaged in making preparations to vacate this place. All the forts and fortified points have been dismantled, and vast quantities of armament have been embarked in vessels and lighters, and sent as far up the river as practicable. About fourteen pieces of light artillery have been detained to cover the retirement of the forces under General Tapia the moment the allied forces appear off the bar.

The civil authorities here, who acted as chiefs in revolt against the late elected Governor, Don Jesus Serna, on hearing of the success of the opposite party at Matamoros and the city of Victoria, closed their offices and disappeared from the place. These occurrences took place on the 17th instant, and on that day General Tapia took formal possession of the offices thus vacated, viz: Collector of customs, Governor of the State, and that of the political chief or prefect.

At the instance of the President of this Republic all the archives of the different offices have been sent to this consulate and to the stores belonging to my premises, which I received as an act of kindness toward these distracted people.

On the 18th instant a schooner, called the Lord Lyons, under the British flag, arrived in this port, in fifteen days from Matamoros. I have ascertained that this vessel was formerly called the Sultan, belonging to Key West, and that her nationality was changed at the British consulate at Havana. She is only $57\frac{18}{35}$ tons burden, laden with 720 pigs of lead and a quantity of goat-skins, with a clearance for Nassau, N. P., notwithstanding she had 9 passengers on board for Havana.

I have intimated to General Tapia the expediency of detaining the lead brought by the Lord Lyons, who assured me that he would consult with the district judge, and if he considered it contraband of war it should not leave the port; but I have lost all confidence in these people, and we must only look to our own resources for the means of our national security.

The sloop Warrior, mentioned in my No. 29, 27th ultimo, has been made over to a Mr. David Jolley, British merchant of this place, and furnished with authority to sail under the flag of that nation by Her Majesty's consul here.

The secession schooner Clarinda, Sherffins master, arrived here from Sabine in the early part of this month with a cargo of lumber and left in ballast on the 18th instant, the exportation of arms and provisions having been denied her.

By the inclosed copy of the letter from John M. Coe, esq., you will be informed of the movements of our enemies in the interior of this Republic.

The people of New Orleans have conceived a plan for the purpose of expediting the transmission of their correspondence with foreign nations through the medium of this port, and to effect that object they have sent Mr. Augustine Leona as commissioner to this place, to provide the means of connecting an express with the monthly British mail steamers. I may add that this port is now becoming the medium for all persons wishing to return to the Southern States who do not like to incur the risk of attempting to force the blockade, and as we are now momentarily expecting the place to fall under the rule of European powers, incalculable injury may accrue to our Government unless this intercourse can be interrupted by the capture and occupation of Brownsville by our forces.

Permit me now to impress upon your mind the importance of having this coast closely guarded by our ships of war, with instructions to communicate with the consulates at least semi-monthly, assuring you that no other means can effectually put a final check to military supplies going into the hands of our enemies.

I am, with great esteem and respect, sir, your most obedient servant,

FRANKLIN CHASE.

[Inclosure.]

ZACATECAS, *January 2,* 1862.

FRANKLIN CHASE, Esq., *Tampico:*

MY DEAR SIR: On my arrival here yesterday I was informed that a certain individual named J. E. Schenck, a German by birth, and an American citizen, was actively purchasing ammunition of war for the Southern Confederacy. To-day I met the same person at one of the commercial houses of this place, where he has purchased 130 flasks quicksilver, some saltpeter, sulphur, and all the percussion caps he has been able to obtain. I have been assured that he leaves in a few days for Matamoros.

I have thought it my duty to communicate this intelligence to you as a representative of the United States.

Hoping you may be able to communicate the same to our Government, I remain, dear sir, yours, very truly,

JOHN M. COE.

. DEPARTMENT OF STATE,
Washington, March 11, 1862.

Hon. E. M. STANTON, *Secretary of War:*

SIR: I inclose for perusal two letters, dated respectively the 5th and 11th ultimo, addressed to this Department by Henry Connelly, esq., Governor of the Territory of New Mexico.

Please cause them to be returned when you may no longer have occasion for them.

I have the honor to be, sir, your obedient servant,

WILLIAM H. SEWARD.

[Inclosure No. 1.]

FORT CRAIG, N. MEX., *February* 5, 1862.

Hon. W. H. SEWARD, *Secretary of State:*

SIR: I arrived at this place to-day, having delayed three days in Socorro waiting the arrival of the first column of the militia called out under my recent order. With that column I came in company. Within four or five days the entire militia force will be in the immediate neighborhood of this post. The exact number I cannot at this time state except by approximation; not less, however, than 1,000, and perhaps as many as 1,500, consisting of our principal citizens.

The Texans have made no demonstrations upon this post since my last, and in fact nothing new has been heard from them.

We expect to hear something certain within two days, as spies are out to ascertain if possible their exact position, and something reliable as to their preparations to move against the forces of the Territory now assembled at this place. Colonel Canby, I think, has not determined whether he will march against them, but most likely will resolve according to the information he may receive by the spies, whose return is daily expected.

There is now, or will be within a few days, a force concentrated at this place of 4,500 men, 3,500 of which are volunteers and militia. This force is fully equal to the protection of the Territory against the forces of Texas north of the desert of Jornada, but it might be a question as to the propriety of advancing upon them at disadvantage at so great a distance from all resources in the event of a reverse to our arms.

The matter will be duly considered by Colonel Canby, and in his good judgment we all have entire confidence. There is something not well understood in the late movements of the Texans; their falling back rather precipitately from all their positions on the Rio Grande north of Robledo, when we all expected a forward movement of the whole force upon this place, has created some surprise, and is attributed to various motives; such as disaffected feeling among the men, to the unexpected force of citizen soldiery arrayed against them, and to the prevalence of small-pox to an alarming degree in their ranks. Perhaps something of all these causes may have contributed to change their program and advised to a defensive instead of an offensive course. I am sure that a few days will lead to new developments, of which you will be duly apprised.

Very respectfully, your obedient servant,
.HENRY CONNELLY,
Governor of New Mexico.

FEBRUARY 6.

After writing the foregoing last night the spies came in and reported the advance of the whole Texan force upon this post. They were at and above Fort Thorn, 80 miles distant, but without a doubt marching forward to determine by a decisive battle the fate of the Territory.

I have no fears as to the result here. We will conquer the Texan forces, if not in the first battle, it will be done in the second or subsequent battles. We will overcome them. The spirit of our people is good, and I have here and *en route* 1,000 and more of the *élite* of the yeomanry of the country to aid in defending their homes and firesides.

Very respectfully, your obedient servant,
HENRY CONNELLY,
Governor of New Mexico.

[Inclosure No. 2.]

FORT CRAIG, N. MEX., *February* 11, 1862.
Hon. W. H. SEWARD,
Secretary of State, Washington, D. C.:

SIR: The enemy are approaching in full force, not, I think, exceeding 3,000 men. They are within 20 miles of this post. To-day our united forces march out to meet them. The battle will most likely take place on the 13th, about 10 miles below. We have no fears of the result. Enthusiasm prevails throughout our lines.

About 800 militia will arrive to-morrow, there being already here and in service 500 of those called out by my late order, issued on the 25th of January. The militia have displayed a commendable spirit in the present emergency, and I have great confidence that they will do good service. We have fully 4,000 men under arms, among them 1,200 regular troops.

Colonel Canby has the entire confidence of the army and of the country. He will be ably assisted by his regular and temporary staff.

I may owe an apology or explanation for having left the capital during the session of the Legislature. It was thought by all that my presence would be very necessary and my example more so, which I think has been the case, as there are hundreds of our best citizens, with their retainers, now present, who might have hesitated had I remained at Santa Fé.

The Legislature had but five days remaining of the session when I left, and but few and unimportant laws to pass; the most of which were sent to me and were signed before the Legislature adjourned.

I learn that Secretary Holmes has left Santa Fé for the States since my departure. He will doubtless explain to the President the necessity that compelled him to leave.

So soon as anything decisive takes place I will communicate the result.

Very respectfully, your obedient servant,
HENRY CONNELLY,
Governor of New Mexico.

FORT UNION, N. MEX., *March* 11, 1862.

Hon. W. H. SEWARD, *Secretary of State, Washington City:*

SIR: Since my last communication, of the 1st instant, there has been no further encounter between the forces under Colonel Canby and those of Texas, so far as heard from. On the 4th instant, Major Donaldson, then commander of the District of Santa Fé, determined to leave that city with the small force he had under his command, say 200 men, and fall back upon this place. It was then said that the advanced guard (500 strong) of the enemy had entered Albuquerque and would proceed immediately to the capital. His departure became the more necessary in order to escort and defend a large amount of Government property then on the way from Albuquerque and Santa Fé to this place. The capital having been abandoned by the United States forces, I came in company with them, and I have for the present established the executive department at Las Vegas, 30 miles west of this post.

Since my last there has been nothing official received from Colonel Canby, but we have reason to believe that he has left Fort Craig and is now on march for this place or its neighborhood. The enemy in full force are said to have entered Albuquerque four days since; if so, Colonel Canby will have an opportunity to make a detour, and march to this place, or to a position in advance of them, by the way of Manzano.

I presume he wishes to avoid a decisive engagement until he can unite with the re-enforcements that are here from Colorado Territory, of whose arrival or near approach he is doubtless apprised. Colonel Slough, from Denver City, arrived here last night, with 950 men, who from all accounts can be relied upon. These, with 300 or 400 that are already here, will give Colonel Canby a force of 2,000 regular troops; that is, American troops. He has still the fragments of three regiments of Mexican Volunteers, I think to the amount of 1,500 men, which would make his force fully 3,500. The militia have all dispersed, and have gone to preparing their lands for the coming harvest, and this is by far the best use that could be made of them.

Should the forces at this place unite with Colonel Canby, of which at this time I have no doubt, the enemy will be driven from the Territory. Should Colonel Canby be attacked by the enemy and suffer a defeat, with considerable loss of men and arms, we will then be in a very precarious condition until re-enforcements arrive. The whole force from this place, say 1,300 men, will leave in a few days to meet Colonel Canby should he be on this side or south of Santa Fé, and if he be still in the rear of the enemy, to engage them between two fires or operate as circumstances may require. I hope by next mail to give you the information that the enemy are either vanquished in battle or are in retreat from the Territory.

Very respectfully, your obedient servant,

·   HENRY CONNELLY,
Governor of New Mexico.

HEADQUARTERS EASTERN DISTRICT,
Fort Union, N. Mex., March 11, 1862.

ADJUTANT-GENERAL U. S. ARMY,
Washington, D. C.:

GENERAL: I have the honor to report that since the battle of Valverde, on the 21st of February, the state of affairs in the Department of·New Mexico has been daily growing from bad to worse. All the militia and a large number of the volunteers (natives) who were called into the service of the United States have deserted and taken to the mountains. A general system of robbery and plunder seems to be the order of the day. There is a general panic in the country, and people are flying from their homes.

Communication with Colonel Canby at Fort Craig has been nearly· cut off, and since the 27th of February, 1862, nothing whatever has been heard from him. On the 27th he dispatched Captains Lord and Howland, each with 50 mounted men, to observe the enemy and to communicate with Maj. J. L. Donaldson, commanding the Santa Fé District, directing him to go to his relief. This order was doubtless given under the belief that regiments of Kansas Volunteers had arrived in the Territory. Major Donaldson, however, had no sufficient force either to go to Colonel Canby's relief or even to hold Santa Fé. He therefore sent all public property that could be transported to this post, and abandoned Santa Fé. His report is herein inclosed.* The supplies reached Fort Union safely. Under these circumstances, as the senior officer, I assumed command of all troops, posts, and depots in the department not immediately under command of Colonel Canby, and ordered Major Donaldson to march all his forces to this post.

The main body of the enemy, about 2,000 strong, is at Albuquerque, N. Mex., and a strong force is near Fort Craig, watching Colonel Canby's movements. I am now organizing a column to march against the enemy and form a junction with Colonel Canby. Should this expedition prove successful—of which I entertain no doubt—the Territory will be saved to the United States; but should it fail, the country will be lost. In either case I cannot too strongly urge the absolute necessity for a re-enforcement of 4,000 men, two batteries of rifled cannon, and six siege pieces. Maj. J. L. Donaldson, whom I have ordered to Washington to represent the interests and wants of the department, will enter more fully into details.

On the arrival of Colonel Slough, with his regiment of Colorado Volunteers, I had the mortification to discover that his commission was senior to mine, and thus I am deprived of a command which I had taken so much pains to organize and with which I expected to reap laurels. Thus, also, an officer of only six months' service, and without experience, takes precedence of one of many years' service, and who has frequently been tried in battle. It is as little as I can ask of the War Department for past and present service to give me such rank as will prevent in future such mortifications. I therefore ask for the rank of brigadier-general of volunteers.

I am, sir, very respectfully, your most obedient servant,

G. R. PAUL,
Colonel Fourth Regt. N. Mex. Vols., Comdg. East. Dist.

NOTE.—At a late hour last night the two inclosed notes were received from Colonel Canby, the express, after many narrow escapes, having made his way safely through the enemy's lines. I also inclose the copy of a letter received by Dr. Baily from Dr. Norris.

G. R. P.

[Inclosures.]

FORT CRAIG, N. MEX., *March* 5, 1862.

DOCTOR: I am not yet prepared to make my official report, and I

See p. 527.

have only to say at present that our department is conducted satisfactorily. We have everything which is needed for the wounded.

Capt. W. A. Van Vliet, assistant quartermaster, has furnished us with 100 blankets and 50 bed-sacks. Fifty-six men killed on the field, including 9 volunteers. One hundred and forty men were brought to the hospitals wounded, 17 of whom have since died. The wounded are treated in five hospitals, established in the officers' and company quarters, and under the charge of the following medical officers: 1st, Dr. B. A. Clements; 2d, Dr. S. Rankin; 3d, Dr. J. H. Bill; 4th, Dr. E. Arnold; 5th, Dr. J. H. Shout. Up to the 2d of March I had charge of Hospital 5, including five amputations in a separate ward. I had also charge of Captain Wingate, Captain Stone, and Captain Mortimore, severely wounded, and Lieutenant McDermott, disabled by a deep flesh-wound in the thigh.

I was attacked on the 2d instant with pneumonia, and was compelled to take my bed, since which time Dr. Shout has been in charge of part of my duties and Dr. Clements with the rest. Dr. Shout remained until very late on the battle-field, and was unable to attend to his duties for several days afterward. Dr. Bill, having been assigned to duty as post surgeon, has been exclusively occupied with the sick of the garrison. His industry and experience have rendered him very useful in that field. I will write you more in full as soon as I feel able. I will forward my report of sick in a day or two. Articles needed for the wounded of another battle are lint, muslin, tow, field stretchers with handles, pulveris licii, and dressings of every description. Mattresses will be very much needed, and I recommend that woolen ones be made. We have been compelled to seize all the mattresses of the garrison. The mattresses allowed by the supply table would not be sufficient for the minimum number of severely wounded to be expected after any battle. Liquors we have found very useful, and I would recommend another supply purchased for future occasions. Ether and chloroform are indispensable, and should be preserved with the greatest care.

I have purchased of the sutler of this post 200 yards of muslin and 40 yards of canton flannel, which is a tolerable substitute for lint. Our wounded are doing well, and if we are ordered to move, all but about 15 could be easily conveyed.

Very respectfully, your obedient servant,

BASIL NORRIS,
Assistant Surgeon, U. S. Army,
Medical Director and Purveyor of Troops in the Field.

E. I. BAILY, *Surgeon, U. S. Army,*
Medical Director, Dept. of New Mexico, Santa Fé, N. Mex.

[FORT CRAIG], *March* 7, 1862.

MAJOR : Our wounded are all doing well and the men are in good spirits. We have supplies of every kind for two months, except flour, and that we can eke out for fifty, or, if necessary, sixty days. Do not trust the Mexican troops. If the Colorado or Kansas or California troops have not joined you, do not risk an engagement until they do.

I have sent you three messengers to advise you of my movements, but they have not returned.

Yours, &c.,

ED. R. S. CANBY.

Maj. JAMES L. DONALDSON.

FORT CRAIG, N. MEX., *March* 7, 1862.

COLONEL: As our communications via Santa Fé will probably be interrupted, I wish you to send me by reliable expressmen, and as frequently as possible, any information that you can gain with regard to the movements of troops coming into the Territory, and any other information that would be useful in our present position.

Our wounded are all doing well, and the men are in good spirits.

Very truly, yours, &c.,

ED. R. S. CANBY.

Col. G. R. PAUL.

———

DEPARTMENT OF STATE,
Washington, March 13, 1862.

Hon. E. M. STANTON, *Secretary of War:*

SIR: This Department has recently had correspondence with the Department of War upon the subject of the occupation of a part at least of the west bank of the Rio Grande, for the purpose of preventing trade between the adjacent region of Texas and the Mexican bank of the river, particularly Matamoros. Though fully appreciating the objections and difficulties suggested by the military authorities against that occupation at this juncture, I cannot forbear to mention a recent marked instance of its importance.

There has in all probability been an extensive importation of merchandise, especially contraband of war, into Matamoros, destined for the insurgent States, and an exportation of cotton from those States through the same channel. Our right to blockade the mouth of the Rio Grande for the purpose of preventing this commerce may be considered as at least questionable. A British steamer, with a cargo of cotton, has recently been captured near the mouth of that river, and has been sent to New York for adjudication. In all probability this Government will ultimately have to pay heavy damages for this capture. A military force, however competent to guard the roads leading toward Matamoros from Texas, might check the carriage of cotton to that port, and consequently the temptation to vessels to proceed thither and exchange it for contraband of war.

I have the honor to be, sir, your obedient servant,

WILLIAM H. SEWARD.

———

HEADQUARTERS EASTERN DISTRICT,
Fort Union, N. Mex., March 17, 1862.

The ADJUTANT-GENERAL U. S. ARMY,
Washington, D. C.:

GENERAL: I have the honor to state that on the 9th instant Colonel Canby was still at Fort Craig awaiting the arrival of re-enforcements. His note to Major Donaldson is herein inclosed.* The enemy has ascended the Rio Grande and taken possession of Albuquerque and Santa Fé. Their main body is at or near the former place, and their advance guard is at the latter. I expect an answer to-morrow from Colonel Canby to a dispatch I sent him proposing a plan for his relief. As soon as it reaches me I shall move forward. I have just written a communication to His Excellency Governor W. Gilpin, of Colorado Territory, urging him to send forward all the assistance he can to the re-

———

* Not found herewith, but see inclosures to Paul's letter of March 11, p. 646.

lief of New Mexico, and I would respectfully call your attention to the situation of our little army here, and assure you of the necessity of large re-enforcements.

I am, sir, very respectfully, your obedient servant,

G. R. PAUL,
Colonel Fourth Regt., New Mexico Vols., Comdg. District.

HEADQUARTERS DEPARTMENT OF NEW MEXICO,
Fort Craig, N. Mex., March 18, 1862.

Col. J. P. SLOUGH,
First Colorado Volunteers :

SIR: Keep your command prepared to make a junction with this force. I will indicate the time and route. Move with as little baggage as possible. Take no tents and only the camp equipage essential for comfort and efficiency. Ammunition, at least 100 cartridges per man and gun. To save transportation, take only bread and meat, coffee and sugar. Reduce the flour and increase the fresh meat ration. Increase the coffee and sugar for guards and pickets. Do not rely upon the New Mexican troops except for garrisons and for partisan operations. Impress upon your men not to place too much confidence in their battery, but to rely upon the musket, and especially upon the bayonet. Be on your guard against attempts to cripple your operations by stampeding your animals. If you have been joined by a sufficient force to act independently against the enemy, advise me of your plans and movements, that I may co-operate. In this you must be governed by your own judgment and discretion, but nothing must be left to chance. There is no necessity for a premature movement on account of this post. We have flour to last until the 10th of next month (April), and it can be made to last until the end. I am jerking beef to serve as bread. Of all other supplies we have enough for three months. The question is not of saving this post, but of saving New Mexico and defeating the Confederates in such a way that an invasion of this Territory will never again be attempted. It is essential to the general plan that this post should be retained if possible. Fort Union must be held and our communications with the East kept open. If you move, a reliable garrison must be left in it. The communication by Fort Garland should also be kept open. If it cannot, that post should be destroyed. All other points are of no importance. While waiting for re-enforcements harass the enemy by partisan operations. Obstruct his movements and cut off his supplies. Use the mounted volunteers for these purposes and keep the regular cavalry in reserve. Feed their horses well.

This post will be retained until the last moment. If forced to abandon it everything will be destroyed, and I will move without incumbrances. The sick and wounded will be left at Limitar. Advise me of the arrival of re-enforcements; what troops are *en route;* when they are expected. Send carriers daily and by different routes—duplicates or triplicates of important communications by different couriers. Reports in relation to plans and movements will be made in cipher. Colonel Paul will give you the key. Keep the Adjutant-General advised of the state of affairs in this department.

Very respectfully, sir, your obedient servant,

ED. R. S. CANBY,
Colonel Nineteenth Infantry, Commanding Department.

WAR DEPARTMENT,
Washington, D. C., March 19, 1862.

Hon. W. H. SEWARD, *Secretary of State:*

SIR: The Secretary of War directs me to acknowledge the receipt of your letter of the 11th instant, inclosing a copy of dispatch No. 3, from Franklin Chase, United States consul at Tampico, recommending the capture and occupation of Brownsville, Tex., by our forces, and in reply to inform you that your letter has been carefully considered, with the conclusion that the condition of the United States forces does not admit at present of the detachment of the troops that such an expedition would require.

I have the honor to be, very respectfully, your obedient servant,

P. H. WATSON,
Assistant Secretary of War.

[MARCH 20–23, 1862.—For Halleck to Secretary of War, March 20, 21, and 23, and to Prince, March 21; and Secretary of War to Halleck, March 20, all in relation to re-enforcements from Department of the Mississippi for New Mexico, see Series I, Vol. VIII, pp. 627–629, 631, 633.]

WASHINGTON CITY, *March* 23, 1862.

Maj. Gen. H. W. HALLECK:

DEAR SIR: I am placed under deep obligation of gratitude for the prompt dispatch of six regiments to the relief of the oppressed people of New Mexico. I am pained to think of the fearful outrages which the Texas forces will heap upon them. The valley of the Rio Grande will be desolated for 200 miles. I feel assured that the re-enforcements sent by you will capture the whole Texas force if they move with rapidity. If they do not do so they might as well not go, for they will find a desolated country and an absent and retreating enemy. Texas will bring up from San Antonio re-enforcements rapidly, and the prospect of plunder will fill New Mexico with this class of troops as fast as they can go. Colonel Canby will no doubt destroy and abandon Fort Craig, and re-enforce Fort Union by a rapid march by Monganos to Fort Union, on the east side of the mountains. Colonel Canby, when at Fort Union with the regiment from Denver, can hold that place until the re-enforcements get to him. Excuse me for urging that at least the mounted portion of the column be urged forward at the most rapid rate possible. The infantry and artillery can follow at leisure. It is probable, if you will look at the map, that the Texas forces will, after taking and plundering Santa Fé, attempt to pass out to Fort Smith by the Canadian River, under the impression that a large column of the Confederates are at that point, threatening Missouri. I hope that in selecting the head of this expedition it will not be forgotten that the rapidity of the movement is the most important requisite of leaders. I shall trust with the utmost confidence to your judgment. Major General Harney, Major Steen, General Davidson, who is well known to the country and people of New Mexico, and others have been suggested to me as suitable persons, but I shall be perfectly satisfied with any one that your judgment dictates as most suitable to insure success. I have been twenty-six times across the plains; feel a deep interest in the rescue from destruction of the people of New Mexico, who have been my friends for many years, and if my services should be required I will leave my place here vacant, and without money and without price aid all I can to forward the movement. I do not wish any command, but will go and aid the command or commandant all in my power if it should be thought best for me to do so.

With kind regards, I remain, yours, &c.,

JOHN S. WATTS,
Delegate for New Mexico.

EXECUTIVE DEPARTMENT,
Las Vegas, March 23, 1862.

Hon. W. H. SEWARD,
Secretary of State, Washington City :

SIR : Since my last from Fort Union, dated 11th instant, there has occurred nothing indicating a speedy encounter with the enemy until this time. To-day the whole force from Denver City, Colo., together with the Territorial forces, numbering 1,400 men in all, will leave this place in the direction of the enemy, but I am informed will go but a short distance until they receive further communications and orders from Colonel Canby, who still remains at Fort Craig. These orders are daily expected, and with them a simultaneous movement of the two forces, so as to reach the position of the enemy on the same day.

There has been some little discord in relation to the movement now made from Union, in consequence of the want of orders from Colonel Canby. Major Paul, in command at Union, was of opinion that the orders of Colonel Canby were essential to an effective forward movement from Union; whereas Colonel Slough, in command of the forces from Colorado, was of opinion that an advance of a day or more march in advance could lead to no evil, and would curtail the limits of the enemy, and mayhap lead to the expulsion of the enemy from the capital, now occupied by about 100 men, with two pieces of artillery. I think this slight difference of opinion and movement will lead to no unfavorable result, as Colonel Slough will advance upon the road that the enemy will necessarily have to march to reach Union, should an attempt be made upon that place, which seems to be the fear entertained by Colonel Paul.

The enemy in force are now occupying a pass in the mountains east of Albuquerque, some 15 miles, called Carnavel, with a view, doubtless, to prevent the junction of the commands from Union and Craig, near which the commands will have to pass in order to form a junction. The forces in either command are nearly equal to those of the enemy, but I presume that Colonel Canby desires to avoid an engagement with them until he unites the two commands. I am sorry to say that the Texans have not behaved with the moderation that was expected, and that desolation has marked their progress on the Rio Grande from Craig to Bernalillo. Exactions and confiscations are of daily occurrence, and the larger portion of those who have anything to give or to lose are here on this frontier, seeking a refuge from their rapacity, and have left their houses and contents a prey to the invaders.

My own house, 90 miles from Santa Fé, was despoiled of its entire contents, including a valuable stock of goods, together with everything in the way of subsistence. On yesterday there arrived at this place some 20 of our most prosperous and respectable citizens from the neighborhood of Albuquerque and Bernalillo, who had fled from the exactions of Sibley; among the number a gentleman of eighty years of age,

Don Pedro José Perea, and his three sons, upon whom a demand had been made for a large sum of money, which they had not in their houses, having advanced all their available means to the disbursing officers of the Government but a short time before. The threat of personal violence in case of refusal so alarmed them, that they left their houses and entire contents at the mercy of the enemy.

It is said that the Texans are preparing for a precipitate retreat from the Territory by way of Fort Stanton and the Pecos River, which I think is not without probability, from the fact of their sudden and mercenary demand for money, and from the fact that they know there is a force superior to their own in the field, to which they must finally succumb. Their position at this time is directly on the road to Stanton, and it is thought was taken with the view indicated.

I hope in my next to give you the news of a more favorable condition of things in this Territory. We have the means now on hand to destroy the Texan forces now among us, except they receive large re-enforcements, of which there exists no probability. I hope in ten or fifteen days more to advise you of their expulsion from the Territory.

Very respectfully, your obedient servant,
HENRY CONNELLY,
Governor New Mexico.

HEADQUARTERS EASTERN DISTRICT,
Fort Union, N. Mex., March 24, 1862.
The ADJUTANT-GENERAL U. S. ARMY,
Washington, D. C.:

GENERAL: I have the honor to state that on the 9th instant I sent a dispatch to Colonel Canby, proposing a plan to form a junction with him (copy of dispatch marked A). In a dispatch from Colonel Canby, of the 14th, instant he approved of the proposed plan, and on the receipt of his note I completed the organization of a column, which I turned over to Col. John P. Slough, First Colorado Volunteers. On the 21st I received another dispatch from Colonel Canby (marked B), in which he concludes by saying: "Do not move from Fort Union to meet me until I advise you of the route and point of junction." Notwithstanding this order Colonel Slough determined to leave two days sooner than the original plan contemplated. I then addressed him a note (marked C), to which he replied, through his acting assistant adjutant-general (marked D). Believing that the best interests of the Government demanded it I wrote again, urging upon him to leave me a part of the troops for the defense of this post (letter marked E). To this letter he paid no attention whatever and left with his column. I am thus left with a feeble garrison and no suitable artillery for the defense of the principal and most important post in the Territory.

My object in this communication is to throw the responsibility of any disaster which may occur on the right shoulders. The position of affairs in the Territory is, with the exception of the occupation of Santa Fé by a small force of the enemy, the same as stated in my last communication. Colonel Canby is still (March 16) at Fort Craig, with 1,600 men; Colonel Slough is now at Bernal Springs, with nearly 1,400 men and eight pieces of artillery. The enemy's main force is now at and near Albuquerque, say 1,900 men and fifteen pieces of artillery; about 120 men and two pieces of artillery are at Santa Fé, and numerous pickets will swell their number to 2,500 men.

I once more urge upon the War Department strong re-enforcements of at least 4,000 men and several batteries of the best cannon.

I have the honor to be, very respectfully, your most obedient servant,

G. R. PAUL,

Colonel Fourth Regiment, N. Mex. Vols., Comdg. Dist.

[Inclosure A.]

MARCH 9, 1862.

COLONEL : I shall move from Fort Union with 1,200 Americans and four guns on the 24th, and be at Anton Chico on the 26th. If you leave Fort Craig on the 20th you can be at Punta del Agua on 24th and Berenda Spring on the 25th; on 26th make a forced march, and on 27th we can unite our forces. If no danger threatens I shall await you at Anton Chico, but if it does I shall move to meet you. I shall have provisions for you. 'Do not fail to meet me at the time designated, for everything depends on your uniting with me. To throw the enemy off his guard move your mounted men and two guns 30 or 40 miles up the river above La Joya, to convey the idea that you are about to attack his rear. This will compel him to concentrate, and under cover of this move by Socorro and road to Abo Pass and Punta del Agua, and before the enemy can unite and attack us separately we can form a junction. Send your express to meet me on the road to Anton Chico. Leave your sick and wounded at Fort Craig if they impede your march.

G. R. PAUL.

[Inclosure B.]

MARCH 16.

Place no reliance on the New Mexican troops except for partisan operations, and then only when the main operations will not be affected by the result. Concentrate all your reliable troops until the re-enforcements from Kansas, Colorado, and California arrive. If in sufficient force to operate directly upon the enemy, advise me of your plans, in order that I may co-operate. Fort Union must be held and our communication with the East kept open. Fort Garland is not so important. If it cannot be held, it should be destroyed. All other points are of no importance. While awaiting re-enforcements harass the enemy by partisan operations; obstruct his movements, and remove or destroy any supplies that might fall into his hands. This post must be held in order to cut off his retreat. Our supplies will last until the 10th of next month (April), and can be made to last until the end. If it is necessary to abandon the post, everything will be destroyed. I will move from the post at the last moment, and without incumbrances of any kind. The sick and wounded will be left at Limitar. In this case it will be necessary to effect a junction with your command. I will indicate the route and point of junction verbally and by several messengers. Keep the Adjutant-General advised of the state of affairs in the department and advise me of the arrival of re-enforcements. Do not move from Fort Union to meet me until I advise you of the route and point of junction.

ED. R. S. CANBY,

Colonel.

[Inclosure C.]

HEADQUARTERS EASTERN DISTRICT,
Fort Union, N. Mex., March 22, 1862.

Col. J. P. SLOUGH,
First Colorado Regiment:

SIR : Although I had organized and transferred to you all the available troops in this district previous to the receipt of the dispatch from Colonel Canby dated the 16th instant, yet you are aware it was done to carry out plans approved by that officer for the relief of and junction with his forces, to the end that when united the entire force should be used to drive the enemy from the Territory. Colonel Canby's dispatch of the 16th instant directs that the movement from here be delayed until further instructions from him, and urges the maintenance of this post at all hazards as of vital importance to all. I fully coincide with him in his views regarding this post. If, therefore, you are determined on moving toward the enemy, I request that you will do so with your own regiment, one section of Captain Ritter's battery, and one section of Lieutenant Claflin's battery, and the regular cavalry now in your front. The remaining sections of Ritter's and Claflin's batteries and the command of Capt. W. H. Lewis are in my opinion the least force required to garrison this post securely, and I request that they be directed to report to me. Even this force will not be sufficient for the purpose should you meet with disaster or advance so far as to render it impossible to return promptly to my relief in case I am attacked by the enemy.

Hoping that you coincide with me in these views, I remain, very respectfully, your obedient servant,

G. R. PAUL,
Colonel Fourth N. Mex. Vols., Comdg. Eastern District.

[Inclosure D.]

HEADQUARTERS NORTHERN DIVISION,
Fort Union, N. Mex., March 22, 1862.

Col. G. R. PAUL,
Comdg. Eastern Dist., Fort Union, N. Mex.:

SIR : I am instructed by Colonel Slough to acknowledge the receipt of your communication of this date, and to state in reply that the instructions of Colonel Canby are not only to protect Fort Union, but also to harass the enemy. By moving the command to or near Bernal Springs both ends can be accomplished, and as the command will be between the enemy and Fort Union, the latter is as much protected as if the troops remained here. By being at the Springs we can better operate for the double purpose of harassing the enemy and protecting Santa Fé from depredation.

If the enemy at San Antonio are no stronger than reported by Captain Walker, the troops under my command will be sufficient to control their action and to defeat them in case of an attack.

Thinking that the command assigned by you can be spared for the purpose named, the colonel commanding cannot consent to leave any portion behind.

I have the honor to be, sir, very respectfully, your obedient servant,

GURDEN CHAPIN,
Captain, Seventh Infantry, Acting Assistant Adjutant-General.

[Inclosure E.]

HEADQUARTERS EASTERN DISTRICT,
Fort Union, N. Mex., March 22, 1862.

Col. J. P. SLOUGH,
First Regiment Colorado Volunteers:

COLONEL: Yours in answer to mine of this date is received. You must be aware that no part of the regular force of this district would have been turned over to you had the instructions of Colonel Canby of the 16th instant been received twelve hours earlier. I had trusted that this knowledge and the fact that your movement is in direct conflict with Colonel Canby's positive orders and in disregard of his anxiety for the safety of this department that my request would have been answered differently. The force offered you in my first note was ample to answer all purposes of annoying and harassing the enemy, as you state that as the object of your advance. You, however, indicate that an attack upon the enemy's position at San Antonio is within your calculations. This most certainly is or will be in violation of Colonel Canby's instructions, and, if unsuccessful, must result in the entire loss of the Territory, at least for a time, and render its reconquest much more difficult. I must urge upon you to reconsider your decision and to submit to the plan of the department commander. The arrangements I proposed in my first letter on this point give you sufficient force to comply fully with Colonel Canby's orders to "annoy the enemy." With due deference to your superior judgment I must insist that your plans do not meet either of these ends, but must inevitably result in disaster to us all. Colonel Canby must have had good reasons for the change directed in the plans he at first approved, and his anxiety to have the change made known is indicated by his sending duplicates of his instructions by different messengers, both of which have been received.

In the name of the department commander, of the best interests of the service, and of the safety of all the troops in this Territory, I protest against this movement of yours, made as it is two days before the time first agreed upon, and as I conceive in direct disobedience of the orders of Colonel Canby.

I am, colonel, very respectfully, your obedient servant,

G. R. PAUL,
Colonel Fourth N. Mex. Vols., Comdg. Eastern District.

WAR DEPARTMENT,
Washington City, D. C., March 24, 1862.

Hon. W. H. SEWARD, *Secretary of State:*

SIR: The Secretary of War directs me to acknowledge the receipt of your letter of the 13th instant, relative to the occupation, by United States troops, of the left bank of the Rio Grande, with a view of preventing trade between the adjacent region of Texas and the Mexican bank of the river, particularly Matamoros, and in reply to inform you that your letter has received careful consideration, with the conclusion that the condition of the United States forces does not admit at present of the detachment of the necessary troops for such an expedition.

I have the honor to be, very respectfully, your obedient servant,

P. H. WATSON,
Assistant Secretary of War.

KANSAS CITY, *March* 24, 1862.

Hon. E. M. STANTON, *Secretary of War:*

Major Donaldson is here *en route* to Washington. Furnishes the following:

Santa Fé evacuated on the 5th. Troops and supplies withdrawn to Fort Union. Colonel Slough, of Colorado, arrived at Fort Union with 950 men, making total strength of that place 1,500. They would form junction with Colonel Canby. Colonel Canby was at Fort Craig on 7th, with 800 regulars and about same number Mexicans, with supplies for sixty days. Advance guard of Texans was at Algodones, 45 miles from Santa Fé, on 4th instant. Another battle expected before April 1.

JAS. ROBERTS.

CONSULATE OF THE UNITED STATES OF AMERICA,
Matamoros, March 24, 1862.

Hon. W. H. SEWARD,
Secretary of State, Washington, D. C.:

SIR: * * * In a conversation with the colonel commanding this line he informed me that a force was being organized of Mexicans on the Texas side to capture Matamoros, and that many Texans were joining, and that the real object was the capture of all the Americans on this side, and on observing everything in relation to it I find such to be the facts without a doubt.

The colonel here (Colonel Quiroyo), who is a warm advocate of the Union, and has been throughout the war, has assured me that he will protect all American citizens in Matamoros to the extent of his power, and for my own personal safety and the safety of my documents he has several times offered me apartments in his own quarters, but as I have a small force of true Americans constantly around me I have declined, thinking that I can fight my way out if attacked.

A collision is becoming more imminent every day, and hundreds of heartfelt wishes are uttered both by Americans and Mexicans that a Government force may appear at Brazos Santiago and restore order.

The Texan troops are becoming demoralized and disorderly in the extreme, declaring that they will burn and destroy everything of both friend and foe.

A force of 1,000 men could conquer the entire line of the Rio Grande, as most of the German and the old United States soldiers would immediately turn at sight of the Union flag.

The difficulty in our mail facilities being now obviated and a regular line being established to Tampico, I am relieved of the expense of my own courier, my great difficulty now being in procuring stationery.

I am, sir, very respectfully, your most obedient,
L. PIERCE, JR.,
United States Consul.

[MARCH 28, 1862.—For Halleck to Secretary of War, in reference to re-enforcements for New Mexico, see Series I, Vol. VIII, p. 647.]

EXECUTIVE DEPARTMENT,
Las Vegas, N. Mex., March 30, 1862.

Hon. W. H. SEWARD,
Secretary of State, Washington City:

SIR: In my communication of the 23d instant I informed you that

Colonel Slough, with the troops from Colorado Territory, together with the small regular force at Union, had advanced through this place in the direction of the enemy.

On the 26th the advance guard of our forces, making a reconnaissance and without anticipating any encounter with the enemy, came in contact with his advance guard of 600 men, neither, it would seem, being aware of the presence or near approach of the other. This took place at the Cañon del Apache, the east end thereof, on the road to and about 20 miles from Santa Fé. An action ensued, in which the enemy were entirely routed, with a loss of 25 or 30 killed and wounded and 62 prisoners. A flag of truce was sent in at night by the enemy asking a suspension of hostilities for the purpose of burying their dead and taking care of the wounded. The 27th was occupied in these acts of humanity. The main body of their forces being at the cañon, only about 7 miles distant, they advanced on the 28th in full force to the attack of ours, which had all been called to the scene of action. The engagement commenced at about noon and lasted until sunset, without any decisive result. The cause of this indecision as to result was that early in the day Major Chivington, with 500 men, had been ordered to make a detour on the heights (mesa) and observe the operations of any forces that might approach in that direction. His position on the table-land, and parallel to the whole length of the cañon, gave him a full view, part of the way, of everything that was in it, and to his joy and surprise when he reached the lower end of the cañon he found the enemy's whole train parked, together with the mules and horses necessary for its transportation, guarded by 200 men. The nature of the country enabled him to approach very near without the observance of the guard. He made a sudden and unexpected attack upon them, and captured the whole train of 80 wagons, with all the stock except the few upon which some of the guard made their escape. He also captured 40 prisoners, and after burning the train, with all its contents of provisions and ammunition, he returned to the command late at night by the way of the same table-land over which he had advanced

Meantime and before his arrival at the train the enemy had advanced 1,200 strong to attack our forces at the east end of the cañon and about 7 miles distant. The absence of Major Chivington from the field gave the enemy a greatly superior force, ours not passing 700 men, and hence the contest was delayed and became very obstinate and doubtful until dark. Both armies remained upon the field a short distance from each other, but Major Chivington having returned and rejoined our forces made our numbers nearly equal.

There were some reports that General Sibley was moving by another road upon Fort Union with the balance of his forces. It was thought best to fall back to a point at which he must necessarily pass in order to reach that place. This was done, and our forces will to-morrow take a position at Bernal Springs for the purposes indicated. Our loss in killed, wounded, and missing in the two days' encounter will reach 150; that of the enemy fully double that number. It is the opinion of those who are better capable of judging that the enemy lost their entire stock of provisions and ammunition in the train that was burnt, and hence that he will have to fall back on Santa Fé or scatter in confusion through the country seeking subsistence. A few days will determine his future movements. I had forgot to state that the enemy lost three pieces of artillery in the engagement, two with the wagons and one on the field.

We have reliable information to-day that General Sibley left Albuquerque five days since for Santa Fé, with 500 men, but at the distance of 20 miles was informed of the approach of Colonel Canby from Fort Craig, and returned to meet him. This I think is reliable, and as Colonel Canby has full 2,000 men with him, there can be no doubt as to his entire rout or capture by Colonel Canby.

From the facts above stated you will see that our Territory will soon be liberated from the further progress of the desolating foe. Our forces here are fully equal to the encounter and dispersion of the enemy we have before us, and Colonel Canby will soon dispose of Sibley and come to our aid, should any be necessary.

I am pleased to be able to give you this flattering account of our affairs, and hope in my next to say that we have not a Texan in arms within our limits.

I have the honor to remain, sir, very respectfully, your obedient servant,

HENRY CONNELLY,
Governor of New Mexico.

HEADQUARTERS DEPARTMENT OF NEW MEXICO,
Fort Craig, N. Mex., March 31, 1862.

The ADJUTANT-GENERAL OF THE ARMY,
Washington, D. C.:

SIR: I have the honor to inclose a copy of a communication* from Colonel Slough, of the First Regiment of Colorado Volunteers, reporting an engagement in Apache Cañon on the 26th instant, and announcing his intention to move against the enemy with his entire force. This movement is, in my judgment, premature, and is at variance with my instructions, but as it may involve serious consequences, I have determined to move to-morrow with the force under my immediate command, leaving a garrison of volunteers for this post, and effect a junction with the troops in the northern part of the department. There are two routes by which this junction may be effected: First, by the Abo Pass and Anton Chico; second, by the river to Albuquerque, and thence by San Antonio and Gallisteo. Both of these routes are liable to interruption by an enterprising enemy; but the latter, as the boldest, will be the least suspected, and I shall move directly upon Albuquerque, for the purpose of occupying that place if it can be done without serious loss, and holding it until the junction can be effected, or, if it cannot be, making such demonstration against it as will draw the main force of the Confederates from Santa Fé and enable the columns to unite without opposition. When united, the force under my command will be sufficient to expel the enemy from the country north of this post, but not to follow them into the Mesilla Valley, unless in the mean time re-enforcements from the East sufficient for the occupation of the upper country should arrive. The New Mexican Volunteers cannot be relied on for any purpose of this kind.

Very respectfully, sir, your obedient servant,

ED. R. S. CANBY,
Colonel Nineteenth Infantry, Commanding Department.

---

* See Slough's report of March 29, p. 533.

HEADQUARTERS DEPARTMENT OF NEW MEXICO,
Fort Craig, N. Mex., March 31, 1862.

Col. C. CARSON:

COLONEL: You are charged with the duty of holding this post. Your command will consist of seven companies of your own regiment, two of the Second, and one of the Fourth Regiment New Mexico Volunteers. The convalescents, as they become effective, will add to your strength.

I am instructed by the colonel commanding to say that the objects in view and the plan of operations require that it should be held to the last extremity. The manner of doing this is left to your judgment and discretion, in both of which he has the utmost confidence. The force of the enemy in the Mesilla will not allow him to make a regular attack upon the post, but it may be attempted by surprise. To guard against this he desires that you will exercise yourself and exact from all of your command the most unremitting vigilance.

The sick and wounded left in your care will of course receive every attention, and the colonel commanding desires me to say that any expenditures that will add to their comfort or conduce to their recovery will be fully authorized.

Very respectfully, sir, your obedient servant,

WM. J. L. NICODEMUS,
Captain, Twelfth Infantry, Actg. Asst. Adjt. Gen.

[APRIL 2, 1862.—For Denver to Halleck, in reference to expedition to New Mexico, see Series I, Vol. VIII, p. 653.]

[APRIL 5–6, 1862.—For Halleck to Denver, April 5, and to Sturgis, April 6, in reference, among other matters, to New Mexico expedition, see Series I, Vol. VIII, pp. 664, 668.]

EXECUTIVE DEPARTMENT,
Las Vegas, N. Mex., April 6, 1862.

Hon. W. H. SEWARD,
Secretary of State, Washington City, D. C.:

SIR: In my communication of the 30th ultimo I informed you that our forces had fallen back to Bernal Springs, 20 miles from the place of our late encounter with the enemy.

On the day of their arrival at that place the adjutant-general of Colonel Canby, Lieutenant Nicodemus, arrived in camp, bringing news and orders from Colonel Canby. The first was that he had not on the 25th of March left Fort Craig, and the orders were for the whole force to fall back on Union.

These orders were obeyed, and on the 31st ultimo the troops passed this place *en route* to Fort Union.

Since the late encounter with the enemy we have had occasion to learn much more of the particulars and consequences of that engagement than I could write you in my last communication.

Two days having been given for the burial of the dead and taking care of the wounded, an opportunity was thereby offered to ascertain the loss of the enemy and their subsequent movements. As I had anticipated, they fled in confusion from the field and returned to Santa Fé, not having on an average 10 rounds of ammunition to the man, the whole of the ammunition having been destroyed in the train that was burned by Major Chivington on the day of the battle. So it turned out that had our troops advanced the day after the battle it would have led to the entire capture or dispersion of the enemy's force in the neighborhood of Santa Fé.

This opportunity has been lost, and we have again to try the fortune of another battle. Upon hearing of the defeat of the troops under the command of Colonel Scurry and their retreat to Santa Fé, General Sibley sent a re-enforcement of 500 men from Albuquerque, which re-enforcement reached Santa Fé two days since, together with as much ammunition and provisions as could be spared from that quarter. These troops, united with those lately routed from the Apache Cañon, I do not think will pass 1,500, and perhaps not reach that number. With these I have no doubt that an attempt will be made either to defend Santa Fé or make a stand again in the cañon 15 miles this side, which can be defended by a smaller against a superior force, acting only on the defensive.

We have certain intelligence that Colonel Canby has left Fort Craig, and on the 1st of this month, so that by to-day he must be at or on this side of Albuquerque. The troops from Union will also leave to-day for Santa Fé or to form a junction with Colonel Canby by concert. The junction will be formed as the situation of the enemy and his strength will permit. It may be at or near the cañon before mentioned, say at Gallisteo, 15 miles south of Santa Fé, or in the more immediate neighborhood of that city.

Certain it is that we are on the eve of another battle, which will be decisive, as all our forces, save a few left at Craig, will be in the field and also the whole available force of the enemy. I do not doubt the result. We shall triumph. Our troops are more in numbers, buoyant with the late success, and resolved to drive the enemy from the Territory.

The loss of the enemy in the late encounter does not fall short of 400 men in killed, wounded, and missing. Many officers of high grade, 1 colonel, said to be Green or McNeill, 2 majors, 1 captain, and 2 lieutenants killed on the field. Three captains (Shannon, Wells, and Scott), 8 lieutenants, names not given, taken prisoners. Their wounded are in a hard condition on the late field of battle, without medicine, medical aid, or the necessary subsistence, and are said to be near 200 in numbers.

By next mail I hope to give you the welcome intelligence of a final and decisive victory over the enemy.

I have the honor to remain, sir, very respectfully, your obedient servant,

HENRY CONNELLY,
Governor of New Mexico.

DEPARTMENT OF STATE,
Washington, April 8, 1862.

Hon. E. M. STANTON, *Secretary of War:*

SIR: I have the honor to transmit herewith for your information an extract from a dispatch (No. 3), dated March 21, received this day from Mr. Leonard Pierce, jr., United States consul at Matamoros, Mexico, relative to the prospect of a battle near Austin, Tex., between loyal and disloyal citizens of that State.

I have the honor to be, sir, your obedient servant,

WILLIAM H. SEWARD.

[Inclosure.]

CONSULATE OF THE UNITED STATES OF AMERICA,
Matamoras, Mexico, March 21, 1862.

Hon. W. H. SEWARD,
Secretary of State, Washington, D. C.:

SIR: * * * The Union men in Texas are becoming bolder, and a battle is expected in the neighborhood of Austin and San Antonio.

I am continually besieged with refugees and deserters; most of them without funds, who expect me to send them North. For many I have procured situations, where they can earn a subsistence, and others I have to provide for to the best of my ability.

I am, sir, very respectfully, your most obedient servant,

L. PIERCE, JR.,
United States Consul.

———

WAR DEPARTMENT,
Washington City, D. C., April 9, 1862.

Hon. W. H. SEWARD, *Secretary of State:*

SIR: By direction of the Secretary of War, I have the honor to acknowledge the receipt of your letter of yesterday, inclosing an extract from a dispatch of the United States consul at Matamoros, Mexico, and to say that the suggestion contained therein will receive the consideration of this Department.

Very respectfully,

P. H. WATSON,
Assistant Secretary of War.

———

EXECUTIVE DEPARTMENT,
Las Vegas, April 11, 1862.

Hon. W. H. SEWARD,
Secretary of State, Washington, D. C.:

SIR: I informed you in my communication of the 6th instant that the troops from Union had marched forward in the direction of the enemy, at that time in and around Santa Fé, having been re-enforced by the remnant of their forces under General Sibley from Albuquerque. On the 7th and 8th instant all our forces had concentrated at Bernal Springs, 20 miles west of this place, and from there marched on the 9th toward the capital. At San José, 7 miles distant, they were met by a flag of truce, borne by Maj. A. M. Jackson and another officer high in rank, the object and purport of which have not come to my knowledge. Enough is known, however, to enable me to say that nothing asked for under the flag of truce was granted, and our troops marched hastily on, Colonel Paul having disposed of the bearers of the flag in a very short conference. But a few hours after leaving San José Colonel Paul received information direct from Santa Fé that the whole Texan force had evacuated that place and were then marching hurriedly toward Albuquerque, leaving behind them all their wounded. The information also confirms the intelligence that I gave you in my last as to the great loss of the enemy on the 28th ultimo in the engagement with our forces on that day. It now appears certain that their loss exceeded my calculation, not falling short of 450 in killed, wounded, and prisoners, so that when they had collected the fragments of their dispersed forces together in Santa Fé (and this was not done until at the end of three days) it was ascertained that out of 1,200 men that had been engaged in the conflict of that day not more than 750 could be found ready for duty. This number, united with the force brought by Sibley from Albuquerque—say 400 men—constitutes the whole Texan force now in the Territory.

Colonel Canby left Albuquerque on the 7th instant, and is presumed to be on his way to the capital either by the way of the river or on the east side of the mountains by the way of the Placer. In either event an encounter with the enemy is inevitable. His movements are all now in concert with those of the forces from Union under Colonel Paul. The enemy is between them, and but a short distance from either. A desperate effort will be made either to defeat Colonel Canby or elude his forces before Colonel Paul's command arrives in their rear and to Colonel Canby's assistance. The force of Colonel Canby now with him is about equal to that of the enemy—say 1,100 or 1,200—900 of whom are regulars, so that we may not fear any serious reverse before Colonel Paul can arrive upon the ground and aid in the capture of the entire Texan force now in the Territory. It is very sure that the Texans are now in full flight, but if not permitted by Colonel Canby to pass round him, I have no doubt but that they will give him battle, and attempt to force their passage down the river to Fort Craig, and thence out of the Territory.

The road to the capital is now clear of the enemy and his spies, and there is not a Texan in Santa Fé except the wounded, one surgeon, and a few attendants. I have this from a gentleman direct from Santa Fé, who left there the day after the evacuation by the enemy, and to whom every credence can be given. I shall leave to-morrow for the capital, and from there, by next mail, I hope to be able to give you the intelligence that the enemy are either captured or dispersed.

We are greatly indebted to the command under Colonel Slough, from Denver City, for this favorable result in our struggle with the Texan invaders. Their defeat and utter annihilation is now sure, and I think it will be the last attempt upon the Territory from that quarter.

I am sorry to say that the Indians during the last three months have entirely desolated the Territory of all the stock within their reach, having advanced as far east as the Canadian, a point far in advance of all their former depredations.

I have the honor to remain, sir, very respectfully, your obedient servant,

HENRY CONNELLY,
. *Governor New Mexico.*

[Copy furnished to War Department by Secretary of State May 6, 1862.]

EXECUTIVE DEPARTMENT,
Las Vegas, N. Mex., April 13, 1862.

W. H. SEWARD, *Secretary of State:*

SIR: I have the honor to inform the Department that on the 11th instant Colonel Canby formed a junction with the command under Colonel Paul at Gallisteo, 15 miles south of Santa Fé, and proceeded by forced marches on to Albuquerque, at which place the enemy with their entire force had concentrated. On his march upwards and in the town or neighborhood of Albuquerque Colonel Canby had an encounter with either the whole or a part of the enemy's forces, in which it is said he took several pieces of artillery, and that Major Duncan, of our cavalry, was wounded in the head.

Colonel Canby made the detour by way of the Cañon Carnavel, and came on the east side of the mountains to the junction at Gallisteo. To-day he will arrive at Albuquerque, and doubtless decide the question of the occupancy of this Territory by the Texans. It is thought the Texans are in hasty retreat, and have full three days' march the advantage. Should that be the case, it will not be easy to overtake them. Col. Kit Carson, with his entire regiment, and some auxiliary forces, is still at Craig, and may offer some embarrassment to the safe retreat of the enemy.

I think there can be no doubt as to the result of any action between the forces under Colonel Canby, now united with the late victorious troops from Denver, and the enemy, with all the forces they have in the Territory.

The cavalry and means of transportation on both sides are completely broken down, and neither a retreat nor pursuit can be effected with any degree of rapidity.

The Territory has been completely exhausted of grain on the route of the military movements, and nothing can be obtained of forage for animals.

I give you herein the latest news from and the positions of the different forces. Not having left for the capital the day mentioned in my last, of the 10th instant, has enabled me to do so. I leave on to-morrow for that place, and will by next mail give you the result of the impending conflict.

I am, sir, very respectfully, your obedient servant,
HENRY CONNELLY,
Governor of New Mexico.

P. S.—The inclosed communication from Colonel Paul was received after the above was written. I forward it for the satisfaction of the Department.

[Copy furnished War Department by Secretary of State May 6, 1862.]

[Inclosure.]

HEADQUARTERS EASTERN DISTRICT,
Gallisteo, N. Mex., April 12, 1862.

His Excellency HENRY CONNELLY,
Governor of New Mexico, Las Vegas, N. Mex.:

SIR: It affords me great pleasure to inform you that Santa Fé is now in our possession, and that Your Excellency will hazard nothing by returning to the seat of government and resuming the duties of your office whenever it may suit your convenience.

I tender to you, sir, the best guarantee of the future prosperity of New Mexico in assuring you of the junction of my command at an early hour with the forces under General Canby, and I am confident that the rebel troops will be driven before us.

Your Excellency will be glad to know that the Union troops on entering Santa Fé were received with public demonstrations of joy.

I have the honor to be, sir, very respectfully, your obedient servant,

G. R. PAUL,
Colonel Fourth Regiment New Mexico Vols., Comdg. Dist.

GENERAL ORDERS, }   HDQRS. DEPT. OF NEW MEXICO,
No. 30.   }   *Camp near Peralta, N. Mex., April 16, 1862.*

I. Col. G. R. Paul, Fourth New Mexico Volunteers, is assigned to the command of the first column, and Colonel Chivington, First Colorado Volunteers, to the command of the second column, of the Union Army of New Mexico.

II. Col. B. S. Roberts, Fifth New Mexico Volunteers, is assigned to the command of that part of New Mexico including the Central, Northern, and Santa Fé Districts, and charged with the duty of establishing garrisons and taking such other measures as may be necessary for the security of public property and the restoration of order at the point recently occupied by Confederate forces.

III. Capt. R. M. Morris, Third Cavalry, is assigned to the command of all the cavalry force with this command except Graydon's Spy Company.

IV. Two companies of the Second Kansas Regiment will re-enforce the garrison of Fort Union; the remainder of that regiment will join this command with as little delay as possible.

V. Capt. J. C. McFerran, senior quartermaster, will proceed to Fort Union, for the purpose of collecting and forwarding supplies and superintending the operations of his department on his arrival at Fort Union. H. M. Enos, assistant quartermaster, will report in person at the headquarters of the Army.

VI. Surg. E. I. Baily, medical director of the department, will proceed to Santa Fé and to Fort Union, and is charged with the duty of providing the supplies and making arrangements for the comfort of the sick and wounded. He will establish such general hospitals and purchase such supplies as may be necessary to secure the comfort and speedy recovery of the wounded. Surg. J. M. Whitlock, First New Mexico Volunteers, will report for duty to Surgeon Baily.

VII. Capt. Chacon's company of the First, Sena's, Eaton's, and Sanchez's, companies of the Second, and Hubbell's company of the Fifth Regiment, will report for duty to Col. B. S. Roberts.

VIII. Col. M. S. Howe, Third Cavalry, will report in person at these headquarters. The officers accompanying him will join without delay their regiments or companies in the field or at the stations at which they may be found.

IX. The senior paymaster will make immediate arrangements for the payment of the troops, commencing with those that have been the longest unpaid.

X. The chief commissary will [make] the necessary provision for the supplies pertaining to this department.

By order of Col. E. R. S. Canby:

WM. J. L. NICODEMUS,
Captain and Acting Assistant Adjutant-General.

EXECUTIVE DEPARTMENT,
Santa Fé, N. Mex., April 20, 1862.

Hon. W. H. SEWARD, &c.:

SIR: In my communication of the 11th instant I informed you that a junction had been made between the forces under General Canby and those under Colonel Paul at the place called Gallisteo, 15 miles south of Santa Fé. I have learned since that the main body of the two forces did not unite until they reached the Cañon of Carnavel, directly east of and about 15 miles from Albuquerque. General Canby, having left his position on the river below Albuquerque, at which place he had a slight skirmish with a small force of the enemy, left a garrison, and taking the position to which I have referred, in the Cañon of Carnavel the two commands were united on the 13th instant.

The fugitive forces of the Texans had meantime reached Albuquerque from this place, and, uniting with the small force there, took up their line of march down the river on the east side, not being able to cross the stream at Albuquerque. They had progressed only 20 miles, when they were overtaken by General Canby at and in full possession of my residence. It being late at night when General Canby arrived within hearing of their position, his ears were saluted with the "sound of revelry by night." The violin was in full blast, accompanied by other and more noisy instruments. The enemy seemed to be entirely unconscious of his approach, nor was his presence known to them until next morning.

My residence is surrounded by quite a dense forest of trees, extending in every direction for at least half a mile, and the only approach for vehicles is by the main road. The ditches (asequias), for the purpose of irrigation, running across and parallel with the road, offer no small impediment to the operation of artillery.

During the day after General Canby had reached the position of the enemy, as related, a cannonading was carried on from both sides without any serious result. The position of the enemy was a strong one and dangerous to be approached by infantry, having high walls, made of adobes, which constitute our inclosures of farming lands. Against this position General Canby did not think prudent to make any demonstration.

During the night, however, the enemy silently left their position, and passed below a mile or two to a ford in the river, where they attempted to cross, but their teams being weak and the river swollen by the spring floods, the whole of their train, consisting of 60 wagons, was left in the river and on the banks, the mules alone having been crossed over to the opposite shore. I am not informed that any of their artillery was either left behind or captured by our forces, with the exception of one piece the day previous, together with seven wagons and the contents.

The latest news from General Canby by Colonel Roberts, who arrived in town this evening, is that our forces were still in pursuit of the enemy, and had taken a position in advance of him at La Joya, 30 miles, where they crossed the river, but on the east side, where the enemy could not pass except under the direct fire of our artillery.

Colonel Paul, with the forces from Colorado, was harassing the enemy in the rear, having crossed the river to the west side. There can be no doubt of the entire capture of the Texans, with all their train of artillery, numbering some eighteen pieces, and this closes the scene of this devastating Texan invasion.

I have the honor to remain, very respectfully, your obedient servant,

HENRY CONNELLY.

[Copy furnished War Department by Secretary of State May 14, 1862.]

HDQRS. CENTRAL, SANTA FÉ, AND NORTH. MIL. DISTS.,
Department of New Mexico, Santa Fé, April 23, 1862.

Brig. Gen. LORENZO THOMAS,
Adjutant-General U. S. Army, Washington, D. C.:

GENERAL: I have the honor to report myself in command of the Central, Santa Fé, and Northern Military Districts, Department of New Mexico, and that I have re-established and garrisoned the posts at Albuquerque and at this place, recently occupied by Confederate troops of General Sibley's brigade.

It will gratify you to know that the Texan troops are in retreat out of the country, having been compelled by our operations to abandon most of their supplies of all kinds, and to take the mountain route behind the Socorro Range, to avoid the capture of the small remaining force of the 3,000 troops that invaded the Territory.

They have abandoned their sick and wounded everywhere on their line of retreat, and are leaving the country in a state of demoralization and suffering that has few examples in any war. The long line of their retreat over Jornada and wastes of country without water, and that furnish no supplies, will render their march extremely difficult, and aggravate the ordinary suffering of a disorganized army under defeat. The broken-down condition of all our animals, the want of cavalry, and deficiencies in all our supplies will make a successful pursuit equally impracticable, if not impossible.

My report of the operations of my division in the field from the 1st to the 16th instant will reach you in time through the proper channel. I effected a junction with Colonel Paul's command at San Antonio on the 13th, after a demonstration on Albuquerque and artillery combats there on the 8th and sharp skirmishing on the 8th and 9th. The last engagement was at Peralta, on the 15th; that drove the main Confederate forces from that position and put their army in utter rout.

We have great numbers of their prisoners, but I am unable to give the figures with accuracy, and some 60 wagons of their supply train and two pieces of artillery have fallen into our hands.

Colonel Canby is on the pursuit with both the Northern and Southern Divisions of the Army, and this information is communicated to you indirectly, because it will be many days before his official reports can be made.   •

According to the most reliable information, General Sibley has not left 1,200 men of the army of 3,000 that appeared before Fort Craig on the 13th of February, and his retreat is the complete annihilation of his remaining forces.

I am, general, very respectfully, your obedient servant,
B. S. ROBERTS,
Colonel, Commanding.

GENERAL ORDERS, }   HDQRS. DEPT. OF NEW MEXICO,
    No. 34.   }   *Fort Craig, N. Mex., April 23, 1862.*

I. Col. G. R. Paul, Fourth New Mexico Volunteers, is assigned to the command of the field force operating in this neighborhood. The cavalry force under command of Capt. R. M. Morris, Third Cavalry, will report to Colonel Paul for duty as soon as possible.

II. The companies of the Seventh Infantry and Claflin's battery will form part of the garrison of this post.

By order of Col. E. R. S. Canby :

WM. J. L. NICODEMUS,
Captain, Twelfth Infantry, Acting Assistant Adjutant-General.

DEPARTMENT OF STATE,
Washington, D. C., April 25, 1862.

Hon. E. M. STANTON, *Secretary of War:*

SIR : I inclose a telegram to this Department from the United States consul at Halifax, announcing a change of the destination of certain British steamers believed to contain contraband of war, from Charleston to Tampico. This change was undoubtedly with the view of transferring their cargoes from Tampico to Matamoros or adjacent points on the coast of Texas.

On several recent occasions I have done myself the honor of suggesting to the Department of War the necessity of occupying Brownsville with a competent military force. The objections to that course at this juncture which have been offered by the Department of War are duly appreciated. Permit me, however, in view of the peculiar position of our boundary on the Rio Grande frontier, the impossibility of blockading the mouth of that river, at least without the consent of Mexico, and consequently the impunity with which arms and munitions of war may be introduced into Texas in that direction, again to urge the importance of posting a military force for the purpose of endeavoring to check such proceedings.

I have the honor to be, sir, your obedient servant,

WILLIAM H. SEWARD.

[Inclosure.]

• HALIFAX, N. S., *April 23,* 1862.

Hon. W. H. SEWARD, *Secretary of State:*

I am advised by consul at Bermuda English steamer Stellia arrived there with cargo destined for Charleston, but has changed destination for Tampico. Will probably be accompanied by steamers Bermuda and Herald.

M. M. JACKSON,
Consul.

KANSAS CITY, *April 28,* 1862.

E. M. STANTON, *Secretary of War:*

Through Santa Fé mail, with dates to 12th, has arrived. Colonel Slough and General Canby formed junction at Gallisteo on 11th. Major Duncan, who was in command of General Canby's advance guard, encountered a large party of Texans and routed them. Major Duncan was slightly wounded. The Texans were 30 miles south of Gallisteo, in full flight from the Territory. General Canby designs giving immediate pursuit. No doubt is entertained of the speedy capture of Sibley's command, as they are entirely destitute of everything.

JAS. ROBERTS.

HEADQUARTERS DEPARTMENT OF THE PACIFIC,
San Francisco, April 30, 1862.

Brig. Gen. LORENZO THOMAS,
Adjutant-General U. S. Army, Washington, D. C. :

GENERAL : Major Drum is still absent inspecting the troops at and
near Fort Yuma. My latest dates from him are of the 14th instant.
It is probable that Colonel Carleton is now at or in advance of Fort
Yuma. Colonel Bowie's Fifth Infantry, California Volunteers, is concentrating at Fort Yuma as a reserve. Carleton's movement will
sweep the predatory bands of Baylor and Reily out of Arizona and
break up their plan of obtaining a foothold in Sonora; and then, with
the well-appointed force under his command, strengthened, if necessary,
by the fine reserve regiment of Bowie, I have no apprehension as to
the result in any conflict with the rebels this side of the Rio Grande.
Outwardly everything is quiet in this country, but I know that there
are many men on this coast who are traitors at heart, and who are at
this moment writhing under the defeats of the rebels. They are harmless now, because so greatly in the minority; but such men require close
surveillance. In the southern portion of this State there are more
sympathizers with the rebels than anywhere else, and I have now
ordered Colonel Forman, of the Fourth Infantry, California Volunteers,
now in camp at Sacramento, to proceed by the next steamer to San
Pedro with his headquarters and three companies. The colonel will
take post at Camp Latham, near Los Angeles, where we have already
four companies of the Second Cavalry.

It has been my aim not to create any unnecessary alarm in the public
mind on this coast, but to watch closely the progress of events, and be
ever ready to crush any attempt to raise the standard of rebellion on
the Pacific. You will observe, by my General Orders, No. 17, that I
am gradually drawing the cords a little closer around treason.

Very respectfully, your obedient servant,

G. WRIGHT,
Brigadier-General, U. S. Army, Commanding.

•

———

HEADQUARTERS, U. S. MIL. DEPT. OF THE PACIFIC,
San Francisco, Cal., May 3, 1862.

His Excellency Señor DON IGNACIO PESQUIERA,
Governor of the State of Sonora :

SIR: By the last steamer from the Gulf of California I received a
copy of a communication addressed to Your Excellency, under date of
December 16, 1861, by H. H. Sibley,* the rebel chief in command of a
body of insurgents in New Mexico; and although I did not receive a
copy of Your Excellency's reply, yet I was much gratified by the assurances of my correspondent that Your Excellency had declined entering
into any arrangements proposed by the rebel commander. Considering
the friendly relations subsisting between the Government of the United
States and that of the Republic of Mexico, as well as between the
citizens of the contiguous States of Sonora and California, any other
decision than that which Your Excellency has made would have been
deeply regretted.

———

* Not found. Sibley's reports of his communications with the Governors of Chihuahua
and Sonora are printed in Series I, Vol. IV, pp. 167, 174.

I need not point out to Your Excellency the utter ruin and devastation which would inevitably befall the beautiful State of Sonora should the rebel forces obtain a foothold within its limits, as in that event it would be indispensably necessary that the frontier should be passed by the United States forces and our enemies pursued possibly to the city of Guaymas.

I beg Your Excellency to rest assured that under no circumstances will the Government of the United States permit the rebel horde to take refuge in Sonora. I have an army of 10,000 men ready to pass the frontier and protect your government and people.

With the greatest respect, I have the honor to be, Your Excellency's most obedient servant,

G. WRIGHT,
Brigadier-General, U. S. Army, Comdg. Dept. of the Pacific.

HEADQUARTERS DEPARTMENT OF NEW MEXICO,
Santa Fé, N. Mex., May 4, 1862.
The ADJUTANT-GENERAL OF THE ARMY,
Washington, D. C.:

SIR: I have the honor to report that I left Fort Craig on the 27th ultimo, and reached this place last night, making arrangements on the road to facilitate the transmission of supplies to the troops in the South. The Confederate force, in rapid retreat, had taken the route by the Renesco through a mountainous and difficult country exceedingly destitute of water. They will probably reach the Rio Grande in the neighborhood of Santa Barbara, where Colonel Steele would probably meet them with supplies. . Scouts and prisoners report this force as greatly demoralized, and that they have abandoned everything that could impede their flight. The sick and wounded have been left by the wayside, without care and often without food. Many of them have been collected and are properly cared for, and arrangements have been made to bring in the others and secure any valuable property that has been abandoned by the enemy.

I shall accumulate as rapidly as possible at Fort Craig and at Peralta the supplies that are necessary for a movement below the former place. This will occupy some time, as with our extremely limited means and the length of the line it is very difficult to meet the current wants of the troops.

Very respectfully, sir, your obedient servant,
ED. R. S. CANBY,
Colonel Nineteenth Infantry, Commanding Department.

HEADQUARTERS DEPARTMENT OF NEW MEXICO,
Santa Fé, N. Mex., May 4, 1862.
ADJUTANT-GENERAL OF THE ARMY, *Washington, D. C.:*

SIR: I have learned through the newspapers that five regiments of volunteers have been ordered from the East to this Territory. If this force is intended only for the defense of New Mexico and the reoccupation of Arizona, the whole of it will not in my judgment be necessary. Two regiments, in addition to the troops now here, will, I think, be amply sufficient, if at the same time arrangements are made to secure our communication with the East by arming and garrisoning strongly the posts between Fort Union and Fort Riley.

The difficulty of procuring supplies of all kinds in this country makes it important that no greater force should be sent here than is absolutely necessary. No operations can be carried on with advantage from New Mexico against any part of the South, as all the supplies for such operations must be brought from the East, as no reliance can be placed upon the resources of this country, Arizona, or Chihuahua.

I have the honor to be, very respectfully, sir, your obedient servant,

ED. R. S. CANBY,
Colonel Nineteenth Infantry, Commanding Department.

SAINT LOUIS, MO., *May 9, 1862.*

General LORENZO THOMAS,
 Adjutant-General U. S. Army:

General Halleck telegraphs me he can give no orders in reference to the troops for New Mexico.

I reiterate my recommendation that not more than 500 infantry, 500 cavalry, and two batteries of light artillery be sent. All their subsistence will have to go from the Missouri River.

JAS. L. DONALDSON.

WAR DEPARTMENT, *May 10, 1862.*

Hon. E. M. STANTON,
 Secretary of War, Fort Monroe:

The following telegram, received by General Meigs from quartermaster at Saint Louis, namely:

Colonel Donaldson decidedly of opinion 1,000 men and two batteries ample force to send to New Mexico. General Canby's force now superior to enemy. If original order* carried out expedition will cost probably $10,000,000, three-quarters of which can be saved by reducing expedition to needed force.

Watts, Delegate from New Mexico, Colonel Donaldson, and General Meigs all think force should be reduced, to save expense and expedite its leaving. Have you any orders to give?†

P. H. WATSON,
Assistant Secretary of War.

HEADQUARTERS DEPARTMENT OF NEW MEXICO,
Santa Fé, N. Mex., May 10, 1862.

The ADJUTANT-GENERAL OF THE ARMY,
 Washington, D. C.:

SIR: I have the honor to report that the Confederate troops, after passing the Nugales, broke up into small parties, and reached the river from the mountains at different points between Cañada Alamosa and Santa Barbara (Old Fort Thorn). They made no stay at this place, but continued their retreat, and crossed the river at San Diego, near

---

* Of April 23, for six regiments.
† No record of the Secretary's orders found. The only re-enforcements sent to New Mexico in this and the following month was one battery of light artillery (Ninth Wisconsin) from Fort Leavenworth, Kans.

Doña Aña. The Rio Grande is unusually high, and has added greatly to our embarrassments in supplying the troops at Fort Craig. I hope, however, to accumulate a sufficient quantity of supplies at that place to enable me to resume active operations by the 1st of next month. Two companies of mounted Colorado Volunteers reached Fort Union on the 8th instant. I am now making arrangements to reduce and consolidate the New Mexican Volunteers, and expect, by the discharge of incompetent officers and inefficient men, to have one serviceable regiment.

Very respectfully, sir, your obedient servant,

ED. R. S. CANBY,
Colonel Nineteenth Infantry, Commanding Department.

HEADQUARTERS DEPARTMENT OF NEW MEXICO,
Santa Fé, N. Mex., May 12, 1862.
The ADJUTANT-GENERAL OF THE ARMY,
Washington, D. C.:

SIR: I have the honor to report that before the receipt of the regulations published in General Orders, No. —, I had given instructions to parole and send out of the country as soon as possible all the prisoners of the Confederate Army who had been or should be taken in this department.

The two reasons that influenced me in giving these instructions were:

First. The difficulty of supplying our own troops with provisions. The troops at the most distant stations have for some time past been and are now upon reduced rations—12 ounces of flour—and this cannot be materially increased until additional means of transportation are received.

Second. My inability to furnish guards, if they are held as absolute prisoners.

Under these instructions 240 have already been sent out of the country and about 240 remain. Of these last two-thirds are sick or wounded men and their attendants.

Before leaving Fort Craig for this place an officer was sent to propose an exchange of the officers and men (about 30) of this command who were taken prisoners, but he returned without effecting his object, having been unable to overtake the Confederate troops.

There are still many stragglers and deserters and abandoned men in different parts of the country who are now being collected, and will probably make the whole number of prisoners about 500.

The consolidated return will be forwarded as soon as the correct reports are received.

Very respectfully, your obedient servant,

ED. R. S. CANBY,
Brigadier-General, Commanding Department.

POLVADERA, N. MEX., *May* 14, 1862.
Colonel PAUL, *Commanding:*

SIR: Last night I reached here from Salada. On the 8th I reached Nugales Spring. From there the road ran between the hills for about 15 miles, then took toward the Magdalene Mountain, where they found water, distance from Nugales about 29 miles; road very rough. On the road they deserted one wagon and a camp and left three dead bodies half buried. In another place found bones of a man's arm, half eaten by wolves. I had all buried. From there the road took to Feather Springs. I called it so on account of feather-beds being strewed around; distance from Dead Man's Spring 17 miles. They encamped there. From there they took the road to Ojo del Pueblo, distance 15 miles; road very rough. Here they blew up a caisson, burned three wagons, hospital department, medicines, &c.; left a few shell and round shot. From there they took to the Salada, distance from Ojo del Pueblo about 30 miles; road very rough. On this road, near and at Salada, they blew up and burned six caissons, one 12-pounder howitzer, and two mountain-howitzer carriages. I found out where they had buried some 40 shell, loaded, in one place, and 38 in another; 78 in all. I took them up and hid them in another place. To-morrow the quartermaster from here sends for them. They burned up about 19 wagons, 10 ambulances, 6 caissons, and 3 carriages. I think they left 3 howitzers, one 12-pounder and two mountain. I had with me a man who came with them, who saw them leave the howitzers. I believe the Mexicans have the large one buried, and by offering a reward we could find out. They destroyed six 100-pound barrels of powder at Salada and a great deal of camp equipage. The road from Ojo del Pueblo is strewn with old harness, iron ovens, and in fact everything but small ammunition. It seems they destroyed very little, if any, of that. It appears that the Mexicans have carried off a great deal. There is nothing worth sending for in the shape of ammunition except the shell. The distance from Nugales to Rio Puerco is about 109 miles; road very bad. Sibley's command made it in five days. Left dead on the road about 60 or 70 mules and horses. Inclosed I send a letter* I found about hiring the wagons.

I am, sir, very respectfully, your obedient servant,

JAS. GRAYDON,
Captain, New Mexico Mounted Volunteers.

EXECUTIVE DEPARTMENT,
Santa Fé, May 17, 1862.

Hon. W. H. SEWARD,
Secretary of State, Washington City:

SIR: A few days since I returned from a visit to my place of residence near Peralta, and 90 miles from this city. The visit was made to see in what state the Texans had left my house and its contents. I am sorry to say that all I had heretofore been informed of as to the wanton destruction of property proved to be true.

They remained in entire possession for near forty-eight hours; all of which time was devoted to the destruction of everything of value about the premises. The same would have happened no doubt to my neighbors of Peralta had it not been for the timely arrival of General Canby, who gave them no time for further depredations upon private property.

My loss has been very heavy, not less than $30,000, and much of this through a pure vandalic spirit. There was much about the house

---

* Not found.

of goods and furniture that they could put to no useful purposes, yet all was taken or wantonly destroyed.

The last thing heard of the Texans they had arrived with about one-half of their original number, in a perfectly disorganized condition, at the Mesilla, on the west side of the river, where they hurriedly crossed it and continued their flight without delay to El Paso, driving before them every quadruped that was upon the borders of the river or in the possession of the inhabitants of that valley. That they have suffered intensely by thirst, starvation, and fatigue we have every evidence by those who voluntarily came into Fort Craig seeking succor, and by one or more contrabands who have returned from Mesilla, after having accompanied them that far. This is the second invasion our Territory has suffered from Texans, both of which have proved equally disastrous, and it is to be hoped we will never witness another.

I have the honor to remain, sir, very respectfully, your obedient servant,

HENRY CONNELLY,
Governor of New Mexico.

[Copy furnished War Department by Secretary of State June 9, 1862.]

HEADQUARTERS DEPARTMENT OF NEW MEXICO,
Santa Fé, N. Mex., May 18, 1862.

The ADJUTANT-GENERAL OF THE ARMY,
Washington, D. C.:

SIR: I have the honor to state that since my report of the 10th instant no material changes in the state of affairs in this department have occurred. The Confederate troops are scattered along the Rio Grande from Doña Aña to El Paso, Colonel Steele with 500 men (the re-enforcements that attempted to reach General Sibley about the 20th of March) occupying their most advanced position. They reached the Mesilla with six guns and seven wagons. The remainder of their guns and wagons and the caissons of all their guns were abandoned or destroyed. The command sent out for the purpose of collecting them has not yet returned. The Confederate troops in the Mesilla are now collecting the means necessary to enable them to leave the country, and many of the citizens who had embraced their cause are preparing to leave with them. I have succeeded with some difficulty in getting to Fort Craig a sufficient quantity of subsistence to prevent any suffering among the troops now there, and hope to accumulate within the next twenty days sufficient to warrant a movement below.

Very respectfully, sir, your obedient servant,

ED. R. S. CANBY,
Colonel 19th Inft., and Brig. Gen. Vols., Comdg. Dept.

DEPARTMENT OF STATE,
Washington, May 24, 1862.

Hon. E. M. STANTON, *Secretary of War:*

SIR: I have the honor to inclose for your information an extract

from a dispatch received at this Department on the 23d instant from
Leonard Pierce, jr., United States consul at Matamoros, Mexico.

I have the honor to be, sir, your obedient servant,

WILLIAM H. SEWARD.

[Inclosure.]

CONSULATE OF THE UNITED STATES OF AMERICA,
Matamoros, March 1, 1862.

Hon. W. H. SEWARD,
Secretary of State, Washington, D. C.:

SIR: * * * It has been with the greatest difficulty that I have
established myself here, as the Confederates had used every possible
exertion to get me driven out, and succeeded so far that none of the
authorities, with the exception of the commanding general, would acknowledge my right until after the receipt of my exequatur. When I
say the Confederates, I mean the military; most of the citizens of
Brownsville being really Union men. The prefect (Martin Lougona,
who was among the slain in the final assault), a man unknown to me
personally, endeavored in every possible manner to show his authority,
and went so far as to enter my room with ten armed men to search (as
he said) for gunpowder. Although he would not acknowledge my
right as consul until the arrival of my exequatur, still he had seen my
passport and appointment, and knew that the general-in-chief had
recognized me and had also given me permission to hoist my flag, which
was flying over my house at the time.

The Confederates occupy both the Texan and Mexican side of the
Rio Grande at its mouth, and use every exertion to prevent me from
communicating with the U. S. ship Portsmouth.

The general commanding here, with most of his officers, are much
against the people of the South, and, in fact, are all the better class of
Mexicans. The general has said to me that he will endeavor to protect
his side of the river, in which case I can then communicate freely.
There are now in port fourteen vessels, among them one American
only, from New York. As the only lighters here bear the rebel flag,
they were unable to unload them while the ship of war may lay there,
but the merchants have now purchased three steamboats and put them
under the Mexican flag. The difficulty is obviated.

Matamoros is now the great thoroughfare to the Southern States.
They pass their coffee, flour, and in fact all the supplies they receive
through here. They have also a large pile of cotton on the east bank
of the river, to take out when an opportunity offers, or, as they say,
burn, in case of an invasion.

There are at Brownsville and Brazos Santiago about 1,200 men,
among them some German companies, whose loyalty to the Southern
Confederacy is much doubted in Texas.

*   *   *   *   *   *   *

There are many of the citizens of Texas leaving since the Governor's
proclamation calling out the militia, and some that have been prisoners
and escaped; nearly all without friends or means to take them North.

I am, sir, very respectfully, your most obedient,

L. PIERCE, JR.,
Consul.

DEPARTMENT OF STATE, *Washington, June* 5, 1862.

Hon. E. M. STANTON, *Secretary of War:*

SIR : I have the honor to submit for your perusal the inclosed original note, with annexed translation, dated the 2d instant, from Señor Romero, chargé d'affaires of Mexico, in relation to the incursions committed by the insurgents of Texas upon the Territory and citizens of Mexico.

I will be very glad to know that the disposition of our forces will enable you to give assurances that such aggressive acts will hereafter be prevented.

Requesting the return of the inclosures, I have the honor to be, sir, your obedient servant,

WILLIAM H. SEWARD.

[Inclosure No. 1.—Translation.]

MEXICAN LEGATION IN THE UNITED STATES OF AMERICA,
Washington, June 2, 1862.

Hon. W. H. SEWARD, *Secretary of State:*

Mr. SECRETARY : The Mexican citizen Juan Bustamente, a deputy from the State of San Luis Potosi to the General Congress of Mexico, and who is now in this capital, to which he has come on personal affairs, informed me upon his arrival here of the unsatisfactory state of things at present upon the eastern frontier of Mexico and the United States, and of the assaults which, in violation of treaties and the rights of sovereignty of Mexico, the insurgents of Texas have made upon the Mexican territory.

I requested him to communicate to me in writing this information, and I have to-day received the communication of which I have the honor to transmit you a copy for the information of the Government of the United States.

Through other channels I had received notice of the incursions made by the insurgent Texans against the defenseless towns of Mexico, and I had abstained from communicating them to you owing to the want of official data confirming them. The situation of the frontier is represented in general to be very dangerous to Mexico. The dissenters of the South maintain considerable bodies of armed men upon the frontiers of Chihuahua and Sonora, and it appears that they desire to make common cause with the traitors of Mexico, which will cause great injuries both to the Government of that Republic and to the United States. I deem it, therefore, my duty to call your attention to this subject, requesting of you that the Government of the United States may take the proper measures to prevent armed bodies from passing over to its territory with a view of invading a friendly republic.

I shall take great pleasure in transmitting to my Government the assurances which you may be enabled to give me upon this matter.

I avail myself of this opportunity to renew to you, sir, the assurances of my distinguished consideration.

M. ROMERO.

[Inclosure No. 2.—Translation.]

WASHINGTON, *May* 31, 1862.

To the Citizen Licentiate M. ROMERO,
Chargé d'Affaires of the Mexican Republic in Washington, present:

SIR : I avail myself of my arrival in this capital to address you the present, with the view of bringing to your knowledge that, in April last past, the people of Piedras Negras were assaulted by a party of Texans, numbering some 200, who robbed and set fire to said town. This outrage will not be the last one, since the Texans are badly disposed toward the Mexicans in consequence of our government not having received the representative which the insurgents of the South sent.

This circumstance and the facilities which the former have for invading our territory will cause these incursions to be repeated if the Government of this Republic does not send a respectable force to prevent not only robberies but also the Texans from giving some aid to the retrograde faction of Mexico, who has offered them to recognize the independence of the Southern States. This is sufficient for believing that the Texans referred to will assist them as far as they can in overthrowing the government, which, by the vote of the nation, to-day governs our destinies.

From what I have stated you will perceive that it is most important to remedy such serious evils, and I have no doubt that, as the representative of Mexico in this Republic, you will do all in your power that this Government may determine upon what is necessary to prevent the Texans from carrying on hostilities, by making an agreement to that effect with the clerical faction.

Upon addressing you the present it gives me pleasure to tender you my respect and consideration.

Liberty and reform.

JUAN BUSTAMENTE.

WASHINGTON, June 3, 1862.

This is a copy.

ROMERO.

HEADQUARTERS DEPARTMENT OF NEW MEXICO,
Santa Fé, N. Mex., June 21, 1862.

The ADJUTANT-GENERAL U. S. ARMY,
Washington, D. C.:

SIR: The inclosed report from Colonel Chivington, commanding the Southern Military District, of the 11th instant, and note from El Paso, old Mexico, of the 10th instant, give the last information from Arizona. This last comes from a gentleman who has heretofore furnished very reliable information, and gives, I believe, a nearer approximation to the actual facts than any of the previous reports.

My letters to Colonel Chivington, of the 16th, 18th, and 20th instant, copies of which are inclosed, indicate the operations proposed in the direction of Arizona. Delay in the arrival of necessary supplies, the unexampled flood in the Rio Grande, which has flooded the valley and destroyed the roads, and the inertness and inefficiency of the flour contractors, have deferred these movements much beyond the time when I expected to commence them, but I believe that I will in a few days have the control of means that will enable me to carry them on without interruption. Heretofore it has been impossible to accumulate a supply of flour at Fort Craig beyond what was required for daily consumption, and it was with great difficulty that a supply to that extent could be kept up.

The movement directed in my instructions of the 20th instant will be a few days in advance of full supplies for the force at Fort Craig, but it is necessary in consequence of the unexpected contingency of the approach of troops from California, which may require support, and it will be followed up as rapidly as possible.

I do not propose to occupy the interior posts in Arizona until after the arrival of the troops that are expected from Colorado Territory and Kansas, but will establish the main body of the force to be sent into that Territory in a strong position in the neighborhood of El Paso, and will not weaken it by detachments until affairs in this Territory have assumed a more settled shape.

A change in the manner of supplying posts that may be established in Arizona west of the Rio Grande is suggested, adopting for all the posts west of that river the route by the Gulf of California and the post of Guaymas for a'l supplies that cannot be procured in the country.

In this Territory there has been no material change since my report by the last mail. About one-half (521) of the deserters from New Mexican Volunteers have availed themselves of the conditional pardon offered them in Department General Orders, No. 43, of May 7. The remainder are still at large, and are giving much trouble to the frontier settlements.

Very respectfully, sir, your obedient servant,
ED. R. S. CANBY,
Colonel Nineteenth Infantry, Brig. Gen. Vols., Comdg. Dept.

[Inclosure No. 1.]

HEADQUARTERS SOUTHERN MILITARY DISTRICT,
Fort Craig, N. Mex., June 11, 1862.
Brig. Gen. E. R. S. CANBY, U. S. A.,
Commanding Department New Mexico, Santa Fé, N. Mex.:

GENERAL: I have the honor to state that five men arrived here yesterday from the Pino Alto mines in Arizona, and fully confirmed what the two Mexicans last week reported about the California forces and the movements below. They saw the California captain at the mines before Hunter took him over to Mesilla. They say that Colonel Baylor has been appointed Governor of Arizona, and his first act was to publish Jefferson Davis' conscription proclamation, and they are impressing all white men in Arizona into their service; also all in the Mesilla Valley. Those men all fled to keep from being forced to fight against the Government. The Arizona Guards, who were raised for the protection of the settlements against the Indians, and who are more than half Northern and Union men, are pressed into the Confederate service. Colonel Reily had been to Sonora, and reports that he had made a favorable treaty with the authorities there. But one of these men is just up from Sonora, and he asserts that they only obtained the privilege of buying for cash anything the citizens had to dispose of, and that they will not touch the Confederate scrip. The name of the California captain who was captured by Hunter is McCleave. His company is independent or unattached, and used exclusively for picket and scouting purposes, named "California Mounted Grays." When he was taken several of Hunter's men were taken by his company. The names of these men from whom this information is obtained are James S. Chase, James Cranston, John McLaughlin, A. J. King, and Patrick Connell, and one of them has been a soldier, and has his discharge with him.

I am, general, with much respect, your obedient servant,
J. M. CHIVINGTON,
Col. First Colorado Vols., Comdg. Southern Mil. Dist., N. Mex.

[Inclosure No. 2.]

The skeleton of Sibley's brigade, consisting of 1,250 men, returned from New Mexico to Doña Aña on or about the 3d of May. General Sibley made his headquarters at Fort Bliss; Colonel Green and Colonel —— [probably Reily] at Fort Fillmore. Colonel [Lieutenant-Colonel] Scurry is now in San Antonio. Major Pyron left Fort Franklin [Bliss] with his command about twenty days ago. Since then parties of 15 and 20 men of infantry companies have been leaving and are now on the road to San Antonio. Those that were left of the Second Regiment have been leaving on the road to San Antonio. Most of their artillery has passed San Elizario on the way down. General Sibley was ready to move this morning. Colonel Steele, it is said, will remain until further orders. He is at Doña Aña. He has between 300 and 400 men. Colonel Herbert, with two or three companies, remains, also under Colonel Steele; but it is believed that these movements are to cover their retreat.

The Second Regiment (Green's) is scattered in parties of 15 or 20 along the road between Doña Aña and Franklin, committing outrages upon the inhabitants they meet upon the highway. They are almost on the point of starvation, receiving as a ration one pound and a quarter of beef and twelve ounces of flour. The Mexican population are much enraged against them on account of their rude treatment. There are no provisions to be bought in this valley, for they are not to be had. Sibley has pressed all the spare provisions on the American side of the river, and has given orders to take all the necessary transportation and provisions from the villages below. No army can subsist in this valley this year unless they bring the necessary supplies along, for there is no supply, not even of live stock, and there will be a scanty wheat crop to say the best of it. It is believed here that there will be a famine among the people at Mesilla, Las Cruces, Doña Aña, and Picacho.

*The Confederate money (paper) is selling at 20 cents on the dollar, and large amounts could be bought for less if there were any purchasers. Captain Hunter's company has returned from Tucson. They report a large Federal force near that place when they left.

[Indorsement.]

This information is furnished by a merchant of El Paso, old Mexico, and sent to the commanding officer at Fort Craig.

ED. R. S. CANBY,
Brigadier-General Volunteers, Commanding Department.

[Inclosure No. 3.]

HEADQUARTERS DEPARTMENT OF NEW MEXICO,
Santa Fé, N. Mex., June 16, 1862.
Col. J. M. CHIVINGTON,
    1st Colo. Vols., Comdg. Southern Mil. Dist., Fort Craig, N. Mex.:

COLONEL: Your communication of the 11th has been received. The information is certainly very circumstantial, and seems probable, but I cannot think that any large force would have been sent from California without being advised of it. It is more probable it is a detachment from the force at Fort Yuma, sent to Tucson for the purpose of acquiring information. The Mesilla produces but little beyond what is required for its own population, and it is certain that there is no surplus at this time. It is necessary, therefore, that we should have supplies for at least forty days after reaching the valley, as it will take that time to get there from Chihuahua (or that we should have sufficient means of transportation to keep up the supply from this country) or Sonora.

I expected confidently to have been prepared in this respect by the 1st of this month, but the inefficiency of the contractors, the destitution of the country, and the flooding of the river have all concurred to delay this; but I hope that these difficulties will be overcome in a few days, and I wish your command to be kept in readiness to move the moment that the state of the supplies will permit it. I do not anticipate any future difficulties, as abundant supplies from the East are near at hand, and with them are considerable means of transportation that will be available for our operations.

Very respectfully, sir, your obedient servant,

ED. R. S. CANBY,
Brigadier-General, Commanding Department.

[Inclosure No. 4.]

HEADQUARTERS DEPARTMENT OF NEW MEXICO,
Santa Fé, N. Mex., June 18, 1862.

Col. J. M. CHIVINGTON,
1st Colo. Vols., Comdg. Southern Mil. Dist., Fort Craig, N. Mex.:

COLONEL: The force intended for the movement against the Confederate troops in Arizona will be composed of the sixteen companies of infantry and eight companies of cavalry and one or two batteries. These troops will be organized into two or three columns, as may be considered most expedient by the immediate commander. The headquarters and eight companies of the Fifth Infantry will form one, and the headquarters and eight companies of the First Colorado Volunteers the other infantry column. The cavalry force will be composed of two companies of the First, three companies of the Third Cavalry, one company of the First Colorado and two companies of the Second Colorado Volunteers. The cavalry force now at Fort Union will be sent down as soon as the troops from Kansas are in striking distance of that post. If it arrives in season the battery attached to the Second Colorado Volunteers will form one of the batteries, and it is intended to replace the pieces in McRae's battery by four 12-pounder guns and two 32-pounder howitzers, now on their way to this country; but as these pieces may not arrive as early as they are expected, the present battery should be put in the most perfect condition for the field that is possible, so that there may be no delay in the movement after the supplies have been received.

The garrison of Fort Craig will be composed of four companies of infantry and two of cavalry. Two companies of infantry and two of cavalry will be posted temporarily at Santa Barbara, to give additional security to the communication between Fort Craig and the Mesilla. These garrisons will be in addition to the field force designated above.

Mule transportation for the baggage train has been ordered and is being prepared as rapidly as possible. Clothing is expected at Fort Union from the East in three or four days, and will be sent down at once. Corn for the cavalry and artillery horses is being sent as rapidly as possible.

A section of mountain howitzers to move with the cavalry should also be prepared. Some pack saddles for the use of detachments that move rapidly, or when wagons cannot be taken, will be necessary.

Very respectfully, sir, your obedient servant,

ED. R. S. CANBY,
Brigadier-General, Commanding Department.

[Inclosure No. 5.]

HEADQUARTERS DEPARTMENT OF NEW MEXICO,
Santa Fé, N. Mex., June 20, 1862.

Col. J. M. CHIVINGTON,
1st Colo. Vols., Comdg. Southern Mil. Dist., Fort Craig, N. Mex.:

SIR: I have received a telegraphic dispatch from Captain Nicodemus, to the effect that Colonel Carleton, with 500 California Volunteers, was on this side of the Pima Villages on the 7th of May, moving in the direction of the Mesilla Valley. I wish you to advance a portion of your command, say 1,000 men, if you have the means of moving and supplying that number, in the direction of Santa Barbara, open a communication with Colonel Carleton, if possible, and hold yourself in readiness to support him if he should be advancing on this side of Tucson. Unless it should be absolutely necessary, in order to support Colonel Carleton, I do not wish the command moved into the Mesilla Valley until I have the means of subsisting them there. This will be arranged in a few days, and in the mean time the force at Fort Craig must be held in readiness to move at any moment and at any sacrifice, if it should be necessary.

Very respectfully, sir, your obedient servant,

ED. R. S. CANBY,
Brigadier-General, Commanding Department.

———

HEADQUARTERS DEPARTMENT OF NEW MEXICO,
Santa Fé, N. Mex., June 27, 1862.

Col. J. M. CHIVINGTON,
Comdg. Southern Military District, Fort Craig, N. Mex.:

SIR: The general object of the expedition to Arizona is the re-occupation of that country and the restoration of the authority of the United States in and over it. In carrying out these instructions I wish to leave you as untrammeled as possible by special instructions, and shall indicate in general terms the particular objects to be accomplished, leaving the details of execution to your own judgment and discretion.

The force that will be under your command has already been indicated in my instructions of the 18th. It is probable that the cavalry may be somewhat reduced by the non-arrival of troops that were expected. This force will be kept as mobile and complete as possible. No other baggage than is necessary for the comfort and efficiency of the troops will be taken. No incumbrances, as laundresses or other persons not immediately necessary for the service, will be permitted to move with the troops. Many persons will no doubt attempt to go with the command, but all persons not directly connected with the Army by enlistment or employment will be vigorously excluded. The only exception will be in the case of civil officers going to their duties in that Territory or contractors and their necessary employés. If the condition of the road or other circumstances of the route should render it necessary to subdivide your command, the columns should always be kept within supporting distance, and no operations should be undertaken that are foreign to the main object of the expedition, and until that is accomplished everything else will be subordinate.

Immediate operations against the enemy must be governed by circumstances and your own judgment.

As soon as possession of the country is secured the main body of your command will be established in eligible position for defense, for supplies, and for facility of movement in any direction. It will be made your depot of supplies, and strengthened so as to be held by a small force when your main body is engaged in active operations.

Doña Aña, or that neighborhood, is suggested as suitable for that purpose, as it commands the road leading into Arizona and the approach to the country from crossing of the Pecos. The position to be selected should be strengthened so as to be held by a small force whenever the main body of the force is in the field, and should be made the depot for your supplies.

It will be your duty to secure the inhabitants of the Territory in their civil rights, and to protect them in their persons and property as far as the means in your power will permit. They will also be secured as far as possible from the aggression of hostile Indians, but any operations undertaken for this purpose will of course be subordinate to the main object of the expedition. If there should be no civil authorities in the Territory the administration of civil affairs, so far as may be necessary to prevent anarchy and confusion, will devolve upon the military authorities, employing as subordinate the civil functionaries authorized by the laws of the United States. Collectors of customs, &c., will be provisionally appointed by the commander of the district, subject to the approval of the department commander; the territorial officers by election, in accordance with the laws of the Territory, commissioned by the Governor, unless in the mean time a separate Territorial government is organized for Arizona, care being taken that no one is allowed to enter upon the discharge of their functions whose loyalty is at all questioned. If it can be procured, a copy of the Territorial laws will be sent to you.

The question of supplies for your command will be one of great importance and difficulty; they should be drawn as far as practicable from Arizona or the neighboring Mexican States of Chihuahua and Sonora. After the necessary arrangements have been made these will no doubt supply you with fresh meat and breadstuffs, bacon, &c., for subsistence, and forage for the animals, and you will at once send agents into the neighborhood from which these supplies can be procured for the purpose of making these arrangements. Until these are definitely fixed your requisitions will be made upon the depot at Fort Craig.

It is apprehended that many disloyal and lawless individuals will be found in Arizona, both in the native and foreign population. These should be vigorously dealt with. The provisions of martial law, as promulgated in General Orders, No. 53, of October 20, 1861, furnishes the necessary power for controlling this part of the population. This order, modified in some particular, will be republished, and furnished you for distribution.

The country south of Santa Barbara will constitute the District of Arizona, to be commanded by the senior officer of the troops serving there.

Very respectfully, your obedient servant,

ED. R. S. CANBY,
Brigadier-General, Commanding Department.

HEADQUARTERS DEPARTMENT OF NEW MEXICO,
Santa Fé, N. Mex., July 6, 1862.

The ADJUTANT-GENERAL OF THE ARMY,
Washington, D. C.:

SIR: I have the honor to report that the party sent for the purpose of opening a communication with General Carleton's command met his advance (130 cavalry) at the Ojo de la Vaca, 140 miles southwest of Fort Craig. This command and the advance forces of that post will meet at Santa Barbara to-day.

General Carleton was at Tucson on the 17th ultimo, with ten companies of infantry, five of cavalry, and one field battery of four pieces. In addition to this, some companies of infantry and one of cavalry are posted at different points (not mentioned in the report) in Arizona.

The force designed for the reoccupation of Arizona, and assembled at Fort Craig, consists of about 2,000 men, but upon information arriving from the commander of the Department of Kansas of the movement of a rebel force against Fort Wise and the supply trains coming to this country I have diverted a part of this force for the purpose of re-enforcing Fort Wise and guarding the supply trains reported to be coming out by the Cimarron route.

The squadron of Kansas cavalry which came to this country as the escort of the paymaster will halt at Fort Wise and report by letter to the commander of the Department of Kansas. The squadron of Colorado cavalry which was on the road to Fort Craig has been ordered back to Fort Union for duty on the Cimarron route. I have requested General Blunt to issue the order given by General Hunter, at my request, directing all trains to come by the way of Fort Wise, as this division of the trains multiplies the chances of loss, doubles the duty of guarding them, and weakens the command by detachments that would not be necessary if only one route is used.

Very respectfully, your obedient servant,
ED. R. S. CANBY,
Brigadier-General, Commanding Department.

HEADQUARTERS DEPARTMENT OF NEW MEXICO,
Santa Fé, N. Mex., July 9, 1862.

Brig. Gen. JAMES H. CARLETON,
Commanding District of Arizona:

GENERAL: The reported movements of the rebel force threatening our communications with the East and the supply trains *en route* to this country has rendered it necessary to divert a portion of the command heretofore designated for operations in Arizona.

A part of the force at Fort Craig has accordingly been ordered to Fort Union for service on the plains, and another part will be held in reserve at Fort Craig to meet further contingencies, reducing the strength of the command that will report to you for duty in Arizona to about 1,000 men. This, with the part of your command not required for duty in the interior of Arizona, will, I have no doubt, be amply sufficient for the purposes intended in the instructions heretofore given, and of which copies have been furnished you.

In consequence of the scarcity of water in the direct route from Cook's Spring to Mesilla, I have supposed the most eligible point for the junction of the two commands would be on the Rio Grande, at or near Santa

Barbara. The commander of the sub-military district was accordingly instructed to advance 1,000 men to that point for the purpose of opening a communication with you and supporting your movements, if the scarcity of water on the route should render it necessary, as is probable at this season, to move your command by mule detachments.

If you should consider it expedient that the junction should be made at any other point you will give the necessary order to the commander of the troops in the neighborhood of Santa Barbara, without waiting for them to come within the limits of your district.

Until the reoccupation of the country and the restoration of order are secured your headquarters and main body of your command will be kept in the neighborhood of the Mesilla Valley.

The force that is ordered to report to you will be deficient in artillery and cavalry horses. Every deficiency I hope to remedy soon. Two heavy field batteries (12-pounder guns and 32-pounder howitzers), completely equipped, are now on the way out, and one of them will be sent down as soon as it arrives. Eight hundred cavalry and artillery horses are also on the road, and a sufficient number to mount the cavalry to complete the equipment of the cavalry batteries will be sent to you as soon as possible.

The staff department are throwing forward to Fort Craig additional supplies to meet the positive wants of your command. The order now in force requires 200,000 rations in depot of subsistence; and, in addition to this, a daily issue of 5,000 rations at and below Fort Craig is provided for, to meet unexpected contingencies. One hundred thousand rations will be in depot at Peralta, and other supplies in the same proportion will be sent down as fast as they are received from the East or can be procured from this country.

I have received no information as yet as to the state of your supplies the sources from which they are drawn, and the arrangements made for procuring them. Please advise me in this respect as soon as possible, in order that the arrangements for supplying your command may be completed as soon as possible.

The chief paymaster has estimated prospectively for funds for the payment of your command, but if there are any arrearages which have not been provided for, you will cause the estimates (if you have a paymaster with your column) or the data for preparing them to be forwarded as soon as practicable.

It is hoped that arrangements will be made by which the greater part of the subsistence and the forage required for your troops can be supplied from that country and the neighboring State of Mexico, but the necessity of depending for some time upon the depot at Fort Craig is anticipated and will be provided for.

Very respectfully, your obedient servant,

ED. R. S. CANBY,
Colonel Nineteenth Infantry, Brigadier-General.

HEADQUARTERS DEPARTMENT OF THE PACIFIC,
San Francisco, July 10, 1862.

Brig. Gen. LORENZO THOMAS,
Adjutant-General U. S. Army, Washington, D. C.:

GENERAL: My latest dates from the Department of Oregon are to July 1, when all was quiet. My latest dates from General Carleton are of June 18, which I inclosed yesterday to you, with certain other papers.

The expedition has thus far been a perfect success. Our army, with all its supplies, has advanced and passed many deserts without loss of men or property. Arizona is recovered and now held under martial law, waiting for the re-establishment of the civil powers, and the Column from California is advancing eastward to co-operate with the forces in New Mexico.

In preparing the expedition under General Carleton, as well as the one under Colonel Connor, for the protection of the mail route, we have been compelled to make large purchases, principally of mules and means of transportation; but I can assure the Department that in all cases the greatest economy, consistent with the good of the service, has been practiced.

The great difficulty is to guard the public interests on such a vast extent of country, with many small posts, some a thousand or more miles distant. However, the losses which the Government will sustain in this department, I am happy to say, will be small; and but a small portion of that can be set down to the unfaithfulness of officers or agents.

Very respectfully, your obedient servant,

G. WRIGHT,
Brigadier-General, U. S. Army, Commanding.

DEPARTMENT OF STATE,
Washington, July 11, 1862.

Hon. E. M. STANTON, *Secretary of War:*

SIR: I have the honor to inclose a copy of two letters to this Department, one from the United States consul at Matamoros and the other from the consul at Monterey, written at the former place. The condition of the loyal inhabitants of Texas in that neighborhood is represented to be so miserable, that it occurs to me those of them of a suitable age to bear arms might be most readily and effectually relieved if they would accept service in our Army. It is consequently suggested that an arrangement be made with the Secretary of the Navy for receiving any such persons on board the blockading vessel or vessels in that quarter as recruits, in order that they may be transferred to the nearest United States military command.

I have the honor to be, sir, your obedient servant,

WILLIAM H. SEWARD.

[Inclosure No. 1]

CONSULATE OF THE UNITED STATES OF AMERICA,
Matamoros, Mexico, May 5, 1862.

Hon. W. H. SEWARD,
Secretary of State, Washington, D. C.:

SIR: In my last (No. 5) I informed you of the arrest and imprisonment of American citizens. After their release I had thought that I should be troubled no more with such outrages; but on the evening of the 2d, as Mr. Alfred Westrop, a young man in my employ, was coming from the United States steamer Montgomery with several letters, he was seized by four Texas Rangers, who had crossed the river (for the purpose) and waited for him, and, with his letters, taken across and to Fort Brown. Mr. Westrop is an English citizen, the only one that I knew that I could put any confidence in, twenty-three years of age, and has resided nine years in this country, his father and mother now living in the neighborhood of Monterey.

Immediately on hearing of his arrest the commander of this city demanded him, and he was released, but the letters were retained. I had addressed a letter to the commander, urging him to demand the release of the prisoner and whatever documents he might have with him. Since this I have not pressed the matter further, as it would only bring a collision between the two cities.

The crowds of refugees from Texas do not diminish in the least, although it is very difficult, owing to the strict watch kept upon their movements, for them to get out. Many are arrested; some are hung; others are taken and pressed into service.

False dispatches of the most ridiculous kind are circulated throughout the country and through Mexico; but even this mode of encouraging the masses is failing, and throughout the counties bordering on the Rio Grande there exists a perfect reign of terror.

At Austin there is a strong Union party, headed by Ex-Senator Hamilton, who will probably resist all attempts that may be made by the rebels to subdue them. At San Antonio nearly all the stores are closed, and many of the merchants are now residing here, waiting patiently for their time to come when they can return.

I am, sir, very respectfully, your most obedient servant,

L. PIERCE, Jr.,
United States Consul.

[Inclosure No. 2.]

MATAMOROS, MEXICO, May 23, 1862.

Hon. W. H. SEWARD, Secretary of State, Washington, D. C.:

SIR: I arrived in the country the 26th instant. Of course I have no business and nothing really worthy an official letter, yet, sir, I hope to make it worth reading. I have seen much that my Government at Washington should know, then correct as fast as their many duties shall afford.

Captain Hunter, of the United States steamer Montgomery, is all that the Government can ask or expect; yes, more; his position is difficult; he lays in a fleet of all nations. To take a prize is out of the question. Smuggling is apparent, but the neutral river affords excuses, &c.

There is no harbor; exposed to gales, in many of which he has at great risk saved vessels and lives. The Mexicans have been laid under obligations by his saving 9 of them from drowning in the surf. They appreciate it, and are on the shore furnishing beef, &c.; also giving shelter and feeding the destitute Union men that make their escape from Texas. They do it, sir, to the risk of their lives against the threats of the Texas army, to which the little Mexican villages will be exposed, especially if our ship is removed.

Captain Hunter had brought off through the surf 70 of these refugees. There does not appear to be provision for the protection of this class of our citizens.

I hope it may be consistent for you to give me some special instructions or advice. I have been for the past two days with Mr. Pierce (consul here), and from what I see it is evident that he should expend treble his salary upon the worthy Union citizens. It is really painful for a consul to see men driven from home and the comforts of life, not even allowed to bring an article of clothing; the only cause of complaint in many cases that they were Northern men (had never killed any one), and refused to fight against the United States. O; sir, would that I could show cases vividly before the Department! Must this thing be, that our best, truest citizens must be turned into the streets, from the door of an American consul upon a population poor themselves, not able to speak their language, also threatened by the soldiers from Brownsville for harboring them? It is not uncommon for complaints and favors asked from Government, but, sir, I am confident no portion of the United States has been so badly oppressed as the Union men of Texas, and I can learn nothing is yet done to relieve the refugees or avenge the oppressors. I have received reliable information that within one week 6 of those refugees have been hung on the frontier of Texas on trees and left hanging.

I have conversed to-day with a secessionist to find out both sides of this hanging business. To excuse it, he alleged that 4 of them were deserters and the other 2 alleged to be suspicious characters; not improbable they may have joined the Home Guard for peace or to save hanging previous, but learning they could get onto a United States steamer, made the attempt, for which they have been hanged.

Let me urge that a force be sent onto this frontier; it may not be very large, if they have plenty of arms. I am assured that there could be 3,000 enlisted from Texas as soon as it was known. I am informed that there is over 300 men at Monterey fed by charity; that they have been impatient for the United States consul to arrive. A merchant of high standing from Monterey says the merchants there have been paying the expenses of this number for months; that when the consul arrived they expected to turn them over, &c.

My office is [not] a rich one; expensive place to get to; fees not half enough to pay my board; more callers than at an almshouse. I shall not turn back. I have been since April 5 on the route to my appointment; shall get there after 300 miles farther, or thereabouts [on] the stage route. I am willing my country shall have my time and all I can do for her during this rebellion, but I have been so badly robbed by it that I cannot contribute much more.

May I hope that some provision will be made for those sufferers, that the United States consul may not be a disgrace in the eyes of other nations by driving away from his presence honorable citizens that seek the protection of his and their country; honorably for their country's welfare thus reduced that they cannot feed themselves.

If this matter cannot be redressed through the Government, then petitions should be circulated through cities. Those who contributed to feed foreign nations I know will not withhold from those Union refugees in Mexico.

I am aware I have not followed rules in this long and hearty letter, but I shall expect an answer, and hope prompt action may be had.

I have the honor to be, sir, very respectfully, your obedient servant,

C. B. H. BLOOD,
U. S. Consul, Monterey, Mexico.

HEADQUARTERS DEPARTMENT OF NEW MEXICO,
Santa Fé, N. Mex., July 20, 1862.

ADJUTANT-GENERAL OF THE ARMY, *Washington, D. C.:*

SIR : I have the honor to report that the advance of General Carleton's command (two companies of cavalry) reached the Rio Grande near Santa Bárbara on the 4th instant. Two companies of the Third U. S. Cavalry from Fort Craig reached the same point on the 6th instant.

The Confederate forces under Colonel Steele, variously represented at from 500 to 800 men, commenced their retreat on the 6th as soon as advised of the near approach of the United States troops. The Rio Grande is still so high that our troops were unable to cross, and consequently any attempt to pursue was impracticable. The latest accounts from the Mesilla Valley represent that the Confederate troops left in great destitution, and that more than 100 of their men were left at different points on the road from the want of transportation to move them. The American part of the population that had taken part with the rebels left the country with them.

I have no information yet as to the orders under which General Carleton is acting, but presume that his force will be available for the reoccupation of Arizona, and have given orders· accordingly. The presence of these troops will render a portion of the force now in this department available for service elsewhere if they should be needed, and I propose as General Carleton's troops come into position to withdraw the First Regiment Colorado Volunteers from the southern part of the Territory and order them to report to the commander of the Department of Kansas for service on the route from Fort Leavenworth to Fort Union, on which, in my judgment, there should be at least 1,000 men.

I inclose herewith a copy of General Carleton's proclamation* and of a letter from Colonel Steele, of the Confederate Army.

Very respectfully, sir; your obedient servant,

ED. R. S. CANBY,
Brigadier-General, Commanding Department.

[Inclosure]

FORT FILIMORE, *July 5*, 1862.

COMMANDING OFFICER UNITED STATES FORCES:

SIR: As I am about to leave this Territory under circumstances which have caused ill-feeling between white men and Mexicans, and as I have many Americans, some with their families, in some degree at the mercy of the Mexican population, I have entered into a covenant with the principal Mexicans of Mesilla, who have bound themselves to protect the Americans remaining in the country, the consideration being the release of one Domingo Cebeno, who is my prisoner under circumstances which would ordinarily cost him his life. The citizens are those remaining here as having taken no part in the struggle now going on between the Confederate and United States of America. All those who have by holding office or otherwise compromised themselves with your side of the question having already withdrawn, I trust that, for the sake of humanity, you will inquire into the manner in which the agreement has been kept.

Your obedient servant,

WM. STEELE,
Colonel First Texas Mounted Volunteers,
Commanding in Arizona. ·

---

* For the proclamation see p. 561.

HEADQUARTERS DEPARTMENT OF NEW MEXICO,
Santa Fé, N. Mex., July 27, 1862.

Brig. Gen. JAMES G. BLUNT,
Commanding Department of Kansas, Fort Leavenworth, Kans.:

SIR : I have the honor to acknowledge the receipt (during a temporary absence) of your communication of the 26th ultimo,* and to express my thanks for the measures you have taken to secure the supplies coming to this country.

General Carleton, with about 1,500 California troops, is now between Tucson and the Rio Grande. This advance and the advance from Fort Craig united at Santa Barbara on the 7th instant. The Confederate force in the Mesilla Valley commenced their retreat on the same day. Unfortunately the Rio Grande was so high that our troops were unable to cross until the rebels got beyond the reach of pursuit.

As General Carleton's force will be sufficient for the occupation of Arizona, I propose, as soon as his troops get into position, to withdraw the Colorado regiment to Fort Lyon, and place them under your orders, as I do not think they will be needed longer in this country.

I do not think that an invasion of this country by the Rio Grande will again be attempted, but it may be by the Canadian or the Arkansas, if our troops in the South should meet with any serious reverses.

A copy of the latest returns of the Colorado troops serving in this department will be sent to you by the next mail.

I have directed copies of the most important orders issued in this department to be sent to you.

Very respectfully, your obedient servant,
ED. R. S. CANBY,
Brigadier-General, Commanding Department.

SPECIAL ORDERS, }   WAR DEPT., ADJT. GEN.'S OFFICE,
No. 181.   {   *Washington, August 5, 1862.*

*   *   *   *   *   *   *

7. Brig. Gen. E. R. S. Canby, U. S. Volunteers, is relieved from duty in the Department of New Mexico. He will turn over the command to the next officer and repair without delay to this city and report to the Secretary of War.

*   *   *   *

By order of the Secretary of War :

E. D. TOWNSEND,
Assistant Adjutant-General.

HEADQUARTERS DEPARTMENT OF NEW MEXICO,
Santa Fé, N. Mex., August 6, 1862.

ADJUTANT-GENERAL OF THE ARMY,
Washington, D. C.:

SIR : The instructions from the War Department and the Headquarters of the Army, of August 15, 1861, contemplated the withdrawal of

---

* Not found.

the regular force in this department upon the organization of the additional volunteer force then authorized. I have already (May 17, 1862) conditionally recommended the withdrawal of a part of the regular force now here, and the near approach of General Carleton's force, understood to be about 2,000 strong, justifies the opinion that the original instructions of the Department may be carried out without detriment to the service.

I do not apprehend another invasion of this country by the Rio Grande, but in the event of any serious reverses to our troops in the Southwest it may be attempted by the Canadian, or an attempt may be made to cut off or destroy the supply trains coming to this country. This last I regard as the most probable danger, and since the renewal of the disturbances in Missouri have made arrangements to send a portion of the troops now in this department upon that line, believing that they could be better spared from New Mexico than from Kansas. One regiment of Colorado Volunteers will be sufficient in my judgment for the occupation of Fort Lyon (Wise) and to keep in check the Indians of Colorado Territory. The Second Regiment for Fort Union and the northern part of New Mexico, the California troops for the southern part of this Territory and for Arizona, while the New Mexican Volunteers will be sufficient for the Indian frontiers. This will give for New Mexico proper about 4,000, with an additional thousand (in Colorado) within reach, if their services should be needed. If this force should not be considered sufficient, re-enforcements may, I suppose, be drawn from California with more ease than from the East.

I have received no report from General Carleton, but have learned unofficially that he expected to leave Tucson about the middle of last month. As he will be obliged, in consequence of the scarcity of water, to move by detachments, his entire force will not reach the Rio Grande until some time in this month.

Very respectfully, sir, your obedient servant,

ED. R. S. CANBY,
Brigadier-General, Commanding Department of New Mexico.

HEADQUARTERS DEPARTMENT OF NEW MEXICO,
Santa Fé, N. Mex., August 10, 1862.
The ADJUTANT-GENERAL OF THE ARMY,
Washington, D. C.:

SIR: I have the honor to report that I have just received reports from General Carleton, but too late to copy them by this mail.

He left Tucson on the 17th ultimo and was at Ojo de la Vaca (about 60 miles from the Rio Grande) on the 27th. He would wait at that place for the rear of his command to close up. He is now probably in the Mesilla Valley. He reports his command in fine condition, and that his effective force in the valley will be 1,273. This is independent of the garrisons of the posts established in the interior of Arizona and the command (four companies of infantry and two of cavalry) sent from Fort Craig.

His command is generally well supplied, and any deficiencies can be furnished from the depots in this country.

With the exception of the sick and some deserters and a few who have taken refuge in old Mexico, none of the Texan troops are now in the neighborhood of El Paso.

The Indians in this department are exceedingly troublesome, and give constant employment to the troops in this neighborhood, thus far with but little success. The depredators are the Navajoes and Mescalero Apaches.

Serious Indian troubles are reported in Colorado Territory, and upon an application for assistance I have sent a company of infantry and one of cavalry to Fort Lyon, and have ordered two companies of infantry upon the road between Fort Union and Fort Lyon, for the protection of the trains. Two companies of infantry and one of cavalry have been ordered from Fort Craig to Fort Union to replace the companies sent from that place, and two companies of infantry have been ordered to this place to relieve companies of New Mexican Volunteers, which will be sent into the Indian country.

Very respectfully, sir, your obedient servant,

ED. R. S. CANBY,
Brigadier-General, Commanding Department.

DEPARTMENT OF STATE, *Washington, August* 16, 1862.

Hon. E. M. STANTON, *Secretary of War:*

SIR: I have the honor to inclose a letter of the 6th ultimo and the accompanying papers, addressed to this Department by Benjamin C. Cutler, who styles himself " Military Secretary of State of the Territory of Arizona." As that Territory has not been organized by act of Congress, and consequently no civil officers have been appointed therein, it is presumed that the communication of Mr. Assistant Adjutant-General Cutler would have more properly been addressed to the War Department.

I have the honor to be, sir, your obedient servant,

WILLIAM H. SEWARD.

[Inclosure No. 1.]

EXECUTIVE DEPARTMENT, TERRITORY OF ARIZONA,
Tucson, Ariz., July 6, 1862.

His Excellency W. H. SEWARD,
Secretary of State of the United States, Washington, D. C.:

SIR: I have the honor to transmit herewith certain documents, marked A, B,* C, D, E, which relate to matters in this Territory, and which it may be important for you to know.

Other copies, with additional papers, together with a mass of evidence in the cases of Mr. Sylvester Mowry, will reach Washington through the headquarters of the Department of the Pacific. These, to save time, I send direct.

Very respectfully, Your Excellency's obedient servant,

BEN. C. CUTLER,
Acting Assistant Adjutant-General, Military Secretary of State.

[Inclosure A.]

HDQRS. DISTRICT OF SOUTHERN CALIFORNIA,
Fort Yuma, Cal., May 2, 1862.

His Excellency DON IGNACIO PESQUIERA,
Governor of State of Sonora, Ures, Sonora, Republic of Mexico:

SIR: Your Excellency is doubtless aware that for certain military considerations the general commanding the United States forces on the

---
* Inclosure B is a copy of proclamation printed on p. 561.

Pacific coast interdicted the crossing by any person of the Colorado River unless such person had a passport signed by himself.

This excluded many of the citizens of the State of Sonora, in the friendly Republic of Mexico, from coming to work in the rich mines recently discovered on the Colorado River, in California, and also excluded others from coming to Fort Yuma to sell provisions and other of the products and commodities of your State.

The restrictions as to the crossings of the Colorado applied no less to citizens of the United States than to citizens of our sister Republic. Thus you will see that no invidious distinction was made favoring Americans in preference to the people of Your Excellency.

It is now my good fortune to be able to say to Your Excellency that the prohibitions about crossing the river are removed, and the people of Sonora are at liberty to come and work in our mines, or to sell their provisions, forage, fruits, &c., within our lines. The forces of the United States under my command now passing up the Gila River to the Pima Villages and thence on to occupy the Territory of Arizona, though abundantly furnished with every necessary article of subsistence and forage, with adequate means of transportation for all additional supplies from the depot at Fort Yuma which they may need, yet if the people of Sonora desire to bring flour, pork, beef, mutton, sugar, coffee, wheat, barley, fruit, vegetables, &c., to the Pima Villages or Tucson, after I have occupied it, they will be paid a fair price in gold and silver coin for what they sell.

It is our sincere desire as well as our true policy to maintain the most friendly relations with the citizens of all nations, but more particularly with those who, like ourselves and like our neighbors of Mexico, are endeavoring to prove to the world that any brave and intelligent people are capable of being governed by laws made by themselves and by rulers chosen by and from among themselves.

Therefore Your Excellency may rest assured that nothing will be done on our part to disturb the kind feelings which happily subsist between your people and those of the United States.

The people in the South, who are in open rebellion against the Government of the United States having an unjust cause, can never succeed in establishing themselves as an independent nation. As the war which they have wantonly commenced is an unrighteous one, they have not the sympathies of a single Christian nation in the world. Such being the case, you can judge how incredulous I was when I heard that an officer of rank of the so-called Confederate States Army, who has recently been to visit you, had stated publicly in Arizona, on his return from Sonora, that he had made such arrangements with Your Excellency that what supplies he might need for his troops could be landed in the ports of Sonora and be transported without let or hinderance thence through that State to Tucson. I know that Your Excellency is well aware that the very people whose emissary, it is alleged, thus comes to ask of you these commercial privileges would, as fillibusters, usurp the power you yourself hold, and subjugate your own State if they had but the ability to do so. Therefore you can judge of my astonishment at such intelligence. I will not even ask Your Excellency if what I have heard is true, as such an utter want of faith toward a friendly neighbor would be so unworthy of your position as a governor, and so much against your integrity as a man, that I should shrink from wounding your sensibility by such a question. I merely mention the rumor that has reached me to show Your Excellency how much you have been maligned.

Wishing Your Excellency health and good fortune and your people happiness and prosperity, I have the honor to be, Your Excellency's obedient servant,

JAMES H. CARLETON,
Colonel First Cal. Vols., Major U. S. Sixth Cavalry, Comdg.

[Inclosure C.]

EXECUTIVE DEPARTMENT, TERRITORY OF ARIZONA,
Tucson, Ariz., June 11, 1862.

To all whom it may concern:

Be it known that under the authority assumed by the undersigned in the proclamation placing the Territory of Arizona under martial law, which proclamation was dated at Tucson, in Arizona, June 8, A. D. 1862, I hereby appoint Acting Assistant Adjutant-General Benjamin Clarke Cutler to be secretary of state of the Territory of Arizona while the said Territory remains under martial law or until the time when a successor may be appointed to take his place.

His duties shall be to record and to preserve all the acts and proceedings of the Governor in his executive department, and to transmit an authentic copy of these acts and proceedings through the general commanding the Department of the Pacific to the President of the United States on the last day of every month.

And be it also known that the secretary of state of the Territory, while it is under martial law, is hereby empowered to administer oaths.

Given under my hand at Tucson, Ariz., June 11, 1862.

JAMES H. CARLETON,
Military Governor of Arizona.

[Inclosure.]

EXECUTIVE DEPARTMENT, TERRITORY OF ARIZONA,
Tucson, Ariz., June 11, 1862.

To all whom it may concern:

Be it known that by virtue of the authority vested in myself as Military Governor of Arizona I hereby empower the following officers with the right to administer oaths within this Territory while it shall remain under martial law; that is to say:

Lieut. Col. Joseph R. West, First Infantry, California Volunteers.
Lieut. Col. Edward E. Eyre, First Cavalry, California Volunteers.
Maj. Edwin A. Rigg, First Infantry, California Volunteers.
Maj. Theodore A. Coult, Fifth Infantry, California Volunteers.
Maj. David Ferguson, First Cavalry, California Volunteers.
Capt. Tredwell Moore, assistant quartermaster, U. S. Army.

Also the presidents and judge-advocates of military commissions, when such commissions are in session.

JAMES H. CARLETON,
Colonel First Cal. Vols., Major, U. S. Sixth Cavalry.

By the Governor:
BEN. C. CUTLER,
Actg. Asst. Adjt. Gen., Military Secretary of State.

[Inclosure D.]

EXECUTIVE DEPARTMENT, ARIZONA TERRITORY,
Tucson, June 12, 1862.

To all whom it may concern:

Be it known:

I. That from and after this date a monthly tax of $5 for license to trade shall be levied on all merchants in Tucson, Ariz., including those who shall traffic within a mile in every direction from its suburbs, whose monthly sales of merchandise amount to $500 or under, and an additional tax of $1 per month for each additional monthly sale of $100.

II. That every keeper of a gambling house within the aforesaid limits shall pay a tax of $100 per month for each and every table in said house whereon any banking game is played.

III. That every keeper of a bar, where wines, spirituous or malt liquors are to be sold, shall pay a tax of $100 per month to keep said bar.

IV. All keepers of gambling houses, for the non-payment of license for gambling tables, will be fined $50 for the first offense; for the second offense he shall have his money, implements, tools, &c., seized, and the same shall be confiscated, and he shall pay a fine of $100 and be forbidden to again gamble in this Territory.

V. Any person who after this date shall sell without a license any intoxicating liquors or drinks shall be fined $50 for the first offense; for the second offense he shall pay a fine of $100 and forfeit all the liquors in his possession.

VI. The commanding officer at Tucson is hereby empowered to grant licenses under these rules, and collect all taxes, fines, and forfeitures. The moneys thus collected shall be turned over to the medical director, who shall receipt for the same and add it to the hospital fund, to be used exclusively for the benefit of the sick and wounded soldiers belonging to the Column from California until further orders.

VII. All sales made by the Government of the United States shall be exempt from taxation, and no license is necessary for the sale of forage, subsistence stores, fruits, or vegetables.

By order of Colonel Carleton:

BEN. C. CUTLER,
Actg. Asst. Adjt. Gen., Military Secretary of State.

[Inclosure E.]

SPECIAL ORDERS, }   HDQRS. COLUMN FROM CALIFORNIA,
No. 17.   }   Tucson, Ariz., June 16, 1862.

I. A board of officers, to consist of Lieut. Col. Joseph R. West, First Infantry, California Volunteers; Capt. Charles A. Smith, Fifth Infantry, California Volunteers, and Capt. Nicholas S. Davis, First Infantry, California Volunteers, will assemble at this post at 4 p. m. to-day, or as soon thereafter as practicable, to investigate certain charges and facts tending to show that Mr. Sylvester Mowry, of the Patagonia mines, in this Territory, is an enemy to the Government of the United States, and that he has been in treasonable correspondence and collusion with well-known secessionists, and has afforded them aid and comfort when they were known publicly to be enemies to the legally-constituted authority and Government of the United States.

The board will be duly sworn to the faithful performance of its duty, and will examine witnesses on oath, and will examine and make certified extracts from such documents as may be laid before them which may have immediate or important bearing on these points, and the board will report in writing and in full the evidence it receives on all these matters, and its opinions whether or not there are sufficient grounds to restrain of his liberty and bring to trial before a military commission the said Mr. Sylvester Mowry.

II. The board will also inquire into the truth of a report that a respectable German citizen was recently murdered at or near Patagonia mines, in this Territory, and report in writing the evidence in the case and their opinion, in the event they find the report to be true as to who are probably the guilty parties.

The record of this investigation will be made up separately from that ordered in the first paragraph hereof.

III. Second Lieut. Erastus W. Wood, First Infantry, California Volunteers, is appointed secretary of the board, and will be duly sworn by the president thereof to a faithful discharge of his duties as such.

By order of Colonel Carleton:

BEN. C. CUTLER,
First Lieut., First Infantry, California Vols., Actg. Asst. Adjt. Gen.

HEADQUARTERS COLUMN FROM CALIFORNIA,
Tucson, Ariz., June 16, 1862.

Lieut. Col. JOSEPH R. WEST,
President of a Board of Officers convened by Special Orders,
No. 17, current series, from these Headquarters:

COLONEL: The colonel commanding the column directs me to inclose to you, as one of the charges against Mr. Sylvester Mowry, the original of a letter directed to General Carleton from the Mowry silver mines on the 11th of May, 1862, and signed by one "T. Schumer, metallurgist, M. S. M.;" also a paper in your own handwriting, purporting to be a statement of one William Pyburn, which seems to touch on the matter of the alleged furnishing of Captain Hunter's men at the Patagonia mines with percussion caps.*

The board will also examine such documentary evidence as Lieutenant-Colonel Eyre may have brought from the Patagonia mines and placed in your custody.

The board will examine into the facts touching the known political character of one Robinson, and whether he has been a guest and received aid and comfort recently from Mr. Mowry, and in all matters touching this case the board will question the persons brought by Colonel Eyre from the Patagonia mines and such other persons as may be thought to be important witnesses in this matter not herein named, but who may become known to the board during its investigation.

The testimony and evidence you will receive will be *ex parte,* and your inquiry will be analogous to that made by a grand jury in the administration of justice by the civil authorities.

I am, sir, respectfully, your obedient servant,

BEN. C. CUTLER,
First Lieutenant, First Infantry, California Volunteers.

HEADQUARTERS COLUMN FROM CALIFORNIA,
Tucson, Ariz., July 6, 1862.

The board having examined the foregoing personal testimony and documentary evidence, as directed by Special Orders, No. 17, and by the letters of the colonel commanding the Column from California to the

---

*Not found.

president of this board, which said order and letter are copied on and made part of these records, are of opinion that said Sylvester Mowry is an enemy of the Government of the United States, and that he has been in treasonable correspondence and collusion with well-known secessionists, and has afforded them aid and comfort when they were known publicly to be enemies to the legally-constituted authority and Government of the United States, and that there are sufficient grounds to restrain the said Sylvester Mowry of his liberty and bring him to trial before a military commission.

J. R. WEST,
Lieut. Col., First Infantry, Cal. Vols., President.
CHARLES A. SMITH,
Captain, Fifth Infantry, Cal. Vols.
NICHOLAS S. DAVIS,
Captain, First Infantry, Cal. Vols.

ERASTUS W. WOOD,
Second Lieut., First Infantry, Cal. Vols., Secretary.

HEADQUARTERS DEPARTMENT OF NEW MEXICO,
Santa Fé, N. Mex., September 14, 1862.
ADJUTANT-GENERAL OF THE ARMY,
Washington, D. C.:

SIR: I have the honor to transmit a report from General Carleton, of the 9th instant, which gives the latest information in relation to affairs in Arizona and Northwestern Texas. The commanding officer at Fort Garland reports that his spies have discovered the rendezvous of a party of guerrillas on the Huerfano, and that he has detached a force for the purpose of destroying or capturing them. This party is composed of gamblers and desperadoes from the southern mines of Colorado, and it is understood that their object is to reach Arkansas or Texas. They will probably be intercepted by the troops operating east of the Raton Mountains. The regular troops are being concentrated at Fort Union preparatory to going East, and, with the exception of the companies of the Fifth Infantry, will be in readiness to march by the end of this month. Upon the representation of Colonel Leavenworth of the danger of Indian hostilities on the Arkansas, I have ordered the companies of the Tenth Infantry to proceed at once to Fort Lyon.

I will leave for the East in two or three days after the arrival of General Carleton.

Very respectfully, sir, your obedient servant,
ED. R. S. CANBY,
Brigadier-General, Commanding.

[Inclosure.]

HEADQUARTERS COLUMN FROM CALIFORNIA,
Fort Craig, N. Mex., September 9, 1862.
General E. R. S. CANBY:

I received the order to go to Santa Fé to relieve you in the command of the Department of New Mexico at Franklin, Tex., at 10 p. m. on the 2d instant, and started the following morning for that city.

I arrived here last night, and shall leave this post this evening and endeavor to arrive at Santa Fé, say, by the 16th or 17th instant. Since

I wrote to you on the 15th of August I marched with a small cavalry force down the Rio Grande to a point below Fort Quitman, where the San Antonio road leaves the river. I had heard that Colonel Steele, C. S. Army, had left some 50 or 60 wounded, sick, and disabled men at Fort Davis, on the Limpia River, and that these men were guarded by a company of troops of Mexican lineage, under command of a Captain Mararro, from San Antonio. I detached a portion of my command to proceed to Fort Davis to look after the wants of the sick, to capture the company, and to hoist the colors upon the fort. This force has returned, having found not a single living person at the fort, but having found one dead soldier in the hospital, who had evidently been left by his comrades and had afterwards been butchered by Indians. He had been shot in the head, and an arrow was still remaining in his body. The fort was very much dilapidated and had been left in great disarray.

It is said that Colonel Steele destroyed much of his ammunition and some of his wagons at Fort Bliss and more at Eagle Springs in his hurried flight, as he had heard the California troops were in pursuit of him, and that you had sent a force to intercept him somewhere near the Pecos. The force which I sent to Fort Davis had a fight with some Mescalero Indians near that post. We had 2 men and 1 horse wounded. The Indians had 4 killed and 20 wounded. Capt. Edmond D. Shirland, First Cavalry, California Volunteers, commanded the handful of men sent to Fort Davis. I recovered at El Paso some 12 wagon loads of hospital and quartermaster's stores which had formerly belonged to the United States. The Texan prisoners, 26 in all, which I found at Franklin, I sent to San Antonio, starting them from Franklin on the 1st instant. They were furnished with provisions, transportation, and an escort.

I have the honor to be, general, very respectfully, your obedient servant,

JAMES H. CARLETON,
Brigadier-General, U. S. Army, Commanding.

Abstract from return of the Department of New Mexico, Brig. Gen. James H. Carleton, U. S. Army, commanding, for September 20, 1862.

Commands.	Present for duty.		Aggregate present.	Aggregate present and absent.
	Officers.	Men.		
Cubero	2	74	89	90
Fort Craig and vicinity	7	176	216	281
Fort Garland	6	86	137	147
Fort Marcy and vicinity	14	311	431	478
Fort Union and *en route* to	29	571	869	1,064
Fort Union Depot	1	15	16	18
Gallisteo	2	52	71	80
Los Lunas	8	119	152	176
Peralta	10	283	362	450
Polvadera	6	138	172	173
The California Column	56	1,232	1,503	1,725
Total	135	3,057	4,018	4,680

CONFEDERATE CORRESPONDENCE, ETC.

[FEBRUARY 2, 1862.—Requisition made by the Confederate authorities upon Texas for fifteen regiments "for the war." The requisition and resulting correspondence appears in Series IV, Vol. I.]

HEADQUARTERS DEPARTMENT OF TEXAS,
Houston, Tex., February 5, 1862.

Hon. J. P. BENJAMIN, *Secretary of War, Richmond, Va.:*

SIR: I have the honor to transmit copy of instructions issued to the different commissaries of this department by the chief commissary of subsistence, by direction of the Commissary-General at Richmond.

I am inclined to believe that a strict compliance with these instructions will much trammel the operations of the Subsistence Department.

This military department is a large one and the posts far apart. The headquarters of the chief commissary are at San Antonio, and the general commanding, considering himself in the field, is obliged to establish his headquarters where he thinks his presence most needed, and at this time within striking distance of the seaboard, exposed at any moment to the attacks of the enemy. This necessarily must frequently, if not always, place the general commanding and chief of subsistence at different and distant stations.

The instructions require that receipts and certificates given by subcommissaries be approved by the commanding general, and then to be presented to the chief commissary of the department for examination and payment. This is very inconvenient. For instance, troops on the Rio Grande or at the distant frontier posts may run short of provisions. In this event the difficulty of purchasing supplies upon certificates, which, to be paid, would oblige the holders to first find the general commanding to get his approval, and then to repair to San Antonio to have these accounts examined and paid or refused payment, as the case may be, is very apparent.

The sub-commissaries report to me that it will be impossible to obtain supplies under these difficulties, as parties selling would be unwilling to be put to the expense, trouble, and traveling involved in getting paid by the Government.

Besides, it imposes more or less commissary duties upon the general commanding in a department, where the duties are already very onerous on account of its vast geographical extent, the number of its posts, and one where, owing to many causes, the general commanding is obliged to almost create resources and means of defense.

Again, it subjects receipts and certificates approved by the general commanding to the examination and approval of an inferior officer, the chief commissary of the department.

I would, in conclusion, respectfully remark that these instructions shift responsibility from the chief commissary and his assistants, disbursing officers, to the general commanding, who in most cases will be unable, especially at distant posts, to judge of the nature and necessity of supplies purchased by the different commissaries.

Respectfully calling the early attention of the Secretary of War to the subject of this communication, I have the honor to be, very respectfully, his obedient servant,

P. O. HÉBERT,
Brigadier-General, P. A., Comdg. Dept. of Texas.

[Inclosure.]

OFFICE OF THE ACTG. ASST. COM. OF SUB.,
Galveston, Tex., February 1, 1862.

General P. O. HÉBERT, *Comdg. Dept. of Texas, Houston, Tex.:*

GENERAL: I have the honor to inclose a certified copy of an order this day received from Maj. S. Maclin, chief commissary Department of Texas.

As I interpret the order, I have no authority to purchase supplies for the troops on this island without your approval of every purchase being indorsed thereon.

You are fully aware of the difficulty in procuring supplies for the troops. Would respectfully submit that, if this order is strictly complied with, it will be impossible to subsist the troops, from the fact that parties having subsistence stores for sale will be unwilling to visit you for the approval of their certified accounts, and then go to San Antonio to receive the money from the chief of subsistence.

I will be pleased to receive instructions from you at your earliest convenience.

I am, general, very respectfully, your obedient servant,
DAN. C. RICHARDSON,
Captain, and A. A. C. S., C. S. P. Army.

[Sub-inclosure.]

PRINCIPAL COMMISSARY OFFICE,
San Antonio, Tex., January 24, 1862.

SIR: In furnishing provisions to officers and others you will be governed by the following instructions, received from the Commissary-General.

Respectfully, your obedient servant,
SACKFIELD MACLIN,
Major, C. S. Army, Chief Com. Sub., Dept. of Texas.

RICHMOND, VA., *December* 5, 1861.

Maj. S. MACLIN,
Chief Commissary of Subsistence, Dept. of Texas, San Antonio:

SIR: The Commissary-General directs me to say to you that you will please instruct the commissaries in your department that when it becomes necessary to purchase supplies in the vicinity of their station the approval of the general commanding the Department of Texas must be expressed upon the receipts or certificates given to the persons from whom the stores are obtained, and that all such accounts must be presented to you for examination and payment.

That no account for subsistence furnished picket guards or other detachments will be allowed unless on the order of the general commanding, setting forth the circumstances rendering the purchase necessary, and these accounts must be submitted to you for examination and payment.

You will also cause instructions to be given to the commissaries of your department who receive "due-bills" from officers to whom provisions are sold to take up the amount of these bills (remaining unpaid) when their accounts current are rendered on that account, and forward the bills to this office as vouchers, with "abstract of sales."

Very respectfully, your obedient servant,
T. WILLIAMS,
Major and Commissary Subsistence, C. S. Army.

[Indorsement.]

OFFICE OF COMMISSARY-GENERAL OF SUBSISTENCE,
Richmond, March 6, 1862.

Respectfully returned to the Adjutant and Inspector General.

The circular within referred to was modified by substituting "officers commanding separate commands" for the words "general commanding," the object being to check, as far as practicable, unnecessary and extravagant purchases, and to prevent certificates from being given for provisions furnished to parties who were otherwise provided for or might have been, and who are not authorized to buy stores or create claims against the Department. The regulations of the C. S. Army fix the responsibility upon the commanding officer of a department, requiring him to enforce a rigid economy in the public expenses, and to promptly correct all irregularities and extravagancies which he may discover. This circular does not add to the responsibilities of commanding officers, nor does the circular require accounts approved by the commanding officer to be afterward approved by the chief commissary of subsistence or "an inferior officer," but simply their "examination," a clerical one, and that the party holding the account is the one to be paid, and finally the payment.

The circular does not apply to commissaries who are furnished with funds and are authorized to buy stores.

L. B. NORTHROP,
Commissary-General of Subsistence.

SPECIAL ORDERS, } ADJT. AND INSP. GEN.'S OFFICE,
No. 33. } *Richmond, February* 10, 1862.

* * * * * * *

III. The State of Texas is hereby divided into two military districts, to be called the Eastern and Western Districts of Texas. The country embraced between the northern and eastern boundaries of the State and the eastern shore of Galveston Bay and left bank of the Trinity River to its intersection with the Cross Timbers at Alton, thence following Cross Timbers to Red River, will constitute the Eastern District. All other parts of Texas will constitute the Western District.

* * * * * * *

By command of the Secretary of War:

JNO. WITHERS,
Assistant Adjutant-General.

WAR DEPARTMENT, C. S. ARMY,
Richmond, Va., February 13, 1862.

Brig. Gen. P. O. HÉBERT, *Galveston, Tex.:*

SIR: It is stated here that you have made calls for troops in Texas for a less period than three years or the war. It is not known whether this statement is correct, as the Department has no official communication on the subject. If it be true, however, it is in entire opposition to the whole policy of the Government, and tends to defeat all its measures for raising a permanent body of troops for the defense of the country. You are therefore instructed under no circumstances and in no emergency to accept troops into the Confederate service for a less period than three years or the war, and if any such have been accepted at once to disband them.

If any emergency arises you may call out the people *en masse* for defense; but you will muster no troops whatever into the Confederate service, under any pressure, for less than three years or the war.

Respectfully,

J. P. BENJAMIN,
Secretary of War.

FEBRUARY 24, 1862.

Brig. Gen. P. O. HÉBERT, *Galveston, Tex.:*

SIR: Our recent disaster in Tennessee has greatly exposed our line of communication with the West, and the importance of this line is so great that it must be held at any sacrifice.

You are therefore instructed at once to send forward to Little Rock, there to report to Maj. Gen. Earl Van Dorn, all the troops in your command, for the defense of the coast, except such as are necessary to man your batteries. No invasion of Texas is deemed probable, but if any occurs its effects must be hazarded, and our entire forces must be thrown toward the Mississippi, for the defense of that river and of the Memphis and Charleston Railroad.

I do not desire that you withdraw such troops as you may have on the Rio Grande or Western frontier, but only the troops you have gathered for defending the Gulf coast. If at any point where you have batteries you deem that there is danger of losing the guns by the withdrawal of the land forces you will remove the guns, but the men are to be pushed forward with all possible rapidity to Little Rock by such route as you may deem best.

I am, your obedient servant,

J. P. BENJAMIN,
Secretary of War.

SPECIAL ORDERS, }   HEADQUARTERS DEPT. OF TEXAS,
No. 221.   }   *Houston, February 25,* 1862.

I. Until further orders the command of Col. H. E. McCulloch will be styled "Sub-Military District of the Rio Grande;" headquarters, for the present, San Antonio.

II. The command of Col. John C. Moore, "Sub-Military District of Houston;" headquarters, for the present, near Houston.

III. The command of Col. E. B. Nichols, "Sub-Military District of Galveston;" headquarters, for the present, Galveston.

By order of Brig. Gen. P. O. Hébert:

SAML. BOYER DAVIS,
Major and Assistant Adjutant-General.

Abstract from morning report of the First Brigade of Texas Volunteers, commanded by Col. E. B. Nichols (Galveston, Tex.), February 28, 1862.

Troops.	Present for duty.						Aggregate present.	Aggregate present and absent.
	Infantry.		Cavalry.		Artillery.			
	Officers.	Men.	Officers.	Men.	Officers.	Men.		
Kirby's battalion infantry...	8	186	......	....	......	....	221	250
Nelson's regiment infantry	33	603	......	....	......	....	760	816
Nichols' regiment infantry	41	526	......	....	......	....	803	911
Oswald's battalion infantry	7	76	......	....	......	....	119	143
Spaight's battalion infantry	11	190	......	....	......	....	292	322
Debray's mounted battalion.	......	....	35	681	......	....	791	879
Cook's artillery	......	....	......	....	24	347	508	622
Edgar's light battery	......	....	......	....	5	58	86	94
Grand total	100	1,581	35	681	29	405	3,580	4,037

Abstract from field return of Confederate forces on the Lower Rio Grande, commanded by Col. P. N. Luckett, for February, 1862.

Troops.	Present for duty.		Aggregate present.	Aggregate present and absent.
	Officers.	Men.		
Fort Brown	38	392	505	557
Ringgold Barracks	5	48	62	88
2d Regiment Texas Mounted Rifles (three companies)	13	264	290	313
Grand total	56	704	857	958

HDQRS. SUB-MILITARY DIST. OF THE RIO GRANDE,
San Antonio, Tex., March 3, 1862.

Maj. SAMUEL BOYER DAVIS, *Assistant Adjutant-General:*

SIR: Since I wrote you respecting the filling up of the mounted regiment I think I have discovered a pretty considerable under-current at work through this country against our cause. It does not occur to me that it can be very strong, yet it may amount in the end to something which will require force to be used. Men have been heard to say, when we (the Confederates) lost a battle, that "We" (the Union men) "have gained a victory." Others have sent up small balloons, while others have fired guns by way of rejoicing over these victories. Others are and have been using their utmost exertions to break down the currency of the country, and some others have arms and other supplies for sale, and ask us twice as much for them in our currency as they would in gold or silver, and then refuse to let us have them unless the cash is paid in hand, although assured that they would be paid in sixty days or less. Our friends do not act in this manner, and these men are our enemies. They cannot be reached by civil law, yet they are damaging our cause every day; and if the enemy should land in force on the coast, or invade us on the north (which I think it likely Jim Lane will do in the spring), it will be necessary to take charge of these men in some way, or it will not be safe for our friends to go into the service and leave their homes, their families, and property, without an armed force could be left to protect them.

Under these circumstances I look to the time that it will be necessary to declare martial law, in order to effect that by force which the Governor, with all his energies, cannot effect through the civil laws of the land; and while I would deplore such a necessity among our people as much or more than any other man, and as my home, my family, and all my interests would be jeopardized by such a step, I am ready to take it, as far as I am personally concerned, whenever I see there is a necessity for it, in my judgment, and have commenced the preparation for it by assembling the regiment here, and, if it is necessary, shall resort to it, unless the general commanding declares emphatically that it must not be done.

I have but one object in being in the service, which is to advance the interest of my country, and, according to my judgment, I shall strive to do that regardless of personal sacrifices or danger.

Most respectfully, &c.,

H. E. McCULLOCH,
Colonel First Regiment Texas M. R., C. S. P. A.,
Comdg. Sub-Military District of Rio Grande.

CAMP ESPERANZA,
Near Saluria, Tex., March 4, 1862.

Col. R. R. GARLAND,
Commanding Sixth Regiment Texas Infantry, Victoria, Tex.:

COLONEL: I have the honor to state that on the night of the 27th ultimo a steamer appeared off our bar and made the usual signal-lights. She remained at anchor until the morning of the 28th. It was hazy; I could not see the course she had taken, but since ascertained she was the Lincoln mail steamer, in search of the blockaders.

About 3 p. m. same day two barks, the Midnight and Arthur, hove in sight, coming from the west. They came to anchor off our bar, about 2½ miles from the light-house. The weather has been so boisterous they could not land conveniently until yesterday morning, when the norther subsided.

About 9 a. m., 3d instant, two launches from the bark Arthur approached the shore, each one bearing a white flag. I caused a white flag to be raised in answer. I met the captain at the Point when he came on shore. He stated to me that he wished to release a prisoner on parole whose wife was also a prisoner, but an invalid. The prisoner was Captain Hopper, owner of the schooner McNeil, which was captured 12 miles to the westward of this bar in January. He said the lady was so ill he could not send her to New York, and she required the assistance of her husband to wait on her; she is badly afflicted with rheumatism.

In my last communication I informed you of the gentleman's bombastic style; he bragged what he could do with his ship; pointed out the position he would occupy if he wished to shell me out of my position, but said he had no orders to fire on the coast unless he was fired on by us, then he would retaliate. He said he knew the caliber and number of guns I had; my exact position and force. His orders are to blockade and break up all commerce inside, and particularly through the bays; he had the means of doing so. He asked, "Where is Hébert now?" After answering his pert questions mildly, I asked him how he got all his information, and remarked at the same time, "Your informant is not as well posted as you imagine." The captain replied that the Government has provided to have persons gather information and to keep him well informed of our movements. This I told him I doubted. He answered, "I get your latest papers; I can show you the Brownsville Flag and Houston Telegraph," and then said, "If I can get my hands on Lieutenant Maltby I will treat him harshly; he has stated that he chased my two boats' crew 3 miles; this is not so; here is his muster roll." · I looked at the document, and saw the names of four men whom I knew, and I learned belonged to Maltby's party. He said Maltby's statement reflected very much on the action of his crew in that instance, and used hard language against the unsoldierlike conduct. He said in a short time there would be 100,000 men in the Gulf, and his party intended taking Galveston immediately. I remarked that his party might take the island with a large army and naval force, but the main-land was close by; "there from under your ship's fire we would measure bayonets with your armies."

We conversed for a space of a half hour. He changed to politics, and was at the close of the conversation very agreeable. We agreed a white flag would be respected; its absence a fight.

I had the lady carried to a house in Saluria, and the gallant captain not exacting a parole from the poor afflicted woman. I am glad to state what she lacks in strength in her lower extremities is concentrated in her upper. She cannot walk, but she has good use of her tongue, and has given me several items of interest. I would not state that her husband whispers in her ear occasionally. She says her memory is not very good.

There are 2,400 men at Ship Island, intended for Galveston, to be attacked with 10,000 men, time not mentioned. Overheard talk between Kittredge and the captain of the three-masted schooner Kitty Taney. There are thirty bomb-proof gunboats to ascend the Mississippi.

The bark Midnight has six 32-pounders and one Parrott pivot 20-pounder. She has about 66 men, and draws 7 feet water, light; 250 tons burden. Station Pass Cavallo; has four boats, and is a good sailer.

Bark Arthur, station Aransas Pass, at present here. She has the same armament: One Parrott rifle 30-pounder; draws 14 feet water. She has 74 men, well equipped with small-arms, pikes, &c. The attack upon Pass Cavallo is expected, but only the men report it. There are 2 men on the Santee who have wives and families in Galveston; one of them piloted the attack on the Royal Yacht. Captain Kittredge made a speech to his men, and said as there were no prizes outside he would take them inside. He took a sloop in Aransas Bay, with medicine.

There has been a great deal said about my blockading Saluria Bayou. My object in causing this pass to be closed was to prevent the enemy from getting our light-draught vessels and arming them against us. There are but few in our bays, and if the proper officer intends the trade and commerce to continue through the west bays he will have to arm a few of our best schooners. Whether he does or not, it is my duty to guard well my exposed position and keep such property out of the enemy's possession that he might use to advantage against me.

I informed some speculators who have been here to see me about our blockade at Saluria that I would now let vessels pass with cotton, corn, &c., while there was a chance for them to get down safe. The troops at Aransas have not communicated with me, as I requested Captain Neal to do.

I have reported some of the leading facts above stated in my last communication, and Major Forshey has kept the headquarters at Houston posted.

I have not received an order of any character relative to the command of the West. I earnestly request the colonel commanding to issue an order relative to the blockade of Saluria, &c.

The captain of the bark Arthur inquired of the men who had lost the medicines why the schooner did not come down as usual. He said, mentioning my name, I had stopped all vessels going west. He said he would come here and break up my blockade immediately; he has not attempted to do so yet. He said emphatically that he must have two of our best and light Aransas vessels. This history, in connection with my last communication, I thought best to let you know in full and submit to your superior judgment.

I have the honor to be, very respectfully, your obedient servant,

DAN. D. SHEA,
C. S. P. A., Major, Commanding Saluria, &c.

[Indorsement.]

HDQRS. SUB-MILITARY DIST. OF THE RIO GRANDE,
San Antonio, Tex., March 12, 1862.

Respectfully referred to the commanding general for his consideration, as it gives information (although not altogether reliable) that may be of service to him, and I must say that I think the suggestions of arming a few schooners or light-draught steamboats necessary for the defense of the commerce in those bays.

H. E. McCULLOCH,
Col. First Regiment Tex. M. R., C. S. P. A., Comdg. Dist.

HDQRS. SUB-MILITARY DIST. OF THE RIO GRANDE,
San Antonio, Tex., March 25, 1862.

Col. SAMUEL BOYER DAVIS,
Acting Assistant Adjutant-General:

SIR: I find that many of the most notorious among the leaders of the opposition, or Union men, are leaving the country, principally in the direction of Mexico. Some of them, I have no doubt, are going simply to avoid the draft, and under its operations a participation in the present struggle with the North, while others are going to co-operate with a considerable number that have already entered Mexico, and are now at Monterey and other points, doing all they can to prejudice our cause with the authorities of that country, and prepare the minds of the common people to take part against us in case there ever is a time when they dare call on them to do so, and to act in concert with men of like feelings about Austin, this place, Fredericksburg, and other points where they are still living among us.

I have said, and I repeat, that there is, in my opinion, a considerable element of this character in this section that will have, ultimately (if the war becomes any more disastrous to us), to be crushed out, even if it has to be done without due course of law, or this country—the section in which I am stationed to protect and in which my family reside—will suffer.

In view of these things I have taken steps to prevent as far as possible the passage of these men out of the country into Mexico, by instructing the military under my command not to let any man go unless he is known to be our friend, and not then unless he can produce satisfactory evidence that he is not going to avoid the draft with which the State is threatened and which will come upon it.

I am fully aware of the responsibility of the step I have taken, and how much it perils my reputation as an officer, and how much it exposes my person and my domestic interests—my home, my wife and little ones—to the malignant acts of these cowardly traitors, but I believe it my duty to my country, and in her case I am willing to peril my all.

The force that I will have congregated here in a few days more will be sufficient to enable the State authorities to enforce the draft or do anything else that a military force may be required to do, and while I assure you that I shall take no step rashly or without reflection, I shall use it for the benefit of my country upon traitors at home if needs be.

Most respectfully, &c.,

H. E. McCULLOCH,
Col. First Regiment Tex. M. R., C. S. P. A., Comdg. Dist.

HDQRS. SUB-MILITARY DIST. OF THE RIO GRANDE,
San Antonio, Tex.; March 31, 1862.

Col. SAMUEL BOYER DAVIS,
Acting Assistant Adjutant-General:

SIR: Inclosed you will find a copy of a notice stuck up in a prominent place in this city, written in a German hand, and showing plainly that it was written by a foreigner.

It may have been by some to array opposition to that character of the population, but it speaks the sentiments of a large portion of the population here, many of whom are doing all they can to injure our cause secretly, and would do so openly if they dared.

Many Germans and some Americans are leaving here to avoid a participation in our struggle. I have directed the troops to permit none to go to Mexico, unless they have a pass from me, or can produce evidence that they are our friends, and not leaving to avoid doing their duty to the country.

I have indicated plainly on other occasions that I deemed it advisable to declare martial law here at some time, and I think the time has about arrived when it will have to be done.

I have force sufficient in the vicinity to enforce it if I declare it; and if I could know that it would not displease the commanding general it would be declared to-day.

Most respectfully, your obedient servant,

H. E. McCULLOCH,
Col. 1st Reg. T. M. R., C. S. P. A., Comdg. S. M. D. of Rio Grande.

[Inclosure.]

NEWS.

German brothers, are your eyes not opened yet? After the rich took every picayune away from you, and the paper is worth only one-half what you so hard earned, now that you have nothing left, now they go about and sell you, or throw you out of employment for Dunhauer, who left his wife and children, wants to do the same with you to the poor you might leave. Now is the time to stay the heads of Dunhauer, Maverick, Mitchel, and Menger to the last bone. We are always ready. If the ignorant company of Newton fights you, do as you please. You will always stay the God damn Dutchman. Do away with that nuisance, and inform everybody the revolution is broke out.

. It is a shame that Texas has such a brand. Hang them by their feet and burn them from below.

[Indorsement.]

This was found sticking up since the letter was written; it was in German, and this is the translation.

McCULLOCH.

Abstract from field return of Confederate States forces stationed on the Lower Rio Grande, commanded by Col. John S. Ford, for March, 1862.

Troops.	Present for duty.		Aggregate present.	Aggregate present and absent.
	Officers.	Men.		
Fort Brown	33	369	504	566
Ringgold Barracks	3	12	20	81
2d Regiment Texas Mounted Rifles.............................	12	284	310	321
Grand total...	48	665	834	968

WAR DEPARTMENT, C. S. ARMY,
Richmond, Va., April 14, 1862.

Col. JOHN R. BAYLOR,
Governor of Arizona Territory:

SIR: You are authorized to enlist volunteers in Arizona Territory and to muster them into service, singly and by companies, for three years or the war, to be organized as soon as a sufficient number of companies are mustered into a regiment, electing field officers. You will continue to organize regiments under this authority until a brigade has been raised for the defense of the Territory.

Very respectfully, your obedient servant,
G. W. RANDOLPH,
Secretary of War.

GENERAL ORDERS, } WAR DEPT., ADJT. AND INSP. GEN.'S OFF.,
No. 23. } *Richmond, April 15, 1862.*

Parties who have been authorized by the War Department to raise troops in Texas are prohibited from enlisting or receiving twelve-months' men; and all authority heretofore granted by this Government to raise troops in any State is hereby revoked, unless the organization is completed and the muster rolls returned to this office within sixty days from the date of this order.

By command of the Secretary of War:

S. COOPER,
Adjutant and Inspector General.

HEADQUARTERS DEPARTMENT OF TEXAS,
Houston, April 19, 1862.

Hon. GEORGE W. RANDOLPH,
Secretary of War, Richmond, Va.:

SIR: On the 14th of March last I received an order, dated February 23, from the Secretary of War, directing me to send all the forces under my command, except such as were necessary to man the coast batteries, to report to General Van Dorn at Little Rock, Ark.

I have since acted in accordance with these instructions, and have moved troops as rapidly as the necessary transportation could be obtained.

Recent events in the Mississippi Valley and telegraphic statements as to the movements of General Van Dorn have left me in doubt as to the position of his command. I shall in consequence, until further orders, forward the troops to their destination according to the orders referred to, but by such a route as to place them on the march within striking distance of the Mississippi—that is, direct to Alexandria, La.—thence on by water transportation.

I have the honor to be, very respectfully, your obedient servant,

P. O. HÉBERT,
Brigadier-General, Provisional Army.

HDQRS. SEVENTH REGIMENT TEXAS MOUNTED MEN,
Camp above Doña Aña, April 20, 1862.

General S. COOPER,
Adjutant and Inspector General:

GENERAL: I have the honor to inclose to you the within letter from Captain Hunter, C. S. Army, now at Tucson, N. Mex.

Respectfully, your obedient servant,

WM. STEELE,
Colonel Seventh Texas Mounted Men.

[Inclosure.]

TUCSON, ARIZ., *April* 5, 1862.

Col. JOHN R. BAYLOR:

SIR: After a march made as speedily as practicable from the Rio Grande, attended by some violently-stormy weather, but without any accident or misfortune save the loss of one of my men (Benjamin Mays), who died at the San Simon, I have the honor of reporting to you my arrival at this place on February 28. My timely arrival with my command was hailed by a majority, I may say the entire population, of the town of Tucson. I found rumors here to the effect that the town was about being attacked by a large body of Indians; that military stores of the Federal Army to a large amount had been landed at Guaymas, and that troops from California were on the march up the Gila River for this place; and these reports were so well accredited that a few of the citizens more ultra in their Southern feelings than the rest were about [leaving] rather than fall into the hands of their Northern foes, to sacrifice all of their interests in this place, and look for safety among their Southern brethren on the Rio Grande.

Immediately after the departure of Colonel Reily, on March 3, for Sonora, accompanied by an escort of 20 men, under Lieutenant Tevis, I started with the rest of my command for the Pima Villages, where after my arrival I negotiated friendly relations with the Indians; arrested A. M. White, who was trading with them, purchasing wheat, &c., for the Northern troops, and confiscated the property found in his possession; a list* of which I send you. Among the articles confiscated were 1,500 sacks of wheat, accumulated by Mr. White, and intended for the Northern Army. This I distributed among the Indians, as I had no means of transportation, and deemed this a better policy of disposing of it than to destroy or leave it for the benefit (should it fall into their hands) of the enemy.

While delaying at the Pima Villages, awaiting the arrival of a train of 50 wagons which was reported to be *en route* for that place for said wheat (which report, however, turned out to be untrue), my pickets discovered the approach of a detachment of cavalry, and which detachment, I am happy to say to you, we succeeded in capturing without firing a gun. This detachment consisted of Captain McCleave and 9 of his men, First California Cavalry. The captain and Mr. White I send in charge of Lieutenant Swilling to the Rio Grande.

I learned also while at Pimo Villages that at every station, formerly Overland, between that place and Fort Yuma hay had been provided for the use of the Federal Government, which hay I have destroyed at six of the stations thus provided. My pickets on yesterday reported troops at Stanwix's Ranch, which is on this side of Fort Yuma 80 miles.

Allow me to say, in conclusion, that I have no opinion to offer in relation to all of these rumors that are afloat, but give them to you as I received them, knowing that your judgment and experience will dictate the proper course to pursue.

I am, sir, your obedient servant,

S. HUNTER,
Captain Company A.

GENERAL ORDERS, }   HDQRS. SUB-MIL. DIST. OF RIO GRANDE,
No. 3.   }   *San Antonio, April 24, 1862.*

I. By virtue of Special Orders, No. 525, from headquarters of the Department of Texas, the undersigned assumes command of the Sub-Military District of the Rio Grande.

II. The military posts north, west, and south of San Antonio, including the posts at Victoria and Saluria, are embraced in the Sub-Military District of the Rio Grande. Headquarters for the present at San Antonio, Tex.

III. Maj. E. F. Gray, Third Regiment Texas Infantry, is assigned to duty as acting assistant adjutant-general, and will be obeyed and respected accordingly. All official communications from posts within the Sub-Military District of the Rio Grande will be addressed to Maj. E. F. Gray, acting assistant adjutant-general, San Antonio, Tex.

---

* Not found.

IV. Called by the President to this important position, the general commanding relies with confidence on his fellow-citizens to assist and sustain him in the discharge of his duties. In the belief that they will do it, he will to the best of his ability maintain the honor and dignity of our Government and require a zealous and cordial support and respect for her institutions. Military discipline will be strictly enforced, and no obstacle allowed to encumber the progress of our country to independence.

H. P. BEE,
Brig. Gen., Comdg. Sub-Military District of the Rio Grande.

SPECIAL ORDERS, }　　　ADJT. AND INSP. GEN.'S OFFICE,
　　No. 101.　 }　　　　　*Richmond, Va., May 2, 1862.*
* 　 * 　 * 　 * 　 * 　 * 　 *

XVI. Brig. Gen. Hamilton P. Bee will report for duty to General P. O. Hébert, commanding Department of Texas, at Houston, Tex.
* 　 * 　 * 　 * 　 * 　 * 　 *

By command of the Secretary of War:

· R. H. CHILTON,
Assistant Adjutant-General.

SPECIAL ORDERS, }　　　HDQRS. MIL. DIST. OF GALVESTON,
　　No. 471.　 }　　　　　*Galveston, May 14, 1862.*

SIR: In case the enemy should make his appearance off our harbor it will probably become necessary to withdraw the troops from our batteries. Commanders of batteries will therefore make every arrangement to spike the guns of their batteries, destroy the houses and gun-carriages by fire, and fall back to the Houston and Galveston Railroad depot in good order and await further orders. All the ammunition and things belonging to the men that can be removed will be taken away as means of transportation will be furnished. They will not evacuate or spike the guns until they receive orders from these headquarters, unless they are suddenly attacked, in which case they will use their own discretion.

By order of

JOS. J. COOK,
Colonel, Commanding Military Sub-District.

Lieut. Col. J. H. MANLY,
Commanding Regiment Artillery.

AITO, CHEROKEE COUNTY, TEX.,
May 15, 1862.

Hon. JOHN H. REAGAN,
Postmaster-General C. S. of A., at Richmond, Va.:

DEAR SIR: I have to acknowledge receipt of your official report, which came to hand a few days since, and for which I am very grateful and much pleased. But I fear, from present indications, with the Federals in possession of the Mississippi River, that in future all mail facilities between Richmond and this country will be cut off for a time. We have varied rumors of a great victory for our forces in Virginia and at Corinth, but for want of through mails all rest on rumor.

Although I am now writing you, yet doubt whether it will be able to reach you, but, at all hazards, will risk its running the blockade, in order that I may, through you, call the attention of the Government at Richmond to the fact that notorious outrages are at this time being practiced in the way of plunder through this section from good citizens by an armed party of the citizens of Texas, professing to be Confederate soldiers, and under the command of one Colonel Carter, from Hempstead, near Houston; but all of those professing to be officers acknowledge themselves void of any commissions authorizing them to draft on the Government for supplies, but notwithstanding they are marching eastward slowly with a force of from fifteen [hundred] to 3,000 men, remaining in each neighborhood just long enough to ravage the corn-cribs and smoke-houses of the defenseless surrounding country, and even the defenseless widow meets with no mercy at their hands, as I am credibly informed. They on yesterday, with ax and sledge-hammer, broke into the smoke-house and corn-crib of Judge Baxter, near the Neches (with whom you are acquainted), and took therefrom a quantity of corn and meat, as I am credibly informed, and that against the wishes and kind remonstrances of the judge and family. They offer pay at their own price by draft on some individual at city of Houston, and in all probability an irresponsible character. They on yesterday made their boasts that they found an old widow lady in possession of only 280 pounds bacon. They took half.

The good citizens left at home for the protection of families of those gone to the war are in perfect dread for selves and families, and know not what may come next. Instead of our own citizens being a protection, they have become our hourly dread, and while I write I have seen them prowling about from house to house, evidently seeking whom they may devour next.

I trust your Government will take immediate notice of such conduct, and take measures for a speedy suppression of all such unlawful and unwarrantable conduct.

Your friend and obedient servant,

W. W. FRIZZELL.

Respectfully referred to the Secretary of War. Mr. Frizzell is a respectable citizen.

JOHN H. REAGAN,
Postmaster-General.

GALVESTON, TEX., *May* 17, 1862.
Brig. Gen. P. O. HÉBERT :

Received following from commander of frigate Santee :

U. S. FRIGATE SANTEE, *off Galveston, Tex., May* 17, 1862.
To the MILITARY COMMANDANT,
    Commanding Confederate Forces, Galveston, Tex.:

SIR : In a few days the naval and land forces of the United States Government will appear off the town of Galveston to enforce its surrender. To prevent the effusion of blood and destruction of property which would result from the bombardment of your town I hereby demand the surrender of the place, with its fortifications and all batteries in its vicinity, with all arms and munitions of war. I trust you will comply with this humane demand.

I am, respectfully, &c.,

HENRY EAGLE,
Captain, Commanding Naval Forces off Galveston, Tex.

Bearer of message stated answer any time within twenty-four hours.

JOS. J. COOK.

HOUSTON, TEX., *May* 17, 1862.
Colonel COOK, *Galveston, Tex.:*

Will send answer in the morning. In the mean time prepare quietly to evacuate in the event of an overwhelming force making its appearance to bombard as threatened. Send up Major Kellersberg by morning train.

P. O. HÉBERT,
Brigadier-General.

HOUSTON, TEX., *May* 17, 1862—9 p. m.
Colonel COOK, *Galveston, Tex.:*

The company at Pelican Spit should be removed quietly. Spike the gun. Act so that the enemy's attention will not be called to your movements. Call upon the president of the railroad for rolling stock. Let there be no excitement. Let the flag stand at the Spit. Don't burn anything for the present to excite attention of the enemy.

P. O. HÉBERT,
Brigadier-General.

GALVESTON, TEX., *May* 18, 1862.
Brig. Gen. P. O. HÉBERT :

I desire to communicate to the commander of the frigate that whenever the naval and land forces of the United States shall make their appearance off Galveston I shall answer their demand.

JOS. J. COOK, *Colonel.*

GALVESTON, TEX., *May* 19, 1862.
Brig. Gen. P. O. HÉBERT :

I communicated to the commander of the frigate yesterday that the proper time for an answer to his demand will be when the land and naval forces referred to shall have arrived, and such an answer will then be given. This morning she has up a white flag, and I have sent out. I am making the preparations advised as well as I can.

JOS. J. COOK, *Colonel.*

GALVESTON, TEX., *May* 19, 1862.
Brig. Gen. P. O. HÉBERT :

Answered the flag of truce. Nothing for ourselves. The foreign consuls received the following :

U. S. FRIGATE SANTEE, *May* 19, 1862.
To the Foreign Consuls residents of the Town of Galveston, Tex.:

GENTLEMEN: To prevent the effusion of blood and destruction of property which will result from a bombardment of the town of Galveston, I have demanded of the military commandant the surrender of the place, with its fortifications, &c. This demand having been refused, I have the honor to inform you that four days will be allowed you from this date in which to remove your families and property. After that time the bombardment will commence at my earliest convenience.

I have the honor to be, your obedient servant,

HENRY EAGLE,
Commanding U. S. Naval Forces off Galveston, Tex.

JOS. J. COOK, *Colonel.*

HEADQUARTERS DEPARTMENT OF TEXAS,
Houston, May 19, 1862.

Col. J. J. COOK,
Commanding at Galveston:

From the tone of Captain Eagle's dispatch the inference is that he may again send a peremptory demand of surrender. There is to be no surrender on any circumstances. There may be an abandonment in face of a superior force, but nothing else, when it would be folly to attempt resistance.

P. O. HÉBERT,
Brigadier-General, Provisional Army.

GALVESTON, TEX., *May 21, 1862.*

Brig. Gen. P. O. HÉBERT:

There are several hundred tons of coal here, besides other articles, ordered to be removed to a place of safety. The laboring classes refuse to do duty, though offered large pay. The only way to reach them by force will be to declare martial law in this place, which I think needs this alternative to an imminent degree. Will you declare the city under martial law?

JOS. J. COOK,
Colonel.

GALVESTON, TEX., *May 21, 1862.*

Lieut. GEORGE R. WILSON, *Aide-de-Camp:*

I have received dispatch about not surrendering the city and will carry it out.

JOS. J. COOK,
Colonel.

GALVESTON, TEX., *May 22, 1862.*

Brig. Gen. P. O. HÉBERT:

This communication received from frigate to-day to the consuls:

It is not in [my] power to give you any assurance of security during the bombardment, for it is impossible to tell what direction the shot and shell will take.

I am making preparations to give the frigate a warm reception. The frigate and one bark off the bar. Steamer went eastward this morning.

JOS. J. COOK,
Colonel.

SPECIAL ORDERS, }
No. —.   }

GALVESTON,
May 25, 1862.

I. You will require every citizen subject to military duty, residing on Galveston Island, over the age of thirty-five, to be forthwith paraded, with the best arms and ammunition they can procure.

II. You are required, with the forces so organized, to co-operate with the commanding officer in the defense of the city of Galveston.

III. Should an emergency arise, in the opinion of the commanding officer, rendering the evacuation of the city of Galveston expedient, you will see that no citizen subject to military duty be permitted to remain.

IV. The object of this order being to aid as far as practicable in the defense of the city and to guard against the capture by the enemy of citizens whose services the State has a right to claim, you will see that these orders are rigidly enforced and observed.

By order Governor and Commander-in-Chief:

J. H. HERNDON,
Colonel and Volunteer Aide.

To Col. T. B. HOWARD.

RICHMOND, VA., *May* 26, 1862.

General P. O. HÉBERT,
Commanding in Texas, &c.:

GENERAI: A military department has been formed, comprising the States of Missouri, Arkansas, and that portion of Louisiana west of the Mississippi, and Texas. Maj. Gen. J. B. Magruder will be assigned to the command as soon as relieved from his present position. In the mean time, as senior officer of the department, its command devolves upon you. You have already been instructed as to the disposition of the armed troops organized in Texas and not wanted in that State. I presume those ready for the field are *en route* for Arkansas. I have to-day received information that the enemy, in possession of the city of New Orleans, are endeavoring to attract to that city provisions from that part of the Southern coast west of the Mississippi, which must not be allowed, nor can any commerce between him and our citizens be permitted. It may be necessary to send troops to Opelousas to prevent this illicit traffic, but as a camp of instruction has been established at that point, and Colonel Marigny appointed to the command, it is hoped that he will soon organize a sufficient force to control the operations of the enemy in that part of the State. Should this not be the case, and he call upon you for aid, you are requested to send one or more of the organized regiments of Texas, according to the number he may be able to arm, to report to him.

I have the honor to be, your obedient servant,

R. E. LEE,
General.

GENERAL ORDERS, } WAR DEPT., ADJT. AND INSP. GEN.'S OFF.,
No. 39.   } *Richmond, May* 26, 1862.

*   *   *   *   *   *   *

IV. The boundary of the Trans-Mississippi Department will embrace the States of Missouri and Arkansas, including the Indian Territory, the State of Louisiana west of the Mississippi River, and the State of Texas.*

*   *   *   *   *

By command of the Secretary of War:

S. COOPER,
Adjutant and Inspector General.

---

* Holmes was assigned to command July 16 and assumed command July 30, 1862. See Series I, Vol. XIII, pp. 855, 860.

Brig. Gen. H. P. BEE,
Commanding Western District, Department of Texas:

SIR: The mail of last week brought unofficial reports from various sources of the intention of the Government to re-enforce this army with one or more regiments; that Col. Debray was already on the march, and finally, as the postmaster at San Antonio expresses it, as derived from you, that New Mexico and Arizona are to be held at all hazards.

In the absence of all official communication on this subject, either from the Government in Richmond or from local departments nearer at hand, I was constrained to abandon New Mexico, our provisions, forage, and ammunition being completely exhausted. In this vicinity I find myself but little better off.

The army is absolutely subsisting on poor meat and bread, with a limited supply.

Under these circumstances the safety of the army depended upon a movement in some direction to the nearest point of supply.

The order has consequently been given for the movement down the country of the mass of the forces.

The unofficial information received by the last mail of course embarrasses me very much, especially as, from the information I have, no hope can be entertained of such supplies being thrown forward as will serve the purposes of an army in active campaign.

Without a dollar in specie, nothing can be purchased on the Mexican side of the river, and our sick even on this side are suffering for the want of articles which can only be procured with specie. Of sugar and coffee we have scarcely a pound; all other small rations are alike deficient; whilst of salt meat we have not an ounce.

Our ammunition may be said to be exhausted. For heavy guns we have perhaps 100 rounds. Clothing completely exhausted, with no means of renewing the supply.

My purpose in addressing this communication to you is to inform you distinctly of the resources of this country and New Mexico.

Any forces sent to operate in this quarter should not depend upon the productions of the country, except, perhaps, the single article of flour.

I have written briefly and to the point. I have made report after report to the Government, but up to this date have received not a single line of acknowledgment or encouragement, having been left to act entirely upon my own judgment and the pressure which momentarily surrounded me.

My volunteer aide, Captain Wager, will hand you this communication. I bespeak for him your kind attention and courtesy.

Very respectfully, your obedient servant,
H. H. SIBLEY,
Brigadier-General, Commanding.

HOUSTON, *May* 27, 1862.

Brig. Gen. P. O. HÉBERT, *Commanding, &c.:*

SIR: In obedience to your Special Orders, No. 596, April 24, 1862, I proceeded toward New Orleans, but ascertained at New Iberia that it was probable that New Orleans was occupied by the Federal forces.

I therefore directed myself toward Baton Rouge as the nearest place from whence I could communicate by telegraph with the War Department.

I reached Baton Rouge on the 2d of May and immediately telegraphed to the Adjutant-General. I awaited an answer until the 4th May. None having reached me and the Federals approaching Baton Rouge, I proceeded to Camp Moore, at Tangipahoa Station, on the New Orleans and Jackson Railroad, where I repeated my dispatch from Baton Rouge, herewith attached and made part of this report.

On the 7th May, being still without an answer, I requested by telegraph to be informed whether I should still await an answer or return to Texas.

On the 12th May I received the answer by telegraph hereto attached, and immediately started on my return to Houston.

I was much delayed by interruption in stage route and crevasses on the Mississippi River and high water generally through that part of Louisiana I had to travel over. I reached here to-day and report for duty.

I have the honor to be, very respectfully, your obedient servant,
·   SAML. BOYER DAVIS,
                              Captain and Assistant Adjutant-General.

[Inclosures.]

TANGIPAHOA STATION, *May* 5, 1862.
General S. COOPER, *Richmond:*

The Federals being in possession of Baton Rouge, I have come to this place, as I have not yet received an answer to my dispatch of the 2d, which I repeat:

BATON ROUGE, LA., *May* 2, 1862.
General S. COOPER,
·   *Adjutant and Inspector General C. S. Army, Richmond, Va.:*

I have been ordered here by Brig. Gen. P. O. Hébert, commanding Department of Texas, for the purpose of communicating with you and obtaining instructions.

General Hébert some time since received orders to send all his available troops to Little Rock. Recent events may make it necessary to change their destination, and he therefore applies for further instructions.

General Hébert has several infantry regiments on the march or ready to march; also a regiment and a battalion of mounted men. The infantry he sends via Alexandria, La.; the cavalry by the inland route. He advises the dismantling of the cavalry under marching orders, unless wanted in Arkansas.

Transportation is being rapidly obtained, and the want of it delays the troops. I am prepared to give any information the Department may require.
                                          SAML. BOYER DAVIS,
                              Captain and Assistant Adjutant-General.

RICHMOND, *May* 12, 1862.
Capt. SAMUEL BOYER DAVIS:

Return to Texas. No definite instructions can be given from here in answer to your dispatches of the 2d and 5th under present state of things.

S. COOPER.

———

GENERAL ORDERS, } HEADQUARTERS DEPARTMENT OF TEXAS,
     No. 45.   }   *Houston, May* 30, 1862.

I. The following proclamation is published for the information of all concerned:

PROCLAMATION.

II. I, P. O. Hébert, brigadier-general Provisional Army, Confederate States of America, do proclaim that martial law is hereby extended over the State of Texas.

Every white male person above the age of sixteen years, being temporarily or otherwise within the aforesaid limits, shall, upon a summons issued by the provost-marshal, promptly present himself before said provost-marshal to have his name, residence, and occupation registered, and to furnish such information as may be required of him. And such as claim to be aliens shall be sworn to the effect that they will abide by and maintain the laws of this State and the Confederate States so long as they are permitted to reside therein, and that they will not convey to our enemies any information whatever or do any act injurious to the Confederate States or beneficial to the United States.

Provosts-marshal shall order out and remove from their respective districts all disloyal persons and all persons whose presence is injurious to the interests of the country.

All orders issued by the provosts-marshal in the execution of their duties shall be promptly obeyed. Any disobedience of summons emanating from them shall be dealt with summarily. All officers commanding troops will promptly comply with any requisitions made upon them by provosts-marshal for aid or assistance. Any attempt to depreciate the currency of the Confederate States is an act of hostility; will be treated as such, and visited with summary punishment.

No interference with the rights of loyal citizens or with the usual routine of business or with the usual civil administration of the law will be permitted, except when necessary to enforce the provisions of this proclamation.

By order of Brig. Gen. P. O. Hébert, Provisional Army, C. S., commanding Department of Texas:

SAML. BOYER DAVIS,
Captain and Assistant Adjutant-General.

HEADQUARTERS,
Richmond, Va., May 31, 1862.

Brigadier-General HÉBERT,
Commanding Department of Texas:

GENERAL: Communications have been received by the President reporting the very destitute and critical condition of General Sibley's command now operating in New Mexico. You were perfectly right in sending the two regiments of cavalry, which had been previously ordered to Little Rock, to his relief. You will also cause to be sent to the western frontier of Texas all the supplies you can for the use of General Sibley's forces. Call upon the Governor of Texas to aid you in this work. The very remote and isolated position of General Sibley's command makes it necessary that you should promptly afford him all the aid you can in men and supplies.

I am, sir, very respectfully, your obedient servant,

R. E. LEE,
General.

GENERAL ORDERS, } HEADQUARTERS DEPARTMENT OF TEXAS,
    No. 46.   }   *Houston, June 2*, 1862.

1. By authority from the executive department of the State of Texas, all State, military, and civil officers are placed at the disposal of the Confederate Government, for the purpose of enforcing the provisions of the act approved April 15, 1862, and entitled "An act to further provide for the public defense."

2. In virtue of this authority, brigadier-generals of the State militia are directed to appoint an enrolling officer for each county included in the geographical limits of their brigades.

3. The enrolling officers will immediately enter upon the discharge of their duties, and comply with the published regulations from the War Department.

4. County enrolling officers will make their reports, with duplicate rolls of conscripts, to such enrolling officers as may be appointed from these headquarters to certain districts or specified limits, and in the absence of these directly to these headquarters, addressed to Capt. Samuel Boyer Davis, assistant adjutant-general, Houston, Tex. .

By order of Brig. Gen. P. O. Hébert:

SAML. BOYER DAVIS,
Captain and Assistant Adjutant-General.

SPECIAL ORDERS, } HEADQUARTERS DEPARTMENT OF TEXAS,
    No. 819.   }   *Houston, June 3*, 1862.

I. The counties of Austin, Harris, Galveston, Liberty, Chambers, and Jefferson will constitute the Sub-Military District of Houston, Department of Texas.

II. Col. George Flournoy is assigned to the immediate command of the Sub-Military District of Houston, and will for the present establish his headquarters at Houston.

III. The senior officer present on duty at any post within the sub-military district is the immediate commander thereof.   ·

IV. All official communications will be addressed to the commander of the district, with the form and mode prescribed by the regulations.

By order of Brig. Gen. P. O. Hébert:

SAML. BOYER DAVIS,
Captain and Assistant Adjutant-General.

EXECUTIVE OFFICE,
Richmond, June 7, 1862.

General H. H. SIBLEY,
    Commanding, &c., San Antonio, Tex.:

GENERAL: I avail myself of an opportunity of communicating with you in a speedy and direct manner through your aide-de-camp, Captain Ochiltree. I rejoice in being able to congratulate you on the distinguished successes of your command, and when I consider your field of operations, the superior number and means of supply of the enemy, and the other difficulties under which you have labored, the conduct of yourself and the army under your command is recognized as most praiseworthy.

With the assistance of the two regiments sent to you from Texas I trust that you will be able to meet the more immediate and pressing exigencies that may arise, and that your own ability and military resources and the valor of your troops may supply comparative inferiority in numbers and munitions of war. Captain Ochiltree will inform you of our condition in this region, and this will be to you a sufficient explanation for failure to re-enforce you to the full extent of your necessities.

With best wishes for your continued success, and with the hope that we may hereafter meet to enjoy in peace the independence for which, you are struggling, I am, very truly and respectfully, yours,

JEFFERSON DAVIS.

GENERAL ORDERS, } HEADQUARTERS,
No. 5. } *Tyler, Tex., June* 12, 1862.

I. By virtue of a commission as brigadier-general in the Provisional Army of the Confederate States, the undersigned assumes command of all the troops within the State east of the Brazos River and north of the old San Antonio road.

II. The commanders of regiments, battalions, and companies, within these limits, will report by express to these headquarters as early as possible, giving arm of service, strength of command, character, quantity, and condition of arms, ammunition, camp and garrison equipage, hospital and medical stores, and transportation.

III. I announce as a portion of my staff Maj. John Henry Brown, assistant adjutant-general; Capt. Ben. E. Benton, aide-de-camp, and Capts. A. W. Terrill, E. S. C. Robertson, C. L. Robards, and W. A. Pitts, volunteer aides-de-camp, who will be respected and obeyed as such.

IV. All twelve-months' volunteers, who have not reorganized under the furlough and bounty law or the conscript act will reorganize as early as practicable, and all officers not re-elected will be relieved from duty, and their names reported to these headquarters.

V. All enlisted men under eighteen and over thirty-five years of age, who desire it, will be discharged from the service, and no person who is to be discharged under this order will take part in the reorganization.

VI. All regiments, battalions, and companies north and east of this place (Tyler), including those of Col. Edward Clark, Col. W. B. Ochiltree, Col. Richard Waterhouse, and Col. Horace Randal, will take up the line of march, with as little delay as possible, for Little Rock, Ark., proceeding by the most practicable route from Marshall and Jefferson, and will report to the commander of the army west of the Mississippi River.

VII. All official communications for these headquarters must be indorsed "Official business," and directed to Maj. John Henry Brown, Assistant Adjutant-General, C. S. P. A.

H. E. McCULLOCH,
Brigadier-General, C. S. P. A.

JOHN HENRY BROWN,
Assistant Adjutant-General.

HDQRS. TRANS-MISS. DEPT. SOUTH OF RED RIVER,
Houston, June 18, 1862.

General R. E. LEE, *Richmond, Va.:*

SIR: I have the honor to acknowledge at the hands of Major Bryan your dispatches bearing date May 28.

Being informed that Major-General Hindman, who ranks me, was in command of the "Trans-Mississippi Department north of Red River," I have assumed command until further orders of the district south of this river.

Such troops as can be equipped and armed I am and have been for some time forwarding toward Little Rock.

The great difficulty, almost an impossibility, is in getting arms; men we can command.

We have now several regiments, both of cavalry and infantry, entirely unarmed. Even when shot-guns are obtained there is a difficulty in preparing suitable ammunition for such a variety of calibers.

I have ordered buck-shot to be made, the men to prepare their own ammunition. All possible means are used to collect and repair such arms as may be found in the country.

I had to some extent anticipated your instructions in regard to Western Louisiana, by ordering a battalion of mounted men to New Iberia, on the Teche.

I would respectfully advise the dismounting of nearly all the troops west of the Mississippi.

There is an excess of cavalry, badly mounted and worse armed. As infantry, if not more efficient, would at least be less expensive.

Captain Davis, my assistant adjutant-general, the bearer of this communication, may give you valuable information in regard to the troops, equipments, armaments, means of transportation, &c.

Very respectfully, your obedient servant,
P. O. HÉBERT,
Brigadier-General, Provisional Army.

[Inclosure.]

GENERAL ORDERS, {   HDQRS. TRANS-MISS. DISTRICT
                          SOUTH OF RED RIVER,
No. 1.   }   *Houston, Tex., June* 18, 1862.

In virtue of instructions from General Headquarters at Richmond, bearing date May 28, 1862, I assume command of the district comprising the State of Texas and all that portion of the State of Louisiana west of the Mississippi River and south of Red River, and of all the posts, camps, and troops within the limits of the district.

P. O. HÉBERT,
Brigadier-General, Provisional Army.

———

FORT FILLMORE, *June* 26, 1862.

General H. H. SIBLEY:

GENERAL: I inclose herewith some dispatches taken from one of Carleton's expresses.* You will see from them that my stay here must be very short. Canby has already crossed his forces to the east side of the river, and the rains having already commenced, he will in a few

---

* Not found.

days be able to cross the Jornada. In this state of affairs I find subject to my control less than thirty days' breadstuff, and the idea which is prevalent that we are about to leave renders it very difficult to get anything. My means of transportation are entirely inadequate to hauling the requisite amount of supplies. Something must be done, and that speedily, or the troops with me will be in a state of starvation. Could not a portion of the supplies with Green and Hardiman be left on the road and supplies sent in time to meet them. The flour and corn-meal I now have would have lasted until the new crop came in. But it is not likely that I shall [be] able to stay that length of time. The hospital at Franklin will be left in a destitute condition.

Let me know soon what you will do. I have been sick for several days, and am scarcely able to be about, and would not be under other circumstances.

Respectfully, your obedient servant,

WM. STEELE,
Colonel Seventh Regt. Texas Vols., Commanding in Arizona.

Abstract from return of the District of the Lower Rio Grande, Texas, commanded by Col. P. N. Luckett, for June, 1862.

Troops.	Present for duty. Officers.	Present for duty. Men.	Aggregate present.	Aggregate present and absent.	Artillery, pieces of.
Fort Brown	10	140	182	211	......
Ringgold Barracks	35	446	567	614	10
Carracitos, Tex	3	77	88	104	......
Resaca de la Palma	3	72	97	114	......
Edinburg	4	70	74	77	......
Camp near Ringgold Barracks	3	60	69	107	......
Carrizo, Tex	4	65	69	81	......
Grand total	62	930	1,146	1,308	10

CAMP NEAR THE DREDGE-BOAT,
[*July* 8]—5 p. m.

Colonel LIVENSKIOLD, *Provost-Marshal:*

COLONEL: I send Mr. Leonard down with this communication. On leaving the Breaker and Rebecca late last evening I came around through the cut to the dredge-boat—saw two launches of the enemy near the shell bank; one very large. With a spy-glass observed every movement. They landed 200 or 300 yards above the fort and formed on the beach. About 25 marched up to the fort and immediately hoisted the American flag upon the ramparts. I counted 15 or 20, who got up upon the fort and acted like they were rejoicing over their capture. They remained at the fort late last night and crossed over the bayou and encamped, so I was informed, all night. They were at the houses (?) early this morning. To-day the schooner came up to the shell banks and anchored in front of the channel. I left the dredge late last night, and reached my camp early this morning, about an hour before day. Fearing the enemy might land at the dredge and cut us off, I concluded to bring a detachment down, with two pieces of artillery; about half way I discovered the schooner and a large launch gone up Aransas Bay. I immediately sent back men and some of the teams to remove my camp equipage and ammunition into the interior, as I have no guns to compete with the one on board the schooner, from the appearance of its bulk as seen through a glass, being covered with a tarpaulin. It is amidship. I fear they will make an attack upon my encampment. 1 shall save all of my artillery, but shall lose a portion of things. There has been no boat down from Saluria for the last few days, and I fear they have a gunboat up there and blockaded the inland communication.

I understand from Captain Hawley that the enemy has placed a gun on this bank, but I think it doubtful. They sounded the channel to-day with one of their launches as far down as Hog Island, and Conklin [was] at anchor in a mile of them, but it appears he did not see them.

If I to-day had the gunboats the launches could have been driven from the shell bank, but it seems impossible to do without means to act with. I think they have captured this evening the Monte Christo and cargo. I ordered the captain to burn his cotton and boat as soon as the enemy appeared in sight; whether he will do so or not I cannot tell. I am at a loss what to do with my force, situated as I am. The steamer A. B. and two other boats are at the dredge; Captain Dunn and Cherry, the engineer, left to-day for Lavaca by land, having abandoned the boat, there being no chance to get out. What the intention of the enemy is can only be determined by future events. I shall have to fall back with my artillery, as it is of no use against their gunboat; besides, I have no ammunition suitable for 12-pound howitzer. Should they attempt to come up the cut I shall give them fight. I look for them to-night. I shall order these boats to Corpus Christi, and am now trying to signalize Lieutenant Conklin, who is laying at anchor just below the dug-out. Leonard will give you further information. I have written to General Bee to-day.

Yours, respectfully,

BENJ. F. NEAL.

P. S.—Let no boats start for Saluria.

GENERAL ORDERS,   HDQRS. MIL. SUB-DIST. OF HOUSTON,
   No. 5.   *Houston, Tex., July 8, 1862.*

I. In obedience to Special Orders, No. 6, from headquarters Trans-Mississippi District South of Red River, the undersigned assumes to-day command of this military sub-district.

*   *   *   *   *   *   *

X. B. DEBRAY,
Colonel, Commanding Military Sub-District, Houston.

HEADQUARTERS FORCES OF ARIZONA,
El Paso, July 12, 1862.

S. COOPER, *Adjutant and Inspector General, Richmond:*

GENERAL: Having recently abandoned the Territory of Arizona, and being on the point of starting with my whole command for San

Antonio, I deem it advisable to give you a brief statement of the various causes that have compelled me to this step.' Of the strength of the force with which I was expected to hold the Territory—about 100 men—you will be able to form a just estimate from the within field report.*

After General Sibley had withdrawn from the country the greater portion of his command, the Mexican population, justly thinking our tenure very frail and uncertain, showed great unwillingness to sell property of any sort for Confederate paper, which would of course be valueless to them should I be compelled to retire, which was at any time probable; and as I was without specie with which to make purchases, I was obliged to seize upon such supplies as were required for the subsistence of the troops and such means of transportation as would enable me to move my command whenever the necessity might arise for so doing. This occasioned so much ill-feeling on the part of the Mexicans that in many instances armed resistance was offered to foraging parties acting under my orders, and in the various skirmishes which took place one captain and several men of my regiment were killed by them. Besides this, the troops with me were so disgusted with the campaign and so anxious to return to Texas that in one or two instances they were on the point of open mutiny, and threatened to take the matter in their own hands unless they were speedily marched back to San Antonio.

In the mean time the forces from California, about 1,500 strong, were steadily approaching, and on the 6th of July their advance was at Fort Thorn, on the Rio Grande. Troops from Fort Craig had been seen the day previous moving toward the same point. Knowing this, and that the enemy, after leaving competent garrisons behind, would be able to bring 3,000 troops against me, independent of a recent re-enforcement which they received—of 500 men—from Pike's Peak, and 250 more, with six rifle cannon, who escorted the paymaster from Kansas, the necessity of moving my force became imperative.

I was then at Fort Fillmore, with but little ammunition, and, notwithstanding the efforts I had made, with very inadequate means of transportation. I, however, abandoned the Territory on the 8th of July and marched for Fort Bliss, at which point I now am. As soon as this move had been determined on the sale was ordered of all public property at Fort Bliss which was too bulky for or not worth transportation. This sale was held for specie and breadstuffs. The specie was turned over to the general hospital which I am compelled to leave at Franklin. There was besides a considerable quantity of stores that could not be sold and which were too weighty for transportation, such as horse and mules shoes, cannon ammunition, tents, &c. To conclude, I am now about to start for San Antonio with very limited means of transportation, and insufficient supply of breadstuff and beef, depending on the contingency of meeting provisions forwarded from San Antonio, and with troops in many instances almost naked.

The general hospital at Franklin, under the charge of Dr. Southworth, has been provided with $830 in specie and credit to a larger amount with parties in Mexico. This I submit to you as a true representation of the condition of affairs in this country.

Very respectfully, your obedient servant,

WM. STEELE,
Colonel, Commanding.

---

* Not found.

HDQRS. SUB-MILITARY DISTRICT OF HOUSTON,
Houston, Tex., July 14, 1862.
Capt. C. M. MASON,
   Acting Assistant Adjutant-General :

CAPTAIN : I have the honor to inclose to you a report, with accompanying documents from the provost-marshal at Matagorda informing me of the endangered condition of Matagorda and vicinity. I have issued orders to one squadron of my regiment to march from the San Bernard to Matagorda, to lend assistance to the provost-marshal, if necessary, and also to meet such emergencies as may arise in case of a landing by the enemy. Please find herewith a copy of my answer* to the provost-marshal of Matagorda, and also a copy of the order* issued to Debray's regiment to detach a squadron to the coast and to keep in readiness to move in case of necessity. I hope that these dispositions will meet the approval of the general commanding. I may yet, if necessary, move Brown's battalion from the Chocolate to Matagorda Bay, but I have no infantry. I do not deem it expedient to call on Bates' battalion, which covers Brazoria County, one of the richest in the State in cotton and negroes, the population of which has been considerably thinned by volunteering. I have here but two companies of Griffin's battalion, one of which is unarmed, and they are necessary to guard the powder magazine and the provost-marshal's office. I have not been able as yet to receive reports from Elmore's battalion, stationed at Hempstead. I am, however, informed that it is considerably reduced by sickness—measles and flux—and that it is very indifferently armed. Some infantry, however, shall have to be sent to the coast, if, as it appears, the enemy intend to inaugurate a warfare of forays on our weak points. I am informed by Mr. Clements, of Galveston, who just arrived from Matagorda, that it was reported that the enemy had landed and planted a piece of artillery on the shore of Aransas Bay.

I am, very respectfully, captain, your obedient servant,
X. B. DEBRAY,
Colonel, Commanding Sub-Military District of Houston, Texas.

P. S.—I do not believe that the enemy can approach Matagorda with large boats. We should guard only against predatory parties in launches and yawls.

[Inclosures.]

MATAGORDA, TEX., *July* —, 1862.
Col. X. B. DEBRAY:

DEAR SIR : I wish to inclose to you a document† addressed to me by the best and most influential citizens of Matagorda, regarding the defense of the place and vicinity against the demands of the pirate Kittredge. His object seems to be to send out small parties on light-draught boats, with a few pieces of artillery on each, which would enable him to land, under cover of his guns, for the purpose of foraging on the small towns and rich vicinities along the coast. As I said in my last communication, only light-draught boats can reach this place. The channel 3 miles below this place is only 60 yards wide and not over 3½ or 4 feet deep. You can judge of the style of launches and

---

*Not found, but see letter of July 15, p. 726.   † Not found.

quantity of men which might be forced upon us under the circum-stances. I do not think, from the best information I can glean, that Kittredge's forces at this time amount to over 150 or 200 men, but he seems to be well supplied with boats and launches of light draught, yet sufficient to carry a few pieces of artillery. In his language he is threat-ening and his manners impudent. After seeing a map of the locality you can judge of the necessity of artillery or the fitting up of boats, as I understand the major commanding has proposed. He has fitted up two boats, one to convey forage and subsistence to the force stationed at the neck of the peninsula and mouth of Old Caney, composed of 24 enlisted men, under command of an officer, with an extra detail of 2 men to assist the sailor to run his boat. They are sent out to re-main nine days. This brings the men on duty every third night, two sentinels on post at the same time. This is the point I spoke of in my last as being the suspicious place where vessels of the enemy stopped from two to seven days; also the outlet of the rich valley of Old Caney; from Matagorda to the canal 20 miles; by the route the horses go 30 to 35 miles. From this suspicious locality to the extremity of the peninsula (on account of loyal citizens, so I am informed by the best citizens) no system of espionage can be carried on. From the extremity of the peninsula (the pass into Matagorda Bay) the water is good in the channel to within 3 miles of the town of Matagorda. This is the reef as described in the previous part of this communication. In this channel I have a light, fast-sailing vessel, which is manned by 6 privates and 2 non-commissioned officers, besides the sailor, with a detail of 1 man to assist him. These pickets are relieved every twenty-four hours. The protection from surprise by this means seems evident. Every vigilance is enforced on the officers and men on duty, in whom I have confidence. Should you think fit to keep a gunboat in the bay or establish a battery on Dog Island I shall require one or more companies, as the reserve will be too small.

Our forces, both below and above this place, have acted (according to the best authority here) in a shameful manner, and I hope to be able to prevent any reflections being cast on our regiment by any injudicious conduct on the part of our squadron. I find the citizens here are hos-pitable people, and the ladies pay every attention to the wants of the sick in hospital, both in regard to diet and clothing. Too much cannot be said for them. Our soldiers are orderly and respectful in their conduct.

Since writing the above I learn by a passenger from the coast that Kittredge has received a new light-draught gunboat, propelled by steam, to be used in this bay. We may possibly hear from him if this report be true. Major Chinn may visit you this week and give you full details.

G. W. OWENS,
Capt., Comdg. Companies E and F, Debray's Regt. Tex. Cav.

PROVOST-MARSHAL'S OFFICE,
Matagorda, Tex., July 12, 1862.

Maj. R. L. UPSHAW,
Acting Assistant Adjutant-General, Houston, Tex.:

SIR: Inclosed you will find a copy of the communication from Major Shea, of Indianola, the commander of that post, [and] a copy of my communication* to J. D. Hawkins, major of our battalion of infantry

---

* Not found.

of militia. I would respectfully call your attention to the following statistics:

Number of inhabitants in our town, about	400
Number of families on the peninsula, about	24
Number of families in the rest of the county	
Number of negroes in the county, over	2,000
Number of bales of cotton here, about	700
Number of bales shipped since January 1, 1862	3,850
Number of ·bushels of salt now here	1,000
Number of bushels received since January 1, 1862	16,000
Number of sheep on the peninsula	10,000
Number of goats on the peninsula	100
Number of cattle on the peninsula	1,500

The peninsula is about 65 miles long. The lower Matagorda Bay is from 15 to 30 miles wide, affording access to vessels drawing from 8 to 12 feet of water. Below the city of Matagorda the Dog Island Reef affords a natural obstruction, over which not more than 4 feet can at any time be obtained. The peninsula is about a mile in width, and as the bay runs up to the mouth of the Caney, which is emptied into the bay by an artificial canal, a force might be landed at the mouth of Caney, take possession of the bay and peninsula, and have free access to the whole of the Caney region. I regard it necessary to place these facts before you for your consideration, and to ask instructions and orders how to proceed in this matter. There is among some of our citizens a great and growing aversion to leaving their homes and residences, and if evacuation of any one point is necessary I think it ought to be general, complete, and thorough, and not by any means partial, as those who are left behind will often, almost imperceptibly to themselves, give information and comfort to the enemy. Let me urge on you that I cannot at present regard such harsh means as necessary. It may be so on the lower part of the peninsula, but certainly not here. The inhabitants of the peninsula are left without a military force, guard, or protection. The inhabitants are too few and far between to guard themselves, and require some force of that kind, as 8,000 to 10,000 head of sheep and 1,200 or 1,500 head of cattle and 100 goats would subsist a military force for some time.

Very respectfully, your obedient servant,

R. H. CHINN,
Provost-Marshal, Matagorda City, Tex.

[Sub-inclosure.]

HEADQUARTERS CAMP OF OBSERVATION,
Indianola, Tex., July 10, 1862.

R. H. CHINN,
Provost-Marshal, Matagorda County, Tex.:

SIR: I am just in receipt of an express from Lamar, stating that a large schooner, heavily armed, is now lying in Aransas Bay. She has captured one vessel loaded with cotton and 300 bales at Lamar, and [will] doubtless attempt to capture others. This schooner is accompanied by a large bark, supposed to be the Arthur, commanded by Captain Kittredge (a bold and daring fellow), who will probably follow up his success by making forages in this bay. You will therefore prevent any vessel from leaving Matagorda for the lower bay until further orders from these headquarters. Take such steps as you may deem necessary to prevent cotton or any species of property that may be useful to the enemy from falling into their hands. I would advise that you call on the State troops of your county to hold themselves in readiness to assist in the defense of your city if any demonstration is made by the enemy in their launches.

I am, very respectfully, &c.,

DAN. D. SHEA,
Major, Commanding Indianola, Tex.

HDQRS. MILITARY SUB-DISTRICT OF HOUSTON,
Houston, Tex., July 15, 1862.

Maj. R. H. CHINN,
Provost-Marshal, Matagorda, Tex.:

SIR: Your report* of the 12th instant has just been received. It is impossible for me to give you any positive instructions for your government, as I cannot anticipate all cases which may arise. It is of absolute necessity that the inhabitants of Matagorda and vicinity shall place all their property—negroes, cotton, corn, and cattle—out of reach of the enemy. Such cotton as cannot be removed must be destroyed. If patriotism does not dictate this course to the citizens, force must be resorted to in order to carry out the policy generally adopted by our government and to prevent the enemy from receiving aid and comfort. Should our citizens feel any repugnance in leaving their homes and remain at the approach of the enemy, they have but two alternatives left—insults or abject submission. I have ordered two companies of my regiment to march from Camp Clark L. Owen, on the San Bernard, to Matagorda, with instructions to lend you assistance. The commanding officer is instructed to concert his action with you. Your duty is a very responsible one. Its discharge requires all your discretion, energy, and patriotism. Appeal first to the citizens. Cause them to understand that they owe to their country the sacrifice of their comforts, and that their mere presence would be an aid and comfort to the enemy. Should they be deaf to the voice of patriotism and sound policy then you will have to make use of force. Harsh means should, however, be resorted to only at the last extremity. I desire you to inform me of every interesting event that may transpire within your jurisdiction.

I have the honor to be, very respectfully, your obedient servant,

X. B. DEBRAY.

PROVOST-MARSHAL'S OFFICE,
Matagorda, Tex., July 17, 1862.

Col. X. B. DEBRAY,
Commanding Sub-Military District of Houston:

SIR: Your dispatch dated the 15th instant has just been received, and I hasten to reply to it. The enemy's vessels have captured several bay lighters, and by that means can command the entire bay. Whether we require any artillery or not I am perfectly incapable of informing you, but we rejoice in the acquisition we possess in having two companies of Debray's regiment. Our fellow-citizens are very patriotic, and we rejoice in having it in our power to render all the aid we can to our cause. There is a determination to remove all that

---

* See p. 724.

would aid and assist the enemy in any way from our midst, and we will exert ourselves to our utmost to get rid of this cotton or other means that they may recognize. Would it be consonant with the public interest or the wishes of the department that if we require more aid and assistance we may call on Lieut. Col. R. R. Brown?

Respectfully,

R. H. CHINN,
Provost-Marshal, Matagorda County.

CAMP CHARLES RUSSELL, *July* 19, 1862.

General H. P. BEE, *Commanding :*

GENERAL : Your official communication of the 16th,[*] ordering me to repair at once to the different points on the bay and take command of the troops there stationed, was received to-day, and in obedience to that order I shall leave to-morrow. After making the necessary investigation I shall inform you at once of the true state of affairs, and under your approval press with energy whatever measures I may deem advisable in ridding our bays of the enemy. The rumors afloat of their strength and position I think exaggerated. Their impudence is great. Dr. Dill can give you my views, but personal examination may change them. Before receiving your orders I had detailed 50 men, fully armed, to proceed at once to the bay and lie in ambush for the enemy, who I heard were in the habit of landing at certain points. I have carried out the design, feeling that it did not in any way conflict with the execution of your orders. I intended to accompany them myself. I made a requisition on the ordnance officer of this county for ammunition, being without it ourselves, which was at once complied with. Do not let Dr. Dill resign, if you please.

I am, very truly, your obedient servant,

A. M. HOBBY.

P. S.—In Captain McCampbell's company there are 100 privates, about half of whom are Mexicans, and they are very anxious to form another company exclusively of Mexicans. This change meets the hearty wish of all who compose the organization. I regard it almost as a military necessity, and feel it would mutually advance the interest of both parties. Orders have to be repeated in Spanish by a non-commissioned [officer], causing delays; besides, in close company association their modes of life, &c., are dissimilar. This matter I respectfully submit for your consideration and trust that it may receive your attention.

HDQRS. SUB-MILITARY DISTRICT OF HOUSTON,
[*July* 25, 1862.]

Capt. C. M. MASON,
Acting Assistant Adjutant-General, Houston, Tex. :

SIR : I have the honor to inclose herewith reports of Captain Owens, Debray's regiment, and the provost-marshal of Matagorda upon the state of affairs at Matagorda and vicinity.

I have the honor to be, sir, very respectfully, your obedient servant,

X. B. DEBRAY,
Colonel, Commanding Sub-Military District of Houston.

---

[*] Not found.

[Inclosures.]

MATAGORDA, TEX., *June* [*July*] 20, 1862.

Lieut. R. [M.] FRANKLIN:

SIR: I arrived here with my command on Friday, 18th instant. I found no probable danger of an attack here at this place. Captain Kittredge, of the bark Arthur, blockading vessel at Aransas Pass, has created some considerable alarm from here to that Pass, and has been, to say the least of it, exceedingly impudent, landing and displaying Federal colors, making extravagant threats, &c., and has succeeded in taking some cotton. From the best information I can obtain he has not more than 150 men all told. He has not erected a battery at Lamar, as was reported. He is nevertheless a troublesome neighbor, landing at all unguarded points where there is an interest sufficient to invite his attention. One of the most important points is the mouth of Caney River, which once emptied into the Gulf, but now, by the aid of a canal a few hundred yards in length, empties into the upper extremity of Matagorda Bay, where the peninsula puts out some 20 miles from this place. There, I am informed, the Federal vessels never pass without stopping and lying off for from one to six days. It is not known, however, that any troops have ever landed at this place, no watch ever having been kept. I intend to send a detachment of men, under command of a commissioned officer, to be relieved once per week, by the aid of a boat from this place, carrying subsistence and forage from this place, and by a short ride down the peninsula to a resident's house I can communicate with the detachment in a few hours. Three miles below the city is a reef extending entirely across the bay. I there can establish a picket post, which will render a surprise impossible. The health of the command has improved since leaving Camp Clark L. Owen. Our horses can have no grass here, but I can supply them, I think, with full rations of corn and fodder. I have also made arrangements to have them stabled. I think we can probably subsist here as cheap as where we left. I have obtained a beautiful little place for a hospital, good water, &c., without cost. I am promised the services of one of the best physicians here, if I need him. From present prospects I expect the command to fare as well as usual. Some are suffering for clothing. Our men behave themselves creditably. I shall promptly report all that transpires of interest. All plans have been concerted with Major Chinn, provost-marshal.

I have the honor to be, &c., yours, very respectfully,

G. W. OWENS,
Captain, Commanding Squadron at Camp Matagorda, Texas.

PROVOST-MARSHAL'S OFFICE,
Matagorda, Tex., July 22, 1862.

Capt. ROBERT M. FRANKLIN,
Acting Assistant Adjutant-General:

SIR: I regret much that my information is so meager, and that I cannot detail it with any degree of certainty. All the passes between Aransas Bay and Corpus Christi Bay have been temporarily blocked up. The enemy still have possession of Aransas Bay, and have within the past week removed some cotton from Lamar, Refugio [Aransas] County, to Mercer's Landing, Aransas Town, Saint Joseph's Island, where it is under the guns of the vessel blockading that Pass. Captain Owens' command is here in good health and high spirits. They have been called on to perform some police duty—the removal of a suspected person to Wharton County. There are no blockading vessels at present at Pass Cavallo, and we learn here that a portion of the military force stationed there has been removed to some point on Aransas Bay.

Respectfully, yours, &c.,

R. H. CHINN,
Provost-Marshal Matagorda County, Texas.

ENGINEER DEPARTMENT,
Harrisburg, July 30, 1862.

Col. X. B. DEBRAY,
Commanding Sub-Military District of Houston, Tex.:

SIR: In accordance with your Special Orders, No. 95, I have examined the defensive works of Sabine Pass and vicinity, and have the honor to report the following: About 2 miles south of the town of Sabine, and on same side of the river, there is an earthwork thrown up not sufficient to protect the four guns that are in it. The shape and figure is also not according to the proper defense, the ground itself about 2 feet too low, and therefore subject to occasional overflow. The location itself is a good one, and has command over vessels that can cross the bar, which has about an average depth of $6\frac{1}{2}$ to 7 feet, with soft, muddy bottom. The armament consists of four guns, of which two are 32-pounders and two 18-pounders. All four are [on] old and unwieldy truck carriages. The powder magazine is not bomb-proof, and also subject to overflows. The whole work is in a dilapidated condition. There is ammunition enough for all four guns, but they have no fuses for shells, nor port-fires, neither gunners' level, tangent scales, pass-boxes, friction-tubes, lanyards, &c. About 35 miles up the river there are two 24-pounders on barbette carriages mounted on a shell bank. They are there of no use whatever, as there is a bar with but 3 feet of water at the mouth of Sabine River into Sabine Lake. No vessels of any amount can therefore go up to these guns. They can therefore be employed somewhere else. The pass at Sabine is certainly a very important point, and in fact the only port from where we receive our powder and other articles. It is the nearest point to the West Indies and easy of access. I would therefore recommend the erection of a strong open battery in place of the old one, for five guns (three of 32 and two of 24-pounders), all on barbette carriages. Then take those two 18-pounders and place them half way between the battery and the town, so that they may flank the lower works.

All of which is respectfully submitted.

J. KELLERSBERG,
Major, Engineer in Charge.

HEADQUARTERS DEPARTMENT OF TEXAS,
San Antonio, Tex., August 8, 1862.

General H. H. SIBLEY,
Provisional Army, C. S., San Antonio, Tex.:

GENERAL: I have the honor to acknowledge your favor of the 1st instant requesting information in regard to the troops, military resources, &c., of this department. Please find inclosed a statement of the number of organized regiments, the arm they belong to, stations, and destination. The regiments raised by my authority in the State are mostly armed. The regiments authorized directly from the War Department by orders to individuals and not passing through the headquarters of this department are, I fear, very deficient in arms. Every effort has been made to procure arms and munitions both here and from abroad, but with little or no success. Contracts have been made with responsible parties, with permission given to ship cotton for the purpose, but with meager results. It has been found impossible to procure arms in Mexico or at any of the Gulf ports. I am now making an effort to try importation from Europe by furnishing cotton. Arms of every description are purchased by the ordnance department as they are picked up here and there throughout the State. Mr. J. R. Jefferson, of Seguin, is Government agent to purchase arms, and is assisted by agents at different stations. The State of Texas is making efforts to procure arms by means of cotton, and has an agent already in Europe. Please also find inclosed a report of arms, ordnance, &c., at the San Antonio Arsenal.*

In regard to the quartermaster's and commissary departments, the estimates were of course based upon the number of troops in the department. Arrangements, however, it is supposed, can be made to provide for your brigade by the period of its reorganization. In the matter of clothing the quartermaster's department is only deficient simply owing to the difficulty and impossibility of procuring it. There is an existing contract with the State penitentiary by which a limited monthly supply is obtained. In this respect I may mention that there are now in this department, destined for the army east of the Mississippi, some 500 bales (400 yards each) of gray cloth, in care of Captain Sharkey, quartermaster, C. S. Army. In view of the great difficulty in transportation across the Mississippi, I have directed Captain Sharkey to store the cloth at Houston and to proceed to Richmond for further orders in regard thereto. Should it be found impossible to place the cloth across the river, it might be advisable to appropriate a portion of it to the use of the troops on this side.

Please find accompanying two letters of instruction* from General Lee, commanding the army.

In conclusion, general, I beg leave to say that any assistance in my power to render, as commander of this department, to your command will be cheerfully extended.

I have the honor to be, very respectfully, your obedient servant,

P. O. HÉBERT,
Brigadier-General, Provisional Army.

[Inclosure.]

Mounted troops.—Colonel Ford, Second Regiment Texas Mounted Rifles, nine companies, furloughed September; Colonel Parsons' regiment, Arkansas; Colonel Debray's regiment, San Bernard River; Colonel Woods' regiment, San Marcos; Colonels Randal's, Carter's, Wilkes', Gillespie's, Burnett's, and Burford's regiments *en route* to Little Rock; Colonel Gurley's regiment, Partisan, Waco.

Raised under authority of General Hindman.—Major Yager's battalion, Rio Grande; Major Brown's battalion, near Houston; Major Waller's battalion, New Iberia; Major Taylor's battalion, Fort Mason; Captain

---

* Not found.

Bowles' company, unattached, Galveston; Captains Andrews' and Durant's companies, unattached, Virginia Point; Captain Daly's company, unattached, Galveston; Captain Martin's company, Partisans, *en route* to New Iberia; Captain Rountree's company, Partisans, San Antonio; Captain Duff's company, Partisans, Fredericksburg; Captains R. Benavides', S. Benavides', and Rhodes' companies, unattached, Rio Grande; Captain Ware's company, unattached, Corpus Christi; Captain Brackenridge's company, unattached, Indianola, and Captain Navarro's company, unattached, special service.

Artillery.—Colonel Cook's regiment, Galveston and main-land; Major Shea's two companies, Indianola; Captain Creuzbar's company, Rio Grande; Captain Neal's company, Aransas; Captain Wilson's light battery, Houston; Captain Haldeman's light battery, *en route* to Little Rock; Captains Willke's and Maclin's light batteries, Rio Grande, and Captain Hill's Partisans, organizing.

Infantry.—Colonel Luckett's Third Regiment, seven companies, Rio Grande; Colonel Garland's Sixth Regiment, *en route* to Little Rock; Colonel Nelson's regiment, Arkansas; Colonels Flournoy's, Young's, Spaight's, Roberts', Hubbard's, Clark's, Waterhouse's, Ochiltree's, and Allen's regiments ordered to Little Rock; Colonel Elmore's regiment ordered to Hempstead; Major Griffin's battalion, Houston; Major Hobby's battalion, four companies, Aransas; Captain Ireland's company, unattached, Corpus Christi; Captains Newton's, Toole's, Penaloza's, and Boise's companies, unattached, San Antonio.

Mixed commands.—Colonel Waul's Legion, *en route* to Little Rock; Lieutenant-Colonel Bates' battalion, Velasco, and Lieutenant-Colonel Spaight's battalion, Sabine Pass.

> [P. O. HÉBERT,
> *Brigadier-General, Provisional Army.*]

GENERAL ORDERS, }   HDQRS. TRANS-MISS. DEPARTMENT,
No. 5. }   *Little Rock, Ark., August* 20, 1862.

The Trans-Mississippi Department is divided into districts, as follows:

1st. The District of Texas, composed of the State of Texas and the Territory of Arizona, Brig. Gen. P. O. Hébert commanding.

2d. The District of Louisiana, composed of all the State of Louisiana west of Mississippi River, Maj. Gen. Richard Taylor commanding.

3d. The District of Arkansas, composed of the States of Arkansas and Missouri and the Indian country west thereof, Maj. Gen. T. C. Hindman commanding.

By command of Major-General Holmes:

> R. C. NEWTON,
> *Assistant Adjutant-General.*

GENERAL ORDERS, }   HEADQUARTERS DISTRICT OF TEXAS,
No. 1. }   *San Antonio, Tex., September* 12, 1862.

In virtue of the above order I assume command of the First District of Texas.

> P. O. HÉBERT,
> *Brigadier-General, Provisional Army Confederate States.*

HEADQUARTERS DEPARTMENT OF TEXAS,
San Antonio, Tex., August 26, 1862.

CHIEF OF STAFF OF MAJOR-GENERAL HOLMES,
Commanding Trans-Mississippi District, Little Rock, Ark.:

SIR: I have the honor to report, for the information of the major-general commanding, as follows:

The evacuation of New Mexico and Arizona by General Sibley's command leaves the northwestern frontier of this State and its line of posts exposed. Colonel Carleton has joined General Canby, with a force from California, consisting of one regiment of infantry, a battalion of cavalry, and a battery of light artillery, and by intercepted dispatches we are informed intended to occupy Fort Bliss. Under the circumstances it will be necessary to evacuate the line of posts down to Fort Clark. Whether an invasion from that direction is contemplated by the enemy further movements will develop. Some time since Captain Eagle, commanding the frigate Santee, off Galveston, demanded, under a threat of bombardment and the speedy arrival of land and naval forces, the unconditional surrender of the city of Galveston, batteries, &c. This was refused. Since then nothing has been done by the enemy, and matters remain as they were. A few days since the blockading force at Corpus Christi, after removing the obstructions in the channel, entered the bay, bombarded the town, landed a small force, which was repulsed, and then retired to their former anchorage. Another attack is expected by General Bee, whom I dispatched to that point. The enemy's force is too small to justify an attempt to penetrate into the interior. The landing of lumber on Saint Joseph's Island may, however, indicate future occupation.

I have the honor to be, very respectfully, your obedient servant,

P. O. HÉBERT,
Brigadier-General, Provisional Army.

CORPUS CHRISTI, TEX., *August 28, 1862.*

Captain MASON:

DEAR SIR: Nothing of interest has occurred since my letter by the express from Ringgold. I have no news as yet of the schooner, but think she is a war vessel, as she cruised yesterday around the Aransas Bay as if learning the way. Upon her depends my stay here, as without an increase of force Captain Kittredge will not renew the attack; but as it is the post of danger as well as honor, I shall not leave without a word from the general that he needs me at San Antonio. I shall await an answer to this before I leave. Say to the general that I will be glad to get the two Nichols guns sent to me. The Adjutant-General of the State gave me an order for them, or promised to do so, and the guns were supposed to be at Alleyton. Wherever they are they will be very serviceable here and of no use where they are, and I hope he will send an officer or agent to bring them here. You know what their weight is and how many horses it will take.

Yours, truly,

H. P. BEE.

HEADQUARTERS DEPARTMENT OF TEXAS,
San Antonio, Tex., August 28, 1862.
His Excellency F. R. LUBBOCK,
Governor of State of Texas, Austin, Tex.:

MY DEAR SIR: Although I had made my arrangements to that effect, I found it impossible to leave in time to meet you in Marshall on the 24th ultimo. Matters not anticipated accumulated at these headquarters so as to preclude my leaving at that time: The enemy's demonstration at Corpus Christi, since realized by actual landing and bombardment; the reports of disloyalty in certain counties, since proved well founded by armed resistance to our troops; the evacuation of New Mexico and Arizona by General Sibley, leaving our Northwest posts exposed, and the arrival of his command, with other matters, made my presence here absolutely necessary about the time that I should have been absent. Furthermore, I had some faint fears that the result of the conference might have involved the taking of more troops from this State (a military exodus), which I think it behooves us to at least put a stop to if possible, unless, in the language of the Secretary of War, Mr. Benjamin, "No invasion of Texas is deemed probable; but if it occurs, its effect must be hazarded." The landing of lumber on Saint Joseph's Island is either for barracks for troops or for a naval hospital for the blockading squadron. On the latter presumption, it means but little; on the former, much. Saint Mary's—only 113 miles from San Antonio—and Corpus Christi are no doubt the landing points for an invasion by sea to reach and support the disaffected portions of the State. The evacuation of New Mexico and Arizona by General Sibley's command leaves the way free from that direction. Colonel Carleton, with his California troops, or a portion of them, has no doubt ere this occupied Fort Bliss; an intercepted dispatch of his showing this to be his intention. One line of forts will have to be abandoned to Fort Clark. To invade in that direction the enemy have a desert, without water, to cross, and must get their provisions from Missouri. When, nearly a year since, I assumed command of this department I immediately set to work to place it in a defensive position. This, I think, I was in a fair way of accomplishing when my best troops were·ordered away. Our intention at the time was no doubt a military justification of the orders issued, yet the effect has been to paralyze my efforts and strip me of means of defense. Tired of negotiating here and filling the position of general recruiting officer for other commands and departments, I have applied to Major-General Holmes, commanding Trans-Mississippi District, to be assigned in the coming campaign to the command of the Texas regiments raised by me, now in Arkansas, and whose commanding officers desire to be under me, from written and verbal communications. In the mean time I will stand at my post and do all I can to defend this department. Should the enemy land or invade from any quarter he shall be fought in some way and with success if we can only get him into the interior. The troops I now have are disposed to the best advantage for the general protection of the coast and frontier, and, owing to the extent of both, are necessarily somewhat scattered. Our best troops having gone, and the conscript law leaving the alternative to persons under and above certain ages, I am calling out partisan rangers of the class above thirty-five years of age to serve in the State. To troops of that kind no doubt the military board would not object to extend assistance when necessary and practicable in the way of arms. The infantry regiments stationed near

Austin I thought advisable to order east, for reasons which Your Excellency no doubt appreciates, as the order was principally the result of a communication from Your Excellency to General Bee. Should Your Excellency think it advisable, I can order a mounted battalion from the east to Austin. Colonel Ford appears to think such a force very necessary. Please advise me in regard to this. The battalion is a good one, composed of brave, true, and loyal men, and can march at once.

I have the honor to be, very respectfully, your obedient servant,

P. O. HÉBERT, •
Brigadier-General, Provisional Army.

RICHMOND, VA., *September 2, 1862.*

Brig. Gen. H. E. McCUILOCH,
    Commanding, Tyler, Tex.:

GENERAL: I am instructed by the Secretary of War to inform you, in reply to your communication of July 28, that the War Department has ordered 18,000 stand of arms, 20 pieces of artillery, and a supply of ammunition to the Trans-Mississippi Department; that 10,000 stand, with the artillery and ammunition, must be now crossing the Mississippi; that $18,000,000 have been sent to Texas and $14,000,000 to Arkansas, and that a list of the persons who receive the money will be sent to General Holmes, in order that it may be accounted for.

I am, general, very respectfully, &c.,

J. S. WHITING,
Assistant Adjutant-General.

VELASCO, TEX., *September 4, 1862.*

Capt. C. M. MASON, .
    A. A. A. G., Trans-Miss. Dist., South of Red River,
            San Antonio, Tex.:

SIR: I desire again to call the attention of the commanding general to the fact that this post is unprovided with any gun larger than an 18-pounder smooth-bore. I will repeat that in my opinion there is not a more important point upon the Gulf to be defended, a large negro population of many thousands being immediately in the rear of my position in this and adjoining counties. Three engagements had with the enemy at this point only tend to confirm my opinion that any demonstration on this portion of the coast should be resisted at its inception. This cannot be done with success without I am furnished with a piece or pieces of heavy ordnance. I have so often urged this view of matters that I hesitate to do so now for fear of an intrusion, and would say no more upon the subject; but knowing as well as I do the absolute want of a better kind of ordnance than I possess, with two more guns for my light artillery and at least 100 more muskets, with bayonets, rifles, or shot-guns, to complete the arming of my force, I am prompted to forward this communication, hoping that it may be more successful than former ones. This I urge, to enable me, if possible, while I have the honor to command at this place, to keep the Yankees and negroes from uniting in the midst of a population which has paid every dollar of its war tax, and in which almost every family has sent some member to the battle-fields of Virginia, Tennessee, and Louisiana. The recent bombardment at Corpus Christi proves a determination on the part of the enemy to invade Texas. If injury and annoyance to us be their object, and it can be accomplished by a bombardment of Corpus Christi, surrounded as it is by a desert, how much more terrible would the destruction be here, where the fairest portion of the State lies open and inviting attack. Again permit me to call the attention of the general commanding to our wants upon the coast here. Let him give me an order for a long-range gun or more of those lying in the streets of Houston, and, if to be spared, two 6-pounders and 100 muskets with bayonets, and I indulge the boast that they will be placed in hands that will use them well.

Very respectfully, your obedient servant,

J. BATES,
Colonel, Commanding.

[Indorsements.]

HEADQUARTERS, Velasco, Tex., October 5, 1862.

Lieut. R. M. FRANKIIN,
Acting Assistant Adjutant-General, Houston, Tex.:

This communication, was forwarded direct to San Antonio, and returned, as you see it, without comment. I respectfully submit it for consideration and hope acquiescence of the proper department.

Respectfully,

J. BATES,
Colonel Bates' Regiment.

——— —, 1862.

Respectfully referred to the general commanding. I have here no ordnance to send to Colonel Bates.

X. B. DEBRAY,
Colonel, Commanding Sub-Military District of Houston, Tex.

———

ADJUTANT AND INSPECTOR GENERAL'S OFFICE,
Richmond, Va., September 12, 1862.

Brig. Gen. P. O. HÉBERT, Commanding, &c.:

GENERAL: Your proclamation extending martial law over the State of Texas has been laid before the President, and is disapproved by him as an unwarrantable assumption of authority and as containing abuses against even a proper administration of martial law. I am directed by the Secretary of War to inclose herewith a copy of General Orders, No. 66, current series, by which your proclamation is annulled.

Very respectfully, &c.,

S. COOPER,
Adjutant and Inspector-General.

[Inclosure.]

GENERAL ORDERS, }   ADJT. AND INSP. GENERAI'S OFFICE,
No. 66.   }   Richmond, September 12, 1862.

I. Agreeably to paragraph 1, of General Orders, No. 56, current series, declaring that "military commanders have no authority to suspend the writ of habeas corpus," all proclamations of martial law by general officers and others assuming a power vested only in the President are hereby annulled.

 * *

By order:

S. COOPER,
Adjutant and Inspector General.

INDEX.

Brigades, Divisions, Corps, Armies, and improvised organizations are "Mentioned" under name of commanding officer; State and other organizations under their official designation.

*For prior orders, see California Column.

---

* For subsequent orders, see District of Arizona.

* Organizations designated without regard to arm of service.

*Embraces New Mexico and Arizona.

Page.

*Embraces also Territory of Arizona.

* May 31, 1862, consolidated and known as First Cavalry.

*Includes commands where arm of service could not be determined.

○

Lightning Source UK Ltd.
Milton Keynes UK
UKHW022200211118
332759UK00023B/785/P